A Life of
Albert Pike

A Life of
Albert Pike

Walter Lee Brown

THE UNIVERSITY OF ARKANSAS PRESS
Fayetteville 1997

Copyright © 1997 by Walter Lee Brown

All rights reserved
Manufactured in the United States of America

01 00 99 98 97   5 4 3 2 1

Designed by Liz Lester

♾ The paper used in this publication meets the minimum requirements of the American National Standard for Permanence of Paper for Printed Library Materials Z39.48-1984.

Library of Congress Cataloging-in-Publication Data

Brown, Walter Lee, 1924–
    A life of Albert Pike / Walter Lee Brown.
       p.   cm.
    Includes bibliographical references and index.
    ISBN 1-55728-469-5 (alk. paper)
    1. Pike, Albert, 1809–1891. 2. Journalists—Arkansas—Biography. 3. Politicians—Arkansas—Biography. 4. Freemasons—Arkansas—Biography. 5. Authors, American—19th century—Biography. 6. Arkansas—Biography. I. Title.
CT275.P6426B76   1997
366'.1'092—dc21
[B]   97-19116
                                                                                     CIP

Frontispiece photograph courtesy of the Supreme Council Library.

For

Carl C. Eubanks
Barnes F. Lathrop
Jane Richart Brown

Acknowledgments

Grateful acknowledgment is made for encouragement and fruitful advice to Barnes Fletcher Lathrop of the University of Texas and for his generous use of the Littlefield Fund for Southern History in aid of acquiring research materials for this book and to R. Baker Harris, Librarian of the Library of the Supreme Council 33° of the Scottish Rite, Washington, D.C., for consenting to and expediting my effort to secure microfilm copies and interlibrary loans of much of the Pike Collection; to John Netherland Heiskell of Little Rock, senior editor of the *Arkansas Gazette*, for gracious and unrestricted use of his important collection of Arkansiana; to Ted R. Wooley, executive secretary of the Arkansas History Commission, Little Rock; to Margaret Smith Ross of the *Arkansas Gazette*; to the staffs of the Arkansas History Commission, the Texas History Center at the University of Texas, Austin, and the Arkansas Collection of the University of Arkansas Library, Fayetteville (especially to director Samuel A. Sizer and his successor Michael J. Dabrishus); also for help of every kind to Jane Richart Brown, Alberta Smith Richart, Denyse Stigler Killgore, James D. Carter, C. Fred Kleinknecht, the late William L. Fox, William L. Fox Jr., Beverly S. Jefferies, Joan Kleinknecht, and Dwane F. Treat.

Contents

I.	They Bade Me Good-bye	1
II.	Falstaff's Ragged Regiment	13
III.	Down to the Hard-Pan of Life	29
IV.	A New Hand Applies the Bellows of the Crittenden Organ	47
V.	A Great Man in Israel	59
VI.	The Editor's Table	69
VII.	A Real Fat Job	87
VIII.	Emerging Whig Partisan	107
IX.	A Dark and Disastrous Season	123
X.	Days of the Humbuggers	139
XI.	Bank Politics, Violence, and a Legal-Printing Mission	147
XII.	A Cleaver Made Expressly to Seek Satisfaction of Pike and Reed	159
XIII.	There Walks, Majestic, the *Immaculate* Pike	167
XIV.	The Greatest Law Reasoner in the State	177
XV.	Blows to Take as Well as Blows to Give	195
XVI.	Saving the Real Estate Bank Assignees	205
XVII.	To Mexico and Back	227
XVIII.	Slavery, Sectionalism, and the Pacific Railroad	241
XIX.	Nobly Did He Vindicate the Union	255
XX.	Renewel of the Bank War	269
XXI.	Let the South Build Her Own Railroad to the Pacific	281
XXII.	Indian Claims and Personal Affairs, 1852–1855	293
XXIII.	Indian Claims: Successes and Failures	303
XXIV.	Know-Nothing Leader	319
XXV.	Political Disruption and Secession	337
XXVI.	Commissioner Pike Makes a Decision at North Fork Village	353
XXVII.	Winning the Confederacy's Indian Allies	361

XXVIII.	To Richmond and Back	375
XXIX.	Mars in the Ozarks: Pea Ridge	383
XXX.	An Interlude of Atrocity	395
XXXI.	Pen-and-Ink Campaigning in the Territory	401
XXXII.	The Scottish Rite Ritualist of Greasy Cove	417
XXXIII.	From the Bench of Arkansas to the Memphis Bar, 1864–1865	425
XXXIV.	Postwar Life in Memphis, 1866–1868	433
XXXV.	Rebel Lawyers in Washington, 1868–1878	443
XXXVI.	Last Years	453
	Notes	469
	Bibliography	559
	Index	583

I

They Bade Me Good-bye

ON A DECEMBER DAY in 1832 a bearded young giant of twenty-two years, with four stalwart companions, came walking along a trail through the Choctaw Nation west of Arkansas Territory. He wore the garb of a mountain man: buckskin trousers, leather jacket and vest, checked-cloth shirt, and moccasins. His clothing was rumpled and scorched and spotted with grease. Tattered, multipatched moccasins barely clung to his feet. Long black hair hung in twisted, sun-reddened mats upon his broad shoulders, and a once-flowing beard fell upon his thick chest in wild, profuse tangles. If he appeared footsore and weary, there was good reason for it. He and his companions had walked over 650 miles in the past sixty days, through the Comanche-infested wilderness of present-day West Texas and Oklahoma.

Early in October they had abandoned a New Mexican hunting party that had foolishly gone from Taos to the headwaters of the Brazos River, on the Great Plains of Texas, to trap beaver. Finding no beaver and nearly starving for want of water and food, the young giant and his companions left the party and set out across Comanche country for the United States. After a narrow escape from Comanches and a desperate bout with starvation, during which time they had to resort to eating wild-horse flesh, they entered what is now Oklahoma in November. On December 10, 1832, they arrived at Fort Smith, the westernmost outpost of civilization in Arkansas Territory. Here among kindly settlers, the weary men found respite from their long travail.

Our bearded young giant stood out from his companions. He spoke in the down east accent of a Massachusetts man, and in his talk and manner revealed that he was no ordinary frontiersman. Indeed, he was no frontiersman at all. He was Albert Pike, late a Yankee schoolmaster, who had come west to seek his fortune. For nearly two years he had searched for it in vain, and now fate had set him down penniless, among strangers, in an out-of-the-way corner of the South. It was as though he were being tested for the role he was destined to play in the history of this colorful Indian border country of the Old Southwest. For whether he knew it or not, Albert Pike had arrived on the stage upon which the main drama of his long life was to be acted out.

If, as many Americans like to believe, "good blood always tells," then Albert Pike was sure to triumph in his struggle for success on the Arkansas frontier. He belonged to a distinguished American family that traced its lineage in the New World back to John and Dorothy Daye Pike, who in 1635 with two grown sons and three daughters migrated from Landford, Wiltshire, England, to Massachusetts Bay Colony. They went first to Ipswich, but soon afterward moved to the newly settled village of Newbury on the little Parker River. Here and at Salisbury, where he later lived, John Pike achieved a certain measure of eminence. As an attorney and surveyor, he accumulated a considerable estate, which upon his death in 1654 he left to his children and grandchildren. He seems to have been a man of intelligence, strong convictions, and liberal views—the town records of Newbury reveal that he was fined on May 5, 1638, for departing "without leave and contemptuously" from a town meeting to which he objected. But it was his destiny to be best known as an ancestor, for he became the patriarch of a famous New England and American family.[1]

Among John Pike's descendants were several men notable in the early history of Massachusetts and of the United States. His son Robert Pike was a representative in the general court, a member of the governor's council, and one of the leaders in the overthrow of Gov. Edmund Andros in 1689. Robert Pike holds a high place among the defenders of religious and civil liberty in colonial Massachusetts. He courageously maintained the right of Quakers and Baptists to preach in the colony and was temporarily disfranchised by the general court for doing so. He denied the validity of "spectre testimony" used to secure convictions during the witchcraft trials. "Is the devil a competent witness?" he pointedly asked the deluded prosecutors of the accused sorcerers.[2]

The patriarch's eldest son, Capt. John Pike, won fame as a colonial Indian fighter and as the progenitor of a distinguished family of soldiers. He migrated in 1666 from Massachusetts to New Jersey where he helped found the new town of Woodbridge. From him descended Maj. Zebulon Pike of Revolutionary War fame and Zebulon's still more famous son, Gen. Zebulon Montgomery Pike, the soldier-explorer who gave his name to Pike's Peak in the Colorado Rockies and who died a hero's death in the War of 1812.[3]

Still other descendants of the original John Pike became scholars, ministers, sea captains, merchants, magistrates, and councilmen. One of the best known of all was Nicholas Pike, who published in 1788 the first popular American textbook in mathematics. His book, as well as an abridgment of it for elementary schools published in 1793, stressed the orderly presentation of the subject to students, gave the first adequate treatment of the new American money as opposed to the British system, and emphasized the application of arithmetic to business. His texts went through numerous editions, made an enduring contribution to American education, and won Nicholas high honors as a fellow of the American Academy of Arts and Sciences.[4]

Albert Pike descended from the original John Pike through Capt. John Pike, whose eldest son, Joseph, remained in Massachusetts when the captain sailed for New Jersey in 1666. This Joseph Pike, a deputy sheriff, was shot down by Indians between Haverhill and Almsbury in September 1694. He left a thirteen-year-old boy, Thomas, who in 1709 married Sarah Little. She gave birth the next year to a son, John, who in his twenty-first year married Sarah Moody, to whom was born in 1739 Thomas Pike, the grandfather of Albert Pike.[5]

Thirty-six years of age when the British marched on Lexington and Concord in April 1775, Thomas Pike then lived in the village of Rowley, eight miles south of Newburyport. He was a farmer, but he was also a sergeant in Capt. Thomas Mighill's company of Rowley Minutemen. When the alarm of April 19 reached Rowley, Sergeant Pike marched with his company to Boston, where it joined in the colonial siege of the city. He was a lieutenant in Mighill's company at the battle of Bunker Hill, June 17, 1775, and shortly after that engagement was promoted to first lieutenant. Serving at that rank in the same company until the end of the war, he then settled down on his Rowley farm and died in 1833, at age ninety-four.[6]

Of the life of Benjamin Pike, Albert's father, we know very little. He and his twin brother Richard were born at Rowley during the Revolution, May 23, 1780, and were baptized in the Byfield Church at Rowley on September 24 of the same year. The boys were reared on their father's farm and most likely were given a public-school education, a common thing in Bible-reading New England. As young men, they left the farm and became apprentices in the shoemaking trade, either in Newburyport or in Boston. Sometime before 1808 they opened their own cobbler's shop in Boston. Their business was profitable enough by then to allow Benjamin to think of matrimony, and we accordingly find in the Boston marriage records for 1808 that he and Sarah Andrews, daughter of Amaziah Andrews, were married on May 3.[7]

Possessed of striking beauty and a gifted mind, Sarah became a devoted wife to Benjamin. She was, in contrast to carefree, fun-loving Benjamin, serious and quiet; and her ideas on child training were seemingly rather severe. A strong, healthy woman, she outlived her husband and all of her children except Albert. She had a fine ear for music and an excellent voice which was doubtless a source of great delight to music-loving Benjamin, who was an accomplished player of the bass viol.[8]

According to Albert his parents resided in a house on Green Street when he, their eldest child, was born on December 29, 1809. This may be true, but the *Boston Directory* of September 10, shows them and Richard Pike residing in a house in Gouch Lane, a short street running northeast off Green Street to the town's mill pond. The directory shows, also, that the Pike brothers' shop was situated on Court Street, a few blocks to the southeast. Three years later, in 1813, Benjamin's family lived some two blocks to the southwest on Chambers, a short street running north from Cambridge Street to Green. Chambers Street, lying a few blocks north of the Boston Common and a few blocks east of Charles River, was in the heart of the workingmen's residential district. It contrasted sharply with the opulence of Beacon Hill, forming the north boundary of the Common, where Boston's proud and wealthy families lived. But the contrast, in 1813, was not as great as it was to be in later years. The Pike house was, for instance, almost in the shadow of the lofty tower of beautiful West End Church, built in 1806 on Cambridge Street. And next to this imposing edifice stood the stately hip-roofed mansion of Harrison Gray Otis, renowned Federalist leader.[9]

By 1813 Benjamin and Sarah Pike had three children, four-year-old Albert, two-year-old Ann, and one-year-old Sarah. The Jefferson Embargo and the War of 1812 had brought Boston's commerce to a standstill, and Benjamin was hard-pressed to make a living for his expanding family. He gave up the struggle in 1814 and moved his family to Byfield-Rowley, near Newburyport, where early in 1815 a second son, Benjamin Jr., was born. By the fall of 1816, when their fifth child, Adeline, came, Benjamin had settled the family permanently in Newburyport. And there in 1821 their last child, a girl named Frances Haskell, was born.[10]

At Newburyport Benjamin Pike was forced to work brutally hard to eke out a precarious living for his family. His small wages as a cobbler were supplemented by farming some of his father's land at Rowley and by doing odd jobs for his neighbors. Though his earnings were slim, they enabled him and his frugal wife to enjoy a comfortable living, pay their taxes, and give their children the benefit of a public-school education.[11] A pious, schoolmaster cousin reported many years after Benjamin's death that Benjamin had been not only poor, but also "not very temperate."[12] This, we assume, meant that he indulged in strong drink, but there is no evidence that he was a drunkard. He seems to have been a merry, good-natured fellow, fond of playing the bass viol and listening to Sarah sing. He early taught Albert to read music and to play the violin, and the son later remembered many gay evenings he and his father and mother had playing and singing together. Benjamin was an Episcopalian, and he brought his children up in the same faith. Albert remembered accompanying his father on the violin in the choir of the Episcopal Church, where his mother sang.[13]

Under five when his family moved from Boston, Albert Pike could never recall anything of his life in that city. But he had vivid memories of his boyhood in Newburyport, the quaint little coastal town lying where the Merrimack River comes to the sea. In the last decade of the eighteenth century the town had prospered from shipbuilding, fishing, West Indian and European trading, distilling, domestic manufacturing, and internal improvements. It was the third town in Massachusetts in 1801, and its commercial and political importance were everywhere admitted. There were months around the turn of the century and afterward when over a hundred vessels were under construction in a half-dozen shipyards. Its trading fleet in 1806 boasted 176 vessels, a total of thirty thousand tons. Nearly all the cordage, sails, blocks, ironwork, and fittings for the fleet were made locally. Newburyport was noted for rum and whiskey distilleries, for ale and porter breweries, and for goldsmithing. It was the principal market, also, for lumber, firewood, and country produce of northeast Massachusetts and of south New Hampshire, which came to her by way of the Merrimack.[14]

This was the golden age of Newburyport, when her wealthy merchants and shipmasters built palatial homes and entertained lavishly. Today High Street, winding along the crest of a low ridge that skirts the south bank of the Merrimack, contains the finest surviving examples of Federal architecture—square, three-storied, hip-roofed houses set in ample grounds and gardens among towering trees. On High Street stood the lavish house of eccentric "Lord" Timothy Dexter, with ornate chimneys encases in wood, a watch-tower surmounted by a gilded eagle, and a yard full of statues of the mythological and historical great, his own included. Little Albert Pike and his playmates often walked by and puzzled over these strange images. They enjoyed, also, the many tales told about the strange man who had lived there in these bizarre surroundings, who had beat his wife for not grieving sufficiently at a mock funeral he gave for himself. Everybody laughed when he, with every appearance of insanity, had shipped to the West Indies a cargo of warming pans. But Dexter had the last laugh. The items were snapped up for molasses ladles, he reaping a tidy profit. Young Pike saw, also, Dexter's book *Pickles for the Knowing Ones*, published in 1802, in which all the punctuation was printed at the end of the volume as pages of "stops and marks" together with instructions to the readers to "Salt and Pepper to Taste."[15]

The Newburyport of Albert Pike's boyhood contrasted sharply with the Newburyport of Timothy Dexter. For by the time Albert's father settled his family permanently in the town, probably early in 1815, it had begun to decline as a port. Enterprise, first checked by the Napoleonic wars and the Jeffersonian Embargo, was dealt an almost fatal blow by the great fire which, in 1811, wiped out sixteen acres in the heart of the commercial section and left over ninety families homeless. From these joint adversities Newburyport never fully recovered, at least in Albert Pike's day. The fog of economic depression settled down upon the town with the coming of peace. Merchants and investors, made timid by cumulative disasters, failed to meet the competition which other cities now began to show. Society, following the War of 1812, was in a state of lethargy, sleepy and unprogressive. In its physical aspects the old town, then as well as now, reflected the wealth and finery of its golden age, but to the son of a poor shoemaker it was plain that the economic opportunity afforded by an earlier, glorious age had departed. In Newburyport Albert Pike's every step was to be dogged by a gnawing sense of poverty, of limited opportunity, of frustration.[16]

And yet his memories of life in the old river town were neither unpleasant nor bitter. He vividly remembered the wild abandon with which, on February 13, 1815, the townspeople received news of the peace with Great Britain. The roaring of cannon, the popping of firecrackers, the ringing of church bells, and the hallooing of drunken celebrants were heard all afternoon and far into the night. The excitement of that event burnt itself into the memory of five-year-old Albert Pike.[17]

There were two other incidents in his boyhood that Pike never forgot. One was the visit, July 12, 1817, of President James Monroe to Newburyport. On this occasion the school children were "arranged with much order and regularity" into two lines forming "an avenue of youths" beside Bartlett Mall on High Street. Albert was in line, and he, like the rest of the children, stood silent and unsmiling as the president rode horseback down the "avenue" between the rows of scholars. It must not have been much fun for Albert, but he had seen President Monroe, a fact that he afterwards recalled with pride.[18]

Albert's other unforgettable experience came during Lafayette's visit to Newburyport in 1824. In the hope of catching a glimpse of the old hero, who was leaving that morning for Portsmouth, he had gone early on the morning of September 1 to the house where the famous Frenchman was staying. When Lafayette came out to his carriage, he stopped to shake hands with all who had come to see him. We can scarcely imagine the thrill of the moment for Albert, who had been brought up to revere the Revolutionary heroes as saints. Surely the lad must have thought it the proudest day of his life: he had shaken hands with Lafayette![19]

Except for these events we know very little about Pike's boyhood in Newburyport. When not in school he helped out in his father's shop, running errands and doing odd jobs. Every summer he and his father walked eight miles along a winding country road, lined with stone walls and neat red-painted houses, to Grandfather Pike's farm at Rowley. There he helped his father with the harvest of crops that they had planted during weekly trips in the spring. Swinging scythe and cradle and rake under a warm New England sun, Albert developed the muscular strength and physical endurance for which he was to become famous.[20]

Pike's grandparents lived on the farm in a large two-storied house, and when there Albert always slept alone in the upstairs chamber, "a great spacious room." From his bed, if he lay quietly, he could hear "the steady ticking of the tall clock in the room below." And in the room with the clock was a fascinating little wheel rigged with a treadle, on which his grandmother, "a little ole bent woman, over ninety when she died," spun flax into linen thread. The boy Albert idled away many an interesting hour watching her operate this small spinning wheel.[21]

An affable man and understanding father, Benjamin Pike does not seem to have tied Albert down with excessive demands on his leisure time. The boy was free to enjoy sports and play with boys and girls of the community. Tramping and hunting in the woods near Newburyport and on the sand dunes of Plumb Island, lying along the coast east of the town, Pike acquired a permanent love for outdoor sports. In the woods he and his friends shot squirrels, gathered walnuts, and picked wild fruit and berries. They rowed and fished the Merrimack, shot yellowlegs and sandpipers, gathered horseshoe crabs, dug clams on the beaches of Plumb Island, speared flounder off the coast, and skated on Frog Pond in Bartlett Mall. Albert also had friends in nearby Rowley. With them he hunted and fished, went huckleberrying, and crossed over the bridge to Plumb Island to pick "the red plums from the low bushes on the sand-hills with the romping girls from Rowley."[22] Strange to say, Pike never learned to swim, even though swimming in the harbor at Newburyport was supposedly a common summer pastime with the boys of the town.[23]

Pike had time, too, in those "golden years that fill the space" between boyhood and manhood to loiter and daydream:

> often on the sea-beach of Plumb Island, listening to the grand solemn harmonies of the never silent sea, watching the white sails far-off upon its bosom, going to and coming from foreign lands that I longed to see, watching the waves that when the sea was placid followed each other in long wrinkles up the broad gentle slope of hard sand, and rising higher and higher as they glided up, into long ridges; with combs of white foam, curled over and fell, with deep grave resonant intonation on the beach, and still ran up it in shallow sheets of liquid crystal, until it flowed around my feet.[24]

Soon after his family settled in Newburyport, Albert was placed in a local "dame" school kept by a "Miss" Ellis, who taught him the ABC's, the catechism from the *New England Primer*, and the rudiments of reading, writing, and spelling. From the time he finished her primary school until he was fourteen or fifteen, he attended the public grammar school held in a brick building at the east end of the Mall. Here he studied under a series of masters, learning advanced reading and writing from Lindley Murray's *English Reader* and *English Grammar* and Noah Webster's *American Spelling Book*, learning how to cipher out of his cousin Nicholas Pike's *System of Arithmetic*, and learning to read elementary Latin from Alexander Adams's *Latin Grammar*.[25] Instilled in young Pike in this school also was a profound respect for the Constitution of the United States, which was read and studied frequently.[26]

Some time before he completed the grammar school, Albert demonstrated signs of precocity that attracted the attention of his cousin, Alfred W. Pike, a Dartmouth graduate and ateacher in the Newburyport Academy after 1818.[27] Though the academy, a preparatory school for admission to college, was a private school and beyond the means of Albert's father, Alfred Pike tutored Albert privately and lent him books to satisfy an omnivorous appetite for reading. Albert's intellectual power was extraordinary. He read rapidly and had exceptional retentive capacity. He never required over four or five hours of sleep a night, and when stimulated by intellectual pursuit he could go for days without sleep. Alfred Pike often related a story concerning one of Albert's mental feats. "Albert," he said, "once borrowed from me a history in 13 volumes, and a few days later brought back the books. I was surprised, supposing that he had not read them; but Albert said he had, and asked to be examined on the history and was found satisfactory in it."[28]

Alfred Pike left the Newburyport Academy in 1823 or 1824 and moved to Framingham, Massachusetts, twenty miles west of Boston, where he became preceptor in Framingham Academy, one of the finest in the state. But the conscientious pedagogue could not forget the gifted boy he had left behind in Newburyport. He wanted Albert to go to Harvard, and he accordingly arranged with Richard Pike, Alfred's and Albert's wealthy Newburyport cousin, to share with him the expense of enrolling and boarding the youth for a term at Framingham Academy.[29]

Albert went to Framingham probably in January 1825, just after his fifteenth birthday. He remained at the academy seven or eight months, preparing himself for the Harvard examination. He did well in his studies, and in August Alfred took him and several other boys to Cambridge for the crucial test. Fulfilling Alfred's confidence in him, Albert "passed a *splendid examination*" and was granted permission to enter the freshman class in the fall of 1825.[30]

But Albert did not matriculate at Harvard in 1825. He was unable to pay the required fees, and there was no one with the necessary security to sign his bond with the college treasurer guaranteeing payment of his bills. An appeal for help from Alfred to President John T. Kirkland failed, though Kirkland did promise to try to secure university assistance for him if by the next August Albert could, as Alfred suggested he might, pass an advanced standing examination for the junior class and secure someone to sign his bond.[31]

Albert took the disappointment in stride. Borrowing the necessary books from his cousin, he returned to Newburyport to begin study for the junior-class examination. He went home hoping to find a teaching position that would enable him to earn money for a year's tuition at Harvard while carrying on his studies. He found nothing in Newburyport, but hearing of a vacancy at Gloucester, twenty miles to the south on Cape Ann, he walked to the place, was interviewed by the school board, and got the job.[32]

Pike taught for three months at Gloucester. He was sixteen years old. He probably stood short of the more than six feet to which he ultimately grew, and as far as is known, he went clean shaven. A silhouette of him, cut in 1825, indicates as much. The silhouette shows also that he wore his hair long but not flowing, though it was black and curly and stood in thick ringlets over his ears and down the back of his neck. His face was handsome, with fair skin, long slender nose, high forehead, large steady black eyes, and generous mouth.[33]

His schoolhouse at Gloucester was a square one-room frame building situated beside the main road that led to the harbor. His students were primarily young men, "tall fellows, hardened, sturdy and strong," who followed the Labrador and Newfoundland fishing fleets except during the winter. Resentful of the confinement and discipline of school, they were a terror to timid schoolmasters. But Pike was not timid, and he must have looked more than a little imposing from the top of his high schoolmaster's stool that stood in the front of the room behind a pulpitlike desk. He asserted and maintained authority over these rude fishermen's sons, many of them older than he, and taught out the term with general satisfaction.[34]

He boarded that winter a half-mile from the school with an old ship's captain who lived in an ancient farmhouse overlooking the sea. Because the weather was too cold for any outside activity, Pike in the evenings and on weekends stuck close to the great wood fire that always blazed in the captain's living room. He pored over the Harvard textbooks he had brought with him, his school duties requiring little work outside of hearing recitations during school hours. His life was not, however, completely devoid of diversion. In the household were two girls older than he, one the captain's vivacious, golden-haired daughter and the other the daughter of an invalid sea captain who was a fellow boarder. Pike flirted with both, and afterwards considered that between teaching, studying, and courting he had passed the harsh winter pleasantly and profitably enough.[35]

Near the end of winter, the school term at Gloucester ended, and Pike went to Knowlton's Cove, eight miles away, where he taught another school for three months. Spring came while he was there, and he forsook his books for duck hunting, clam digging, flounder spearing, and lobster fishing with the boys and girls of the community. He found the sports and society of these youngsters especially gratifying after having been shut-in with his studies through the long bleak winter. It was, therefore, not strange that years later in recalling his experiences as a teacher at Knowlton's Cove he could remember only the good times he had there and nothing at all of his school or students.[36]

He returned to Newburyport in the late spring of 1826 with enough money in his pocket to see him through a year at Harvard. Full of enthusiasm over his prospects, he settled down to three months of intensive study.[37] The freshman and sophomore requirements at Harvard then included grammar and reading in five foreign languages—Latin, Greek, French, Spanish, and Italian; mathematics courses in plane, solid, and analytical geometry, algebra, plane and spherical trigonometry, and calculus; and special courses in Lowth's *English Grammar*, Adam's *Roman Antiquities*, and Blair's *Lectures*. Pike had probably gone over these subjects during the winter, and he now made himself master of them. In August he went to Cambridge, passed the examination, and was given permission to matriculate with the junior class.[38]

An unforeseen difficulty arose when Pike presented himself for registration. The statutes of Harvard University stipulated that any student entering an advanced class, except transfers from other colleges, must pay a hundred dollars for each year's advancement in addition to the regular tuition for matriculation in the university. Pike was incensed over this requirement, believing that the Harvard authorities were seeking to charge students for services not rendered. He had driven himself for a year to prepare for the advanced class and to earn a year's tuition, only to have his hopes blasted by what he considered to be an unreasonable and unwarranted demand. But the regulation stood, and he had not the money to meet it even if he had had the inclination. Heartsick and angry, he left Cambridge and abandoned all hope of ever attending college.[39]

That fall of 1826 Pike returned to Newburyport and secured a job as assistant teacher to the headmaster of the public "grammar," or high school, where only two years before he himself had been a student. He taught there most of two years, during which time the seventy-odd unruly boys in the school ran off a succession of headmasters. After one of these incidents, when he was acting as headmaster and serving as sole teacher, the eighteen-year-old Albert asked to be made headmaster, but was refused because of his age. Angry over the rebuff, he promptly resigned. He had, however, been idle but a month when the students rebelled and rid themselves of their new principal. This left the school without a teacher, and the contrite trustees came to Albert and requested him to take the headmastership. He accepted, becoming not only principal but also sole teacher, but at the headmaster's salary of six hundred dollars a year.[40]

Pike's tenure as headmaster apparently began during the winter of the 1827–28 school year. He laid down the law to the hitherto ungovernable boys, backed it up with courage and physical intimidation, and restored peace and discipline to the stormy schoolhouse on Bartlett Mall. Though he "earned twice over" the salary paid him for keeping order and hearing recitations among these spirited youngsters, Albert in his old man's memory looked back pleasantly enough on the arduous duties performed there as headmaster. He remembered on cold winter mornings wading through the snow to his schoolhouse, where "half-frozen" he "kindled a fire in the great stove, with the help of a tinder box." He also recalled declaiming to his students from "the stage in the corner of the school-room" and setting "traps for the mice in my desk."[41]

Albert no longer lived at home during the years he served as assistant teacher and headmaster of the public high school. He roomed and boarded at a house on State Street near his school and was on his own, free to come and go as he pleased of evening and weekends. Joining a young men's social club that met evenings in a building on Pleasant Street, Albert and a circle of boyhood friends "'drove dull care' away with many a merry symposium." Among the members were Luther Chase, Pike's closest and dearest friend who later moved to Arkansas to be near him; Joseph Titcomb, to whom Pike dedicated his first book; Rufus Titcomb, Joseph's brother, who accompanied Pike and Chase to New Mexico in 1831; Edward L. White, "pianist, organist, and composer" who, along with Jo Titcomb, was Pike's musical friend; Thomas Bayley Lawson, later a New England portrait painter of some note, among whose clients Pike would number; and George Lunt, afterward a distinguished writer and journalist of Boston but who at the time had given up schoolmastering at Newburyport for reading law with a local attorney.[42]

A gay crowd, the club members defied with the disdain of youth the social mores and pious views of the town's elders. And in a hundred humorous pranks they satirized and poked fun at Newburyport Society, such as causing brave Luther Chase to go on a dare "one Sunday to good old Dr. Andrew's Unitarian Church, wearing knee-breeches with black-silk stockings and shoes with silver buckles." What response Chase's "Pilgrim" costume drew from the Unitarians we, unfortunately, are not told. But that Pike remembered it as a capital joke on the most liberal congregation in town bears evidence that he and his young friends spared no one and no institution their youthful scorn.[43]

Pike, Jo Titcomb, and Ed White formed a musical trio at the club, and they frequently practiced together and spent many a musical evening entertaining others in Pike's room in his boarding house on State Street. Pike was evidently a violinist of some ability as a young man, though he was always chagrined by the fact that he could never play unless he had notes before him and that he had no talent for composing—and, so, after "twenty years or more" he brought his "musical practice to a sudden close." Yet he probably had more skill as a musician than this bit of self-criticism implied, for he played the violin in the choir of St. Paul's Episcopal Church, and he recalled playing privately with Louis Ostinelli, the Italian violinist who had helped found the Boston Philharmonic Society, when that famous musician came from Boston to Newburyport in the twenties and gave concerts. Ostinelli's still more famous daughter, Eliza, afterwards married to the Italian Count Biscaccianti and one of the prominent prima donnas of Europe, was then, Pike remembered, but "a pretty, bright and innocent child" who sat "upon my knee and chattered."[44]

That Albert played the violin in church on Sunday mornings was perhaps to his credit in the eyes of the school trustees, but that he and his companions were having musical Sunday evenings together in Pike's room was definitely not approved behavior for a schoolmaster. When at the end of the school year in 1829, Pike asked the board to give him an assistant teacher to help with the onerous duties at the high school, the trustees declined his request and took the opportunity to upbraid him "for playing the fiddle on Sunday." In the exchange that followed Pike was "turned out." The real reason, apparently, was that he insisted too strongly upon the assistant being given him, but the reason seemingly given by the school authorities for his dismissal was a "lack of early piety" or "dissipation" in playing the violin outside the church on Sunday.[45]

For a few months after his dismissal from the grammar school, Pike taught in an academy at Fairhaven, on the far-south coast of Massachusetts. The town was only a "long street of houses" built on "a sluggish arm of the ocean" that thrust itself up into "the bowels of the land." On the opposite side of this inlet lay the smelly whaling-fishing town of New Bedford. Pike had really gone south to be near Ed White, who had moved to New Bedford, and while at Fairhaven Academy passed half his evenings "musically with White in New Bedford." He also cured himself of a "boy's love" for a Newburyport girl that was too old for him by finding "a new angel to adore" in the daughter of a Fairhaven skipper. At the academy he did not have to punish a single student, and he found the time during school hours to try his hand at poetry, composing at his desk at least six of his latter famous "Hymns to the Gods."[46]

When the term at Fairhaven Academy ended, Pike returned to Newburyport. There in the fall of 1829 he secured enough subscribers to open a private school for the winter, teaching at five dollars for the term per student all "the studies commonly taught in High Schools and Academies." He seems to have taught the first and second terms of this school in a room over Henry Titcomb's store on State Street.[47] In May 1830, he organized a new school in "an old framed wooden building near the Post Office on Pleasant Street."[48] Here he instructed "youth of both sexes, in the various branches of English education—in the Latin and Greek languages—Algebra and the higher mathematics."[49]

The first term of his new school ended in August, and Pike was seemingly unable for a month or two to secure sufficient subscribers for a second term. He still did not have the requisite number when he began advertising in late September an evening school that he planned to hold in addition to the second term of his day school. Eventually he got enough students in both day and evening classes and commenced teaching apparently on Monday, October 17, 1830. His schools this time were located in a spacious room under the Masonic Hall on Green Street. In addition to the subjects that he had taught in previous sessions, he now offered to teach reading and speaking of the Spanish language.[50]

While teaching on Green Street Pike made something of a clubhouse out of his schoolroom. It became "a centre" at which gathered "'a somewhat genial circle of friends, whether musical, poetical, anecdotal or scandalistical.'" The "genial circle" seemingly included "three or four young mad-caps" from the former social club—Pike, Luther Chase, Joseph and Rufus Titcomb, and Thomas Lawson. Pike furnished the meeting place and presumably was the master spirit behind the new club, which was organized for "Musical, Literary, and Gastronomic exercises and amusements," three activities that Pike found time for throughout his long life.[51]

By 1830 Pike had completed on his own the studies for the junior and senior years at Harvard.[52] Meanwhile, he was reading intensively the poetic works of Coleridge, Shelley, Keats, Byron, and Scott. Their poems, especially "the mighty spell of Coleridge," "waked the tide" of poetry within Pike's soul and cast a Romantic spell over his life. In 1828–30 he was overwhelmed by a desire to express himself in verse like that of the English poets. Writing feverishly, he burst into print in these years with numerous poems—twenty-two in Katherine A. Ware's little Boston magazine, *The Bower of Taste*; four in John Neal's popular *Yankee and Boston Literary Gazette* of Portland, Maine; fifteen in George W. Light's *The Essayist* of Boston; and fifteen more in Nathaniel Parker Willis's stately *American Monthly Magazine*, also of Boston. Six of the contributions to Willis were Pike's "Hymns to the Gods," which reflected an interest in Greek mythology stimulated obviously by his reading of Keats's *Endymion*.[53]

"For *such* poetry we are always ready to make room," wrote the congenial Yankee critic and writer John Neal in early 1829 of one of Pike's poems, "The Ice Ship."[54] Having won such attention and praise for his verse, Pike was ambitious to win fame as a poet—was positive that he would achieve it if only he could find the time and solitude he needed to set down "in measured rhyme" the feelings, passions, and thoughts that swirled within his soul. Inspired by his English models, writing poetry had become a passion with him. He no longer wanted to teach, to toil, to jostle with the crowd in the busy world to gain "the scanty pittance of a livelihood."[55]

Yet he required an income if he were to have the leisure necessary to develop his talent as a poet and writer, and none was forthcoming from the magazines that had carried his poems. He continued to teach, hoping apparently that he would get an opportunity to enter upon a literary career, but a "transitory" attempt by him and his friend George Lunt, also an aspiring writer, to publish at Newburyport a little magazine, *The Scrap Book*, failed in 1830.[56]

Pike was now profoundly discouraged and frustrated over the utter hopelessness of his situation. He began to think of leaving New England where, he tells us,

> The hand of poverty has chilled his hopes,
> closed up their rainbow wings, and bid them brood
> no more upon his heart, to comfort it.

There was the west. Perhaps he could find somewhere out there

> . . . a fairer lot,
> And friends less faithless, and a world less cold.[57]

Up to the winter of 1830–31 Pike had only thought of going to the West. He had made no definite plans to do so. But that winter a new motive impelled him to leave. He fell in love with one of his students, "fair-golden-haired" Elizabeth Perkins. She was, he said later, his "first sure-enough true love and sweetheart," and he wanted to marry her but was too poor to tell her of his love. Overcome with anguish from this frustrated love affair, Pike made up his mind early in 1831 to put both Elizabeth and New England out of his life. He had heard that Tennessee was a country of liberal people and of opportunity. He thought he would try his chances there. His friends Luther Chase and Rufus Titcomb decided to go with him.[58]

Pike's last evening in Newburyport was spent in his schoolroom under the Masonic Hall, where a group of his friends gave him and Chase and Titcomb a going-away party. Pike was sad, for he

> had seen Elizabeth for the last time, had told her sister Caroline that I was going away because I was too poor to hope to marry her, but had not said to herself a word of my intention, had kissed her sister, for her, because she pitied me, and was to take the stage to Boston on my way west, the next morning. It was a night of wassail and carousal, of song and wine, and all the greater gayety and laughter for the heartache that I could not hide, and the cause of which they knew; and when the morning-star rose, they went with me home and bade me good-bye at day-break of that cold cheerless morning of the tenth of March, 1831.[59]

II
Falstaff's Ragged Regiment

BY STAGE, BY BOAT, AND BY FOOT, Pike and his companions made their way via Boston, Albany, Rochester, Buffalo, Cleveland, and Cincinnati to Nashville, Tennessee. Pike had hoped to find a school to teach near Nashville, but nothing turned up and he and his friends again took to the road. They walked across Kentucky to Paducah, caught a keelboat down the Ohio to Cairo, and went by steamboat up the Mississippi to St. Louis.[1]

At St. Louis they fell in with a party of Rocky Mountain trappers and were preparing to join them in a winter's expedition to the Yellowstone River when they met Charles Bent, a prosperous Santa Fe trader who with his business associate in Santa Fe, Cevan St. Vrain, operated the largest merchandising and fur trading firm in New Mexico and the Southwest under the name of Bent, St. Vrain and Company. When Pike met him in early August 1831, the black-haired, gray-eyed, stern-faced, thirty-two-year-old Bent, who stood but five-feet seven-inches tall, was already a veteran fur trader of the Great Plains and northern Rockies and had captained at least two trading caravans to Santa Fe in 1829 and 1830. Captain Bent at St. Louis in August 1831 was organizing a third trading expedition to Santa Fe from Independence, Missouri, and needed extra guards. Pike, Chase, and Titcomb accepted his offer of jobs.[2]

Before leaving St. Louis Pike sold his winter clothing and bought himself a horse and a rifle. He was reluctant to sell his heavy clothing, but Bent insisted that he could not take it along and assured him they would be in Santa Fe before cold weather came. Furthermore, a horse and a rifle were essential tools for a guard on the Santa Fe Trail.[3]

Thus properly outfitted for his new job, Pike set out with Bent, his two Massachusetts friends, and a dozen other men for the rendezvous at Independence. Pike singled out a few members of the heterogeneous party for special mention. There was a little Frenchman, an ex-sergeant of the French army, who not only cooked and tailored for Bent's men but entertained them on the flute as well. On reaching Santa Fe, this versatile individual "turned confectioner." There was also a one-eyed French Canadian, called "Batiste something," who was a complete "imbecile." He drove an old white mule hooked to "a little swivel" and sang Canadian boat songs for the party. His antics kept the men wary of what fool thing he might do next. Next came Antonio, a tall, dark, scowling Catalonian, who was "lazy and useless." And, finally, there was a New Mexican Spaniard, whom Pike then thought the best rider he had ever seen. He proved to be a valuable member of the group. A few days out of St. Louis several of the men who had signed on with Bent as guards but who had no mounts purchased some unbroken mules and attempted, with various degrees of failure, to break them for riding. The New Mexican, displaying his bronc-busting talents, rode and broke the mules for the hapless men.[4]

In traveling to Independence Pike saw part of the richest agricultural region in the frontier state of Missouri, the fertile Missouri River Valley. He was struck by the neat farmsteads, by the general appearance of prosperity of the people and the country, and by the intelligence and hospitality of the inhabitants. That part of Missouri, he learned, had been settled mostly by sons, or sons of sons, of Virginia and Kentucky—men who took pride in their descent from the "sons of the 'Old Dominion' and 'Old Kentuck.'" Most of them, he found, had "much of the chivalrous, open, and hospitable nature" so commonly associated with those two older southern states; but, not strangely, Pike described them as westerners and not as southerners:

> I love a Western man. There is so much open, brief, off-handed kindness—so much genuine honesty, excellence of heart, and steadiness of purpose in them, that they always claim, from him who knows them well, the utmost affection and respect. You, who have never left the shores of the Atlantic, cannot appreciate, you know nothing about their character.[5]

The trip across Missouri also gave Pike his first view of the western prairie of which he had heard and read so much. He fell in love with it. "There is," he declared, "no sight on which the broad sun looks that is more beautiful and more magnificent." He attempted to describe if for his eastern readers in as honest a way as he could.

> You emerge from a deep, heavy body of timber, of that solid, massy, continuous greenness, that we never see in the east, and you gaze upon a broad, undulating plain, covered with grass mingled with flowers of the most gaudy colors,—extending away—away—north, south, and west—with here and there a long line of timber on the edge of some water course, or a solitary grove standing like a lone castle in the garden-like greenness around it. Let not the reader imagine, however, that there is in *these* prairies any of that illimitable extent of vision which he has upon the ocean. By no means. The horizon is rather limited, because the prairie is generally a succession of long, undulating, swelling ridges—and in traveling over them you are like one riding over the long, heavy swells of the sea—at one moment you see only the summit of the next ridge, and at the next you have a broad sea of a thousand colors before you.[6]

It was in the prairie of western Missouri that Pike saw his first mirages, those peculiar optical illusions for which the prairie, the plain, and the desert are so famous. He found the mirages he viewed in the sunny Missouri prairie to be especially beautiful. Sometimes he would "see, far ahead, upon a long ridge, a running flame, and a smoke, as though the grass on the ridge were burning." The fire and smoke appeared to him to "curl, and wane, and float up spirally and quiver" until the deception was perfect. Then they would suddenly vanish. At other times he would see what appeared to be "a broad lake of rippling water" or on a slope ahead what seemed to be "a thick, green grove of trees—promising shelter and fire for the night." On approaching, he found these to be mere phantoms also. These mirages, he found afterwards, when he was "hungering and thirsting," often deceived him "with the empty promise of water."[7]

Near the end of August, Bent's party arrived in Independence, where fifteen other men were added to the group. Bent's wagons were now carefully packed for the long, jolting passage to Santa Fe, and oxen were procured to pull the cumbersome vehicles. Everything being ready by September 10, the caravan rumbled out of Independence and took up the slow march "toward the desert."[8]

Two weeks later the wagon train arrived at Council Grove, on the Neosho river, 120 miles southwest of Independence. Because here was located the last hickory trees to be found along their route, the men were put to work for a day or two cutting spare gun rods to take with them. At Council Grove Bent organized the night guard. The usual number of watches was eight, but because his party was small, the number was reduced seemingly to three, with each watch standing a third of the night. The watches were rotated daily, each member completing a cycle of three different watches every third night. It was the "common law of the prairies" that every able-bodied man in a train, whatever his condition of employment, had to take his turn at guard. So Pike got his first taste of sentry duty here at Council Grove. Though the Santa Fe trading expeditions usually got underway in May, it was now late September and Pike observed that blankets had already become necessary at night.[9]

Bent's train left Council Grove about the last week in September. It made good time to the Great Bend of the Arkansas River, reaching there before the middle of October. But once on the Arkansas, which the caravan followed for several days, it ran into trouble. Depending on ample grass and water along the trail for his oxen, Bent now discovered that he had made a serious mistake in leaving Missouri so late in the season. The short plains' grass along the Arkansas was burned to powdery stubs, and water was unavailable for several days. Suffering from hunger and thirst, the oxen began to fail. Every day or so one had to be left behind to a pack of wolves that now followed continually in the wake of the train in anticipation of feasting on the hapless beasts. The men suffered, too, from "a constant, fierce, dry wind" that blew upon them from the north now for several days. It baked their faces and parched their tongues until, said Pike, they were "as dry as the 'Aunciente Marinere's'" crew.[10]

After following up the Arkansas some eighty miles the train turned south across the valley and forded the river. The water was muddy but sweet, and the men slaked their thirst, filled their empty kegs, and watered the oxen. Near the ford several buffalo were killed, and the party feasted, said Pike, "regally on humps and various other savory morsels."[11]

The passage from the Arkansas to the Cimarron was across fifty miles of waterless desert, the most dreaded stretch of ground on the trail to New Mexico.[12] It was composed, Pike said, of a series of "immense undulations, as though it had been the bed of a tumultuous ocean—a hard, dry surface of fine gravel, incapable almost of supporting vegetation." In crossing this wasteland, Bent's oxen suffered severely. Already emaciated by the dry run on the Arkansas, they now decreased daily in numbers while the wolf pack that now followed them continued to grow in size, howling mournfully about the wagons at night. By the time the caravan reached the Cimarron, described by Pike as the "saltiest, most singular, and most abominable of all the villainous rivers of the prairies," the oxen that remained in the train were so exhausted that they could pull the wagons scarcely eight miles a day. Pike's description of the "villainous" Cimarron was doubtless a result of the angry mood he was in at this time. His horse having run away in a windstorm during the crossing of this desert, he was now on foot and was to remain so for the rest of the trip to Santa Fe.[13]

Bent's haggard party reached the Middle Spring of the Cimarron on November 1, where sweet water was available. On their arrival a light snow was falling, accompanied, said Pike, "by a keen, biting north wind, fresh from the everlasting ice-peaks that guard the springs of the Arkansas." They encamped early and immediately began to gather the dry dung of the buffalo for fuel. A great quantity having been collected and piled under the wagons, the men built a fire and cooked a meal. They then wrapped themselves in their blankets and went to sleep.[14]

That night Pike had the morning watch. Routed out of a sound sleep at one o'clock, he wrapped and tied his blanket about his body, shouldered his rifle, and grudgingly took his post. Only "the wise commander of the expedition knew," Pike complained sarcastically, "for what purpose" sentry duty had to be kept up in such weather. "Indians," he said, "never attack on such nights." As the night wore on Pike noticed that the snow fell thicker and thicker and that the cold grew more and more intense. By morning his feet were so swollen and frozen that he could hardly walk, and he discovered to his horror that a horse had frozen to death within ten feet of him. "Great God!" he exclaimed, "how those animals suffered."[15]

The storm let up next day, permitting the caravan to move in the following several days forty miles along the Cimarron and across it to the Upper Spring. Here they filled their kegs and turned southwest toward the Canadian River. The train now found easier going on the downhill grade that sloped from the Cimarron toward the Canadian, and the hard surface of the trail allowed the wagons to glide along almost without exertion from the worn, gaunt oxen. Blessed with balmy weather, the men's spirits began to rise again as they moved forward in good time.[16]

But on November 18 at Point of Rocks, in eastern New Mexico above the Canadian, they were hit by a blizzard that was to become famous in the annals of the Southwest. They saw signs of the storm—banks of rolling, black clouds to the north—that afternoon before reaching Point of Rocks. Quickly reading the meaning of these signs, Bent ordered the wagons run into a straight line and stopped. He then put the men to work cutting small cedars from the sides of Point of Rocks and carrying and piling them along the north side of the wagons to serve as a windbreak. The large mess tent was pitched, and before dark the oxen and the one or two horses still left in the train were driven up a hollow so that they might have the protection of its walls.[17]

Gathering in the large mess tent, the men ate a hot supper and smoked. Pike was outraged to learn that Bent expected the guard to be posted that night as usual. Angry, too, because he had listened to Bent's advice about selling his winter clothing, which he sorely missed, Pike was convinced now, if he had not been before, that Bent was stupid and that he had been victimized by the man's brainlessness.[18]

In the morning of November 19 Captain Bent ordered the train to move on in spite of the intense cold and deep snow. A half dozen carcasses of dead oxen, frozen to death the previous night, were left behind. To keep warm Pike spent the day running back and forth in the tracks of the creaking wagons. He had on heavy shoes, but his socks were worn out, and by night he found that his feet were so swollen that he could not remove his shoes.[19] His friends finally got them off, and Pike spent several hours alternately sticking his frozen feet into a snow bank and pulling them out to rub them. "I don't think I ever had any worse pain," recalled Pike, "than I had while my feet were thawing. The next day I put on deer skin moccasins, and walked all day without my feet getting cold at all and without any socks. I was walking the day after my feet were frozen."[20]

November 24 found Bent's train across the Canadian River and encamped some twenty miles west of it on the main route to Santa Fe, which looped south and threaded Glorieta Pass before entering the city from the southeast—a distance of roughly 130 miles. They were now, however, 60 miles due east of Taos, and from where they were camped a direct but rugged pack trail crossed the Sangre de Cristo Mountains to the town. A party was leaving to take this trail to Taos and thence south by way of a valley road to Santa Fe, apparently to announce to St. Vrain that Bent's hapless train would arrive as soon as possible by the regular wagon trail. Pike, Chase, and Titcomb and a few others made up the party. They left the wagons early on the twenty-fifth and took the trail to Taos.[21]

The party made twenty-five miles that day and camped for the night in a grove of hemlock and pine high in the mountains. It snowed heavily on the twenty-fifth and snowfall continued at intervals on the twenty-sixth and twenty-seventh, slowing the small column on those last two days to a weary trudge. Two pack mules beat a path of sorts for them through the deep snow. When the snow now and then let up, a cold "blue mist hung about the mountains" and froze into icicles on Pike's beard. His deerskin moccasins wore thin, causing him again to suffer painful but not disabling frostbite on the twenty-sixth. "The climate in which I was born is cold enough," he said of the weather on the twenty-sixth, "but I never experienced anything equal to the cold of this day. All of our . . . party except one or two froze their feet."[22]

Late afternoon of the twenty-seventh brought the party out of the mountains into the valley of the Rio Fernando de Taos that led to Taos. They pressed on into the night, and arrived about ten o'clock at a stillhouse in the valley three miles from Taos.[23] "I think the most delightful sound I ever heard . . . was the sound of a pig grunting in that distillery," remembered Pike as an old man.[24] Thawed out and refreshed by a night's rest with the owner of the stillhouse, where they ate red chili peppers mixed with their food and washed it all down with raw corn whiskey, the party entered Taos next morning.[25]

Trudging into Taos with his companions, Pike presented the appearance of "a tall, wild, smoked, Indian-like fellow." "I think my dress," he later wrote to a Boston editor,

> would have excited considerable attention in your fair City of Boston. A cap of fur covered a long and tangled mass of hair—leggins of blanket protected my nether limbs—and thin moccasins my feet—and round me was wrapped a buffalo robe, out of which appeared my whiskered and mustachioed face, black as a Comanche's with pine smoke.[26]

Pike stayed at the Alcalde's house in Taos. He was impressed by the friendly, hospitable old Mexican couple, with whom he spent a week before traveling on to Santa Fe with the party from Bent's train.[27]

Pike spent the next nine months in New Mexico, but his movements after leaving

Taos for Santa Fe are not fully recorded.[28] At Santa Fe he continued in the employ of Bent, St. Vrain and Company, clerking in their store. Except for a trip or two west to Jemez Pueblo, probably on a trading mission for his employer, he seems to have remained in or near Santa Fe until August 1832.[29] In these months he still owned no horse, but he seemingly fell heir at Santa Fe to a large, yellow, lionlike, stray dog. He called him Tigre and allowed the animal to accompany him wherever he went. Tigre was a fine watch dog and, unless Pike exaggerated, more than a match for any other dog in a fight. "Poor Tigre!" he lamented. "I gave him away when I left the country. They chained him up, but he moaned and whined after me with a despairing tone which I shall never forget."[30]

Pike's experiences in traveling from St. Louis to Taos and Santa Fe, in living at Santa Fe, and in journeying to Jemez Pueblo furnished him material which he later used in his book *Prose Sketches and Poems Written in the Western Country* (Boston, 1834). The editor of a recent edition of Pike's rare little book credits him with being a pioneer in the development of a southwestern literature, a view that is shared by others in the field.[31] Pike's knowledge of Spanish, which he spoke fluently, gave him an easy access to the New Mexicans not open to the average American traveler of the day. His natural curiosity about the strange land and the life and speech of the people, his keen sense of observation, his gift for writing, and his intellectual honesty gave him a sound understanding of New Mexico and made him a good and faithful reporter.

Pike was naturally amazed by what he saw in New Mexico. Viewing the village of Taos for the first time, he felt as if he had been set down in some "Oriental town." Everything about it appeared "new, strange, and quaint" to his New England eyes and ears. The narrow, winding dirt lanes; the generally drab appearance of the winter landscape; the colorful and distinctive clothing of the people; the unfamiliar Spanish language of the inhabitants; the habitually slow pace of life; and the pulsating animation of the Mexican fandango, which he first saw in Taos—all reminded him that he was in "a different world."[32]

Approaching Santa Fe for the first time, it looked to Pike "like a whole city of brick-kilns," the square, flat, adobe buildings at a distance appearing more like neat stacks of dried bricks than like houses.[33] Yet Pike found "more of splendor" in Santa Fe than in Taos. Situated in an amphitheater surrounded on three sides by mountains and watered by the sparkling Rio de Santa Fe, the provincial capital occupied a magnificent setting. There was a certain degree of charm in the formality of the small central public square, surrounded by blocks of adobe buildings with covered porticos in front, pillared by rough, peeled logs of ponderosa pine. Though he was not favorably impressed with the rude architecture of these "mud buildings," Pike did point out that the shuttered windows of the porticos on the square had panes of glass unlike those in other parts of the city and of the province which generally were "of the mica of the mountains." Santa Fe's central plaza throbbed with life and commerce by day except between the hours of one and three in the afternoon, when all its stores and private and public offices, by common consent, closed for the customary siesta.[34]

Pike had been led by the writer Timothy Flint, for whom he had a great regard, to believe that the Governor's Palace, forming the entire north side of the small central plaza, was a stately building with grand staircases, formal gardens, and gushing fountains. At least Flint, who had never sat foot in Santa Fe or New Mexico, had so described the edifice in his novel *Francis Berrien, or the Mexican Patriot* (1826), which Pike had read. Disappointed to find that the so-called "palacio" was nothing "more than a mud building, fifteen feet high, with a mud-covered portico, supported by rough timbers," Pike corrected Flint: "The gardens, and fountains, and grand stair-cases, &ct., are, of course, wanting. The Governor may raise some red pepper in his garden, but he gets his water from the public spring."[35]

Pike was, likewise, none too impressed with the New Mexicans as a people. He found them to be unclean, unkempt, lazy, gossipy, sinful, promiscuous, ignorant, and superstitious. He described the women as being generally unattractive. The most common daily pursuit of the people, both men and women, as he observed, seemed to be "lounging on the blankets and smoking the *cigarillos*," while by night they usually were engaged in drinking whiskey, gambling, and, when such were held, in dancing the fandango. Like other early American visitors to New Mexico, he brought with him a built-in prejudice against Roman Catholicism and its priests, whom he found to be poorly educated and far too worldly for his own tastes, and was astonished to learn that they tolerated a considerable measure of skepticism upon the most common articles of their faith. The government officials, whom he named and described quite accurately, were, without exception, ignorant, immoral, and corrupt. He discovered that the masses lived in squalor, poverty, and illiteracy, and smiled to think that they were "a people who called themselves republican."[36]

Yet Pike was not an altogether hostile observer, and he tried to be, and was, exceedingly accurate. His fabulous memory enabled him many months later to recall and set down names of persons and towns, and correct distances and dates, with extreme precision. He revealed, also, that he could be charmed by the customs of the people and the beauty of the land. He marveled at the majestic beauty of the blue-green Sangre de Cristo Mountains, the summer greenery of Taos Valley under cultivation, and the sheer vastness of the desert. And he generously admitted that whatever vices the New Mexicans might have, they were at least friendly and hospitable to strangers. He even offered his frank opinion of one priest in particular who was grievously addicted to a love of good liquor and occasionally to a forgetfulness of his vow of celibacy, and who therefore taught his flock, "better by precept than by example." Had the man not been a priest "he would have been a bon vivant, and a very good fellow, as the world of New Mexico goes, and no crime or sin would have been laid at his door."[37]

Fortunately, we have a description of Pike as he appeared that winter of 1831–32 at Santa Fe and a record of his friendship with Alexander Le Grand, a colorful American frontier figure who had lived at the New Mexican capital since about 1822. William Waldo, nineteen-year-old younger brother of Santa Fe trader Daniel Waldo, was in Santa Fe that winter. He made Pike's acquaintance, later saw him in Arkansas, and greatly admired him for his talents and what he made of himself. But Waldo recalled as an old man that Pike at Santa Fe in 1831 looked anything but impressive or successful. "Pike was at this time," he said, tall, slim and of sallow complexion, with nothing remarkable in his appearance, but a large rolling black eye; he was shabbily dressed, in a well-worn seal cap, common forty or fifty years ago, which may have cost when new, fifty cents, and other clothing to match, and everything about the young man's appearance, indicated both destitution and despondency.[38]

Young Bill Waldo, who also met Alexander Le Grand at Santa Fe in 1831–32, frequently saw Pike and Le Grand together. The scion of a well-to-do Franco-American family of Maryland, then in his early thirties, Le Grand was slender, handsome, debonair, well-educated, and had once been a Baltimore lawyer. He had, however, thrown over his law practice at the age of twenty-one or twenty-two, abandoned family and friends, gone to the frontier and entered upon the life of a drifter. For a year or so he lived an adventurous life as a hunter and trapper, traveling the pathless plains and exploring the mighty mountains of the Far West, and finally settling in Santa Fe. There he so charmed the married daughter of the governor that she fell desperately in love with him and pledged an endless devotion to him. These feelings the amorous Le Grand passionately reciprocated, and he established a liaison with her that continued throughout his years in New Mexico. This arrangement seemingly caused him no trouble with the lady's husband and lost him no status in Santa Fe society. Indeed, her influence opened doors to him that otherwise might have remained closed, and her bounty allowed him to lead the life of a gentleman. We have Waldo's word for it that Le Grand's affair with the governor's daughter "mattered little, as conjugal fidelity was not at a premium of more than fifty per cent, in that isolated country fifty or sixty years ago."[39]

Le Grand was not a gigolo, however. His excellent knowledge of Spanish, which he spoke, wrote, and read superbly, his training in law, and his experience as a Santa Fe trader and a Mexican surveyor caused him to be much in demand as an interpreter in the courts of justice and as a translator of business for the swarming American traders. His accommodating disposition, his affable manners, his reputation for honesty and fair-dealing, and his quick retribution when he felt himself aggrieved made him respected by the Americans and New Mexicans alike. He therefore enjoyed considerable power and prestige in Santa Fe by 1831 when Pike met him. He might well have gone on to high position in New Mexico had he remained there until after the American occupation in 1846. Instead, he threw up everything he had built for himself there and went off to Texas in about 1836 and joined the Texan army for independence. He survived the war, became a Texas Indian negotiator to the Comanche but having somehow crossed Sam Houston, president of the Texas Republic, was never paid for his service. He left Texas in 1839 disappearing from history.[40]

Insofar as we know, Pike's connection with the colorful Le Grand extended no further than a scholarly, and perhaps gastronomic, friendship. They were both fond of intellectual companionship and good food and drink and were attracted to each other. Waldo recalled that Le Grand bespoke a high regard for young Pike's learning and talents. Le Grand was steeped in the history and lore of the land, and Pike acquired much knowledge from him about New Mexico and its people that he later used as a basis of stories for his book *Prose Sketches and Poems Written in the Western Country* and for newspaper and magazine articles and poems.[41]

Evidently embarrassed over Le Grand's past life, or possibly by his open liaison with a married woman, Pike nowhere named his friend in his writing about New Mexico, which was in marked contrast to his usual openness about such matters and to his general practice of identifying and giving careful pen portraits of the many famous men and characters that he met in his western travels. However, he did make the romantic figure of Le Grand the hero of his story "Refugio," which may have been the Marylander's familiar Mexican name. In Pike's story, possibly based on a true incident in Le Grande's life, Refugio successfully defends himself before a New Mexico court against rigged evidence that he had been involved in the murder and robbery of an American trader. There is not the slightest doubt that in sketching Refugio's character and his mysterious American past that Pike drew heavily on intimate knowledge of Le Grand's background in Maryland and New Mexico. Yet there is nothing in the narrative dishonorable to Le Grand and no apparent reason for Pike's failure to describe him.[42]

The closest Pike ever came to identifying his friend was in the introduction to his story "The Inroad of the Nabajo," based on the tragic love story of a pretty, black-eyed young Indian widow that Pike supposedly had seen in Taos. He recounts her story against the background of a Navajo raid on Taos and of a subsequent punitive expedition by Taos warriors against the Navajo. Le Grand seemingly told the story to Pike in Santa Fe, and Pike afterward related it in Le Grand's own words. In introducing his friend as his source, Pike hints at faults in him which, we think, explains why he chooses not to name him outright. "Among my acquaintances in Santa Fe," Pike says in a veiled passage, was one

> American in particular, by the name of L——. He had been in the country several years; was a man of much influence there among the people, and was altogether a very talented man. Of his faults, whatever they were, I have nothing to say. It was from him, some time after my arrival [from Taos], and when the widow had ceased almost to be a thing of memory, that I learned the following particulars respecting her former fortunes. I give them in L.'s own words as nearly as I can, and can only say, that for the truth of them, he is my authority—true or not, such as I received them, do I present them to my readers.[43]

By the late summer of 1832 Pike and his two Massachusetts friends had had their fill of Santa Fe. Chase left Pike and Titcomb about this time and in the employ of Bent returned to St. Louis and ultimately to Newburyport; he and Pike were still the dearest of friends and were destined to be together again in Arkansas.[44] Meanwhile, Pike and Titcomb learned in Santa Fe in early August of 1832 that John Harris of Missouri, a prominent trapper and Santa Fe trader, was collecting at Taos a party for the purpose of trapping beaver in the Comanche country upon the headwaters of the Red and False Washita rivers. They journeyed to Taos with the intention of joining Harris. After their arrival there, however, they joined Richard Campbell, who proposed to trap beaver in the same region to which Harris was going. Pike purchased of Campbell a horse, a mule, six traps, and a supply of powder and lead and tobacco, giving him a promissory note for the entire outfit.[45]

Campbell's expedition was doomed to early failure. Crossing the Sangre de Christo Mountains to the east and descending the Pecos River to the area of present-day Fort

Sumner, New Mexico, they met a party of New Mexican traders returning from a visit among the Comanches of the east. These traders so frightened the Mexicans and Indians in Campbell's party with tales of the horrible fate that awaited them if they went with Americans among the Comanches that they refused to go any further. Campbell therefore disbanded his expedition and returned to Taos. He permitted Pike, however, to keep his trapping outfit, and he and Titcomb now joined the expedition of John Harris, who up to this time had been traveling with Campbell's party and was camped nearby. Pike's note of hand for his equipment was transferred to Harris for collection.[46]

The Missourian Harris had not changed his plans for leading his expedition into the Comanche country to trap beaver on the upper reaches of Red River. Among several other Americans in his party, whom Pike met at this time, were Aaron B. Lewis and Bill Williams. Lewis, who resided in Arkansas Territory and who had crossed the plains to New Mexico in the fall of 1831 for a season of trapping in the Rockies, had been caught in the same November snowstorm that Pike had suffered through the previous fall. After hearing his stories of the experiences, Pike persuaded the Arkansas trapper to write down a day-to-day account of his adventure, which Pike later incorporated into his own "Narrative of a Journey in the Prairie."[47]

Pike's meeting with Lewis at this time was fortunate in one other respect. From Lewis, who had been a member of a Rocky Mountain trapping party out of Taos led by the famous Thomas L. (Peg-leg) Smith, Pike learned details that later allowed him to sketch briefly many interesting facts about the life and adventures of the mountain man. Although it is likely that Pike himself had seen Peg-leg Smith in Taos and drew on his own observations for personal description of the bald-headed, stout, middle-sized, one-legged, old trapper, it was from Lewis that he gleaned the information that went into his account of how the "Bald Hornet" Smith lost his "pin" and gained a wooden leg. Pike's sketches of Smith give us much of the authentic information we have about this unique character, who, as Pike said, "still stuck to the old trade, and stumped after beaver nearly as well as the best of his trappers."[48]

Pike met Bill Williams at the same time he met Aaron B. Lewis, which was truly fortunate, for he was thus able to provide us with what one writer says is "the best contemporary description of the well-known Old Bill Williams."[49] Pike had naturally heard of Williams, one of the most famous of the early mountain men, and was of course fascinated to find that circumstances now afforded him the opportunity of seeing the old trapper in the flesh and of accompanying him on the upcoming expedition. Pike thought that Williams stood "foremost" as " a specimen of the genuine trapper." He was, Pike wrote, tall, gaunt, and red-headed, "manifestly of Scotch descent," with a sharp, long, hard, weather-beaten, and pockmarked face. Lean and muscular and absolutely tireless, he was "the most indefatigable hunter and trapper in the world." "Neither is he a fool," pointed out Pike. "He is a shrewd, acute, original man, and far from illiterate. He was once a preacher, and afterwards an interpreter in the Osage nation." Williams was the best man that Pike had ever seen for enduring hunger and thirst on a hunt. He was also a thoroughly good man, completely unselfish in putting the safety and the necessities of his companions before his own. Yet Bill had one consuming ambition: to shoot more game and trap more beaver than any man about him. Pike reckoned this was not necessarily a fault in the man, and laughed at stories of how Bill outwitted his comrades in the woods to obtain "the best set for his traps."[50]

Not even Bill Williams's skill as a hunter and experience as a woodsman would keep the Harris party from hunger and thirst in the days ahead, as Pike was to discover. Leaving the Pecos on the twenty-first of September, the expedition entered the dreaded Llano Estacado, that expansive, high, flat tableland that today forms the high plains of the Texas Panhandle and eastern New Mexico, from whose eastward tilting surface and out of whose eastern escarpment, the Caprock, flowed the streams which Harris sought. The Llano Estacado was an almost waterless and timeless region, shunned alike by the buffalo and the Comanche, and many a bleached skeleton scattered over its desolate landscape bore mute witness to the hard toll it had exacted of the Comancheros, those hardy new Mexican traders who dared its many perils to wage an uncertain commerce with the Comanches east of it.[51]

Harris's route across the Llano Estacado was the road used by New Mexico's Comancheros, which took the party by way of the Portales Valley of present-day eastern New Mexico to the head of Yellow House Creek, a stream that rises on the Great Plains on the western border of Texas and flows east and southeast some fifty miles before joining the Double Mountain Fork of the Brazos near today's Lubbock, Texas. Harris understood from his New Mexico guide, Antonio, that fourteen days travel due east across the Llano Estacado would bring them to the headwaters of a branch of Red River, which was wrong, of course, and which was an error that later led him to mistake the Double Mountain Fork of the Brazos for the branch of the Red that he was seeking.[52] Actually, "the road" they were taking turned out, as Pike said, to be no more than several parallel horse paths across the plains, and in many places even these dim traces disappeared among blowing sand or thick grass. What Harris was undertaking, to say the least, was a perilous journey. It was the first time that a New Mexico based trapping party, or any other for that matter, had dared to cross the Llano Estacado to reach the fur-bearing streams of western Mexican Texas. Whether young Pike found any beaver or not, he was about to undergo the adventure of his life in a land in which no other Americans had yet set foot, and his account of that adventure, later publicized as his "Narrative of a Second Journey in the Prairie," made him the only historian of the Harris expedition.[53]

For the first five days, from September 21 through the 26, the Harris party were able to follow the intermittent trail of the Comancheros, but, expecting to live off the land, as was the custom of trappers, they found game and water exceedingly scarce. There were forty-five men in Harris's party, and Bill Williams and other hunters, one of whom was Pike, who fanned out by day along the flanks of the column to hunt, were hard pressed to kill an antelope and a few cranes to divide among the party during the first two days. When no game at all was shot on the twenty-third, Harris killed and butchered an old mare, of which Pike and a few others "refused to be partakers." Bill Williams and another hunter each killed an antelope on the twenty-fourth, dividing the meat among the whole party and saving Pike from having to eat any of the horse meat. Meanwhile,

Pike seemed not at all surprised on the twenty-second at seeing two human "skulls bleaching in the sun."[54]

Though buffalo rarely ventured into the semiarid Llano Estacado, preferring instead the broken plains east of it where grass and water were more plentiful, scattered small herds were to be found. Likewise, as Pike discovered, where the buffalo wandered the Comanches were sure to follow. Hunting to the right of the main party on the twenty-fifth, Pike's party of six men came upon five old buffalo bulls lying down in a grassy swale. Sending back to Harris for reinforcements, they approached to within a hundred yards of the animals before the beasts were up and running. Mounted on his mule, Pike was left far behind in the two-to-three-mile chase that followed, but his companions, riding horses, managed to kill three of the bulls. The meat was divided among the whole party. Pike found it very tough, later pointing out that the meat of fat buffalo cows was much to be preferred to that of bulls. He also found the meat difficult to cook since the only fuel to be found was some tall weeds whose strong, stinking smoke made the half-done meat taste bitter. It "required the utmost influence of that stern dictator, hunger, to induce us to eat it," Pike said.[55]

Losing their way completely on the twenty-seventh, when the trail they were following evaporated before their eyes into a wide belt of wind-blown sand dunes, Harris's men fanned out in search of the route and of water and timber. Pike, Bill Williams, and a Frenchman were far ahead of the others, pushing on to locate water and timber. It was a cold, windy day, the deep soft sand made walking difficult, and their eyes smarted from the blowing grit and dust. Late in the afternoon, emerging from the last of the dunes into an uneven plain, they thought they saw buffalo far ahead on the horizon. They pressed forward eagerly, hoping to kill a fat cow, only to find that the animals were horses and that they belonged to Comanches camped beside a water hole. They retreated and waited for the rest of the Harris party to come up, then discussed what course they should pursue. Williams strongly opposed going to the village for water, and several of the men agreed with him, but most of them, including Harris and Pike, voted to proceed and encamp near the water hole.[56]

A parley with some of the Indians who came out to meet them revealed that they were in luck. The chiefs and braves were away from the village to the north hunting. An old chief invited them to camp near the village and to help themselves to the water. Accordingly they accepted, although they noted with apprehension that the few young men left in the village had mounted and ridden off in different directions, as they suspected, to warn other villages and their own scattered warriors of Harris's party's presence.[57]

On close examination, Pike found that the village contained about twenty tepees, or as he called them, "lodges," each about "fifteen feet high, made with six or eight poles, and in the form of a cone, covered with dressed buffalo hides." When following the buffalo herds, he noted, these nomadic people dragged their "lodge poles" along on the ground suspended along the sides of their horses. The villagers were poor, having no blankets, no buffalo robes, and very little meat, and Pike described them as being the most unattractive Indians he had seen. "The old women, particularly, were hideously ugly," with "high cheek-bones—long black hair—brown, smoked, parchment-like skin—bleared eyes."[58]

Pike concluded from what he had heard and seen that they were in a village of the hostile northern Comanches, who traded with the Spanish of New Mexico but who hated and warred on Americans. His own party was safe only because the village warriors were away and the Indians left in the village feared Harris's fire power. The fear was mutual, but that evening Harris accepted the old chief's invitation to eat with him in the village. Pike, Bill Williams, and a clerk went with him, all well armed.[59]

They found the old chief's family in front of his tepee, seated round a fire over which a small brass pot was hanging. They were motioned to seats in the circle "with true Indian gravity," and the contents of the pot were emptied into a communal wooden bowl and placed before them. It was the boiled meat of a fat buffalo cow, freshly killed, and said Pike, "a most delicious meal it was to us." He estimated that he and his famished companions ate at least four pounds each of the meat, as kettle after kettle was prepared and emptied into their bowl, it taking only about five minutes to boil the fresh meat.[60]

The meal over, Harris presented the chief with tobacco and a knife or two, and Pike filled and lighted his pipe. With it "a general smoke" was held, Pike's pipe going "once or twice round the whole party, women and all."[61]

Next morning, September 28, the chief sent word inviting Harris to lay by and hunt buffalo on a lake nine miles to the northeast. Harris refused, fearing treachery, and led his party eastward, "following," Pike said, "the trail by which the chief and his party had come a day or two before." This posed some problems because the trail was through intermittent loose sand and hard ground, and in addition it rained, obliterating the marks left by the dragging lodge poles. But just before dark they came "into a break in the prairie, which opened into a long hollow, in which we encamped by the side of a ford, which is the head of one of the chief branches of . . . Brazos de dios River." [62] This "hollow" was Yellowhouse Canyon through which flowed Yellowhouse Creek.[63]

Traveling down Yellowhouse Canyon to the southeast for the next several days, they passed down from the Llano Estacado into the broken plains country to the east of it. They visited two Comanche camps, one on September 29 and the other on October 3, and bartered for some meat and a supply of meal made from the ground beans of mesquite trees. Again, they were in luck, for the warriors were away and only women, children, and old men were present in the villages. Pike noted that several of the younger women in both camps had recently lost their husbands and were in mourning. These women had horribly cut and mangled their legs with knives, as was their custom in such cases, and were woefully crying out lamentations over their dead men. Their plaintive cries, kept up by day and by night, made it impossible for the men in Harris's party to sleep. Pike was unable to learn how the men had been killed but speculated that they had lost their lives in an attack on an American wagon train to the north on the Santa Fe trail.[64]

Continuing down the Yellowhouse until they reached its confluence with the Double Mountain Fork of the Brazos and thence down this stream to a point near the present city of Post, Texas. They suffered ten days of severe hardship, as thirst, hunger, and the gnawing fear of a Comanche attack dogged their every step. October 11 and 12 found them on the Double Mountain Fork searching for fit drinking water. The men were in a bad mood, Pike remembered. For almost a month they had wandered through a perfect desert, starved for food and water, lived in daily fear of a Comanche ambush, and were now on a stream as salty as brine and unfit to drink.[65] "We had," said Pike, "found no beaver and we had no hopes of finding any. The very aspect of the country forbade it."[66] Pike himself began "scolding" with Harris, who was now convinced, of all things, that they were on a branch of the Canadian River, which was at least a hundred and fifty miles north of them, above Red River.[67]

Under the circumstances, Pike, Aaron B. Lewis, and three other men by the name of Irwin, Ish, and Gillet, whose first names Pike does not give, made up their minds to leave Harris's party and head east for Fort Towson on the Red River. Pike's friend Rufus Titcomb seemingly remained with Harris, and what became of him is unknown. He may have returned to Taos with a party of six men led by Bill Williams, who left Harris soon after Pike's group departed. Or he may have gone to Fort Gibson with Harris, who reached that post above Fort Smith in January, 1832. Unfortunately, Pike makes no further mention of Titcomb, and he drops from his life and the pages of history.[68]

Pike and his four companions, with Pike mounted on a horse and the others on mules, departed Harris's party about noon of October 12 on their journey toward Fort Towson. Lewis we have met. Of the remaining three, Irwin was an Englishman who had just come by land from California to New Mexico before joining Harris. He was a brave, good-humored fellow, whose only weapon was a double-barreled English fowling piece. Ish and Gillet were young Missourians who had hired on with Harris in Santa Fe. Gillet was a "mere boy," but Ish was "much of a man, brave as a lion, active and industrious in the woods." Each man, except Irwin, had a rifle and a pistol or two, while Pike carried his rifle and wore two pistols in his belt. They had, also, "plenty of ammunition and Spanish blankets."[69]

They reached the Salt Fork of the Brazos, which Pike is credited with naming,[70] about noon of October 13 and traveled down it, crossing and recrossing the briny stream in search of drinkable water. Next day they found a hole of water less salty than the rest and lay by to drink and to water and rest their famished animals. The following morning, October 15, they left the Salt Fork and struck an eastward course across a broken prairie. Before noon they came upon "a large clear limestone spring of water," drank generously, and proceeded down the small stream fed by this spring in search of game. Horse tracks and other Indian signs were plainly visible all about them now, and they lived in fear of being attacked. Still, the sight of some large catfish in the water beneath the shelving rocks was enough to cause them to fire a shot or two at them, at the risk of bringing the Comanches down on them. They killed no fish, of course, and soon abandoned the stream and took up their eastward course across the prairie.[71]

Game and water were scarce along their route, signs of Comanches were plentiful, and they and their mounts had suffered terrifically for two days. Finally, on the seventeenth, they were forced to shoot and butcher a wild horse, herds of which they saw frequently. Pike had no qualms about eating the meat on this occasion, so intense was his hunger, and was pleasantly surprised to find the roasted meat to be tender, sweet, and very fat, even better than lean deer meat. His choice piece of horse flesh was in the neck directly under the mane, which he wrapped in the hide and left roasting overnight under a hot bed of coals.[72]

Pike was impressed by the vast herds of wild horses that he saw on the prairie. Hardly a day passed without his "seeing a herd of them, either quietly feeding, or careening off wildly in the distance. They are the most beautiful sight to be met with in the prairie."[73]

Daily, as October drew to a close and November came, Pike and his companions found themselves descending the Wichita River of Texas, which enters Red River northeast of today's Wichita Falls, Texas. Water was plentiful and game more abundant in this prairie country, especially buffalo, deer, bear and turkey, which made traveling easier. Their fear of the Comanches was behind them, although they continued occasionally to see a vacated village site. By November they had crossed the mile-wide, dry bed of the Red River in what is now southwest Oklahoma and were traveling eastward in the open prairie north of and parallel to that stream. They now began to see and pass "through immense herds of buffalo," the largest that Pike had ever seen. The first two weeks of November found them in the briars, brush, gravel and oak trees of the Cross Timbers, and their pace was slowed by the almost impenetrable timber and undergrowth. Turning his jaded horse loose, Pike made a back pack of his blanket and began walking. He made better time on foot but was much bothered by the gravel and briars which severely punished his feet through his worn moccasins.[74]

Near the western edge of the Cross Timbers they came upon a large camp of Osage Indians, who welcomed them as friends. The Indians had come to the prairies bordering the Washita River of Oklahoma to hunt and dry buffalo meat, and it was from them that Pike learned the name of the river, a tributary of the Red. Pike was impressed with the Osage, who were "generally fine, large noble-looking men, supplied with immense Roman noses. Young Claremore, the chief of the party, was a very fine, noble-looking fellow." Speaking later from experience, Pike describes the Osages as being "much more generous and friendly, too, than the Choctaws and Cherokees, in their treatment of strangers." Claremore's party, he said, "fed us bountifully on the meat of the buffalo, bear, deer, and pole-cat; of the latter of which, however, we partook merely out of compliment." Pike noted the difference between the "conical" tepees of the Comanches and the "round" lodges, or wigwams, of the Osages, the tops of the latter, he explained, being supported by bent saplings and covered on top with dried buffalo jerky. He reported, nevertheless, that the Osages managed to steal nearly all of their tobacco while he and his companions were among them and consumed most of what had not been stolen in after dinner smokes.[75]

On leaving the Osages and completing their trip through the Cross Timbers, the footsore Pike and his comrades, who still had their mules but who were now walking and driving them ahead, made better time. They were now in the Choctaw Nation and had been since crossing Red River. November 28 brought them into the Fort Smith-Fort Towson road, which they intended to take south to Fort Towson and thence down Red River and the Mississippi to New Orleans, where Pike hoped to either find work or catch a ship to South America. But the day was cloudy and foggy and the road crooked, and the weary travelers were disoriented. They unwittingly turned north toward Fort Smith and before discovering their mistake had gone so far that they refused to turn back.[76]

The afternoon of December 1 brought the party within earshot of a half-dozen Choctaws chopping a bee tree. Their offer to buy some of the honey was refused, leading Pike to remark that "A Choctaw is, without exception, the meanest Indian on earth." Next day Pike traded his rifle to a Choctaw for a dozen pounds of meat, and Ish disposed of his in the same way. They now pressed on, traveling thirty to thirty-five miles a day and driving their mules before them. On the ninth of December they reached the Choctaw Agency, eighteen miles west of Fort Smith, where Lewis renewed acquaintances with the sub-agent Capt. David McClellan, "whose heart," Pike reported, "was not quite big enough to allow him to invite us to dine with him." They accordingly went on to the ferry at the Poteau River, arriving after dark on the ninth. The half-famished men spent the night with a little Frenchman, "who had nothing to eat but pounded corn, and nothing to cook it in but a kettle that held about a pint and a half." They were far into the night cooking three kettles full of corn, each man getting only a few spoonfuls from each kettle.[77]

The next morning, December 10, 1832, Pike and his companions took the ferry over to Fort Smith. "Falstaff's ragged regiment was nothing to us," Pike said,

> I had on a pair of leather pantaloons, scorched and wrinkled by the fire, and full of grease; an old greasy jacket and vest; a pair of huge moccasins, in mending which I had laid out all my skill during the space of two months, and in so doing, had bestowed upon them a whole shot-pouch; a shirt, which, made of what is commonly called counterpane, or a big checked stuff, had not been washed since I left Taos; and to crown all, my beard and mustachios had never been clipped during the same time.[78]

Pike estimated that he had walked the last 650 miles of the 1,400 miles they had traveled since leaving Taos in September.[79]

III
Down to the Hard-Pan of Life

IN FORT SMITH Pike found himself in a frontier village "containing three or four stores and some half dozen houses," that had sprung up adjacent to the military post of the same name.[1] Both the fort and the village were "very prettily situated" on Belle Point, a wide angle of moderately high bluff on the east side of the Arkansas River which crossed the Indian line into Arkansas Territory immediately west of the village and turned north against the foot of the bluff on which stood the settlement. The clean, blue, sweet waters of little Poteau River flowed northward into the "muddy, red and brackish" current of the Arkansas at the precise point where the larger river bent north against the base of Belle Point bluff so that the east bank of the Poteau and the east bank of the Arkansas formed a straight north-south line along the west face of the prominent escarpment.[2]

The fort itself had been established in 1817 to keep peace between the Osages and Cherokees, between whom there was bad blood, and also to protect whites against Indian depredations. The post had occupied since 1825 only a narrow slice of Belle Point lying between the east bank of the Poteau and the Choctaw-Arkansas boundary, which as surveyed in 1825–26 began on the south bank of the Arkansas a hundred paces east of the fort stockade and ran due south to Red River. Hence Fort Smith post lay just west of the territorial line in the Choctaw Nation while Fort Smith village, occupying the remainder of Belle Point to the east and north, was in Arkansas Territory.[3]

The fort that had spawned the village had had no garrison since 1824, and when Pike visited it in December 1832, "the only appearance of a military post about it, were some few old buildings which had served as barracks."[4] But it was about to be regarrisoned and put into habitable condition by a company of infantry on detached duty from Fort Gibson, from up river in the Cherokee Nation. On arriving in February 1833 these troops would be assigned the unconventional military duty of blocking the smuggling of whiskey up the Arkansas River and across the territorial line into the Indian country, an event known in the fort's annals as the "white lightnin' war" of 1833–34. Outnumbered and outmaneuvered by Arkansas's swarming bootleggers, the soldiers, whose hearts were not in their work since their own supply of illicit liquor was involved, lost the war and again vacated the post in 1834.[5]

Though small, Fort Smith village had considerable claim to commercial importance because it lay at the main head of steamboat navigation on the Arkansas—"at low water . . . the worst river of the West, except Red River, for snags and difficult navigation," Pike would write in 1835.[6] Here supplies were unloaded and stored before being shipped by wagon to the numerous Indian agencies and military posts lying beyond the territorial boundary. Merchants, traders, and bootleggers were naturally attracted to the place as a consequence of the Indian and military trade, and the settlement flourished, too, as a result of being situated in a thriving agricultural region in western and northwestern Arkansas, an area then being rapidly settled. Yet the town's true historical significance lay in its use as a federal center for administering Indian removal and the Indian Service, and in its long, though intermittent, use throughout the nineteenth century as a U.S. Army post. From the end of the Civil War on, the federal district court for Western Arkansas, with jurisdiction over the Indian country to the west, was located there.[7]

On arriving in Fort Smith village Pike met the man who was most responsible for first seeing the commercial possibilities of the site. This was Capt. John Rogers, a large, affable man with the magnificent head and face of the godlike Daniel Webster. Born in 1780 on the Pennsylvania frontier, Rogers gained the rudiments of an education in reading and writing and early on mastered the arts of bookkeeping and careful business methods, which he put to good use as a trapper, hunter, and fur trader in his father's employment. He saw service in the War of 1812, and in 1817–18 was purchasing agent for supplying Gen. Andrew Jackson's military expedition into Spanish Florida. Four years later, in 1822, he arrived at Fort Smith, Arkansas Territory, as military storekeeper of the Seventh United States Infantry Regiment, commanded by his good friend Col. Matthew Arbuckle. In addition to his military duties, Captain Rogers entered into a profitable merchandising business with the civilian population of the region about Fort Smith, and in due course acquired title to a large tract of land adjoining the military post that included within its metes and bounds the entire Belle Point settlement east of the Choctaw line of 1825. This splendid piece of Arkansas real estate in 1838 became the 160-acre town site of Fort Smith, incorporated by the legislature in 1842, as well as the site of the second Fort Smith post, established also in 1838 on a 306-acre military reservation that the enterprising captain sold to the federal government for the tidy sum of $15,000.[8]

By 1832, when Pike made his acquaintance, Captain Rogers had retired from the army and was easily the wealthiest man in the settlement. Merchant, ferryboat owner, fur trader, cotton ginner, land speculator, farmer, slaveholder, postmaster, and agent for the *Little Rock Arkansas Gazette*, the territory's oldest newspaper, the captain had a hand in nearly all the business activity in the community, including being suspected by federal authorities of furnishing much of the illicit whiskey that got into the hands of the Indians and soldiers. He and his wife Mary also headed the rustic sort of society that had developed in the village. Apparently Rogers's interest in fur trading ventures into the headwaters country of the Arkansas in the Rocky Mountains attracted him to young Pike, whose experience in New Mexico and in the Campbell-Harris expeditions gave Pike valuable information to relate to the captain. But whatever the reason—perhaps it was nothing more than the old man's kindly heart—Rogers and his wife took the penniless Albert into their home for a month and treated him with warm hospitality. Pike still remembered their kindness as an old man himself.[9]

About the first of January 1833 Pike took a job with George M. Aldridge, a farmer who owned a small place on Garrison Creek northwest across the Arkansas River from

Fort Smith in a narrow wedge of fertile bottom land lying between the Cherokee line and the Arkansas. In return for his board and lodging he chopped trees, sawed logs, grubbed cane, split rails, and did other odd jobs around Aldridge's farm.[10] Yet his experiences there proved invaluable because for the first time Pike observed the real meaning of the American agricultural frontier. To a newly arrived Yankee the pioneering process in the impenetrable forests and canebrakes of the Arkansas bottoms was an impressive sight. And Pike, in describing it for his eastern readers from his firsthand experience on Aldridge's homestead, has left us an unmatchable description of it. "The soil of the Arkansas bottoms," he wrote in 1835,

> is inferior to none in the world; and the facilities offered a man for making a living and a fortune there, are nowhere equaled. A poor man comes here, whose necessities have driven him from the States. He has not a cent in the world—nothing but his axe and his rifle. He goes into the Arkansas bottom, cuts a few logs, and his neighbors help him raise a hut, with a wooden chimney, daubed with mud. If it is summer, he leaves the crannies open; if it is winter, he *chunks* them with bits of woods, and daubs them with mud. He chops out a hole for a door, and another for a window; splits and hews out some thick slabs, or, as we call them here, *puncheons*, for a floor; hires himself out for a month or two, till he earns some corn and two or three hogs, and then "turns in to work" on his own farm. He cuts his hogs' ears in some mark or other, turns them out to *root* for themselves, and goes resolutely to work, chopping timber, grubbing up cane, and performing the various operations necessary to clearing up land. Then you may hear a mile off, the continual musketry which the cane keeps up in burning, as the air contained in the joints expands and explodes. Having burned up the underbrush and the smaller trees, he *girdles* the larger ones—that is, cuts off a girdle of bark around them, for the purpose of deadening them; breaks up his ground a little, and throws in his corn. In four or five years that man will raise twenty bales of cotton and a thousand bushels of corn, and be steadily enlarging his crop and increasing his income.[11]

Pike narrowly escaped with his own life in one incident which he and Aldridge shared during the January rise. On a day late in that month, when the water on the Arkansas was at its highest and had backed up Garrison Creek until the stream was bank-full, he and Aldridge got in a small boat and floated down to the town of Van Buren, which lay a few miles northeast of Fort Smith on the north bank of the Arkansas. Once there they began to discuss—something they had not considered before leaving home—how they were to get back. Rowing up river against the swift current of the flooded Arkansas was, of course, out of the question. They secured their boat and set out on foot. Reaching the flooded canebrakes of Garrison Creek bottom, they plunged into the icy water and headed in what Aldridge believed was the general direction of his cabin. Aldridge soon confessed that he was lost, upon which Pike, "as the oldest woodsman," undertook to lead them. Pike could not "swim an inch," and had two narrow escapes from drowning before leading them out upon the bank of Garrison Creek opposite Aldridge's. The swollen stream was sixty feet wide. Gathering fallen logs and tying them together with green hickory bark, which they slashed from young saplings with their knives, they fashioned a crude raft. But it was no sooner launched than it broke up, ducking Pike again. He next tried floating across on a short log, but it rolled over in the current giving him "another bounteous dunking" and nearly drowning him.[12]

Safely back on shore, the pair discovered it was growing dark. A feeling of desperation now gripped them, for they were soaking wet and the night air was getting intensely cold. Suddenly across the creek they heard a settler chopping wood. Their yells for help brought the man down to the opposite bank, and Aldridge swam over and hired him to chop down a tall tree on which Pike could cross. Surprisingly enough, Pike did not get sick from this ordeal, but he did learn "never to go down river again, in an overflow, without knowing how I was to get back."[13]

By late February Albert had had enough of farm work and decided to look around for a school to teach. At Fort Smith he heard there was an opening for a schoolteacher at Fort Gibson, in the Cherokee Nation above Fort Smith. Still penniless, he walked the eighty miles to the army post only to learn on reaching it that the position had been filled. He returned to Van Buren, where late in March 1833 he opened a private school a few miles east of town on Flatrock Creek.[14]

The hardships of the past year had made something of a stoic of young Albert. He had become reconciled to his fate, accepting the situation in which he now found himself "with the resignation of indifference and apathy." He had, he tells us, entered Arkansas unintentionally, "an utter stranger to every human soul in it, a very waif and stray, friendless, with only useless knowledge and no power to be of any service to any but the common people of the backwoods and their ignorant children." His "classical education" was worthless to him on the frontier, where "a wild-hog running in the bottom was better off than I." He had, he concluded, "gotten down to the hard-pan of life, and was myself at school." There was, if he survived, no way to move but up.[15]

Young Pike may not have been happy, but teaching did not vex him and his reputation as a scholar and his friendlessness won him a deference of sorts among the crude frontiersmen and their women. He boarded on Flatrock Creek with "little Andy Mansen and his wife." She was "tall as a grenadier" and large and strong enough to have lifted her tiny husband with one hand and cuffed him with the other. The thing that saved Andy from this fate, which Albert thought he richly deserved because of his lazy worthlessness, was the little man's "unvarying good humour." Andy kept his family supplied with corn meal from a nine-acre patch that he "pretended to cultivate" with the aid of one lean pony. For meat "he shot wild swine running the bottom." The family had no milk nor butter, but drank a "pale decoction" called coffee and also tea made of sassafras and the spicebush. "I have not seen such food," Pike complained years afterward, "except towards the close of our civil war, when we were reduced to corn-bread and commissary beef, of oxen too lean and weak to walk without tottering, or stand without being propped up."[16]

Albert did not permit time to hang too heavily on his hands on Flatrock Creek. He frequently "wandered off into the woods, if the day was pleasant, and lay musing under the trees." On other days he walked to "the cluster of three or four houses called Van Buren" and conversed with the merchants and chance acquaintances in the village. Two or three times a week he crossed a little prairie to the house, "half a mile from Mansen's of the widow Bell." She was the mother of three boys, Albert's students, and of a pretty rosy-cheeked, dark-haired "sweet Huldah Bell," a girl of "sixteen summers, bright-eyed and mischievous." Albert "half-loved" this girl, who bragged afterward, when he was well-known in Arkansas, that if she had chosen she could have made him love and marry her. "I am not so sure," Pike later confessed, "she said so without reason."[17]

On one of his trips to Van Buren about this time Albert posted an urgent letter dated Van Buren, March 16, 1833, to Secretary of War Lewis Cass. He had learned, probably on his visit to Fort Gibson, that Sam Houston of Tennessee had been commissioned by the War Department to make a treaty with the Comanche Indians. Albert informed Secretary Cass that Houston was making a mistake. The Tennessean proposed making a treaty with the already friendly southern Comanches, while it was the northern Comanches, inhabiting the upper reaches of the Canadian River, that were hostile and were committing depredations among Americans on the Santa Fe Trail and elsewhere. Houston would be "immediately scalped" if he went among the northern Comanches, Pike told Cass, and the U.S. Army could never make war on them; for possessed of numberless horses and having a prairie to flee into "as barren and dry as the Sahara," they absolutely defied pursuit. There was, however, one chance of success with these people. A treaty party should be sent to the northern band despite the grave risks. Pike volunteered himself and Aaron B. Lewis as guides for the negotiating party. His own knowledge of Spanish, which many of the Comanche spoke, would, he added, enable him to serve also as interpreter if a better one, fluent in the Comanche tongue, could not be found.[18]

Albert failed to say to Cass why it was that Sam Houston would be scalped by the northern Comanches and he and Lewis and the whole party would not be if they presumably led Houston's party. In any case Pike's madcap proposal was ignored by Cass, an act that seemingly disrupted a still wilder plan which the young man had helped hatch. Pike and Lewis, who was a brother-in-law of Andy Mansen and who frequently visited there while Pike was boarding with Andy, had talked of leading a party of men into the Comanche country on the headwaters of the Brazos, stealing horses from them, and driving them back to Arkansas for sale. Secretary Cass's failure to reply to Pike's impertinent letter many well have shot down the Pike-Lewis horse-stealing expedition. If so, it may also have prevented Pike's flowing locks from gracing a Comanche warrior's tepee.[19]

As opportunity offered that winter and spring, between mauling rails for Aldridge and hearing recitations at Flat Rock Creek, the young New Englander busied himself with his writing. In late February he sent to the *Arkansas Advocate*, an anti-Jackson newspaper in Little Rock, the first canto of his long autobiographical poem "Los Tiempos." Published anonymously on March 13, 1833, canto 1 presents a conversation between Pike's "Muse" and "Time" concerning the question of whether the present age in America is better than former ages in world history that "Time" had shattered. This literary vehicle gives a cynical Pike an opportunity, after repeating the standard American brags of the day, to indict Americans. Americans, he allows, are proud of their piety and religion, their freedom, their union, their wisdom, their inventions and enterprise, their peddlers and politicians—"the four, / Or five great men that are our nation's teachers, / Whose names thou may'st have heard at every door, / Our Websters, Clays, Calhouns, Van Burens, Beechers." But Americans, "Time" responds, are guilty of vast crimes. They have broken numerous Indian treaties, robbed and murdered the helpless Indians, and allowed themselves to become the slaves of scheming and unprincipled politicians. They have fostered a two-party system based not upon consistent creeds but upon vacillation and self-interest. Three verses, twenty-six through twenty-eight, catch the spirit in which Pike wrote:

XXVI

Hartford Convention, was, short time ago,
South Carolina's only cri de guerre;
And he who loved Calhoun, could hardly show,
Too much of horror at New England's blur,
This, chimed in every key, from high to low
Was to their loyalty a noble spur;
But now they hold it a right good precedent
Ay! good enough to write, and die, and bleed on't.

XXVII

State rights, state sovereignty, 'tis now four years
Was Georgia's motto—and her clamorous cry,
For war and self defence, was in our ears,
Her point is gained—fulfilled the robbery,
Visions of justice give her now no fears—
now ask her creed. She preaches piously
Union and patience to the nullifier—
They who are fouled can well point out the mire.

XXVIII

Clay and New England—dog and cat made friends;
New Hampshire, Jackson—something of the same—
And thus each party in its forces blends,
The oil, the ice, the water, and the flame,
All meeting, joining for their various ends
Like tigers by a strange enchantment tame.
Their claws cut short, or sheathed in transient rest,
By that magician named self-interest.[20]

Beyond marking his first appearance in an Arkansas newspaper and revealing a Pike who has taken some pains in the past three months to catch up on the political history of the Jackson administration and to keep abreast of the nullification movement in South Carolina—which achieved crisis proportions and an ultimate peaceful solution during the three months that spanned Pike's arrival and sojourn on the Arkansas border—the first canto of "Los Tiempos" is important in his life more for what the poem promises to become, which will be considerable, than for any significance its initial subject matter contains.

Meanwhile, Pike's most ambitious writing project that winter and spring was the manuscript of his book *Prose Sketches and Poems, Written in the Western Country*. He mailed it from Van Buren to George W. Light of Light and Horton, Boston publishers, on May 25, 1833. In a letter accompanying the manuscript and in a separate letter, mailed at Van Buren on May 26, young Pike confessed to his friend Light that he hoped to make enough from his proposed horse-stealing expedition among the Comanches to return to Boston. "I am confident," he vowed, "that when my book has been published I can obtain some business in New England which will support me."[21]

He had, he confided in Light, been taking lessons from his own heart. "Do you," he asked, "ever study your own?"

> Mine is a tangled wilderness whose paths I cannot tread—I know not its powers or abysses of thought—Still, the more Time, Place and Circumstances—of which latter are Desolation, Poverty, Wandering—throw me back on it, the stronger and wealthier I find it to be—You observe a change in my poetry—It has grown from a boy's to a man's—and if God gives me life for ten years more I will tear fame and honor from the world—I have been tossed about wearily on its breakers—the poems which I send you shall be my first stepping ground—Let me get hold once more—and I will have what I want from the world—
>
> What is life worth to a wanderer—to a poor man—to a slave—better the desert and the lonely life of the hunter—I go to make one effort for home and if I do not succeed in that—and if I fail in raising any thing from my book—why "then my native-land good night!"—I would not return after death and marriage had left me nothing to wish for—[22]

The death he referred to was that of his sister Frances, and the marriage was doubtlessly that of his beloved Elizabeth Perkins. But Albert had long since ceased to grieve over them. "I am poor but strong as a lion at heart—and some day I will," he said, "ride the world." "Establish the Essayist again," he begged in a postscript, "and let me come and edit it—what do you say (I am not joking now) *I will do it if you say so.*"[23]

In late June Albert's school on Flatrock Creek ended, and, paying his last penny to Andy Mansen for board, he went to Van Buren. There he met Irwin, his companion on the trip from New Mexico, who told him they could find jobs in Fayetteville, fifty miles north. Albert quickly agreed to go, and they set out on foot across the rugged but beautiful Boston Mountains for the little Ozark town. On their arrival, a peace officer from Van Buren overtook them with a warrant for their arrest on a charge of stealing otter skins. Irwin had taken the pelts from his Van Buren employer without telling Albert they were stolen. Humiliated by the entire episode, Pike insisted that they return at once to Van Buren with the officer. He was, at the trial, completely exonerated of any wrong doing on the testimony of Irwin, who was apparently publicly whipped for his crime. Albert had, however, not heard the last of the otter skin affair.[24]

In July, following his arrest and trial, Albert left Crawford County and, alone, went sixty miles down the Arkansas to Little Piney Creek, then in Pope County but later in Johnson County, where he hoped to take up a new subscription school. His account of this experience, which he later sent to a Boston publisher, while appearing ludicrous, was perhaps not far from the truth of the matter. Arriving, Pike said, at a settler's cabin to which he had been directed, he found the owner sitting in front of the rude house dressed in buckskin, and "playing lustily on the fiddle." To Pike's inquiry about the prospects of getting a school in the neighborhood, he offered encouraging if colorful advice.

> "Why," said he, "if you would set in, right strait, I reckon thar' might be a right smart chance of scholars got, as we have had no teacher here for the best end of two years. Thar's about fifteen families on the creek, and the whole tote of 'em well fixed for children. They want a schoolmaster pretty much, too; We got a teacher about six months ago—a Scotch-man, or an Irishman, I think. He took up for six months, and carried his proposals round, and he got twenty scholars directly. It weren't long, though, before he cut up some ferlicues, and got into a primary; and so one morning he was found among the missing."
> "What was the trouble?"
> "Oh! he took too much of the essence of corn, and got into a chunk of a fight—no great matter to be sure; but he got whipped and he had to leave the diggins."
> "And how am I to manage to get a school?"
> "I'll tell you. You must make out your proposals to take up school; tell them how much you ask a month, and what you can teach; and write it out as fine as you can, (I recon you're a pretty good scribe,) and in the morning there's to be a shooting match here for beef; nearly all the settle*ment*," (laying the accent on the last syllable) "will be here, and you'll get signers enough."[25]

Pike took his new found friend's advice. He attended the shooting match, obtained twenty scholars, and opened his school. His schoolhouse on Little Piney "was a small log house, with a fireplace the width of one end—no floor—no boarding, or weatherboarding—a hole for a window, and one for a door." For teaching reading, writing, and arithmetic to the twenty youngsters, Albert was to receive three dollars a month per student, but his pay was to be half in cash and half in pigs.[26]

He found life in the settlement "superlatively dull. There was no town to go to, and but one man of intellect and education in the neighborhood, Judge Andrew Scott, once of the Superior Court of the Territory." Judge Scott had joined the superior court in 1819, the year the territory was organized, and because he had killed a fellow superior court judge in a duel in 1824, had been refused reappointment by the U.S. Senate in 1827. His river bottom farm "Scotia," to which he had retired, was located along the north shore of the Arkansas River in Pope County ten miles below Pike's school. The young schoolmaster walked down once or twice to visit and talk to him.[27]

Pike boarded on Little Piney with Abram T. Smith, a farmer who had an avid interest in territorial politics. Smith was particularly excited that summer of 1833 over the race between Robert Crittenden and Ambrose Hundley Sevier for territorial delegate to Congress. Pike had learned something of these two politicians while still in Crawford County, and he now acquired from Smith, and doubtlessly from Judge Scott, both of whom were Crittenden partisans, a fuller history of the two leaders and of the two political factions they represented.[28]

The history went back at least to 1827 when the voters became divided into two camps. One faction was led by Crittenden, a Kentuckian who had been appointed the first territorial secretary in 1819 and served until 1829. The other was led by Sevier, an affable young Tennessean who had arrived in Little Rock in the fall of 1820. He clerked in the lower house of the legislature in 1820 and 1821, hung up his lawyer's shingle, and entered upon a political career. Elected to three consecutive terms in the territorial house of representatives in 1823–27, he made himself a powerful force in that body, serving as speaker in 1827. He was ambitious to rise still higher when Arkansas should become a state.

By virtue of his office as territorial secretary Crittenden served as acting governor during much of the time prior to 1829, since the regular governor appointed up to that time had found malaria-ridden Arkansas with its torrid summers an unbearable place in which to live. Consequently, Crittenden, a younger brother of Kentucky's influential John Jordan Crittenden, who had secured Robert his position and sustained him in it, used territorial patronage to build himself a loyal political following. Even Henry Conway, Sevier's first cousin, who was elected territorial delegate to Congress in 1823 and 1825, had Crittenden's blessing and was his friend, as was Sevier.

For several years, then, Crittenden's authority in Arkansas went almost unchallenged, but in 1825 a quarrelsome martinet, Gen. George Izard of Pennsylvania came to Little Rock as governor. He found fault with nearly every subordinate officer in the territory, especially with young Crittenden, who was some twenty years the fifty-year-old general's junior. Izard afterwards denied having anything to do with the course that events now took regarding Crittenden and was perhaps telling the truth. Yet he attracted to his official, as well as his social, circle a group of Little Rock men who were ambitious to strip Crittenden of his power. They naturally found in the strained relationship between the governor and the secretary an opportunity to realize their goal. The chief leaders of this anti-Crittenden cabal were Chester Ashley, William Edward Woodruff, Sevier, and Conway. The first three would play important roles in Pike's life.

A native of Westfield, Massachusetts, born in 1790, Ashley moved with his parents to Hudson, New York, while still an infant. He was educated in the Hudson public schools, graduated from Williams College in Williamstown, Massachusetts, in 1813 and completed the law course under Tapping Reeve at Reeve's famed school at Litchfield, Connecticut. He began practicing law in Hudson, and, following short residences in Illinois and Missouri Territory in 1818–19, settled permanently at Little Rock late in the latter year. One of the founders of Little Rock, he was instrumental in getting it created the territorial capital in 1820–21 and was a principal real estate holder in the new town. A brilliant lawyer, whose partner at one time was Crittenden himself, and a land speculator on an enormous scale, Ashley was by 1827 reputed to be the wealthiest man in the territory. He also coveted the power of a political king maker and by 1826–27 obviously found Crittenden in his way.

Ashley's bosom friend and his lifelong political ally was William Woodruff, a New Yorker born in 1795 and owner of the territory's only newspaper, the *Arkansas Gazette*, founded in 1819 at Arkansas Post but moved to the new capital Little Rock in 1821. So small of stature and physique as to be called "Little Billy," Woodruff nursed numerous petty grievances against Crittenden growing out of their differences over territorial printing and over Woodruff's continual refusal to conduct his paper to Crittenden's liking.

With an eye constantly on the main chance, especially when there was the likelihood of a dollar in it for himself, Little Billy obviously saw in Ashley's anti-Crittenden cabal an opportunity not only to even old scores with the secretary but also to make it pay.

Sevier and Conway, who were loosely identified with Crittenden, may not have been privy to the movement in its early stages, but both soon found themselves involved and, willy-nilly, helping it along.

Ashley, Sevier, and Conway early on became social friends of Izard. All three became lieutenant colonels and aids-de-camp on the new governor's military staff, and all three would, as a result, be called "colonel" the remainder of their days. Ashley, who dissolved his law practice with Crittenden in late 1826, just as the cabal was getting underway, had become so close to the governor as to be his legal and personal aide. In this latter capacity he was aware of, if he did not have a hand in, a quarrel that erupted between Izard and Crittenden in the fall of 1826.

Governor Izard planned to spend the winter of 1826–27 with his family in Philadelphia, and he objected to Crittenden's plan for leaving Arkansas in his absence. He then pulled strings in Washington to have Crittenden's leave canceled. Crittenden was up for reappointment to a third four-year term as territorial secretary that winter and wished to go to the national capital to settle some private accounts and lobby for his reappointment. He could be forgiven if he secretly feared, which he did, that Izard, who left Arkansas in November 1826, was headed to Philadelphia by way of Washington City to use his influence there against his reappointment. Crittenden's fears were groundless, for Izard went straight to Philadelphia, and so far as is known made no effort to interfere with the Kentuckian's reappointment.

Be that as it may, Crittenden was plainly galled by Izard's interference in having his leave canceled, and after waiting a decent interval, defied the absent older man by going to Washington anyway. His departure from Arkansas in January 1827 left no acting governor, which, to be sure, had hitherto been the case in territorial history. This time, however, the occurrence was a signal for an all-out attack on Crittenden by anonymous writers in the columns of Woodruff's *Gazette* that continued all spring and summer and into the fall. Chester Ashley had covertly fingered the lanyard that activated the *Gazette* barrage, though he and Woodruff secretly screened themselves behind the curtain of fire that now fell all about Crittenden. In Washington Conway, responding, he said, to outraged constituents, introduced in February in the House of Representatives a resolution looking toward the provision for an acting executive in the absence from the territory of both the governor and the secretary.

When Crittenden returned to Little Rock in March 1827, he learned, if he did not already know, of the war against him in Woodruff's *Gazette* and of Conway's apostasy. He ignored the newspaper attack at first except to announce that he might horsewhip one or two of the more scurrilous writers, and he failed, if he tried, to settle the difference with Conway. That summer he supported Robert H. Oden against the incumbent Conway in their race for delegate. Smarting under the fierce treatment he was getting in Woodruff's newspaper and fully aware that he himself, and not Oden, was the chief target of the men managing Conway's race, Crittenden struck back by secretly passing word to Oden that Conway back in 1824 had made improper personal use of several hundred dollars of federal money. Conway publicly admitted to using the funds in question, which he said he had later accounted for to the Treasury Department in Washington, but he publicly denounced Crittenden for his political dirty trick in revealing the private matter to Oden.

Conway then indulged in some political dirty tricks of his own. He permitted Ashley and Woodruff and Sevier, who was now privy to the anti-Crittenden cabal if he had not been before, to enlist Dr. Matthew Cunningham of Little Rock to attack Crittenden in the *Gazette* over the signature of "A Voter of Pulaski County." The trio together fed the doctor information derogatory of the Kentuckian—among other things the charge that Crittenden for years had been making private use of public funds. Conway also tried to shield himself with the voters by announcing that Crittenden, as acting governor, had given him permission back in 1824 to use the public funds in question. This the Kentuckian hotly denied, and Conway and he publicly gave the lie to each other over the point.

After the August election, which Conway easily won, Crittenden challenged him to a duel, an affair that might never have come off had it not been for Ashley's and Woodruff's continued irresponsible agitation and for the clumsiness of Conway's and Crittenden's friends in trying to work out a settlement between them. Crittenden killed Conway but not the faction that had now risen against him. Feeling deep remorse over Conway's death, he abandoned plans to challenge the hated Ashley, whom Crittenden and his friends rightfully blamed for the bloody course that events had taken. In the special election held in December to fill the vacancy caused by Conway's death, Sevier (who had himself fought a bloodless duel with Thomas W. Newton, a Crittenden partisan, over issues growing out of the Conway-Oden campaign) was narrowly elected.

Sevier's victory in 1827 marked the ascendancy in Arkansas politics of a succession of Conways and Conway relatives, a domination that carried over into the period after statehood in 1836 and lasted until the time of the Civil War. The related families owed their rise in part, at least, to the fact that Sevier was a friend of President Andrew Jackson, in 1829–37. Sevier and Sevier's relatives, the Conways and Rectors and Johnsons, came to Arkansas Territory as federally appointed officials. Sevier's father-in-law was Benjamin Johnson, territorial and federal judge, wealthy planter, and brother of Kentucky's Richard Mentor Johnson, the slayer of Tecumseh and later vice president under President Martin Van Buren. Sevier's brother-in-law was Robert Ward Johnson, later state attorney general, congressman, U.S. senator, and Confederate States senator.

Sevier's first cousins were Henry Conway's brothers James Sevier and Elias Nelson Conway, whose mother was a Rector. James became the first governor of Arkansas in 1836–40 and Elias the fifth in 1852–60. Sevier through the Conways was also related to the powerful Rector family. William Rector, as surveyor general of Missouri, Illinois, and Arkansas Territory, gave his Rector and Conway relatives their start in Arkansas. Wharton and Elias Rector, cousins of the Conway brothers, supported both Henry Conway and his successor, Sevier, in territorial politics, and themselves held several minor offices. Another cousin, Henry M. Rector, was governor in 1860–62, though he was not then a member of the Sevier-Conway-Johnson-Rector "family dynasty." The strength of the clan, which was referred to by its detractors as the "Bourbon Dynasty," "Sevier's hungry kinfolks," or simply as "the family," has been best summarized by an Arkansas historian who calculated that its members held office an aggregate of 190 years among them and "constituted the reigning dynasty in Arkansas from 1820 to 1860, and held all the great offices with some exceptions."

We shall hear more of the "exceptions" in due course, as they are an important part of Pike's life story. For the time being it is necessary to know that from 1827 until Crittenden's untimely death in 1834 Crittenden and Sevier waged political war against each other. In 1829 President Jackson's political ax fell on Crittenden, who was removed as secretary in favor of a stalwart Jacksonian, Alabama's William Savin Fulton. Crittenden seems to have been a victim in 1829 not of Sevier's intrigue but of national politics; he was John Jordan Crittenden's brother, a noted Henry Clay partisan, who was axed by Jackson at the same time. That same year, 1829, Jackson named Kentucky's John Pope as territorial governor.[29] Pope in 1831 thwarted Crittenden's scheme of exchanging his costly Little Rock home for ten sections of land that Congress had given Arkansas for building a statehouse.

Outraged over Pope's veto of the exchange bill, an act that was warmly applauded by Ashley and Woodruff and other Sevierites, Crittenden had his backers in the legislature appeal to Congress to make the offices of governor and of secretary elective. His intent was clear. He was still a potent force in territorial politics, as his control of the 1831 legislature demonstrated, and he intended to have Pope defeated if the outsider dared run for office. But Sevier, on duty in Washington and ever alert to an opportunity to gouge Crittenden, interceded with his Jacksonian friends in Congress to kill the measure. Sevier doubly punished Crittenden by getting Congress to put the matter of locating and selling the statehouse bonds and of erecting the new building in the hands of Governor Pope, who then made Ashley, his chief surrogate, the agent of the statehouse project.

In 1833 Crittenden himself announced as a candidate for delegate, a bold departure from his usual past conduct as a political wire puller. The same day the Kentuckian announced, March 27, 1833, Sevier proclaimed his intention of seeking a fourth term to the office. Meanwhile, Crittenden and his friends had already embroiled Delegate Sevier in a most critical political crisis. They had, the previous January, brought charges of impeachment in the national House of Representatives against Sevier's father-in-law, Judge Benjamin Johnson, for abuse of judicial power and drunkenness on the bench. Sevier defeated the impeachment proceedings, and returning to Arkansas that spring, opened a blistering campaign against Crittenden.

Pike was still teaching in Crawford County when the 1833 territorial canvass opened. Besides the absorbing race between Crittenden and Sevier, there were the important contests between rival Crittendenites and Sevierites for seats in the legislature and for county offices. From the accounts that he later gave of the electioneering scenes he witnessed that June in Crawford County, Pike indicated that he was not a little surprised at the intense excitement among the local populace. There was, he wrote, "a stir in the country on the subject of politics": candidates began "riding in every direction, electioneering; and now and then a hot quarrel took place among the excited partisans." Riding into the little village of Van Buren on a June day, he found the place, which normally numbered about a dozen inhabitants, jammed with a vast crowd of country people. They had come in to hear the rival candidates speak. Pike inquired if Crittenden and Sevier were present, and was disappointed to find that they were not.

It was a meeting for the legislative and county candidates, whom Pike observed "busy among the people, shaking them by the hand, and making themselves boon companions. The noise arising from the throng, among which whiskey flowed freely, "was a perfect Babel."[30]

> Hurra for Sinclair! He's a horse. Who'll drink Crittenden's liquor? Here goes for Sevier! Good morning 'Squire; how's your family? Come up and drink with an old acquaintance, who's a candidate. Bates forever! the people's candidate. He's a horse in a cane-brake! Go ahead steamboat! Brown's a roarer! Five dollars on Martin! Such were some of the cries that struck my ear.[31]

The electioneering among the crowd was preliminary to the speaking. A board placed across an empty barrel served the candidates as a platform on this occasion rather than the usual tree stumps. Pike later assured his new England readers that the oddity of such makeshift platforms as empty whiskey barrels and stumps and of such open-air gatherings soon disappeared, and one became quite accustomed to them. He also commented that one might "hear as much oratory in the west on a stump, as in the East in a Court-house, or in old Faneuil itself." Moreover, he was inclined to believe that the "Western manner of electioneering is to the full as proper, and more honest and open-handed than the silent canvassing in the East." He heard that day three lawyers and two farmers, who were rivals for the county's three seats in the legislature. "I had expected," he said, "a display of bombast and was agreeably surprised by good strong sense, keen satire, and almost an entire freedom from violence or affectation in all the speeches." Indeed, the two farmers proved to be abler offhand speakers, Pike discovered, than all but one of the lawyers, while the lawyer who spoke best was a man "who had quit brick-laying for brief-making and special pleading" and was a master at "sarcastic and satirical humor, which tells well in a candidate."[32]

The contest between Crittenden and Sevier reached its climax about the time Pike moved to Pope County in July 1833. There on Little Piney Creek he listened to Abram Smith's endless chatter on the rivalry between the two men, which since Smith was a Crittenden supporter had to do mostly with the alleged evils practiced by the Sevierites and with wrongs committed by them against the Crittendenites. Besides listening to Smith, Pike also followed the campaign in the *Arkansas Gazette* and the *Arkansas Advocate*, the territorial capital's two newspapers, which in itself amounted to a liberal education on territorial politics.[33]

Pike found these two Little Rock papers a most interesting pair. The *Gazette* was still, in 1833, owned and edited by the Sevierite, Little Billy Woodruff, a native of Long Island, New York, who had as a boy served an apprenticeship, arranged by his widowed mother, on New York papers. He afterward worked as a journeyman printer in New York and in Kentucky and Tennessee before grasping an opportunity in the fall of 1819 of coming to Arkansas Post and establishing his *Gazette* as the newly formed territory's first newspaper. For twelve years running he enjoyed a monopoly on territorial printing, practiced careful business methods and, craftily choosing sides in 1827, put his paper behind his friend Ashley's anti-Crittenden cabal and thereafter became identified with the rising Sevier faction. He accordingly prospered as a newspaperman and job printer, subscription agent and book dealer, and debt collector and land speculator.[34]

Little Billy was thirty-eight in 1833. He had foolishly favored John Quincy Adams for president in 1828, believing General Jackson not qualified for civil administration. But the coming of Jackson to power in 1829 and Sevier's increasing identification with the Jacksonian party in the intervening years, had caused the calculating editor to drift quickly into an alliance with the new party. This was especially noticeable after 1830 when the *Advocate*, in an attempt to make trouble between Sevier and Woodruff, charged that Woodruff was anti-Jackson.

Meanwhile, Woodruff, who obviously despised the somewhat imperious Crittenden, had made himself a master of the art of invective and, being a fierce political competitor, became a force to be reckoned with not only in the Crittenden camp but also in the private councils of the Sevier faction, where he had the powerful support, indeed, of Chester Ashley. Though Woodruff refused to accept challenges to duels, preferring, he always said, to defend himself in court, he did frequently go armed in self-defense and was suspected of having killed one man who attacked him and Ashley in his newspaper office. The charge was never proved, nor was either he or Ashley, who was involved, ever indicted for the act. Yet Woodruff was blamed, not unjustly, for having incited several bloody encounters between other men because of the libelous and vituperative letters that he freely admitted to the columns of his paper.

The *Advocate*, founded in 1830, was owned and edited by young Charles Pierre Bertrand, the stepson of Dr. Matthew Cunningham. He was born in 1808 in New York City, the son of Eliza Wilson and Pierre Bertrand, younger brother of Napoleon's Grand Marshall of the Palace, Count Bertrand, who followed the French emperor into exile at St. Helena. Charles's father, who had extensive landholdings and sugar planting interests in Saint Domingue (Haiti), lost his life during an insurrection while visiting the troubled island in 1809. Charles's widowed mother soon afterward married Dr. Cunningham, a graduate of the University of Pennsylvania Medical School, who practiced in New York City. Charles and his younger sister Arabella June Bertrand began their educations in New York City, where the Cunninghams lived until 1817, and continued their schooling in St. Louis, where the family lived from about 1817 to 1820. In the latter year the mother and two children joined Dr. Cunningham at the new town of Little Rock in Arkansas Territory.

The Cunningham-Bertrand family became famous in Little Rock history as the result of a number of "firsts" being credited to the physician and his wife.[35] He was the town's first doctor; Eliza and her young daughter were the first white women to arrive there; Eliza's son by the doctor, Chester Ashley Cunningham, was believed to be the first white child born in the rustic village; and Dr. Cunningham, after Little Rock was officially incorporated a town in 1831, was elected its first mayor in January 1832.

Charles Bertrand was a boy of twelve when he came to Little Rock in 1820. There being no school in the primitive settlement until Jesse Brown arrived and opened a private school early in 1823, Charles probably studied under the supervision of his parents until he began attending Brown's school, which by 1825–26 was known as the Little Rock Academy.[36] In 1824 his stepfather arranged with Woodruff to take the fifteen-year-old boy into his house as an apprentice on the *Gazette*, a period of training that lasted until his twenty-first birthday in November 1829. During these years Charles probably continued his education at Brown's academy at least part of the time, for schooling was a common enough arrangement in the case of apprentices in the printing trade.

Charles and Dr. Cunningham had identified themselves politically with the Sevier faction in 1827, during which year the doctor, with material furnished him by Ashley and Sevier and Woodruff, contributed anti-Crittenden letters to the *Gazette* over the nom de plume of "A Voter of Pulaski County." Meanwhile, before he completed his apprenticeship under Woodruff, Charles had begun to read law with Crittenden. When soon after Charles launched his *Advocate* in March 1830 and he made a fierce attack on Woodruff and the *Gazette*, it became apparent that Bertrand had gone over to the Crittenden forces. His strategy seemed to be to drive a wedge between Governor Pope and Sevier on the one hand and between Woodruff and Sevier on the other.

Thanks to the support of Crittenden, whose friends controlled the legislature of 1831, Bertrand was elected official printer to the territory that fall, ending Woodruff's twelve-year monopoly. It rankled young Bertrand, nevertheless, that Governor Pope and Secretary Fulton, now loosely identified with the Sevierites, continued to bestow on their friend Woodruff whatever printing patronage the executive branch of the territorial government controlled. This led to perpetual editorial wrangling between him and his former master and to a private resolution on Woodruff's part to leave no political stone upturned in electing a legislature in 1833 that would restore him to his accustomed position as territorial printer.

Bertrand and Woodruff perpetually quarreled also over personal issues and politics, and their columns bristled with partisan writings of their numerous pseudonymous contributors. These correspondents were uncommonly canny at the art of applying nicknames to their enemies. Clever Chester Ashley wielded one of the most potent pens for the *Gazette* and was himself a principal target of the writers in Bertrand's paper. They identified Ashley as the malign influence behind the *Gazette* attacks on Crittenden, blamed him for the Crittenden-Conway duel in 1827, and charged his friend Woodruff with being his "jackal and pimp" in that tragic affair and others. Because Ashley had been "prime minister" to Governor Izard and Governor Pope, both of whom had displayed hostility to Crittenden, he became known by the apt title of "Talleyrand" in the columns of the *Advocate*.

Ashley returned as many blows as he received. Writing in 1830 over his nom de plume "Jaw-Bone," he gave Crittenden and Bertrand their respective titles of "Cardinal

Woolsey" and "Beau Charley." Cardinal Woolsey of England, Ashley wrote, "desired the seat of a *Pope* in Rome" whereas Crittenden merely coveted "the seat of a *Pope* in Arkansas." As for Bertrand, the college-bred Ashley declared, he was young, uneducated, inexperienced, and was more devoted to his "toilette" and "the arts of dandyism" than "to books and the company of the wise and virtuous." "Beau Charley" he was known as thereafter in the Sevier ranks. Sevier himself was easily identifiable as "Don Ambrosia," a play on his supposed Spanish ancestry and a slap at his pretense of being a gentleman.

Pike himself thought that his later good friend, young Thomas Willoughby Newton, received the most colorful title at this time. During the anti-Crittenden cabal of 1827, Newton was living in Crittenden's Little Rock home while reading law under him. He rashly undertook to reply to a letter of the polished James Woodson Bates, the "Junius of the West," Crittenden's temporarily estranged friend who wielded a poisoned pen against the Kentuckian. Newton wrote that unlike Bates he was not college bred but had been reared and educated "on the barren heath among the commoners of our country" and that he walked fearlessly there, defying all liars, oppressors, and backbiters. The merciless Bates retorted that Crittenden's "page of the household" had indeed been educated on a barren heath, that his "predilection for piracy on character" induced him to believe that the name of that heath was Hounslow (an allusion to the famed Hounslow Heath in England, the haunt of pirates and highwaymen) and pointed out that Newton should have written: "Like my predecessor of old, I walked the Hounslow Heath, seeking whom I might devour." Poor Newton after that put down was, Pike said, promptly dubbed "the Knight of the Hounslow Heath."

Pike had the good fortune of meeting Crittenden that summer of 1833, and it was, he tells us, quite by accident. His landlord, Abram Smith, had gone one day in mid-July to nearby Spadra to hear the candidates for office speak. On returning in the evening he brought Crittenden home with him to spend the night. Pike and Crittenden became acquainted and talked late into the night, the Kentuckian being fascinated by what the young schoolmaster had to relate about his travels to Santa Fe and his hardships on the Great Plains, the Spanish, the Indians, the buffalo, and the wild mustangs. Crittenden was "kind, indulgent, and gracious; and as he was one, to know whom was an honor and to hear whom a pleasure, to meet him so was quite an event in my life."[37]

Pike did not exaggerate. Meeting Crittenden proved a turning point in his life, for the Kentuckian sometime after returning to Little Rock recommended to Bertrand that the young schoolmaster be invited to the capital to work on the *Advocate*. Pike made it appear that the invitation came immediately on Crittenden's reaching Little Rock, but such was not the case. Crittenden was supposedly impressed with Pike all right, but he obviously had other things on his mind in the weeks that followed—among other things the crushing defeat he suffered on election day, August 5, 1833, when Sevier polled 4,476 votes to his own 2,520.[38]

From what we know of the circumstances it must have been mid-September or later before Pike received Bertrand's offer to work on his newspaper. Meanwhile, leaving nothing to chance, Pike revived his Byronic Don Juan–like poem "Los Tiempos" and mailed canto after canto to Bertrand. Following publication of the first canto back in March, Pike had turned to other writing and work and had suspended work on the epic poem; now between August 14 and September 25, 1833, eight additional cantos, numbers two through nine appeared in Bertrand's paper. It was hardly a coincidence that canto 3, published in mid-August but probably written soon after Pike met Crittenden in Pope County, contained two sarcastic gibes at the political expediency of "Little Billy Woodruff." Appearing in Bertrand's last weekly issue in August was, besides canto 5 of "Los Tiempos," Pike's anonymous four-verse propagandistic poem entitled "Epitaphs Conned in a Church-Yard, AD 1901." In it he furnished mock epitaphs for the four principal anti-Crittenden villains—Woodruff, Pope, Ashley, and Sevier. The leading authority on Pike's poetry, Susan B. Riley, who praises his spunk for undertaking to become America's Don Juan in "Los Tiempos"—she says it was "an extraordinary achievement and as successful as any effort among American poets of the day"—declares that it was this piece of writing that "was to be the means of his leaving the backwoods for the territorial capital of Little Rock where opportunities for him to use his education and native abilities opened up rapidly."[39]

She is undoubtedly correct. Pike meant this latest rash of poetry, both the formal verses of "Los Tiempos" and the informal and derisive ones of "Epitaphs Conned in a Church-Yard," to remind Crittenden of the gifted schoolmaster on Little Piney. His efforts this time did not go unrewarded, for, as he later said, he soon received a letter from Bertrand inviting him to Little Rock to work on the *Advocate*.[40]

Bertrand's joyful letter found Pike prostrated by "an attack of chills and fever." He struggled out of bed and made the rounds of the neighborhood to collect what money he could. Three dollars in cash was all that he could raise. He neglected to mention the pigs due him, but in after years, speculating freely on the population growth among his swine running loose in the woods along the Little Piney, he facetiously boasted that he was the biggest pig owner in Johnson County, which when created in the fall of 1833 included that portion of Pope County in which Little Piney lay.[41]

He left for Little Rock about the first of October. He was fortunate enough to meet a man who wished to send a horse to Little Rock and allowed him to ride it. On the way down the road that skirted the north bank of the Arkansas River and passed through the settlements of Lewisburg and Cadron, now ghost towns, Pike fell in with an old soldier from New England who knew the country and served as guide. Fifty miles above Little Rock they crossed the track of a tornado, which impressed Pike. Its force, he reported, must have been tremendous. Hardly a tree was standing in its path, a mile and a half in width. "The largest hickory and oak trees were twisted and *broomed* up by the blast; and a thick growth of vines and briars had grown up in place of the forest."[42]

Pike arrived at the Little Rock ferry with barely enough money to pay his fare across. But he landed safely on the Little Rock shore, delivered his horse, and sought out the *Advocate* office.[43]

IV

A New Hand Applies the Bellows of the Crittenden Organ

AT THE *ADVOCATE* OFFICE Albert met Bertrand and learned what was expected of him. He was to familiarize himself with every aspect of getting out the weekly paper—typesetting and composition, printing and mailing, news gathering and reporting, editorial writing and handling correspondence, and billing and bookkeeping. In return Bertrand would furnish him a bed in a back room of the newspaper office and he could take his meals with Bertrand's family, but he was to receive no wages for his work on the paper. Doubtless surprised to find that he was to be no more than an apprentice, Albert, as time went on, grew more than a little annoyed at Bertrand's tightfistedness. When it was absolutely necessary for him to have money, he had to go to Bertrand and ask for it. Bertrand kept, Pike said, a meticulous record "of every little sum of money furnished me, and some ten or twelve years afterward presented it to me and I paid it."[1]

For almost a year Albert lived in a tiny unventilated shed-room at the rear of the *Advocate* office. Debilitated by his bout with fever in 1833, he suffered a more serious attack of "bilious fever and ague" in the summer of 1834. He dosed himself on "calomel and tartar-emetic by the half tea-spoonful" and eventually "acclimatized" himself to the fevers of Arkansas. But, racked with chills, he found his cramped quarters "hot during the summer of 1834 beyond the power of words to describe."[2]

Getting used to Little Rock's July temperatures was obviously tough on Albert. "Oh," he exclaimed in July 1834, "for an hour of the climate of Nova Zembla or Spitzbergen—and thence upward to the North Pole!—avalanches, glaciers, ice islands, any thing to temper this overwhelming heat!" He was "thin" and he feared he might "evaporate into thin air." Yet if he were "fat," he would drown himself in the Arkansas "for fear of being fried in his own substance." "Lo, you, now—it is but seven of the morning, and we are already stifling!" His room, he added, was "a purgatory in the evening."[3]

Despite his enervated condition, Albert entered joyfully and vigorously into his new job. He knew something about typesetting from his brief, ill-fated connection with the *Scrap Book*, but he was almost totally unfamiliar with the rest of the routine of getting out a weekly newspaper. He quickly became proficient at typesetting and printing and, a fast learner, soon mastered the then simple art of news gathering and editorial writing. Before long he was in complete charge of Bertrand's paper.

As a newcomer to Little Rock, Albert was interested in the history of the town. It lay on the south bank of the Arkansas, just below the point where the mighty river dropped out of the Ouachita highlands into the coastal plain. Rocks cropped out of both banks at the site, a circumstance not unlike the fall line separating the Piedmont from the coastal plain in other southern states. But the rocks along the south bank were dwarfed by the north shore's Big Rock that towered above the river two or three miles above the town. The more modest bluff on the south bank, above overflow, sloped gently upward away from the river to the south and west. It received the humble but descriptive pioneer name of "the little rock."[4]

On this site, in 1821, the territorial capital of Arkansas had been located, removed from the less accessible settlement of Arkansas Post. Two sets of claimants had located "town sites" at the place overlapping each other, one set calling its town Little Rock and the other giving its town the pompous classical name of Arkopolis. The dispute was compromised, the capital was retained at the site, and, thanks to the good sense of the rival parties, the familiar homespun name Little Rock was kept.[5]

The town was only twelve years old in 1833, when Pike settled there. It had not quite a thousand inhabitants, but the dirt streets were, he said, "laid off with tolerable regularity . . . running at right angles." Its houses were " a motley mixture; consisting of every variety, from brick blocks of two stories to log cabins—standing in juxtaposition." By far the greatest number were, however, "shingle palaces." Except for one brick church and two wooden ones and the partially completed State House, there were no public buildings to distinguish Little Rock from any other village on the frontier. The State House stood on the free eminence overlooking the river, in plain view of water traffic, but it faced south toward the town. It was, as Pike described it in 1835, "a great, awkward, clumsy, heavy edifice, of brick, with a smaller building on each side—one a court house, and the other for the secretary's office, &c." The main building was, he said, in something less than impartial terms, "partly covered with *tin*; and is commonly called 'Pope's folly.'" When finally completed after 1840 the building, designed as a great, gleaming-white Grecian temple, was nonetheless as magnificent a public building as there was in the country.[6]

The rough-hewn little town had big ideas and obvious advantages. Steamboats gave easy access, at least at high-water mark, to the outside by way of the Arkansas and the Mississippi. And several important roads converged here at a key crossing on the Arkansas—among them the great Southwest Military Road running from southeast Missouri to Fulton on Red River, the Memphis and Little Rock Road, and the Little Rock and Fort Smith Road, down which Pike had journeyed on his way to the capital. Attracted by the land boom of the early thirties, land speculators, lawyers, merchants, saloon and inn keepers, cotton factors, steamboat captains, roustabouts, gamblers, and prostitutes gathered in the ambitious town. Soldiers passed that way, too, on their way to and from their posts in the West, and the hapless Indians plodding their "Trail of Tears" to new lands in the Indian country west of Fort Smith.

Into this active small river port once every two years, in the fall of odd-numbered years, came the tobacco-chewing, whiskey-drinking Arkansas legislators, some with their families and hangers-on. Though a meeting of the territorial legislature was in itself a solemn affair, Arkansas's lawmakers were rugged men with pistols in their pockets and bowie knives in their belts. "The greater portion of the members," Pike said in 1835, "were rough, but sensible and honest; but there were some two or three who would in the East have secured themselves a place in a hospital for idiots."[7]

The territorial legislature was already in session when Albert arrived in Little Rock in 1833, meeting in two rooms of "the long row of frame buildings" belonging to Charles Caldwell. Crittenden got his friends in the council, the upper house of the legislature, to appoint young Pike as assistant secretary beginning the fifth of November.[8]

The young man's position carried considerable responsibility. He assisted in the important task of keeping an accurate council journal and in seeing to it that the whole legislative process in the upper chamber moved smoothly along. Across the clerk's desk flowed an endless stream of bills, resolutions, joint resolutions, and committee reports. It was Albert's job to help make sure that they all moved in proper order day by day from floor to committee, from committee back to floor, from council to house, and finally on to the governor. He learned valuable lessons in lawmaking, got well-acquainted with the members of the council, and was paid a small per diem for his services.

Listening to the picturesque speech of the councilmen, Albert wrote up choice items for the *Advocate*. His amusing report of the debate that fall on a wolf-bounty bill won him a wide audience in papers throughout the country. Councilman Amos Kuykendall of Conway County had proposed a bounty for killing wolves, "a kind of wild fowl, which," as he testified, "had been immensely injurious to the well-being of his pigs." A number of the old man's friends, when the bill came up on the floor of the council, gleefully offered a number of absurd amendments to it in an attempt to make the bill appear ridiculous and thereby to defeat it. Their amendments added bounties for all kinds of wild animals—mink, opossums, panthers, wildcats, catamounts, and even rats. But Kuykendall was deadly serious. Advancing to the secretary's desk, he delivered, said Albert, "the following comprehensive, classical, energetic and nervous speech."

> Mr. President—If I'm in order I want to say this and thus on this here subject. I think it one of the most important, and one of the most glorious, one of the most valuable, frontier works that can be done. Don't treat it with quite that much contempt, for I'm a frontier man. Give it a little! Give it a half dollar! Do, my sons! We are all frontier men. If I want a worthy thing, I'll give it a reason. Now, as to minks, I ha'n't no objection. I've seen a mink catch a chicken—I'll catch a chicken, too, if my wife tells me to, and treat a gentleman. And as to 'possums, I ha'n't no sort of objection. I've seen Virginians climb a persimmon tree, ninety feet high, after a 'possum, and bring back his load on his back home. I don't eat 'possums—I eat hogmeat—that's good—that makes sop. I ask for a wolf first—he's a big fellow—he catches a big hog. Let them that wants a 'possum, catch him and eat him. All them things catches chickens. I only ask a liberal price. May-be you want to treat me with contempt. You daren't do it—you daren't'—I'll meet any of you on even ground. But I'll moderate a lettle—I'll come on a more moderate scale. Understand me, my Sons! You all know *Uncle Amos*; some of you twenty-five year. Now don't let him be brutified! Don't treat him with contempt.[9]

Despite his forensic efforts the old man's bill was defeated, Albert said sorrowfully.[10]

Three years later, in 1836, Albert confessed that he was no longer capable of "marking down and particularizing the peculiarities in the language of the West." Western speech and words had "ceased to be odd or quaint" to the New Englander. "I use them myself." he said.

> For example, the word *mind* is still used here in its meaning of *remember*. Thus, "do you *mind* the time?" &c. "Splurge" is a common word, meaning tumult, noise, &c. "Surrygorous," and "survenomous," are common words. *Husking* is called "shucking." A *throng* is called a "whang." A place where liquor is sold, "a doggery." Hair, bear, stair, id omne genus, are pronounced *har, bar, star,* &c. Contrary is always pronounced with the accent on the second syllable. villain is pronounced vilyain. The word "seen" and "seed" are often used for "saw."[11]

Albert's job as assistant secretary to the council was not permitted to interfere with his duties on the *Advocate*. He found, on joining the paper, that Bertrand was involved in a spirited exchange with Woodruff of the *Gazette* over the public printing. Not only had Sevier defeated Crittenden in the recent election, but Sevierites had gained narrow control of the legislature and, once in session, had promptly awarded the lucrative public printing contract to Sevier's friend Woodruff. Bertrand claimed that the *Advocate's* bid was *"nine and one-quarter per cent"* lower than the *Gazette's* and that "partizan feelings" had influenced the legislature to select Woodruff, which was true enough. But Woodruff quickly denied Bertrand's assertion, claiming his own bid was 5 percent lower than Bertrand's. Bertrand promised to make a thorough exposition of the whole matter.[12]

Bertrand permitted Albert to cut his editorial teeth on this quarrel. Pike executed the assignment with admirable aplomb, and though his powers of invective were as yet in their infancy, he demonstrated that he could compete with the veteran Woodruff at swapping insults.

Woodruff had, Albert maintained, purposely made his bid on the public printing ambiguous so that the legislators could not detect that it was actually higher than Bertrand's. He gave some examples and then declared that it would, of course, do no good for the *Advocate* staff to contend with Woodruff; "they had a character to lose and Woodruff had none."

> We may prove him a liar and a perjurer a hundred times, but it injures him not — nay it renders him more valuable to the *party*, for upon that capacity depends his employment. Let him become honest, and they discard him. — But let him be ready to invent whatever falsehood — to assail whatever character — and to prostitute his paper to whatever ends — and they hug him to their heart. In proportion to the degradation of his moral worth, is the increase of his worth to them.[13]

Albert had not signed his insulting editorial, but Woodruff in the next issue of the *Gazette* scornfully drew attention to it. A "new hand," he said, "applies the bellows of the Crittenden organ." His editorial, "whose song was the loss of the public printing," abounded with more "scurrility and abuse" against the *Gazette* editor than Woodruff ever recalled meeting with before in the columns of the *Advocate*. The "new hand" had performed his task well and no doubt to the satisfaction of his masters; and we congratulate the faction on their acquisition of a writer who bids so fair to sustain the unenvied reputation which their Organ has heretofore maintained for unparalleled effrontery and licentiousness.... In a controversy with an adversary so utterly destitute of moral principles, even a triumph would entitle the victor to no laurels. The game is not worth the ammunition it would cost. We therefore leave the writer to the enjoyment of the unenvied reputation which the personal abuse he has heaped on us will entitle him to from the low and vulgar herd to which he belongs.[14]

When Woodruff refused to debate further the subject of public printing, Albert stung the veteran editor with the satirical doggerel verses of his "Intercepted Letters." The first of these appeared in the *Advocate*, November 20, 1833, and continued from time to time during the next year and a half. The earliest of them purported to be confidential but servile reports from "Old Billy" Woodruff to his master Sevier, who was in Washington. In the first one, Woodruff, after reporting on local affairs, says to Delegate Sevier:

> And now let me give you a little advice,
> Buy golden opinions at whatever price,
> Flatter Members of Congress, and turn every stone
> To help us, your Friends—make the People your own:
> Swear alliance to J[ack]s[o]n and all of his friends,
> And not heeding *principles*, look to the *ends*.
> Should the Hero e'er mention the *Tale of the Tree*,
> When he tells how he shot, be the loudest in glee:
> If he hint at the love that you once bore for C[raw]f[or]d,
> Swear loudly, you left *him*, when J——s——n first offered,
> But say not a word, (do you hear?) that you never
> Left C——f——d, until he was floating down river,
> And tell not that [Chester] A[sh]l[e]y and I never knew
> Any creed until lately but that of John Q. [Adams]
> In short tell the truth when it answers out ends—
> But what is the Truth when compared with your Friends?[15]

Albert's fourth letter in the series, published February 28, 1834, dealt with Sevier's reversing his stand on statehood for Arkansas. In their 1833 race for delegate, Crittenden had favored statehood when Arkansas had the requisite population but Sevier had kept silent on the subject. Yet in December 1833, without informing his friends Woodruff and Ashley, Sevier did an about-face, asking Congress "to inquire into the expediency" of permitting Arkansas to form a constitution preparatory to admission to the Union. Gleefully pouncing on Sevier's turnabout, Pike pictured Billy Woodruff addressing the following anxious lines to Sevier:

> Dear Master! methinks you have taken a course
> That might have been better, could not have been worse.
> For, spite of our wants and our infantile years,
> You are just about lugging us in, head and ears,

> To the Union. Methinks we were better to wait
> For a year or two yet, ere we grow to a State;
> For this I have reasons, so many and strong
> As will surely convince you that you're in the wrong.
> In the first place when once we have grown to a State,
> You'll be shorn of your glory, on colleagues must wait
> And sometimes be guided by them—while at present,
> You rule all yourself—which you know is quite pleasant.
> And very convenient for filling one's pocket;
> If the big chest is shut, we can shortly unlock it—
> But a State—Lord preserve us! our power is over,
> And we feed upon straw where we once fed on clover.
> Let us stay as we are, dearest Master, and best!
> Till we get once or twice more our hands in the chest.[16]

Pike now had both feet planted firmly in the Crittenden camp and was serving his readers weekly helpings of political pabulum both in prose and poem. Woodruff remained silent. Woodruff, it must have appeared to Albert, did not know how to deal with his cleverness. He was about to discover just how tough "Old Billy" could be. On March 4, 1834, only five days after the appearance of his most recent "Intercepted Letter," Pike read in a prominent place in the editorial column of the *Gazette* an anonymous letter signed, "Vale."

> Mr. Editor—Permit me through the medium of your paper, to say to the *fellow* of *otter skin* memory, who has figured so largely of late, in the Advocate, both in *prose* and *verse*, from *Los Tiempos* down to his more recent publication, that it would be *well* for him to keep an ear to the windward, lest a tale should be told that would make even him blush. The *otter* and *mules*, and also the *whipping post*, may be brought up in judgement against him.[17]

Anger mixed with anxiety as young Albert read and reread the letter. Woodruff, he concluded, had made himself a party to a move calculated to destroy his character, drive him from the *Advocate*, and perhaps run him out of Arkansas. The insinuation that he had stolen mules from Harris and otter skins at Van Buren, unless disproved at once, would ruin him. Unburdening his soul to Bertrand, who accepted his word, he was permitted to print in the *Advocate* a lengthy reply to the public. First of all, he described in full his debt to Harris and his innocent involvement and acquittal in the otter skin case; he had, he said, "never before known that to be suspected, and to be honorably and fully acquitted, was a crime." The truth was, he concluded, that he was being attacked by "an underhanded slander" because he had exerted "the little talent which I possess, in defending a course which I embraced when interest could not have swayed me." He would not, however, be frightened from his course by either "insinuating slanders or open attacks." "I am not," he declared, "so easily put out of the way. I have buffeted too many storms, to heed such a slander."[18]

He wrote off at once to the prosecuting attorney, to John Harris, and to others at Van Buren asking for written evidence of his innocence and good character. Their statements came in due course and were published in the *Advocate*. But Woodruff curiously offered his readers no correction nor explanation of the charges against young Pike.[19]

Meanwhile, Albert learned "through intermediaries" that "Vale" was probably James W. Robinson of Logan's Post Office, Pope County. He inquired of Robinson through friends if it was true, but received no satisfactory answer from him. On April 11 young Albert did what was expected of an Arkansas gentleman; he published Robinson as "a base *liar* and *slanderer*." Though a duel was in order, so far as is known Robinson sent no challenge. Out of it all, Albert had learned an important lesson in frontier journalism. It was a hazardous business, especially so with crafty "Old Billy" Woodruff as an opponent. On the other hand, he had demonstrated to "Old Billy" that he could stand the heat and that he was prepared to defend himself on the dueling ground if the need arose—as well it might in Arkansas.[20]

Under Albert the *Advocate* remained what it was meant to be, an anti-Sevier sheet. But he moved the paper in new directions and molded it to fit his own personality and breadth of interests. In it he voiced opinions and expressed views on topics of the day as well as on what he considered to be the needs of the people: the "hard money" chimera—"a great commercial people must have a more transferable currency, than one which is to be carried from one point of the Union to the other in wagons or on pack mules."[21] Western superstitions—the people were superstitious because of a "lack of diffusion of knowledge" among them. They believed that if a man drowned his body could be found by throwing one of his shirts into the stream—the shirt would settle to his body! They believed that every event had its omen, that peculiar noises were always associated with, or preceded, death. In one case, which Pike witnessed, a strange noise was heard, and it was quickly prophesied that the man of the house was sure to die. He did not. The man's fiddle, stored in a trunk, had popped a string![22] Tobacco chewing—an irate Little Rock hostess wrote to Pike that she would give no more parties for the young people of the town unless the young men could refrain thereafter from spitting tobacco juice on "my wainscots and finely papered walls, and my sideboards."[23]

Having encountered firsthand the "lamentable want of facilities of education" in Arkansas, Albert wrote again and again on the subject. He blamed both the lack of school buildings and the poor quality of the available teachers on "the people." They had not organized to support a general system of schools, and they did not pay enough to attract competent teachers. He proposed that each county be divided into a number of school districts, each district having a centrally located schoolhouse to be built at county expense. A county committee of school examiners would visit each school regularly to check on standards and efficient operation. Above all, he would have every teacher paid at least forty-five dollars a month, a fund for that purpose to be created from the sale of federal sixteenth-section school lands and from fines collected for certain specified crimes and misdemeanors.[24]

In Massachusetts the public school system was, Albert argued, supported by a direct annual tax on property. There was no injustice in this, for "education is a general blessing." Other states, he continued, operated schools out of income from a general school fund built and maintained from various sources—school lands, taxes, and fines. Arkansas could use any of these methods in time, but at present it was believed by many that none was possible in a territory. Meanwhile, if adopted by the people in the counties, his own county-district plan was feasible and would give them a good start until a more permanent general system could be enacted after statehood.[25]

Nothing came of Albert's school proposal, but his New England conscience would not permit him to drop the subject. He had no patience at all with those who argued that Arkansas was too new a territory or too poor to afford good schools. "If we do live within a mile or two of sunset," he protested in January 1835, "it is no reason why we should be worse supplied with schools than any part of the Union or its Territories." He would welcome, he said, "any communications" on the subject of education. "There is no more important theme on which men can write—there is none which should be more continually urged upon the community. We shall certainly urge it upon the consideration of the next legislature."[26]

If Arkansas's schools were almost nonexistent, Little Rock's stump-strewn streets were in full view of Editor Pike, and he never ceased reminding the town council of the need for repairs. He complained, in June 1834, that his "editorial dignity" recently had been nearly laid low by "certain old acquaintances of ours, in the shape of stumps, that greet us every rod or two." Moreover, the "grass grows and the gullies deepen—although certain ordinances hang over them in *terrorem*—and have hung for months." There was also a "certain ordinance covering dogs" which the mayor and council might well enforce. A month later Albert invited his fellow citizens to stand in the middle of the town and look up Main Street. It was filthy, filled with gullies, and littered with rubbish swept or thrown into the street; yet the town officers did nothing. "One thing we are resolved on," he declared. "The town shall be improved, or they shall not soon hear the last of it."[27]

Albert's efforts on behalf of certain cultural improvements at Little Rock were more fruitful than his attempt at securing street improvements. He joined the Little Rock Debating Society, which in 1834 had charge of the city's important Fourth of July celebration. His first known speech in Little Rock was his "Independence Day Address" delivered before the Debating Society that year. He spoke in the Presbyterian Church with a public dinner following at the Eagle Hotel and with Governor Pope and other territorial and city functionaries in attendance.[28]

Published by the *Advocate* "by request of the Society," Albert's oration was not unlike other long addresses expected of Independence Day speakers of the time. He demonstrated that he had been brought up in a venerable tradition, speaking with reverence of the Declaration; the writers of the Constitution—"the noblest work of the power of the human intellect" under which "we have become a great and mighty nation"; and the American people—"the freest people in the world and they should remind themselves of their blessing."

But there was, young Albert warned his audience, afoot in the land a threat to America's freedom—the "spirit of disunion." He saw men at work in the North and the South stirring up the people, inflaming their minds against one another, and threatening thereby the unity of the nation. He believed the people would see through this demagoguery, but they must be ever vigilant and never surrender their birthright to demagogues. If the American people lived up to their destiny, and he felt confident they would—for "the spirit of '76 lives yet" in their hearts and minds—there was no limit to their progress.

He turned, in closing, to the women in his audience and to his fellow Debating Society members. On woman, "beautiful woman," depended the fulfillment of "our dream" and the fate of the nation. He asked them to teach their children love of country and the meaning and worth of freedom. He thanked them for honoring him as their speaker. Men like them, concerned with America's destiny, had a duty to country and to society and were fulfilling it. Together they could guarantee to posterity education, a free press, and liberty.[29]

A would-be magazine editor, Albert gave the *Advocate* a more literary character. He reprinted in its columns many of his own poems and prose pieces as well as publishing many of his own original writings. He got immense personal satisfaction from his column "The Walking Gentleman," which permitted him to indulge his fondness for literary criticism and his desire to instill in his readers a love for and knowledge of literature.[30]

In two numbers of his column, in August 1834, Albert took a perceptive look at American poets. America had, he said, no great poets: it was not because America's poets did not have "imagination and fancy" but because they lacked the "industry and application necessary to produce a sustained and powerful work." Unlike their counterparts in England, American poets and writers were not patronized by a "powerful moneyed aristocracy." Accordingly, American writers had to look to the professions for livelihoods and gave only passing attention to literary efforts. There was likewise small inducement in the United States held out "to the exertion of intellectual labor." "The country," he concluded, "is too new, as yet, to offer the same reward as is offered in England, either in money or fame—and this applies particularly to the West." There was, he confessed, "no hope in the West at all."[31]

But Albert was determined that his fellow westerners in Arkansas should, at least, be taught to appreciate America's literary efforts. "Let no man scoff at or depreciate literature—and especially poetry. It is the purifier of the human heart—the concentration of the best and most exalted feelings of humanity." He pitied anyone who had in his soul no appreciation for poetry.[32]

Sketching for his readers the leading American poets, Albert singled out five. He named William Cullen Bryant, Fitz-Greene Halleck, James Gates Percival, Nathaniel Parker Willis, and Mrs. Lydia Sigourney, who was to become famous afterwards as editor of *Godey's Lady's Book*.

A newspaperman, Bryant was, Albert said, not as free as he should be to cultivate his talent for poetry. Albert nevertheless wanted from Bryant a "connected poem," and declared that he "owes" it to his country and to his "own character." Albert did not know Halleck's profession—he was a clerk in the counting house of John Jacob Astor—but felt that his poetry possessed more spirit and fire, though less stateliness and dignity, than Bryant's. The public had a right to demand of Halleck that he "add something substantial to the stores of literature." Percival was, Albert felt, "without a doubt the most deeply imbued with poetic feeling of any man in this country." A professor at Yale College, Percival had of late allowed his "muse to sleep." He also wrote too fast and failed to "polish and correct" but had great promise as a poet. At first overrated and then condemned by the public, Nathaniel Parker Willis, editor of the prestigious *American Monthly Magazine*, had been most unfortunate. His advice to Willis, who was and would remain his close friend, was that he study for "at least five years," for he had "many faults but also many beauties." Finally, there was Mrs. Sigourney, "one of our best writers," who while she never "rises very high" also never "falls below herself." But Albert thought she had added much to "the character of our country," even though her poetry lacked "intensity and life"—he might have added that it was characterized by a sickening sentimentality and morality.[33]

To be sure, Pike's literary criticism in the "Walking Gentleman" was neither brilliant nor profound, but it did reveal that he was reading America's poets, that he was aware of their handicaps and limitations, and that he was concerned about their problems. A proud American nationalist, he wanted his country's writers to produce a body of literature in which the country could take great pride. He also wanted Arkansans to be as aware of it as easterners, and the *Advocate* afforded him a means of communicating this knowledge.

The town Debating Society offered Albert an additional forum for advancing interest in literature. What is believed to be his second appearance before this group was his reading of an "essay" on "the comparative genius" of Shakespeare and Byron. Assigned the subject, Albert complained affably if modestly to his fellows that they had asked a "thrush" to judge the flight of "two eagles." Bulwer's *England and the English* furnished him, he acknowledged, "some few of the thoughts" for the comparison. In his essay he concluded that Shakespeare's "delineation of character" and "language and versification," written in blank verse, were superior to Byron's; but that Byron's "fancy and imagination" and "diction" were "not inferior" nor less "brilliant" than the old master's. Yet it was Albert's eloquent reading of comparative samples of their poetry that impressed his listeners, and at their request he printed the essay in the *Advocate*.[34]

Albert's first year in Little Rock coincided, not accidentally, with the organization of a "little theatre" movement in the town. A backer of the project, possibly a prime mover in it, he devoted a third of a column to the announcement of the organization meeting of a "Thespian Society" to be held at "early candle-light" on Saturday, September 27, 1834. The organizers approved a constitution, named themselves "The Thespian Society," and made plans to fit up for their theatrical uses "that large room of Mr. Caldwell's, opposite Dr. Cunningham's."[35] A month afterwards, in late October, Albert happily announced that "the corps" of the Thalians had the room ready and would perform the comedy of the "Soldier's Daughter" on opening night, Monday, November 3. An address would precede the play, while songs, recitations, and good music would conclude the evening's program. Tickets were a dollar—children and servants half-price. Albert especially urged the ladies of Little Rock to give the Thalians their encouragement.[36]

If all his activities made it appear that Albert had settled permanently in Little Rock, the observation was correct. Sometime during the winter of 1833–34 he came to an important decision about what to do with himself. Teaching was out of the question, finding a suitable literary position in New England seemed hopeless, and newspapering in Little Rock offered little hope of a livelihood. Most of his friends and acquaintances in the capital were lawyers, and there appeared to be no end to the need for them in the rapidly settling land. He would, he decided, remain in Arkansas and become a lawyer.[37]

His decision made, Albert borrowed, most likely from Robert Crittenden, Kent's *Commentaries on American Law* and Blackstone's *Commentaries* and began to read. In August 1834, after he had completed Kent and the first volume of Blackstone, he sought out Judge Thomas J. Lacy of the Superior Court of Arkansas Territory and requested a license to practice law.[38]

A Kentuckian who had read law under Governor Pope back in the Bluegrass State, Judge Lacy owed his appointment to the Arkansas court to Governor Pope rather than Sevier. Albert had noted this editorially at the time of Lacy's appointment, in the spring of 1834, seeking to expose the fact that Governor Pope and Delegate Sevier had broken politically.[39] Young Pike's flattering notices of Judge Lacy, who unlike many other territorial officials moved his family to Arkansas and took up residence, were obviously not calculated to hurt his chances for the upcoming bar examination. The affable judge quizzed him perfunctorily and awarded him his license, commenting off-handedly that giving a law license was not like granting a medical license: a lawyer could take no one's life, while a doctor could. Albert had good reason to recall the judge's words, for soon afterward he and another new attorney were appointed to defend an indigent man for murder. The jury convicted him and he was hanged. "I have defended twenty," Pike later said, "and he was the only one among them all that was convicted, and the only one that ought *not* to have been hung."[40]

A short but ardent poem, "To Miss Mary ———," appearing in the *Advocate*, December 18, 1833, intimated that Albert had something besides newspapering and law books on his mind that first winter at Little Rock. Supposedly the poem was meant for the eyes of pretty Mary Ann Hamilton of Arkansas Post, a tiny settlement on the north bank of the Arkansas River some eighty miles below Little Rock. Albert first met her in the fall of 1833, when she accompanied her guardian Terence Farrelly, who was a councilman, to Little Rock for the legislative session. Deeply impressed by the beauty of the tall, shapely brunette maiden, Albert is said to have fallen in love with her at first sight. He may have begun courting her that fall, when he was assistant secretary of the council, and he seemingly continued to shower his affection upon her by letter and verse after her return to the Post.[41]

They became better acquainted in the summer of 1834 when Mary Ann came back to Little Rock to appear before the superior court in the case dealing with her deceased father's estate. According to Pike, Judge Lacy was their mutual friend and helped further their romance. The kindly judge delivered the opinion of the court in her favor, and, struck by the beauty of the young girl and the tragedy that had marked her life, looked upon her thereafter as a sort of ward.[42]

Mary Ann Hamilton was a beautiful girl, and she was considered something of a catch. Born in 1816, she was the third daughter of James and Drusilla Hamilton, who had settled at Arkansas Post before 1820. Her father, one of the founders in 1821 of the town of Arkansas Post, had been a well-to-do planter, slaveholder, and land speculator, a member of and a friend of the ruling clique in Arkansas County. He died in the early twenties and her mother afterwards married William H. Lenox of the Post. Left an orphan in 1828 when her mother and two older sisters were drowned in the Arkansas River, Mary Ann and her eleven-year-old sister Margaret had gone to live with a court-appointed guardian, Terence Farrelly, a wealthy Irish immigrant who owned a cotton plantation near the Post. There the two girls grew to womanhood, loved by their father's friend Farrelly as if they were his own daughters.[43]

By the time Albert was admitted to the bar in August 1834, his courtship of Mary Ann had proved successful. He accordingly wrote to his Boston friend George W. Light, August 18, 1834, that he was "just on the eve of committing *matrimony*. Here then I shall be a Western lawyer, with a Western Wife."[44] Three days later, on August 22, his first card appeared in the *Advocate*:

ALBERT PIKE
ATTORNEY AT LAW—Resides in Little Rock, and will practice in the 1st and 4th Judicial Circuits and the Superior Court of the Territory.

V

A Great Man in Israel

ALBERT PIKE was a very happy young man in 1834 as August and September gave way to a balmy October. He had been admitted to the bar and had the promise of a lucrative partnership with William Cummins, an established Little Rock attorney with good family connections in the territory. Consequently, Albert quit his position on the *Advocate* and early in October announced that he would be "obliged to go to the Post and remain in that vicinity for three months."[1] He was going to claim his bride.

Crossing the ferry at Little Rock, he set out alone on horseback down the river road to Arkansas Post. Already debilitated by a summer's bout with malaria, he now suffered recurring attacks of chills and fever. He dosed himself with quinine, conquered the fever, and in due course arrived at Terence Farrelly's plantation, fifteen miles above the Post at Farrelly's Bend on the Arkansas. He was greeted by Mary Ann and a host of Colonel Farrelly's friends and neighbors. They had gathered to celebrate the Pike-Hamilton wedding, which, as young Pike discovered, would consist of a month's round of "festivities."[2]

Albert was marrying into a circle of landed, close-knit Arkansas Post families. Colonel Farrelly, Col. Frederick Notrebe, and Capt. Benjamin Desha headed the most prominent families. All three of them had come to Arkansas as poor but enterprising men. By hard work and ability, a measure of good luck, and careful attention to opportunities, they had prospered. They acquired vast acreages. Among them slaves became more numerous, livestock multiplied, and the cotton raised on expanding plantations crowded their steamboat landings. By the thirties they enjoyed luxuries, a leisure, and much power. The wilderness, for them, had given way to a prosperous plantation society. An ambitious young attorney could hardly have had three more influential friends.

Terence Farrelly had been born in Ireland about 1795, but as a lad of five immigrated with his parents to America and settled in Pennsylvania. He grew up there and became a merchant. Seeking his fortune in the West, he formed a partnership with another Irishman, Thomas Curran, and immigrated to Arkansas Post. They arrived in 1819, the year Arkansas Territory was created.[3]

Circumstances favored Farrelly. His partner married and moved away, while he bought out their mercantile establishment and remained at the Post. One of his competitors was pretty Mary Mosely, the young widow of a Scotch merchant. Farrelly courted and married Mary in 1820, acquiring thereby not only her store and its stock, but also a considerable amount of real estate. From the profits of his mercantile establishments and land Farrelly acquired more land, bought slaves, raised cotton, and grew wealthy. Outgoing and friendly, he formed valuable social and political friendships in

Arkansas County, which he represented in the territorial legislature, first in the house and afterwards in the council, from 1823 until the time of statehood. He also served as adjutant general of the Arkansas militia and in 1836 became a delegate to the constitutional convention.[4]

Farrelly was the father of eight children, borne him by Mary, but he worshipped his foster daughters, the Hamilton sisters, whose estate he had carefully watched over since 1829. He welcomed young Pike into his family as though he were a beloved son. Albert, after his marriage, would spend many a pleasant day in the company of "dear old Terence Farrelly."[5]

Col. Frederick Notrebe, Farrelly's close friend and neighbor, was a Frenchman by birth, a foot soldier of the First Republic who had fled both the army and France during Napoleon's antirepublican regime and made his way to New Orleans. He settled at Arkansas Post about 1810, operated a trading post and a cotton factoring business and made large profits from both. Investing in the cheap but rich lands about the Post, he became a wealthy land speculator and planter. By 1833 he owned large brick homes both at the Post and on his plantation three miles below the Post, entertained lavishly, and was by all odds, "the great man" of the area. Washington Irving, passing through the Post in 1833, observed that the Frenchman Notrebe lived the life of a Don, taking his own servant and his own personal wine with him when he traveled by steamboat—the "steam boat wine" did not suit the colonel's sensitive palate.[6] Pike became very fond of Notrebe, was a frequent guest at his home in Arkansas Post and at his plantation, where he enjoyed his good wine and food. Notrebe's daughter, Francine, was married to Pike's prospective law partner, William Cummins.[7]

Capt. Benjamin Desha, a descendent of French Huguenots, owned an 800-acre plantation at Desha's Bend on the Arkansas adjoining Farrelly's. A Tennessean by birth, he had during his youth been taken to Kentucky where his father, Joseph Desha, became a prominent politician. Ben served as a captain of dragoons in the War of 1812, farmed afterward in Kentucky, and was several times sent to the state legislature. His brother-in-law, Hartwell Boswell, register of public lands at Batesville, secured him the office of receiver of public moneys at Little Rock in 1824; he replaced no other than Henry Conway who had just been elected delegate to Congress.[8]

In Little Rock, Ben became a close friend and supporter of fellow Kentuckian Robert Crittenden, served as Crittenden's second in his duel with Conway, and was an unsuccessful candidate against Ambrose Sevier in 1831. By 1831, when he left the receiver's office, Desha had acquired a plantation and a sizable slave force in Arkansas County. He was, said Pike, who first met him at Farrelly's in 1834, "a large, stately man, fitted to be an emperor. I never saw such eyes in any human head as his . . . large, luminous, brilliant, terrible in anger." Pike saw Desha "once at the Post of Arkansas drive a faro-dealer, who menaced him with a Bowie-knife, out of the room by advancing upon him with a penknife, his eyes blazing. . . ." Unless provoked, he was nonetheless a peaceful, good-natured man, "a king among men," Pike said.[9]

On November 18, 1834, in the presence of a throng of Farrelly-Notrebe-Desha relatives and neighbors, Albert and Mary were wedded.[10] James H. Lucas, judge of the

Arkansas County probate court and a man of no little political influence himself, solemnized the rites.[11] The couple made an impressive picture. Pike, at almost twenty-five, was tall and broad shouldered, though much slenderer and more muscular than he was afterwards to be. His military erectness and patrician bearing gave him the appearance of being formal, stiff, unbending, standoffish. His large head, his long, black, flowing, wavy hair combed back from a broad forehead, his handsome face with its sallow skin, its neatly trimmed black mustache and beard, its long, prominent nose, its generous mouth and full lips, and its large, clear, rolling black eyes suggested a refined romantic nature that made Pike so impressive to those about him. The flowing hair and beard were, however, the trademarks that most distinguished him. Mary Ann, at eighteen, tall and dark with raven curls and fine black eyes, made an equally impressive sight on the occasion of their wedding.

A round of dinners and parties followed the wedding, after which Albert and Mary Ann returned to reside at Little Rock. Pike had expected to enter at once into partnership with Cummins, but he was disappointed. The politically ambitious Cummins, hoping to use Pike's connections with the *Advocate* to promote his career, reconsidered his offer and declined to make Pike his partner on learning that he had quit the newspaper.[12]

On top of this misfortune came the sad news about the of January 1, 1835, that Crittenden had died suddenly in Vicksburg on December 18. The loss of his influential friend at this particular time must have been a severe blow to Pike, for he had been robbed of the one man who might have guided him through the early, tough years of establishing himself as an attorney. Bertrand, suffering from ill health himself, took Crittenden's death hardest of all. He decided to sell the *Advocate* and apply himself fully to his own law practice. He offered the paper to Pike for $2,650.[13]

Anxious to obtain the *Advocate*, Albert agreed to Bertrand's terms. Under his contract, signed the sixteenth of January, he was to pay $1,150 within four weeks, $750 more in six months, and the final $750 in twelve months—the entire debt to be paid within one year. He mortgaged to Bertrand Mary Ann's undivided one-half interest in her and her sister Margaret's slaves to guarantee the debt, and he sold enough of her lands to meet the first payment and possibly to also meet the other two payments. For his investment Pike received Bertrand's entire "printing establishment" together with the indentures of Bertrand's apprentices George W. McSweany and Baptiste Suggett, but not the house nor the lot upon which it stood. Though it was not in his contract, he also acquired with the paper an experienced journeyman printer and assistant editor, Charles E. Rice.[14]

Pike brought out the first issue of the *Advocate* under his own name on the twenty-third of January. In an editorial note Bertrand explained that he had sold the paper to Pike because of his own "continued bad health, and by that cause alone." He assured his readers that under Pike the paper would "undergo no change in its principles."[15]

As for his own statement, Pike took a full column to affirm his loyalty to "the measures and men ever defended by the paper of which we now assume the entire control." As a territory, Arkansas could not participate in national elections, and consequently, had little concern with "the general politics of the country." But Pike wanted to make his own position clear. He had identified his own prosperity and his future with Arkansas and the West and "the cotton growing States." He would, consequently, support the national system of policy which would most benefit his region. "We would," he said, "have no Land Bill, and no Tariff for the protection of the North-east. We would have a National Bank, and a Western President—and finally, we would have no public officer who had not talent, and as much honesty as is consistent, in these days, with the character of a public man."[16]

He would, he said, be bold and unflinching but courteous in support of all the measures he had hitherto supported. He emphasized the need for "proper courtesy" thereafter in Arkansas's press in order to help rescue the territory "from some of the reproaches which have been cast upon her." He was sure the Advocate would be tagged as "the organ of a party or of a man." It certainly would not be such. "We buy this paper," he declared, "with our own means, and owe nobody any favor therefor. It is our own—wholly and entirely—and if we choose to support any man for any office, it will be more through affection than through obligation."[17]

He added a sincere paragraph about his ambitions for the Advocate. He wished to enlarge it if he could get adequate subscriptions, to use his "best exertions" to make it a good newspaper, and to give it "a more literary character." "We only ask," he said in closing, "'no jockeying, and a clear track.'"[18]

Pike owned the Advocate for slightly over two years, and found it to be less than a paying proposition. But in another sense it succeeded.[19] It brought him into personal contact with the leading men of the Crittenden faction, many of whom, like Jesse Turner of Van Buren, David Walker of Fayetteville, Hiram A. Whittington of Hot Springs, and Terence Farrelly of Arkansas County, were agents of the Advocate. And it won him, in March 1835, the coveted partnership with Cummins. "I am now," he wrote March 8, 1835, to New England, "Sir, Attorney and Counsellor at Law—Editor—Benedict—and a great man in Israel. I imagine I am settled here for my life time. After all there is something to being looked up to—even in Arkansas."[20]

Pike's purchase of the Advocate may well have grown from a secret ambition for a political career. Admission to the bar and ownership of a newspaper were the normal means for seeking political preferment, yet Pike never announced as a candidate for any office in Arkansas, and he always denied having any desire for a political career. But he was a political animal, and he came to exercise more than a little political power in Arkansas. Through the Advocate he rallied the dispirited Crittenden faction and became a major voice in shaping Arkansas's antebellum two-party system.

For us, however, since Pike did not keep a diary and because his personal correspondence of the period is, for the most part, missing, the Advocate opens a window on his life. There is a fascination in looking through it, in observing how he lived, how he conducted the paper, and how he felt about the local and national issues of the day.

That he and Mary Ann were living in a house to themselves during the years 1835–39 may be deduced from a notice which Pike inserted in the Advocate, May 22, 1835:

> Whereas certain unprincipled hogs have contracted a vile habit of making forcible entry into my garden, by demolishing the fence—to the great injury of the vegetables therein—And whereas, also, I have read the riot act to them sundry times

without its producing any salutary effect—This is to give notice, that after tomorrow, I shall be in the habit, for my own recreation, of discharging sundry guns, pistols, etc. on my premises—loaded with shot and powder—and that it is very possible that some of the said shot might by accident hit some of the said hogs, unless the owners would take some care of their four legged property.

When his vegetable garden succumbed either to the hogs or to the hot summer weather, Pike complained in late July about the high cost of "vegetables and produce" in the Little Rock market. "We are forced," he said, "to give . . . a dollar a bushel for Irish potatoes, (and be it known, we are a lover of praties,) two dollars a bushel for onions, two bits a pound for butter, a bit a dozen for tomatoes; and every thing in the same proportion—prices which we do not find at all congenial to our poor editorial pocket." He expressed a wish that a colony of "Yankee farmers" would settle near Little Rock. At those prices they could, he said, be rich in a year.[21]

The tomato was one of Pike's favorite vegetables, though he found there were in the country at large many unfounded prejudices against it. This led him, in September 1835, to defend the tomato editorially as a cure for "the Liver Complaint." It had, he testified, been effective personally for him, and he cited medical evidence to support his case for the much-maligned vegetable. From the *Medical and Surgical Journal* he reprinted an article that castigated the silly superstitions about the tomato, and from an "interior" paper he copied an article that appraised the wonderful curative powers of tomatoes in treating disease.[22]

Newspapermen in rural Arkansas were notorious beggars of fresh vegetables, and Pike fostered the tradition. In the late fall of 1836, complaining again about the high cost of "provisions," Pike noted that the editor of the *Gazette* had acknowledged receipt of a bottle of champagne and a single potato that was so large it "supplied two dinner parties." The *Gazette* editor, in an expansive mood, had requested "a turnip to do for a week." Pike hoped his own friends would not "permit themselves to be outdone in civility."[23]

A circuit-riding lawyer, Pike traveled on horseback in the spring of 1835 as far southwest as Hot Springs and as far west as Van Buren on the Indian border. The road to Arkansas's famous watering place he found well settled along either side, and he was impressed with the Hot Springs and the settlement that had grown up there. It was destined, he believed, to be a great and fashionable resort for the Southwest. He probably sampled the water and baths, for he spoke knowingly and positively of their curative powers. "In all chronic diseases and bilious attacks," he wrote, "these waters are of great use. Bath houses and sweat houses are already built—and experience is daily showing the value of these waters." Speaking of the "natural magnet" in the earth at nearby Magnet Cove, Pike explained that it so affected compasses that much of the land about Hot Springs had not been surveyed. Moreover, he noted that the title to the Hot Springs themselves was in dispute between the U.S. government, who had reserved the lands from public sale, and conflicting private claimants.[24] Pike may well have gotten his information about Hot Springs and the land claims from Henry M. Rector, whose own claim to the springs he later handled.

Pike's trip to Van Buren, in late August–early September of 1835 took him through the fine "upland" country north of the Arkansas River in Johnson County. He was much impressed with the upland and praised it in his paper. Covered with post oak and luxuriant grass, it was, he said, easier cleared than the heavily timbered and cane-infested bottom land. The upland was bedded on hard clay which permitted it to hold moisture better than the bottom land, and it was healthier because, as he explained, plowing up the bottoms opened a "miasma" of decayed vegetable matter into the air and contributed to the sickness so common among settlers there.[25] Pike did not know, of course, that the mosquito was the primary cause of spreading sickness along the rivers.

When legal business concerning his wife's estate took him in November to Farrelly's plantation in Arkansas County, Pike apparently accompanied Farrelly and other Arkansas County planters to New Orleans. He was gone three weeks and on his return to Little Rock the first week of December had much to report on the cotton crop but nothing about his trip. This was not strange, for cotton was what his friends talked about most of the time and what his readers were immensely interested in also. In Arkansas, Pike reported, there would be only half a crop of cotton raised, in Tennessee about the same, in Mississippi a "common crop," while South Carolina and Georgia would have "good crops." The price of cotton was, he said, down from about sixteen to eighteen cents a pound to twelve and one-half to fourteen cents from the previous year, and planters were holding back their crops in anticipation of a rise. Pike was pessimistic about their chances, for advice from Europe did not favor a rise in price.[26]

Pike returned to Little Rock in time for the birth of his and Mary Ann's first child on December 2, 1835. The baby was a boy, and they named him Ben Desha after their good friend who had died in Arkansas County on the twenty-first of November. A proud new father, Pike on the evening of the second treated his friends to champagne. The boisterous celebration, held downtown in the surveyor general's office, involved Pike unexpectedly in a mild social scandal.[27]

The new editor of the *Times*, John H. Reed, who was either a prude or a meddlesome joker, published a pseudonymous account of the "*frolic in the Surveyor General's Office*" and of the "comical looking genius" who hosted it.[28] Pike probably would have ignored the article had it not been for the fact that a clerk in the surveyor general's office, Pike's friend, had foolishly permitted the party to be held there without thinking of the consequence. The surveyor general was none other than James Sevier Conway, who less than a year later became Arkansas's first governor, and Pike may well have feared that Conway would fire the clerk for involving the office in a scandal.

Consequently, Pike marched to Reed's office and angrily demanded the author's name. Doubtlessly surprised at Pike's reaction, Reed stalled. He would, he said, consult with the author. Scurrying about town, Reed tried to persuade several of his friends to acknowledge authorship of the piece. At last he found one, but not before Pike learned from a mutual friend that Reed was the author. Accordingly, Pike blasted Reed for his "scurrilous article" against the surveyor general's office and against his friend the clerk, and revealed the "secret history" of Reed's "communication": "If men have courage enough to *write* and publish such effusions of private malice," declared Pike, "they should also be brave enough to acknowledge them. To make other men father such foundlings, is worse than throwing them on the parish." Pike had the good sense not to challenge Reed over the matter.[29]

Presumably it was in the small "humble" house, molested by the town's wandering hogs back in the spring of 1835, that Mary Ann gave birth in December to Ben Desha. Here also were born Albert on February 23, 1837, and Luther Hamilton on August 20, 1838. Ben Desha lived but fifteen months, while Albert lived only two days. But Luther Hamilton, called Hamilton by the Pikes, grew to manhood and survived his parents, dying in Washington, D.C., January 9, 1895. He was named after Mary Ann's family and after Pike's close friend Luther Chase, who, it will be remembered, had been with Pike on their trip to Santa Fe and back and who had since moved from Massachusetts to Arkansas to be near Pike.[30]

Before their fourth son, Walter Lacy, was born, June 29, 1840, Pike had erected in southeast Little Rock the famous mansion that stands to this day as a mute symbol of his legendary life. Occupying extensive grounds of more than a city block in area, the house was built by a private contractor at a cost of $7,500, which Pike raised by selling some of Mary Ann's property. The two-story structure, fifty-four feet wide and forty-two feet from front to rear is built in the classic style of the period. Its imposing portico, supported by six large white Ionic columns, rises two stories high and extends completely across the front of the house. There is no pediment but the front facade is capped by the chaste lines of a wide cornice above the pillars.

Facing north and shaded by the Greek portico, nine large shuttered windows and a great classic doorway look out through the columns upon a broad level expanse of lawn studded with giant oaks, magnolias, and locusts. A wide brick walk extends straight as an arrow from the front steps to the street—Seventh Street today—which the mansion faces.

The sash windows, the shutters, and the classic doorway are beautiful in their workmanship. Fitted with a giant lock requiring an eight-inch key, the massive front door opens into a broad central hallway, flanked on either side by two large rooms, each twenty feet square with thirteen-foot ceilings. At the rear of the hall a stairway, simple and plain in its design but handsome in its fine craftsmanship, rises to the wide central hallway of the second floor. Here there are also four rooms, two on each side of the hall, equal in size to those below, except with twelve-foot ceilings. Four chimneys, two at each end of the house, accommodate the eight fireplaces which, in Pike's day, heated the eight rooms. The large attic had no fireplace.

The eighteen-inch outer walls and the narrower inner walls along the halls were built of brick, laid on a stone foundation. Under the southwest room a stone-lined wine cellar seven feet deep and twenty feet square held, in Pike's day, many "a bottle of bright, sparking wine, / From sunny France." As was common in such houses, there were no bathrooms. The Pikes used a toilet detached from the house and chamber pots at night and in inclement weather. Their weekly baths on Saturday afternoons were taken in basins or tin tubs brought to them by black servants. Likewise, the kitchen was also detached from the house, and their food was carried by servants to the dining table located in the back room above Pike's wine cellar. Water for drinking, cooking, and bathing was drawn from a shallow hand-dug well situated a few yards southwest of the house, near the kitchen. Their slaves' quarters were some distance behind the house; and far to the rear in the southeast corner of the grounds were the barn and stables where Pike's horses, carriages, milk cows, and chickens were kept. A cistern built at the stable furnished water for the animals.[31]

Of Pike's life in this house we know but little. Try as hard as we can to ferret out the facts that might be pieced together to give us a picture of his life there, we must admit that we catch no more than fleeting glimpses of him at the place.

Certainly by the mid-forties Pike was a successful, prosperous lawyer. Times were improving after the long dark years of the depression that set in in 1837. He still, it is true, indulged in an occasional outburst against certain unavoidable and unpleasant features of living in "this out of the world region." But he owned a fine, well-furnished home, kept his cellar well stocked with French wines and his larder stored with good food, had a steady and sufficient income for his family's needs, owned a number of household slaves to serve and wait on his and his family's every whim, and had the love and esteem of a number of friends and neighbors.

Therefore, living in the big house with Mary Ann and the children was pleasant, as one of the many poems he wrote at this time reveals:

> Here will I make myself a golden age,
> Here live content, and happier than a King.
> Nor bird that swings and sleeps in his small nest,
> Nor bee that revels in the jasmine-blooms,
> Nor humming-bird, that robs the honeysuckle,
> Nor cricket, nested under the warm hearth,
> Shall sing or work more cheerfully than I.[32]

Of the three sons born to them in the thirties, only Luther Hamilton, born in 1838, survived infancy. Seven more children were added in the forties: Walter Lacy, June 29, 1840; Isadore, January 20, 1842; Lilian, February 22, 1843; Albert Holden, October 4, 1844; Clarence, August 18, 1846; Eustace, February 20, 1848; and the last, a son Yvon, September 10, 1849. Clarence and Eustace both died in 1848, the former on February 20 and the latter on July 24.[33]

Pike's poem "An Invitation," written for Mary Ann in the spring of 1845, gives us a glimpse of one fleeting moment in his life with her and the children. It was just before sunrise on a clear morning in May. Pike was sitting beneath a circle of tall oak trees in his yard. Around him Mary Ann's roses and flowers—yellow jasmine, wild honeysuckle, and the coral woodbine—bloomed in profusion. A martin sang "a merry note upon the ivied eaves," hummingbirds and bees darted like "tiny thieves" among the sweet-scented blossoms, and far above, perched near his mate's nest, a southern mockingbird, Pike's favorite, trilled forth his "many voiced song."[34]

To this idyllic scene Pike addressed "An Invitation" to Mary Ann:

> Come out and sit with me, dear wife, beneath these branching trees,
> And let our little children come, and clamber on our knees.
> It is a sweet, soft, pleasant morn, the loveliest in May,
> And their little hearts are beating fast, longing to be at play.[35]

There were, he said to Mary Ann, five "sturdy oaks" clustered around them among the many trees he and she had planted on their grounds. He proposed to her that they name the five oaks after their five children:

> This tallest one for HAMILTON, our little manly boy,
> Whose dark and thoughtful eyes are now so radiant with joy;
> This, WALTER's, whose bright, dancing ones with merry mischief shine,
> But still, affectionate and kind, are images of thine.
>
> This, for our silent little girl, the quiet ISADORE,
> Who sits demurely working at her doll's new pinafore;
> This, for our blue-eyed LILIAN, the merriest of all;
> This smallest, for the babe, that by his father's name we call.[36]

Having named the trees, Pike turned to Mary Ann, told her how happy she had made him for more than ten years, how fast their years together had passed, but how happy their future years will be if these "dear" children "all are spared." Together he and Mary Ann would, he said, make their children "virtuous, honest, true, kind, generous"; and when they have grown "to lovely women, and true-hearted, gallant men," he and Mary Ann could die content knowing that "In our sweet children's virtues we shall live and love again." It was pleasant to think also, he said to Mary Ann, that the five green oaks he and she had planted on their grounds and named after their children would bless their children's children "with their shade."[37]

"An Evening Conversation," a poem written in 1845, depicts Pike playing with his children beneath the trees of his expansive lawn. It was late afternoon on a sunny spring day. Since noon, Pike had lain on his lawn beneath "a pillared circle of old trees" reading by turns from "this and that old book" of his favorite writers—"Fuller, Montaigne, and good Sir Thomas Browne, Feltham and Herbert." His children played around him on the grass—"Sad rogues that interrupted my thought, and did perplex my reading." One of them in particular, Isadore, a "little chattering girl with bright brown eyes," was his pet, knew it, "and of it took advantage."[38]

In a quiet interlude, when Pike had turned idly from his children to his reading, he heard a step along the shaded front walk. Looking up, he saw that it was Luther Chase, "the dearest of my friends." After briefly relating the hardships and dangers he and Chase had endured together in the desert and mountains of the Far West, Pike described how, on this occasion, they warmly greeted each other and stretched out on the grass to talk.[39]

The picture we get of these two men is entirely believable. They lay, each with a little girl of Pike's nestled on their arm, and talked endlessly. Pike's purpose in the poem was to tell his friend Chase of his hatred for the political strife of the day, of his contempt for the gladiatorial demagogues who held sway in the public political arena, of how he had eschewed for himself a public career as an officeholder, but of how he had vowed to continue working in his own way for his stern mistress Truth:

> But henceforth I shall labour in the peace
> And quietness of my beloved home.
> No good is wrought by mingling in the fray
> Of party war. Under these kingly trees,
> Encouraged by my children's loving eyes,
> Soothed to serene and self-possessed content,

> By all the sights and sounds that bless me here,
> Will I work ever in her noble cause.[40]

As Pike and Chase conversed, they lost all sense of time. Darkness came on, their "little audience" fell asleep in their arms, and they arose and carried the children into the house. Still talking, the two friends made their way to Pike's study, the large west front room of the house, and sat

> Near the large windows, where the moon shone in
> Upon the carpets, and the Spring's warm breath,
> Sweet as a girl's, came heavy with perfume;
> And, with a bottle of bright, sparkling wine,
> From sunny France, and fitful conversation,
> Sustained awhile, then dying into silence,
> Prolonged our sitting far into the night.[41]

VI

The Editor's Table

FOR US THE *ADVOCATE* opens yet another window upon Pike's life in 1835–37. Getting out the paper was bothersome to him in its mechanical aspects. Good printers were hard to find and harder still to keep, and he fretted much over the fact that apprentices were never in adequate supply.[1] But in another respect, getting it out was a great joy for Pike. He exulted in writing for the paper. It gave him an outlet for boundless mental energies. It furnished him a means for speaking his mind on the momentous questions of the day for which he deeply cared, as the lover cares for his sweetheart. The *Advocate* was for Pike no mere organ of anti-Sevier propaganda nor was it a mere business proposition. It was his schoolmaster's desk, his pulpit, his tripod, his voice—as much so as the *Evening Star* of New York was the mouthpiece of Mordecai Noah, Pike's "beau ideal" of a Whig editor, or as the *Louisville Journal* was the organ of his example George D. Prentice.[2]

The very month that he took over the *Advocate*, Pike revived his "The Editor's Table," a column he had begun the year before under Bertrand and in which he imitated the role of an editor receiving and conversing with an imaginary caller, his reader. The column became his outlet for speaking his mind on what ever overwhelming issue or insignificant subject was in his thoughts at the moment. It is worth examining if we are better to understand Pike, for running through the column, like a kaleidoscope of ideas, is a sort of summary of his public thinking at the time.

In "The Editor's Table" of January 30, 1835, the first published under his ownership, Pike set the tone of the column in an easy, rambling, chatty style. "Of these cool pleasant evenings in winter, we love to stir up the fire, and enjoy our ease with our friend. We are but newly seated in our chair editorial, and we have hardly shaken ourself in it, and become well at home."

Pike then called attention to his "editor's table," which was "spread with various fare," and discussed item by item what he and his reader found there. There was the "late election in New York." It seemed to secure Van Buren the succession to Jackson, but Pike thought the Mississippi Valley would be "unwise" to follow Van Buren and New York, for the "selfish and sectional character" of Van Buren would "induce him to aggrandize New York at the expense of the West." The papers from the West and the South were "stirring in support" of Hugh Lawson White of Tennessee, and these movements would injure Van Buren. "We respect Judge White," Pike said, "as an honest and liberal man,—and if he supports the principles with which Jackson *went into* office, we go with him. If he is disposed to extend the Executive power, and to continue abuses,—we'll none of him. We know of no man now, that we would prefer to him."[3]

To his reader friend Pike had nothing to say about Arkansas politics, although he was sure time would see him buckling on his armor "to take to the field." "If our friends choose a candidate for any office, we will aid him to the best of our ability—if we like him,—for confound the man who would not stick to his friend, right or wrong." In supporting his friends, Pike was sure he would find himself "now and then in a minority. It was ever our luck to get on the weak side,—and that, we take it, is a tolerable sign that we have been honest in our politics."[4]

Turning from politics, Pike told his listener that he intended "to give our citizens now and then a hint on the subject of education." He noticed, also, that the Missouri legislature had appointed a committee to revise the laws of the state. "This is what Arkansas will have to do, whenever she becomes a State." He would, he says, welcome "a revision of the whole code, by competent hands."[5]

In closing, Pike, an inveterate smoker himself, invited his visitor to take a cigar, relax, think of nothing—"then smoking is a luxury. How beautiful is the night! The stars are clear, keen, and glittering—the air is cool—and the heaven behind the stars, is blue and deep." How he enjoyed Arkansas's mild winters! "This is," he says, "the climate for an epicure,—a mental epicure, we mean. The snow has small dominion here—and this winter especially, we have had such weather as men boast of in Italy."[6] Pike was to find, however, that Little Rock's weather could be unpredictable. Two weeks later, on February 13, he complained bitterly that no mail had arrived from the East since the fourth—the extremely cold weather had frozen the Arkansas solid, and subsequent thawing had resulted in "floating ice hazards to navigation."[7]

Another week in his editorial chair found Pike arming himself and taking to the field for Hugh Lawson White. Perhaps, Pike said, he should explain why he, "being simply a *Territorial* Editor," had endorsed Judge White. He could do it "in a few words." The *Advocate* "has ever been stigmatized and reviled, as being anti-Jackson in its principles." The charge was untrue, certainly insofar as it applied to him, said Pike. He had favored most of the principles with which Jackson went into office, but disagreed both with Jackson's "conduct" and many of his "public acts" as president.[8]

Pike listed his differences with Jackson in a revealing paragraph. He believed a president should serve but one term, that a national bank "under proper restrictions" was necessary to the country, and that internal improvements "for the benefit of a single State" were unconstitutional but that those for the benefit of the nation were not only constitutional but necessary. Pike confessed that he was and always had been "what General Jackson *was*, a democrat." When Pike lived in New England he was for a protective tariff. A tariff, he explained,

> was for the interest of that country, a manufacturing community. Now, we are against it, for the same reason. It is a simple question of interest. There is no great principle involved in it. A Southern man, belonging to a cotton-growing State, would be a fool to be a Tariff man—and we are an Arkansian, and that not for a year or two, but for our lifetime.[9]

Yet Pike professed to see "principle" and "not interest" involved in his personal choice of White for the presidency. "He is," said Pike," "an honest, bold, decided man, and no political Machiavelli—and we believe him to be in character, much like Monroe and Madison." Pike condemned the recent Democratic National Convention, which had nominated Van Buren, President Jackson's personal choice for the succession. "We are," declared Pike, "in favor of no Convention of political jugglers. We believe all parties to be corrupt—and therefore we are for laying aside party, and choosing an *honest man*."[10]

In the same column in which he endorsed White for president, Pike applauded Jackson for payment of the national debt. He said he had never agreed with those, like Alexander Hamilton, who believed that "a national debt was a national blessing." He hoped, now that the United States had no debt to pay, that the price of public land would be reduced. He had found, he said, in traveling in New Mexico, that Mexicans paid less than Americans for public land. "We doubt," Pike wrote, "if there is any innate justice in making the native of any country pay any price at all for his land." At any rate, Pike felt that the American settler should never have to pay any more for land than what it would take "to defray the expense of surveying."[11]

Accordingly, Pike opposed, in early 1835, Henry Clay's land bill which called for the distribution of the proceeds of the public lands to the states. Pike was careful to explain that he was "no friend of the veto," but he hoped President Jackson would veto Clay's bill if it passed Congress. "Arkansas will soon be a State," he said, "and the Land Bill would as certainly be a curse to her." It would keep the price of land up, when what Arkansas needed was low-priced land to attract settlers.[12] Eighteen months later, however, Pike endorsed the Surplus Revenue Bill which called for a distribution of the Treasury surplus as a loan to the states. Under the new bill, which he erroneously attributed to Clay, the newer states would get 10 percent over and above their regular share, a provision that pleased Pike. "The amount which would fall to Arkansas would," he explained, "establish a system of common schools throughout the State, and construct many important and much needed roads."[13]

At the same time that Pike announced his support for the Surplus Revenue Bill, he proposed a federal system of public schools. "The Constitution of Mexico established," he related, "a system of common schools throughout the country—even in the Territories—and the teachers are paid by the General Government." He had seen two of these schools in Santa Fe, one a common school and one a Latin, or high school—"where any boy, rich or poor, can be educated at the expense of the Central Government."[14]

He would "rejoice" to see this in is own country. "We for one, would like to see Congress establish the common school system in every State, if it could be done constitutionally, and pay the teachers." If it could not be done, he wanted the federal revenue divided among the states, and Arkansas with its share would "give the people in every county three or four common schools, whose teachers shall be paid out of the common fund. An educated people are not likely to be enslaved."[15]

When the surplus revenue measure became a law in the late summer of 1836, Pike repeated his approval. Arkansas could, he reasoned, use its share to good advantage. By then his fertile mind had sprouted a new proposal. Arkansas should use part of her share, he said, to promote construction of a railroad from Little Rock to Helena.[16] This, incidentally, was not his first suggestion for railroads in Arkansas. He had mentioned them almost a year before in August 1835 noting that the East was "making great strides in building railroads, that New York, Philadelphia, and Baltimore are contending for the trade of the West by building railroads from their cities into the interior all the way to the Mississippi."[17]

These eastern railways, he thought would be a great boon to Arkansas's growth in population and in giving her products a ready outlet. He predicted, in a wild flight of his imagination, that in twenty years one could "jump into a locomotive" and travel to any city in the East at the speed of fifty miles an hour. He expected he would be able to write then that a train pulled by the engine *Little Rock* had left the Arkansas capital for Boston, that Gov. Stephen F. Austin had been reelected governor of the state of Texas, that the treeless Grand Prairie of Arkansas between the Arkansas and White rivers had been settled, that Arkansas had a million and a half population, and that she was producing a million bales of cotton a year.[18]

Taking command of the *Advocate* in early 1835, Pike knew the Second Bank of the United States was comatose, and there was practically no chance for its survival. He had never been a confirmed supporter of the bank as run by Nicholas Biddle, but had always expressed himself, it seems, in favor of a modified recharter of the institution. Accordingly, he had been much perplexed, even incensed, when President Jackson, having vetoed a recharter bill in 1832, undertook the bank's destruction in 1833–34 without so much as suggesting a restructured national bank in its place. Pike was likewise vexed in these years by arguments put forth by men around Jackson on "hard money" theory.[19]

Writing for the *Advocate* of February 13, 1835, Pike expressed himself fully and clearly on the "currency question." He came out solidly for paper money, local banks, and a national bank with power to regulate the issuance of local bank notes. Paper money was, he argued, essential to carrying on the commerce of the country; it could not be abolished "without altering the character of our nation, and changing its whole business in extent and manner." He believed banks were also necessary, and was impatient with those who argued that "hard money" could replace the need for banks. "We believe," he declared, "that a hard money currency is all a chimera—and that we must have banks." But since he believed "that a multitude of local banks would be a curse without a national bank," he advocated chartering a new national bank. He was careful to point out that he opposed Biddle's Bank of the United States. That institution had, Pike declared, "acted corruptly," and he was for a "new bank, with additional restrictions, when the present one expires." "Time and experience," he thought, "will bring the whole nation to this way of thinking."[20]

This was a sober enough defense of his own views on banking and paper money, but his response to the hard-money policy of the Jackson administration was neither sober nor just. The Jackson policy proposed to establish a "metallic currency" for the ordinary transactions of the people and to limit bank paper to commercial affairs of the business world. It also proposed to exclude banks from control over the currency and to confine banks to the functions of deposit and discount, gradually withdrawing from them the power of issuing bank notes or paper money. Pike was aware of both the details and the merits of the hard-money policy. He apparently approved the principle that gold coins would circulate among the people and that bank notes would be restricted to large denominations and circulate primarily in large commercial transactions and in transferring money from one place to another through the mails. But the theory failed to work out in practice, and Pike quickly denounced it.

First of all, Pike joined the opponents of the hard-money policy by lending his voice to the denunciation of the Coinage Act of 1834. Sponsored by that stalwart Jacksonian Sen. Thomas Hart Benton, this measure revised the valuation of silver to gold to sixteen to one and provided for the minting and circulating of gold coins. It won Benton the name of "Old Bullion" among his hard-money friends, but his enemies called him "Gold Humbug." Pike by February 1835 was among Old Bullion's enemies. He denounced "the gold bill" as a "humbug," declaring that it had been a complete failure.[21]

Pike was correct. Benton's and Jackson's "new eagle coins" were simply not circulating. They had found their way into the vaults of state banks, and the banks, retaining the gold, circulated their notes in place of coins. Jackson tried to suppress bank notes of small denominations, in keeping with hard-money policy, but was powerless to do so in face of the great boom that had now begun.[22]

Pike permitted his correspondent "Hamilton" to explain to the *Advocate's* reader's in April 1835 the consequences of the Jackson-Benton gold policy for Arkansas. "Nine months have now elapsed since the mint commenced the new coinage," said Hamilton, "and to this day there is not one in five hundred of our population that ever saw a piece of the new coin." The reason, he explained, was simple. The coins had gone into bank coffers in the neighboring states, and Arkansas had received instead of coins a deluge of bank notes, many of which were not accepted at land offices in the territory in payment for federal land. Hamilton found that the legislatures were increasing the number of state banks, while the legislators themselves confessed to a belief in Jackson's and Benton's "metallic currency." He wanted the Arkansas legislature to pass laws guarding against the "approaching evil" of the increased circulation of state bank notes in the territory. He professed to be no friend of the banking system, but he thought that the day might soon come when Arkansas itself might have to establish its own bank as a means of controlling the circulation of unsound bank notes in the territory.[23]

Curiously, Hamilton's suggestion of a territorial bank for Arkansas was based on a premise that both he and Pike agreed on, that is, that the Jacksonian hard-money policy was a failure. It had failed precisely because Jackson, by abolishing the bank, had destroyed the power of Biddle's institution to control paper money and because Jackson had not set up in its place an agency powerful enough to deal with the problem. The state deposit banks, called by Jackson's enemies "Pet Banks," into which federal funds were put, could be controlled by Treasury Department orders, and the Jackson administration ordered them to cease issuing bank notes of a denomination of less than five dollars. But these orders were ineffectual in the general banking situation, and Jackson's personal appeal to the state legislatures to outlaw small bank notes fell largely on deaf ears. Old Hickory had led in putting down the Bank of the United States only to give rise to an uncontrolled wilderness of state and local banks. He had replaced the paper currency of Biddle's bank not with gold coins but with a flood of paper currency from a mass of unchecked local banks.[24]

Pike and his correspondent Hamilton analyzed the failure of Jackson's hard-money policy for the *Advocate*. Not only was Benton's gold bill of 1834 a failure, but Pike went so far as to charge that the hard-money men wished the complete prostration of the banking system. That was unfair and untrue but perfectly understandable in one, like Pike, who believed a national bank with power to control the currency was the best solution to the money question. He would have good reason to express himself on the issue again and again in the years immediately ahead, as Arkansas groped for a solution to its currency problem.[25]

Prominent in Pike's mind in his first months as owner of the *Advocate* was the subject of statehood for Arkansas. In his "The Editor's Table" of February 27, 1835, he told his readers that with statehood being the talk of the territory, he felt compelled to speak to them upon some very important things about "the nature of government," about the powers of the executive, the legislature, the judiciary, and the freedom of elections. His discourse, he advised, would deal with the momentous question of "how free shall we make ourselves so as not to be too free." He said later on in discussing the problem of defining the power of the executive that his purpose was to stir in Arkansas a discussion of government and constitution making, "a particularly interesting topic to a territory about to become a state."[26]

Anticipating criticism, Pike prefaced his "discourse" on government by a few pertinent remarks on his New England background. He was sure some of his Arkansas readers, on perusing his views on the nature of government, would be heard "to expatiate loudly" upon "Federalism and Jeffersonian democracy" and upon "bluelightism and New England Aristocracy—as sententiously as though they did of a truth know something."

"Whip me such knaves!" exclaimed Pike. Would his readers like to know what kind of aristocracy existed in New England in his youth? In Newburyport where he was brought up, "the rich were taxed, in proportion to their property, to support free schools for the poor, and to buy their children books." No, if New England had been a country of aristocrats, "we had never been an editor." He was, he said, "no friend to Northeastern politics, in many respects,—but let us acknowledge, for it is but the simple truth, that the people there are better educated—that their rights are better understood, and protected by the very safeguards which our Mobocrats wish to break down."[27]

"Mobocrats!" There was the rub. "The people's *friends*, those who *love* the people, are of the opinion," sneered Pike, "that they cannot be too free—that there is no office which ought not to be conferred directly by the people, by a popular expression of their will."[28] Pike vehemently disagreed. For over a year he had been reading Chancellor James Kent's conservative views in *Commentaries on American Law*, and, though Pike called himself a Jeffersonian Democrat, a republican of the "old school," he agreed with much that the confirmed Federalist Kent had to say about government and the law. Kent praised the most conservative features of the U.S. Constitution, those which removed the Senate, the president, and the entire federal judiciary from direct election by the people. Kent feared democracy, the power of universal suffrage, and the fumings of "a licentious press" and freely dropped warnings to his readers about the necessity in a republic of protecting the Constitution and the laws from the encroachments of the people and from the "tyranny of faction."[29]

Though Kent came to have doubts about the future of republican government in the United States during the Jackson administration, he expressed himself in his *Commentaries* to believe that an independent federal judiciary was the bulwark of the American republic. But if the judiciary were to remain independent, it would be necessary to retain the presidential appointment, the life tenure for judges, and a requisite salary. In no case should judges be elected by the people or by Congress. "The fittest men would," he believed, "probably have too much reservedness of manners, and severity of morals, to secure an election resting on universal suffrage. Nor can the mode of appointment by a large deliberative assembly, be entitled to unqualified approbation."[30]

For a man who resented being called a Federalist or a "blue-light" New Englander, Pike took little pains to conceal his own admiration for Kent as well as his own revulsion for too popular democratic state government. Kent despised the unicameral legislature, praised the two-house Congress, and admired the concept of the indirectly elected American Senate.[31] When Pike undertook in 1835 to defend the U.S. Senate against "those theorists" who would abolish it and set up a unicameral national assembly, he quoted Kent to them and his readers. The chancellor had observed, said Pike, the weakness of the Italian republics with their unicameral legislatures and had noted that Rome fell when the "Senate" was attacked. "Let the people beware of every attempt to make them distrust the Senate," warned Pike in his best Kentian style.[32]

When Pike undertook at the same time to answer those who declared that the federal judiciary was antirepublican and aristocratic, he again found his authority in Kent. The Supreme Court was not a "dictator." It could annul an act of Congress only by ruling it to be "unconstitutional." "The constitution, then, is the master of the court—and the court is only its interpreter," said Pike in an echo from Kent.[33]

Thus when Pike came to set down in "The Editor's Table" his own views on "the nature of government" he not surprisingly drew heavily on the misanthrope, Kent. He wanted Arkansas to draw up a state constitution that would safeguard liberty, that would give the people freedom—but not too much freedom. Universal manhood suffrage he apparently accepted without complaint. It was in denying power to the people to exercise the franchise too freely and in distributing power among the three branches of government which furnished for Pike the key to guaranteeing liberty in a state, that is, in Arkansas.[34]

Pike began with the judiciary because, like Kent, he was convinced that an independent judiciary was the greatest safeguard of liberty. The problem here, as Pike approached it, was how to go about ensuring "learning in our judges," for which he had a ready Kentian answer. The people must not elect them. "The experience of all men teaches us that an unlettered populace cannot be capable of judging the legal qualifications of a judge." The people would not look for "intelligence, learning, nor political honesty" in a candidate, but would be swayed by the "popular man" in a race whose "necessary qualifications . . . are, a faculty for demagoguery, for mixing with and flattering the people." The best lawyer in Arkansas, Pike warned, would not stand a chance against "one of your ignorant, noisy, vaporing demagogues."[35]

How should judges be chosen? Here Pike parted company with Kent, who was a strong advocate of the federal method of executive appointment with senatorial advice and counsel. Though Pike liked that method for the federal judiciary, he was unwilling to bestow such power on the future executive of the state of Arkansas. He apparently believed that executive appointment would not work with the popularly elected state governor, that is, that the judiciary could not remain independent under such a system. The judiciary, he argued, must be protected against both the people and the executive. "Law and justice would be empty words" if the executive could "remove and appoint judges at will," and it would be the same if the judges held office "at the irregular will of the people."[36]

Pike concluded, then, that the legislature should elect judges. "Learning in a judge is important to our freedom, and what difference should it make whether we or our representatives choose the judge," he asked. To Pike the question needed no answer, but he argued that the legislature was "better qualified than the whole body of the people to judge of the legal knowledge and fitness of a candidate for judicial office." Legislators were more likely than the people to be acquainted with "the prominent men of talents in the State," and were less likely than the people to be impressed by demagoguery in a candidate. "Popular elections would," Pike believed, "ever bring forward a multitude of candidates, always creating risk that some incompetent person would obtain the office." But legislative elections would "diminish the number of applicants."[37]

To Pike these were convincing arguments. The collective wisdom of the representatives of the people would do a better job of electing judges than the "whole body of the people." He was not unaware, however, that ignorant men would be elected to the legislature. Yet he preferred taking a chance on the wisdom of the deliberative body rather than on the ignorance of the "unlettered populace." The influence of an ignorant man in a legislature could be bad, he declared, but never as bad as one on the bench. "In vain are we free, if we have not talented, honest, impartial, and bold judges," he proclaimed in a ringing Kentian summation to his proscription of popular election of judges.[38]

Taking up the problem of delineating the power of the executive, Pike demonstrated that he had been brought up in the venerable American tradition of hostility to a strong executive. A state, he advised Arkansans, was "a powerful division of government" and "the power of its chief magistrate should be well and carefully defined." His argument postulated the inherent evil of executive government—dictatorship. "It is in the common course of human events," he said, "that power should concentrate, and at length gather into the hands of one man." In that moment the executive became so popular that the people would not "scrutinize his acts," "our liberty is in danger—it lies in the power of that man's hand." And if that man possessed the veto power, he could "oppose the will of the representatives of the people"; then liberty was in further danger.[39]

The constitutional remedy, then, for executive dictatorship was to take away the executive veto power. Here again Pike parted company with Kent, who saw the presidential veto as a valuable check on the power of the legislature. Sparked by his own hostility to President Jackson's use of the veto, Pike, an emerging Whig, refused to see any good in the veto. Good might come occasionally of a veto, but that was like "doing evil that good may come. It is letting loose an unconquerable fire." The veto power had no place in a republic. "It is anti-republican. It is monarchical. It is saying, in effect, that one single man is more capable of judging for and governing the people than the whole body of a representation." No man should have the power to set aside the will of the legislature by veto.[40]

Unfortunately, Pike never bothered to define the powers of the legislature. But we may assume that, while he had serious doubts about the caliber of Arkansas's future lawmakers, he was ready to risk legislative government under statehood. His experience with the territorial legislature had convinced him that Arkansas legislators were no worse than those in the older states. If anything, he was too optimistic about the quality of the future legislature, for if he had his way, it not only would elect judges but also would be unchecked by the customary governor's veto.

Pike assumed that he had taken the minority side of Arkansas public opinion in opposing the popular election of judges, an assumption that was without support as things turned out at the time of the constitutional convention in 1836. But in 1835, when he was expounding his conservative views on state government, he conjectured in "The Editor's Table" that his stand on legislative "appointment" of judges was unpopular and that he might be called "a federalist" for opposing their popular election. He would, he said, "leave to office holders and office seekers the praiseworthy employment of accommodating their principles to suit their interests," to take the popular side of the question. But he had something to say to those who carelessly bandied about such vague words as "federalist," and undertook to give them a lesson in etymology. The word "federalist" was, he said,

> a word without an idea. Like *many* other *cant* words, it means every thing and nothing. If it means we are a consolidationist, we deny its applicability to us—for we are inclined to the doctrine of State rights. If it means we are no nullifier, we agree to it. If it means the desire of strengthening the Executive—we deny it again, for we would rather his power should be diminished.[41]

As a lawyer and humanitarian, Pike was absolutely horrified by Arkansas's antiquated criminal code, by her lack of a territorial penitentiary, by her public hangings, by her public whippings, and by her other barbarous punishments. He found that whipping was tolerated in the territory as a punishment only through necessity because there was no territorial prison for the confinement of criminals. He had, he reported on April 24, 1835, seen two public whippings in Arkansas and needed to witness no more to convince him "that every such infliction is an injury to the country." Such harsh punishment merely hardened and rendered more reckless the offender, taking from him his sense of dignity, robbing him of his character, and disgracing him in the eye of the public.[42]

Witnessing the first public hanging of his life in Little Rock on May 16, 1835, Pike was sickened by the event. He was moved to denounce the practice, suggesting that capital punishment should be carried out behind prison walls at midnight accompanied by the tolling of a bell or the roll of a muffled drum.[43]

His first recommendations in the spring of 1835 for amending the harsh criminal code in order to provide for a territorial penitentiary and to abolish public whippings and hangings may well have drawn heavy fire. Taking up the subject again in August 1835 he wrote in an editorial that there was much difference of opinion in America with regard to the results to be had from establishing "the penitentiary system" for the confinement of criminals. But the consensus was, he reported, that imprisonment was "far preferable" to the "whipping, branding, cropping, and the whole catalogue of punishments which grow up under the common law."[44]

Pike favored the penitentiary system for Arkansas. It was, he maintained, far better than "those punishments" which allowed criminals to be "let loose on society" with a feeling of anger and of disgrace in their hearts. But he quickly confessed that he was no utopian, no follower of New Harmony or of Robert Dale Owen. These "theoretical" writers believed that reform among criminals was very likely and had persuaded themselves "that mankind are much better than they really are." Pike assumed, however, that no "rational legislator" looked to criminal reformation "as the ultimate object of Penitentiaries." "It would be a chimerical and visionary idea. The true object is, to confine and keep apart those who prey upon and injure society—and to do that with the least possible expense to the community."[45]

Calling for an end in Arkansas of the whipping of criminals and the turning of them loose upon the world, where robbery and murder were often the immediate results, Pike endorsed what was then an up-to-date penitentiary system—secure prison walls with a penal farm attached on which prisoners would work and support themselves. Penal farms had been set up in some of the eastern states, said Pike, and had "elicited the admiration of the Commissioners sent over by the French and British governments." He recommended a memorial to Congress for funds and, that failing, a tax on the people of Arkansas Territory with which to establish such a prison.[46] His humanitarian plea fell on deaf ears, and Arkansas, when it established a penitentiary in 1838, confined its prisoners behind walls but auctioned off their labor to the highest bidder under the disgraceful convict-lease system.

Of the national issues to which Pike addressed himself, none was more important in his mind than the abolition movement in the North. In August 1835, expressing the wish that his voice could be heard "in every nook and cranny" of the nation, Pike warned that "unless these fanatics abandon their wild schemes, civil war and immeasurable misery will be the consequence." He had been "raised in a free state—even the old State of Massachusetts," but his experience in Arkansas had convinced him "that the black slaves of the South are infinitely better off than the white slaves of the North." The South's black slaves were, he continued,

> as well clothed, as well, ay, ten times better fed—as well treated, and their work equally as light—and we do know that multitudes of them—even the few we have, would consider it their greatest misfortune to be cursed with such freedom as is possessed by the poorest class of the population in the North.[47]

He wished to be understood. He was speaking only to the abolitionists of the North. "If the Southern States themselves, or their people, see fit to abolish slavery, it is another thing. If the people of Arkansas are against slavery, we, for one, say let it be abolished." But he desired "to tell these Northern miscreants, once and for all, that we will brook no foreign intermeddling with our rights, our property, our lives." He was sure that William Lloyd Garrison (who like Pike was from Newburyport) and his followers wished to be martyrs. They could be accommodated if they would "come this way," allowed Pike.[48]

A month later, in September 1835, Pike was pleased to note that antiabolition meetings were being held in the North to oppose the Garrisonian fanatics. He had a word, he said, for his readers in the North. "The revolutionary heroes of the North fought for their liberties and their possessions. So did those of the South, and they have a right to keep both." Moreover, the abolitionists, if they had had the sense of a "blinking owl," might have known that their intermeddling would end in injury to the slaves. This was the case throughout the South, he said, especially in Mississippi, where whites had just hanged black accomplices of the white outlaw John Murrell.[49]

In his opposition to the abolitionists, Pike wrote from the viewpoint of a slaveholder as well as a southern partisan. He had brought with him from Massachusetts a feeling of racial prejudice, which he revealed in the fall of 1835. The *Gazette* had called for the enactment of a municipal code to regulate the conduct of Little Rock's free blacks. Pike not only endorsed Woodruff's "very sensible remarks about *free negroes*," but also drew attention to the need for a city slave code as well. The slaves were "equally a curse to the town." He spelled out his complaint: "We mean the number of slaves in and about this city, whose masters suffer them to hire their own time, either openly, or by evading the law in a roundabout way. The masters of these pests to the place, are hereby notified that the laws will be speedily enforced against them. Forbearance has ceased to be a virtue."[50]

Prompted by Woodruff's and Pike's editorials, the Little Rock City Council in December 1835 adopted a long, detailed ordinance "concerning Slaves, and free Negroes and Mulattos." The "black code" was no more severe than that of other cities of the South, but it, like those elsewhere, reflected the fear slaveholders had of free blacks and of town slaves that were permitted to move about too freely. A master of household slaves by way of marrying Mary Ann, Pike shared such fears. He printed the municipal black code in full in the *Advocate*, having already advised careless masters that it would be enforced against them.[51]

Pike was demonstrating in his attack on the abolitionists and in his stand on the municipal black code that he had become attuned to the southern way of life. Yet he was willing to play politics with the slavery question, at least at home. When Delegate Sevier stated in June 1835 that Arkansas would have to fight northern "fanaticism" to get into the Union as a slave state, Pike responded matter-of-factly that the abolitionists were a minority in the north and were treated there with the contempt they deserved. He could not resist asking Sevier if New York would not be one of Arkansas's enemies on statehood, and whether the New Yorker, Van Buren, the Democratic nominee for president, would not be found in the "front lines" against statehood. Pike concluded that Sevier's fear of northern fanaticism was merely "electioneering fears" expressed in Arkansas for the benefit of Sevier's party.[52]

Later the same year Pike attacked Postmaster General Amos Kendall for advising the postmaster at Charleston, South Carolina, that he could stop delivery in Charleston of all publications deemed dangerous to society. "This is fine advice for a Postmaster General to give!" exclaimed Pike. "It is only another link in the great chain of making mob law and private judgment superior to the laws." The "most intelligent papers" in the country were "solidly opposed" to Kendall's instructions, Pike observed.[53]

As it turned out, Pike was reading only the "most intelligent" northern papers, for southern opinion applauded Kendall's action and Pike had to "eat crow" on the issue. He humbly explained that, having read Kendall's letter of explanation to the New York City postmaster, he had withdrawn his own objection. Kendall had, Pike said, told the New Yorker that the postmaster general had no legal power to authorize a postmaster to stop delivery of mail but that a postmaster might well be justified in stopping delivery of "incendiary mail."[54] Five months later, in late February 1836, Pike approved when the Little Rock postmaster took such action. Two copies of *Human Rights*, an antislavery "incendiary paper published in New York," arrived in the Little Rock post office with a request that they be "widely circulated." The papers were "widely circulated," reported Pike, by being torn into bits and pieces and scattered on the streets. "No citizen here would receive such a publication from the office."[55]

The "Texas question" was much in the news in 1835–36, and Pike reflected the attitude of Arkansas toward the issue. When in November 1835 the hero David Crockett passed through Little Rock on his way to Texas, Pike attended a public dinner given in Crockett's honor, announcing later in the *Advocate* that he should now die content, that he had seen the "Hon. David Crockett."[56]

In "The Editor's Table" for December 18, 1835, Pike compared the revolution in Texas to the American Revolution. Americans owed "a considerable debt" to sundry foreign patriots, men like Lafayette, who came to America to help win her liberty. The "first installment" on that debt now "is demanded—to be paid by services rendered to the cause of freedom and free principles in Texas." If Americans refused to pay the debt, "assigned over as it is, too, to our brethren in an enemy's country," the voice of "our fathers" would cry "shame" upon them. "Let us hope," said Pike in closing, "that Texas may become free—be joined to the United States—and becoming another Southern State, offset the future state of Ouisconsin. The whole *South*, at least, will say amen, to that wish."[57]

Two months later, in February 1836, Pike was not so favorably impressed with Texas. He noted with regret that "the inhabitants" of Arkansas Territory west of Red River, an area claimed by Arkansas but most of which she ultimately lost to Texas, had separated themselves from the government of both Arkansas and the United States and were "taking measures to incorporate themselves with Texas." These people had sent delegates to a "Texian Convention," a step which Pike deemed both rash and unadvised. Texas was, he said, in a state of anarchy, it would be a long time before she could get into the Union even if she won her independence from Mexico, and the Americans in Arkansas's Red River country meanwhile would be putting themselves into jeopardy from Mexican retaliation.[58]

Pike was right. These south-of-the-border, sunshine Arkansans soon called on Gov. William S. Fulton for militia protection. The Mexicans, they claimed, were promoting an Indian attack against the Red River settlements. This was in May 1836, when Sam Houston's Texans had on April 21 at San Jacinto defeated the only Mexican force within 500 miles of Red River. Crafty Governor Fulton informed these quasi Arkansans how they might form their own militia under Arkansas jurisdiction, and sat back to watch developments within this troublesome border region, which Arkansas had organized as Miller County back in 1828 and whose people, wavering between Mexican and American citizenship, had been a constant problem for the territorial government ever since.[59]

By this time Pike was beginning to have even greater misgivings about "the Texas question," though, as we shall see later, he got caught up in 1836 in the general excitement in Arkansas over a threatened Indian war on the territory's western frontier which was partly a result of suspected Mexican intrigue. But his full Whig about-face on Texas did not come until March 1837, when he spoke out publicly in opposition to annexation. Texas would be independent: the United States would recognize her as the independent Republic of Texas and would and should "protect" her as a free nation.[60]

"What will be the next step?" he asked. Behind his answers to that question were his knowledge of northern opposition to annexation of Texas as a slave state and his fear of stirring up the slavery question. He believed Texas would not be annexed, and he hoped not. The Union was "already large enough"; it might "some day fall to pieces of its own weight," and it did not need Texas, which should be preserved, he argued, as a "buffer state" between the United States and Mexico. He was thinking of the slavery question but, because of his southern outlook, did not dare broach the dreadful subject. Yet the fear was there—annexation, he warned, "would infallibly dissolve the Union."[61]

Pike's newspaper office, which he moved in mid-March 1835 "to the new brick building nearly opposite the State House" on Markham Street, became a sort of "circulating library" for Little Rock.[62] He gladly lent his books and magazines but became so upset over people taking books and not returning them that in August 1835 he published a long farcical poem about the problem:

> A circulating library
>   Is mine—my birds are flown;
> There's one old volume left, to be
>   Like all the rest, a-loan.[63]

The poem, containing many verses, used the authors' names as puns upon the disappearance of their works from his office. It revealed, if indeed he owned all the books mentioned, that he had acquired a considerable collection of American and English poets as well as works on political thought by Hobbes, Locke, and others.

Book borrowers continued to plague Pike. Two years later, in July 1837 he advertised for some fifteen volumes of prose and poetry "loaned or lost," the "return of which will confer a singular favor."[64] He concluded the notice with a wry bit of humor:

> The gentleman who took the first volume of *Irving's Astoria* from me on the steamboat John Jay, in the Arkansas river, on her trip up, is informed that if he

will send me the book so that I can read it, I will be happy to return it to him—or I will throw up heads and tails to see which of us shall have both volumes—or if that won't do, as the second volume is of no use to me, I will give it to him for the privilege of reading the first.[65]

On the Little Rock scene in 1835, Pike's most interesting editorial crusade concerned the problem of gambling. In mid-July he routinely reported the lynching in Vicksburg of five professional gamblers in open daylight and noted that a nest of runaway Mississippi gamblers had arrived in Little Rock on the steamer *Neosho*. A new paper in town, the *Times* edited by a young Ohioan, Andrew Jackson Hunt, rashly called on the people of Little Rock to follow the example of Vicksburg citizens in ridding themselves of the gamblers. Moreover, Woodruff's *Gazette* endorsed the youthful Hunt's stand. Appalled by this appeal to mob law, Pike declared that he wanted the gamblers to leave town but that he wanted the law carried out by officers and not by a lynch mob as in Vicksburg.[66]

There was considerable hypocrisy in Hunt's and Woodruff's stand because some of the leading men in Little Rock society patronized the gamblers and even invited them into their homes. Pike himself had gambled with them and so apparently had Hunt, and Pike had been present when some of the gamblers were guests in the best homes in town. Accordingly, Pike sold space in the *Advocate* for William Copp, a spokesman of the gamblers, to address a letter to the public in reply to Hunt and Woodruff. Signing himself "Sportsmen," Copp protested the mob action at Vicksburg and attacked Hunt and Woodruff, especially young Hunt whom he called a "lap dog" and not a "watch dog" over the morals of the town. He and his friends, Copp said in a rather eloquent appeal, had come to Little Rock bearing themselves "as gentlemen." They had insulted no man, had committed no outrage against "the good order of the town" nor against "the peace of your society," and were prepared to obey any and all laws that were against them.[67]

On reading "Sportsmen," Hunt sped to the *Advocate* office and demanded from Pike the writer's name. He got it, but substituting goose quill for dueling pistol, wrote a long, testy editorial instead of an invitation to fight. He denounced Copp as beneath contempt and raged at Pike for publishing his letter. Pike had, he charged, sold out to the gamblers for "the paltry sum of fifteen dollars," which was the price of the space in the *Advocate* used by Copp. Heretofore, proclaimed Hunt, he had favored permitting Copp and his crowd to leave Little Rock in peace, but now he would support any measures the townspeople wished to take against them. Again, Woodruff foolishly backed up Hunt in this piece of reckless nonsense, publicly censuring Pike for accepting Copp's ill-gotten money.[68]

Before Pike had time to reply to Hunt and Woodruff, a public meeting convened on July 26 to consider the problem of the gamblers. Pike attended and reported the entire proceedings. Although the city's mayor presided over the meeting, the gathering was strictly voluntary and resulted in the formation of a sort of frontier vigilante body called the Anti-Gaming Association. Its constitution, however, pledged its members to use all "fair and legal means" to suppress gambling; to discountenance all professional gamblers; and, through the investigations of a secret committee of ten men, to work for the arrest and prosecution of all gamblers.[69]

Pike balked at a provision in the constitution which required the society's members to discountenance all officials or candidates for office and to boycott all businesses and persons who thereafter should "game at or frequent gaming houses" or should "connive at or countenance the vice in others." Resenting the hypocrisy in the requirement, he mockingly moved that the words "unless absolutely forced thereto by necessity" be added to the stringent rule. When his amendment was rejected, Pike refused to sign the constitution and, therefore, to become a member of the Anti-Gaming Association. But at a subsequent meeting on the twenty-ninth, his amendment won approval, and he signed the articles and became a member.[70]

Two days after Pike joined the Anti-Gaming Association, on July 31, he uncorked a vintage editorial on law and order. Defending his own stand against lynch law, he blamed Little Rock society for winking at the city's antigaming ordinances and for receiving the Mississippi gamblers as social equals into their very homes, so that in nearly every house one went "*you met a gambler.*" The root of the evil lay as much with the townspeople as with the gamblers, said Pike, but Hunt and Woodruff, to rid Little Rock of the gamblers, had begun a crusade not against the people's customs and morals but against the professional gamblers and against law and order. Hunt and Woodruff had even gone so far as to advocate "mob vengeance" as a means of eliminating the gamblers.[71]

Pike zeroed in on the two editors. He himself detested gamblers as a class as much as anyone, but there was, he said, a class of men in society whom he despised even more. It was those self-righteous men, like Hunt and Woodruff, who would tell the people "that they should have either anarchy, mob law, or a *Despotism.*" Therefore, explained Pike, he had spoken out against such lawlessness in Little Rock out of a "firm belief that where the sanctity of the law is at stake, *the end does not justify the means.*"[72]

This brought Pike to William Copp's letter and to Hunt's and Woodruff's charge that Copp had "bought" and "silenced" the long-haired editor of the *Advocate*. Pike admitted that "fifteen dollars" was important to him, whether such a paltry sum was or was not to the "rich old gentleman who edits the Gazette, or the very liberal, careless and profuse publisher of the Times." But money in Copp's case was not the editor's sole object, added Pike. He accepted the gambler's letter in the spirit of the newspaper "corps," in the sense of fair play. Having been received and treated as gentlemen by Little Rock society, Copp and his friends were entitled to be heard in reply to those who would set aside the law and substitute the "lynch mob" in its place. Moreover, Copp confessed in his letter that he and his friends would leave town when society quit patronizing them and when the laws and the climate no longer favored them.[73]

If Pike had erred in accepting Copp's letter, he was not about to admit it. Nor was he willing to permit Hunt and Woodruff to get away with their outrageous charge that he had sold out to the gamblers. Consequently, he moved to the offensive. He had, he said, done a great service to the community in printing Copp's letter. By allowing these "arrogant men" to stand up and tell the people that they did not execute their laws, that, indeed, their laws are "a mockery and a byword," Pike claimed that he had awakened the townspeople from their apathy. He hammered the point home: "We do aver, and well do the Gazette and Times know it to be true, that the advertisement which we published, was the *sole* cause of the meeting which originated the Anti-Gaming Association."[74]

To be sure, Hunt and Woodruff were unwilling to credit Pike with the meeting on July 26 that resulted in the formation of the Anti-Gaming Association. They even used his quibbling over the society's constitution on that occasion as further evidence of his sympathy for the gamblers and implied either erroneously or dishonestly that he did not join and support the association. In his editorial of the thirty-first of July, Pike had affirmed his membership in and his support of the society and had held out the olive branch of peace to Hunt and Woodruff. He offered to work hand in hand with them in backing the Anti-Gaming Association and in ridding the town of the gamblers. But on the sixth of August Pike, announcing that the gamblers were gone, took further issue with Hunt and Woodruff. They apparently had printed handbills ordering the gamblers to disperse. Pike declared that this had been unnecessary, that the antigaming society was "in full force" and that if its members would stick to their pledges, "as we will," then the gamblers would not return.[75]

In the interim Hunt had permitted an anonymous correspondent to charge that Pike had been seen gambling in public. Bristling at Hunt's invasion of his privacy, Pike on the seventh fired back:

> It is true! We have sometimes been where there was a faro bank—and two or three times we have bet. Who will throw the first stone? One of the few times we were there, we found the editor of the Times, that Phoenix of young gentlemen, *dressed in character*—and personating—we won't be so cruel as to say what. The skill, however, with which he acted his part, induced a belief that he had before practised on such a stage. We remember also betting to the amount of a dollar, that night, which we lost—while our neighbor sat by in pious horror—and—kept calculations.

Closing, Pike warned young Hunt that if his "anonymous goose" honked any more that he could unfold "not one tale, but several." The threat was effective. Hunt said no more, and the matter was dropped.[76]

The antigaming episode revealed several things about Pike. He detested mob rule, he hated narrow-minded social watchdogs, and he was, for a man who eschewed a political career, extremely vain and sensitive about his public image. A proud man, Pike possessed a high sense of personal honor and integrity. If anything, he was too quick to resent insults, far too sensitive for his own good, especially so for one who did not hesitate, as an editor, to insult others. To his credit, he later looked back on his early years as an editor as years of immaturity and poor judgment. But, as a young editor, he pictured himself as a peace-loving, honorable, brave, immaculate man. He was all these things, but he was also opinionated and factious. Thus he constantly paraded before the public his own virtues, while castigating the faults of his enemies. It was a characteristic that he carried to his grave.

But Pike was no public boor. He enjoyed the free, open, tolerant society that he had found in Arkansas, at least among a large part of the planter-lawyer-merchant class in Little Rock and Arkansas. Indeed, his own exploits in that society were to become the sources of numerous legends. He gambled, he drank, he stuffed himself on rich food and wine, and defied those who, like young Hunt, "sat by in pious horror—and—kept calculations," or those like John Reed, who brought before the public Pike's "frolic" at the surveyor general's office in December 1835.

"We are a citizen of Arkansas for life," he had affirmed back in April 1835, announcing the beginning of the sixth volume of the *Advocate*. "Our heart and our hand are with its people, and we commence a new editorial year, with the warm hope that our present connexion may not soon be dissolved."[77] By then he had been long enough in Arkansas to chide his eastern friends about their ignorance of the West and of Arkansas. His old friend John Neal, editor of the *New England Galaxy*, in May 1835 made note of Pike's setting up in Arkansas "in the Great Deep of the Western Wilderness" as editor and proprietor of the *Advocate*.[78] Though Pike thanked Neal for his good wishes, he undertook in July 1835 to educate him and his other eastern friends about Arkansas:

> Our brethren at the East have some queer ideas about Arkansas and its people. This Territory is almost as unknown to them as the Flying Island described by the veracious Peter Wilkins. They talk about our exiling ourselves to this part of the world, as they would if we were exiled to St. Helena—and no doubt some of them take the little town of Helena to be that self same island. It is true we are pretty well to the leeward, but we are not *quite* on the edge of the world.—We have parties and weddings where a hundred people are present—and at length we are in the habit of getting regular mails from the East. All this gives us a claim to civilization.[79]

Our "citizen of Arkansas for life," whose views on national and local issues we have examined, remained in 1835–36 the voice of a dying political faction. It yet remained to be seen whether that faction would be nursed back to health and, if so, what course it would take in the years immediately ahead as Arkansas Territory achieved statehood and began to participate in national politics.

VII

A Real Fat Job

ALBERT TOOK CONTROL of the *Advocate* at a crucial moment in the history of Arkansas Territory. Her people, anxious to be free of the thralldom of territorial status, believed by 1835 that Arkansas's population of some 53,000 warranted her admission to the Union as a state. The year before, in 1833–34, Delegate Sevier had attempted to get an enabling act through Congress authorizing the territory to hold a convention and draw up a constitution. When the bill failed, Sevier abandoned the accepted doctrine that an enabling act was necessary and recommended to his constituents that Arkansas hold a convention, draw up a constitution, and submit it accompanied by a petition to Congress without benefit of such an act.[1]

Favoring Sevier's plan, though he twitted him and Woodruff with being inconsistent on the issue of statehood, Pike joined Woodruff in the spring of 1835 in editorially suggesting to Gov. William Savin Fulton that he call a special session of the legislature to provide for a convention. The governor, fearing privately that Chester Ashley was behind Woodruff's stand and that the two were plotting to steal the senatorship Fulton coveted for himself, refused. His oath of office, he announced publicly, bound him to oppose such a move unless first authorized by Congress.[2]

Impatient with their over-scrupulous chief executive, Pike and Woodruff appealed over his head to the people. A new legislature was to be elected in August. They requested that the people meet locally, in towns and countryside, and express themselves on the question of statehood. The response was highly gratifying. Reports soon flowed in to the two Little Rock papers from across the territory of meetings held and of resolutions passed pledging to vote for no legislator who did not favor statehood and requesting the governor to call a special session of the legislature as soon as practicable after the election. Pike also endorsed Woodruff's suggestion that the August ballots poll the people directly on the question of "For State Government" or "Against State Government."[3]

Except on the issue of statehood there was no territorial-wide canvass in the election of 1835. The Crittenden faction, crippled by the untimely death of its leader, entered no candidate against Sevier for delegate to Congress, possibly thinking that with statehood so near there was little to be gained by opposing him. But in Pike's legislative district, comprising the counties of Pulaski, White, and Saline, which had been swept by three Sevierites in 1833, his law partner William Cummins announced in June for a house seat. Two other Crittendenites, Absalom Fowler and Charles Caldwell, ran on the ticket with him, Fowler for the other house seat and Caldwell for the council. A Little Rock attorney and Crittenden's former law partner, Fowler was a veteran of the territorial party wars. So, too, was Caldwell, who had twice been president of the council in 1829 and 1831 before going down to defeat in 1833. He had since moved from Little Rock to Saline County.[4]

Pike's main task in the legislative canvass, as it turned out, was in defending Fowler against a personal vendetta by Woodruff, who, while he had little use for Cummins and Caldwell, absolutely detested Fowler and concentrated on defeating him. Matching insult with insult, Pike countered Woodruff's anti-Fowler tactics so well that Woodruff accused him of inciting "warfare" with the *Gazette* over the local election. That "warfare" existed was obvious enough, but Pike, pleading innocence to the charge, took pains to explain that he meant nothing personal toward Woodruff in opposing the *Gazette* editor's politics. He had, he reminded Woodruff, acted in concert with him on the statehood question but was not about to stand by and permit Woodruff to assault his political friends and not return blow for blow. This duty, Pike said, he owed to his own "character as an independent editor and freeman. It was to support our principles, and to oppose and put down by every honorable means, those whom we believe to be in the wrong, and to whom we are conscientiously opposed."[5]

Pike was hardly as independent as he professed to be; after all, it was common knowledge, which he afterwards freely admitted, that the ambitious Cummins had made him his law partner solely because Pike owned the *Advocate* and could be expected to bring the paper to Cummins's political support. Pike thus made the first payment on that obligation in the summer of 1835, but while it was to his personal interest to do so, it would be unfair to conclude that Pike was merely a hireling editor. He and Cummins were business, social, and political friends. Though Cummins was nine years older than Pike, they both had served political apprenticeships under Crittenden and had become well known in Little Rock as opponents of Sevier, Ashley, and Woodruff. Therefore Pike, when he brought the *Advocate* to the cause in 1835, continued that paper's anti-Sevier tradition and did it with a spirit, a zest, that no plain mercenary could have.[6]

Pike unquestionably followed this important local campaign with the keenest interest from his vantage point at the *Advocate* office. He was surprised, recalling the rancor and violence that had accompanied the 1833 election, with the peace and good order with which the balloting was conducted in Pulaski County on August 3, 1835. When the local poll books were finally closed and the results announced, a shout went up from the happy Crittendenites. They had swamped the Sevierites, the popular Cummins by a massive majority and the hard-pressed Fowler by a lesser one but by so decisive a majority that his old enemy Woodruff admitted to "a Waterloo defeat." It was obvious, as Woodruff reported, that Cummins, Fowler, and Caldwell had carried on a better organized campaign than the Sevierites; that is, in Woodruff's words, the trio had "by dint of intrigue and superior management, out-maneuvered us, and obtained a temporary majority." Pike's equally partisan summary was that his friends had won a victory over "party spirit," a contagion of which only Sevierites were apparently guilty.[7]

Hardly less important than the victory of his friends was the thundering endorsement of statehood by the voters on August 3. Pike had hoped that such a demonstration of the popular will would move the cautious Fulton to action. He was disappointed, therefore, when the governor on the fourth of August published a long legal document explaining why he could not call a special session of the newly elected legislature. Pike accepted Fulton's action fairly calmly, giving him credit at least for acting from a sense of duty but expressing regret over the delay. He believed that the governor could call the lawmakers into special session without alluding to the subject of statehood. If they saw fit, on assembling, to pass a convention bill, the governor could veto it. The legislature might then override the executive veto, thus freeing Fulton from any responsibility in the matter.[8]

The governor refused, however, to be budged and there was nothing to do but await the regular session of the legislature on October 5. In the interval, Pike filled the *Advocate* with prostatehood correspondence and reports and permitted no word of Fulton on the subject to go unchallenged. Late in August the governor turned up a congressional speech of South Carolina's William Lowndes, delivered back in 1820, declaring as a doctrine that Missouri was a state from the time it formed—with prior congressional consent—a state constitution and a state government even though Congress had not admitted it to the Union. Missouri's electoral vote for president in 1820 was counted as a consequence of Lowndes's doctrine, Fulton claimed, and he cited it as evidence for the necessity of Arkansas's first securing an enabling act. If so, he concluded, Arkansas could form a constitution and a government and vote for president in 1836 even though Congress, as in the Missouri case, had not finally admitted it to the Union by election time.[9]

Historians have never decided whether Missouri's vote was or was not counted in 1820, but Pike resented his use of the Lowndes's doctrine to justify waiting for a congressional enabling act for Arkansas and pounced on it with ridicule. He pretended to see the possibility of Fulton's "State of Arkansas" being in a very anomalous position under the South Carolinian's doctrine if Congress, having once consent to Arkansas's forming a state government, still refused to admit her. Arkansas would, laughed Pike, cease being a territory without becoming a member of the Union, sort of suspended between heaven and earth "like Mohemet's coffin."[10]

As September gave way to October, Pike watched anxiously as the assemblymen gathered at the Rock. He, Woodruff, and Jefferson Smith and John H. Reed, the new owners of the *Times*, were all calling for prompt attention to the passage of a convention bill. But they and the legislators alike were wondering what Governor Fulton would have to say on the subject in his biennial message. There was not long to wait. The legislature organized on the fifth of October and next day received Fulton's written message delivered by his private secretary.[11]

Setting new standards for verbal obfuscation, Fulton told the legislators that since Arkansas had the necessary population it would be unjust for Congress not to allow her to become a state; that he would support any action of the legislature tending "to urge" Congress to a speedy admission of Arkansas Territory; that he had "no desire to check the tide of popular opinion in favor of a State Government"; and that "as the people have willed it, I now feel it to be my duty to forward this important object, by all the means competent to be used by the Executive power of this Territory." There were enough loopholes in Fulton's language to do credit to a Philadelphia lawyer, but Pike and Woodruff, interpreting it for the Arkansas public, declared that he no longer opposed a convention bill. Woodruff reported that he "recede[d] from" his stand against state government, while Pike, only slightly more optimistic, reported that his message "leans in its favor." The truth was, as they doubtlessly knew, that the sly governor had nowhere in his labyrinthian passages stated that he supported a convention bill in the absence of a congressional enabling act.[12]

By Pike's own count there were no more than five to eight members of the legislature opposed to forming a state government, and he expected speedy action on a convention bill. He was about to learn an important lesson in Arkansas politics. A joint committee of fourteen members, chaired by his friend Absalom Fowler, took under consideration the governor's message as it related to state government. A week later, on October 14, the committee majority, citing the governor's message as evidence of his support, reported in favor of statehood and requested authority from the legislature to bring in a convention bill. The committee minority, citing the governor's message and also his previous "public" statements, reported that it was "unnecessary, impolitic and inexpedient to Legislate on the subject of a State Government, at this time."[13]

Voting triumphantly for statehood, the house and council members approved the majority report, and Fowler's joint committee spent five days hammering out a bill. Reported back to the house on the nineteenth of October, Fowler's convention bill was immediately tied up in an acrimonious debate over the basis of representation for the proposed convention. The planters of the south and east and the small, nonslaveholding farmers of the north and west each wished their particular interests protected. Almost evenly divided between the two sections, the legislators found themselves involved in a quarrel that cut across the recognized Sevier-Crittenden factional lines and threatened to disrupt the session. The outstanding leaders on the two sides in 1835, as it turned out, were all Crittendenites. Pike's partner Cummins and a wealthy Hempstead County planter, James H. Walker, spoke for the southeast. Pike's friend Absalom Fowler and the conservative David Walker, a rising anti-Sevierite in populous Washington County in the northwest, spoke for the northwest.[14]

The discord grew out of Arkansas's two great topographic regions, the lowlands of the southeast and the highlands of the northwest, or rather out of the sectional interests represented by these two geographical areas. Slaveholders had settled on the alluvial soils of the coastal plains and on the fingers of rich soil extending up the river valleys into the highlands, while mostly nonslaveholding yeoman farmers had settled in the picturesque hill country of the Ozark Plateaus and the Ouachita Mountains.

These two groups, the cotton planters of the southeast and the corn and hog farmers of the northwest, were distinct in several ways because of different origins. The southeast planters came mainly from the older cotton states of the lower South, while the northwest farmers came mostly of yeoman stock from Tennessee and the upper South. In the southeast cotton production and slaveholding flourished, and the people there—whether planters and their retainers, yeomen farmers with a handful of slaves, or squatters with none—all developed a community of interests attuned to the spreading cotton-slave culture. In the northwest, on the other hand, the corn-hog-hay-cattle-fruit subsistence farmers lived in a world apart. These hardy men had few if any slaves and mistrusted whites who did own them.

Out of these differences based on geography and soils rather than on politics, arose Arkansas's internal sectional conflict. Broadly it became a struggle of lowlander against uplander, of planter against farmer, of slaveholder against non-slaveholder, of a wealthy minority against a less prosperous majority. Not political in origin, it nevertheless profoundly affected politics; and politicians, trying to effect statewide alliances and winning majorities, were constantly aware of the hostile sectional feelings bubbling just beneath the lid of the Arkansas political kettle. It was, of course, the task of the politicos, if they were to construct their workable majorities, to keep the lid on the pot.[15]

Pike looked on in October 1835 as the lid blew off and angry legislators gave vent to sectional feelings over the basis question. Southeastern slaveholders, led by James H. Walker of Hempstead County, stoked the fire beneath the pot. They objected to the apportionment of delegates in Fowler's bill, which called for the election of forty-two delegates—one for each of Arkansas's thirty-four counties and the remaining eight to be portioned out among the larger counties according to the number of white persons or of white adult males. According to Fowler's later explanation his committee had worked out this basis as a compromise giving equal representation to each of the sections. Thus twenty-one of the delegates were to come from the southeast, including Pulaski County's three, and twenty-one from the northwest, a ratio which left the populous white northwest under-represented in comparison with the less populous southeast but which the northwest committee members under Fowler's prodding had accepted in the interest of harmony.[16]

A zealot for statehood, Pike seemingly favored Fowler's basis as a reasonable solution to the thorny question. Writing for the *Advocate* of October 23, while the house was still considering the convention bill, Pike interpreted Walker of Hempstead's amendment to the Fowler bill as an attempt to prevent any convention bill from passing. Walker of Hempstead's amendment, providing that each county elect to the convention delegates equal in number to its representatives and councilmen in the current legislature, would have given control to the southeast without including Pulaski County. Moreover, he defended his basis on the grounds, as Pike reported, "that were it not for the slaves in the Territory, we have not the requisite population to entitle us to admission into the Union."[17]

Pike on the twenty-third accused Walker, a known opponent of statehood, of deliberately raising the "unfortunate question" of slave representation in order to divide the legislature and to scuttle the convention bill. Pike expressed genuine alarm over the "animated, violent and acrimonious" debate stirred by the amendment. "The Northern and Western section of our Territory," Pike warned, "is now arrayed against the South and East. Sectional feelings of the utmost bitterness have sprung up, which may jeopardize the best interests of Arkansas." He regretted that such feelings had arisen and pleaded with the lawmakers not to permit statehood to be endangered by the question of whether one section or the other should have "a little more or a little less influence" in the convention. "Compared with our entrance into the Union, all such considerations shrink into insignificance," he concluded.[18]

Meeting his editorial deadline for October 23, Pike probably was not aware of the complete legislative history of the convention bill. He had implied that the backers of Walker's amendment were, like its sponsor, all advocates of slave representation. The truth was that Pike's partner Cummins had carried the amendment in the house on the twentieth by a skillful appeal for what he called "district representation." Under Walker's amendment, Cummins argued, each county would have at least one delegate as a "district representation" irrespective of population and one additional delegate for each 500 white males as a popular representation. Cummins allegedly opposed slave representation or the federal three-fifths ratio but in support of "district representation" cited the compromise adopted in forming the federal Constitution whereby each state had equal representation in the Senate and popular representation in the House. He thus equated the counties in the territory with the states in the Union, declaring that to destroy county representation in the convention and to assume any other basis for apportioning delegates would place the right of the less populous counties in the hands of the more populous ones. "This," he proclaimed, "would not be justice, would not be republican in principle, and would really be tyranny, that a small district [in area] should govern the whole because it happened at the moment to be the most populous."[19]

Swayed by the polished Cummins, one or two northwest house members went over to the southeast and helped carry the Walker amendment on October 20. Cummins had convinced them that "district representation" was a completely different principle than Negro representation when in fact it amounted to the same thing. At least Fowler and Walker of Washington believed this, and, breaking with their friend Cummins, fought a successful battle to restore the Fowler basis in place of Walker of Hempstead's. In doing so they educated northwestern legislators on the real meaning of "district representation" and won the stragglers back. Walker of Washington minced no words in denouncing it as an attempt to give one white southeasterner with five slaves a voice equal to four white adult male northwesterners with no slaves, a sarcastic slap at the Federal three-fifths ratio. He also rained ridicule on Cummins's "district representation," declaring that the plan proposed the hitherto unheard of principle in America of giving districts of uninhabited country representation, and that it held out the possibility of permitting trees of the forest in Cummins's "geographical districts" to represent as many American citizens because such unpopulated districts "might one day be peopled." And in any case, "district representation" gave the southeast slaveholders what they wanted—control of the convention.[20]

Fowler agreed with David Walker of Washington County that Cummins's "district representation" was nothing more than a clever scheme to secure southeast control of the convention by substituting "district" for "negro" representation. But Fowler exercised a mediating influence with the angry Walker of Washington, and together they became the architects of a successful compromise. They mustered the votes in the house on the twenty-second to substitute the original Fowler basis of forty-two delegates for Walker of Hempstead's amendment. Cummins contested them on the issue, but on the twenty-third surrendered and actually voted with them in favor of the convention bill on its final passage in the house.[21]

When the southeast-controlled council on the twenty-fourth again restored the basis of the Walker of Hempstead amendment, the house, led by Fowler and Walker of Washington, proposed a compromise measure approved by both houses on October 26. This final bill, which cautious but cagey Governor Fulton permitted to become law without his signature, provided for a convention of fifty-two delegates instead of the forty-two originally proposed by Fowler and approved by the house or the sixty-two proposed by Walker of Hempstead and approved by the council. The contemporary view, which seems to be valid, was that the bill gave equality to the two sections, twenty-six to the southeast including Pulaski County and twenty-six to the northwest.[22]

Between the twenty-third and the thirtieth Pike was obviously subjected to considerable pressure by his partner Cummins and by a number of southeast legislators. They had not, they insisted, voted for Walker of Hempstead's amendment on the twentieth because they were advocates of slave representation but because they were backers of Cummins's idea "that districts of country, as well as people by numbers, should be represented in Convention." Accordingly, Pike on October 30 published a correction. He was glad, he said, to do so. He had no fear of "compromising" his "independence" and was more than ready to make the correction "because although we ourself are thoroughly opposed to slave-representation, we are, and ever have declared ourself, in favor of a representation of districts, as being absolutely necessary to the existence of any Republic, or Republican state."[23]

Pike's endorsement of Cummins's "district representation" revealed two things. First, it was consistent with his published views on government, especially his recent defense of the U.S. Senate as a bastion of republican government and of the minority South. Second, it revealed his true sympathies in the Arkansas sectional dispute of 1835. This came out when John Reed of the *Times* asserted that Pike had become the official apologist of the southeast. Pike's southeast friends, according to Reed, had tried to ram through a bill based on "negro representation" but, growing alarmed at the opposition aroused by that hateful doctrine, had switched over to "the undefinable substitute of *District* representation." Pike on the twenty-third, Reed said, had "freely" admitted that "the question was slave representation." But now, on the thirtieth, Pike was trying to screen his southeast friends by making it appear to the public that they were all along in favor of "district representation," which Reed described as a "covert" scheme to throw the balance of power to the southeast. It was, he proclaimed, "as great an outrage on the rights of freemen, as any arbitrary principle which could be fostered upon them, except indeed, the original proposition of slave or property representation." It was bad enough, Reed concluded, for the representatives of the people to run into such error, but for Pike to use "the press" to conceal the selfish designs of such men was "a curse to the community."[24]

So far as is known Pike was satisfied with the compromise basis included in the convention bill. His partner Cummins had voted for it in the house, and it gave the southeast planters a larger proportion of the delegates than they were entitled to on the basis of the southeast's white male population. But Pike took umbrage at Reed's charge that he was shielding his southeast friends. Reed had asked how he got his facts as to how southeast members had truly stood on Walker of Hempstead's amendment. By their speeches in the house and by "their solemn declarations afterwards to us personally," Pike bluntly answered. Only Walker of Hempstead and Cummins, Pike explained, had spoken for the amendment on the house floor, and Cummins "denied going for slave representation—and many members from the South[east], in private conversation with us afterwards, averred the same thing." "It is not our habit to doubt the word of *gentlemen*," enjoined Pike. "It may be otherwise with the publishers of the Times."[25]

The election of the delegates was scheduled for December 14 and the meeting of the convention for January 4, 1836. Pike left Little Rock for some three weeks in late November–early December of 1835. He returned to town a few days before the election to find that Cummins, Fowler, and his friend John McLain, a partner in Little Rock's largest mercantile establishment, were assured of election as delegates. But at the *Advocate* office he learned from his assistant editor that John Reed of the *Times* was demanding that Pike "get *off the fence* and take sides either for or against *free white male representation*."[26] He discovered, also, in looking through the back files of the *Times*, that Reed had opened his columns to a hostile correspondent who used the signature "A.B.C." The gist of both Reed's editorials and A.B.C.'s long letters was that Pike's paper was "the ostensible organ of the southern doctrine," that is, that Pike's southeast friends had abandoned Negro representation and were now contending for "what they call district representation." Defining district representation, A.B.C. declared that "it is precisely the same in effect as the negro basis. One is an aristocracy of a species of property largely owned in the south—the other is an aristocracy of land and cotton farms, &c., &c." Of the two, A.B.C. considered district representation the more dangerous and the more oppressive. As for Reed, he wanted representation in each chamber of the future state legislature to be based solely upon free white male inhabitants, a system that would give the populous white counties of the northwest control of both chambers.[27]

Pike debated the basis question with Reed and A.B.C. in a series of essays on representation, a study of which shows that he had examined with great care both the U.S. Constitution and the *Federalist Papers*. He saw Arkansas as a miniature United States. Southeast Arkansas, he contended, stood in relation to northwest Arkansas exactly as the South stood in relation to the North, "asking certain rights and powers to be guaranteed to them before they sign the compact of united government." The Senate of the United States, based on equal representation for each state, had become the bulwark of the minority South. The senate of Arkansas must offer the same protection to the minority southeast, else there could be in the state no republican government, which Pike defined as "a compact between the minority and the majority." A state senate based on districts of equal numbers of white male inhabitants, as contended for by Reed and A.B.C., would merely make the upper house a facsimile of the lower house on a smaller scale. The majority northwest would control both bodies, and there would be no way for the minority southeast to obtain justice from the majority in such an assembly. "Let it be remembered," he pleaded, "that the House of Representatives will be the people's *agent. We want another agent to act as a check upon them*—a Senate. The Senate is not an agent to control the people. *It is an agent to control another agent.*"²⁸

Pike solemnly denied that district representation was the same as Negro representation or that district representation, for which he spoke, was "aristocratic, outrageous, and not to be thought of" as asserted by his opponents. Reed and his correspondent had, said Pike, labored "assiduously to convince the poor men of this country that district representation is only another plan for giving the rich man from six to a hundred votes to the poor man's one." "Let us see," reasoned Pike,

> "how the matter really stands." It was plain from the recent contest in the legislature that the southeast had been placed in open opposition to the northwest, that there are two great divisions in this Territory—and there will be two in the future State. One of these, the South, is in a minority as to numbers. Now it is of course agreed by every one that the House of Representatives in the State Legislature shall be elected, one for so many free white males—on the popular basis. Here then the North will have the majority. If the State Senate is elected in the same way, the North will have a majority there too. *Where then is the protection for the minority?*²⁹

There would be none, Pike answered, unless the senate were apportioned so as to give the southeast at least an equal voice with the northwest in that body. Pleading for protection of the southeast, Pike appealed to the federal Constitution which afforded the less populous states an equal voice with the more populous ones in the U.S. Senate. The southern states depended upon this same basis, equality in the Senate, for the protection of their minority rights in the Union, said Pike. "Let these men who gabble so loudly about patriotism," he sneered, "answer if it is patriotism to take away from the minority every check against the rapacity and greediness of the majority."³⁰

"Yes," asserted Pike, "we are 'the ostensible organ of the Southern doctrine.' If that means that we wish to see a Senate formed by members elected from Senatorial districts of equal extent, it is our doctrine, and we will sink or swim by it." He spelled out what he meant by "districts of equal extent." He would have the territory divided into senatorial districts of equal geographical areas without consideration of the number of white or black inhabitants in each. Such a scheme would, he argued, provide for the future as well as the present. "Equal extents of country may be supposed to be capable of supporting equal numbers of inhabitants," he asserted, in denying that he was motivated by sectional feelings in advocating district representation. "It is," he maintained, "a doctrine for the whole country—for the benefit of the thinly settled portions of the North, as of the South."³¹

Closing, Pike said that he was sure that those who opposed district representation would say that it favored the southeast. For this he had but one answer. The southeast was presently more sparsely settled than the northwest, but there was no reason to believe that this would always be the case. "Any man who can make the discovery," he countered, "that the population of the South and East is about to decrease, is a fit candidate for Bedlam." He also had a final word for Reed, who had been "lustily calling on us during our absence" to take a stand "either for or against free white male representation." Charging that Reed had known since October his position on district representation for the senate, Pike accused the *Times* editor of irresponsibility in agitating the question of "free white male representation," this "cross of fire" which had been carried through the northwest by two or three "patriots" at "the expense of the peace and happiness of Arkansas." Yet these same "patriots," were, he noted, very desirous of Arkansas's entering the Union and sending "two senators to Congress for our fifty thousand—negroes and all." He thought it ironic that Reed and his "patriots" were unwilling to give the southeast equal representation with the northwest in the senate, although they were quite satisfied for Arkansas's "fifty thousand" to send two senators to Congress to match the two sent by "the mammoth State of New York."[32]

However mistaken Pike may have been in defining republican government as a compact between the majority and the minority, however partisan he may have been in defending the minority rights of the southeast section, however undemocratic he may have been in ignoring the revered principle of white-male representation for the senate, it cannot be denied that he had made out a good case for using the bicameral system to afford protection for the minority. He would grant control of the house to the majority but would give the minority at least an equal voice in the senate. Whether his gridwork of senate districts of equal land area would have accomplished this is beside the point; what he proposed was a senate whose members represented sections and not people, interests and not population. No one living at the time would probably have believed that the southeast half of the state would one day be the more populous section, yet by the beginning of the next century, that was the case. Pike was no prophet, but he recognized that, if such were the case, the northwest would then have the power that he, in 1835, asked for the southeast. Constitutions were made, he said, for the future as well as the present.

He was accused of being undemocratic, which he was, but he did not argue the point. He replied bluntly that he had "always been opposed to the ultra democratic principles with which so many are enraptured." Accordingly, he had no compunctions whatever about telling the John Reeds of Arkansas that the northwest should not control both houses of the legislature simply because that section contained a majority of the free white males in the territory. If he thought about it, Pike must have known that such a stand was unwise politically. But, as he had said months before, in expounding his views against the popular election of judges, he would leave it to office seekers and officeholders to trim their sails to ride with the political winds. He would speak for what he believed to be right and wise, not what he believed to be expedient and unwise. He was no trimmer.

Pike's December editorials did not, however, make him unpopular in the convention that assembled in Little Rock on Monday, January 4, 1836. His friends among the delegates, especially genial Terence Farrelly, Mary Ann's foster father and representative of Arkansas and Jefferson Counties of the southeast, got him elected printer to the convention over the formidable Woodruff by a vote of twenty-seven to twenty-three. This "real fat job" as Woodruff would come to call it, was a reward to Pike for his defense of the southeast on the basis question and a rebuke to Woodruff, Pike said, for Old Buck's "pretended" neutrality on the question publicly while privately supporting the southeast.[33]

It was Pike's responsibility as convention printer to copy and print the day-to-day proceedings and reports, a duty that gave him a good vantage point from which to study the work of the convention. He also printed the proceedings in the *Advocate* and commented in his editorial column on the reports and debates. All went smoothly and peacefully, he observed, until on January 19 the committee on the legislative branch submitted adverse majority and minority reports on the basis question. The southeast planters threatened to adjourn the convention *sine die* and return to their homes unless their senate district plan was adopted, but in the end, thanks to the hard work of Little Rock's Absalom Fowler, they gave way to a compromise plan that gave them temporary control of the senate while giving control of the house to the northwest farmers. Pike was pleased with Fowler's success, even though the adoption of his plan meant that the southeast would probably lose control of the senate after 1838, when a new census would be taken and a reapportionment would take place. The session, Pike announced to his readers in reporting Fowler's compromise, "will terminate amicably in the great object desired—giving a Constitution to a free people. The vexed question of Representation has been settled by a compromise between the friends of a District representation and those opposed to it."[34] The northwest victory over the southeast lay in the fact that representation in both houses of the legislature would be based on white adult males and that neither slaves nor senate districts of equal land area would be considered in apportioning seats in future legislatures. Pike's insinuation that the northwest had compromised with "friends of a District representative" was meaningless unless he meant it as a gesture of concession."

In addition to following developments in the exciting basis question, Pike kept an interested eye on the work of the committee on the judiciary. When the committee submitted its report to the convention on January 9, Pike expressed himself editorially on the details. He was pleased that the committee recommended legislative election of judges, but was appalled at the short term of office for supreme court judges. He preferred, he said, "to see them elected to serve during good behavior. If not, they should serve ten years, and the circuit court judges six at least." When his friend Judge Thomas Lacy, a delegate from Monroe County, moved on a subsequent day in the convention to change the term of office for supreme court judges from six to twelve years, Pike showered praise on the judge both for his amendment and for the "fervid eloquence of language" with which he defended it. Judge Lacy's motion carried but later was reversed and a new amendment substituted changing the term to eight years.[35]

Expressing keen disappointment, Pike described the ground on which Judge Lacy's amendment was reversed "to be radically wrong." To his horror, Pike had now discovered that legislative election of judges, which nine months before he had learnedly defended over either popular election or executive appointment, also had its evils. If subjected to too frequent reelection by popularly elected legislators, the judges would not be free from popular prejudice after all. He swore eternal opposition to the provision, declaring that his "feeble efforts" would "never be remitted to place the Judiciary on a basis not to be shaken by Legislative favoritism or revenge, or popular fickleness." Time would shortly reveal that Arkansas judges, as Pike suspected in 1836, could indeed be shaken by "popular fickleness" and "Legislative revenge."[36]

All in all, Pike was satisfied with the work of the convention. He praised the clause in the Bill of Rights guaranteeing freedom of religion. "Let no man," he proclaimed, "interfere between another's conscience and his God." An enemy of the veto, he liked the provision which permitted a simple majority in each house of the legislature to override the governor's veto. And he was happy with the authority bestowed on the legislature to establish chancery courts when it was deemed expedient, although he himself had called for the immediate establishment of a separate system of such courts together with a "High Court of Chancery." Summing up his views on the work of the convention and the constitution, which he printed in full in the *Advocate* the week following final adjournment, Pike gave the document his "almost unqualified" approval. It was true, he said, that he had opposed some of its features. But he had not expected that all his "notions and views" would be enacted, and he stood ready to defend the document "and to live under it." "The convention has," he concluded, "done honor to itself and to Arkansas."[37]

The final adjournment of the delegates brought into the open a Pike-Woodruff quarrel over convention printing that had been smoldering for a month. Back in January Pike, editorially thanking his friends for electing him printer, took the opportunity to insult Woodruff. Pike was especially proud of his election, he crowed, "coming to us, as it did, by a fair vote, without any huckstering or auctioneering, than we could have been of even 'a fat job' coming from the hands of Government."[38] To be sure, Woodruff did not take his defeat kindly, and as he was about to demonstrate, he keenly resented Pike's gratuitous insult about past "fat jobs" of printing which the territorial and federal governments had bestowed on the *Gazette* editor.

Woodruff was peeved, also, because his old enemy Absalom Fowler had, in the convention, persuaded the delegates to deduct five dollars from Woodruff's bill of ten dollars for "hauling furniture to and from Convention House, Servant hire, &c." It was a petty, vindictive act on Fowler's part, but typical of the low level on which Absalom and Old Billy carried on their personal vendetta. Young Pike, thinking his friend Fowler's act a capital joke, printed Woodruff's bill in the *Advocate* and needled him about it. Woodruff had been grumbling about "high prices and fat jobs." What did he think, asked Pike, of his own bill for drayage and servant hire? "We understand," prodded Pike, "that the negroes are about *striking* for an increase in wages since the Editor of the Gazette has raised the price of *Drayage*. That valuable class of citizens think our neighbour good authority."[39]

There is no evidence in the *Gazette* of January 1836 to indicate that Woodruff had been editorially grumbling, as Pike said, about "high prices and fat jobs." But Woodruff secured a copy of the new constitution, worked furiously to set it in type, and published it as a *Gazette* extra on February 4, the day before Pike's regular weekly issue of the *Advocate* was to carry it. Woodruff not only had deliberately scooped Pike but was obviously proud of his feat. "Although not *smart* enough to secure *fat jobs* of the Legislature and the Convention," he crowed, referring to his defeat back in October by the publishers of the *Times* and his loss in January to Pike, "our readers shall ever find us, as usual, not behind our competitors in *industry*, in laying before them, at the earliest period, the result of the labors of those bodies."[40]

Pike must have been annoyed over Woodruff's scooping him on the constitution since he undoubtedly had the document set in type, and perhaps already printed, even before Old Buck's extra went to press. It was Woodruff's reference to "fat jobs" in his extra of the fourth which seemingly impelled Pike, at least in part, to publish on the fifth Woodruff's drayage bill, a little joke that was soon to backfire on the long-haired *Advocate* editor.[41]

On the eve of adjournment, the convention had generously ordered Pike to print and distribute 5,000 copies of the Constitution of the State of Arkansas and 500 copies of the Journal of the Convention. Pike had billed the territorial auditor for $177 for day-to-day printing ordered during the convention session, and after the final adjournment, he billed the auditor for $1,050 for the work to be done on the constitution and the journal. Neither of his bills was protested by the auditor, who promptly paid over to Pike a total of $1,227 for all the convention printing. But Woodruff, after Pike's drayage-bill joke of the fifth, called at the auditor's office to examine Pike's printing bills. He undoubtedly got a friendly reception, since the territorial auditor was none other than Elias Nelson Conway, Woodruff's close political friend and a younger brother of the deceased Henry Conway.[42]

In the *Gazette* of February 9, Woodruff treated his readers to a prize editorial, entitled "A REAL 'FAT JOB.'" Since Pike had "thought proper" to publish a bill of his, Woodruff hoped the editor of the *Advocate* would not "take it unkind of us" if he exposed a bill which Pike "made out for fat jobs given him by the Convention, and which has been paid before the work was done, or even commenced." Woodruff then printed Pike's bill item by item. He declared Pike's charge of $850 for printing 5,000 copies of the constitution to be "the most extravagant one ever made for such a job of printing—either *fat* or *lean*—in Arkansas or elsewhere," and concluded that Pike had received $1,227 for convention printing "for which $475 would have been a very liberal compensation."[43]

Woodruff was "sorry that the yeas and nays" on Pike's "extravagant allowments" were not spread upon the convention journal "so that the people could see who were so lavish of the public money." "Where," he asked, "was *honest* Absalom—who is always so eager to pounce on our bills? Why did he object to a bill of our's, and get it curtailed $5, and at the same time vote for giving Mr. Pike nearly $800 of the people's money without rendering any equivalent for it?" Fowler could answer in only two ways, thought Woodruff. Either he was disposed to tax the people to pamper "*his* favorite, or else . . . he was deceived by Mr. Pike, as, we have, no doubt, were a large majority of the members of the Convention—for we can hardly believe that any of them (*honest* Absalom excepted) would have been so dishonest as to have voted for such extravagant allowances, had they been aware of the deception which was practised on them."[44]

Closing, Woodruff thought there was a lesson to be drawn from the matter: Pike could not be trusted. None of the men who served as delegates would be likely ever to vote money to him again, "without scrutinizing his accounts a little more closely than was done by the Convention—and it would have been well had they done so on the late occasion."[45]

Well burned by Old Buck's able bit of journalism, Pike evidently chose to ignore the political implications of the convention printing. It was plain that his friends who had elected him printer had rewarded him liberally, even though the convention itself had not, as Woodruff suggested, approved the amounts specified in Pike's bills. The convention had merely ordered a certain amount of printing, leaving it to Pike to bill the territorial auditor for the money and to the auditor to approve and pay him. If it was true that Fowler had voted for Pike's printing, so had all the rest of the delegates. If there was anything amiss concerning Pike's charges for printing or his being paid before part of the printing was completed, it could not have been lost on Woodruff that his good friend Auditor Conway was as culpable as Pike.

Consequently, Pike's rather weak reply to Woodruff's charges of extortion was that, yes, he had got the money and would do the printing. "Our neighbor is welcome to grumble," gloated Pike. "It is the prerogative of disappointed men and old women to scold, and he may enact Xantippe to his heart's content. A man who has been beaten as often and as badly as he has, should be allowed that privilege. So grumble away, neighbor!"[46]

But Pike may have felt that his readers deserved a more reasonable explanation. Admitting that he got "a good price for the printing," he declared boldly" "We work for nobody, and little as any for the Territory, without being paid. We could have got more, had we asked it." He had, he said, "got too little for copying and printing the Journals," and the convention members had said "we got too little for printing done during the session." If he got "too much for printing the Constitution," which he confessed was "perhaps" true, it was only fair. "On the whole," he concluded, "the account is about balanced." He was certain that the *Gazette* editor, who "wishes the yeas and nays had been taken," would not be satisfied to learn that there had not been "one dissenting voice against either of our bills." "No body grumbles but our neighbor of the Gazette." It was "a pity," said Pike, the delegates had not allowed his drayage bill "as a sop to this Cerberus. He is an interesting guardian over the public crib."[47]

That ended the matter of the convention printing insofar as Pike was concerned, although Woodruff kept the subject before the public all through February and into March. John Reed of the *Times* reported on February 15 that his neighbors Pike and Woodruff were still after each other, but he promised not to interfere. Woodruff threatened in the *Gazette* of the sixteenth to "demolish" Pike in his next issue, whereupon Pike mockingly asked for mercy. "We fight single handed," he told Woodruff. "The Times says it won't interfere." He hoped, however, that Woodruff would not retain "his venom too long" and end up, as David Crockett had once said, "so full of *pison*, that if he bites himself he'll die." To which Woodruff replied that Pike had "constituted himself the 'guardian of the public crib'—and the way he guards it is a 'sin to Crockett.'" Yet when Woodruff's "outpourings of . . . wrath" fell on Pike in the *Gazette* of the twenty-third, they were nothing but repetitions of his earlier charges of extortion. Albert refused any further reply to Old Billy on the subject of the convention printing, and Woodruff, unable to draw Pike into further exchange on the subject, soon dropped it also.[48]

While Pike and Woodruff debated the weighty subjects of drayage charges and printing bills, Fent Noland conveyed a certified parchment copy of Arkansas's constitution to Washington City. Traveling by boat to Mobile, thence overland by stage to Washington, Noland arrived shortly before noon on March 8, exactly a week after Woodruff's *Gazette* extra of February 4 had reached Delegate Sevier by mail. Indeed, Sevier had apparently used the uncertified document in Woodruff's extra to obtain committee approval in the House for a bill admitting Arkansas as a state. Sevier expressed himself to be perturbed by the fact that Noland had brought only a single certified copy of the Arkansas constitution, which was addressed to the Secretary of State rather than to himself. Nevertheless, President Jackson, anxious to obtain Arkansas's electoral vote for Martin Van Buren in the fall election of 1836, prodded the Secretary of State to submit the document promptly to Congress.[49]

There Arkansas's statehood bill was tied up in a heated and somewhat prolonged debate over the slavery clauses in her constitution. The clauses were eventually accepted, but only after the antislavery and proslavery forces had compromised by agreeing that the admission in 1836 of Michigan as a free state and Arkansas as a slave state was calculated to keep the sectional balance in the Senate even.[50]

In Arkansas that spring there was great excitement in anticipation of the first state election on August 1, that is, if the statehood bill got through Congress. Pike assumed that it would and laid plans for organizing a state political party that he hoped would wrest control of Arkansas from the Sevierites. He had been flying Hugh Lawson White's presidential flag for a year, and now, on March 4, 1836, put his readers on notice that the Van Buren forces were organizing to carry Arkansas for their man and to fill all the state offices. He suspected Sevier, Ashley, Woodruff, and "half a dozen schemers" at Little Rock had already made up a ticket "for the people to swallow" and sent orders to the "out counties" for "caucuses and conventions" to be held and "demonstrations on the enemy's flank." He wanted to know who the people were expected to vote for, and then bragged: "We will beat you, man by man, in detail and in mass—for every office, when you make Van Burenism the question."[51]

Since Arkansans had never voted in a national election, there had been no clear distinction between the territorial factions on national issues. But 1836 was a presidential election year, and it was expected Arkansas would be admitted in time to cast three electoral votes in the contest. Sevier had, of course, cast the lot of "the Dynasty" with Jackson, which for nearly eight years had paid them handsome dividends in offices and power. He committed himself in 1836 to work for Jackson's candidate, Martin Van Buren, and he had dutifully informed the federal secretary of state that under no circumstance should that official appoint Pike as a publisher of the laws in Arkansas. Pike's *Advocate* was, reported Sevier, in "opposition to every thing in the name or shape of Jackson and democracy."[52]

The charge was true. Pike had attacked Jackson, and he had plainly gone on record as opposing "ultra-democratic principles." But Pike also knew that Jackson's candidate, Van Buren, was not very popular in Arkansas. The New Yorker had voted for the Tariff of Abominations in 1828, and he was suspected of being an abolitionist. On the other hand, Judge White of Tennessee, a heretofore loyal Jackson man, was supposedly very popular in Arkansas. The Sevierites would have a tough time explaining to Arkansas voters why they should vote for a protariff, abolitionist rather than a hitherto loyal Tennessee Jacksonian. Or so Pike thought. Accordingly, on April 29 he placed at the masthead of the *Advocate* his personal choice for the presidency, "Judge Hugh Lawson White of Tennessee."[53]

In backing Judge White, Pike had two objects in mind: to defeat Van Buren in Arkansas, and, thereby, to lend support to the national Whig strategy of forcing the election into the House of Representatives. Henry Clay and northern Whig leaders had adopted this strategy in 1835, and by early 1836 Daniel Webster in the North, Judge White in the South, and Gen. William Henry Harrison in the West had won local nominations and were conducting campaigns. Tennessee in early 1836 gave every indication of deserting Jackson for White, and it was obvious to Pike that Arkansas might follow suit.

Though Pike was not fully aware of the intimate details, the Sevierites were badly worried over White's candidacy. Governor Fulton had told President Jackson in the summer of 1835 that he opposed statehood because he felt that "Whiteism" was behind it, and that Little Rock's powerful lawyer Chester Ashley, a national bank and a White man, would be able to carry Arkansas for White. In February 1836, with statehood far advanced, the governor reported to the president that Jackson's friends were "endeavoring to organize the Jackson party in Arkansas" and to make the new state an "administration state." He thought Arkansas, "in spite of Whiteism," could be carried for Van Buren. The people were still Jackson men, but they were opposed to Van Buren, who "must place us in possession of facts, to meet all the charges made against him." The governor also requested "all the materials necessary" to carry on a "vigorous" newspaper campaign. The Little Rock press had the governor much concerned. The *Gazette*, because of Colonel Sevier, would support Van Buren, but editor Woodruff's principles were "decidely opposition, so that we cannot trust him and we must therefore act under restraint in communicating with the public." Ashley was not mentioned, but it was obvious that Fulton's distrust of Woodruff stemmed directly from his own personal knowledge of the close tie between Ashley and Woodruff.[54]

Whiteism was not Sevier's only concern that spring of 1836. In Washington in April, he addressed a serious letter to President Jackson. He reminded the president that he had told him "some months ago" that his cousin James Sevier Conway "was a candidate for the office of Governor in Arkansas." At that time Sevier, Conway, and others had recommended that another cousin, Col. Wharton Rector, replace Conway as surveyor general of Arkansas. But now, in April, Sevier had learned that Edward Cross, a federal judge in Arkansas, wanted the surveyor general's post. Sevier thought it best to appoint Cross, stating his reasons in a revealing paragraph on "the Dynasty."

> Col. Rector at this time is agent for the Creek Indians—His brother Elias Rector, is now Marshall and will expect a reappointment under our state, as soon as it is admitted—James Conway, who is now the incumbent, is Rector's cousin, and is the democratic candidate for governor—Conway is my relation also—I am held up for the Senate in Arkansas, and my father in law Judge Johnson, I desire to be appointed federal Judge—I am thus particular, in order to show you that if Rector

is appointed in the place of Conway to the exclusion of Cross, who wants it, the people of Arkansas will consider that there is too much monopoly in the offices of Arkansas by my relatives and intimate friends—And this impression may injure the cause in Arkansas, and on that account, I desire the appointment of Cross—[55]

The president appointed Cross, Johnson would get his judgeship, and Elias Rector would get his marshal's badge. For Jackson's "readiness ever to conform to the wishes of your friends in Arkansas," Sevier pledged himself to "a fortunate issue to the administration in the coming contests in Arkansas."[56]

Matters did not improve, however, for Van Buren with the Little Rock press. In May John H. Reed bought complete control of the *Times* and joined Pike's *Advocate* in supporting White. The same month Woodruff, it was noticed, took on a new man at the *Gazette*. He was Thomas Jefferson Pew, former editor of the *Gazette* of Lexington, Kentucky. Though no notice was ever given, the appointment was doubtlessly dictated by Sevier and Fulton. Pew's name appeared alone on May 17 over the *Gazette's* editorials, but it was July before Woodruff publicly announced that "since the change of editors" he was not responsible for the paper's editorials. The *Gazette* had been rescued for Van Buren.[57]

Pike obviously enjoyed the embarrassment that White's candidacy had brought to the Sevierites, and he would in time seek to make the most of it. But as May gave way to June, uppermost in his mind was the first election for state officials and for congressman coming up on August 1. Not yet ready to call himself a Whig but feeling the need for both a party organization and a new name for the Crittendenites, Pike adopted the prosaic name of "People's Party" for the Arkansas anti-Sevier, anti–Van Buren party in 1836. He also used for his party's slate the label "People's Anti-Caucus Candidates," a reference to the Baltimore Democratic national convention of 1835 which Whigs claimed was a rigged caucus of Jackson's corrupt friends. Nor did he object to the name "People's Republican Party," a title preferred by his ally Reed of the *Times* and which referred to Jefferson's Republican Party, from which both Democrats and Whigs now imagined they were rapidly emerging.

The People's Party was as tightly organized as Sevier's Democrats, with a small clique of Little Rock lawyers and merchants determining, in private conference, its views, policies, and measures; dictating to packed conventions its candidates; and conducting through the *Advocate* and *Times* vigorous propaganda campaigns in support of their cause. Since, however, Pike's and Reed's papers had a limited circulation and since the population of Arkansas was sparse and scattered, the principal method of getting out the vote was stump speaking to mass meetings of the people at county seats and other settlements.

Pike owed his commanding position in the People's Party directly to the fact that he owned the oldest and most powerful anti-Sevier, anti-Jacksonian newspaper in Arkansas. His paper, his partnership with the ambitious Cummins, his marriage into the Farrelly-Notrebe-Desha circle, bound him intimately with the anti-Sevier forces. Most prominent in the Little Rock clique, besides Cummins, was Absalom Fowler. Cummins was a Kentuckian and Fowler a Tennessean; Cummins had married the daughter of Frederick Notrebe and Fowler the daughter of Ben Desha; Cummins was Pike's law partner while

Fowler had been Robert Crittenden's. Both Cummins and Fowler had represented Pulaski County in the constitutional convention, both had voted for Pike as convention printer, and both had political ambitions.

On June 24 Pike announced in the *Advocate* that a People's convention of the voters of Pulaski, White, and Saline counties would meet at the Pulaski County courthouse in Little Rock on Saturday night, June 25, to nominate candidates for the legislature and for county offices. Supported also by Reed's *Times*, the convention met on schedule. It endorsed White for president, nominated Cummins for Congress and Fowler for governor, and named a full ticket for the legislature and for county offices. It appointed Pike chairman of a committee of twelve to draw up an address to the people of the state and of Pulaski, White, and Saline counties on behalf of the local candidates.[58]

A week before, on June 18, a packed meeting of Sevierites, calling themselves the "Jackson Republican Party," had held a pro–Van Buren convention in Little Rock. It had dutifully approved a slate, as Woodruff later confessed, which Sevier, Ashley, Woodruff, and a few others had agreed to several months before at "a sort of oyster party" gathering at the Rock.[59] Van Buren was endorsed, Archibald Yell was named for Congress and James Sevier Conway for governor, and Delegate Sevier and Governor Fulton were commended in such a way as to indicate they would be the party's choice in the legislature for U.S. senators.[60]

Campaigning moved at a snail's pace as anxious eyes turned toward Washington for news of the fate of Arkansas's statehood bill. At last, on July 1, a message reached Little Rock that the bill had passed Congress. Pike had charge of the city's Fourth of July arrangements. He joyously published the glad tidings and requested a grand "illumination" of all the houses in town on the evening of Independence Day in honor of the new "Sovereign State."[61]

The campaign now gained momentum, with the People's candidates stumping the state and Pike and Reed editorializing on their honesty, sincerity, and superiority. Pike was kind at first to Yell and Conway. Yell was, he wrote, an amiable, warmhearted, skillful campaigner, but unlike Cummins had not lived long enough among Arkansans to have a claim for office, and he was no orator, writer, or deep-read lawyer. With Conway, Pike was "personally friendly," but Conway would probably laugh in anyone's face who would call him "a statesman, an orator, or a writer." Cummins and Fowler, on the other hand, possessed "high talents" as speakers, writers, and leaders. They were better qualified for office than Yell and Conway; therefore, Pike gave them his warm support.[62]

Cummins was vulnerable on the basis question in the northern counties, since he had supported in the convention the slaveholders' district plan in apportioning representation. Yell was vulnerable there on the White question, and cagily avoided committing himself to Van Buren in his first campaign circular. But Yell outfoxed Cummins. In the north, where he resided, he campaigned on his own popularity and secretly attacked Cummins on "the old basis question." In the south, where Cummins was popular and ex-Tennesseans were less numerous, Yell relied on his Van Burenism and dictated that his friends say nothing on the basis question, getting out a "secret circular" in the *Gazette* office late in the campaign that was circulated only in the south.[63]

The election was but ten days away when a copy of Yell's secret circular fell into Pike's hands, and he discovered Yell's strategy. His kind feelings toward the judge turned overnight into scorn and vituperation. Exposing Yell's duplicity in reviving the basis question, he asked the people if they would "permit a Janus-faced politician" to deal with them in such a demagogic way, saying one thing in one part of the state and another in another part. When Pew bragged that Judge Yell in a joint debate had "used up John McLain," Pike's friend who was running for the senate from the district made up of Pulaski, White, and Saline counties, Pike scoffed, "Judge Yell can not use any body up. He speaks just about as well as he writes, and uses nothing up but the English language."[64]

Pike's anger over Yell's treatment of Cummins turned to outrage when the *Gazette* printed as a last-minute campaign extra an attack on Fowler by a "A Voice From the North." This correspondent charged that Fowler was no friend of the "North," that he had "apostatized" and betrayed it to the "South" on the final settlement of the basis question in the convention. Pike exploded in wrathful indignation. He and Pew had both made public stands against agitating this troublesome question, but the *Gazette* had, Pike said, broken faith by reviving the question against Cummins in the north and had now compounded the evil by "a deliberate and infamous slander" against Fowler's public record on the basis question. Fowler in the convention had boldly defended "a free white male basis," and as an architect of the compromise on apportionment had preserved for the "North" the free white basis of representation. The apportionment that gave Arkansas its constitution and got her admitted to statehood was to last but two sessions of the legislature, said Pike. After that the "North" would be in full control of both houses of the general assembly.[65]

Whatever chance Cummins and Fowler had had were doomed by such tactics—Pike called it the "business of trickery and management." Yet he remained hopeful. When Pew predicted Conway-Yell majorities in practically all the counties of the state, Pike good-humoredly replied that Pew's friends should shave his head and put him in a strait jacket: "Much learning hath made him mad." Conway, said Pike, would lose by 1,000 votes and Yell by 500.[66]

Election day results on August 1 deflated Pike considerably. Conway beat Fowler by a majority of 1,831 and Yell swamped Cummins by a thumping majority of 3,715 in a total of some 7,500 votes.[67] As for the legislature, the People's men won only a handful of seats in either house. Pike took some pride in the fact that Pulaski County returned majorities for Fowler and Cummins and for the People's legislative and county slates—his Kentucky friend Dr. John H. Cocke had been elected to the house and John McLain to the senate. But Pike could not deny that in the state at large the People's Party had suffered a stunning defeat; his partner Cummins had carried only eight slave counties in the "South."[68] "The Humbuggers," Pike confessed, "have knocked us into the middle of next week. Our best friends wouldn't know us, so long a face have we put on."[69]

At the end of August, Pike could not resist replying to Pew's editorial on the "Glorious Victory." Yes, he admitted, the Democrats had won. But not a single question had been settled by the election. Van Buren's "regency" lieutenants in Arkansas had concerned themselves "with *ends* not *means*, that is with *victory* not *methods*."

The *ends* the Regency were determined on—the *means* they were not so scrupulous about. Judge Yell and his friends were electioneering in the North on the basis question, as early as January last. That was the great moving power in that section. The plan of the campaign was sketched out, and the subaltern officeholders in the different counties received their orders from headquarters in what way to conduct the contest—in the North, on the basis question—in one County, on Van Burenism—in another, on Sevierism—in all, aided by the cry of Federalism and Nullification, raised-slanderously against our friends—and by the potent name of Jackson, disgraced by being evoked by their assistance. Judge Yell, in his northern circular, was carefully non-committal as to Van Burenism, in his southern, he became an avowed partisan. The whole of it was a business of trickery and management. . . .[70]

Pike thought "our friends" had erred in allowing local questions to predominate over national ones, that outside money had flowed in to publish "Baltimore speeches" in aid of the opposition. "With candidates confessedly superior to their opponents, we are shamefully beaten." He hoped, nevertheless, that his party would remain active. "For ourself, we shall fight on, '*on our own hook.*' When this becomes a reading and reflecting community—and when men who are striving against corruption and party drilling, learn to be united and energetic, we shall be conquerors."[71]

VIII

Emerging Whig Partisan

THE AUGUST ELECTION OF 1836 failed to produce a calm in the political storm for Pike. The first session of the legislature would convene September 12 to organize the new state government, inaugurate Governor Conway, select U.S. senators, fill the supreme court and circuit judgeships and state executive offices, and approve important public issues. Beyond that lay the presidential election in November.

Pike instructed the upcoming legislature on its duty to Arkansas, laying down a six-point program which became for him a state political platform of sorts for the next several years. It called for electing the judiciary on a nonpartisan basis, establishing a state university, founding a free common school system, chartering two state banks, building railroads with state aid, and codifying the laws of Arkansas.[1] The nonpartisan judiciary, state university, system of free public schools, and consistent, systematic law code—these spoke for themselves. It was the two banks and the railroads that caught Pike's imagination. In them lay not only the nation's destiny but also the state's:

> Give us two good banks, with a proper number of branches—open the country with rail-roads, and in twenty years not a State shall compete with us. Our progress in population, wealth and comfort, will astonish even ourselves. Imagination in its highest flight may not be able to keep pace with the reality—if we take the proper steps—but if we pursue a niggardly, penurious, and timid policy, years may pass away, and the resources of Arkansas await a development under the superior energy and broader policy of another generation.[2]

Pike's three years of observation from the editor's office, of listening to old Crittendenites and Sevierites, of riding the circuits and drinking and gambling with the lawyer-politicians of Arkansas had given him a practical education in political matters. Severism, he had concluded, was a bubbling cauldron of personal ambitions, jealousies, and intrigues. It defied analysis in terms of principles, issues, or patriotism. Only by looking at its chief leaders could anyone gain an idea of the uneasy political alliance over which Sevier presided. Lust for power and for private gain among these leaders constantly threatened to destroy it, but in the first state election their greed for federal patronage had united them behind Van Burenism.

The view from Pike's window was clear. He sized up Sevier's party pretty accurately. Hawk-nosed, cunning, unscrupulous, wealthy Chester Ashley was the ablest and most powerful man in the Democratic Party. This talented Little Rock attorney was also the most disreputable individual among the party's elite, and craved, Pike believed, public office more to restore his tarnished name than to exercise power. Ashley controlled William E. Woodruff, who owned the *Gazette* but whose loyalty to Van Buren had been so suspect that outside pressure had been brought to bear to import Pew as editor for the 1836 campaign. Fulton sparked this move, but Sevier, whose relatives the Conways, Johnsons, and Rectors nursed inordinate appetites for feeding from the public trough, had to work things out with Ashley and Woodruff. The upshot was that Conway had run for governor; the interloping but personable Tennessean, Judge Yell, a friend of Jackson and powerful friend indeed of House Speaker James Knox Polk, had been allowed to stand for Congress; and Sevier was to be the "first" senator. There were vague hints from time to time through the spring and summer of 1836 but no confirmation from Sevier, Pike observed, that Governor Fulton should be Sevier's colleague in the Senate.[3]

Pike was positive that Ashley coveted the other senatorship and that he had the power to force Sevier to aid him in his quest. Pike could abide Conway, Yell, and Sevier, but the very thought of the contemptible Ashley being elected to an office of honor and trust maddened him. In August he had begun in the *Advocate* a series of political letters signed "Casca," after the blunt, malicious, envious conspirator of Shakespeare's *Julius Caesar*. He now put Casca to good use in exposing Sevier's alleged sordid plan for knifing Fulton. Sevier secretly desired, he said, neither Fulton nor Ashley but another "more apt, docile and unscrupulous instrument of your will." This was obviously William McKnight Ball, state senator-elect from populous Washington County and a rising leader in Arkansas politics. Casca nevertheless believed Sevier would be unable to "exercise that choice," for he had just learned from one of Sevier's voluble friends that Ashley could force Sevier to his assistance.

Could this actually be true Casca asked. Could this pariah, this discredited man have the "unblushing impudence and shameless effrontery" to "dare offer himself as a candidate for the United States Senate?" Could Sevier be forced to his support? Casca confessed that he was "reluctantly compelled to believe it. I wait now with a feverish anxiety for news from the Capitol. I am in a wide ocean of doubt to which I can see no shore." He knew, he said, that Sevier did not wish Ashley elected. He knew that Sevier's friends had grossly betrayed Governor Fulton, an event that would be recorded hereafter as one of the blackest pages in the political history of the state. But a still "darker page" was possible: Ashley's elevation from Fulton's political ashes. He appealed to Sevier, if there was a spark of decency left in him, to take no hand in such an odious business.[4]

Unsure of Sevier and unwilling to take the heat off Ashley, Pike opened his columns to "Grand Jury," a correspondent that exposed the details of one of the darker episodes in Ashley's checkered career. A federal grand jury of Pulaski, White, and Saline counties had charged him with "subornation of perjury." Ashley sued it for libel and damages of $10,000. The grand jury pleaded the truth in justification and offered proof of his guilt in three instances. Trying to save himself, Ashley resorted to a sly lawyer's trick. He pleaded for a dismissal, arguing in a demurrer that even if the grand jury's pleas were true they were defective in "legal form." When the court overruled his demurrer, Ashley dropped his suit, paid the court costs, and hoped the matter would be hushed. Pike chose the first week of the legislative session in September 1836 to print grand jury's account.[5]

How much, if any, influence Pike's attacks on Ashley had is uncertain. But Sevier definitely felt Casca's sting. For it was about this time that he said to Pike in the street one day: "Look here, Pike, if that fellow Casca who is writing for your paper gets more severe, I shall have to ask for his name." Pike replied that he would get it when he called for it and returned to his and Cummins's office. He laughingly related the encounter to Cummins, who despised Sevier and would have welcomed a duel with him. "Tell him I wrote them! Tell him I wrote them!" he shrilled at Pike. Sevier never meant, of course, to ask for Casca's name, and nothing came of it.[6]

The second week of September 1836 found the sleepy little river town buzzing with activity. The legislature was gathering for its first session, and the streets, saloons, and public houses were crowded with lawmakers, office seekers, and lookers-on. At the unfinished State House, the steady pounding and ringing of carpenters' hammers bore witness to frenzied efforts to render the weathered structure usable for the session. Old Crittendenites, remembering the Ten Sections's controversy and recalling Governor Pope's elaborate promises, must have laughed over the makeshift arrangements—"Pope's Folly" they called the unfinished building. Pike himself, a few weeks after the 1836 session started, reminded the public that not only was the building uncompleted but also that a debt of $6,000 was owed the builders. Yet he was pleased that Congress had given another five sections of land to finish the building and landscape and fence the grounds and that the legislature had charged Governor Conway with selling the land, paying all arrears, and completing the project. At the same session money was appropriated to furnish and decorate the interior.[7]

On Monday morning, September 12, the lawmakers strolled up Markham Avenue to their improvised legislative rooms and organized themselves, listened to Fulton's farewell address as territorial governor, opened the gubernatorial returns, and announced to no one's surprise that James S. Conway had been elected governor. Next day an elaborate military parade escorted Conway to the State House where a crowd of assemblymen and townspeople listened to his inaugural message. That over, Pike administered the oath of office to him, and as first lieutenant of the newly organized First Artillery Company of Arkansas Militia joined his fellow officers and men in firing a grand national salute of twenty-six guns, the twenty-fifth for Arkansas and the twenty-sixth for Michigan.[8]

Pike's "wide ocean of doubt" over the question of the senatorial election vanished quickly. Ashley was not nominated, and the legislature was permitted a free hand in electing Sevier and Fulton. Pike praised the legislature for refusing to bow to the "drilling" of "party leaders" in the election. But looking back at the session three months later and considering things that he had "seen and heard" during the session, Pike concluded that the slippery Ashley had not only lost none of his power but had forced the legislators to endorse his character after all. Losing the senatorship, Ashley next schemed, said Pike, to get on the supreme court as a public affirmation of his respectability. When the legislature balked at that, he left no stone unturned in his quest for a seat on the State Bank directory.[9]

On the banking question and on the relationship of the ubiquitous Ashley to it, Pike was something of an expert. A year before, in the fall of 1835, Ashley had written a charter for a Union Bank of Arkansas Territory and rammed it through the council. Pike at the same time expressed serious objections to the measure, especially to a territorial government establishing a bank, and his partner Cummins, who detested Ashley and suspected him of an attempt to charter and gain control of the institution, defeated the bill in the house. Not only that, but Cummins and Pike were so incensed with Charles Caldwell for managing Ashley's bill in the council that they broke with him politically and helped elect John McLain over Caldwell in the contest for delegate to the constitutional convention in December 1835. Pike denounced the defeated Caldwell as a "nag" who had been ill-used and "poorly raced" by the Ashley-Woodruff crowd in the bank bill matter.[10]

But in 1836 matters were different insofar as banks were concerned. Pike's closest political friends in the legislature were working hand-in-glove with Ashley's probank Democratic friends to charter the state banks that had been authorized by the state constitution. Indeed, two People's leaders, John Ringgold and Anthony Davies, sponsored the bills that chartered both banks. Senator Ringgold was a Batesville merchant, steamboat owner, and rising entrepreneur on the White River, where he owned much rich land and a number of slaves. He was highly respected in the legislature for his honesty, ability, and forthright manner. Though he was a White man and favored a national bank, Ringgold seemingly suffered little loss of popularity among Van Burenites in the legislature who might oppose reestablishing a national bank but favored "sound" state banks.

Across the hall in the house chamber sat Ringgold's banking twin, the wealthy, able Chicot County planter, Anthony Davies, who commanded equal respect and power in the legislature. They easily took charge of the joint senate-house banking committee, secured quick committee approval of the bank charters, and shepherded them through their respective chambers in record time.[11]

State banks were not unfamiliar to men like Pike, Cummins, Ashley, Woodruff, Ringgold, and Davies, nor to most Arkansans. Practically all of the older states had had them for years, especially Tennessee whence most Arkansas settlers came. State legislatures in these states issued limited-liability charters to banking corporations which had the power to print and issue their own bank notes, or paper money. These notes were merely certificates bearing on their face a promise by the issuing bank to pay on demand gold or silver coin—"specie" was the popular term of the day for such coin. As long as the people had confidence in a bank's ability to redeem its notes in specie, they were seldom presented for redemption. These stock banks, like our present banks, made profits by loaning money; but unlike our present banks they made loans in their own bank notes. And since they were permitted in most cases to issue far more notes than they usually had in specie reserves, these banks fostered a wild expansion of credit and a still wilder speculation—in the South at least—in land, cotton, and slaves.

As we have seen Pike supported the idea of a national bank. But he had not been a blind supporter of the Second Bank of the United States, which he felt had abused its power. Yet he did believe that a national bank "under proper restrictions" was essential to the control of state banks and the regulation of the currency. He, like his contemporaries, knew the history of the Second Bank of the United States. Chartered by

Congress in 1816 for twenty years, it had had a capital of $35 million and the power to open branches anywhere. With all federal funds deposited without interest in its vaults, it was permitted to issue as many bank notes as its president and cashier deemed expedient. Because the federal government received the bank's notes in payments due it, they circulated at or near face value, or par, everywhere in the country. In return for its privileges, the bank had paid the government a bonus of $1.5 million and had received, transferred, and disbursed federal funds without charge.

The national bank under the presidency of Nicholas Biddle had performed a useful function in operating as a central banking institution and in helping regulate the state banks. It acquired a multitude of state bank notes in federal deposits, and when it desired could return them promptly to the issuing bank for redemption in specie. This had had a tendency to force state banks to keep adequate specie reserves on hand and to restrain their note issues. By expanding or reducing its own issues, the bank could encourage the state banks to follow suit. In times of inflation it could restrain the state banks; in times of tight money it could come to their aid with larger issues and loans and a loosening of restraint.

Pike and his friends had approved these national bank measures, and they would have welcomed the establishment of a branch of it in Little Rock after statehood. But the bank had had its enemies. It was essentially a private, profit-making institution, four-fifths owned by private stockholders, who elected twenty of the twenty-five directors. The branch banks of the central bank had been still further removed from federal control. Indeed, except for the presidentially-appointed five directors, the only check the government had had on the bank was the secretary of the treasury's authority to remove the federal deposits from its vaults.

Many people believed the national bank had had too much power, especially the wildcat state bankers who resented Biddle's restraining hand and the enterprisers-on-the-make who preferred to operate in an atmosphere of easy money and credit. Some westerners had felt the easterner Biddle ran the bank for the benefit of eastern capitalists, that while it might furnish an adequate and sound circulating medium for business in the East it failed to do much for the West. New Yorkers like Martin Van Buren were said to have opposed the bank because it was in Philadelphia as much as for any other reason.

Farmers, planters, and settlers in Arkansas had found it almost impossible to obtain specie or U.S. bank notes to pay for lands and make purchases. Out-of-state bank notes circulated more freely but never in adequate supply and always below par.[12] Much of the paper money Arkansans used in local transactions was in the form of territorial and county scrip, which carried severe discounts in most cases. Mechanics and artisans resented receiving wages in paper notes at face value and then suffering 10, 20, or even 50 percent loss when their money was discounted at the grocer's. Failing to see the intricacies of the money market or of the expanding national economy, many confirmed "hard money" men had become convinced that all banks and all paper money were evil, were a conspiracy of the moneyed class against the poor, or some such thing. If they could have their way all banks, all paper money, would be abolished.

By the end of President Jackson's first term the Bank of the United States had had more enemies than friends, and Jackson possessed both the power and the will to destroy it. His plans for the bank had not been altogether clear until Biddle, alarmed over Jackson's expressed hostility toward the institution, embarked upon a scheme to force Jackson's hand. The charter was to expire in 1836, but Biddle early in 1832 had secured from Congress a bill for renewal of the charter. The bill reached Jackson's desk in early July, and he promptly vetoed it on the grounds that the bank was unconstitutional, monopolistic, and undemocratic. He then carried his antibank fight to the people, won reelection, and also, in his opinion, a mandate to destroy the institution. In 1833 he inaugurated the policy of spending all federal deposits in the bank and placing all new federal deposits in selected state banks—"pet banks" his enemies called them. This "removal of the deposits" seriously crippled the bank, whose federal charter lapsed in 1836.

Pike cut his editorial teeth on the *Advocate* during these momentous years. Though he admired Jackson for his patriotism and nationalism and for his tough talk to the nullifiers in 1832–33, he scolded his destruction of the national bank, his disastrous "pet bank" scheme, and his "hard money" ideas. He applauded Henry Clay's action in 1834 in leading the Senate to adopt resolutions of censure against Jackson for removal of the deposits; he likewise condemned Arkansas's legislature in 1836 for instructing Senators Sevier and Fulton to vote for expunging the censureship, which was done in 1837. He blamed Arkansas's "money crisis" of 1836–37 on Jackson's fiscal blunders, especially the wild inflation and land speculation sparked by his "pet banks" in 1834–36, and on the ruinous consequences of his 1836 Treasury Circular requiring that public lands be paid for in specie only. "We wait for the time," Pike wrote in November 1836, "when the people of this state will begin to wince under the Treasury Circular. They have got their fingers in the trap. It remains to see how they will get them out. Nothing but a sound appeal to the purse will eradicate the disease of Van Burenism."[13]

Though Pike was firmly committed to a national bank and adamantly opposed to the Jacksonian "pet bank" and Treasury Circular policies, he championed the movement in Arkansas in 1836 for state banks. He saw nothing inconsistent in this. The Second Bank of the United States was dead, and Arkansas's chance for securing a branch of it was dead too. Arkansas's perennial money shortage could, he believed, be alleviated only by founding its own banks. State banks would bring its people a circulating medium in the form of her own bank notes backed by specie; banks would also bring the safety and convenience of banking to the people, and profits both to the state and to stockholders which would be good for the growth and development of the young state.[14]

Pike championed a winning cause. His friends Ringgold and Davies in 1836 quickly presented the legislature two bank bills, one creating the State Bank of Arkansas and the other the Real Estate Bank of the State of Arkansas. These two measures were interesting examples of frontier logrolling. In part they reflected the unsettled conditions in the realignment between Arkansas's political factions accompanying statehood. Sevierites were trying to rally the state behind Van Buren, but this hardly meant that the people and their legislators were ready to endorse the vague Jacksonian-Van Buren fiscal policies. The "pet bank" deposit system had led to a proliferation of credit, flooded Arkansas with a variety of state bank notes, and fueled a land boom, but Jackson's

Treasury Circular threatened a drastic restriction in public land sales. This bred uneasiness on the financial front. Moreover, there were still hard feelings in Arkansas over the basis question, as the recent state election had plainly revealed.[15]

Ringgold and Davies ignored the antibank diehards and concentrated on working out a compromise between the probank men in the legislature. Two principal issues divided the probank men: the power which the state should exercise over the banks and the sectional antagonism aroused by the basis question. Ringgold and Davies met the first issue by having the State Bank completely owned and operated by the state and by having the other, the Real Estate Bank, owned and operated by private stockholders. They met the second issue by locating the branches of the State Bank in north Arkansas and the branches of the Real Estate Bank in south Arkansas; the principal bank of each was, of course, to be at Little Rock.[16]

The State Bank's capital was to be $1 million, all of which the state would raise by selling bonds. Its principal bank was to be at Little Rock with branch banks at Fayetteville and Batesville in the north. All of the presidents, officers, and directors were to be elected by the legislature. It was permitted to issue paper bank notes at a ratio of three to one, that is, three dollars in paper for every dollar in specie on deposit in its vaults. The bank's original capital was to be increased by requiring the state to deposit in its vaults all state funds, such as, the seminary fund, the 5 percent of the sale of federal public lands, and Arkansas's share of the upcoming distribution of the federal surplus revenue. Pike estimated, incorrectly as it turned out, in December 1836 that Arkansas's share of the federal surplus would be a whopping $469,500 in specie! Interest would be paid on many of these funds and added to their principal, but in any case all the profits of the State Bank would go to the state and would be subject to the control of the legislature.[17]

The Real Estate Bank was chartered for twenty-five years.[18] Its capital stock of $2 million, none of which was to be owned by the state, was to be subscribed in mortgages on real estate, which would be both a guarantee to the state and to the bondholders that the bank would retire the $2 million in state bonds that were to be sold to raise the bank's operating capital. The bank was to pay off the principal and interest on the bonds and was to pay the state a bonus of $5,000 a year for ten years.

The Real Estate Bank was in essence a privately owned corporation, though the state exercised some supervisory power over it. The governor was to appoint a board of managers whose duty it was to award the stock of the bank to subscribers. Assisting in the elaborate process of organizing the bank were boards of superintendents of stock subscription and boards of appraisers. The superintendents, named in the charter, were to receive subscriptions at the principal towns in the state, while three-man boards of appraisers in each county, appointed by the governor, were to determine the actual market value of real estate mortgaged by the stock subscribers.

The board of managers, once they satisfied themselves that the mortgages for stock subscriptions were perfected and in good order and that the state would be fully protected for its $2 million in bonds, would so certify to the governor and publish a list of the stockholders of record.

As soon as the stock was awarded, the stockholders of the principal bank and of the branch banks were to elect directors of their respective banks while the governor was to appoint two state directors to each of the four banks. The four directors of the three branch banks were to elect their respective presidents, but the president of the principal bank was to be elected by a central board of directors of twelve members. This central board, which was to oversee the operation of the entire Real Estate Bank, was composed of three members from each of the four banks—three directors of the principal bank and the president and two directors of each of the branch banks. Four of the directors on the central board, one from each bank, had to be a state-appointed director. The central board was to elect one of its members as president, who also served as president of the principal bank at Little Rock.

The central board had the responsibility of putting the Real Estate Bank in operation. It was to receive from the governor's board of managers all the books, papers, titles, mortgages, and documents relating to the stock and business of the bank. It was also to receive from the governor the bonds of the state and was to appoint two commissioners to "negotiate and effect a sale of the same." The charter specified that "nothing less than the par value" should be received for these bonds, a requirement that would be of much importance in the future history of the bank.

Because of Pike's later close personal and political involvement in the affairs of the Real Estate Bank it is perhaps well at this point to examine the nature of the institution. The stockholders were by the charter "created a corporation and body politic" for a period of twenty-five years and were invested with the full property rights of any citizen of the state. The state owned none of the stock. It had only four directors on the twelve-member central board of directors, and even these four state directors must be stockholders in the bank to be eligible for appointment. In effect, then, the Real Estate Bank was a private banking corporation. Yet the state was handing over $2 million in bonds to the bank to be sold for raising its operating capital. True, the governor was required, as we have seen, not to release the bonds to bank officials until he and his board of managers were satisfied that ample real estate was mortgaged by the stockholders to protect the state's interest. The governor's culpability if things went amiss could be enormous. But the legislature's responsibility could be even greater, chartering a bank on the unsound feature of having all its stock subscribed in mortgages on real estate. Still, it would be the central board that would be on the firing line if the experiment failed.

Nobody thought much about that in the fall of 1836. Ringgold and Davies pushed their bills through in record time, beating down attempts to add more branch banks. The first bill Governor Conway signed into law was the charter of the Real Estate Bank of the State of Arkansas, the second was the charter of the Bank of the State of Arkansas.

The signing of the State Bank bill by Governor Conway on November 2 touched off the same day a spirited contest in the legislature for control of the presidency and the directory of the principal bank at Little Rock. Terence Farrelly's friends made strenuous efforts to make him president, but Chester Ashley blocked this and had his friend Capt. Jacob Brown of the U.S. Army placed at the head of the new bank. Pike was infuriated over Farrelly's defeat and was soon charging that Ashley headed a Little Rock "cabal" to whom all Arkansas Democrats must bow and scrape.[19]

Ashley had capped his defeat of Farrelly by placing himself on the directory, though not without a supreme effort. Twelve directors of the principal bank were to be elected, and on the first ballot, November 2, Ashley came in twelfth in a slate of twenty nominees, and he had but one vote to spare. Overnight a vote was withdrawn, probably with some artful pressure, and on the morning of November 3 Ashley faced a new election. All his opponents of the previous day withdrew and Pike's partner Cummins, who up to now had not been a candidate, entered the contest. A ballot was taken, and the two arch enemies ended in a dead heat, twenty-seven each. Fighting desperately, Ashley rousted out the necessary votes on the second ballot to defeat Cummins thirty-one to twenty-seven. If Pike can be believed, Ashley personally searched out legislators who were either drunk or in hiding and forced them to turn out to vote for him.[20]

Fent Noland, who had replaced Independence County's Townsend Dickinson in the house when Dickinson was elected to the supreme court, agreed with Pike's estimate of Ashley's election. In a public letter to his constituents from Little Rock, Noland declared that "intrigue, corruption, bribery and threats" had been used to defeat Farrelly. Capt. Jacob Brown, who was absent on official army business and who was not even qualified to vote in Arkansas, had been chosen president because "*Chester Ashley* wished *him* elected— and the knowledge of that fact influenced *some votes*." When Noland rose to object to Ashley's own nomination for the directory of the State Bank, he was quickly ruled out of order. "I knew," he afterward related, "that if Chester Ashley was appointed to the Directory, all confidence in the institution would be destroyed both at home and abroad."[21]

Recounting for his constituents several of Ashley's shady private acts and his bad public character, Noland denied, though not convincingly, that politics had anything to do with his opposition to him. "Whiteism and Van Burenism are not the question," he said. "There is a party here, the head and front of which is Chester Ashley—an individual with whom many Van Buren men refuse to associate." Yet Ashley, who "is not nor ever was a Jackson man," was rapidly rising to power under "the mask of Van Burenism." He had wealth, talents, and cunning, controlled the *Arkansas Gazette*, and was "the most dangerous man in the community."[22]

Pike taunted prominent Democrats with their cowardly subservience to Ashley and kept up a steady stream of abuse of Ashley himself in the process. He published in capital letters a list of the legislators who had voted for Ashley for director: "We wish their constituents to see it." He singled out Sam C. Roane, president of the senate and a respected attorney, for special treatment in one of his most memorable Casca letters. Roane was a prominent man in Arkansas, knew intimately and personally of Ashley's shadowy past as a land speculator, and had as a federal attorney publicly charged him with corruption. Pike reminded Roane of these things, and of his supposed reputation for political independence, in an angry reference to his vote against Farrelly: "I have not learned whether you voted gratuitously against your old acquaintance Farrelly, or whether you were forced to give him up by the proscription of the Triumvirate." The "Triumvirate" was, of course, Sevier, Ashley, and Woodruff.[23]

But Pike's main "presentment" against Roane was his support for Ashley. It was a withering attack not only on Roane but also on Ashley:

> I find your name recorded as having voted three times for Chester Ashley, when he stood before the Legislature a candidate for the Directory of the State Bank. Did you do so because you believed him to be honest, trustworthy and true to his country? I imagine that I see you start and turn pale. You well know the character of that man. Cunning, artful, unscrupulous, rich in all the resources of villainy, unencumbered with either principle, honesty or gratitude, a blot upon the face of creation, hung on the highest gibbet of public infamy, with the wind of popular contempt and indignation blowing through the skeleton of his character, he was still enabled, by means of his wealth and talents, to set public opinion at defiance, to walk the streets proudly in unblushing impudence, and to infest society with the contamination of his presence.[24]

In the midst of the fight over control of the State Bank came the presidential election—on November 7, 1836. Pike had been flying Hugh Lawson White's name and attacking Van Buren since early 1835, and he went valiantly down to the end with White's cause. He helped name the three People's Republican electors in September, he published the People's Party address of October 8 which denounced Van Buren as a tool of antisouthern, antiwestern interests, and he praised in one editorial after another White's prosouthern, prowestern views. "Hugh Lawson White is," Pike summed it all up, "a son of the West—an old, venerable, wise and honest man. His supporters are the common people of the South and West."[25]

A careful examination of Pike's fall editorials on the presidential race reveals that he was more than a White partisan. "White first, Harrison next" was his punch line for a long editorial in reply to Harrison's critics. He carefully avoided attacking Richard M. Johnson, Van Buren's running mate. After all, Johnson's brother, Benjamin Johnson, was the new federal district judge at Little Rock while Benjamin's popular son-in-law was Senator Sevier. Sevier's "Uncle Dicky" Johnson was also the reputed killer of Tecumseh and a popular man in the West; in Arkansas, because of his powerful relatives, he was absolutely unbeatable.[26]

By the end of October Pike was convinced that White and Harrison, the "Western" candidates, had enough electoral votes between them to block Van Buren's election. He therefore urged the friends of White and Harrison to unite after the election behind whichever one was strongest against Van Buren. If so, "White or Harrison is elected." By then Pike had become a Whig. "The Whigs are awake throughout the Union," he cried, and even in Arkansas "the Tories tremble." "We say to the Whigs in Arkansas—up and be doing." But he kept at his editorial masthead the old label "People's Anti-Caucus Candidates," and he urged Jackson's friends in the "Western states" to vote for White, not Van Buren.[27]

Again, Pike's optimism went for naught. Van Buren swept Arkansas by a decisive majority of 2,547 to 1,251, winning twenty-one of the thirty-four counties. White carried only six river counties along the Arkansas, White, and Mississippi. Van Buren even carried Pulaski County, including Pike's Big Rock township. This, Pike explained, was "owing to the fact that the whole Legislature voted here, and the Lawrence Company of Volunteers which was passing through the city on its way to duty at Fort Towson. The two gave a majority of at least sixty for Van Buren."[28]

Pike conceded Arkansas to Van Buren on November 25. The state vote had been light, but this hardly hid the fact that the Democrats had trounced the Whigs. Yet out of the elections of that summer and fall, Pike's People's Party had emerged as the Whig Party and was on the threshold of affiliating with the national party. In the years ahead the Whigs would be a constant threat to Arkansas's Democrats. They could always be counted on for a heavy vote, most of the time a majority vote, in the slave counties of the southeast and along the inland rivers. But they would also continue to pull a third or more of the votes in the rest of the state.[29]

The Whig threat hardly worked any major changes in Arkansas's political map from that of 1836, for the Democrats won about the same geographic areas in 1840, 1844, and 1852 as they had in 1836. But in those same years the Whigs won from 37 to 45 percent of the statewide vote and kept the Democratic leaders busy patching up factional disputes within their ranks. For any division within Democratic ranks meant potential victory for the Whigs, that is, if the Whigs could remain united, which was by no means certain.[30]

Pike's *Advocate* had been a commanding force in shaping Arkansas's Whig Party, and he would personally remain a steadfast leader of the party until its demise in the early fifties. The men who led the Arkansas Whig Party were in part held together by the more basic demands of geography, economics, and society. The lawyers, merchants, planters, farmers, artisans, mechanics, and laborers who voted the Whig ticket year after year found in the party various appeals.

Some liked Henry Clay or William Henry Harrison or Zachary Taylor; some were attracted by the conservative appeal in Whiggery, some were ardent supporters of a national system of internal improvements, and some, like Pike, thought a Whig national bank was a saner solution to the money question than the Democrat Independent Treasury. Yet at the heart of the Whig cause in Arkansas were the lawyer-merchant, probusiness leaders of the river towns of Little Rock, Helena, Batesville, Van Buren, and other smaller settlements. They had economic ties that extended outside Arkansas into the business community of the North and especially to the commercial centers of Memphis and New Orleans. They had economic and social power that extended widely into the hinterland from their own local seats of power.

These lawyer-merchants brought to Arkansas's Whig Party financial resources, sustained a Whig press at Little Rock and at other towns, and furnished talented leaders. Pike knew them all. He depended on them to support his *Advocate* and, still later, his efforts to maintain a Whig newspaper at Little Rock.

The most conspicuous figures among them at Little Rock were the trio of Pike, Cummins, and Fowler.[31] But there were other outstanding Whigs at the capital: James B. Keatts, a planter-slaveholder, merchant, and land speculator, whose home on the outskirts of the city was the scene of lavish social events; Thomas Willoughby Newton, "the Knight of the Hounslow Heath," a lawyer and cashier of the Real Estate Bank, the only Arkansas Whig ever to serve in Congress; handsome Frederick Trapnall, a brilliant lawyer, polished orator, and expert student of English history; homely John W. Cocke, Trapnall's law partner, who in Kentucky had been married to Governor Pope's daughter, a spellbinder on a stump or on an Independence Day platform; and Dr. Lorenzo Gibson, the perennial Whig candidate of Pulaski County and later of Hot Spring County.[32]

Pike was very close to all of these men. He was attorney of the Real Estate Bank at the same time Newton was cashier. He sat with Trapnall on the vestry of Christ Episcopal Church. His favorite traveling companion on the judicial circuits was the genial Kentuckian John W. Cocke. At one time or another, Pike was associated with every one of them in contesting cases before the Little Rock courts, in lobbying before the legislature, or in waging political warfare on the Democrats.

The most important Whig leaders in the rest of the state were Jesse Turner and John Drennen of Van Buren; David Walker of Fayetteville; John Ringgold and Charles Fenton Mercer ("Fent") Noland of Batesville; Capt. John Preston Jr. of Helena; Terence Farrelly and Frederick Notrebe of Arkansas County; Anthony Davies of Chicot County; John Clark of Union County; and John Linton of Conway County.

Pike knew and worked with all these men at the different circuit courts in Arkansas, but he was especially close friends for life with Turner, Drennen, Walker, and Noland. A North Carolinian born in 1805, little Jesse Turner of Van Buren had settled in Crawford County in 1831. When Pike met him in 1835–36 at Crawford Old Courthouse, the diminutive Turner was already an established attorney and a popular public figure. He represented his county in the constitutional convention of 1836, served it in the lower house of the legislature in 1838, was appointed as a Whig U.S. district attorney for the new federal court at Van Buren in 1851, and in 1861 was sent as a Unionist delegate to the secessionist convention at Little Rock. Whiggery was a religion with Turner, a devoted follower of Henry Clay who stumped for Harrison and Tyler in 1849 and served as Whig presidential elector in 1848, when his friend and long acquaintance Zachary Taylor won election. Pike and Turner became close associates politically, professionally, and socially, and corresponded intermittently the rest of Pike's life. One of Pike's great disappointments was that he failed to obtain for Turner the federal judgeship at Little Rock on the death of Judge Benjamin Johnson in 1849.[33]

John Drennen, the Van Buren merchant and Whig leader, was also a prosperous planter, slaveholder, whiskey distiller, Indian trader, and charterer of the abortive Chihuahua Trading Company, through which he planned to open trade with the states of Mexico south of Santa Fe.[34] A sociable, convivial man who kept his cellar well stocked with fine whiskey, champagne, and rare wines, Drennen lived on top of the high ridge at the west edge of Van Buren. His house faced southeastward across the village and down the picturesque Arkansas Valley. Pike had met Drennen in 1833 and, after he was admitted to the bar and began riding the circuit to the courts at Van Buren, always stayed with him. "Five hundred times," Pike recalled, he and his Van Buren friend Phineas T. White, "climbed the steep hill to Drennen's house together, where for a long time he lived, to be greeted on arriving by the hospitable and genial host with great solid silver tumblers, filled with invigorating liquid, heaped up with crushed ice from which the green leaves of mint protruded, or with breakers of champagne; and with kindly words of frank glad witticism."[35]

Drennen was elected to the first legislature in 1836, strongly supported the creation of the state banks, and secured in 1837–38 the establishment of a western branch of the Real Estate Bank at Van Buren, of which he became president. As a Whig editor in 1835–37 and as attorney for the Real Estate Bank after 1840, Pike was obviously more than a social acquaintance of Drennen. Yet Pike, in recalling his days with Drennen, set down only the social good times he had while a guest in Drennen's home.[36]

David Walker, a Kentuckian, was the spearhead of Whiggery in northwest Arkansas. This conservative Fayetteville attorney, born February 19, 1806, had settled there in the fall of 1830 and prospered as a lawyer, land speculator, and bankite (a supporter of the state bank). A large, stern-faced man, with big eyes, ample nose, and a high, broad forehead, Walker went clean shaven but allowed his sideburns to grow to the bottoms of his ear lobes. His large downcast mouth gave the impression of unyielding grimness and perpetual bad humor, but he was, in fact, good natured and friendly and capable of sparkling good humor, such as his self-effacing stories of how Arkansas's unconquerable Democrat, Archibald Yell, his fellow townsman, beat him for Congress in 1844. The versatile Yell, Walker related, had outstumped, outdrank, outshot, outsung, outkissed all the babies, and publicly outprayed him in their joint canvass of that year.[37]

Pike's fishing and hunting crony, Fent Noland, a year younger than Pike, was a Virginian.[38] He had flunked out of West Point in 1825, and his father, seeking to take the high-spirited sixteen-year-old boy in hand, had brought him to Arkansas in 1826 to serve as his assistant as federal receiver at Batesville. The father returned to Virginia in 1827, but young Fent remained in Batesville, read law, traveled and wrote about Arkansas, became a Crittendenite, killed Gov. John Pope's nephew in a duel, served for a long time in the army in the old Northwest, contracted tuberculosis which plagued him the rest of his life, left the army in 1835 and returned to Batesville, where he practiced law, looked after his large landholdings, and married wealthy old John Ringgold's daughter.

Fent Noland had been a staunch supporter of Andrew Jackson, despite being a Crittendenite, but in 1836 broke with the Democratic Party, voted for White, and thereafter identified himself as a Whig. Elected to fill a vacancy in the lower house in the fall of 1836, he, as we have seen, was already a firm opponent of Ashley, Woodruff, and Senator Sevier. Pike may have met him before 1836 at the Little Rock racetrack, for Noland, a horse breeder and racer, annually made the Arkansas racing circuit at Little Rock, Fort Smith, Van Buren, Carrollton, Batesville, and at other places in the state. Pike loved the consumptive, skinny, hollow-cheeked, boyish-looking Fent and fished and hunted with him in the streams and the mountains of north Arkansas. Many of their experiences together on such occasions became the theme of Noland's famous letters to William T. Porter's *Spirit of the Times* which he signed "Pete Whetstone of Devil's Fork."

In Arkansas, where Fent was known as Colonel Noland because of his lieutenant colonel's commission in the state militia, he and his father-in-law John Ringgold were very prominent Whigs and bankites. Fent was reelected to the house in 1838, 1840, and 1846 and in the last year ran for Congress to fill the vacancy created by the resignation of Archibald Yell. In announcing his candidacy for the office, he said the six-week term was too short for him to do either much good or much harm and "should you elect me, I will be grateful; if you don't I have the consolation to know you leave me in no worse fix than you found me." Losing the race to his fellow Whig, Thomas Newton, Fent drolly attributed his defeat to a "lack of votes."

This handful of Whig leaders dominated the few large slave counties of the southeast and along the river valleys, and exercised considerable power throughout the state. They were particularly apt at lobbying and maneuvering in the legislature, and none of them was abler at this science than Pike who had learned it directly from his old master Crittenden. But oddly enough, or perhaps it was not so odd after all, the southeast was also home to most of the Democratic leaders of the period.

The Sevier-Conway-Johnson-Rector family clan, who constituted the "reigning dynasty" of antebellum Arkansas were southeast based planters and slaveholders.[39] Senator Sevier began at Little Rock, but marrying Judge Johnson's daughter, lived after 1836 on one of Johnson's large plantations in Chicot County. He was a planter, speculator, and maximum stockholder in the Real Estate Bank. Sevier's mother was a Conway whose brother Thomas Conway, who married Ann Rector, was father of the numerous Arkansas Conways who formed the backbone of the Democratic dynasty prior to 1860. The Conway brothers lived mostly in Lafayette County in the southwest where they prospered on fertile Red River plantations.[40]

The personable Robert Ward Johnson, son of Judge Johnson and brother-in-law of the powerful Senator Sevier, was a law student at Yale when Pike met him and became friends with him at Little Rock after 1833. Finishing his law studies and marrying a Kentucky girl, Johnson first lived in Little Rock, served as prosecuting attorney to the Pulaski County circuit court and ex officio state attorney general until 1843, when he moved to his splendid cotton plantation near Pine Bluff in Jefferson County. Tall, blonde, blue-eyed and handsome, he became a spellbinder on the political stump and a coming politician. He went to Congress in 1847–53 and served in the Senate from 1853 to 1861.[41]

The Rectors, cousins of Sevier and the Conways, descended from William, Wharton, and Elias Rector, whose sister Ann Rector, as we have seen, was married to the progenitor of the Conway brothers of Arkansas. As surveyor-general of Illinois, Missouri, and Arkansas Territory, William Rector took care to see that his relatives—the Conways, Seviers, and the Rectors—got lucrative positions from the U.S. Land Offices in Arkansas.[42]

Archibald Yell, who lived in populous, Democratic Washington County in the far northwest corner of the state, was one of the founders of the Arkansas River town of Ozark, a dabbler in Real Estate Bank stock, a land speculator, and a money lender—among his chief borrowers was his lifelong friend and future President James Knox Polk of Tennessee. Yell came to Arkansas as a Jacksonian appointee to the territorial superior court and by his own strength of personality and popularity made himself into an independent Democratic force that the dynasty Democrats always had to reckon with until his life was cut short on the Mexican War battlefield of Buena Vista in 1847.[43]

Chester Ashley, the brilliant but badly scarred Little Rock Democratic boss, made most of his fortune in questionable land deals, but as attorney and speculator came to possess numerous slaves and plantations. He held much land in the preeminent cotton county of Chicot in the far southeast corner of the state.[44] His best friend and loyal supporter was his fellow New Yorker, William E. Woodruff, the patriarch of the *Gazette*, who made a success of his paper through contracts for public printing. But Woodruff made most of his money as a ferry operator, mill operator, land agent, and debt and bill collector.[45]

These southeast-based Democratic leaders, though slaveholders and planters themselves, were not as popular in the southeast as in the northwest. Southeast conservatives had a tendency to vote Whiggish, while northwest yeoman farmers voted Democratic. And since northwest small farmers greatly outnumbered the southeast planters, the Democrats had a great advantage over the Whigs in the state. "Hurrah for the north," Pew's *Gazette* had exclaimed in 1836 as the Democrats swept the section against the Whigs.[46] Yet the Whigs were not without strength in the northwest. The truth was they polled a larger total vote in the northwest than they did in the southeast. Sweeping the Whig planter votes in the slave counties, where few whites lived, had little effect in statewide elections. The key to winning elections in antebellum Arkansas was to turn out the voters in the populous white counties of the northwest, and the Democrats whose chief leaders resided in the southeast, were simply more adept at that than Whigs.[47]

The unpopularity of Whigs and their lack of success in north Arkansas is best illustrated by a story Pike afterwards told. A county was formed in north Arkansas and "was called Randolph County. They cast about six hundred votes in that county and I think that there was not more than fifteen or twenty Whigs—it was no use for a Whig to run for office. All the candidates were Democrats." But one year, two Democrats announced, he said, for the same office, and, there being no Whig in the race, they agreed not to tell any stories, or lies, against the other unless they were both together and could defend themselves. Shortly one of them heard that the other had gone to a township and said that his opponent was a hog thief. The accused was angry, and, when he met his rival, asked why he had told that story. "Well, it was true, was it not?" "Yes," was the reply, "it was true. But look here, if you go and tell that story again—if you dare—damn it, if I don't tell everybody that you're a Whig!"[48]

IX

A Dark and Disastrous Season

THE YEAR THAT FOLLOWED the close of the first legislative session was a busy one for Pike. He found himself more and more absorbed in his and Cummins's expanding law practice, and he, as junior partner of the firm, rode most of the circuits. He was, therefore, frequently away from Little Rock, which made getting out the *Advocate* burdensome to him.[1]

When Pike bought the paper in 1835, he had acquired with it two young apprentices and a dependable journeyman printer and assistant editor, Charles E. Rice, who relieved him of much of the worrisome details associated with putting out the weekly issues and conducting business and job printing.[2] But this happy arrangement lasted only ten months. After Rice shouldered his rifle in November 1835 and went off to Texas to join Sam Houston's army, Pike was over a year finding a dependable man to replace him. This was Archibald Coulter, who in February 1837 became Pike's partner "in the printing business" and in conducting the *Advocate*.[3]

By then, however, Pike was anxious to rid himself of sole responsibility for the paper. He obviously had found it to be less than a paying proposition, as we shall see, and was much troubled by the constant problem of recruiting and keeping apprentices.[4] His *Advocate* and John Reed's *Times* were already in agreement politically, since both had been White supporters and since both were anti-Sevierites, and the two publishers quickly came to terms when Pike suggested a merger. In a joint statement to their respective patrons and subscribers on April 29, 1837, Pike and Reed explained the "many and cogent reasons" for consolidating their papers. They each had about seven to eight hundred subscribers. A single paper with 1,500 would be "a more powerful engine" in behalf of their political cause. Moreover, Pike wished to be honest with the *Advocate*'s patrons. His other "avocations" made it impossible for him "to be longer burthened with the business of a printing office," and he had, therefore, "gladly joined in a plan which, without working injury to his patrons, w[ould] relieve him of a large amount of labor and attention not now in his power to bestow upon its details."[5]

Pike called himself "senior editor" of the *Times and Advocate*, but he did not actually edit the new paper. When the *Gazette* announced the merger of the Whig papers, it stated that Pike would "continue the Editor" and Reed would "take charge of the business department of the concern." Reed promptly corrected the *Gazette*. "So far from relinquishing the editorial department of the *Times*, I shall be sole editor, as it were, in consequence of Mr. Pike having little or no time to devote to this business. Every thing intended for the columns of the 'Times and Advocate,' will be under my supervision, and must receive my sanction before insertion."[6] But Pike reserved the right of writing for the paper, a privilege he did not fail to exercise when he was in town and felt the urge to express himself.

The fact that he and Reed often, but not always, initialed their respective editorials seemingly did not reflect a difference of opinion on editorial tastes or views. An examination of their respective editorials indicates not only that they were both hard-hitting writers but also that they were in complete harmony on skinning Democrats.

Pike's merger of his paper with Reed's came at a crucial time in the history of Arkansas. Her leaders early in 1837 were attempting to set on foot the two state banks chartered the previous fall. But disquieting reports began to reach Little Rock as early as January of financial distress in the East. In mid-January President Jacob Brown of the State Bank received word from New York bankers that "the press of the money market" made it impossible to sell the state bonds for raising the capital for his institution.[7] Even more disturbing reports followed in March and April of failing banks and businesses and of a drop in cotton prices on the New Orleans market, which had been at fifteen cents in December, skidded to half that price by March. By May, when Pike bemoaned the "dark and disastrous season, in this land," the truth was clear. The country was in the grip of an economic panic. Businesses were failing, banks were suspending specie payments, bank notes were losing value, cotton was having trouble finding a market, unemployment was growing, and a curtain of gloom and fear fell upon the land.[8]

For over a year Pike had been debating Tom Pew, the imported Van Buren editor of the *Gazette*, on the subject of Jacksonian monetary policies. Pew ably defended President Jackson's efforts to suppress paper notes of small denominations and to induce gold dollars to become the circulating medium of the people — "the People's money," in Jackson's words. Pike could not quarrel with the aim of Jackson's hard money policy, but when its ends were not achieved, he became its severest critic in Arkansas.[9] In June 1836, Congress at long last passed the distribution bill, providing for the distribution of the federal revenue surplus to the states. Pike strongly backed the measure and was relieved when Jackson approved it.[10] Yet Jackson fretted over the inflationary nature of the distribution act, which called for selecting new state depositories and making still more millions in federal funds available to the states and the state banks. Consequently, in July 1836, he issued the Specie Circular, or Treasury order, as an antidote to the inflationary tendency in distribution and, also, as an attempt to call a halt to the wild speculation in the public lands.

Jackson's reasons for the Specie Circular were commendable. He wished to repress alleged frauds in land transactions, to place the government on the side of actual settlers by withdrawing all government countenance from large speculators and capitalists, and "to discourage the ruinous extension of bank issues, and of bank credits."

Displaying typical Democratic loyalty, Pew brought the *Gazette* to the defense of the circular. It would, he prophesied, put a stop to speculators from the East, who, armed with blank checks and certificates of credit from deposit banks in Mississippi and Louisiana, had been monopolizing land sales in Arkansas. It would, on the other hand, benefit the actual settler by curbing bank credits to large speculators and by halting land speculation.[11] Just how this miracle was to come about Pew did not explain. There was, of course, the distinct possibility that Jackson had thrown out the baby with the bath. His Treasury order might make it tougher for the actual settler, who after December 15 would have to get his hands on enough specie to pay for his land.

Since Pike professed, sincerely it seems, to be on the side of the actual settler, he could not argue with the intent of Jackson's circular. But he replied to Pew's defense of it with a withering attack. The circular was, he said, "calculated to injure the poor settler, and benefit nobody but the speculator." He admitted that the opposite was Jackson's stated purpose, but the president's action was like "shutting the stable door after the horse is stolen." Here Pike spelled out his argument in the terms of his rural reader's experience, a thing that he was a master at. Eastern speculators, commanding easy credit and bank paper, had already made off with the best tracts of land in Arkansas; the effect of the circular would be merely to reduce the sales of public lands and increase the price of speculator-held land. Actual settlers would be at a big disadvantage in acquiring gold and silver, while the demand for gold would depreciate what paper currency they had still further. Not being able to command specie, the settler would be forced to use his depreciated paper currency to purchase the higher-priced land of the large speculator.[12]

The months immediately ahead proved Pike right. Jackson's Specie Circular sharply reduced speculation in public lands, while specie began to command higher and higher premiums. By late November 1836, when Pike was grieving over Van Buren's victory in Arkansas and when business trouble in England had reversed the flow of specie to the United States and curtailed English credit to America, Pike spoke out bitterly on the growing money crisis. He waited, he snapped, for the time when the people of this state will begin to wince under the Specie Circular. They have got their fingers in the trap. It remains to see how they will get them out. Nothing but a sound appeal to the purse will eradicate the disease of Van Burenism.[13] By March 1837, when actual settlers were paying at Little Rock $110 in U.S. Bank notes, and very much more in depreciated state bank notes, for $100 in silver or gold with which to enter their federal lands, Pike noted their "groaning" under the "incubas of the Treasury Circular [Specie Circular]." "Good!" he exclaimed. "It is a fit reward for their Van Burenism and Bentonism."[14]

Pike's indictment of the Specie Circular was good Whig doctrine and sound up to a point. The circular had doubtlessly worked a hardship on settlers wishing to buy public land, but the real problem there was that public receivers could no longer accept bank obligations in payment for land. The depreciated bank currency lay, then, at the bottom of the settler's problems, and a dozen reasons could be given for its depreciation. A loyal Whig, Pike preferred the anti-Jackson reasons—destruction of the national bank, inflation and speculation associated with state deposit banking, and pretension and deception involved in hard-money policy—whereas the more important reasons seemed to be economic recession in England, outflow of specie to England to satisfy American debts and other obligations, and restriction on credit associated with tight money, the Specie Circular, and distribution of the surplus revenue which went into operation January 1, 1837.

Nevertheless, there was the ring of truth and conviction in Pike's attack on Jacksonian monetary policies, and he hammered home his version of the history of those policies to Arkansas's Van Buren constituency. It went like this: Jackson took the deposits from the Bank of the United States; this produced scarcity of money and brought distress; he remedied this situation by putting the deposits in the state "pet banks"; this brought on a deluge of speculator's notes; Jackson grew fearful of the wild speculation in the public lands and the inflated paper money and issued his Specie Circular; and now the settler, whom Jackson proposed to help by his Treasury order, must now hire gold and silver at 10 per cent premium to enter his land with. Pike's conclusion: "We sat again good! It will open the people's eyes."[15]

But Pike did not really enjoy the plight of the settlers exchanging their hard-earned paper money with the sharp money-changers of Little Rock, and he called loudly for the repeal of Jackson's "outrageous Treasury Order" which was "grinding the face of the West and Arkansas in particular." His most bitter personal attack on General Jackson came when the old man, on the eve of his final departure from the White House in March 1837, applied one of his infernal pocket vetoes to a measure granting relief from the circular. "Instead of signing it," proclaimed Pike, "he put it in his pocket, and stamped off to the Hermitage. He would have done the same thing if the lives of half the country had depended upon his signing it."[16]

The onset of the panic in May only intensified Pike's opposition to Democratic money policies, which he blamed for all the hardship in the country. He enjoyed reminding Democrats of Jackson's pledge to give the country a "better currency" than the notes of the defunct Second Bank of the United States. All of Jackson's state deposit banks had now suspended specie payments, and the general's "better currency" turned out to be the depreciated state paper which had flooded the country. He particularly poured contempt on Van Buren for sticking by the Specie Circular, under which gold and silver were drained from Arkansas in land payments while at the same time the government was paying Arkansas her share of the surplus revenue in federal drafts on deposit banks in Mississippi that could be cashed only in the depreciated paper of the Magnolia State, an issue that Pike pounced on with glee.[17]

Thereby hung still another tale of the long Pike-Woodruff rivalry. The great issues in Arkansas that spring and summer, as we have seen, were the hoped-for opening of the State Bank and the collection of Arkansas's share of the federal surplus revenue, two questions that became badly tangled in the thorny thicket of Arkansas politics. Pike's attitude toward the State Bank was excessively complicated. He defended it, as well as the Real Estate Bank, as a way of protecting Arkansas from a flood of Jackson's "better currency," that is, the depreciated state bank notes flowing into the new state from Jackson's deposit banks. He assumed, of course, that Arkansas's two banks would be sound, specie-paying institutions. Yet his editorial views in 1837 regarding the State Bank were, to say the least, strictly partisan. All its stock was owned by the state, and the Democratic-controlled legislature had elected a solid slate of Democrats as officers and directors. Most nauseating of all to Pike was the fact that Chester Ashley controlled the directorship of the principal bank at the capital. Pike disliked Ashley intensely and bore an open grudge against him for having pulled wires to defeat Terence Farrelly for the presidency of the principal bank.[18]

The man elected president was Ashley's close friend, Capt. Jacob Brown, of the United States Army. Brown was a disbursing officer for the Indian Office in the War Department, a Jackson-Van Buren Democrat, and a seemingly popular man. He got into state news most often by making trips up the Arkansas River with huge sums of specie and currency to be doled out to the Indians. He was absent from Little Rock, his apparent home, on official army duty in the fall of 1836 when the legislature elected him president of the State Bank, and Pike and the Whigs, believing he was not actually a citizen of Arkansas, charged that he had been illegally elected to a state office while holding a federal one.[19]

When Captain Brown did not promptly resign his army commission as promised and devote himself to opening the State Bank, Pike and Reed, who were raising serious questions about the State Bank on several counts by the late summer of 1837, repeatedly pointed out the anomaly of the captain's holding two jobs at once. When Brown, infuriated by their eternal sniping, reportedly bragged that he intended to "hold *both jobs for life*," Pike made the most of the remark. "We shall see about that!" exclaimed Pike, who thought the people might have something to say to a legislature that would permit the captain to stay on as bank president while remaining in the army.[20]

Pike's attack on Brown was closely connected with his complaint that the directors and officers of the State Bank were dragging their feet in capitalizing and opening it. To be sure, those individuals were facing almost insurmountable odds in trying to organize the principal bank at Little Rock and the branches at Fayetteville and Batesville. The $1,000,000 in 5 percent bonds issued the State Bank in the fall of 1836 for the purpose of raising the needed capital had not found a market early in 1837 in the East, which was in the throes of the oncoming panic.[21] Captain Brown, however, persuaded the War Department in May to invest $300,000 of Choctaw Indian trust funds in the bonds, the money to be paid in lots of $50,000 each, beginning apparently in July. But none of the remaining $700,000 in state bonds would sell until, as was hoped, the legislature should increase the interest rate to 6 percent.[22]

The chief hope, therefore, of obtaining specie for capitalizing the principal bank, which was to open using the first capital raised for the State Bank, lay in collecting specie for Arkansas's share of the surplus revenue. This distribution began in January 1837, when the Treasurer of the United States announced that Arkansas's share of the surplus to be distributed that year came to $382,335.31 and was to be paid, beginning January 1, in four quarterly installments of $95,583.83 each.[23] Under a law passed the previous fall, in anticipation of the distribution, the legislature directed State Treasurer Woodruff to collect the surplus and deposit it with the State Bank as a supplement to its capital.[24]

The installment payable January 1, 1837, reached Woodruff in early February, in the form of two transfer drafts from the U.S. Treasurer, one for $45,583.83 drawn on the Planter's Bank of Mississippi and the other for $50,000 on the Agricultural Bank of Mississippi, both federal deposit banks at Natchez. Woodruff exchanged the smaller draft for specie at the Little Rock office of the receiver of federal monies, who, unfortunately, did not have enough specie on hand to cash the larger draft. Biding his time and wishing to make "one trip suffice for the collection of the whole," Woodruff retained this larger draft until the second installment, consisting of two drafts of identical amounts on the same two Natchez banks, arrived on schedule April 1.[25]

Still winding his leisurely way, Woodruff waited until after the middle of April to leave for Natchez, where he finally arrived April 23 to find the banks suffering a severe run from traders on the Mississippi River. Instead of getting in line and demanding Arkansas's specie, Woodruff allowed himself to be fast-talked into what turned out to be a fiasco for his state. He accepted the Agricultural Bank's pledge to pay $100,000 to him in specie at Little Rock on July 1, 1837, which was the amount due on the two drafts from the first and second installments. In return for this generous indulgence, he got from the Planter's Bank bills of exchange on banks in New Orleans for $45,583.33 in specie called for by the draft on that bank from the second installment.

After a successful trip to New Orleans, where he secured the $45,583.33 in specie, Woodruff returned home. Arriving at the Rock on May 8, Old Billy Buck took a sense of pride in his trip. He had collected another $45,583.33 in specie, making a total of $91,167.66 collected to date and had "the guaranty of the Agricultural Bank" to deliver to him on July 1 the $100,000 due in specie, "free of charge for transportation or risk." This latter feat alone, he allegedly boasted, had saved Arkansas at least $1,000 of transfer costs.

Alas, poor Woodruff had hardly brushed the dust of Natchez and New Orleans from his clothes when the shocking news reached him about the twelfth of May that the Mississippi banks had all suspended specie payments. He caught the next steamboat down river to Natchez, where he arrived on the seventeenth to learn that the Agricultural Bank had indeed suspended and would neither honor nor renew its April pledge to him. Woodruff then got the two $50,000 drafts protested and on May 20 set out "across the Mountains" for Washington City. He hoped to arrive in time to get new drafts issued on New York or Philadelphia banks that would pay him in specie. He was too late. Secretary of the Treasury Levi Woodbury, whom Woodruff visited personally on June 6 and 7, declined the Arkansas treasurer's request for drafts on the hard-pressed and suspended northern banks but presented him some new drafts drawn on deposit banks in Cincinnati, Louisville, and New Orleans.

On his way back to Arkansas, Woodruff collected in Ohio paper currency a draft of $33,000 on the Commercial Bank of Cincinnati and, in Kentucky paper notes, a draft of like amount on the Bank of Kentucky at Louisville. Since both had suspended, they scorned his request for specie. Accordingly, he reached home on Independence Day with $66,000 in paper notes and a $34,000 draft on the Commercial Bank of New Orleans which together represented the $100,000 that the Agricultural Bank had promised to pay in specie on July 1 at Little Rock.

Awaiting the harassed state treasurer at his Little Rock office was the third installment of the surplus revenue. This was in the form of two federal drafts on his old friends the suspended Natchez deposit banks, one for $50,000 on the Planter's Bank and the other for $45,583.33 on the Agricultural Bank. The State Bank was, he found, making gestures of opening for business, and he asked its officers and directors if they would not take these two drafts, together with one for the $34,000 on the Commercial Bank of New Orleans, off his hands. This brought a curt note that the State Bank was not authorized to receive such drafts, whereupon Woodruff dispatched "a special and trusty agent" to collect the three drafts.

There was no hope now of obtaining specie on any of the drafts, but Woodruff to save face instructed his agent to demand specie anyway. Neither did he want the badly depreciated Mississippi paper and told his agent that, in event of the refusal of the Natchez banks to pay specie, he should accept up to half the face value of the drafts in the notes of the Natchez banks providing they should agree to pay the balance in notes of certain banks in New Orleans. When the Natchez banks refused to pay in anything but their own notes, Woodruff's agent retained the federal drafts. Proceeding to New Orleans, he collected $16,800 in notes of the Commercial Bank and the balance of the $34,000 in a credit to the State of Arkansas with authority to draw. In early August, Woodruff again tendered the unpaid Natchez drafts to the State Bank which this time accepted them and afterwards collected them in Mississippi paper.

This closed Woodruff's part in the collection of Arkansas's share of the surplus revenue since the fourth installment was canceled by the government and never paid. Of the $286,751.49 represented by the three installments actually paid the state, Woodruff collected only $91,167.66 in specie, and he and the State Bank together collected the remainder in depreciated paper money of four states. In settling with the State Bank, Woodruff in late July and early August deposited with the bank $90,000 in specie and $196,156.49 in Ohio, Kentucky, and New Orleans bank notes and in federal drafts on the Natchez banks. This came to $286,156.49, while the three installments totaled $285,751.49. The difference between the two sums is $595, the amount which Woodruff charged the state for his travel expenses in trying to collect the surplus revenue. He had collected $91,167.66 in specie but had paid over only $90,000 in specie. Of this $1,167.66 in specie, $595 of it is accounted for by his travel charges and $572.66 by bank notes of his own which he substituted for that amount of specie in settling with the State Bank. Nothing was ever said about the $572.66, but the $595 for travel charges formed part of a later legislative investigation into Woodruff's conduct as treasurer, which investigation was to have important consequences for Arkansas Whigs.[26]

Long before Woodruff returned from his May-July mission, Pike and Reed had learned of his "April arrangement" with the Natchez "pet banks" and were making political capital of it. They knew neither the details of, nor the motives for, Woodruff's granting an indulgence to the Agricultural Bank. It was enough for them to know that Billy Buck of the Little Rock Democratic regency did not get the specie on demand in April. Therefore, they concluded that he had botched the collection of the surplus from beginning to end, and, with Pike wielding the editorial pen, set out to discredit him in the eyes of the public.[27]

Pike characterized Woodruff's "April arrangement" with the Agricultural Bank not only as an unauthorized act by the state treasurer but also suggested, in an editorial of May 22, that perhaps Mississippi's Sen. Robert Walker and other good Van Buren men at Natchez had convinced Woodruff that he should not demand specie of the "pets." Removing the specie might force the banks to suspend and thus hurt the Democratic cause in Mississippi. Or perhaps, Pike thought, the Natchez bankers had persuaded Old Billy that it would be dangerous for him to remove so much coin while the streets of Natchez were filled with angry men demanding specie—he might be robbed and lynched trying to carry the money back to Arkansas.[28]

By the twenty-ninth of May, Pike expressed as a matter of conviction that Woodruff had "lost sight of the interest of Arkansas" and had violated his obligation as treasurer by "his sympathy for a *Pet* Bank in Mississippi." He denied Pew's charge in the *Gazette* that he wished merely "to disparage" Woodruff. "We wish him to do his duty," Pike told Pew, "and when he fails in it, we shall take particular pains to tell him of it." The specie that Woodruff had gone after in April was needed by the first of June, Pike reminded the public, "in *order* that the Bank of the State might get into operation at that time, if Capt. Brown should happen to recollect that he has been elected president—which he seems entirely to have forgotten."[29]

There it all was. Woodruff had bungled the collection of the surplus, imperiling both the possibility of obtaining the specie now that the Mississippi "pets" had suspended and of getting the State Bank open. Pike made Woodruff out to be a fool. If the Agricultural Bank "was *hard run* when Mr. Woodruff was there" in April, was that "not so much more reason that he should have demanded the specie." Was Billy blind? "Cotton was at 6 cents—failures in New Orleans for 30 or 40 millions—the paper of that very bank at a discount of 25 per cent in New Orleans; and yet Mr. Woodruff, good, kind, easy soul, acting for the best [for his party], gave the Bank *time* on the draft." He was convinced, too, that Woodruff would fail in May to get the specie in Washington. "If he does not get the money," quipped Pike, "we see no chance for him except to go to Texas."[30]

Pike's version of Woodruff's kind treatment of the Natchez "pets" caught on. Was it true, a correspondent signed "Q," wanted to know of the *Gazette* in early June, that Woodruff on his second trip to Natchez in May cashed the drafts for the surplus revenue in Mississippi and Louisiana paper notes and had since made $10,000 clear money by lending it to Arkansas planters at 10 per cent interest? "If so," said Q, "The Times men will sit under their vine and fig trees a long time, waiting for the State Treasurer to go to Texas." Pike noted that the *Gazette* had replied neither "yea nor nay" to Q. Q was, said Pike, a fool for asking such a question. Nothing of the kind had been done. When the treasurer went the second time to Natchez, he got the drafts on the Agricultural Bank protested and "hurried on to Washington to get other drafts, *if he c[ould].* before [the] Government hears the true version of his conduct."[31]

Pike's reply to Q gave him the opening he needed to elaborate on and refine his own version of Woodruff's clumsy handling of the collection of the surplus revenue. Woodruff should have collected each installment at once on the federal drafts. Instead, he held them at Little Rock for a long time, and then when he finally did go to Natchez in late April had agreed to give the Agricultural Bank until July to pay him. The bank could have paid him in April since it had not then suspended, but Woodruff "was fearful of causing a run upon the Banks which might injure the party in Mississippi." Billy generously granted the Agricultural Bank "time," the bank subsequently suspended, and now Woodruff was on his way to Washington to try to save the specie for Arkansas. "One thing is certain," Pike told Q. "We shall not get the money." There was no specie in the country to be distributed; the banks had all suspended. "We cannot expect a dollar [in specie]."[32]

Pike and Reed, in Woodruff's absence, allowed their correspondents to express the most despicable of rumors. One had it that he made $10,000 for himself by lending out the $91,000 in specie in his custody. Another, that he allowed his pal Ashley use some of the specie to settle his accounts with the federal land offices. The Whig editors gleefully copied stories from the Whig press in Ohio and Kentucky of Woodruff's failure to collect Arkansas's share of the surplus. "The Ohio State Journal, and some of its kindred prints," the *Gazette* noted, had "given a croaking groan of sorrow because 'the young state of Arkansas has lost all share of the surplus revenue,' on account of a *faux pas* made by its treasurer."[33]

George D. Prentice, famed Whig editor of the *Louisville Journal*, with whom Pike had for several years exchanged papers, told Kentuckians that the people of Arkansas were "without bounds" in their indignation against Woodruff. With Pike as his main source, Prentice gave his readers full details of the Arkansas treasurer's indulgence to the Natchez "pets," of the subsequent suspension and loss of Arkansas's specie, and of Woodruff's flying trip to Washington City "to get his friend the Government to help him out of his perplexities." "He was entirely successful," reported Prentice: the government took back the drafts on the Democratic banks of Natchez and gave him new ones on the Whig deposit banks of Ohio and Kentucky.[34]

Woodruff was now on his way from Cincinnati to Louisville, Prentice warned Kentuckians on June 28, armed with federal authority "to take a large amount of the public funds from Kentucky and carry them to Arkansas." Kentucky already had less than her proper share of the public deposits, but she was a Whig state and the administration in Washington City was resolved to rob her of what she had for the sake of a Van Buren state, Mississippi. Prentice admonished the Kentucky bankers "to consider well" what course to take with the Arkansas treasurer. The Mississippi legislature had forced the Natchez banks to satisfy its demands under the distribution bill, and those banks, to protect Mississippi's share of the surplus, had refused to pay federal drafts in favor of Arkansas. Should Kentucky "send to Arkansas the sum due from Mississippi" was the question Prentice posed. He apparently wished the Louisville bankers to spurn the drafts completely, but the Kentucky bankers were, of course, willing to oblige Woodruff in Kentucky paper money, which was all the Arkansas treasurer got at Louisville. Pike and Reed happily quoted Prentice's warning to Kentuckians in order that Arkansans could see "in what light the conduct of our Treasurer is held in our neighboring states."[35]

Pike appeared to be in good humor that summer, as he expressed himself on Woodruff's travail as treasurer and on the affairs of the Little Rock regency. His view of the state Democratic power structure was by now fixed, which was that the wealthy lawyer-speculator, Ashley, not only bossed the capital "junto" but also made the state Democrats—even Sevier, Fulton, Yell, and Governor Conway—dance to his command. He believed that Ashley, with the backing of Woodruff's and Pew's *Gazette*, had laid plans in the winter of 1836–37 to elbow Congressman Yell aside and run the ambitious Fayetteville Democrat, state senator William McKnight Ball, in his place. Yell allegedly got wind of the plot and sent a friend riding horseback across north Arkansas to assure his friends he wished to run again, and, according to Pike, when Congress adjourned in

March, Judge Yell returned to Little Rock and angrily confronted the conspirators. The judge convinced them that, if forced to it, he would run against Ball and do his best to beat the Little Rock regency. This stormy session, reportedly taking place in Ashley's "political parlor," became a theme of Pike's "Political Life; or, The Reason of Democracy," a "Political Dramma" that he published in the *Times and Advocate* of June 12 over the name "Scene Shifter."[36]

A bit of the background is necessary to an understanding of Pike's dramatization. When President Van Buren on May 15, 1837, called Congress to meet in special session on the first Monday in September, Yell's term had expired in March and the regular congressional election in Arkansas was not scheduled until October. Therefore, Governor Conway, who had drawn some fire for reappointing Sevier to the Senate until the legislature could meet to reelect him, on June 5 proclaimed a special congressional election for the first Monday in July. Pike and Reed professed to be surprised at Conway's action, called it "election by proclamation," complained that a month was "short notice to the people in an emergency like the present," and announced that the Whigs would "select a candidate at the regular election in October, and leave the Gazette & Co., to take care of Judge Yell themselves."[37]

Shortly before this, Pew, who dabbled in law practice at Little Rock, was associated with two other lawyers in the unsuccessful defense of William F. McKee for murdering his Little Rock brother-in-law, Beaufort P. Scott, a sensational case that found Pike and Fowler aiding the prosecution in securing McKee's conviction. On applying to Governor Conway for a pardon for McKee, who was nevertheless hanged on May 26 at Little Rock, Pew charged in his petition that Pulaski County sheriff Dr. F. A. McWilliams had improperly influenced the jury in its verdict. Offended, Dr. McWilliams published in the *Times and Advocate* that Pew had "basely lied" about him, and, when Pew ignored the customary recourse to a duel, the doctor confronted Pew in the street in what Pike's and Reed's paper jokingly reported as a "Fatal Affray." Pew refused to fight the sheriff, turned pale, became inarticulate with fright, and "died without a struggle, or a groan," read the mock obituary. "As there was no sign of blood, even in Mr. Pew's face, and as no deadly weapons were seen or used by either, and as Mr. Pew showed no signs of violence, either towards the Doctor or himself, the Doctor is esteemed guiltless."[38]

Pike's "Political Dramma," was built around this "Fatal Affray." His first scene pictured four Arkansas Democratic officeholders discussing the dismal outlook for their party now that the economic panic had struck. They confessed to be amazed that so much ruin had been wrought by "that damnable little bulletin in the shape of a Specie Circular" and the "the 'experiments' of our late ruler, our beloved Andrew, upon the currency." The people were grumbling, and newly-crowned "King Martin begins to tremble on his throne." But they agreed among themselves that such pessimistic talk was dangerous, especially if any Whigs were in earshot, and roused themselves to consider their Democratic duty "to save the person as well as the reputation" of King Andrew and "henceforth smother and hide the vile stratagems and treachery of our Rulers from the world." They vowed to lie, cheat, and delude the yeomanry of Arkansas, with whom "those naughty fellows of the 'Times and Advocate'" were "ingratiating themselves into the confidence of."

Indeed, the four officeholders feared that while their cause in the Union was safe their cause in Arkansas looked more and more hopeless, as expressed by the "1st Office Holder:"

> The People are beginning to open their eyes, since Billy [Woodruff] lost or fooled away their draft for a round hundred thousand. I don't wonder at it. He has gone to beg Uncle Sam's pardon, and get absolution from sin; but I fear he won't be paid for wear, fare and travel. We are beset on all sides. A rascally fellow calling himself "A Silent Monitor," has had the audacity to tell at this late day, of the frauds and the peculations, and misbehavior of John Pope and others; and the fellow has told the truth; (*but this is among ourselves.*) I am sorry the best of our party were associated with the Ex-Governor; or I would join in with the "Monitor" and help abuse him; but as it is, I cannot without endangering the Democratic cause in Arkansas, which has already received some fatal stabs from, as I thought, its truest votaries. It is to be hoped that our beloved Ambrose [Sevier] may escape censure for taking the superintendence of the public building out of the hands of the Legislature, and putting it into the hands of that old Pontiff [Pope]. . . .

But again, they convinced themselves that Senator Sevier was "too omnipotent" to be hurt by "Monitor" and swore to help him by any means "until every heart in all the realm is warped and biased in favor of the evil doers who pride in misrule."

At this point the carrier of the *Times and Advocate* appeared on the scene, hawking his papers and shouting "Mournful tidings . . . Deaths—Broken Banks, and Proclamations." An officeholder took a copy of the paper and read to the others of a "Fatal Affray" in which the editor of the *Gazette* had been killed. They all four drew their Bowie Knives and ran off shouting: "The Murderer! Vengeance! Retributive Justice!"

Pike's next scene was set in Ashley's "political parlor," where Yell ("The Congressman"), William McKnight Ball ("Mr. North"), Ashley ("1st Attorney"), Judge Charles Caldwell ("Judge"), and others were discovered in close confab. Yell was still angry at Ashley, though Ashley had by now seemingly agreed to Yell's reelection. Yell was advised to hold his temper and not to start a quarrel, but he could not refrain from expounding in a voice loud enough to be heard by Ashley and Ball:

> I hold my temper when my most deadly (*tho' secret*) enemy is bearding me with indirect threats to put me down? Not I. I, who was elected your Representative not a year ago, and only waiting the Gov's Proclamation, to be elected again; stand by and quietly submit to the insults of the vilest of his sex . . . I . . . be moderate and restrain my passion, when attempts are making by a few to array Mr. North against me for a seat in Congress. Never. I am the favorite of the party. I paid, out of my pocket, the expenses of a friend, . . . while he rode through the North and stirred up a feeling in my favor, and I am determined at least to get my money back.

Ball interrupted Yell to deny that he himself had any "ambition to go to Congress" or that he had exerted "secret means to become the Nominee instead of our worthy Representative now standing dumb with fury." Yell was about to say to Ball that Ball could not deny being approached to run, when Ashley, interrupting abruptly, said to Yell, "But I, sir, deny your right to monopolize a seat." This brought an exchange of oaths and a fist fight. While Yell and Ashley continued their fight, the four officeholders entered, waving their Bowies and relating the sad story in the *Times and Advocate* of the "Fatal Affray." This shocking news saddened them—"our Oracle is gone"—and, after interceding to separate Yell and Ashley and to restore friendship between them, they adjourned to the courthouse. There a coroner's jury and coroner were to examine Pew's body and the prisoner, Sheriff McWilliams, was to be arraigned.

Pike was at his best in the final scene in the courtroom, with Judge Caldwell presiding. The clerk intoned to the prisoner the arraignment: "You are looked upon as the supposed author of a bloody deed. All eyes single you out, as the fell destroyer of your fellow man. Our lamented Organ, the Editor of the Gazette. They say he lives no more. . . . Then are you guilty or not guilty?" The prisoner pled not guilty, saying Pew "was standing mute in the crowd and suddenly fell dead from causes unknown. I had no agency in his death, more than every other good citizen." The prisoner was told that he would be discharged if he could "prove an Alibi," which brought a murmur from the crowd: "No let him be tried in a regular way."

To see, as one unknown character said, "how for to proceed," they now brought in the coroner, coroner's jury, and Pew's body. A physician also entered and was asked to "extract the ball and dress the wounds." The physician discovered that Pew still lived: "His pulse yet beats, but slightly." Yell advised, "Wash his face with camphor. Do! Quick. He may not be dead." Revived, Pew explained that, of course, he had not been murdered: "I was sick from a relaxation of my system, nothing else. I am now almost able to walk."

Pew's friends were now satisfied "that violence has neither been done or offered," a sarcastic reference to the theme of the "Fatal Affray," and the prisoner was released. "Our Oracle is safe, and we should rejoice," cried Yell. They all agreed, and after "mutually pledging" themselves "to play our parts well in the next Congressional Election (*for the Gov. has issued his Proclamation.*) . . . ," they all marched off rejoicing to the tune of "Hail Columbia."

Interestingly enough, Pike's little political farce contained more truth than fiction. The Whigs fielded no candidate against the popular Yell, whom Pew dutifully backed in the July election. Pike and Reed denounced Yell as a man who was opposed to any "redress of the present grievances—ha[d] helped to injure the currency by voting for the Deposit Banks last session, and by shouting loud against the United States bank." The people believed, however, that a national bank was "the only remedy for the present distress" and would not vote for Yell. Yet the people were robbed, by the governor's short notice, of any opportunity of selecting a candidate who would support a new national bank. With the people sitting out the July election, Pike and Reed blustered that the Whigs could hardly wait to take after Yell in October.[39]

When Pew interpreted the Whig decision to sit out the July election as a challenge to Governor Conway's legal authority to call such an election and as a threat to contest Yell's seat in the National House, Pike and Reed expressed great amusement. They had no plan to investigate the governor's power nor to challenge Yell's election to the called session of Congress. "By all means," they said, "let him in the halls of Congress, aid in perfecting the work which the 'experiment' has so favorably begun, and in carrying out Gen. Jackson's 'humble efforts to improve the currency.'" Yell's skill, sagacity, and genius in "financial matters, making dim the fame of Necker and throwing Webster, Clay, and Calhoun far into the shade," would be of incalculable help to the Bentons and Polks and those other Democratic "tinkerers" and "quack-salvers" in completing the ruin they had begun under Jackson. It would be "time enough for the Whigs to step forward" after these men had brought the country to its "last gasp." Meanwhile, they were willing to see no Whig in the House from Arkansas, and trusted that the Whigs already there would leave the Democrats "to the prodigious resources of their own brains."[40]

Pike and Reed were quite aware of the growing division within Van Buren's national ranks on the subject of a national bank and did what they could to sow discord on the topic among Democrats at home. Pew declared in late June that the congressional trio from Arkansas—Sevier, Fulton, and Yell—would continue to oppose "any National Bank of whatever nature, and in whatever emergency." Alluding to ancient Whig rumors that Van Buren and Tammany Hall Democrats had meant all along to replace Nicholas Biddle's Philadelphia-based Bank of the United States with a new national bank in New York, Pike and Reed predicted that Van Buren would make the current distress and the "consequent general cry for a National Bank" an excuse for "consummating" their intended object. Party and self-interest would then see the Arkansas trio turn a somersault on the national bank question.[41]

There was, of course, no basis for the Whig charge that Van Buren favored a national bank in New York or anywhere else and thus no chance that Arkansas's congressional trio would be called upon to break the pledge that Pew made in their names. But Pike and Reed claimed they had good evidence—from a Sevier neighbor in Chicot County—that Senator Sevier was ready to vote for a national bank. And in late July–early August, the *Gazette* was bombarded with a series of anonymous letters advising Sevier on what course he should take on the issue. A correspondent signing himself "C." began the campaign and sounded for all the world like Pike, who had just revived his Casca letters in the *Times and Advocate*. So far as is known Pike never revealed himself as the author, although his later use of the C. letter strongly supports it, and it fitted his views precisely. It would have been like him to plant the letter in Pew's *Gazette* through an intermediary, and there was not the slightest doubt that Pew violated every canon of partisan journalism in admitting the letter to his paper.[42]

C. told Sevier that he was Arkansas's "leader of leaders"; that the state could look to him alone to bring forward in Congress "the great measure which is to save the country"; that neither Fulton nor Yell, whose watchword was "our party, right or wrong," would vote for it unless it was brought up by a friend of the Van Buren administration like Sevier; that he was sure Sevier by now recognized the failure of President Jackson's "experiments" and the stupidity of "the recent attempts made in Congress to force upon the nation a metallic circulating medium"; and that it must have occurred to Sevier that "the only remedy for the pending evil" was the chartering of a national bank by Congress. Declaring that such an institution was needed to save the country, C. launched into the standard Whig argument in defense of a national bank. It would give the people a currency that would "pass as well in Maine as in Arkansas." It would exercise a proper control over the local banks which were so essential to the business of the country. And it would facilitate commerce and exchange, restore a vigorous tone of prosperity to all the economic pursuits of the people, and unshackle the nation's "traveling intercourse."[43]

Turning to the "empirics" and "fanatics" of the day, who clamored vehemently "against banks and the banking system," the anonymous writer was positive that Sevier was too knowledgeable of commercial affairs and too independent of the encumbering chains of political "faith" to be "gulled" by such arguments. He believed Sevier would draw his own conclusions from the past and present, that when the senator did conclude that a national bank was necessary that he would "have the manliness to act, 'though opposed by an army of banners.'" Arkansas esteemed Sevier for being such a man, exhorted the writer "and as such she is proud of you. Do not suppose I flatter; I was never one of your flatterers. In days gone by, I opposed you; but you have since 'bought golden opinions of all sorts of people,'" a reference to Sevier's vote against Van Buren's anti-Western land bill in the recent session of Congress while Fulton and Yell had voted for it strictly on a party-loyalty basis.[44]

The letter prompted a barrage of letters to the *Gazette* condemning the anonymous writer of it for calling on Sevier, as "Old School" declared, to save the country by administering "the *specific* of the Whigs." This gave Pike and Reed the opportunity they may have been fishing for, that is, if Pike was, indeed, C. If not, it was a situation made to order for them. Accordingly, the *Times and Advocate*, with Pike obviously wielding the editorial pen, noted on the fourteenth of August that *Gazette* correspondents differed widely among themselves on what course Senator Sevier should pursue regarding a national bank.[45]

Calling "Mr. Old School's" reply to "Mr. C." "truly a curiosity," the Whig editor pounced on him for putting party above the good of the country and for praising the party regularity of Fulton and Yell. He accused "Old School's" party of ruining the currency by supporting Jackson, asserted that the Democrats had defeated themselves by their own fiscal blunders, and dealt at length with the charge that "a United States Bank is the specific of the Whigs." The Whigs, he said, wanted the country to have a sound currency that would be "cash at par value every where." They believed that such a currency was necessary to insure the rights of a free people. They cared not in the least how this object was to be accomplished and were not fatally attached to the idea of a national bank, knowing that such a bank was liable to being abused; but they asked, "can the interest and rights of the people be preserved without one?" Finally, the Whigs of Arkansas saw no good for the country, in "Mr. Old School's" advice that the Arkansas congressional trio should look to the Van Buren administration alone for relief, and that the Arkansas trio should make themselves slaves to their national party masters. "We of Arkansas might as well not send representatives to Congress at all—but just send word to the party to do what they please with us," he closed.[46]

Noting the silence of the *Gazette* on what it proposed as a substitute for a national bank but remarking on the "abortions" which that newspaper had "of late been putting forth on plans, cooked up by the schemers in Washington," Pike and Reed on August 28 commented that they would like to know where Pew stood. The *Globe*, Van Buren's

Washington City organ edited by Frank Blair, seemingly could not make up its mind, said Pike and Reed, although its most recent proposal was that the government should be separated from "the banking principle." Under this plan the government would divorce itself from all banks, set up its own depositories and become its own banker, and use Treasury drafts payable in specie for paying the government's bills. Pike and Reed objected strongly to this plan, believing all the government's specie would be stored on the seaboard and that only Treasury drafts bearing a premium, that is, a discount, would circulate in the West. They thought the proposal was thrown out merely to feel "the public pulse" on what was plainly a crackpot scheme, that the men behind the *Globe* "mean soon to bring forward a plan for Treasury Bank, in order, of course, 'to separate the Government from the banking principle,'" a sarcastic reference to a Democratic-controlled bank. They expressed amusement at Pew's dilemma of trying to keep abreast of party developments at the national capital, and at his floundering hopelessly in a sea of mad schemes.[47]

It was true that Pew did not know where to turn, for both Van Buren and the Democratic press had been undecided about a solution to the government's fiscal problem. Van Buren took all spring and most of the summer to feel out party leaders and make up his mind. He never seriously considered a national bank. On the other hand, the state bank deposit system was in ruins, and he was unwilling to try to prop it up by making improvements and changes, That "experiment" was over. In the end, he fell back on the idea of relieving the government from any further financial embarrassment by ceasing to rely on the deposit banks. Indeed, he had already instigated such a system by refusing to use the suspended deposit banks and by ordering all government funds to be collected, stored, and disbursed through Treasury agents and postal employees. He decided, therefore, to ask Congress to make this arrangement permanent, that is, to divorce the government from all banks. In doing so, he would leave the deposit banks to their own fate, with the hope that the states might then act to solve banking abuses within their jurisdiction.

Pike and Reed, therefore, were dead wrong in late August when they denounced the divorce plan put forward in Blair's *Globe* and reprinted in the *Gazette*. President Van Buren had made up his mind to ask Congress for a divorce, or Independent Treasury, bill, which would become the great party issue for the next several years. It took Arkansas's congressional trio in Washington City a few days in September and Pew in Little Rock until October to learn this. When they did find out, they all, including the hitherto inscrutable Sevier, lined up solidly behind the president. Inevitably, Arkansas's Whigs denounced the Independent Treasury as a separation of the Treasury and the government from the people and prepared to do battle on the issue.

X

Days of the Humbuggers

AT THE TIME the Democratic congressional trio went off to Washington in August 1837, Pike and Reed were locked in a battle with Pew over the upcoming regular congressional election in October. Judge Yell had won reelection in July unopposed and, understandably enough, did not relish standing again in October — "presenting the unusual spectacle," as he affably phrased it, "of a candidate being before his constituency three times in a little upwards of one year."[1] Hints by Pew that Yell had been elected in July not only for the special session but also for the next regular term beginning in December brought a howl from Pike and Reed. To quiet matters, Pew on August 22 again placed Yell's name at his masthead and announced that "we are determined to run Judge Yell again; notwithstanding he is not legally bound to do it." Yell was then on his way to Washington, but he had, said Pew, authorized him to say that if a majority of his constituents expressed themselves against him in October that he would resign his seat. Yell had also enclosed his "circular for use in the event that the republican party proposed him as their candidate in October, "which they will undoubtedly do," added Pew.[2]

Pike and Reed deemed this act the height of impudence on Pew's part, that is, to place Yell's name at his masthead — "Jackson Republican Ticket"/"For Congress"/"Hon. Archibald Yell" — to announce that "we are determined to run him" and then meekly subjoin the condition, "if the republican party propose him as their candidate in October." This was to say, the Whig editors snidely remarked, that "Messrs. Ashley & Co. have concluded to run him again, as they are a little afraid they may not be able to elect anybody else this time." They also had some choice words for Yell's as yet unpublished "circular." They suspected that it had not been "enclosed" at all but that the judge had "requested the Directory to write one for him, if it is necessary." Would Pew oblige their curiosity by exhibiting "the circular to the people in manuscript when it is finished, so that they may judge whether it is really the Judge's handiwork?" Yell's "own writing requires so much correction as a foul 'proof-sheet' to fit it for the press," they "should like to see the 'dockument.'"[3]

Pew inferred from all this noisy bustle that the Whigs meant to challenge Yell. Accordingly, he asked them in the *Gazette* of September 5 to please "trot out their nag and let us have a look at him." In the same issue, Pew published Yell's circular, a production that took up two full columns in the paper and which blamed the panic on the "wild and ruinous" banking system and on the fact that the people had forsaken the habits of "republican simplicity" for the vanity of "show, magnificence, and extravagant dress and notions of every description." Promising nothing definite, he believed that

Congress would do what it "legitimately" could to help the state legislatures correct the banking evil, suggested nothing more exceptional than a currency bill to coerce the deposit banks into either closing their doors or resuming specie payments, but vowed that his "uncompromising hostility to our whole system of banking" would guarantee that he should "do nothing to prop it up longer than to relieve the pressure it has been the main instrument in producing."[4]

He attacked the Specie Circular for its unequal and unfair enforcement against settlers in the new states but was careful to neither criticize President Jackson nor say what he would do about it in Congress. Concerning land policy, the judge explained that he voted for the abortive land bill in the recent Congress because "it was better, with all its faults, *than none at all*," a rather weak defense in light of the fact that Sevier had voted against the anti-western measure in the Senate and that it was defeated in the House by western votes. Yell was vulnerable on this issue, since Pike had roasted him and Fulton for putting their party loyalty to the administration-sponsored bill above the interests of Arkansas. Turning to the subject of internal improvements, Yell promised to continue to press for federal appropriations to open Arkansas's navigable streams and to complete all roads and navigation projects already begun. He ended by saying he favored a strong military force on the state's "exposed" western border from Missouri to the Sabine and would "act so as to anticipate and prevent the horrors of an Indian war in the midst of our thinly settled and scattered population."[5]

Pike and Reed, in reply to Pew's request to "trot out their nag" for the October race against Judge Yell, noted that Pew's own "nag" was an interesting one to observe. "He is already harnessed, and between the shafts, drawing the Little Rock Regency at his heels.— We will see how he will trot with the load." Meanwhile, they would be sure to let the *Gazette* know when the People decided on a candidate, if any. They wished for now to congratulate the party on Yell's circular—the "gentlemen employed to concoct it" had done the judge "some credit." They were glad to see that Yell had magnanimously agreed to run for the regular session after all; were happy to note that the judge acknowledged that there was "some distress 'among the farming interests'" since the *Gazette* had constantly pictured the farmers and working men as well off under the current panic; were not surprised to find that Yell made no mention of a national bank since he had not yet got to Washington and learned from Van Buren "what plan the party had fixed upon"; were pleased to see that Yell now admitted that the Specie Circular, which the *Gazette* and loyal Democrats had ever defended, was working a hardship on the West; but were disappointed to read that Yell's only remedy was a currency bill to prop up the deposit banks under which speculation would continue to run rife. "The truth is," they closed, "the Judge and his friends did not know what to propose—and if they had no better plan to offer, than the abortion they had produced, they had better let it alone altogether."[6]

Pike's law partner, Cummins, pleading the press of "private business," declined to run for Congress, but was so slow in letting it be known that the Whig leaders had trouble finding a willing candidate.[7] The election was only two weeks away when on September 18, the *Time and Advocate* put at their masthead: "The People's Ticket"/"For Congress"/"John Ringgold." In an editorial endorsement of the Batesville state senator, Pike and Reed called him "a firm and undeviating republican of the school of Jefferson,

Madison, and Monroe;" a "man of character, capacity, and firmness, opposed to the misrule of party and the ruinous effects of Van Burenism."[8]

In the same issue, "Long John" Ringgold addressed a circular "To the Independent Voters of Arkansas," dated Batesville, September 9. He blamed "Executive action" and "untried 'Experiments'" with the currency of the country for the bankruptcy of the government. He carefully avoided mentioning a national bank but indirectly endorsed one by proposing to restore the government to that "former settled policy" which for "the last twenty years" had secured to the people "a sound, good and healthy circulating medium." As for his other planks, he pledged to contend for the rights of the states, to restrict executive power and patronage, to oppose all efforts to create a Treasury Bank that would concentrate the power of the purse and the sword in the hands of a party government, to work for a land bill that would combine preemption and graduation in price "agreeable to quality" and that would award "the poor man with a large family a donation under salutary conditions," and to support internal improvements by the general government, as allowed by the letter and spirit of the Constitution. Spelling out his program for internal improvements, Long John called for appropriations for the hitherto neglected Black and White Rivers, for further improvements on the Arkansas and Red Rivers, and for completing all public roads in Arkansas and particularly for extending the National Road from St. Louis through Arkansas to Fulton on Red River. His reference to those "much neglected streams" the Black and the White, in which he was personally interested, became a standing Democratic joke in Arkansas politics since thereafter no platform was considered to be complete without a mention of Ringgold's two rivers.[9]

Ringgold called on his friends to be magnanimous to his absent opponent but ruefully referred to the dilemma in which his fellow Whigs had placed him. "The limited time allotted me by my friends in announcing myself a candidate for your suffrages, will prevent my visiting any section of the State, and having a personal interview, and free communion with the people,—a matter of much regret on my part, if time would admit, and my competition were present." As it was, he thought Judge Yell's friends could hardly complain about any advantage or disadvantage "on the score of absence." In a personal note, Ringgold stated that he had resided in Arkansas fifteen years, had come to the Territory as a poor man, and all that he now possessed was in the state, none of it the result of "Executive patronage or Federal Commissions"—a direct allusion to the fact that Yell and other Democrats had come to Arkansas as federally-appointed officials. Ringgold closed by announcing that he was resigning as state senator from Independence and Jackson counties.[10]

The congressional campaign that followed, what there was of it, found Pike and Reed stooping to the same despicable tactics that Pike the year before had so strongly condemned in Yell. They believed that Ringgold from north Arkansas would divide that section of the state with Yell, but that for Long John to win the election he must carry the slave counties of the south and east by overwhelming majorities. They consequently adopted the strategy of the forked tongue, appealing to the south to vote against Yell because he had put his party interests above the slaveholding interests in the recent session of Congress while trusting that the panic and other grievances of the north would pull votes away from Yell there.[11]

To implement this strategy, Pike dug up an old issue he had raised in the *Advocate* back in February, which was that Yell, as a party gesture, had then refused to attend a caucus of slave-state members of Congress called for the purpose of working out a method of stifling the receipt in Congress of antislavery petitions. He and Reed now charged that Judge Yell should have attended and spoken for the slave interests of Arkansas and even went so far as to say that Yell in refusing to attend the caucus had "virtually" sided with the old abolitionist, John Quincy Adams![12]

Meanwhile, they had every reason to believe that their "*seventy-four inch candidate*" from the north would divide the vote of that section with the popular Yell. For one thing the north was hopping mad over the State Bank and might well vote against Yell out of spite. That section's grievance stemmed from the fact that the principal bank officials had used all the surplus revenue funds to capitalize and open their bank in Little Rock, had made no serious move to open the branch banks, and, meanwhile, had distributed the loans and benefits of the principal bank to twenty-two counties in the south on the ground that the branches would, when opened, benefit only the twelve counties of the north. Enraged over being omitted from any benefits of the principal bank and from the surplus revenue, spokesmen of the north had raised serious questions about the legality of the principal bank's authority and demanded that the branches be opened in order that the general board of the State Bank—a body which would represent and govern all three banks—could be created and begin setting policy for the State Bank at large. To be sure, Pike and Reed had opened the *Times and Advocate* to these northern complaints. They perhaps thought, too, that Ringgold's sectional appeal for navigation improvements on those "much neglected" northern streams the Black and the White would aid the Whig cause against Yell.[13]

Pew quickly caught on to the Whig strategy, but was plainly worried over it. He labeled the slavery issue a distortion of Yell's moderate position, declared the judge safe on the question, and charged quite correctly that Pike and Reed had raised the absurd issue to injure Yell on the old "basis question" in Arkansas. Declaring that conflict "an exploded local question in Arkansas," he admonished southeast Democrats to remember that Conway, Sevier, and Fulton from south Arkansas had been in 1836 "warmly supported by the democracy of the north and west." It would now be, he warned, "illiberal, absurd, and anti-national" for the south and east Democrats not to support the northwest's candidate, Judge Yell, in the October election.[14]

Whether based on pure bravado or conviction born of certainty, Pike and Reed expressed the view a week before the election that Ringgold would carry every county south of the Arkansas River. "If this be the case," they said, "his election is sure—for in several of the northern counties his majorities will be overwhelming." What made them so optimistic was the intelligence that Ringgold would divide with Judge Yell the votes of Washington, Carroll, Van Buren, and Pope. They appealed to the Whigs of Pulaski County to turn out in record numbers and "give the Tory leaders here a drubbing long to be remembered."[15]

Election day, Monday, October 2, revealed that Yell had outpolled Ringgold by something over a thousand votes in the state. There was no doubt, though, that the trumped up slavery issue had hurt Yell in the south. Pike and Reed blamed the heavy rain falling across the state on election day for the light Whig turnout—"as the counties where Ringgold would have got the largest majorities, were visited with the heaviest rains." Though they conceded victory to Yell, they took pride in the fact that the Whigs had cut his large majority of 1836 by two-thirds and took renewed hope for their cause from the additional fact that a number of southeast counties had been "regenerated"—Phillips, Crittenden, Jackson, Monroe, Arkansas, Jefferson, and Hempstead—all of which had gone to Yell the year before. It was the "*turn-coats* of Washington county," they regretted to say, who not only failed to deliver the promised votes to Ringgold but who had, instead, actually turned out for Yell, giving him a stronger majority in that populous county than he had had in 1836.[16]

Pew did not disagree with this interpretation but put things in better perspective when he gave the northern counties credit for Yell's reelection. "*Nine cheers* for the North!" he exclaimed when the results were in. "But for their patriotism, promptness, and energy . . . the Jackson candidate for Congress might, by a secret movement and active combination, have been defeated. These counties are the PILLARS OF DEMOCRACY!" Pew implied, but did not dare articulate it, that the slave counties had been won by the Whig sectional appeal to the slavery interests. But Pike and Reed could take little consolation from the truth of the matter, which was, that the trumped up slave issue, if it hurt Yell in the south, had seemingly gained him new strength in the northwest. All they could do was to curse the "*turn-coats*" of that region for betraying a northern brother, "Long John" Ringgold.[17]

The congressional campaign of August-September drew from Pike's facile pen another of his incomparable "political dramas," this one entitled, "The Review, or The days of the Humbuggers."[18] That it was not published until two weeks after the election is perhaps indicative of the disorganization in the Whig effort against Yell. Written over the signature of "Bob Handy, Junior, of Ozark Vicinage," a reference to Yell's financial interest in the new Arkansas River town of Ozark, Pike built his one-act play around the high drama of Congressman Yell presenting his famous "Cirkular" to the Little Rock Regency for approval.

The strongest evidence that Pike was the author of the C. letter to Sevier published earlier in the *Gazette* came in the first scene of this drama, when Sevier ("Bombastus"), Fulton ("Mr. Risible"), and Yell ("Robbin Roughhead") were gathered in a private room in Little Rock on the eve of their departure in August for Washington City to attend Van Buren's called session of Congress. Pike presented Fulton and Yell as suspecting that their "masters at Washington" had played havoc with the currency and the country but as being afraid to lift a finger in opposition. Indeed, Yell denied that the Arkansas trio had any "right to oppose what Andrew, or Benton or Martin may think for the good of the party." But Sevier, in whom he had seen some hope, Pike pictured as having enough spunk to blame Jackson and Benton for landing "us in the Abyss of ruin which Benton had prepared for the whole democratic fraternity." Sevier also made fun of Fulton and Yell for what that fellow C. had said about them:

> He doesn't seem to think you are like to do much to relieve the country, because he says you are Hard Metal men, and so you are, if I understand your views, for you say you are bound to do what your taskmasters set you at; consequently you

are opposed to a National Bank, for Benton won't let you vote against his Gold Bill. (Laughing) Huzza for Mr. "C." He says that I'm the boy what fears no noise; neither do I. He tells you to a gnat's heel what I'll do, which by the way will be regulated a good deal by what Uncle Dicky [Vice President Richard M. Johnson] says. Damn the difference I'm safe, for I'm looked upon by Whig and Tory as an advocate of a National Bank, and If I don't go for one, I'll patch up some tale to tell the boys why I opposed the only institution (as I believe) that will serve a nation of such diversity of interest and pursuits as ours; (laughing) but my boys he don't seem to calculate upon much from you. . . .

Fulton interrupted Sevier here, damned "Mr. C." and the *Gazette*, called Pew "a dog—whelp—a dirty lickspittle" for publishing the letter and, remembering Sevier's treachery the year before in scheming to rob him of his Senate seat, accused Sevier of being up to another plot to replace him. He shook his fist in Sevier's face and invoked the sacred name of Jackson—"there is one, who'll veto all your dastardly attempts to supplant me, and rear up some one else les[s] worthy, upon my ashes." So "long as a certain personage lives at the Hermitage," Fulton reminded Sevier, "I'll be provided for, and that well, too; for he told me when he sent me here as Secretary, that if I kept along in the good track, he would be a sure prop, and so he will."

Yell intervened in their quarrel and, after some discussion of their disagreement on the land bill in the previous session, told the two senators that he was greatly worried about the October election. He was haunted by "a dream last night that I was in the middle of the river straddle of a rail, floating down stream." He awoke but could not "persuade myself for an hour, but that the dam'd Whigs had me bound hand and foot and were about kommitting me to the mercy of the Kurrent." His friends discussed with him his strange dream, which brought the question from Sevier as to whether Yell had dreamed "that some rascally Whig" had got hold of a private letter Yell had written earlier from Tennessee stating that his true motive for being "a whole hogge Jackson man" was to get the general to appoint him to a judgeship in Arkansas. Yell admitted that it, unfortunately, was true, and that moreover he had in the same letter explained how he chose to "settle in Washington Kounty on akkount of its dence population." Sevier teased Yell about what the Whigs could "construe these words to mean" and recommended that they all three "consult our great leader Talleyrand, and I'll underwrite that his prolific brain will devise some way for you to get out of the scrape."[19]

Yell jumped at the suggestion of conferring with Ashley and advised his two friends that Tom Pew ("Mr. Pica") thought, in any case, that he should submit his "Cirkular" to the Little Rock Directory of the party for "revision and kerrection, which I will do, as the meeting is solely for that purpose." Fulton and Sevier then remarked on Yell's legendary circular. Fulton wanted to know whether the judge was really going to have it before the meeting, "or is it a joke?" "It's no joke, I can assure you," replied Yell. "It will be there, if it's done, I wrote about half of it myself and got our friend Billy Buck [Woodruff] to Kontinue it.—He says he can make it a prime dockument." Sevier warned that they "must keep a sharp eye out[,] for it will be fatal if the orthography be bad," an allusion, of course, to Pike's and Reed's charge that Yell had not written the circular and to Pike's long tradition of poking fun at Yell's spelling.

The meeting for the consideration of Judge Yell's circular was presided over by Ashley ("Talleyrand"), who warned his followers before Yell arrived that they must listen carefully and make sure that the judge said nothing "that's incorrect or tends to impugn the character of land speculators, all of whom you know are good democrats and do much to keep up this party." Wealth insured political power, lectured Ashley, and land and money were the source of both. He asked them to consider himself and his partner in land speculation, "Mr. [Roswell] B.[eebe]." "What can we not accomplish with two hundred thousand acres of the richest of your soil, o'er which you could not tread without our will and pleasure?" Therefore, Ashley's henchmen must "beware that nothing is said or done in disparagement of us."

To complete his picture of the powerful but corrupt Ashley, Pike at this point had the officers of the State Bank appear carrying the "Bank Chest" with all the institution's money in it. Ashley explained that it was the bank's money, "but it's for our friends who are going to Washington and some for me; there are 1000 acres of prime land and I must enter it by sun to-morrow." A bank officer assured all present that this, indeed, was the case, but not to worry as "the money will not be lost to you, if it is to the State."

With Yell, Sevier, and Fulton on hand, Sevier explained the problem to Ashley of Yell's letter having gotten into Whig's hands, which, as Sevier worded it, revealed the judge's true "motives for supporting Jackson." Ashley's simple remedy was, "Swear it's a forgery." Next, Yell read his "Cirkular," which was signed "Robbin Roughhead, Back Woods, Aug. 20, 1837." It was proclaimed a masterpiece by Yell himself, who pointed out that he had been careful to say nothing about what he was going to do about anything. Ashley gushed over it for its "chasteness of style," for the fact that it contained "nothing *offensive* or *defensive*," and for the fact, therefore, that it "breathes the sentiments of a true democrat."

But Yell in private, told his friends what he really meant to do in "Kongress." He would first cut the pay of all Whigs there.

> I'm then agoing to move Washington City to some place on the Ohio or Mississippi.—If I get that to take, there will be no danger but what we'll have Kongress meeting in this State after a while; near Ozark [Yell's new town] for instance, for let me once get the City started I'll have to put it smack along side of Ozark, and then we can go to Kongress whenever we please.

Yell also would "have a separate Land District up about Ozark" and had already promised the offices of receiver and of register to five or six different men each; then "You dogs you, you shall have farms at your own prices. Don't you see into it?"

This pleased all present, and Ashley, after checking again to make doubly sure that Yell had mentioned neither "that *letter*" nor "Land Speculators," ordered Pew to get out the circular in the next *Gazette*. The question then came up of keeping Ashley on as leader in Arkansas while the congressional trio was absent in Washington. Sevier assumed the chair from Ashley, whereupon Fulton moved "that the house appoint the most grave and wily Talleyrand the '*Great Leader and Head of the Jackson Republican Party in Arkansas*.'" Jackson was the man, said Fulton, because he had "strength and popularity." Yell thought the party name was a capital idea and told Pew to announce him as the "Jackson Republican Kandidate for Kongress," to which Pew replied that Yell had "anticipated me for already have I got those burning words in type: "Jackson Republican Ticket"/"For Congress"/"Robbin Roughhead." Pew explained that he "left the name of Van Buren out, as he does not seem to take with the sovereigns as well as we could wish, but by "good management" Pew thought the Arkansas Democrats could "entail him upon the people of this state under the corner of *Jackson Republicanism*.'"

Finding no objections to Ashley's election as "generalissimo of the democratic forces" of the state, Sevier pronounced him elected and installed him. The congressional trio's boat arrived at this juncture, and the whole party, commanded by Ashley, prepared to leave for the river landing. Ashley expressed his regret that there was not time for him "to confer" with the trio as to how they should act in Congress "in the coming struggle between bank and anti-bank men and a hundred other things, upon which I might give you much prudent counsel." Ashley, however, had watched "with pleasure, that at home" as the trio had demeaned themselves in a manner befitting good Democrats and in accordance with "my advice." He regretted only "the foolish little fight that myself and Mr. Roughhead got into on this spot not long since" but was pleased that all had "blown over" and that he and Yell were at peace. Yell fell at Ashley's feet and begged forgiveness, to which Ashley replied that the judge should have no fear "that my vengeance will be wreaked upon you." With this they all went off to the steamboat.

On board the "Steamer Little Rock" Ashley had his political lackeys—Pew, State Bank officers, et cetera—store away the baggage of "the noblest trio that ever held in their hands the liberties and destinies of any sovereign and confiding state." To this flattery the cocky Yell promised that the "tumultuous halls of Kongress" would ring with the trio's "eloquence." "Ay Sir, but few Kongresses will be held in Washington hereafter," he repeated, "for I am strong in the hope that I'll have Washington City brought westward this fall and merge it into Ozark. Then I'll have land offices and cheap farms for all my constituency." The scene ended with Ashley telling the trio not to worry but "that the affairs of this State will be regulated by me" and that he would do his best "to elect Mr. Roughhead at the next election." "Already are my slaves at work. Some misrepresenting the Whig Doctrine, some crying out persecution and some cheering and invigorating our brethren through the state for the coming conflict."

Pike's "The days of the Humbuggers" was about the last thing he wrote as an editor for the *Times and Advocate*. He had now decided to sell his share of the paper to Reed, who had a chance at this time to resell an interest in it to John J. Budd. Pike got $1,500 for his share, considerably less than the $2,650 he had paid for the *Advocate* in 1835. Afterwards, looking back on his experience with the *Advocate* and the *Times and Advocate*, he recalled it as an unprofitable business adventure. When he sold out to Reed in early October, he had been trying for six months to collect back subscriptions due on the *Advocate*. He tried for six months more and gave up. Sometime late that winter of 1837–38, he "one day put the books into the stove, where they served for fuel, and I had no further trouble with the accounts."[20]

XI

Bank Politics, Violence, and a Legal-Printing Mission

THE MONTH AFTER PIKE SOLD his share of the *Times and Advocate* found the legislature meeting in special session at Little Rock to deal with a host of problems. But foremost of all was the problem of the two state banks. As for the State Bank, there were the issues of Capt. Jacob Brown's questionable presidency, the animosity of north Arkansas toward the principal bank in Little Rock, the problem of getting the branches open, and the necessity of increasing interest rates on the remaining bonds if they were to be marketed. State Bank Democrats, especially those connected with the principal bank in Little Rock, were plainly sore over the fact that Pike and Reed had made a political issue of the State Bank by their eternal sniping at Captain Brown and the Ashley directory and by their constant meddling to arouse the wrath of the leaders of the branch banks against the Little Rock central bank.[1]

At the same time Pike and Reed had expressed nothing but editorial praise for the Real Estate Bank, whose founders had been working since early spring organizing it.[2] Beginning March 1, 1837, boards of superintendents, named in the charter, for forty days took subscriptions for stock at the principal towns in the state. Land and property to be mortgaged in guarantee of the stock subscribed for were in turn appraised by boards of appraisers, appointed by the governor, in each county. Finally a board of managers consisting of five men, appointed by the governor, met in Little Rock in a laborious session of eighteen weeks to make the stock awards. The board examined land titles, certificates of record stating that certification of entry had been duly filed, the property appraisals, and in general the adequacy of the mortgages offered in security of the stock. The board of managers, once it was satisfied that the land titles and the mortgages for stock subscriptions were perfected and in good order and that the state was fully protected for its $2,000,000 in bonds, awarded the stock to individuals, published a list of stockholders of record, and certified to the governor that the state bonds could be issued to the Real Estate Bank.[3]

As we have seen earlier, the Real Estate Bank was to be established for the benefit of the "great agricultural interests" of Arkansas which, when translated into economic and political reality, meant the raising of ready cash to be lent to Democratic and Whig large landowners of south and east Arkansas. Money for the loans was to be acquired by the sale of state bonds, while mortgages on real estate of its stockholders and creditors were to secure the state and the bank from any loss. A unique feature of this rather strange corporation was that not a dollar of stockholders' money was paid over to the bank, only paper promises to pay in the form of real estate mortgages registered in the several courthouses of the state. But stockholders had privileged positions as borrowers. They could borrow for twenty years, nonstockholders for only ten—in other words stockholders could borrow first and pay back last.[4]

Under the broad language of the charter, any citizen of the state might qualify as a stockholder up to the maximum amount of $30,000 on offering approved security. And being a stockholder, he might then borrow up to $15,000, or half the value of his stock. In actuality, however, only 184 lucky individuals in thirteen of the state's thirty-two counties received stock in 1837. These men were concentrated in Pulaski County, home of the principal bank, and in five Mississippi and Red River Counties. For example, twenty-eight large landowners in the premier slave-cotton county of Chicot on the Mississippi River in the southeast corner of the state got 6,286 of the 22,500 shares of stock awarded in 1837 by the board of managers.[5]

Pike subscribed to none of the stock himself, but he saw nothing wrong with the system of privilege on which the Real Estate Bank was founded. Indeed, he had urged the legislature to charter the bank, defended it against its detractors, and in time became so personally involved with the institution that his name became inseparable from it. His tie with the institution, as we have said, came directly from his intimate connection with the leading Whig stockholders. His law partner, Cummins, subscribed for and received the maximum amount allowed an individual—300 shares worth $30,000. Half of this was in Cummins's own name and half in a 300-share partnership with his wealthy father-in-law, Frederick Notrebe, who also held 150 shares in his own name, giving him a total of 300 shares. Anthony Davies, Chicot County representative and father of the Real Estate Bank charter, was chairman of the board of managers that awarded the stock. On the board with him was another Whig, William D. Ferguson, a planter and state senator from Crittenden County on the Mississippi River in northeast Arkansas who had been read out of the Democratic Party by Pew and the *Gazette* for failing to faithfully support Sevierites in the legislative session of 1836 and for being too friendly to Pike and Cummins. These two powerful Whigs were kind to themselves, each getting 300 shares. While Pike was intimate with both Davies and Ferguson, he was even closer to John Drennen, the Crawford County representative and merchant-adventurer of Van Buren, who later received 100 shares in the so-called Western Branch of the Real Estate Bank established there in 1838. Another Crawford County Whig friend of Pike's, the merchant-whiskey distiller John Dillard, also got 100 shares in the same branch.[6]

Beyond a doubt the Whigs had a powerful voice in establishing and controlling the Real Estate Bank. But they by no means had exclusive, nor even majority, control in the management. The three Democrats on the board of managers with Davies and Ferguson were Thomas T. Williamson, a planter and state senator from Lafayette County on Red River; Samuel Hutchinson Hempstead, a prominent Little Rock lawyer; and William Field, a nephew of Gov. John Pope who had risen high in the intimate circle of Little Rock Democrats led by Chester Ashley and William Woodruff. These three men—Williamson, Hempstead, and Field—exercised enough influence on the board of managers to see that the interests of Democrats were not neglected in handing out

Real Estate Bank stock. Indeed, the list of stockholders read like a Who's Who of Democrats. Senator Sevier was awarded 300 shares, Senator Fulton 70, Governor Conway 300, Judge Benjamin Johnson 300, Congressman Yell 51, William E. Woodruff 300, Chester Ashley 299, Edward Cross, the surveyor general of Arkansas and Ashley's brother-in-law 100, and James DeBaun 97. These men would have much to say about the affairs of the bank.[7]

The very fact that stock in the Real Estate Bank was given to so few and to such prominent Whigs and Democrats involved the institution in controversy. A number of men had subscribed for shares but were awarded none, and ugly rumors sprang up at once that Davies's board of managers had shown great favoritism and abused its power. Pike himself had not helped matters by his abuse of the State Bank as a Democratic machine and by his unqualified praise of the Real Estate Bank as a bank of the people. He and Reed had made it appear that the Whigs opposed the State Bank but supported the Real Estate Bank, and though this was not the case, it was a dangerous position for a bankite like Pike to be in and it made needless enemies for the Real Estate Bank.

The Real Estate Bank certainly needed friends by the fall of 1837. Not only had disappointed would-be stockholders spread dark rumors against the stock awards, but also a chorus of opposition had arisen charging that the land mortgaged by the privileged few who had received stock were grossly overvalued. When Governor Conway's called session of the legislature met at Little Rock in November, there was hell to pay. Breathing fire, angry legislators descended on the capital determined to investigate both the State Bank and the Real Estate Bank and to look into Treasurer Woodruff's conduct in collecting the surplus revenue.

The State Bank escaped with relatively few scars. Captain Brown, responding to widespread Whig and Democrat pressure, resigned as president, but not before he had submitted a report to the governor intended to soothe the ruffled feelings of north Arkansas legislators on the matter of the branch banks. He told the public that $100,000 of the $300,000 worth of bonds sold to the War Department on behalf of the Choctaw trust had arrived and had been set aside to put the Fayetteville and Batesville branches into operation. Books and bank note paper ordered for the branches had, he announced, already been shipped from New York, and as soon as these arrived "both branches will, doubtless go into operation." He also reassured the public that the principal bank had kept its own issues of bank notes well within the confines of "*its specie capital*," and expressed the belief that the legislature would approve the entire course that the principal bank had taken.[8]

The possibility that Whigs and Democrats would enter into another divisive brawl over the presidency of the State Bank was likely enough, for the friends of Pike's foster father-in-law, Terence Farrelly, were determined to elect him in order to avenge Ashley's insult to the kindly Irishman the year before. But as it turned out, Farrelly and his Arkansas County neighbors were more interested in securing a branch of the State Bank at Arkansas Post than in electing him president of the State Bank. Accordingly, they adopted the strategy of preventing an election for Brown's replacement until their bill for the Arkansas Post bank could be guaranteed. Ashley's choice for the presidency of the State Bank was said to be William Field. The nephew of former territorial Gov. John Pope, Field had resided in Little Rock several years, but, unlike his uncle who had returned to Kentucky and allegedly had become a Whig, he had become a Democrat in Ashley's intimate circle.[9]

When Field's friends tried on November 21 and again on December 8 to bring up his election prematurely, Farrelly ran against him and both times a tie vote of thirty-four votes each resulted. The vote late on Friday, December 8, had almost caught Farrelly's forces by surprise, but they had rallied in the nick of time. The next vote was postponed until Monday the eleventh, by which time a compromise had been agreed on, the terms of which were that Farrelly would withdraw in opposition to Field if Field's backers would vote to create the Arkansas Post branch and elect Farrelly president of it. As a consequence, Field was elected president of the State Bank on the eleventh without opposition, the Arkansas Post bank bill cleared the legislature on the twelfth, Governor Conway signed it into law on the fifteenth, and Farrelly, also without opposition, was duly elected president of the branch bank on the sixteenth. The nine directors elected the same day included several of Farrelly's Whig friends, including his wealthy neighbors, Frederick Notrebe and Dr. Bushrod W. Lee. This had to be a significant victory by Whig bankites because for the first time they breached the solid Democratic control of the State Bank. It could not have been without interest to Pike either, for he soon got Farrelly and the directory to name his Massachusetts boyhood friend, Luther Chase, then living in Little Rock, as cashier of the new bank.[10]

Meanwhile, the Real Estate Bank had not been so lucky. Sen. Mark Izard of St. Francis County, a staunch advocate of the State Bank but an implacable foe of the Real Estate Bank, early in November introduced a joint resolution that, in its preamble, gave a not inaccurate description of the institution. It was, he said, "unequal, unfair, and unjust, and ... calculated from its nature, to enrich the few at the expense of the many." He demanded a full report from President Wilson on the stock awards, the land appraisals, and the condition of the mortgages. Sen. Robert McCamy of Washington County, a director of the Fayetteville branch of the State Bank, also pounced on the Real Estate Bank in a partisan gesture. He introduced a resolution asking the governor to suspend emission of the state bonds until the grave charges of abuse against the institution could be investigated.[11]

Alarmed over this turn of events in the senate, the Democratic and Whig bank forces quickly united to beat back the antis. Pike's friend Senator Ferguson, who was now an active Whig, gutted Izard's resolution with a series of successful amendments and killed the McCamy resolution outright. With Ferguson calling the shots, the senate courteously requested a general routine report from the president of the Real Estate Bank by December 1.[12]

Over in the house, the Real Estate Bank forces appeared to be in complete control. Its speaker was John Wilson, who also was the bank president. But in that chamber affairs quickly took on the character of high drama. Rep. Joseph J. Anthony of Randolph County, a Democrat, nursed an inordinate grievance against the Real Estate Bank and against President Wilson, which stemmed largely from the fact that the house had killed, on November 13, Anthony's motion to have the joint banking committee inquire into the expediency of establishing a branch of the bank in his northeast part of the state, while it had approved resolutions to have the committee investigate the possibility of establishing a branch in the western part of the state and of creating a branch of the State Bank at Arkansas Post. Whatever else rankled Anthony is uncertain, but on November 25 he submitted a preamble and set of resolutions which, charging that the Real Estate Bank was undemocratic and organized not to promote the majority agricultural interests of the state, called for a vote of the people on the institution. His resolution was promptly refused by the house, but Anthony vowed on the streets to strike the Real Estate Bank again and again. Friends of his and of the bank tried to dissuade him, but he would not listen, and put himself on a collision course with Speaker Wilson.[13]

On November 30, President Wilson, alias Speaker Wilson, complied with the terms of the watered-down Izard resolution and reported on the Real Estate Bank. He boldly defended the work of the board of managers, the land appraisals, the stock awards, and the bank directors. Denying all the charges of the bank's enemies, he declared the security of the state's financial interests to be more than adequate, repeated the bank's request for an increase in the interest rate on the unmarketable state bonds from 5 to 6 percent, and expressed the urgent necessity of bringing into the state's economy the capital to be realized from the Real Estate Bank bonds. Absolutely no time should be lost, he exhorted, in putting the entire system into operation "to impel forward and support all the various interests of the state."[14]

Wilson's glowing report on the condition and expectations of the Real Estate Bank was submitted on Thursday, November 30. Four days later, on Monday, December 4, Representative Anthony clashed violently with Speaker Wilson. About one o'clock that afternoon a senate bill providing for a bounty on wolf scalps had come to the house for concurrence. Two Whig bankites, Anthony Davies and Fent Noland, amended the bill to provide that certificates for wolf scalps when accompanied by the proper magistrate's signature circulate as "good currency throughout the State, and be receivable for all dues to the State." They were perfectly serious, intending that the certificates be signed by local justices of the peace, but Representative Anthony was not when he moved to amend their amendment so as to require certificates to "be signed by some great dignitary"—the "President of the Real Estate Bank."[15]

Bristling with anger at Anthony's gratuitous motion, Speaker Wilson demanded to know if Anthony intended it as an insult. Anthony tried to pretend that he did not and, scorning Wilson's order to take his seat, insisted on his right to the floor to explain that he "merely 'thought that the certificates should be signed by a man of great dignity.'" At that pointed remark, Wilson flew from his speaker's desk down the aisle toward Anthony. Hunting knives flashed in their hands. They closed on each other, striking and thrusting, deaf to the cries of "Order! Order!" Receiving a severe cut on his left wrist that "cut his hand about half off," Wilson stepped back to recover. Anthony retreated a few steps and threw his heavy knife, the blade hitting Wilson's right arm two inches above the wrist and cutting it to the bone. As Wilson again moved forward to the attack, either a member shoved a chair between them or Anthony picked up a chair with which to protect himself. Wilson grabbed the chair with his mangled left hand and, pushing it up and out of the way, plunged his knife upward "to the hilt" into Anthony's stomach and chest. The chair fell to the floor, and the stricken Anthony gasped and pitched forward, his life's blood gushing forth upon the new scarlet carpet of the house floor.[16]

There was a moment of stunned silence as the members, gazing on the bloody scene, became conscious of what had happened. Someone laid Wilson down to prevent him from fainting, and, after a moment, Rep. James Smith, of Arkansas County, speaker pro tempore, moved to the chair. The wolf scalp bill was tabled "until next Saturday," and on motion of Fent Noland, the house adjourned.[17]

So tense was the atmosphere surrounding Anthony's death that Little Rock's newspapers for several weeks dared give but a few factual lines to the fatal fight. On December 6, two days after the bloody encounter, the house spurned Wilson's resignation as speaker and expelled him for committing "a flagrant violation" of its "dignity, rules, and regulations" and for "casting a stigma on the House of Representatives." Taken before a local justice of the peace court, Wilson, following four days of testimony, was permitted to post bail in the amount of $10,000 pending a hearing before the Pulaski County grand jury, which, curiously, did not hear the evidence in Wilson's case until the next April.[18]

With Anthony buried at state expense and Speaker Wilson replaced by Democratic representative Grandison D. Royston of Hempstead County, the friends of the Real Estate Bank watched nervously as the legislature resumed proceedings. Governor Conway had recommended an increase in the interest rates on the bank's 2,000 bonds of up to 6 percent, and the bank's forces had so far beaten down all attempts to investigate charges against the institution. The bill authorizing the interest increase easily passed both houses and was approved by Governor Conway on December 19, when the legislature recessed for six weeks. Carried over to February was a bill authorizing the stockholders of the Real Estate Bank to establish a branch in the western part of the state, which John Drennen of Crawford County wanted for Van Buren. Also carried over to February was a bill allowing the State Bank to increase the interest rates on its bonds to 6 percent.[19]

Meanwhile, a strange new threat to the Real Estate Bank loomed on the horizon. The *Gazette*, beginning in late November, had opened its columns to the enemies of the bank. Pike no longer owned an interest in the *Times and Advocate*, but Reed and Budd, depending on Whig and Real Estate Bank patronage to make the paper go, brought their sheet to the defense of the institution. There could be little doubt that Pike, whose partner Cummins was now a director of the principal bank at Little Rock, as well as Cummins and other Whig friends of the Real Estate Bank supplied Reed both the incentive and the information with which to meet this new threat to the institution.[20]

Reed's explanation of the *Gazette* assault on the Real Estate Bank was plausible enough. The Ashley-Woodruff junto, the "monied power" of the state Van Buren party, had, he said, won control of the State Bank and turned it into a machine to advance their political cause, a view that Pike had presented for more than a year. Naturally, said

Reed, the junto wished to control the Real Estate Bank and use it in the same way. They brazenly determined to take their attack to the legislature in 1837, bring the bank and its leaders into general disrepute, prevent the sale of its bonds, and, after the bank was dead, step in and "raise a new institution upon the ruins" of the old one.[21]

Reed claimed to have inside information on Woodruff's complicity in the Ashley plot against the Real Estate Bank. Old Billy Buck had been elected a director of its principal bank at Little Rock back in October, the other directors being Roswell Beebe, William W. Stevenson, James C. Anthony, James Erwin, Charles Rapley, and William Cummins, while the state-appointed directors, who were also stockholders, were Judge Benjamin Johnson and Sam C. Roane. This principal bank board, controlled by Ashley's Democratic friends, had in turn named Woodruff, Beebe, and State Director Roane to represent the principal bank on the central board, the governing body of the entire Real Estate Bank system. According to Reed, who obviously got his information from Pike and Cummins or from their Whig friends on the central board, Woodruff threatened to resign from the central board and open the columns of the *Gazette* against the Real Estate Bank unless the board elected a "certain individual" from Little Rock as president of the central board who would also serve as president of the principal bank under the charter. This person, who had to be Roswell Beebe, was not elected; Woodruff and Beebe resigned and on November 22, 1837, were replaced on the central board by Charles Rapley and William W. Stevenson. Woodruff thereupon immediately opened the columns of his paper to the enemies of the Real Estate Bank.[22]

Chester Ashley was known to be critical of the Real Estate Bank charter—because he did not write it, snapped his enemies. Yet he held stock in it, and so did Woodruff, and their main complaint was against the provision that prevented the principal bank directors from electing their own president. That officer, as we have seen, was elected by the central board, and was president of both the board and the principal bank. Friends of the charter, which was written by Anthony Davies, argues that this provision gave a healthy cohesiveness between the branches and the principal bank, even if it did, as happened in the fall of 1837, allow the central board to elect a president who was not a director of the principal bank. Yet Ashley could be forgiven if he saw the provision as a political obstacle to his desire to control the principal bank and he was right if he suspected that the sly Davies had that "intention" in mind when the Whig planter wrote the charter. If Reed's facts were straight, and they appeared to be, the main attack of the *Gazette* did not come until after Ashley and Woodruff lost their October 1837 bid to make Beebe president of the Real Estate Bank.[23]

In any case, there was no doubt that the Real Estate Bank was getting a bad press in the *Gazette* from November to February and beyond. Pew gave full coverage to the Izard-McCamy-Anthony resolutions, and, while he also reported Ferguson's and Wilson's defense of the stock awards and the bank's management, he opened the paper's columns to anonymous, bitter critics of the bank. "A Stockholder," "A Stockholder's Friend," and "Pulaski" all wrote critical letters which Pew displayed prominently on the editorial page of the *Gazette*. All three attacked the charter, the stock awards, and the management of the bank. "A Stockholder" replied to Ferguson's answer to Izard, charging him with being an enemy of the people and a friend of the privileged few. "A Stockholder's Friend" declared that the directors and officers were fully authorized "to loan the whole amount of bank capital to the 180 stockholders and their friends, at their direction," which raises the question of whose "friend" he was. And "Pulaski" on January 2, 1838, directed to the central board a list of seventeen hostile questions which were, in effect, suggestions of charter flaws, charter violations, corruption, and special privilege.[24]

If Reed interpreted these attacks as an attempt to destroy the Real Estate Bank, he seemed to be justified. He never named Ashley directly, but he made it plain that the Little Rock lawyer was "Pulaski." "The sole object of 'Pulaski,'" Reed charged on January 8, "is to injure, or prevent the sale of the State Bonds, and thereby to break down the Bank, that *he* and *his friends* may raise a new institution upon the ruins of this one." Ashley's object was to put the Little Rock Regency in control of the Real Estate Bank and, since they already controlled the State Bank, "to WIELD THE MONIED POWER OF THE BANKS" for the benefit of their party. Reed even suggested at one point that Ashley's clique perhaps had in mind having the legislature "abrogate" the charter of the bank, and issued a ringing call to the stockholders and the friends of the institution to rise to the occasion and strike down these "unhallowed attempts . . . upon the Real Estate Bank." And he went so far as to say that Representative Anthony, becoming an "innocent disciple" of "Pulaski's" war on the bank had lost his life as "a martyr of the cause," which brought a sharp rebuke from Pew and an equally sharp rebuttal from Reed that did both a disservice.[25]

As it turned out, the Real Estate Bank weathered this puzzling Ashley-Woodruff attack in good shape. When the legislature reassembled in February 1838, John Drennen and the western bankites secured easy passage and approval of a bill establishing a western branch of the Real Estate Bank at Van Buren, with an additional half million in state bonds appropriated for raising its capital and with the stock, as for the original branches, to be subscribed in real estate mortgages. Also at the February session, the State Bank forces, with the help of the Real Estate Bank's friends, secured its bill for increasing the interest rate to 6 percent on its bonds; and the same alliance beat back a Royston-sponsored bill establishing a branch of the State Bank at Washington, in Hempstead County.[26]

From all appearances it would seem that Terence Farrelly and his backers had secured the Arkansas Post branch of the State Bank by agreeing to support the Van Buren branch of the Real Estate Bank, but by helping to kill any additional branches of the State Bank. Involved in this, of course, was the compromise by which Field became president of the State Bank and Farrelly president of the branch at the Post. Yet the most curious fact of all that came out of this session was that the Whigs had breached the solid Democratic control of the State Bank and secured a southeast-based branch of it, while allowing a small band of western Whigs to set up a branch of the Real Estate Bank at Van Buren. As for Ashley, he still had control of the principal bank of the State Bank and he and Cummins, with Cummins backed by Pike, were about to launch their historic battle for control of the principal bank of the Real Estate Bank.

Meanwhile, the central board of the Real Estate Bank had met in Little Rock on

February 5, 1838, and elected Anthony Davies to replace John Wilson, who had resigned as president in January. Seeking a quick sale of the bonds and hoping to silence the *Gazette*'s attack on the bank, President Davies appointed Thomas T. Williamson, president of the Washington branch, and Senator Sevier to serve with him as the commissioners to sell the bonds. This strategy worked wonders. Sevier now had both feet in the camp of the Arkansas bankites, even though he had disappointed Pike and Reed and the other Whigs by spurning a national bank in the fall of 1837 and endorsing President Van Buren's Independent Treasury. The senator, in Washington City, had become truly alarmed by the reckless course of the *Gazette* and its correspondents in regard to the Real Estate Bank. Notified of his appointment as bond commissioner, Sevier in March accepted with alacrity, agreeing with President Davies that it was "important to shut the mouth of our anti-bank adversaries and to give character and stability to our banks." The senator also forecast a ready market for the Real Estate Bank bonds, and frankly admitted to Davies his "*great anxiety to get our banks in operation*" because he personally would "*want all the facilities that it can afford me*"—which would be a loan of $15,000 since Sevier held the maximum stock of $30,000. Sevier was dead serious, for he ultimately borrowed $14,000 of the bank.[27]

Pike's part in the affairs of the Real Estate Bank that winter came through his partnership with Cummins, who was a maximum stockholder, a director of the principal bank, and also attorney for the principal bank. Pike himself had laid down the Whig pattern of defense of the bank in his *Advocate* and later in the *Times and Advocate*, and he doubtlessly fed, if he did not write, information for Reed's use in fighting the *Gazette*'s attacks on the bank that winter. It must have delighted his soul when, with Pew assaulting the Real Estate Bank, Davies appointed Sevier one of its bond commissioners. After that Pew did not last long as editor. Just why he left the *Gazette* has never been explained, but it could have been Sevier's dissatisfaction with his role in the fight against the bank. Woodruff remained noticeably quiet about the reasons for Pew's departure but, with Billy Buck sitting again in the editorial chair by mid-May, 1838, and with Sevier serving as bond broker, the Real Estate Bank began at once getting favorable treatment in the *Gazette*.[28] Reed explained in June 1838 the remarkable transformation of the paper, implying that Pew had been made a scapegoat of Ashley's and Woodruff's lost war against the bank and that he had been "re-shipped to Washington" for the purpose of getting a federal office as a reward "for his services in insulting the people of this state" and for the purpose of giving Woodruff "a chance, if possible, to resuscitate" the paper's "broken down energies" by going over to the side that "pays best."[29]

Meanwhile, Pike had the personal satisfaction of watching as his Whig friend Absalom Fowler, who had replaced the deceased Pulaski County representative, Dr. John H. Cocke, went after Woodruff for his conduct as state treasurer. Fowler himself had been much in the state news the past year since his defeat in the governor's race in 1836. As captain of a Pulaski County company of volunteer mounted gunmen, he had in September 1836 been elected lieutenant colonel of a battalion of five companies of Arkansas Volunteers called up for six months duty in the Indian country on Red River, where it was feared the Mexicans in Texas were attempting to arouse an Indian war. A month later at Fort Towson on the Red River, with two additional Arkansas companies in his ranks and with James Conway in the governor's office in place of Fulton, Fowler refused an order instigated by Conway to hold a regimental election for colonel and major and to organize the seven companies as a regiment. Fowler saw this for what it was, a plot by his Democratic enemies in Little Rock to supplant him as commander and, being a ready battler and a skillful lawyer, he decided to make a fight of it. Naturally, he found two willing supporters in Pike and Reed, who had not yet consolidated their papers.[30]

Though Fowler refused either to notice Conway's order or to call a regimental election, his politically minded company commanders held one anyway and sent an officer galloping back to Little Rock with the happy results. These showed that Capt. Laban C. Howell of Pope County and John Kavanaugh of Randolph County, both Democrats, had been elected colonel and major respectively, and, moreover, that a Sevier County Democrat, Capt. Charles Pettigrew, had been elected lieutenant colonel in place of Fowler, who allegedly had stood for the colonelcy against Howell. Though Fowler protested the election in writing and, at last, in person, declaring that he had not authorized it and denying that he had been a candidate for colonel, Governor Conway, while acknowledging the truth of Fowler's protests, held it to be a valid election and issued commissions to Howell and Kavanaugh but not to Pettigrew, leaving Fowler as lieutenant colonel.[31]

Thereafter, the Arkansas public was treated to ten or twelve months of absorbing reading, as Fowler and Conway and their partisans took to the newspapers to wage the battle of what was variously called "the Fowler affair," the case of the "*quondam* Lieutenant Colonel of the Mounted Volunteers*,*" or "The Conway-Arbuckle conspiracy." Called out to quell an Indian war or possibly a Mexican invasion of the southwest border, the Arkansas troops never saw a "hostile" Indian or Mexican, but they had a lively time observing the ludicrous conduct of militia officers engaged in a classic conflict over command.[32]

Losing his appeal to Conway in Little Rock, Fowler boned up on military law and concluded that the governor's authority over the militia did not extend to volunteers once they were mustered into federal service and were beyond the state's borders. Accordingly, he appealed his case to Brigadier General Arbuckle, commander of the Army of the Southwest Frontier at Fort Towson and took command of his battalion before Howell's commission as colonel arrived. When Howell, whose commission meanwhile had reached him, objected to the lieutenant colonel's authority and attempted to take command, Fowler placed him under close arrest for "trying *to incite a mutiny.*" But General Arbuckle refused to assume responsibility for deciding on the legality of the regimental election and, taking the safest course available, released Howell and put him in command until, as was hoped, Arbuckle's own superior should decide the case or the troublesome Arkansas volunteers could be discharged.

This episode took place in November-December. Apparently sick of the entire controversy, Arbuckle in December transferred the Arkansas volunteers northward to Fort Gibson. With Howell in command and Fowler now in arrest, the regiment got to Fort Gibson in late December. Released from arrest by General Arbuckle, Fowler in January

1837 took his case before a court of inquiry at that post. This body, composed of three regular army officers, reported an opinion so vague as to allow both sides to cite it as evidence of victory.

Back in Little Rock by February, his military duty over, Fowler published in Pike's *Advocate* and Reed's *Times* a lengthy account of his mistreatment at the hands of Conway, Howell, Arbuckle, and "a few reckless schemers at Little Rock." He boasted of his "acquittal," quoting the court's opinion as proof of it and grossly insulted Conway and Arbuckle. Conway had usurped "authority not given by the laws" and had found in Arbuckle a "pliant subject" and "co-worker" in his misdeeds. Conway's conduct, motivated by politics, could be understood, said Fowler, but for the general there was no "*sort* of apology" to be offered. Arbuckle was, Fowler had concluded, "unfit to command," and he charged the old soldier with, among other things, "Imbecility and Incapacity" as well as "Subserviency to a political party, at Little Rock."

Not to be outdone by the "*quondam* Lieutenant Colonel of the Mounted Volunteers," Governor Conway sent a copy of Fowler's "slanderous production" to General Arbuckle, requesting a statement from him on "the conduct" of Fowler and a copy of the records pertaining to the court of inquiry. Arbuckle's brisk letter, together with the desired documents, arrived in due time, and Conway published them in the *Gazette* in order, as he said, that the public might "judge how far the *late* Lt. Col. may pride himself on his acquittal." Conway's own conclusion was, of course, that he had been sustained by General Arbuckle and by the court.

Neither Fowler nor Conway had been fully sustained by the court, which exonerated Fowler for arresting Howell but declared that he erred in not preventing the "informal" election of regimental officers. Fowler admitted that he erred in not prohibiting the election, offering the rather lame excuse that he believed an appeal to Conway would set it aside since it took ten companies to form a regiment and only seven were on hand. Once Conway turned down his appeal, Fowler could depend only on General Arbuckle, who really refused to decide the question of the disputed election; and seemingly no appeal to Gen. Edmund Pendleton Gaines, the department commander, was ever made. Fowler was not hurt politically in Pulaski County by the squabble because his own company had been made up exclusively of Whigs, but he came home with a new nickname among Democrats—"the *Knight of the Wooden Horse*," an allusion to the fact that he, while battalion commander, had a wooden horse erected in the horseless Arkansas camp with which to teach his men the basics of mounting and dismounting.

Elected by Pulaski Whigs to fill the house vacancy created by Dr. Cocke's death, Fowler won laurels on the legislative battlefield that winter of 1837–38 denied him on the Southwest border.[33] First of all, he pounced on Billy Woodruff's conduct as state treasurer, leading an investigation which revealed that Woodruff had illegally retained $2,100.43 as a commission on state land redemptions and that he was not entitled to the full $595 withheld by him for his travel expenses in collecting the distribution of the surplus revenue. In all this, Fowler was aided by Reed's *Times and Advocate* which kept a steady fire under Woodruff's feet for his failure to collect the surplus in specie and for granting a dispensation of time to the Natchez "pets."[34]

The happy result for the Whigs was that Woodruff was ordered by the legislature to return $294.75 of the $595 charged for travel and the entire $2,100.43 retained on the sales of state lands. When Woodruff refused to pay back the money promptly, pending an appeal to the courts, Fowler next sponsored a bill that, when finally passed, required Old Buck to pay 25 percent interest per year on the $2,395.18 retained by him. Fowler's attempt to bring impeachment proceedings against Woodruff for "malversation and misconduct in office" failed, but the treasurer's "default" in not restoring the money at once was a clear victory for the Whigs over a hated Democrat, and marked the beginning of a serious split in the Democratic ranks. Woodruff had naturally expected his fellow Democrats to allow his commission on the sale of state lands as well as his travel expenses; when they voted not to sustain him, he never forgave them, a breach that would in the long run benefit the Whigs.[35]

Fowler's second attack on Woodruff and the Democrats resulted from Fowler's and Fent Noland's legislative assault on William McKnight Ball and Sam C. Roane for their alleged sloppy work in codifying the Arkansas law. This fight indirectly involved Pike. As an editor and a concerned lawyer, Pike had long urged the codification of Arkansas's statutes and had been pleased when the legislature of 1836 provided for the work and when Governor Conway assigned the two respected lawyers, Ball and Roane, to the task. Pike had editorially applied gentle pressure on them to have the job finished in time for the special session of 1837. But his Whig friends, Fowler and Noland, attacked the content of the manuscript code presented to the special session, angrily demanded its rejection, and unsuccessfully tried to block an appropriation compensating Ball and Roane for their labor and to prevent Treasurer Woodruff from paying them.[36]

Complicating legislative action on the Ball and Roane code was a quarrel over whether Woodruff and Pew of the *Gazette* or Reed and Budd of the *Times and Advocate* should print the book. Neither set of printers was properly equipped for such an undertaking, and the legislature, tired of the hassling, decided to put the entire problem of the code in Pike's hands.[37]

Pike obviously dictated the terms of his assignment. He was "to index, arrange, annotate, and superintend the printing" of the Ball and Roane code. He was also authorized to have the work executed at any place he thought proper, "under the direction of the governor." When Pike, with Governor Conway's blessing, chose to have the work done in Boston, his friend Reed expressed keen disappointment. "Albert Pike, Esq.," he coldly announced in his paper, "was elected by the Legislature, Agent to *correct* and superintend the printing of the REVISED CODE—*the printing of which is to be done at the city of Boston!!*" Pike's compensation for his services and travel as "superintendent" of the printing of the revised statutes was to be $1,500.[38] At the same session, Pike was appointed reporter of the decisions of the Supreme Court of Arkansas, which paid him $500 a year and gave him the discretion of awarding the printing for which $2,555 was appropriated.[39]

XII

A Cleaver Made Expressly to Seek Satisfaction of Pike and Reed

PIKE LOOKED FORWARD to the trip to Boston and to the opportunity it afforded him for a brief visit with his mother at Newburyport, but over three months of hard work lay ahead before he could depart. Occupied not only with preparing the revised statutes for the Boston printer, he was also giving time to Whig preparations for the coming presidential campaign of 1840 and readying himself for two important murder cases in which he had been retained.

February found him at Little Rock active in his party's councils. Many Whig leaders were present in the capital city attending the legislature and looking after other matters, especially Real Estate Bank business, when on February 14 there took place a "Great Whig Meeting," what editor John Reed described as "the largest and most respectable assembly of citizens and strangers that had ever taken place in the city."[1] Colonel Terence Farrelly presided, William Cummins, who was tuning up to run for Congress in October, explained the necessity of preparing the state Whig Party for the coming presidential election of 1840, a set of anti–Van Buren resolutions was read, and Pike was named chairman of "a committee of ten" appointed by Farrelly "to draft an address to the People of Arkansas, explanatory of our principles, to accompany and be published with these resolutions."[2]

Pike reported his committee's address to an adjourned meeting of the Whig leaders a week later, on February 21, "in an able and eloquent manner." Two thousand copies, with the party resolutions appended, were ordered printed in pamphlet form for use by the state party during the next two years.[3]

The address which Pike undoubtedly wrote, placed the blame for the economic distress of the times directly on the Van Buren administration. It damned the president's stubborn adherence to the Specie Circular, excoriated his decision to abandon the deposit banks, fumed at his open threat to Congress to veto any national bank charter, and vowed eternal Whig opposition to his proposed Sub-Treasury System. It went on to recount how conservative Democrats in Van Buren's own New York had broken with him over his abandonment of the state deposit banks and his proposed "divorce" of the government from all banks, how the New York conservatives "falling back upon the true Whig principles, had joined with Whigs to deal the president embarrassing political defeat, how similar Conservative-Whig alliances in Massachusetts, Kentucky, and Tennessee had carried additional "defeat and dismay" into his ranks, and finally how the "blaze of Whig and Conservative victory" promised to light up "the whole political heaven" of the country. Pike's address called on Arkansas's "brother Whigs and Conservatives" to unite, to take their anti–Van Buren message to the people, and to light up the state's own fair sky with the same "fires of triumph" and "rejoicing" that were "breaking out on every hilltop and in every valley heretofore darkened by Van Burenism."[4]

Though Reed was already flying the name of Henry Clay for president at the masthead of his paper, Arkansas's Whig leaders in their February resolutions avoided endorsing any candidate. Instead, they merely declared their willingness "to sustain for the Presidency any true Whig who may be fixed upon by the great body of our brethren in the Union; and for Congress, any one recommended by our brethren throughout the state."[5] They did, however, pledge Arkansas's Whig voters in the presidential election of 1840

> to no other man than he who will support principles, give us a currency uniform and equal all over the Union, arrest the rapid and insolent march of Executive power, retrench the enormous expenditures of Government, diminish the patronage of the Executive, cleanse out the Augean stable at Washington of its corruptions, provide that members of Congress shall no longer be bribed with office, and, in a word, bring back the Government to the principles on which it was originally administered.[6]

The two murder cases that demanded Pike's attention that spring of 1838 were those of David S. Douglass for killing Dr. William C. Howell and of John Wilson for killing Representative Anthony. David Douglass was Senator Fulton's nephew and scion of a prominent family of Gallatin, Tennessee. Dr. William Howell and Dr. Thomas Howell, brothers, practiced medicine at Little Rock and Hot Springs and conducted a wholesale and retail drug business in Little Rock. Early in 1838, Dr. William Howell had trouble with David Fulton and Dr. John T. Fulton, the father and brother respectively of Senator Fulton, who was in Washington attending Congress. Their conflict concerned a road the elder Fulton was opening across Dr. Howell's farm at the south edge of Little Rock and resulted in Howell whipping the old man with a switch. When Dr. John Fulton and his nephew, David Douglass, orally and publicly insulted the unoffending Dr. Thomas Howell over the matter, Dr. William Howell on the morning of March 16, 1838, purchased a new double-barrel shotgun at a downtown store, loaded it with buckshot, and set out to locate Dr. Fulton.[7]

On the street near the Howell drugstore, some of Dr. Howell's friends, seeing his new shotgun, asked if he were going "birding." The doctor replied, yes, that he was looking for "a very foul bird," Dr. John Fulton. About this time, Douglass, armed also with a loaded double-barrel shotgun, confronted him saying: "Dr. Howell, if you abuse my uncle I will kill you." Dr. Howell turned to James B. Keatts and William C. Pope, who were standing within earshot of Douglass's remark, and stated, "Gentlemen, I want you both to take notice that he says if I abuse his uncle he will kill me." While saying this, Dr. Howell cocked the hammer of one of the barrels of his weapon, threw the piece into the hollow of his left arm, and turned to face Douglass, saying as he turned, "Dr. Fulton is a contemptible puppy."

Accounts disagree as to what happened next. A newspaper reported at the time that both men fired at about the same time, that both shots missed, that the youngster instantly discharged his second barrel into Dr. Howell's right groin, and that the doctor died that afternoon from his wound. A later account by William Pope, written when he was an old man with faulty memory, said Douglass was untouched by the doctor's first shot but that both of Douglass's shots took effect, the first in Dr. Howell's right hip and the second blowing the lower part of his abdomen away, from which he died at four o'clock that afternoon. Pope recalled, also, that Dr. Howell's only shot went wide, striking and mortally wounding a young slave girl belonging to William Woodruff. This latter part of Pope's version agreed with the contemporary news report.

Douglass was promptly arrested, brought before "an examining magistrate," and bound over to the county sheriff to await trial for murder in April. The Fultons and Douglasses hired for the youngster one of the most impressive defense counsels ever assembled in Arkansas. It included Col. Washington Barrow, a renowned criminal lawyer of Nashville, Tennessee, a "Judge Anderson of Mississippi," and four of Little Rock's best lawyers—Ashley, Pike, John W. Cocke, and John M. Steuart. John Clendenin, the local prosecutor, engaged William Cummins and Absalom Fowler to assist him against this mighty array of legal talent. The trial, of which we have only the barest details, lasted ten days, April 26 to May 3, and ended with the jury deadlocking in a vote of five for murder and seven for manslaughter. Continued to the next term of the Pulaski County Circuit Court, the defense got the case removed to the circuit court in Phillips County, where it was continued from term to term until November 1839. Another hung jury resulted, and the local prosecutor, growing tired of the troublesome case, dropped any further prosecution of the youngster under a declaration of nolle prosequi. Douglass returned to his father's home at Gallatin, but afterwards, in 1849, went to California, where he became a U.S. marshal and an important figure in that state.

Meanwhile, Pike and three other prominent Arkansas lawyers had been engaged by Clendenin to help prosecute John Wilson, who had been indicted in April 1838 for murdering Representative Anthony. These three lawyers were William C. Scott and John M. Taylor of Little Rock and Colonel Bennett H. Martin of Pope County. Defending Wilson were a battery of Arkansas's ablest criminal lawyers—Chester Ashley, Absalom Fowler, John W. Cocke, John M. Steuart, and Robertson C. Childress. The defense, deciding that the Little Rock community was prejudiced against Wilson, moved for a change of venue, and though the prosecution opposed the motion, Judge Charles Caldwell quickly granted it, ordering the case to be taken to the May term of the circuit court in neighboring Saline County over which he also presided.[8]

Pike, Clendenin, and the other prosecution and defense lawyers were in Benton, the seat of Saline County, the first week of May for Wilson's trial. The prosecution attorneys hoped to convict Wilson on the plea that Anthony, while performing his duties as a representative of the people, had been assassinated by Wilson. The selection of the jury on May 7 went against them, as was always the case in regard to counsel for the state, for Arkansas law limited the state to but six challenges while permitting the defense up to twenty challenges.[9] Hence, the prosecution soon exhausted their permissible challenges, while Wilson's attorneys went on to challenge sixteen prospective jurors before the jury was completed. Although the prosecution produced eyewitnesses who testified that Wilson initiated the fight with Anthony on that fateful day back in December, and that Anthony was faced with the choice of running or defending himself, they were unable to sway the jury that Anthony had not provoked Wilson. Indeed, the defense produced eyewitnesses, friends of Wilson, who testified that Anthony not only defied parliamentary procedure and rules of good order by insulting Speaker Wilson, but also had shown equally as much aggressiveness as Wilson on the occasion of their fight. The jury took only two or three hours, on May 11, to return a verdict of "*excusable homicide.*"[10]

The testimony at the Wilson trial, printed in the *Gazette* on May 23 and reprinted from that paper in the *Times and Advocate* of May 28, resulted in several weeks of bitter correspondence in the *Gazette* concerning the trial. The testimony and correspondence revealed the interesting fact that Representative Anthony had had his long knife, "his cleaver, weighing one pound and three ounces, . . . made expressly to seek satisfaction of Pike and Reed, for attacks made by them upon him, on some former occasion, in their paper, the *Times and Advocate.*" The testimony also revealed that Wilson's trial reverted at times into a controversy over the Real Estate Bank, leading one to speculate whether it was not Pike and Ashley who were responsible for this trend in the proceedings. Made public for the first time, too, was the fact that Wilson was carrying a loaded pistol for the purpose of seeking either an apology or "satisfaction" from Sen. Robert McCamy of Washington County.[11]

The clash over the Real Estate Bank came when the house clerk, Samuel H. Hempstead, a state witness, testified that Anthony had offered a resolution in the house reflecting on "the character" of the Real Estate Bank and conveying "a censure upon Wilson, the president." An unnamed defense lawyer promptly interceded to ask Hempstead whether Anthony had not "offered to prove by parol testimony the substance of said resolution," to which an unidentified prosecution attorney quickly objected "on the grounds of its irrelevancy and illegality." But Judge Caldwell, after hearing argument, overruled the objection, although Hempstead's answer to the defense question, as reported in the *Gazette*, stated only that Hempstead went on to say that the resolution reflected on both the Real Estate Bank and President Wilson and adding nothing whatever about Anthony's offer to prove the truth of it. Judge Caldwell also permitted Hempstead to testify that Speaker Wilson had told him on Saturday morning, December 2, that Sen. Robert McCamy had stated on the senate floor that President Wilson's bank report of November 30 "contained falsehoods." Wilson had then told Hempstead that that "was what no man could say of him," and he went with Hempstead to Hempstead's office where he "got powder and ball to load his pistol."[12]

The plain fact was that Wilson was angry enough to fight Senator McCamy. Anthony Davies, a state witness and the man who had succeeded Wilson as president of the Real Estate Bank, corroborated Hempstead's evidence on this point. Davies was the first person to tell Wilson of McCamy's remark in the senate against Wilson's bank report. "Wilson seemed a good deal angry" at this news, and vowed, said Davies, to make McCamy "retract as publicly as he had done the insult" or that he "would have satisfaction." On the other hand, Davies stated that he saw Anthony and Wilson together on the street on Monday shortly before the fatal session and heard Anthony say to the speaker that "he was going to give the Real Estate Bank another touch." Wilson had replied good-humoredly, "only show us your hand and we will meet you." Davies expressed surprise that the fight between them developed later that afternoon, though he did testify that Wilson's manner that afternoon at the speaker's desk in ordering Anthony to take his seat "was preemptory and positive."[13]

Sen. William D. Ferguson's testimony for the defense rounded out the evidence on the involvement of the Real Estate Bank. He said that McCamy's harsh words in the senate on Saturday, December 2, against Wilson's bank report caused "some excitement." Knowing that Anthony was "hostile" toward the bank, and fearing trouble between Anthony and Wilson over the issue, he took Anthony "out on Saturday evening, and talked to him." Anthony refused to stop his attacks on the bank, and, said Ferguson, "he almost angrily observed that he would not cease, that the bank should fall, or he would, and if he did, others would fall with him, that he was armed and prepared to meet the consequences." Ferguson stated that he told Anthony "that threats would not avail against the bank, and we parted." But Ferguson, like Representative Davies, testified that on Monday morning before their fight the two antagonists had "seemed jocular" in their remarks to each other about Anthony's statement that "he was going to come out on the bank again." Ferguson did not actually witness the fight, but it was he who, entering the house chamber just as it ended, laid his friend Wilson down to keep him from fainting.[14]

Long before interest in Wilson's acquittal dropped from the columns of the *Gazette* and from public view, Pike had departed for Boston. He arrived by July 12, when he signed a contract with Weeks, Jordan and Company, Publishers, for printing and binding the *Revised Statutes of the State of Arkansas*. He visited his mother in Newburyport at this time, but it could not have been for long because he put in seven or eight weeks of arduous work in Boston reading and correcting proofs, and compiling a lengthy index. In September he left for Arkansas, reaching Little Rock on Friday, September 28. He brought with him an unbound copy of the printed code and reported that he expected a thousand bound copies by early November.[15]

At Little Rock Pike learned the details of his partner's race for Congress, the election for which was to take place in three days, on Monday, October 1. Yell had not sought reelection since he planned to run for governor in 1840, and the Little Rock Regency, headed by Ashley and Woodruff, had put Edward Cross forward as a successor. A former judge of the territorial superior court, Cross was the federal surveyor general of Arkansas, was married to the sister of Ashley's wife, and, reputedly, was deeply involved with Ashley in land speculation. Cummins entered as a Whig, and his chances appeared good when Judge Lewis B. Tully of Carroll County, a Democrat who had been elected judge of the third circuit in 1836, insisted that he was in the race long before Cross and would withdraw for "no man."[16]

In July John Reed, Pike learned, had sold his interest in the *Times and Advocate* to Eli Colby and Michael J. Steck. A newcomer to Little Rock, Colby became editor. He was a stalwart Whig and Clay partisan but had quickly demonstrated too much independence to please Cummins. He backed Cummins against Cross, to be sure, but he did it in his own way, picking and choosing what should and should not be admitted to his columns. Cummins resented Colby's attitude, feeling that the new editor was only lukewarm toward the Whig cause and completely indifferent to the old animosities which governed Whig-Democratic partisanship in Little Rock and the state.[17]

In time the Cummins-Colby breach would widen into an open break, but in the summer of 1838 Colby fell in with the Whig strategy of keeping Tully in the race, splitting the Democratic vote and, it was hoped, sending Cummins to Congress. Ashley and Woodruff were not about to allow that to happen. In late August, Judge Tully withdrew from the race. Some said he was "bought off," either with money or with promises of being sent to Congress from the northern district when Arkansas should have two congressional districts, an eventuality expected after the 1840 census but which was not realized until after 1850.[18]

Thus by the time Pike returned home from his New England journey, Cummins's chances of election, once so pregnant with hope, had totally miscarried. Not only that, but the Whig paper in Little Rock had gotten into the hands of an outsider who showed abominable ignorance of Arkansas politics and alarming indifference to Cummins and his close friends.

On election day, October 1, 1838, Cross swept the state on an anti–national bank, pro–Independent Treasury platform, which also endorsed gold and silver money and state bank notes convertible into specie; opposed any future accumulation of a Treasury surplus; promised to work for improving the navigable streams of the state, opening roads, graduating the price of public lands, passing a liberal preemption law, defending Arkansas's western frontier, and adjusting the boundary between the United States and Texas, and supported Martin Van Buren for the presidency in 1840 in the event that he and Henry Clay were the candidates. Cummins carried only Pulaski and the usual handful of Whig river counties, running on a platform favoring "a well regulated and governed National, or Bank of the United States, with branches in each State"; opposing Van Buren's "Sub-Treasury bill"; promising to labor for "fortification and protection of our frontier," for graduation of the price of public lands, and for preemption rights; and declining to endorse any candidate for the presidency in 1840 while pledging himself to abide by "the will and instructions of the people of Arkansas" in case "the election of a president should devolve on the House of Representatives."[19]

Pulaski voters sent two Whigs, Absalom Fowler and Dr. Lorenzo Gibson, to the house, but they helped send a Democrat, Richard Byrd, to the senate in place of the Whig incumbent, John McLain. Byrd was a "union" candidate of sorts, that is, his name appeared on both the Democratic and Whig tickets. This was a Democratic "trap" that caught the naive Colby completely off guard. On election day, Colby realizing what had happened, issued an urgent warning for Whigs to vote the straight Whig ticket and cautioning them against the "Independent Ticket," which, he said, was "designed" to split the Whig vote. Colby expressed wide-eyed amazement at seeing William Field, the president of the State Bank at Little Rock, descend "from his high, responsible, and influential station" so far "as to be seen leading voters by the arms to the polls, and urging them to vote the Democratic ticket; and also to stand at the polls shouting for the democrats, and calling upon them to come forward and vote." Colby lamely explained Byrd's victory as a Whig success, but the Whig friends of McLain remained unimpressed—especially with Woodruff bragging that Byrd's election was a Democratic triumph and forecasting a Democratic sweep of Pulaski County in 1840.[20]

For the moment, Pike did not have much time to think about the problem of the new Whig editor or the election. He had returned from Boston thinking the shipment of bound *Revised Statutes* would follow in a month. It did not, and he had no completed copies on hand when the legislature assembled the first week of November. His report to the general assembly, dated November 10, described the extraordinary labor he had expended on the code. He had, he admitted, made the broadest possible use of the authority given him to "correct errors" in the work. Ball and Roane, he obviously had discovered back in the spring, had done a bad job of codification. They had not arranged the laws by chapters and had not bothered to delete the unnecessary enacting clauses of the various statutes. Moreover, their manuscript, as Pike originally found it, was filled with "bad grammar," "artificial construction of sentences," and "manifest mistakes in the use of words."[21]

Laboriously editing the bulky, unorganized Ball-Roane manuscript, Pike performed a Herculean task. He condensed it by striking out the enacting clauses. He gave it order by arranging the laws into chapters, by completely remodeling the section on militia law, and by correcting egregious errors in the law on insane persons and their estates. And he did his best to cast the code in a consistent and readable style. To accomplish this, he confessed, "he found it necessary to strike out or add words, to re-mould the sentences, and sometimes write them over entire." This he always did "in order to avoid ambiguity, and to express clearly the intention of the Legislature." Finally, he prepared an exhaustive index of 186 pages and personally wrote out two full copies of it.[22]

Having put in so much time on the manuscript, index, "headnotes," and the printer's proofs, Pike naturally took a paternalistic interest in the *Revised Statutes*. He asked that the legislature pass a resolution "putting the book in force, *as printed*, as the law of the land, upon the proclamation of the Governor." This was necessary, he explained, because "the work as printed will vary considerably from the enrolled copies in the office of the Secretary of State." He might well have said, but did not, that Ball and Roane had not codified the law but had compiled it from other state codes and from the enrolled copies of Arkansas statutes, enacting clauses and all. Whatever utility or value the new code would have was due to him more than to Ball and Roane.[23]

If Pike expected quick approval of the code, he was in for a surprise. The joint committee on the judiciary, with Fowler and Noland present to settle old scores, scrutinized it for three weeks. The committee's majority report, written by friends of Ball and Roane, recommended approval of the code as printed, but Fowler and Noland, writing for the minority, proposed its rejection. Pike's two Whig friends were careful to praise his "arrangement" and "index" of the statutes as being "excellent and highly worthy of approval." It was Ball's and Roane's "matter" that they objected to. In his best "Pete Whetstone" style, Noland insulted both the committee majority and the codifiers:

there seems to be one thing certain, that if it be found to be the invaluable system of jurisprudence, contended for by some, Arkansas will have carried away the palm from all law-givers, ancient or modern; and two of her sons, by a few months' labor, or recreation, will have nullified and thrown into the back ground the fame of Solon and Lycurgus, as well as that of our own Wythe, Jefferson, and Livingston.[24]

Three weeks of angry debate and parliamentary maneuvering followed. Fowler and Noland cogently argued their case against the code and won many of the legislators to their side, but the majority of the Democrats remained unconvinced that the two Whigs were engaged in any more than a political assault on Ball and Roane. At last the legislature approved the code "as printed and reported" by Pike to go into effect when the governor should issue a proclamation for that purpose. The printed copies of the code began to arrive in late December and were distributed to the counties over the next three of four months. Though the delay in receiving the entire number printed proved something of an embarrassment to Pike, they all had arrived by late March 1839, when Governor Conway proclaimed the new code of laws to be the "law of the land."[25]

XIII

There Walks, Majestic, the *Immaculate* Pike

IN JANUARY 1839 Pike found himself caught up in a new clash between Cummins and Ashley over control of the principal bank of the Real Estate Bank at Little Rock. Having sold $1.5 million of its bonds, the central board at its Little Rock meeting back in November laid final plans for putting the principal bank into operation, which was done a month later, on December 10.[1] During its November 1838 session, the central board also adopted an ordinance equalizing the stock of the entire Real Estate Bank between the principal bank and the branch banks in such a way that either all or portions of the stock of several large Whig stockholders were transferred from the branches to the principal bank.[2]

At the same meeting, the central board ordained that the next election for directors of each of the four banks should be held on the first Monday in January 1839 and annually thereafter on the same day. The election ordinance provided, also, that each of the four directories should be elected by local stockholders voting in the district served by their respective bank, a provision based on an erroneous interpretation of the Real Estate Bank charter as was later revealed. If a partisan Democratic view was correct, the November stock transfers were made to give Whigs control of the Little Rock bank. Chester Ashley himself had no doubt that President Davies and William Cummins hatched the scheme to enable them to wrest control of that bank from him and his Democratic friends.[3]

What followed was the hottest fight yet between Cummins and Ashley over control of the principal bank. The first directory of the bank, elected in 1837, consisted of Cummins, Roswell Beebe, William W. Stevenson, James C. Anthony, James Erwin, Charles Rapley, William E. Woodruff, and two state-appointed directors, Judge Benjamin Johnson and Sam C. Roane. Richard C. Byrd, a wealthy Little Rock commission agent and slave trader, had replaced Woodruff, who resigned in the autumn of 1837 but who went back on the directory in November 1838 as a state director in place of Roane. We have Cummins's word for it that Byrd, Rapley, Stevenson, Anthony, and President Davies were the "gentlemen associated with him in the old directory," by which he obviously meant that they were the directors friendly toward his cause in the fall of 1838 and afterwards. However, on election day, January 3, 1839, President Davies was not present in Little Rock and not all of Cummins's alleged friends on the principal bank directory stood with him. The result was, as Pike later recounted, a crushing defeat of Cummins by Ashley.[4]

Ashley's triumph over the hapless Cummins began early in the morning of January 3, when the principal bank directory met to prepare for holding the annual election of directors. According to the rules laid down by ordinance of the central board of the Real Estate Bank, the directory of the principal bank, and that of each of the branches, was to appoint three commissioners from among the stockholders to conduct the balloting and make the return to their respective bank president, who thereupon should promptly issue certificates of election to the winners. Taking advantage of Davies's absence, Ashley's friends on the morning of January 3, 1839, promptly organized the old directory of the principal bank by naming Roswell Beebe president pro tempore. Beebe then packed the election commission with a majority of Ashley men who quite naturally refused to receive the votes of the transferred Whig stockholders, thus blocking the election of Cummins and some of his friends while assuring victory for Ashley and a majority of his friends. Consequently, on the basis of the returns handed him that day at the close of the balloting, President Beebe issued certificates of election to himself, Ashley, Stevenson, Byrd, James L. Dawson, James DeBaun, and Elijah H. More. The new board, with State Directors William Woodruff and Judge Benjamin Johnson, two stalwart Ashleyites, sitting in, immediately met and organized. It continued Beebe as president pro tempore and took control of the bank from the former directory.[5]

When Cummins promptly hailed Ashley and the new directors before the state supreme court in the famous quo warranto case of 1839, Pike, who never owned any Real Estate Bank stock, found himself deeply involved in his partner's continued war with Ashley. Up to January 3, 1839, Cummins had been not only a director of the principal bank but also its attorney, a position which now had been awarded to Ashley. It galled Cummins immensely that the new directory paid Ashley $500 of the principal bank's funds in defending himself and them against Cummins's quo warranto proceeding, and he and Ashley quarreled endlessly over this "fee" alone.[6] Pike learned a good deal more about his partner's personality before the quo warranto case was over and was plainly embarrassed by his conduct. What bothered Pike most about the Cummins-Ashley fight over the principal bank in 1839 was that these two "gladiators" put their own personal desire for power over it above the best interests of the Real Estate Bank as a whole. They "convulsed it" to its core, Pike afterward noted in explaining the quo warranto proceeding of 1839.[7]

Yet Pike stood loyally by his partner in 1839. They, with the help of several other Little Rock Whig lawyers, got the Ashley directory ousted all right, but on the grounds that the Cummins-Davies bank packing election ordinance of 1838 and the subsequent separate elections held under it were invalid. The complicated legal history of the quo warranto case need not distract us. Four times it went before the supreme court between January and May before the final decision was handed down on May 7. Cummins and Ashley took seven days between them to present their oral arguments in the final trial before the high court, "in which," as Pike later recalled, "the one addressed the Supreme Court for four, and the other for three, mortal days, and each was fined for vehement zeal in his own cause."[8]

The end result was that the court upheld the constitutionality of the Real Estate Bank charter; ruled that the institution was one single bank and not four separate ones;

and declared that the central board—"the bond of union, which binds its separate parts together"—alone must conduct directory elections. In keeping with the decision, the central board ordered new elections for July 8, 1839, for directors of all local boards at which each stockholder should be entitled "to vote for seven other stockholders as Directors of the Principal Bank, and for seven others for each of the branches at Columbia, at Helena, and at Washington." All voting was to be at the banking house of the principal bank in Little Rock, was to be viva voce, but voting by attorney was permitted.[9]

Cummins was so overjoyed with the quo warranto triumph over Ashley that he hired a band and paraded the streets to celebrate his enemy's defeat.[10] Over the signature of "An Old Observer" he published in Colby's *Times and Advocate* a long, gloating account of "Mr. Cummins's" victory. It was mainly an attack on the *Gazette*, "Ashley's organ," which got him involved in a protracted and rancorous newspaper exchange with the new owner-editor of the *Gazette*, Edward Cole, an ambitious New Yorker who had worked as a printer on the paper since 1834. When James DeBaun, one of the Ashley directors attacked by "An Old Observer," demanded and got from Colby, Cummins's name a duel was narrowly avoided, and Cole mercilessly exposed and ridiculed Cummins in a blistering editorial. He especially laughed at that part of Cummins's communication wherein "he gravely tells the public of the large quantities of gratitude which they owe him for his vast exertions in behalf of himself and his associates in the controversy."[11]

At the heart of Cummins's exchange with Cole was, of course, the fact that the Whig leader was trying to defeat the Democrats, especially Ashley and his Little Rock crowd, in the approaching elections for directors of the principal bank and of the branches. His strategy backfired badly. The nervous stockholders, leery of both Cummins and Ashley, in July 1839 put the principal bank in the hands of a group of neutral Democratic and Whig directors—Simon Buckner, Richard C. Byrd, Richard Decantillon Collins, James L. Dawson, and Sam C. Roane—with the Democrats in control. The new directory elected Collins, Dawson, and State Director Judge Benjamin Johnson to the new central board, which in November elected Collins president of the Real Estate Bank in place of Anthony Davies.[12]

This denouement had important results for Pike, who resented his partner's willful handling of the quo warranto proceeding and his bad judgment in afterward making a political issue of the court victory.[13] The new principal bank directors determined to drop Cummins as their attorney but decided, apparently, that Pike should not be punished for his partner's rashness. In July 1839 they retained Pike as the principal bank's attorney but only on the condition that he and not Cummins conduct all of its legal business. (This event, as time would reveal, marked the beginning of Pike's break with Cummins.[14])

Meanwhile, against the background of the bank war of 1839, Arkansas's Whigs at Little Rock suffered an internal struggle that flared into the open in the early summer of 1839. In December 1838, when Whig legislators and other out-of-town party members were at Little Rock, a Whig meeting nominated three delegates to the Whig National Convention when it should be held and drew up an address to the Whigs and Conservatives of the state asking them to hold local meetings and ratify the nominees if they approved of them.[15] Pike's Little Rock Whig Central Committee was largely responsible for this event, but Colby, asserting his independence, disagreed, at least privately, with the strategy of connecting Arkansas's Whigs with Conservatives, that is, Democrats who had broken with Van Buren over the Independent Treasury and who were getting a bad press nationally. Cummins, who looked on himself as the father of Arkansas Whiggery, resented both Colby's independence and his impertinence in questioning party policy.[16]

By the spring of 1839 Cummins decided that he could no longer abide Eli Colby as editor of the *Times and Advocate*. He nursed personal grievances against the Whig editor which are not altogether clear. But among them were his belief that Colby had not wholeheartedly supported him against Cross in 1838 and, as the *Gazette* later alleged, that Colby had in June 1839 cravenly revealed Cummins's identity to DeBaun and to Cole of the *Gazette* as the author of "An Old Observer." Whatever else he believed or did not believe about Colby, Pike at least shared his partner's view that Colby was not vigorous enough in the local Whig cause and backed the move to remove him as editor.[17]

David Lambert arrived in Little Rock on April 1, 1839, opened a law office, and soon won Pike's confidence as a loyal Whig. That Lambert had served an editorial apprenticeship of sorts on the *New York Evening Star* under the famed editor Mordecai Manuel Noah was recommendation enough to Pike of Lambert's obvious ability as a politician and an editor. Not surprisingly, therefore, Lambert's prospectus for an *Arkansas Star* for Little Rock was soon circulating among Pike's and Cummins's friends in the state as they quietly began raising funds for the enterprise. With enough cash and promised credit on hand to buy a half interest in the *Times and Advocate*, Pike, on behalf of the Whig Central Committee, addressed a letter to Eli Colby and his partners.[18]

There are two versions of Pike's letter—his and Colby's. Pike said his committee offered to buy a half interest in the *Times and Advocate* "for the purpose of getting Lambert to edit it." Colby stated that Pike's committee requested him and his partners "to *unite* with the *is to be*, 'Arkansas Star,' promising us if we did so, 'a large accession of patronage,' and threatening us, if we did not comply with their request, to do all they could to injure us and assist Lambert." "They write us in reply," reported Pike, "a damned insulting letter." Colby's version of their response was "To this 'proposition' we replied that their *threats* and *promises* were alike regarded by us, that we considered the one as vain and futile as the other was officious and domineering."[19]

In consequence the Whigs at Little Rock decided to establish a new party organ at Little Rock. Active in the movement, besides Pike and Cummins, were Charles Bertrand, Absalom Fowler, Frederick Trapnall, and John W. Cocke. They furnished Lambert enough money to order a press, type, and supplies and began writing letters soliciting contributions and subscriptions. "It will be a *thorough* Whig paper," Pike assured Jesse Turner of Van Buren,

> and sustained by us all, by the pen, as well as in other ways. I hope you will do all you can for it. Lambert is an experienced politician—has served an apprenticeship in editing, under Old Noah, and will do us much good. You will now understand the meaning of the Times about dictation. The fact is, we found we must have a new paper or give up the contest. The Times is asleep, or worse. And by their letter to us, they forced us into establishing another paper.[20]

Lambert's weekly *Arkansas Star* began publishing on July 25, 1839, but the new editor hardly lived up to Pike's estimate of his abilities. He was sensitive, hotheaded, and imprudent and within a month engaged in a street brawl with Colby of the *Times and Advocate* and got himself publicly cowhided by genial Edward Cole of the *Gazette*.[21] He was much ridiculed by *Gazette* correspondents for the attack on Colby, who had haughtily declined his challenge to a duel.[22] On June 6, 1840, when a tornado struck Little Rock, the *Star* office was badly damaged.[23] Five days later, from Batesville, Fent Noland wrote Jessie Turner, "Lambert has fled. And the storm has blown down the office. Sic transit gloria mundis. Pike, Bertrand, Trapnall & others *hold the bag* for about $4500."[24]

Exactly what happened remains a mystery. The *Star* backers at Little Rock dug deeper into their pockets and came up with the money to repair the office and press, and seemingly allowed word to pass that Lambert had gone to Louisville to purchase a stock of paper. If so, he did not return, and two new men, Cornelius Stone and Samuel McCurdy, began getting out the *Star* again late in June.[25]

Cole of the *Gazette* greeted the revived Whig paper with a brief history of its unfortunate career. It was founded, he explained, by Little Rock's Whig clique who were unhappy because of the independence of the *Times and Advocate* and because Colby gave up William Cummins's name "as the author of a communication that was near bringing his person in jeopardy," a reference to the DeBaun-Cummins quarrel of a year before. Lambert was imported to write for the *Star* and "do all the fighting, and stand all the beating," allowed Cole. After the recent storm blew down the office, Lambert, with money to buy paper, went to Lexington. There he hung up his shingle as a lawyer and "coolly wrote back word to his employers that they were a pack of scoundrels, and the he would have no more to do with them." "Whether the successors of Mr. Lambert are to fulfill his bond entire, remains to be seen," concluded Cole.[26]

This was on July 1, 1840. A week later on July 8, Cole informed his readers that Lambert had written to the *Batesville News* to explain his unexpected departure from the *Star*. The men who began the paper, because of the unsettled state of the economy, had been unable to keep their promises to him. He decided to retire but left the paper in responsible hands to attend to all business that remained unsettled. Cole commented he hoped so, else the young men now running the *Star* might find themselves in the "same suck, without having the opportunity of 'retiring,' with their hands full, on a trip to Louisville, to purchase paper, the ostensible motive given out when he sloped."[27] Colby believed, too, that Lambert had fled Little Rock leaving the "disaffected few" "minus four or five thousand dollars."[28]

Lambert's departure from the *Star* may well have come as a relief to Pike, who was by June 1840 so deeply absorbed in the Whig campaign that he probably had little time to think about Lambert's flight. Since January Pike had thrown himself into the Whig cause, so much so that if his anonymous critics in the *Gazette* are to be believed he was the generalissimo of Arkansas Whiggery that year.

On January 25, 1840, some seventy-five Pulaski Whigs gathered at Little Rock and formed a Tippecanoe Club in honor of their presidential candidate, William Henry Harrison, who had been nominated the previous December at the Harrisburg National Whig Convention. Pike opened the Little Rock meeting, and he, John Cocke, Absalom

Fowler, and William Cummins spoke. "Phocion" observed the proceedings and reported them to the *Gazette*. Pike's "Hymn to the Gods" had just been published in *Blackwood's Magazine* of Edinburgh, a fact that Phocion noted; but it was his reference to Pike's birthplace in this article as "Bostin," a play on Pike's lingering Down East accent, that won for him the title "Bosting" or "Capting Bosting."[29]

Pike became a regular speaker at the Saturday night meetings of the Tippecanoe Club and thereby became the target of much rough treatment at the hands of Edward Cole's correspondents. Pike denied that he himself was politically ambitious and prided himself on his honesty and integrity, themes which seemingly sprinkled his speeches. "Timon," who heard a number of Pike's talks that winter, called him a "censorious Cato" and declared that in his "secret soul" Pike lusted after office. But Pike was, said Timon, an "instructor" in politics on public occasions such as the meetings of the Tippecanoe Club.

> These, too, are the occasions he takes to abuse office-holders, whilst he himself sits ensconced behind three offices, viz.: Attorney for the Bank of the Post of Arkansas, salary $1,000; Attorney for the Real Estate Bank at Little Rock, salary $500; Reporter to the state [supreme court], salary $200 and perquisites; besides which he is a member of the town council, President of the Bar Association, or perhaps Vice President, and a Captain to boot. Now what more has he to say of office holders? If holding an office be a temptation to dishonesty, how shall his friends endorse for him who tells them so, whilst he himself holds so many?[30]

Timon refused to let go of Pike, who had, he wrote, denounced Governor Conway and all Democrats as "scum." This "Solomon from Bosting," this "fishy son of Yankee land" believed himself, said Timon, to be "immaculate, and unlike all other public men, beyond reproach." But Timon was not prepared to accept all that Pike said, "or that he is all, and more than all the imagination of man can picture" in his immaculateness.

> You would not say, would you, if you saw him walking up street, "There walks, majestic, the *immaculate* Pike; or riding, "there rides, O grandeur! the immaculate Pike;" or drinking, "there, gulping liquids, the immaculate Pike."[31]

When the Whig state convention met at Little Rock in March 1840, Absalom Fowler was nominated to oppose Edward Cross, who in February had accepted a Democratic bid to stand for reelection to Congress. No Whig nomination was made for the gubernatorial office, the convention "being of the opinion that no great principles are involved in the election of governor," for which Archibald Yell has been campaigning since November 1839. But three Whig presidential electors were chosen—John Ringgold of Independence County, John W. Cocke of Pulaski County, and Lewis Evans of Washington County—who were to stump the state for Harrison and John Tyler.[32] For the committee appointed to respond to the Harrisburg nominations, Pike wrote and delivered the response, while his resolution calling for a Young Men's Whig Convention at Little Rock in July met with enthusiastic approval.[33]

The Tippecanoe Club of Pulaski County, attempting to quiet statewide charges of Little Rock dictation, had been largely responsible for calling the Whig state meeting. But Cole of the *Gazette*, who said the printed proceedings listed only forty-six delegates from nine counties, charged that several of those named were not in attendance and insinuated that, as always, Little Rock's "Whig clique" controlled the affair.³⁴ If his self-appointed critic, the ubiquitous Phocion of the *Gazette*, is to be believed, Pike deserved full credit, or blame, for this "leading Convention." It was, Phocion proclaimed,

> a *poor abortion* from the loins of its fecund father, Capting Bosting, *who begot this child of wonderful promise*. Bosting moved to organize the Convention, March 16th, 1840. Bosting was appointed one of a committee so to do March 16th, 1840, whereupon Bosting organized the Convention, and appointed the independent ex-minister [Dr. James Walker] President, March 16, 1840. March the 17th, 1840, Bosting appointed member of committee to nominate candidates; and March the 17th of the same year, Bosting appointed member of committee to respond to Harrisburg nomination—Bosting, with the cold document in his pocket, which doubtless had been prepared a month before, responded to the Harrisburg nomination. March 18th, 1840, Bosting submitted a resolution, calling a Whig Young Men's Convention, in July, to rescue the State from that odious Van Burenism, which, it seems, prevents Bosting from acquiring a *sixth office* in his own proper person, besides those that have expired on him. In fact, it is Bosting, Bosting, and all is Bosting. The history of the convention is the history of Bosting.³⁵

Meanwhile, the Pulaski Whigs, still badly divided by the Cummins-Colby strife, were having much trouble settling on a three-man slate for the house of representatives to which the county was entitled in 1840. Meeting March 7, a county convention nominated Absalom Fowler, Emzy Wilson, and a man named Brown, whom Phocion of the *Gazette* identified as being, respectively, a lawyer, a farmer, and a mechanic.³⁶ Fowler withdrew, apparently on being nominated for Congress, and neither Wilson nor Brown remained in the race. According to Editor Cole, "a very stormy session" of the Tippecanoe Club on March 27 ended in a failure to fill the ticket. When William Cummins, Charles P. Bertrand, and Sterling H. Tucker were named on April 11, Cole reported that Colby took "the nominations very coolly," that he published the proceedings without drawing attention to the nominees, and that he failed to "puff the candidates, nor emblazon their names on the Tippecanoe Democratic Whig flag" of his paper. The *Gazette* editor predicted, however, that Colby would soon print their names. He was mistaken, at least in part. Colby never placed the detested Cummins's name on his masthead, though he did eventually post Bertrand's and that of Dr. Lorenzo Gibson, who was designated to replace Tucker on the ticket when the latter moved out of the county and declined to run.³⁷

Gazette correspondents amused themselves endlessly that year poking fun at the sessions of the Tippecanoe Club and reporting the latest developments in the Cummins-Colby feud. For example, "Paul Pry" speculated at length whether Colby's *Times and Advocate* or Lambert's *Star* was the "organ" of Arkansas Whiggery.³⁸ Phocion suggested that the key to this particular riddle was Pike, or "Bosting, the ex-editor of the *Times & Advocate*." To illustrate the point, he related a story then circulating in Little Rock about Pike, whose "Yankee speech" and alleged "Yankee ways" were the butt of so much of the humor, both good and bad, that came his way. Phocion said:

> A malicious wag remarked, the other day, that Bosting knew too well the system of old clothes dealing, pursued by the thrifty Yankees of his native place, to neglect it here. In Bosting, when a Yankee's clothes are pretty well worn out, he starts for an old clothes store, and sells them on the principle that he will cheat the buyer, if he can, in a trade for new clothes; and the purchaser buys on the principle, if he can't cheat the seller, that a stitch in time saves nine, so he will furbish them up and sell them for new to the next man. The skillful dealer in old clothes sometimes puts back the same garment on the same individual that sold it to him, but this never occurs, except where the visitor is a stranger or green. An old Yankee can never be deceived by that trick. He will "guess" at it and around it, till some peculiarity strikes him which he will "guess" was the same rent or stain for which he sold it.—So Bosting knows the old paper [the *Times and Advocate*] well; he sold it, he knows the old stains and rents about it well; he guesses you can't fool him with it again. . . .[39]

Undaunted by his critics, Pike remained active in the Tippecanoe Club, which, to stir interest in the campaign, announced plans for a log cabin and liberty pole raising for the morning of May 13. The event was well advertised by handbills bearing the emblems of a log cabin and cider barrel. Accordingly, a large crowd turned out for the occasion at Maj. Nicholas Peay's vacant lot on the corner of Cherry and Scott streets. After first raising the liberty pole and running up the Whig banner, the thirsty men tapped the cider, three barrels of which were consumed before their cabin was completed that day. A disgruntled correspondent in the *Gazette*, "Cyrus," deemed it, withal, a pretty inefficient piece of work; he thought a dozen Democrats with a gallon of "good Democratic whiskey" would have done a better job of it.[40]

The climax of the Whig campaign that year for Pike was the mammoth Young Men's Whig Convention held at Little Rock on July 13. Pike had suggested it to the state convention in March and, winning approval for it, poured enormous energy into making it a success. People came from all over the state and camped out during the meeting. A party of 150 to 200 men and women from Independence County brought with them in a wagon from Batesville a giant disassembled canoe. Put together at Little Rock and mounted on wheels, the canoe was the principal attraction in a great parade that was staged on the morning of the convention. In the canoe were seated twenty-six Arkansas beauties, representing the states of the Union, each wearing Harrison and Tyler badges. The prow of the enormous craft contained a miniature log cabin with a live raccoon tied to its roof.[41]

This unique float, followed by a procession of 3,000 singing and shouting Whigs, paraded the principal streets and then proceeded to the grounds of the U.S. Arsenal. There beneath "the flag of Old Tip and the Country" the Tippecanoe Club of Pulaski County treated the throng to free barbecue and hard cider. After the feast Pike, the temporary president, called the crowd to order, a "suitable arbor" having been erected to protect them from the summer sun. Jesse Turner of Crawford County was elected president and twenty-four vice presidents, one from each county in attendance, were designated. Pike read a letter of regret from Sargent S. Prentiss, famous Whig orator of Mississippi, who had been invited by the committee to attend and address the convention. The nominations of Harrison and Tyler were then ratified, and Turner appointed Pike chairman of a committee to draw up an address to the voters of Arkansas on behalf of the convention. To conclude the day, the candidates for the electoral college and for the state and national offices spoke to the crowd, and Pike read the address he had written for his committee.[42]

Enthusiastic campaigning on the part of Arkansas's Whigs in the months that followed made inroads into hitherto immovable Democratic counties but failed to shake the ironclad grip of the Democracy on the state's voters. Though Fowler had the congressional field virtually to himself since Cross did not return from Congress until late August and was in such poor health that he made but one speech in Little Rock and toured only the neighborhood about his Hempstead County home, Fowler lost in October to Cross by a statewide majority of 2,088, getting 5,788 to Cross's 7,876. Popular Archibald Yell, with no Whig opponent, rolled up 10,554 votes to 392 for Bryan H. Smithson, a rebel Democrat whose name seemingly was not before the voters in most of the counties. Pulaski's Whigs were cheered when their county's voters gave Fowler a clear majority over Cross, and elected a solid Whig slate to the house—Cummins, Bertrand, and Gibson. A month later, in November, the Democrats swept the state for Van Buren by a popular vote of 6,048 to 4,663. Again, Pulaski's Whigs rejoiced that their county had given the Harrison-Tyler electors a large majority over the Van Buren electors.[43]

In the final reckoning for the nation, Harrison defeated Van Buren, an event that prompted prolonged celebration among Arkansas's Whigs, who in Fent Noland's words had "skinned" the Democrats.[44] When news reached Pike that Old Tip had won, he was attending court at Van Buren. He was the house guest of his good friend Phineas H. White and his wife Emeline, both of whom were natives of Massachusetts with a special liking for Pike.[45] A prosperous merchant on the Indian border at Van Buren, White was known to his close friends as "Old Festivity" because of his fondness for using the word "festivities" to "designate every jollification, of whatever kind."[46] News of Harrison's victory gave White the excuse, as Pike remembered, for a "festivity" at which he and Pike and twenty others celebrated the glad tidings until sunrise.[47]

XIV

The Greatest Law Reasoner in the State

PIKE WAS ONLY THIRTY-ONE YEARS OLD that December of 1840 as he celebrated old Tip's victory over Van Buren. He could reflect contentedly on the past seven years. There had been struggles to prove himself on the Arkansas frontier. Writing for the eastern market, schoolteaching in the backwoods, and newspapering at Little Rock had all ended in failure. His hard work for the Whig cause in Arkansas had been anything but a success, although he could bask in the reflected glory of his party's national success in 1840 and in the brilliant sunlight of continued Whig triumph in his hometown and county. But most important of all, he had found his life's work in the law, had established himself among the leaders of the Arkansas bar at the same time that he was establishing his place in the society of the new state, and was just now entering upon his most productive years as a lawyer and citizen. He had come a long way since those first wretched months of 1832–33 in Crawford County.

There had been hard work to prove himself as a lawyer. From 1835 to 1837, the years that spanned his attempt at newspapering, he was a circuit-riding lawyer. He traveled, he estimated in 1836, about 1,200 miles a year on the two circuits in which he and Cummins practiced. His saddlebags crammed with papers, a book or two, spare clothing, and "always a flask or bottle," his blankets rolled and tied behind his saddle, Pike mounted his horse "Davy" and rode off through the dense canebrakes of the river bottoms or over the winding hill roads to the primitive county seats where log buildings served as courthouses and split logs as benches for the spectators.[1]

Court day brought large crowds to the county seats, and during election years it was the custom of the time for the lawyers, before and after court hours, to address the people on the political issues of the day. Most of Pike's early training as a political speaker took place in these impromptu circumstances.[2]

Riding circuit had its discomforts and dangers. Being unable to swim, Pike especially feared "crossing the deep rapid streams at rocky fords," where at flood stage man and horse could easily be swept into the current and drowned.[3] In the winter of 1835–36 he accompanied a party of Little Rock lawyers to Crawford Courthouse, the original county seat of Crawford County. The Arkansas River was frozen over at the time and the men walked across on the ice leading their horses. Judge Archibald Yell of Fayetteville, crossing to the south bank with them, barely escaped drowning when the ice broke through with him and his horse. At Crawford Courthouse that term Pike and eighteen other lawyers slept in an improvised courtroom, under which, he said, a faro table operated at night when the court was not in session.[4]

Pike enjoyed the comradeship of the lawyers and judges on circuit, but his favorite companion was John W. Cocke of Little Rock. They were both hard drinkers and prided themselves on their great capacity for holding their liquor. Setting out one day from the capital to a court at Hot Springs, they agreed, Pike recalled, "to stop at every 'branch' we came to and drink together." They found "the little creeks and rivulets" so numerous and the content of their whiskey bottles dropping so fast that they were quite drunk by the end of the first day's ride and "hardly in a presentable condition." Next day, as they rode on, they abandoned their drinking bargain for the remainder of the journey.[5]

John W. Cocke, a widower, had been married in Kentucky to the eldest daughter of former territorial governor John Pope. After his young wife's early death in 1835, he came to Little Rock in 1836. Coming with him was Frederick W. Trapnall, who was married to Cocke's sister, Martha Frances Cocke. The brothers-in-law early in 1837 formed a partnership, opened a law office, and became well connected in law, political, and social circles, since Cocke's sister Mary Ann was the wife of the chief justice of the Arkansas supreme court Daniel Ringo, also a Whig. Pike liked Cocke and Trapnall, these two well-bred Kentuckians, who were, he said, so unlike in physical appearance. Cocke was a tall, lean, homely, slouchy fellow, who, like Pike, was careless and somewhat slovenly in his dress. He was, however, an able, eloquent speaker and a ready debater. Outgoing and friendly, his bright blue eyes sparkled with laughter and good humor. "He was," Pike remembered in old age, "a man whom you could not help loving, and in those days of fun and frolic was the most delightful of companions."[6]

Trapnall, on the other hand, was tall, handsome, well formed, with a finely chiseled face, whose bold thin features gave him the air of an aristocrat. He dressed immaculately and carried himself proudly. "He was," Pike recalled, "well read, especially in English history, an excellent lawyer, ready and quick, never taken at a disadvantage, never at a loss, never confused, and always alighting, when he fell, on his feet, like a cat. He was the best, readiest and most efficient Circuit lawyer in the State."[7]

A favorite story of Pike's in later years concerned Trapnall and a Kentucky horse jockey named William Triplett who lived at Little Rock. Pike had first seen Triplett in 1833 in Pope County, where Pike was teaching school and where Bill had brought a "quarter-nag" that he was taking over the territory and challenging all comers for a straight quarter-mile race. Later Triplett settled in Little Rock and became a town loafer, frequently borrowing money of Trapnall, Pike said, "on the strength of both being Kentuckians and old acquaintances."[8]

In 1844 Trapnall and Charles Bertrand, from whom Pike had bought the *Advocate* in 1835, were Whig candidates in Pulaski County for the house. Two or three days before the election, Pike related, "the Democrats at Little Rock got up a hand-bill, with some lying report or other in it against our candidates Trapnall and Bertrand." They hired Triplett to distribute them. Trapnall and Bertrand were elected despite the report, and soon afterward Triplett came to Trapnall and asked to borrow twenty dollars.

"See here, Bill," Trapnall remonstrated, "why don't you go to your Democratic friends and borrow? Whenever I am a candidate, you do all you can to beat me, and then come to me and borrow. You have just got back now, after going all over the county and distributing a hand-bill that you knew was full of lies."

"Fred," said Triplett, with grotesque solemnity and a queerly contorted visage, "politically I am your enemy; but financially I am your friend."

He got the money, Pike said, "which of course he never repaid."[9]

Bill had a brother, Hedgeman C. Triplett, who lived at the Mississippi River town of Columbia, the county seat of Chicot County, and who in 1838 represented the county in the lower branch of the state legislature. "He was," Pike remembered, "a huge, tall, strong, ungainly, ugly man, who pretended to practice law." Always broke, he stole wood of winters for his office stove from either the courthouse supply or his neighbors' woodpiles. Pike landed at Columbia one cold December night, after ten o'clock, to attend court there. At the clerk's office in the courthouse, he found the clerk, Triplett, and one or two others. An hour later they were all hungry and thirsty but knew that all the stores and saloons were closed.

"Come with me," said Hedge. "I can find liquor."

He led them to a grocery store in front of which, against the wall, stood a long rick of firewood. Seizing a stick near the middle, he worked it loose and brought the whole pile tumbling noisily down. In a flash, said Pike, the front door flew open and the proprietor rushed out with a pistol in each hand.

"Hedge Triplett, you ——," he cursed, "let my wood alone, and be off."

"Hedge was behind him in a moment," Pike said, "pinioned his arms, and invited us all in to drink." Heartily welcomed, they "found champagne and a barrel of oysters just from New Orleans inside, and made a night of it."[10]

Amusing as such reminiscences are, they were the exception rather than the rule in Pike's professional life. He took his practice and "self-education" in the law seriously. He invested much of the money from early fees in law books and reports, especially in the English Common Law and in American equity practice, read, studied, observed, and soon was spoken of as one of Little Rock's crack lawyers.[11]

He early acquired a reputation as a scholar in Arkansas law circles. Though he rightfully refused to take any blame for the much criticized *Revised Statutes*, which Lawyers Ball and Roane had badly botched, Pike's work as indexer was generally recognized as having given the code what little utility it possessed.[12] Responding to the need and popular demand for a work that would illustrate and explain the proper legal forms for deeds, wills, mortgages, and other legal instruments, Pike in 1842 published *The Arkansas Form Book*. It sold for $3.00 a copy and, remaining in print for at least ten years, must have made a nice supplement to his income.[13]

Pike served as the first official reporter of the decisions of the Arkansas Supreme Court, a position to which he was appointed by that court in February 1838 and which he retained through 1844. In this capacity he had to report the cases for the January and July terms in 1838, when there seemingly had been no reporter, and, thereafter, for all terms through that of July 1844.[14] The office paid him only $200 a year but carried with it the not unwelcome power of awarding the lucrative printing contracts for the different volumes. Handling this part of his responsibility with the aplomb of a born partisan, Pike gave all but two of the volumes to Whig printers, withholding these two only because he was at odds with Colby of the *Times and Advocate* after 1839.[15] The reportership also afforded Pike an additional means of building up his law library, allowing him to exchange the *Arkansas Reports* through eastern book houses for legal works that he needed; and besides giving him a familiarity with Arkansas law second to no other lawyer in the state, the reportership added to his prestige in the legal profession.[16]

Pike's skill at appeals to the supreme court won him a larger and larger practice before the state's high court. By 1841 he was participating in four out of every ten cases that came before that court.[17]

His energy and capacity for hard work became legendary. During twenty years he was "on the circuit" for seven months in every year. For the first ten years he traveled on horseback, and afterwards by buggy, to the courts of the interior counties of south Arkansas and by steamboat to the river towns along the Arkansas and the Mississippi. When not riding circuit or otherwise absent from home, his office work and law reading engaged so much of his time, he complained, that he could find little time except late at night and "occasionally on Sunday" to devote to other reading and writing. It was his habit at this time to work, read, and write at his office eighteen or nineteen hours of the twenty-four, not counting time out for eating.[18]

His formula for storing up energy for such heavy stints of work was camping, hunting, and fishing. Having applied himself at his office four or five months, it was his custom in the thirties and forties to close his office; load his fishing rod, gun, and camp equipment into his buggy; ferry across the Arkansas River; and with a slave servant drive off to the Grand Prairie east of Little Rock to relax for a week or two. This almost treeless level grassland began twenty-five miles from town and extended to White River. It was threaded by bayous and small streams that teemed with fish, and the prairie land swarmed with grouse and wild pigeons and in winter with geese, ducks, and plover. Deer also fed there, and Pike fished and "hunted and camped all over it." Sometimes he went with a companion or two but most often with only a black servant. There was "no such remedy for an overworked brain," Pike believed and, returning to his office "refreshed and invigorated," he would settle down for another term of labor at his law desk.[19]

Life was not all work for our busy lawyer. He somehow found time to participate in such social and cultural activities as the town afforded. From 1837 on, he commanded the Little Rock Guards, better known as "Captain Pike's Artillery," in parades and at various public celebrations, where because of his reputation as a man of letters he frequently delivered addresses.[20] Beginning in 1843 he belonged to the "Club of Forty," founded the year before "by those who were fond of literary pursuits." Its members contributed money for subscriptions to "the various reviews and periodicals" of the United States and Great Britain.[21] Donor of many magazines and books to the organization, Pike served as president of the club in 1843 in which capacity it was his duty to direct the "conversational discussions" at its Saturday night meetings, where political topics were not infrequently the order of business.[22]

Between 1838 and 1841 Pike lent his pen, pocketbook, and name to the abortive effort by Sam Waters to establish a "Little Rock Theatre." Waters, who brought to the state capital its first traveling professional theatrical companies, opened the 1838–39 season in a warehouse on an alley between Main and Louisiana streets but moved his operations in January 1839 into the renovated Arcade Building, standing on the north side of Markham Street between Main and Scott. For opening night at the new site, on

January 16, 1839, described as "a brilliant and gala" social affair with the town's "most beautiful and fashionable women" in the "dress circle," Pike composed a poetic "Address" especially for the event.[23] Read by Mrs. Waters, Sam's talented actress wife, it expressed Pike's sincere belief that the new theater was a sign of Little Rock's growing cultural maturity. Here, he wrote, where "late the Indian held undoubted sway, and where"

> a dense, dark forest stood,
> And the Arkansas rolled its troubled flood,
> Through pathless wilderness, to the ocean.
> All now is changed. Life, with its constant motion,
> Is eddying here, and wit, and grace, and beauty,
> Approve our humble efforts, while we engage,
> The first time here, to introduce THE STAGE.
> . . . .
> We are resolved to please—and we will do it;
> And now, kind friends, say—*shall Sam Waters rue it?*[24]

By early 1840 the Arcade Building, "originally constructed for a stable" and then converted to a saloon and coffee house "before it was devoted to the drama,"[25] no longer suited the convenience or taste of Pike and the town's playgoers. Plans for erecting a new theater building at the corner of Rock and Cherry streets for Waters's use had begun that spring when the great fire of April 26, 1840, which destroyed the Arcade and every other building on the block on which it stood, rendered their work a necessity.[26]

Pike gave money to help erect the new "Little Rock Theatre" and served on the committee that received subscriptions for and superintended construction. The work was dogged by bad luck. The tornado that wrecked the *Arkansas Star* office on June 6, 1840, also demolished the skeleton framework of the new theater building, but Pike and his friends, beginning over, got the edifice up in time for Waters to open his third season in it in October 1840. Unfortunately, Waters was forced to close in late January 1841, citing as reasons a lack of patronage and the many expenses "attendant upon such an establishment." The fact was that Little Rock's first attempt at having a theater had fallen victim to the economic depression that was blighting the state and the nation by early 1841.[27]

Meanwhile, Pike's reputation as poet and man of letters came about primarily through the publication in 1839 of his "Hymns to the Gods" in *Blackwood's Edinburgh Magazine*. While owning the *Advocate* and sharing ownership of the *Times and Advocate*, he had continued from time to time to amuse himself by writing poems, many of which appeared in the *Boston Pearl* and the *American Monthly Magazine* during 1835 and 1836. By the latter year, however, he was finding it necessary to devote more and more of his time to the law. "This poring over law books, and arguing demurrers, and writing declarations and deeds," he complained in 1836, "is but dull business; and does not tend to exalt the imagination, or to fit a man to write for a magazine."[28]

But his friends back in Boston kept urging him to make further attempts at writing, and during his brief visit among them in the summer of 1838, while he was in Boston having the Arkansas *Revised Statutes* printed, he either read or showed them revised versions of his "Hymns to the Gods," the eight long classical poems he had first written and published before leaving New England. Now, encouraged by the praise of his friends, he arranged to have Isaac C. Pray, former editor of the *Boston Pearl* but in 1838 a rising New York journalist, dramatist, actor, and theatre manager, recommend them to *Blackwood's*.[29]

The editor of this famous magazine was the distinguished Scottish literary critic John Wilson, better known at that time by his pen name of "Christopher North." Either on Pray's advice or on his personal initiative, Pike addressed a cover letter to Wilson designed to intrigue and charm the Scotsman out of his socks. Though Pike was then still in Boston, he dated his cover letter "Little Rock, State of Arkansas, August 15, 1838," as if to have Wilson believe he was sending "the accompanying trifles in verse from this remote corner of the Union—beyond the Mississippi." The backwoods poet went on to say to Wilson that he

> would fain believe them worthy a place in your estimable maga, which regularly reaches me here, one thousand miles from New York, within six or seven weeks of its publication in Edinburgh, and is duly welcomed as it deserves. Should you judge them worthy of publication, accept them as a testimonial of respect offered by one resident in south-western forests, to him whose brilliant talents have endeared him, not only to every English, but to multitudes of American bosoms, equally dear as Christopher North and Professor Wilson.[30]

Pike's poems, apparently held up for several months by Pray in New York, did not reach Scotland until the following May. Wilson published them in the very next issue of his magazine. In a footnote signed with his famous initials "C. N.", he praised Pike's poetry and explained the delay:

> These fine hymns, which entitles their author to take his place in the highest order of his country's poets reached us only a week or two ago, though Mr. Pike's most gratifying letter is dated as far back as August, and we mention this that he may not suppose such composition could have lain unhonored in our repositories from autumn to spring. His packet was accompanied by a letter—not less gratifying—from Mr. Isaac C. Pray, dated New York, April 20, 1839, and we hope that before many weeks have elapsed the friends, though perhaps then almost as far distant from each other as from us, may accept this, our brotherly salutation· from our side of the Atlantic.—C.N.[31]

With such praise from one of the most renowned critics of the time, it might have been expected that Pike would have given more attention to writing poetry. The evidence is, however, that while he continued to dabble in poetry in the forties, he did so with no serious, sustained effort. "I have been seriously contemplating for some time the gathering into one heap and publishing such of my scattered rhymes as are worthy of it—but having no acquaintance among your fraternity of publishers, it has, up to this time remained a mere floating and undefined idea," he wrote Carey and Hart, a Philadelphia publishing house, in the summer of 1841. He expected "no profit from the work," he said, nor did he "want to incur any great expense," but wished to learn on what terms they would be willing to "undertake it in good style."[32] Their terms, whatever they were, were obviously beyond either his means or his inclination.

Two years later, in the summer of 1843, he was still toying with the idea of gathering "my stray leaves into a book which I could preserve for their amusement [those] who are to bear my name after me—and if I can do it without wasteful expenditure of coin, I intend to do it."[33] It was 1854 before Pike finally contracted with a Philadelphia printer, C. Sherman, to execute the work *Nugae*, meaning "trifles," a 363-page collection of his poems. His preface stated that only 150 copies were published for private distribution and that he should "never consent that they be published in any other way."[34]

But Pike was not forgotten as a poet. When Rufus Wilmot Griswold compiled his famous anthology *Poets and Poetry of America* (1842) for the Philadelphia publishing house Carey and Hart, he accorded Pike a place in it, praised his "Hymns to the Gods" and a few poems in his *Prose Sketches and Poems*, but opined that Pike's "later poems had failed to measure up to the promise indicated by his earlier poetry."[35] Griswold was correct. Pike published not over a dozen poems in the next decade, and none of them equaled his earlier exertions.[36] Pike was the first to agree with his critics: "My poetical days are well nigh over, if not quite gone," he wrote in 1843. At the same time he declared that he had "not the slightest sensitiveness in regard to anything I ever wrote. No one thinks less of my productions than myself. . . ."[37]

If Pike's "poetical days" were "well nigh over" by 1840–43, he was by then just reaching manhood as a lawyer. By "mutual consent" he and Cummins dissolved their partnership, effective March 1, 1840, and for nearly two years Pike practiced alone, while Cummins took in as a partner his twenty-two-year-old younger brother, Ebenezer Cummins, who had been reading law with Pike and Cummins since 1838.[38] Then, beginning January 12, 1842, and lasting until March 20, 1848, Pike took as a partner David J. Baldwin. This young man, born at Orange, New Jersey, January 17, 1818, had come to Little Rock in about 1838 and had begun a careful four-year preparation for the Arkansas bar in the distinguished law office of Chester Ashley and George C. Watkins. A fellow Whig, Pike made him his partner apparently on his admission to the bar in January 1842. Baldwin afterwards, in about 1850, moved to Galveston, Texas, where he practiced as a lawyer and ultimately became U.S. Attorney for the Eastern District of Texas.[39]

By 1842 the Real Estate Bank was occupying so much of Pike's professional time that he had been forced to seek Baldwin as a partner. He had become attorney of the principal bank in July 1839, when its directors declined reappointing Cummins, and soon after that Pike was also named as attorney for the Columbia branch of the bank. Two years later, in November 1841, Pike was elected by the central board, "as a matter of economy," sole attorney of the Real Estate Bank, that is, of the central board and principal bank as well as of all the branches. From that date his salary was $2,000 a year, with an office furnished him in the new principal bank building at Little Rock but with him to supply his firewood and stationery.[40]

It was a good salary for the time amid the depression that had settled down upon the country in the wake of the Panic of 1837, but he would in due course have cause to complain that the workload was a heavy burden, imposing upon him the responsibility of bringing suits to collect bank debts "in half the courts of the State," preventing him from attending to other professional business and after 1842 consuming much of the time of Baldwin, who was supposed to be looking after the balance of their private practice.[41]

The Real Estate Bank was in political and economic trouble during these years, and its troubles multiplied as the new decade progressed. Forced to suspend specie payments in the fall of 1839, when there was a general suspension throughout the nation and when it was necessary for the Arkansas state banks to suspend to prevent a drainage of their specie to other states, the Real Estate Bank nevertheless remained open for business on a nonspecie basis. It even extended its paper circulation in order, as Carey A. Harris, cashier and secretary of the central board, said, to avoid a "too stinted accommodation to the public" and, thereby, to increase its loans and discounts.[42] Unfortunately, the depression worsened, the bank's notes rapidly depreciated, its debtors began to default, and by the fall of 1840, the bank's officials could not collect enough to pay interest on the state bonds and to meet other obligations.[43]

The Real Estate Bank met bond payments due in January and July 1841 in part by borrowing the money from North American Trust and Banking Company, in New York City. This loan involved the Arkansas bank in the great "Holford bond" controversy at home and abroad and became so important an episode in Pike's professional and political life that it is necessary to relate its history in some detail.[44]

The trouble originated when Real Estate Bank agents at New York in the early fall of 1840 signed a contract by which North American Trust lent the bank $250,000 to be repaid in two annual installments due in July 1841 and May 1842. As collateral the Arkansas agents hypothecated, or signed over and deposited as security, to the New York bank 500 state bonds issued the Real Estate Bank for capitalizing its Van Buren branch and for which there was no buyer in the tight money market of 1840. The Arkansans understood that North American Trust was not to make use of a power of attorney given it for transferring the bonds to a third party unless the Real Estate Bank defaulted on repayment of its loan and that half the bonds would be returned to them on payment of the first installment and the other half on payment of the second and final installment.

All did not go as planned. North American Trust, allegedly violating its pledge to the Arkansas bankers, transferred the 500 state bonds late in 1840 or early in 1841 to James Holford and Company, a London, England, banking house, in return for a loan to itself in an amount variously estimated as between $325,000 to $375,000. The New York bank endorsed the bonds payable in sterling at Holford's in London.

Real Estate Bank officials, who had requested in early 1841 an extension of their loan, at first seemingly acquiesced in North American Trust's arrangement with Holford, thinking perhaps the New York bank was merely raising money for the Arkansas bank. But growing suspicions that North American Trust was looking after its own interests rather than those of the Real Estate Bank, the Arkansas bankers by late spring fell back on the letter of their 1840 agreement, proffered payment of the scheduled first installment of their debt at New York in July 1841, and demanded half the 500 hypothecated bonds. When told that none of the bonds were attainable, as they had been deposited with Holford and Company, the Arkansas bankers dropped payment to the New York bank; apprised Holford that the transfer of the bonds to him by North American Trust, being a fraud upon the Real Estate Bank, would not be recognized by the Arkansas bank; and published in the *New York Herald* a "Caution to the Public" warning all persons against purchasing or becoming interested in the 500 Arkansas bonds "believed to be in the hands of Holford & Co., bankers, London," since the Real Estate bank would not hold itself liable for the principal or interest on them, nor did the Arkansas bankers believe that the state would, "under the circumstances, consider itself bound to provide for them."

When North American Trust, on August 31, 1841, became insolvent and assigned its assets to a trustee for collection and payment of its debts, it failed to assign adequate assets to secure payment of its debt to Holford or to redeem the Arkansas bonds, leaving them still in the hands of the London banker. James Holford in the fall of 1841 applied to the Real Estate Bank for payment of the amount plus interest that he had lent North American Trust on the 500 bonds. The Real Estate Bank, as he expected, spurned his claim, and he appealed to Governor Yell, who also spurned his claim on behalf of the state. Yell contended that the Real Estate Bank had no legal right to dispose of the bonds by hypothecation and, therefore, that the state was not liable because of the bank's illegal act. The Real Estate Bank contended that while it did have the power to hypothecate the bonds with North American Trust as security for its loan, the New York bank had fraudulently transferred them to Holford. To his credit, Yell did declare that North American Trust had committed a breach of trust in violating its contract with the Real Estate Bank, and lectured Holford about not being an "innocent purchaser" of the 500 bonds.

The result was that the Real Estate Bank repudiated the Holford debt, and the state indirectly backed it up in that action. The Arkansas bank, as it turned out, had expected to receive $250,000 from North American Trust on the hypothecated bonds, but obtained in reality only $121,336.50.[45] The bank did acknowledge this amount as its liability on the Holford bonds, and its official position from the fall of 1841 on was that it would pay the $121,336.50 if all 500 of the bonds were delivered over to the bank by Holford, who, of course, refused to do so, and began legal proceedings against the Real Estate Bank.[46]

The Holford bond affair hit Arkansas newspapers in October and November of 1841. For several months prior to that time Colby's *Times and Advocate* and George Burnett's *Gazette* had been demanding that Governor Yell call a special session of the legislature to deal with the state banks. In July 1841 Yell had released to the public a summary report of an investigation of the Fayetteville branch of the State Bank which revealed a shocking scandal. William McKnight Ball, Democratic state senator for Washington County and cashier of the Fayetteville bank, had juggled the books, reported more specie than was on hand, and could not account for some $21,544.17 of bank funds. Ball at first denied the charges, but to save himself, soon gathered his family and slaves and fled to Texas. He was never returned to stand trial, and the missing money, which turned out to be $46,199.60 on a final accounting in 1842, remained a loss on the State Bank's books.[47]

Colby and Burnett, up to the time Yell released the report on the Fayetteville bank, had been merely puzzling and raging over the badly depreciated Arkansas bank money. The Ball embezzlement, the Holford bond controversy, and an alleged unsound speculation in cotton in the fall of 1841 by both state banks convinced the two editors that bank management was responsible for the depreciated state currency and that the bankers more than ever needed the attention of the legislature. But Governor Yell had no use for the holdover legislature, which he claimed had not supported him against the banks at its regular session in 1840–41. Therefore, he refused to call a special session and announced that he would await the election of a new legislature in 1842 when, as he hoped, the people would send him antibank legislators to deal properly with the banks.[48]

Consumptive young George H. Burnett, for whom the Vermont newcomer Sterling H. Tucker, a twenty-nine-year-old lawyer, filled in at the *Gazette* most of late 1841, died in December 1841.[49] Woodruff again took control and became temporary editor of the paper. Old Buck and his correspondents defended Yell's position on the Holford bonds and Yell's decision not to call the legislature, and Woodruff, a maximum stockholder in the Real Estate Bank, remained personally sympathetic toward the financial plight of that bank as 1841 gave way to 1842.[50]

Eli Colby, of the *Times and Advocate*, on the other hand, kept up a steady drumbeat for a called session of the legislature, and, by mid-January 1842 when he realized there was no longer any hope for Yell's summoning one, opened a wholesale attack on the governor and the Real Estate Bank. Begging the questions of the Real Estate Bank's strong claim that it had the legal right to hypothecate the bonds, of its just contention that North American Trust had committed a fraud in transferring the bonds to Holford as it did, and of its official position that it stood ready to pay what it believed to be rightfully due on the bonds, Colby took the high moral ground that the faith and credit of the state was behind the Holford bonds, which, he asserted, had been "pawned" by Real Estate Bank agents and then "repudiated" by the bank and the governor. Declaring that Holford and Company were "innocent purchasers" of bonds illegally hypothecated by the Real Estate Bank, Colby laid all the blame for any fraud involved at the door of the Arkansas bank. The State of Arkansas was the bank's security on the bonds; therefore, the state was bound to redeem the Holford bonds if the bank did not. But Colby wished the state to compel the bank to pay the bonds, stating that anything less would tarnish the name of the state with repudiation. "*Let justice be done though the* BANKS *fall*," he proclaimed.[51]

Though Colby was attacked by correspondents and editors friendly to the positions of the Real Estate Bank and of Governor Yell, the Whig editor righteously clung to his moral stance that the state was "legally" and "equitably bound" to redeem the Holford bonds. And in the campaign for the legislature that year, he called for antibank Whigs and Democrats to vote for men "without regard to party politics" who would "go for a judicious and economical winding up of the Banks." Though Yell was calling for a Democratic legislature that would also vote to liquidate the state banks, Colby continued to denounce the governor as a repudiationist of the Holford bonds and to advise the people that they should support no Democrat or Whig for a legislative seat who was not "*against* Repudiation, in all its forms."[52]

Just as the preliminaries to the antibank campaign of 1842 were getting underway in Arkansas that spring, Pike found himself front and center in a new controversy that now swirled about the Real Estate Bank.[53] Defaulting outright on bond payments due January 1, 1842, the harassed central board of the institution met in emergency session at Little Rock in late March to discuss the fate of the bank.[54] Unable to collect its debts, oppressed on every hand by angry creditors and note holders who were attaching its available means in New York and New Orleans and bringing suits against its individual debtors in Arkansas, and unable to continue banking without in fact perpetrating a daily fraud upon the public, the troubled institution actually faced a complete collapse if it went on operating any longer.[55]

To prevent this collapse and the ruin and oppression that would inevitably follow in its train, the central board on April 2, 1842, made a deed of assignment of the property and assets of the entire Real Estate Bank to fifteen trustees. The objects of this assignment, as stated in the deed, were threefold—to secure and pay the creditors of the bank, to call in and redeem the circulation, and to protect the debtors of the bank and enable them to pay their debts. Under the terms of the deed, the trustees were to apply all money accruing to the trust in payment of the bank's debts, but in a preferred "manner and order," as follows: First, all balances due officers of the bank; second, the deposits; third, the calling in and redeeming of the circulation; fourth, the interest upon the state bonds except those hypothecated to North American Trust and Banking Company; fifth, the bonuses due the state; sixth, the principal of all the state bonds except those hypothecated; and, seventh, whatever amount, with interest and exchange, was actually received by the Real Estate Bank upon the hypothecated bonds in the event they were delivered up to the trustees, or "whatever legal amount shall be found to be due upon the bonds...."[56]

This legal instrument, which Pike recommended to the central board, was a deed of trust, a time-honored means by which insolvent persons and corporations could assign all their assets to trustees for benefit of their creditors and, as in the case of the Real Estate Bank, in a preferred order of payment. Under the deed the trustees became the medium through which the bank's debts were to be collected and all of its assets to be applied to the settlement of its debts.

Pike had very valid legal and practical reasons for recommending a deed of trust. It would put all the available and collectible assets of the Real Estate Bank in the hands of trustees, placing the funds beyond the immediate reach of creditors and noteholders and preventing them from being eaten up by a multiplicity of private suits. More important, it allowed the bank to protect its debtors from ruin by extending to them a reasonable period of eight years in which to settle their debts and save their mortgaged estates from foreclosure, and by extending to the indebted stockholders the life of the charter for this purpose as provided by law. Finally, the deed of assignment offered the most likely prospect in sight of guaranteeing payment of the creditors with as little loss as possible to the state.

As the attorney of the Real Estate Bank, Pike had the responsibility of drafting the deed of assignment. Among the various provisions of the instrument was one that designated him as attorney for the trustees to serve during good behavior at a stipulated annual salary of $2,250 and with an office to be furnished him in the banking house at Little Rock while the building remained "undisposed of." Although Pike was instructed by the central board to write this into the deed, as well as a position for Thomas W. Newton as cashier and secretary to the executive board of the trustees at Little Rock at a yearly salary of $1,200, Pike was afterwards soundly denounced by his political enemies for becoming attorney to the trustees, denunciations, to be sure, that had their origins in Democratic-Whig partisanship.[57] Be that as it may, Pike at the time kept silent on the subject of his attorneyship and salary and proceeded with the task of carrying the trust into execution.[58]

The deed of assignment, becoming effective on April 2, 1842, immediately involved Pike in a prolonged and bitter contest with his former partner. Though Cummins in 1842 was neither a member of the central board of the Real Estate Bank nor a director of the principal bank at Little Rock, whose stockholders had dropped both him and Ashley as directors because of their eternal bickering over control of that banking house, Cummins was never one to hesitate about intruding on the central board where Real Estate Bank matters were concerned.

In March 1842, therefore, just before leaving Little Rock for a few weeks, Cummins impertinently wrote President Carey A. Harris protesting the rumored assignment and declaring the law to be that the central board had no authority to deed the property of the bank. He also suggested giving out to the creditors of the bank the promissory notes of its nonstock debtors, exempting, however, the notes of stockholders—a self-serving recommendation of the first order since Cummins himself owed the Real Estate Bank some $25,000 on his own stock debt.[59]

Pike had, of course, studied his law books carefully before recommending a liquidation by deed of assignment and, holding fast to his considered opinion, told the central board that the decision in the quo warranto case of 1839 had settled the question of the board's power over the whole bank and that, furthermore, the authorities on the law governing deeds of trust were with them. The board accordingly ignored Cummins and voted to have Pike draft the deed of assignment. They also ignored Cummins's proposal of giving out the notes of nonstock debtors, it being their policy to protect all debtors from harassment by giving nonstock debtors a period of eight years from January 1843 to pay their debts and stock debtors the life of the charter as provided in the same.[60]

But Pike had not heard the last from Cummins on the matter of the assignment. A main stipulation of the deed was that the principal bank and branch banks were to turn over all their records, property, and assets to the three trustees at each of the five respective banking houses. The banks at Helena, Columbia, and Van Buren promptly demonstrated a willingness to comply with the deed of assignment, but those at Washington and Little Rock ignored it. At Little Rock a majority of the directors of the principal bank banded together with other opponents of the trust and resolved to not turn over the effects of that banking house to the trustees and to challenge the assignment's legality.[61]

The chief instigator of this movement was William C. Field of Little Rock, a Democratic state director of the principal bank, whose principal objection to the trusteeship seemed to be that no state directors were elected to the trust. He had attended the March meeting of the central board, had voted to put the bank in liquidation by assignment, but, failing to secure the election of the five state directors whom he had nominated, had angrily walked out and declared soon afterwards that he would not "regard the deed."[62] Cummins returned to town furious over news of the assignment and eager for a place in the ranks against the trustees. Field quickly arranged to oblige the angry Whig leader. Judge Benjamin Johnson, the other state director of the principal bank, suddenly resigned, and Governor Yell appointed Cummins in his place.[63]

This political volte-face by Governor Yell was only the beginning of other strange new developments, as Pike was quick to recognize.[64] Colby of the *Times and Advocate*, who was personally calling for the election in 1842 of a legislature of antibankites "without regard to party"—a move that had orthodox Whigs and Democrats alike greatly puzzled—had violently and irresponsibly attacked the assignment as the work of self-interested stockholders and bank debtors. Colby now took up Cummins as a long-lost friend and, overlooking his old enemies more-than-obvious faults as a Real Estate Bank stockholder, bank debtor, and perverse Whig, began lavishing personal praise upon him for his war against the trustees. This reversal in enemies-become-friends was soon climaxed by the revelation that, of all things, Cummins had engaged the hitherto loathed Ashley as cocounsel for the rebellious directors.[65]

Pike's first challenge as attorney for the trustees came when Cummins fathered a set of resolves by the principal bank declaring the deed of assignment fraudulent and invalid and ordering the bank's cashier not to recognize the trustees nor to turn over the bank's effects to them. These resolves contained three principal objections to the deed of assignment: First, they denied the power of the central board to deed the assets of the Real Estate Bank to trustees. Second, they argued that the deed on its face was an invalid contract because there was no second party to it: the members of the central board, this argument ran, had turned over the effects of the entire bank to themselves as trustees, ten of whom had been on the central board. Third, the resolves made the serious allegation that the trustees, being debtors to the Real Estate Bank, were too "interested" in the trust to enable them impartially to administer it.[66]

Shown a copy of the resolves, apparently by Woodruff who was asked to publish them in the *Gazette* for April 27, Pike requested and received permission from Old Buck to publish a rebuttal to them in the same issue. Signing himself "Publius," a signature that fooled no one, Pike gave the public a masterful explanation of "the law" and "the legal rules" governing "cases of Assignment," plus a withering critique of the law contained in "the different positions in the resolutions." To the three principal objections to the deed of assignment contained in the resolves, he answered: first, that the central board certainly did have the power to speak for the whole Real Estate Bank, a question that had been settled by the quo warranto case of 1839; second, that the deed of assignment most surely was a valid contract between two distinct parties—the central board, representing the whole bank, deeded the property to fifteen trustees, acting for themselves as individuals; and, third, that however improper it might appear to the public for members of the central board to deed the bank to some of themselves as trustees, it was lawful for them to do so, and there was ample precedent in corporate law and history for them to do it.[67]

Nevertheless, Pike admitted that he could not defend this last action of the central board on grounds of perfect propriety. But he refused to admit that there was anything wrong or fraudulent about the fact that the trustees, as debtors, were "interested" in the Real Estate Bank and the trust. "They are interested," he pleaded, "in so managing the affairs of the Bank, as to save the greatest amount to the institution, and to wind up its affairs with as little loss as possible, in order to protect their estates from ruin."[68]

He carefully avoided dealing in personalities or in impugning the motives of the refractory Little Rock directors but made it plain that their real objection was not to the liquidation of the Real Estate Bank under a deed of trust but to the fact that more trustees from Little Rock had not been appointed. Indeed, Pike declared that an attempt had been defeated in the central board to put the bank in the hands of trustees from Little Rock. This would never have worked, he argued: Too much "jealousy exists in regard to this city and its citizens, in banking matters, and . . . a measure which had for its object to transfer the whole affairs of the Bank to this place, would never have been sanctioned. It would have produced (I speak in perfect sobriety), riot, confusion, and *bloodshed*."[69]

He had no hesitancy, however, in informing the public that the principal bank directors were wrongfully interfering with the execution of the deed of assignment. There could be, he asserted, "no earthly doubt that in holding to the property with the strong hand, they are acting illegally." The property simply was not theirs. Moreover, if they had desired to proceed legally, they should have already applied to the chancery court at Little Rock to set aside the assignment or, if the present trustees could not legally serve, to have the chancellor remove them and appoint others in their place. "Whenever they do that," wrote Pike, "if I am not grievously mistaken, it will be promptly decided that the deed is legal and valid."[70]

Pike and the trustees were not completely without public support. Denying that he had formed an opinion as to the directory's charges, Woodruff editorially tried to persuade the warring bank parties to settle their dispute without a resort to legal proceedings. A worried stockholder himself with much valuable real property mortgaged to the bank in guarantee of the state bonds, he warned that a continuation of the dispute stood to ruin the Real Estate Bank, to deal serious injury to the stockholders, and to bring heavy monetary losses to the note holders and the community at large. He did, however, venture the view that the deed of assignment, while it might contain errors, was honestly designed to wind up the affairs of the bank without loss to anyone and was not, as alleged, designed to help only the central board and the trustees. He sanely recommended "a spirit of compromise among the contending parties" in order that the rights of both debtors and creditors would be protected.[71]

But Cummins, his pride hurt by Pike's biting criticism of the lack of law behind the directory's case, refused to heed Woodruff's sober advice. Indeed, he was highly incensed that Old Buck had carried Pike's "Publius" article in the same issue of his newspaper with the principal bank's resolves. To placate the ruffled attorney and to preserve his own neutral stance, Woodruff agreed to put out a *Gazette* extra carrying Cummins's reply to Pike over the signature of "One of the People."

Written in his best self-serving "Old Observer" style, Cummins repeated in this extra his arguments against the validity of the deed of assignment and, hot with wrath, pounced upon its author.

> Mr. Pike whose celebrity as a lawyer has been so very precocious as to make his legal acumen to be much overrated, drew this contract. As by it, however, his nest is to be feathered with the real *hard down* of $2250, every year for the next nineteen years, when the charter will expire, he probably thought it was all right.

But it remained "to be seen," warned Cummins, whether the stockholders and the state would submit to this "unparalleled usurpation" or would "vindicate their rights."

Closing, he blustered that he would reserve for another time what "I have to say touching the impropriety, impolicy, injustice, and indelicacy of this conveyance, and the features therein which tend so strongly to corruption."[72]

At this point Colby reprinted all the communications from the *Gazette* in his *Times and Advocate* and took up Cummins's side of the dispute. He praised his "One of the People" letter as "a plain and true statement of the matter." Unlike Woodruff, snapped Colby, "We *have* formed an opinion 'as to which is right and wrong,' and do not wait to see which is the popular side before we give it."[73] To be sure, the politically ambitious Whig editor *had* decided which was "the popular side" of the dispute, and it was not Pike's. "The article signed 'Publius,' it seems to us," judged Colby, "contains as long a string of *legal nonsense*, as we ever saw put together." And he gleefully clipped soon after this what a wit, Francis M. Van Horne of the *Arkansas Intelligencer* at Van Buren, had to say on Pike's article:

> A writer signed "Publius," (Col. [sic] Pike,) comes forth with a long argument citing nine hundred and ninety-nine law books, all of which prove that if the assignment is not legal it may be made so by as many suits in chancery. We have an idea that this same Publius must be of kin to the member of the English Parliament who recommended the confinement of that scourge of crowned heads, Napoleon Bonaparte, in a court of chancery....[74]

Though Cummins and Colby had hammered him hard over his professional and financial stake in the deed of assignment, Pike wisely ignored their lure for further public exchanges. He now applied himself to the work at hand of enforcing the trust against the refractory directors. Failing to persuade Cummins and Ashley to initiate a test of the assignment, which they shrewdly recognized would put the burden of proof upon themselves, Pike at last petitioned Judge John Clendenin of the Pulaski Circuit Court, sitting in chancery, for an injunction against further interference on the part of the principal bank with the execution of the trust. This was in late April. Judge Clendenin, on hearing arguments by Pike for the trustees and by Cummins and Ashley for the directors, refused, May 2, 1842, the injunction on grounds of "want of jurisdiction."[75]

Pike was now prepared to appeal at once to the supreme court for a mandamus ordering Clendenin to issue the injunction. Two choices were open to him in May. He could apply at once to a single judge of the high court or he could wait two months and apply to the full court of three judges at the July 1842 term. Since the only supreme court judge available to him at the moment was Chief Justice Daniel Ringo, whose capricious views of the common law and of equity pleadings he did not trust, Pike had no trouble deciding to delay his application until July when Judges Thomas J. Lacy and Townsend Dickinson would be sitting with Ringo. In the interval, it was rumored, Pike later said, not only that Ringo was against the assignment but also that Pike "feared to bring the question before the Supreme Court, and had abandoned the case."[76]

Cummins, if he fostered such misrepresentations, knew better, and he and Ashley prepared to fight Pike's appeal. Cummins even arranged to have the principal bank declare its office of attorney vacant and to have his law firm, W. and E. Cummins, elected to the post, a rather despotic and ironic act considering the fact that Pike was attorney of the entire Real Estate Bank and would doubtlessly remain so in the event that the deed of assignment was not sustained. Cummins was, of course, allowed to retain newfound friend Ashley as cocounsel in the case.[77]

Still claiming to be neutral, Woodruff found Clendenin's decision surprising, creating, as he expressed it, "a singular state of things" within the Real Estate Bank. Two or three of the branches, he explained to the public, had willingly assented to the trust, while those at Van Buren and Columbia had actually forwarded all their records to the executive committee of the trustees at Little Rock. But the directory of the principal bank at the capital, he went on, had by Clendenin's decision been confirmed in its continued control of that house's effects. Woodruff understood that Pike would apply to the supreme court for a writ of mandamus to require Clendenin to grant the injunction. Meanwhile, Old Buck, remaining silent as to how he felt about Pike's expected appeal, clung to the fading hope that an "amicable arrangement" could still be worked out "for winding up the bank so as to protect her debtors from oppression and ruin—but we do say that a continuance of the contention is most unfortunate for the Bank and the community." The circulation of the bank, he pointed out, could only be hurt by a prolongation of the controversy.[78]

The mandamus case of 1842, when it came on for argument before the supreme court in late July, was a contest between Arkansas's legal giants. Pike was not unmindful of the fact that he would be going up against two of the state's most experienced and most feared lawyers. "Squire" Cummins, so small in size as to be called "Little Billy," was at forty-two and at the height of his mental and physical powers. While not as talented, acute, plausible, or dexterous in argument as Ashley, he was, in Pike's opinion, a far better speaker and had the virtue "of an indefatigability" in pursuit of a cause.

A college graduate who had later completed the course at Judge Tapping Reeve's renowned law school at Litchfield, Connecticut, Ashley was perhaps the best-educated lawyer in Arkansas. Tall, blue-eyed, hawk-nosed, and at fifty-one, heavy of body and completely gray-headed, he was a man of commanding physical presence. Universally called "Colonel Ashley" as a result of his early Arkansas militia rank as lieutenant colonel, Pike thought, however, that he was too portly to look like a "colonel" in a state well stocked with the Kentucky variety. In court Ashley was cool, unexcitable, professionally aloof, while Cummins was in debate, fiery, emotional, dogmatic, sensitive, and animated. If Ashley never admitted to being convinced by an opponent's argument, said Pike of the two men, Cummins never doubted but that he was always right and was incapable of being convinced otherwise. Together, therefore, they were an awesome pair to contend with.[79]

As for Pike, he was confident that his cause in 1842 not only was right and just but also was "fraught with consequences . . . grave to the community at large."[80] He was positive, too, that he had the law and the authorities on his side. These beliefs, as well as his own high confidence in his ability, instilled in him the conviction that he could beat Cummins and Ashley if his case were decided on the basis of law. Yet in his mind he had a gnawing fear that the court, bending to popular pressure and prejudice, might well rule against him and hand down a decision based on the expediency of current bank politics.[81]

There was every justification for Pike's anxiety. Cummins had tried the case before the court of popular opinion and obviously had won, turning the intrabank quarrel over the deed of assignment into a public political debate. And Colby, who since June had been an announced candidate to represent Pulaski County in the house on an antibank "union ticket," had kept the cauldron of public opinion bubbling merrily all spring and summer against the assignment. Indeed, this erratic Whig editor not only had attacked the deed as a fraud and the trustees as public thieves, but also in May had stirred a minor crisis among businessmen in Little Rock by urging a march by the people on the town's two state banks to demand redemption of their depreciated Arkansas money half in specie and half in certificates of deposit bearing interest. Charged by some of his own friends with threatening the banks "with the violence of a thunderbolt, and the destruction of a tornado mob," Colby moderated his position but not his antibank rhetoric, explaining that he merely wished the directors of the banks to "pay out what specie they have in their vaults, before it is consumed by Bank officers, Bank Attorneys, and Bank thieves."[82]

The erstwhile Whig editor likewise openly urged keeping the Real Estate Bank out of the hands of the trustees. "Racoon Fork" of the *Washington Telegraph* had "very properly" asked, Colby remarked in late May, why Governor Yell should not intercede in the assignment case and save the whole property of the bank until the legislature could meet and place its affairs "in proper and legal liquidation."[83]

Though nothing came of Colby's wild suggestions, they did serve to exacerbate public opinion against the trustees and to create the crisis atmosphere in which Pike's case went before the high court of the state in the summer of 1842. As a result of Colby's work, Pike had come to be pictured as the champion of a corporation owned by a wealthy minority who was being charged with mismanagement, corruption, deception, and outright fraud. If Pike correctly viewed the deed of assignment as an honest and sincere effort by the corporation's directors to wind up the hapless bank's business in the best interest of the community at large, Colby and his correspondents had caused the people to come to look on the assignment as a swindle—an attempt by a corrupt few to milk the insolvent institution of whatever assets were left. In consequence, Pike's name became permanently identified with the unpopular Real Estate Bank and its trustees, an association that would bring him endless criticism and trouble.[84]

The details of the complicated legal arguments in the famous mandamus case of 1842 need not concern us here, since our proper subject is Pike's conduct of his case and of himself before the supreme court in what had to be his greatest challenge to date as a lawyer. Knowing this, he left no book untouched, no page unturned, no case or point or rule unconsidered, that he might bring to bear on sustaining the deed of assignment, which he had to do to win his case. Even Ashley paid him a backhanded sort of compliment on his thorough preparation. That guileful attorney drolly told the court that while he had found no case directly against the deed that Pike had found only three or four supporting it, and, therefore, that he ought to succeed against Pike. "'We all know,' as Ashley told the court, 'that such is the industry and research of that gentleman, that if there had been one other case in the books, he would have found it and brought it here.'" Commenting later on Ashley's statement, Pike disclaimed the compliment but thought the lawyer's argument deserved to be noticed "for its originality."[85]

If Pike's research had been exhaustive, his careful organization and logical presentation of his case for the deed was a brilliant piece of legal work. And his reply in rebuttal to the arguments by Cummins and Ashley against the deed was, in the words of an eyewitness, "a masterful effort" by "the greatest law reasoner in the State."[86] This same witness, besides recording his profound regard for Pike's rebuttal, also captured for us something of the tense atmosphere surrounding the trial before the supreme court.

> I listened attentively to his speech. It was a masterly effort—not remarkable, at all, for eloquence, for the lawyer, I am told, has none—but abounding in the richest gems of logic. He laid down premises, which, to me, appeared just and incontrovertible, and his conclusions flowed from them with the ease, brilliance, and power, which always characterize the greatest efforts of the accomplished logician. The speaker waded through a pile of authorities with an equanimity and familiarity indicative of previous application.
>
> "That man has a great mind," said I to the mob man, "Yes," replied he, "what a pity he's on the wrong side. If we have a mob, he will be one of the principal sufferers—the bank could not get along without him. No other lawyer could carry it through such a storm of opposition as he has done. It would, therefore, be necessary to get rid of him."[87]

Pike's worry about the supreme court judges bending to popular pressure was, as it turned out, needless. In a two-to-one split decision, with Chief Justice Ringo dissenting on grounds of a lack of jurisdiction by the lower court but not on the validity of the deed (on which he refrained from expressing his opinion), the court sustained the deed of assignment. It issued a "preemptory mandamus" commanding Judge Clendenin to take equity jurisdiction of the case, ordering him to grant the injunction and requiring him to see to it that the effects of the principal bank be immediately surrendered to the trustees.[88]

Judge Lacy's opinion, which when printed would fill fifty-one pages of Pike's 1842 *Arkansas Reports*, followed Pike's cogent arguments so closely that it amounted to a repetition of them. Lacy sustained Pike in every single contention against Cummins and Ashley, upholding the power of the central board to deed the entire Real Estate Bank, affirming the legality of the deed in ruling that the central board and the trustees constituted two distinct parties to the contract, and denying every allegation of fraud in the provisions of the assignment. The judge's ruling against the charges of fraud—expressed in strong, clear language—was as much a rebuke to Cummins and Ashley as it was a compliment to Pike:

> The deed, upon its face, carries, to our minds, strong and persuasive evidence, that it is not only free from the imputation of fraud, but that it was executed in good faith, and under the firm belief that it would cure the evils to be remedied, which were that its creditors should be secured and paid, its circulation called in and canceled, and its debtors protected against injury and oppression. It proposed to do this, because the Bank was unable to meet its immediate demands, to pay specie upon its notes, or to discharge the interest upon the bonds of the State. These objects were, certainly, just and equitable, and the reasons adduced in support of them, cogent and conclusive.[89]

XV

Blows to Take as Well as Blows to Give

PIKE HAD SUSTAINED the legality of the deed of assignment and, in the month that followed the supreme court decision, wrested control of the principal bank from Cummins and its angry directors. He did not accomplish this easily or painlessly. Governor Yell, throwing the weight of his office into the fight against the assignment, at the end of August requested Cummins and Ashley, as attorneys for the principal bank, to move the supreme court for a rehearing of the case. The motion was promptly denied, and Judge Dickinson, delivering the court opinion for himself and Ringo (Lacy being absent), severely chastised Yell for executive interference with the independence of the judiciary.[1]

Battling still more fiercely, Cummins and Ashley next undertook to persuade Judge Clendenin of the Pulaski circuit court, sitting in chancery, to disobey the appellate authority of the supreme court, and, thus, to refuse Pike the injunction ordered by the high court's mandamus. This farcical legal procedure ended in failure but not until feelings were further exacerbated and not until after Judge Clendenin threatened to throw out of his court a scurrilous cross-bill penned and filed by Cummins. The angry judge allowed Ashley, red-faced with embarrassment, to withdraw it. "Thus departed the glory of the cross-bill," reported the *Gazette*, "and with it some of the finest specimens of chancery eloquence, which have ever been written since the days of Bacon!"[2]

Meanwhile, Cummins began denouncing in Colby's *Times and Advocate* the "unaccountable act" of Judges Lacy and Dickinson in legalizing the deed of assignment. Writing over the signature "X.," Cummins declared the "whole mass of the community" and every "legal man" in the state save for "the Attorney for the Trustees" were opposed to the decision. He also threatened that "the approaching Legislature" would find itself duty bound "to look into the conduct of these judges, and see that the laws of the land be thoroughly enforced."[3] Pike believed Cummins's attack to be an attempt to break down his professional reputation in the state and his attack on Lacy and Dickinson to be an effort to destroy the independence of the judiciary. Seeking vindication, he replied in the *Gazette* to Cummins without naming him except to say: "The paternity of the article cannot be doubted. No one could have written so violent a tirade, except one of the counsel employed in the case."[4]

Signing himself "V. V.," meaning apparently *Vice Versa*, Pike began by expressing regret that there was to be found in the community any man who would publicly assault and attempt to destroy the independence of the judiciary and that there was any editor so heedless of public responsibility as to publish it. He then defended the court decision in the mandamus case, cited legal support for it among some of the best lawyers in the state, denounced the selfish and illegal act of the directors for trying to retain control of the principal bank, declared the people were likely to agree that fifteen trustees from across the state were as competent to manage the liquidation of the Real Estate Bank under the jurisdiction of Judge Clendenin's chancery court as a clique of four or five self-appointed men at Little Rock, and ridiculed the Yell-Cummins-Ashley-Field cabal to address Lacy from office and to defeat Dickinson at the approaching legislative session.[5]

Pike closed his lengthy reply with a few pointed words of advice to this foursome. They might as well understand, he warned, "that attacks upon the court will not be suffered with impunity." If continued, the people would be informed of the motives which induced them to oppose the deed of assignment and "to desire to control the bank." There would be in such a conflict "blows to take as well as blows to give." He did not allude, he said, to two or three of the directors. "I mean especially those who have owed the bank for years, and never in their lives paid it a dollar." "If this new coalition of old enemies suddenly converted into warm friends, desires now to commence public war on the judiciary, they had better supply themselves with defensive armor," was Pike's final word.[6]

Pike's article drew from Colby, who identified V. V. as "alias the Attorney of the Real Estate Bank Assignees and the special defender of Judges Lacy and Dickinson," the editorial charge that Pike was "writing letters" to different candidates for the legislature urging them to pledge themselves not to go against the two justices in the coming session. "Is he confident the opinion is wrong, and therefore afraid of *public* opinion," Colby asked, "or is he *deeply interested* in having these two judges remain on the bench?"[7]

Pike's V. V. article also drew from Cummins a second crisp article. The people of Arkansas, he declared, would soon "show V. V. that it is no crime to show corruption in a judicial officer." "Mr. V. V.," had no doubt alarmed the public "very much by his threat to show men's reasons for opposing his assignment, and to expose their private affairs," Cummins continued. He wished him to know that he would "find all persons concerned very ready to settle any *private affairs* he may be concerned in with them of every character." Finally, Little Billy assured V. V. that he could rest assured Governor Yell would "answer fully" to the people for all the charges made against his excellency.[8]

Since Cummins was determined to continue his crusade against Lacy and Dickinson in Colby's paper, Pike now began an exchange with his former partner that lasted all through October and into November. His motive, besides seeking personal vindication, was to educate the public on the history of the Real Estate Bank and to try to forestall a legislative vendetta against Lacy and Dickinson. He accordingly published in the *Gazette* over his signature V. V. a full account of the origin and organization of the bank; elaborated at length on how Cummins and Ashley, the "Caesar and Pompey of this little republic" the principal bank, had fought each other for personal control of it and in the process had kept the entire Real Estate Bank convulsed in constant litigation; gave the intimate legal history of the quo warranto proceeding of 1839 that had sustained the power of the central board as the governing agency of the Real Estate Bank system; explained how the central board in early 1842 had come to make the deed of assignment; expounded and defended the supreme court's decision in the recent mandamus case; and buttressed his defense of that decision by soliciting and publishing the personal opinions of Chancellor James Kent of New York and Associate Justice Joseph Story of the U.S. Supreme Court, two of America's foremost authorities on chancery law, who fully concurred in the opinion of the Arkansas court.[9]

For good measure, Pike prepared and printed a pamphlet containing their opinions, and distributed it to the members of the gathering legislature. He also presented their opinions in the final number of his V. V. series, which appeared in the *Gazette* of November 16, just after the legislature assembled. In this same number he was permitted to announce that Judge Benjamin Johnson of the federal district court at Little Rock concurred fully in the state supreme court's opinion and also that George S. Yerger, "the most eminent lawyer in Mississippi," likewise concurred.[10]

The exchange between Pike and Cummins over the assignment case and the destiny of Lacy and Dickinson meanwhile got caught up in the congressional campaign of 1842, which reached its climax the first week of September with Colby's announcement that Cummins "at the request and solicitation of prominent Whigs" had become his party's candidate for the national House of Representatives.[11] Little Billy entered the race because Edward Cross, standing for a third term, had drawn three independent Democratic opponents, and it appeared likely to Cummins that a Whig would have an excellent chance for a plurality and a victory. But, as in 1838, fate was unkind to Cummins. His announcement prompted two of Cross's Democratic opponents quickly to withdraw, leaving the field to Cross, Cummins, and an ineffective but disgruntled Democrat, Lemuel D. Evans of Washington County, whose chief claim to the office was that he had entered the race before Cross, had not expected Cross to run, and had blamed Ashley and Woodruff and the rest of the Little Rock junto for putting Cross in the field.[12]

The main contest was, therefore, between Cummins, who approved the 1841 Whig repeal of the Independent Treasury and favored reestablishment of a national bank, and Cross, who opposed a national bank and supported Democratic reenactment of the Independent Treasury. They both had backed establishment of the state banks in Arkansas and both had become stockholders in the Real Estate Bank, which was a political liability to each of them in the antibank atmosphere of 1842 in Arkansas. Consequently, they both professed to be opposed to the state banks in 1842 and favored winding them up, the chief difference between them that fall being the momentous political question of which one had come out first against the state's banks. Much energy and printer's ink was expended over this ludicrous issue. From the beginning, however, especially after two of the Democrats dropped out of the race, the advantage seemingly lay with Cross whose endorsement of the Independent Treasury had more voter appeal in Arkansas than Cummins's declaration for a national bank.[13]

The *Gazette* editor, Cyrus W. Weller, whom Woodruff had hired to take charge of his paper beginning July 13, 1842, ably backed Cross while scorning Cummins. The Whigs, according to Weller, had laid a careful plan to defeat Cross by backing one of his Democratic opponents, but "the every-busy little Cummins" had dashed his party's hopes by putting himself in the race. So astonished and so vexed were the Whigs at Little Rock at Billy's rash act, allowed Weller, that they had "resolved not to vote for the intruder."[14]

Weller scoffed, too, at the new political friendship between Cummins and Colby, who himself was seeking a house seat in the legislature on a nonpartisan, antibank pledge. He especially laughed at Colby's efforts to foist Billy off on the public as an enemy of the state banks. A lawyer himself, Weller editorially condemned Cummins's despicable attack on Judges Lacy and Dickinson in the Real Estate Bank mandamus case. Proclaiming the high court's decision as having settled "the legality of the assignment," the Democratic editor denounced Little Billy's attempt in the circuit court "to interrupt" that decision. Weller cautiously refrained from taking sides in the quarrel over the rumored defeat of Dickinson and the forced retirement of Lacy but did say that the movement allegedly was "to appease the wrath of such bank divinities as WILLIAM CUMMINS and others" and declared himself to be skeptical "in regard to the rectitude of conduct, which is said to be characteristic of the entire anti-assignment denomination."[15]

With his former law partner and Colby bearing the brunt of Weller's editorial blows, Pike enjoyed something of a favorable press in the *Gazette* that fall. Weller printed his V. V. articles in reply to Cummins, and in a memorable article of his own the second week of September, entitled "Colloquial Beauties," the Democratic editor made Pike's version of why Cummins was warring on the assignment the central theme of his piece. This Weller article, presenting "a supposed conversation" between Cummins and Colby, revealed the terms of an alleged "bargain" struck between the two former Whig enemies by which Cummins agreed to "apologize for certain things" in the past if Colby would "write in favor of my being a Congressman."[16]

The agreement reached, Cummins then instructed a still somewhat reluctant Colby as to how to handle his "connexion with the local banks." Weller had Cummins say:

> You must go it blind ... about my connexion with the local banks. You must not say that I am largely indebted to the Real Estate Bank. You know we have always considered that a Whig bank, until it became unpopular. There is one thing you must urge in my favor, and that is my opposition to the Real Estate Bank assignment, and my abuse of the Supreme Court, on the streets.
>
> Ed.— That's a ticklish business. Every body about Little Rock knows the reason why you are opposed to the assignment.
>
> Cum.—Ah! Indeed! What is that?—[*with a knowing grin.*]
>
> Ed.— [*Grinning, also.*]—Why, sir, if the Deed of Assignment can be bursted up, and the Directors of the Principal Bank get hold of the money again, they will constitute you their attorney, at two or three thousand dollars a year.
>
> Cum.—[*Laughing scientifically.*]—Ah! Ha! ha! ha! I wish that would be the case. I would get well paid, then, for my big speech in the Supreme Court, against the assignment.
>
> Ed.— You are inconsistent. You cry down with the Real Estate Bank, although you are a State Director in it; and the whole object of your cry is, to get the Local Board re-instated, that they may have a chance to employ you as their attorney. You are death on the assignment, now, and the conduct of the Bank generally; but, when you become attorney in Pike's place, you will eulogise the Bank incessantly!!

Cum.— True—but I am a candidate for Congress—I must have a hobby—the banks are the most unpopular things in the State—I will oppose the banks and get the people to vote for me.

Ed.— But what in the name of sense, can a member of Congress do with the banks?

Cum.— Nothing. I admit—but the people don't know that—half of the voters can't read, and the other half are not as intelligent as we lawyers and editors.

Ed.— You are a plausible humbugger.

Cum.— Ah! But you must not write what you think.

Ed.— No—certainly not—I will merely say that you were opposed to the banks in 1838—(the reason was, though, because they would not employ you as their attorney—but I won't say that), and Cross was in favor of the banks at the same time. I will also say that Cross has not done any thing for us since he has been in Congress.

Cum.— Well—go it—you are a more clever fellow than I had supposed. Can't you praise me a little in the next paper? Can't you say, for instance, I am a great lawyer, smart man, and good judge of great national questions?

Ed.— No, Cummins. I can't go the figure quite so strong. I don't want to say any thing that nobody would believe.

Cum.— Ah! Well—good-morning, Colby.

Ed.— [*With great coolness.*] Good day, sir.

Finis.— Cummins departs and writes an address to "the whigs of Arkansas," which Colby altered a little, and put in his paper as an editorial.[17]

Weller's prediction in September that the Whigs of the state would not unite behind Little Billy proved, as it turned out, quite groundless. Election day, on October 3, which saw Cross carry the state with 9,413 votes to 5,315 for Cummins and 1,686 for Evans, found rank-and-file Whigs across Arkansas turning out for Cummins in customary fashion.[18] Colby crowed that Cummins had defeated Cross in Pulaski County, a standard brag since the county uniformly voted the Whig ticket, and that Billy had, without conducting a statewide campaign as Fowler had in 1840, received almost as many votes as Fowler.[19]

This, indeed, was true. Yet in analyzing still further "the late election for Congress" in the cool light of All Hollow's Eve, Colby indirectly acknowledged that matters had not gone smoothly among Arkansas Whigs that fall. Some "pretended Whigs, and some who style themselves *leaders,*" had not bestirred themselves for Cummins. "This treachery to the party," declared Colby, "prevented much activity in certain portions of the State." There were, besides, "several individuals whose course in the late election" the Whig editor promised to comment on more fully "at a proper time." These heretics had "labored to direct votes to Judge Cross, and against the Whig candidate." If such men wished "to go over to the other party, the Whigs can very well spare them; for they have always manifested a determination to rule or ruin the Whig party," said Colby.[20]

So far as is known, Colby never carried out his threat to name the "several individuals" who allegedly had worked to throw Whig votes to Cross in 1842. Hence, we have no way of knowing whether Pike was numbered among those guilty of such action. To be sure, Pike was estranged from Cummins and had every reason in the world neither to work nor to vote for him that fall, but Pike probably did not work nor vote for Cross, whose opposition to a national bank made him unacceptable to our Whig leader. Yet there could not be much doubt, now, that Cummins and Colby had become personally reconciled and were warring on Pike over the bank assignment and over his defense of Judges Lacy and Dickinson and that Colby's pointed remarks about traitorous Whigs were aimed at Pike, among others.[21]

Pike and other Pulaski Whigs separated as they were from the Cummins-Colby faction, had every reason to be puzzled in 1842 over just who it was who was attempting to "rule or ruin" the local Whig Party. Now that the *Arkansas Star* was dead, Colby owned the only Whig organ at Little Rock, the *Times and Advocate*. But he used it in the state election that year to promote a "union movement" of farmers and mechanics who would, as he hoped, nominate candidates for the legislature unconnected with the state banks and pledged to go for winding them up. Charging that state bankites controlled Pulaski's Whig and Democratic Parties and, besides, that the national parties and national political issues had nothing whatever to do with electing the state legislature, Colby's union movement amounted to a revolt of antibankites in the county against the leaders of both major parties.[22]

This was a most anomalous position on Colby's part, for he continued to speak out simultaneously as a national Whig—denouncing John Tyler's treachery to the party, praising Henry Clay, and opposing Arkansas's solid Democratic delegation in Congress. For example, when the state's Democratic editors lied that the state's Whigs were responsible for the rotten condition of the state banks and denied any Democratic culpability, the fiery Colby quickly set the record straight. The banks were, he said truthfully, the joint liability of Whigs and Democrats, and, having been mismanaged, should be liquidated.[23]

Yet Colby's local antibank revolt, as it turned out, could not be separated from national politics, and hurt the Whigs while playing into the hands of Democrats. His movement, which began in the spring of 1842, was fairly well organized, apparently, at the township level in Pulaski and resulted in a county nominating convention which met at Little Rock on June 18. The delegates, torn by doubt about abandoning the two established parties in favor of an "Anti-Bank party" ticket, voted to make no nominations. But showing their distrust for local bankite party leaders, they resolved against any regular party nominations and called instead for individual candidates to announce and run on their personal merit for the legislature.[24]

Accordingly at the end of the meeting on June 18, Colby, Middleton H. Hill, and Jared C. Martin announced to the gathering their respective candidacies for Pulaski's three house seats, and Richard C. Byrd, the incumbent, declared for the county's single seat in the senate. Since Colby and Hill were Whigs and Martin and Byrd were quondam Democrats, since all four favored legislative liquidation of the state banks, and since Colby and Hill and the independent but popular Democrat Byrd all favored a national bank, this foursome's simultaneous announcement at the antibank convention gave some appearance of being the "union ticket" that Colby may have hoped would be nominated at the meeting. Barring that, he seemingly hoped the ticket would win recognition and be supported as such.[25]

The Democrats of Pulaski, agreeable to the spirit expressed at the antibank meeting on June 18, dropped plans for a county nominating convention announced for June 30, but only after two antibank Democrats, Peter T. Crutchfield and James Fletcher, put themselves in the race for house seats. This, as Woodruff of the *Gazette* explained, gave the Democrats of the county a solid four-man legislative slate—Martin, Fletcher, Crutchfield, and Senator Byrd—and rendered it unnecessary to proceed with the party meeting called for June 30. Though two other Democrats, acting on their own, afterwards announced—one for the house and the other for the senate—Woodruff's paper continued to back the ticket named above.[26]

This partisan Democratic strategy isolated Colby and Hill, who were also personally unsatisfactory to many of the Pulaski Whigs. Consequently, four additional Whigs—John W. Cocke, Richard C. Fletcher, John F. Gorham, and John K. Taylor—in due course announced themselves for house seats, and William Scott Sr., likewise a Whig, declared himself for the senate. By election day, therefore, ten candidates in all, six Whigs and four Democrats, were contending for the county's three house seats; and a Whig and two Democrats were contesting for her single seat in the senate.[27]

Unlike the veteran Woodruff, who sagely put the weight of his paper behind a Democratic legislative ticket of his choice, the beginner Colby remained stubbornly opposed to endorsing a Whig slate. Freewheeling as ever, the Whig editor blindly insisted that the voters should select from among all the candidates, regardless of party affiliation, the four individuals most likely to go for depriving both state banks of their charters and putting the institutions into liquidation. The Real Estate Bank's charter provided, he declared, the test by which the voters could judge a candidate's true grit, for even "many honest anti-Bank men" doubted, he said, that the legislature could deprive that "swindling" corporation of its charter. "Such men are," he warned, "more to be feared than the open advocates of the Bank." Cast no vote for any candidate who would not pledge himself to deprive the Real Estate Bank of its charter and to put it into proper liquidation, was Colby's advice.[28]

By late July, Weller of the *Gazette*, Woodruff's hired editor, expressed alarm lest Colby's "coy use" of antibankism might not lull antibank Democrats into electing Whigs to the legislature not only in Pulaski but in other counties as well. Senator Sevier would be before the coming legislature for reelection, and it would not do, Weller pointed out, for Democrats to elect antibank Whigs to seats under the guise that, as Colby maintained, the national parties had nothing to do with electing legislators. Senator Sevier's return to Washington after March 4, 1843, depended upon the Democrats controlling the next legislature; therefore, Weller asked Democrats to vote for no candidate for a seat who would not pledge himself to go for the colonel's return to the U.S. Senate for a new six-year term.[29]

On August 1 at Little Rock, John W. Cocke declared in a speech that if elected to the house he would vote for the reelection of Senator Sevier, who himself was not present in Arkansas since Congress was still in session. Cocke's cautiously worded statement was a parody of sorts on the muddled status of the Arkansas Whig Party that summer and on the strange pattern the Pulaski legislative canvass had taken under Colby's whimsical direction. Cocke explained that he understood "the Whigs of Pulaski

County did not design to run candidates for the Legislature on national party questions," that it was a principle of the legislative campaign that only state and local issues should be discussed, that he personally believed the agitation of party feuds between Whigs and Democrats was most "pernicious," that he thought Senator Sevier was the most popular Democrat in the state and no Whig could ever beat him, and, therefore, that if elected he would vote to return Sevier to the Senate. But almost as if he had had tongue in cheek in reciting the above points, Cocke closed by proclaiming himself to be "still a true and uncompromising Whig—that if the Whigs of Pulaski required the candidate to run on the strength of their whigism or democracy—he would boldly take the party ground and vote for a Whig to fill the place of Mr. Sevier." He believed, however, that national politics had been, and should continue to be, discarded from the canvass, and "that the candidates must stand or fall on their own merits or demerits." Hence, he would act in keeping with that belief and conduct himself accordingly.[30]

Declaring that he had already "thrown a bomb-shell" into Colby's ranks by calling for Sevier pledges, Weller now threw in a second. He printed in the *Gazette* a letter from one of Cocke's Little Rock Whig friends, who told Weller that Colby's recent editorial against Whig pledges to Sevier was a dirty deed. It was executed, the writer said, with foreknowledge of Cocke's intention to announce publicly for Sevier. Cocke's friend then charged Colby "with the *selfish* and *malignant* intent" of injuring the Kentuckian's prospects for election. Calling upon "all true Whigs" to spurn Colby's "invidious attack" upon an "honorable opponent," the writer bluntly warned the Whig editor to "Let Mr. Cocke alone." "If not," he threatened, "I know much, dear friend, that sickens, and I'll see you again."[31]

What chance there now was for Whig unity went down the drain of intraparty feuding. Colby shamelessly allowed Cocke to be attacked in the *Times and Advocate*, in an anonymous guest editorial, as a fence straddler, as a man who professed belief in the Whig doctrine of a national bank and sound national currency but who had now pledged himself to vote for Senator Sevier, the inveterate foe of a national bank. Having permitted this national issue to be injected into the local canvass against a fellow Whig, Colby simultaneously furled the flag of truce between Whigs and Democrats in the contest for the legislature.[32]

The Whig editor blamed the *Gazette* for this unhappy turn of events, repeating the charge that Weller had put Sevier's reelection above the interests of the state in general by insisting that all candidates, if elected, pledge themselves to vote for the senator's reelection. Henceforth, declared Colby, the legislative contest would be waged on the issues of Sevier and "depreciated currency" versus a national bank candidate for the Senate, of establishing a national currency in "the place of our depreciated one," and of liquidating the state banks. "If the people prefer Col. Sevier and the present currency, or no currency at all, to a national currency, without him, we say let them have it," concluded Colby.[33]

Unfortunately, the Whigs of Pulaski were too divided to do what was now needed, that is, to meet, compromise their differences in face of Democratic solidarity, agree on a Whig legislative ticket, and nominate a candidate to oppose Sevier. They attempted such a meeting, but there is no record that it ever assembled, and, if held, it certainly failed in its purpose.[34] By election day the quixotic Colby had reverted to his earlier nonpartisan stance. In Weller's last issue of the Gazette before the polling date, that confident editor, noting the Whig "quarreling among themselves," called upon Pulaski's Democrats to unite upon Martin, Crutchfield, James Fletcher, and Senator Byrd. "We can elect them," he said, "without the least difficulty."[35] Though this was merely sound political strategy, Colby denounced it. "The candidates have all, Whigs and Democrats, been running on their own merits, and not on the party question," he naively retorted, "and we hope they will continue so to run, notwithstanding the attempted dictation of the Gazette."[36]

Election day, on October 3, was a disaster for the Whig legislative candidates. Two years before, in October 1840, the united party had, with Colby temporarily bridled and Pike's central committee directing the cause with the assistance of the Star, sent a solid Whig delegation—Cummins, Bertrand, and Gibson—to the house. Now, in 1842, with the Whigs splintered and dividing their votes among six party members for the county's three house seats, only the popular John W. Cocke was elected to a seat. The other two house seats went to Democrats Peter T. Crutchfield and Jared C. Martin. Richard Byrd, polling the largest vote of any of the legislative candidates, swamped his two opponents for the senate to give the Democrats a three-to-one majority in Pulaski's legislative delegation.[37]

As for Colby, who polled 294 votes and ran sixth among the ten house candidates and fourth among the six Whig candidates, he had by his divisive tactics helped assure the Democratic triumph. Having the last word, since he owned the only Whig organ, he declared the election a Democratic sweep. Cocke was a Democrat, he proclaimed, because he had pledged himself to vote Democratic on the only party test that would come before the fast-approaching legislature—the reelection of Colonel Sevier.[38] Colby also had a word about his own defeat. He felt proud, he allowed, that a clergyman and the working men of Little Rock had voted for him, while "the would-be aristocrats and those that live without work" had voted against him. He thus consoled himself: "With the clergy and honest working man in his favor, who would not rather be beaten, than be elected by the votes of a mushroom aristocracy, speculators, and Bank officers!"[39]

As the next few months would reveal, Pike had been gravely concerned about Colby's destructive party leadership in the legislative campaign of 1842. He would, in due course, act to establish a sound Whig paper at Little Rock. For the moment, however, the legislative session was at hand, and he was too preoccupied with business to come before that body to apply himself to the problem of the divided local party.

XVI

Saving the Real Estate Bank Assignees

THE FOURTH GENERAL ASSEMBLY of the State of Arkansas, meeting from November 7, 1842, to February 4, 1843, was the most important session to date in Pike's experience. Elected at the height of the antibank reaction in the state, in October 1842, it contained many new faces. "Scarcely an individual of us who was in the legislature of 1837 [1836] when the banks in the state were chartered is now permitted to occupy a public station," wrote Anthony Davies, a Real Estate Bank trustee, in early December; "we are left in fact perfectly powerless."[1]

As usual Democrats controlled both chambers, outnumbering the Whigs fifteen to five in the senate and forty-one to twenty-five in the house.[2] Party affiliation would mean little apparently, for Democrats and Whigs alike were pledged to liquidating both state banks and for reelecting Senator Sevier. A majority of the members of both parties appeared to be determined, too, to defeat Judge Dickinson and to address Judge Lacy from office.[3]

As attorney for the Real Estate Bank trustees, Pike that fall was giving much thought and time to the expected movement in the legislature to investigate the bank, to try to revoke its state charter, to ignore or set the assignment aside, and to place the institution's liquidation in the hands of either new legislative trustees or state receivers. It would be his duty to defend the assignees and to explain the trusteeship to the hostile governor and legislators, that is, that under the present trustees the bank was already in the process of being liquidated under as safe and sound a system as the law and the wisdom of English and American jurisprudence and experience could provide. If successful, he would be able to convince the legislature that a state liquidation act was not only unnecessary but also a needless waste of legislative energy and time. He was not yet prepared to say so publicly in behalf of the trustees, but he saw them, under the law and under the assignment fully entitled to the property and assets of the bank, just as he saw the state as not being in the slightest degree entitled to seize the property of the bank. Moreover, he saw the trustees themselves as being free of any scandal attached to the bank management prior to the assignment, and he had no intention of recommending to them that they obey a state liquidation law that should replace them as trustees.

Pike's dander was up over the renewed fight against the assignment, and he prepared to do battle to sustain it before the legislature or, failing that, in the higher courts of the land. Governor Yell had already interfered to try to get the supreme court to rehear the assignment case and was said to be smoldering with suppressed anger over Judge Dickinson's reprimanding him for trying to compromise the independence of the judiciary in the matter. It was widely rumored and even discussed in the press that Yell had boasted that he would "beat" Dickinson whose term was up and who would be before the 1842 legislature for a renewal, and that he would move to purge Judge Lacy for having the legislature address him from office under the 1836 Constitution.

Expecting the worse from Yell and the legislature, Pike as early as August sent copies of the deed of assignment and the full record of the case together with the supreme court's decision to Chancellor James Kent of New York State and to Justice Joseph Story of the U.S. Supreme Court, then the two leading authorities in the country on civil jurisprudence and corporate law. He asked each of them to express his opinion on the case. Both declared the bank assignment valid and sustained the state high court's decision. Pike then had copies of Kent's and Story's letters printed in pamphlet form, adding for good measure the concurring opinion of U.S. district judge of Arkansas Benjamin Johnson and and had them laid on the desks of the members of the legislature on opening day, November 7, 1842, the day before Governor Yell's biennial message was to be read for him to a joint session.[4]

This maneuver, Pike thought, had caused the anticipated charge "from the gubernatorial blunderbuss" to be drawn, and had "certainly operated a dreadful discomfiture of all that small fry of small lawyers and small politicians, who expected to thunder by day against the decision." But just how effective Pike's piece of strategy was is dubious. He later claimed credit for it for blocking Governor Yell from openly denouncing either Dickinson or Lacy in his message to the general assembly and for preventing the governor from making a harsher attack on the Real Estate Bank assignment. But the fact is, as we shall shortly see, that the legislature nevertheless cooperated with Governor Yell in chastening the court.[5]

Meanwhile, Pike's presumed lobbying activity came under attack from Colby from the opening day of the legislative session. On the day the legislators assembled, on Monday, November 7, 1842, the Whig editor gleefully put them and the public on warning as what to expect from Pike during the session. He allowed as to how he had received a communication on the previous Saturday morning, the author of which was "left to conjecture; and whether there is any truth in what he says, or whether to hoax somebody, we are equally ignorant." But as the communication could "do no harm, if it does no good," Colby had decided to publish the piece "as we received it, without vouching for its correctness." It read:

> Mr. Colby:—I picked up this morning in the street a small bundle of papers in a very good handwriting, but so blotted and torn I could not get beginning or end of them, or what they were intended for, but they seemed to be letters and memorandums. Some things are so strange. I think it would be well to publish something of their contents, to let people have a hint of what is doing.
> The first I can read is a set of eatables, drinkables, sic.:
> Champagne, 4 doz.,
> Brandy,
> Whiskey,
> 1 cask, (I think hams, but it is not plain.)
> Parties, dinners, snacks, are plain, but the number is blotted out.
> Then there is something about Lacy and Dickinson. "Burnt brandy will not save them" is pretty plain—then "unless we keep down investigation" is plain—

then it goes on "say to the members there is nothing in all the noise—the public is not interested—it is a private quarrel to get possession of the Bank. If they begin to look into the conduct of our two friends on the bench, everything is lost—all must act together to prevent this—all our friends must be here early, and make the proper impressions on the members, (some body will give parties,[)]" but it is so blotted, the name cannot be read. "Good eating and drinking are the best arguments" is very plain[.] "Entertain well and we can do as we please—a few thousand is nothing to us all if we get every thing settled quietly. Tell our friends to use their money freely—money must not be spared. The salaries are splendid for these times, and besides that two million of dollars is a large sum—we can have plenty of opportunities to make up any outlays—another thing, more salaries can be made. The *Gazette* is with us and will defend all we do at a proper time. It can control the State. Another thing, our friends should not forget with this Bank in our hands we will have influence enough in the State to control some of the best and highest offices—our friends should know these things and reflect—of course our friends will not be forgotten."

Another piece, very much torn, says something about Judge Lacy—that he will be here—has a room provided—will see much company—he will have great effect—invite the members to his room—he can shed tears like a child about any thing—he will affect their feelings.

From all this I infer there must be something ahead new to me at least, as I have not yet been in town for some time, and perhaps new to others—I therefore send you all I can pick out of it. I shall not be in town again for some time.

OLD SNOOKS

P.S. A remark which we heard yesterday, induces us to believe there may be some truth in the above. The remark was that a certain gentleman deeply interested in the assignment of the Real Estate Bank, wrote to a Stockholder informing him of the assignment, and ordering a quantity of his best champagne, which he knew to be superior to any in the State. It is an old saying, and perhaps a true one in this case, that "straws show which way the wind blows." The names of the parties were not mentioned.—Ed.[6]

Colby's mischievous piece of "inside" information could well have been the product of his own imagination, although it might well have been, as he craftily implied, the result of a bit of carelessness on Pike's part in dropping the packet of letters and notes that Old Snooks so luckily had stumbled upon in the street. Yet Colby was the one person who was accusing the *Gazette*, under Weller's editorship, of being with Pike and the trustees in the assignment case, and he was well acquainted with the art of legislative lobbying and the consummate skill brought to that ancient practice by Pike, who had acquired his knowledge, in part at least, from observing Crittenden and Ashley and other well-known wizards of the craft at the Rock; hence, the Whig editor could have been engaging in mere speculation when he so cleverly described Pike's frenzied efforts to see that the friends of the Real Estate Bank and of Lacy and Dickinson should be on hand with food and drink and parties to woo the hostile members of the legislature.[7]

Colby's meddlesome article, whether written by Old Snooks or himself, was nevertheless on target. The legislative session was but three weeks old when a worried Colby correspondent, signing himself "Observer," confessed that he was highly uncertain whether the legislature would do anything in regard to the banks. The public wanted the banks wound up, but Observer feared that bankite legislators, of whom there were several, would put their own private interests ahead of the public's, that they were unlikely to work to expose themselves and their bankite friends. "The Bankites... have their parties nightly," he said. "The poor debtor is sued without one grain or mixture of mercy, while the rich one is invited to the champagne frolics, and egad! the invitation extends to both Houses of the General Assembly...."[8]

Our "Observer" hardly had a clear view of the hostility of the legislature toward the banks. In the first place, Governor Yell in his message of November 8 furiously attacked both banks and called on the legislature to liquidate them. The State Bank, he indicated, was chartered by and owned by the state, was a public corporation, and there was not the slightest doubt that the legislature had the power to put it into liquidation.[9]

He also believed the Real Estate Bank to be a public corporation and subject to the will of the legislature. Singling out the assignment for special attention, Yell declared that it had placed the assets and their management beyond the control of the state government and this had the effect of throwing back upon the state and the taxpayers the immediate responsibility of paying accrued and future interest on the state bonds before the trustees as required under the assignment, could pay. "We are left either to suffer in credit," growled the governor, "or oppress the citizens, to sustain a worthless corporation."[10]

There was a way, however, to avoid taxing the people, which he opposed, and making the bank assets available to pay interest on the bonds. His premises were, Yell repeated, that the act of assignment was unauthorized by the Real Estate Bank's charter, that the charter itself had not created a private corporation conferring individual rights, and moreover that the bank had willfully perverted facts in its last report to the legislature [1840] concealing the fact that it had hypothecated five hundred state bonds at far less than face value and at what amounted to a fraud upon the state and another violation of its charter. If correct in these propositions the conclusion was unavoidable, Yell, an ex-territorial judge, pressed, that the act of assignment "was illegal without sanction of law, and void."[11]

The only indication that the willful governor had noticed Pike's stratagem of printing the Kent-Story-Johnson opinions on the assignment case was his caution to the legislature at this point that he might be in error upon his "opinion in relation to the power of the Legislature to act upon the charter of the Real Estate Bank." "I am disposed to distrust my own judgement, upon legal questions, when it conflicts with the opinions of some of the most enlightened and wisest jurists of our country," said the governor in a rare attempt at modesty. The state supreme court, he reminded the legislature, had decided that the assignment was legal, and it was reasonable to infer that the court would likewise "decide that the assignment did not work a forfeiture of the Bank charter, for the Bank cannot be presumed to have forfeited its charter, in doing a legal act." Accordingly, the legislature might well doubt its "power or policy" of legislating "some remedy for the existing evils."[12]

If this were true, the governor suggested, as a minimum, that the legislature appoint "a committee, or commissioner, to examine and take an inventory of all assets and liabilities of the Bank, and to report immediately to the Legislature" that the lawmakers might have data to govern their future action. The governor found it difficult to let go of his subject. The interest of the state demanded, at least, that some summary remedy be enacted to control the action of the Real Estate Bank or the trustees, so that the trustees might be removed at once whenever the deed of assignment was not strictly complied with or, if the assignment should thereafter be set aside, provision be made to put the bank into liquidation.[13]

Before closing his remarks on the Real Estate Bank assignment the governor interjected a personal, partisan piece of advice that drew attention to his own hard feelings toward the supreme court. "In your deliberation upon this subject," he coaxed,

> I am sure you will act like statesmen, and avoid, if possible, any collision with a co-ordinate branch of the government, and reconcile, if possible, conflicting opinions, where it can be done without a surrender of the great sovereign power with which you are clothed by the Constitution.[14]

Pike and the trustees obviously expected nothing but hostile treatment from the lawmakers toward the trusteeship. Pike's fear of this was driven home when Senator Sevier's reelection for a full six-year-term after March 3, 1843, got caught up in antibank politics. The Whigs had learned of a potential scandal affecting Sevier's character and reputation in connection with his conduct as bond commissioner for both the State Bank and the Real Estate Bank and moved immediately for a thorough investigation in the hope that a full airing of the alleged irregularities might prevent his reelection. Rep. Dr. Lorenzo Gibson, a thirty-eight-year-old Whig of Hot Springs and a veteran anti-Sevierite, and Rep. John Field, a twenty-six-year-old Hempstead County Whig lawyer, led the attack.[15]

On November 9, by a vote of sixty two to one, Gibson secured a resolution appointing a house committee of seven members to investigate Sevier's role as bond commissioner for the State Bank. Tied to the resolution was a proviso for suspending the senatorial election until the committee should report. The proviso was promptly killed by Sevier's friends, and the committee, which ordinarily would have been appointed with Gibson as chairman, was raised by ballot. Consequently, it was packed with five pro-Sevier Democrats against two Whigs and was chaired by a friendly Democrat, Thomas B. Hanly, twenty-nine, a lawyer of Helena, Phillips County. Gibson and Alfred W. Arrington of Washington County were the two Whig members, but Arrington was pledged to vote for Sevier and worked hand-in-glove apparently with the Democrats on the committee.[16]

Senator Sevier was present on the floor of the house during this artful maneuvering and did himself a disservice by forgetting his elevated position as a senator and at its conclusion personally confronting Gibson on the floor in the house chamber. In the partisan opinion of Colby, Sevier used the most "violent gestures, strong and vulgar language," and displayed a "most undignified excitement of feelings," in his oral assault on Dr. Gibson. When Weller of the *Gazette*, in an equally partial opinion of the confrontation, blamed Gibson's biased language and concluded, "We view the presence of such men as Dr. Gibson, in deliberative bodies, as a public misfortune," Colby replied that he personally viewed Weller as *Gazette* editor as a "private misfortune."[17] We don't know Pike's reaction to the Sevier-Gibson confrontation, but he considered the good doctor a high-toned, learned gentleman and must have regretted Sevier's rude handling of his Whig friend. As for Sevier, both his friends and enemies were seeing for the first time a new unwelcome side of his personality.

The next day, November 10, Field introduced a long resolution calling for a thorough investigation of the Real Estate Bank by a joint committee of five house members in conjunction with a committee to be appointed by the senate, to meet such committee as might be appointed by the "Stockholders of the Real Estate Bank" for winding up that institution. Tabled until November 11, when several amendments were added, Gibson secured one that called for a special investigation of Sevier's role as bond commissioner without mentioning him by name. The Gibson amendment to the Field resolution pointedly asked the joint committee to make this subject "one of special investigation and first upon entering upon the duties, and that they report specially to the House before the election of U.S. Senator shall take place on this day week." The senate concurred and ultimately six representatives and four senators composed the Field Committee. No committee of stockholders ever met with the committee.[18]

The senatorial election, which had been scheduled and postponed three times was still unscheduled on November 22. Early that day the Hanly Committee reported to the house completely whitewashing Sevier's agency in selling State Bank bonds and in retaining $10,000 of the capital funds for his own use during several months in 1839. Though he later paid interest on the money, there was no creditable evidence that the cashier of the principal bank at Little Rock had authority from the directors to handle bond receipts, which were capital funds, as a loan; nor was there any real evidence that Sevier had actually solicited the use of the funds. Glossing over this and other matters, the Hanly Committee found no grounds to censure either Sevier or the cashier. Indeed, the committee report had attached to it a glowing resolution of thanks to Senators Sevier and Fulton, who had merely helped deliver the bonds but was not implicated in personally retaining any of the money received for them, for the important public service they had performed in arranging the sale of the bonds. The report, minus the resolution of thanks, which was tabled, was adopted by a thunderous majority of fifty-seven to six. Seventeen of twenty-five house Whigs supported the report, two failed to vote, and six voted against it. Gibson and Arrington, the two Whigs on the committee, split their votes, with Gibson opposing and Arrington favoring the proposition.[19]

Sevier's Democratic friends succeeded in some sharp parliamentary tactics immediately following adoption of the Hanly report to prevent the Field Committee report from coming before the house. At the earliest opportunity Rep. John Selden Roane of Jefferson County, a member of the Hanly Committee and a loyal Democratic ally of Sevier, gained the floor and secured a motion to have the senatorial election take place at one o'clock that day. The concurrence of the senate being necessary, a messenger stepped across the hall to request it. In the brief interval required for this, Field won the floor and asked consent of the house to report from his committee concerning Sevier's agency in selling Real Estate Bank bonds. His request was denied by the pro-Sevier

Speaker Williamson Simpson Oldham of Washington County on the grounds that Field was unready to make a full report with instructions from his whole committee, whereupon Field angrily demanded that his committee be excused from reporting at all. His motion was at first granted but on reconsideration was denied and further time was granted to allow the committee to complete its investigation.[20]

A last-ditch Whig effort to hear from the Field Committee now came from John Cocke, Pulaski County Whig and perhaps Pike's closest friend, who was pledged to go for Sevier but who may have been seeking an honorable way out of delivering the vote. He moved that the committee's "papers prepared as a report" be read for the house's information. The ayes and nays were called for and ordered on the controversial motion, but before the roll was begun a message arrived from the senate notifying the house that it had concurred in the resolution to proceed with the senatorial election at one o'clock. The message was read, disrupting and preventing the vote on Cocke's motion. The vote was never taken, for a motion to recess to have the house chamber prepared for the reception of the senate interceded.[21]

A short while later the senators filed into the hall of the house of representatives. and the joint session proceeded with the senatorial election. Rep. Jared C. Martin, Pulaski County Democrat, nominated Sevier. Rep. William Byers, Independence County Whig, nominated Pike. There were no other nominations. When the respective rolls of the two bodies were called and the joint vote was announced, it was found that Sevier had trounced Pike seventy-one to ten, with three votes thrown away to a Col. John Miller, a Democrat from Independence County. A check of the Whig balloting revealed that fourteen of the twenty-five house Whigs, and two of five Whig senators, all previously pledged to him, voted for Sevier. "The attempt of the member from Hot Springs for some time past, to asperse the character of Col. Sevier, proved to be worse than a failure, and recoiled upon him with overwhelming force," crowed Weller over Gibson.[22] Colby in the *Times and Advocate*, November 7, urged the Whigs to vote against Sevier, arguing that they were not "instructed," as Weller maintained, to vote Democratic; Weller prevailed.

Meanwhile, Pike had become alarmed over the difficulties the Real Estate Bank trusteeship was encountering in the legislature and proposed to the trustees that they memorialize the legislature in an attempt to reconcile the differences in regard to the assignment and to the movement to abolish the charter and proceed with a liquidation act. They acquiesced, and he drafted a memorial, which, when finally approved, was presented to the house on November 14, 1842. The trustees, activated by a sincere desire to perform faithfully the important trusts confided to them, wanted, he wrote, to remove all causes of complaint, doubt, or suspicion in the mind of the public, and lay open to the closest scrutiny every transaction with which they might have been or might thereafter be concerned. And being authorized by the deed of assignment to accept and conform their action to any law of the land that might be enacted concerning the trust conferred upon them, they had prepared and desired to present certain propositions for the legislature's consideration.[23]

In making these propositions they were governed solely by a spirit of concession and an ardent desire to compose the existing differences affecting the bank, to enable the trust to be carried out with entire faithfulness, and to give assurance to the state that its interests and the interests of the people would not be jeopardized. The highest tribunal in Arkansas having declared the deed of assignment to be valid, a decision whose correctness had been attested to by "the highest living luminaries of the land in the United States," the trustees did not feel at liberty, even if they desired, to renounce the trusteeship. But they were willing to submit to all such "checks and guards, as shall secure on their part a full and perfect accountability, and guarantee a faithful administration of the assets of the Bank."

Accordingly, they proposed to the lawmakers five propositions:

> First, that as trustees and stockholders, believing that they spoke for a large majority of the stockholders, they were willing and assented to a surrender or forfeiture of the charter for the purpose of ending the corporate existence of the bank so far as related to their banking privileges.
>
> Second, that the legislature create a board of commissioners to whom the books and papers of the bank should always be open for inspection and which should have all the powers of "a board of visitation and inspection"; and that the trustees should annually make out and publish a full disclosure of the condition and disposition of the bank's assets and the manner in which the trust property had been administered.
>
> Third, that suitable provisions be made by law to effect the speedy removal of any of the trustees, whenever they might become liable thereto, and to cause a settlement and account at any time in a manner more speedy than ordinary proceedings in chancery.
>
> Fourth, that the bonds executed by the trustees should be filed with the secretary of state's office for security, and that the five residuary trustees to succeed to the trusteeship under the deed of assignment should execute bonds of $50,000 each to the governor and his successors in office to be filed also in the secretary of state's office.
>
> And, fifth, that the trustees be fully empowered by law to continue all its legal powers and rights under the deed of assignment to liquidate the bank "in and by the name and description 'The Real Estate Bank of the State of Arkansas.'"

Pike repeated the trustees' appeal to the Arkansas lawmakers in a sincere entreaty to approve the propositions so as to enable the trustees to do what they under the present difficulties could not do, that is, "in carrying said trust into full operation" and thus saving the state, the stockholders, and the debtors and creditors from further jeopardy. He then closed the memorial with an invitation to the legislature to make "the most ample and minute scrutiny into all the affairs of the bank and the conduct and transactions of the directors, officers, and agents, and also of themselves, in such manner as the legislature should think proper."[24]

The trustees' memorial was presented to the house at a most inauspicious time. Gibson's and Field's committees had just been created, the senate had just ordered its judiciary committee to inquire into the sufficiency of the trustees' bonds, and other measures were in the works to liquidate the banks.[25] Action on the memorial was accordingly imperative and insulting. A Democratic, antibank motion to postpone any action on it for a week was lost, and one by Gibson the Whig to have the house judiciary committee report as soon as possible on whether the Real Estate Bank assignees had "any existence in law, and therefore any right or authority to submit propositions" which would be binding on the trustees if assented to by the legislature was deferred until Field's Committee should report. Gibson's motion was eventually referred to that committee for action.[26]

"Publius" in Colby's hostile *Times and Advocate* attacked the memorial in the most sarcastic terms. The "pretended trustees" of the Real Estate Bank who had taken into their hands the funds and assets of that institution and who seemed to think that they could manage its two million dollars worth of property better than any persons the state or the stockholders could select, had, he understood, petitioned the legislature to grant them "a sort of charter" to sue and be sued in their "corporate names, and to do business in the same manner a corporation could." "This would remove their individual liability to a great extent," Publius declared, "and give us a new name for the old evil." And the same men would continue to manage the bank, leaving the public just where they were before.[27]

But Publius, who was probably William Cummins, was happy to report that the legislature was not "duped by this movement." Rather than grant the trustees "such favors" they referred the memorial to an appropriate committee to investigate their powers to represent the bank and the state. This "discreet course" on the part of the lawmakers "produced quite a chilling effect on the trustees."[28]

On another subject, the state supreme court, Publius was certain that the trustees had "determined to elect Judge Dickinson whether the Legislature are willing or not." The first week of the session, "it was found that scarce any members would vote for him. He then declined, but within the past few days, he is again out at the solicitation of his friends, (the Trustees of course.)" They showed considerable confidence in being able to do as they pleased with the bank funds if they could "retain Lacy and Dickinson on the Bench." This was their great object, for if they can accomplish this, "they want no additional charter."[29]

But Publius believed that the legislature was "inclined to select judges of the Supreme Court to declare the law, rather than to select or maintain them merely to oblige the pretended Trustees of the Real Estate Bank." Though the trustees were making every possible effort to control the legislature, that body was proving "difficult to manage." The "older members" and the "calculating and practical men" of the legislature were quietly maturing and adapting a plan to secure management of the banks and to ease the burden of the bank debtors. This plan, as he understood it, would for the next year or two require from debtors of both state banks no more than would pay the amount of the interest on the state bonds and the calling in of the circulation of the banks.[30]

When the judicial election was held on November 30, Dickinson permitted himself to be nominated for a second term even though he knew his cause was hopeless and wished to withdraw. Put in nomination, also, were George Washington Paschal of Van Buren, Crawford County, Thomas Johnson of Independence County (not related by blood to Robert W. Johnson but by marriage to the Conways), John Joseph Clendenin of Little Rock, the chancery judge Pike had sued in the assignment case, William Conway B of

Hempstead County (who added the B to his name to distinguish him from a cousin in the county who bore the same name), and William King Sebastian of Phillips County. They were all Democrats, including Judge Dickinson of White County, the incumbent.[31]

Though Pike and the trustees worked hard to muster support for Dickinson, they were able to obtain but nineteen votes for him on the first ballot, seventeen of them cast by Whigs. The real contest, as it turned out, was between Paschal of the northwest and Sebastian of the southeast, each of whom also polled nineteen votes on the first ballot. Ballot after ballot continued until on the ninth and final one Paschal received forty-five votes, a majority, to Sebastian's thirty-five and Conway B's six.[32]

Paschal owed his election to the fact that the Democrats on the final ballot divided twenty-six to twenty-six between him and Sebastian and cast four for Conway B. And the Whigs, having abandoned the hopeless Dickinson, cast nineteen of their thirty votes for him. Of course, Paschal was decisively aided by the fact that Conway B, a dynasty Democrat like Sebastian, was kept in the contest through the final ballot. The Whigs by remaining united in the face of a Democratic split had hit on a strategy that gave them the balance of power.

Under the old sectional division of 1835–36, the legislature of 1842–43 consisted of forty-three northwest members, forty southeast members, and four central, or Pulaski County, members. Paschal, from the northwest, polled thirty-six northwest voters, eight southeast voters, and one Pulaski vote, Senator Byrd's. Sebastian, from the southeast, received twenty-eight southeast votes, five northwest votes, and two Pulaski votes, John W. Cocke's Whig vote and Jared C. Martin's Democratic vote. Conway B, from Hempstead County, got three southeast votes, two northwest votes, and one Pulaski vote, Peter T. Crutchfield's Democratic vote. Paschal's vote was truly sectional all right, but the fact that nineteen of thirty Whigs (with five crossing sectional lines to vote for him) had gone for him to break an even Democratic division accounted for his final success.[33]

Pike was personally bitter over the purging of Dickinson, and did not soon cease reminding the public of the true meaning behind the rotten deed. The good judge, Pike declared, had been defeated "upon the sole ground" that he had concurred in the decision upholding the Real Estate Bank assignment, thus establishing the base principle "that whenever a judge makes an unpopular decision, or one that does not chance to suit the Legislature, he is to retire from office. . . ." This was surely "a most admirable plan" by which "to secure an independent judiciary and prevent judges from electioneering on the bench," he went on. "What a debt of gratitude does the State owe to the patriots who have done this good work! I trust she will sometime discharge it to the uttermost farthing."[34]

Pike's view of Dickinson's defeat was strictly that of the minority. Colby no doubt expressed the popular view of the matter in declaring it a "triumph of the people over the Bank" as well as over the trustees. Paschal was "wholly unconnected" with the bank and his elevation to the supreme bench in Dickinson's place had deprived the trustees "of all hope of having the assignment legalized."[35]

With Judge Dickinson disposed of, the legislature soon turned its attention to Judge Lacy. Anonymous letters in Colby's *Times and Advocate* of December 5 and 12 praised the legislature for defeating Dickinson and shamelessly attacked the alleged conduct of Lacy. The writer of both letters, who signed himself "Y.X." was undoubtedly Pike's former law partner Cummins, who repeated old charges he had earlier made of Pike's being Lacy's special "pet." In his letter of December 12, Y.X. suggested that the remedy he had in mind for Lacy's misconduct was the constitutional provision whereby "for reasonable cause, which shall not be sufficient ground of impeachment, the Governor shall, on the joint address of two-thirds of each branch of the Legislature, remove from office the Judges of the Supreme and Inferior Courts: *Provided*, the cause or causes of removal be spread on the journals, and the party charged be notified of the same, and heard by himself and counsel, before the vote is finally taken and decided."[36]

The day after Y.X.'s second letter appeared, on December 12, Representative Field of Hempstead County moved the election of a house-selected committee of five to look into the judicial and private conduct of Lacy. The committee, according to the resolutions of the lengthy Field motion, were to find and report answers to several questions: Had Lacy actively promoted the election of certain members of the legislature or of any officers of the Real Estate Bank? Had he manifested on the bench individual partiality or favor towards any persons, suitors, or others before the supreme court? Had he falsely stated the law in giving opinions? Had he in any case, and especially in the decision in the Real Estate Bank mandamus case, extended his decision beyond points properly before the court? Had he not in his opinion in that case attempted to forestall future or further adjudication on the subject, and were the authorities cited in that opinion adequate to sustain the court decision? Had he intentionally misstated the law or facts, or both, in that case? Had he consented to, or had he knowledge of, material changes and additions to his opinion after it was delivered, and after a motion for a reargument was disposed of and refused?[37]

If so, when, how, and by whom, and by what authority, were such changes made, and was the altered opinion read in open court after the changes were made? Had he not shown evidence of partial or interested feelings on his part in his decision in the mandamus case? Had he not written congratulatory letters to certain persons, who were parties to the application for the mandamus, revealing the result of the case before it was read in court? Had he not frequently intimated the opinion of the court before such opinions were delivered?[38]

Furthermore, had he given legal advice before the assignment of the Real Estate Bank was made touching upon the manner in which the bank should be put into liquidation? Had Lacy not received a large loan from the Helena branch of the bank, when that bank was not making loans to anyone else, and, if so, upon what terms had he received the loan? A final clause in Field's resolution authorized the committee to investigate any other matters as might be deemed necessary and that "the committee report accordingly by either preferring charges or specifications."[39]

Before the ballot raising the committee could be taken, Rep. Charles A. Stewart, Desha County Whig, added an amendment to Field's all-encompassing resolution concerning Lacy to require the committee to give the same detailed scrutiny to the judicial and private conduct of Chief Justice Ringo and called for it to extend its investigation to Governor Yell. A native of Maryland and a twenty-eight-year-old lawyer, Stewart was visibly upset by the dragnet the bombastic Field was launching against Lacy and judicial independence. His words dripping with sarcasm and mimicking Field's petty, personal, and vindictive style, Stewart reserved his best questions for Yell to be required to answer: Had Yell written letters published in the *Gazette* concerning the manner in which the banks should be liquidated and thereby "forestalling or attempting to forestall public opinion?" Had he written letters to certain persons to induce them to stand for seats in the legislature to carry out the measures of the governor? Had he not been present in the courtroom at the time the supreme court's opinion in the assignment case was read, and had he not "immediately thereafter declared that the judge whose seat was about to be vacated, should be beat?"[40]

Moreover, had Yell not written letters to various persons urging upon them that a judge should be elected in Dickinson's place who would oppose the Real Estate Bank assignment? And had he not declared, both before and after the legislature assembled, that no man should be elected in Dickinson's place unless he should be pledged to reverse the opinion in the assignment case? Closing, Stewart, using the same insulting language employed by Field concerning Lacy, called for the committee to inquire "into such other acts of the Executive" as might be "derogatory to the dignity of his office," and to "report by articles of impeachment or otherwise."[41]

Before the Field resolution as amended by Stewart was voted upon, it was divided into three separate questions so that the parts relating to Lacy, Ringo, and Yell were voted upon independently. That part of the resolution relating to Lacy was adopted by a vote of fifty-seven to one, that relating to Ringo by fifty-five to five, and that relating to Yell by fifty-four to six. Only Harris Flanagin, a Clark County Whig, voted against all three resolutions; he was joined by a few Democrats in opposing those related to Ringo and Yell. Raised by ballot, the select committee that was to carry out the investigation consisted of Field, as chairman, Alfred B. Greenwood of Benton County, Thomas B. Hanly of Phillips County, Jared C. Martin of Pulaski County, and Charles A. Stewart of Desha County, giving two Whigs, Field and Stewart, to three Democrats.[42]

The Field Select Committee spent several weeks investigating Lacy. On December 21 it received house permission to send Representative Hanly as a sort of subcommittee of one to examine "material witnesses" relating to the Lacy investigation and residing in or near Helena, to take testimony under oath, to send for persons and papers, to employ a competent assistant at the expense of the state to execute process and make return thereof, and to pass over to the committee such testimony as he might obtain. Having enjoyed a paid legislative leave with his family over the Christmas holidays, young Hanly reported back to the house, January 2, 1843, that he had performed the special duty which report and accompanying documents he referred to the select committee.[43]

The Field Select Committee, meanwhile, were examining witnesses in secrecy without Judge Lacy being present or being represented by counsel.[44] On January 5 Chairman Field surfaced in the house to report that a fellow Whig, Rep. John W. Cocke of Little Rock, who had been called before the committee to testify, "did refuse, and still refuses to answer" a "question propounded to him by your committee": "Have you ever heard Judge

Lacy speak disparagingly of any attorney who practices before him in the supreme court?" Cocke replied that if the committee would "specify any particular charge against Judge Lacy, of improper language or conduct used toward any member of the bar" he would gladly answer whether he knew the same to be true and would give the committee any information he might be able to furnish in regard to the "particular charge preferred."[45]

Field wanted Cocke brought before the bar of the house the next morning, January 6, and compelled to answer the question or be cited for contempt. Representative Gibson, coming to his Whig friend Cocke's aid, moved to reject Field's motion. He was sustained by a whopping vote of fifty-one to nine, and the Lacy investigation dropped from sight until January 28 when Field reported to the house that, after careful inquiry into the conduct of Lacy, Ringo, and Yell, the committee had found no evidence "against Judge Lacy" that would warrant "impeachment or address" nor had it "examined any testimony concerning the Hon. Daniel Ringo, or his Excellency Governor Yell, calculated to cast any reflection, or the slightest shade of suspicion upon them." He asked that his committee be discharged from further consideration of the matter, but there is no record that the report was ever acted on, and the subject disappeared from sight.[46]

If Pike had been angry over the defeat of Judge Dickinson, he was furious over the shameful way Judge Lacy's good name had been dragged through the mud of partisan politics and over the shabby manner in which Representative Field had conducted the investigation. We have Pike's informed word for it that Field's biased report was meant to imply that the committee had examined witnesses and taken testimony regarding Ringo and Yell. Pike declared that the committee had not "examined a single witness in regard to either of them," that it had given its full attention to Lacy, and he concluded that Lacy "must have been innocent, indeed," if the "ingenuity" of the vindictive men on the committee could not torture or prevent something that he had done into ground of address."[47]

Though Pike was relieved that "the persecution of Judge Lacy" was over, he went on, in the days to come, to denounce the committee as "a kind of American branch of the Spanish inquisition, whose business it was to hunt in every direction for cause of address, to inquire into Judge Lacy's private conversations, to haul their drag-net over the whole country, and see what they could gather up and bring to shore therewith." The investigation, he continued, was a disgrace to "the free State of Arkansas," "a great outrage" upon the law and the "private rights and private reputation" of a citizen, and "a precedent which, if followed up by acts of a like nature, will make its inventors to stink in the nostrils of all mankind."[48]

The attack upon Lacy was also, Pike declared, "a most disgraceful and outrageous attack upon the independence of the judiciary, calculated to degrade it in the eyes of the people, and to expose it to general scorn and contempt?" Pike regretted upon reflection that he had not called upon the judiciary to decide the question of whether the committee had the right "to compel witnesses to appear and respond to an illegal investigation," to ask the courts "to decide whether the legislature is omnipotent." "I pledge myself," he promised, "that if the opportunity ever again occurs to me, I will teach them that they are *makers* and not *breakers* of the law." To Pike's credit, his was the lone voice, except for Cocke's brave defiance of the committee's authority, to be raised in protest against the Lacy investigation, which as he said, did "stink in the nostrils of mankind."[49]

Against the background of Sevier's election, Dickinson's defeat, and the Lacy investigation, Field's Joint Committee on the Real Estate Bank conducted its work. Chairman Field appeared before the house on December 17 to report on the committee's first order of business, the inquiry, sparked by Gibson's resolution of November 11, into Senator Sevier's agency in selling 500 Real Estate Bank bonds in 1838 to the Treasurer of the United States on behalf of the Smithsonian legacy and the subsequent disposition of the $500,000 in specie, or its equivalent, received for the bonds.[50]

The Field report severely criticized Sevier and Thomas T. Williamson, the bank's bond commissioners in 1838. They converted the specie of the Smithsonian bequest into southern and western bank funds which were at various rates of discount in New York where they carried out the transaction. They failed to turn over to the Real Estate Bank, or accounting for, the full amount of these premiums and discounts. They each retained and appropriated to their personal use a little over $14,000 of the funds. They loaned to four fellow Arkansans then visiting in New York City (namely, Peter Hanger, Chester Ashley, James L. Dawson, and Lambert Reardon) a total of $9,050 of similar funds. They paid a Washington banker and broker, William Corcoran, a fee of $5,000 to negotiate the sale of the bonds to the U.S. Treasurer. And, finally, they paid themselves a fee of like amount, of which $2,000 went to Sevier and $3,000 to Williamson.[51]

The most damaging aspects of the report, insofar as Sevier's public reputation was concerned, came with the revelation that he and Williamson had personally speculated with the half million dollars "in *gold* or its equivalent" and had reaped rich, though concealed, dividends for themselves on the corrupt transaction. The two "brokers" in New York City had converted the $500,000 of par funds into depreciated southern and western bank paper that was at the time of the exchange being discounted in the city banks at from two to twelve and a half percent. But in settling with the Real Estate Bank they had accounted for, and turned over to the bank, total funds which included a discount, or premium, of but three and a half percent. In other words, the two Arkansas brokers had received southern and western bank notes whose face value exceeded by several thousand dollars the original half million of par funds and had obviously pocketed a large part of the difference.[52]

The committee would "leave to be determined by this house and an enlightened people" the degree to which Sevier and Williamson had personally "participated in the emoluments of this speculation." The committee closed its report, however, with a recapitulation of the facts evolved by them which amounted to a severe censure of the two men. Their conduct was, it read, in direct violation of the trust reposed in them and "was most fatally disastrous to the interests of the institution and of the state."[53]

The Field report censuring Sevier and Williamson was the subject of heated committee in-fighting. Representative Field, a violent, bombastic Whig partisan, drafted the first report back in early November and intended to use it against Sevier in the senatorial election. He was rebuffed in this effort by Sevier's friends, as we have seen. The committee continued its investigation, and Representative Gibson wrote out the next report and submitted it for committee approval. Several members objected to Gibson's harsh language. Senator David Walker, Washington County Whig and a known moderate, got it referred to his subcommittee. He then wrote a report acceptable to the whole committee but which was nonetheless highly critical of Sevier and Williamson.[54]

Walker's draft was unanimously adopted by the committee and reported to the house by Chairman Field on December 17. It was tabled and not again taken up until January 6, 1843, when two Sevier Democratic partisans, Albert Rust of Union County and Abram G. Mayers of Crawford County, withdrew their names from it. They then submitted a minority report that amounted to a complete whitewash of the two bond commissioners. According to one Democrat, Mayers refused to support the censure of Sevier as a Democrat because "he would be signing his political death warrant."[55]

The rest of the committee, composed of seven Whigs and two Democrats, stood their ground. Gibson moved the next day, January 7, that the report of December 17 be adopted by the house. It carried by a close vote of thirty-three to twenty-seven. Voting with the majority were twenty-two Whigs and eleven Democrats. Voting with the minority were no Whigs and twenty-seven Democrats. For some unknown reason John Field and two other Whigs did not vote; three Democrats also failed to vote.[56]

By late December Pike knew that the legislature would likely pass a bill to liquidate the Real Estate Bank. His lobbying to have the legislature legalize the deed of assignment, retain the original trustees, and name a board of bank commissioners to examine and ride herd on the work of the trustees and the bank's agents intensified as December gave way to January.

A bill to liquidate the Real Estate Bank passed the senate on January 5 and went to the house. This bill, ignoring the pleas of the trustees and Pike's arguments for legalizing the assignment, opined that, indeed, the bank by the act of assignment "forfeited its right to a corporate existence." Yet the report accompanying the bill argued that "this was a question to be decided by the courts," which had the effect of enacting a lawsuit and not a law. Sen. David Walker's report accompanying the senate bill went on to confuse matters by declaring it the duty of the legislature to the people "to cause a forfeiture to be declared, to place the effects of the bank in the hands of responsible and faithful agents, to be collected and preserved, to cause the circulation to be taken in, and the state indemnified against loss."[57]

Action in the house was long and heated. Pike drafted a bill containing the objectives favorable to the trustees, that is, declaring the trusteeship a private corporation and legalizing the assignment under the watchful eye of a "Bank Commissioner of the State of Arkansas." Pike got Rep. Alfred W. Arrington of Washington County, a gifted Whig orator, to propose his bill as a substitute for Senator Walker's measure and to defend it in the committee of the whole house. The Arrington substitute—Pike's bill—was defeated, but the debate had the effect of changing the minds of a majority of the house to favor a sort of compromise measure. A new house substitute bill, drafted by a select committee of five and chaired by Whig Rep. John W. Cocke of Pulaski County, was approved by the house on January 25. It declared the assignment legal but called for replacing the old trustees with a new set of trustees: five state trustees, one for each of the five separate banking houses in the system, to be elected by the legislature, and ten to be chosen by the stockholders. It also called for a state bank commissioner who should visit the Real Estate Bank and examine the work of the new legislative trustees. Representative Field, a member of Cocke's committee, objected to the bill's recognition of the Real Estate Bank as a private corporation and to its allowing the stockholders a majority of the trustees. He submitted a minority report, which the house ignored and passed the bill based on the majority report.[58]

The senate approved this house substitute bill on January 27, and Governor Yell signed the so-called Real Estate Bank liquidation bill into law on January 31. Pike had valiantly fought the measure and had declared openly in the name of the trustees that they would not recognize the new law. He even threatened to carry the question of the state's attempt to replace the old trustees to the Supreme Court of the United States.[59]

Under the act of January 31 the legislature proceeded with its enforcement. On February 2, two days before it permanently adjourned, the legislature elected a bank commissioner and five state trustees. These five were to join ten new trustees elected by the stockholders on Monday, March 6, 1843, to whom the old trustees were to convey the entire Real Estate Bank property. Fighting furiously, Pike and the original trustees interceded to secure proxies from a majority of the stockholders, and exercising these, prevented an election of new trustees on March 6.[60]

A month later, on April 5, the old trustees, meeting at Little Rock, published a protest against the Real Estate Bank act of 1843. Drafted by Pike, it cited two reasons why the law was neither binding nor obligatory upon them:

> first, because, it is void, and a palpable usurpation of private rights upon its face; an attempt on the part of the State violently to seize upon property which was and is as much beyond her reach as the property of any private individual; and directly impairs the obligation of the contract entered into between the State and the Bank, as well as the contracts created by, and contained in, the deed; and, second, because, by the decision of the supreme tribunal of the State, the property conveyed by the deed and vested in the Trustees, and the deed is legal and valid; while the act of assembly, being upon its face a reversal of the decision of the Supreme Court, and an attempt to wrest the property from those to whom the ministers of the law have solemnly decided it belongs is a gross usurpation of power, and a direct defiance of, and attempt to override, the judiciary, until this time unknown in a free State.[61]

Closing, they defiantly declared that they were prepared to stand under the deed of assignment of April 2, 1842, and the state supreme court decision declaring the deed valid and also legalizing the trusteeship created under it. If proceeded against by the state under the liquidation act of 1843, they would appeal to their private rights under the assignment decision of 1842.[62]

The 1843 liquidation act provided that if no election of trustees by stockholders was held, it would be the duty of the prosecutor of the fifth judicial circuit at Little Rock, who also was ex officio state attorney general, to procure by writ of quo warranto a forfeiture of the Real Estate Bank charter and the appointment by the chancellor of the ten trustees. Robert Ward Johnson of Little Rock, son of Judge Benjamin Johnson and brother-in-law of Senator Sevier, had just been reelected fifth judicial circuit prosecutor by the legislature. And Eli Colby, *Times and Advocate* Whig editor, promptly reminded him and the public of his duty under the liquidation act.[63]

Engaging the able Little Rock attorney George C. Watkins to aid him, Johnson secured by writ of quo warranto, issued from the state supreme court by Judge Thomas J. Lacy in August 1844, a forfeiture of the bank charter. This ended any possibility that the old trustees could exercise any of the franchises under the state charter to the bank to carry on a banking business. But Pike shrewdly secured in consenting to the forfeiture an admission by Johnson and Watkins that the deed of assignment of April 2, 1842, was valid. Indeed, Judge Lacy had ruled that the Real Estate Bank by her deed had transferred and assigned so much of all her rights, credits, and effects to certain trustees that she had extinguished all her powers and corporate franchises and that the state by her writ of quo warranto had the right "to have that fact ascertained and declared by a judgement of this court, and to seize the franchise into her own hands."[64]

It would appear that Johnson never attempted to secure the appointment of stockholder trustees, for the old trustees retained control of the Real Estate Bank, with Pike as their attorney, until 1855.[65]

Meanwhile, Pike had helped revolutionize the party press in Arkansas. William Woodruff back in November and December 1842 had again lost an appeal to the Democratic-controlled legislature to have his name cleared as a defaulter to the state and relieve him of the heavy financial burden. Furious at the Sevier-Conway-Johnson-Rector Democratic dynasty for not supporting his appeal, Old Buck decided to sell the *Gazette*.[66]

Pike at the time was estranged from Eli Colby and his former law partner Cummins, who, according to Colby, had renounced his sins of 1838–39 in trying to break down the *Times and Advocate* with the ill-fated *Star* episode, and had been welcomed back by Colby as a loyal Whig in the fall of 1842.[67] Pike had not renounced his sins against Colby and his paper, and, indeed, held the aberrant, independent-minded editor in enormous contempt for his outrageous attacks on Lacy and Dickinson and on the independence of the state supreme court in the Real Estate Bank case of 1842.

Accordingly, Pike was primed to act when he learned that Woodruff wanted to sell the *Gazette* and was willing to sell it to the Whigs. He had no desire whatsoever to return to the newspaper business after his earlier losing experience with the *Advocate* and *Times and Advocate*. But when he now heard that his young friend Benjamin J. Borden—a graduate of the University of North Carolina and Little Rock attorney with good family connections, and, as Woodruff would soon describe him, "a gentleman of very respectable pretensions as a writer"—was interested in purchasing the paper, Pike became perhaps the main intermediary with Woodruff to make it possible for Borden to consummate the bargain.[68]

Woodruff wanted $1,000 in cash and the assumption of $5,000 worth of his debt to the Real Estate Bank. Pike and Tom Newton, attorney and cashier-secretary respectively to the trustees of the Real Estate Bank, bolstered Borden's sometimes flagging confidence as to whether he would be making a paying proposition by holding out to him the promises of bank patronage in the form of job printing and legal advertising. But because of their personal ties to the institution neither of them signed as securities for Borden on the notes he gave the bank. Pike easily solved this problem. His oldest and closest friend from Newburyport days, Luther Chase, and his new law partner of less than a year, David J. Baldwin, signed one note with Borden for $2,500. The other note, for a like amount, was signed by Borden's stepfather, James Lawson Sr., and by his brother, William S. Borden. Pike probably raised the $1,000 in cash among Whig friends, although Borden later admitted in 1844 in a public statement that Pike had personally lent him a "small sum" to help him buy the Gazette and that he had long since paid Pike. On December 30, 1842, Pike's law partner delivered the $1,000 in cash to Woodruff, and a bill of sale was executed and signed, but Woodruff did not publicly surrender the Gazette office to Borden until January 4, 1843.[69]

In announcing the transfer in that issue of the Gazette, Woodruff praised Borden's ability as a writer and expressed his hope that he would "conduct" the paper so as to give satisfaction to the public. This was hardly reassuring to Democrats, since everyone with the slightest claim to being informed about political affairs knew that Borden was a Whig. Moreover, Woodruff's Democratic editor, young Cyrus W. Weller, who already suspected Pike of leading a Whig plot to buy a Little Rock newspaper and to use it to try to divide the Arkansas Democracy was shocked by Woodruff's announcement. In a valedictory editorial, Weller scarcely concealed his hurt feelings and suspicions. The Gazette, he tersely announced, would be in new editorial hands after the current number. As for himself, he had been left completely out of the negotiations as to "the object of the transfer." He would remain in Little Rock and practice law, and remain "a Democrat of the strictest order."[70]

Weller went on to say, however, that he suspected a "secret," "infamous conclave" between Arkansas Whigs and "diverse doughface democrats" was behind the purchase of the Gazette.[71] Borden avoided any mention of his own political affiliation in his salutatory editorial of January 11, 1843, but it was common knowledge that he was a Whig. And almost from the beginning he allowed Pike to publish his "History of the Real Estate Bank" and "The Evil and the Remedy." The former work was Pike's defense of himself and the trustees against their alleged mismanagement of the Real Estate Bank. In it he revealed the old, long fight between Ashley and Cummins for control of the central board and of the directory of the principal bank, his own connection with the central board and the trustees as their attorney, and Sevier's and Williamson's shameful roles in mishandling the funds from the Smithsonian legacy in 1838–39 by exchanging them for depreciated western and southern "rags" to serve as capital funds for the bank.[72]

"The Evil and the Remedy," published in the Gazette over the pseudonym "Sabinus," between February and late July 1843, was a work designed by Pike to support his idea for a new organization called a "Republican Society of the State of Arkansas." As conceived by Pike in the fall and winter of 1842–43 and as expounded by him to social gatherings of friends and acquaintances at his home, it was to be strictly nonpartisan and had as its central goal the attempt "to moderate the rancor of party strife, to reform the press, and to make virtue and qualification the only tests in election to office. It was not a secret order but it did not publicize its meetings and affairs, and soon rumors began to be spread about Pike's organization.[73]

On December 21, 1842, Weller of the *Gazette*, a highly partisan Democrat, published what is believed to be the first public mention of the new order. Under the heading "The Hotchpot Party" he declared a number of Whigs and "disaffected Democrats" then in Little Rock "have agreed to go into irrevocable hotchpot, with a view to establish a newspaper to advocate a political-educational spirit throughout the State." "The ulterior design is to create divisions in the Democratic ranks, and to promote the interests of the concern," said Weller. Their "heaviest artillery" was to be directed at the governor and the *Gazette*. "So says rumor, 'We shall see what we shall see.'" A week later Weller quoted a correspondent as referring to "the new party lately formed at the house of the Attorney for the Trustee of the Real Estate Bank, to break down all parties."[74]

No wonder then that Weller was shocked when he learned at the last hour that Woodruff had sold the venerable Democratic *Gazette* to the Whigs and that he suspected a "secret conclave" between Whigs and "diverse doughfaced democrats." The fact that Borden placed the phrase "The Constitution and the Laws" at the head of his editorial column reminded members of the Republican Society that he was probably a member, for Pike used this same phrase in expounding on the purpose of the society. Borden followed this on February 8 by publishing a "Declaration of Principles of the Republican Society . . . in the State of Arkansas." He explained that it had been published some weeks ago in "circular form" designed at that time for the author—"one of the ablest writers of Arkansas"—to be used in the formation of societies in the different counties of the state to carry out "by all honorable means, the high and noble purposes therein promulgated." Pike was not identified as the author, undoubtedly because he felt that to draw attention to himself would detract from its possibilities to succeed.[75]

His readers not on the inside remained skeptical for over a year about whether he was trying to use "The Evil and the Remedy" to divide and breakdown the Democratic Party. He was not, of course, for he remained a Whig. Typical of public reaction was that of his old nemesis Eli Colby who on February 27, 1843, attacked the "design" in Pike's first number of Sabinus to "establish societies for the formation of a 'no party party' in Arkansas." He also derided Pike's efforts as an attempt to form a new third party as a "Hotch Potch," a play on the word first used by Weller: "Hotchpot." Finally, Colby fell back on an ancient practice in Arkansas of a personal attack for Pike's critical remarks on Arkansas. "It slanders Arkansas, makes it appear lawless, says the judiciary is no longer respected (Pike's way of abusing the people of Arkansas because they would not submit to judicial abuse), and abuses the press and the legislature."[76]

The dynasty leaders from January to September 1843 were without a press, and were extremely distraught. From Washington City Sevier wrote long, angry, scurrilous letters denouncing Whigs and Democrats alike for his censure by the house of representatives. He sent these to this brother-in-law Robert Johnson, who persuaded Borden to publish them. This gave Borden all the editorial ammunition he needed to discuss the scandal concerning Sevier and Williamson, to defend the members of the house committee that investigated and censored them, and to give them in turn free access to his columns to reply to Sevier.[77] When Sevier returned home from Congress that summer, he went on a whirlwind damage-control speaking tour. Preparing for the 1844 state election, he now demanded that the people instruct the members elected to the legislature in that year to vote to purge the censure against him.[78]

The dynasty leaders by September 1843 established a new Democratic organ, the *Little Rock Arkansas Banner* and before the end of the year imported the colorful and belligerent Dr. Solon Borland, a Tennessee Democratic editor, to edit it and, as it turned out, to do the fighting and dueling for the paper against Borden and the *Gazette*.[79] One thing was clear: if the Whigs believed by acquiring the venerable *Gazette* they could convert the divided Whig Party into the majority party in Arkansas, they were doomed to failure.

When 1843 gave way to 1844, a presidential-election year, the Whigs vigorously organized, held a state convention in Little Rock in January, and put a full slate of state candidates in the field: Dr. Lorenzo Gibson, the voluble Whig from Hot Springs, who was suspected by Democrats of being an infidel, for governor; David Walker of Fayetteville, a popular state senator and Whig, who though he had voted for Sevier in 1842 had worked to censure him for bank scandals, for Congress; and John Cocke of Little Rock, William Byers of Batesville, and Alfred Arrington of Fayetteville for Whig presidential electors. The Whigs of Pulaski County, seemingly reunited and with Colby supporting the convention and the nominees, named Newton for state senator and Absalom Fowler, Fred Trapnall, and Charles Bertrand for the house.[80]

That year the Democrats were badly split by factionalism. The older dynasty bosses had late in 1843 decided to make room for a new generation of leaders, and held a packed convention at Little Rock. It nominated Elias Nelson Conway for governor and David J. Chapman of Batesville for Congress. Immediately there was an outcry from unhappy Democrats with independents cropping up as candidates. Dynasty leaders quickly accommodated the soreheads by agreeing to hold a new convention. It named Archibald Yell for Congress; Dr. Chapman for governor; and Mark W. Izard of St. Francis County, Chester Ashley of Little Rock, and Williamson Oldham of Fayetteville for electors. Dr. Chapman, a colorless, inept candidate, withdrew in July, and the Democrats soon named dynasty hanger-on Thomas Stevenson Drew of Randolph County for governor. In the meantime the wealthy commission agent and slave trader Richard Byrd of Little Rock had announced as an Independent Democrat for governor, and defying all party factions, remained in the race. The joyful Whigs, who hoped Byrd and Drew would so divide the Democrats, as to give Gibson a plurality of the votes and the election, cheered Byrd's cause.[81]

Under attack by both the *Banner* and the *Times and Advocate* as a divisive force in the state and as using the attorneyship of the Real Estate Bank as the means to his own evil ends, it was perhaps with a sigh of personal relief that Pike left behind the turmoil of Arkansas politics at the end of that hectic summer of 1844 and entered upon the arena of national campaigning for the first time. At Nashville, Tennessee, on August 31 he spoke before a vast Whig convention. His speech was, according to the partisan editor of the Nashville *Whig Banner*, "in no wise to be condemned except for its brevity. Mr. Pike is a whole-souled, eloquent Whig, and with such spirit to lead the van of the party, we must sooner or later triumph even in benighted Arkansas."[82] Five days later, Pike, having journeyed north to Louisville, Kentucky, was the star of another giant Whig convention. On entering the Whig Pavilion there, his fellow Arkansan William H. Gaines of Chicot County, surprised Pike by loudly calling his name and demanding that he be called on to speak. He went forward to the podium and entertained the multitude with a stem-winding oration that he had by now become the master of on the stump in his home state. The handsome, bearded Arkansas giant, hailed because of his militia rank as "Captain Pike," was presented by the women in the gallery with several scarfs and a ring for his heroic effort. Pike later remembered this incident as one of the three happiest moments in his life.[83]

This hurrahing failed, however, to enable Pike to stay the ever onward marching Democratic phalanx in Arkansas. Returning home, he learned that in the midst of the canvass, on August 15, 1844, Senator Fulton had died suddenly at his home near Little Rock. Fulton's term in the Senate was to end in March 1847, and the popular Yell was already on record that he planned to challenge Fulton for the seat before the legislature of 1846. Yell was now embarrassed, for, having resigned as governor to stand against the popular Whig David Walker for Congress, he could not very well withdraw from that race and enter the contest to succeed Fulton before the coming session of the legislature in November, 1844.

Chester Ashley, Democratic presidential elector at once announced as a candidate to succeed Fulton. It was said that Sevier did not want Ashley elected to succeed Fulton, but Sevier, under a cloud himself because of the scandal concerning his own record as Real Estate Bank bond broker, was in no position to raise questions about Ashley's checkered record as land speculator and crooked lawyer that had heretofore been used to keep him from elective office.

Historians have never figured out whether Ashley boldly lied to Yell's friends or not in 1844. But he and his perpetual pal Billy Woodruff let the word pass to Yell's friends that Ashley wished to be elected for the two years left in Fulton's unexpired term as a sort of exercise in the rehabilitation of his reputation and character and his place in history. Therefore, Ashley told Yell's friends that the popular Yell would be able to run in 1846 to succeed to the full six-year term in Fulton's place, and Ashley would not stand in his way. Ashley also appealed to his own age; he was fifty-three and by 1846 would be ready to retire. All this was very vague and was not put in writing, and Yell's friends would in due course regret being taken in by the wily old New Yorker's honeyed words. Sevier was quoted as saying that if Ashley were elected in 1844 "even the popular Yell could not unseat him two years later." These were propitious words though an element of good luck intervened to make them so. Ashley was elected overwhelmingly in 1844, and when 1846 came Yell was in Mexico, and Ashley had virtually a free hand in winning reelection to a full six-year term.[84]

In the October 1844 state election, Drew and Yell were elected governor and congressman respectively, while the Whigs of Pulaski sent their solid party slate of a senator and three representatives back to the legislature of 1844. When the legislature met on November 4, outgoing acting governor Sam Adams of Johnson County in his farewell address to the lawmakers drew attention to the fact that the old assignees of the Real Estate Bank had in effect nullified the liquidation act of 1843 and recommended they investigate why this was the case. He and Drew, who made a similar recommendation in his inaugural message, seemingly did not understand that Pike had saved the assignees from further state interference.[85]

By the time the legislature met the Democratic *Banner* was charging that Pike as attorney to the trustees was not only the boss of the Whigs and Borden's *Gazette* but that he was using the funds of the Real Estate Bank to finance his grab for power, that he had the state "well-yoked" and the debtors of the bank fell over each other in doing his bidding, and, finally, that it had been Pike after all who had secretly secured the censure of Sevier and Williamson in 1843. Though nearly all of this was patently untrue, it was undoubtedly part of the Democratic strategy to secure Sevier's petition to the legislature that fall reversing his censure in 1843, for he was now haughtily threatening to resign his Senate seat unless this was done. Speaker of the house John Selden Roane, a rising Democrat in the good graces of the dynasty who would soon touch Pike's own life in a dramatic way, used the full power of his position to accommodate Sevier. The Whigs opposed the measure, which had the effect of repealing the resolution of censure of 1843 but also of praising Sevier for his service to his state. Borden's *Gazette* regretted this action and drew attention to the fact that Sevier's friends had neglected to include Williamson in the whitewash. The Whig editor speculated that this oversight resulted from their view that a private citizen's reputation was less important than a senator's.[86]

Meanwhile, James K. Polk of Arkansas's mother state of Tennessee, carried the state in November over Clay.[87] The main issue of the election, the reannexation of Texas, was accomplished by President John Tyler and John C. Calhoun during the lame-duck session of Congress of 1844–45 before Polk could take office; it soon resulted in a crisis which was to send Pike upon a new adventure—this time into the wilderness of northern Mexico as a volunteer officer in the service of the United States.

XVII

To Mexico and Back

MILITARY MATTERS were in a measure familiar to Pike almost from the time of his entry into Arkansas. During the summer of 1836 President Andrew Jackson withdrew all U.S. troops from the Indian Territory to fight the Seminole War in Florida.[1] Pike became a first lieutenant in the First Company of Arkansas Artillery formed that fall to protect the citizens of Little Rock in case of an attack from the Indian tribes then migrating, under the auspices of the federal government, through Arkansas to their new home in the Indian Territory. While there was perhaps little real danger from these peaceful tribesmen, Pike thought an attempted massacre not unlikely. Over his card describing the formation of the artillery company and the election of its officers was printed the following note:

> With at least 15,000 Indian warriors on our frontier, and the tide of forced Indian migration still flowing past us to the new abode of the Redman, we cannot expect to be always secure. The exiled barbarian, his limbs still sore from the chains that galled them, his mind still brooding on defeat and dishonor, concentrated, and enabled in concert to mature and carry into direful effect his plans of bloody revenge, it will be strange if the war whoop does not soon sound among us. These fears are not chimerical. The Seminoles and Creeks have dared to wage war against us, when hemmed in and surrounded by a dense population. What is to keep them from it now?[2]

Soon after the formation of the First Artillery, Pike was chosen to replace John T. Fulton, who had resigned.[3] Equipped with rifles and two six-pounder field guns, the company was drilled in infantry as well as artillery tactics. The uniforms, of which there were two, were furnished by the members themselves: The winter uniform consisted of full suits of black broadcloth, the coats being of the swallow-tailed variety, faced with red. The trousers had a wide gold band of braid running down the outside seams, and the headgear were black shakos, with red pompons. In the summer the men wore gray blouses with red trimmings, duck trousers, and gray fatigue caps. The uniforms were purchased in New York City by a member of the company who went there for that purpose.[4]

The company, known to the townsmen as "Pike's Artillery," became expert under his leadership in both mounted and foot drill and was much in demand for parades and displays on special occasions. The dawn of Independence Day was always shattered with a salute of "thirteen guns to the old States" by Pike's battery; and at the inauguration ceremony of Gov. Archibald Yell in 1840 the company fell out for a full dress parade to give a military air to the affair. Another memorable display of Pike's Artillery came in June, 1841, when Gen. Zachary Taylor passed through Little Rock on his way to take command of Fort Gibson. On that occasion Pike posted his men on the bluff at the back of the statehouse, which overlooked the Arkansas River. As General Taylor's boat, the *Artizan* steamed up the river Pike's company fired a general's salute, receiving an answer from a battery on board the boat. Music was furnished by a band of the Fifth Regulars, in company with General Taylor on the *Artizan*.[5]

The Fourth of July was no small day in the lives of the Arkansans who lived in the 1830s and 40s. An account of the celebration of Independence Day, 1845, by Pike's company, then popularly known as the "Little Rock Guards," may serve to give us an idea of the importance of the holiday to the members of the Guards and their fellow townsmen. As July approached that year numerous committees met to make arrangements for the program to be carried out on the holiday and to send letters of invitations to various dignitaries—the governor, U.S. senators, and congressmen. On the afternoon of July 3, Pike's men assembled at the U.S. Armory in Little Rock and after being fully equipped, marched under Pike's command to the country home of Euclid L. Johnson of the dynasty, who lived approximately two miles from town. Encamping beneath the shady grove fronting the Johnson home, the men were placed under strict military rules. "Officers of the guard were regularly appointed, and sentinels stationed at the main gate, denying admittance to all, who could not give the countersign, or who was not passed by the officer." At sunset that evening a national salute of twenty-seven guns—one to each state in the Union—was fired.

Shortly before dawn next day—July 4—a thirteen gun salute in honor of the "Old Thirteen" ushered in the activities. At approximately ten o'clock in the morning the ladies of the "Guards" arrived from Little Rock.

> A collation was spread for them underneath fine shade trees, which adorned the yard, and then it was that Mars seemed to be temporarily dethroned by the Graces—mirth, wit and beauty bringing all present under their potent spell.

The "fair visitors" soon departed, however, leaving the men with their invited guests to themselves. Noon brought another national salute, and at two in the afternoon the men "sat down to a sumptuous dinner." Pike presided at the table, with the invited guests, officers, and men seated in order of their rank on either side of him. Speeches, toasts, and a reading of the Declaration of Independence accompanied the food and drink.

Late in the afternoon the company struck tents and marched back to town, where a final salute to the nation was fired. The guards then repaired to the Anthony House for a dinner given in their honor by the proprietor, John Brown. Among the guests present at the dinner was one of unusual interest to the members of Pike's command. This was Qm. Gen. Thomas S. Jesup, then en route to an inspection tour of the frontier military posts. General Jesup was introduced to Pike, who in turn presented the general to the guards. In a short speech General Jesup complimented the men upon their fine appearance and the precision of their drill and went on to describe the bravery of volunteer troops throughout the military history of the country. Later that night the men "broke up in good condition," thus ending the two-day celebration without a single mishap "to mar the general joy."[6]

In April, 1846, the United States went to war with Mexico over the disputed question of the Rio Grande boundary. To vindicate the shedding of "American blood on American soil," Congress on May 13 gave President James K. Polk authority to call into service up to 50,000 volunteers.[7] Two days later Secretary of War W. L. Marcy addressed a letter to Gov. Thomas S. Drew of Arkansas, requesting him to organize immediately one regiment of cavalry, or "mounted gunmen," and one battalion of infantry. The cavalry regiment was to rendezvous at Washington, Hempstead County, Arkansas, where the men would be mustered into the service of the United States. The infantrymen were to report to Fort Smith as replacements for the troops on the frontier, now all ordered south to the Rio Grande by Gen. Zachary Taylor.[8] Governor Drew's proclamation calling for the volunteers was issued on May 27.[9]

Pike, absent from Little Rock attending a session of the Hempstead Circuit Court, when the request for volunteers came, received the news with little joy. He knew that his men would be anxious to go to Mexico and that he would be expected to lead them. He also knew that it would mean a great personal sacrifice to surrender his valuable law practice for a year; but greater still must have been the humiliation he felt at the thought of serving in a Democratic war with which he had little sympathy.[10] With these things in mind, Pike immediately dispatched a letter to the chief executive of the state offering him the "service of one company of infantry."[11] But when Pike returned to Little Rock a few days later, he discovered that his men would not be satisfied to sit out the war at Fort Smith. At a special meeting on June 7 the Guards voted to volunteer a company of "Flying Artillery" for duty in Mexico. Should their services as artillerists not be accepted by the governor, they requested to be sent as a company of horse in the Arkansas cavalry regiment.[12]

Notified by the governor that his company would be received in the service of the United States only as mounted gunmen, Pike hurriedly converted the Guards into a cavalry corps. By June 15 his command had acquired its full complement of horsemen and had held a new election of officers. In the voting Pike was the unanimous choice for captain, while Hamilton Reynolds and William H. Causins were elected first and second lieutenants respectively. On June 19, while Pike's men were being equipped at the armory in Little Rock for the march to Washington, the ladies of the city presented the company with a banner upon which was embroidered an "elegant wreath" containing the words "Up Guards and at 'Em." In response Pike thanked the women and vowed that his men would ever remember the honor paid them.[13]

On June 20 Pike's company left for the rendezvous in Hempstead County. Pike seems to have had little trouble with the new recruits until July 4, when several of them rode off to their homes without his leave. But he was well able to cope with such problems. As a warning to other would-be deserters, he wrote a scathing exposition against two brothers, William and Alford Stacy of White County, who neglected to return at all.[14] As to those who returned to the company following Independence Day, we may get an idea of Pike's discipline of them from a correspondent in the *Gazette*, who was visiting the volunteer camp at Washington and observed that

> Pike is a strict disciplinarian, and in consequence, has incurred the dislike of several of his *holiday* soldiers who have returned. But those who remain with him know and feel that he is not the man to undertake a thing without doing it well,

and admire him for it. . . . Capt. P. takes great interest in his men, sees that their wants are provided for, and gives himself up, with unwearying assiduity, to the task of making them good soldiers. He certainly possesses great versatility of talent, as he has shown himself to be as completely at home in the camp, as he is in the courts, or on the hustings, or at a musical *soiree*, or when cultivating the Muses.[15]

All ten companies of the Arkansas regiment were assembled at Washington on July 7 when the election of regimental officers took place. Pike was nominated for regimental colonel to oppose Archibald Yell, who had resigned his seat in Congress and returned to Arkansas to enlist as a private in Solon Borland's company. Pike was easily the most experienced and capable leader in the Arkansas cavalry, but ability counted for little in the eyes of the volunteers. Pike's Whig affiliation and aristocratic air had done nothing to enhance his personal popularity during the past score years, and his reputation as a "strict disciplinarian," as well as his respect for military forms, most surely gave the citizen soldiers of Arkansas a dark view of what they might expect from him. In the balloting for regimental officers only the officers participated. Pike was passed over in favor of Yell, who was popular as a politician if he knew nothing whatever of military matters.[16] Two other Democrats, John Selden Roane and Solon Borland, were elected lieutenant colonel and major, respectively. Pike's men, who petitioned him not to participate in the election on the ground that they had enlisted in his company solely because it was expected that he should remain in command, were pleased with the results of the election if Pike was not.[17]

The regimental election over, the Arkansas volunteers were mustered into the service of the U.S. government on July 13. Pike's company had arrived at Washington with 111 men, but was reduced to 78 upon examination by the mustering officer.[18] Five days later the regiment marched with 800 men and a train of forty wagons for Shreveport, Louisiana, 110 miles away, the first lap of the journey to San Antonio, Texas, where they were to report to Brig. Gen. John E. Wool, then busily engaged in training and organizing an expedition against the State of Chihuahua. General Wool's army was to act in conjunction with Gen. Zachary Taylor and Gen. Stephen W. Kearney, who were then moving against Santa Fe and Monterey respectively, as part of a grant strategy of the government of the United States to invade Mexican territory in several directions for the purpose of "conquering a peace" from the enemy.[19]

After a six day march the Arkansas column reached Shreveport, where it was learned that they were to march overland to San Antonio. The march from Shreveport got underway on July 26. Eleven days later the column arrived at Robbin's Ferry on the Trinity River, some 165 miles southwest of Shreveport. Here the regiment lay by to receive supplies which had been shipped up the Trinity by steamboat. Bad weather and incessant rain delayed the departure from Robbin's Ferry until August 10, when the regiment again took up the march. Sunday, August 16, found them ferrying across the Brazos River at the town of Washington, a former capital of the Republic of Texas situated just below the mouth of the Navasota River. At last on August 28 the column reached the general rendezvous at San Antonio.[20]

General Wool ordered the Arkansas regiment to encamp at a point some four miles from San Antonio on the small stream that ran through the town.[21] In getting the companies into camp Colonel Yell placed them in reverse order. Likewise, he made no provisions for sanitation in the area. When General Wool came out to inspect the Arkansas regiment a few days later, he noted the unorthodox position of the companies and the unusually poor condition of the camp and immediately ordered them out. "We broke camp," said Pike, "and marched out on a ridge a mile or two away where there was no water. It was a hotter place than 'purgatory'. My company dwindled to sixteen men fit for duty."[22] Another officer in the Arkansas cavalry, while highly pleased with the first encampment, described this last campground as lying "in an open plain, without a particle of shade . . . during an excessively hot time." "We have suffered terribly," he went on," . . . [and] one morning had nearly 200 on the sick list."[23]

Such stern measures on the part of General Wool did little to make him popular among the "Arkansas Devils," as he soon came to call the Arkansas volunteers. A glimpse of the esteem in which "Old Wool" was held by Colonel Yell's men may be had from the diary of a private in one of the Illinois companies:

> General Wool is liked less every day by the volunteers because of his aristocratic manner and his harsh treatment of them. The Arkansas Volunteer Cavalry, which General Wool calls Colonel Yell's Mounted Devils, if provoked by him, would at the first opportunity blow out his life. Recently an Arkansas volunteer passing the General's tent, stopped and out of curiosity looked in. It displeased the General, and he told him to leave; as he did not leave immediately, he told his orderly to point his gun at him. The Arkansas soldier pointed his gun at General Wool and said, "Old Horse, damn your soul, if you give such orders I will shoot you for certain." General Wool withdrew quickly. Another Arkansas soldier who met the General wearing civilian clothes in his tent, asked him, "Stranger, have you seen my bay horse this morning?" although he knew it was General Wool. Another time General Wool sent his orderly to the Arkansas camp with the request not to make so much noise. The Arkansan replied, "Tell Johnny Wool to kiss our ———."[24]

For his part, Pike held such conduct among the Arkansas volunteers to be contemptible. He maintained, with probable truth, that their treatment at the hands of General Wool was a direct result of poor leadership by Colonel Yell, whom Pike thought "totally incompetent and unable to learn. . . . [He] is the laughing stock of the men—for as yet he has never undertaken to give an order without making a blunder."[25] It would seem that only two of the company commanders—Pike and John Preston—had attempted to drill their men since their arrival at San Antonio. Indeed, Pike had the distinction of being the only officer in the regiment who drilled his men while en route from Arkansas.[26] Doubtless much of Pike's criticism of Colonel Yell was for political consumption on the home front, and it may have been in part the result of soreness over the defeat which Yell had handed him in the regimental election. But even such a good Democrat as Major Borland reported from San Antonio that "things in our regiment [have not] been well managed."[27]

By the middle of September General Wool's army was collected at San Antonio. With preparations as complete as he could make them, Wool marched September 26 with some 1950 men upon his assigned mission of going to Chihuahua. Four companies of the Arkansas regiment remained behind under Major Borland to come up with the rear party with additional supplies. Pike's company, its sick left with Major Borland, marched with the advance column under Colonel Yell.[28] On October 21 the Arkansas cavalry, along with the remainder of General Wool's column, crossed the Rio Grande opposite the Mexican town of Presidio.[29] Once across the river the army encamped to await orders from General Taylor, who, it was learned, had taken Monterey and signed an armistice. A member of Pike's company wrote home:

> Since the news of the Armistice, and our peaceful and bloodless entry into Presidio, all are convinced that the war is quite concluded, are anxious to return—none more so than myself.
>
> I am sick of ranging over uninteresting country, looking for an enemy we cannot find.... Capt. Pike... would, himself, gladly be on his way home. He is most anxious for our immediate discharge, which may take place.[30]

But the Arkansas volunteers were not destined to return home at this juncture. General Wool, taking advantage of the armistice terms following the fall of Monterey, determined to move on to Monclova. Pike's and Preston's companies were separated from the Arkansas regiment and formed into a squadron under command of Pike, the senior captain. Pike was then ordered to go ahead of the main army with the squadron as escort for the topographical engineers, who were to reconnoiter the route to Santa Rosa, which was to be the first stop for the main army on the road to Monclova.[31] Pike's party left Presidio on the morning of October 15. Four days later the detail reached Santa Rosa, 105 miles west of Presidio. The next morning, October 20, Pike's "squadron marched into town with flags flying and sabres drawn" to accept its surrender. He then waited for the main army to come up on October 24.[32]

From Santa Rosa General Wool's army moved on to Monclova, a town of some 8,000 and the former capital of Coahuila, situated 200 miles south of the Rio Grande. Reaching Monclova on October 29, General Wool was halted by the Monterey armistice terms. Delayed until November 23, he took advantage of the layover to drill his men, improve the organization of his services, and scout the route toward Chihuahua.[33] Discovering that the only feasible route was by way of Parras, a town 120 miles west of Saltillo, he wrote General Taylor asking him what was to be gained by going to Chihuahua. His troops, he thought, would be of more use to General Taylor at Parras than at Chihuahua.[34] Taylor, acceding to Wool's request, issued orders for him to advance to Parras, which, Taylor reported, would complete the occupation of the State of Coahuila, Gen. William J. Worth's division being at Saltillo already.[35] Thus General Wool marched for Parras on November 24 arriving there on December 5.[36]

At Parras Pike's squadron was again placed under command of Colonel Yell, where it remained until December 17, when word was received from General Worth at Saltillo that the enemy was moving on that town.

> We immediately struck our tents [said Pike], started at 4 P.M., and in twenty-four hours marched forty miles—the day after twenty-five, and the next day, artillery, cavalry, infantry and trail all reached Agua Nueva, twenty miles south of Saltillo, on the San Luis Potosi road; where having found the alarm to be false we

encamped.³⁷ On the 24th I started with my squadron for Monclova, by order of General Worth, to bring up a train containing specie and clothing for our Regiment; but on reaching Saltillo, Maj. Gen. Butler directed me to remain there until he could see Gen. Wool. On the next day [Christmas Day], while I was walking about with some officers and preparing to drink divers tumblers of egg nog, a report came in that Gen. Wool was attacked and retreating. The long roll was beaten, and the troops ordered to join Gen. Wool; so in hot haste, we saddled, mounted and marched first out of the city, expecting every instant to hear the roar of cannon; but after marching ten miles, met an express and found it a false alarm.³⁸

Thus ended the battle of Agua Nueva, of "clear water," as John C. Peay, one of Pike's men, called it.³⁹ Four days later Pike, again with the Arkansas regiment, was at Patos, "a large Hacienda, thirty-five miles from Saltillo, on the road to Parras." He wrote on December 31 that he did not believe they would be attacked; nor did he imagine they would advance upon the enemy. But if they did have to fight he was sure that he knew "how to place and manage" his squadron to the "best advantage." "They know how to do what I order," Pike said, "and are of good stuff."⁴⁰ On January 31 Pike's squadron was detached from Colonel Yell's command and ordered to report to General Wool at Saltillo. From Saltillo Pike was ordered on February 8 to Las Palomas, "a narrow pass through the mountains" twelve miles northeast of Saltillo, on one of the less direct roads to San Luis Potosi. Here Pike relieved the Kentucky cavalry regiment posted there. From Las Palomas on February 14 Pike reported that his force consisted of ninety-two men fit for duty, with thirteen more absent on detached service, one lieutenant on leave, and four men absent sick.

> Having so small a force [said Pike] I am putting up a small fortification—a redoubt 24 yards square, with a small lunette covering the entrance, which will be done in a few days, and then if Gen. Minon⁴¹ comes here I shall stay and fight him.
>
> We do not know whether Santa Anna is at San Luis, or marching this way as reported: but we are instructed to use all possible vigilance and make daily and nightly reconnaissance of the roads. So, with picket and camp guard, inspection at Reveille, dress-parade at Sunset, and brick-hauling and port-building all day besides, our men are pretty busy: but they have all hardened into good soldiers and stand it admirably.⁴²

Meanwhile the remainder of the Arkansas cavalry had been faring poorly. Major Borland—who had rejoined the regiment at Monclova in October—and thirty-four of the Arkansas volunteers were captured on January 22 while on a reconnaissance detail to La Encarnacion, a town forty miles south of Agua Nueva, on the San Luis Potosi road.⁴³ And during the first week of February one of the men in Capt. Christopher C. Danley's⁴⁴ company was murdered by Mexican civilians. In retaliation a secret party among the men in Danley's and Edward Hunter's companies rode forth to Cantana, two or three miles distance from the volunteer camp at Agua Nueva and killed and wounded several innocent people suspected of the murder. The affair was investigated, said Josiah Gregg, but "owing to the difficulty of identifying the men," who were, it seems, not accompanied by any of the officers of the regiment, nothing was done with them.[45] General Taylor made a diligent attempt to discover the Arkansas men connected with the atrocity, threatening for awhile to discharge the two companies as an example to other volunteers; but at last changed his mind out of fairness to the innocent men in the commands involved.[46]

With such adverse reports as the capture of Major Borland's and other reconnaissance parties in the vicinity of Saltillo reaching him at Monterey, General Taylor himself marched for Saltillo on January 30. In company with him were the Mississippi infantry regiment under Col. Jefferson Davis, a squadron of dragoons under Lt. Col. Charles May, and two batteries of artillery commanded by Capt. Braxton Bragg and Capt. Thomas W. Sherman. Reaching Saltillo on February 2, Taylor determined to move on to Agua Nueva, where he established his headquarters, being joined three days later by General Wool's forces. Here the American army remained until Santa Anna advanced upon it to initiate the hostilities that resulted in the battle of Buena Vista.[47]

Santa Anna began his advance from San Luis Potosi late in January. By February 20 his entire force was gathered at La Encarnacion, less than forty miles from General Taylor's Agua Nueva headquarters. At noon on February 21 Maj. Ben McCulloch, who had passed through the Mexican lines during the preceding night, reported to Taylor that Santa Anna was approaching with an army of some 20,000 men. Then it was that Taylor abandoned the camp site at Agua Nueva and withdrew nine miles to a more defensible position selected by General Wool. Covering the American retreat was Colonel Yell's regiment. Sometime near midnight, when his advance pickets were driven in, Yell ordered the buildings and remaining grain stacks fired, while the train of supply wagons "moved off with furious speed" for Buena Vista. Colonel Yell then fell back in good order and reached the American lines at daybreak on the morning of February 22.[48]

The rancho of Buena Vista was located seven miles south of Saltillo near the opening of a narrow valley—La Angostura—through which the main road from Saltillo to San Luis Potosi ran. Pike has given one of the few firsthand descriptions of the terrain:

> Standing at Buena Vista, and looking [south] to the front, you see first the two parallel ridges of mountains—that on the east, a lofty and impassable ridge, on the west a lower, relieved against a higher one behind it, with a valley between them, and at intervals a pass way or two across into that valley; then southward, along the foot of the eastern slope, running along their base as far as the eye can reach . . . a ravine, narrow but traversable by cavalry. An open plain stretches upward for half a mile south and east of the village. On the west, by a steep descent, the ground sinks into a lower plain . . . [which] is cultivated in wheat, as also is the ground . . . in rear of the village. In front the ground rises in ridges.[49]

Across the valley at La Angostura (the narrows), three miles south of Buena Vista Ranch, General Wool deployed the American army. Directly in the road, which was but a narrow defile, he placed Capt. J. M. Washington's battery. On each side of this "key position" were the men of the First Illinois Regiment under Col. John J. Hardin. Immediately to their left was the Second Kentucky Infantry commanded by Col.

William McKee. And then trailing away to the left in more or less dispersed positions came Col. William Bissell's Second Illinois Regiment and Brig. Gen. Joseph Lane's Indiana brigade, whose two commands composed the left center of the American line, while far against the eastern mountain were Col. Humphrey Marshall and Col. Archibald Yell with their regiments of mounted gunmen, now operating on foot. In reserve and slightly to the rear of left center were the batteries of Sherman and Bragg and Capt. Enoch Steen's squadron of First Dragoons. With General Taylor, who had gone on from Agua Nueva to check the defenses of Saltillo, were May's squadron and Davis's Mississippi Rifles. This small army of some 4,500 men were to attempt to hold its position against an estimated 20,000 Mexicans.[50]

Pike was still at Las Palomas when he learned on February 20 that Santa Anna had reached Encarnacion. The following afternoon he was ordered to fall back to Saltillo to reinforce Maj. Charles B. Warren of the First Illinois Regiment, who was in charge of the city's defenses. Reaching town after dark, Pike found the streets "barricaded with wagons." He was assigned quarters for his men and ordered to defend the hospital in case of an attack, which was expected hourly from Gen. J. V. Minon's cavalry. During the night Pike's men "manned the tops of the houses, and kept up regular guards and advanced piquets on the roads to Monterey and Palomas." The next morning Pike was ordered to march to Buena Vista with General Taylor but was ordered back to Saltillo before the party reached their destination. Returning to town, Pike dismounted his squadron, deploying them upon the housetops along the central plaza. Throughout that day the enemy's cavalry could be seen maneuvering in the plain four miles to the west, but no attack was made.[51]

That afternoon the Mexican army attacked at Buena Vista, but nothing except light skirmishing and indefinite movements occurred before dark. In the evening General Taylor returned to Saltillo, the central depot of the American force, reported still in danger of an assault from General Minon. Taylor provided for the city's defense and the next morning returned to Buena Vista, taking with him beside May's squadron and Davis's regiment, Pike's squadron.[52]

By the time Taylor reached the battlefield on the morning of February 23, Santa Anna's forces had turned the American left flank and were threatening the rear supply train at Buena Vista Ranch. At dawn Colonels Yell and Marshall at the extreme left flank had received the main shock of the Mexican charge, and their inexperienced men, along with the Second Indiana Regiment and four companies of Arkansas volunteers under Lieutenant Colonel Roane, who before daybreak had been transferred to the left center to support the Indiana brigade, had been routed. Exactly what happened to the Arkansas troops during this early morning action is a matter of controversy. James Henry Carleton, an officer and eyewitness to the battle, reported that the four Arkansas companies at the left center retired almost at the first firing. He thought that as individuals "they were as brave as any men in the world. But their being entirely without discipline, or any habit of strict military obedience, and their consequent want of confidence in their leaders and in each other, may be fairly assigned as the principal reasons for their precipitate retreat."[53] Augustus F. Ehinger, a private in the Second Illinois Regiment, who had been shocked, and therefore prejudiced, by the unsoldierly conduct of the Arkansas volunteers who murdered the innocent Mexicans at Cantana,[54] recorded on March 7, 1847, that "The Arkansas Regiment, just as Gen. Taylor predicted, though they boasted, were very cowardly in battle. The most of them left their brave Colonel when he made his charge on the Lancers, where he met his death."[55] Josiah Gregg, another eyewitness, said that he did not "expect raw volunteers to stand the severe fire" of the superior numbers of the Mexican force. "In truth," he said, "the 4 companies of Ark. riflemen (commanded by Col. Roane), were, I believe, almost entirely dispersed."[56] And Pike, airing past and present grievances, wrote home to the Arkansas public a week after the battle that the men under Colonel Yell at the extreme left behaved poorly. Exposed to the fire of a Mexican eight-pounder battery, said Pike,

> Col. Yell ordered . . . [his men] to retreat a little way, in order to avoid the cannon range, intending then to wait a charge of the lancers supporting the battery. But the men untaught to maneuver and totally undisciplined, understood the word *retreat*, to be an order to make, each man, the best of his way to the rear . . . turned and ran off in great confusion. Col. Yell, who behaved most gallantly, the *adjutant*, [Major Gaston] Meares . . . and others, succeeded in rallying a portion of them . . . but a great many of them ran to Saltillo.[57]

Others reported, however, that Marshall's and Yell's men put up a stubborn fight for several hours before being driven from the mountainside by a Mexican force which outnumbered them three or four to one.[58]

Seeing the critical state of affairs along the left flank, General Taylor ordered Davis's regiment to the left to meet the advancing Mexicans; while May, with Pike's squadron added to his command, was sent to reinforce Colonels Yell and Marshall, who with their partially rallied troops were withstanding a severe charge immediately to the east of the Buena Vista buildings.[59]

> As we were approaching the village [said Pike], Cols. Marshall and Yell formed their men to receive the army. They waited until they came within forty yards, when each man raised his carbine and fired . . . the fire did but little harm . . . Col. Yell's command was routed. He himself, facing the foe and trying to rally his men was killed with many wounds—so disfigured that hardly one could recognize him. . . .[60]
>
> Just then Col. May's command, of his squadron and ours, came down the road at a gallop, by fours—formed platoons, and then completed at that gait, halted an instant to let the dust blow off, so that we could see the enemy, and our men might not kill one another with their sabres; and charged in heavy column. I had a momentary glimpse of the enemy, who, taken by surprise seemed wild with fear, and not awaiting our charge, fled precipitately in every direction. We charged through them and then formed in line on the other side of the Rancho. They made their way across the ravine to the west, descended into the cultivated plain below, and huddled together there for a few minutes as if undecided what to do, and finally commenced ascending the mountain by a narrow pass—by which time our piece of artillery under Lieut. [John F.] Reynolds was up, and flung its balls among them with great precision, until they scampered over the hill and we saw no more of them.[61]

This ended the threat to the American supply train at Buena Vista. In the meantime Col. Jefferson Davis's Mississippi Rifles, Col. Joseph Lane's Third Indiana Regiment, and Sherman's and Bragg's batteries had repulsed an even heavier charge somewhat southeast of Buena Vista, putting the Mexicans in full retreat along the eastern mountain. An unexplained flag of truce, which passed between the two armies at this time enabled the imperiled Mexican soldiers to regain the main army. But late that afternoon, Taylor's artillery under Captains Bragg and Sherman and Lieutenants John Paul Jones O'Brien, George H. Thomas, and John F. Reynolds repulsed a Mexican charge at the extreme left. When night came, Santa Anna retreated, leaving Taylor's army victorious.[62]

During the afternoon of February 23 Pike had continued, under May's command, in support of Lieutenant Reynold's artillery pieces on the American left. But when firing ceased at dusk that evening, Pike was sent with his squadron to the right flank to reconnoiter the mountains and to see that the Mexicans did not establish a battery there during the night.

> The night was cold, the men had left their blankets and great coats in Saltillo; but we mounted, our horses and ourselves half fed, and proceeded to our position—where with the horses half in line, and the men lying by their bridles, we, half frozen, passed the night.... Just before day the Mexican fires died out; and at daybreak, two large ones, where we had supposed the Generals to be, appeared to die away likewise. At broad-day, we discovered they had retreated, and we returned to camp, where a tumult of joy had succeeded to gloom and uneasiness. We then knew we had gained a great victory, for the army had fled from the field and acknowledged his defeat.[63]

During the afternoon Pike was ordered to ride south along the road to Agua Nueva to observe the movements of the enemy. He remained on this duty until it was established that Santa Anna was in full retreat for San Luis Potosi; then on February 28 Pike's squadron was ordered back to Saltillo and again placed under command of Major Warren, now military governor of the city.[64]

Because there was some degree of jealousy and friction between the officers and men of Pike's squadron and those of the Arkansas regiment, the two commands remained separated after the return to Saltillo. Pike's corps was encamped at Arispi's Mills, one mile south of Saltillo, on April 8, when Pike and twenty-five of his men were directed to accompany Lt. J. L. Collins and a party of twelve who were returning to Chihuahua with orders from General Taylor for Col. Alexander W. Doniphan to bring his regiment to the main army, whence they would be sent to New Orleans for discharge.[65] Pike, the ranking officer, took command of the party. They went by way of Parras and Lorenzo to Napimi, a town of some 3,000 inhabitants, which surrendered to Pike on April 16.[66] The band then moved on through San Jose to Jimines, where, although the town was swarming with Mexican soldiers, they rode "directly to the Prefect's," from whom Pike demanded and received quarters and supplies for his men and forage for the horses. The Americans passed the night with a good deal of anxiety, however, and the next morning, April 20, moved off relieved that not a single mishap had marred their stay. Three days later Pike's fast-riding party reached Chihuahua, having traversed over 500 hostile miles in fifteen days.⁶⁷ The anxious men of Doniphan's command, guided by Pike, all departed from Chihuahua before April 28. On the return trip were not only Pike and Josiah Gregg, but John T. Hughes, historian of the Doniphan expedition, the three making up what Robert Selph Henry calls the "most distinguished literary trio" to make any of the marches of the Mexican War.⁶⁸ Reaching Saltillo on May 22, Doniphan's Missourians moved on to the Rio Grande, thence across the Gulf to New Orleans for discharge.⁶⁹

By the time Pike returned from the Chihuahua mission the twelve months' enlistment of his squadron was almost up. Consequently near the end of May the squadron was ordered to Monterey, where Pike and his men were on June 7 paid and mustered out of the service.⁷⁰ Anxious to return home, Pike and the majority of the squadron immediately went on to the coast and took deck passage on a ship to New Orleans, thence by steamboat up the Mississippi and Arkansas Rivers to Little Rock. Arriving at the hometown landing on July 9, the volunteers were welcomed by a large crowd. On the same boat with Pike and his men were Colonel Roane and several members of the Arkansas regiment. William F. Pope tells that as the men were debarking the father of one of Colonel Roane's men, J. D. Adams, greeted J. D. and said, "I hear you all fought like h—l at Buena Vista." But J. D., who was still in his teens, gave "one of his characteristic laughs [and] replied: 'We ran like h—l at Buena Vista.'" "The joke," said Pope, "was greatly relished by some, but not by all."⁷¹ Within two weeks the joy of the homecoming was to be marred by a much more unpleasant occurrence—a duel between Pike and Roane.

In order to understand the quarrel whence this fight developed, it is necessary to go back to Saltillo, where, on March 8, Pike wrote home to the editor of the *Gazette* a description of the battle of Buena Vista. In his account Pike passed up no opportunity to criticize the leadership of the regimental officers—Yell and Roane—during the action of February 23.

> It is a sad thing that brave men, for they were brave, should be . . . destroyed for want of discipline. In the first place, the companies of our Regiment engaged there, had been hardly drilled at all, except what little the company officers had done. The Colonel and Lieutenant Colonel had never drilled them since they left San Antonio. Their order once broken could not be restored, and a retreat was bound to be a rout. . . . Had they . . . possessed that mobility and facility of changing front which only discipline could give, they could not have been routed as they were. Poor Yell! He atoned for his error with his life; but other brave men died with him, who were not in fault. . . .
>
> It must not be understood that I intend to accuse any, much less officers, of a lack of bravery—on the contrary, the universal testimony is that the officers behaved with great gallantry—but the astonishing confusion for want of discipline, utterly broken up, dispersed and disorganized their commands, so that they could not be collected together. Many of the men behaved heroically, but their individual courage and conduct could not restore confidence or order to the mass. . . .
>
> This battle, glorious in its results, has proven several things. It will not answer to take undisciplined troops, and especially undisciplined cavalry, into the field.

It is murderous. Men must not only be *drilled*, but disciplined. They must not only like, but respect their superior officers for their superior knowledge, and fear them because they have been taught to obey.[72]

Soon after writing this letter Pike went to Chihuahua, but on his return to Saltillo on May 22, he was confronted by certain members of the Arkansas regiment with a complaint that he had not only made false statements concerning the conduct of the regiment during the action of February 23, but had also accused the corps of a lack of courage in face of the enemy. Chagrined because he felt the regimental officers had spread these reports among the men, Pike immediately wrote General Wool requesting him to appoint a court of inquiry for the purpose of investigating the false complaints. The gravity of the situation may be seen by the fact that Pike told the general that unless the matter was looked into it would result in "great difficulty and perhaps loss of life."[73]

The court, consisting of Colonels William H. Bissell and William Weatherford, Maj. William A. Richardson, and Lt. W. B. Franklin, Judge Advocate, assembled on May 24 at General Wool's Buena Vista headquarters. Colonel Roane, who had succeeded the deceased Yell, and Captains Hunter, Inglish, Desha, and Dilliard were called before the body for examination, as was Pike. In a statement before the court Pike reiterated that he had never "accused the regiment of cowardice." He said that he had also learned since the battle that Colonel Yell's men retreated from the mountainside on February 23 in better order than was first thought, but Pike repeated that the regiment had been "badly managed, owing to want of discipline, and lack of military skill in the commander, which exposed it to great disadvantage." The men, however, "acted as well and did as good service as any volunteer cavalry in the same state of discipline." Apparently Roane and his subordinate officers did not welcome a full scale investigation of the behavior of the Arkansas cavalry, doubtlessly fearing that such a procedure might uncover unpleasant truths. They declared themselves satisfied with Pike's statements and announced to the court that all matters in dispute between "Capt. Pike and the Regiment have been amicably adjusted." The official opinion of the court was that the "difficulty between Captain Pike and the officers of the Arkansas regiment, grew out of a misunderstanding, and that neither party are at all to blame in the matter."[74]

When Pike returned to Little Rock in July, he discovered—that which had been concealed at the hearing on May 24—that both Colonel Roane and Capt. Edward Hunter had asserted in letters to the *Banner* not only that Pike's squadron had been separated from the regiment on February 22–23, but also that it had taken no part in the battle on either of those days, being, as Hunter declared, "without the range of gunshot."[75] So vexed was Pike at this deception that he promptly issued a challenge to Roane.

Most writers have attempted to lay the principal blame for this duel upon Pike, whose criticism of the Arkansas regiment, according to these accounts, grew out of the fact that he was brooding over the defeat that Colonel Yell handed him in the regimental election the year before.[76] Surely no one can deny that bad political feelings prompted both Pike's and Roane's statements. The records indicate, however, that Pike's assertions are supportable by evidence, while Roane's statement that Pike's squadron was not at the battleground on February 23 was a willful lie. It may be that Roane intended to embroil Pike in an editorial dispute and thus allow the truth of Pike's case to be confused and destroyed in the eyes of the anti-Whig Arkansas public. But whatever Roane's intention, his plan was disrupted by Pike's decision to fight, this time with weapons instead of words.

Pike and Roane met on July 29, 1847, on a sandbar in the Arkansas River opposite Fort Smith, in the Cherokee Nation. Only a few spectators were present. Pike was accompanied by Luther Chase of Little Rock and John Drennen of Van Buren serving as seconds; Dr. James A. Dibrell of Van Buren, acting as surgeon; and William H. Causins, Pat Farrelly, and Dr. R. Thurston of Little Rock, present as friends. Henry M. Rector and Robert W. Johnson of Little Rock acted as seconds for Roane, while Dr. Phillip Burton of Little Rock, served as his physician. Their positions determined by lot, Pike stood upstream and Roane down. Henry M. Rector said many years afterward that Pike's "indifference and deliberation impressed me." He smoked a cigar "enjoyably" up to the very moment for the firing to begin. At the "call" both parties stepped forward ten paces, and a pair of beautiful dueling pistols was loaded and placed in their hands. At the word both fired, but neither was hit. The second fire proved no more damaging than the first. According to Doctor Dibrell, whose account of the meeting appeared in the *Gazette*, April 2, 1893, an unorthodox procedure for the *code d'honneur* took place while the seconds were preparing for a third fire.

> Pike and myself were sitting on a cottonwood log on the edge of a forest that fringed the bar, when Dr. Burton was seen approaching us, with his usual slow and dignified step, and when within a few paces of us, beckoned to me to meet him. I did so. He remarked: "Dibrell, it's a d——d shame that these men should stand here and shoot at each other until one or the other is killed or wounded. They have shown themselves to be brave men and would fire all day unless prevented. The seconds on neither side can interfere, because it would be considered a great disparagement for either to make a proposition for cessation of hostilities. So, let us, as surgeons, assume the responsibility and say they shall not fire another time; that unless they do as we desire we will leave the field to them helpless, however cruel it might seem."
>
> I replied that I knew nothing about the code, but would consult my principal. I stated Dr. Burton's proposition word for word as made to me. Pike remarked, "I want one more fire at him and will hit him in a vital part; I believe he has tried to kill me; I have not tried to hit him."
>
> After reflection, he said, "Do as you think proper about it, but do not by anything compromise my honor."[77]

The good offices of Doctors Dibrell and Burton, however contrary to the dueling creed, were effective. The combat was stopped; Roane and Pike shook hands and agreed never to refer to the difficulty again.[78] Thus it was, said Rector, that the affair which he had "calculated" to end with a funeral resulted in a "banquet."[79] Pike returned unharmed to his family and friends in Little Rock, where at thirty-eight years of age he was just coming into his own as a useful citizen both to Arkansas and the South.

XVIII

Slavery, Sectionalism, and the Pacific Railroad

IN 1844 PIKE HAD PROFESSED to be no defender of states' rights, declaring, with South Carolina nullification in mind, that it was treason for a state to refuse to obey an act of Congress. He also denied that the states had the right to decide when a Federal law was or was not constitutional: "*That* question the supreme judiciary alone is competent to settle." And he solemnly warned that if the Constitution and Union were to be preserved, the time had come when the national government must never again yield to the states.

> If the general government had coerced South Carolina [in 1833] into obedience, as Jackson would have done, if he had been let alone, (and that, too, without any bloodshed), instead of allowing herself to be bullied into a compromise, that would have been the last attempt to set the national authority at defiance. Clearly in the wrong as South Carolina was, as Webster proved her to be, she could not have stood a week against the moral forces of the government; and if she had attempted to withstand it, a few traitors less in the world would have wrought no harm.[1]

Yet from 1848 on, if Pike was not so rabid an advocate of states' rights as men like Calhoun, Rhett, and Yancey, he indicated clearly enough that he was moving further and further away from his strong national beliefs of the past and closer to the states' rights camp. His course was not only natural but quite typical. Southern Whigs who professed to be nationalists were becoming scarce, and for two reasons. Firstly, the South had become sectionally minded; and, secondly, politics was in a state of flux as a result of sectionalism. The South had developed a sectional-political platform of sorts during the congressional debates in the 1820s over internal improvements, public land, the national bank, and tariffs. Her sectional consciousness was intensified in the 1830s and 1840s by the virulent attack of northern abolitionists not only upon slavery but upon southern society in general. Thereafter, no matter how much southern Democrats and Whigs might disagree on national political issues, they inevitably mustered to the defense of their way of life. And although they were unable to devise an effective way to stop the growth of the abolition movement, or to reason with its adherents, they evolved a wonderful apologia for nearly every phase of southern life.

This apologia grew in remarkableness as the abolitionists grew in viciousness. Southern society, so the antislavery argument ran, was polluted throughout by slavery. Southern defenders answered that slavery was good, that slavery was perfect, that slavery was the builder of the noble character and leadership qualities of the slaveholder, that slavery was the only sound and permanent basis for republican government, that slavery was the only truly beneficial relationship between capital and labor ever devised, and, finally, that the South, like ancient Greece, was a perfect society because it was based upon the institution of slavery. Thus it came to pass that even though many southerners might dislike the society in which they lived, their dissatisfaction was usually voiced in condemnation of the North, which they came to blame for all their evils and their shortcomings.

As a society the South was anything but homogeneous, though it had certain distinguishable characteristics that set it aside from the rest of the country, among which was its distinctive weather, generally warmer than that of the North, and basically responsible perhaps for the southern way of life; its ruralism; its dependence upon the cultivation of the important staple crops, tobacco, cotton, rice, and sugar; and its peculiar institution of slavery. The routine of daily living throughout the South was tied to the annual cultivation-cycles of the staples, and in Arkansas, at least in the part of Arkansas where Pike lived, the local culture was attuned to the production of cotton.

The river bottoms and the lowlands of southern and eastern Arkansas were being filled in the 1830s and 1840s by planters from the older slave states. They came in search of new fertile land and found it plentiful and cheap. These men became Pike's friends. He drew up their deeds, handled their claims and lawsuits, wrote their wills, and defended some of them on charges of murder. He spent many nights in their homes while on the circuit, ate their food, drank their liquor, smoked their cigars, swapped yarns, and argued politics with them. Those of the planters who came to Little Rock as legislators in turn visited Pike, stayed with him, played cards with him, and drank and ate off his board. Pike's real property at this time consisted of his mansion and a few city lots in Little Rock; he had no slaves except a handful of household servants.[2] But it was evident that he saw nothing radically wrong with the system of using slave labor in producing cotton. Fees from cotton planters composed most of his income, and anything that affected them adversely affect him likewise. Truly enough, as ex-Yankees were usually wont to do in the South, Pike kept to himself his thoughts about "the propriety of slavery in the abstract, or as to man's right to hold another in bondage."[3] But there was one thing, he said in 1844, on which he could speak positively.

> The Constitution recognizes slavery, and bases Congressional representation in the southern States, in part upon it. By that great contract, the right to hold slaves, which the south possessed before it was framed, is amply reserved, guaranteed and protected and the north has nothing at all to do with it, nor northern men any right whatever to meddle with it.[4]

Arkansas slaves also represented an immense financial investment, and Pike had a great respect for property. As a lawyer, steeped in the writings of Blackstone and Story, Marshall's decisions, and the common law, and entertaining the traditional nineteenth-century American concept of the sacredness of property, he distrusted change, worshipped stability, and revered the past.[5]

Above all else Pike loved and revered the Union. It was always his boast that he was born in Boston in "the shadow of Faneuil Hall, the cradle of American Independence."

In his youth he imbibed the romantic nationalism of his beloved New England. As a young man struggling to establish himself in the practice of law he absorbed from the texts of Blackstone and Story an intense veneration for the common law and the American Constitution, which in turn increased his admiration for the Union.[6] This nationalism was strong in Pike, and it would be hard to down. Nevertheless, the forces molding Pike's mind and ideas in the 1840s were converting him into a southerner.

Pike worked hard in the 1840s, spending seven months of each year "on the circuit" and the other five in his office at Little Rock, reading, writing, and talking law. He put in eighteen or nineteen hours a day while at home, month after month.[7] But life was not all work for Pike. He somehow found time at night and on Sundays for reading and study outside the law. With great expense, he greatly expanded in the 1840s the number and variety of volumes in his library.[8] He found time, too, to participate in such social activities as the town afforded. He commanded the Little Rock Guards in parades and at various public celebrations, where, because of his reputation as a man of letters and his popularity as an orator, he was frequently called upon to deliver addresses. Beginning in 1843 he belonged to the "Club of Forty," founded the year before "by those who were fond of literary pursuits." Its members contributed money for subscriptions to "the various reviews and periodicals" of the United States and Great Britain.[9] Pike, donor of many magazines and books to the organization,[10] served as president of the club in 1843 and as such directed the "conversational discussions" at its Saturday night meetings, where political topics were not infrequently the order of business.[11] Diversion from the regular order of things came also by way of business and political trips to New Orleans, Memphis, Louisville, Nashville, and the East.[12] The decade of the forties was perhaps the happiest of Pike's life. He might, it is true, indulge in an occasional outburst of living in "this out of the world region."[13] But he owned a fine home, had a comfortable income, and was esteemed by a host of friends and acquaintances. Living in the big house with Mary Ann and the children was pleasant.

Pike was, then, an Arkansan, with an Arkansan wife and a family of little Arkansans, and Arkansans were southerners. Not all Arkansans depended on slavery and cotton. The men of the hill country in the northern and western part of the state had hardly any slaves, grew little cotton, had little money, raised hogs and corn, voted Democratic. But Pike had nothing to do with the mountain boys. He lived in Little Rock, went by steamboat to the courts along the Arkansas, Mississippi, and lower White Rivers, and by two-horse buggy to those in the southern counties along the Red and Ouachita Rivers. This was cotton country in the main; most of the counties had strong Whig minorities, some occasionally gave Whig majorities. Because planters grew cotton and sold it for cash, they paid fees when the year's crop was sold. For this reason Pike liked to handle cases for wealthy planters.[14] Because his interests were so closely tied to their interests, Pike came to have the same outlook on southern rights as planters, and when the sectional squabble began over the lands that had been won from Mexico, his basic loyalty to the South readily disclosed itself. Almost overnight he discarded Webster's nationalist theory for Calhoun's compact theory. He went over, however, with reservations. His patriotism, and love for the flag and the Union were still dearer to him than southern rights, and were to be for several years to come.

The quarrel over the new territory began before Pike reached Mexico, even, in fact, before the United States had acquired it. In August, 1846, President Polk sent a special message to Congress, requesting an appropriation to be used in negotiating peace with Mexico. It was understood in Congress that the money would be used to purchase territory from Mexico, since it had nothing else with which to indemnify the United States. But the proposition of acquiring new territory revived the slavery question. On August 8, David Wilmot, a Pennsylvania Democrat, amended the bill in the House with a proviso that none of the territory to be acquired from Mexico should ever be open to slavery. The amendment passed in the House, but was defeated in the Senate. The issue, winning fame as the Wilmot Proviso, was renewed, however, the next year in Congress and though defeated was not vanquished.

In the debate over the organization of Oregon Territory in 1848 it again waxed strong. Proslavery leaders, holding a majority in the Senate, refused to organize Oregon as a free territory, while the House, where Free Soilers held the balance of power, would consent to nothing less. The political status of California and New Mexico came under discussion at the same time and added oil to the flames. Southerners, fearing the North might not agree to allow them more room in which to extend slavery, were hesitant to join with the North in extending freedom. Week after week in the spring and summer of 1848 the debate continued. Southern extremists, led by Calhoun, denied that either Congress or the territorial inhabitants could prohibit slavery in a territory; Calhoun believed that slavery could not be prohibited in a territory until it was about to enter the Union. When it was suggested by southerners and northern moderates that the Missouri Compromise line be extended to the Pacific, southern and northern diehards refused to be appeased. Free Soilism and the Wilmot Proviso had so angered the followers of Calhoun that they would accept nothing less than the principle that slavery might go into any territory of the United States, whether it be north, south, east, or west. northern radicals, led by Sen. John P. Hale of New Hampshire, were equally stubborn. They demanded not only a free Oregon but the enactment of the principle of the Wilmot Proviso respecting all the territory acquired from Mexico.

At last reason was tried. On July 12 the whole controversy was placed in the hands of a select committee in the Senate, headed by John M. Clayton of Delaware. Six days later Clayton reported a bill providing that the territorial legislature in Oregon should decide the question of slavery there, while the problem would be left to territorial courts in California and New Mexico. All cases arising over slavery in any of the three new territories would, explained Clayton, thus be referred to the Supreme Court. The bill passed the Senate but was tabled in the House. Nevertheless, a separate bill for organizing Oregon under the Northwest Ordinance of 1787 passed the Senate on the last day of the session. The question of New Mexico and California was postponed to the short session of 1848–49.

Meanwhile the presidential campaign had temporarily taken the mind of the country off the wrangling in Congress. At the appointed times the three national parties had met in conventions and nominated candidates for president and vice president. The Whigs chose Zachary Taylor of Louisiana, the Democrats, Lewis Cass of Michigan, and the Free-Soilers, Martin Van Buren of New York. Neither the Whig nor the Democratic platform mentioned the highly explosive question of slavery expansion. As a consequence the state campaigns were left to be fought primarily along local lines.

General Taylor had been stationed at Fort Smith before the Mexican War and was well known and generally liked by the people of Arkansas. Catapulted into fame by his brilliant victories in northern Mexico, he was the idol of the Arkansas troops, whether Democratic or Whig, who had fought under him at Buena Vista, and Arkansas Whigs thought that he might be the one man who could break the stranglehold of the Democrats upon the state. It was, therefore, with great optimism and zeal that Pike, a close friend of Taylor,[15] began early in the summer of 1848 to marshal the Whig forces for the coming contest. Long accused of being the boss of the Whig Central Committee at Little Rock and thereby the dictator of the Whig Party in Arkansas, Pike hoped to avoid such criticism in the campaign by holding a state nominating convention.[16] But correspondence among the party leaders soon revealed the impracticability of the proposal. In consequence the Whig Central Committee at Little Rock was again called upon by editors and leaders over the state to select an electoral ticket for the party. The committee readily accepted the invitation. Pike's hand was clearly discernible in the ticket announced on June 15. It consisted of Capt. John Preston Jr. of Helena, Jesse Turner of Van Buren, and John W. Cocke of Little Rock. Preston had been Pike's junior officer in Mexico, and both Turner and Cocke were his intimate friends.[17] Each presidential elector was promptly notified of his selection and urged to "take the field at once" in order to aid Whig candidates running for the legislature as well as to win support for the presidential election in the fall. They were requested to communicate with each other immediately to determine which counties each would visit and were asked "to attend personally" to the formation of Taylor clubs in each county.[18] Having helped make preliminary arrangements for the canvass of the State, Pike threw himself into the work of arousing enthusiasm for Taylor in Little Rock and Pulaski County. On June 21 he addressed at Little Rock a large meeting of Whigs from Pulaski and Prairie Counties who had gathered to ratify the nominations of Taylor and Fillmore and to choose candidates for the state legislature.[19] A month later, on July 24, he helped form a "Young Men's Rough and Ready Club"[20] in the city for the purpose of supporting the Whig cause, and he soon made numerous addresses to the club. On August 1, four days before the county election, he delivered what the editor of the Whig *State Gazette* called "a most excellent and admirable speech.... The tinsel of office and station was stripped from the putrid and festering corpse of Locofocoism, [which was] ... displayed to view in all its hideous corruption."[21]

Aside from the presidential canvass the most important contest in the state in 1848 was the election of Arkansas's sole member of the national House of Representatives. The Whigs ran Thomas W. Newton, who had previously on account of a division in Democratic ranks at a special election, December 14, 1846, been elected to fill out the remaining two and a half months of Yell's term. His choice was something of a political anomaly, since at the time Robert W. Johnson had already been elected the previous August to succeed Yell on March 4, 1847. Now Newton undertook to oppose Johnson in the regular election, and was severely beaten. Johnson polled on August 7, 1848, over five thousand more votes than Newton,[22] though in "Old Pulaski," "the Palladium of

Whiggery," Newton received a majority and a full Whig slate was elected to the legislature.[23] The victory in Pulaski helped mitigate the discouraging results elsewhere in the state, and during the late summer and fall the Whig leaders redoubled their efforts to carry Arkansas for "Old Zack" in November. Jesse Turner stumped the counties of northern Arkansas while Preston and Cocke covered southern and western Arkansas for the Whigs.

Pike also lent his voice to the Whig cause. At Van Buren in early August he asked "the honest portion" of the Democracy to join with him in support of General Taylor, and in the enthusiasm of the moment—perhaps as an argument that Taylor's military experience was a valuable asset for the presidency—went so far as to declare that General Jackson had "possessed the elements of greatness."[24] The Democratic editor of the *Van Buren Intelligencer* in reply reminded the people that "eight or ten years ago the Captain could see no strong points in the character of Gen. Jackson to qualify him for President; now he has progressed and discovered that Gen. Jackson possessed the elements of greatness." But even this, the editor continued, was proof that Pike had progressed only to the point where the Democrats were twenty years before.[25] Back in the Whig stronghold of "Old Pulaski" by October 6, Pike addressed a called meeting of the Rough and Ready Club. His speech was declared by a friendly editor to be "one of the most able whig speeches we have heard in many a day." "Pike dissipated several Locofoco humbugs, refuted sundry Locofoco calumnies, and pointed out . . . clearly and indisputably the fatal consequences which have resulted from Locofoco competition and misrule," but the admiring editor failed to say how he went about it.[26]

The Whig efforts in Arkansas were in vain, for the state's three electoral votes went to Cass; yet Taylor's popularity had narrowed the Democratic majority to seventeen hundred votes, making the election one of the closest presidential contests in Arkansas before 1860.[27] The success of Taylor elsewhere in the country prompted the Whigs at Little Rock to long and lively celebrations, and Pike brought forth two victory songs for the occasion.[28]

With the presidential contest out of the way Pike was for sometime engrossed in seeing that Democrats were removed from federal offices in Arkansas and replaced by loyal and deserving Whigs. Because the Arkansas delegation to Congress was made up solely of Democrats there would be no one in Washington to urge the cause of the Arkansas Whigs. Pike, who wished to go to Washington to apply for admission to practice before the Supreme Court of the United States, decided to attend in person to the matter of federal patronage while in the city. He was in Washington by March 6, when he wrote President Taylor of his mission.[29] He was probably referred to Thomas Ewing, Secretary of the Interior Department, on whom Pike and John Bell called soon after.[30] Pike submitted a long list of recommendations to Ewing,[31] but was told that the Arkansas Whigs would have to be satisfied with the offices within the state. Ewing did consent, nevertheless, to bestow one of the Indian agencies on an Arkansan. But letters must be mailed to Washington showing that the Democratic incumbents had "meddled in elections."[32] When Pike returned to Arkansas early in April, he set about getting the needed statements.[33] Accordingly, Ewing's promises were fulfilled. John Drennen of Van Buren got the Choctaw Agency, and Pike's recommendations for the land offices were followed to the letter. For the office of U.S. District Attorney at Little Rock, Pike suggested either Absalom Fowler of Little Rock or Jesse Turner of Van Buren, the former being selected by the administration.[34] Pike hoped, however, to place Turner in an expected vacancy on the bench of the U.S. District Court at Little Rock; it was rumored in Little Rock in early June that Judge Benjamin Johnson was at death's door.[35] But when Judge Johnson died his place was filled by Daniel Ringo, a former Kentuckian, late chief justice of the state supreme court, and an attorney of Little Rock. On December 20 Pike wrote Turner that

> Ringo & his friends did (with Kentucky help I suppose) out manage us. How I do not know. I only know that I used every possible fair endeavor to defeat him and secure you the appointment—and I regret bitterly, for your own sake, and more, for that of the public that I did not succeed.[36]

A more important question than political patronage was on Pike's mind during 1849. This was the all-absorbing topic of a railroad to the Pacific. First suggested as early as 1832,[37] in 1844 a clearly defined plan for building such a road had been presented to Congress by Asa Whitney, a New York merchant. He saw the Pacific railroad as part of a great international highway from the Far East to England and western Europe. Since Oregon was the only U.S. possession fronting on the Pacific in 1844, it was logical that Whitney should have advocated a northern route from Oregon to the Great Lakes, and thence either down the St. Lawrence River or along the system of east-west railways to the Atlantic.[38] No sooner was Whitney's plan made public than others came forward with alternate routes. Stephen A. Douglas, representative in Congress from Illinois, issued in October, 1845, a plan that would have Chicago as the eastern terminal of the road and perhaps San Francisco as the western terminal "if that country could be annexed in time." The Southwestern Convention, which met at Memphis in November, 1845, primarily to encourage the construction of a chain of railroads from the Atlantic to Memphis, took occasion to suggest the possibility of an extension of the line from Memphis to the Pacific, terminating either at San Francisco or Mazatlan.[39]

It was inevitable that the subject of the Pacific railway should become involved in the sectional dispute between the North and South. In the early rivalry for the road the northern route appeared, however, to have the advantage over the southern, in that it would lie entirely within the American boundaries, while the southern, no matter how superior in terrain and climate its advocates claimed it was, would run through Mexican territory.[40] But by 1848 the conquests of the Mexican War had secured the intervening territory between Texas and the Pacific and had added strength to the argument for having the road run along a southern route. The discovery of gold in California in early 1848 increased a thousand-fold the already enthusiastic national demand for the transcontinental railroad. Accordingly, the sectional contest for the political and commercial advantage of controlling the eastern terminal of the railway was greatly intensified.

Behind the desire of southern leaders to secure the construction of a Pacific railroad along a southern route was the hope of effecting an economic regeneration of their section. Long conscious of what they termed "Southern decline," the people of the South were becoming increasingly aware in the late forties that the North was fast outstripping their section in economic development. The South was in large measure dependent upon cotton, the most important of her staples, and though cotton was being grown in ever increasing amounts in the forties, the section found itself little wealthier. The North had long before captured the commercial, or money-making, end of the cotton business, and the planters seemed helpless to free themselves. Northern factors handled their cotton, advanced them credit on it, shipped it to northern and English mills for them, sold it for them, and pocketed, so southerners claimed, the profits of the sale. Northern merchants in turn sold the planters most of their goods, imported and domestic. And while the South remained tied to agriculture, the North diversified its economy, exploited its natural resources, built factories, expanded and improved its transportation facilities, and rapidly outgrew the South in wealth and population. Southerners were irritated at their economic vassalage, but they were downright frightened at the thought that the North was gaining predominance in Congress. By the late forties the North, which had long had command of the House, was threatening to wrest control of the Senate from the South. Moreover, northern leaders in Congress were showing a determination to prevent slavery from extending into the territory acquired from Mexico, while northern abolitionists, a minority group, were striving to destroy slavery itself. Southerners, seeing little difference between those who would destroy slavery and those who would limit it, jumped to its defense and tried frantically to devise ways to keep control of the general government and to render themselves economically independent of the North. The demand to have the Pacific railroad built along a southern route was one of the methods by which they hoped to free themselves from the grasping Yankees and revive their prosperity. Pike became the great spokesman of this cause.[41]

The Pacific railroad had particular interest for Arkansas. As early as 1847 William E. Woodruff, editor of the *Little Rock Democrat*, advocated in his paper the construction of a railroad along the thirty-fifth parallel from Memphis through Arkansas to the Pacific, though nothing came of his recommendation.[42] The people of the state, while anxious that the road should run through Arkansas, and seeing in the prospect visions of increased wealth to her landowners, made no attempt to translate thoughts into action.[43]

Pike was the first Arkansan to take positive steps for bringing the Pacific railroad through the state. On January 6, 1849, a meeting attended by citizens of Pulaski County, members of the legislature, and other interested persons from over the state, was held at Little Rock to get up a petition to Congress for survey of a military road from Memphis to San Francisco. Pike was present and suggested petitioning not for a wagon road but for a railroad, and inviting the people of the South to send delegates to a general convention to meet at Memphis in the course of the summer for the purpose of discussing the matter further. Resolutions embodying Pike's proposition were drawn up by a committee and adopted at an adjourned session of the meeting January 8, 1849. Regarding it "important for the interest of the southwestern States" that the proposed railroad should begin at Memphis and run either to San Francisco or Monterey on the Pacific coast, the resolution declared that the southern route was shorter and more direct, less likely to be "obstructed by snow or ice in winter, or extreme heat in summer," cheaper to construct than any that had been put forward, and was needed as a military communication to the western frontier. Since it was the duty of the general government to construct this "great national work," Congress was asked to initiate the project by having the right of way surveyed by the Corps of Engineers. Finally, to further the views set forth in the resolutions, the meeting invited the people of the southern states to send delegates to a convention at Memphis on the following Fourth of July for considering the subject of the Pacific railroad. Pike was one of twelve delegates selected by ex-governor Drew, chairman of the meeting, to represent Arkansas at the proposed convention.[44]

The citizens of Memphis heartily accepted the Arkansas proposal. At a meeting held February 22, 1849, they endorsed the invitations already issued by Arkansas and appointed a committee to prepare an address upon the subject.[45] The committee's "Circular to the Citizens of the United States," which was distributed widely throughout the country, attempted to avoid the sectional aspects of the Arkansas plan. The Tennesseans appealed to the truly national interests that would be served by reestablishing the eastern terminal at, or opposite, Memphis. Here was the one location where the welfare of "the whole country, north, south, east and west, foreign and domestic," would be taken into consideration. But in

> advocating one of the proposed routes, over all others, we would deeply regret to excite sectional jealousies or prejudices, or that it should be considered that the magnitude of the question had been lost sight of by local consideration. The road to be built must be located. The friends of each of the several routes, which have been proposed, have appealed to the public—we do the same, with entire confidence and willingness to abide by their decision.

They invited all advocates of the railroad, no matter what their favorite route or scheme for the construction might be, to attend the convention, assuring each "a sincere and cordial welcome."[46]

Reaction of southern states to the proposed convention was varied. The editor of the *Richmond Enquirer* recognized the value of the Pacific railroad "to the Union and to our own State, if carried out," but wondered how it could be financed by the general government "consistently with the Constitution." He hoped "to see the great work effected by the enterprise of States and individuals."[47] At New Orleans the editor of the *Daily Crescent*, noting the preparations being made in "the towns of the south and west" for sending delegates to Memphis, recommended that his own city not fail to send a full delegation.

> No matter at what point on the Mississippi the railroad from the Pacific is to terminate, the subject is one of vast and incalculable interest to New Orleans. [But] . . . there are many considerations which might lead us to prefer the southern road—say from San Diego or Monterey to Memphis or Vicksburg—before the northern route from San Francisco to St. Louis. If the Memphis convention is properly conducted, it may furnish the next Congress with a clue as to what the will of the west—including by that term all the States of the Mississippi—is in regard to the proposed road, and as to which route will be the most advantageous for the country at large.[48]

The editor of the *Little Rock Banner* observed the local and sectional interest of the various delegates that were to attend at Memphis and urged his fellow citizens in Little Rock not to forget that their city had originated the idea of the convention. "Having given birth to the bantling, we must not abandon it in its infancy, we must follow it up and foster it, and see that it is trained in the way that we think it should go."[49]

> The establishment of this road through our State will be to us the precursor of untold prosperity. It will develop our vast resources, increase our population and productions, and the value of our lands. It will aid materially in placing Arkansas in that rank among her Sister States, where, by her geographical position, her unrivaled soil and inexhaustible mineral wealth, she is destined to shine. We must not stand idly by listening to the distant roar of the enthusiasm that is expressed elsewhere, and watching the vigorous efforts of our neighbors in Tennessee. . . . A great enterprise like this can only be effected by popular enthusiasm. . . . As we value success, we must be zealous; we must be prompt and active. . . . Since this proposition was first agitated here, it has been circulated far and wide. Every State, South and West of the Alleghanies, has eagerly caught up the idea.

Arkansans were to publicize the superiority of the route through their state. Virginia, Kentucky, North and South Carolina, Georgia, Alabama, Mississippi, and Tennessee would be its advocate. The delays in completing the Panama railroad, the danger of the proposed route through Mexico, and the recent disastrous failure of John C. Fremont's party in its attempt to find a pass through the Rockies at the headwaters of the Arkansas River would "do the rest."[50]

In June the meeting of the Memphis Pacific Railroad Convention was postponed from July 4 until October 23 because of the "ravages of cholera in the South and West."[51] Both the *Banner* and the *Gazette* sought to keep up the interest of Arkansas in the convention. At a meeting in Little Rock in June the Arkansas delegation was increased so as to include all the leading state and federal officials. As the time for the meeting approached arrangements were completed with James Timms, proprietor of the Great Western and United States Mail Line, to make available the steamboat *William Armstrong* for the trip to Memphis. He proposed a fare of ten dollars each way, or five dollars on the return trip from Napoleon to Little Rock.[52] As a result of these efforts, eighty-one of the four hundred delegates who assembled at Memphis in October represented Arkansas.[53] Though Pike was a delegate, and the originator of the idea for the convention, he was greatly overshadowed by the eminent officeholders in the Arkansas delegation, which numbered in its ranks Gov. John Selden Roane, Pike's recent antagonist, ex-Governor Drew, and U.S. senators Solon Borland and William K. Sebastian. Nevertheless, Pike's close friend, Col. Absalom Fowler, for whom Pike had just secured the post of federal district attorney at Little Rock, was given the honor of presiding over the convention pending the arrival of the permanent president, Matthew F. Maury. This was in recognition of the fact that Arkansas had fostered the idea in the beginning.[54]

As the work of the convention progressed there was little doubt that a majority of its members were there to test the strength that would be brought to support the southern route for the Pacific railroad. A few days before a convention at St. Louis, evenly divided between the partisans of Benton's "central national highway" route running from St. Louis and Douglas's northern route beginning at Chicago, had adopted a compromise plan calling on Congress "to provide for" a great trunk railway from the Mississippi Valley with branches to Memphis, St. Louis, and Chicago. Before adjourning the meeting selected a committee of fifty to attend the Memphis convention in order to secure the acceptance of the same resolutions by that body. But the Memphis convention was in no mood to concur in the St. Louis plan. It adopted a resolution recommending the "particular attention of the General Government" to the "special advantages" of the route from "San Diego, on the Pacific Ocean, crossing the Colorado of the West, running along the Gila river . . . in a direction to the Paso del Norte, thence across the state of Texas . . . between 32° and 33° of north latitude, terminating at some point on the Mississippi between the mouth of the Ohio river and the mouth of the Red river." The resolution declared that it was the duty of the government to make explorations and surveys of all the proposed routes and to select the best and shortest one, and it asserted that "the public lands of the United States" constituted a legitimate fund for financing the railroad.[55]

Pike was dissatisfied with the plan adopted at Memphis. As a Whig he had long held that Congress had the constitutional right to construct internal improvements within the states. But the convention, "to protect the tender feelings" of certain delegates, had ruled against injecting the controversial subject into its discussions and while it declared in its final resolution that the public lands were a proper fund for constructing the railway, it had made no outright request for the federal government to grant lands to construct the road within a state. Pike was opposed to their noncommittal policy. He regretted, too, that sectional feelings had been projected into the assembly and deplored the fact that the convention had made no effort to conciliate such feelings by responding to the St. Louis Proposal with a "really national plan" for the Pacific railroad.[56]

Having mulled over these shortcomings, Pike formulated what he chose to call a "National Plan of an Atlantic and Pacific Railroad." On November 21, 1849, he presented the plan to the public in an address before a large audience at Memphis. The speech, aside from its relation to the Pacific railroad, was of particular importance as the earliest evidence showing how the great sectional issues then before Congress had affected Pike's thinking. He summarized his dissatisfaction with the results of the late Memphis convention, explaining that the convention rules and his own consciousness that his humble name and local position could command no support for any argument he might offer had prevented his expressing his views to the convention. Now, however, his thoughts were fully matured, and the grave dangers that beset his country encouraged him to speak out. The St. Louis and Memphis conventions had clearly demonstrated that the Pacific railroad had become a sectional question. No one could ignore that fact, though the members of both of the recent meetings had attempted to shape their courses as if it did not exist. There was no doubt that the road would be built. "*Where* and *how* it is to be built, are the only questions." The important fact that had to be considered in dealing with these two questions was the political situation of the country. All minor political differences of the Union were "about to be merged in the great question of North and South." The "great free-soil party" of the North had raised the cry of free territory as a blind for a movement "to transfer the political dominion to the North, and there to retain it. It is the commencement of a strict alliance of the northern States, for the purpose of swaying the whole political power of the Union." The Pacific railroad had become involved in this struggle.[57]

In examining the question of locating a transcontinental railroad Pike expounded what he believed to be the true basis of the Union. The Constitution and the Union could only exist if the North and South could be maintained on terms of perfect equality; yet everyone knew that the free states would soon control Congress. The key to the preservation of the Union lay, then, in the exercise of congressional power by the northern majority. If the North recognized the difference between its power and its right to do an act and used its power always to place the South and the North on terms of equality the Union could be preserved. Therefore it was of no importance, Pike said, whether or not Congress

> has the mere power to exclude slavery from any territory obtained by the joint means or arms of the North and South. They have no *right* to do it, against the will and without the consent of the South. When the North inserted the Wilmot Proviso in the Oregon Bill, and at the same time positively rejected the proposition to extend the Missouri Compromise line to the Pacific, it said distinctly to the South, "We will not admit of any compromise, but we will assert and maintain our *right* to exclude your property from this territory, and to settle affirmatively the question of power." When the South once submitted to that, it conceded all. There is no longer room for question as to the power of Congress over slavery in California, New Mexico or the District of Columbia and the moment this power was exercised, the North assumed the attitude of a master over the South, and asserted such a power as is wholly inconsistent with the terms of equality on which the Union rests, and on which alone it can be maintained.[58]

Pike held that in supporting the Wilmot Proviso the North had been regardless of patriotism and heedless of the welfare of the Union. He warned that if the free states continued to exercise such power over the South the bonds of the Union would constantly weaken and end in dissolution. It was, therefore, the duty of every patriot to restrict and narrow the means by which the North might abuse the rights of the South. If the South was weaker than the North there was so much the greater reason why northern statesmen should labor to maintain the South in a condition of equality and independence. The welfare of the Union should be the paramount object of every American. But the Union could be preserved and perpetuated only by adhering to the spirit of compromise which created the Constitution and breathed in every line of it and by maintaining and cherishing in every state and section of the Union the feeling of state pride, self-respect, and perfect equality.[59]

Anyone who would vote to build the Pacific railroad solely within one or the other great sections of the Union would be doing incalculable injury to his country, continued Pike. Where then should it be built? The "enlarged and patriotic principle" which had "led Congress always to admit one northern and one Southern State at the same time" furnished an admirable basis for locating the road. It seemed to Pike that it should start at one and the same time from two points on the Mississippi, one at St. Louis, or some other point in the northern States, connected or to be connected by railroad with the northern Atlantic cities, and one at Memphis, or some other point in the southern States, connected or to be connected by railroad with the southern Atlantic cities; that these two roads should be carried forward simultaneously, unite at some point west of Missouri or Arkansas, and one line thence proceed to the Pacific, by such route . . . as shall afford equal facilities and advantages to the South and North, and to the southern and northern Atlantic cities, and that whenever, therefore, another one shall be built from a *terminus* in the North, one shall be built simultaneously from a *terminus* in the South. I do not see how any one who wishes to strengthen the bonds which bind the States together, whether he lives in the North or in the South, can object to this proposition. It seems to me eminently national, patriotic and anti-sectional. And it seems to me that the whole South ought to take its stand upon it, and present it as an *ultimatum* to the North. If they do so, there cannot be a doubt that every Whig and democratic lover of his country in the North will cheerfully assent to and approve it.[60]

Pike would leave to the Corps of Engineers the task of determining the course the main road would take. All he asked was that it be a practicable route and one that would offer equal advantages to each section of the country. The general government had the power and the right, and it was her imperative duty to build the road. But to protect states' rights and to prevent undue expansion of national power once the railway was completed he proposed that "the States, as separate sovereignties" should be granted the privilege of purchasing it, paying for it out of their shares in the proceeds of the public lands and in the profits of the road. Whatever stock the states did not choose to take, could be taken by cities and American citizens. Once, however, the road was out of the hands of the general government he thought its board of directors should be appointed either by the states or by the President of the United States and that freight and passenger rates should be fixed by Congress. For advancing the funds and building the road the general government should be given perpetual free passage for troops, munitions of war, and mails.[61]

Here was Pike's compromise plan for the Pacific railroad. In conclusion and in defense of it he declared that he was not presumptuous enough to imagine that it had no faults but could not help believing that it anticipated many objections. He did not see how any man, of the North or South, could object to its setting out simultaneously from two terminals unless he was opposed to the spirit of compromise by which alone the Union could be preserved. It could not be objected to by state righters, for the road was ultimately to belong to the states. The strictest constitutionalist could not object to its being built by the general government, because the funds expended were to be repaid by the states. He sincerely hoped that the South would unite behind his plan or some similar national one. If it should not and should foolishly urge an exclusively southern route, the North would unhesitatingly vote the South down and build the road entirely within its own limits. But if a plan such as his was presented and the North was frankly told the South wants only equal advantages and facilities and asks no more and will accept no less, there are in every northern state true friends of the Union, honest and patriotic lovers of this country, enough to control public opinion and the votes of their States, who will assent at once, and cheerfully say that the South demands no more than she has a right to ask.[62]

Though his speech was fraught with southern bias, Pike's audience at Memphis was struck with his oratory and the eminent fairness of his plan. They adopted his proposal, drew up a petition to Congress in favor of it, and voted a series of resolutions calling upon the legislature to memorialize Congress upon the subject and recommending that "primary meetings" in Tennessee and neighboring states do likewise.[63] In spite of their enthusiasm, Pike's efforts failed. The approaching session of Congress was to be too busy with the great sectional debate over slavery expansion to have time to devote attention to the Pacific railroad.

XIX

Nobly Did He Vindicate the Union

WHEN PIKE RETURNED FROM MEMPHIS to Little Rock in December 1849, he found the people and the editors of the town filled with misgivings over the sectional trouble brewing in Congress. As the old year gave way to the new his and their apprehensions increased. In October the Mississippi legislature had issued, at Calhoun's instigation, a call for a southern convention to meet at Nashville the first Monday in June 1850 to seek a remedy and formulate a common policy for defending the South against "Northern aggression." To many it appeared that unless Congress could in the meantime find a favorable solution to the slavery controversy, secession would be high on the agenda of the meeting. But Congress was divided. Separate bills were pending before it in relation to the admission of California, New Mexico, and Utah; the abolition of slavery and the slave trade in the District of Columbia; the fugitive slave law; and the Texas–New Mexico boundary. Free Soilers were determined to prevent the extension of slavery to the Mexican cession and southern die-hards were set on maintaining their equality there. President Taylor had alienated southern Whigs by messages in which he recommended the admission of California as a free state without committing himself on the slavery issue. The stage was set for the great drama of 1850.

From the nation's capital "Molaska, the Cosmopolite" wrote January 27, 1850, to the *Little Rock Banner* that he felt "fully authorized" to state that the Arkansas delegation in Congress would make every effort "to head" the Wilmot Proviso. Especially, he informed the editors, was this true in the case of Arkansas's member of the House, Robert W. Johnson, who was a "whole lion" and who would "most assuredly lock horns with it."[1] Johnson, now attending his fourth session of Congress, had won his spurs as an aggressive defender of southern rights by drawing blood from the person of Representative Ficklin of Illinois during a general affray upon the floor of the House in February 1849.[2] A Democrat of long standing, he had just inherited a leading role in the councils of the party in Arkansas through the recent deaths of his kinsman Senator Sevier and his father. He was, therefore, in a position to sway a large portion of the Arkansas populace toward any course that he might choose in the coming struggle. Nor was he long in deciding what that course should be. A week after President Taylor sent to Congress his special message of January 21 on the subject of California statehood, Johnson penned a letter to the "Citizens of Arkansas." "There are," he began, "few Southern men in this Congress who will not subscribe to it when I assert that the union of the Northern and Southern States, under a common Government, for a period beyond the present Congress, is a matter that may be seriously questioned." What had brought things to this perilous juncture? The immediate difficulty was the admission of California, from which by its Constitution, slavery was excluded. But there were other causes. The northern states had

> instructed their delegations . . . to *exclude the South and her property* from our new Territories; to abolish slavery in the District of Columbia; to abolish the slave trade between our Southern States, and to exclude slaves from all forts, arsenals, dock yards, and all other national possessions. They not only give us through Congress, no adequate power . . . [to] recover . . . [our] fugitive slaves, but many of their people engage with impunity in decoying them off, whilst the Legislatures of many free States encourage and support such conduct, with enactments . . . to obstruct all recovery.[3]

The free state constitution of California was, declared Johnson, "a *shameless* fraud upon the South," a trick whereby northern leaders sought to avoid the direct issue of the Wilmot Proviso by throwing themselves "upon the policy of the Cabinet—admit the new States in detail—adopt no policy by which Southern property can be protected in the Territory, and admit none but free States." The plan, warned Johnson, had been admirably conceived. It would give southerners no excuse to break up the Union while northerners destroyed the rights, and circumscribed the limits of the South. He was determined, therefore, to vote against the admission of California, to do everything in his power to defeat the measure, because he firmly believed that "with her admission, unless all other questions be first settled, the Union ought and will dissolve." The North had the erroneous idea that the South would submit to anything, however ruinous or degrading, for the welfare of the Union.[4] If the Union was to be placed in

> the scale, to be weighed against degradation to our people and posterity, and ruin to our country, it will be wise that we shall estimate the nature of this Union, and its actual value. Discuss, then, these subjects at large. Discuss them as freemen. *You have a right to discuss them.* A Government whose acts, whose benefits and evils, will not bear investigation and the searching light of discussion, and which consequently, is sustained upon something other than its equal justice, and the confidence and affection of the people, *should* be destroyed.[5]

A number of the legislatures of southern states had approved the southern convention that would meet at Nashville in June to discuss the formulation of a policy for defending themselves against the encroachments of the North.

Johnson sincerely hoped that Arkansas would not be unrepresented at that convention and that every county in the state would express its sentiments freely and take such steps as would ensure for Arkansas a full, faithful, and able delegation. Since the subject to be discussed was above all party issues he advocated "*that the delegation shall be composed equally of both political parties.*"[6]

Shortly after sending this letter to the editors of the *Banner*, from whose columns it was copied widely by other Democratic editors of the state, Johnson wrote Pike asking him to attend the proposed Nashville convention as a representative of Arkansas. As an enticement to gain Pike's support he held out the prospect that Pike "might gain some reputation by a bold utterance in behalf of the South."[7] A less just man than Pike might have made political capital at the expense of an opponent for making such an offer, but in spite of the implications of Johnson's offer Pike took no offense. Notwithstanding their political differences Pike liked Johnson. Their acquaintance and friendship extended back to 1835 when both were struggling young lawyers in the village of Little Rock, from whence they had ridden forth together upon the circuits. Though since those days Johnson's political star had risen with the Democracy, Pike still esteemed him as a dear friend and ever considered him an upright and honorable man. Thus it was that Pike overlooked features in Johnson's letter which ordinarily he might have spurned outright.

> My dear Friend: You have been kind enough to express to me a flattering wish that I should attend the contemplated Southern Convention . . . where you think, and thank you for it, I might gain some reputation by a bold utterance in behalf of the South. I have also received and carefully considered your address to the people of Arkansas. I so much regard and esteem you, and value your friendship so highly, as very sincerely to regret that I am compelled to dissent from your views. Allow me frankly and kindly to define my position.
>
> I mean only to express my own views not to assail yours. . . .
>
> Nor shall I be understood to speak for any but myself. I am a Whig, it is true, but I am not about to write as a partizan—others can speak for themselves when they choose—and will do so, I do not doubt, at the proper time.[8]

Pike agreed with Johnson that the North was principally responsible for the fact that the Union was in danger. Too many people there had been too "busy gazing at the mote in our eyes, to attend to the beam in their own" and had felt themselves called upon to crusade against the sin of slavery, with which they had no business to meddle. This movement was inconsistent with peace and concord among men or nations, and it was obvious that if public opinion had been right at the North the miserable fanatics from Garrison and Whittier down to "the basest cur that yelps in the pack" would long before have been overwhelmed by general contempt. He believed, therefore, with Johnson that the South would be justified in severing all connections with the northern states because they had fostered and protected abolitionists and had intentionally refused to comply with obligations to the South in returning escaped slaves. Likewise, he agreed with his friend upon the right of slaveholders to carry their property to the new territories, and justified his belief by repeating the argument given at Memphis in November. He cared not a fig whether Congress could find the constitutional power to prohibit slavery in the territories, it had no right to prevent slavery from going to any territory, for to do so would undermine the foundation of the Constitution by destroying the perfect equality among the states and between the sections, and "make of the South an inferior and degraded people."[9]

Yes, he would admit to Johnson that northern hostility to slavery and to southern expansion were two of the major evils which beset the South, but it was equally clear, asserted Pike, that some of the difficulties which faced the section had been produced by its own acts and that others were the results of natural causes. Struggle as it might, the South would always be in a minority in the Union. Rapid growth of population in the Northwest and the vast emigration from Europe to the North had already transferred political control in the nation to that section. What was particularly unfortunate about the future aspects of the whole situation was that in acquiring Texas the nation had gotten California and New Mexico and a huge country between, all of which was "as certain to be free-soil as Destiny, Death and the Taxes are concerned." A half-dozen free states would in time be carved from this new territory, and Oregon, Nebraska, and Minnesota would soon be calling for statehood. Then the free states could annex Canada by joint resolution, a precedent the South could thank herself for setting in connection with the annexation of Texas, and bring in innumerable free states from that vast land. And all the while the South's power in the national government would be shrinking, no matter what might be thought or said.[10]

These were, said Pike, some of the evils that faced the South. Was there no remedy for them short of disunion? He thought there was, and he thought that "disunion would be such a remedy only as the *death* of the patient, which no doubt cures all his diseases." Granted that the South must hereafter be in a minority within the Union,

> I am in a minority here at home. For all practical purposes there might as well be a law in Arkansas that no whig should vote at all. If the South should be justified in severing itself from the Union, because it is in a minority, so would a single state be justified in severing itself from the rest of the South; one county from the rest of the State, one township from the others of the county—on the homeopathic system of infinitesimal division.[11]

No, the South must not secede. She must submit to the inevitability of her minority position but she must be ready to make the most of that position. A united and coherent minority could always make its voice heard and would, at least half the time, wield decisive power in the nation. The North and West would disagree and conflicting interests would divide the free states; then, if the South was found in phalanx and acted in concert, it could dictate its own terms. A more auspicious time for uniting the South behind such a policy had never before presented itself, for now she could unite, "while if more States were added to her, division of feeling and conflict of interests would soon render her powerless."[12]

He failed to see that disunion would remedy anything. It would not restore the relations of amity and good humor between the sections. It would not prevent the emigration of escaped slaves across the Ohio. On the other hand, what little restraint that then existed would be gone, and "there would be a general Hegira of negroes toward the Great Lakes." The South certainly would lose California. The only result from secession would be war, and what an unutterable curse and horror a war between the North and South would be. No, there was nothing to gain and everything to lose by disunion. He was not for gratifying a set of fanatical abolitionists by allowing them to drive the South out of the Union. Let the South, to the contrary, say

> to them that we are in the Union, and that there we mean to stay. Let us forget all our stupid and senseless quarrelings and dissensions, lay aside party names, meet on some conservative middle ground, and determine to go together and vote together; and so by holding the balance of power, and *using* it, too, *force* the North to do us justice.... *There must be one party in the South*, if the South intends to assert its rights—and when there is but one, its vote and its aid will be too potent to allow her to be insulted or neglected.[13]

It might be said that the Nashville meeting was to form such a party as Pike contemplated, but in his mind the southern convention would not meet on a "conservative middle ground." He opposed it because he thought many hot-headed men would go there, who would increase rather than allay the excitement. Men smarting under wrongs grew more and more angry by conversing about them, and with everyone in the convention attempting to outgo his neighbor in zeal and devotion to the South, the body would commit the southern people and states to a program which they might repent when too late.

Furthermore, he was opposed to the manner in which the delegates were being chosen. He thought that the practice of transferring the most important constituent powers of government into the hands of delegates selected by small squads of politicians or by legislatures had gone far enough: "It is neither whiggery, democracy, nor republicanism." He claimed on behalf of the people of Arkansas, who desired, he believed, to remain in the Union, that before any man should go from the state to sit in a convention such as the proposed Nashville convention the people should have a vote in the selection of that person. The people had delegated no such power to any man or to any body of men; on the contrary, they had surely reserved to themselves the privilege of voting for those whose action might endanger the Union and plunge Arkansas into "a gulf of despair and horror darker and deeper than any that ever opened since the world began."[14]

Pike did not care what the North might do, he would not urge the people of Arkansas to take any step tending toward dissolution of the Union. If matters ever came to that juncture, and they certainly had not in the current crisis, the people would need no more urging than a man needed to be urged to throw off a rope that was strangling him. If, however, the position of the state became unbearable, there was a just and equitable method to remedy it. The legislature, declaring such the case, should provide by law for selecting at a general election delegates to a state convention. Such a convention, deriving its powers directly from the people, might, if so empowered, appoint delegates to a southern convention if other states took the same course. When that was done Pike should gladly abide the fortune of his state, for in Arkansas was all he had or loved on earth. There his children had been born and some buried, and there for weal or woe he would take his stand under the flag of the state. But knowing that he should have at present no legal power to speak for Arkansas in the Nashville convention and believing that the convention was not only unnecessary but dangerous, he could not consent to go there as Johnson wished. He was, however, sure that he and Johnson felt alike on one point.

> I desire, and so do you, I am very certain, to see such a settlement of these difficulties as that the South may honorably and with due regard to her dignity remain in the Union. So desiring, and so most ardently hoping and trusting, join me, (I know you will do so,) in saying of this our glorious Union, which has made us great, a prosperous and enlightened and a happy nation, *Esto Perpetua!*[15]

While Johnson and Pike were declaring their positions on the Nashville convention a new issue arose between them. On January 29, the same day that Johnson had sent his appeal to the people of Arkansas, Henry Clay introduced in the Senate his famous compromise plan. It offered a series of mutual concessions. In return for a free

California, the abolition of slave trade in the District of Columbia, and a limited western boundary for Texas, the North should concede to the South a more rigorous fugitive slave law, the abandonment of the Wilmot Proviso in organizing the territories of Utah and New Mexico, the assumption and payment of the Texas public debt contracted prior to annexation, the continuation of unrestricted slave trade between southern states, and a pledge that slavery would not be abolished in the District of Columbia without compensation and the consent of Maryland and the people of the district. For two months Clay's plan was the main consideration of the Senate, though other sets of resolutions and "Taylor's plan" were injected into the "Great Debate" from time to time. Senator after senator discussed the crisis day after day, while all other legislation was stalemated upon the rock of slavery. Tempers flared, pistols were drawn, and lives threatened during the all-absorbing debate, which saw the most venerable statesmen of the country as participants—Webster, Clay, Calhouin, Benton, Cass.

Reason, nevertheless, was tried. On April 18 a select committee of thirteen senators, headed by Clay, was appointed to examine the whole controversy and report a plan of settlement. Clay reported on May 8 the results of the committee's hearings, three bills and a detailed argument that virtually incorporated the original propositions of the Great Compromiser. The first provided for the admission of California as a free state, the settlement of the Texas boundary, and the organization of Utah and New Mexico as territories with no mention of slavery. The second dealt with the problem of runaway slaves, while the third abolished the slave trade in the District of Columbia. But Taylor threw the weight of the administration against the compromise, and a stalemate resulted while he and Clay battled for supremacy in Congress.

Clay's propositions were to Johnson a total surrender of the most vital contention of the South. In a letter of February 1 to the "Corps Editorial of the State," he warned that the spirit of abolition at the North had risen to the pitch of fanaticism and declared that the South could accept nothing less than an equal division of the new territory—that is, the extension of the line of 36° 30' to the Pacific—if she were to defend her property and maintain her rights in the Union. Once the North excluded slavery from expanding into the new lands, the fate of the South would be sealed forever. Her future history could be written at once. It would all be embraced in the words, "*down, down, down*, and at the admission of each new State, and at each decennial census, it will be deeper and deeper, down." In a quarter of a century southern representation would "amount to a mere squad in the House, and less than one third in the Senate." Then the Constitution would be amended to suit the free states, and the South would be unable to resist. Its property would "be liable to constant destruction—her institutions to constant reproach—her people to constant insult and shame." The editorial and political leaders of Arkansas had failed to do their duty toward the people of the state in not discussing the sectional controversy in the press and from the stump. No time must be lost; these issues must be discussed weekly in order that the people might be informed of the grave dangers that faced the South. The Arkansas public must understand that the territorial question must be settled so as to preserve the equality of the South or the South must form a separate republic. He did not believe the North would force the South to a separation, but he was positive that it would take all the territory if northerners believed that southerners would submit to it.[16]

The editors of the principal Johnson organ in the state, the *Little Rock Banner*, promptly complied with the wishes of their leader. On March 5 they attacked Clay's plan as "an undignified attempt at compromise" when no compromise could be effected unless the South yielded her equality within the Union. They paid their compliments to Clay's effort in a piece of doggerel verse:

> He wriggled in and wriggled out,
> And left the people still in doubt,
> Whether the snake that made the track
> Was going North or coming back.[17]

The influential *Gazette and Democrat*, owned by William E. Woodruff, who had repurchased and merged the *Gazette* with the *Democrat*, came to the support of the compromise and opposed Johnson's strong southern stand. (Interestingly, Woodruff's hired editor of his new paper from March until August 1850, when he fired him for anti-Democratic zeal, was John Elliott Knight, a native of Newburyport, who like Pike was undergoing a metamorphosis from Yankee to southerner at this time. Ross, *Gazette*, 271-76.) In March the editors of the *National Intelligencer* at Washington, D.C., printed extracts from Woodruff's sheet to demonstrate the indecision in Arkansas on the crisis, whereupon Johnson promptly informed the Washington editors by letter that they had misrepresented public opinion in the state. The views of the *Gazette and Democrat* were, Johnson proclaimed, not a reliable index to the true southern spirit in Arkansas.[18]

This letter was reprinted in the *Banner*, whose editors proudly asserted that Johnson had not mistaken the views of his constituents. No matter what "a few whigs, no-party democrats and abolitionists" might tell the *Intelligencer*, Arkansas would stand by the South in the hour of trial; and if the South was forced to dissolve the Union, there would be "willing hands and hearts enough, to resist any unholy aggression."[19] On April 30, a week before the compromise committee of the Senate reported, Johnson warned the editors of the *Banner* that a false impression had gone forth that Clay's committee would arrive at a satisfactory settlement to the slavery controversy. "But little hope exists here in the under current," he said, "that it will, or can [,] originate a settlement of the matter, otherwise than of sacrifice to the South." He hoped, therefore, that nothing would hold Arkansas from the Nashville convention in June. "It is the only thing that staggers Northern pertinacity."[20]

Believing Clay's compromise plan a wise and sincere effort to solve the sectional dispute and to preserve the Union and fearing Johnson's advocacy of the Nashville convention and opposition to the compromise, Pike took a bold stand against Johnson. Encouraged by the determined opposition of the *Gazette and Democrat* to Johnson, Pike sent in March, a copy of his letter to Johnson on the southern convention to that paper, where it was published. Pike had spoken for himself alone, as his letter read, but from the start he probably intended the letter for publication and circulation in Arkansas to arouse opposition against the convention.[21]

Both Pike and Johnson must have perceived that there was no middle ground upon which the leaders of the Whigs and the Democrats in Arkansas could meet to form a strictly southern party. Consequently, from the time of the publication of his Johnson letter, Pike entered actively into the campaign against the Nashville convention. He spoke and wrote and used his influence at the head of the Whig Party in opposition to the convention and in favor of the compromise.[22] Though the absence of a Whig paper in Little Rock at the time meant that his labor left but a scant record, yet he soon achieved notable success. On April 19 the *Banner*, its editorial page edged in black because of the recent death of Calhoun, observed that "a large portion of the whig press and the whig party" had arrayed itself against the vital interests of the South by refusing "to co-operate with us . . . in the earnest endeavor to protect ourselves from aggression and to maintain the Union." The writer consoled himself with an exercise in the historical method to prove to his satisfaction that Whigs had ever been traitors: Loyalists in the Revolution, Hartford Conventionists in 1814, and slackers in the Mexican War. Three weeks later in answering a query from the Whig organ at Washington, Arkansas, as to the position of the Whig Party on "the Southern question," the *Banner* editors pointed out that "every whig paper in the State is opposed to the views of R. W. Johnson on the southern question, while every true democratic paper advocates the sentiments he has sent forth."[23] The Whigs, the *Banner* editors contended, were opposed to the Nashville convention because they feared it would weaken the national strength of their party.[24] Johnson himself noted by late April the opposition being aroused against the convention by "newspapers and wiseacres" of the state and furiously denounced the whole combination as traitors to the South. He trusted that such disloyal action would not prevent Arkansas from doing her duty for the South by sending a large delegation to Nashville in June.[25]

Pike must have been amused at Johnson's discomfiture and doubly so at the *Gazette and Democrat*'s trenchant reply to Johnson's accusations: "Because a large majority of the people of Arkansas differ with their representative in reference to the peculiar mode by which the Union is to be preserved, is certainly no good reason . . . to denounce them as traitors."[26] The "Great Debate" in Arkansas had developed into a political wrangle with recrimination heaped upon recrimination, but beneath the tumult it was abundantly clear that the southern convention would be discredited in the eyes of a large portion of the population. Not only did Pike and the Whig Party have their own followers solidly behind them, but they were also gaining many Democratic adherents through the able and vigorous support of the powerful *Gazette and Democrat*.

As the time for the convention approached, Pike stepped up the tempo of his campaign. On April 15 he participated in a widely publicized debate at El Dorado in Union County. The editors of the *Banner* warned "our friends in Union" that Pike was "a very plausible speaker" and hoped that while "admiring his talents and eloquence" they would also remember "his Whiggery, and the position of the Whig party on the Southern question."[27] At El Dorado Pike and his opponents debated the twin problems of the compromise and the Nashville convention. According to a Whig editor Pike's opening speech

> was a profound, patriotic, eloquent, and every way masterly effort. He took—in reference to the great sectional question of the day—the same identical ground

with Webster, Clay, and other master spirits of our country. His were broad and national grounds—not limited, sectional or partizan in their nature; and nobly did he vindicate *The Union*, against the insidious wiles of Ultraism—both Northern and Southern—so predominant at the present day. He discountenanced and utterly repudiated the projected Nashville Convention. It could do no good, and was almost sure to do injury. He went upon broad and more comprehensive grounds. He was for the *Union*—the whole Union—and nothing else than the Union!

After Capt. Pike had concluded . . . [his opponent] rose and addressed the assembly. "Oh, what a *falling off* there was, my countrymen!" Narrow, contracted, bigoted, partizan and sectional, he floundered about, like a wounded terrapin, in the mud and slough of political selfishness—unable either to attain or aspire to the pure air of a healthy nationality! Pike's rejoinder was seething—lacerating! We really pitied the Judge—but nothing more. He *ought* to have suffered *some*, for his Temerity.[28]

During the last days of May it was plain that the people of Arkansas were looking more to Congress than to the Nashville convention for a solution of the sectional crisis. The *Banner* stated on May 14 that everyone was looking with eager anxiety to Clay's committee "for the scheme of compromise by which the great agitation upon the slavery question is to be settled, the North to be pacified, the South to be satisfied, and the Union guarded for all time to come." The editors doubted, however, that a plan would be presented that would be acceptable to both sections.[29] When the committee report finally reached Little Rock the *Banner* objected strenuously to it, echoing Johnson's complaint that the sacred line of 36° 30' had been disregarded.[30] The *Gazette and Democrat*, on the other hand, warned the members of the Arkansas delegation that "the voice of their constituency" was in favor of the compromise. Let the members offer a better plan if possible, but if not then they must support the one reported by Clay and bring "about a settlement of those questions which have so fearfully disturbed the public mind, and by the continued discussions of which the stability of the Union is considered by many to be jeopardized."[31]

By June 1 it was quite obvious that Pike had won the fight against the convention. So discredited, in fact, was the movement in the state that only two delegates attended from Arkansas,[32] and even their authority was disputed. The *Gazette and Democrat* indignantly declared that the two delegates might "speak for the few individuals who gave them their credentials, but no one will contend that Arkansas is bound by their votes."[33] Even the obstinate editors of the *Banner* admitted that the "humbugging cry of 'disunion'" had diminished the size and influence of the southern convention, though they were happy to say that "it is not a *failure*, as was so confidently predicted by the enemies of Southern rights."[34] "It has adopted," the *Banner* boastfully announced, "as the *ultimatum* for the South, the Missouri compromise line of 36° 30' and suggests, that should Congress fail to make an adjustment satisfactory to the South . . . the Convention again meet on the sixth Monday after the adjournment of Congress."[35] But the *Gazette and Democrat* gave a fairer view in declaring that the men at Nashville did not represent the southern people and that the South would, therefore, never give credence to the resolutions of the majority report.[36] The editor thought, moreover, that Congress would reach a decision on the compromise favorable to the South, and thus give no excuse for a second meeting of the convention.[37]

Pike was delighted that the menace of the convention was past, but there were anxious days of waiting to see what Congress would do. As July approached it looked as though the stalemate in Congress over the compromise might be broken by armed conflict between Texan and federal forces in the disputed border region east of the Rio Grande in New Mexico. Southern Whigs besought President Taylor to give in and support the Senate plan, but Taylor would not budge from his stand against slavery extension. He not only refused to countenance the mongrel bill put forth by Clay but also warned that he would meet force with force in preserving the Union. Then suddenly in early July Taylor died and was succeeded by Vice President Milliard Fillmore, a Henry Clay compromiser. With the administration reorganized along more conservative lines and solidly behind the compromise, Sen. Stephen A. Douglas, an Illinois Democrat, in August took up Clay's shattered bill, reintroduced it piecemeal, and secured its passage through the Senate. In the House Robert Toombs of Georgia led southern Whigs in support of the measures and they were rapidly approved. By the middle of September the Compromise of 1850 was complete.

Would the southern people approve the compromise and uphold the Union or repudiate it and move for secession? The answer to the question lay primarily in the state elections of 1850 and 1851. Southern Whigs returned home as soon as Congress adjourned in September to mend political fences and to get the compromise accepted. The first important trial came in Georgia and resulted in a victory for the compromise. A convention early in December adopted the famous "Georgia Platform of 1850" accepting the compromise but warning the North in stern terms that the finality of that adjustment and the preservation of the Union itself depended upon strict enforcement of the fugitive slave law and abstention from further aggression against the South. Georgia's action was an important influence toward moderation in the other southern states.[38]

Pike probably never had reason to fear that there would be resistance to the compromise in Arkansas. Johnson, who had fought the Clay omnibus bill tooth and toenail in the House and had supported only the fugitive slave bill of the final measures, announced in September 1850 that he would not be a candidate for reelection to Congress in 1851, indicating thereby that he had no desire to carry the anticompromise fight before the people of Arkansas.[39] With Johnson apparently out of the picture, the editors of the *Banner* came out in the fall in favor of accepting the compromise acts as the law of the land, and later in the year they endorsed resolutions of a "Union Meeting" at Van Buren that declared that the compromise did not present sufficient cause for secession or resistance but that a dissolution of the Union would be inevitable unless the fugitive slave law was enforced.[40]

Highly pleased with the conservative tone of Johnson's organ, Pike believed by early 1851 that Arkansas was well on the way to a tranquil acceptance of the compromise. But in April the Democratic State Convention met at Little Rock and drafted Robert W. Johnson to run for reelection, an event that did not in the least surprise Pike. He was, however, chagrined when the editors of the *Banner*, in jumping on Johnson's bandwagon, proclaimed that the action of the convention would meet the approval of nine-tenths of the Democracy and asserted that they had never doubted for a moment that Johnson's constituents would fully endorse and sustain his views on the compromise. Pike could hardly have blamed Whig editors for seeking to make political capital from Johnson's anticompromise stand in Congress and from the stupidity of the editors of the *Banner* for reopening old wounds of the previous year. Yet he soon professed to be horrified at the secession sentiment he thought he saw developing in the state as a result of the editorializing of the Whig and Democratic editors. He was, however, considerably relieved when Johnson, who had quickly accepted the Democratic nomination on May 7 upon his return from Washington, announced on June 11 in a letter to the *Banner* that he would support the compromise acts as the law of the land.[41]

But the Whigs to Pike's utter dissatisfaction continued to denounce Johnson as a disunionist. In June the party selected Pike's old friend Capt. John Preston Jr. of Helena to oppose Johnson. Their platform was "the Union" and "the Compromise," and they immediately began an intensive propaganda campaign against Johnson. They openly accused him of being a secessionist and, to support the claim, reprinted damaging, if not garbled, extracts from his speeches and letters of the previous year. Pike naturally favored and voted for Preston, but he refused to sanction the unfair and dishonest tactics employed against his friend Johnson. He frankly declared in a letter to the *Little Rock Whig*, established in May, 1851, that Johnson was no disunionist and got involved in a bitter quarrel with other Whig leaders that eventually led either to his withdrawal or to his dismissal from the state party.[42] In consequence Pike steered clear of the state politics until the rise of the Know Nothing Party in 1854. However, he remained in a measure a member of the national Whig Party until 1852.

The independent position which Pike assumed in the campaign of 1851 can be explained only in the light of his own political frustration resulting from the events of 1848–51. A Henry Clay nationalist Whig until 1848, Pike had supported his personal friend Taylor that year in an Arkansas campaign that revealed little sectional feeling. In his Pacific railroad speech at Memphis in the fall of 1849 he had first revealed strong southern and states' rights proclivities, although it was clear that he still placed the Union above sectional interests. Hence in 1850 he had been at the forefront in organizing the Whigs and conservative Democrats against the southern convention and the anticompromise stand of Johnson.

But the division between the northern and southern wings of the national Whig Party during the crisis of 1849–50 had kicked the props from under Pike and had left him without a party. Consequently, he had while refusing Johnson's invitation to go to Nashville recommended an alternative, the formation in the South of a new party of conservative Democrats and Whigs. There could be, he had said to his friend, only one party in the South if it wished to preserve its rights in the Union. In Pike's mind Whiggery was dead and Democracy was synonymous with knavery, but there were men in each party who could meet "on a conservative middle ground" to form this new party. It would command a majority of the southern vote, would secure the election to Congress of conservative men, who could there join with moderate northerners in upholding the Constitution, in protecting southern property, and in making the compromises requisite to preserve the Union in an age of fanaticism. This was what Pike preached during the Johnson-Preston canvass in 1851. He had no real hope, though, that he would be heeded. The South would "still go on in the old track, jabbering incoherently about Democratic platforms, and the old faith—everything in the meanwhile, going to the devil as fast as possible."[43]

While Pike occupied himself in his role of prophet, party builder, and defender of the Union, Johnson and Preston met a series of joint appointments in the western and northern counties of the state.[44] From their first meeting at Perryville, Perry County, on June 16, until the close of the tour at Little Rock on July 9, it was evident that Preston, a man of considerable ability, with the aristocratic bearing and polish of a wealthy Whig planter, had blundered seriously in agreeing to go into a Democratic stronghold in company with Johnson.[45] As one of their hearers put it, Preston's well turned periods and studied mannerisms, his graceful action and smiling address were "better fitted for a drawing room than the open wild wood where he addressed the rough boys who . . . gathered to hear him."[46] Johnson was, like Preston, a wealthy slaveowner, but he was also an accomplished stump speaker already popular in northwest Arkansas. He long ago had observed that backwoodsmen came to political rallies more to be entertained than to be swayed by reason. Knowing, too, that there was hardly a man in Arkansas, Whig or Democrat, who did not believe that the compromise had been passed at a sacrifice of southern rights, he could safely indulge in stringent criticism of the measures, and of the North. But he never lost sight of the important point which he must hammer home to the Jacksonian stalwarts of the northwest, that is, that he did not favor, or advise, resistance to the acts, now the law of the land. With masterly skill he gauged the feelings of the people, answered or evaded Preston's questions, and entertained his listeners with bitter ridicule of the Whigs for their attempt to steal the election on trumped up disunion charges.[47] Wherever he went he proved, in the words of one of his admirers, "that he was *no disunionist*; but that he was a true and patriotic friend of the South, a genuine democrat, and an honest man."[48]

On August 4 Johnson was returned to Congress by a majority of over three thousand votes.[49] Clearly he had carried the election not by an anticompromise stand but by traditional Democratic strength and by his promise to abide by those acts as the settled policy of the country. A few days before the election Woodruff of the *Gazette and Democrat*, who had remained noticeably inactive in Johnson's behalf during the campaign, wrote that the Democratic Party in Arkansas "was willing to give the highest possible proof of devotion to the Union" by abiding by the compromise. "But the settlement, if one at all, must be final, and they are not willing to be continually harassed by farther hostile legislation against what they . . . do honestly believe, are their constitutional rights." Johnson, he understood, had not approved the measures but did not "avow himself in favor of any sort of resistance to them unless they should be disturbed by the North."[50] Johnson's reelection, crowed the editor of the *Banner* on August 12 after the results were definite, will be hailed by the whole south as a signal triumph for the democratic southern rights party. It will teach the oppressors upon the constitutional rights that the people of the south will sustain their faithful representatives in voting for the constitution, and will show our whig opponents that they must adopt some more artful dodge than the false cry of "Union."

The Whig editor of the *Helena Southern Shield* proclaimed on August 30 that the results showed plainly "that Arkansas is true to the Union" and that Johnson, "the friend and ally of the secessionists," had been "driven to deny his creed. On more than one occasion did Col. Johnson claim to be a better Union man than his competitor. The man that calculated the value of the Union . . . dared no longer avow his old . . . principles." The principles of the Georgia Platform had become, then, the basis of the Democratic as well as the Whig Party in Arkansas. Elsewhere in the South, Union candidates were meanwhile triumphing over southern rights men to end the secessionist threat that had loomed so ominously over the country since 1846. Pike could rest assured that the Union still stood firm.

Schoolhouse in which Albert Pike taught on Flat Rock Creek, Crawford County, in early 1833. It now stands on the courthouse lawn in Van Buren, Crawford County, Arkansas.
COURTESY BOB'S STUDIO OF PHOTOGRAPHY, FAYETTEVILLE, ARK.

Above: Pike home as it looked in about 1900, when it was owned by John Gould Fletcher.
COURTESY J. N. HEISKELL HISTORICAL COLLECTION /UALR ARCHIVES.

Below: Pike's home built by him on a city block in Little Rock, Arkansas. It is now owned by the Arkansas Arts Center Decorative Museum.
COURTESY ARKANSAS ARTS CENTER DECORATIVE ARTS MUSEUM.

Pike, thirty-four years old in 1844, from an oil portrait by Charles Eliott Loring. It is owned by the House of the Temple, Supreme Council of the Scottish Rite.
COURTESY OF THE SUPREME COUNCIL LIBRARY.

Pike, about 1850.
COURTESY OF THE SUPREME COUNCIL LIBRARY.

John Seldon Roane (1817–1867), who succeeded the deceased Yell as the commander of the Mexican War volunteers and who accepted Pike's challenge to a duel in 1847.
COURTESY OF THE LIBRARY OF CONGRESS.

Pike, in a regalia of the thirty-second degree, Scottish Rite of Freemasonry, about 1853–54.
COURTESY OF THE SUPREME COUNCIL LIBRARY.

Pike wearing a hooded fur coat, about 1850.
COURTESY OF THE SUPREME COUNCIL LIBRARY.

Sen. Robert Ward Johnson, probably about 1857, who headed Arkansas's powerful Democratic dynasty but who remained to the end a friend of Pike's.
COURTESY NATIONAL ARCHIVES.

Sen. William King Sebastian, Pike's fast friend in the 1850s. He was Bob Johnson's Democratic twin in the U.S. Senate.
COURTESY NATIONAL ARCHIVES.

Pike, in a portrait painted by Arkansas painter Edward Payson Washbourne between 1850 and 1854.
COURTESY SPECIAL COLLECTIONS DIVISION,
UNIVERSITY OF ARKANSAS LIBRARIES, FAYETTEVILLE.

Albert Pike, about the time of the Civil War.
COURTESY CHICAGO HISTORICAL SOCIETY.

Photograph of Brig. Gen. Albert Pike by Matthew Brady, Washington, D.C.
COURTESY NATIONAL ARCHIVES.

Maj. Gen. Earl Van Dorn, the earliest of Pike's military enemies in Arkansas, a friend of President Davis's, though unsuited for high command. He lost at Pea Ridge, stripped Arkansas of men and supplies, and returned to Mississippi. COURTESY CHICAGO HISTORICAL SOCIETY.

Brig. Gen. Ben McCulloch, Pike's division commander at the battle of Pea Ridge, where he was killed.
COURTESY THE CENTER FOR AMERICAN HISTORY, THE UNIVERSITY OF TEXAS AT AUSTIN.

Maj. Gen,. Thomas C. Hindman, controversial from the first, became Pike's most virulent military enemy. Pike carried on a war against Hindman's regime in Arkansas.
COURTESY SPECIAL COLLECTIONS DIVISION,
UNIVERSITY OF ARKANSAS LIBRARIES, FAYETTEVILLE.

Another of Davis's incompetent friends, Lt. Gen. Theophilus H. "Granny" Holmes, against whom Pike filed charges for endorsing Hindman's usurpations in the Trans-Mississippi.
COURTESY LIBRARY OF CONGRESS.

Pike, about 1875, as Grand Commander, in the Matthew Brady Studio in Washington, D.C.
COURTESY OF THE SUPREME COUNCIL LIBRARY.

Vinnie (Ream) Hoxie, Pike's dear friend in the Washington years, 1868-91. His *Essays to Vinnie* form the best autobiographical information on his long life.
COURTESY OF THE SUPREME COUNCIL LIBRARY.

Pike as Grand Commander in Baltimore about 1880.
COURTESY OF THE SUPREME COUNCIL LIBRARY.

Pike, about 1880, enjoying one of his many exotic pipes.
COURTESY OF THE SUPREME COUNCIL LIBRARY.

Pike, in about 1889, note decoration from the king of Hawaii and cigar.
COURTESY OF THE SUPREME COUNCIL LIBRARY.

The Supreme Council in Washington, D.C., in which Pike lived the last years of his life.
COURTESY OF THE SUPREME COUNCIL LIBRARY.

Pike in his library in the former House of the Temple in Washington, D.C.
COURTESY OF THE SUPREME COUNCIL LIBRARY.

Pike lying in state with an honor guard in the House of the Temple.
COURTESY OF THE SUPREME COUNCIL LIBRARY.

Albert Pike statue, dedicated October, 23, 1901. The sculptor was Gilbert de Trentove. The monument stands near the intersection of Third and Indiana, near the site of the House of the Temple where Pike lived and died.
COURTESY OF THE SUPREME COUNCIL LIBRARY.

XX

Renewal of the Bank War

O N RETURNING TO LITTLE ROCK from Mexico in the summer of 1847 Pike resumed his place in the law firm of Pike and Baldwin and his duties as attorney to the trustees of the Real Estate Bank, a position he had held continuously since 1842. By the late forties Pike had become dissatisfied with circuit riding and the never-ending business of drawing up legal documents; his preference leaned increasingly in these years toward the more interesting and more profitable cases that came before the state supreme court.[1] Hard work and diligent study had won him a reputation as the ablest equity lawyer in the state,[2] and his success before the highest court of the state encouraged him to make an important advancement in his law career. Having dissolved the partnership with Baldwin in March, 1848,[3] he applied and was admitted to practice before the Supreme Court of the United States on March 9, 1849.[4] But Pike must soon have realized that he could not abandon his Arkansas practice while establishing himself in a national practice. Accordingly he formed in the summer of 1849 a partnership with Ebenezer Cummins, brother of the William Cummins who had been his first law associate.[5] This arrangement promised Pike the advantages of both a steady income and the freedom for the numerous absences from the state that his public life and Supreme Court cases entailed.

The first two years of the new firm were, as it turned out, decidedly unprosperous. Heavy rainfall and floods and an attack of "the worm" in 1849, and a cold, wet spring in 1850 dealt harshly with the cotton planters of Arkansas. Pike's income was as a consequence seriously diminished.[6] By 1850 he had six children—Luther Hamilton, twelve; Walter Lacy, ten; Isadore, nine; Lillian, seven; Albert Holden, six; and Yvon (the Pikes's last child), one—to provide for in addition to the upkeep of an expensive private estate.[7] In debt and faced with a great reduction in income, Pike was discouraged. For a while in 1851 he considered removing to New Orleans and opening a law office[8] but decided against it probably because he had no training in the equity law or Roman law, which made up a large part of the legal code in Louisiana. He kept the possibility of moving under advisement, nevertheless, and began in his spare time to study and read the *Equity Code of Louisiana* and to translate the French *Pandects*. In the meantime with the rise of cotton prices in the early fifties prosperity returned to Arkansas and the South, and Pike became occupied with other matters.

Pike's most important U.S. Supreme Court cases in the fifties were concerned with the inert Arkansas Real Estate Bank, which had, since Pike's deed of assignment in 1842, been in the hands of a trusteeship. Pike was for thirteen years attorney for the trustees of the bank, a position which furnished him a steady salary but which also brought much criticism and ill feeling his way. As the years passed the trusteeship and Pike's connection with it came to be looked upon by the people of Arkansas with much distrust. Many wondered what was going on at the trustees' meetings, if they were making honest attempts to liquidate the affairs of the bank, collect its debt, and pay the interest and principal on the bond issues, all long overdue. The trustees in refusing to make public their transactions left themselves open to invidious attacks. Gov. John Selden Roane, elected in 1848, the year after he and Pike fought their duel, pronounced the defunct institution "a sealed book to all those uninitiated" and "a mystic monument of modern banking."[9] The editor of the Democratic Banner in 1850 took obvious delight in making public a letter from an irate but anonymous English bondholder of the bank. The correspondent, signing himself "A Victim," imagined Pike (this was when Drew was governor) presiding over a dinner party at an official meeting of the five trustees,[10] Henry L. Biscoe, John Drennen, Sandford C. Faulkner, George Hill, and Ebenezer Walters, "the fortunate youths" who had been appointed eight years before:

> The cloth being removed, and grace said,
> Mr. Pike gave "the Healths of the most patient, mild, and suffering bondholders in existence—the Arkansas creditors." He would venture to affirm that no other set of men had been more successfully humbugged for the period of eight long years, and he had no doubt that he could still continue to evade all demands and keep the trustees in the reception of their salaries at least eight years more to come.
> The toast was drunk with much applause. At the conclusion of the cheers,
> Mr. Walters rose, and gave "the health of the Governor of Arkansas, and long life to him."
> Mr. Biscoe responded to the toast, as the Governor was a friend of his and also of the company's. "It is true," said Mr. Biscoe, "the State is responsible for the debt, and that it was in the power of the Governor to enforce the realization of the mortgages, stock notes, &c., by which all the creditors might have been paid eight years ago. But it must be obvious to the company that any such liquidation (although they [the trustees] were especially appointed for that purpose) would be a great loss to the State, inasmuch that if they continued receiving the interest on the mortgages and the stock notes, and reinvesting it, it was quite obvious in a few years the bondholders could be repaid their capital from the accumulated interest, and the creditors would be glad enough to get back what they had advanced. As the Governor did not enforce the liquidation he was obviously the best friend of the trustees and the State."
> Mr. Faulkner gave, "Our worthy selves." To which
> Mr. Hill remarked, that "charity began at home"; "that he had read with much interest the report of Governor Drew, who indignantly refused to countenance repudiation, and who declared he would uphold the honor of the State. It was evident the case could not be in better hands, and he proposed to continue in the course they had followed.
> Mr. Drenen [sic] felt it his duty to offer a few remarks. They had enjoyed a handsome salary, it was true; but he had passed many a sleepless night in pondering over the best way to avoid repudiation—and to keep his salary. Bondholders were very foolish people; they expected to be paid, as if the money

was to be picked up like California gold. It required a long time to investigate claims, and his learned friend, Mr. Pike, agreed with him in the advantage of the law's delays. In conclusion, he would add, that no star of the States was more unspotted than that which designated Arkansas; that the honor, integrity and honesty of the State was entrusted to them; and he proposed not to let it pass into the hands of those who might advocate repudiation on the one hand, or be too incautious by a hasty liquidation on the other.

At the conclusion of this speech the different gentlemen shook hands with much cordiality, and agreed to meet again next quarter day; Mr. Pike remarking that he thought every man in debt must have credit, and that therefore Arkansas and the trustees were entitled to every credit."[11]

Under the influence of such criticism, the legislature passed an act, approved January 12, 1853, directing the attorney general of the state to file a bill in chancery against the trustees to divest them of the assets of the bank. The second section of this act authorized Gov. Elias N. Conway to employ "two efficient and eminent lawyers" to assist the attorney general in the cause.[12] The filing of the bill in chancery was delayed over a year because of Conway's difficulty in finding a lawyer who would prosecute the case for the state and because of the refusal of the trustees to furnish the requisite information on which the bill could be based. Finally in the spring of 1854 James M. Curran, a Whig attorney of Little Rock, drew up a bill of complaint against all those living who had been trustees or employees of the bank and against the executors and administrators of the estate of all those dead who had been connected officially in any way with the institution.[13] The document set forth the history of the bank before it was assigned to the trustees; described in detail the duties of the trustees under the assignment of 1842 and under the liquidation act of 1843; charged the trustees not only with failure to perform their duty but also with serious, if not criminal, misconduct in executing the trust; demanded answers from the trustees and their agents and officers to all such charges and queries; requested that all records of the bank be placed in the custody of the court; and, finally, petitioned that the trust be taken from the trustees and placed in the hands of a receiver to be appointed by the court and that the trust henceforth be executed by the court and its receiver. Among the gravest charges were those declaring that "although said deed purports on its face to have been made for the purpose of securing the creditors of said Bank, and to indemnify the State against the payment of said bonds," actually "the principal and real object was to place the assets beyond the reach or control of the State, and in such position that the authorities of the State could have no voice in the management or administration thereof," and that the deed was "fraudulently made" by the trustees in order that they might delay or prevent collection of their own large debts to the bank and enjoy further credit as well. Furthermore, the trustees were charged with flagrant breach of trust: they had not paid the interest due on the state bonds issued for the benefit of the bank; they had shown great favoritism toward certain persons in collecting debts, in allowing too liberal terms, and in overevaluating lands taken for debts; they had increased the liabilities of the bank tremendously so that in 1854 the assets were some $170,000 less than the liabilities; they had paid themselves large accounts for travel and expenses of at least $750 per year; and they had not kept proper records of the transactions of the institution, had not accounted for vast sums received, and had lost large amounts by indulgence to debtors, lapse of time, and the statute of limitations.[14]

The trustees and their agents had not answered the bill of complaint by October 6, 1854, when Curran died.[15] But Conway had Curran's bill of complaint printed at the *True Democrat* office and had copies of it laid before the members of the legislature when they assembled in November 1854. In his message to the legislature, November 7, Conway requested that the legislature give him full power to execute the suit against the trustees and to have a thorough accounting made of the bank's records. If the trustees and their officials had acted correctly it would be no great hardship to require an account from them, while if they had acted incorrectly it would be only right that they should be held to account for all losses to the creditors and stockholders of the bank and to the state. He was fully aware of the virulent opposition he would encounter in warring on those who controlled and had "in charge millions of assets of a bank," but no matter how strong the opposition might be, he was determined that no governor of Arkansas should ever again have reason to say that the transactions of the institution were a "sealed book" to the authorities and people of the state.[16]

The legislature cooperated fully with Conway, passing "An act to aid in bringing to light the true condition of the Real Estate Bank of the State of Arkansas" that empowered the governor to prosecute the pending suit against the trustees, to employ special attorneys to aid in the cause, and to appoint two accountants for the purpose of "investigating the books, accounts, and all other matters connected with the said suit, and the accounts and answers of all parties who are or shall be made defendants in said suit." All reports of the accountants were by the act to be "taken and received as evidence of the facts stated therein, in any and all courts of law or equity" of the state.[17] The measure was approved by Conway on January 15, 1855. On the same day he signed an act to establish a separate court of chancery at Little Rock with special jurisdiction to handle the suit of the state against the trustees and officers of the Real Estate Bank and all other cases in chancery pending or arising thereafter in Pulaski County. The court was to meet on the first Mondays of February, May, August, and November and was to be presided over by a chancellor appointed by the governor for a term of four years.[18]

Special state attorney Samuel H. Hempstead promptly filed in the new court a bill in chancery against the four surviving residuary trustees, Biscoe, Drennen, Walker, and Faulkner, charging them with fraudulent breach of trust and demanding that they be divested of the records and assets of the bank.[19] The trustees' answers to the complaint were filed by April 16, 1855,[20] when an adjourned session of the court opened at Little Rock. Four days later Chancellor Hulbert F. Fairchild delivered an opinion on the case and issued a decree removing the records and funds of the bank from the hands of the trustees and placing them in the hands of a court-appointed receiver, C. F. M. Noland.[21] Fairchild, in reaching his decision, refused to consider the charges and denials of fraudulent dealing with the trust fund but confined himself strictly to the answers of Biscoe, Drennen, Walker, and Faulkner and to the law governing trusts. The four respondents had not pretended, he said, that the trust had been performed, but had stated several reasons—injudicious legislation, executive hostility, fluctuating and unintelligent judicial decisions, popular prejudice, drought, and flood—why it could not be done. Finally the trustees had admitted that they did not desire "to incur the price and odium" of executing the trust. Then, said Fairchild, "it must be done by a receiver, as the arm of this court."[22]

Under Fairchild's decree the assets and records of the bank were transferred to Noland on April 25, 1855. Soon afterwards Governor Conway directed William M. Gouge and W. R. Miller, state accountants appointed under the act of January 15, 1855, to examine the records of the institution seeking "answers" to certain questions proposed by Conway. A disagreement between Noland and the accountants stalemated the investigation until the fall of 1855, when Chancellor Fairchild, under pressure from Conway, removed Noland and appointed Gordon N. Peay, ex-cashier and secretary of the trustees, to the position.[23]

Conway and Noland had had an exchange of letters in October over Noland's refusal to cooperate with the accountants. Upon Noland's dismissal by Fairchild the editor of the anti-Conway *Gazette and Democrat* charged the governor had used "jesuitical" methods to obtain Noland's removal. To defend the governor, his private secretary, Richard H. Johnson, editor of the *True Democrat* and brother of U.S. senator Robert W. Johnson, printed in his paper the Noland-Conway correspondence. Johnson charged that Noland had neglected his duty and had been disrespectful toward the chief executive of the state.[24] On November 24 Noland sent "a card" to the *Gazette and Democrat* denying the assertion that he had neglected his duty and indignantly protesting that Conway had allowed the correspondence between them to be published to make political capital. "Governor Conway has, politically, fed and fattened upon the poor old Real Estate Bank. It has been his standing theme by day—and at night, its ghosts [a reference to the debts of the Johnsons and the Conways to the bank] give him feverish dreams." Furthermore, Conway had not only "humbugged" the people but also had "humbugged himself into the belief, that the late Trustees thirst for his blood." In consequence the governor was for "any thing and every thing, that can make prejudice against the Trustees, and at the same time advance the political fortunes of Elias N. Conway." However, there would be a time, he said, and he did

> not think it very distant, when it will be made to appear that, in a pecuniary point of view at least, neither his Excellency Elias N. Conway, nor his kith and kin and his particular friends have been set back any by the Real Estate Bank; and that his zeal in prosecuting the suit against the Trustees, increased considerably after certain persons arranged their indebtedness with the bank.[25]

The break between Noland and Conway was a phase of the political quarrel over the bank that had been going on for months before October 1855. Conway, who was primarily responsible for bringing an end to the trusteeship, had, as Noland remarked, taken every opportunity to make "political capital" out of the suit against the trustees and the investigation by the accountants. Pike, founder and leader of the Know-Nothing order in Arkansas in 1854–55, was especially abused in the summer of 1855 by the Conway organ, the *True Democrat*, for his connection with the bank. It was said that he had used the funds of the institution to foster the former Whig Party and that he had persuaded James Yell, also a Know-Nothing, to resign as state attorney rather than bring suit against the trustees in the spring of 1855.[26]

Incensed by such outrageous charges, Pike replied to them on August 31, 1855, in a long letter to the editors of the Know-Nothing *Gazette and Democrat*. He began with a summary of his official and financial connection with the bank. He had served as attorney from April 2, 1842, to January 2, 1855, when he resigned, had received a salary of $2,250 a year, had owed the bank when he resigned "an Arkansas money debt, of about $16,000," which had been "contracted like other debts due by the debtors, and amply secured," and which he had since reduced by nearly one half. He declared that he had answered under oath the charges of "malfeasance, corruption or intentional wrong" in the bill of complaint against himself and had filed it together with his accounts and papers in the chancery court in April 1855. Challenging "the world to show" one of his statements untrue, he then quoted a long extract from his reply to the bill to display his statements before "the world." Following this exposition Pike got down to the business at hand, his response to his enemies, asserting that

> it is not of the least importance to me how many Receivers, Clerks and Accountants are employed and set to examining the affairs of the Bank. Nor is it the slightest importance to me how many lawyers, or who, are employed to prosecute the suit. It does not in the least concern me, so far as my accounts as attorney are concerned, or my transactions with or for the Trustees. Gen. Yell might have continued Attorney for forty years, for aught that I should have cared....
>
> The Governor is perfectly welcome to have as much investigation made as he pleases. I know that the war he and others are waging, is aimed chiefly against myself. I defy them all; I scorn and despise them all, by far too much to hate them.[27]

Whether Conway was behind Johnson's attacks on Pike and whether he had waited until the Conways and other "kith and kin" were out of debt to the bank before pressing the case against the trustees, as Noland had alleged, is beyond certain determination today, though a recent historian thinks there was a basis for Noland's charges.[28] It would seem that the governor was guilty of a breach of good conduct in allowing Johnson to print the correspondence between himself and Noland; and Pike publicly declared that Conway, in printing the bill of complaint after it had been filed in 1854, and in sending it over the state and placing it before the legislature, was "guilty of a contempt of Court, and an interference with the course of justice, that in any other country would have been at once stamped with public reprehension."[29]

Moreover, it is apparent to one who reads today Conway's instructions to the accountants that he framed many of his questions to make damaging implications whether alleged malfeasance on the part of Pike and the trustees could be proved or not. Accordingly the report of the accountants, printed in 1856, was a less than impartial exposition of the conduct of the trustees and the officers of the bank. Gouge and Miller, the accountants, severely condemned the control and management of the bank under its original directors as well as under the trustees, who were of course selected by and from the directors in 1842. They bestowed equal censure, if not contempt, upon the deed of assignment, which they characterized as having been "made by debtors to themselves, for their own benefit," with "the State and bondholders, the parties most deeply interested in its good management, deprived of all share in the trust."[30] Their general conclusion was that the trustees had failed to collect the debts and pay the interest due the stockholders because neither the state nor the bondholders had representation on the board.[31] There were good

> causes why the trustees should not be too vigorous at the beginning in enforcing the payment of debts. But there is reason in all things. They ought to have collected at least enough to have paid the expenses of the trust. That they did not do so, was owing to the peculiar constitution of the board. They, and their particular friends, were among the greatest debtors to the bank. They paid nothing, or next to nothing, of what they themselves owed to the bank, and under these circumstances it was with ill grace that they could enforce payment on others.[32]

This sweeping condemnation is hardly justifiable in light of certain details of the report. The answer to question five showed that all the trustees, owed large personal debts amounting in all to $155,661.99 and had signed notes with other debtors for an additional total of $152,641.75 at the time of the assignment in 1842. But by comparing this grand total of $308,303.84 charged against the trustees with the reply to question ten it is seen that by April 25, 1855, five of the trustees had paid their debts in full and the total indebtedness, of the others, personal and surety, amounted to only $87,526.60 in Arkansas money and $10,126.45 in specie.[33] Pike's individual debt in 1842 had been $4,563.19, and he had acted as surety for others for debts amounting to $19,560.00. The accountants' report showed that during his service, which ended January 2, 1855, Pike had collected $28,687.50 in salary; that he owed the bank on April 25, 1855, $17,753.79; and that he decreased this debt to $9,996.24 by November 1855.[34] By October 1, 1858, he had paid it in full.[35]

Query twelve posed by the governor was supposed to bring to light part of the secret machinations of Pike and the trustees. It read, "Have the trustees or officers of the bank assumed debts in bank for debtors, and received from them moneys, notes[,] property, real or personal? How were the debts assumed secured, if secured at all, and what profit or loss to such officers or trustees by the transaction, and what profit or loss to the bank?" The answer was that "in all cases where the trustees or attorney collected money from debtors to the bank and did not pay them over immediately to the cashier or secretary, they may be said to have assumed such debts, at least temporarily."[36] The accountants did not, however, submit specific proof that the officials had not immediately turned over all monies from debts collected, or that they had not amply secured and accounted for all debts assumed for others. Pike's account, under this question, was presented first. It showed that on January 1, 1848, he had purchased half of Sandford C. Faulkner's plantation in Chicot County, assuming $45,000 of Faulkner's debt to the bank and mortgaging property in Little Rock as security. But Pike had been unable to complete the purchase, and in July, 1850, Faulkner "re-assumed the debt of $45,000 together with the interest that had accrued on it from the 1st of January, 1848." The accountants called this transaction "a more formal assumption of debts owing the bank." Pike "also made a formal assumption" of debts of twelve men listed in the report amounting to $10,263.07. This sum "went into his general account, and may be said to have constituted the greater part of the claim of $18,914.18 which the bank had against Mr. Pike on the 20th April, 1855."[37] The report did not state how, when, or where these latter debts were taken over by Pike, how secured, "if secured at all," nor whether he profited and the bank lost by the transaction. They were probably surety debts which he had been forced to pay. The trustees' accounts were no more incriminating than Pike's.[38]

In response to question thirteen, whether the trustees and officers had "severally accounted" for all funds of the bank that came to their hands, the accountants said that they had no reason to believe that the bank officials had failed to report to the cashier and secretary all money and other assets received from debtors. The accountants declared, however, that rents and profits from bank property were very small and that they could not find that any money had been received for the hire of sixty-six slaves which had at intervals come into and temporarily remained in the hands of the trustees, though they presented no evidence in the report that any of the trustees had ever hired out any of the slaves.[39] A similar injustice was done the trustees in the accountants' answer to the inquiry as to whether or not they had speculated with the bank's funds. In some instances, said the accountants, some of the trustees had not promptly paid over money collected from debtors of the bank and specie placed in their hands for special objects. The accountants "presumed" that the trustees had employed such funds in their own business, though the records contained no entries from which it could be inferred "that they, in any other way, speculated in the funds of the bank."[40]

At the time the bill was passed to provide for the accountants' investigation, Pike and Cummins had suits pending in the Pulaski Circuit Court against the State of Arkansas involving nearly a million and a half dollars.[41] The cases were on behalf of the estate of James Holford, an English investor who had purchased two hundred and fourteen bonds of the Real Estate Bank issued before 1840 and who, as we have already learned, had acquired in 1841 five hundred more from a New York City bank.[42] On October 7, 1840, the cashier of the central bank at Little Rock had, at the authorization of the board of directors, deposited five hundred $1,000 bonds with the North American Trust and Banking Company, New York City, as security for a loan of $121,336.59 to the Real Estate Bank. The next year the New York bank pledged the bonds to James Holford, a private banker of London, as collateral for a loan of $325,000. Not long after this transaction the North American Trust and Banking Company became insolvent, and in the fall of 1841 Holford applied to Governor Yell for advice on recovering the interest and the principal advanced by him on the bonds. He implied that he was looking to the state for payment or guarantee of payment. But Yell, leader of the antibank movement in Arkansas, sternly replied that the central board of the Real Estate Bank had violated the provisions of the bank's charter in hypothecating the bonds below par, and that the state was, therefore, in no degree responsible, morally or legally, for the Holford claim. The directors of the Real Estate Bank had already refused to redeem the bonds, claiming that the New York bankers had had no authority to turn the bonds over to a third party. As a consequence Holford's case looked unpromising, but for several years afterwards he kept stressing in memorials to the legislature and in correspondence with the governors that he had accepted the securities because he believed the faith of the state was pledged for them. It was apparent, however, that the legislature did not have any intention of taxing the people to pay the claim, and as time went on it became obvious, moreover, that the bank itself, if able, had no disposition to pay Holford.[43] It was this condition of affairs that led William A. Platenius, administrator in the United States of Holford's estate—he had died in the interim—to engage Pike and Cummins to file suits in November, 1854, for the hypothecated bonds of 1841 as well as other bonds of the bank that Holford had purchased before 1840.[44]

Pike and Cummins as solicitors for Platenius filed suits on November 21, 1854, to recover the interest due and unpaid on the bonds held by Holford's estate, 214 purchased before 1840 and the 500 received from the North American Trust and Banking Company in 1841.[45] The two suits were in the form of actions of covenant, declaring that the State of Arkansas had failed to carry out the contract implied by the act under which the bonds were originally issued to the Real Estate Bank, that is, that the state was responsible for paying 6 percent interest semiannually on the bonds from date of purchase.[46] The arrearage in interest on the Holford claim amounted to $1,500,000.[47] The legislature, which met the same month the suits were filed, and before the cases were taken up by the court, circumvented the efforts of Pike and his partner by passing a bill which required that, in all state suits brought to enforce the payment of principal or interest of bonds issued by the state, the original bonds would have to be filed with the clerk of the court before the case could be heard and judgment rendered; and if this was not done, the court should dismiss the case. Governor Conway approved the act on December 7,[48] and the following summer the Pulaski Circuit Court dismissed the suits with costs because Pike and Cummins had not filed the bonds.[49] The partners appealed to the state supreme court in July, 1855, but the cases were not heard until the January term, 1856, by which date Pike and Cummins had dissolved their partnership.[50] Thereafter Pike had sole charge of the cases. He argued in the Arkansas supreme court that the act of December 7, 1854, was unconstitutional because it had impaired the contract, or law of 1839,[51] by which he had assumed he had every right to sue the state.[52] The court at its January term, 1856, overruled Pike's argument, declared the act of 1854 constitutional on the basis that the legislature as competent "to obstruct and impair" the rights of bringing suits against the state, and upheld, therefore, the judgment of the Pulaski Circuit Court by dismissing the suits for want of jurisdiction.[53] Pike carried the cases to the U.S. Supreme Court in 1856; they were heard on April 20, 1858. Pike's chief point in the appeal was that the Arkansas courts had ruled erroneously and that their decisions and the act of 1854 should be nullified because they impaired the obligation of contracts between the state and his client not only under the act of 1839 but also under statements in each of the bonds issued by the state on behalf of the Real Estate Bank.[54] Chief Justice Roger B. Taney delivered the unanimous opinion of the court on May 14, 1858. He declared that the law of 1839 authorizing suits against the state was not a contract but an "ordinary Act of legislation" and that the legislature was perfectly within its rights in prescribing and limiting the terms upon which the sovereign State of Arkansas could be sued. It was not in the sphere of the U.S. Supreme Court to inquire whether the law of 1854 "operated hardly or unjustly upon the parties whose suits were then pending. That was a question for the consideration of the Legislature." Consequently, Taney upheld the decision of the state supreme court. Since there was nothing either in that decision or in the act of 1854 "which in any degree impairs the obligation of the contract, and nothing which will authorize this court to reverse the judgment of the State Court. *The writ of error must, therefore, be dismissed for want of jurisdiction in this court.*"[55]

Pike was severely criticized by the Democratic press for his part in the Holford bond cases. Editor Johnson of the *Little Rock True Democrat* congratulated the legislature in the summer of 1856 on its success in disposing of the cases in the state courts and in preventing "Capt. Pike" from "ruining many honest debtors to the Real Estate Bank and injuring the State materially."[56] A joint committee of the general assembly on the affairs of the Real Estate Bank made a long report in 1857 defending and commending Governor Conway's investigation of the bank and complimenting the legislators of 1854 upon their promptness in protecting the people of the state from suits brought against them "by able and ingenious lawyers."[57] But the committee used more than allusive phrases to hit at Pike. In praising the legislation of 1855 setting up the chancery court to handle all cases concerning the collection of debts due the Real Estate Bank, the committee concluded it had been "high time" for doing something to prevent the exhaustion of the whole assets of the institution by the expenses paid to special collectors of the trustees and their officers. To document their allegation the committee then related a single and admittedly extreme case that had come to their attention.[58] James Gibson, who owed the bank a debt of "some thousands," had gone to Texas. Pike, acting in his capacity as attorney for the trustees, hired H. K. Brown "to pay him a visit, and collect . . . if possible, what was due the bank." Brown collected from Gibson, in cash and other valuables $6,033.33 1/3 and retained $3,194.26 "in requital of his own services." How much Pike had agreed to allow Brown is not stated, but the committee to be "fair" to Brown inserted an extract from a letter dated September 6, 1854, from him to Pike concerning a dispute over the fee. The substance of the letter was that Pike had not agreed to give him half of the amount collected in "the Gibson and Spear claims" but had in "the Curll case." Successful in his mission, Brown apparently grew greedy and demanded half in the Gibson case also. "I think," said he to Pike,

> the bank can well give me half, as I am satisfied that it was through me and my friends and acquaintances in Texas, that it was got at all. The job has paid well, but if I had failed, I should have lost a full year's time, as I could not undertake anything else on account of the bank business. It is tolerably *fat*, but if old Jim had taken my scalp, it would not have been so fat. I think the bank men will say I should have half when they know all about it.[59]

Brown further supported his claim by informing Pike that the State Bank of Arkansas had been giving half for collection of debts within Arkansas as well as in Texas. He was "willing to do right in the matter, but would not undertake it again for less than half, all expenses paid." We do not know the outcome of the disagreement, nor were the reporters interested in presenting it. Rather, they gleefully assumed that Pike and "the bank men" no longer had the power "to decide what is justly due to Mr. Brown for his services in the case, and for the personal danger to which he was exposed from the supposed ferocity of Mr. Gibson."[60]

Pike's connection with the Real Estate Bank is still a great question mark. We may see in reading between the lines of the report of the accountants that opportunities for large illicit gain had been open to him. Through his hands as attorney passed great sums of money from debtors. He could have retained much of this for long periods if he chose. He could have used or hired out slave and real property received on foreclosures of mortgages; as far as the accountants could find the bank had received not a cent for the hire of Negroes and only token rents on the land which had come from time to time under its control.[61] He could have benefited to a great extent in the total expenses of $215,207.59 paid out by the bank from 1842 to 1855.[62] There is no proof, however, that either he or the trustees speculated with the bank funds or failed to report every amount that came to hand. Considering the political nature of the investigation, the probable personal hostility of the accountants, and the way the investigation was slanted by the "set" questions propounded by Conway, it is likely that if Pike and the trustees had been found culpable they would have been prosecuted. As far as is known not a single case was ever brought against the trustees or their officers.

A recent writer has condemned the control of the bank under its original directors and under the trustees as "a system which increasingly concentrated the benefits of the bank while keeping the public in ignorance of its affairs."[63] Undoubtedly Arkansas's first and only state experiment in banking was unfortunate. Founded in response to a popular demand for the increase of the circulating medium in the state during a period of expansion and inflation, her banks had opened at an inauspicious time and had failed in the general financial debacle that accompanied the panic of 1837. Yet the question whether the Real Estate Bank was justified in suspending specie payment in 1839 had little to do with the significance of the war begun in 1840 between Governor Yell and the bank directors. Their contest was actually a struggle between those who advocated outright repudiation of bank debts and state debts and those who sought to keep the business of the banks out of state hands and temporarily prevent repudiation in the hope that the honor and faith of the state might be salvaged and the debts paid. The deed of assignment was made in the face of a threatened investigation by a hostile legislature, and Yell later went beyond the bounds of executive propriety in attempting to override the judicial decision that had declared Pike's assignment constitutional.[64] Once the bank was beyond the reach of its enemies in the state government it became an easy target for anyone who wished to abuse it. The fact that the trust was a "sealed book" must have been gratifying to its leading abusers, many of whom were heavily in debt to the bank.[65]

The trustees were guilty of being debtors and controllers of the bank and of being lenient to its debtors in the depressive decade of the forties, but much can be said for them on the ground both that they prevented repudiation in 1842 and that they thereafter made honest efforts either to collect or to secure the majority of the debts due the bank.[66] Conway's accountants in 1856 reported that at the time of the assignment the assets of the institution were $2,231,624.92 and the liabilities $2,257,558.32, a deficit of $25,933.40.[67] Soon after the bank passed into the hands of the state receiver in 1855, its total assets were reported to be $5,006,507.53, or net assets of $2,492,007.53, while its total liabilities were only $2,415,759.26.[68] That Arkansas did not realize enough out of these assets to pay off the Real Estate Bank debt was no fault of the trustees; on the other hand, it is by no means certain that the trustees would not have paid the debt had not the state taken it out of their hands. In the absence of sources more impartial than slanted public documents and partisan editorials, a biographer of Pike must refrain from indicting either Pike or the trustees for their conduct of the bank from 1842 to 1855.

XXI

Let the South Build Her Own Railroad to the Pacific

HOWEVER MUCH PIKE might be criticized or damned for his politics and his bank connection, he was greatly respected and admired in Arkansas for learning and scholarly attainments and for his zeal in working for civic and internal improvements in the state during the fifties. He repeatedly though unsuccessfully advocated the establishment of a system of free, tax-supported public schools in Arkansas.[1] He helped organize an "Industrial Association" at Little Rock in 1852 in an attempt to encourage the development of manufactures in the town and state, worked for and secured increased and improved mail service for Arkansas the same year,[2] and labored to bring railroads to Arkansas.

In the fall of 1851 Pike made a long trip through several of the northern states. He was struck by the rapid progress made there in railroad building and industrialization and was even more impressed with the advantages the northern people had over those in Arkansas. When he returned to Little Rock in December, he was nominated by Governor Roane to represent Arkansas at the Southern and Western Railroad convention to meet at New Orleans in January 1852.[3] To perk up interest in the subject he wrote over the signature "The Plain Truth" a series of articles for the *Little Rock Whig* extolling railroads. The main source of his information was his recent trip, but he supported personal observations with an array of facts and figures and statistical tables to prove that great prosperity awaited Arkansas if only she too would build railroads. The title of his articles, "Starvation, Emigration or Railroads," indicated not only Pike's conclusions but also the state of mind that had led him earlier that year to consider removing to New Orleans to try his fortune.

> One thing is certain. If the condition of things here cannot be improved, we must leave the State, and seek a home elsewhere. When a man gets beyond our borders and travels eastward, he finds the whole country in a stir, like a hive of industrious bees. Every where he hears the hum of industry, the rattle of machinery, the puffing of the locomotive. Every where else property is increasing in value, towns and villages are springing up in every corner, new lands are opened and cultivated, and old ones rejuvenated. Men are cheerful, earnest, energetic, hopeful. In September last, I was in Ohio, New York, Pennsylvania, Connecticut, Massachusetts. In Ohio, there were 29 railroads, including branches, 830 miles of railroad in operation, and 1,519 in course of construction: In New York, 52 roads, 1,867 miles in operation, 1,052 in course of construction: In Pennsylvania,

52 roads, 1,224 miles in operation, and 608 in course of construction. In Connecticut, little as she is, 13 roads, 551 miles in operation, 65 miles in course of construction: and in Massachusetts, 38 roads, 1,142 miles in operation, and 73 miles in course of construction. I came home through Michigan. She came into the Union when we did, and she has four railroads, and 447 miles in operation, the cost of which was nine million of dollars. At St. Louis I found the people all astir about the great Pacific railroad: at Memphis nothing was talked of but the Charleston and Memphis road. Every where I found plenty of occupation for young men, abundant openings for employment for men of information and talent, fair prospects for men's children to become useful citizens and respectable men. I found that every where except here, if a man chose to educate his sons, to give them proper practical knowledge, they could find respectable occupations, and profitable, too, without making lawyers or doctors of them, and so condemn them to linger through life in the condition of semi-starvation and semi-respectability.

I found that education and knowledge as well as enterprise and comfort, kept pace with railroads. . . .

At last I reached the mouth of "that beautiful but neglected stream," White River; and so, by way of Rock Roe, at considerable expense and trouble, managed to get home. The contrast was enough to make one heartsick. A dull, stupid apathy broods over the whole State like a great leaden-colored cloud. All along our roads are abandoned huts, shattered fences, deserted fields overgrown with weeds. Except a few cotton-planters, nobody seems to have any energy, confidence, or hopefulness. *"Home,"* I called it! Yes, such a home as a tavern is,—round which not a single recollection clings, which we enter without a single thought of pleasure, and leave without a single thrill of emotion. Not a foot of railroad; not even a foot of plank-road or turnpike in the State. No manufactories; hardly one public school to a county; the roads almost impassable; and half the people of the State ready to leave it whenever the "range" gives out, or the "mast" yields but a short crop.

Even the roads which the General Government made for us we have been too lazy to keep up. Within two miles of this very town, this place called in mockery a *city*, the great Southern Road is in winter an almost impassable bog. . . . So . . . [is] the old military road from Little Rock to Fort Smith. It is a perfect miracle if a man gets a hundred miles on any road in the State, without breaking his carriage to pieces, or laming the horses. Last spring I lamed three, upon old rotten causeways, in one trip, at a cost, in the long run of over four hundred dollars:—a tolerable large tax, one would say, to pay in a single year on account of bad roads.[4]

The cure for all these ills, argued Pike, was a system of railroads and internal improvements in the state. He realized there was little available capital in Arkansas, but the general government would give land, and enterprising citizens in Memphis and New Orleans would give aid, if the people of Arkansas would only wake up and show enterprise in the matter. Arkansas must make Memphis and New Orleans compete for its trade.[5]

At the New Orleans convention in January 1852, Pike attempted to rouse fear in the Louisiana delegates by warning that the trade of Arkansas might be shifted to Memphis if Tennessee took the initiative in building railroads into his state. But his most important work in the convention was to urge the construction of "a national road to the Pacific," with a terminal each for the North and South, a plan vaguely similar to the one he had presented at Memphis in 1849.[6] For political reasons no eastern terminal was designated in the resolutions, but Pike knew that Arkansas would benefit only if Memphis secured it. Furthermore, he recognized that the Pacific railroad question had now entered a new phase. Enterprising citizens in Missouri and Illinois were securing state and federal aid to build east-west railroads in their states in the hope that Congress would attach the National Pacific railroad to the most successful "first link."[7] At a railroad convention at Little Rock in July, 1852, Pike took the opportunity to encourage the South to join in the race for "first links."

> Missouri is rapidly pushing forward the Atlantic and Pacific railroads towards her western boundary, preparing strong inducements to the General Government to adopt *her* road as the eastern *terminus* of the great highway that is to connect the two oceans. The South must not be behind in that race. She must offer to the Government equal inducements to place the *terminus*; or at least one of the *termini* in the South. We must offer her a railroad, either on Red River or the Arkansas, running to and connecting with the roads to Charleston and Richmond and the more Northern and Southern ports. That road must run from Memphis, either to Fulton or a little higher on Red River, or to Fort Smith or Van Buren on the Arkansas.[8]

The Little Rock convention adopted Pike's plan and voted to petition the legislature to memorialize Congress for a land grant in aid of the road and to request the legislature to charter the Arkansas Central Railroad Company to build via the Memphis, Little Rock, and Fulton route.[9] Representative Johnson, heeding the railroad talk among his constituents, got a bill through the House on August 27, 1852, for a grant in aid of a road running from Cairo, Illinois, to Fulton by way of Little Rock with branches from Little Rock to Fort Smith and from Little Rock to the Mississippi at a point not designated.[10] Borland, who had a few months before secured in the Senate a grant for the Memphis, Little Rock, and Fulton road tried diligently to get Johnson's bill through the Senate, but that body refused to consider it in the few days left in the session.[11]

Much bad feeling developed in Arkansas over Johnson's bill. A northern route to Cairo had hardly been mentioned in the state, and the failure to designate an eastern terminal for the extension from Little Rock to the Mississippi threatened damaging rivalry between Memphis and Helena, Arkansas. The action of the legislature, which met in November, indicated the divided feeling in the state. It chartered two companies to build roads from Memphis to Little Rock, the Memphis and Little Rock and the Arkansas Central, though the latter was to extend from Little Rock to Fulton and to be built on a scale suitable to the standards "for an integral portion of the main trunk, or a southern branch of the national Atlantic and Pacific railroad." It also chartered the Cairo and Fulton Company[12] but instructed the state's delegation in Congress to work for a grant in aid of the Memphis, Little Rock, and Fulton, and the Gaines Landing (Chicot County) to Fulton routes, making no mention of the road to Cairo.[13]

When Congress reconvened in December, 1852, Borland, swayed by public opinion in Arkansas and fearful of political repercussions, refused to have anything to do with

Johnson's bill, though Johnson had told him that no better measure could be got through the House and that even the same bill could not be passed there again. William K. Sebastian, junior senator from Arkansas, convinced by Johnson and others that the House would kill the bill if it was amended by Borland and sent back, took advantage of Borland's absence from Washington during the first week of February 1853 and with able help from Pacific railroad enthusiasts William M. Gwin, Californian, and Thomas J. Rusk, Texan, pushed Johnson's bill through the Senate.[14] On February 9 President Fillmore signed the measure, and ten days later Borland, on his return to the city, accepted it with reservations, making a somewhat ambiguous attempt to keep in the good graces of both the friends and the enemies of the act.[15]

In Washington at the time on another matter, Pike probably exerted influence on Sebastian to get the bill through. Two days after President Fillmore signed the measure Pike wrote John M. Butler, editor of the *Little Rock Whig*, that Sebastian had "dexterously passed it" in the Senate. "I have, as you know, approved this bill, as at all events the best that could be got—and as, in my humble opinion, the very best possible bill for Arkansas."[16] Pike assumed that there was no doubt that the legislature would confer the lands for the eastern branch on the Arkansas Central, and optimistically wrote John T. Trezevant, Memphis railroad promoter, that grants had been made "for roads from Cairo and Memphis to Little Rock and from Little Rock to Fort Smith and Fulton. We regard this as settling, in point of fact, that Pacific Rail Road question, and as securing the ultimate adoption of the southern route."[17] The people of Memphis received the news with enthusiasm, voting in April by an overwhelming majority to subscribe $500,000 to the Arkansas Central. The editor of the *Memphis Appeal* proclaimed that the successful and speedy completion of the Memphis to Fulton road would "materially determin[e] the question as to whether or not we shall have a connection with the great Pacific road."[18]

But Pike and the Tennessee friends of the Arkansas Central had failed to take into consideration serious trouble brewing in Arkansas. Railroad fever was at such a pitch that practically every hamlet in the state had come forward with its favorite project. The jealousy and spite engendered by these movements combined to tie up the Arkansas Central in a political dispute. Pike was well aware that sectional and factional politics in the state menaced internal improvements. As early as 1851 he had declared himself independent of the Whig Party, and he had repeatedly urged that both parties put the question of internal improvements above politics.[19] At the railroad convention in Little Rock in July, 1852, he had restated his views and besought the people of the state to forget sectional and political interests and unite behind the Arkansas Central in order to assure the rapid completion of Arkansas's "first link."[20] The *Whig* and *State Gazette and Democrat*, an anti-Johnson and anti-Conway sheet, supported him,[21] but the *Little Rock Banner*, edited by Lambert J. Reardon and Richard H. Johnson, brother of Robert W. Johnson, suspecting that Pike was urging the Pacific railroad solely to gain popularity, opposed him. Internal improvement, declared the hostile editors, was "a cause of too great magnitude and importance to be made subservient to the advancement of ambitious demagogues, or sacrificed for the triumph of a selfish and unprincipled faction."

"When," they continued, "we hear men, for any end or object under the shining sun, advocate 'no-party' doctrines, and profess themselves in readiness to sacrifice their principles, we begin to suspect their motives, if not their virtue." Moreover, the editors thought the Memphis–Little Rock–Fulton road, advocated by Pike, too local in character; it failed to offer any incentive to the "whole northern, western and southeastern portion of the State," and consequently those sections had declined to send delegates to the convention. This short-sighted policy was detrimental to the cause of internal improvement and did not, therefore, deserve the support of the *Banner*.[22]

Governor Conway, dubbed by his enemies "Dirt Road" Conway because of this advocacy during the gubernatorial campaign in 1852 of "good dirt roads" rather than railroads for Arkansas, was strongly urged in 1853 by friends of the Arkansas Central and the Cairo and Fulton to call the legislature into special session to confer the lands upon the companies and thus get work on the roads underway.[23] Economy minded and suspicious of the motives of the Whigs and opposition Democrats who were leading the railroad movement, Conway refused. As a consequence the lands were not conferred until January 1855 at the regular session. In the final struggle in the legislature the Arkansas Central got nothing; the lands that it had counted upon were given instead to the hitherto inconspicuous Memphis and Little Rock Company. Long before this Pike had lost all interest in either the Arkansas Central or the state's "first link."[24]

The wrangling over the calling of the special session and the legislative battle over the land grants in Arkansas killed Pike's interest in the Arkansas Central, but did not affect in the least his determination to see the South obtain a railroad to the Pacific. By early 1854 he was, however, convinced that the sectional strife which had theretofore defeated every Pacific railroad measure introduced in Congress, and discredited the Pacific railway surveys made in 1853 under the direction of Secretary of War Jefferson Davis, would prevent the South's ever getting a bill through Congress for the construction of the road. The reopening of sectional wounds as a result of the Senate debate on the Kansas-Nebraska bill in the spring of 1854 had increased his conviction. If the territorial bill passed Pike saw that it would mean not only the reviving of the ancient slavery question but also that the North would have organized territory through which to construct a Pacific railroad.[25] Moreover, the rapidly expanding population at the North would soon fill up the new lands and in no long time give the northern states a large enough majority in Congress to pass a federal act to locate the route and to finance it as they pleased. Pike was satisfied, therefore, that if the South was to have a Pacific railroad she would have to build it herself. And the medium for putting the question before the southern states was at hand, for the third session of the Southern Commercial Convention was to meet in April 1854 at Charleston. Pike formulated his sectional plan for the road and went to Charleston to present it.

The Southern Commercial Convention which met annually from 1852 to 1859 at different cities of the South was a phase of the movement begun in the forties by which certain southern leaders sought to accomplish the economic regeneration of the South and to bring an end to her commercial vassalage to the North. Pike and others had, as we have seen, long believed that if the South were again to prosper she must diversify her industry, build cotton factories, exploit natural resources, establish direct trade with Europe, and encourage agricultural and educational improvements. The plan for securing a Pacific railway along a southern route, proposed at Memphis in 1849 and at the 1852 and 1853 sessions of the Southern Commercial Convention, was an aspect of the same movement.[26] But these meetings had concluded that the national government was the only proper agency to build the road. Pike hoped in the spring of 1854 to convince the members of the convention that the South could no longer depend upon Congress to provide for a road along a southern route, and that if the South would have the railway she must build it herself.

By 1854 Pike was widely known in the South. His reputation as a lawyer, poet, and orator preceded him wherever he went, and his grand physique and flowing hair and beard made him stand out in any assembly. The aura of romance that hung about his earlier life—his western travels, his hardships on the Great Plains, his "Hymns to the Gods," his Mexican War experiences, and his duel with Roane—lent picturesqueness to his name. By his admirers he was always referred to as the "poet-soldier" or the "poet-statesman" of Arkansas.[27] His exquisite taste for fine foods and wines, his scholarly attainments, and his wit and conversational powers, made him a splendid entertainer as well as a welcome guest at the tables of a host of friends throughout the country.[28] At Charleston in April, 1854, he found a setting in which he could indulge his talents to the fullest, for the meeting of the Southern Commercial Convention was more than a sober business affair. Its sessions were occasions for gala social entertainment, and the people of Charleston wished to make theirs the most memorable of all. The Charleston committee on entertainment planned a series of balls and banquets and concerts, even a night cruise upon the moonlight waters of the bay. The Histrionic Theatre engaged a Spanish dancer for the week, while the hotels and inns of the city prepared to receive "the immense concourse about to gather." Nor were they disappointed. Nearly nine hundred delegates from thirteen states attended the convention, many bringing their wives with them.[29]

Amid much fanfare the convention assembled at eleven o'clock in the morning April 10, and spent the entire first day in organizing. On the second day Pike, sole delegate from Arkansas and one of the numerous vice presidents of the session,[30] presented a series of resolutions embodying his new plan for the Pacific railway. He proposed that Virginia as the oldest southern state charter a Southern Pacific Railroad Company "with a sufficient capital" to finance construction from some point on the Mississippi between New Orleans and St. Louis through Texas and along the Gila River route to the Pacific. Southern states, cities, railroad companies, and individuals, and the Cherokee, Creek, and Choctaw Nations, would subscribe to the stock. The charter should provide, in event the Senate did not ratify the Gadsden Purchase Treaty then pending, that the company officials be authorized to bargain with Mexico for "a right of way through her territory" and for permission to maintain military posts along the route in that country.[31]

In a speech on April 12 Pike employed arguments of extreme sectionalism to urge upon his southern brethren the importance of rushing the proposed project. In his opinion the South could not afford delay. Drawing the attention of his listeners to the

Northwest, he pointed out that it was being settled and populated giving the North a "political preponderance over the whole South." To draw foreign immigrants to the region the right of suffrage was given aliens even before they had declared their intention of becoming citizens of the United States. The Kansas-Nebraska bill and homestead legislation then before Congress were other northern bids to acquire foreign voters. Before many years this immigrant vote would be represented by "twenty members of Congress." And with this continued increase in foreign and northern influence was it not obvious, he asked, that the prospect of the South's ever getting the Pacific railroad was put further and further off every year? Moreover, he was confident that the Gadsen treaty, then before the Senate, would receive no northern support because it was to provide a southern route to the Pacific over former Mexican soil. He then examined the motives of northern men:

> Suppose we went to Northern men, and said to them: 'We can demonstrate that our route is five hundred miles shorter than yours; that it is cheaper on the score of grades; that we can get cheaper labor and cheaper building materials; and we want you to go along with us for our route because the result will be that the trade of India and China will come to New Orleans and Charleston, and Savannah and Richmond, instead of going to Philadelphia, and New York, and Boston, and we want you to help us get it?' Would he [sic] not answer: 'Do you think I am a fool? Are not these the very reasons why I should not go for it?' Most undoubtedly such would be the answer.[32]

Any further inaction on the part of the South in the matter of the Pacific railroad would, Pike believed, simply be giving aid to the North in building a northern road. The South should be ashamed to ask Congress to build the railway and should understand by now that even if the government did build it, it would be along a northern route. His plan proposed, therefore, that the southern states confederate "in a legal union," build the road with their own funds and deal "as independent States, negotiating if need be with Mexico" for the right of way. After it was completed the South could tell the general government, "if you want your mail carried over our road, you will have to pay us the price that we charge, or build a road for yourselves." The project should be "a partnership of all the Southern States," and he felt that the aid of the Choctaws, Chickasaws, and Cherokees should be earnestly sought. In closing he remarked that he did not care about the details of the plan: a committee could work those out. His whole purpose was that "the Southern States should confederate together and build the road."[33]

Gen. Leslie Combs of Kentucky and Gen. James F. Gadsden of South Carolina supported Pike's plan. Combs in an able speech urged the southern people "to put both shoulders to the wheel and build the road." He thought that by building through Texas they should have the advantage of running through slave territory and also of receiving twenty sections per mile donated for such a road by the Texas legislature in 1853.[34] No doubt the North would build a similar road, but he believed that its traffic would have to pass over the southern railway from three to six months of each year because of snow and ice in the gorges of the mountainous northern route. If it should become necessary to negotiate with Mexico for a right of way, he thought that they should request the executive branch of the general government to do it for them.[35] Gadsden, negotiator of the treaty then before the Senate, declared that there was no constitutional doubt that the southern states could unite behind such a corporation as that proposed by Pike and "treat legitimately with Mexico for a right of way, if denied us, or rejected, after being secured" by him in the late negotiations with Mexico.[36]

But Pike's plan did not go unchallenged. Several of the ablest men in the convention opposed it. N. D. Coleman, railroad promoter from Mississippi, declared the whole scheme was "visionary, utterly impracticable, and unmanageable" in its details. He disapproved of the sectional aspects of the proposition and firmly denied the power of any state to incorporate a company with power to negotiate with a foreign country.[37] T. A. Marshal, another Mississippian, attacked the resolutions on the ground that the work would tax the people too heavily and that consequently no southern state would join in the undertaking.[38] Lt. Matthew F. Maury, distinguished director of the Naval Observatory at Washington, maintained that no state could treat with Mexico nor could a corporation chartered by one of the states acquire real estate in a foreign country without permission of Congress. He thought the whole scheme verged on unlawfulness. In his opinion the U.S. government was the only proper agency to construct the road, and it was the duty of the government to do so.[39] Judge E. A. Nesbit, Georgian, protested that Pike's suggestion was "Quixotic," that it was "emphatically sectional in its character," and that it was absurd to think of asking the merchants and people of the South to enter "an *ad libitum* partnership" with Indians. The whole thing would fall to pieces.[40] U.S. senator W. C. Dawson of Georgia, convention president, left the chair at the end of the series of opposition speeches to speak against Pike's plan. He informed his listeners that there was no need for a new company. Any one of several companies already chartered could, if given adequate support, build the road to the eastern border of Texas, whence it could be continued across that state to El Paso under the Texas land grant and charter of 1853. West of El Paso the aid of the federal government should be secured both in financing the road and in obtaining land from Mexico, for only by the guarantees of a solemn treaty pledged by the United States would Mexico, in his opinion, surrender its soil or control along the route.[41]

On the final day of the convention the ten-minute rule was suspended for Pike, and he arose to reply to his critics. He was aware, he said, that he had "a hard task to fulfill, in answering the arguments of so many distinguished gentlemen, concluded as they have been by one from the President of the Convention." But had they been "ten times as numerous, and ten times as strong, unless they were better founded in fact and in reason" he "should not dread the conflict." His measures had been attacked as being impracticable. Similar remarks had been made against every worthwhile project in the history of the human race. The rivalries and jealousies of southern men were, in his opinion, the principal obstacles to be overcome. Disagreements about the location of the terminal on the Mississippi, and "difficulties in regard to different notions concerning politics," were the basis of much of the dissatisfaction with his scheme. "Of course, no man," he said, "expects that we will all unite. But in setting forth these difficulties, you tell the North that we are weak, and should we lay our whole secret open to them?"

He asked how the general government was to build the road and remain consistent with the constitutional and states' rights scruples of many southern men. He felt, knowing the financial condition of the southern railway companies, that it would be impossible for them to furnish capital for constructing the road. But "we are told about this munificent grant of land by the State of Texas. There may be ten millions of acres of land granted by Texas, yet more than two-thirds of it is not worth a farthing an acre." He had also been in New Mexico. "Except the valley of the [Rio Grande] Del Norte, there is hardly a single foot of land worth a cent in New Mexico, on the line of this road." If the road was to be built money must be secured. The government had no power to appropriate money to construct a road, and grants of land would be insufficient.

His resolutions had been drawn up with all these problems in mind. His plan proposed, therefore, that to provide for the road the convention earnestly recommend that a southern organization be formed "for the purpose of obtaining the right of way, if necessary, from Mexico." He did not expect all the states to unite, but he would have Virginia grant a charter involving a certain amount of capital. Once the company was organized the states could enter and take stock as they chose. Declaring that the U.S. Supreme Court had already settled the constitutionality of such a corporation, he added that the directors would be able to go to Mexico and buy land as if the corporation were an individual. Furthermore, he disagreed with Senator Dawson and others on the method of getting the right of way from Mexico. That country would rather deal with a private company than with the United States. The U.S. government was bound by international law to protect the property rights of her citizens in foreign countries. But even if she refused to protect the interests of this company he "could take the road with 3,000 Creeks and Choctaws, and keep it forever. (Great applause)."

In conclusion he made a strong appeal to the men on the floor and to the women spectators in the gallery to use their influence to support his plan, which, he said, "is the first attempt to see whether we are not capable of combining for the accomplishment of any great work." He wanted the project to be a "sort of declaration of independence on the part of the South."[42]

Pike took his seat amid prolonged and enthusiastic applause, and it was abundantly clear that he had won his case. The "Pee Dee Ladies" presented him with a bouquet in appreciation of his brilliant effort.[43] When the vote was taken, his resolutions were unanimously adopted.[44] A correspondent of the *Memphis Eagle and Enquirer* wrote that Pike's "lucid and powerful exposition" of his plan and his able defense, which "Clove through . . . all the doubts, fears and misgivings of the opponents of the proposition," had won the day. "No man in the convention has gained so much reputation as Captain Pike. His speeches have gained for him, at once, an equal rank with the men of first ability in the country."[45] Others concluded, however, that the "sectional nature" of the plan was as important as Pike's convincing oratory in securing its adoption.[46]

In spite of Pike's splendid efforts at Charleston, his plan was poorly received in the South. As chairman of the Pacific Railroad Committee, he drew up a charter for the proposed railroad and presented it to the legislature of South Carolina in November, 1854.[47] The bill was never reported from the House Committee on Incorporations.[48] In the interval between the meeting of the South Carolina legislature and the next session of the Southern Commercial Convention, Pike returned to Little Rock, where an important state railroad convention met in November. George D. Prentice, admirer of Pike and renowned editor of the *Louisville Journal*, attended the convention to urge the importance of establishing railway connections between Kentucky, Tennessee, and Arkansas as a possible link for a road to the Pacific. While in town he published an article over the signature "Arkansas" in which he denounced the chief engineer of the Little Rock and Helena Railroad Company, M. Butt Hewson, for having spitefully and jealously delayed the important Memphis to Fulton road by putting his company's interest above the more important Arkansas Central Company. Hewson called on the editor of the *True Democrat* for his assailant's identity and then issued a challenge to Prentice. Mutual friends of the two men appointed Pike, C. F. M. Noland, and Philip H. Raiford to settle the dispute. The committee worked out a satisfactory adjustment between the two men, though Prentice had, in a masterly denunciation of the dueling code, already refused to fight Hewson:

> I would not call a man to the field unless he had done me such a deadly wrong that I desired to kill him, and I would not obey his call to the field unless I had done him so mortal an injury as to entitle him, in my opinion, to demand an opportunity of taking my life. I have not the least desire to kill you or to harm a hair of your head, and I am not conscious of having done anything to entitle you to kill me. . . . I might yield much to the demands of a strong public sentiment, but there is no public sentiment nor even any disinterested individual sentiment that either requires me to meet you or would justify me in doing so.
>
> I look upon the miserable code . . . with a scorn equal to that which is getting to be felt for it by the whole civilized world of mankind.[49]

During the second week of January 1855, Pike was on hand at the fourth session of the Southern Commercial Convention, meeting in New Orleans, to urge a second endorsement of his Pacific railroad plan. The lack of success with the South Carolina legislature had resulted in a modification of his former proposition. The road still was to be built along a southern route and owned by a southern corporation, but he would now "demand the aid of the General Government" in financing the road. The convention accepted with little argument the revised resolutions, and Pike was appointed chairman of a five-man committee to wait upon the Louisiana legislature to secure a charter for the Southern Pacific Railroad Company.[50] In a brilliant speech before the legislature on February 10 Pike won the support of that body.[51] An act approved March 15, 1855, chartered the company, but it was never organized.[52] Southern interest had now been attracted to the Vicksburg and El Paso Company, or Texas Western, organized in December 1854 for the specific purpose of taking advantage of the Texas grant for constructing a Pacific railroad. In October, 1856, the Texas Western Company met the requirement of the Texas law and was reorganized under a Texas charter as the Southern Pacific Railroad Company. Later the same year work was begun on a branch of the road in East Texas.[53]

As a result of the apparent success of this new company, Pike's Louisiana company was all but forgotten. He did not, however, give up the fight. From the fifth session of the Southern Commercial Convention at Savannah in December 1856, he procured a reendorsement of his plan and company. The endorsement was ineffective, and Pike himself seems to have acknowledged defeat after the session.[54] Many reasons besides overshadowing interest in the Texas company might be assigned for the failure of Pike's scheme. Perhaps the principal one was that he was working against insuperable odds in presenting his plan to the southern states through the Southern Commercial Convention. Jealous of their own prerogatives, the states and communities of the South never heeded the advice of the convention, and it was a tribute to Pike's personal ability and influence that the Louisiana legislature chartered the company at all. An anonymous correspondent of the *Little Rock Whig,* May 25, 1854, declared that he feared Pike's very desirable plan would "not take at all," and made a very accurate prediction of its failure:

> The South desires to do a great many things—practicable and impracticable; but between politics, chivalry, jealousy, and the have-all-or-none disposition, together with her real, comparative, disadvantages, growing out of her peculiar institution—she is in first rate train to do nothing at all. . . .
>
> We are fine exemplifications of the jealous members in the fable—the hands would not work, the feet would not walk, the mouth would not eat, &c., because each conceived itself imposed upon—therefore the whole perished together—a chivalrous, uncompromising, independent set of members they were. Charleston determines, Savannah takes a stand, New Orleans will not give an inch. Every one planks down his sine quo non; and "non" comes off victorious all round.[55]

XXII

Indian Claims and Personal Affairs, 1852–1855

PIKE'S ROLE AS A MAN OF PUBLIC AFFAIRS was always secondary to the law business by which he made a living. He might dabble in many things—poetry, politics, economics—but he did so only at moments of leisure or at a sacrifice to his practice. In the 1850s he was primarily absorbed in the prosecution of claims of the Creeks and Choctaws at Washington, attending every session of Congress but one between 1852 and 1861. As a claims attorney he was more lobbyist than lawyer, his principal labor being to convince congressmen of the justness and honesty of the demands, to correct misstatements, misinterpretations, distortions, and falsifications of facts rather than to point out the law of the cases, His authorities were not court reports nor the commentaries of Chitty, Blackwood, Kent, and Story, but documents, receipts, and correspondence in the files of the offices of the Interior and Treasury Departments. These records gave him the facts with which to argue before the Indian affairs committees and to win supporters to his cause on the floor of Congress. More important than facts, however, were influence and acquaintance with the leaders of the Senate, where Pike's cases were initiated. What Senators Robert M. T. Hunter of Virginia, Robert Toombs of Georgia, and Benjamin Fitzpatrick of Alabama, implacable foes of nearly all claims that came to the Senate in the fifties, had to say about an appropriation to pay a Creek or Choctaw claim was more often than not the deciding factor between defeat and victory. Such "watchdogs" of the Treasury were equivalent to prosecuting attorneys in the trial of the measures before the Senate; Pike's friends, and those convinced by him of the justice of his causes, the defense[1]

Pike had become well acquainted with the Creeks and Choctaws by defending a number of them in the courts of western Arkansas and by the fact that he had gone into Indian Territory on numerous hunting expeditions.[2] In 1852 Philip H. Raiford of Alabama, Creek agent, while on his way from Washington to the Creek Nation stopped in Little Rock and discussed with Pike the claim of the tribe against the United States for lands taken by Andrew Jackson under the treaty of Fort Jackson, August 8, 1814. The Creeks wanted Pike to prosecute the claim, and he promised to go to Washington and look into the matter. Upon investigating the claim he was at once convinced that it was just and agreed to accept it.[3] He made an oral agreement with Raiford, who had managed the claim since 1850 and was about to resign as Creek agent in order to engage openly as an advocate in the matter, that they would prosecute the case together and divide the 25 percent contingent fee, Pike to receive two-thirds and Raiford one-third.

But before Pike came into the case Raiford had engaged the services of three other men, John T. Cochrane and Joseph Bryan, from a Washington law firm, and Edward Hanrick of Alabama, speculator in Texas lands and claims agent before Congress.[4] Raiford had pledged to Cochrane and Bryan one-half of his interest in the fee and had later promised Hanrick a half of the residue. After the Pike-Raiford agreement, this meant that Cochrane and Bryan would get one-sixth of the total fee, Raiford one-twelfth, and Hanrick one-twelfth. In 1852 Pike also employed Cochrane and Bryan, agreeing to make up their interest in the final fee to one-fourth; and he later augmented Raiford's and Hanrick's interest in the fee, as we shall see.[5] Though not a lawyer himself, Cochrane was familiar with the records and employees of the Indian Office, where he had been a clerk, and his ability as a writer made him a valuable assistant. Cochrane's partner, Bryan, was an able attorney.[6]

The Creek claim was almost as involved as the agreements and subagreements of the attorneys. Before the war of 1812 the Muscogee or Creek Nation of Indians owned nearly all of what is now Alabama and approximately half of present-day Georgia. The southern portion of the tribe was friendly toward the United States. But the northern portion of the nation was hostile and fell under the influence of Tecumseh in 1813, taking up arms against the United States and the southern Creeks. The Creek war was in reality a civil war and resulted in the permanent division between the Friendly, Loyal, or Lower Creeks and the Hostile, Red Stick, or Upper Creeks. The Lower Creeks defended themselves heroically against the Upper Creeks and gave valuable assistance to the U.S. troops sent to the region from Tennessee to chastise the hostile Indians. In the decisive battle of Horseshoe Bend on the Tallapoosa, March 14, 1814, a large body of them forded the river "with Coffee, set the town on fire, and attacked the Red Sticks from behind, while General Jackson stormed the breastworks in front."[7]

In April following Jackson's victory Gen. Thomas Pinckney of South Carolina reached the country, took command of the U.S. forces, and set about making peace with the hostile Creeks. Enough land was to be retained from the conquered lands of the Red Sticks to indemnify the United States for the war and to pay all damages and injuries sustained by its citizens and the friendly Creeks. But before Pinckney's treaty was completed Jackson replaced him as commander. At Fort Jackson in early August the Tennessean dictated a treaty to thirty-six chiefs of the Creek Nation, only one of whom was a "hostile chief." He demanded and received from friend and foe over twenty-four million acres of choice land, "seven-eighths of the present State of Alabama," and over seven million acres "in the southern part of Georgia." The friendly chiefs signed the treaty August 8, 1814, under vigorous protest and only after Jackson agreed to have an instrument drawn up and sent in with it which declared that they were the sole owners of their confiscated land, that they alone could dispose of it, and that "they had received no equivalent for cession which they made by the capitulation." When Pike became their attorney in 1852 the Loyal Creeks had never been compensated for any of the land surrendered at Fort Jackson, though they had received under the treaty terms $82,925 in 1819 and $110,417.90 in 1852 in compensation for the destruction of their homes, livestock, and personal property by the Red Sticks.[8]

After laborious research Pike prepared a history and memorial on the Creek claim, had it printed at Little Rock,[9] and in December 1852 got his friend, Robert W. Johnson, to present the matter to the House.[10] On December 27 the petition was referred to the Committee on Indian Affairs, of which Johnson was chairman.[11] The committee sent a copy of the memorial to the Department of Interior on December 28, asking verification of the statements of fact therein and an estimate of the number of acres, if any, on which compensation was due. In the department the subject was referred to the Office of Indian Affairs, headed by Luke Lea, probably a friend of John T. Cochrane.[12] Commissioner Lea reported, January 17, 1853, to Johnson that the friendly Creeks were due compensation on 8,849,940 acres of land as their petition prayed, but he did not say how much should be paid the Indians.[13]

The committee sent Lea's report to the secretary of the interior, requesting an estimate of the amount which should be appropriated for the land. On January 21 Lea, to whom the matter was also referred, reported that twenty cents per acre would be a moderate price and one which would probably satisfy the Indians.[14] A. H. H. Stuart, secretary of the interior, endorsed the commissioner's estimate of $1,769,880 and recommended that if Congress saw fit to appropriate the money that it be "specially provided that the money shall be paid, per capita, to the Indians themselves, and that it shall be taken and received by them in full and complete satisfaction of all demands of whatsoever nature, both legal and equitable, they may be supposed to have against the United States."[15]

In keeping with Lea's and Stuart's recommendation, the committee drew up an amendment to the general appropriation bill for Indian affairs which Johnson moved in the House on February 22. The committee report was unanimous, but this was true only because Volney E. Howard, Texas, had not attended the final hearing on the amendment and had not, therefore, registered his opposition in the committee vote. Once the measure got before the House and was taken up in committee of the whole Howard became the chief opponent of the measure. He pleaded that the statute of limitations should bar consideration of the forty-year-old claim, that to open up the claim would set a dangerous precedent for other tribes, that the land assigned by Jackson to the friendly and hostile Creeks between the Coosa and Tallapoosa Rivers was equivalent to that taken from the friendly Creeks, and that the money paid them in 1819 and at the previous session of Congress in 1852 had more than compensated them not only for personal but also for land claims.[16]

Johnson replied to Howard on February 23. He denied that the United States could plead the statute of limitations against anyone, pointed out that in 1821 the Creeks had been forced to pay white claims against their tribe dating back to 1773, asserted that the money paid the Loyal Creeks in 1819 and 1852 was specifically for personal damages and not for land claims, and declared that the land left the Creeks between the Coosa and Tallapoosa was short of being an equivalent to the lands confiscated in southern Alabama and Georgia by nearly nine million acres. He ended in a strong appeal to the House to pay the amount recommended by the Interior Department and asked for in the amendment before them. "I believe," he said, ". . . if there can be such a thing as a person knowing what is a just conclusion from, his premises, when they are laid down before him on the record, I will say I *know*, that I have demonstrated the title of the Creeks to the land that was taken. I know that I have also demonstrated the fact that they have not received compensation for it." A few minutes later the Johnson amendment was rejected without a division.[17]

Notwithstanding the defeat of the Creek claim Pike had a good time during the session, which he afterwards remembered with pleasure. He boarded at a house on Fourth Street with Luther Chase, his "more than a friend," then U.S. Marshal for Arkansas and Indian Territory, and William M. Burwell, a Virginian who was urging a claim before Congress concerned with the Tehuantepec railroad and who was later editor of *De Bow's Review* at New Orleans. Maj. Elias Rector of Fort Smith, Democratic aspirant under the incoming Pierce administration to the place held by Chase, boarded only a house or two away and was constantly with them except for a few hours each night. Despite their political differences, Rector, a Virginian who had immigrated first to Missouri and thence to Arkansas while it was still a territory, was one of Pike's oldest and warmest friends. A fancy dresser, Rector usually wore a suit of "black silk velvet," immaculate ruffled linen, "a costly Mexican sombrero," and morocco boots,[18] but he was, said Pike, a man "of great intelligence, and of an excellent and most quaint wit; one of his peculiarities being that he wore his hair long, and put up with a comb, like a woman's."[19] Pike blamed an attack of pleurisy he had at Washington that winter on "the incessant laughter" provoked by Rector and Burwell.[20]

Other Arkansans were in the city, and because most of them were in one way and another connected with Indian matters they formed a "Wigwam Club" with headquarters at Pike's house.[21] Pike was "Principal Comanche," or president, of the club, and each of the members, or "chiefs" was appropriately named for different tribes. At the most notable of the numerous dinners of the club, Pike and seven of his chiefs invited over thirty men to a banquet given in honor of Robert W. Johnson, each host signing his last name, X-mark, and tribe to the invitations.[22] Among the guests was Alfred Bunn, an English traveler then stopping in Washington, who wrote and printed an account of the affair.

> At this repast were assembled some of the choicest specimens of the land, including senators and representatives of contending politics, some retiring placemen, and several expectants; the planter from Arkansas and the merchant from New Orleens (as it is pronounced) fierce Democrats and spouting Whigs, loud in speech, and ready, it would seem, to eat each other up; and while courtesy forbids our introducing the names of individuals, strictly of a private station, we do not consider ourselves bound to observe any such delicacy toward public men of public repute.[23]

Since Pike, in Bunn's estimation, fell under the latter category, he singled him out for special attention.

> We had the further pleasure of becoming known to one whose literary and social qualifications are of the most enviable distinction—we allude to Albert Pike, of Little Rock, Arkansas,[24] one of America's distinguished poets, whose name heads the list of chiefs.... To his brilliant conversation the table owed a great part of its diversion and to his wit the fullest amount of its hilarity.[25]

Pike's song, "The Fine Arkansas Gentleman," a rollicking burlesque on the life and times of Elias Rector, who was present, "was introduced, for the first time, at this festival."[26] In its day the piece was very popular and was published widely. Pike's friend William T. Porter, editor of the *Spirit of the Times*, a sporting journal, copied "the exceedingly clever song" from the columns of the *Missouri Republican*, whose editor had praised the author as "the most versatile genius, the ablest lawyer, the best hunter, the most distinguished orator and poet,—and last, though not least, the jolliest good fellow in the South-west."[27]

To his friends Pike had become, indeed, "the jolliest good fellow of the South-west," but to say with the enthusiastic Missourian or with Bunn that he was "one of America's distinguished poets" in the fifties or at any other period of his life, before or after, would be overstatement. Whatever youthful promise he had shown of becoming a truly great poet had now long since passed. He had published, as we have seen, a few new poems in the forties, and he reprinted many of the old ones and composed a few new ones in the early fifties,[28] but he never valued them highly. When, early in 1854, he collected and reprinted in a single volume called *Nugae* the best of his poetry up to that time, he passed judgment on the lot as being "trifles" which he wished to preserve for his "children and a few friends."[29]

"I am too conscious of their great defects," he said in the preface to the book, "not to know that they would be of no value or interest to any other person in the world; and not to be aware that if I were to publish them for sale, I should justly incur the wrath of all critics and reviewers, who might think that they were worthy of notice at all."[30] He told William Gilmore Simms in September, 1854, when requested by him to write a short biographical sketch to be included with a selection of his poetry in the Duyckinck brothers' forthcoming *Cyclopaedia of American Literature*, that he was "not ambitious of reputation as a Poet—shall never publish a *book* of poetry—shall never write any more of it; that is if mine is worth being called poetry at all."[31] "I have written," he told an intimate friend in 1855, "no verses for a long while. When I had Nugae printed, I said goodbye to the Muses. The courtship, conducted for many years, was not a very successful one."[32]

Pike merely reasserted here in the mid-fifties a resolution that he had made as early as the late thirties. He had been ambitious then of winning fame as a writer, of making his livelihood with his pen, but the harsh realities of life soon crowded such aspiration—he would have said "nonsense"—from his mind. The law and public affairs left him little time in the busy years of the forties and fifties to "dream of rhythm and rhyme." Maurice Thompson, who believed Pike had shown true poetic genius in his youth, felt that he was

> ambitious and yet as retiring and shy in some directions as he was bold and aggressive in others. He gave the impression that he regarded literary art as something to be wrought at in some remote nook and under polite protest. Disappointment doubtless had much to do in shaping this attitude. His early success did not hold; it broke and was dissipated, while yet his footing on Parnassus needed wise and careful attention. He had too many irons in the fire; that glowing one, ready to be beaten into the divine forms of art, cooled hopelessly, while grosser interests clanged on the anvil.

An intelligent look at conditions in the South during old slavery days will help to an understanding of Pike's course. William Gilmore Simms found literature as a stumbling block at the vestibule of social and political favor in Charleston. It was not an isolated case. Southern life demanded a certain cast of virility in men which was felt to be above the sentimentalities of poetry and the unrealities of fiction. Moreover, there was no recognition of the "nobility of labor," and somehow literary work did not rank with that of the lawyer, the politician, the priest and the doctor, as of polite consideration. Pike was of too sane a temper to resent openly, as did Simms, this manifest injustice; he simply and wisely embraced the surer opportunity, and so did not die at starvation's door along with Timrod and Hayne. He bade good-by in stately fashion to the Muse's graves.

> "I would, sweet bird, that I might live
>   with thee amid the eloquent
>   grandeur of the shades,
> Alone with nature; but it may not be.
> I have to struggle with the stormy sea
>   of human life, until existence
>   fades
> Into death's darkness."[33]

Another critic saw in Pike's own nature the limitations that prevented him from winning fame as a great poet:

> In studying the poetic work of Albert Pike, I have found that he is the singer of himself, seldom in a large, suggestive, representative way, as truly great lyric poets must be, but rather with a gift which seems to be circumscribed and confined within bounds, personal moods, and feelings. This flavor of self in his work is too marked, as he truly recognized himself, to give him a high rank among men of poetic fame. He communed with his own soul in writing, he tells us,[34] but unfortunately it was his soul too concerned with its own joys or sorrows instead of with those of the human spirit as such. One hears in his utterances a constantly recurring plaintive wistful note that would have more of an appeal if it came out of deeper depths. His work, therefore, like most of the Southern poetic work of his day, lacks ultimate seriousness,—that seriousness which is the result of universality of feeling.

Yet, said this writer, when "the occasion really demanded the soul-animating and trumpet-like, "Pike" could make adequate response. Of this kind was his "Dixie." It shoots flame and emits heat." There was no "metrical hesitancy," no groping "for the rhyme," for the lines of "Dixie" had forthrightness; "they are energized by the occasion, and throb and leap in the consciousness of imminent crisis."[35]

"Dixie," written in 1861,[36] was Pike's only attempt at earnest poetry from the time *Nugae* came from the press until the outbreak of war. But during the same period he occasionally amused himself and his friends with humorous verses: "The Fine Arkansas Gentlemen"; "After Dinner"; "Cruiskeen Lad," a drinking song; and "Oh, Jamie Brewed a Bowl O' Punch," a parody on Robert Burns's "Willie Brew'd a Peck O' Mout," being his best known productions. "An Aunciente Fytte Pleasaunte and Full of Pastyme of a Dollar, or Two," first published in the *New Orleans Daily Picayune*, December 7, 1854, and later revised and printed in a small pamphlet, at once reflects Pike's indifference to the art of poetry and exemplifies his knack for writing the catchy pieces which won him popularity and endearment among the undiscriminating, carefree men with whom he was associated at this time.

> Do you wish to have friends who your bidding will do,
> And help you your means to get speedily through?
> You'll find them remarkably faithful and true,
> By the magical power of a Dollar, or two.
> > For friendship's secured by a Dollar, or two;
> > Popularity's gained by a Dollar, or two;
> > And you'll ne'er want a friend
> > Till you no more can lend.
> And yourself need to borrow a Dollar, or two.
>
> If a claim that is proved to be honestly due,
> Department of Congress you'd quickly put through,
> And the chance for its payment begins to look blue,
> You can help it along with a Dollar, or two.
> > For votes are secured by a Dollar, or two,
> > And influence bought by a Dollar, or two;
> > And he'll come to grief
> > Who depends for relief
> Upon justice not braced with a Dollar, or two.[37]

Pike went to Washington at the opening of Congress in December 1853 to urge the Creek claim.[38] Since William K. Sebastian, Arkansan, member of the Wigwam Club, and close friend of Pike, was chairman of the Senate Committee on Indian Affairs, and since his good friend Bob Johnson had been appointed to the Senate during the summer,[39] Pike decided to try his luck in the Senate. He had rewritten and condensed the lengthy memorial of the previous year, had added a section answering the charges brought against the measure in the House in February, and had, in support of his plea for the $1,769,880 payment, printed and appended to the petition the correspondence between Johnson's committee and Lea and Stuart of the Interior Department.[40]

Introduced in the Senate by Johnson on December 14, 1853, Pike's memorial was referred to Sebastian's committee,[41] where it was again put to the test of authenticity.[42] The committee, satisfied as to the facts and as to the justness of the claim in every particular except the price per acre recommended by the Interior Department, arbitrarily reduced the amount to six and one-fourth cents per acre and the number of acres to eight million.[43] The only apparent excuse for their action was that it gave them a round figure of $500,000.[44] On May 3, 1854, Isaac P. Walker of Wisconsin, committee member, moved in the Senate to amend the House bill on appropriations for the Indian service to include payment of the half million dollars in full settlement of all Creek claims.[45]

The amendment was debated intermittently during the following three weeks. Walker and Sebastian of the Indian committee led the van in defense of the measure, and John Bell, Tennessean; Lewis Cass, Michigander; Albert G. Brown, Mississippian; and Johnson of Arkansas were valiant supporters of the claim. They were not, however, able to overcome the prejudice which the Virginian, Robert M. T. Hunter, manager of the appropriation bill; James Dawson, Georgian; and Benjamin Fitzpatrick, Alabaman, aroused against it.[46]

Justice and facts were on the side of Pike's friends, but the majority opinion probably agreed with Hunter's views that the Senate could not afford to "rip up old Indian treaties" in order to correct past mistakes, that because the claim was an old one and the evidence was cloudy it was impossible to "make a fair decision," that the Indians in "abandoning the right to rove over the land and catch game" certainly did not deserve "the consideration which we would pay to the fee-simple proprietor," and that the Creeks had been amply compensated already, "better paid than almost any other tribes of Indians that ever had dealings with the United States."[47] A month later, June 26, Walker brought in a separate bill and a committee report in favor of the claim.[48] The bill was passed to a second reading but was not acted upon again that session.[49]

The claim had been dealt a terrific blow, but there was still hope that it might pass as a separate bill at the next session of Congress. In the meantime Pike had picked up a new Indian claim. Having heard, probably in 1852 or 1853, of Choctaw and Chickasaw claims against the United States for treaty violations, Pike asked his friend Luther Chase, whose jurisdiction as U.S. Marshal included Arkansas and Indian Territory, to inquire about securing their claims for prosecution. Chase discovered, perhaps in the summer or fall of 1853, that the Chickasaws had employed Luke Lea, ex-Commissioner of Indian Affairs, to handle their claim,[50] but nevertheless he made an oral agreement with the Choctaw claims' delegation headed by Peter Perkins Pitchlynn, Choctaw statesman and later principal chief of the nation, to place in Pike's hands a claim that had arisen out of the removal treaty of Dancing Rabbit Creek of 1830.[51] At Washington, D.C., March 13, 1854, the oral agreement was transferred into a written contract. Pike was made sole attorney of the Choctaw Nation to prosecute their claim with a contingent fee of 25 percent.[52]

Nominally he was "sole attorney," but in fact it was understood between him and the interested parties that Pitchlynn, John T. Cochrane, and Douglas H. Cooper of Mississippi were each to have one-fourth of Pike's fee, after all expenses were deducted. Cochrane was working with Pike in the Creek case and the Choctaw delegates requested Pike to employ him in their case; Cooper was Choctaw agent for the United States. By this oral arrangement Pike and Cochrane were to prosecute the case in the name of the Choctaw delegates, while Cooper as agent was to aid in securing favorable consideration by the government.[53] Since Pike and Cochrane were involved in both the Creek and the Choctaw claims, they made an agreement that Pike would conduct the Creek claim and Cochrane the Choctaw. Soon after this Pike returned to Arkansas, stopping at the Charleston commercial convention on his way.

On his return to Arkansas in the summer of 1854 Pike determined to move to New Orleans and open a law office. He had first considered the idea in 1851 but had found that he was not prepared to handle cases involving the civil law. In the intervening years he had purchased all the authoritative works in the field and had begun an intensive study. The task was no small one, for he was forced to relearn both Latin and French, having lost through "twenty years' disuse" his ability to read them. Once he became proficient in them he read diligently, and by the end of 1854 he felt he was ready to pass the examination at the Louisiana bar. In February, following the commercial convention at New Orleans and his trip to Baton Rouge to urge the Pacific railroad charter by the legislature, he returned to New Orleans for the examination.

> It was required then that an applicant for admission to the bar of the Supreme Court should be first examined by a committee, and then in open court. In the former, the examination in regard to the Civil Law consisted of the one question, put by the venerable old French jurist (I cannot recollect his name),[54] who was the representative of that law on the committee: "What works have you read on the Roman law?" I answered: "I have read the Pandects and made a translation into English in writing of the first book."[55] He was perfectly satisfied with this, and it was true. I had also read the twenty-two volumes of Duranton, several volumes of Pothier, the five volumes of Marcade (the highest authority of all—higher than all the courts of France—and out of sight the most admirable of all writers of the law) and other works.[56]

Having completed the examination successfully, Pike was admitted to practice before the supreme court and in the other courts of Louisiana on February 19, 1855.[57] Soon afterwards he formed a partnership with Logan Hunter, a prominent Louisiana Whig and attorney, who had served as U.S. District Attorney at New Orleans during Taylor's administration.[58] Pike did not, however, establish himself at once in New Orleans. He returned in the early spring to Little Rock, where he continued his civil law studies.[59] This was the year of the great upheaval over the Real Estate Bank. Five days before the trustees were deprived of the assets of the trust Pike wrote his intimate friend John F. Coyle, editor of the *National Intelligencer* at Washington, of his thoughts and future plans:

> I am annotating the Civil Code of Louisiana with extracts from Pothier, Duranton and the Pandects, which latter I am sturdily engaged in translating. You wonder what I am wading about after, in the Civil Law. I anticipate the question. I am about to encamp in New Orleans, and see if I can make a living there. I am weary of Arkansas—weary and worn out, and must get out into the world, somewhere. It is nothing to me that I am in a minority here; because I have no tendency towards office; but I am sick of the constant squabbling and snarling that goes on around me, and of the antediluvian notions of Boobydom. The government of the State is in the fullest sense of the word a Boobyocracy, and itself lies supine like a lean sow in a gutter, "with meditative grunts of much content," waiting for the good time to come when railroads, school houses and other public improvements will build themselves, and nobody have it to pay for. That's their idea of the millennium.[60]

Pike returned in May 1855 to New Orleans, where he participated in the spring session of the courts.[61] He then went to Washington to look after the Creek claim but found that the Senate had not considered the measure and that he could do nothing in the business until the next session.[62] In late June he passed through New Orleans on his way to Little Rock to handle the Holford Bond cases, then before the Pulaski Circuit Court, and while in the Crescent City expressed the intention of permanently establishing himself there in the fall.[63] In consequence of his final determination to leave Little Rock, Pike and Ebenezer Cummins dissolved their partnership in December, 1855.[64]

From the fall of 1855 until the summer of 1858 Pike's residence was in New Orleans, though Mary Ann and the children remained at the family home in Little Rock. During this time he considered himself a citizen of Louisiana and was so considered by others.[65] But whatever hopes Pike had of rising to an eminent place at the Louisiana bar were not to materialize. The courts of that state met at the same time as the Congress and the Supreme Court of the United States, and he was unable to shuttle back and forth successfully between his New Orleans and his Washington cases. He attempted it in 1855–56 and 1856–57 but gave up in 1858,[66] when he apparently dissolved the partnership with Hunter and brought the experiment to an end.

As a result of his sojourn in New Orleans Pike was induced to prepare two manuscripts, neither ever published. The first, *Notes on the Civil Code of Louisiana,* over two hundred pages long, he prepared in 1855. It is a detailed annotation of the Louisiana law code with extensive abstracts of opinions of eminent French jurists and decisions of courts bearing on the different articles and clauses of the code. The work was intended for use in his own practice. The more pretentious work, *Maxims of the Roman Law and Some of the Ancient French Law, as Expounded and Applied in Doctrine and Jurisprudence,* intended for publication, totals 3,340 pages bound in thirteen manuscript volumes, and contains over 3,000 maxims with comments by Pike on each. In the preface, written in 1876, he defines a maxim as "that which briefly states what the law of the case is" and adds that he began to collect the maxims "many years ago, when I studied the rudiments of the Roman and French law." In his autobiography Pike remarked that the *Maxims*

> would make three volumes of goodly size; but it remains, with other unpublished works of mine, in the Library of the Supreme Council, because it would not pay a book-seller to publish such a book; and I have had since the war no means wherewith to publish it myself.[67]

Judge Charles S. Lobingier, an outstanding American authority on comparative law, believes that if the work had been published it would have placed Pike "in the front ranks of American writers on civil law."[68]

In light of what Pike accomplished during his intermittent stay in New Orleans it was perhaps unfortunate that the Choctaw and Creek claims forced him to abandon his practice in civil law. But the claims were bread and butter and more to Pike, and we must turn now to examine their prosecution.

XXIII

Indian Claims: Successes and Failures

DURING PIKE'S ABSENCE FROM WASHINGTON from the summer of 1854 until the late spring of 1855 Cochrane had been actively pushing the Choctaw claim. In accordance with his and Pikes's agreement that he should handle the correspondence and initial prosecution of the Choctaw case and Pike that of the Creek case, Cochrane began in the spring of 1854 to collect information and data on the Choctaw claims arising under the treaty of Dancing Rabbit Creek of 1830 whereby the Choctaw Nation surrendered to the United States the remainder of its lands in Mississippi and removed to the tribal lands west of Arkansas[1] Cochrane found that the Indians had many complaints. They charged that the United States had not fulfilled treaty and legislative promises to pay for cattle and property abandoned at the time of the Choctaw removal, to reimburse those who paid their own removal expenses, and to compensate those who had been prevented by hostile white men from becoming citizens of the United States and settling on individual allotments set aside for them out of their Mississippi lands. Finally, the United States in making and keeping large profits, that is, the "net proceeds," from the sale of the Choctaw lands in Mississippi to white settlers had shown bad faith; according to the Indians the tribal delegates who negotiated the treaty in 1830 had understood that the United States would seek no financial gain, above the expenses of Choctaw removal, from the lands.[2]

After a brief examination Cochrane saw that it would be next to impossible to collect evidence and proof of each of the individual claims. He discussed the problem with Pike, and it was decided that the wisest and cheapest course would be to sound out the Interior Department on the possibility of a new treaty making a full settlement of the financial and political complaints of the Choctaws. Accordingly Cochrane wrote, April 5, 1854, with Pike's approval,[3] a letter to George W. Manypenny, commissioner of Indian Affairs, in which the Choctaw delegates set forth the Choctaw claims, declared the necessity for a new treaty to settle these and other difficulties, requested an investigation and report by the Interior Department of the amount due them, and suggested that since the "esteemed agent" of the tribe had not been consulted on the subject he was "free to be first consulted by the department thereon."[4] At Manypenny's recommendation Robert McClelland, Secretary of the Interior, approved the investigation and it was referred to Cooper on April 20, after Pike had left the city.[5]

Concealing the fact that Cooper was an interested party, Cochrane and Cooper worked hand-in-glove in preparing as advantageous a case as possible for their clients. Formal correspondence pertaining to the investigation was carried on between Cooper and the delegation, but Cochrane not only wrote all the letters of the delegates but also had a hand in Cooper's final report, submitted on May 25.[6] This document declared that the only satisfactory settlement would be either to pay the Choctaws the net proceeds of their lands or to give them "a reasonable sum of money, as a compromise, in lieu of all claims under the treaty of 1830." A "comparative estimate" submitted by the Choctaw delegates (Cochrane), and in the main endorsed by Cooper, indicated that approximately $2,380,701 would be due if the principle of the net proceeds were adopted.[7] Secretary McClelland decided against the net proceeds claim, as it was henceforth styled, on June 20, refusing at the same time to "re-open" the private claims under the treaty. In answering a plea for reconsideration prepared by Cochrane for the delegation, McClelland on September 25, 1854, again firmly denied the right of the Choctaws to the net proceeds, though he did recommend that the Choctaws take the whole subject to Congress where money could be appropriated for the extra clerical help that would be needed to make the investigation called for by Cooper's report and the Choctaw petition.[8]

Cochrane had expected nothing favorable from McClelland. Consequently he had written on September 14 to Pike, then in Little Rock, proposing that Pike appeal to the Senate in its executive capacity to secure a resolution for making a new treaty with the Choctaw Nation "on the principle of allowing them the proceeds of their lands."[9] Pike's refusal to approach the Senate in the manner suggested, and his absence from Washington from April 1854 until May 1855[10] were undoubtedly handicaps to Cochrane and may have been the principal cause of the new course which Cochrane now took in prosecuting the claim. Having convinced the Choctaw delegates that Pike had virtually abandoned their cause, Cochrane persuaded them to revoke the Pike contract and to sign on February 13, 1855, a new contract making himself sole attorney for the Choctaw claims with a contingent fee of 30 percent.[11] This maneuver eventually became, as we shall see, a source of much trouble among the Choctaw attorneys, but at the time, or soon afterwards, Pike, who later claimed not to have read the Cochrane contract until 1871, accepted Cochrane's explanation that it had been necessary to draw up a new agreement in order to raise the fee so that other attorneys might be brought into the case.[12]

After signing the new contract, Cochrane gave up the idea of taking the case to the Senate, and in March 1855, appealed McClelland's decision to President Pierce. But the President refused to review the opinion of his subordinate.[13] This unfavorable action temporarily brought the case to a standstill. It was, however, given a new lease on life when negotiations between the Chickasaws, the Choctaws, and the United States were opened at Washington in April 1855. The U.S. government desired to settle a grievous political quarrel between the Chickasaws and Choctaws by separating the two tribes and allowing the Chickasaws to set up an independent government over its hitherto leased district in the western part of the Choctaw Nation; to limit the disputed western boundary of the Choctaw Nation to the hundredth meridian in order to avoid possible trouble with Texas; and to secure a permanent home west of the new Chickasaw district for the Wichitas and other bands who were intruding on Choctaw lands. Manypenny wrote Cooper during the first week of April, requesting him to confer with the Choctaw claims delegation to obtain their views on the possibility of a treaty between the tribes.[14]

Cooper and Cochrane could hardly have asked for a better opportunity to reopen their case. They bought off Luke Lea, attorney and adviser of the Chickasaws, by granting him a full share in the Choctaw fee, and they and Lea became the silent spokesmen of the disputing delegations.[15] They had the Choctaws present as a sine quo non the reference of all their claims to the Senate for final adjudication and decision whether the Choctaws should have the net proceeds of their lands in full settlement of all claims or a lump sum to pay the private claims under the treaty of 1830. After Manypenny and the secretary of the interior reluctantly agreed to this, and after other difficulties were ironed out, the negotiations were completed.[16] The treaty, signed June 22, 1855, separated politically the Chickasaws and the Choctaws, set up an independent Chickasaw government over their district in the Choctaw Nation, established the western boundary of the Choctaw Nation at the hundredth meridian, provided for a permanent lease to the United States of the area between the ninety-eighth and hundredth meridians west of the Chicakasaw district, and referred the Choctaw claims to the Senate for adjudication. For surrendering the claim to the area west of the hundredth meridian and for leasing the area west of the ninety-eighth meridian as a home for the intrusive Indians and others whom the United States might wish to locate there, the Choctaws and Chickasaws were to receive $800,000 divided between them in a ratio of three to one.[17]

When Congress met in December, 1855, the treaty was pending before the Senate; it was Pike's responsibility to see that they ratified it. Leaving New Orleans before the fall term of the courts had ended, Pike rushed to Washington early in February 1856 and immediately went to work on Sebastian, whose Committee on Indian Affairs had had the treaty under consideration since January 28, to get a favorable report.[18] His efforts were successful. On February 19 Sebastian reported the treaty without amendment, and two days later it was approved by the Senate by a vote of thirty-one to two.[19]

After a brief absence at Philadelphia in late February, Pike returned to Washington to look after the Creek case. Neither house of Congress had given the claim favorable consideration, though it had been before one or the other body since December 1852. But now a new way was open to Pike to present the matter. Delegates from the Seminole and Creek tribes had been called to Washington by Manypenny to make a treaty looking to the separation of the two tribes and to the establishment of territorial and political independence for the Seminoles, who since 1845 had been a minority adjunct to the Creek Nation. The United States believed an independent status for the Seminoles in Indian Territory would be an inducement to hostile Seminoles still in Florida to remove to that region. Pike had the Creek delegates propose to Manypenny as an indispensable condition of negotiation that their claims under the treaty of 1814 be incorporated into the talks. The commissioner at first refused this demand, but Pike took up his pen for the Creek delegates and in an exchange of letters between May 20 and July 28, 1856, convinced Manypenny that for ceding the Seminoles a country between the Canadian and North Fork of the Canadian extending to the hundredth meridian and for surrendering all claims to their territory east of the Mississippi the Creek Nation should be paid a million dollars.[20] In consequence the treaty, concluded August 7, 1856, separated the Seminoles and Creeks and settled the forty-two-year-old claim of the Creek

Nation against the United States. President Pierce referred the treaty to the Senate on the day it was signed, and Sebastian's committee took it under consideration on August 13. Reported three days later with minor amendments, it was unanimously ratified.[21] Immediately afterward Sebastian introduced and got a bill through the Senate to fulfill the stipulations of the treaty, but the House did not take up the measure before adjournment in September.[22]

In spite of the lack of action on the Creek bill in the House, the year had been one of great success in the advancement of the claims. It now looked as though both cases would be speedily closed, and the attorneys to ease their financial strain were to receive a fee of thirty percent of the $400,000 already appropriated by Congress for the Choctaws under the treaty of 1855. But Cochrane, the new principal attorney, apparently planned to exclude Pike from a share in the fee, notwithstanding Pike's original connection with the case and his assistance in getting the treaty ratified. On October 2, 1856, before Cochrane left Washington for the Choctaw Nation to collect the money, he wrote Pike that he thought Pike had no "just claim to participate in" a division of the amount due on the $400,000 claim, though he readily conceded that Pike was entitled to a full interest in the fee to be collected on the award yet to be gained before the Senate. Cochrane probably perceived that Pike would be displeased at such treatment, for he added that Pike should, if dissatisfied for any reason with the contemplated settlement, "make me out a memorandum of your views on the subject, which I can have when I reach the Rock." "For myself," he concluded, "I want to do not only what is just and right but what is liberal towards you."[23] There can be little doubt that Pike believed he had every right to share in any and all fees connected with the Choctaw case, and he said in 1872 that he "indignantly and energetically" answered Cochrane's letter, "asserting my rights as in all respects equal to his."[24] The upshot was that Cochrane forwarded to Pike from Fort Towson November 18, 1856, "a full and equal share" of the sum collected, two $5,000 certificates of deposit of the Southern Bank, New Orleans. He also hoped Pike would be in Washington when Congress met "to aid us with the big Choctaw claim."[25] If Cochrane had intended to cheat Pike, he had changed his mind.

Pike went to Washington in December 1856 and remained until Congress adjourned on March 4, 1857, when James Buchanan was inaugurated. Early in the session he prepared a documented argument, "Notes Upon the Choctaw Question," in defense of a net proceeds award and filed it with Sebastian's Committee on Indian Affairs, which had before it the subject of adjudicating the claims of the Choctaw Nation under the treaty of 1855. But because of the brief session no action was taken on the case.[26] Congress did, however, appropriate on March 3, 1857, $800,000 of the Creek money under the treaty of 1856, stipulating in the act that no treaty money should be paid by the Indians to "any agent, attorney, or other persons, for any service or pretended service in negotiating said treaty." By this proviso Pike was left to depend solely upon the honesty and integrity of the Creeks for the payment of his fee.[27]

The treaty money was to be paid over to the Creeks in the course of the summer by Elias Rector, who had in 1857 taken office under Buchanan as superintendent of the southern superintendency headquarters Fort Smith. Pike planned to be on hand when it was distributed to demand his fee. He returned to New Orleans after Congress adjourned, thence to Little Rock in early May 1857.[28] He spent the rest of the month with Mary Ann and the children before going on to the Creek country. His preparations for the trip, which was to be, as was always true of Pike, for pleasure as well as business, were noticed by his old friend Fent Noland, temporary editor of the *Gazette and Democrat* in the absence of the regular editor. A great sportsman himself, Noland was particularly interested in Pike's camp chest.[29]

> It is a curiosity—a living practical demonstration, of what may be achieved in the way of economy of space. It is made of substantial English oak, is 2 feet and scant three inches long—and 1 foot 4 1/2 inches deep, and is wide as it is deep—contains decanters, 12 ivory handle knives, 6 steel forks with ivory handles, 6 ditto of silver, 6 tumblers, 6 wine glasses, 6 coffee cups, 6 egg cups, 6 big spoons, and 6 small ones, 6 plates, dishes, coffee pot, tea pot, sugar dishes, all kinds of contraptions for carrying sugar, tea, coffee, salt, pepper, &c.
>
> There is also, outside and separate from it, a circular bucket, 1 foot in depth, and 2 1/2 in circumference, containing tea-kettles, tea-pots, stew-pans, frying-pans, chafing dish, with the most complete spirit lamp we have ever seen, together with vessels to hold the spirits of wine. The whole affair can go in an ordinary buggy, and with it in the woods, there is every thing that is necessary, to set a table for six persons in the very best style.[30]

After a short visit with friends in Van Buren in early June,[31] Pike went on to the Creek Nation before the middle of the month.[32] He spent three leisurely months there hunting, loafing, and studying the various languages of the Creek Indians. Through the help of George W. Stidham, an intelligent and educated Creek who had been one of the delegates sent to Washington to aid in negotiating the treaty with the Seminoles in 1856, and Stidham's sister, a teacher in the Creek schools, both of whom spoke English well, Pike collected that summer a lengthy vocabulary of the Muscogee or Creek language. From the Stidhams, who were half Muscogee and half Hichitis, Pike also gathered a vocabulary of the Hichita tongue; and from other Indians he collected lists of words of the dialects of the Uchee, Natchez, Co-os-au-da or Co-as-sat-te, Alabama, and Shawnee tribes, all belonging to the Muscogee Confederation. For the sake of comparison Pike arranged the different vocabularies in parallel columns. In the left hand column he gave the English words and in the other columns, one for each of the Creek tongues, he gave the Indian equivalents, spelling all the words phonetically. This, he said, enabled him "to pronounce any word correctly, upon seeing it, and without having any recollection of it." Besides this table, which fills fifty-six pages and contains fifteen to seventeen hundred words, Pike made up a twenty-one page table of verb forms in the Muscogee language, in which he ran seven verbs through various tenses and moods in that language. A third table of twenty-seven pages contains comparative verb forms of the Muscoki (Muscogee), Yotchi, Hichitathli, and Natchez languages.[33] In 1861 while on his Indian mission for the government of the Confederate States Pike added "partial vocabularies" of the Comanche, Caddo, Wichita, Kichai, Delaware, Toncawa, and Osage languages to his work.[34] These later supplements were, however, on a very minor scale, occupying only twenty-five of a total of a hundred twenty-nine pages.

Pike compiled the Indian vocabularies because of his own curiosity and interest in linguistics; and it is doubtful if they were ever of great benefit to him or if he ever mastered any of the languages included in the work. He always used interpreters while in the Confederate Indian service in 1861 and 1862; nor did he ever pretend that he spoke or understood any of the Indian tongues, though others have claimed that distinction for him.[35] The work has, nevertheless, been of some value to American ethnologists who have investigated the Creek Indians.[36] Sometime in 1874 or 1875 Pike, then residing in Washington, submitted the manuscript at the director's request to the Smithsonian Institution, where Maj. John Wesley Powell, chief of the Bureau of Ethnology, got hold of it and promised Pike that he would publish it. Powell was very careless with the work, did not fulfill the promise of publication, and eventually loaned the sheets to Prof. John Hammond Trumbull of Hartford, Connecticut, who copied and used the vocabularies without Pike's permission. Learning of Powell's irresponsible conduct and breach of promise, Pike reclaimed the manuscript from Trumbull in 1880. A few years before his death, he presented it to the Supreme Council under the express stipulation that neither the U.S. government, the Smithsonian Institution, nor the American Bureau of Ethnology should ever be allowed to have or copy any part of it. It still remains unpublished.[37]

In August the treaty money of $800,000 was paid the Creeks.[38] Pike and Cochrane, who had joined Pike at the Creek agency in the course of the summer, were on hand to receive their fee.[39] The Creek chiefs and delegates apparently never hesitated about paying,[40] although there seems to have been a compromise on the amount of the fee. Pike testified before the Senate Committee on Indian Affairs in 1887 that he was due $160,000 in 1857 but that he accepted $120,000 since he had not obtained in the treaty of 1856 as much as he and the Creeks had originally expected.[41] He received an additional $10,000 on money appropriated in 1858, and another large sum, possibly $50,000, on $200,000 appropriated in 1859.[42] In the absence of an accounting of the fee, it is impossible to determine either how much Pike realized out of it. After payment of all costs probably including clerical help, printing, entertainment, and perhaps the personal expenses of the attorneys, Pike divided the residue according to oral agreements with Raiford and with Cochrane. One-third of the net amount went to pay Raiford's share, which was divided equally between Raiford, Hanrick, and Cochrane and Bryan. Pike then paid from his two-thirds enough to bring Cochrane and Bryan's total interest to a sum equivalent to one-fourth of the net fee. Whatever Pike's portion finally came to, it was beyond doubt the most lucrative case in which he ever participated.[43]

Pike returned from the Creek Nation to Little Rock in the latter part of September[44] and then went on, after a short visit with his family, to New Orleans for the fall session of the courts. In late January, 1858, he traveled to Washington to aid Cochrane and John B. Luce of Arkansas with the Choctaw claim. Luce had entered the case in December 1855; and to conceal the fact that Pike and Cochrane were connected with the case, thereby hoping to prevent any prejudice that might develop over the fact that the two had recently collected large fees from the Choctaws and Creeks, Cochrane gave him formal management of the claim in 1857.[45] Against the backdrop of "the eternal Kansas excitement" that absorbed most of the energy of Congress,[46] the Choctaw attorneys made a vain attempt to force their claim to a final settlement in the Senate. But neither Luce nor Pike, both of whom had great influence with Sebastian,[47] could convince their friend or his colleagues on the Committee of Indian Affairs that they should recommend to the Senate the award of the net proceeds. The most serious obstacle in the minds of the committee members to a decision on the issue was the fact that the attorneys were unable to present any more than a vague, undocumented estimate of the personal claims of the Indians under the treaty of Dancing Rabbit Creek. Without such facts Sebastian's committee quite justly refused to report in favor of either of the alternatives placed before them by the treaty of 1855. The matter would lie over till the next session.[48]

At the end of the session in the summer of 1858 Pike closed his law office in New Orleans and removed his effects to a new office in Little Rock.[49] We have no record of his homecoming other than a brief note in a local paper,[50] but the initial meeting of the family must have been a sad occasion. Albert Holden, a promising lad of thirteen who, it has been said, inherited the "versatile mind" of his father, was no longer present to greet Pike. He had drowned in the Arkansas River on May 16 and had been buried at Mount Holly Cemetery while Pike was absent in Washington.[51]

Pike's stay at home was short. In September he made a hunting excursion to the Indian country to collect $10,000 in fees due him on money appropriated for the Creeks at the past session of Congress.[52] Having received such a large sum the previous year and knowing that Congress had again stipulated that the money should be paid per capita and that none of it should be used for fees of counsel, Pike apparently expected trouble from the Creeks. On the evening before Superintendent Rector started the Creek payment Pike arrived at North Fork Village, situated at the forks of the Canadian above Fort Smith. Next morning he went

> to the pay-ground, and was told it was arranged that the chiefs had appointed a clerk, who would stand at the pay-table, on the outside, and when the money of each individual or head of family was pushed over to him would take out so much per centum towards payment of my fee.
>
> When the payment was about to commence, I stood on the inside of the pay-table. I had looked at the roll and seen that Opothli yahola's Town would be called first, and his name stood first on the roll. . . . He was a tall, large man, with large head and features, somewhat more heavily moulded than those of Daniel Webster, and coarser, but resembling them, and indicative of power of will, indomitable firmness, quick decision, self possession and strong intelligence,—the face, in every way, of a man whom one would not seek to have for an enemy. . . .
>
> I knew him well in 1858 . . . and when the payment was about to commence he sat in front of and near me, silent, and with the same expression of profound melancholy that was so habitual to Daniel Webster. I could not catch his eye. He would not look at me, and I concluded that he did not intend to permit the clerk to take the per centum out of his money. Of course I knew if he set the example it would be followed, perhaps by all.
>
> His Town was called. The Town-Chiefs, and he with them, came out and sat on a bench close to the table, to identify the persons called to be paid. His name was called, and he rose, and stood in front of the table, facing it and me, his arms folded on his chest; and still he would not look at me. I could read nothing in his

> face. It was as inscrutable in its massiveness and melancholy gloom, as the face of the Egyptian Sphynx.
>
> The amount to be paid him was named, counted in gold and silver, and pushed towards him. He did not stir to touch it. The clerk was afraid to move his hands towards it. Then the old man shot a quick, keen look at me, reached his left hand and slowly, to take the money I thought, and pushed it towards the clerk, then folded his arms again, looked full at me, and a smile lighted up his face, full of glee at having deluded and played upon me. I never saw a human face so changed in my life. It lighted up all over.[53]

Following this encounter, Pike, satisfied that there would be no more trouble, left the pay-ground. Next day his friend Stidham and one of the McIntoshes brought him ten thousand dollars in gold.[54]

With the Creek fee secured Pike remained in the Indian country until December to enjoy the fall hunting. During his stay, word got out in Arkansas and elsewhere that he had been accidentally killed. The report, apparently not the first that year,[55] was corrected on his safe return to Arkansas,[56] but news of the happy fact traveled slowly. When he reached Washington in late December, 1858,[57] his friends in the "Roast Oyster Club,"[58] a Thursday-night convivial group, a successor to the Wigwam Club he had helped organize the previous session, had not heard it and consequently could hardly believe their eyes. John F. Coyle, Irishman, charter member of the new club and editor of the *National Intelligencer*, meeting Pike unexpectedly in the street, asked, "What right have you to be walking about, looking for all the world like a live man, when you're d— d— dead?" "Because," answered Pike, "I've not been waked ... and until that how could I keep quiet in the grave?" "You shall be waked, then," Coyle declared.[59]

But before Coyle's "wake" came off, an unidentified member of the club, at a meeting on Tuesday night, January 18, 1859, honored "the departed" with a banquet. Robert Shelton Mackenzie, noted British writer and historian of *Blackwood's Magazine* who had been residing in the United States since 1852,[60] was a guest at this repast. He wrote an account of it which was published in the *Philadelphia Press*, January 22, 1859.[61] After the host and guests were seated at the table

> the parlor-door opened, and a stalwart figure, large and lofty, with keen eyes, a nose reminding one of an eagle's beak, a noble head firmly placed between a pair of massive shoulders, and flowing locks nearly half-way down his back, entered the apartment, looking as like a living man as anything I had ever seen. But the company, who did not appear frightened in the least, at this apparition, one and all assured me that he was dead, that he had been killed in the newspapers, that he was wandering about, wishing some one to say, "Rest perturbed spirit." ...
>
> He behaved remarkably well—for an apparition. A good spirit in his day, he very naturally took a nip of "old rye." ... When Mr. Coyle sang a touching melody, narrating the adventures, at home and at New Orleans, of a fine Arkansas gentleman, the Defunct politely informed him that he had better make himself more fully master of the words which *he* (the Defunct) had an interest in.
>
> We took wine with him, conversed with him, enjoyed his stories, anecdotes, and songs; but strictly under protest. A Departed man he was, and could not be

recognized in any other capacity. He con-versed freely upon the published incidents of his death, and was indignant only upon one point—the newspapers, he said, had libelled him by declaring that he had died rich! For, he was, in life, a sort of humanized Cerberus—three single gentlemen rolled into one, as Mrs. Malaprop has it—Poet, Soldier, and Lawyer. In the first capacities no man gets wealthy (save in fame), and our friend was a trifle too honest, too free-handed, to become rich in the third.[62]

Three days after the banquet, Friday evening, January 21, some 150 people gathered at Coyle's house on Missouri Avenue, two doors from one rented by Pike,[63] to "keen" Pike "in the Hibernian manner."[64] According to the "Programme of Obsequies" Pike's "corpse" was in charge of "Superintendent of Ceremonies" George S. Gideon, Washington printer, and twelve "Mourners in Chief," all members of the Roast Oyster Club. One of these, Prof. Alexander Dimitry, a Louisianian then serving as an interpreter in the state department,[65] opened the ceremony by reading a highly eulogistic obituary written by him when he believed Pike dead but which he had not published after Pike had arrived on the capital scene alive.[66] William M. Burwell followed Dimitry's encomium with an announcement "that the distinguished defunct had burst the cerements with which the newspapers had enshrouded him," and Coyle then recited Burwell's farcical poem, a jovial parody entitled "The Arkansas Gentleman Alive Again!" relating how Pike had accomplished this rare feat. The first four verses described Pike's visit to the Indian country to hunt with his Indian friends, who had "welcomed him with all the sports well known on the frontier."

> Now whilst he was enjoying all that such adventure brings,
> The chase, the pipe, and bottle, and such like forbidden things,
> Some spalpeen of an editor, the Lord had made in vain,
> Inserted in his horrible accident column, amongst
> > murders, robberies, thefts, camphene accidents,
> > collisions, explosions, defalcations, seductions,
> > abductions, and destructions, under a splendid
> > black-bordered notice, the lamentable news that
> > he was dead *again*.
> This fine Arkansas gentleman
> Who died before his time.

> The other papers copied it, and then it was believed
> That death at last had taken him, so recently reprieved;
> They mourned him as a warrior, a poet, and a trump,
> And with elegies, eulogies, biographies, reviews,
> > articles, criticisms on his productions, doubts
> > whether he had ever fought, wrote, hunted buffalo,
> > or indeed lived at all—And one incredulous pagan
> > "Johnson Hooper," of the Montgomery Mail, always—
> > denied his dying plump.
> This fine Arkansas, &c.

The Masons and the Odd-fellows prepared to celebrate
His obsequies with every form of grief appropriate,
So sad the tavern-keepers and the faro-bankers feel,
They craped the bell a half an hour and intermit a deal
    For this fine Arkansas gentleman, &c.

But far above the common grief—though he was good as gold—
His creditors, like Jacob's wife, refused to be consoled;
They granted him a poet and a warrior, if you will,
But they said they had extensive experience in generals,
    commodores, orators, statesmen, Congressmen,
    actors, editors, letter-writers, route-agents,
    conductors, and other public characters who—
    rarely paid a bill
    This fine Arkansas gentleman, &c.

Behold in this excitement our distinguished friend arrive,
We "knew from a remark he made" that he was still alive;
Then every journal joyously the contradiction quotes,
The tailors take his measure, and the banks renew his notes.
    This fine Arkansas gentleman, &c.

But Johnny Coyle—an Irishman, the news refused to take,
He swore "no gentleman alive should chate him of his wake;"
So he called his friends together, as here you plainly see,
And he has set out the spirits, and the tabacey to lay the body *under*—
    the table dacently.
    This fine Arkansas gentleman, &c.

So now when he must surely go the way that all must pass,
Don't hold a feather to his lips, nor yet a looking glass;
But whisper that a friend's in need of either purse or hand,
And he'll make a move to aid him—if they hav'nt got him damned.
    This fine Arkansas gentleman, &c.

Or try another certain test, if any doubts remain:
Just put within his pallid lips a drop of whiskey-plain;
And if he make no mortal sign, just put him in the ground,
And let his Maker raise him at his final trumpet's sound.
    This fine Arkansas gentleman, &c.[67]

    Pike was deeply moved by all this and when called upon to give assurance that his "mortal body was not yet tenantless" declared that however out of place it was at such a merry celebration he could not find it in his heart "to respond with jest and levity" to the "touching testimonials of friendship and esteem." It was, therefore, with sincere humility that he thanked his friends for the "wealth of kind recollection and charitable opinion that has been so unexpectedly and so gratefully . . . bestowed upon my memory."

But this serious vein did not prevail long, for at the conclusion of his remarks Pike called upon Jack Savage, Washington journalist and author,[68] one of the Mourners in Chief, to chant a lengthy song, "Spree at Johnny Coyle's," sung to the air of "Benny Havens, O!" which Pike had dashed off as a contribution to "the fun and frolic" of his "wake."

> A gentleman from ARKANSAW, not long ago 'tis said,
> Waked up one pleasant morning, and discovered he was dead;
> He was on his way to Washington, not seeking for the spoils,
> But rejoicing in the promise of a spree at JOHNNY COYLE'S;
>   One spree at Johnny Coyle's, one spree at Johnny Coyle's;
>   And who would not be glad to join a spree at Johnny Coyle's?
>
> He waked and found himself aboard a rickety old boat;
> Says the ferryman, when questioned, "on the Styx you are afloat;"
> "What! dead?" said he;—"indeed you are," the grim old churl replied;
> "Why, then, I'll miss the spree at Coyle's, "the gentleman replied.
>   One spree at Johnny Coyle's, &c.

After he had gotten across the Styx and by Cerberus, the three-headed canine gatekeeper of Hades, Pike went before Pluto and Proserpine, king and queen of the infernal regions, of whom Pike asked permission to return to earth for "one frolic more at Johnny Coyle's." Pluto attempted to convince Pike that he should remain in Hades to consort with the numerous worthies of all ages, such as Homer, Tully, Horace, and Montaigne, who were there. But Pike declared that he could "match the lot" if Pluto would let him go to Johnny Coyle's and "fetch" the crowd who would gather at the "spree." Whom would he bring, asked Pluto, and Pike replied in a series of flattering verses in which each of his dearest friends, most of them perhaps members of the Roast Oyster Club was mentioned.[69]

> "Enough!" old Pluto cried; "the law must be enforced, 'tis plain;
> If with those fellows once you get you'll ne'er return again;
> One night would not content you, and your face would ne'er be seen,
> After that spree at Johnny Coyle's, by me or by my queen,
>   One spree at Johnny Coyle's, &c.
>
> And if all these fellows came at once, what would become of us?
> They'd drown old Charon in the Styx, and murder Cerberus;
> Make love to all the women here, and even to my wife;
> Drink all my liquor up, and be the torment of my life.
>   One spree at Johnny Coyle's, &c.

Pike was almost ready to make a rash reply to Pluto's refusal when the hitherto silent Proserpine, "very much elated . . . at the promise of unbounded fun with this good company," interceded for Pike.

> And so at last the Queen prevailed, as women always do,
> And thus it comes that once again this gentleman's with you;
> He's under promise to return, but that he means to break,

And many another spree to have, besides this present wake.
One spree at Johnny Coyle's one spree at Johnny Coyle's;
And who would not be glad to join a spree at Johnny Coyle's?[70]

The gaiety of the party increased in tempo as the evening advanced. When the crowd broke up next morning, they tottered from Coyle's house singing Burwell's and Pike's songs. At the time the unusual celebration received much editorial attention. Willis Gaylord Clark, editor of the *Knickerbocker* magazine, published a lengthy account of the affair. "Our old correspondent," he said, "was honored at his 'wake' by the presence of some of the first men in the nation: and he must have been as much flattered as he was when Christopher North pronounced so candid an euloguim upon his admirable contributions to 'BLACKWOOD'S Magazine.'"[71] And the memory of the evening lived on in the minds of Coyle's guests. Twenty-five years afterward Ben Berley Poore, a close friend of Pike, remembered it as one of the outstanding social events at the capital in the decade before the Civil War.[72]

In the meantime Pike was occupied with the Choctaw claim. After the failure before Sebastian's committee in 1858 he and Cochrane had almost despaired of the case. Cochrane, according to a subsequent statement by Pike, was extremely discouraged because he and Luce could not obtain sufficient data to establish the losses and treatment of individual claimants under the treaty of 1830; Luce was so disheartened that he quit the case early in 1859 and returned to Arkansas.[73] Before he left Washington he deposited with Pike the material he had collected in the Indian office, apparently unaware that it held the key to the solution of their problem.[74] With indefatigable energy Pike went through confused piles of papers, organized them, and made notes to see if he could document the Choctaw losses. He soon saw that he could, and on completing the research prepared a forty-two page "Memorandum of Particulars" itemizing claims, national and individual, arising from Choctaw removal.[75] He filed the brief with the committee and soon afterward went before them to argue the case. Convinced by Pike's written and oral argument of the immense personal claims of the Indians, the committee saw that the cheapest course for the government was to pay the net proceeds. Pike wrote Sebastian's report accompanying the committee resolution that called for the award of the net proceeds and for an account to be made by the interior department of the amount due the Indians under that principle. On March 9, 1859, a famous date in the history of the Choctaw claim, the Senate approved the resolution, stipulating that in addition to the net proceeds on all lands sold up to January 1, 1859, the Choctaws should be allowed twelve and one-half cents per acre on all their former lands remaining unsold on that date.[76]

The account was to be taken during the recess of Congress. Pike returned in April to Arkansas[77] and went on in May to the Creek Nation to collect a fee from the Creeks on $200,000 appropriated for them under the treaty of 1856.[78] From Little Rock his sons Walter Lacy and Luther Hamilton accompanied him for the adventure of hunting with their father in the Indian country. At Fort Smith they joined a party under Elias Rector, who was about to leave for the leased district, west of the Chickasaw land, to establish an agency for some Texas Reserve Indians.[79] The trip offered every promise of being very pleasurable for all, but tragedy and violence attended it almost from the beginning. In the Cherokee Nation two slaves were killed and six or eight others wounded by an explosion of gunpowder belonging to the men in the expedition.[80] At the Wichita Agency, in the leased district, on July 4, Asa P. Hurst stabbed and killed Wharton Rector and seriously wounded his brother Frank, nephews of Elias Rector. Caught soon after by pursuing Indians, Hurst was taken by a Deputy U.S. Marshall to Van Buren, Arkansas, and placed in jail to await trial. Elias Rector remained in the leased district to locate the new agency and the Pikes stayed also. They returned in early August by way of the Creek Nation, where Rector paid the remaining treaty money and Pike collected his fee.[81] On August 20 the Pikes arrived in Little Rock.[82]

Pike returned to Washington that winter to help secure the appropriation for the net proceeds award.[83] Because of unforeseen delays in the interior department the account was not submitted to Congress until May 8, 1860.[84] It showed that $2,981,247.30 was due the Choctaw Nation; but Alfred Burton Greenwood, of Bentonville, Arkansas, commissioner of Indian affairs, suggested in a letter accompanying the account that the total would be reduced to $1,851,247.30 if Congress deducted the $530,000 paid the Choctaws by the Chickasaws in 1837 and $600,000 paid the Choctaws by the United States under the treaty of 1855. He furnished, however, no evidence that either amount could be deducted as a payment under the treaty of 1830. He also pointed out that Congress might desire to subtract the price of 2,292,776 acres of former Choctaw lands given by the United States to Mississippi under the swampland act and under acts for railroad and school purposes.[85]

Pike was highly indignant at Greenwood's suggestions, believing that since he had found no basis for the deductions he had merely injected them into his report to cloud and prejudice the claim in the eyes of Congress. Pike declared in 1872 that he went before Sebastian's committee to oppose Greenwood's report, that he convinced the members of the unjustness of the proposed deductions and wrote the report for Sebastian which rejected each of them, but that after his report was completed the committee inserted in it without his knowledge a deduction of $648,686.15. "We could not get the report changed," he said, "but we could and did prevent action being had on it, and it never was adopted."[86] This statement, made twelve years after the events and in defense of his rights as attorney for the Choctaws against men who were attempting to exclude him from the case, is not only very general but very misleading. Indeed, it leaves so much unsaid that were it not for Pike's impeccable record of honesty one might suspect him of concealing details in order to strengthen his argument. He really had no reason, however, either to conceal facts or to lie, for the truth was as good evidence as he needed to prove his valuable services in obtaining the net proceeds award; his omissions were probably a result of bad memory. The report which Pike alleged he wrote for Sebastian was not submitted to the Senate until June 19, 1860, six days after Sebastian had moved the payment of $2,332,560.85 as the final award.[87] No committee report accompanied the motion, which was in the form of an amendment to the House general appropriation bill, but Sebastian in a brief speech explained that the amount requested was the sum reported in the interior department account minus $648,686.15 deducted by the committee.[88]

Sebastian's motion touched off a furious two-day debate in the Senate. Frugal-minded Robert Toombs of Georgia, showing abominable ignorance of the facts of the case while demonstrating the forensic ability that made him one of the most dreaded opponents of claim agents,[89] attacked not only the appropriation and the award of 1859 but the treaty of 1855 as well. He had examined the account of the interior department at the request of "the very able gentleman who represents the Indians," meaning Pike,[90] and declared that he disagreed with both him and the committee about the merits of the claim. Toombs's argument was that the lands granted the Choctaws in 1820, a part of which they had in turn ceded away in 1837 and in 1855 for $1,130,000, could and should be charged as an expense of removal under the treaty of 1830 and deducted, therefore, from the net proceeds. Moreover, he reasoned that since the United States was entitled to that credit that it was also due a credit for the land still in possession of the Choctaw Nation. Under this principle he thought the Choctaws would "find themselves on the wrong side of the balance sheet."[91]

Though Toombs's argument was quite untenable, Sebastian and his committee were unprepared to refute it convincingly. They fell back on the feeble principle accepted in committee that the $1,130,000 in question was not deductible since it had not been so specified either in the treaty of 1855 or in the Senate resolution of March 9, 1859. Sebastian, Daniel Clark of New Hampshire, and James R. Doolittle of Wisconsin, all of the Indian committee, pointed this out and asserted that the Senate could not go behind the treaty or the award and that both were final and were of higher sanctity than a judgment at law. They were ably supported by others.[92] Jefferson Davis of Mississippi suggested a compromise payment of $1,851,247.30—that is, the sum recommended by the interior department minus the disputed $1,130,000—but the proposal was voted down.[93] Toombs, stubbornly refusing to accept either a compromise or the plea of finality, managed with the help of R. M. T. Hunter of Virginia and one or two others to arouse enough suspicion to defeat the amendment by a vote of 24 to 22 on June 14.[94]

On the following June 19 Sebastian introduced a separate bill calling for the payment of the same $2,332,560.85. A long report—the one that Pike later asserted he had written for Sebastian—accompanied the bill. The report was ordered printed, and the bill was passed to a second reading but was not taken up again in the few days that remained of the session.[95]

Pike told the Choctaws in 1872 that he and the attorneys prevented further action on the bill after he had "demonstrated to the chairman that, at all events, the deductions were too large by several hundred thousand dollars."[96] But if Pike did prevent action on the measure because he believed it unfair to the Indians, he had a change of mind by the next session. A great drought devastated the Indian country during the summer of 1860, and crops failed completely, leaving the Indians almost destitute. Most of them were forced to appeal to the United States for aid.[97] The Choctaws petitioned Congress for relief under the award of 1859, and their attorneys, who may have devised the petition plan, were on hand to urge the appropriation.[98] The attorneys were now willing, whatever their attitude the previous session, to accept the amount recommended by the committee in June 1860. Furthermore, they had Sebastian propose on February 2, 1861, that the $1,202,560.85, "being the undisputed balance" due the Choctaws, be appropriated at once and that the $1,130,000, so vehemently questioned the previous summer, be allowed to lie over for further consideration.[99] The framers of the proposal, which was submitted as an amendment to the House Indian appropriation bill, obviously sought to obscure the fact that Toombs and his friends had questioned the whole award. At the same time they may have believed that in the absence of Toombs—then at Montgomery, Alabama, helping form a provisional government for the Confederate States—there would be no strong opposition to the "undisputed balance." William P. Fessenden of Maine remembered, however, what Toombs had said, and reminded the Senate of it.[100] The attorneys then threw in their reserve: Robert W. Johnson, armed with indisputable facts furnished by them, made on February 9 a long speech that routed the opposition. He demonstrated that the treaties of 1820 and 1830 were entirely distinct, that the Choctaws were given a clear title to their land west of Arkansas in 1820, and that money received in 1837 and 1855 for lands ceded to them in 1820 could not be deducted from claims arising under the treaty of 1830. Johnson's argument swayed enough votes to carry the amendment, which passed the same day without a division.[101]

In the House John Sherman of Ohio, chairman of the Committee on Ways and Means, to which the Indian appropriation bill was referred, and John S. Phelps of Missouri,[102] of the same committee, secured the defeat of the Choctaw amendment on February 28, 1861, by a thumping 104 to 56 vote. They objected to the tying of the net proceeds appropriation to the Indian bill and believed the whole claim needed further investigation. Phelps thought that the Senate award was unjust, that there was no basis for the claim under the treaty of 1830, and that the treaty of 1855 was not binding upon the House. When Horace Maynard of Tennessee, defender of the amendment and a proponent of the theory that ratified treaties bound the House, asked Phelps if he thought the House could examine an award under the treaty of 1855, Phelps cried, yes— that the principle was as old as the debate on the Jay treaty in 1794. Maynard and John Stevenson of Kentucky countered Phelps's argument with assertions that the award was final and no longer a claim but a just debt which the United States was obligated to pay. Sherman regained the floor in the closing minutes of the debate to support Phelps. He argued that neither the treaty of 1855 nor the award was final until the House had been consulted and thought that no appropriation should be made for the Choctaws until it was certain "whether they belong to this Government or to the southern confederacy." But after the whole bill was considered, a conference committee of three from each house of Congress was appointed at Sherman's motion to study and report on the rejected amendments.

The report of the conference committee on March 2 contained a five-to-one recommendation in favor of restoring the Choctaw appropriation. Because of this Sherman and Phelps defeated the entire report and got a new committee appointed to restudy the matter. This second committee reported, March 2, unanimously in favor of a compromise payment of $500,000, one-half to be paid in cash and one-half in U.S. bonds with a proviso attached that the amount would be charged against any future adjustment of the claim. Sherman vehemently opposed the compromise, protesting that it recognized "the validity" of the net proceeds claim and compelled the House to pay the money "as an entering wedge for the whole claim." William A. Howard of Michigan, member of the second conference committee, explained that the report recognized only the treaty of 1855, not the award of 1859. To reject the report would defeat the whole Indian bill, and there was not enough time left in the session to initiate and pass a new bill. Howard's admonition was successful. The House approved by a narrow 70 to 61 vote the compromise appropriation and the same day, March 2, forty-eight hours before Lincoln's inauguration, the Senate concurred in the action and President Buchanan approved the Indian bill.[103]

Pike was in Washington from sometime in January until March 26, 1861, lobbying for the appropriation for the net proceeds claim.[104] He told the Choctaws in 1872 that Johnson argued and won the case for him in the Senate, and that Vice President John C. Breckinridge of Kentucky allowed him to name the Senate members of the conference committees.[105] He had Daniel Clark of New Hampshire placed on the first and James R. Doolittle on the other "without consulting either of them, but knowing that I had long before convinced them of the justice of your claim. The Senate members on the first committee insisted on the original appropriation; and those on the last would only consent to a compromise, and the $500,000 was appropriated."[106] He concluded, therefore, that he "alone" procured the appropriation for the Indians.[107]

To buy corn for the drought-stricken Choctaws the Treasurer of the United States paid Agent Cooper $50,000 on March 22 and $84,515.55 on April 5. The remaining $115,484.45 in cash, out of which the attorneys were to receive their fee, was turned over to the Choctaw delegates, Peter Perkins Pitchlynn and Israel and Peter Folsum, April 12, 1861, the fateful day on which Confederate forces opened fire on Fort Sumter in the harbor of Charleston, South Carolina.[108] Because of the war and the uncertainty about which side the Choctaw Nation would choose, the bonds, which were ready to be issued in early April, were not delivered.[109] Cooper became involved in a great scandal over the "corn money," and the attorneys had a difficult time getting their fee paid as a result of the general confusion of the war. But these stories and the subsequent history of the Choctaw case, which occupied so completely Pike's later years, must be postponed until after the war.

XXIV

Know-Nothing Leader

FOLLOWING THE BITTER CONGRESSIONAL ELECTION of 1851 Pike withdrew from active participation in the Whig Party of Arkansas. His statement in the party organ during that campaign that Johnson was not a disunionist, a statement that may or may not have aided in Johnson's triumph over Preston, was in any event an unforgivable sin in the eye of partisan Whigs. For it Pike was roundly denounced and "read out" of the party.[1] He continued, however, to think of himself as a national Whig until 1852. In the presidential election of that year Pike was extremely disappointed that the Whigs passed over both Fillmore and Webster to nominate Winfield Scott, who was suspected of being unfriendly to the Missouri Compromise. Pike preferred Fillmore, whose stand on the compromise and whose enforcement of the fugitive slave law he admired, and he would have been pleased with Webster. As for Scott, Pike did not believe for a second the charges that the general was lacking in patriotism or was really a tool of Free Soilers, but because he felt with many other southern Whigs that Scott's nomination was in a sense the result of "the schemes of Seward, Greeley, *et id omne genus*," Free Soilers in the northern wing of the party.[2]

His disappointment was great enough that he refused to support Scott, though his feeling was not sufficiently intense to seduce him into the hideousness of supporting the Democratic nominee, Franklin Pierce of New Hampshire. He looked upon Pierce's victory in 1852 "as a good thing for the country *per se*."[3] The Whigs, he said shortly before the new president's inauguration, were almost "universally . . . inclined to wish well to General Pierce's administration" and would offer it "no factional opposition." There was, however, "already a great deal of restrained but muttered indignation" at the prospect that both John A. Dix, ardent New York Free Soil Democrat, and Jefferson Davis, "representing the ultra Secessionists of the South," would "hold honorable posts in the Cabinet."[4] "I rather think" concluded Pike, "that a small earthquake may be looked for in a month or so. Should Gen. Pierce possess the requisite firmness and determination, he will cow the rampant elements into submission, but should he not, his administration will prove a disastrous failure; and the Democratic party will go to pieces like a ship in a storm."[5]

The "earthquake" which Pike foresaw came rapidly, for Pierce possessed neither the intelligence, the determination, nor the nerve to have a strong administration. During the summer of 1853, while Pike was in Washington looking after the Creek case, two groups of squatters on the public domain in the vast Nebraska country north of Indian Territory and west of Missouri and Iowa elected delegates to Congress to petition for territorial organization. Their action represented the desire of the people for territorial government, official sanction of settlement, and organized territory through which to build a Pacific railroad.

Stephen A. Douglas, Illinois Democrat and chairman of the Senate Committee on Territories, sympathized with their wishes and had a special interest in the Pacific railway. But there were formidable complications to be dealt with. Nebraska was north of the Missouri Compromise line; yet slaveholders in Missouri, which lay east of the southern section of the Nebraska country, known as Kansas, would not agree to organization unless it were provided that slaves could be taken there. Consequently, when Sen. Augustus C. Dodge, Iowan, introduced in December 1853 a bill for the organization of Nebraska, Douglas, who had lost a similar bill in the Senate the previous session, was prepared to appease all critics of the measure. Dodge's bill came out of Douglas's Territorial Committee with a section that proposed that the question of slavery in Nebraska be decided by the settlers thereof, a principle identical with that established by the Utah and New Mexico Acts in 1850. The veiled sop was not enough for certain plain-spoken southerners and Missourians, who now demanded the outright repeal of the Missouri Compromise restriction. Douglas, pressed from all sides, reluctantly gave way to the imposition of the slaveholders. He also agreed to almost equally strong demands from Iowa that the territory be divided in two in order that the state might compete with Missouri for the Pacific railroad and the development of the new land. Accordingly the final bill called for the formation of two territories, Kansas and Nebraska, and provided for the repeal of the limitation on slavery north of 36°30' established in 1820.

In this shape the bill was supported by Pierce and thus became an administration measure. He had been persuaded to this dangerous course by Jefferson Davis, his secretary of war, and Caleb Cushing, Massachusetts proslavery Democrat, his attorney general. Instead of controlling the "rampant elements" of his party Pierce had fallen under the influence of slavery expansionists. With presidential backing the bill was forced through Congress after months of tumultuous debate and was signed into law by Pierce on May 30. The results were disastrous. The debate over the legislation had revived all the fear, anger, and strife of the dreadful crisis of 1848–50 and more. It had forced upon Kansas an abnormal interest in an abstract question that ordinarily would not have bothered the territory. It had split the Democratic Party; it had given the Whig Party its final blow; and it had handed the opponents of slavery extension at once the incentive and the excuse to create the Republican Party as a purely sectional party, finding ready recruits among the dissenting elements of the old parties. The struggle had in short unleashed the dogs of war, and no man would be able to call off the pack.[6]

Southern Whigs after 1854 had three choices politically: to remain neutral, to join the Democrats, or to cast about for a new party. Because Democracy was still anathema to Pike he temporarily chose to remain neutral or, as he was fond of explaining, an "impartial observer" of the Pierce administration.[7] That the great Whig Party to which he had belonged since its inception in the mid-thirties and now lay dismembered and powerless, was in his eyes a national misfortune. He had seen in its conservative membership and national unity the strongest force in the country for averting the dangerous possibilities of disunion and sectionalism. Yet in all but name he had been estranged from Whiggery since 1850. He had seen then that he could not remain in the party whose northern wing advocated doctrines dangerous to slavery, and in the intervening years, though he had given token profession to Whig principles, he had longed desperately for the formation of a new party, one that would put national above sectional interests and would suppress the infernal questions of slavery expansion and abolition. Therefore, no matter how much Pike may have regretted the final collapse of the Whig Party he probably was neither greatly surprised nor unduly pained by it.[8]

It was while Pike was in Washington in the fateful spring of 1854 that he first became interested in the American Party, popularly labeled the "Know-Nothing Party" because of the supposed common response, "I know nothing," with which its members met inquiries about the principles and objects of the order. In his various trips to the East in the late forties and early fifties, Pike had observed the spectacular rise in the foreign-born population. He resented the manners, habits, tastes, and usages of the foreigners with whom he came in contact in Boston, New York, Philadelphia, and other Eastern cities, and he had a genuine fear that allowing so many aliens and naturalized citizens to vote and to hold office was a serious threat to American institutions. He found it particularly objectionable that the Democracy catered to the foreign element in order to gain political strength. And he saw and voiced the fear of southerners that the northwestern and western bid for immigrants was a menace to sound views on slavery in those regions. To make America safe for Americans, and to make the population of the Northwest and West safe on the slavery question, he would have immigration drastically restricted, the period for naturalization greatly extended, and the privileges of voting and office-holding permanently denied to naturalized citizens except in rare cases of special merit.[9] He readily agreed, therefore, with the antiforeign plank of the American Party, but with the other great tenet of the order, hostility to Roman Catholicism and resistance to Papal interference in temporal affairs in the United States, Pike never had more than a minor interest. Religious intolerance was certainly no part of his belief. He later admitted that when he joined the order at Washington during the spring of 1854 it

> had but two great tenets in its creed—that native born citizens only ought to share in the government of the country, and that the attempts of Pope and Priest to meddle with that government and exercise temporal power here ought to be resisted and defeated. The former, in my eyes, was the great cardinal principle—the latter a mere accessory. I took it to gain the other.[10]

At the time Pike entered the new party, these two principles and the oath of secrecy, which bound the initiate never to reveal the ritual and secrets of the order, were set down in the first degree. This degree controlled the member as a voter, but the second degree, conferred on Pike at the same time, was administered only to those worthy of holding office and directing party affairs. It bound the candidate to enforce party principles and required that an officeholder should remove all naturalized citizens, aliens, and Roman Catholics from positions within his power. In November 1854, the National Council of the party adopted a third, or "Union" degree, apparently conferred only on those who held the second degree. To take this degree the member swore to discourage and oppose anything which tended either to dissolve or to weaken the Union. Its adoption was a concession to slaveholding Whigs who had infiltrated the party and who with its author, Kenneth Rayner of North Carolina, wished not only to build the American Party upon the ruins of the former Whig Party but also to draw into its folds nativistic and Union Democrats. By avoiding old party issues and maintaining neutrality on the dangerous slavery question, Rayner and other prominent leaders felt that the appeal of American nativistic doctrines might bring the party to victory and unite the nation upon a "sterling union" platform.[11] Pike took this degree and came in time to look upon it as the most important principle of the party. "The country needed," he said at New Orleans in 1855, "a great national party—one loving our country better than any other, and believing it to be the best under the sun, and that party is the American Party." At Baltimore the same year he stated that he saw "no hope for the south or for the Union in any *other* party."[12]

At the head of the new party was the National Council, composed of seven delegates from each state council. It drew up the ritual and degrees, established the various signs, grips, and passwords employed by the brethren in their intercourse, issued charters to state, territorial, and district councils, served as the high court and arbiter of the entire party, and framed the platform of the party. The National Council is to be distinguished from the National Convention, the body that made presidential nominations, even though many or all of the members of the National Council could be, and usually were, delegates to the National Convention. Below the National Council were the state councils and one for the District of Columbia, which was given a rank equivalent to that of a state. Before a state council could be formed and chartered, there had to be at least five district or subordinate chapters within the state. The state council, consisting normally of two delegates from each subordinate council, chose its own officers and might levy taxes, grant dispensations to found new local councils, establish passwords, and make its own bylaws, but all these functions were subject to the approval of the National Council. Its principal business was the nomination of state candidates and the election of delegates to the National Council and to the National Convention.[13]

At the time Pike took the first two degrees of the order in the spring of 1854, apparently from the District of Columbia Council, he was given dispensations from the National Council for establishing local bodies and a state council in Arkansas. On returning to Arkansas early in the summer of 1854, he set to work organizing the local chapters in the state.[14] The work was carried on under such a veil of secrecy that would-be opposition editors did not get wind of the new movement until the spring of 1855. In the state election of August 1854, there may have been members of the American Party running on either the Democratic or Whig ticket, for undoubtedly several were elected to the legislature. When the legislature met in November, Pike used his influence with American Party friends in that body to help elect, over a hostile Democratic faction, Robert W. Johnson to the U.S. Senate for the remainder of Solon Borland's unexpired term, and for a full six-year term beginning the following March.[15] The editor of the *Gazette* stated on November 17, 1854, that Johnson's election was "a *Know-Nothing* victory, and as corroborating this report, we have been pointed to the fact, that he received the entire Whig vote." "We," he remarked "*Know Nothing* about it." Later in the year American Party papers outside the state hailed as a party victory the voting down in the legislature of "a resolution condemning the American Party."[16]

By April 1855, the order had secured a substantial membership in Arkansas, and a provisional state council had been formed with Pike serving as president, an office he accepted in order to complete the organization of the state party. On April 30, 1855, Pike summoned delegates from the subordinate councils to meet at Little Rock to organize a permanent state council. The session was apparently conducted in secrecy, for neither of the Little Rock papers noted it.[17]

Pike opened the meeting with a long address. The party was growing everywhere, he said, and had "ample assurance of carrying every slave State in the Union."

> And even here in Arkansas, where no one imagined the Order could gain a foothold, where our political differences have been so bitter, party allegiance so staunch and true, and party prejudice so strong—even here, in seven months, we have seen our Councils swell to more than sixty in number, and our members to between eight and ten thousand. In a year and a half from now, you will be able to speak to your Senators in Congress in a tone that they will be compelled to obey.... And I hope to see them instructed to carry out our principles or resign.[18]

He would have them instructed to work for laws which would deny the right of aliens and naturalized citizens to vote or to hold office and cited figures purporting to illustrate the power of foreign-born voters in the country. In fourteen major cities of the United States, including New York, Philadelphia, Boston, Baltimore, Cincinnati, Louisville, St. Louis, and New Orleans, the nonnative population was 664,000 to 1,000,000 for natives; therefore, in a closely contested two-party campaign "foreigners" held the balance of power. It was ample time, he warned, that their political power be curbed, for they not only might decide presidential elections but might ultimately modify all American laws. Speaking briefly of the anti-Catholic features of Americanism, he denied that the party had made "a religious test as a qualification for office." "We simply decline," he explained, "to vote for them, thinking their peculiar tenets to be hostile to freedom." He advocated the establishment of a party press in the state and advised the Arkansas council to recommend to all subordinate councils that their members cancel all subscriptions to opposition papers and support only American organs. This, he thought, would teach "a salutary lesson" to the editor of the *True Democrat*, "that unscrupulous sheet" which "teems weekly with wholesale slander of the Order" and which "never corrects a falsehood, nor atones for an injury."[19]

Pike concluded his address with an outline of the work which the delegates must accomplish. They must draft a permanent constitution and establish a permanent state council, elect state officers for the ensuing year, and choose delegates to the National Council.

> The office of President, which was conferred upon me against my will, I accepted solely because I knew of no one here who would do the labor necessary to organize the Order in this State. When your Constitution is adopted, that will have been done.... The order has assumed shape and consistency; and I shall

gladly retire from an office, honorable enough to satisfy the ambition of anyone; but which, considering the antecedents of parties here, ought to be filled by one whose former political creed and associations have been different from mine.[20]

He urged them to select seven delegates to the National Council who would be certain to attend its sessions, declaring that upon its deliberations "the destiny of this country depends." He sincerely hoped that the slavery issue could be kept out of the discussions of the National Council and that a platform could be adopted based solely upon the three great principles of the American Party, namely, to secure control and management of the government by native citizens, to resist papal interference in temporal affairs of the country, and to preserve the Union. The National Council must, however, "give us of the South ample assurance that, so far as the power of the Order goes, the slavery agitation shall cease; and on that question, we must act, though firmly, yet with great prudence and judgment." Finally, he hoped the National Council would make a definite attempt "to settle whom we are to support for President and Vice President." He himself believed Daniel S. Dickinson, ex-Democrat of New York, would be the wisest choice, for his nomination would avert all allegations that the new party was only "Whiggery in disguise," an accusation, Pike said, which Americans must make every effort to avoid and one which he himself had in mind when he stepped down from the presidency of the state council to permit the election of a former Democrat, Andre J. Hutt.[21]

Pike was selected by the state council to head the Arkansas delegation to the National Council scheduled to meet in Philadelphia on June 5, 1855. He went to Washington in May, thence to Philadelphia in the early days of June. On the morning of June 5, when the council organized, the Arkansas delegation was refused admission because of imperfect credentials. Pike was greatly vexed at this deference to technicalities and, according to one reporter, "exhausted the language of 'our army in Flanders,' in invective" on the exclusion of his delegation. A committee was appointed to study the problem, and the next day Pike's Arkansans were seated.[22]

Another bitter controversy developed over the seating of the partially Catholic delegation from Louisiana, whose state council had adopted a ritual and constitution admitting French Catholics to the order. It had then sent Charles Gayarré, a Catholic, as one of six delegates in an effort to test the strength of the Catholic proscription.[23] Pike favored admission of the entire delegation and told the National Council that if he had "to choose between the order at large and the order in Louisiana" he would "adhere to the latter." He deprecated the religious quarrel and intolerant views brought out in the debate, which to him "seemed better fitted to be addressed to a conventicle of Scotch Presbyterians, looking upon the Pope as Antichrist, than to an assembly of American gentlemen met to discuss matters of political consideration only."[24] Since much of the northern opposition to seating American Creoles seemed to stem from a desire to weaken the slaveholding vote in the National Council, Pike concluded his appeal on behalf of the Louisiana Creole delegates with a proposal "that no Council shall discuss subjects that are distasteful to other Councils." The correspondent of the *New York Tribune*, June 8, 1855, asked:

> Is Albert a Quaker? What a set of dumb shows the meetings would be under this rule! The question of Catholicism would be tabooed as well as Slavery, for both are equally obnoxious to the sensitive "lords of the lash" and worshipers of the most holy Catholic Church of Louisiana.

Pike's efforts failed. Kenneth Rayner recommended a strict adherence to the party principles, and Gayarré was refused a seat. The five Louisiana delegates who were not Catholics were accepted, but declined to take seats and retired from the hall with Gayarré.[25]

The heated debate over seating the Louisiana delegation brought the issue of slavery into prominence. Pike had gone to Philadelphia with the sincere hope that slavery could be kept out of the discussion, but the unfavorable reception of his resolution on June 6 aroused his fear lest the National Council not maintain a sane view upon the fearful question. Nevertheless, he still hoped that the delegates would allow the subject to die. On the evening of June 7, speaking at a banquet given the delegates by the people of Philadelphia, he appealed for the party to unite on the great American principles of the order and to put the welfare of the country above sectionalism. He pledged Arkansas to the support of these ideals and declared it would never utter one word that would "wound the sensibilities or excite a feeling of hostility in any other man." "If you will present us a platform upon which every citizen of this Union can stand firmly planted," he declared, "we will help to build it with you, and stick by it as long as a single inch of it remains together."[26]

Two days later Pike was selected to serve on the important platform committee.[27] It was evident by then that the National Council was badly divided. Unless the platform committee could work out a compromise between the northern and the southern delegations on the slavery issue, the American order was very likely to break up. Northern abolitionists under the leadership of Henry Wilson of Massachusetts had joined the order and had come to Philadelphia with the set purpose of either making the party abolitionist or destroying it.[28] The activity of such men in the ranks of the order in New England and the Northwest had placed the southern wing of the party in an embarrassing situation. They felt they must drive the Wilson crowd out of the order or forsake it themselves. Between these two factions stood the men of the stamp of Rayner and Pike, who still hoped the National Council would revert to its original principles and persuade the northern wing to do likewise. "I believed," said Pike a month later,

> that the continued agitation of the slavery question would end in a dissolution of the Union. I was content, nay anxious, to leave the whole question, in all its aspects, out of our creed, if the National Council would declare that its incorporation into that creed in the North was unauthorized, and a perversion of the organization of the Order to improper uses. Others thought . . . that it was necessary for us [the southern delegates] to take clear and distinct constitutional grounds in regard to the rights of the South. I thought to do so would break up the Order. . . . I . . . fondly hoped that the more intense and overpowering feeling of native Americanism would drive anti-slavery out of the field.[29]

The thirty-one members of the platform committee were almost evenly divided between the hostile factions, with New York and Pennsylvania, unknown quantities, holding the balance of power. Assuming the role of peacemaker, Pike proposed at the first meeting of the committee a series of resolutions excluding "all sectional doctrines" from the platform. He urged their adoption and warned the committee "that to incorporate any anti-slavery or pro-slavery plank in the platform would sever us asunder."[30]

His resolutions were voted down, whether by southern or northern delegates is not clear. Pike himself said shortly afterward that they were defeated by New England and the Northwest with the support of New York and Pennsylvania; but in the light of the committee reports, which saw New York supporting the majority platform, Pike may have been in error.[31] Whatever the facts of the case, the issue was now clear. There would be two reports, two platforms, and a split in the National Council. Henceforth Pike felt he had no choice but to uphold the rights of Arkansas and the South. He joined, therefore, with the southern members in drawing up the notorious "twelfth section" of the majority report. This section deplored "Whig and Democratic agitation of the slavery question"; pronounced it "the imperative duty of the American Party" to give peace and perpetuity to the Union; declared that the best warranty of this was "to abide by and maintain the existing laws upon the subject of slavery as a final and conclusive settlement of that subject in spirit and in substance"; asserted that Congress had no power to legislate upon the subject of slavery in any state or territory, or in the District of Columbia without the consent of Maryland; and denied that Congress could exclude any territory from admission as a state because its constitution "does or does not recognize the institution of slavery as a part of her social system." The corresponding section of the minority report demanded the restoration of the Missouri Compromise, or, if that should prove impracticable, the rejection by Congress of any slave state formed in the area formerly excluded by the provisions of that act. New York, California, the District of Columbia, and the Territory of Minnesota and seventeen delegates representing fifteen slave states signed the majority report, and fourteen delegates from twelve states signed the minority report.[32]

During Monday afternoon, June 11, the two reports of the platform committee were submitted to the National Council. A fiery debate that consumed the next two days found the Massachusetts delegation vying with that of Alabama in presenting the extremist views of North and South, while the New Yorkers occupied themselves in explaining their vote in favor of the majority report. Rayner of North Carolina shocked the sensibilities of his southern brethren on June 12 by declaring the repeal of the Missouri Compromise an uncalled-for outrage. He still held the forlorn hope that the National Council would come to its senses and ignore completely "the Slavery and Kansas question," but a plan incorporating his wishes was defeated on June 13 by a vote of 92 to 46. Late in the evening of the same day a motion to substitute the minority for the majority report was lost 51 to 92, followed immediately by the adoption of the majority resolutions 80 to 59. "The Black Power," declared the reporter of the *New York Tribune*, "in secret midnight conclave, was triumphant."[33]

Pike voted against Rayner's compromise plan and united with the southern delegates and their northern friends in defeating the minority report and in adopting the majority report.[34] Apparently he made no speech during the debate of June 11 and 13; but on the morning of June 14, when the supporters of the minority report withdrew from the National Council, Pike spoke in answer to the protests of the retiring delegates.[35]

He told the National Council that he thought the cancellation of the Missouri Compromise by the Kansas-Nebraska Act "unwise and inexpedient," but he wanted it understood "that the South *had paid the price* for its repeal." It had agreed to help buy out the Indian titles in Nebraska and Kansas, "including 500,000 acres in the latter" owned by slaveholding Cherokees and which, though lying north of 36°30', was slave territory. It had given the North and Northwest "an uninterrupted route for a northern Pacific railroad" and had consented to allow both Kansas and Nebraska to be subdivided into unlimited numbers of free territories, thus acquiescing in a settlement that might ultimately secure to the North ten additional U.S. senators and perhaps two more from Kansas. "And for all this," exclaimed Pike, "we received the repeal, the *empty* repeal of the Compromise, and squatter sovereignty, itself a greater outrage upon the South than the Wilmot Proviso: and, now having received the full consideration, the North impudently claims to take back the miserable so-called *equivalent* which they gave for this great boon—the repeal of an act that was itself an outrage on the South and miscalled a *compromise*." The revocation of that act was, he asserted, neither an injury nor a wrong to the North, and the South and "Middle States" would never consent to its reenactment. The majority platform had been made, he declared, to "drive off New England." "We did it. We meant to do it; for we found that they had come into the Order for the purpose of making it an Anti-slavery party, or breaking it up."[36]

Following the retirement of the antislavery delegates on June 14, the National Council took up other details of the platform. Pike was particularly anxious that the eighth section, that on Catholic proscription, be modified so as to comprehend the French Catholics of Louisiana and Maryland. "I wished," he said two months later,

> to have these gentlemen with us in the Order. I wished to leave out of the Ritual and Constitution the words *"Roman Catholic"* altogether, and to substitute in their place definite expressions that should show our objection to those only, who, whether Catholic or not, recognized any power in any foreign Prince, the acknowledgement of which is inconsistent with the character of an American Republican.[37]

Pike planned to offer such an article in committee but found it unnecessary when the committee adopted one presented by another member that did not bar American Creoles. This eighth section of the platform was taken up by the council June 14. Rayner moved and secured an amendment to it providing for "Resistance to the aggressive policy and corrupting tendencies of the Roman Catholic Church in our country" and for a general prohibition against any Catholic entering the order. Pike asked that the words "Roman Catholic Church" be struck out or that "an explanatory clause" be added which would exclude American Creoles from the general prohibition. By implication Pike's proposal involved a change in the ritual of the first degree as well as in the eighth section of the platform. A committee of three appointed to study his proposition reported that it was too late in the session and that too many delegates had gone home for it to be proper to make "radical changes" in either the ritual or the platform. Satisfied that he could do nothing further at this session of the National Council, now extremely weary and greatly diminished in numbers after two long weeks of exhausting debate, Pike decided to drop the subject. Therefore, Rayner's amendment stood in the final platform.[38]

The adoption of the twelfth section was a victory for the South, but it held grave portents for the future of the American Party. If the seceders, representing all New England and the Northwest, remained permanently out of the order then it was not at all likely to recover its national status. Henry Wilson, who led the northern delegations from the convention hall, was determined to "shiver" the party "to atoms" if it persisted in hostility to freedom.[39] Under his radical leadership the dissenters published an appeal to the people of the country, demanding the unconditional restoration of the Missouri Compromise principle and congressional protection for all voters in the territories.[40] The reporter of the *New York Tribune*, June 15, 1855, was exultant over the bolt of the anti-Nebraska delegates.

> Freedom has won the greatest moral victory [over slavery] which the whole history of the controversy between those two great elements of the Republic has recorded. Henceforth there is to be a new era in that controversy. The great importance of the results of the past twenty-four hours lies not in the fact that they compass the destruction of the great [K]now-Nothing party . . . but in the . . . fact that it has inaugurated a North, and formed a rallying point for those who would gather into one triumphant host all [in] the nation who henceforth would make Slavery sectional and Liberty national.

The months after the adjournment of the National Council in June were a busy period for Pike. On June 16 he went to New York City at the invitation of the New York delegation to attend a ratification meeting of the party, held in Central Park on June 18. In the presence of five to ten thousand enthusiastic followers the Philadelphia platform was ratified. Pike did not speak, though he had been scheduled to do so.[41] Two days afterward he and Rayner appeared and spoke at a similar mass meeting in Baltimore.[42] Later that same month he spoke at American meetings in Washington, D.C., and Mobile, Alabama.[43] At the end of June he arrived in New Orleans.[44]

His two weeks' visit in that city was marred by an unpleasant dispute with the editor of the *Daily Delta*, who was a bitter critic of the anti-Catholic plank of the Philadelphia platform. Under the title "A Peripatetic Orator" the *Delta* editor published a bitter article insulting Pike and attempting to discredit him in the eyes of Louisiana Catholics. He ridiculed Pike's professed modesty for refusing to give his poetic meditations to the world, derided his fatherhood "of a certain Pacific railway which was never born," and scoffed at his reputation for eloquence; Pike had "more of Cicerowhaccio than the original Cicero in him." Perhaps, the editor said, some of his readers were not acquainted with" Albert Pike of Arkan*sas*, or Col. Pike of Arkan*sas*, or Mr. Pike of Arkan*saw*." "He is an admirable Crichton, a bearded phenomenon, a kind of patriotic Hamlet, a merry Rabelais, with a cross of the dreamy Swedenborg. He is the hope of his country in the coming years—her young Ascanius—her pride, her glory and her joy.

Hunter, Warrior, Planter, Poet, Patriot and Know Nothing, he is not one, but all mankind's epitome." Pike's latest feat, sneered the editor, was to save the Union at Philadelphia and then to take a tour of the country "to acquaint the people with the miracle." Drawing "upon his imagination for his facts, and upon his memory for his wit" and acting the deceiver and the hypocrite, Pike had chosen his words to suit time and place and had thrown consistency to the winds on this speaking excursion. He had voted for the Catholic test at Philadelphia and had spoken in praise of the whole platform at New York, but at Mobile, where the whole platform was again ratified, the chameleonic Pike had taken thought of the feelings of New Orleans and announced that he was opposed to the proscription clause of the eighth section and would work for its removal at the next annual session of the National Council. The Roman Catholics of Louisiana, proclaimed the writer, would not be deluded by such "gross and deliberate quibbling." They knew and Pike knew that the Council could never repeal the clause without destroying the strength of the party at the North. Furthermore, Pike was committed to the national platform and it was "useless for him to attempt any apologies in Louisiana for the peculiar manner in which it is constructed."[45]

Two days after this editorial came to his attention Pike wrote an answer published on July 12 in the morning issue of the sympathetic *Daily Picayune*. He declined to reply "to the refined wit and graceful personalities" of his assailant, stating merely that he "should be sorry to learn that they suit the taste of the people of New Orleans." But the attack upon him was of public interest and must be answered publicly. He related his efforts to have the Louisiana delegation seated and to amend the eighth section. He had not spoken at New York at all, and in his speeches at Baltimore, Washington, and Mobile, his stand on the eighth article was the same as it had been in the National Council.

> I said at Mobile, and I say now, that I had foreseen that what was at first opposition to the assumed *temporal* power of the Church of Rome, would degenerate into hostility to the Catholic Church, *as a church*, and become a *religious* quarrel; and that there was a mighty anti-Catholic feeling in the country, which was a great fact to be dealt with in some way or other; and that feeling would be prevented from doing great harm, only by the exertion and influence of the discreet and moderate men *of the Order itself*, and intended, and I believed would be able . . . to modify and liberalize the feature of the platform to which I objected.
>
> I said that I adhered to the Order, notwithstanding my objection to that single feature, . . . for the purpose of aiding in changing it; and that I felt certain it would be changed at the next session. I do feel certain of that. . . . It is new to me that I must adhere to the platform as it is, without saying how I desire to see it amended.

In the evening issue of the *Delta*, July 12, the editor responded to Pike's statement. He thought Pike should have corrected the mistaken report of his speech in the *Mobile Advertiser* if he had desired to escape misrepresentation. But he doubted that even Pike's "thrilling eloquence" would convert such party stalwarts as Andrew Jackson Donelson, John Cunningham, President E. B. Bartlett, Kenneth Rayner, Neil S. Brown, and Felix Zollicoffer, to repeal the notorious test act, because such action would be political suicide. Moreover, he feared that Pike, who was at present "in a minority of one" in opposition to the proscription clause, was "blessed or cursed with a sanguine disposition and that in this instance the wish (for we give him credit for his wishes) is father to the thought."

A "Grand Know-Nothing Demonstration" was held in Lafayette Square in the city on the night of July 11 to ratify the nomination of candidates for state officers. Before some ten thousand people Charles Derbigny, nominee for governor, George Eustis Jr., and Pike spoke. Pike defended the twelfth section of the platform as "adequate protection to slavery" and brought the crowd to laughter and applause when he took a parting shot at the dogged obstinacy of the *Delta* editor, declaring that it was an established principle that newspaper editors never corrected a mistake nor admitted an error. He defended his position at Philadelphia, and his views on the eighth section found favor with his audience since they were identical with those adopted by the Louisiana State Council and approved by the state convention.[46]

From New Orleans Pike went on to Little Rock for the July term of the Pulaski County Circuit Court. By the time he reached home the American Party was the chief topic of discussion among Democratic politicians and editors in Arkansas. Though it was an off year politically, the Democratic leaders of the state, not sure what to make of this new factor in politics nor how to combat it, were noticeably concerned at its rapid expansion in Arkansas. Richard H. Johnson of the *True Democrat*, the principal organ of the administration party, exhibited great indecision in taking a stand against the Philadelphia platform. Arkansas was overwhelmingly Protestant; consequently he must have feared a strong defense of Catholicism would injure his own party by creating new adherents for the American cause. He cited statistics to show the hopeless minority of the Catholic faith in Arkansas and suggested to his readers that if they were Protestants they "already hated the Catholics enough" without being prompted to hostility by a party. Moreover, he thought Arkansas had nothing to fear from foreigners; there were 160,000 natives to offset the 1,500 foreigners in the state. But he declined to comment on the slavery plank of the platform.[47]

If the platform and tenets of the American Party were dangerous to assail, personalities were not. On July 24 he reprinted in full the attack of the *New Orleans Daily Delta* on Pike. Near the end of July or the first of August a copy of Pike's April message to the state council fell into Johnson's hands. Pike's recommendation in that address that the subordinate councils be instructed to cancel subscriptions to the *True Democrat* furnished Johnson ammunition for a terrific barrage against Pike. Pike had "secretly and bitterly" attacked and maligned editor Johnson without giving an opportunity of defence." "He sent his 'address' clandestinely around, under thick wrappers, to the 'subordinates,' who were to act upon his skulking suggestions, but he shrank from the manly act of delivering a copy to me."[48]

Johnson construed Pike's wish that the Arkansas delegation to Congress be instructed to support changes in the naturalization laws as a personal attack against the delegates. He accused Pike of inconsistency in adhering to the order and to the principles of the party platform. He reprinted from papers across the country editorial criticisms of Pike's American activities. Finally, he attempted to impugn Pike's reputation by dragging up and reprinting vicious gossip concerning Pike's connection with the Real

Estate Bank, implying that Pike had pilfered from the state to fill his own pocket and to foster the now defunct Whig Party.[49]

Pike was deeply wounded by Johnson's accusations. He had patiently borne the vicious slander circulated against him since 1842 in regard to the Real Estate Bank and had by this time made up his mind to remove to New Orleans, but he did not intend to allow editor Johnson and Governor Conway to discredit the American Party in Arkansas by trumped-up charges concerning his former attorneyship for the bank. On August 31 in a long letter to the *State Gazette and Democrat*, recently acquired as the chief organ of the American order,[50] Pike answered Johnson's charges. He gave full details of his work as attorney, his debt to the bank, his resignation from that institution, and his prosecution of the Holford bond cases. He explained that there was nothing personal in his request that Americans withdraw support from the *True Democrat* nor in his desire to have the Arkansas congressman instructed to vote for changes in naturalization process. He regretted that Johnson, "a gentleman, by birth, training, and habits," had seen fit to make "gross and offensive" charges against him when based "upon mere idle rumor and vague suspicion." But he understood the motive, for it was a maxim in Arkansas politics "that to make a party or a measure unpopular, it is only necessary to say that *I* belong to it."

> It is not important to me whether I am popular or not. But I do desire to be believed to have acted honestly and to speak truthfully. In a very brief time, I shall cease to be a citizen of the State, severing forever a connection of nearly twenty-three years. It no longer concerns me to whom the political offices of the State may be divided. They never had any charms for me; for political life is not to my taste. I prefer my books; and peace and quietness. . . .
>
> There was a time when I would have answered with bitterer words. But I am weary of strife and controversy, and do not desire to assail any one. Indeed, the attack of the editor of the True Democrat has only pained and not angered me. . . . I feel too entirely above it to be more moved by it than I am by the idle wind. . . .
>
> I shall leave Arkansas with the consciousness that if, in a momentary glow of passion I have ever done an injury, I have been ready to atone for it. In a law practice of near twenty years, I have sacrificed no man's property for my own benefit under execution. I have made no man poorer that I might become richer. I have done more favors to my enemies than to my friends. I have *earned* here and expended over a hundred and thirty thousand dollars, and have not needed to pilfer from a Bank to live. . . . I entertain no animosity or ill will towards a soul on earth that I would not freely reconcile, if I found in him a corresponding disposition.[51]

Having stated his case fully and having bidden farewell to the people of Arkansas, Pike declined further participation in the editorial warfare that now waxed strong between the editors and correspondents of the *Gazette* and those of the *True Democrat*. In late August and during September he spoke at several American rallies over the state, but before October 1 he was on his way to Washington for the fall term of the U.S. Supreme Court and for the approaching session of Congress.[52]

As a result he was not present when the Arkansas State Council met in Little Rock at the end of October to nominate delegates to the National Council and to the National Convention. There was a question at this session whether or not Pike had ceased to be a citizen of the state and doubt about the propriety of selecting him as a delegate. At last, however, he was chosen to represent Arkansas in both bodies, his nominator asserting, if the *True Democrat* did not exaggerate, "that his bare presence in the national convention, *without opening his mouth*, would be worth more than a hundred common Know Nothings."[53]

Pike's absence from Arkansas in the fall of 1855 saved him from an embarrassing dispute with the Catholic bishop of Arkansas, Andrew J. Byrne. On August 24 Pike had published a statement in the *Gazette* explaining his views on the eighth section of the American platform. He said that with the exception of American Creoles it was a general rule that Roman Catholics permitted "the power of the Pope to direct their conduct in civil and political matters" and that he was for admitting the Creoles and excluding other Catholics from the order. No matter how absurd he might think the papal claim of succession from St. Peter and the doctrine of the infallibility of the Pope, who was after all "but a man . . . and often a very ordinary, a very narrow-minded and unprincipled man," he wished it understood that he made no war upon the Catholic faith. He blamed "the arrogance and impudence" of certain Catholic bishops and "their attempts to obtain control of a separate share of the school fund in New York" for the hostile spirit of the "Protestant feeling of the country."[54] Bishop Byrne undertook to refute Pike's charges, addressing "to the Unprejudiced People of Arkansas" four letters over the name of "Petricula." He declared in the first letter, dated Little Rock, September 22, that "after mature reflection" he had reached "the conclusion that the character, influence and standing of Captain Albert Pike in Arkansas" had given too much weight to certain "historical blunders and gross misrepresentations of Catholic doctrines" made in his "studied and written apology" of August 24. The bishop impugned Pike's poor taste in making a public issue of religious freedom by his unbridled and calumnious statements about the Catholic Church. Byrne denied that the Pope possessed, or claimed, any temporal power outside the "patrimony of St. Peter," declared that it was no doctrine of the Roman Catholic faith that the Pope was infallible, and defended the constitutional right of New York Catholics to petition for a share of the common school fund to which they had long contributed without receiving any benefits. It was, asserted the bishop, the bigotry of Know-Nothingism alone that had brought about the present unhappy state of affairs. Pike was welcome to his personal and private views of the Pope, and "no Catholic" as far as the bishop knew had ever disputed the right to express such opinions. He was puzzled, however, "to discover where, or in what school, the noble Captain should have *read* his theology."

Perhaps Pike was lucky in not being on hand when Byrne's letters appeared, for it was obvious that the writer had made an able and telling defense of his faith. But it was also obvious, and doubtless would have been to Pike, that Bishop Byrne's views were not those of the Catholic Church generally. The truth was that the leaders of that faith were by no means of one opinion on the temporal powers of the Pope. Moreover, it was conceded by many of the clergy that the layman could determine the matter for himself.[55] Whatever the truth of the matter, it was quite evident that if Bishop Byrne and his followers in Arkansas actually believed the doctrine to be that stated in the Petricula letters then they had no reason to fear Pike's opposition. Despite Pike's indiscretion in publicly expressing personal contempt for the Papacy, his interpretation of the eighth section would not have excluded any Catholic who accepted Byrne's views of the temporal power of the Pope.

Pike's political thinking on the slavery question had undergone a positive and permanent change at the meeting of the National Council in June, 1855. Prior to that time he had hoped and worked to keep the issue out of the American Party, but the bitter hostility of the Wilson anti-Nebraska faction at Philadelphia drove him to support the adoption of the proslavery twelfth section. Thereafter he was determined that the plank must stand, declaring that the "only safety" for the South "consisted in placing our candidates upon the platform as it was."[56] But a movement was now under way to revise the platform. In November 1855, the northern state councils had sent delegates to a convention at Cincinnati to see if they could work out a plan for reuniting with the proslavery wing of the party. Though the meeting was poorly attended and badly divided, a majority of those present rebuffed the antislavery extremists and proposed a special session of the National Council for the purpose of attempting to compromise the differences between the two wings of the party. These overtures of peace were successful. President E. B. Bartlett, Kentuckian, acted on the request and called a special session of the council to meet in Philadelphia on February 18, 1856.[57]

Pike opposed the special session of the National Council. He believed with other southerners that it was but a scheme of the antislavery wing of the party to remove the twelfth section. Slavery had now become the great curse of southern Americans and of Pike. He and they were committed to the sectional platform, and there was no turning back. "Were it not in," said the reporter of the *New York Tribune*, February 20, 1856, "the South would not insist now that it should be put in; but having once got it, they cannot consent to part with it without self-destruction."

The special session of the National Council convened at Franklin Hall on Sixth Street at noon February 18. Philadelphia was in the clutches of a severe cold wave. A furious gale roared along her streets, rattling windows, slamming shutters, and chilling to the bone the few pedestrians who dared venture forth. Everywhere frozen fireplugs lay entombed in mountains of ice.[58] To the shivering southerners who gathered there that day, the warm interior of Franklin Hall proved little more cheerful than the blizzard howling outside. Moderate Americans took control of the council during the organization on February 18–19, and after two days of debate secured on February 21 the repeal of the platform of 1855. A new one was then adopted which repudiated the twelfth section of the former platform, replacing it with an obscurely worded pledge of neutrality upon the subject of slavery.[59] This done, the National Council adjourned on February 21 to make way for the assembling of the National Convention in National Hall, in Market Street, at ten o'clock the following morning. The row over a statement of principles was resumed in the convention, but at last, on Saturday, February 23, it was agreed to begin nominations and to allow the subject of the platforms to lie over. On Monday Millard Fillmore and Andrew Jackson Donelson were nominated for the first and second places on the ticket, and the convention adjourned without renewing the debate on principles, thus tacitly accepting the council's platform.

In the meantime Pike had withdrawn from the National Council on the question of the repeal of the old platform. Having gone to Philadelphia firmly determined to oppose the repeal of the twelfth section and suspecting that the northern delegations intended that very thing, he had joined Charles Mathews of California in keeping before the council the subject of repeal once it had been proposed on February 20.[60] On the evening of February 20, Pike and Mathews and other southern members met in caucus and agreed to withdraw in a body from the National Council if the twelfth section were deleted. Next day the old platform was voted out, and Pike and Mathews retired from the council with other southern delegates. But by February 22 most of the southern members had changed their minds and had taken seats in the National Convention. Absalom Fowler, James Logan, and perhaps S. L. Anstell, of the Arkansas delegation entered the convention and cast Arkansas's four votes for Fillmore.[61] As for Pike, he and Mathews refused to take seats in the convention and issued a joint statement to the people of their states explaining their conduct. They said that they had withdrawn from the council as a result of the agreement in the southern caucus and that they now resigned their commissions as delegates to the National Convention because they could not stand by the new platform.[62]

Pike attached to the joint statement a larger private letter to the American Party of Arkansas, had both printed as a pamphlet, and sent the pamphlet to Arkansas for circulation. After relating in detail the action of the council and his reasons for withdrawing from the body, Pike said that he blamed no one.

> My only object is to be *rectus in curia* myself. I cannot stand on the new platform. I cannot defend it, so far as it touches the matter of slavery. The 12th article was my *ultimatum*. I would stand on no platform, *now*, on which those who represented Ohio and Pennsylvania in the council could stand.... Now, I am satisfied that we and they cannot be the members of one and the same party.
>
> I decline to defend, but I shall never attack the platform. So far as it relates to slavery, and so far as it abandons the 12th section it is not my creed; and, that being the case, I cannot act under it when I mean to repudiate it....
>
> I therefore request you to accept my resignation as delegate to the national council and nominating convention. And in surrendering into your hands the last political trust with which I ever intend to be clothed, ... I wish only to add, that I desire to belong to no other party *in* the South, so long as the 12th article forms part of its creed; but hereafter and forever, I decline any affiliation or connection with those who repudiate that Article, and the principles, essential, in my opinion, to the salvation of the Union, which it contains.[63]

Following the nominations of Fillmore and Donelson by the National Convention, Pike advocated the outright revolt of the whole southern wing of the American Party. In support of his views he wrote a pamphlet, entitled *To the American Party South*, which he had printed in Washington and mailed to various political leaders at the South. In it he objected to "the Platform adopted by the National Council at its called session, and the candidates placed upon it by the National Convention." Both were hostile to the true interests of the South and to the American Party in general. The new platform had left the northern men who stood upon it quite free to agitate the slavery question as much as they pleased. Moreover, the nomination of Fillmore was a serious error. He had no personal dislike for the ex-president, whose administration he had supported, but "when we formed the American party, we assured our democratic friends who joined us, that it was *not* meant to be a whig party in disguise. They joined us in that belief." As matters stood the platform justified former Democrats "in leaving the party, and the *whig* nomination will *urge* them to do it." Entering the Democratic Party might be well enough, but its northern wing was "no more reliable than ours." As an alternative Pike called on the state councils of the South to assemble, form on the conservative principles of the twelfth section, nominate a northern Democrat acceptable to all, and campaign on the platform of 1855.[64]

Southern American Party members were not long in relegating Pike's suggestions to the limbo of lost causes. Once the delegates left Philadelphia and their tempers had time to cool, they came to realize that the new platform itself was not so very dangerous and that Fillmore, a northern man with southern sympathies, was platform enough for those who took such statements of principles seriously. By far the vast majority entered actively into the campaign in support of the platform and Fillmore. Only in Arkansas did Pike's apostasy embarrass the American cause. American editors in the state had praised the decision of Fowler, Logan, and Anstell to enter the convention, but they attempted for some time to conceal Pike's action. However, Johnson of the *True Democrat* got hold of Pike's addresses to the American Party and gleefully reprinted them in his columns. The editor of the *Gazette*, apparently assuming that Pike was behind the Johnson stories, bitterly assaulted Pike, declaring that no one in Arkansas had ever had any confidence in him as a political leader, charging him with attempting to betray the American Party to its enemies and asserting that, since his very name was "death to any political party, his desertion is regarded as a certain presage of the success of Americanism; and for that reason it has been the cause of rejoicing among true Americans."[65] The *Gazette* even accused Robert W. Johnson of mailing Pike's circulars "to Arkansas under his senatorial frank" and dug up and reprinted the debate on the Creek appropriation in 1854, hinting that Senators Johnson and Sebastian were "the special sub-attorneys for this claim of Capt. Pike's in Congress."[66]

Pike's absence in Washington during the summer of 1856 saved him from the brunt of this unjust criticism. He had no intention of opposing the American candidates, much less of going over to the Democratic Party. But he definitely refused to support Fillmore. While he was on his way to New Orleans from Washington in October 1856, the *Memphis Appeal* announced that he would speak in Memphis at a Fillmore rally. In denying the report Pike stated that he had laid his

> views before the American party in March last,[67] and they not being approved, I forbore to reply to any attack upon me, because I did not mean to become the assailant of Mr. Fillmore or the party; but not because I was without the means of defense.

What the country wants is not so much a *candidate* who is right, as a party that is so, on the great question of the day. The American party north is, in a great measure, not so; for in Maine, Vermont, Connecticut, Pennsylvania, and elsewhere, it fuses with the black republicans, and is acting in concert with those who assail the constitution and endanger the Union. I impugn the propriety of no man's course in the south; but for myself alone, I cannot feel it right to be the ally of those who are in the north the allies of black republicanism.

If Mr. Fillmore could be elected by the votes of men who adhere to the principles enunciated in the twelfth article of the platform of June, 1856, [1855] I should rejoice; for that would demonstrate that a majority of the people of the Union were true to the constitutional rights of the south. But his election . . . [is now] impossible. . . .

And, while the democratic party is, in my view, right, on the questions that grow out of the existence of slavery, . . . yet there are other things in its creed and platform to which I cannot assent. I shall, therefore, not vote for Mr. Buchanan; but as I believe, that he and the democratic party alone can defeat Mr. Fremont and the republican party, (if indeed, even they can,) and so delay for a brief time that imperative dissolution of the Union which mutual hatred and ill-will, every day becoming more intense in the north and south, must inevitably and soon bring about, I cannot conscientiously do any act or say any word that could in the slightest degree tend to defeat him.

I am, therefore, content, for the present, to stand aside and belong to no party, until the south, forgetting its insane dissensions, shall see how necessary it is for it to become a unit in the assertion of its constitutional rights against northern fanaticism and foreign radicalism, which must assuredly soon be the case.[68]

The results of the election of 1856 revealed how intense the sectional feeling of the country was. James Buchanan, Pennsylvania Democrat with a safe record on slavery, carried every southern state except Maryland, which alone of all the states gave its electoral vote to Fillmore. John C. Fremont, Republican, swept the New England states and Ohio, Michigan, Missouri and Iowa; and Pennsylvania, New Jersey, Indiana, Illinois and California went to Buchanan by slim margins. Buchanan won, and Democrats exulted that they still held the presidency, the Senate, and the Supreme Court. But the Republicans, having gained the House and seeing that Indiana, Illinois and Pennsylvania, the northern states that accounted for Buchanan's election, were moving closer to the Republican fold, looked longingly toward 1860, when a solid sectional vote might give them victory.

XXV

Political Disruption and Secession

IN THE YEARS between 1856 and 1860 Pike was torn between his love for the Union and his love for the South, much of the time undecided and confused over what went on about him. The country was agitated by the aftermath of the Kansas-Nebraska Act. Since 1854 Kansas had been settled by rival groups of proslavery and antislavery men, neither willing to accept the authority of the other. They charged one another with fraud and violence, went armed, and involved in their bloody strife for political control the peaceful and disinterested settlers who had gone there solely to establish new homes. By the opening of 1856, each group of extremists had set up a separate government in the territory: one headed by a governor appointed by President Pierce and dominated by the slavery element, the other directed by a small cluster of Free Soil fanatics, who in the spring of 1856 petitioned Congress to admit Kansas to the Union under a free-state constitution drawn up and adopted at Topeka the previous fall.

Badly divided, Congress rejected the Topeka constitution after months of angry debate, leaving the territory still torn between hostile factions. And while Congress was making up its mind to do nothing about the Kansas situation, a proslavery force had sacked the Free Soil capital of Lawrence, John Brown had made his vengeful raid on Pottawatomie Creek, and Rep. Preston Brooks, South Carolinian, had caned Sen. Charles Sumner into insensibility on the floor of the Senate. The outlook this year was anything but cheering. It was becoming more and more difficult for conservative men to ignore the sectional agitators; it was becoming less and less easy for them to remain sensible, rational, and calm. Northerners and southerners in ever-increasing numbers were looking on Kansas as the Armageddon of America, on whose outcome depended the continuation of their way of life.

At the height of the Kansas controversy in 1856, Pike wrote and printed anonymously in Washington for distribution in the North a series of *Letters to the People of the Northern States* in which he attempted to look impartially at the slavery controversy and to see where it was leading.[1] He was, to be sure, hardly in a position to examine the problem without prejudice, but he was better able to do so than were most other southerners of his day. To begin with he professed that he was positive the repeal of the Missouri Compromise was just, and thought it only fair that the people of Kansas should have slaves if they desired them; he presented a legal argument to show that the federal government, both by statute in 1830 and by treaty in 1833, had actually opened territory north of 36° 30' to slaveholding Cherokee Indians. Yet he thought the North had little reason to fear that the South would take and hold Kansas for slavery. The land was simply not suited to the institution, though it might temporarily be taken there "by way of bravado, and in assertion of disputed right." He did not doubt that unlawful acts had been committed in Kansas. That was always the case when men quarreled and became exasperated. But the moderate people of the South did not justify lawlessness, and he was sure that conservative and wise counsels in Congress would settle the whole difficulty if given a chance. Congress should be allowed to supervise the next elections in Kansas to insure their legality, and the people of the territory should not make another attempt to form a constitution until Congress directed it.

In the meantime the people outside Kansas should "let things there take their natural course, without forcing them from any quarter." Settlement should be equally open to people from North and South who desired to make homes there, "to see which can go in greatest numbers, and which can fairly out-vote the other."[2]

In taking up the moral, economic, and political aspects of plantation slavery, Pike outlined the qualifications that enabled him to think "dispassionately" on the subject. He had been born and bred to manhood in New England, had been educated in Massachusetts, and had lived exactly half his life "in the extreme Southwest," where the dust of four of his children now mingled with southern soil. He had owned such slaves only as he needed for household servants. He was not "one of those who believe slavery a blessing." It was evil and abusive and necessarily gave power that could be misused:

> It involves frequent separation of families. It, here and there, prevents the development of a mind and intellect that might, *perhaps*, rival that of the white man, it if were free to expand. . . . The slave toils all his life for mere clothing, shelter, and food; and the lash is heard sometimes upon the plantation, and in rare cases, cruelties punishable by the law are practiced.[3]

Slavery was not, however, the "unmitigated curse and evil," the "greatest outrage upon humanity," the "crime in the sight of God," that its enemies proclaimed it to be.[4]

> Do you imagine that we have no affection for those wards? If you dared to strike one of them, you would see. Do you imagine that we *like* to punish them? If you knew how reluctant we are to do it, . . . you would not think so. When misfortune compels us to part with them, do you suppose it causes us no pain? Why, we are men, like you, and not brute beasts, devoid both of humanity and reason! . . .
>
> The interest, as well as the feelings, of the master *compel* him to treat his slaves with humanity; and except in rare-cases [sic] he does so. There are exceptions to this, of course. There are brutes everywhere, in the shape of men; and some will be found to violate our laws, and even escape punishment, as sea-captains and masters of apprentices have done before them. But none can do so and escape condemnation by that public opinion which is the corrector of abuses everywhere.[5]

While slavery offered opportunity for abuse, Pike believed that the institution furnished no more occasion for it than did the relation between child and parent, husband and wife, master and apprentice, employer and employee, officer and soldier, captain and seaman. It was said that any system which permitted abuses ought to be abolished, but could you, asked Pike, abolish the institutions of family, of commerce and industry, of the military and naval service simply because they were abusive? He did not think so. Furthermore the abolition of slavery involved problems to which northern reformers were blind. They proposed that slaves be emancipated but did not offer to take charge of the freedmen. They "would have them freed *and left so,*" when it was obvious "that the same powers which the *master* has over them, would have to be vested somewhere under another name." The "iron law of wages," expounded by David Ricardo, English political economist, governed slavery. By this law, "enacted by God," it was ordained that capital should rule and labor obey. It was ordained that the masses should toil, not for fortune, not for a competence, not to leave something to their children, not to educate them, not even for comfort, but for bare subsistence "of the rudest, commonest and cheapest kind." Was it fair, then, demanded Pike, for northern editors and politicians to compare the position of the slave, who toiled all his life for coarse food, rough clothing, and a bare shelter, with the independent farmer and mechanic of the North? If these self-constituted critics would compare the slave's position with that of the laboring classes of the world they would soon see the unfairness of their views. Pauperism and poverty in the industrial centers of the North inflicted hardships on white laborers and their families as degrading as those imposed by slavery on the blacks. Both systems offered room for reform, but by the time the philanthropists of the northern states had corrected the evils in theirs they would have "little of life left them in which to follow out fine theories" in respect to the South. He did not mean "to undervalue an enlarged philanthropy—a desire to see all men free and happy"; yet he was no extremist and "would not endeavor to *force* freedom upon any other race, to which freedom would be but anarchy and another form of servitude." Therefore, he would not undertake to emancipate southern slaves unless he could first see "they were *fit* to be free, and that from such freedom they would reap substantial benefits, and increased happiness and comfort."[6]

Suppose for the sake of argument, said Pike, that southern slaveholders agreed to lose the value of their bondsmen and set them free. They would not give them the ballot, would not intermarry with them, would not admit them to their social circles, would feel obligated to hire them only so long as they were able to work, and would pay them as low a wage as possible:

> With you, they are shoe-blacks, servants, porters. Do you imagine that with us they would rise to any higher rank as laborers, or become mechanics or small farmers? That has never yet happened anywhere. They would be Pariahs among us. Do you imagine that they would not have to work as many hours in the day to earn wages enough to live on, as they now do for a better living than they would get then? Do you imagine that we would establish public schools for them, employ and pay teachers, build churches for them? *We should lose too much in setting them free, to be able to do it.* They would sink below their present level, and be as much under our power as they now are, *with no right to require us to support them when they ceased to be able to work.* I cannot conceive a more horrible condition than that in which they would be placed if set free, and left to take care of themselves. *Liberty to starve is no great liberty anywhere in the world, after all.*[7]

Setting the slaves free would not, argued Pike, destroy the forces which had caused them to be enslaved. And the one great force that must be considered in dealing with the slavery problem was the intellectual inferiority of the black to the white man. This inferiority was responsible for his original bondage, and it stood in the way of his enfranchisement. Opponents of slavery protested, however, that it "prevents the intellectual development of the race, presses it down relentlessly to one common level, crushes, the intellect that, if free, would rise, and so perpetuates the necessity for its own continuance." Pike preferred to deny this. The slow progress of the blacks was owing not so much to his inferior intellect as to "the depth of brutality and degradation from which he had to rise." The black was intelligent; he was capable of advancement; he was progressing slowly toward "the level of the white man"; and he would "be free in God's good time." But it was impossible to hasten the arrival of that day, notwithstanding the efforts of "those philosophers and philanthropists to whom his present condition causes so much concern." Men too often flattered themselves that God had selected them to serve as his instruments, when he perhaps was only making of them "examples of the feebleness of human efforts, and the vanity of human self-conceit." Blacks, declared Pike, were fulfilling their mission on earth. He could not be legislated into freedom, for such law would not be expressive of the general will and sentiment of the southern people and would not, therefore, be of any force. They would be free only when they was fit to be free and when they gained their freedom by their own exertions. "Until then, if you make [them] free in law, [they] will be instantly enslaved again in fact."[8]

In the meantime, while blacks were fulfilling their destiny, their servitude was not unbearable; nor did it "embody *all* the evils under which poor humanity suffers." They neither starved nor froze, did not fear that they would not have food and medicine when ill, and were protected by law from being turned out to shift for themselves after their services ceased to be of any value. This security was certainly valuable. Pike did not mean to degrade or undervalue "the blessings of liberty;" indeed, he fervently wished that "every living soul on earth could be free." But until the slave was capable of exercising freedom, "that man would be his worst enemy who should give him liberty."

Moreover, the problem of slavery was "a great *practical* question, not to be settled by the simple enunciation of the supposed axiom, that every man has a *right* to be free, and that it is a crime to hold a human being in bondage." The slave system, interwoven with every fiber of southern life, needed to be considered in the light not of what was right or wrong at the beginning, but of what was now practicable, what would be safe, what would be of the greatest actual benefit to the bondsman, whether he was fit to be free, and if not how he was to be made so. The northern people must recognize that the people of the South had the deepest personal interest in the subject. To abolish slavery would impoverish great numbers of masters and make drones and paupers of the vast body of the freedman. Then the antislavery leaders would see that freedom and the right were not the greatest blessings that could be bestowed upon the black race. The people of the North must, above all, cease to agitate the subject of slavery, must cease to sow discontent in the minds of the bondsmen if they would truly benefit him.

> Then the southern laws would soon make the institution of marriage more sacred; the gospel would be more generally preached to them; the children would be taught to read; additions would, from time to time, be made to their privileges, and they would be allowed a portion of their earnings; until, at some time in the future, when by long training they were fitted to be free, the transition from servitude to liberty would be so slight and insensible a change as to produce no con-

vulsions in the State, no loss of property, no pauperism, and no annihilation of the inferior race.[9]

In closing his appeal to the northern people Pike directed their attention to the critical point that slavery agitation had reached. The South had become so much a unit upon the question that she was preparing to forsake all national political connections and form a purely sectional party in defense of slavery. Meanwhile, the leaders of the Republican Party, their ranks swelled by recruits from the former national parties which had been shattered by the slavery question, were daily growing bolder and bolder in their attacks on slavery. Unless this utter senselessness ceased, in both North and South, the Union would surely break up and its people be caught up in the holocaust of civil war. He looked upon the strife, antipathy, bitterness, and hatred between the two sections, between which his heart's allegiance was divided, with "the profoundest sorrow and the gloomiest apprehension." It was time, he solemnly warned,

> for us all to pause and reflect. For if, when the coming tempest strikes the good ship the Union ... those who could have prevented the calamity, and *would* not, must be responsible for that most awful of shipwrecks, and for all the disastrous, bloody consequences that will inevitably follow.[10]

There were fallacies in Pike's justification of slavery in these letters, but they were fallacies accepted by the South as universal truths. Hardened in defense of their peculiar institution by the attacks of abolitionists, southern extremists shut their eyes to its inhuman aspects and came to look upon it not only as a system of labor and of race control but also as a necessary, honorable, and beneficent institution justified by history, scripture, economics, sociology, biology, and political science. Pike rejected this extreme proslavery point of view as readily as he condemned the violent antislavery argument. His views were in the main moderate and equitable. Though he considered blacks biologically and intellectually inferior to the white man, a common tenet of the proslavery argument and a not uncommon belief of white men everywhere at that age, he believed them capable of learning and looked ultimately to the emancipation of the entire race. In this sense, and in the fact that he openly admitted and impugned the harshness of slavery and hoped to see the amelioration of its abuses, he was extremely liberal for his time and section. Whether for the sake of argument or from the result of sincere conviction, Pike blamed, perhaps justly, the threats of abolitionists for the laws of southern states which drew tighter the chains of thralldom and prevented enlightened planters from granting periodical additions to slaves' privileges that would eventually make possible for them "the transition from servitude to liberty."

In Pike's eyes the southern extremists were as dangerous as the abolitionists. At the southern Convention held at Savannah, Georgia, in December 1856, he helped defeat a resolution calling for an endorsement of the movement to reopen the slave trade. Its proponents, led by Leonidas Spratt, a South Carolina editor, and ably supported by James D. B. De Bow of *De Bow's Review*, argued that the move would bring down the price of slaves and enable the small farmers of the South to buy black labor, thus democratizing the system of slavery and resulting more quickly in sectional solidification in defense of the institution.

When the subject came up at Savannah, Pike, who was there to secure an endorsement for his Pacific railway project adopted the previous year at New Orleans, made a vigorous speech against the slave trade resolution. He confessed that he had recently written and published a series of letters to the people of the North in defense of slavery, but that he "would suffer himself to be torn by wild horses before he would justify the renewal of the African slave trade." To reintroduce the barbarities of that vile commerce would damn the South in the eyes of the world and make her position indefensible. "We could no longer say to the world that our slaves were valuable, were born and brought up with us, and by association were dear to us." Moreover, he thought that there was not a "slaveholder present who would not be glad to believe that in some good time every man on the face of the earth, who was fit to be free, would be free." The framers of the Constitution had implied that "by degrees we should make our slaves more persons and less things." He himself considered slaves more than mere chattels, but human beings with souls to be saved and minds "to be cultivated and improved" looking to the day when they would be free. All the progress made by the black race would be lost if the country was flooded "with slaves from those barbarous regions." There were, besides, financial interests to be considered. Great losses would be suffered if cheap slaves were placed on the market.[11]

Almost all of the men who answered Pike at Savannah said that they felt there was nothing immoral in the slave trade even though a majority of them opposed its reopening. John Cochran of Alabama felt so. He argued that to bring the African to America would advance him in civilization and certainly would not retard the advancement made by those already here. But he opposed the measure because it would be only a temporary solution and would eventually create a "redundancy" of laborers, a greater evil than the current shortage. John A. Calhoun, a South Carolinian who favored the measure, ridiculed Pike for his "sickly sentimentality . . . as to the horrors that would attend the . . . trade if re-opened." R. B. Baker, Alabamian, voted against the resolution, but he severely attacked Pike for "expressing the hope, that the time might come when all men might be free." Freedom was desirable for whites, but he did not "believe God intended the African to be free, and if republican institutions were to be preserved, it must be by preserving the institution of slavery." And William B. Gouldin, Georgian, also an opponent of the proposal, declared that he saw no moral difference in buying a slave in Virginia and in Africa.[12] Thus the measure was defeated not so much because of compassion as because of the pecuniary interests of the large planters.

After its Savannah meeting in 1856 Pike broke entirely with the Southern Commercial Convention. He felt that its former conservative membership had given way to dangerous radicals, and he had no desire to be associated with men who were, in his opinion, striving to break up the Union.[13] He told the delegates at Savannah that commerce not the political condition of the country had brought them together. Yet even he gave vent to strong feelings on the recent campaign, warning his listeners to look "at the formidable proportions of the [Republican] party at the North." Every New England state "had gone against the South," and Pennsylvania and Indiana had been saved only by narrow margins. This was, he hastily advised, no reason to dissolve the

Union, though he professed to believe in the right of secession and thought that nullification of the fugitive slave act by the North "would warrant the South in doing so." Determination of what the South should do when and if the breakup came must be deferred, however, until that deplorable event should take place. A commercial convention was, in his opinion, no proper body to discuss such questions. Instead it should take steps to make the South independent of the North in commerce and manufacturing. It should urge the South to build the transcontinental railroad and bring the wealth of China and the East Indies to its people. It should make every effort to have the southern people "forget their intestine feuds and struggles" and unite in a great crusade to throw off northern economic dominance. The South could never hope to be in a majority in the national councils, but as a vigorous, united minority it could continue to govern the country. "We could then remain in the Union which we love so much, but unless some such steps . . . [are] taken . . . the days of this Union . . . [are] numbered."[14]

This was Calhoun's talk with reservations, and it carried an undertone of hollowness; for Pike did not really believe the convention would do any of the things that he urged. He looked on southern unity as the one hope for preserving the Union, or so he said; but he knew that the North had already formed a sectional block, almost a majority block too. Yet he naively asserted that the South could govern the country as a strong minority. He probably knew better, otherwise he would not have been such an outspoken advocate of preserving the national status of the Democratic Party between 1857 and 1860.

In the summer of 1857 Kansas again occupied the attention of the country. An election, called by the territorial legislature, was held for delegates to a constitutional convention. The Free Soilers, angry and disappointed because Congress had spurned their Topeka constitution in 1856, refused to participate in the election. As a result the convention was captured by the proslavery element, now identified with the national Democratic Party. The national leaders of the party were convinced, however, that Kansas would not become a slave state, though they hoped it would be a Democratic one. To further the interests of the Democracy, President Buchanan had sent to Kansas in the spring of 1857 a new governor, Robert J. Walker, a strong Unionist of Mississippi. His principal task was to persuade the proslavery group to submit the constitution, which would, of course, be proslavery, to the people for ratification, hoping thereby to effect a just settlement of the Kansas slavery question as well as to win Kansas and northern Democratic support for Buchanan. In his inaugural address Walker plainly implied that he believed Kansas would be a free state, and he virtually promised the people of the territory that Congress would not admit Kansas under any constitution that had not been concurred in by a majority of the legitimate voters of the territory. In all this he had Buchanan's support. The result of Walker's efforts was a compromise by which the delegates, who met at Lecompton in September and drew up the proslavery constitution, refused to submit the constitution proper to the people but agreed to a referendum on a separate section allowing a choice between "the constitution with slavery" and "the constitution without slavery." Whatever the result, the constitution would preserve existing slave ownership in Kansas.

Walker's inaugural pledge raised a fierce opposition from southern radicals, who refused to accept the view that Kansas was destined to be free. But Pike, who understood what Walker and the administration were up to and who also believed Kansas was lost as a slave state, readily acquiesced in it. Calling himself a "Southern State Rights Democrat," Pike told southern Democrats in August of their mistaken view of Walker's policy. Because Walker had expressed a personal opinion that Kansas would probably be free and because he had warned the people there that Congress would reject any constitution not submitted to popular ratification did not make him at once a traitor to the South and a dictator to the people of Kansas. "He did not go to Kansas to make it a slave State, nor to make it a free State." He went to guarantee to the people the enjoyment of their rights; and when he found that a majority were in favor of making the territory a free state, that the law-abiding proslavery men had abandoned their efforts to establish slavery there, he proceeded with commendable devotion to his party to win the new state to the "faith and creed of Democracy" and thus to save it "from the despotic rule of Abolitionists and Black Republicans."

While he was engaged in this work southern editors and politicians had opened their vituperative assaults, undertaking thereby to dictate to the people of Kansas what institutions they should or should not have, instead of leaving them free to regulate their own affairs. This unwarranted attack, born of ignorance and fed on misunderstanding, had seriously embarrassed Walker and had, perhaps, driven many Kansas Democrats into the Republican ranks. Pike believed that he had presented the question in its true light, and he hoped that southern Democrats would cease warring on the administration policy in Kansas, that they would allow the legitimate residents of the territory to settle the question of slavery, and that henceforth they would cooperate in winning the new province to the Democracy.[15]

In December, 1857, the special referendum on the Lecompton constitution was held and the "constitution with slavery" was ratified. The election was, however, boycotted by free-state men, who early the following January held a separate balloting in which they overwhelmingly defeated the constitution. Hoping to get the Kansas question settled, and influenced by threats of secession from southern firebrands, Buchanan overrode Walker's plea of illegitimacy and sent in to Congress on February 2, the Lecompton constitution, declaring it just and legal and recommending that Kansas be admitted under it in order that the sectional trouble would be ended forever.

Douglas, father of the doctrine of popular sovereignty, the theory that the people of the territory had the right to decide at any time all questions of internal policy, revolted and led the northern wing of the Democratic Party in rebellion against the Lecompton constitution. Administration men and southern radicals, who held that neither the people of a territory nor the Congress could exclude slavery from a territory until the very moment that it was ready to become a state, opposed Douglas. Pike looked on in horror at the impending split in the great party, the last hope, he believed, for preserving the Union. Convinced that the Lecompton instrument was a fraud, he was delighted when Congress refused to admit Kansas under it and sent it back to the territory for a popular referendum. When the vote was taken in August 1858, his suspicions of fraud were borne out; the constitution was condemned by nearly a ten-to-one majority. "The Democratic party occupied," he said, "an untenable position from the beginning. Kansas was *always* lost to the South, and it was a great error not to see this at first." He hoped the "attempt to *force* a constitution on the people of Kansas" had not seriously weakened the party, though he was sure it had done considerable damage. The American people, with their "natural and inherent dislike of what is unfair," simply would not stand by, declared Pike, and see unfairness perpetuated; and to the "Democratic party, relying as it does on the instincts and impulsion of the people, fairness is not only its wisest, but an indispensable policy."[16]

The struggle over the Lecompton constitution in 1857–58 had done a great deal more damage to the Democratic Party than Pike realized. The break between Douglas and Buchanan was irreconcilable. In 1858 when Douglas ran against Lincoln for reelection to the Senate, Buchanan in defiance of the majority will of his party allowed administration forces to war on Douglas in what amounted to an alliance with Republicans to crush the Little Giant. Douglas was, however, strong enough to overcome these odds, but at the Freeport debate with Lincoln he had announced that the people of a territory could lawfully shut out slavery prior to statehood. This was anathema to southern extremists, who claimed that the Dred Scott decision of 1857 denied to the territorial governments as well as to Congress the power to prohibit slavery in a territory.

From this time on the rift in the Democratic ranks was final and catastrophic. Many predicted defeat for the party in 1860 and a consequent breakup of the Union. "Probably," Pike admitted in 1859, "it will be defeated at the next Presidential election; but those who imagine that such a defeat will destroy it, or be of vital injury to the South and disastrous to the Union, are simply mistaken." He thought that the party would be strengthened by the cathartic of defeat, that once in power the incongruous elements of the Republican organization would fall to pieces, and that the Democracy, reorganized and revitalized, would then rise triumphantly to power.[17] Even as he wrote, his words were being belied by events, for Buchanan was nursing his wrath and waiting to avenge himself on Douglas at the Democratic nominating convention in Charleston the next year. And at the same time southern firebrands were maturing a scheme to block Douglas's nomination or, failing that, to leave the Democratic Party and take the South out of the Union.

On April 23, 1860, the Charleston convention opened in an atmosphere of anger, suspicion, and name-calling. A determined group of southern radicals, led by William L. Yancey of Alabama and Robert B. Rhett of South Carolina, tried to force the party to accept their doctrine that it was the duty of Congress to protect slavery in the territories. But the Douglas men, who were in a majority, refused and adopted the Cincinnati platform of 1856 which merely provided for noninterference, or neutrality, on the question of slavery extension. Declaring this was in effect an endorsement of popular sovereignty, Yancey and Rhett bolted and were followed from the convention hall by enough southern delegates to prevent Douglas from being nominated under the two-thirds rule. The rump of the convention, unable to nominate a candidate, adjourned to meet in Baltimore on June 18; and the bolters, meanwhile holding a separate convention in Charleston, adjourned to reconvene in Richmond on June 11.

Efforts were made to patch up party differences in the interim but with Buchanan, who was pleased with Douglas's discomfiture, refusing to interfere in the quarrel, the attempts were all ineffective. The reassembled convention of Democrats at Baltimore saw the return of many seceders and a heated dispute over the seating of rival delegations that had been chosen since the Charleston fiasco. When the issue was decided in favor of the Douglas men, a new walkout of the seceders occurred, whereupon the remnant promptly nominated Douglas and Benjamin Fitzpatrick of Alabama. Conventions of southern bolters meeting separately at Baltimore and Richmond nominated John C. Breckinridge of Kentucky and Joseph Lane of Oregon on a platform calling for federal protection of slavery in the territories. Lincoln was already in the field for the Republicans, and John Bell of Tennessee, Constitutional Unionist candidate, rounded out the four-party campaign of 1860.

Pike had professed to be a neutral in national politics ever since his withdrawal from the American Party in 1856, but as we have seen, he had endorsed Democratic principles since that year and had moved closer and closer to the party. "I regard it today," he confessed in 1859, "as the party of the Union and the Constitution; and though I do not join it, it is because I am weary of politics and mean hereafter to lead a quiet life."[18] The smash-up of the Democratic Party in 1860 abruptly ended Pike's fanciful political existence, inducing him to renounce his neutrality and to assume an active role in the campaign that year. In July 1860, after his return from Washington, where he had been for six months, Pike received an invitation to address a Breckinridge-Lane rally at Pine Bluff on August 9. He reported that he could not attend the meeting but took advantage of the opportunity to announce his resumption of active participation in the political affairs of the country.

His reply was also a cogent argument on behalf of the states' rights theory of the Union and a legal review of the question of popular sovereignty. Briefly condensed, his argument, a refinement and independent commentary on the Calhoun compact theory, was that the Constitution was a compact made up by "the distinct people of *each* of the States"; that the government thus created was a corporation entitled "the United States"; that this corporation held "in law" the legal title to the territories; but that "in fact and for all beneficial purposes" the territories were the joint property of the states, "the corporators." Having established the nature of the general government, he then proceeded to examine the constitutional aspects of citizenship, popular sovereignty, and congressional power over slavery in the territories. He concluded that no person could be a citizen of the United States "except *by* being and *because he is*, a citizen of some one of the States"; that a citizen of a state removing to a territory remained a citizen of the state whence he came; that no territory, "a mere collection of citizens of the several States, living upon lands which are the common property of those States," possessed sovereignty or the power to legislate upon any topic with the exception of those powers specifically granted to its legislature by the states "assembled in Congress"; that it was the plain intent of the Supreme Court in the Dred Scott decision that neither Congress nor a territorial legislature could deny the right of a slaveholder to carry his slaves into a territory; and that it resulted from this that Congress was bound to "protect and enforce that right, *if necessary*, by proper legislation," and if it did not do so "it ought to abdicate."

But Pike refused to rest his case solely on the right of individuals to go to and remain in the territories with their slaves, for he pointed out that if the right was an individual one, there would be plausibility in the doctrine of popular sovereignty, since "majorities may sometimes dispose of individual rights for the general benefit." He rested his argument "on the rights of the States—the joint owners of the territory." He refused, accordingly, to agree that part of the states could "virtually appropriate the territory, to the exclusion of the others"; and he declared that it was not only absurd but most "insolent and impudent" for the people of a territory to attempt "to deny the right of fifteen of the joint owners of the territory" an opportunity to settle there with their slaves and to have a fair chance to make it a slave state. "There can," he protested, "be *non-intervention* by *Congress*, without *non-intervention* by the territorial legislature." Why, then, he demanded, would southern men continue to be blinded by their admiration of Douglas and not see the potential danger of his doctrine to the South? The only safe candidates for the South were Breckinridge and Lane, and "so I cannot choose but vote for them."[19]

Pike received an enthusiastic welcome into the ranks of the "constitutional party" by the editor of the *True Democrat*, who printed his Pine Bluff letter and praised it as "the great paper of the campaign."[20] "It is a masterly effort," declared the editor of the *Fort Smith Times*, who also printed it and proclaimed it the solemn duty of every man in Arkansas to read it. He who could not be convinced, by Pike's argument, of the evils to be entailed upon the South by Douglas's doctrine of "squatter sovereignty" was, asserted the editor, "unable to comprehend anything, or is too much prejudiced to listen to plain reason and good hard common sense."[21] The editor of the *Washington Telegraph*, former Whig, then American, but now Constitutional Union sheet, regretted that Pike "had crossed the Rubicon" and had joined "the ranks of those whose success we must believe would be fatal to the peace, if not the integrity of the country."[22] This was "a new tack," answered the editor of the *True Democrat*, who admitted that it had been mooted about that Lincoln's election would have fatal consequences for the peace and integrity of the Union but this, he said, was "the first time we have ever heard that the success of Breckinridge and Lane would endanger the peace."[23]

In spite of his southern-rights views and his support of Breckinridge, Pike was still devoted to the Union, though those who professed to be supporters of the national theory of the Union must have felt his views on the Union and the constitution were considerably strained. He made his position clear in his Pine Bluff letter by affirming that he was no tool of Yancey and that his future adherence to the southern Democratic Party depended upon its continued loyalty to the Union: "I will," he warned, "stand by them while they vindicate the Constitution.... If they assail that Constitution, or without ample cause march, shaking their spears, against the Union, there will be no obligation rest upon us to be their allies in that war."[24] He was not, however, opposed to the doctrine of secession, having professed his belief in the right as early as 1850 and reaffirmed it from time to time thereafter. In 1859 he had made a thorough examination of the controversial question and had concluded that a State has the right, for grave violations of the Constitution, to secede from the Union; but it is not possible to maintain, that when she decides to do so, the other States are barred and precluded to deny that right and by force prevent the exercise. As it is her right to decide whether she ought to and will secede, so it is theirs to judge for themselves also for her right, and to decide for themselves whether they will prevent it by force.[25]

It was inconsistent with Pike's views on constitutional law and politics to believe that Lincoln's election in November 1860 was ample cause for the secession of the southern states. He had foreseen as early as July the probability of a Republican victory and, so far from seeing any danger to the Union in such an event, had gloried in the salutary effects which a defeat would have in uniting the South upon a sectional party basis.[26] Arkansans in general, though they had voted for Breckinridge by a large majority, did not take Lincoln's election to mean all hope for the South within the Union had ended. Even Gov. Henry M. Rector, suspected of being a radical secessionist, counseled moderation in his inaugural address to the legislature on November 15 and alluded to the possibility of cooperation with "conventions assembled by the northern and southern portions of the Union" in an attempt to settle the sectional dispute over slavery. Rector thought, however, that if any one of the southern states left the Union and was coerced by the general government, Arkansas ought not to withhold her sympathy and active support from the seceded state.[27]

The legislature, predominantly conservative, proceeded in a leisurely way with routine work, paying little heed to the crisis that now threatened the Union. Not until December 11 did the house committee on federal relations respond to the governor's inaugural. The committee recommended a state convention to select delegates to a general southern convention that it proposed should meet at Memphis on the second Monday in February. The committee urged early action because "South Carolina will secede immediately, unless she can be induced to take counsel with her Southern sisters."[28]

Before the house acted on the proposed bill, Rector submitted on December 12 a special message. He had had a complete change of mind since his inauguration. The Union could "no longer be regarded as an existing fact," for the people of South Carolina, Georgia, Florida, Alabama, Mississippi, Louisiana, and Texas were firmly determined to leave it. Arkansas tended, he said, to side with the more conservative slave states, Maryland, Virginia, Kentucky, Tennessee, and Missouri, but it must recognize the inanity of such an unnatural position. The "status, the destiny, the fortunes, right or wrong, of the cotton states is [sic] her legacy"; therefore, he believed that she "must in ninety days, seek an alliance, as a necessity, with a confederacy of southern states." If consummated before Buchanan left office it might be done in peace, but the possibility of war should be considered. To meet the crisis he recommended that the legislature call a convention with full powers, pass measures of defense, prohibit the importation of slaves from the border states, and refrain from electing a U.S. senator to succeed Robert W. Johnson, who had declined to run again and whose term was to expire on March 4, 1861.[29]

Knowing that Rector spoke solely for the cotton-slave counties of the state, the conservative members of the house refused to be hurried by his secessionist appeal. They relegated his message to a routine place on the calendar, where it still was on December 20 when South Carolina seceded. Stirred by this news, they passed on December 22 a bill providing for a vote of the people upon the question of the advisability of holding a convention and for an election of delegates at the same time. The bill as reported from committee called for cooperation in a southern convention, but an amendment proposed from the floor and adopted immediately before the bill passed the house provided that the convention also should be empowered to "decide upon the course to be taken by this state in the present crisis."[30]

Pike had maintained a noticeable silence on the crisis to this point, but he was alarmed by the secession sentiment that had developed in the state following the action of South Carolina, and he feared the result if the upper chamber should impulsively pass the convention bill. The hall of the house of representatives was tendered to him on the evening of December 27, the day the bill was reported in the senate,[31] and he addressed the members of the legislature and a large audience of Little Rock citizens who crowded in to hear him. He thought Arkansas should exhaust every possible means of preserving the Union before availing herself of the extreme remedy of secession, and he earnestly besought the people and the legislature to put aside all ideas of hasty and ill-considered action, such as those that inspired them to follow South Carolina headlong out of the Union. The wisest policy for Arkansas was to cooperate with the border slave states, and he advised the legislature to elect delegates to a convention of those states, and of all other southern states that would participate, for the purpose of consulting together on the dilemma which had been forced upon them by South Carolina. Whatever course the general convention decided upon should be referred to the people of each state for ratification.[32]

Among conservatives who deplored South Carolina's rashness Pike's speech and recommendations were widely applauded.[33] But by the first week in January it was generally conceded that cooperation in a southern convention was hopeless.[34] The Gulf states had all called separate conventions in order to follow the example of South Carolina, and the governors of Alabama and Mississippi had each sent a commissioner to Little Rock to work for secession. Both men were tendered seats in the legislature and allowed to speak before it. Still the senate hesitated. The confused people of the state were flooding it with memorials expressing their numerous views on the crisis. Some denied the right of secession, some hoped for cooperation with the slave states in securing a redress of grievances, some looked to Congress for a compromise settlement, some advised waiting to see what Lincoln would do, and some demanded immediate and unconditional secession.[35]

Finally, on January 5 a majority of the senate committee on federal relations, ignoring the house bill before it, reported a bill calling for the election in April of delegates to meet in convention the first Monday in May. The minority dissented because the bill did not allow the people to vote for or against the convention. After a week of consideration in committee of the whole, a bill was reported which moved the election date back to February and the assembly date back to March. An entirely new bill was proposed from the floor and substituted on January 12 for the committee bill. It provided that the people should vote February 18 for "convention" or "no convention" as well as for delegates. This substitute measure passed the senate on January 13 and the house on January 14. The next day, after the senate had confirmed a minor amendment made by the house, Governor Rector signed the bill.[36]

When the campaign for the Arkansas convention began, Mississippi, Florida, and Alabama had already seceded, and by February 1, Georgia, Louisiana, and Texas were out. Arkansas was torn in sympathy between the border states and cotton states. The cotton counties of the southern and eastern portion of the state naturally felt drawn to the states of the cotton belt, while the upland counties of the north and west were in sentiment tied to the border states. Pike had been identified with the cotton counties in temperament, profession, and politics almost since his entry into Arkansas, and he did not turn from them now. Convinced that all hope of cooperation was gone and equally certain that all hope of Congress reaching a compromise was dead, he went over to the secessionists near the end of January.

To announce his decision he wrote and printed probably at Washington, where he had gone on Choctaw business, a stirring pamphlet entitled *State or Province? Bond or Free?* which he distributed in Arkansas as a secessionist campaign document.[37] It was another elaborate discourse on the Calhoun doctrine of states' rights and the final declaration of his belief in the right of secession. The time for resorting to that extreme remedy had arrived, he said, and if Arkansas and the border states acted promptly and joined the seceded states in forming a constitution and setting up a new government, there was a bare possibility of peace and perhaps a remote chance of reconstructing the Union. There would then be not just a half-dozen seceded states, but a "powerful confederacy, to attempt to coerce which would be simply fatuity." If the southern states adopted the old Constitution with no amendments but those that were absolutely essential for their protection and refrained from inserting therein any unfair or injurious thing to the northern states and if they established and set on foot a government under the Constitution thus amended and invited the other states to ratify it and unite with them under it, a restoration of the Union, a better Union, was possible. But the fourth of March was near at hand, and if Arkansas was then found in the Union she would be a party to whatever acts of aggression the North might commit against the seceded states. Arkansas, he asserted, was inexorably tied to the cotton states; "as well expect a limb severed from the human body to live" as to expect her to remain separate from them. Let Arkansas concur, therefore, in amending and adopting the Constitution and in

> establishing a Government for the Southern States. Let us arm and perfect our military organization. Let us invite the North again to unite with us, and offer them, if they decline, a treaty of amity and reciprocity, peace and the mutual benefits that flow from friendly intercourse. And having then done our duty, and provided for every emergency, we may tranquilly await the result, sure in any event that we shall not be dishonored.
>
> If war results from it, it will not be by our fault; but in consequence of Northern avarice reluctant to let those who have so long been its tributaries go free, and resolute to substitute another government for that which our forefathers made. And whatever their determination, if the present Union be not restored, and we are such men as have heretofore built up empires, we shall establish a new Republic, that shall outlast us and our children, and vying with its Northern Ally

or rival in arts and arms, surpassing the proudest glories of their common Ancestor, shall still prove to the world that the great experiment has *not* failed, and that men are capable of governing themselves.[38]

The secessionist tide which swept Pike from the ranks of the Unionists found less tractable minds among a majority of the Arkansas populace. Contrary to telegraphed warnings from Washington by Pike, Senators Johnson and Sebastian and Representatives Thomas Hindman and Albert Rust, Governor Rector in early February attempted and badly bungled a *coup de main* against the U.S. arsenal at Little Rock; his action threw pivotal Pulaski County into the Unionist ranks and damaged the disunionist movement throughout the state. In the face of overwhelming odds the peace-loving and much-respected Capt. James Totten was forced to withdraw his small garrison from Little Rock on February 8. He left amidst the plaudits of the ladies of the capital who presented him with a sword in gratitude of his "gallant and humane conduct" in saving the city from bloodshed. In the only public act of her life that has come to the writer's attention Mrs. Pike joined in this tribute to the departing officer.[39]

Though generally conservative and scornful of emotional appeals, the Union candidates were not without stirring arguments. They played upon the fears of the people by pointing out the dangers of Indian and abolitionist attacks from Indian Territory and Missouri if Arkansas left the Union. They warned the merchants of the Arkansas Valley, and especially those along the western border, that the profitable Indian trade would collapse if Arkansas seceded and the Indian tribes were left under the protection of the United States.[40] Governor Rector's failure to obtain from John Ross, able and crafty principal chief of the powerful Cherokee Nation, assurances of friendship and military aid in case Arkansas seceded, forestalled any adequate denial by the disunionists of the gravity of the border situation.[41] And some Unionists argued convincingly that Arkansas as the sole remaining cotton state would be in a position to gain a monopoly of the northern cotton market and thus "occupy one of the highest positions in the Union instead of becoming the weakest state in the Confederacy."[42]

Pike was still in Washington urging the appropriation for the drought-stricken Choctaws on February 18 when the people of Arkansas approved the convention. In choosing delegates to represent them, they elected a majority of Union men, who in the convention which assembled in Little Rock on March 4 blocked every attempt of the secessionists to carry Arkansas out of the Union. Finally, however, they agreed to a concession to the radicals by providing for a popular referendum on the issue of immediate secession or cooperation with the border slave states.[43] When Pike returned to Little Rock in early April, the convention had adjourned to await the outcome of the referendum on August 5. He had bought with him from Washington a supply of his pamphlet *State or Province?* to which he now added a twenty-one page appendix for distribution as an argument for immediate secession.[44]

While leaders of both sides were completing plans to canvass the state, Confederate forces fired on Fort Sumter and Lincoln called on Governor Rector to furnish Arkansas troops to aid in suppressing the rebellion. Rector immediately denounced the request as an insult and was applauded throughout the state. Convention president David Walker,

Washington County Unionist, waited a week in order to feel out the delegates on the new crisis, then called them to reassemble at Little Rock on May 6. One jubilant Arkansan predicted April 21 that the state would "go out 6th of May before breakfast."[45] It was actually ten minutes past four in the afternoon when the ordinance was passed by a loud sixty-five yeas to five nays, whereupon all but one of the negative votes, that of Isaac Murphy, staunch Unionist of Madison County, were changed at Walker's request.[46] Earlier in the morning Pike had had an unidentified delegate introduce for him the draft of a declaration of independence which he hoped the convention would adopt to express its belief in the justness of its revolutionary action and to arraign the northern states "*at the bar of the civilized world.*" He had the declaration withdrawn when someone tried to amend it but later published it by request of several delegates who thought he had ably expressed the causes that had compelled them to vote for secession.[47]

The ordinance of secession was formally signed by the delegates on May 7. Three days later the convention ratified the provisional constitution of the Confederacy and proceeded to elect delegates to the provisional congress of the Confederate States. Pike was nominated by Jesse N. Cypert of White County, but he received only five votes on the first ballot, which resulted in the election of Robert W. Johnson, Augustus H. Garland, and H. F. Thompson. Albert Rust and W. W. Watkins were elected on the second and third ballots to complete the five-man delegation. Thus Pike could still say he had never held a public office and was left free to accept an important mission the Confederate government had in mind for him.[48]

XXVI

Commissioner Pike Makes a Decision at North Fork Village

WITH ARKANSAS SAFELY in the Confederacy, Pike turned his attention to a problem that was of vital concern to the safety of his state. This was to secure Indian Territory for the Confederate States. By the end of the first week of May all the U.S. posts in the territory had been abandoned.[1] Pike believed these posts should be occupied by Confederate troops before Federal forces regarrisoned them, and he expressed his views freely to Robert Toombs, Confederate secretary of state, and to Robert W. Johnson, Arkansas delegate to the provisional congress. He told Johnson on May 11 that 3,500 troops could be raised to help defend Indian land against a Federal invasion if the Confederate government would guarantee them their lands, annuities, and the treaty rights which they then had with the United States and would arm and advance each recruit a bounty of twenty-five dollars. But white troops were absolutely essential to the safety of the territory and should be sent at once as visible evidence to the Indians "that they will be seconded by us."[2] Pike consulted Brig. Gen. N. Bart Pearce, responsible as commander of the first division of the Arkansas militia for the defense of the state's western frontier, and they agreed that no time should be lost if Indian cooperation was to be obtained and the work of Federal emissaries among the Indians forestalled.[3]

The provisional government of the Confederate States had made no determined effort to secure the Indian country and to obtain the military assistance of the Indians therein before Arkansas seceded. When on March 15, 1861, the provisional congress created a Bureau of Indian Affairs in the War Department, the Confederacy had no Indians to administer, though Secretary of State Toombs was trying in leisurely fashion to get some. A resolution proposed by Toombs and passed by the Congress on March 4, authorized President Davis to send a special agent to the Indian tribes west of Arkansas. Toombs, who was well aware of Pike's influence with the Creeks and Choctaws, recommended him for the position, and sometime in early May forwarded him a commission signed by Davis. Pike was to visit the Indian tribes, to assure them of the friendship of the Confederate States, and to induce them to join the Confederacy.[4]

Pike had implied to Johnson on May 11 that the job he half expected to get, but did not seek, was that of commander "of the department to be formed of the Indian country."[5] Toomb's civil appointment may, therefore, have come as something of a surprise to him. But Pike accepted the assignment, even though he was not sure what he was expected to do. Toombs did not specifically instruct him to negotiate treaties with the Indians. Pike was convinced that they could not be budged without formal negotiations. In replying to Toombs on May 20, he regretted that neither arms, money, supplies, nor authority to guarantee Indian treaty rights had not been sent. He urged that at least a thousand rifles and $60,000 be forwarded to him at once and that another thousand rifles and perhaps $40,000 more be sent "as soon as possible." The money to pay twenty-five dollars bounty for each Indian who enlisted would be "indispensable" to success in raising Indian troops for the defense of the Territory. "Provisions, commissary stores of all kinds, except flour, and medicines" were also necessary and should be shipped before the Arkansas River fell too low for steamboats to reach Fort Smith. Finally, Pike informed the secretary of state that since he had been directed to act at his discretion and since he had not been forbidden to give the Indians "formal, full, and ample" guarantees that the Confederacy would maintain their existing rights under treaties with the United States, he would give such guarantees if possible, by treaty. "It cannot be expected they will join us without them, and it would be very ungenerous, as well as unwise and useless, in me to ask them to do it."[6]

While the secretary of state was thus preparing to win the friendship and military assistance of the Indian tribes, secretary of war, Leroy P. Walker, in whose department the Bureau of Indian Affairs had been placed, was planning, quite independently of Toombs, to occupy Indian Territory and place its population under the military protection of the Confederacy. On May 13 he assigned Brig. Gen. Benjamin McCulloch, redoubtable Texas ranger, to the command "of the district embracing the Indian Territory lying west of Arkansas and south of Kansas." To defend the district against invasion from the north, McCulloch was to have two mounted regiments, one each from Texas and Arkansas, a regiment of foot soldiers from Louisiana, and two regiments of Indians if he could engage their services.[7] On May 14 Walker ordered commissioner of indian affairs David Hubbard, an Alabamian totally without Indian experience,[8] to proceed immediately to the territory. Hubbard should strive to bring the Indian country under the protection of the Confederate States. He should inform all the tribes that it was the intention of the Confederate government to defend them and their property from Federal invasion and abolitionist attacks, but he must not commit the Confederacy to any financial obligations to the Indians. No mention was made of making treaties; Walker apparently believed that Hubbard could secure Indian acquiescence in the protectorate without formal negotiations.[9]

Meanwhile the provisional congress, sitting in secret executive session, was pursuing yet another course in regard to the Indians. On May 17, three days after Walker outlined to Hubbard his comprehensive scheme for establishing a virtual protectorate over the Indian tribes, Congress passed an act, approved May 21, annexing Indian Territory to the Confederate States and placing all the Indian tribes within it under the protection of the Confederacy. The act authorized President Davis to take military possession of the territory and to issue commissions to all the U.S. officers therein who would take an oath in support of the Confederate constitution. It granted the Confederate government full power of trustee over all Indian funds invested by the United States in bonds of the states of the Confederacy. It conceded that Confederate control over the territory would be subject to the rights and privileges guaranteed to the Indians under U.S. treaties and statutes but stipulated that this concession would not commit the Confederate government to the expenditure of money for financial obligations contracted by the United States.[10] Pike may have been surprised on learning that McCulloch had been given the military assignment which he himself had probably hoped to receive, but he could not have been extremely disappointed at the War Department's action. He had told both Toombs and Johnson that he would accept the command but did not seek it, that he preferred "the selection of a regular officer of experience and rank," and that "above all" neither of them should "out of regard for me, in any way embarrass President Davis or the Secretary of War if other arrangements are thought of."[11] They apparently took Pike at his word. But from the circumstances it would appear that Pike was eminently pleased with the choice of McCulloch, who was highly respected in Arkansas and Texas for his daring exploits as a Texas ranger and for his great energy and enthusiasm.[12]

By the time McCulloch, en route to his new command, reached Little Rock, Pike had received from Toombs his instructions and appointment as commissioner of the Confederate States to the Indians west of Arkansas. Pike consulted McCulloch and received the Texan's hearty approval of the terms he intended to offer the Indians in return for their cooperation with the Confederacy. Pike trusted that Commissioner Hubbard, said to be on his way from Alabama to the Indian country, would also acquiesce to his plan.[13] Pike was, however, without funds and without an escort for the journey to the Indian country. Both were supplied on May 21 by the state convention which appointed Pike commissioner from Arkansas to Indian Territory, appropriated $500 toward his expense, and authorized the state military board to assign a company of Arkansas militia as his escort.[14] The Capital Guards, Pike's Mexican War company, now commanded by his good friend Capt. Gordon N. Peay of Little Rock, was ordered to accompany him. Pike was directed by the state convention, which furnished transportation, to convey a consignment of military stores from the arsenal at Little Rock to Fort Smith for the use of Brigadier General Pearce, defender of the frontier.[15]

With preparations as complete as he could make them, Pike took the steamer *Tahlequah* for Fort Smith on Thursday evening, May 23, 1861. Sandy Faulkner, W. Warren Johnson, and Pike's son, Walter Lacy, accompanied him as permanent members of the treaty party. General McCulloch, anxious to secure Pike's influence in enlisting the military aid of the Indians, also went with the party. They reached Fort Smith Saturday night.[16] With the state supplies off his hands Pike set about making final preparations for his expedition. He saw Elias Rector, late Superintendent of the Southern Superintendency, and Samuel M. Rutherford, U.S. agent for the Seminoles, both Arkansans, and each agreed to continue under the Confederate States, the discharge of his former duties. He also saw William Quesenbury, Arkansan, who had refused in April Lincoln's appointment to the Creek Agency, but who now agreed to accept the office from the Confederacy.[17] On May 26 Pike wrote Matthew Leeper, a Texan who was agent for the Wichitas and other Indians of the leased district in the far southwestern corner of the territory, requesting Leeper to continue in his place under the Confederacy and to persuade the Indian leaders under his jurisdiction to gather at Fort Washita to await the arrival of the treaty party. Desiring to allay any undue excitement or apprehension in relation to his mission, Pike directed Leeper to tell the Reserve Indians for him that the Confederate government would fulfill all obligations of the United States to them, would pay all reparations due them for injuries, and would continue to supply them with rations.[18] He asked Douglas H. Cooper to retain the Chickasaw and Choctaw Agency and hoped John Crawford, an Arkansan, whom he expected to see shortly, would continue as Cherokee agent. For incidental expenses he borrowed $300 from Charles B. Johnson, Fort Smith merchant and Indian contractor, giving in return a draft on the commissioner of Indian affairs. He also instructed Johnson to continue furnishing rations to the Reserve Indians under that merchant's contract with the United States, which would expire June 30, 1861. General McCulloch having procured transportation for him, he was ready by May 29 to leave Fort Smith on his assigned mission.[19]

On the morning of his departure, Pike reported to Toombs. He had, he said, no official information that the Bureau of Indian Affairs was not a part of the State Department and did not address the commissioner of Indian affairs because he understood that officer was on his way to Fort Smith. In case of mistake he asked Toombs to forward his letter to the proper department. He reiterated the immediate necessity of sending rifles before the Arkansas fell any lower. "Not one in ten of either of the tribes" had a firearm, and these were generally double-barreled shotguns. To raise Indian troops and "keep them long without arms would disgust them, and they would scatter over the country like partridges, and never be got together again." No funds had been remitted to him, and he had no authority to draw any for the expenses of the councils he would have to hold and which the Indians always expected in their talks with whites. He had borrowed $300 from Johnson for incidentals and received $500 from the state of Arkansas, but at least $1,000 more, to meet contingent expenses, should be placed at Fort Smith subject to draft. "And, as I have several times urged, money should be placed in the proper hands to pay a bounty to each Indian that enlists." He requested that his action in regard to the employment of Rector and the agents be confirmed. "If we have declared a protectorate over these tribes and extended our laws over them we have, I suppose, continued in force there the whole system. Even if we have not we cannot dispense with the superintendent and agents." To allow their places to become vacant or to make changes at the present would throw the Indians into confusion and make much mischief for the Confederacy. He wished, he said in closing, that he

> had more definite instructions and power more distinctly expressed, especially power in so many words to make treaties and give all necessary guarantees. For without giving them nothing can be done, and I am [not] sure that John Ross will be satisfied with my statement or assurance that I have the power, or with anything less than a formal authority from Congress. He is very shrewd. If I fail with him it will not be my fault.[20]

As his statement implied Pike's first destination was Park Hill, the residence of John Ross, principal chief of the Cherokees. He had particularly strong reasons for giving priority on his itinerary to the Cherokee Nation. Not only was it the most powerful tribe in the territory, not only did it lie directly opposite the Arkansas line north of Fort Smith, but it was also divided between southern and northern sympathizers and in danger of civil strife. As Pike pointed out in his report to Toombs on May 29, there had since 1835

> always been two parties in the Cherokee Nation bitterly hostile to each other. The treaty of that year was made by unauthorized persons, against the will of the large majority of the nation and against that of the chief, Mr. Ross. Several years ago [John] Ridge, [Elias] Boudinot, and others, principal men of the treaty party, were killed, with, it was alleged, the sanction of Mr. Ross, and the feud is to-day as it was twenty years ago. The full-blooded Indians are mostly adherents of Ross, and many of them—1,000 to 1,500 it is alleged—are on the side of the North. I think that number is exaggerated. The half-breeds or white Indians (as they call themselves) are to a man with us. It has all along been supposed, or at least suspected, that Mr. Ross would side with the North. His declarations, are in favor of neutrality. But I am inclined to believe that he is acting upon the policy (surely a wise one) of not permitting his people to commit themselves until he has formal guarantees from an authorized agent of the Confederate States. These I shall give him if he will accept them. General McCulloch will be with me, and I strongly hope that we shall satisfy him, and effect a formal and firm treaty.[21]

In case he could not convince Ross to negotiate, Pike was seriously considering the possibility of treating separately with Elias Boudinot, and Stand Watie, leaders of the minority, anti-Ross party. In fact a delegation representing Watie and Boudinot visited Pike and McCulloch at Fort Smith and asked point-blank if the Confederacy would protect them from the Rossites if they organized and took up arms for the South. They assured the delegation it would, and Pike dispatched letters to the leaders of the hostile group asking them to meet him at the Creek Agency two days after he was to talk with Ross.[22]

Incessant rain and high water hindered Pike in getting to Park Hill. It was June 4 before he got across the Illinois River, a tributary of the Arkansas lying immediately east of Park Hill. His arrival at Ross's residence without an escort and apparently with only a single companion, Col. Mark Bean of Boonsborough, Arkansas, deflated a rumor spread among the Cherokees that he was advancing with 2,000 men upon Tahlequah, Cherokee capital, located a few miles north of Park Hill, for the purpose of making Chief Ross a prisoner if he refused to join the Confederacy.[23] On June 5 Pike and McCulloch, who had gone in advance to the Cherokee Nation to look for a suitable location for a permanent post for his command,[24] interviewed Ross. They were told in polite but no uncertain terms that it was still his intention "to maintain the neutrality of his people" and that he would neither enter into a treaty with the Confederate States nor allow either Union of Confederate troops to occupy his country. Ross did agree, nevertheless, to call his executive council together later in the summer and confer with them on the terms which Pike offered. McCulloch informed Ross that he would respect neutrality of the Cherokees and would not send troops into the nation unless it became imperative in order to protect it from Federal invasion.[25] The conference over, Pike and McCulloch separated, Pike going on to the Creek Nation and McCulloch returning to Fort Smith.[26]

Accompanied by his mounted escort, which came up with him at Park Hill, Pike left Tahlequah on June 6. He took the military road west to Fort Gibson, crossed the Arkansas below the mouth of Grand River, and continued westward along the south bank of the Arkansas to the Creek Agency, which he reached sometime before June 12. His men and horses were greatly troubled on the march by swarms of flies which brought blood from the animals and threatened as one man reported, to consume both riders and horses.[27]

Pike had anticipated no trouble in dealing with the Creeks, but once among them he discovered that they were as badly divided as the Cherokees.[28] The Upper and Lower Creeks were nominally united in the Creek Nation under a common principal chief and national council and administered to by a single U.S. agency. In reality they were strongly divided by an old feud precipitated when leaders of the Upper Creeks assassinated William McIntosh of the Lower Creeks for negotiating the fraudulent treaty of Indian Springs in 1825. Now that the North and the South had gone to war, the ancient enmity between the Upper and Lower Creeks threatened to flare into open warfare. Fortunately for Pike's cause both Principal Chief Moty Kinnaird, who was also first chief of the Lower Creeks, and Icho Hacho, first chief of the Upper Creeks, were slaveholders and men with southern leanings. A large segment of the Upper Creeks were, however, opposed to an alliance with the South. They had an able leader and spokesman in Opoth le Yahola, reputedly one of the assassins of William McIntosh.[29]

When Pike reached the Creek Agency, he learned that Opoth le Yahola, whom he had good cause to remember since the Creek payment of 1858, had, acting at the suggestion of John Ross, sent delegates to meet representatives of the Cherokee, Kickapoo, Delaware, Seminole, Caddo, Anadarko, Ione, Wichita, Kichai, Comanche, Tonkawa, and Tawakoni tribes at the Antelope Hills in the leased district.[30] This council, an effort of Ross and Opoth le Yahola to form a great Indian confederation for the purpose of maintaining their neutrality and independence, met June 22–24 and made a general declaration of neutrality.[31] Anticipating the outcome of the convention, Pike was determined to forestall Ross's and Opoth le Yahola's action by treating with the friendly Creeks. Pike undoubtedly learned from William H. Garrett of Alabama, the Creek agent,[32] that both Moty Kinnaird and Icho Hacho were dissatisfied because the U.S. Indian Office had suspended payment of all Indian allowances and because the two chiefs themselves in a mission to Washington in the winter of 1860–61 had failed to secure adequate guarantees from the United States that Creek integrity would be maintained if war came between the North and South. In fact at the very time Pike entered the Creek Nation, the Creek leaders were anxiously awaiting the return of a delegation sent to Montgomery for the purpose of obtaining assurances that Creek trust funds invested by the United States in securities of the several southern states would not be canceled.[33]

Though Pike was still without definite instructions from the Confederate States to treat with the Indians, he knew that no time should be lost if he was to take advantage of the propitious circumstances which he found among the Creeks. He sent word, therefore, to their chiefs and headmen to meet him at North Fork Village, principal town of the Upper Creek settlement. He also dispatched messengers to the leaders of the Choctaws and Chickasaws, whom he had planned to meet at Fort Washita, requesting them to come to North Fork Village in order to expedite negotiations.[34] With these preliminaries out of the way he waited at the agency a few days expecting the leaders of the disaffected Cherokees to appear. But on learning that they were afraid of being murdered by pro-Rossites if they treated with him, Pike left for the rendezvous with the Creek chiefs. Before leaving he sent his escort back to Fort Smith.[35]

North Fork Village was situated some twenty-five miles southeast of the Creek Agency in a heavily wooded area between the North and South Forks of the Canadian River. Pike reached there in the latter part of June. Soon afterward he received communications containing a copy of the Confederate act of May 21 for the protection of the Indian tribes and instructions of the secretary of war for conferring with the Indians. Neither the act nor the secretary of war granted authority to make treaties, while both positively forbade him to incur in the name of the Confederate States any financial obligations to the Indians. The secretary of war would have him tell the Indians of the Five Civilized Tribes that it was the intention of the Confederacy to advance them toward a system of "holding lands in severalty under well-defined laws, by forming them into a Territorial government," but with no promise of statehood or independence.[36]

Only abysmal ignorance of Indian affairs could have prompted such advice. The Indians feared and opposed above all else territorial organization and distribution of their lands in allotments among the individual tribesmen. A similar proposal by the United States in 1860 not only had been flatly refused but had created lingering mistrust among the Indians.[37] The prohibitions against incurring financial obligations was equally absurd. Pike's trump card in negotiating with the Cherokees, Creeks, Choctaws, Chickasaws, and Seminoles was adequate financial guarantees. Without it his hands would be tied. He also believed the Indians would support the Confederacy in a war against the United States only if the Confederacy would guarantee their political and civil rights under treaties with the United States, and he perceived that the Indians were too shrewd to accept these guarantees unless they were set down in new treaties.

Since Pike had no intention of risking his or the Confederacy's reputation by presenting to the Five Civilized Tribes the ill-advised terms outlined in the communications, two courses remained open to him. He could send dispatches to Richmond explaining the recent developments in the territory and asking for full authority to make treaties granting the Indians adequate financial, political, and civil guarantees in return for military cooperation, or he could disregard the instructions already at hand. If he waited for further instructions he would run the risk of complete failure. Ross's and Opoth le Yahola's council was then in session at the Antelope Hills, and their plans for forming an independent Indian confederation were well underway. Pike decided, therefore, to disregard his instructions and to assume the responsibility of negotiating treaties.[38]

XXVII

Winning the Confederacy's Indian Allies

PIKE CARRIED THE NEGOTIATIONS at North Fork Village without difficulty. There was hardly a white man in the whole Indian country who dared speak for the United States, and with Opoth le Yahola's leading supporters away attending the Antelope Hills conference, there appears to have been little, if any, opposition among the Creeks to the liberal terms that Pike offered them.[1] No one seems to have suspected that he had no authority to make treaties. The final draft was formally signed July 10 by Pike, commissioner of the Confederate States to the Indians west of Arkansas; Motey Kinnaird, principal chief; Icho Hacho, first chief of the Upper Creeks; a host of other less prominent town chiefs; and the members of Pike's party.

The treaty provided for perpetual peace and friendship between the Creeks and the Confederacy and established an offensive and defensive alliance between the two parties. In return for becoming a protectorate and an annex of the Confederate States and for raising in conjunction with the Seminole Nation a mounted regiment for Confederate service, the Creeks were conceded a perpetual right to hold their tribal lands in common and a guarantee that all money due them under laws, treaties, and trust funds of the United States would be paid by the Confederate States. The Creek troops would be armed and paid by the Confederacy, and they could not be moved out of Indian Territory without their consent—a significant restriction as it turned out. There were besides these major points notable minor concessions to the tribe in the form of enlarged civil, political, and judicial rights. Among the most prominent innovations under this classification were those bestowing upon the Creek Nation the rights to determine the conditions of tribal citizenship, to expel white intruders from their lands, to control their own trade, to sue, plead, and be held as competent witnesses in state courts, to subpoena witnesses and to employ counsel if brought before a state court, and to send conjointly with the Seminole Nation to the Confederate House of Representatives a delegate who would "claim their rights and secure their interests without the intervention of counsel or agents." The institution of slavery was, of course, recognized as legal, property rights in slaves were guaranteed, and mutual rendition of fugitives, slaves or freemen, between the Creek Nation and the states of the Confederacy was provided for. And as a general rule, all former laws and treaty rights of the United States not specifically annulled by the Pike treaty were continued in force under the Confederate States. For instance, the Confederacy assumed the right of eminent domain, readopted the agency system, and reinserted the usual clauses promising agricultural and industrial assistance.[2]

Two days after the Creek treaty was finished a joint treaty with the Choctaws and Chickasaws was completed and signed. From the beginning of the secession movement these two slaveholding tribes had indicated that their fortunes lay with the South. On February 6, 1861, the Choctaw National Council, meeting in special session, instructed its net proceeds delegation at Washington to consult with the U.S. Treasury concerning the safety of their trust funds, authorizing the delegation to withdraw and to redeposit the funds in southern banks if necessary.[3] The council issued next day a message to the governors of the southern states, announcing that should the regrettable controversy between the North and South end in permanent dissolution the Choctaw people would be released from their connection with the United States and left free to effect a union with the southern states, to whom they were indissolubly tied by "natural affections, education, institutions and interests."[4]

After the abandonment of Indian Territory by U.S. forces, the defection to the Confederacy of their respected and trusted agent, Douglas H. Cooper, and the suspension of Indian allowances by the Office of Indian Affairs, secession sentiment rapidly crystallized among the Choctaws.[5] George Hudson, principal chief, and P. P. Pitchlynn, head of the net proceeds delegation, may still have been for neutrality as late as June 1861, but they were in a hopeless minority.[6] Assured by Pike in May that he would soon be among them with full powers from the Confederacy to guarantee their national finances and perpetual right to hold their land in common,[7] the leaders of the Choctaw National Council proceeded to prepare for his arrival. At a special session which assembled at Doaksville the council on June 20 declared, the nation independent of the United States, appointed commissioners to make a treaty of alliance with Pike, and authorized Chief Hudson to organize at once seven companies of mounted men to serve in the First Regiment of Choctaw and Chickasaw Riflemen under Col. Douglas H. Cooper, Provisional Army of the Confederate States.[8]

The legislature of the Chickasaw Nation had meanwhile met at Tishomingo and had on May 25 adopted resolutions announcing that the Union no longer existed, indicting the dangerous pretensions of the Lincoln government, declaring the Chickasaws independent of all foreign government, and expressing an "abiding confidence" that all their tribal and individual rights formerly secured by treaties with the United States would be guaranteed by the Confederate States. Geographically, institutionally, and socially attached to the people of the Confederate States, the Chickasaws were, declared the resolutions, free to ally themselves politically with the Confederacy.[9]

Thus Pike's request that Choctaw and Chickasaw commissioners meet him at North Fork Village fell on willing ears. His intimate acquaintance with the history, leaders, and affairs of these two tribes must have made his talks with their delegations especially pleasant. The joint treaty of alliance and friendship. formally signed July 12, not only awarded them terms almost identical with those granted the Creeks, but also made two important concessions in which Pike departed radically from his instructions. First, the treaty conceded the right and outlined the method by which the Choctaw and Chickasaw Nations could become a state in the Confederacy, and second, it freed the Choctaws and Chickasaws from the injustices connected with their dependence on the former federal court at Fort Smith by conceding that a Confederate States court would be established at Boggy Depot, Choctaw Nation, a small settlement on the Clear Boggy near the Chickasaw line. Long familiar with the expense, delays, and unfair treatment of Indians at the Van Buren court, where only white juries sat, Pike considered this a reform well overdue. All cases involving violations of treaty rights and Confederate criminal and civil law would be tried in the Indian court and, of course, before juries of the vicinage. As in the case of the Creeks, all the annuities, trust funds, debts, and claims of the two nations against the United States and the states of the Confederacy were guaranteed. While there was no specific mention of the Choctaw net proceeds claim, it was obvious to both Pike and his clients that it came within the meaning of the treaty.[10]

With the work at North Fork Village completed Pike, left immediately for the Seminole country to confer with the Seminole National Council. He hoped also to treat with the Indian leaders of the leased district, whom he had invited to meet with him at the Seminole Agency on July 22. Because Superintendent Rector had supervised the settlement of the Reserve Indians in the leased district and understood their problems, Pike wanted Rector present for the negotiations with them. On July 5 he requested Rector to be at the Seminole Agency by July 22 if possible and to be prepared in case the Indians should not appear, to accompany Pike's party to the leased district. In a second letter the same day, Pike directed Rector to make a new contract with Charles B. Johnson for feeding the Reserve Indians or to renew the old one (it had expired June 30) if no better terms could be obtained.[11] Pike thought on July 5 that he would be ready to leave North Fork Village on July 10, but it was the twelfth before the Choctaw and Chickasaw treaty was finished. Once underway Pike led his small party without escort southwestward down the military road to Fort Washita, thence up the Washita River road to Fort Arbuckle. There they turned northward across the prairie to the Seminole Agency, located on the north bank of the Canadian ten miles above the site of old Fort Arbuckle. En route Pike and his companions camped in the open prairie, "displaying the Confederate flag."[12]

The Seminoles, who numbered less than twenty-three hundred people in 1861,[13] were, like the Creeks, Choctaws, and Chickasaws, a slaveholding tribe. They had been a part of the Creek Nation until 1856, when they were given an independent government and territory. But they were in 1861 still highly responsive to Creek leadership, and they reflected, accordingly, the divided sentiment of the Creeks in regard to a Confederate alliance. When Pike reached the Seminole Agency he discovered that those Seminole chiefs who had attended or been represented at the Ross–Opoth le Yahola conference at the Antelope Hills in June favored neutrality. Moreover, they had probably 50 to 75 percent of the tribe behind them.[14] The atmosphere now took on an ugly aspect. Rumors were drifting up from the Creek Nation that Opoth le Yahola and other nontreating leaders of the Upper Creeks would not accept the Pike treaty. They had called a convention of the disaffected portion of the tribe for August 5 to decide the issue, and there appeared to be little doubt that the convention would reject the treaty. Would civil strife result? The same indefinable system of communication, "the grapevine," by which news was carried in Indian Territory, had also brought and spread reports that Col. J. H. Lane, Kansas jayhawker, was raising a brigade to invade the territory and drive out all secessionist sympathizers. What would Ross and Opoth le Yahola do if Lane came? Would they throw off the mask of neutrality and proclaim their allegiance to the Union?

All these questions must have been in Pike's mind as he viewed the unfavorable state of affairs among the Seminoles. Fortunately, he was prepared to make the most of a bad situation. Besides his permanent staff of Quesenbury, Faulkner, Johnson, and Walter Lacy Pike, he had at the Seminole council the able and influential assistance of Superintendent Rector; Samuel M. Rutherford, the Seminole agent, Charles B. Johnson, a popular Indian merchant who had come with Rector from Fort Smith; James M. G. Smith, interpreter, a resident of the Creek Nation; and Moty Kinnaird and Chilly McIntosh, principal chief and war captain, respectively, of the Creeks. But even with this array of talent aiding him, it took until August 1 to induce John Jumper, principal chief of the Seminoles, and twelve of his town chiefs, headed by Pas-co-fa and George Cloud, who represented approximately half of the people, to sign a treaty. Billy Bowlegs, who had removed from Florida with his hostile band in 1859, and a dozen other town chiefs chose to remain neutral.[15]

By the treaty the Seminoles did not become outright allies of the Confederate States, though they virtually accepted such a status by agreeing to raise two to five mounted companies for Confederate service under the usual proviso against being taken out of Indian Territory without their consent. In all other respects the nationality of the Seminoles was recognized as in every sense equal to that of the Creeks, Choctaws, and Chickasaws, and they were conceded the same liberal terms that had been given the Creeks. Yet, as in the case of the Creeks, the Seminoles were not granted a separate Confederate States court.[16]

Pike dispatched other important work at the Seminole Agency. Affairs in the Creek Nation needed to be watched. To do this he authorized James M. C. Smith, his interpreter at the Seminole council to raise and command a company of friendly Creeks to be stationed at North Fork Village. Smith was ordered to guard the Canadian River ford on the great Missouri-Texas road and "act as a police force, watch and apprehend disaffected persons, intercept improper communications, and prevent the driving of cattle to Kansas."[17] On July 31 Pike advised Secretary of War Walker of the enlistment of his Indian escort and offered advice on the military situation in the territory. Eight companies of the Creek regiment had been reported organized, but he had received complete rolls for only three. These he had accepted and forwarded to General McCulloch to be mustered into Confederate service. He recommended that an additional battalion be raised among the Creeks, that the battalion offered by the Seminoles be received, and that Colonel Cooper's Choctaw and Chickasaw regiment, which Cooper had reported organized, be armed and mustered in immediately. If Colonel Lane invaded the country with his jayhawkers these Indian troops would "be a force not to be despised" and were especially needed in view of dangerous "condition of the Cherokee country."[18]

It was August and the leaders of the Reserve Indians still had not reached the Seminole Agency. With misgivings Pike prepared to go to the leased district in an attempt to persuade them to meet with him. It would be a dangerous mission. Many of the bands settled on the reserve were semiwild and the Comanches of the Great Plains, whom Pike hoped to persuade to come in and settle on reservations, were not only wild, but also were carrying on intermittent warfare with their white enemies in Texas. To protect his small party and to enable him to present a show of force, Pike organized a company of mounted Creeks and Seminoles for escort. The organization was commanded by Chilly McIntosh and John Jumper. He also took Moty Kinnaird, Rector, and Charles B. Johnson with his party, and a trusted friend, Jesse Chisholm, half-Cherokee and half-Choctaw, who had traded among the Reserve Indians and the wild tribes of the Great Plains and knew their various tongues.[19]

Soon after the first of August Pike left the Seminole country. His destination in the Leased District was the Wichita Agency, Leeper's headquarters, situated just south of the Wichita Mountains. Lying sixty miles west of Fort Arbuckle and thirty miles south of Fort Cobb the agency occupied the heart of the leased district and commanded the passes through the Wichitas and the military road along the north fork of Red River to the southwest. Pike had sent dispatches ahead to Leeper to do everything possible to collect the reserve leaders at the agency house, but he must have doubted that Leeper would be successful.[20] He was in for a pleasant surprise. Waiting for him at the Texan's headquarters were not only the reserve chiefs but also chiefs of four bands of wild Comanches, among them the celebrated war leader, Buffalo Hump, a fugitive from the Texas agency which Leeper had formerly held.[21]

The council with the chiefs and braves of the wild Comanches, Pike thought particularly impressive. Informed that Pike was ready to open the first session,

> they approached in state, marching in single file, with due regard to precedence, having among them a corpulent and brawny warrior who was the jester of the band. When within twenty feet of the arbor under which were the seats for the council, they halted and formed a semicircle, and I (the Commissioner or Big Captain [)] followed by the Superintendent, the agent for the Reserve Indians, and others, advanced in single file to where they stood. Each ... shook hands with each. ... Then the chief that had precedence [Qui-na-hi-wi] folded me in his arms, with a hug like that of a bear, which I returned after the same fashion. Each Comanche seemed to endeavor to force from each of us some ejaculation of discomfort ... and the jester succeeded with Major Rector, the Superintendent, who said afterwards it was like being squeezed in a cotton-press. Then the fellow challenged me, and I found the Major's simile just; but being myself pretty strong, and heavier than the jester, I returned his hug with interest, which avenged the Major by forcing the Indian to explode with a vehement grunt, welcomed by the universal laughter and jeers of his fellows.[22]

With the introductions completed, the Comanches were seated. Pike then made his talk. He explained to them "the nature of the war between the States" and told them it was the desire of the Confederate States that they should not take up arms in the conflict. The Confederacy wished only that all the Comanches would come in and settle on reservations in the leased district. It would feed and supply them with cattle and other useful presents and grant them the right to hunt anywhere north of Red River. Texas was one of the Confederate States; the Comanches must cease all depredations into it. Pike pronounced these terms a sentence at a time in short, plain statements. At the end of each sentence a half-dozen interpreters, all talking at once, repeated it in the different dialects of bands. Half the talk had been so repeated when Pike "noticed two or three young men of the Comanches laughing and chuckling from time to time." He was relieved of a feeling of vexation at their apparent discourtesy when he found that an old Indian "near them had fallen asleep, and they were amusing themselves by pricking him into wakefulness by sharp-pointed thorns. They are merry fellows enough, among themselves, and fond of rough practical jokes."

At the end of the talk, Pike had beeves given to the Comanches and directed the interpreters to reread each of the bands the proposed treaties. The wording of the treaties would, he told the Comanches, be so plain that they would, having but one tongue, "speak the same thing always." Among other things the treaties provided that it would be in the future "disgraceful to steal horses."

The day after Pike's talk, the wild Comanches gathered at the council place to hear talks by the Creek chiefs. Among the Comanches was an old emaciated man, evidently intelligent, with a thin, keen face. His nakedness was hidden apparently by only a worn and dirty blanket. "He had been a great chief, but becoming too old to lead his people on the war-path, he had been, according to their custom, deposed." Seating himself on a buffalo robe spread on the ground, the ex-chief listened attentively to the Creek chiefs, who advised the Comanches to settle on reservations, relating the experience of the Creek Nation in leading a settled life and especially calling to the attention of the Comanches the facts that the Creek chief had been driven to the leased district in his own four-in-hand coach and that Pike's "well-armed and well-clothed escort of sixty-four men were Creeks and Seminoles."

When the Creek chiefs had finished the ex-chief of the Comanches, still sitting upon his buffalo robe, began to speak to the chiefs and braves of his tribe, who were seated upon benches at each side of the council place:

> He used no gestures and spoke about twenty minutes, earnestly, almost vehemently at times, the language sounding wonderfully like Spanish. I did not understand a word, but I never in all my life heard a speech more fluently and impressively delivered, more musically, with better emphasis and more perfect intonation. At times there was a singular pathetic sadness in his voice; and in a sentence or two the words rang out like the tones of a trumpet. He spoke of me, and of Kekarewa, as his glances toward us showed, and I thought he was advising the rejection of the treaty, accusing me of meaning them harm, and denouncing Kekarewa for having abandoned the nomad life . . . [for life] in a house.[23]

But Pike was mistaken. The ex-chief was "advising his people to come in and settle," telling them to trust in Pike, and pointing out to them that Kekarewa "had tried the experiment and had found it good." The old man's eloquence carried the negotiations; next day, August 12, the treaty was signed. On the same day Pike signed a treaty with the Reserve Indians, obtaining their promise to live in peace and friendship with the people of the Confederacy in return for Confederate rations and gifts. To encourage the cultivation of their lands both the Reserve Indians and the wild Comanches were promised agricultural and industrial assistance, and the prohibition against horse stealing applied to both groups of Indians.[24]

Discussion of the "horse stealing" clause in the Comanche treaty brought up a quarrel that almost disrupted the peace council. Some of the Seminoles of Pike's escort had discovered that part of the wild Comanches had ridden to the agency on mounts stolen from them two years before. They now demanded restoration of their property. Considering possession ten-tenths of the law the Comanches refused. Bloodshed threatened, but Pike with the help of Rector, Chisholm, and Moty Kinnaird worked out a peaceful settlement. He got the horses returned to their Seminole owners by agreeing that the Confederate government would compensate the Comanches for them and, to prevent future trouble, agreed that thereafter the Confederacy would pay for all horses stolen from Comanches within the limits of the Confederate States, meaning the leased district. In the same agreement Pike promised compensation to all Seminoles who could not find their horses among those at the agency. That neither the Reserve Indians nor the wild Comanches might attach the wrong meaning to this settlement and take advantage of its liberal terms, Pike made it clear in the treaty that stealing was dishonorable practice and would never again constitute lawful title of possession nor enable a thief to claim compensation for surrendering stolen property.[25]

After the treaties were signed Pike's party, accompanied by the Seminole and Creek escort and the Comanche chiefs, set out to examine the country north of the Wichitas for the purpose of selecting reservations for the wild Comanches, who were to come in during the fall and settle. Pike led the party around the east end of the mountains and westward along their northern slope to the north fork of the Red River, where they camped in the bottom and spent several enjoyable days hunting buffalo on the prairies near the stream. While engaged in the sport one day Pike drank some gypseous water from a small creek. Within a moment he became deathly sick. Too weak either to ride horseback or to sit up, he was carried in an ambulance to the Wichita Agency, where under the "womanly care" of Jesse Chisholm and Tosawi, a chief of the Comanches, he soon recovered. He was afterward fond of relating a story in connection with his illness. To make the six-day trip back to the agency his companions had hired from Tosawi's men three ponies at two dollars a day each. When it came time to settle with them, Pike learned an amusing lesson on the mental processes of the Comanches. He sent for Tosawi and the owners of the horses, who came accompanied by several other braves, as was their custom. After the usual silent smoke Pike

> said to Chisholm, "three ponies at two dollars each a day is six dollars a day, and I have had them six. Here are thirty-six gold dollars. Pay them." Then he talked to them, and they to him, until I was weary, and as he still held the money, I asked why he did not give it to them and let them go. "O," he said, "they don't know whether it is right, and they want to figure it out." "Figure it out!" I said, "what figuring does it need?," and I repeated the calculation. "O yes, I know," he said, "but they don't. They can't count anything up in their heads." So they talked again, and then Jess[e] pulled up some blades of grass, divided and subdivided them, and put them in little piles, and then together in a less number, for more

than five minutes; and finally tossed them away, saying, "They say yes, it's all right;" and handed them the money.[26]

As soon as Pike recovered from his illness, he left for the east. He delegated to Leeper the unaccomplished task of locating reservations for the Comanches and instructed him to send word to the nontreating bands of wild Comanches and to the Kiowas to meet him at the Wichita Agency "at the falling of the leaves," when he would return with gifts and goods for all his red friends of the leased district and the Great Plains. Leeper wanted Confederate troops stationed at the agency to defend it against hostile Indians and to aid in enforcing regulations and keeping order among his own wards. Pike had no troops and no authority to order any sent there, though he promised Leeper that he would try to secure a white garrison for the place as soon as possible. In the meantime Pike arranged with H. P. Jones, a white employee at the agency, to enlist and command, as lieutenant, thirty Indians. Jones's force would protect the government men and their families from raids and act as a "spy company" among the hostile Comanches and Kiowas and warn Leeper of any impending danger.[27]

It must have been the middle of September before Pike reached Fort Arbuckle on the return trip from the Wichita Agency. There he received a messenger from John Ross bearing resolutions of a mass meeting of the Cherokee people of August 21 and a request from Ross to repair at once to the Cherokee Nation and make a treaty with him.[28] What caused this sudden change in Ross? Several factors entered into it. In keeping with his promise to Pike on June 5, Ross had called his executive council together in the last days of June. They gave him a rousing vote of confidence in his policy of neutrality.[29] Ross advised Pike of this, and at the same time sent him copies of letters to Hubbard and McCulloch in which he refused to budge from his settled course of strict neutrality.[30]

But neither Pike nor McCulloch allowed Ross to rest in peace. Pike had forestalled his plans for a neutral Indian confederation by drawing all the neighbors of the Cherokees into alliance with the Confederate States, and McCulloch had surrounded the Cherokee Nation with Confederate white and Indian troops in order to "force the conviction on the Cherokees that they have but one course to pursue—that is, to join the Confederacy."[31] Added to Ross's uneasiness over this unfavorable external situation was serious apprehension over internal matters. He was faced with bitter criticism by the Watie-Boudinot faction, which grew louder and louder in denunciation of his administration, as outside pressure for a Confederate alliance increased. To check the opposition Ross decided that he needed a vote of confidence from the nation; consequently, his executive council met August 1 and arranged for a mass meeting of the Cherokee people at Tahlequah on August 20.[32]

On the same day that Ross's council issued the call for the Cherokees mass meeting, Pike, at the Seminole Agency, indicted a warning to Ross. He did not complain, he said, that Ross had elected to keep his treaties "with those States only that still compose the United States of America" nor that the Cherokee chieftain had implied to General McCulloch that armed intervention of United State troops in the Cherokee Nation would not be deemed an act requiring Cherokee resistance. On the contrary, the Confederacy would, so far as his advice could avail, leave the Cherokees free to test this "supposed neutrality." It would not send troops into the Cherokee Nation unless it became necessary either to expel the enemy or to protect the friends of southern rights among the Cherokee people. But Ross must not think that the Confederate States would "hold themselves bound by, or bound to renew any of the guarantees or any of the propositions" offered in June, especially the proposal to pay the Cherokees for the neutral land on the Kansas and Missouri borders "plundered" from them by the North. They could not expect to stand by and risk nothing, wait until the Confederacy succeeded and then ask it to pay what the northern states owed them. "If you owe to *them*, alone, allegiance, loyalty, or friendship, *they*, alone, can owe you money and protection." He concluded with the hope that Ross's policy would not prove at once disastrous to the Cherokee people and regrettable to their leaders.[33]

Pike's letter, circulated in printed form among the Cherokees, reached Ross at about the same time as the news of the Federal defeat at Wilson's Creek, Missouri, August 10, 1861. The two events together convinced Ross that it would be unwise to delay any longer forming an alliance with the Confederacy. When the mass meeting of the Cherokees assembled in the capitol square at Tahlequah on August 21, he announced that the permanent disruption of the United States was now probable and declared that neutrality was no longer possible. Cherokee interests were inseparable from those of Arkansas and the adjacent Indian nations, and it was not desirable that the tribe stand alone. He believed, therefore, that the time had come when his people should consent to "preliminary steps for an alliance with the Confederate States upon terms honorable and advantageous to the Cherokee Nation."[34] Resolutions embodying his plans were adopted, and Ross promptly dispatched the message to Pike already alluded to. At the same time he ordered a regiment of mounted men raised and tendered their services to McCulloch, who out of regard for Pike's position quite properly refused to accept them until the proposed alliance could be consummated. Ross's feelings probably were not soothed by McCulloch's announcement that Stand Watie was already in the Confederate service, commanding a Cherokee battalion on the northern border of the nation.[35]

Delighted with the news brought by Ross's messenger, Pike immediately agreed to go to Park Hill to treat with the Cherokees. In a letter by return messenger he fixed a meeting date and requested Ross to invite the Osages, Quapaws, Shawnees, and Senecas, small tribes located north of the Cherokee Nation, to meet him at the same time. Discharging his Indian escort at Fort Arbuckle about September 20, Pike and four companions left soon after for Park Hill. They traveled by a direct route across the Chickasaw and Creek Nations to Fort Gibson. There they were received by Col. John Drew's newly raised Cherokee regiment and escorted with much pomp and ceremony to Park Hill. Chief Ross met the procession en route and formally welcomed Pike to the nation.[36]

Unprotected by a guard or an escort, Pike encamped at Park Hill near the Ross's residence. Over his tent flew a Confederate flag containing a red star for each tribe with which he had completed a treaty.[37] In response to his and Ross's requests the chiefs of the Osages, Quapaws, Shawnees, and Senecas gathered at Park Hill in the last days of September to council with him.[38] Negotiations with the Osages were delayed because of a dispute in the tribe. Clermont, band chief and popular war leader of the tribe, was challenging the leadership of White Hair, blood heir to the tribal chieftaincy of the Osages. He had planned a coup d'etat to be sprung at Park Hill as a final bid for supremacy. When the Osage chiefs filed up to Pike for the first time to be introduced, White Hair, young, immature, and short of stature, led the column with Clermont second. Pike put out his hand to clasp White Hair's, but Clermont, a tall, powerful man, quietly and swiftly took Pike's hand first. White Hair retained his composure and forced a smile as he grasped Pike's hand next, though he was visibly humiliated by Clermont's public insult. After the Osages returned to their camp, the quarrel between the two leaders waxed strong, and they eventually sent a request to Pike asking that he decide between them. Pike refused to interfere in the matter, explaining that the Confederate government "claimed no power to make or unmake chiefs." After a second request he did suggest, however, that the warriors themselves should decide the issue. Agent Dorn believed White Hair would never agree to such a vote, but both he and Pike were gratified to receive word next day that White Hair had yielded to Clermont.[39]

This removed the major stumbling block to negotiations, and on October 2 the Osage treaty was signed. Two days later a joint treaty with the Senecas and Shawnees and a treaty with the Quapaws were signed. These three treaties form a distinct class among the Pike treaties. That these tribes ranked higher than the bands and tribes of the leased district but lower than the Five Great Nations is clearly discernible from the fact that Pike, in placing them under the protection of the Confederacy, asked that they become a party "to the existing war between the Confederate States and the United States" and agree to raise and furnish troops for the Confederacy if called upon to do so. But this was neither an alliance nor a recognition of the nationality of these tribes. They were not, for instance, given delegates to Congress, nor control over their trade, nor the prospect of becoming a part of the proposed Indian state. Slavery was, however, recognized, and they were guaranteed all land and financial rights they had possessed under the United States. To encourage the cultivation of their lands, Pike promised the same generous agricultural and industrial aid he had offered the tribes of the leased district. Their procedural rights were to be respected by courts of the states of the Confederacy, and as far as Confederate States law was involved they were placed under the jurisdiction of the Confederate district court to be established at Tahlequah, Cherokee Nation. Pike granted increased financial assistance to these tribes for building schoolhouses, hiring and paying teachers, and purchasing books and instructional equipment. As a special concession to the Quapaws, who in 1824 had been removed from Arkansas after selling their lands "for a grossly inadequate price," Pike admitted their wrongs and promised that the Confederate States would, in reparation, expend for the benefit of the tribe $2,000 per year for twenty years, the money to be used by the superintendent of Indian affairs for the purchase and distribution among the Quapaws of blankets, clothing, tobacco, household furniture, utensils and "other articles of ease and comfort."[40]

Meanwhile Pike and Ross had been working on a preliminary draft of the Cherokee treaty, and sometime before October 6 they went to Tahlequah, Cherokee capital, to consult with Ross's executive council and three special commissioners, Lewis Ross,

Thomas Pegg, and Richard Fields, on the final terms. The negotiations were completed and the treaty was formally signed at Tahlequah on October 7. The same day it was submitted by Chief Ross to the upper house of the Cherokee legislature, where it was debated article by article and ratified without amendment.[41]

The terms of the treaty need not be discussed at length. As in the case of the Creeks, Choctaws, Chickasaws, and Seminoles, the Cherokees were made allies of the Confederate States in the war against the United States, agreeing to raise a regiment and two reserve companies for Confederate service in Indian Territory. Pike gave full recognition to the rights of the Cherokees to hold their lands in common, to send a delegate to the lower house of Congress, to control and regulate their trade, to regulate tribal citizenship, to expel trespassers, and to govern themselves. A Confederate States district court, to be established at Tahlequah, was to have jurisdiction over all cases involving violation of Confederate States laws and treaties in the Cherokee Nation and in the country of the Osages, Senecas, Shawnees, and Quapaws. Full procedural rights in all Confederate and state courts were promised the Cherokees. Pike also guaranteed all financial obligations of the United States to the Cherokee Nation, and agreed that if the Cherokee neutral land was ultimately lost the Confederate States would pay for it. No mention of prospective statehood was made in the treaty; it had, however, been provided for in the Choctaw and Chickasaw treaty.[42]

The Cherokees were at last allies of the Confederate States, but they were still sharply divided in spite of Pike's efforts during the negotiations to reconcile the bad feelings between Watie and Ross. Watie, who in September was commanding a small independent force of Cherokees under McCulloch,[43] had been especially worried that once a treaty was made he and his men would be forced to serve under Colonel Drew and hence be subject "to Ross's tyranny."[44] He came to Park Hill to discuss the matter with Pike, who was fully aware of the animosity between the two factions and who hoped to prevail upon Watie and Ross to settle the old feud or, above all, to prevent armed clashes between their followers. Pike met with considerable success as mediator between the men, though he must soon have realized that the breach between them was too great, too old, and too complicated to admit of permanent settlement. It was agreed that Watie should raise and command a regiment for Confederate service independent of the one already raised by Drew.[45] After the treaty was signed at Tahlequah, Ross and Watie shook hands and expressed hope for union and concord in the nation.[46] But time was to show that harmony between the two men was impossible.

From Tahlequah Pike went to Fort Smith, where he spent two or three weeks putting Indian affairs in shape before he left for Richmond with the treaties. While at Fort Smith in June he had given drafts on the State Department to various traders and individuals for incidental goods and services connected with his mission. But the secretary of the treasury had refused to honor his drafts, announcing that all money disbursed for Indian service would have to be charged to the Bureau of Indian Affairs in the War Department. Confronted by his apprehensive creditors, Pike wrote on October 13 to Judah P. Benjamin, secretary of war, explaining his embarrassment. Fortunately Toombs had already advised the War Department of the difficulty and Benjamin had forwarded

$20,000 to Fort Smith for Pike's use. The money reached Pike on October 22. He deposited it with William B. Sutton, Fort Smith merchant, and notified the holders of his drafts to present them to Sutton for their money.[47]

Pike received official notification at Fort Smith that he had been commissioned a brigadier general in the provisional army of the Confederate States to command the Indian troops raised under his treaties.[48] He accepted the appointment on October 14, sending the same day to the secretary of war and to Adj. and Insp. Gen. Samuel Cooper reports on the forces then organized in the territory and recommendations for additional troops.[49] In other dispatches to the War Department on October 13–14 Pike reported the successful completion of his Indian mission, urged immediate payment of his escort to the leased district, and recommended confirmation of his appointments to the Indian agencies and his contract of August 14 with Charles B. Johnson for furnishing rations to the Reserve Indians.[50]

The new general was at once faced with a grave crisis among the Creeks. The nontreating faction of the tribe, signers of the neutrality pact at the Antelope Hills council in June, had refused to accept the Confederate alliance. Pike had assurances in the summer from their leader, Opoth le Yahola, a wealthy slaveholder, that they were friendly and did not wish to war against the Confederate States. But in August trouble had developed between the McIntosh secessionists and Opoth le Yahola; fearing the vengeance of his ancient enemies, Opoth le Yahola encamped the families and warriors of his followers under armed guard at the junction of the Deep and North Forks of the Canadian above North Fork Village. Desiring to settle the dispute, Pike asked Ross in September to invite Opoth le Yahola and his chiefs to Park Hill to discuss the Creek differences, but Opoth le Yahola refused the invitation. Yet he assured Ross and Pike that he was at peace with the Confederacy, with the Cherokees, and with Colonel Cooper, commander of the Choctaw and Chickasaw regiment, who also had been endeavoring to establish peace between the Creek factions. He could not feel secure in the Creek country, because "a party in his own nation was against him and his people, who would not allow him to be at peace."[51]

After the Cherokee treaty was completed at Tahlequah, Ross sent at Pike's request Assistant Chief Joseph Vann and a Cherokee delegation to Opoth le Yahola's camp, then situated just south of the Cherokee line between the Red Fork and Arkansas Rivers, 115 miles above Fort Gibson.[52] Ross and Pike both sent messages by Vann asking Opoth le Yahola to "disperse his people and send them home ad by no means to fight." They also requested him and his leaders to come under letters of safeguard to Tahlequah and discuss with Cherokee officials the Creek dispute.[53] Having in the meantime communicated with federal agents in Kansas and received promises of aid, Opoth le Yahola courteously declined to give any assurance that he would abide by Ross's and Pike's advice. He would call his tribal council together and discuss the matter with them.[54] But soon after this, feeling emboldened by the prospect of federal support, Opoth le Yahola threw off the mask of friendliness and made an armed raid against stock and property in the Cherokee Nation. He then marshaled his forces apparently with the intention of attacking the Creek troops under Col. D. N. McIntosh.[55]

When Pike received work of Opoth le Yahola's action he was greatly perplexed. Except for a detachment of horsemen under Lt. Col. William Quayle of the Ninth Texas Cavalry he had only Indian troops; and he knew the danger of using Indians against Indians, especially Creeks against Creeks. Still he had no choice but to protect McIntosh from attack. He placed Colonel Cooper of the Choctaw and Chickasaw regiment in command of all the troops in the territory and ordered him to march to the assistance of McIntosh. Hoping that this show of force would overawe Opoth le Yahola and cause him to disperse his men without resorting to battle, Pike cautioned Cooper to make every effort to settle the Creek quarrel by peaceable means if possible.[56]

Having thus temporarily disposed of affairs in his new command Pike left Fort Smith about October 22, stopped for a week's visit with his family in Little Rock, and reached Richmond after the middle of November.

XXVIII

To Richmond and Back

WHEN PIKE REACHED the Confederate capital in November 1861, the provisional Congress had probably already begun its session.[1] Anxious to have the treaties ratified as soon as possible, he submitted to Secretary of War Benjamin on November 25 his report accompanied by the nine treaties.[2] That done, he waited for executive and legislative action on his handiwork, holding himself in readiness to answer any questions that might come from President Davis or Congress.

In the meantime he was not idle. On November 22 by Special Orders No. 234, Confederate Adjutant and Inspector General's Office, the "Indian Country west of Arkansas and north of Texas" had been constituted the Department of Indian Territory with Brigadier General Pike assigned to command it.[3] He accepted the appointment and threw himself into the work of organizing the new department. Before the end of November he sent in recommendations for his staff, asking and receiving commissions and assignments for a group of Arkansans: William Quesenbury, major, brigade quartermaster; Francis Lanegan, captain, assistant quartermaster; George W. Stidham, captain, assistant commissary; G. A. Schwarzmann, captain, assistant adjutant-general; and William Warren Johnson, first lieutenant, aid-de-camp.[4] His request for engineer officers was met by assignment to him of Captains R. H. Fitzhugh, a Virginian, and Thomas J. Mackey, a South Carolinian.[5] Apparently without Pike's concurrence or knowledge Maj. N. B. Pearce of Kentucky was made chief commissary for Indian Territory and western Arkansas, and Maj. George W. Clarke of Arkansas became depot quartermaster at Fort Smith with the duty of supplying all troops in Arkansas and the Indian country.[6]

The orders creating Pike's department specified that the troops of the command should "consist of the several Indian regiments raised or yet to be raised" within its limits.[7] Was he to have no white soldiers? Determined that he should have, Pike told Benjamin in a letter of November 27 that he did not desire "to be merely a general of Indians." A force of three or four thousand mounted Indians would be valuable only if sustained by white infantry and artillery. The Indian country would be invaded in the spring; to defend it two or three important points should be fortified. Only white infantry and artillery could construct and garrison such works, though Indian riflemen would efficiently aid in defending them. Would the secretary of war grant him authority to receive into Confederate service three regiments of white infantry, two companies of white artillery, and enough Indians to bring the Indian force to a total not exceeding 7,500 men?[8] Benjamin's answer came promptly. Pike must muster "into the service as many companies or regiments of Indians as you may be able to find arms for; also two regiments of infantry and two companies of artillery in the same manner, as soon as you can procure the arms."⁹ It was not what Pike asked and hoped for, but it would have to suffice for the time being.

Pike had chosen a location for his brigade headquarters before leaving Indian Territory. The site, which now became departmental headquarters, was in the Creek Nation, situated on high ground just south of the Arkansas River, "nearly opposite to and a little above the mouth of the Verdigris River." Healthful, well watered, and well timbered, it overlooked the Great Road from Missouri to Texas which crossed the Arkansas a few hundred feet below. Quesenbury, on the spot, was already engaged in erecting temporary quarters for the brigade offices, kitchens, and other necessary buildings. Pike named the place Cantonment Davis. He planned to make it a permanent military post and, if guns and men could be had, to construct fortifications to command the ford on the Arkansas.¹⁰

Though fully occupied with preparations for organizing, supplying, and defending the Department of Indian Territory, Pike was still encumbered with duties connected with his civil position of commissioner to the Indian tribes west of Arkansas. The treaties were yet to be ratified, and the monies and goods promised under them yet to be secured and paid over. Funds for the pay of Indian troops enlisted under the treaties must also be obtained. These matters would have to be attended to by Pike personally, for the success of his military mission would depend upon the faithful execution by the government of his financial promises. Moreover, he hoped to make treaties with the remaining bands of the wild Comanches and with the fierce Kiowas, whom he had invited to meet him at the Wichita Agency "at the falling of the leaves."¹¹ On November 21 he wrote Rector, Confederate superintendent of Indian affairs, that he would be unable to meet the Indians as planned and asked him to send Richard Pulliam, Rector's clerk, to explain his delay and to tell them that he would meet them later in the winter. Pike sent the letter to S. S. Scott, acting commissioner of Indian affairs, who forwarded with it orders to agent Leeper "to use all the government laborers in putting up houses for the Comanches who are coming in, and not to use them for any other purpose." "If it is possible to send up additional laborers," Pike advised Rector, "it had better be done." The Bureau of Indian Affairs had transmitted $25,000 to New Orleans to be used by Rector in purchasing articles for the Comanches and Reserve Indians. Would Rector immediately assure the Indians that the supplies should be forthcoming?¹² Pike secured through the secretary of war funds to pay Charles B. Johnson for rations furnished the Reserve Indians up to August 16, to pay his mounted escort to the leased district, and to buy clothing for the Indians of the district under his treaty with them. These were turned over to Rector for disbursement.¹³ To obtain money for paying the Indian troops, Pike got his friend Augustus H. Garland, Arkansas delegate to the provisional Congress, to introduce a bill for their relief, which was referred December 9 to the Committee on Military Affairs.¹⁴ On the same day Pike followed up Garland's action with a letter to Delegate Miles of South Carolina, chairman of the committee, urging the importance of the measure. It was necessary, said Pike, to enlist more Indians for the defense of the Indian country, but unless those already serving were paid, no more would volunteer for Confederate service.¹⁵

Meanwhile the executive department was acting on Pike's treaties. Benjamin accepted Pike's explanation of why he had disregarded Secretary Walker's instructions and in communicating to President Davis in early December spoke highly of the "zeal, energy, and fidelity" with which Pike had conducted the difficult mission.

> He has made treaties with the entire Indian population of the Territory in question; has secured their alliance; has enlisted several regiments of their warriors in our service, and has shown a rare and admirable combination of the qualities chiefly required for success in such a mission, namely, sympathy and friendship for the Indians, blended with devotion to the interests of his Government.[16]

In his message of December 12, 1861, transmitting the treaties and Pike's report to Congress, President Davis recommended that the financial obligation incurred as a result of Pike's departure from instructions be assumed in full. But in regard to the contemplated changes in the political and judicial status of the Indians, Davis refused to support Pike.

> That their advancement in civilization justified an enlargement of their power in that regard will scarcely admit of a doubt; but whether the proposed concessions in favor of their local governments are within the bounds of a wise policy may well claim your serious consideration. In this connection your attention is specially invited to the clauses giving to certain tribes the unqualified right of admission as a State into the compact of the Confederacy, and in the meantime allowing each of these tribes to have a delegate in Congress. These provisions are regarded not only as impolitic but unconstitutional, it not being within the limits of the treaty-making power to admit a State or to control the House of Representatives in the matter of admission to its privileges. I recommend that the former provision be rejected; and that the latter be so modified as to leave the question to the future action of Congress; and also do recommend the rejection of those articles in the treaties which confer upon Indians the right to testify in the State courts, believing that the States have the power to decide that question, each for itself, independently of any action of the Confederate Government.[17]

Legislative action on President Davis's recommendations for ratification was set in motion by Robert W. Johnson, delegate from Arkansas and chairman of the Committee on Indian Affairs. No doubt Pike worked closely with Johnson, for the two were old friends and both were interested in consummating the Indian alliances at once in order that Pike could return to his command.[18] At Johnson's motion the treaties, Pike's report, and Davis's message were referred on December 13 to his committee.[19] On the nineteenth Johnson reported the Choctaw and Chickasaw treaty with amendments in line with President Davis's views.[20] Article 27 giving the two nations jointly a delegate in the lower house of the permanent Congress had been amended in committee to limit the delegate's action to initiating and speaking in support of measures for the benefit of the two tribes and to "such rights and privileges" as might be determined by the House of Representatives. Even as amended this article remained a substantial contribution to the Indians, since it gave them about all any territorial delegate in the U.S. Congress ever had. Article 28, which provided for ultimate statehood, was amended in such a manner as to leave final determination to the permanent Congress, "whose consent it is not in the power of the President or of the present Congress to guarantee in advance." Both articles as amended in committee were adopted unanimously, Johnson having complete control of the situation on the floor.[21] On December 20, Articles 42 and 44, granting procedural rights in Confederate and state courts to the Choctaws and Chickasaws, were taken up under Johnson's tutlege. Unanimous consent was given to amendments which left the Indians full rights before Confederate courts but which modified the terms in regard to state courts so as to leave final decision to the individual states. It was stipulated that the Confederate government would request the states to make Indians competent witnesses before their courts.[22]

The alterations of December 19–20 in the Choctaw and Chickasaw treaty set precedents that pointed the way to successful ratification of all the treaties, though consideration of them dragged on into January. After December 21 Pike was invited to be present during sessions at which the treaties were to be discussed in order to answer questions connected with their terms. The Osage and the Seneca and Shawnee treaties were ratified on December 24, the Creek, Choctaw and Chickasaw, and Quapaw on January 2. The treaties with the Reserve Indians and with the Comanches, ratified December 31, had no political or judicial provisions; but two articles in each, providing that the Confederate States furnish rifles and ammunition to all unarmed braves and that Texas troops be withdrawn from the leased district, were struck out. All financial obligations under all the treaties were approved.[23]

Meanwhile back in Indian Territory, Col. Douglas H. Cooper was trying to put down an insurrection among the Creeks. He had attempted in vain to obtain an interview with Opoth le Yahola, and then had received information that the Creek chief was in correspondence with the federal agents in Kansas. As a result Cooper advanced upon him with the intention of either compelling him to submit to the Creek authorities or driving him from the Indian country. On December 8 Cooper found Opoth le Yahola's force encamped behind strong entrenchments in a bend of Bird Creek, a small tributary of the Verdigris River approximately thirty miles north of the Creek Agency. Cooper prepared to attack next day. On the night of the eighth most of the First Cherokee Mounted Rifles deserted, many of them to the enemy, it was reported; only Colonel Drew and twenty-eight company officers, sergeants, and privates were left. Cooper, with the remainder of his force, attacked the Creek position and drove its defenders into the hills beyond, but lack of ammunition forced him to break off pursuit. Despite his temporary success the engagement was not decisive and great alarm was felt in Indian Territory and in Arkansas that once word of the desertion of Drew's regiment reached the Cherokee Nation the whole tribe might go over to the Union.[24]

News of the Cherokee disbandment at Bird Creek reached Pike shortly before Christmas.[25] He was then engaged in legislative work on the treaties and in lobbying for the passage of appropriation bills for the Indians and remained so occupied until December 24 when Congress took a six-day recess for the Christmas holidays. Fortunately the appropriations for the payment of the Indian troops and for complying with the financial obligations of the treaties passed before the adjournment even though all the treaties had not yet been ratified.[26] Pike determined, in view of the danger threatening his command, to leave for Indian Territory as soon as the monies under these acts could be obtained. He spent Christmas Day writing a report to Benjamin on the critical state of affairs among the Indians, recommending remedies, and requesting the cooperation of the War Department. The desertion of Drew's regiment Pike attributed not to disloyalty to the Confederacy but to a natural "reluctance of the Cherokee to fight against their neighbors, the Creeks." This feeling he had found "strong among them in October" when he had been forced by lack of white troops to send the Cherokee to the aid of the friendly Creeks. He had always considered white troops essential to the good order and security of the territory and intimated that much of the present trouble stemmed from General McCulloch's decision not to place his white regiments there. Failure to arm, supply, and pay the Indian troops promptly was equally responsible. Delays in negotiating and ratifying the treaties and in appropriating and transmitting the monies due under them had caused suspicion and discontent among the Indians. Since the Confederate treaties had been negotiated federal emissaries from Kansas had gone among the Indians promising them their monies and trying to convince them that the Confederacy could neither maintain itself, protect the Indians, nor secure them their monies. Congress had now ratified the treaties and had appropriated the monies to be paid under them. He had procured funds to pay the Indian troops, to meet the expenses of his quartermaster, and to purchase arms. He would leave for the Indian country within three days if everything he had to do could be effected.

But it would be of no use for him to go there without the treaty monies. Could the secretary of war not procure them immediately from the Treasury and forward them to Superintendent Rector at Fort Smith? Pike thought the specie provided for could be obtained in New Orleans. He was going by that city and could, if the secretary pleased, take charge of it and the other monies and convey all to Rector. The payment by Rector of the treaty monies would settle much of the discontent among the Indians and keep them in Confederate service. These payments alone would, however, not suffice to restore order in the territory. Now more than ever it was essential that at least three regiments of white infantry and two companies of white artillery, all well armed and supplied, be placed there. Col. Frank A. Rector's Seventeenth Arkansas Infantry, recently raised and assigned to McCulloch, could easily be transferred to the Indian Department. Two thousand rifles should also be given to Pike to arm the two white regiments already authorized by the secretary of war to be recruited for service in the territory. Guns for two batteries of artillery, already authorized, eight fortification guns, and supplies of cannon and rifle ammunition, shoes, clothing, and blankets ought also to be sent to him.[27]

Benjamin refused to transfer Rector's regiment to Pike but did promise him 2,000 Enfield rifles, or "minnie muskets" if the rifles could not be had, as soon as they could be procured.[28] The secretary of war consented, "indeed proposed,"[29] to send the treaty money by Pike and promptly requested the Treasury Department to prepare the funds and turn them over to him for transmittal to Superintendent Rector.[30]

It would take a week for the Treasury Department to make out the accounts and secure the sum of money demanded. Meanwhile, Pike was busy with final preparations for his trip. He saw Lt. Col. Josiah Gorgas, chief of ordinance, signed requisitions for the rifles, was told that there were none available but that some were expected soon via the *Gladiator*, a blockade runner, and that he could have them when they arrived.[31] Capt. A. L. Rives, acting chief of the engineer bureau, furnished him $5,000 for engineer service, which Pike turned over to Captain Fitzhugh and Mackey of his staff.[32] At an interview with Col. Lucius B. Northrop, commissary general, Pike learned that Northrop had made a contract with George E. White, a Texan, giving him a monopoly of furnishing fresh beef and bacon to the troops of Arkansas and Indian Territory. According to the agreement White was to get six and a half cents per pound for beeves on the hoof and fifteen cents for bacon. Pike exploded, told Northrop the contract "was an immense swindle," that he "could buy beef in the Indian country at 3 1/2 cents, and did not want anybody to buy it for me except my own commissary." He was in for a worse surprise. To obtain funds for his commissary he would, said Northrop, have to make requisitions upon Maj. N. B. Pearce, chief commissary for Indian Territory and western Arkansas, headquarters Fort Smith, who had been granted $350,000 for operations. Pearce had absolute control over all commissary business in the district assigned him and had been instructed to enforce the White contract to the letter. Pike left empty handed, but with definite opinions of pig-headed Col. Lucius B. Northrop.[33]

Desiring to expedite business on his arrival in Indian Territory, Pike wrote letters from Richmond to the Indian chiefs and leaders informing them that their treaties had been ratified and that he would return shortly with their monies. He invited them to meet him at Cantonment Davis by February 1 and to come with full powers to ratify the amendments and to receive the monies.[34] These letters Pike dispatched by special messenger to Rector on December 29 instructing Rector to forward them to each tribe by express. He outlined to Rector the late developments in Richmond and in his immediate plans. Congress having ratified the treaties and appropriated the monies under them, the secretary of war had agreed to send the money to Rector by Pike, who would go by New Orleans for the specie. Pike's own compensation for negotiating the treaties Congress had fixed at $3,750.[35] He meant to be at Cantonment Davis by January 25. He hoped the Indians would ratify the treaty amendments at once in order that Rector could pay them soon afterward. He wanted the Comanches to meet him at Cantonment Davis and thought Rector should buy all the goods possible to give them. "I hope when we pay the Indians their money, and I get some white troops in the Country, we shall settle the difficulties there. God knows."[36]

Under the appropriation act[37] no money had been provided for the expense of holding Indian councils in connection with securing ratification of the amendments to the treaties. On December 31 Pike notified the Bureau of Indian Affairs of the oversight. Acting Commissioner Scott promptly obtained $3,000 from the War Department and had it placed to Pike's credit in the Treasury Department.[38]

The Confederate States treasurer, Edward C. Elmore, had the Treasury notes ready on January 1.[39] When Pike went to pick them up he discovered that he would have to go to Columbia, South Carolina, for $95,000 of the gold. He expressed the Treasury notes to the Planter's Bank, Memphis, Tennessee, and left for Columbia on January 2.[40]

When he reached there on the fifth, he found that the sub-treasurer at Charleston had not transferred the coin.[41] An exchange of telegrams brought no results, and Pike went to Charleston to see the official. Back in Columbia on January 8, he obtained the money and shipped it by the Southern Express Company to New Orleans. At the Crescent City, Pike got the residue of the specie, shipping it on January 15 to the Planter's Bank in Memphis. On his arrival in Memphis about the eighteenth Pike found the Treasury notes awaiting him. With the coin and notes boxed, strapped, and under armed guard he took a steamboat on January 22 to Napoleon, Arkansas, thence by another steamer to Duvall's Bluff on White River.[42]

Pike reached Duvall's Bluff at an auspicious time. The final link in the Duvall's Bluff-Little Rock section of the Memphis and Little Rock Railroad was to be completed on Sunday, January 26, and a special train was to run from the Bluff to the capital. Pike arranged to get his men and freight on the train. At a point ten miles east of Little Rock Pike's train met the "down train" from the capital and all piled off to watch William Woodruff, "oldest representative of the press in Arkansas," drive the last spike. With the ceremony over, both trains proceeded to Little Rock, where "a most excellent dinner at the Anthony House" awaited the officials and their guests.[43]

After dinner Pike went home to his family. He had seen little of his children in the past year. Hamilton was away serving as aid-de-camp on McCulloch's staff. He had been at Wilson's Creek in August, had rendered valuable assistance under fire, and had been officially praised in McCulloch's battle report.[44] Walter Lacy, who had been with his father on the Indian mission the previous summer, was still at home. When Pike's aid-de-camp, Lt. William Warren Johnson, resigned at Little Rock, Pike appointed Walter to the place and secured a first lieutenancy for him. Yvon, aged twelve, was too young for service; he and Isadore and Lilian were left behind to solace their mother as father and brothers went off to war.

XXIX

Mars in the Ozarks: Pea Ridge

HEAVY RAINS FALLING about the time Pike reached home, turned the road from Little Rock to Fort Smith into a quagmire, nullifying his plan to transport the Indian monies and supplies to the territory in wagons.[1]

At the same time the rains had done little to improve navigation on the shoal-filled Arkansas, now at low watermark. The outlook was disquieting, but it did give Pike a brief respite from the strain of travel and an unexpected excuse to continue the visit with his family.

His stay at Little Rock must also have given him an opportunity to hear the latest news and gossip concerning affairs in Arkansas. The chief topic of conversation among armchair generals about town was the controversy between Brigadier General McCulloch, Provisional Army of the Confederate States, and Maj. Gen. Sterling Price, Missouri State Guard, over military policy in Missouri and Northwest Arkansas. McCulloch, who had no personal dislike for Price but mistrusted his ability as a commander, believed his own main concern was the defense of northwest Arkansas. He had, therefore, only a secondary interest in recovering Missouri from Federal control, while Price's sole aim appeared to be the liberation of his state. Taking a selfish view of the dispute, many Arkansans severely criticized McCulloch for refusing to cooperate with Price. The editor of the *Little Rock Daily State Journal* expressed unutterable surprise when he learned that McCulloch had withdrawn his division from Springfield to Arkansas in November. He hoped that McCulloch's men would be sent back to Price immediately. So long as Missouri is free, Arkansas is safe, and so long as Missouri is bound Arkansas is in danger.[2]

President Davis had become so alarmed over the dispute between McCulloch and Price by the beginning of the new year that he decided to intercede in behalf of the Confederacy. On January 10, 1862, the War Department issued orders announcing the organization of the Trans-Mississippi District of Department Number 2. It comprised Louisiana north of Red River, Indian Territory, and Arkansas and Missouri west of a line formed by the Mississippi and St. Francis rivers. Maj. Gen. Earl Van Dorn of Mississippi, West Pointer and division commander under Lee, was assigned to command the new district. At long last McCulloch and Price, who retained their respective commands, were to have a master.[3]

Pike, too, had a master, and one he did not relish. In October 1858, Van Dorn, then a captain of U.S. Cavalry in Texas, had crossed the Red River and made a brutal and vengeful attack upon a defenseless Comanche camp in the leased district. The Indians at the time were under a flag of truce, conferring peacefully with the Wichitas and under the protection of the commander at Fort Arbuckle; moreover, Van Dorn was completely out of his department and jurisdiction. Though the captain was praised in Texas for the massacre of some sixty men, women, and children at the camp, Pike was infuriated on hearing the details of the act and wrote the War Department severely criticizing Van Dorn's murderous foray. Pike's letter found a convenient pigeonhole, and Van Dorn was commended by General Winfield Scott, chief of the army, for his "gallant exploit." Thereafter, as can be well imagined, Pike and Van Dorn had little regard for each other.[4]

The captain of cavalry was now a major general and Pike's commanding officer. Pike might well look to the future with doubt if Van Dorn still held the grudge and was the vengeful sort. Pike must also have wondered about Van Dorn's jurisdiction. Indian Territory had been placed under the commander of a military district, which was itself merely a section of another department. Officials in Richmond had bungled badly if they had intended to abolish Pike's department or to make it subordinate to Department Number 2, commanded by Gen. Albert Sidney Johnston. Neither Pike's authority nor the name and organization of the Department of Indian Territory was explicitly superseded by the orders which assigned Van Dorn to the head of the new district. If disagreement ever came, such vagueness could only breed confusion and disorder.

Van Dorn assumed command of his district at Little Rock on January 29, announcing that henceforth his headquarters would be at Pocahontas in northeast Arkansas, fifteen miles south of the Missouri border.[5] Since Pike was in the city at the time, he reported in person to Van Dorn. Their interview apparently went smoothly, though there is no record of what was said or done. From what both subsequently stated it appears that Pike received permission from Van Dorn to have three regiments of infantry and two companies of artillery, then being raised in Arkansas, for service in the Indian Territory; that Pike informed Van Dorn the Indians were intended for defense alone and could not be moved out of their country without their permission; and that Van Dorn left Pike "sole control of the Indian Country."[6]

Van Dorn reached his supply depot at Jacksonport, on White River, in early February. On the seventh he wrote Price of his preparations for opening a spring campaign in Missouri. He had called on the governors of Arkansas, Louisiana, and Texas for troops and hoped to get enough to organize at Pocahontas a force of 9,500 men. He would order McCulloch's division of 10,000 from Fort Smith to join him, and estimated that with artillery he would then have an army of some 20,000 men. He hoped Price could increase his command at Springfield to 15,000 by March 20, when he expected to begin the offensive.

> I shall order General Pike to take position in Lawrence County near you, say Mount Vernon [Missouri], with instructions to cooperate with you in any emergency. He has, as he told me, about 8,000 or 9,000 men and three batteries of artillery. Three of his regiments are, I believe white. The others half-breed Indians &c. all true men, he says.[7]

Van Dorn elaborated plans for "attempting St. Louis" in a letter to Price on February 14. But his optimistic estimates of a week before were considerably reduced.

With McCulloch he would have only 18,000 at Pocahontas; and Price must not depend upon over 15,000, since Pike's command, which had in the meantime been ordered to Mount Vernon, was "intended for defense alone and as a corps of observation on the Kansas border." Until both armies were ready to move on St. Louis, Price should maneuver between Rolla and Springfield. Pike could aid in this, "but he should not go too far, as he would leave Western Arkansas, the Indian Territory, and the counties west of you exposed too much to the half-savage enemy in Kansas."[8]

While Van Dorn was complacently collecting an army at his headquarters and completing plans for the expedition to St. Louis, Federal brigadier general Samuel R. Curtis, assigned to command the southwestern district of Missouri on Christmas Day 1861, had already undertaken an offensive to drive Price out of Missouri. Curtis moved with five brigades from Rolla to Lebanon in late January. He paused there to await reinforcements and to reorganize his army. On February 9 Curtis ordered a general advance against Springfield. Three days later his forward elements drove in Price's pickets, and on the thirteenth his main force marched into the city on the heels of Price's retreating column.[9]

Outnumbered two or three to one, Price retreated to Arkansas with Curtis in pursuit.[10] On February 18 Maj. Gen. Henry W. Halleck, commanding the Department of Missouri since November 19, wired Gen. George B. McClellan in Washington that "the flag of the Union is floating in Arkansas," and on February 22 ordered Curtis to halt and select and entrench a strong point near Bentonville. Curtis acknowledged receipt of the order on February 26. He was then encamped along an east-west line some two miles south of Bentonville, his left flank resting on Cross Hollows in the White River Mountains and his right on Osage Springs, five miles due west of the Hollow. In this position he commanded the two main approaches to Fayetteville, the Telegraph Road on his left and the Bentonville Road on his right, five miles apart. Sugar Creek Valley, twelve miles to his rear, was a stronger position, and he thought he might fall back to that point and entrench his army. He would wait, however, until his forage at the present encampment was used up. Price had halted on Cove Creek on the south slope of the Boston Mountains, about fifty miles south of Bentonville, where he was joined by McCulloch.[11]

Van Dorn did not learn of the Federal advance and of Price's retreat to the Boston Mountains until February 22. He then ordered McCulloch to join Price. He also requested McCulloch to notify Price to prepare his force for an advance against Curtis. About the same time he sent a dispatch to Pike ordering him to proceed to the Confederate position with his entire force.[12] Two days later, February 24, Van Dorn set out from Jacksonport for the Boston Mountains to take command of McCulloch's and Price's divisions. He reached their headquarters on the morning of March 3, and after a brief inquiry concluded that Curtis had stopped at Sugar Creek merely to await large reenforcements before mounting a new ofensive. He resolved to attack the Federal position at once, and promptly dispatched orders to Pike to press on with his column along the Cane Hill-Fayetteville road and fall in the rear of Price and McCulloch, who were to move for Fayetteville early the next morning. Similar orders went to Colonels Drew and Watie of the Cherokees and to Col. D. N. McIntosh of the Creeks, their commands being at the time, it was supposed, on the Arkansas line. In the afternoon of March 3 Van Dorn sent new orders to Pike. He was to "hasten up with all possible dispatch and in person direct the march of your command, including Stand Watie's, McIntosh's and Drew's regiments," in order to "be near Elm Springs," eleven miles south of Bentonville on the Fayetteville road, by the afternoon of March 5.[13]

In the meantime Pike had had difficulties all his own. On January 28 the road to Fort Smith was still impassable. He wrote Rector that day that he would leave Little Rock on January 31 and requested the superintendent to go at once to Cantonment Davis and arrange to feed the Comanches and other Indians if they should come there. Pike could "take the money there and send by the same messenger who takes this, to Colonel Cooper for an escort." He was enclosing an order requiring passports for admission into the territory; this would keep out some hundred and fifty gamblers who were following the Indian monies.[14] It was, however, after February 4 when Pike took the steamer *Tahlequah* in an attempt to navigate the Arkansas.[15] The boat was six days reaching Dardanelle, half-way to Fort Smith," from which point he "conveyed the money to Fort Smith by wagons."[16]

Pike reached Fort Smith about the middle of February and spent a busy week preparing for the remainder of his trip.[17] Rector, he found, had gone ahead to Cantonment Davis to meet the Indians, but had left at Fort Smith part of the goods purchased for the Comanches.[18] Pike was faced with the problem of procuring teams and wagons to transport the money as well as the goods. While he was occupied with the details of this work news reached town that Price had evacuated Springfield and had been chased into Arkansas by Curtis. At Fort Smith under orders from Van Dorn to march to Pocahontas, McCulloch determined instead to March to Price then camped on Cove Creek near the Crawford County-Washington County boundary; before he left town he called upon Pike to join him with his Indians.[19] Pike's responsibility for the money and supplies on his hands prevented his taking the field, but he agreed to order the Cherokees under Colonels Watie and Drew and the Creeks under Col. D. N. McIntosh to move toward Fayetteville and temporarily take orders from McCulloch.[20] While still at Fort Smith, Pike received from Van Dorn a belated order to march his Indian troops to Mount Vernon, Missouri, and cooperate with Price. The order came through Price who requested that Pike join him at his new camp in the Boston Mountains southwest of Fayetteville. Informing Price that he had temporarily placed the Cherokees and Creeks under McCulloch, Pike told Price that he would proceed to the territory with the Indian monies and supplies, raise all the troops he could find, and then march them to him.[21]

On February 21 Pike started his train from Fort Smith up the south side of the Arkansas toward Cantonment Davis. The teams furnished him at Fort Smith proved unable to stand the strain of a rapid march. It was the night of February 22 before he reached the mouth of the Canadian, some forty miles above the Arkansas line, where Douglas H. Cooper's First Regiment Choctaw and Chickasaw Mounted Rifles and Maj. Sampson N. Folsom's First Choctaw Battalion were encamped. Here Pike found himself in a quandary, for the sustained pull had already greatly weakened his mules, wherefore the rest of the trip would be slower than the first lap. For a moment he considered sending the money on to North Fork Village and letting Rector go there for it. This would leave him free to lead Cooper's and Folsom's men to Price. But discovering that there was only one boat at the camp site determined him to move up to Fort Gibson to put the troops across the Arkansas River. He sent word for Rector to meet him the evening of February 24 at Spaniard's Creek, twenty miles below Fort Gibson, where they could determine what to do with the money.[22] Pike made better time than he expected and was five miles beyond the creek next afternoon when he met Rector together with Samuel N. Rutherford, Seminole agent, and Andrew J. Dorn, agent for the Osages, Quapaws, Senecas, and Shawnees. Rector informed Pike that he was on his way to Fort Smith to look to the safety of his family in the threatened Federal invasion and that he would neither take the money with him nor return to Cantonment Davis and pay it over to the Indians. From the trouble that later arose between Pike and Rector over the disposition of the treaty funds, it would seem that Pike spoke his mind pretty freely to Rector. But whatever Pike said, he did not convince the superintendent that his duty to the Indians and his country came before his duty to his family. Consequently Rector got in his buggy and proceeded to Fort Smith, leaving Pike standing in the prairie fuming.[23]

Rector's behavior was totally unexpected and left Pike, as he said later, "utterly at a loss what to do."[24] When his temper cooled, enabling him to think more calmly, he elected to go on to Cantonment Davis to meet the Indians, who were there waiting to be paid. He reached the encampment February 25. The same day he "received an order from General Van Dorn to join him at Bentonville, with all my force."[25] Pike could not take the treaty monies to Arkansas, and they would be unsafe at Cantonment Davis; on the other hand only Rector was authorized under Confederate law to make the treaty payments. Forced to make an immediate decision, Pike assumed the role of acting superintendent and began paying out the treaty monies in Rector's name on February 25.[26]

Pike's request that the Choctaw, Chickasaw, and Creek troops, who reached Cantonment Davis on the night of February 25, march to Arkansas was answered by a demand that he pay them before they moved. They refused to listen to talk about a postponement; consequently Pike had treaty and troop payment going on simultaneously. As none of the promised Arkansas infantry and artillery had yet arrived, Pike's only white troops were some two hundred Texas cavalrymen organized into a squadron under Capt. O. L. Welch. The treaty and troop payments consumed three days, but by the morning of February 28 Pike had gotten his whole force across the Arkansas to Fort Gibson. Leaving the Choctaws and Chickasaws to bring up the rear, he took the road to Park Hill, accompanied by Welch's Texans and the Creek regiment. The Creeks, still unpaid, he had persuaded to march by the promise that they would be paid at the Illinois River, near Park Hill. March 2 was spent at Ross's residence in paying over the Cherokee treaty monies and in beginning the payment of the Creek regiment. On the morning of March 3, the Choctaws and Chickasaws still had not arrived. Pike decided to delay no longer. Breaking off the Creek payment, he and his staff and Welch's squadron took the road to Arkansas. He came up with Watie's regiment at Cincinnati, Arkansas, on the evening of March 4. That night he arranged to have a detail return the balance of the Indian monies to Fort Gibson, and the next day, Wednesday, March 5, accompanied by

Watie and Welch, he reached Freschlag's Mill. The following day he overtook Drew's regiment at Osage Springs, five miles south of Bentonville on the Fayetteville road. He pushed his column of 1,000 men forward and late in the afternoon came up with the rear of General McCulloch's division. That night Pike encamped his exhausted troops two miles south of Camp Stephens, Van Dorn's headquarters. He found that he was a day late for the preliminaries of the battle.[27]

Van Dorn had moved rapidly, almost secretly, after leaving the Boston Mountains in the early morning of March 4.[28] The advance units of Price's division, which headed the Confederate column, had reached Elm Springs on March 5 before Curtis was aware of their approach. The Federal commander, whose army was organized into four divisions, had then hastily issued orders for Col. Eugene A. Carr's division and Brig. Gen. Franz Sigel's two divisions to fall back to Sugar Creek, where Col. Jefferson C. Davis's division was constructing entrenchments for the army.[29] From information given by prisoners captured on March 5, Van Dorn was convinced the next morning that the enemy was still unaware of his movement, and he moved out of Elm Springs hoping to pounce upon Sigel's troops at Bentonville. Van Dorn's wishes for an accelerated march were futile. Price's men, in poor condition and weary from the exertion of the previous two days, did not reach the southern outskirts of Bentonville until eleven o'clock just as Sigel's rear guard was pulling out northward on the Sugar Creek road. Van Dorn pressed his men through Bentonville and pursued the retreating column, but he was unable to move fast enough to trap Sigel, who with the aid of timely reinforcements from one of his division commanders got his whole force safely behind the Federal line before nightfall.[30]

With the arrival of Sigel's column late in the afternoon of March 6 all four of the Federal divisions, numbering 10,500 men according to Curtis's estimate, had joined Curtis at Sugar Creek, though a number of small detachments were absent on reconnaissance and forage details.[31] Curtis himself had reached the position at two o'clock the same morning and had spent the day preparing his defenses against an assault by Van Dorn. His line of fortification lay at the crest of a belt of high hills that skirted the north side of Sugar Creek Valley, which at that point ran east and west. Telegraph Road from Fayetteville to Springfield crossed Sugar Creek almost at right angles and bisected the left half of Curtis's position in ascending the north slope of the valley on its way to Missouri. The road from Bentonville, some three miles west of, and approximately parallel to, the Telegraph Road, forked just south of Sugar Creek. The right hand road zigzagged eastwardly along the valley in front of the Federal line, connecting with Telegraph Road immediately south of the Sugar Creek crossing. The left branch of the fork, an eight-mile "detour," continued northward on Curtis's right, inclined to the east after a few miles, traversed and passed along the back side of a lofty plateau, called by contemporaries Pea Vine Ridge, or Pea Ridge, and intersected Telegraph Road two miles north of the ridge. Between the hills occupied by the Union troops and Pea Ridge was a flatland two miles in width. Heavy timber and dense undergrowth covered the uneven surface of flat, though an occasional glade or cleared field broke the continuity of the almost impenetrable woods, allowing limited visibility. In the middle of this flat, a mile behind the Federal center and halfway between the Bentonville detour and Telegraph Road, lay the hamlet of Leetown, which was connected by a network of small roads and lanes with both the detour and Telegraph Road.[32]

Curtis expected Van Dorn to make a frontal assault against his works at Sugar Creek. Accordingly, he sent out details to obstruct the roads leading into his position from the south. He especially ordered Col. Grenville M. Dodge to take a large detail from the Fourth Iowa Infantry and block the Bentonville detour by felling trees across it. By the night of March 6 Curtis, his men and guns deployed behind formidable earth and timber breastworks, was ready to receive the anticipated attack.[33]

At nightfall on the same day Van Dorn halted his column in marching order along the Bentonville road, Price's advance resting at the road forks two miles south and west to the Federal line. Counting Pike's two regiments of Cherokees and Welch's squadron, which had caught up with the rear of the Confederate army during the afternoon, Van Dorn by his own estimate had 16,000 men, but they were fagged out as a result of the hard march of the previous three days. Nor were they to get the rest they needed that night. Not daring to risk a frontal assault against Curtis's works, Van Dorn consulted McCulloch and James McIntosh, one of McCulloch's brigadiers, and learned of the detour which ran to the left and rear of Curtis's position. He decided at once to employ this route to pass his army behind Pea Ridge and then advance southward by Telegraph Road against the Federal rear. To be successful this turning movement required rapid marching, precise timing, and utmost secrecy, for if Curtis learned of the movement during the night or if Van Dorn failed to get his army in position to attack by dawn, the maneuver would be disclosed to Curtis with possible disastrous results.[34]

To conceal his intentions Van Dorn threw out pickets and bivouacked as if for the night. Soon after dark Price's division, accompanied by Van Dorn and staff, got back into the road and resumed its march. McCulloch followed Price, and Pike brought up the rear. Brig. Gen. Martin E. Green of the Missouri State Militia was left behind at the road fork to protect the Confederate baggage train and to hold the position in case of an attack.[35] The march of the main column was slow. By an unaccountable oversight no provision had been made for bridging the icy waters of Sugar Creek. The few rails and poles that were hastily thrown across the small stream proved inadequate and caused great delay.[36] It was after midnight before McCulloch had advanced far enough to enable Pike to get in motion, and it was after sunrise before the last of McCulloch's troops got across Sugar Creek.[37] Inevitably daybreak found the Confederate column short of its objective. It was ten o'clock before Price reached Telegraph Road and got in position to attack the Federal pickets guarding it. About the same time McCulloch and Pike, still on the detour four or five miles back, and completely unaware of what was taking place elsewhere, received orders from Van Dorn to countermarch and advance against Leetown to the southeast.[38]

Curtis had not learned of the Confederate movement until sometime after sunrise on the morning of March 7. He then immediately called a conference of his division commanders in Brigadier General Asboth's tent and ordered a change of front to meet the new conditions. Sigel, commanding Col. Peter J. Osterhaus's First Division, would turn so as to face west with his left on Sugar Creek. Asboth's Second Division would be to Sigel's right, while Osterhaus with a mixed column of cavalry, light artillery, and infantry would be between Asboth and Davis's Third Division. Carr's Fourth, formerly on the left, would now occupy the right. Curtis directed Osterhaus to form his column and attack at once what was thought to be the Confederate center northwest of Leetown.

After Osterhaus had gone and while Curtis was elaborating the new movement to his officers, a messenger arrived from Elkhorn Tavern, three miles north, with information that the enemy had attacked the Federal picket on Telegraph Road. Colonel Carr was ordered to advance at once with his division to meet this threat.[39] The conference broke up at half past ten. Curtis, hearing heavy firing on his new right, rode to investigate. He found Carr deploying his men "under a brisk fire of shot and shell." Concerned with the size of the Confederate column advancing down Telegraph Road, he ordered Davis to the support of Carr. But soon after this a message came that Osterhaus was in danger of being overwhelmed by superior numbers. Curtis immediately countermanded Davis's orders and sent him to reinforce Osterhaus.[40]

Following the receipt of Van Dorn's order to attack Leetown, McCulloch and Pike had retraced their steps a mile or two and turned left off the detour into narrow lanes that led through heavy woods northwest of the village. They had gone approximately a mile when they plunged into the midst of Colonel Osterhaus's force, deploying in the open fields of Leetown.[41] Pike on the right of the Confederate advance, found himself face to face with an enemy battery supported by cavalry. He hastily posted his men behind a rail fence that extended eastward through the woods on his left, some two hundred yards north of the battery. In the meantime the enemy guns had commenced firing into his line, and he ordered a charge. The Cherokees, accompanied by Welch's squadron and part of a Texas cavalry regiment commanded by Lt. Col. William Quayle, threw down the fence and rushed forward. The hideous war whoops of the Cherokees seemingly terrorized the Federal cavalrymen and artillerists, who abandoned the guns and raced to the rear.[42]

During the charge the Indians got completely confused. For some twenty minutes they milled excitedly around the captured guns, "all talking, and riding this way and that, listening to no orders from any one."[43] Meanwhile, Osterhaus brought up his infantry and deployed it under the protection of another battery.[44] A shell or two from the Federal guns fell among the throng of Indians and sent them scampering into the woods whence they came. There Pike and his staff got control of them, sent Drew's horses to the rear, and ordered his and Watie's troops each to "take to a tree." After they calmed down Pike sent a detail from Watie's regiment to drag the captured battery into the woods, where a Cherokee guard was placed over it. But for the remainder of the day's action the Indians, pinned down by the fire of an enemy battery, were useless.[45]

While Pike was trying to regain control of his muddled troops and protect them from Federal shells, McCulloch had gone into action on the left. Riding at the head of his division the bold leader led charge after charge against Osterhaus's line of infantry and artillery only to have them repulsed with fearful slaughter. At two o'clock in the afternoon Davis arrived on the field at Osterhaus's right and helped drive back the last grand effort of McCulloch's division. In this final charge McCulloch and one of his brigadiers were killed, and the other captured. These untimely tragedies threw the division into hopeless disorder. Davis and Osterhaus moved forward and drove the Confederates from the field, but attempted no pursuit.[46]

About three o'clock in the afternoon, Pike left his dismounted Indians in the shelter of the woods and rode over to the left to investigate a notable silence in that direction. On the road by which he had come that morning he found three regiments of infantry and a battalion of cavalry belonging to McCulloch's division. Maj. J. W. Whitfield of Texas, commanding the cavalry, informed Pike that McCulloch and McIntosh were dead and that the enemy were advancing to turn their left flank. "Totally ignorant of the country and the roads, not knowing the number of the enemy, nor whether the whole or what portions of General McCulloch's command had been detached from the main body for this action," Pike took command and "prepared to repel the supposed movement of the enemy." To the left of where McCulloch had launched his attacks lay the western end of Pea Ridge, which at that point was of no great height. A rail fence ran along the foot of the ridge on the west and northwest, and back of this fence, open and level ground sloped northward to the Bentonville detour, half a mile away. Pike marched the three regiments of infantry, Whitfield's cavalry, Welch's squadron, and Watie's regiment, now mounted, to the ridge and posted them behind the fence. He sent orders for Drew to mount up and join him, but the order was not delivered; and Drew after some time retreated westward to the detour, thence south to Camp Stephens. There Drew joined Colonels Cooper and McIntosh, who had come up with their regiments and Pike's train, in helping Green defend the Confederate train.[47]

Having deployed his small force, Pike rode up Pea Ridge to the left in order to obtain a more commanding view of the enemy's line. He found the Federals in possession of the battlefield and the position of his own men untenable, since the enemy's cavalry could easily cross the ridge and descend on the rear. He determined to withdraw the troops and take them via the detour to Van Dorn. In the retreat Pike placed Captain Welch's cavalry in the lead, threw Watie's Cherokees out along the flanks of the infantry. Following the infantry was a battery of artillery that came up just as Pike was getting under way. Col. B. Warren Stone's Sixth Texas Cavalry, which came up at the same time, Pike ordered "to protect the retreat and preserve our trains." Pike reached Van Dorn's headquarters in the course of the evening and reported the disaster on the right. The units from McCulloch's division were sent into the Confederate line, leaving Pike with only Watie's and Welch's men.[48]

The Federal army had held on the right, but Van Dorn and Price had pushed Carr down Telegraph Road and captured Elkhorn Tavern at the east end of Pea Ridge. When night came on, Sigel's and Asboth's divisions, both idle all day, were moved to the right by Curtis in order to concentrate his army in the open flats straddling Telegraph Road along a line south of Elkhorn Tavern. Once he was convinced that the field west and north of Leetown had been abandoned, Curtis also ordered Osterhaus and Davis to the right.[49]

A similar movement of sorts, though a great deal more disorderly, was enacted by the Confederate army. Pike had brought his column to Van Dorn in the evening, and another officer arrived early the next morning with the remnant of McCulloch's shattered division. Van Dorn's army was, however, hardly in condition to fight longer. Most of the men had had no food since the morning of the sixth, and fought on the seventh without water, and had very little ammunition left. Nor was there any chance of getting fresh supplies. The ammunition and subsistence trains were at Bentonville, with Curtis between them and the Confederate army.[50]

It was, therefore, with "no little anxiety" that Van Dorn awaited the dawn of March 8. When it came, it revealed to him the Federal army in a new and strong position ready for battle. He prepared "to accept the gage, and by 7 o'clock the cannonading was as heavy as that of the previous day."[51] The action on this Saturday morning was short but decisive. The Federal army pushed forward slowly and relentlessly, forcing the Confederate line back all along the front. One by one the Confederate batteries exhausted their ammunition and went to the rear, where, of course, no more was to be had. At ten o'clock Van Dorn saw that his men could not withstand the pressure and gave the order to break off the fighting. The main portion of his army fell back rapidly up Telegraph Road until they came to the Huntsville road, leading through the valley to the southeast, into which they turned. Some ten miles down this road Van Dorn halted his battered column for the night. The enemy made no attempt to pursue, and next day he proceeded unmolested to Huntsville, thence to Van Buren within the following week.[52]

To conceal and protect his retreat Van Dorn left a number of Confederates on the field uninformed of his plan.[53] Pike was one of these. Early Saturday morning Van Dorn had ordered him to divide Watie's regiment and place half of it on each flank of the army to observe the enemy and report any attempt to turn the Confederate position. After directing Welch to join a Texas regiment for the day's action and after detailing Capt. Fayette Hewitt and his son, Walter Lacy, to post the Cherokees on the left, Pike himself accompanied Colonel Watie and the remainder of the Indians to Pea Ridge on the right. Pike remained on the ridge until nearly eleven o'clock, when he returned to the area of Elkhorn Tavern to see Van Dorn.[54] But the commanding general was nowhere to be found, and Pike heard from "one person and another" that the army had been ordered to fall back on Telegraph Road and take a new position.[55] From where Pike stood he could see in front bodies of troops moving from the Confederate right to the left, though it never entered his mind that they were headed for the Huntsville road, or that they were retreating. About the same time he looked to his right and saw "a body of cavalry and a considerable force of infantry" pass up Telegraph Road. "They were," he said, "followed by no others, nor was there any appearance of flight, or of a rout.[56] Pike now sent Major Lanigan and Captain Schwarzman to find Van Dorn and obtain orders, he himself remaining with two batteries which had come up and which he had placed so as to play upon Telegraph Road in case Union cavalry pursued the Confederates who had just gone up it.[57]

Pike's messengers had been gone about fifteen minutes, it being then about half past eleven, when an officer rode up and informed him that the field in front was occupied by Federal troops, that Van Dorn and Price were supposed to be captured, and that the enemy cavalry were but a hundred and fifty yards away. Apparently the men of the batteries overheard this report, for when Pike looked around they had already wheeled their guns about and started for Telegraph Road. Pike and Captain Hewitt and Walter Lacy Pike, who had returned after posting the Indians on the left, attempted to halt the guns in the vicinity of the tavern and bring them into battery facing the rear. They partially succeeded, but after a few moments an enemy shell fell nearby and "the cry 'the cavalry are coming' was raised." Everything became confused. The Confederate troops, two regiments of infantry and a portion of the two batteries that Pike and his officers had stopped, now broke into a scramble down the north side of Pea Ridge. Pike, his son, and Hewitt, thinking the men would turn west on the Bentonville detour, rode west across Telegraph Road, splashed through a small stream on the west side, dismounted and led their horses up a steep hill, remounted at the top, and galloped headlong down Pea Ridge to the detour. From the brow of a hill immediately west of Telegraph Road, where they had hoped to halt the fleeing units, they looked eastward and saw that the Confederates had not turned but had passed to the north up Telegraph Road, "the enemy's cavalry pursuing, en route for Springfield, Mo."[58]

Pike and his two companions were alone now, except for a half dozen stragglers who came up the detour. They waited at the crest of the hill a few minutes, "wondering where the remainder of the army was, and uncertain which way to turn to rejoin it."[59] Suddenly Federal guns on each side of Telegraph Road opened on the valley east of them. They turned and rode westward along the detour, discovering after a mile or so that a detachment of enemy cavalry was following them. They spurred their mounts into top speed and left their pursuers behind. Just past the western end of Pea Ridge, where the detour inclined south, they quit the road, took to the woods and hills, and made their way westward toward the Cherokee line. Next day they turned south, passed west of Bentonville, and reached the road from Elm Springs to Cincinnati on Monday morning. From some troops on the road, probably stragglers from his own command, Pike heard that Colonels Cooper and McIntosh had reached Camp Stephens on Saturday in time to help bring off the Confederate train, which had been taken through Fayetteville toward Van Buren. His own train, brought from Fort Gibson by Cooper and McIntosh, had been taken by them, with Drew's assistance, to the Indian line. Pike overtook his command at Cincinnati. There he found Lanigan and Schwarzman and learned from them of Van Dorn's retreat to Van Buren.[60]

Pike marched from Cincinnati down the line road to Evansville, Arkansas, thence westward into the Cherokee Nation.[61] At Dwight Mission on the Arkansas River, forty-two miles southwest of Tahlequah, he wrote on March 14 the official report of Indian participation in the campaign of Pea Ridge. Since his report has served as the chief source of the preceding narrative, we do not need to discuss it further, except to say that Pike did not consider that his Cherokees had played a very important part in the battle. He did, nevertheless, point with evident pride to the capture of the flying battery, the scout work of Watie's regiment, and the assistance given by Cooper, McIntosh, and Drew in saving Van Dorn's train. That the Choctaws, Chickasaws, and Creeks had been reluctant to march, that the Indians were undisciplined and completely disarranged in the charge against the guns at Leetown, and that he had them dismounted and posted behind trees, Pike frankly admitted. This he did without intending the slightest disparagement of the real bravery of the Cherokees. They simply would not, as he well knew, face shells in the open.[62]

XXX

An Interlude of Atrocity

THE DAY AFTER HE WROTE his battle report Pike heard that one of the Federal dead at Leetown had been scalped.[1] He then called on his surgeon, Dr. Edward L. Massie of Little Rock, who had attended the Confederate and Federal wounded at Leetown. Massie, who had been "over the whole ground" soon after Pike's charge against the Federal battery, reported finding "one body which had been scalped; that it had evidently been done after life was extinct, probably late in the afternoon."[2] Pike himself had seen a half-blood Cherokee shoot and kill a wounded Federal soldier shortly after the capture of the battery, but the Indian had passed too soon from sight to be recognized.[3] As soon as the conference with Massie was over, Pike, "angry and disgusted," issued a special order to the troops of his department. He announced the "barbarous and wanton" killing of the wounded men at Leetown and the fact that he

> learned with the utmost pain and regret that one, at least, of the enemy's dead was scalped upon the field. That practice excites horror, leads to retaliation, and would expose the Confederate States to the just reprehension of all civilized nations. If the Indian allies of the northern states continue it, let retaliation in kind be used to them alone, and those who with them may invade the Indian Territory and sanction it. Against forces that do not practice it, it is peremptorily forbidden during the present war.

This order would "be read and interpreted" to every regiment, battalion, and company of Indian troops in the Confederate service.[4]

A week after the order was issued, Pike forwarded under flag of truce from Cantonment Davis a copy to Curtis, with a statement that "the inhumanities censured and forbidden by it are not likely to be repeated, and are regarded with horror by the Confederate commander." A general court-martial had been ordered to try a person accused of shooting "one of the wounded in the action of the 7th inst., the man so shot being prostrate on the ground, unable to offer resistance."[5] Curtis's reply brought word that the matter of Indian atrocities had already been a subject of correspondence with Van Dorn.[6] Pike's action was "fully appreciated," but it was impossible to expect Indians "to practice civilized warfare" and regrettable that such belligerents had been resorted to in the war.

> The imputation in your order of . . . the use of savage allies on the part of the United States is entirely gratuitous and looks too much like an apology or excuse for what your letter and conscience so strictly condemn. I avail myself, general, of this occasion to assure you I reciprocate the personal regard expressed by you. I would prefer that we were friends rather than foes.[7]

Curtis's implication that the Confederacy had no justification for using Indian troops in the war stung Pike. To justify the Confederate alliance with the Five Civilized Tribes, and to avert criticism in the Confederate States of Indian atrocities at Pea Ridge, Pike sent to Little Rock his order and the correspondence between him and Curtis and had it published. He added to it a "reply to so much of . . . General Curtis's letter, as denies 'the use of savage allies on the part of the United States,'" wishing the people of the Confederacy to know that the United States had aided Opoth le Yahola in his depredations in the Indian country; that the United States was then getting up an expedition, made up partly of Indians, to invade and reconquer Indian Territory; and that Fremont had had a Delaware bodyguard. Pike cited correspondence found in Opoth le Yahola's camp after the battle of Chustenahlah, Cherokee Nation, December 26, 1861 (at which time Colonel Cooper and Col. James McIntosh of McCulloch's division had decisively defeated and driven the disaffected Creeks into Kansas), for proof of a part of these accusations; and he cited other instances, names and sources to substantiate the remainder of his charges.[8] He ended with an accusation that the Civilized Indians had been used by the United States in every war of her history, but it had been left until the present conflict for her "to arm and incite against those of their own race, the savage Caiowas, Comanches, Wichitas and Kickapoos."[9] He wondered at General Curtis, "that he should be ignorant of these facts."[10]

Meanwhile, the Northern press was making such ado over the Pea Ridge atrocities, and Pike was fast winning an unsavory reputation. Word went back to Springfield on March 10 that two thousand Indians were led into the battle by Pike and that eighteen of the Union dead were found scalped.[11] From there the news was spread across the country by telegraph. Imaginative editors needed no more than these bare facts to inspire them. In Pike's birthplace, where he had had before the war something of a reputation as a poet, the editors of the *Evening Transcript* viciously attacked him in an article of March 15, 1862, entitled "The New Indian Warfare and Its Hero."

> Southwestern advices stated, some time since, that Albert Pike was stirring up the Indians of the Plains to fight against the United States. An example of the result of his efforts has come to the world through the battle of Pea Ridge. There were Mr. Pike's copper colored allies, with their scalping-knives, in all their original merciless ferocity. It is hard to believe that such a miscreant could have existence—as one who was willing to reopen the war of the savage, and that upon his own blood and upon his own countrymen. But renegades are always loathsome creatures, and it is not to be presumed that a more venomous reptile than Albert Pike ever crawled upon the face of the earth.
>
> The meanest, the most rascally, the most malevolent of the rebels who are at war with the United States Government, are said to be recreant Yankees. Albert Pike is one of these. He has been called Albert Pike of Newburyport, as he emigrated from that place; but he was born in Boston. His father was a journeyman shoemaker, but he never did his duty to the son, or he would have *strapped* him into a decent observance of the commands of God and the regards of man. There is no pit of infamy too deep for him to fill.

A writer for the *Chicago Tribune*, March 25, 1862, though obviously no closer to Pea Ridge than his desk in the Chicago office, shed "further light" on the "atrocities of the Indians." Some three thousand Cherokees, Choctaws, Creeks, and Seminoles, led by "Col. Albert Pike, a Northern man, who deserves and will doubtless receive eternal infamy for his efforts to induce a horde of savages to butcher brave men who had taken up arms to prevent the subversion of the Republic," had committed "shocking barbarities." They, as rebels were wont to do, fought from behind logs and trees, "anxious to destroy, but fearful of exposure"; and maddened by liquor given them immediately before the battle opened, they scalped "as many as a hundred" Union soldiers, some ten or twelve of whom "were merely wounded."

> The appearance of some of the besotted savages was fearful. They lost their senses of caution and fear, and ran with long knives against large odds, and fell pierced by dozens of balls. With bloody hands and garments, with glittering eyes and horrid scowls, they raged about the field with terrible yells, and so often frightened some of our soldiers for a few moments as to escape the fate that should have befallen every one of their number.

The editor of the *New York Tribune* sketched Pike's life in an article of March 27, 1862:

> The Albert Pike who led the Aboriginal Corps of Tomahawkers and Scalpers at the battle of Pea Ridge, formerly kept school in Fairhaven, Mass., where he was indicted for playing the part of Squeers, and cruelly beating and starving a boy in his family. He escaped by some hocus-pocus of law, and emigrated to the West, where the violence of his nature has been admirably enhanced. As his name indicates, his is a ferocious fish, and has fought duels enough to qualify himself to be a leader of the savages. We suppose that upon the recent occasion, he got himself up in good style[:] war-paint, nose-ring, and all. This new Pontiac is also a poet, and wrote "Hymns to the Gods" in *Blackwood*; but he has left Jupiter, Juno, and the rest, and betaken himself to the culture of the Great Spirit, or rather of two great spirits, whiskey being the second.[12]

Inevitably the alleged atrocities at Pea Ridge came to the attention of Sen. Charles Sumner of Massachusetts, who asked on April 1, 1862, that the "joint committee on the conduct of the war" investigate, among other "rebel barbarities," "the fact whether Indian savages have been employed by the rebels in their military service, and how such warfare has been conducted by said savages against the government of the United States."[13] Sumner's motion was adopted by the Senate on April 1. Next day the committee, a machine of the radical Republicans in Congress which has recently been criticized as a gross example of political meddling in military affairs, and undue interference of the legislative with the executive branch of the government,[14] voted to send to General Curtis for information on the use and conduct of Confederate Indians at Pea Ridge.[15] The chairman, Benjamin F. Wade of Ohio, promptly called on Curtis to furnish evidence on the question, and in the interim the committee occupied itself with taking testimony on other phases of "Rebel barbarities." It was May 21 before Curtis got "the facts" assembled and June 20 before they reached Washington.[16] By that time the committee had already written its report, but it voted to file Curtis's "testimony" with other evidence taken in the investigation. In 1863 it was subjoined to the report and printed.[17]

The material forwarded by Curtis consisted of uncertified statements of Col. Cyrus Bussey, commander of the Third Iowa Cavalry, and John W. Noble, adjutant to the regiment, and affidavits from Daniel Bradbury, first sergeant of Company A, and John H. Lawson, private in Company D. Bussey estimated a thousand Indians were engaged at Leetown; Noble stated "there were Indians among the forces"; Bradbury saw after the charge on the battery "about 300 Indians scattered over the battle-field, without commanders, doing as they pleased"; Lawson judged there were "about 150 Indians" dispersed over the area where the charge was made and declared "they were formed into companies and marched out of my sight in good order." Neither Bussey nor Noble mentioned seeing Indians at the battleground on March 8, but Bradbury saw that day what he "would judge to be about 3,000 Indians marching in good order toward the battle-field, under command of Albert Pike," and Lawson said that on the same day "about 2,000 Indians said to be under the command of Albert Pike and Martin Green, marched towards the battle-ground in good order. These were all mounted, armed with shot-guns, rifles, and large knives." Only Noble and Bussey testified concerning the scalping at Leetown on March 7. Noble declared that he was at the battery when Pike's Indians charged and that he personally inspected "the bodies of the Third Iowa Cavalry" who fell there. Eight were scalped, he attested, and other were "wounded in parts not vital by bullets, and also pierced through the heart and neck with knives," which fully satisfied him that the men had first been wounded by gunshots and "afterwards brutally murdered." Bussey, who was also present at the battery, swore that after the battle he "attended in person to the burial of the dead of my command."[18] "Of 25 men killed on the field of my regiment, 8 were scalped and the bodies of others were horribly mutilated, being fired into with musket balls and pierced through the body and neck with long knives." Suppressing entirely the correspondence with Van Dorn and Pike, Curtis pointed out to Wade that from the facts presented by the four Iowa men "it will appear that large forces of Indian savages were engaged against this army at the battle of Pea Ridge, and that the warfare was conducted by said savages with all the barbarity their merciless and cowardly natures are capable of."[19]

And so the legend of "Pike the rebel renegade" was built. It was to be a source of frequent embarrassment, even bitterness, in his later life. His best friends at the North probably never believed that he could have condoned, much less, encouraged the perpetration of atrocities by anyone. But his enemies, and those who did not know him personally, never forgot what they had read during the war. To these Pike would have to explain and explain.

Even today one can hear not infrequently a thrilling account of how Pike maddened his Indians with whiskey and sent them against the Federals at Pea Ridge. Occasionally some of these legendary stories have gotten into print and been given the respectability of historical fact.[20] The late Anne Heloise Abel, generally reputed to be the outstanding authority on Indian participation in the Civil War, declared as recently as 1919 that Pike deserved the opprobrium attached to his name as a result of the Pea

Ridge atrocities. Pike had "allowed Colonel Drew's men to fight in a way that was 'their own fashion,' with bow and arrow and with tomahawk"; and the Indians had indulged in their hideous warwhoop, "itself enough to terrify."[21] She cites Pike's battle report for evidence that he allowed Drew's men to fight in "their own fashion" and a letter from Curtis to Gen. Henry W. Halleck, commander of the Federal Department of the West, of March 13, 1862, to show that Pike meant by this "with bow and arrow and with tomahawk."[22] As proof that this act brought Pike a well-deserved reputation of infamy, she cites and quotes only a scurrilous editorial in the *New York Tribune* of March 27, 1862.[23]

Pike's order for Watie's and Drew's men to dismount and "join in the fight in their own fashion," that is, from behind trees, was given after the Indians were chased from the captured Federal battery by a second enemy battery. Neither Cherokee regiment was, as a matter of fact, engaged with the enemy after the order was given, for Osterhaus kept them pinned behind the trees with artillery fire during the remainder of the battle at Leetown. The evidence submitted by Curtis to the Senate committee in May 1862 mentions no use of bows and arrows and tomahawks by the Cherokees; therefore it is improbable that Curtis had any basis beyond surmise for his statement to Halleck in March that the Indians had employed such weapons. Whether these archaic weapons were, if used, more barbaric or more brutal than muskets, bayonets, sabers, and rifle butts—especially the last in hand-to-hand combat—would be a matter of opinion; the Cherokees probably considered Osterhaus's artillery damned unsportsmanlike, if not uncivilized. But even if the worst of the charges against the Indians be accepted, it is absolutely impossible to find the slightest evidence to prove that Pike either authorized or countenanced such atrocities. His promptness in condemning scalping and the killing of wounded men, and his sincerity in forwarding to Curtis a copy of his order against such practices, show that he did regard these inhumanities with horror. Not only was Abel's use of evidence unsound, her conclusion was utterly ridiculous.

XXXI

Pen-and-Ink Campaigning in the Territory

LONG BEFORE THE NORTHERN PRESS and Curtis and his men finished damning Pike and the Confederacy for Indian barbarities at Pea Ridge, Pike had settled down to the business of becoming a pen-and-ink general. Pea Ridge was, as it turned out, the only battle in which Pike participated. Henceforth his greatest energy was put forth in administering to the Indians, and in quarreling with superiors. But his life was scarcely ever dull; for where he was there was smoke, and where there was smoke there was fire—or soon would be.

Pike learned on returning to Cantonment Davis that the treaty money which he had sent from Cincinnati to Fort Gibson was safe. He had it conveyed to his headquarters, and on March 20–21 paid the chiefs and national treasurers of the Chickasaws and Seminoles, taking receipts as before in Rector's name. To insure uninterrupted operation of the agencies Pike also delivered funds in Rector's name to the Choctaw and Chickasaw agents and to the joint agent of the Osage, Senecas, Quapaws, and Shawnees, but he was unable to see the agents of the Creeks, Seminoles, and Reserve Indians. On the completion of the Seminole payment March 21, Pike had disbursed in all over half a million dollars, though he still had on hand approximately $200,000 for the reserve and Comanche Indians, the agencies, and the contingent expenses of the superintendency.[1]

With the Indian payments off his hands Pike turned his attention to military matters. He was discouraged over the condition of affairs in Arkansas, concluding that Van Dorn's evacuation of the line of the Boston Mountains had uncovered and exposed the right flank of the Indian country above the Arkansas and Canadian to invasion. Believing Cantonment Davis had thus become untenable, he deemed it necessary to abandon the post for a more defensible position south of the Canadian.[2] Accordingly he issued orders on March 21 for Major Quesenbury to proceed at once to Scalesville, Choctaw Nation, a trading station situated a few miles below the Canadian at the junction of the Missouri-Texas and Fort Smith-California roads (later the site of McAlester), to select and purchase a site and to erect buildings for a new headquarters for the Department of Indian Territory.[3] Pike reasoned that he would have in front of him at Scalesville all the roads north of the Canadian by which the enemy could advance. Van Dorn would protect his right, and he himself could look after his left and front. Moreover, his supply lines to Texas and Fort Smith would be not only safer but shorter.[4]

To garrison his new post Pike planned to use only white troops. He would leave the Indians in their respective nations as home guards to raid and harass the enemy if they should invade the territory. In case such tactics failed to stop and turn back the invaders, the Indians would then join him behind entrenchments to be constructed at Scalesville and aid in defending the line of the Canadian. A secondary advantage to be realized from employing the Indian troops as home guards would be that two-thirds of them could be furloughed to return to their farms to plant corn. This he provided for in orders issued to the Indian commanders on March 22; the men should seize their arms and rejoin their organizations if the enemy entered the territory.[5]

In making the decision to withdraw his headquarters to Scalesville Pike acted upon his own authority, believing he had the sanction of both the War Department and Van Dorn for his independent course. But before Quesenbury had begun work on the proposed headquarters at Scalesville Pike heard from the district commander. Van Dorn had decided to take the Confederate forces in Arkansas to the eastern part of the state and charged Pike with the defense of the state against invasion from the northwest. He did not expect Pike to give battle to a large force but merely to delay, impede, and prevent such a force from entering the state. To assist his Indians in the work of harassing the enemy Pike could have Capt. William E. Woodruff's battery, raised for him in Arkansas, and two Texas cavalry regiments then en route to Van Buren, but he must make every effort to maintain his force independent of the main army of the district, purchasing his subsistence supplies wherever possible and drawing his ammunition from either Little Rock or New Orleans. In case of emergency he could call on southwest Arkansas and north Texas for additional troops, but "in case only of absolute necessity" could he move southward.[6]

Thus began the trouble that was to make the next few months of Pike's long life the most distressing and, in the opinion of many, the least creditable to him. He was stubborn once his mind was made up, and his mind was never more firmly made up than it was in the last week of March 1862. He had devised what he believed to be the soundest possible plan under given conditions for the defense of Indian Territory. Furthermore, he had convinced himself that he was responsible for its defense alone and that under no circumstances should it be attached to Arkansas. To do so would subordinate its interests and the welfare of the Indians to those of the state. McCulloch had tried to defend both the territory and Arkansas and had been forced by pressure of public opinion in Arkansas to keep all his white troops there. It was to quiet Indian dissatisfaction over this unfair situation that the Confederate government had made the territory an independent department and had sent Pike to command it with the promise that white troops would be stationed there. But now the commander of the Trans-Mississippi District, whom Pike had acknowledged as his superior, had again tied western Arkansas to the Indian country and had ordered him to look to its defense. The order was, in Pike's opinion, a clear violation of established policy, and he ignored it.[7]

Pike could ignore the order to defend western Arkansas, but he would not ignore the defenseless condition that the region would be in once Van Dorn moved east. Fort Smith and the roads leading westward from it into the country below the Arkansas and Canadian would then be within the grasp of the Federal army. This meant that the line of the Canadian would be untenable because the enemy could easily place itself astride all communications between it and Texas. Pike concluded that the only alternative was to fall back to Red River Valley; contrary to Van Dorn's orders, he vacated Cantonment Davis and put his men and train on the road toward Texas before the end of March.[8]

Pike had expected criticism of his retreat to the south, and he was prepared to accept it. The result he most feared and hoped to forestall was that the Cherokees would feel that he had forsaken their country and left it open to invasion. At North Fork Village, where he paused April 1, he wrote to Chief Ross and to Colonels Drew and Watie explaining the military necessity of his movement and assuring them that he did not mean to abandon their nation. He would keep Drew's and Watie's regiments there and the Creeks and Seminoles in their respective nations. The commanders of these forces would advise him of the approach of the enemy, "harass his flanks and rear, stampede his animals, destroy his foraging parties, and at last if he still advances, gaining his front join me within my lines and aid in utterly defeating him there." The Choctaws and Chickasaws he would retain in their countries near him, along with his white troops, and he would send his Texas cavalry alternately into the Cherokee Nation to assist Watie and Drew in harassment of any invading force. The Cherokees must not listen, therefore, to any report that he meant to abandon their country, but they must understand the necessity of his retreat. He would not let the enemy gain his rear and compel the territory's destruction or surrender. He would go to the south and, calling to him all the Indian troops, select and "fortify a strong position." There he could destroy any force that should dare attack his works.[9]

From North Fork Village (today the site of Eufaula), Pike continued southward along the Missouri-Texas road, passing through Scalesville, Perryville, and Boggy Depot before he finally halted at Nail's Bridge on Blue River, twenty miles above Red River and approximately forty miles north of Sherman, Texas. Though the Blue flowed in a general southeast direction, it ran due south at Nail's Bridge. Immediately west of the crossing, the Missouri-Texas road passed over a high, flat-topped, treeless hill which was bounded on the north and west by rolling prairie grasslands. The narrow bottom of the Blue was heavily timbered and the area was well watered. Pike selected this eminence for his headquarters, naming it Fort McCulloch in honor of the heroic Texan who had died at Pea Ridge.[10]

Pike planned and began construction of an elaborate set of entrenchments and gun emplacements at Fort McCulloch, but progress was slow. His white troops, two regiments of Texas cavalry under Colonels Robert H. Taylor and Almarine Alexander, a regiment of Arkansas infantry under Col. C. L. Dawson, and two companies of artillery commanded by Maj. William E. Woodruff Jr., probably did not gather at headquarters until late April, and most them appear to have been violently opposed to pick and shovel work.[11] Pike was able to report to the War Department on May 4 that he had overcome their aversion and that work on the entrenchments was underway, though he had less than a thousand men fit for duty. He blamed bad weather and bad cooking for the fact that the remainder were either sick or absent on sick leave.[12]

Pike's report of May 4 also contained full details of his plan to hold and defend Indian Territory. He was confident that he had acted wisely in leaving the Indians in their own nations and in withdrawing his headquarters to Blue River. His works at Fort McCulloch would command the roads to Forts Smith and Gibson, to Forts Washita, Arbuckle, and Cobb, and to the towns of Sherman, Bonham, and Preston in Texas. In north Texas he could procure ample supplies of forage and subsistence, neither of which he could have obtained on the Arkansas and Canadian. His chief problem would be in procuring ordnance and quartermaster supplies. Most of what he had purchased and shipped to his department had been stopped at Fort Smith and taken by Van Dorn, who had gone to Tennessee to aid Beauregard. Major Woodruff had rescued eighteen pieces of artillery, twelve of them Parrott guns, and a hundred rockets, but Van Dorn had gotten the caissons of the Parrot guns, 3,000 pounds of cannon powder, and several pieces of artillery. Pike's staff had managed to salvage his rifle powder, a small quantity of buckshot, and some percussion caps and lead, but they had saved only a negligible portion of his shoes, clothing, and tents, and none of his small arms. Van Dorn had also taken $160,000 intended for the Indian Service, leaving Pike's department quartermaster and commissary completely without funds.

To fill deficiencies in ammunition and quartermaster supplies created by these losses, Pike had sent agents to Memphis and New Orleans, and to keep forage and food coming from Texas he had advanced $20,000 from his own pocket. But this would soon be exhausted, and then he would have infinite trouble unless money were sent to him shortly. Texans, while unwilling to take certified accounts in exchange for provisions, would gladly take Confederate notes. He hoped President Davis would see fit to allow him every possible discretion in the management of the Indian country. If this was granted, he would be willing to assume full responsibility for Indian defense; without it he would be helpless. He asked that the command be restored to the status of a department, that he be given sole control of all Indian troops, that he be allowed to keep a white force to encourage and reassure the tribes, and that his department quartermaster and commissary draw their funds directly from Richmond and thus be freed from the necessity of transacting business through officers at Fort Smith and from the burden of complying with outrageous beef and bacon contracts made by the commissary general at Richmond. He was endeavoring to put an end to swindling by contract and preferred "to purchase corn, flour, and meat of the provider himself."[13]

Meanwhile, Rector had tried to make trouble for Pike over the Indian payments, alleging in reports to S. S. Scott, acting commissioner of Indian affairs, that Pike had improperly disbursed the treaty and agency moneys.[14] Pike explained his conduct to the complete satisfaction of the secretary of war, who accepted Rector's resignation and left Pike to act as superintendent until another appointment could be made.[15]

Disturbed over a report from Leeper that one of the reserve bands had crossed Red River into Texas and returned with stolen horses, Pike decided in early May to invite the reserve and Comanche chiefs to visit Fort McCulloch for a talk. He thought a look at the white troops and "the effect of a rocket or two" might teach them that the Confederacy had "the power either to protect or punish them."[16] Major Woodruff long afterward remembered Pike's powwow with these chiefs as one of the outstanding events that took place at Fort McCulloch. "It was a wonderful thing," he said, "to see them as they sat in a semi-circle in front of General Pike's large office tent all day long, gazing at his striking and majestic person, as he sat writing, or reading and smoking. They seemed to reverence him like a God." Before the council adjourned Pike ordered Woodruff to send a section of artillery to the edge of the camp for the demonstration.

> The effect on an old chief standing near . . . the firing party was amusing. His face had about as much expression as a . . . grindstone, until the first shell exploded about one-fourth of a mile distant. The chief turned to the officer, all wonder and astonishment, and holding up two fingers said, "Him shoot twice," then relapsed as if ashamed, into the grindstone stage.[17]

While Pike was attempting to surmount the difficulties of supplying his troops, of constructing fieldworks at headquarters, and of keeping the good will and friendship of the Indian wards of the Confederacy, new trouble was brewing for him in Arkansas. After Van Dorn moved his army to Tennessee in April to help Gen. P. G. T. Beauregard defend the vital rail junction at Corinth, Mississippi, violent opposition sprang up in Arkansas over the defenseless condition in which he had left the state.[18] To quell this dissatisfaction Beauregard on May 26–27 relieved Maj. Gen. Thomas Carmichael Hindman from the head of a division in his army and sent him to Arkansas to command the Trans-Mississippi District.[19] A resident of Helena and a popular anti-Johnson Democrat, Hindman hastened to Little Rock and began to organize the defenses of his state. He assumed command of the district on May 31, issuing a bombastic address to the citizens and the soldiers of his command that he had come "to drive out the invader or to perish in the attempt." The same day he sent an order to Pike to send his entire white infantry force and Woodruff's battery to Little Rock "without the least delay."[20]

The arrival of Hindman's courier at Fort McCulloch the afternoon of June 8 found Pike already incensed. Van Dorn's official report of the battle of Pea Ridge had turned out to contain not a single line acknowledging that Pike and the Cherokees were in the action or that the Choctaws and Creeks had helped bring off Van Dorn's train. Piqued by the general's ingratitude, Pike had immediately protested to the War Department, adding for good measure accounts of how Van Dorn had plundered him of supplies and money and left his troops unpaid and unclothed.[21] And just a week before Hindman's messenger arrived, Pike had had to refuse a request from Van Dorn through his old antagonist, Brig. Gen. John Selden Roane, to send white troops to Arkansas.[22]

Hindman's order was under these circumstances a blow that Pike could hardly have been expected to accept with equanimity. Though he grudgingly complied with it,[23] he wrote during the evening of June 8 a vigorous protest to Hindman. He related the outrages and misfortune that had been his lot as Indian commander, warned Hindman that his order had destroyed his plan and paralyzed all his efforts to save the Indian country for the Confederacy, and declared that unless he was allowed full power to manage affairs there he would "decline further responsibility for what I cannot help."

> I confess I am discouraged. All my toil ends in nothing. We are confessing our weakness too palpably to these Indians, breaking our promises to them, withdrawing our handful of troops from their country, and telling them we are unable

to arm, clothe, or pay them. They never should have been asked to go out of their own country to fight our battles. They are a little people, and we promised to protect *them*. I promised we would do it; *Congress* promised it; the *President* promised it.

He professed that he did not consider himself "justly or properly treated by being placed under any other officer" and that he meant to have the Indian country restored to the status of an independent department if he could. Hindman would do him an injustice to think, however, that he was merely opposed to being commanded by him in particular or that he desired a promotion to department commander. He only wanted "to save the Confederacy this fine Indian country." He could have done it had he been let alone and believed he could do it yet if he could be free and could have the means to carry out his plans.

If I remain under your command, I beg you to leave, as General Van Dorn promised he would do, this country to my entire control. You . . . will pardon me for saying that, giving orders at a distance, you are more likely to do harm than good. If you can send me back my guns and help me . . . get ammunition, I can take care of the rest. Even if I were left here with no troops but the Indians, I should be reluctant to resign, but it would be wiser and better for me to do so if the singular course adopted by General Van Dorn in stripping me of supplies, without notice or apology, were to be continued. It was a contemptuous indignity to me, personally, and, I think, equally unwarranted by law and justice.[24]

Pike heard nothing from Hindman until six o'clock in the evening of June 24, when he received a curt message dated Little Rock, June 17. The commanding general wanted to know if Pike had sent the artillery and infantry to Little Rock as ordered, and directed him to move his remaining white force "to or near Fort Gibson" as soon as possible. Pike dispatched a reply by Hindman's courier the same night. "As long as I retain my command here," he began, "I shall obey all lawful orders received from any quarter, if I can." Woodruff and Dawson had been ordered to Little Rock on June 8 and were either still en route or there by now. He would move the residue of his white troops to the neighborhood of Fort Gibson, but Hindman must expect delays. Most of the Texas cavalry had been furloughed to help with the wheat harvest and would not be due at Fort McCulloch until June 25. Following that, elections for reorganization and lack of transportation would mean further delay. Half his wagons were unserviceable and a great many of the serviceable ones were scattered among the several Indian detachments. Because neither provisions nor forage could be had at Fort Gibson and because he had had experience enough with quartermaster and commissary officers at Fort Smith to know that he could expect nothing from them, he would have to carry with him what he would need. His twelve Parrot guns, entirely without powder, men, or horses, must be left behind, and other ammunition was woefully inadequate.

It looked to Pike as if he had been "very carefully and very effectively deprived of the men, arms, and ammunition . . . and . . . left with just enough to make it a matter of course that the odium of abandoning the country, when the necessity comes, shall be thrown on me." He assured Hindman that he would "take good care, in advance," that it was not, though he would hold the country as long as possible. But he thought the movement north with his skeleton force foolhardy, believing it would be "no extraordinary result" if it ended in disaster and total loss of Indian Territory. He would not of his own accord leave Fort McCulloch but would stay there, "complete the works commenced, collect and organize, drill and discipline troops, especially infantry, until I was strong enough not to be easily run across Red River, no matter who gabbled, or however loudly, about 'falling back,' and 'staying in intrenchments.'"[25]

From this time on the quarrel between Pike and Hindman never slackened. When Hindman on June 17 put Maj. N. Bart Pearce in supreme control at Fort Smith as commissary, acting quartermaster, and acting ordnance officer for northwest Arkansas and Indian Territory, Pike not only refused to recognize him but informed the secretary of war on June 30 that if Pearce attempted to operate west of the Arkansas line without reporting to him personally he would have him arrested. Other communications from Pike to the War Department during the last week of June and the early days of July carried reports that Hindman had seized at Little Rock and Fort Smith rifles and ammunition consigned to Pike, that Hindman had asserted control over Pike's medical director, and that Hindman had placed Col. J. J. Clarkson of the Missouri state guard, an officer outranked by three Indian colonels who held Confederate commissions, in command of Indian forces north of the Arkansas River. Pike protested that in each case Hindman had unlawfully interfered with and virtually deprived him of his command.[26]

In the intervals between appeals to the secretary of war, Pike was busy preparing to move his supplies and troops to Fort Gibson. Hampered by troop reorganization, horseshoeing, and oppressively hot weather, he made slow progress. On June 29 he ordered Col. J. G. Stevens, new commander of Taylor's regiment, to march for the Arkansas within five days and Colonel Alexander to be ready to move at a day's notice. But on July 3 he reported to Hindman that neither of the regiments had left, though one of his two independent Texas companies had gone. The other was "debating about bounty and pay." If they gave him any trouble, he would open on them with his artillery and drive them across the Red River. "They provoke me beyond endurance." Three of Stevens's companies would march on July 4, but transportation was so scant that the rest of his men would be unable "to move in less than twelve or fourteen days. All our wagon-tires are dropping off."[27]

Meanwhile, Pike had discovered a new "usurpation" by Hindman that ultimately turned out to be the bitterest bone of contention between them. To preserve society and to create and maintain an army, Hindman had at the end of June proclaimed martial law in Arkansas. While this step may have been, as Hindman believed, both necessary and desirable, the fact was that Confederate law vested the power to declare martial law exclusively in the president.[28] On July 3 Pike, calling himself "a private citizen of Arkansas," though he was then commanding at Fort McCulloch, forwarded to the president a printed letter lecturing Davis upon his duties under the act for suspending the writ of habeas corpus and declaring martial law. He then launched into a rhetorical assault on Hindman's regime in Arkansas. Vested with legislative, executive, and judicial powers, Hindman's provost marshal wore "Like a triple-headed Deity . . . the robes of the Senator and the ermine of the Judge, and wields the bloody fasces of the Lictor at once."

Pike asked, "in the name of thousands upon thousands who dare not lift up their voices in condemnation or protest," that the president not only annul Hindman's illegal and arbitrary measures but also mark them with "signal disapprobation." Davis's only reaction was to reprimand Pike for addressing the president through "a printed circular," the publication of which was "a grave military offense" and one of "the slowest and worst courses" that could be taken to secure redress of alleged evils. Pike informed Davis that his letter was not a printed circular and that it was not published until after the president had received it, but the icy chief executive did not acknowledge his explanation.[29]

By early July the Pike-Hindman controversy was fast approaching a climax, for Hindman was badgering Pike to the breaking point.[30] On July 7 he opened a new attack by dispatching Capt. L. P. Dodge to Fort McCulloch to take Pike's Parrott guns. They were badly needed in Arkansas, Hindman explained, and might be "wholly worthless" to Pike. Dodge could hardly have reached the Indian country before Pike received on July 11 a telegraphic message from Hindman dated Little Rock, July 8, ordering him to travel night and day with his staff to Fort Smith and take command of all forces in Indian Territory and northwest Arkansas. Pike had already declined to obey similar orders from Van Dorn in March, and he was, as Hindman undoubtedly knew, in no mood to comply with Hindman's orders in July.[31] Instead of complying Pike wrote out a letter of resignation and sent it to the district commander with the request that it be forwarded to President Davis. He also requested that Hindman relieve him of command and grant him leave of absence until the president could act on his resignation.[32]

The rest of July was epilogue. Pike had gotten his troops as far as Boggy Depot, twenty-five miles from Fort McCulloch, on July 15 when he met orders from Hindman to send his "best battery" and a company or squadron of white cavalry to Fort Smith. He complied with the order and repeated the request for relief, warning that if he had not received notification to that effect within two weeks he would place the command in Colonel Cooper's hands. A week later, on Monday, July 28, Pike received somewhere south of the Canadian orders from Hindman relieving him of command and directing him to report in person to headquarters in Little Rock.[33]

Refusing to go to Little Rock as ordered, Pike showed up at Fort Washita, Chickasaw Nation, on July 31, an eventful day as it turned out, for he occupied part of it in composing and publishing in print an address to the chiefs and people of the Five Civilized Tribes. He told them that he had resigned and been relieved of command of Indian Territory because Hindman had ordered him out of their country to defend northwest Arkansas, "an act of injustice to you which no power on earth could make me do." Moreover, he shifted all blame for the fact that the Indian troops had been left unpaid, unclothed, unarmed, and unsupported by adequate numbers of white troops from himself and from the Confederate government to Van Dorn and Hindman. Promising the Indians that these evils would all be remedied, that he would go to Richmond to inform the president of the manner in which they had been treated, and that he would do everything in his power to see that their annuities for 1862 should be paid, he besought them to remain loyal to the Confederate cause. If he was not again placed in command of their country, some other officer in whom they could confide would be. And no matter what might be told them about him, they would soon learn that he had never made them a promise that he had not expected to be kept and that he "had never broken one intentionally nor except by the fault of others."³⁴

There could be little doubt of Pike's purpose in this address. The Cherokee Nation had been invaded by a Federal expedition in early July and Drew's regiment, never steadfast in its devotion to the Confederacy, had deserted and gone over to the Union. Pike feared that the spirit of defection might spread to Watie's regiment and to the other tribes and knew that he must do what he could to retain their loyalty and good will. Since their confidence in the Confederacy depended almost solely on their faith in him, he cogently reasoned that to vindicate himself against Van Dorn and Hindman would be also to defend the Confederacy against all blame for what those two officers had done, or had failed to do. He thus argued that Van Dorn's and Hindman's deeds were not acts of the government and that they, not he or the president, were guilty of the wrongs done the Indians. Pike's "motives were pure and could not be honestly impugned by anybody. The address was an error of judgment but it was made with the best of intentions."³⁵

But Col. Douglas H. Cooper, who had replaced Pike as commander of Indian Territory, either did not see, or pretended not to see, any good in the address. Suppressing all copies in reach and denouncing Pike as either a lunatic or traitor, he ordered him arrested and conveyed to Hindman's headquarters at Little Rock. Cooper reported to Hindman that if Pike was sane he should be punished for violating army regulations against publications concerning Confederate troops. Hindman approved Cooper's action, ordered Pike sent to Little Rock in custody, and forwarded Cooper's report to Richmond with an endorsement asking to withdraw his approval of Pike's resignation in order that he might court-martial him "on charges of falsehood, cowardice, and treason."³⁶

Warned that an armed force was on its way to Fort Washita to arrest him, Pike escaped into Texas. At Bonham, ten miles below the Red River, he deposited the balance of the treaty monies with C. C. Alexander and proceeded through north Texas to Washington, Arkansas, which he reached on August 18. There he learned that Maj. Gen. Theophilus H. Holmes, a North Carolinian, had replaced Hindman as commander of the Trans-Mississippi Department, as the former Trans-Mississippi District was now called. Pike had apparently planned to proceed to Richmond to present charges against Hindman, but the change in command made him decide to go instead to Little Rock to report to Holmes. On August 19 he sent S. S. Scott, acting commissioner of Indian affairs, a detailed inventory of the disposition of the Indian funds. He desired, he told Scott, to get the money off his hands and to settle his accounts as soon as a superintendent was in office. The same day Pike wrote Leeper that he had forwarded the agent's letters to the Office of Indian Affairs. "Having resigned and been deprived of command in the Indian Country, I am also relieved of duty as Acting Superintendent, for which crowning mercy, God be thanked." However, he expected to settle near Leeper and would "always gladly aid in cultivating friendship with the Indians and enabling you to succeed with them." Pike left Washington for Little Rock on the morning of August 20, looking "well and in excellent spirits."³⁷

Pike arrived in Little Rock before the week was over and reported to Holmes.

Hindman had already convinced Holmes that Pike was in the wrong in their dispute and that his printed address to the Indians was treasonable. The Pike-Holmes interview was extremely disconcerting to Pike. He intended to plead his case and prefer charges against Hindman, but he never got the chance. Holmes was so agitated over Pike's address to the Indians that he could talk and think of nothing else. He related that when he first read it he had exclaimed, "What! is the man a traitor?" and declared that, though he had been prepared to judge Pike favorably before he read it, he was convinced by it that Pike was wrong. When Pike tried to justify the address, Holmes severely upbraided him for censoring Van Dorn and Hindman in print and told him that whatever a commander of the Trans-Mississippi Department did or ordered "was the act of the Government." Pike angrily replied that the diversion of supplies from the Indians was not an act authorized by either the president or the government, that if he had permitted the Indians to think so they would long before have left the Confederacy, and that he had been compelled for three months before the address was issued to explain to the different tribes what had happened to their supplies and how and by whom they had been seized. Holmes agreed "that was right for local explanation" but said that Pike had committed a grave indiscretion in publishing the address and that it had destroyed their confidence in the department commander, whose good faith Pike had impugned. Convinced that Holmes had prejudiced the case and seeing that he could not reason with him, Pike requested and received a leave of absence from the command of Indian Territory until his resignation could be acted upon and stalked out of Holmes's office.[38]

Listening to talk about town that the War Department had never approved Beauregard's action in appointing Hindman to command the Trans-Mississippi District and that Hindman had afterward usurped command of the new Trans-Mississippi Department under the prior, irregular assignment—which, if true, meant that all his acts had been illegal—Pike became incensed. On Saturday, August 23, he drew up formal charges against Hindman for unauthorized assumption of command and power in the Trans-Mississippi District and Department, illegal and unconstitutional declaration of martial law in Arkansas, unwarranted and unjust interference with the property and civil rights of the people of the state, and unlawful enforcement of the conscription and military laws of the Confederacy. Though there were "specifications" of abuse, injury, and atrocity under each of the charges, Pike's principal complaint was aimed at Hindman's declaration of martial law and suspension of the writ of habeas corpus, which Pike understood to be identical in meaning. "For nearly two months and a half, the State government of Arkansas has been deposed, and the constitution of the State stricken with paralysis. It has been no State; because it has been without a constitution, without law, without courts in action; the will of the military commander its only law." Pike thought that President Davis would gladly bring Hindman to justice and hasten to proclaim that

> no military power can annul any part of the Constitution; that martial law can only be declared, when allowed by the Constitution and authorized by Congress; that when declared, it does not suspend the Constitution or the laws, or authorize the General to make laws, but only extends a known code of laws into wider

limits and beyond the immediate precincts of the army, and substitutes, as to certain offenses, the military courts, provided for by law, in place of the civil tribunals; that it does not in any wise warrant the conferring of unlimited triple-headed power upon Provost Marshals, any violation of the sacred obligation of contracts, or an agrarian distribution of private property among the necessitous, and the sweeping confiscation of the whole cotton crop of a State.

Hindman had committed all these "usurpations and outrages" under the plea that they were necessary. "Necessity," exclaimed Pike, "has in all ages been the plea of tyrants."[39]

Two days after he drew up the charges against Hindman Pike learned that Hindman's courier bearing his letter of resignation had been captured en route to Richmond. He immediately wrote a new letter of resignation to President Davis, submitting it to General Holmes on August 28. He requested Holmes to approve and forward it and the "sealed packages accompanying"—one of which doubtlessly contained his charges against Hindman—to Richmond at the earliest opportunity.[40]

General Holmes endorsed Pike's resignation on August 29, recommending that it be accepted. In a letter of the previous day to President Davis, Holmes had expressed himself on the comparative merits of Hindman and Pike. It was necessary that Davis should understand the condition of affairs in Arkansas in order that he might make allowances for Hindman's "numerous violations of law and regulations in the matter of appointments, marshal [sic] law, criminal investigation, &c. &c." He was certain that everything Hindman had done was performed "with a single eye to the public interest and perfectly seekless of unpopularity." He asked, therefore, that Davis confirm everything that Hindman had done, not only on Hindman's account, but "because to disturb the present state of things, otherwise than by modifications justified by future circumstances, would produce a confusion that might be ruinous." And then he came to the subject of Pike: "Genl [.] Pike has ruined us in the Indian Country and I fear it will be long before we can reastablish [sic] the confidence he has destroyed. . . . Please accept Pike's resignation, as he has head enough to do us great injury with the Indians, but he has not judgement [sic] enough to do us good anywhere."[41]

While waiting to hear of his resignation Pike entered upon the most inexplicable adventure of his life. In September he went to Warren, Texas, a small town on Red River some thirty miles southeast of Fort Washita. Just why he settled there is not entirely clear. One reason may have been unfinished business connected with his military accounts, but it would appear from subsequent events that his primary purpose was to keep an eye on developments in Indian Territory.[42]

On October 22 Pike crossed the Red River north of Sherman, Texas, and proceeded to Fort Washita, whence he dispatched next day a formal notification to General Holmes that he had resumed command of Indian Territory. Because the president had sent him oral advice that his resignation "could not and would not be accepted"; because the secretary of war had continued to address him as commander of the Indian Department; because General Hindman had not been the rightful commander of the Trans-Mississippi Department at the time he had relieved Pike from command; and because General Holmes's assistant adjutant-general had, in directing communications to him on October 6 and 8, addressed him as "commanding, &c.," Pike had concluded, he informed Holmes, that his leave had expired and that he had been reinstated to his command. His leave was from his headquarters at Fort Washita, and he had determined that military precedent provided that at its expiration he should present himself for duty at the same post, "there being nothing in the leave to the contrary." He hoped he had not erred in coming to the conclusion to report to General Holmes at Fort Washita instead of at Little Rock, but if he had he stood ready "to obey any lawful orders" that should be given him.[43]

Pike was sincere in thinking that the president had not accepted his resignation and that the War Department had sustained him against Hindman,[44] but he was not sure that General Holmes would accept the feeble excuse that he had offered for returning to Fort Washita instead of to Little Rock. He had good reason to be dubious about Holmes's reaction to his resumption of command, for on his way to Indian Territory on October 22, he had received and evaded an order from the general to report to Little Rock on charges of having detained ammunition in Texas. With the evasion of the order still in mind, Pike wrote a long letter of explanation to Holmes's headquarters on October 26. He had, he said, been ordered to report to Little Rock only on the condition that he had detained ammunition in Texas. Since he had not detained ammunition he had considered it unnecessary to report as ordered. Pike then launched upon "a few frank words" to the commanding general, who "hardly knows me, and has been surrounded by my enemies." General Holmes had, without understanding either Pike's position or the Indians' feelings, severely condemned his printed address to the Five Civilized Tribes. The address was necessary and had effected what Pike desired among the Choctaws, Creeks, Seminoles, and Chickasaws. All four tribes not only had continued loyal but had also increased their forces. They had looked to him alone, and for him to vindicate himself was to vindicate the government. "We lost half the Cherokees solely because their money and supplies were intercepted. If they had been clothed and their pockets filled with Confederate money they would have been loyal yet." If he had been left alone they would have been clothed and paid. It was possible that he had erred in his views on the defense of Indian Territory; if so, the error was persisted in by the president and the War Department, who had done everything possible to furnish what he needed. The president had known and had approved his plans for Indian defense and had condemned the actions of Generals Van Dorn and Hindman in seizing his troops and supplies. Pike believed General Holmes would soon be forced to admit that white troops were essential in the Indian country:

> That, however, does not interest me now. I am here with nothing, and must do with what I can. I do, however, anxiously wish General Holmes to be convinced that I have never dreamed of making a factious opposition to his wishes or his orders. I never sought a controversy with any one . . . I would fain avoid strife and controversy if I could, and I shall certainly obey with promptness and in good faith all lawful orders from any superior officer. At the same time I do not think that Major-General Holmes would respect me . . . if I obeyed unlawful orders, or if, being unjustly assailed, I did not defend myself . . . or if I did not earnestly protest against any invasion of the Constitution or the laws.[45]

By the time Pike resumed command of Indian Territory in October 1862, the fruits of the Holmes-Hindman Indian policy—"impolicy" as Pike described it—were dropping from the tree. In August Holmes had sent Hindman to northwest Arkansas to put things in order there after the Federal expedition into the Cherokee Nation had broken down from internal dissension and retreated to Kansas. Hindman went about his task with characteristic energy but with equal lack of foresight so far, at least, as the defense of Indian Territory was concerned. He removed practically all the white troops to Arkansas, neglected to send supplies to the Indians, and ordered them out of their country without seeking their consent. Meanwhile Holmes had adopted the unfortunate practice of diverting Indian moneys and supplies to the troops in Arkansas. Under these mistreatments Indian discipline rapidly degenerated. By early October, when Cooper was ordered to lead an Indian expedition into Kansas, the Indians declined to assemble on time, and once collected they vigorously protested against crossing the Cherokee line. On October 22, in the midst of this wrangling and while Hindman was absent at Little Rock on temporary duty, a superior Federal force under Gen. James G. Blunt surprised Cooper, who was reported drunk and unfit for duty, routed his divided command, captured all his artillery, and chased his troops across the Cherokee Nation and beyond the Arkansas River.[46]

Such was the state of affairs that gave Pike "infinite concern" as he entered, in late October, upon the business of trying to save Indian Territory for the Confederacy. Convinced that he had the president's sanction for resuming the command, he sent on October 24 a full report to Richmond on the desperate situation among the Indians and asked President Davis's advice for alleviating it. He blamed Van Dorn, Hindman, and Holmes for the defenseless condition of the territory and for the demoralization of the Indians, warning that if the Holmes-Hindman policies were pursued the Confederacy would lose the whole country. He fully expected an advance of the enemy either to Fort Smith and then into Indian Territory or to Texas through Indian Territory. In their present state of mind and destitute condition the Indians would be powerless to oppose the enemy.

> God knows what excuse I can make to them that they will believe. They certainly will not believe that the President cannot compel officers to permit supplies obtained for them to reach their destination. Am I to leave them to suppose that I have lied to them or that the President and Government are in fault? Must I refrain from telling them the simple truth, as I had to do once before, because to do so will impugn the action of my superior officer and subject me to the harsh judgment and denunciation of General Holmes? Shall I recognize the correctness of his proposition made to me on the subject in August, that "the act of the officer is the act of the Government?" I wish I could to-day have the President's answer to these questions. I am also anxious to know whether the President approves of leading the Indians out of their country. I have always been averse to it. I think it unjust and cruel to them and impolitic in the extreme for us.[47]

He was, he said in conclusion, "oppressed with very gloomy forebodings" and deeply regretted that the president had not seen fit to accept his resignation and relieve him from "this horrible condition of responsibility, anxiety, and embarrassment."[48]

Pike was not long in command at Fort Washita. He was arrested near Tishomingo on November 14 by a force of 250 Missouri cavalrymen sent from Fort Smith by Hindman, whose orders were that Pike be conveyed to Holmes's headquarters at Little Rock. He was taken through north Texas to Washington, Arkansas, where apparently he was released by order of General Holmes, who had learned that his resignation had been accepted.[49]

Soon after he was freed, Pike went to Little Rock to visit his family. He had in the meantime preferred charges against General Holmes for disobeying orders and for conduct unbecoming an officer and a gentleman.[50] When Secretary of War Randolph ignored the charges, Pike on December 20, 1862, released to the public his famous *Letter Addressed to Major General Holmes*, a "torrent of verbal denunciation" that "stands to this day as a dreadful monument of its kind."[51] Pike's blistering lines revealed his rage against Holmes and Hindman. Holmes had been sent to Arkansas to end Hindman's misdoings, to restore to the Indian Department what he had plundered from it, and to rescind his declaration of martial law and the regulations adopted to enforce it.

> But when you reached Little Rock, you found him there, and you found that the troops, artillery, ammunition and stores that had reached and were on their way there from the Indian country, under his unrighteous orders, . . . were too valuable to be parted with. . . . Twenty-six pieces of artillery, a supply of fixed ammunition and other trifles, on hand, with $1,350,000 in money, and over 6,000 suits of clothing in prospect, were the bait Hindman had to tempt you withal; and for it you sold him your soul, as Faust sold his to Mephistopheles. Your Lieutenant became your master; you found it convenient to believe his version of every thing, and to justify him in every thing, and you ended in making all his devilments your own, and adopting the whole infernal spawn and brood, with additions of your own to the family.[52]

By Holmes's orders, Pike charged, martial law was still in force in Arkansas, stifling freedom, muzzling the press, trampling on the rights of the people, and making them "a congregation of Helots" unfit to be represented in the Confederate Congress. By Holmes's acts Indian Territory either had been or would be lost to the Confederacy. Holmes would undoubtedly find it desirable to let the blame for its loss fall upon Pike; he probably had that object in mind while pretending in August that Pike's address to the Indians was traitorous and that it had produced ferment among the Indians. Just as power always had its "pimps and catamites" there were "assassins wearing uniforms" who would pretend to see in the address "the desire of a disappointed man to be revenged, even by the ruin of his country," and thus make it an instrument for Pike's murder. But Holmes well knew that it could be proven that he himself "as the pliant and useful implement" of Hindman was solely responsible for losing the territory. "And you may rest assured, that whether I live or die, you shall not escape one jot or tittle of the deep damnation to which you are rightly entitled for causing a loss so irretrievable, so astounding, so unnecessary and so fatal."

> It is *your* day *now*. You sit above the laws and domineer over the constitution. "Order reigns in Warsaw." But bye and bye, there will be a *just* jury empannelled

[sic], who will hear *all* the testimony and decide impartially—no less a jury than the People of the Confederate States; and for their verdict as to myself, I and my children will be content to wait; as also for the sure and stern sentence and universal malediction, that will fall like a great wave of God's just anger on you and the murderous miscreant by whose malign promptings you are making yourself accursed.

Whether I am respectfully yours, you will be able to determine from the contents of this letter.

Albert Pike, Citizen of Arkansas[53]

Pike's letter went to the public at a critical time as far as Holmes and Hindman were concerned. On December 7 Hindman had foolishly engaged a superior Federal army at Prairie Grove in northwest Arkansas, had suffered a staggering defeat, and had been forced to retreat to Little Rock with heavy losses in supplies and arms and widespread desertion. The disaster was Hindman's undoing. Characterizing Prairie Grove as "a battle fought without reason, and directed without ability," the editor of the *Little Rock Patriot* declared January 8, 1863, that "Hindman has been weighed and found wanting." The editor believed he knew now why Holmes had refused a request to send troops from Arkansas in November to the relief of Vicksburg. Such a movement might have taken "along Maj-General Hindman, and thus force him from the State, or into a subordinate position, or deprive him of the opportunity to achieve fame and laurels." Arkansas and the Trans-Mississippi must have new commanders.

With the fall of Arkansas Post on January 12 the clamor against Holmes and Hindman rose to a new pitch. "Hindman and Holmes have played *General* hell—in Arkansas," quipped an admirer of Hindman, "and even women and children are cussing them."[54] Holmes, who quite properly declined to make a public reply to Pike's letter, confessed to President Davis on February 12 that "you cannot imagine how I chafe under it." Though he declared the charges were "utterly false, or garbled misrepresentations and deductions gotten up in malice," he thought it might be wise for the government to send out a new department commander "who is entirely untrammeled." Davis could have "no idea of the degree of discontent" in the state. Pike's letter was only "an example of many that reached me from different directions." Hindman, he admitted, "is exceedingly unpopular and has no friends," and "his enemies are violent and open in their denunciations." He would be relieved as soon as a replacement could be sent out to command his army.[55]

Three days before Holmes wrote this letter to Davis, the president had, under pressure from the Arkansas delegation in Congress, assigned Lt. Gen. Edmund Kirby Smith to replace Holmes as commander of the Trans-Mississippi Department, and ten days prior to that Hindman had been relieved of duty and ordered east of the Mississippi. General Kirby Smith assumed command of the department on March 7, 1863, retaining Holmes, who had the confidence of the president and the Arkansas delegation in Congress, as commander of the District of Arkansas. "Hindman's reign of terror has passed," announced the *Little Rock Patriot*, March 28, 1863.[56]

Pike might well have congratulated himself in March 1863 on the part he had played in the shakeup of the high command and have retired to revel in the degradation of his enemies. But he was determined to try to have Hindman and Holmes punished for declaring martial law in Arkansas. The Confederate act permitting the president to suspend the write of habeas corpus had expired on February 13, 1863. Knowing that the administration would try to secure a reenactment, Pike decided to appeal his case against Hindman and Holmes to Congress while the debate on the habeas corpus bill was underway.

Pike went to Richmond in late March or early April to prepare his case. There he had printed the charges and specifications that he had made in August 1862 against Hindman and wrote and had printed an address to the Arkansas delegation to Congress reiterating the charges against Hindman and Holmes and asking the support of the delegation in bringing the pair to justice.[57] The charges against Hindman were injected into a House debate on a set of resolutions pertaining to martial law on April 13 by Augustus H. Garland, Confederate representative from Arkansas. Garland was ably supported by Henry S. Foote of Tennessee, who recited from one of Pike's pamphlets many "instances of rapacity and bloody violence" on the part of Hindman. Holmes was not mentioned by either, and though Hindman was severely condemned nothing seems to have come of their action.[58] Pike's last word in the matter was a "Second Letter to Lieut. Gen. Theophilus H. Holmes" from Richmond on April 20. He publicly announced to the general that he hoped his efforts in Congress would succeed in bringing him and Hindman to justice or at least in "permanently relieving Arkansas of the affliction of your and his presence." But having preferred the charges he would not pursue the case further. It was for the state to prosecute or not to prosecute as it chose: "I have done all that, as one of her citizens, it was my duty to do."[59] With that announcement Pike's military career and his experience with militarism came to an end; the state did not choose to prosecute. He left Richmond in early May to return to Arkansas.[60]

XXXII

The Scottish Rite Ritualist of Greasy Cove

AFTER A LENGTHY AND CIRCUITOUS JOURNEY Pike arrived in Washington, Arkansas, on May 29, 1863, only to disappear from sight shortly afterward.[1] What he did with himself during the following twelve months is clouded with legend, though most of the important facts can be sifted from the myths. He probably went from Washington to Pike County to get papers and Masonic books from his library, which he had had removed from Little Rock to Pike County for safekeeping.[2] He then proceeded to the mountainous region of southwestern Montgomery County, where in January 1863 he had purchased a small farm on the Little Missouri River. It was in an obscure neighborhood called Greasy Cove some eighteen miles west of Caddo Gap, and on his land on the very bank of the Little Missouri, he had had a cabin built. Here in this "secluded nook" he lived isolated among a handful of his books

> during ten months, with but two neighbors in the whole valley, each more than a mile distant, one above and one below, and wrote undisturbed by any one, among the great oaks and beeches, caring for my little wheat and corn fields and abundant gardens.[3]

The writing Pike was engaged in during his sojourn at Greasy Cove was the revision of the rituals of the Scottish Rite of Freemasonry.[4] He had become a Mason in 1850, when he received in Western Star Lodge Number 2, Little Rock, the three basic degrees of the order. Two years afterward he helped form Magnolia Lodge Number 60 at Little Rock and became its master in 1853. As master and past master of Magnolia Lodge he was active in the work of the Grand Lodge of Arkansas, governing body of the Blue Lodges of the state, rendering valuable service to the order as chairman of committees on Masonic law and usage, foreign correspondence, education, and library and as a supporter and trustee of St. John's College, a senior college that the Grand Lodge founded at Little Rock in 1859 to answer the need of the state for an institution of higher learning.[5]

The three basic Masonic degrees—Entered Apprentice, Fellow Craft, and Master Mason—that Pike took in 1850 were those of Ancient Craft Masonry. They were conferred by a Blue, or Symbolic, Lodge (Western Star Lodge Number 2 in Pike's case), and made Pike a Master Mason. Beyond Blue Masonry there existed then, as now, two separate rites, the York and the Scottish. The York Rite consisted of ten additional degrees and the Scottish Rite of twenty-nine. In the York Rite a Master Mason took four degrees in a Royal Arch Chapter, three degrees in a Council of Royal and Select Masters, and the three final degrees in a Commandery of Knights Templar. In the Scottish Rite the Master Mason received the fourth to fourteenth degrees in a Lodge of Perfection, the fifteenth and sixteenth degrees in a Council of Princes, the seventeenth and eighteenth in a Chapter of Rose Croix Knights, the nineteenth to thirtieth in a Council of the Kadosh, and the thirty-first and thirty-second in a Grand Consistory. Superimposed upon the foundation stone of the Blue Lodge, whose jurisdiction and sovereignty over the three basic degrees of Ancient Craft Masonry was supreme, neither of the advanced rites possessed any power over the Master Mason. He was, and still is, free to enter or to abstain from entering either or both of the advanced rites.[6]

Pike took all the degrees of the York Rite in the years 1850–53; was High Priest of Union Chapter Number 2 of Royal Arch Masonry, Little Rock, in 1852; helped form the Arkansas Grand Chapter of Royal Arch Masonry in 1851, of which he was the Grand High Priest for two terms in 1853–55; assisted in founding Occidental Council Number 1 of Royal and Select Masters at Little Rock in 1853, serving as Illustrious Master of it for three successive terms; and aided in the formation and was First Eminent Commander of Hugh de Payens Commandery Number 1 in Little Rock, 1853–56, of which he remained a member until his death.[7] Though Pike continued active in the work of the various bodies of the York Rite for some time, it was the Scottish Rite that claimed his chief attention from the time that he received its degrees from the fourth through thirty-second in Charleston, South Carolina, on March 20, 1853.[8]

The Scottish Rite was first introduced into the United States from the French colony of Santo Domingo in 1783. That year Isaac Da Costa, a French Huguenot of South Carolina, who had been appointed Deputy Inspector General for his state by a Santo Domingo body, established at Charleston a Grand Lodge of Perfection. The rite flourished in this cosmopolitan center. In 1788 a Council of Princes was founded and subsequent to that "Consistories of Princes of the Royal Secret were occasionally held for initiations and other purposes." In 1786 Frederick II of Prussia, Grand Commander of the Order of the Princes of the Royal Secret, who possessed sovereign Masonic power over the Scottish Rite, ratified the Grand Constitution of the thirty-third degree by which he conferred and surrendered to national Supreme Councils all the Masonic prerogatives that he had theretofore possessed. Since no such national bodies then existed, the constitution stipulated that nine Sovereign Grand Inspectors General in each nation could establish a Supreme Council, and once established it would assume full sovereignty over the Scottish Rite in that nation. Other provisions were that only Inspectors General would hold the Thirty-Third Degree, that no more than nine Scottish Masons could hold the degree at one time, and that all vacancies on the Supreme Council would be filled by surviving members.[9]

On May 31, 1801, John Mitchell and Frederick Dalcho established at Charleston the first Supreme Council provided for by Frederick II's dispensation of 1786.[10] The Charleston Supreme Council, the "Mother Supreme Council of the World," governed the Scottish Rite throughout the United States until 1813, when it established a Northern Supreme Council at New York City. Thereafter the country was divided into a Southern and a Northern Jurisdiction, though no definite boundary was established between the two until 1828. But that year the Southern Supreme Council approved a compromise settlement that delimited the Northern Jurisdiction to the area bounded by the Mississippi and Ohio Rivers and the southern borders of Pennsylvania and Delaware. All states and territories south and west of this line, including the District of Columbia, were reserved to the Southern Jurisdiction.[11]

The Supreme Council of the Southern Jurisdiction was not a thriving institution during the first half century of its existence. Torn by conflict with an intruding council, weakened and almost destroyed by the Anti-Masonic movement of the twenties and thirties, and monopolized until the late fifties by a group of unprogressive South Carolinians, it managed to do little more than remain alive. That it survived at all in face of these obstacles was due primarily to the efforts of two of the South Carolinians, Moses Holbrook, Grand Commander from 1826 to 1844, and Albert Gallatin Mackey, Secretary General from 1844 to 1881. It was their faith in the moral and intellectual value of the Scottish Rite and their dream that it should expand and become a flourishing order that inspired them to labor to sustain it.[12]

Under Holbrook's fearless and conscientious leadership the Supreme Council waged war simultaneously against a spurious council that intruded on its jurisdiction and against the Anti-Masons.[13] It was Mackey, however, who infused new life into the Supreme Council that Holbrook had miraculously saved. He encouraged the election to it of active members who lived outside South Carolina and worked to settle internal conflicts in the Southern Jurisdiction.[14] In 1847–48 he secured the election of William Spencer Rockwell, Georgian; John Robin McDaniel, Virginian; and John Anthony Quitman, Mississippian, to vacancies on the council.[15]

But Mackey's greatest contribution to the Scottish Rite was his sponsorship of Pike, upon whom he conferred the Scottish Rite degrees March 20, 1853.[16] Struck by Pike's interest and enthusiasm for the order and recognizing in him the intellectual curiosity, energy, and leadership that were needed to build and expand it, Mackey worked in the years that immediately followed to make Pike an active member of the Supreme Council. Finally on July 7, 1858, he wrote Pike that "my ardent wish for so many years has at length been accomplished, and . . . I am now enabled officially to inform you that you have been elected an active member of the Supreme Council for Southern Jurisdiction in the place of J. C. Norris deceased."[17] But he was not done. "You must and shall be at its head. McDaniel of Va. is of the same opinion and has written me to that effect. If Rockwell declines the vacant office, as I think he will, you are most entitled to it. I waive *absolutely* my own claim as the oldest member now living."[18] He was, he said, determined that there should "be a revival in the Sup. Council. The old fogy regime has lasted long enough."[19] His wishes were realized on January 2, 1859, when Pike's election as Sovereign Grand Commander was proclaimed.[20]

Pike had merited his advancement in the Scottish Rite. Appointed by the Supreme Council as Deputy Inspector General for Arkansas in 1854, he introduced the Scottish Rite into that state the same year, conferring the lower degrees of the order on numerous candidates and establishing subordinate bodies of the craft in Little Rock.[21] On

August 2, 1858, he capped his work for the Scottish Rite in Arkansas by organizing and setting in operation at Little Rock a Grand Consistory of the Thirty-Second Degree. Its jurisdiction included Indian Territory.[22]

During Pike's residence in New Orleans from 1855–58 he was active in promoting the Scottish Rite in Louisiana; in 1857 he was elected Grand Commander of the Consistory of Louisiana. These were years of great turmoil among Louisiana Masons. The Grand Lodge of Louisiana, the representative body of the Blue or Symbolic lodges of the state, had always recognized and cooperated with the York and Scottish Rites, allowing the lodges under its jurisdiction to work the first three degrees of either or both of the advanced orders. But in 1856 a spurious Masonic organization, claiming the power to confer the three Blue degrees as well as all the Scottish degrees through the Thirty-Third, was formed in New Orleans under the leadership of James Foulhouze, an adherent of Joseph Cerneau, ancient enemy of the Southern Supreme Council. This Cerneau body, which was "at once a Supreme Council and a Grand Lodge," enlisted a number of followers, formed several new Blue Lodges and subordinate Scottish Rite bodies, and enticed at least two Blue Lodges to transfer allegiance from the legitimate Grand Lodge to itself. So much jealousy, suspicion, and bad feeling was engendered by the controversy that Masonry was greatly discredited in that state.[23]

Pike was particularly concerned over the injurious effects the quarrel was having on the Scottish Rite, and after his election as Grand Commander of the Consistory of Louisiana interposed as mediator among the warring factions. His object was to organize the Grand Lodge and the York and Scottish orders against the Cerneau body. In a lecture delivered before the Grand Lodge on February 8, 1858, reputed to be one of the most erudite Masonic addresses ever delivered in the United States, he denounced and exposed the Cerneau council and pleaded that the Grand Lodge and the York bodies of the state unite with his consistory for mutual defense "against those who disturb the Masonic peace."[24] The union was effected, and though it did not immediately destroy Cerneauism in Louisiana the alliance weakened the spurious body and put it on the road to ultimate extinction.[25]

Meanwhile, Pike had undertaken his most valuable contribution to the Scottish Rite, the revision of the rituals. He became satisfied soon after he received the degrees in 1853 that if the order was to be promoted, its rituals would have to be revised. The following year he carried most of the manuscript rituals to Little Rock and later had Mackey send the residue to him. These he copied in an elegantly bound manuscript volume secured by twin locks, a prized possession today of the Library of the Supreme Council. The work has a "fairly complete" ritual of the three Blue degrees, but the rituals of the Scottish Rite degrees "are mostly skeletons," containing mere

> descriptions of the Lodge or other body which confers the degree, titles and dress, opening and closing, obligation and signs of recognition. Occasionally there is a "history" of the degree and a catechism or "lecture" though nothing approaching those which Pike later contributed.[26]

While copying the original rituals Pike was preparing himself for the task of rewriting them. He "collected and read a hundred rare volumes upon religious antiquities, symbolism, the mysteries, the doctrines of the Gnostics and the Hebrew and Alexandrian philosophy," and though many of the degrees even then remained "impenetrable enigmas" to him he was ready to begin writing by 1855.[27] His work was made official on March 8, 1855, when the Supreme Council, sitting in special session at Charleston, adopted a resolution calling for the Grand Commander to appoint a committee of five to prepare new copies of the Scottish ritual of the fourth through thirty-second degrees. Though he held only the thirty-second degree at the time, Pike was placed on the committee; and since it never met he alone executed the work assigned to the five men.[28]

By the fall of 1855 Pike had completed the twenty-first through the thirtieth degrees and forwarded them to Mackey for criticism. He had endeavored, he said, to find and carry out in each a "leading idea," though he had soon discovered that for most of the degrees it was equivalent "to making something out of nothing." He had, however, "retained *all* the signs, words, &c., and generally the substantial parts of the obligations," and he hoped the Supreme Council, especially Mackey, would like what he had done.[29] Pike had not intended to touch the other degrees, but after the revision committee died of inertia, he took upon himself, perhaps at Mackey's insistence and encouragement, the responsibility of redoing the fourth through twentieth and the thirty-first and thirty-second degrees.[30]

Pike completed a draft of a ritual for the fourth through thirty-second degrees by early 1857. Desiring the Supreme Council to adopt his work, and knowing its members would never have the patience to read the massive manuscript that he had produced, he had a hundred copies printed at a cost to himself of over $1,200. On March 31, 1857, he sent a bound copy to Mackey with the wish that he would carefully examine it and get the Supreme Council to act upon it.

> Everything in it has been carefully and well considered, and I have tried to adopt the crude materials of the old rituals, as skilfully as I could, to the great, general, connected purpose of the work. It forms *now*, one coherent system, and I am sure will, if adopted, give astonishing impetus to the movement of the Scottish Rite.[31]

Though Mackey was enthusiastic over Pike's revision, which he called Pike's *magnum opus*, a majority of the Supreme Council, while not rejecting it, did not approve it. As a result the matter of a standard ritual for the Scottish Rite was for several years in serious dispute. Charles Laffon de Ladebat of Louisiana, an honorary member of the Supreme Council, though not a member of the revision committee of 1855, had produced rituals for the eighteenth, thirtieth, thirty-first, and thirty-second degrees that were highly pleasing to himself and to some of the Scottish brethren of Louisiana, where Laffon's work was adopted and used by the New Orleans bodies of the order. Pike naturally preferred his own work to that of Laffon and began to use it in conferring degrees and sent it abroad to Scottish Rite bodies for their use. In consequence of their competition Pike and Laffon became quite cool toward each other.[32]

The Supreme Council still had done nothing to settle the dispute when Pike became Grand Commander in 1859. One of his first acts as the head of the order was to call a session of the Supreme Council for March 25, 1859, to consider "matters of vital importance" to the rite, and "particularly to settle what Rituals shall be used within the jurisdiction and provide against undue multiplication of copies thereof and publication and divulging of the same."[33] The session seemingly accomplished nothing regarding the ritual.[34]

By the next session of the Supreme Council, which met at Washington in March 1860, Pike had reason to believe that he had overcome the two major obstacles to the adoption of a standard ritual. Firstly, he and Laffon, who had been elected an active member of the Supreme Council in 1859, had compromised their differences over the rituals of the eighteenth and thirtieth through thirty-second degrees and Pike had, by combining their two versions, produced new rituals of those four degrees.[35] Secondly, he had in 1858 secured long-needed reforms of the Supreme Council that were likely to create a friendly atmosphere for a revised ritual. Of the nine members of the council only Pike and four South Carolinians—Mackey, Charles M. Furman, Achille Le Prince, and John H. Honour—had attended the meeting of 1859. Pike told them they had two choices: either to disband or to increase the number of members of the council so as to give every state in the jurisdiction one or more representatives on it. He was deadly serious, for at the time a movement was underway to divide the Southern Jurisdiction and create councils for a Southwestern Jurisdiction and for a Pacific Jurisdiction. Some members of the Scottish Rite were even advocating that each state should have a Supreme Council.[36]

The South Carolinians believed Pike and voted to increase the membership on the council from nine to thirty-three and to apportion the new members so as to include every state in the Southern Jurisdiction except Oregon. In order to give the states a voice in the matter of filling vacancies on the Supreme Council, they provided that where a consistory was functioning in a state, the consistory could nominate for each vacancy from its state three persons, from whom the Supreme Council should select one to fill the vacancy.[37]

When the Supreme Council met in 1860, eighteen of the twenty-four vacancies had been filled. The new members had, said Pike, been carefully selected to give "weight and influence" and "intellect and learning" to the proceedings of the Scottish Rite. Headed by John C. Breckinridge, vice president of the United States, the list included Giles M. Hillyer, editor of the *Natchez Courier*, Past Grand Master and Past Grand High Priest of Mississippi; Theodore S. Parvin, professor of natural history at the University of Iowa, Grand Secretary of the Grand Lodge of Iowa; Luke E. Barber, Past Grand Master and Past Grand High Priest of Arkansas, Past Commander of the Consistory of Arkansas, and clerk of the state supreme court; James Penn, a banker of Memphis, Past Grand Master of Alabama; Anthony O'Sullivan, Grand Secretary of the Grand Lodge of Missouri; Benjamin B. French, Federal Commissioner of Public Buildings and Past Grand Master of the Grand Lodge of the District of Columbia; William P. Mellen, Grand Master of Mississippi and an eminent anthropologist of the day; Azariah T. C. Pierson, Grand Master of Minnesota; and Benjamin R. Campbell, Grand Master of South Carolina. There were also E. H. Gill of Virginia, Hugh Parks Watson and J. McCaleb Wiley of Alabama, John R. Batchelor of New Orleans, Charles Scott of Memphis, and Thomas Brown and Edward Ives of Florida, all of whom were prominent leaders in one or more branches of Masonry.[38]

At last, said Pike to the council on the morning of March 29, 1860, the attendance comported in some degree with the dignity, prerogatives, and pretensions of a Supreme Council. There were five states with consistories; he hoped every state in the Southern Jurisdiction would soon have a consistory and subordinate bodies to extend the Scottish Rite. But the order was meant to be exclusive, not popular. The recipients of its degrees should be selected from the most intelligent, studious, and learned Ancient Craft Masons. To exact large fees for the Scottish degrees would not secure the desired result, for often the best candidates would be the poorest while the worst might be the richest. Precaution and the blackball were more effective means of selection, but there was a still better way to eliminate undesirables. A higher and truer value must be placed upon the degrees; they must be made to appeal to the intellect and be "so perfected as to make one consistent and harmonious whole." Until that was done, until the Southern Jurisdiction had adopted a regular ritual for the Rite, it would never prosper. He had completed and had had printed in 1857 a revision of the rituals of the fourth through thirty-second degrees and had since combined his and Laffon's work on the eighteenth and thirtieth through thirty-second degrees to produce a final revision of those four degrees. All of these he would like to submit to the Supreme Council for consideration. If it approved them, it might be pleased to adopt them as the official ritual; if it did not, then it should put all in the hands of a new committee of revision.[39]

Pike's remarks and material on the rituals were referred to the committee on finance. The committee never reported, but on the last day of the session, Hillyer, not a member of the committee, secured the passage in the Supreme Council of a motion to adopt Pike's final revision of the rituals of the eighteenth, thirtieth, thirty-first, and thirty-second degrees but to permit the use of "the others" for the time being.[40] Pike was obviously disappointed because the Supreme Council had failed to adopt his entire ritual. In June, 1860, Batchelor of New Orleans, who was planning to go into southern Alabama to confer some Scottish degrees, wrote Pike asking what ritual to use. "It is," Pike replied,

> wholly optional with you whether to use in your Alabama Proceedings the large Book I printed, or not. *I use it, because I don't know what else to use. I would not read the old Rituals to a gentleman of good sense.* I tried it once, at Memphis—was ashamed of them and myself, and stopped at the 18th.[41]

"Power in our Rite *descends*, from the summit," Pike once said.[42] The same thought must have been in his mind in 1860–61 when he decided to invoke the full prerogatives of his office at the head of the order to force a decision from the Supreme Council on a uniform ritual. He explained his motives and results in a report to the Supreme Council at its meeting at New Orleans in April 1861. If the Scottish Rite was to expand, he said, it was essential that Lodges of perfection should be established among the Blue Lodges to attract "the better and more intellectual class of those Masons who do not care to go beyond the Blue . . . degrees." But to do this it was imperative that a monitor and a ritual of the Lodge of Perfection should be prepared by which "all the degrees of the Lodge, from the 4th to the 14th" could be worked and conferred in full. The old rituals were hopelessly inadequate; they had to be revised so that the idea of each degree could be developed, "the formulas made more full, the absurdities and platitudes of the lectures and catechisms cut away, and the whole restored to something like what it must have been at the beginning, if it ever commanded the respect of intelligent men." The task was one that "it was useless to expect the Supreme Council as a body to undertake"; it had "to devolve upon a few." Furthermore, life was "too short for one to wait *many* years the doing of a single thing," and the leaders of the order had gone too far with the rite to allow it to fail and to be "derided as visionary and inefficient."

To supply in some degree the needs of the rite Pike said that he had requested Mackey to meet him in Washington the previous January. They together had prepared— Pike neglected to say that they had had no authorization whatsoever for doing so—with great care and in complete "accordance with the spirit of the ancient Rituals" a ritual and monitor for the Lodge of Perfection. Moreover, the new ritual was being printed in a limited edition and should be issued by the Supreme Council with great caution in order that it should not fall into improper hands. The ritual of the seventeenth and the monitors of the fourteenth and eighteenth degrees were also being printed, but the secret work of the fourteenth and eighteenth degrees was not to be printed. These printed materials together with manuscript revisions of the degrees from the nineteenth upward he wanted to present to the Council for its consideration.[43]

If Pike had any enemies on the Supreme Council they must have burned with rage at his display of nerve not only in revising the rituals without authorization but also in ordering them printed, without permission, at the expense of the order. But there was apparently no serious opposition to what he had effected. A committee of three appointed to consider his address reported on April 3, 1861, in favor of a full endorsement of everything he had done regarding the rituals. The Supreme Council approved the report and voted a resolution of thanks to him

> for the untiring zeal, the constant fidelity, the patient and elaborate pains, the profound learning and the hearty self-sacrifice in time, in study and in purse— without the hope of fee or other reward than the satisfaction derived from duty well performed—which so eminently distinguished, and still every day mark his services in behalf of Scottish Masonry.[44]

After the session of the Supreme Council in the spring of 1861 two years of war interrupted Pike's work for the Scottish Rite. But on returning from Richmond to his cabin at Greasy Cove in May 1863, he again devoted himself to the task of perfecting the degree rituals and in completing ceremonial rituals for inauguration and installation, baptism, adoption, reception of Louveteau, burial, and the Lodge of Sorrow. He was, however, not allowed to work in peace.

XXXIII

From the Bench of Arkansas to the Memphis Bar, 1864–1865

ALL DURING THE SPRING AND SUMMER of 1863 while Pike was cultivating his gardens and reflecting on Masonry a Federal army of 25,000 men moved from Helena on the Mississippi westward through Arkansas, opposed by an army of 9,000. The larger pushed relentlessly forward, and for the smaller there was nothing to do but retreat. In early September Gov. Harris Flanagin fled with the state archives from Little Rock to Washington, Hempstead County, followed by a stream of refugees; and on September 10 Gen. Sterling Price, who had temporarily replaced Holmes, was maneuvered out of Little Rock. He fell back rapidly to Arkadelphia on the Ouachita, the next line of Confederate defense, leaving his cavalry to harass the enemy between the Arkansas and Ouachita.[1]

Satisfied with occupying Little Rock and the line of the Arkansas from the Mississippi to Fort Smith, Gen. Frederick Steele. commander of the Federal army, moved no further that winter.[2] He made Pike's home in Little Rock his headquarters. In the spring of 1864 he received orders to advance from Little Rock through southwest Arkansas to Shreveport to meet Maj. Gen. Nathaniel P. Banks who was advancing up Red River with an army escorted by Adm. David D. Porter's river fleet. Steele left Little Rock on March 23 with 9,000 men and was joined on the march by an additional 5,000 from Fort Smith. Before he reached the Confederate capitol at Washington in April he learned that Banks had been turned back in engagements near Mansfield, Louisiana, on April 8–9 and was in retreat toward the Mississippi. Deciding it would be hazardous to advance further, Steele turned eastward and occupied Camden, on the Ouachita, on April 15. He remained there until April 26, when he learned that Gen. Kirby Smith had arrived from Louisiana with Confederate reenforcements and was trying to cut his supply lines to Little Rock and annihilate his army. He immediately put his army in motion to escape the trap that Smith had planned, outran the Confederate army, fought a rearguard action at the Saline, and escaped into his lines at Little Rock on May 3. For the remainder of the war he remained on the Arkansas facing the Confederate army on the Ouachita and sending his cavalry on an occasional raid into the no man's land between the rivers.[3]

Pike's farm on the Little Missouri, a tributary of the Ouachita, was virtually in this no man's region. Federal troops had passed through Caddo Gap, eighteen miles from Pike's place, on their way from Fort Smith to join Steele in March 1864, and Montgomery County tradition has it that marauders operating near Caddo Gap about the time the Federal race came through learned of Pike's retreat in the mountains. Believing he had a trunk full of gold hidden there, the marauders laid plans to rob and kill him. But Pike was warned, so the story goes, by a neighbor's son, and managed to escape in the dead of the night with his money and most of his valuable papers and books. Furious because their victim had eluded them, the jayhawkers strewed over the countryside the books and papers Pike had left behind and burned his cabin.[4]

Whether this story is true or not, Pike did leave Montgomery County at about the time alleged. We know that he wrote a deed of trust in Sevier County on March 11, 1864, that he recorded it in Hempstead County on the following April 2, and that he appears to have resided in Washington from that time until late 1864 or early 1865.[5] Pike's wife, Isadore, Lilian, and Yvon lived with him at Washington, where they had come as refugees from Little Rock. His son Hamilton, still a private, was stationed near Washington in one of the Arkansas regiments. Walter Lacy, promoted to the rank of captain, had been killed in Missouri on April 7, 1864. Pike always said he was robbed and murdered after having been wounded in an engagement with Federal cavalry; an obituary in the *Washington Telegragh*, June 8, 1864, supports Pike's statement.[6]

On June 8, 1864, Gov. Harris Flanagin appointed Pike an associate justice of the Arkansas Supreme Court. Pike accepted the position and met with Chief Justice Elbert H. English at the July session of the court in 1864.[7] Four of the opinions Pike delivered before the court at this term are still in the official reports, but the most interesting and most important opinion he prepared was discarded in 1866 when reviewed by the loyal state court.[8] This was his opinion, delivered August 8, 1864, in the case of *Arkansas v. Williams*.

Early in 1864 Arkansas Unionists north of the Federal lines in the state, desiring to take Arkansas back into the Union under President Lincoln's 10 percent plan, drew up and ratified by a vote of over 20 percent of the voting population of 1860 a Unionist constitution, abolished slavery, and launched at Little Rock a working "free state government," claiming to represent the whole state, though it probably represented fewer than half the counties of the state.[9] Samuel W. Williams, attorney general for the Confederate state government, had remained in Little Rock when Steele occupied it. In March, 1864, he took an oath of allegiance to the United States and ran for election as attorney general of the loyal state government. Meanwhile, Governor Flanagin had appointed in place of Williams an acting attorney general who in July, 1864, applied to English and Pike to issue a writ of quo warranto requiring Williams to show by what right he held "the office and franchise of Attorney General of the State of Arkansas."[10]

The vital question involved in the case was that of the legality of the government sitting at Little Rock. Its founders claimed not only that it represented the entire state but also that under it Arkansas had again become a state in the Union, that legally she had never been out of the Union. In examining the pretensions of this loyal state government as against the claims of his own government, Pike was confronted with an interesting constitutional problem. He asserted three years later with unconcealed pride that his opinion was "the only judicial opinion given in the Southern States, during the war, in which the nature of the Government of the United States and the right of a State to secede from the Union, were discussed at large."[11]

It may well have been, but if he had been more precise he might have said that it was the only opinion in which state sovereignty and secession were "defended at large." Essentially his chief concern was to prove that his state was out of the Union and that its government was the only constitutional one in Arkansas. He did this in an elaborate historical discussion, showing that state sovereignty had existed prior to the Union, that it had been conscientiously preserved at the framing and ratification of the Constitution, that it had afterward been jealously guarded by the states, and that it had been, in short, the basis of "the Federal Union," or "Federal compact," until the secession of the southern states in 1861. Arkansas had entered this Union in 1836; and, exercising her right as a sovereign state, had withdrawn and become a constituent of a new nation in 1861. Because no one could be a citizen of the United States without being a citizen of one of the states, because allegiance to the will of the majority of the people of a state was binding upon all the people of a state, and because loyalty to a state was more binding than loyalty to the Union, it followed that all the citizens of Arkansas were bound by her acts of secession and of entering the Confederacy. Moreover, when Arkansas became a party to the war waged by the Confederate States against the United States all the citizens of the state became belligerents in that war.

The Arkansas government sitting at Washington was, continued Pike, the one founded in accordance with the constitutional compact of 1836. It had been in uninterrupted existence since that time. By issue of arms it had been forced to remove temporarily from its regular seat to Washington. But it had by no means surrendered sovereignty over, nor abandoned hope of liberating, those counties held by the enemy. A portion of the people of the state and others had, without authority from the legislature of the state, met at Little Rock and "adopted and promulgated an instrument called a Constitution of Arkansas." By this pretended constitution it had been asserted that Arkansas had returned to the Union and had become a party to the war waged by the United States against the Confederate States. The supporters and officers of this supposed government had taken an oath of allegiance to the Union and had sworn "to regard secession as rebellion."

Those who thus forsook the true government of the state had become public enemies of the Confederacy and Arkansas, subject to prosecution under the laws against treason. The allegation in the petition of the acting attorney general that Williams had taken an oath of allegiance to the United States and had become a candidate for office under this pretended state government therefore afforded proper grounds for the court to issue a writ of quo warranto demanding him to show by what authority he still held the office of attorney general of the regular state government.[12]

Neither of the Arkansas governments, regular or irregular, was ultimately to survive; nevertheless Pike's government struggled for existence and remained in the contest until the collapse and surrender of the Trans-Mississippi Department in May, 1865. Justices Pike and English did all they could to aid Governor Flanagin in keeping the government alive. On July 25, 1864, Flanagin issued a proclamation calling for a general state election on the first Monday in the following October. Knowing his proclamation would not be heeded by the counties occupied by the enemy, and realizing that as a result a quorum of each house of the legislature would not be elected, he requested of the supreme court a written opinion on two points. In case counties failed to choose members of the legislature at the scheduled time, could he order elections when it became possible to hold them? In case a legally competent legislature did not meet at the time appointed by law, could he afterward convene it before the next regular session? Pike and English replied that the terms of the constitution were broad enough to justify the governor issuing writs of election at any time to fill vacancies, that it was the inherent power and duty of the executive to prevent a failure of the legislative branch of the government, and that he had the power to summon the legislature into special session at any time.[13]

Encouraged by this favorable opinion and by public sentiment, Governor Flanagin on August 9 called the legislature elected in 1862 to meet at Washington in special session on September 22.[14] His primary motive seems to have been to secure the adoption of an act to allow refugees and soldiers to elect senators and representatives for the counties held by the Federal Army, though there was other important business to present to the body. As soon as the lower house assembled, a committee was appointed to request the supreme court's opinion whether the houses of the general assembly could organize and legislate with less than legal quorums.[15]

Justices English and Pike sent a reply to the speaker of the house on September 24. The enemy, they said, could not destroy the state government by conquering part of the counties of the state and making it impossible for them to be represented in the legislature. They were of the opinion, then, that a quorum of each house of the legislature would consist of two-thirds of the members from counties not within the Federal lines and of all members who presented themselves from counties within the enemy's lines. This did not mean that the de jure state government surrendered sovereignty over the subdued counties or that those counties were legally out of the state. It only meant that the government would proceed on the principle that the counties were de facto out of the state and that they could not be represented in the de jure government meeting at Washington. Where no members from a county appeared it could be held that that county had elected either to adhere to the conqueror or to the "usurping but *de facto* Government" sitting at Little Rock.[16]

This was probably the last business Pike conducted as a judge of the supreme court. Sometime late in 1864 or early 1865 he moved his family to Lafayette County, probably because it was almost impossible to secure food in the heavily-garrisoned and overcrowded refugee center of Washington.[17] In Lafayette County the Pikes lived in log cabins Pike built on Big Creek, six miles from the village of Rondo. While sitting on the supreme court, Pike had had his library moved from Pike County to Washington, thence to Big Creek, where he continued writing on the Scottish Rite rituals and where he is believed to have completed *Morals and Dogma*, which he had started composing at Washington. Yvon, who had somehow managed to procure powder and shot, kept the family supplied with game, enabling them to survive the winter.[18]

On May 26, 1865, the Confederate Trans-Mississippi surrendered, ending the Civil War. Pike, fearing arrest by Federal authorities, seemingly started with his family to Mexico. But he stopped for some reason at Boston, Texas. Leaving his family in care of

Yvon, Pike went to Shreveport to see Maj. Gen. Francis J. Herron, Federal commander of North Louisiana, about a pass to go north, where he planned to seek aid from Masonic friends in obtaining a pardon.[19]

Pike reached Shreveport sometime after June 6 and interviewed General Herron, who told him that he was free to go to the North without a pass.[20] He took a steamboat from Shreveport to New Orleans, which he reached before June 20 and went thence by another steamboat to Memphis.[21] He had planned to stop in Memphis, apparently to arrange for opening a law office and to secure a petition from friends in the city for his pardon. But an ex-Confederate officer who came aboard his boat informed him that if he stopped there he would not be allowed to resume his journey. Pike was seemingly able to transact his business on the boat. He saw John Jennings Worsham, an honorary member of the Supreme Council who resided at Memphis and perhaps other Masonic friends. Worsham got eighteen signatures to a petition to President Johnson for Pike's pardon and sent it on June 26 to B. B. French, commissioner of public buildings at Washington, a member of the Supreme Council.[22] While at Memphis Pike may have seen Charles D. Adams, with whom he agreed to form a law partnership.[23]

Before he left Memphis Pike sent to French a letter addressed to President Johnson asking for special pardon under the terms of the president's proclamation of amnesty and pardon of May 29. He had served the Confederacy in "a war in behalf of the sovereignty and rights of the states." He could offer no special claim to clemency except that he had, after contending long against the spirit of disunion, obeyed a sincere conviction of right and duty to support a movement that he considered neither treason nor rebellion but the exercise of a lawful right. Rather than aid usurpation he had retired to private life in 1862, and both in the Confederate service and on the supreme bench of Arkansas he had "always condemned irregular warfare, violence to individuals, inhumanities, persecutions and spoilations, and all other acts contrary to the rules of war between civilized nations." He had voluntarily come from beyond the Mississippi to submit to what the president might determine. His sole desire for the future was to practice his profession, to live among his books, and to work to benefit his fellows and his race by other than political courses. He had accepted without reservation

> that construction of the Constitution against which I contended. The war had but done a little sooner that which the irresistable influence of Time were effecting. Power is as legitimate a source of government, as contract. For the future, the States compose one Nation, and the Constitution of its government is enacted by the will of the majority of the American people. Voluntarily accepting the Constitution as thus expounded, I have sworn to support it, and I will legally keep the oath, and bear true allegiance. I accept the decision as final, and shall not seek to disturb it.

Proceedings had, he said, been instituted to confiscate part of his land. He was willing to lose that. Nothing would then be left him but his books. "These, peculiarly dear to me, I pray the President to exempt from confiscation." He was, he stated in closing, unable to advance any other special claim to clemency, but he would like to remind the president that it was not "just to regard as rebellion and treason, what had been claimed by States and parties, for seventy years, as the lawful exercise of a political right, by a State." No graver mistake could ever be made than to shed the blood of southern leaders. It would only "furnish a conquered people with martyrs" to serve as "eternal inciters of future insurrections, apostles of a faith whose vitality can only thus be preserved." It was within the power of the president to prevent this and to immortalize himself by securing "to the country permanent peace, by mercy." Let him remember that "It is not by the proscriptions of Sylla, that the wounds caused by civil war are to be healed."[24]

From Memphis Pike went up river to Cairo, thence by train to New York City. At New York he went before a notary public on June 29 and took the oath of allegiance required by the proclamation and forwarded it to French to file with his application for pardon.[25] His friend A. T. C. Pierson, active member of the Supreme Council from Minnesota, who was in New York, got sixty-seven signatures of Scottish Rite Masons (among them Robert D. Holmes, Grand Master of New York) to a memorial to President Johnson in favor of Pike's pardon and sent it to French about the first of July.[26]

While waiting to hear of French's progress with his pardon Pike did not wish the Federal authorities to know he was in the city and kept himself as inconspicuous as possible. But he was provoked into writing a letter to the editors of the *New York Express* early in July. In their issue of June 30 the editors reported that Pike had stated at Indianapolis a few days before that he was confident he could clear himself of the charge that he had approved Indian atrocities at Pea Ridge. Pike pretended to the editors of the *Express* that he had not known that he had been accused of sanctioning Indian atrocities; therefore, he could not have stated at Indianapolis that he was confident of acquitting himself. Surely he must have been aware of the charges; in any case he took particular pains to deny at length any responsibility for the alleged atrocities. "When a man's life is at stake," he concluded, "a little justice should be shown him. He is entitled to a fair trial, even before the tribunal of public opinion."[27]

The publication of his letter may have exposed Pike's presence in the city. At any rate one of his friends came to him a few days afterward and told him that Gen. John A. Dix knew that he was in New York. Pike and Dix had been friends before the war, and Pike concluded that Dix had sent the warning. That night at ten o'clock Pike took a train for Ogdensburg, New York, on the St. Lawrence. The following day he crossed over to Canada and proceeded to Ottawa.[28]

Pike lived in Ottawa about two months, from the middle of July until the middle of September, 1865, waiting impatiently for news from his pardon. Idle, almost without money, and worried about his property in Arkansas, he almost despaired near the end of July when he received word that it would be three or four months before action could be taken on his pardon.[29] He professed to a friend on July 29 that he did not "expect Masonry to have energy or influence enough to obtain me a pardon. Nor do I greatly care whether it does or not."[30] But he really did care, and he feared that false accounts concerning the alleged Indian atrocities at Pea Ridge were holding up his pardon. To counteract these he sent French on August 4 a long sworn statement describing his civil and military service for the Confederacy and denying all charges of atrocity.[31] Nine days later he wrote a member of the Supreme Council that he had not been pardoned because "my Northern birth, my making treaties with and commanding the Indians and lies in regard to that command are working against me." He was, however, "anxious to be 'restored' to my civil rights, that I may set vigorously to work extending the Rite."[32]

A loan from Masonic friends in Boston relieved Pike's financial worries, and he went in late August on a two-week fishing trip on the Ottawa River.[33] When he returned to Ottawa on September 11, he found a letter from Pierson saying that President Johnson had signed on August 30 an order permitting him to return home and to be unmolested by either civil or military authorities if he would take an oath of allegiance and give his parole of honor to conduct himself as a loyal citizen.[34] Finding that the president's order insured his personal liberty, Pike went to New York City sometime before September 22. He remained there, apparently, for almost two months supervising the printing and reading the proofs of the ritual of the Lodge of Perfection that he had completely revised in 1863–64. In November he attended a session of the Supreme Council at Charleston, and then went on to Memphis about the first of December.[35]

The editor of the *Memphis Daily Appeal* announced December 3, 1865, that he had had a visit from "Albert Pike, the soldier, poet, and jurist," who had, he said, settled permanently in Memphis to practice law. In the same issue was a notice that Pike and Adams had opened a law office at 19 Jefferson Street and would "attend to all business in the courts of Tennessee, North Mississippi and Eastern Arkansas." Pike's partner was Gen. Charles W. Adams, aged 48, a native Bostonian who had migrated in 1835 to Helena, Arkansas. In 1839 he became cashier of the Helena branch of the Real Estate Bank of Arkansas and was admitted to the bar the same year. A Whig, he had served as a circuit judge in Phillips County before the war, had become by 1860 an owner of a cotton plantation and thirty-four slaves, had been an ardent secessionist delegate to the state convention in 1861, had risen to the rank of brigadier general in the Confederate army, and had moved to Memphis after the surrender because of dissatisfaction with the ruling faction of the loyal state government in Arkansas. Tall, slender, erect, with gray eyes, long hair, and beard, he persisted after the war in wearing Confederate gray almost everywhere he went. Like Pike, he was a man of enormous energy and great force of character and, though dignified, was genial, sociable, pleasant in manner, and much loved by his associates for his keen sense of humor and for his hearty and infectious laughter. A self-educated lawyer, he prepared his briefs with meticulous care and was in court an earnest, persuasive, convincing speaker.[36]

Similar as they were in careers, temperaments, and tastes, Pike and Adams had enjoyed an intimate friendship before the war that doubtlessly induced them to form a partnership in 1865. John Hallum, then a fledgling at the Memphis bar, remembered in his old age that often at the end of a day's labor Adams

> would call me to the private rooms of Gen. Pike and himself, open a box of cigars and spread of fine pipes and choice preparation of the weed. We generally chose the latter. Then [followed] an Attic hour, a genial feast of humor and flow of soul, the cream of the day, the nectar of the past. What capacity for intellectual enjoyment those men possessed—and happy the man on whom they shed their light.[37]

As soon as he was settled in his new office Pike went to Little Rock to visit his family. Yvon had brought Mary Ann and Isadore and Lilian back to Little Rock in the course of the year and they were again living in their old home, now vacated by General Steele. Hamilton had formed in Little Rock a law partnership with William E. Woodruff Jr. and was doing what he could to support the family.[38] It was not a pleasant visit for Pike. His city property, valued by him at between $20,000 and $25,000, had been seized and sold for $2,250 under the federal confiscation act of 1862, and he had been indicted for treason in the Federal Circuit Court for the Eastern District of Arkansas, Little Rock.[39] Pike had, after receiving President Johnson's permission to return home, declined to push for a full pardon, believing the president's order would suffice to protect him from arrest and prosecution for treason or alleged atrocity.[40] Now he changed his mind and wrote French requesting him to press Attorney General James Speed and President Johnson for a pardon. His property to the amount of $20,000 had, he said, been sold under decree of confiscation and proceedings were pending against other property. "If I am not pardoned soon, I shall have nothing left."[41] The same day Pike wrote Dennis N. Cooley, commissioner of Indian affairs, asking him to speak to President Johnson in his behalf. A word from Cooley he thought might win him a pardon and give him "the chance of rescuing a little portion of my property from the clutches of a set of official and unofficial harpies, whose appetite for spoil is unsatiable."[42] Five days later Pike forwarded to Secretary of State William H. Seward his oath of allegiance and parole of honor and compliance with the president's order of August 30 and requested that the indictment for treason pending against him in the Federal court be dismissed.[43]

Whether the indictment for treason against Pike and the proceedings against his other property were dropped by presidential order is not known. Pike wrote and printed two briefs for his case, pleading that the president's order of August 30, 1865, amounted to a final pardon at law.[44] If tried, Pike was not convicted, and it would seem that he was able to prevent confiscation of the remainder of his property in Pulaski County.[45] His Scottish Rite brethren, and perhaps others, secured him a pardon in April 1866. It was handed to him by President Johnson when the Supreme Council called on the president at the White House, on April 23, 1866.[46] Pike refused to accept the pardon because it required that he should pay over $300 in costs in the suits by which his property had been confiscated and that he should never claim any property or proceeds from that seized and sold under the confiscation laws of the United States. The court costs had, he told a friend, already been paid out of the proceeds, and "as to the implied conclusion of treason committed, if I were to accept, I care nothing. 'Rebellion against tyrants is obedience to God.'"[47] His conscience and conviction told him that he could do well enough without a pardon, and so it was to be.

XXXIV

Postwar Life in Memphis, 1866–1868

WHEN PIKE RETURNED from Little Rock to Memphis early in January, 1866,[1] his wife Mary Ann remained in Little Rock; she and Pike never lived together again. They had apparently had many difficulties in the fifties, and Pike had from the time he opened a law office in New Orleans in 1855 become permanently estranged from her. He professed to a relative in 1875 that he and Mary Ann

> could not live in peace, nor could the children, even Isadore, [have] lived with any comfort in the same house with her. Her temper was not only terrible, but she was captious, unreasonable, and not truthful, often saying that the children had done this or that, without any foundation for it. When it became intolerable, I quietly made another home.[2]

On October 29, 1857, Pike had conveyed the family home and grounds and all the furniture and household slaves to Luke E. Barber to hold in trust for Mary Ann, allowing her to dispose of the slaves, furniture, and personalty as she pleased but granting her separate and exclusive use of the land and tenements only during her and Pike's joint lives. On Pike's death she would receive fee simple title to the house and grounds, but if he survived her the title would revert to him.[3]

This settlement seems to have marked the official separation of Albert and Mary Ann, though he continued to house his library, which he had retained together with other personalty, in Mary Ann's home, and he apparently lived there during his brief stays in Little Rock from 1857–63. He had his library transferred to Pike County in June 1862, and he lived alone in Montgomery County in 1863–64. Before Little Rock was captured in September 1863, Isadore and Lilian had been taken to reside with a family in Lewisville in Lafayette County. Yvon remained in Little Rock with his mother, who refused to leave her home even though General Steele had made it his headquarters. In 1864 after Pike and Isadore and Lilian had located in Washington, Yvon left his mother and joined his father and sisters. Sometime later that year Mary Ann went to Washington to live with the family, and she was also with them near Rondo and in Texas. The children returned with their mother to Little Rock in 1865 and lived with her until 1868, when they went to Memphis to join their father. Mary Ann lived alone the remainder of her life, subsisting on the interest of a trust fund that Pike established for her and on the rent she received from boarders.[4]

Pike went to Memphis optimistic over his and Adams' chance of building a lucrative practice. The town had suffered less from the war than almost any other southern city. By the fall of 1865 when Pike returned to the city it was bustling with "the rush and roar of business." A Kentuckian then visiting Memphis predicted it would be "the greatest city in the Mississippi, St. Louis not excepted." By the spring of 1866 cotton mills and foundries were back in operation, and wholesale houses were doing a land-office business supplying "a section that had sheathed its sword and was again following the plow."[5] But just when economic recovery seemed assured the blight of reconstruction fell upon Memphis and its hinterland, and for three turbulent years, from 1866 to 1869, it suffered a stagnation in trade. Three banks failed in 1868, and it was reported that five thousand people had left the town that year because of the depression and high rents.[6] "I am doing very good business *on a credit*," complained one Memphis attorney. "I don't get ten dollars in money, although my usual fees are generally two hundred to five hundred dollars per week."[7]

The man held responsible for this economic setback was "Parson" William G. Brownlow, leader of the east Tennessee radicals who had brought the state back into the Union in 1866 under Lincoln's 10 percent plan. It was his heartfelt conviction that the "intelligent and influential men of wealth, who instigated this rebellion have forfeited all rights to protection and life, and merit the vigorous and undying opposition of loyal men."[8] He meant that these "rebels" should never again secure control of Tennessee, and in carrying out his program inflicted upon his state a tragic era all its own. During his administration, from 1865 to 1867, Brownlow established his faction in control of the state. By denying the franchise to all ex-Confederates and by granting it to blacks he and his legislature reduced the electorate until the vote of east Tennessee, formerly a third, amounted to three-fourths of the state's total. By enforcing the laws with hand-picked militia, Federal troops, and a servile judiciary, Brownlow reigned supreme over Tennessee, being reelected in 1867 over Emerson Etheridge, candidate of the indignant Conservative Party, by over a three-to-one majority.[9]

Pike's Tennessee clients were dealt a blow by the economic depression accompanying the political and social turmoil inaugurated by the Brownlow regime in 1866–67, and he found himself absolutely penniless much of the time and barely able to eke out enough to provide for his family.[10] His Arkansas clients were equally hard pressed by nature and reconstruction. Beset by an importunate creditor in the summer of 1867, Pike confessed that he

> *ought* to have received, for my last year's practice, some six thousand dollars, but failure of the cotton crop in the counties of Arkansas where I practice disenabled my clients to pay, and I have found it difficult to collect enough to live on. Meanwhile much of my property has been sold under the Confiscation act, and lands, of which I have an abundance in Arkansas are wholly unsaleable. Every thing here is gloomy, discouragement and apathy. We all hope to struggle up and pay by and by, but times will have to change before we shall be able to do it. With $150,000 worth of lands I am as poor as if I did not own an acre.... I have been endeavoring, by advertisements, to sell part of my lands, for four months; but have no offers to purchase. Surely lands will be valuable after a time. Mine are very fine, but unimproved in the alluvial bottom of the Arkansas, in the western part of the State and above overflow. There is *no* finer land in the world, and yet it is at present worthless to me.[11]

In an effort to enhance his power to "struggle up" Pike had entered upon an editorial experiment early in 1867. Learning late in 1866 that the owner of the *Memphis Daily Appeal* desired to sell the paper, Pike borrowed money from some friends in New York City to enable him to join J. S. C. Hogan and John Ainslie of Memphis in purchasing it. The new firm, known as Hogan and Company, assumed control of the *Daily Appeal* on February 1, 1867. Pike was editor-in-chief and Ainslie was manager. By serving a year on the paper Pike acquired a full interest in the proprietorship, and the name of the establishment was changed, February 26, 1868, to Albert Pike and Company. Pike then continued as editor-in-chief until August 30, 1868.[12]

Pike desired a share in the *Daily Appeal* not only because he believed it would supplement his income from a tenuous law practice but also because he had much on his mind to say to the people of Tennessee and of the South. His first editorial, "The Policy and Duty of the South," appeared February 2, 1867, was continued on the third, and was concluded on the fifth. He advised the southern people to submit calmly but honorably to the punitive measures of the northern Congress, asking them to remember that reverses and distresses were temporary while dishonors were eternal. They would have to yield to the conqueror as a price for having struggled vainly in a crusade for "republican freedom," but no evil, no amount of oppression, could justify southerners in becoming accessories to their own annihilation. He conceived it to be the duty of the South to adopt, therefore, a policy of "masterly inactivity":

> to remain entirely quiescent and let madness and folly run their course; to bear with equanimity what they can neither avoid or remedy; to have no part or lot in removing the old landmarks and changing the nature of government; to oppose nothing and approve nothing, and let no share of the responsibility for what may happen, rest upon themselves; to contract no alliances with any party in the North, and lean upon no broken reeds; to seek to take no part in the national legislation; to give no just occasion for the establishment of a military despotism; to consider the emancipation of the negroes as a finality, for the disastrous consequences of which they are in no wise responsible.[13]

He believed radical leaders in Congress, who had wrested from the president the function of reconstructing the southern states, were deliberately goading the South, trying to create local disturbances that would give them an excuse for raising an "immense army" of blacks to subjugate the section. By adopting Pike's program of "masterly inactivity" the South could avoid provoking the radicals to further violence. If a reign of radical terror came in spite of southern efforts to prevent it, southerners could still look to the federal courts to vindicate the Constitution and their rights guaranteed by it. "It is not the *government* of the United States that is stamping on us, but only one department endeavoring to swallow up the others."[14]

In the months that followed Pike continued to fill the columns of the *Daily Appeal* with a fantastic volume of polemic, expounding the constitutionality of states' rights, defending and justifying secession, sanctifying the "lost cause," and berating scalawags who were aiding the South's carpetbag despoilers. The Southland demanded that her sons should

> never admit that the cause in which they fought and so many heroes died, was not an honorable or a just one; that they shall never admit that their States had not the right to withdraw from the Union of the States, that their Ordinances of Secession were null and void, and secession, rebellion and treason. She demands of them . . . that they shall not apostatize from their ancient faith, and become allies of a sordid Jacobinism, baser and more corrupt than that that ruled at Paris. . . . The man, born in the South, or adopted by it, who gives countenance and currency to the infamous and dishonoring measures of reconstruction, by accepting a seat in the Congress of the United States, under whatsoever thin pretext he endeavors to mask his treachery . . . betrays her into the hands of the Philistines, and is her deadliest enemy.[15]

This moral conviction that the South had engaged in a holy crusade for freedom and independence under the principles of the Constitution, formed the central theme of what Pike considered his proudest achievement as an editor. This was a series of ponderous articles, constitutional, political, and historical, entitled "The Past Teaching the Present and the Future," that appeared intermittently in the *Daily Appeal* from April, 1867, until Pike's departure from the paper. At lucid moments in these articles Pike revealed that he understood the nature of the momentous constitutional change that the conquest of the seceded states had brought about, that is, that states' rights were dead forever. But no one "need mistake the purposes for which these papers are written," he once confessed to his readers, whom he had just bewildered by an admission that the leaders of the South had been partly in the wrong in the sectional feud before the war. "On the great, main questions, the South, in our opinion, was always in the right." Her cause had been political liberty, and she had, in seceding, "only vindicated the right of self-government in States and Nations." Because she had fallen in the struggle did not mean that "she had not the right to make the effort to win independence; for Poland, Hungary and Circassia had also attempted it and failed."[16] Southerners need not fear, he said on another occasion, "that we shall be maligned by History, or misjudged by Posterity. We shall not always be called rebels or traitors. . . . The History of the late Civil War will not always be written by partizans. By and by there will be for us a Tacitus or a Macauley." And that history, no longer "written by parasites, or dedicated with cringing servility to Kings, or lying to gratify the vanity or hatred of a people, or becoming the hired apologist for National crimes, will not fail to record the whole for the benefit of posterity."[17]

Pike claimed at the beginning of his editorializing for the *Daily Appeal* that he would keep the paper clear of politics. And he advised his Tennessee readers that it would be wise for them also to keep outside all political alignments. When the anti-Brownlow faction at Memphis, calling itself the Conservative Party, began talking in February 1867 of allying itself with the National Democratic Party, Pike advised against it. Neither Tennessee nor the South was in a position to enter into such an alliance, for a majority of their people had no political rights and could not be permitted to be heard in Congress.

> Tennessee is endeavoring to deceive herself into the notion that she sneaked into the Union, and is represented in Congress. She has not done so. She is not in the Union. The People of a State are the State, and the majority of the people of

> Tennessee are foreigners in their own State. A negro is not a member of his master's family, because he is permitted to eat in the kitchen the scraps from the family table. Better be a Province forever, than *such* a State in such a Union.

The Democratic Party could not, in face of northern opposition, dare say it would remove the political disabilities of southern men, readmit the conquered states to the Union, and open Congress to duly elected delegates from those states. When these three principles were "distinctly propounded as part of their creed, we shall begin to know our latitude and longitude." Without them "there ought to be no alliance between us and them."[18]

Though disfranchised himself and still professing to be a nonpartisan, Pike supported the candidates of the Conservative Party in the state election of 1867. But he strongly disapproved the efforts of that party to win the vote of the enfranchised blacks, declaring that the ballot "might just as safely be given to so many Southern American monkeys. . . . We do not want their votes and never shall."[19] When the party failed to adopt his views, Pike suggested that economic coercion be used to prevent blacks from voting at all. Why not refuse employment to any colored man who voted the radical ticket? He would print cards at his office which should be issued to loyal blacks; only those owning these passes would be employed by Memphis Conservatives. The Conservatives adopted the plan in modified form, using the threat to force blacks to vote for their candidates. Keenly disappointed over the perversion of his plan, Pike intensified his criticism of the attempts of the Conservatives to outbid the Union League and the Freedmen's Bureau for the black vote.[20]

As time for the polling approached, it was rumored in Memphis that the Brownlow regime intended to move four companies of state troops to the city to prevent disturbances on election day. Pike proposed in the *Daily Appeal* that the Conservatives raise a "Civic Guard" to protect the citizens and property of the city from possible outrage and destruction at the hands of Brownlow's troops, a third of whom, Pike declared, "ought to be in the penitentiary." The editor of the radical organ at Memphis, the *Post*, assailed Pike for this "incendiary" proposal and advised him to "observe his parole." Pike angrily retorted that he had advocated resistance neither to Tennessee nor to the United States in asking that the men of Memphis organize and cooperate in resisting prospective oppression. He still hoped that if it became necessary the civic guard could be formed. In the end Brownlow's troops did not come, but on election day in early August, federal troops marched into the city to preserve order. Of the 3,628 blacks who voted 3,000 supported the Radicals, while only 868 whites of a total of 2,831 voted for the radicals. Pike commended the Conservatives for cooperating with the federal troops in keeping the peace. The Conservatives, he said, might "well be content with all they have done, except the attempt to obtain the votes of part of the negroes, an idle attempt and a mischievous mis-policy, to which we never assented."[21]

Outwardly Pike attempted to pass off Brownlow's one-sided victory with indifference, but inwardly the radical triumph convinced him that a return to a government of reason was further off than ever and caused him to despair of succeeding in either law or journalism at Memphis. In the early fall he took a trip of a month to Louisville seeking an editorial position in that city. He found nothing that suited him and on October 9,

1867, resumed his place on the editorial bench of the *Daily Appeal*. He believed that the recent state elections in the North indicated that a definite reaction had set in there against radical Republicanism and professed, himself, in an editorial of October 12, glad to believe that those who voted the radical ticket in Tennessee would continue to do everything in their power to make radical rule still more odious to northerners. "The beauties of negro rule" would be fully displayed in Tennessee. The roads to Texas and Arkansas were already lined with wagons of Tennesseans seeking a country where blacks and men elected by them would not govern white men, and now a bill had been introduced in the Tennessee legislature allowing blacks to hold office. There was, thank God, not the least chance that wisdom would "rule in the counsels of the State, control the course of the lunatic who is Governor, or influence the extraordinary zoological collection called by courtesy a legislature." No, the epidemic of unreason must be allowed to run its course.

> Let the negroes be made competent to hold office, let the losses of loyal men to the amount of millions be put upon the back of the State, like a burden on a patient camel! The sooner the better. Let the disfranchisement of 80,000 white men, and the abuse of the privilege of voting by 50,000 ignorant negroes be continued: and let the people wait for the reaction that is sure to follow. They can *afford* to wait; for when it comes it will make a clean sweep of Radicalism and misrule. . . . Tennessee . . . will not always bear . . . the disgrace of negroism.[22]

By the time Pike returned from his Louisville trip, there was much talk among Memphis Conservatives of allying themselves with the National Democratic Party for the presidential election of 1868. Pike had, in February 1867, opposed a similar movement, arguing that the Democratic Party had not given proper inducements to the South. Now that these inducements had apparently been proffered Pike found new reasons why he could not support the alliance. The truth was that his old antagonism to Democracy had returned. In an editorial of October 11, 1867, he presented a plan for the organization of a new national party, whose principal aims should be "to reconstruct the Union of the States" and "to reestablish the Constitution, as the supreme law not only in peace but in war, and to deny to each department of the Government any power whatever 'outside that Constitution.'" The new party would unite, in the "great enterprise" of restoring the "Constitutional Republic," all conservative men of all former parties, who should cease to think of themselves as Whigs, Democrats, or Republicans. There were tens of thousands of honest and patriotic men, once Whigs and afterwards Republicans, who could no longer stomach radicalism and "the immense curse of negro suffrage" but could not accept Democracy. These men were prepared, "to maintain the sanctity of the Constitution, and a *Republican* form of government"; they would enroll in a "Constitutional Republican Party." This name should, therefore, be adopted as the name of the new party.

Though Pike continued during the winter of 1867–68 to urge upon the Conservatives his plan for a new party, he was convinced by late February 1868 that the case was hopeless, and he then went over to the Democratic banner. There was, he said in announcing his shift, no national party then existing at the North that was opposed to radicalism except the Democratic. He accepted, therefore, the name of Democrat, and was "also willing to accept Andrew Johnson as the candidate of the Democratic party for the Presidency; and that the more especially, if he shall be impeached and cast out of office for his fidelity to the Constitution."[23] In early June Pike approved the decision of a convention of the Democratic Conservative Party of Tennessee to merge with the National Democratic Party and to send delegates to the national convention.[24] On July 1 he was elected president of the Democratic Club of Shelby County, organized to aid the party's cause in the election.[25] Johnson, Tennessee's own son and Pike's choice for the presidential nomination, was repudiated by the National Democratic Convention, but Pike announced on July 11 that he himself heartily accepted the nominations of Horatio Seymour of New York and Francis P. Blair of Missouri.[26]

As president of the Shelby County Democratic Club Pike took a leading role in the campaign of 1868. He worked hard to collect money to finance the party's effort, making numerous appeals before the weekly Saturday night meetings of the club and before political rallies in Memphis. To him the campaign was a crusade to overthrow radicalism in Tennessee and the South. "We mean that the white race, and that race alone, shall govern this country. It is the only one that is fit to govern, and it is the only one that shall." If the people of his state and section would rise up in righteous indignation against their bondage and degradation, they could, Pike believed, revolutionize their local and national governments. "The man, or set of men, that denies me the right to vote in the State in which I live, is not my political opponent, he is my personal enemy and deadly foe."[27]

Denied access to the ballot box, the disfranchised Confederates turned to extralegal methods to aid the Democratic cause in 1868. They made the Ku Klux Klan, originally a social organization, a vigilante's association and used it to intimidate blacks into absenting themselves from the polls. I have found no contemporary, nor no reliable late evidence that Pike ever joined the Klan. Yet in at least three unreliable histories of the Klan, it is stated that he was either attorney general or a high-ranking official of the order.[28] Allen W. Trelease, the most recent and most authoritative historian of the Klan casts doubt on Pike's membership. The Prescript, or constitution, of the order provides for no such officer, he says.[29]

Pike is believed to have mentioned the Ku Klux Klan only once in his editorials for the *Appeal*. This was April, 16, 1868, in reply to an accusation of the editor of the *New York Tribune* that the southern press had neglected its duty in allowing the Klan's activities to go uncriticized. Pike then left the impression that he neither belonged to the organization nor considered it worthy of his support: "We do not know what the Ku-Klux organization may become, if it ever becomes anything. It is quite certain that it will never come to much on its original plan. It must become quite another thing to be efficient." But Pike definitely saw possibilities for ex-Confederates in an "efficient" Klan.

> The disfranchised people of the South, robbed of all the guarantees of the Constitution . . . can find no protection for property, liberty or life, except in secret association. Not in such association to commit follies and outrages; but for mutual, peaceful, lawful, self-defence. If it were in our power, if it could be

effected, we would unite every white man in the South, who is opposed to negro suffrage, into one great Order of Southern Brotherhood, with an organization complete, active, vigorous, in which a few should execute the concentrated will of all, and whose very existence should be concealed from all but its members. That has been the resort of the oppressed in all ages. To resort to it is a right given by God; and the Brownlows and Meades would find it idle to attempt, by any threats or denunciations, to prevent it, if the people were not so entirely sunken in the apathy of hopeless despair as not to have energy enough to unite for anything.[30]

In spite of hard work on the *Daily Appeal* and in the political contest of 1868, Pike found time for much quiet relaxation in the evenings of this his last summer in Memphis. All his children had now joined him, and he had taken an "old one-storied cottage" at 144 Adams Street. His partner, General Adams, boarded with them to round out the "gay household." Isadore, aged twenty-six, vivacious, cultured, even-tempered, and an accomplished harpist, was the center of the group. Her gentle and winning qualities, sound judgment, and mature thoughtfulness commended her to Pike above all the other children, and he frequently turned to her for advice and sympathy. That "Issy" was Pike's pet was apparently not resented by Lilian and the boys. She was their pet, too, and they readily went to her for counsel, finding in her unselfish love, gaiety, and exuberant energy the solution of numerous personal problems. Though more reserved and less radiant than Issy, Lily (Lilian), aged twenty-five, possessed a quiet charm all her own. She was a talented pianist and a voracious reader. Hamilton, aged thirty, had closed his law office in Little Rock and had taken in July 1868 a place in his father's firm at Memphis. Yvon, eighteen, was fresh out of a year's study at St. John's Masonic College, Little Rock.[31]

The war-impoverished Pikes had adjusted themselves well to living on a shoestring in a new city and state. The children were young and full of life and brought much happiness to their father, who at fifty-nine already thought of himself as an old man. Their love, especially Isadore's, helped him bear up under the struggle for economic security and filled the great void in his life left by his separation from Mary Ann. The children attracted to the family circle other young people whom Pike welcomed and appreciated. During the entire summer of 1868 Isadore and Lilian had three house guests who were particularly dear to him: Annie Merrick, daughter of a deceased lawyer friend of Little Rock; Fannie Borland, daughter of Solon Borland, a girl who wrote poems "of extraordinary merit and ability"; and Mignonne, in whose veins mingled the blood of Greece, France, and Kentucky, "strikingly beautiful, brilliant, fascinating, perverse and wilful, an indomitable coquette, with the finest mezzo-soprano voice in the world."

> So every night there were gay company and music, duos by Isadore and Lilian on the piano, and harp and piano, and ballads wonderfully sung by Mignonne; and little . . . Nora Bradford came constantly, a singer of rare excellence, superb voice and cultivated taste, to delight us all, and to be fond of me and make me fond of her, for all her perverse ways; and Henry Farmer came with his flute, to play the duos for violin and piano of Stauser, and de Beriot, and for flute and piano, with Lilian; and Sabatzky came to sing, a magnificent baritone; and others, some now

dead and some still living, to listen partly, and partly to talk with me, in my own room across the hall.³²

When not talking with the children and their guests, Pike preferred to swing in a hammock that stretched between two great beeches in his front yard. There he would relax with his pipe and listen to the music, song, and merry laughter that drifted out from the open windows of the house. "Ah! those were pleasant days and nights."³³

But all Pike's days were not pleasant. Especially depressing were those on which it was borne home to him that he was not succeeding in either law or journalism. The economy of west Tennessee and east Arkansas had been thrown completely out of order and none of his clients could pay. Forced to compete with a half dozen other papers, the *Daily Appeal* scarcely kept out of the red. And the competition was merciless. At one fell swoop three hundred of Pike's German and Italian readers canceled their subscriptions early in 1868 when they learned from the *Memphis Avalanche* that Pike had been a Know Nothing. Faced with rising costs and a sinking subscription list Pike was compelled to let an able associate editor, Leon Trousdale, go in the first week of 1868. Even drastic economizing did not make the paper pay, and by midsummer Pike, who had expanded his law firm in hope of greater success, decided to sell his interest in the journal. The presidential election was then in full sway and Pike was conducting an editorial crusade against Democratic efforts to secure black votes. Therefore he desired, if he found a buyer, to retain editorial control of the *Daily Appeal* until after the election. On August 30 he sold his share of the paper to John M. Keating. It was agreed that Pike would continue as editor until December, when he planned to go to Washington for the winter. But he demanded a larger salary than the proprietors thought they could afford to pay. As a consequence he gracefully vacated his position on September 2, though he undoubtedly would have preferred to remain. His letter of departure carried a solemn warning against the evils of black suffrage and the Democratic attempts to compete with the radicals for the colored vote.

> Speaking for myself, I emphatically say, that I would infinitely rather be defeated by the negro vote than succeed by means of it, if to gain it, it is necessary to vote. A victory so gained, I am sure, would be in the end far worse than a defeat.³⁴

The week after he left the *Daily Appeal* Pike traveled to St. Louis for the Triennial Convocation of Knights Templar and General Grand Chapter of Royal Arch Masons. He had gone north with a heavy heart fearing that the northern delegations, who far outnumbered those of the South, would resent the presence of the "late rebels."³⁵ But the northern reception of the southerners was deeply gratifying to Pike; not a single incident of bad feeling marred the entire proceedings. On the evening of September 15 Pike attended a lavish banquet given the General Grand Chapter by the Grand Royal Arch Chapter of Missouri. He had scarcely finished eating when the guests began to call loudly for him to make a speech. In response he thanked the northern Masons for the magnanimity that they had shown toward the southern delegates, "who you think erred in the last late civil war, but toward whom you maintained, through that war, those feelings of charity, Masonic kindness, love and affection that becomes Masons to entertain toward one another" at such a time. It was, he believed, a great honor to the teachings of Masonry that its followers could, so soon after a fratricidal struggle, meet as those at St. Louis had met, "with open arms, with no capstone to the noble example set by the northern Masons." Pike proposed that everyone present take with him an oath to bury all ill feelings "under the altar of Masonry" and strive thereafter to make Masonry what it professed to be—"an apostle of peace, good-will, and charity, and toleration."[36]

Before the end of September Pike returned to Tennessee. He made a short business trip to New Orleans late in the same month and returned to Memphis for the last few weeks of the heated presidential campaign.[37] October was an exciting month that year not only in west Tennessee but also in Arkansas. Early in the month a shipment of four thousand rifles reached Memphis en route to the radical governor of Arkansas, Powell Clayton. Since the rifles were supposed to be used to arm Governor Clayton's black militia, no Memphis steamboat captain would "handle the unholy cargo." The governor chartered, therefore, the steamer *Hesper* to go to Memphis and get the guns. The crew of the *Hesper* got the arms aboard and put out from Memphis for Helena late in the afternoon of October 15, 1868. Twenty-five miles down the Mississippi the boat was overtaken by the tug *Nettie Jones* bearing a hundred masked men who quickly and bloodlessly subdued the *Hesper's* crew, threw all the rifles in the river, and set the boat adrift. The *Nettie Jones* then started back toward Memphis. Eight miles below the city the masked men were rowed ashore. There they mounted horses that had been methodically hidden and returned to their homes.[38]

Just who organized and led the raid on the *Hesper* has never been divulged. A special investigator sent to Memphis by the *New York Tribune* reported on November 2 that Memphis Republicans were of the general opinion that the commander was General Forrest, alleged head of the Ku Klux Klan, who then resided in Memphis. He fitted the description of the leader given by the crew of the *Hesper*: "A very large, well-dressed man, very broad shouldered, a little stooping as he walked, and having a sharp, quick voice."[39] But the editor of the *Memphis Public Ledger* replied to the *Tribune* that over fifty people knew that General Forrest was at home the entire evening of October 15.

The raid on the *Hesper* was only one of several incidents that helped keep passions aroused as the people of Memphis moved toward the November polling date. The Ku Klux Klan had joined in a battle for victory against Brownlow's militia and the Union League, and many predicted that the streets would run red with blood before the campaign ended. To preserve order at the polls in face of this threat, federal troops were again marched into the city on election day. Their presence apparently frustrated whatever intention the Klan had of preventing blacks from voting. Grant received over 99 percent of the 4,369 black votes, while getting only 18 percent of the 2,971 white votes.[40] Pike had predicted that the Conservative-Democratic efforts to entice the blacks from the Radicals would come to naught, and the final results had proved him right. The new editor of the *Daily Appeal*, who had given indirect support to the policy of weaning Negroes from the Republican fold, now admitted the wisdom of Pike's staunch stand against it. The attempt had, said the editor, been not only unwise but also disgraceful. "In Tennessee, hereafter, Radicalism will be interpreted [as] negroism, in contradistinction to the Democracy of the white race."[41]

XXXV

Rebel Lawyers in Washington, 1868–1878

PIKE'S TRIP TO WASHINGTON in November ,1868, resulted from business arrangements he had worked out the previous summer with his son Hamilton, General Adams, and Robert W. Johnson, former United States and Confederate States senator from Arkansas. Hamilton and General Adams had agreed to handle all cases of the firm of Pike, Pike, and Adams, at the courts of Memphis and of "the river counties of Arkansas." Pike himself, the senior partner of the firm, would thereafter "especially attend to cases in the Supreme court of Tennessee, and in the Supreme Court and court of claims of the United States at Washington."[1] To assist him in the prosecution of cases before the Supreme Court and the court of claims of the United States Pike then formed a separate partnership with Robert W. Johnson. Pike and Johnson were also to attend to claims before Congress and the executive departments. Johnson agreed to reside permanently in Washington, where he and Pike apparently opened an office in September, 1868. Pike, who was Johnson's senior, was still to reside at Memphis, though he would join Johnson during the sessions of Congress and of the Washington courts.[2]

Pike's partner in the Washington office was an old and dear friend who, like Pike, had been impoverished by the war. Pardoned in late August or early September 1866, Johnson had returned to his former home at Pine Bluff the same fall. He had somehow saved from confiscation two of his Jefferson County plantations, Woodbourne and Chalmette, comprising some 3,788 acres of choice Arkansas River Valley land. But the property was heavily encumbered with debts, and he narrowly prevented foreclosure against it in October 1866 by signing it to Pike and Adams under a deed of trust. This legal loophole kept the plantations in Johnson's hands for two more years, in which time he sank deeper in debt. By the summer of 1868 he was totally without means to pay the annual taxes or to meet other "existing and current expenses of cultivation." A month after Pike and he formed their partnership that summer the property was sold at auction under bankruptcy proceedings. This desperate step, taken apparently at Pike's suggestion, freed Johnson from harassment by his creditors, though it left him practically nothing except the hope that he and Pike could succeed in their new legal undertaking at Washington.[3]

The partnership offered certain possibilities of success. Johnson had practiced law successfully at Little Rock in 1838–40, and had then served as attorney general of the state for five years. As a member of the U.S. House of Representatives in 1846–52 and of the U.S. Senate in 1853–61, he had become intimately acquainted with the investigation of claims in the executive departments and with the prosecution of these claims before Congress. But his chief asset to Pike, who far surpassed Johnson as an attorney, was his wide acquaintances with members of Congress and with the bureaucrats in the executive offices. Pike needed and probably accepted no help from Johnson in drawing up briefs and in prosecuting cases in the courts, but Johnson's influence in urging claims in Congress would be invaluable.

The partnership had one great weakness which was ultimately to strangle it. Pike and Johnson had backed the losing side in the Civil War, and they were yet to learn that "Rebel" lawyers could be discriminated against in Washington. This handicap is illustrated by an article that appeared in the *St. Louis Times*, September 6, 1868. Reverdy Johnson, the distinguished American constitutional lawyer, was about to embark for Europe where he was to replace Charles Francis Adams as minister to England. A client with an important suit pending before the U.S. Supreme Court asked him what attorney could fill his place. The famous lawyer named several but the client found objections to each. Thinking a moment, Johnson said, "If the partisan politics of Albert Pike, who has no superior among American lawyers, might not prejudice your case, I would commend him. This is the only risk you would incur; determine yourself. He will master the facts and the law, and those who hear him are not apt to dissent from his conclusions."[4] After his removal from Memphis, Pike was often to hear people say, as he walked along the streets of Washington, "He is a damned old Rebel."[5]

In spite of this major drawback Pike and Johnson managed to hang on at Washington until about 1878, when Johnson seemingly returned to Arkansas to live. Although their practice was never lucrative, it was a distinguished one. They participated in several of the most important cases that came before the U.S. Supreme Court from 1868–76: *Texas v. White* (1869), *First National Bank of Louisville v. The Commonwealth of Kentucky* (1870), *Wallach v. Van Riswick* (1875), *Pike v. Wassell* (1877), and *Hot Springs Cases* (1876).

The celebrated case of *Texas v. White*, a suit of the state against George W. White, John Chiles, and others, was filed in the U.S. Supreme Court on February 15, 1867. The state sought an injunction to restrain the defendants from using Texas indemnity bonds and to obtain restoration of fifty-one of the bonds, issued to them in payment for Confederate military supplies by an agency of the state government after Texas seceded from the Union. George W. Paschal, chief of the counsel for Texas, was a native Georgian. He had moved to Van Buren in 1837 and opened a law office. The antibank legislature of 1842–43 elected him to replace Judge Dickinson as associate justice of the Arkansas Supreme Court. Having resigned from the court within a few months, he migrated to Texas about 1847 and by 1848 had opened a law office at Austin, the state capital.[6] Pike represented Chiles in the case and was thus pitted against a former rival at the Arkansas bar. Philip Phillips acted for White and J. W. Carlisle and James W. Moore, both prominent members of the Supreme Court bar, were associated with the defense.

The main issue in the case was whether Texas, having seceded and not having been reconstructed, had status in the Union and consequently a right to sue in the U.S. Supreme Court. Pike wrote and filed a brief of ninety-six pages arguing that Texas could not sue in the Court because it was not a state. Texas had, in seceding from the Union and in waging war against the United States, lost its status as a state. Conquered by Federal forces in 1865, it had since been governed by "pro-consuls" under a "title of conquest." This was the very essence of the meaning of the reconstruction acts, by which Texas was not permitted to be represented in Congress nor to have a voice in the national legislation but was ruled as a conquered province. Either the reconstruction acts were unconstitutional and Texas was a state or those acts were constitutional and Texas was not a state. Pike's associates in the case presented similar arguments.[7]

Basing his argument upon the constitutional doctrine that the Union was indestructible and indivisible, Paschal denied the legality of secession. When Texas entered the Union in 1845 she surrendered, he asserted, all rights of self-determination; therefore all acts in contravention of that surrender were null and void. Texas had never ceased, then, to be a state in the Union, although it must be admitted that the state had done everything it could do "to sever the Union and the allegiance of its inhabitants from the nation." The doctrines of states' rights and of secession had, he said, never been more strongly put than in the brief

> of quaint rhetoric and eloquence filed in this case by the scholar, poet, and lawyer, and soldier, Albert Pike. I have read that argument with all the admiration for the genius of the misguided author which I had when we were contestants at the same bar, and when he appeared as advocate and reporter, where I had the honor to be one of the judges of the supreme court in a young State, but far advanced in its jurisprudence.

He had little argument to advance in reply to Pike's "long and able" brief except to say that his and the general's theories were directly and irreconcilably opposed. Pike believed Texas had left the Union. "As I understand it," answered Paschal, "Texas remained a State of the Union all the time." Pike interpreted the reconstruction acts to mean that no legal government existed in Texas, because the state government was subject to a Federal military commander. Paschal agreed this was true but maintained that whether the reconstruction acts were constitutional or not was wholly immaterial to his argument. If those acts were taken away Texas was still a "corporate state" under its constitution of 1866; and should that instrument be taken away "then we fall back to the constitution of 1845 and the act of annexation, and Texas remains a State of the Union."

Though he admitted that Texas was "subject to the national legislation," Paschal rather pointedly declined to reply to Pike's central arguments that Texas, not having a share in making the national laws but being subject to them, was governed as a conquered province and not as a state. A staunch defender of the right of secession, Pike simply could not see how anyone could justify the reconstruction acts and assert at the same time that Texas was still a state in the Union. In his mind the court had but two alternatives: It could nullify the reconstruction acts and deny the legality of secession or uphold those acts and admit the constitutionality of secession. Either choice would have been a moral victory for Pike; he despised the reconstruction acts almost as much as he revered the doctrine of secession. Observing that Pike had set a trap for him on this particular point, Pashcal dexterously avoided being ensnared. He shrewdly perceived that while the court would be reluctant to pronounce judgment on the reconstruction acts it would scarcely hesitate to denounce secession. By refusing to admit any connection between the doctrine of an indissoluble Union and the peculiar status of Texas under reconstruction, he presented the court with a single problem. It must decide between two adverse theories of the Union: either the Union was divisible or it was indivisible. If the court decided that the Union was inseparable, as he believed it was, then Texas had never been out of the Union, its acts while in rebellion were void, and the bonds issued to the defendants must be restored.[8]

The attorneys completed their oral arguments before the court on February 5, 8, and 9, 1868. Chief Justice Salmon P. Chase delivered the opinion of the court the following April 12. He held that the Union was indissoluble and that the acts of secession were therefore null and "utterly without operation in law." The defendants were ordered to restore the bonds to the state. The chief justice reviewed the history of reconstruction in summarizing the facts of the case, but he made an obvious effort to avoid pronouncing judgment upon the reconstruction acts. And in asserting that Texas had never ceased to be a state in the Union, he declined to notice that Texas was not represented in Congress. He had adopted Paschal's argument almost verbatim. This line of reasoning was, states the historian of the case, "very largely an echo of the popular view in the North and it doubtless possessed in the eyes of the court the great weight derivable from the approval of public opinion."[9] Associate Justice Robert C. Grier, dissenting, announced that he was "not disposed to join in any essay to prove Texas to be a State of the Union, when Congress have decided that she is not." Congress not only had not permitted Texas to be represented in Congress but also had made her subject to the military authorities of the United States. The act of secession was, he declared, the act of a sovereign state, and the act of the secession government in assigning the bonds to the defendants was a solemn and irrepealable contract. Justices Noah H. Swayne and Samuel F. Miller concurred in Justice Grier's view that Texas was incompetent to sue in the Supreme Court, but they agreed with the majority upon the merits of the case. Not even Justice Grier offered to question the validity of the reconstruction acts.[10]

Pike was always bitter over the inconsistency of the decision in *Texas v. White*, though he was well aware that it was inevitable that the results of the Federal triumph in the Civil War should be upheld by the Supreme Court. "All the people of Texas were not Texas! There was no secession government de facto of Texas! Such nonsense the Court gravely gabbled. A State, they said, *did* not secede from the Union, because it *could* not: and it *could* not, because it could not *rightfully*: as if what State or Nation actually *does*, it does *not* do, because it has not the *right* to do it." In Pike's mind the case stood unequaled as a memorial of "judicial folly," and no one could have convinced him differently.[11]

The case of *First National Bank of Louisville v. Kentucky* arose out of a Kentucky law which sought to collect a tax of fifty cents per share upon bank stock. When the First National Bank of Louisville refused to pay the tax on its shares, the state brought an action in the Franklin County Circuit Court to recover judgment for the amount of the tax. Upon a demurrer of the bank to the state's petition the court dismissed the case. The state then appealed to the Kentucky Court of Appeals, which reversed the decree of the lower court and awarded judgment to the state. Under a writ of error, the bank appealed to the U.S. Supreme Court. The case was argued March 4, 1870, by John A. Wills and associates for the bank and Pike and Johnson for Kentucky. Will's principal argument was that the bank had been organized under a federal act, that its entire capital had been invested in United States securities that its shares of stock represented but an interest in these securities, and, therefore, that neither the bank, its capital, nor its shares could be taxed by the state. Pike riddled this argument. "The tax sought to be avoided here is," he answered, "neither a tax on the bonds and securities of the government, nor a tax upon the instrument or agent of the government, unless it is the Bank itself that is taxed." As the shares were the property of the stockholders and not of the bank, it was not the bank that was being taxed. Associate Justice Samuel F. Miller in delivering the opinion of the court on March 28, 1870, upheld Pike's views by affirming the judgment awarded Kentucky in the state appellate court.[12]

The cases of *Wallach v. Van Riswick* (1875) and *Pike v. Wassell* (1877) dealt with the important question of "reversionary rights of rebels" under the Federal Confiscation Act of July 17, 1862. Though Congress had passed an explanatory resolution explicitly limiting forfeiture under the act to the offender's life, there had still remained considerable doubt—especially among those who purchased confiscated lands—whether decrees of confiscation involved surrender of the fee simple title or merely the life fee. The Supreme Court decided in the case of *Bigelow v. Forrest* (1870) that Congress had specifically provided that a sale under a decree of confiscation conveyed a title that terminated "with the life of the person for whose act it had been seized."[13] When the offender died the full title would revert to the offender's heirs. In *Wallach v. Van Riswick*, a suit brought in 1873 in the Supreme Court of the District of Columbia, Pike contended that the Confiscation Act and the resolution accompanying it not only reserved the reversionary estate to the offender's heirs but also left the offending ancestor no right to convey the property by deed after it had been confiscated. He buttressed his argument with an exhaustive brief that went deeply into the legal and historical precedents of English common law. However, the court decided against Pike, and he appealed to the Supreme Court of the United States at its December term of 1875.[14] The case was argued December 2 and 3, 1875, and decided January 10, 1876. Pursuing the same line of reasoning he had used in the lower court, Pike won the case in a brilliant argument. In delivering the opinion of the Supreme Court Justice William Strong paid an indirect tribute to Pike not only in using identical citations of American and English law but also in adopting virtually the same language Pike employed in his learned brief.[15]

This decision afforded a precedent that helped Pike win an important case for his own heirs in 1877 in the case of *Pike v. Wassell*. Sometime between 1868 and 1875 Pike had learned that the deed transferring his confiscated property at Little Rock had mistakenly omitted five and a half feet of lot 11 in block 1. Believing he had full title to this segment, Pike deeded it to Lilian on April 10, 1872. Meanwhile the purchasers of Pike's confiscated estate had discovered the error and had, in conveying the property in block 1 to John Wassell in 1871, corrected the description to include the disputed footage. After Pike's deed to Lilian in 1872 Wassell, his title in question, refused to pay the taxes on the disputed land as well as on the other Pike property in block 1. Pike then instituted suit for his children in the U.S. Circuit Court for the Eastern District of Arkansas at Little Rock, demanding that Wassell be ordered to pay the taxes on the undisputed portion of his confiscated estate. He based his case on the fact that his children as his "heirs-at-law" were the owners of the reversionary right to the property. They could, therefore, file a suit to compel Wassell, the tenant for life, to keep down the taxes and "properly care for and preserve the property." Pike alleged in the bill of complaint that Wassell was allowing the taxes to become delinquent in order that the land could be sold in a tax sale. Wassell then could have purchased the land and secured a fee simple title, a procedure that Pike maintained the Confiscation Act had not intended.[16]

The case was argued and decided at the April term of 1873. In an absurd opinion Circuit Judge John F. Dillon ruled that Pike's children were not Pike's heirs while Pike himself was still living. They could not, therefore, bring a suit on behalf of their father's reversionary interest during the father's lifetime.[17] Pike hooted then and long afterward at Judge Dillon's marvelous display of law and logic in asserting that "no one is the heir of a living person," saying once with the "learned" judge in mind: "So there are judges who . . . listen with weary indifference to the reasons of the law, to elaborate discussion of its analogies, to the interpretation of it by the old law, to illustration and explanation, and 'rise' only to a fallacy or a phrase, by which they are inevitably hooked."[18]

Pike appealed the case to the U.S. Supreme Court, and it was argued and decided in the spring of 1877. Since the court had ruled the previous year in *Wallach v. Van Riswick* that the duration of the forfeiture of confiscated land had been intended solely for the benefit of the offender's heirs, the court now had little trouble seemingly in decreeing that "the heirs, apparent or presumptive, of one whose estate in lands has been condemned and sold under the Confiscation Act, may do whatever is necessary to protect it from forfeiture or incumbrance." Chief Justice Morrison R. Waite, delivering the opinion, indirectly rebuked Judge Dillon by defining Pike's children as his "heirs apparent," or, as Pike had maintained, his "heirs-at-law." The case was remanded to Judge Dillon's court with an order to compel Wassell to pay the taxes on the children's "estate in expectancy."[19] Wassell's widow refused, and the property was seized and sold for taxes on January 31, 1882. On March 9, 1882, the purchasers, James H. Hornebrook and Miles Q. Townsend of Little Rock, paid Pike's children $8,800 for their "expectant and restoratory" title to the land. To clear the title and settle the long dispute, Pike himself had executed a quitclaim deed to Hornebrook and Townsend on March 6, 1882. In this way Pike and his children were enabled to benefit from the property prior to Pike's death. On Pike's death the full title of the property in block 1 passed to Hornebrook and Townsend, but Pike's other confiscated land in Little Rock reverted at that time to his children. They sold it on January 31, 1893, for $10,000.[20]

In prosecuting Henry M. Rector's claim to the Hot Springs of Arkansas Pike became identified with one of the most perplexing legal problems that came before the Supreme Court in the nineteenth century. His client claimed the Hot Springs under a New Madrid land warrant issued by the United States to Francis Langlois on November 26, 1818. Langlois's two hundred arpents of land in southeastern Missouri had been injured by the catastrophic New Madrid earthquake of 1811–12, and he had, by the New Madrid Act of February 17, 1815, been allowed to locate a like quantity of land on any of the U.S. lands of Missouri Territory then authorized to be sold.[21]

Elias Rector purchased the Langlois certificate on February 19, 1819. The same year he got the surveyor general at St. Louis to approve an application ordering the two hundred arpents surveyed *"in a square tract, with lines corresponding to the cardinal points of the compass and to include the hot springs, so called upon the waters of the Wachita River, south of the river Arkansas, the said springs to be as near the center of the square as circumstances will admit."*[22] The surveyor general's order was based upon the General Land Office's construction of the act of 1815 to mean that New Madrid warrants could be located upon lands that had not been surveyed by the United States. That office had in mind seemingly the keeping down of trouble that would arise in converting arpents into acres and fitting these acres and fractions of acres into the rectangular surveys of the United States.[23] Accordingly, the survey was made and plats were returned on July 16, 1820, to the office of the surveyor general, who approved and filed them. To complete a title under the New Madrid Act it was necessary that he return a copy of the plat to the recorder of land titles for filing and issuing of a patent. The surveyor general was prevented from sending the plat by an order of the secretary of the treasury. The secretary's action was based upon opinions of Attorney General William Wirt of May 11 and June 19, 1820, overruling the General Land Office's interpretation of the act of 1815. The attorney general decided that the act had not authorized a departure from the established system of surveying, that New Madrid warrants could be located only on previously surveyed lands, that such locations should be limited by sectional lines, and that sales of all irregular and unconformable fractions of land were void. As a consequence no patent was issued to Rector.[24]

The New Madrid Act "is imperfect & requires amendment," Attorney General Wirt had confessed to the Treasury Department in 1820.[25] Congress agreed and on April 26, 1822, passed an act to remove all the attorney general's objections to the location of New Madrid claims. This measure provided that all New Madrid locations made on previously unsurveyed lands of the United States should be perfected into grants "in like manner as if they had conformed to the sectional or quarter sectional lines of the public surveys." All fractions of lands theretofore created by such locations were permitted to be sold, the sale to be binding on the United States "as if such fractions had been made by rivers, or other natural obstructions."[26] Though this law seemingly removed all objection to the location of the Langlois claim, Rector never attempted apparently to perfect his title under it. And on April 20, 1832, Congress passed an act reserving to the United States "the Hot Springs together with four sections of land including said springs."[27]

From 1820 the title to the Hot Springs was in dispute. Elias Rector willed the property to his son Henry on August 9, 1822, and the son fought for over half a century to perfect a title to it. In 1838 Henry got the claim resurveyed and recorded through U.S. officials at Little Rock. A patent certificate was issued him, but the General Land Office at Washington, D.C., ruling that the reservation of 1832 voided appropriation of the Hot Springs, refused to issue a patent. Under an act of March 1, 1843, for perfecting titles to New Madrid locations south of the Arkansas River, the General Land Office again rejected Rector's patent certificate of 1838 because of the reservation of 1832.[28] The claim was, however, kept active, and in 1859 Attorney General Reverdy Johnson delivered an opinion advising the Department of Interior to issue a patent to Rector. But before an order of the secretary of interior was executed another claimant appeared on the scene. Held in abeyance until 1854, Johnson's opinion and the Interior Department's order were annulled by an opinion of Attorney General Caleb Cushing. Cushing ruled that the reservation act of 1832 had rendered void all subsequent locations on the site of the Hot Springs. When the Civil War began, Rector still had not secured a patent to the land.[29]

Pike took Rector's claim sometime between 1866 and 1870. There were then four other claimants seeking to recover the identical property by different and conflicting titles. Pike and the other attorneys appealed to Congress and on May 31, 1870, an act was passed permitting all claimants to bring suit in the federal court of claims against the United States.[30] For the convenience of the court, the five cases were consolidated into a single unit. Each attorney was allowed to argue his client's claim against both the other claimants and the United States, but the court was to dispose of all the suits in one decree.

After various delays for taking affidavits and testimony and for drawing up briefs the cases were argued and decided at the December term of 1874. Pike contended that the actual survey and the approval of the plats and survey by the surveyor general made the Langlois location complete in 1820; that the duty of returning a plat to the recorder devolved exclusively upon the surveyor general and his neglect or refusal to send it could not defeat Rector's rights under the act of 1822; and that the location of 1820, being in contemplation of the laws of 1815 and 1822 complete, should be perfected into a grant in like manner as if it had conformed to the sectional lines of the public surveys. The United States contended that the objections to Rector's right to complete a title to the Hot Springs were, first, that the lands in that region had not been reached by the public surveys and were not, therefore, authorized to be sold in 1820; second, that the location of a New Madrid warrant should conform to the lines of the public surveys, could only include quarters and half quarter sections and consequently that Rector could not locate absolutely two hundred arpents of land; third, that the location being illegal and defective, and not completed before 1822, it was barred from benefit under the act of 1822; and, fourth, that the sale not having been complete and valid, the Hot Springs was reserved to the United States by the act of 1832.[31]

Rector's case actually hinged, then, on the question whether a location had, or had not, been made in 1820. In arguing that a location had been effected Pike distinguished between "perfecting a location" and "completing an appropriation or sale" of public land under the New Madrid Act. He quoted the words of the act itself—"the location made, on the application of the claimant, by the principal deputy surveyor"—and cited several previous land grant acts to demonstrate that a location was made under the New Madrid Act "precisely as it was under other and former laws, by the survey, and the return of it to the . . . surveyor-general." The land claimed and located by the survey was not appropriated until the plat was returned by the surveyor general to the recorder and a patent was issued. But the recorder had, Pike maintained, "nothing to do with making the location." He simply performed "the ministerial duty of issuing the patent certificate" after the surveyor general had forwarded him the evidence (a copy of the plat) that the "location had been made." If accepted by the court, this definition meant that Rector's claim had been located in 1820, and that he had been prevented from securing a patent to the claim in 1820 and again in 1822 by the illegal action of U.S. officials. Under the established rule in equity law "that that which ought to have been done shall be taken as done," Pike concluded that since July 16, 1820, the title to Hot Springs and the land covered by the Langlois location had been erroneously and unjustly withheld from his client.[32]

In its decision the court of claims recognized the "unusual learning and power" of Pike's "cogent argument" that the location had been complete when the survey was made, returned, approved, and filed in the surveyor general's office. It agreed that Elias Rector had done everything that the law required him to do, that everything that remained to be done to perfect his title "was made a statutory duty on the part of the officers of the Government." It accepted Pike's plea "that the Supreme Court has enunciated the principle that things which the public officers ought to have done should be regarded as having been done." But to decree that Pike's definition of a location and construction of the act of 1815 were valid would, concluded the court, reverse not only Attorney General Wirt's opinions of 1820 but also a half dozen decisions of the U.S. Supreme Court. The court of claims admitted that it was not satisfied with the direct and indirect construction given the New Madrid Act by the Department of Justice and by the Supreme Court. It believed Rector's case would present a substantially new question to the Supreme Court, a question upon which it might not be bound by its former rulings in other and essentially different cases. Yet the court of claims did not feel at liberty to disregard the reiterated opinion of the Supreme Court and deemed "it best to leave to that tribunal the duty of correcting its errors, if errors they be." The court decided, therefore, that it must hold that no location was ever made by Elias Rector and that his son had no title, legal or equitable, to the Hot Springs.[33]

Though all the claimants except Rector had been rather hopelessly defeated by the decision of the court of claims, all the attorneys immediately appealed to the Supreme Court. The appeals granted, Pike rewrote and revised the briefs in Rector's case, adding considerably to the argument and "changing some things in which it was untenable." He wrote Rector May 12, 1875, that he had "*no fears of the result.*" Alexander T. Gray, who had written the brief for the United States in the court of claims, had said, "that he never *could* see any way to answer our brief: and the Government has no hope of defeating us." It was "all humbug" about Justice Samuel F. Miller of the Supreme Court having expressed a private opinion on Rector's claim. Miller was "*entirely above* doing anything of the kind. We shall have a fair and unprejudiced decision, and all reports to the contrary are mere lies. He was sorry Rector could not do more to aid with the expenses of prosecuting the case, but thanked him "very heartily for what you did do. We'll pull this 'the season,' *Some* how."[34]

Rector's case was argued with the other Hot Springs cases on January 19 through 21 and 24 and 25, 1876. In his argument Pike pointed out a number of alleged errors and inconsistencies in the opinions of Attorney General Wirt of 1820 and in six Supreme Court decisions that had defined a location under the New Madrid Act and the act of 1822. He knew in demonstrating that the Supreme Court had erred that "all the presumptions are that the court is right and the counsel wrong." But he was convinced that the errors were so patent in these instances that the court simply could not fail to correct them. No diminution of the court's dignity would, he advised, come from correcting an error, no matter how often the error had been acted upon or how many times the error has misled the court. The court could not afford to permit its precedents to prevent its giving a suitor property that was his own if its decisions, founded on misinformation or error, had helped to deny him his right.[35]

Justice Joseph P. Bradley, delivering the opinion of the Supreme Court on April 24, 1876, either did not see or refused to see a difference between perfecting a location and completing an appropriation under the New Madrid Act. He weakly observed that a location under the act "evidently meant a complete location." A "complete location" included the transfer of the plat to the recorder and the issuing of a patent. Because this view had been "repeatedly adjudged" by the Supreme Court and had accordingly "become part of the established land law of the country," he believed the court "should do a great wrong at this late day to shake it." He ruled similarly regarding the opinions of Attorney General Wirt. The New Madrid Act was in 1820 what the attorney general held it to be—that unsurveyed land was not land the sale of which was authorized by law—and as that "doctrine was received and acted upon by the Land Department of the Government, we should not feel authorized at this late date to reverse it." Rector's claim to the land had never been "located within the meaning of the Act of 1815 and the Act of 1822"; therefore it could not "prevent the operation of the Act of April 20, 1832, by which it was reserved to the United States." The decree of the court of claims was confirmed.[36]

"Yes, I did not win my case," Pike wrote a cousin in June. "I *was* disappointed. I thought success was certain. I know that law and fact were on my side. The Court did not decide according to the law, was not governed by the law; but the hot springs were too valuable for an individual to own."[37] He never got over the feeling that a mistake had been made. Nearly a dozen years later he declared that he would have had money to publish his "Maxims of the Roman Law" if the Supreme Court "had not, in violation of all law and justice, deprived Henry M. Rector of the Hot Springs, to which he had as good title as I have to the pen I am writing with."[38]

The Hot Springs case was the last important suit in which Pike and Johnson appeared together. They apparently dissolved their partnership soon afterwards, and Johnson returned to Arkansas to reside. In 1878 Johnson made an unsuccessful bid for a seat in the U.S. Senate. He died at Little Rock on July 26, 1879, and was buried in Mount Holly Cemetery. Pike, too, retired from practice about this time, but the account of his retirement will be related in the following chapter.

XXXVI

Last Years

WHEN PIKE WENT TO WASHINGTON in late November, 1868, to join Johnson for the winter sessions of the courts and Congress, he had no intention of making it his permanent home. He returned the following spring to Memphis and spent several weeks with his children who were still living in the cottage on Adams Street. He attended a court in Arkansas in April and then returned to his Washington office on business before June 10, 1869.[1] He was still in Washington on Wednesday, July 7, when he received a dispatch from Memphis saying that Isadore had died the night before. The message did not give the cause, and he was at a loss to figure it out. "I did not even know she was sick," he confessed.[2]

Isadore was to be taken to Little Rock for burial. Pike could not reach there in time for the funeral, and if he could have, he really had no desire to see her in death. Therefore he remained in Washington to mourn alone over her passing. By a cruel twist of fate Thursday's mail brought him "a letter full of love from Isadore," written on the Sunday before she died. There was no hint of any illness in the happy letter. "She must have been perfectly well then, and have died very suddenly," he confided to a friend.[3]

For days he could not bring himself to realize that Isadore was "*dead*, dead, and that I shall not see her any more." He remained alone in his room in Johnson's house passing through a "Vale of Tears." "God has struck me a cruel blow," he cried out once. "I shall never recover from it. It seems absurd to toil on any longer."[4] But by July 12 he had recovered enough to reply to a note of sympathy from a member of the Supreme Council. He was, he said, used to losses and sorrows, but "I feel this one." It was the hardest of all:

> Isadore was more to me than any one else in the world; and she deserved to be, for she loved me more than any one else did, and thought no one in the world was like *me*. Then she was nearer perfection than any one *I* ever knew, gentle, affectionate, even tempered, never censorious, never angry, never jealous, never ungenerous. In all my life I never had to censure her once even in my own mind.[5]

Two days later he wrote his intimate friend Vinnie Ream, who was then in Europe, the details of Isadore's death. Pained by

> a nervous headache but otherwise in good health and spirits, Isadore took with her a phial of chloroform, when she went to bed, Tuesday evening [July 6], a week ago. In the morning they found her dead, the phial empty, the pillow having been saturated with the chloroform. I suppose that she opened the phial, inhaled the fumes too long, became stupefied, and dropped the bottle close to her face on the pillow. You may imagine the distress of her brothers and sister, who idolized her as I did.

So the "young die and the old live on—How strange a thing that seems!" But who could say "that it was desirable for one to live longer, who is dead? Who can say into what misery, if Isadore's life had been prolonged, she might not have fallen." She had always been "quietly happy," and now she had died "without anticipation of death, or sickness, or pain. 'God laid his finger on her and she slept.'"[6]

With Isadore gone, Pike could not bear the thought of returning to the family home in Memphis, and he decided to remain permanently in Washington. Lilian joined him sometime after the funeral of July 13. "When I have been plunged into the depths of sorrow, I have always gone doggedly to work, night and day. . . . I work, and I have to help others who would suffer if I did not, and I must not indulge in grief," wrote Pike on July 23, and there was work and responsibility enough to occupy his mind now that he had come to think about it:

> I have Lilian left to care for, to comfort, and to love, and she is very dear to me; for almost perfect as Issy was, Lilian has always been a dear good girl and an affectionate and obedient daughter. . . . *Now*, she will be far, far dearer than ever. I have her and Yvon to live and work for; and Yvon is a good son, too.[7]

Pike and Lilian lived until the summer of 1870 in a two-story cottage that he and Johnson had jointly rented in 1868. But it proved too expensive and they gave it up. Pike and Lilian then took "the nicest rooms you ever saw—because it is all books, pictures and easy chairs."[8] The address was 116 C Street. They lived there apparently until the fall of 1873. He and Johnson scarcely earned enough money to pay expenses during these years, and to add to his troubles Pike himself was frequently unwell. "Have had rheumatic gout ever since Christmas morning," he wrote in early January, 1872. "It has given me 'fits.' I don't expect to get out for two weeks longer. It is in my *right* foot this time. First I had it in both in 1868, then twice here, in 1870 & 1871, in the *left* foot. Now in the right. It's impartial. Lord! It's tiresome."[9] Though the attacks became more frequent and more painful in later years, he somehow managed to keep himself cheerful and resigned:

> I have rheumatic gout. Well, I might have a worse complaint. It is a great mercy of God that with inability comes absence of desire; that as I cannot drink wine, I do not want it or care for it; if I cannot run and leap, I do not wish to; if I must keep to my rooms a great deal, I have come to like that best, and that if I cannot have the love that young men can win, I do not need it as the young do, but am content with such quiet affection as the young can have for the old.[10]

Pike did like to have the affection of women, both young and old, one of his maxims being that it was "no small thing to have the good opinion of good women." He thought it absolutely absurd that people often said it was hard for an old man to love the young ardently because the young could not return love to the old. "Thank the good Gods," he wrote in 1871, "that in that respect I am no older than I was forty years ago, and can love and be jealous now, as fiercely as I could then. God forbid I should become *so* old as to be no longer capable of loving beauty and goodness; even if an old man who loves *is* an old fool."[11]

Though he professed to love several women in these last years, his greatest love of all was for Vinnie Ream, the sculptress. She was only nineteen when he met her in the Capitol at Washington in 1866. Born in Wisconsin Territory of poor parents, Vinnie grew up in Washington, D.C., and in Missouri, where her father was employed by the federal government. Returning to Washington with her parents during the Civil War, she obtained a minor clerkship in the Post Office Department at the age of fifteen. One day about 1864 she went with a friend to the studio of Clark Mills, the sculptor. She amused Mills with her childish curiosity in his work, and he handed her a lump of clay, saying, half in fun. "Do a portrait of me!" Vinnie laughingly accepted his challenge, and the result delighted Mills, who recognized great talent in her work and took her as a student. From that moment she gave herself up to the study of sculpture, sacrificing her free time and meager salary in order to master the art of modeling in clay. She could think and talk of nothing but her art, and she was clever enough to talk to the right people, namely, several of the most influential members of the U.S. Senate. It was something of a tribute to her ambition and enthusiasm that before she had studied a year she had executed busts of Senators Charles Sumner, Thaddeus Stevens, John Sherman, and E. G. Ross, of Generals McClellan and Fremont, and Francis P. Blair, Horace Greeley, and Col. Elias Boudinot, the Cherokee chieftain. Her personality was so captivating and her interest so great that within the same year some of her friends spoke to President Lincoln about sitting for her. Vinnie was "young and a poor girl," they told Lincoln. "So she's young and poor, is she," Lincoln replied. "Well, that's nothing against her. You may tell her she can come." Vinnie went to the White House a half hour daily for five months in 1865, but her bust of Lincoln was still unfinished when he was assassinated that spring. When Congress voted in 1866 to have a full-length marble statue of Lincoln made for the Rotunda of the Capitol, Vinnie entered the competition and won. A partisan of one of the older and more experienced artists described Vinnie and her tactics:

> She is a young girl, about twenty, has only been studying her art a few months, never made a statue, has some plaster busts on exhibition in the Capitol, including her own, minus clothing to the waist, has a pretty face, with a turned up nose, bright black eyes, long dark curls and plenty of them, wears a jockey hat and a good deal of jewelry, sees all the members at their lodgings or the reception-room at the Capitol, urges her claims fluently and confidentially, sits in the galleries in a conspicuous position and in her most bewitching dress, while those claims are discussed on the floor, and nods and smiles as a member rises and delivers his opinion on the merits of the case, with the air of a man sitting for his picture; and so she carries the day over Powers and Crawford, and Hosmer and who not.[12]

Vinnie had no studio in which to work on the plaster model of her statue, but her friends in the Senate came again to her rescue. She was assigned a room in a "gloomy recess" of the Capitol.[13] It was in this room, which Vinnie had brightened with basket plants and songbirds, that Pike first saw her. They struck up a conversation and soon discovered, as another of her friends expressed it, that "there were thoughts of our brains and strings of our hearts, which always beat in unison."[14] She conquered Pike, heart and soul, and soon afterwards we find him writing her affectionate notes depicting the "singular charm of your features, and the luminous glories of your wonderful eyes."[15] Vain and something of a coquette, Vinnie thrived on such personal praise, but she was far more ambitious than vain, and she may have thought in the beginning that Pike could be of help to her. She respected and admired him, confided in him, went to him for advice, and she allowed him to love her. Pike was, however, aware of the age barrier between them, and he told Vinnie early in their acquaintanceship that "as I am not so insane as to expect the love which you could feel for one far younger . . . I am not in danger of misunderstanding you: and I shall *try* not to come to love you too much, and so make love a misery."[16]

In this manner and on this basis began a beautiful friendship that lasted until Pike's death. Their relations during this twenty-five years consisted largely in letter writing, for they were frequently separated. When they were together, their favorite pastime was reading poetry. Vinnie's love was the inspiration for Pike's best known poem, "Every Year," for his popular "Ma Triste Cherie," and for five manuscript volumes (2,166 pages) of "Essays to Vinnie," which he began in 1873 upon a bargain with her that he would write them if she would come each week and listen to what he had written.[17] At these meetings they held hands, kissed, and caressed, but their love was never a sensual one. "No lie is on my lips," Pike professed not long before his death, "when I aver that all the endearments, caresses and kisses of the one who has so long been dear to me never inspired in me a thought or emotion of desire. If every man has at some time worshipped Anteros, he is to be pitied who has never worshipped Eros alone."[18]

However much he desired it to be otherwise, Pike was too poor to help Vinnie in her struggle for recognition in sculpture, to "place her works in my library and . . . otherwise encourage her to persevere until she should extort admiration and appreciation of her genius and proficiency in her art from the country, of which she . . . ought to be the pride and idol."[19] To the contrary his status as "a Rebel" probably did her more harm than good with certain influential Republicans in Congress. He could not have blamed her if she had withdrawn from him, but she continued to see him despite unpleasant talk about consorting with "Rebels"—there were other ex-Confederate friends in her life besides Pike. Observing that Vinnie was more independent and brave than wise, Pike generously tried to make their friendship as inconspicuous as possible to the vindictive radicals in Congress. He refused to attend the unveiling of her "Lincoln: and to go to her house for several days afterward, explaining that he did not like "to meet men who have no name for me but 'Rebel,'" and that he was "sure it would not serve you, with them, for you to welcome me before them, as a friend."[20] Even with these precautions a severe critic of Vinnie's statue, learning somehow that Pike had conferred on Vinnie the Scottish Rite degrees of Adoption, wittily played upon the fact in his review. He had been

> informed of the great secret of Miss Vinnie Ream's grand success as a "sculptoress." It appears that she is a Mason, or a "Masoness," as you please. She belongs to a Female Lodge, which has some sort of connection with Male Lodges. . . . However, Miss V. Ream has taken eight degrees in something or other and is very high in the mysteries. This accounts for the elegance, beauty, and generally fine masonwork of the Lincoln statue.[21]

As soon as he saw the above passage in the *New York Tribune*, Pike wrote Vinnie "not to be worried by the miserable effusions of malice and meanness" of the reviewer. "You are a subject of *envy* now, because you are honored and distinguished.... It is merit acknowledged, and success won, that most provokes them."[22]

The prejudice against "Rebels" that he constantly met in Washington induced Pike to move early in 1874 to nearby Alexandria, Virginia, a town where, he explained to a friend, "there were decent people who were rebels and are neither sorry for it nor ashamed of it."[23] Pike commuted by train to his and Johnson's Washington office, but he seldom went to the office at all after the move to Alexandria. Hamilton and Yvon were now living with him and Lilian; Hamilton had joined the firm of Pike and Johnson. Leaving to his son the responsibility of answering correspondence and conducting the routine business of keeping office, Pike took less and less interest in his law practice and increasingly devoted himself, as he had for two or three years before the move, to his duties as Grand Commander of the Scottish Rite and to writing and research for that order and for his own satisfaction.[24]

He had completed the rituals, liturgies, and ceremonies of the Scottish Rite in the years 1863 through 68, and by 1870 they all had been printed and adopted as the official work of the Southern Jurisdiction. The only serious opposition to his revision came from the York Rite bodies in Missouri. George Frank Gouley, Grand Commander of the Knights Templar in that state, had in early 1867 received Pike's Scottish revised work through the thirty-second degree. In August of the same year he wrote Pike objecting that the twenty-ninth and thirtieth degrees of the Scottish rituals had revealed important secrets of the York Rite and demanding that Pike have the Supreme Council decree that no Council of Kadosh, the Scottish Rite body having jurisdiction over the nineteenth to thirtieth degrees, could receive as members any but Knights Templar.[25] For Pike to have complied with this virtual ultimatum would have been to make the Scottish Rite subordinate to and dependent on the York Rite. He replied that he could not see that the Scottish rituals revealed any York secrets—Pike belonged to both orders—and concluded that the accusation and the demand were not only insupportable but also unreasonable.[26]

Whatever the justification for Pike's argument, there can be no doubt that he had erred in underestimating the seriousness of the situation. It is also clear that the tone of his reply was not such as to pour oil on the waters. He should have kept the matter open by making a counterproposal or even by inviting further discussion, but he replied in such a manner as to convince Gouley that the differences between them could not be compromised. But Gouley, as strong-minded and as stubborn as Pike, probably desired no further discussion; for his ultimatum had been flatly refused and his feelings ruffled by Pike's tone of finality. Convinced that Pike had definitely revealed York secrets in the two highest Kadosh degrees, he now appealed to his Commandary and got it to order that no Knight Templar could attend any session of a Scottish Rite body and aid in conferring the Scottish degrees upon any candidates unless these candidates were Knights Templar. Gouley also began a rhetorical attack on the Scottish Rite in a Masonic periodical. Angered by Gouley's conduct Pike preferred charges against him for violating the vows of the Scottish Mason and for defaming the rite. In a trial that followed Gouley was found guilty and deprived of all privileges of Scottish Masonry.[27]

The issue was now clearly drawn, and it was more than a mere quarrel between Pike and Gouley. The York Rite of Missouri was in open opposition to the adopted ritual of the Scottish Rite, and the quarrel had all the possibilities of creating a breach between the two great Masonic orders of the nation. Pike realized this by 1872, and at a session of the Supreme Council that year appointed a committee of three to study the quarrel. The three members were Knights Templar, and their report held out the olive branch of peace. The Supreme Council voted, in keeping with the committee report, to modify the three objectionable passages in the twenty-ninth and thirtieth degrees. Pike readily made the changes, and they were adopted at the next biennial session (1874).[28]

In the interval Pike and Gouley had met in St. Louis in November, 1873, and had quickly settled their dispute. Pike agreed to change the controversial wording of the degrees and recommended and secured Gouley's reinstatement in the Scottish Rite. From that time forward they were fast friends, though their friendship was cut short on April 12, 1877, when Gouley met an untimely death falling five stories from a ladder while trying to escape a hotel fire in St. Louis. Pike's tribute to his memory of April 24, 1877, might well have been what Gouley would have said of Pike if the circumstances had been reversed: Warm and energetic in controversy, he "was placable and easily reconciled, generous and genial, a true friend and a fair foe." As an "Editor and disputant" he had shunned no encounter, had counted more victories than defeats, and had achieved a deserved reputation, "for he was one 'who had convictions,' and followed at all hazards wherever they led."[29]

The Pike-Gouley compromise of 1873 ended the only serious opposition to Pike's ritual, and it healed a threatening breach between the York and Scottish orders. In return for making minor changes in the working of the two degrees, Pike and the Supreme Council had gotten the Missouri Knights Templar to rescind their restriction against the Scottish Rite bodies of the state. Thereafter the two rites worked in peace.[30]

Meanwhile, Pike had completed his second most important contribution to the Scottish Rite. This was the publication in 1871 of his monumental *Morals and Dogma of the Ancient and Accepted Scottish Rite of Freemasonry*, a book of thirty-two lectures (one for each degree of the order) to be studied in connection with the rituals of the degrees that he had been so long in revising. The work was prepared and published for the official use of the Supreme Council to be sold to those who received its degrees; therefore Pike did not share in the income from the sales. He admitted in the preface that he had been "about equally Author and Compiler," having "extracted quite half its contents from the works of the best writers and most philosophic or eloquent thinkers." He apologized for omitting to document the book by stating that it was not "intended for the world at large," an excuse that some scholars cannot accept. Foreseeing that some would criticize him for the neglect Pike pointed out to these with an air of independence and self-respect that he had not cared to distinguish his own writing from that of others and that he was "quite willing that every portion of the book, in turn, may be regarded as borrowed from some old and better writer." *Morals and Dogma*, the "bible of Masonry," is not a book in the sense that each of the thirty-two divisions relate to each other as chapters of a book normally do, and there is a controversy among Masonic interpreters as to whether the work should be studied as a unit. Roscoe Pound insisted that it "must be read and interpreted as a unit," while others maintain that it cannot be.[31] Certainly in its passing from grade to grade in the direction of the highest, Pike's book possesses unity; yet it is not a unit in itself and was not intended by Pike as such. He intended it to be a supplement to that great "connected system of moral, religious and philosophical instruction" that he had developed in his revision of the Scottish ritual. Taken together, Pike's two great works—the revised ritual and *Morals and Dogma*—made the Scottish Rite what he believed "Masonry at first was meant to be, a Teacher of Great Truths, inspired by an upright and enlightened reason, a firm and constant Wisdom, and an affectionate and beloved philanthropy."[32]

While perfecting, in 1870–71, the translations of certain words and symbols in his revised ritual Pike began an intensive study of the religion of the Ancient Hindus as contained in the *Rig Veda* and of the religion of the Ancient Persians as contained in the *Zend Avesta*. Because of these studies a legend has grown up that Pike was a Sanskrit scholar; he was not, and he did not claim to be. In his work on the *Rig Veda* and the *Zend Avesta* he was, he tells us, primarily indebted to the translations of the famous German-English Sanskrit authority, Frederick Max Miller, to H. H. Wilson's translations of the *Rig Veda*, to Dr. J. Muir's *Original Sanskrit Texts*, to Authur Henry Bleeck's translation of Franz Spiegel's famous edition (1852) of the *Zend Avesta*, and to Martin Haug's *Essays on the Sacred Languages, Writings and Religion of the Parsees*, though he used a number of other histories and books in the course of his studies. Many of these books he purchased at great sacrifice to his own welfare, and others he seems to have borrowed from the Library of Congress. Alfred Moore Waddell of North Carolina remembered in 1908 that Pike one day about 1873

> asked me to use my privilege as a member of Congress to order from the Library of Rig Veda so that he could get it from me to verify something he was writing, and of course I readily promised to do so; but when I made the request in the usual way for myself of that wonderful man, A. R. Spofford, the Librarian of Congress, . . . he laughed and said, "Oh, you don't want this book for yourself, but for General Pike, I guess, who is the only man in Washington who wants it; but it cannot be taken out of the Library for anybody."[33]

By 1874 Pike had written three treatises of over six thousand manuscript pages based on an investigation of the *Zend Avesta* and the Vedic hymns: *Ancient Faith and Worship of the Aryans as Embodied in the Vedic Hymns* (1872–73); *Lectures of the Arya* (about 1873); and *Irano-Aryan Theosophy and Doctrine as Contained in the Zend-Avesta* (1874). In the course of his study he had compiled nearly twelve thousand pages of *Translations of the Rig Veda*,[34] consisting primarily of hymns copied from translations of others and used by Pike in his commentaries on the Aryan religion. The undertaking had been a "labor of love," but it had also been a fatiguing one. Moreover, he had been engaged in making meticulous corrections in the Scottish ritual at the same time. This exacting work had sapped his enthusiasm apparently, for on the completion of his *Irano-Aryan Theosophy* in 1874, he confessed to Vinnie Ream that for seventeen years he had constantly labored, in his leisure time, under some self-imposed task. The last was now finished and he thought he would set himself no other. He was content with what he knew of the *Veda* and *Zend Avesta*, "believing that I have learned what the Gods of the Indo-Aryans were to the Vedic Poets, and what the theology and philosophy of Zarathusra were." If he published his three works on ancient religions, as he hoped he would sometime be able to do, he thought he would "imitate the example of the witty and learned Dr. Fuller, who entitled his last work, which he lived not to see printed, 'The History of the Worthies of England; Endeavored by Thomas Fuller.'"[35]

The preparation of his manuscripts on the Aryan religion was the last project of such magnitude that Pike attempted. In fact the year 1874 marks the end of his serious scholarship not only for the Scottish Rite but also for himself. "I am inclined to rest now," he confessed to Vinnie Ream that year, "and to read no longer as a toil or to accumulate knowledge, but for recreation." He had heard it said that Cato had begun to learn Greek at the age of eighty. He was content to admire Cato's example without desiring to follow it.[36] "After many years of diligent labor in compiling and writing books for an ancient association, in the hope of benefiting men thereby, and having consumed the last two years in writing commentaries on the Ancient books of our Aryan race," he desired, he said on another occasion in 1874, "to imitate one who having plied the oars until he is weary, lets the blades swing idly in the water, and floats down the stream in the shadows of the trees."[37]

But Pike's canoe was floating on rough water in 1873–75. The nation was in the grip of a financial panic, and he and Hamilton and Johnson were not succeeding at law in Washington. "For a year I have had all kinds of worriment in regard to means of living, and pretty hard work to get through it all," he wrote on January 26, 1876. "I am over 66 now, and begin to want rest, and a little means *for myself*."[38] But 1876 brought no relief. Before the year was up, he and his children had broken up housekeeping in Alexandria and he had moved alone into the quarters of the Supreme Council at 602 D Street, N.W., Washington. Even with rigid economy he found it impossible to support himself alone, and he borrowed money to live on hoping that his luck would change.[39]

His greatest hope of financial security in these years was that Congress would pay to the Choctaw Nation the residue of the net proceeds award of 1859 and that he would be able to collect his fee. The postwar history of the claim revealed that both propositions were highly questionable. In 1866 the Choctaw Nation went back into the Union under a new treaty that recognized the validity of the net proceeds award of 1859. The same year the Choctaw treaty delegation employed John H. B. Latrobe as attorney to prosecute the claim. In 1869 Pike, who had remained inactive in the case since 1861, sent a memorial to the Choctaw National Council protesting that he was, as the original attorney and surviving partner of John T. Cochrane, the sole attorney of the nation and claiming a fee of thirty percent on the award.[40]

From that time forward the attorneyship was in serious dispute. Pitchlynn and Peter Folsom, ignoring Pike's claim and the Cochrane contract, signed a new contract on July 16, 1870, with James G. Blunt of Kansas and Henry E. McKee of Arkansas. Blunt and McKee were to prosecute the net proceeds claim for a thirty percent contingent fee, of which they were to pay Cochrane's wife one-sixth and adjust the claims of all other parties who had rendered service in prosecuting the case.[41] Learning by February, 1872, that a scheme was underfoot to exclude him from the case, Pike published a *Letter to the Choctaw People* protesting that the Cochrane contract was a fraud and that he considered himself sole attorney of the Choctaws under his contract of 1854 with Pitchlynn and the original net proceeds delegation. Two years afterward Principal Chief William Bryant, acting in part at Pike's request, got the Cochrane contract nullified;[42] but unfortunately for Pike the National Council also revoked all other contracts made by the Choctaw delegation of 1852, Pike's included.[43]

Thus the matter stood until the spring of 1875 when Coleman Cole, Choctaw principal chief, invited Pike to the Choctaw Nation to discuss the attorneyship. Traveling by rail by way of St. Louis and Muscogee to Armstrong Academy, Pike met Cole for an interview. Pike and Pitchlynn had in the meantime an understanding,[44] and when Cole proposed that Pike assist him in depriving Pitchlynn of any share in the fee, Pike replied that he would have no part of any such scheme, and "that Colonel Pitchlynn must not be displaced or interfered with as Delegate." He then presented his own plan to Cole asking to be adopted by the Choctaw Nation, to be recognized as their sole attorney at Washington under his contract of 1854, to be given "some assurance that I and others should be paid for our labour, loss of years of time, and heavy expenses," and to be granted the "power of getting rid of a host of lobbyists and blackmailers" who were prejudicing the claim at Washington.[45]

Since Cole had given him no assurance apparently of presenting his plan to the National Council, Pike, after spending the summer in Kentucky and Washington, returned to the Choctaw Nation in September for a session of the council.[46] Cole declined to support Pike, and the council adjourned without having acted on the attorneyship. Before he left Armstrong Academy for Washington in October, Pike wrote the chief a rather indignant letter stating that he had ascertained soon after the council met

> that the plan which I proposed could not be carried out; that you could not have me recognized as sole attorney; and that it would be impolitic to have any legislation upon the subject of attorneys or their compensation: that, in fact, the Council would not legislate in that direction at all; nor had you advised it, if, indeed, you ever meant to do so.

Pike had concluded, therefore, to continue to prosecute the net proceeds claim, as he had been doing for years, "under my employment by the Delegates, to protect the interests of the Choctaw people in regard to it; and to look to the General Council and Delegates for the moderate compensation which I claim and shall be entitled to." He was a fool who reposed confidence in all men, and he was not wise who suspected all. There were white men quite as honest as Cole who would not for the whole claim wrong the Choctaws out of a dollar. They had been Pike's clients for twenty years and he was always glad and happy when he would do anything to protect their rights.

> If I had wished to be adopted, it has been that I might be able to do more for them. I do not particularly need the honour, and should give full equivalents, I think. You cannot defend their rights more zealously than I will, with or without remuneration. But I cannot be made use of to oust others from their places or prejudice their rights, by helping you or any one to violate contracts or deprive gentlemen of compensation fairly earned. I don't think the Choctaw People will it.[47]

There was an undertone of anxiety in this letter, and there might well be. Pitchlynn's commission of 1852–53 as net proceeds delegate was still in force, and under it he had, in 1872, sustained Pike's argument that the Cochrane contract was fraudulent and had signed affidavits agreeing that Pike deserved a fee of five percent of the net proceeds plus $10,000 for expenses during five winters at Washington before the war.[48] This explains Pike's strong defense of Pitchlynn in his interview with Cole, who hated and distrusted Pitchlynn and desired to break him. The Cole-Pitchlynn feud reached a climax at the council's session in 1877. Pitchlynn was sustained by a thumping vote of confidence and Peter Folsom was elected to aid him in prosecuting the net proceeds claim.[49]

Meanwhile Pike, acting for Pitchlynn, had from 1871 to 1876 annually memorialized Congress for an appropriation under the Senate award of 1859. "This is no longer a claim," he asserted; "it is a debt, ascertained and settled; due under treaty stipulations; a debt of peculiar and sacred obligation."[50] At least thirteen different committee reports recommended an appropriation, but every year Congress seemed to move further and further away from a final settlement. At last Pike and the other attorneys, acting for Pitchlynn and Folsom, appealed, in 1876, that Congress assign the case to the court of claims. The bill was held up for five years because of a dispute among the attorneys. Pike got a bill introduced into the Senate that would refer the case to the court with the right of impeaching the award of 1859 but not of going behind it. McKee and others got a bill introduced into the House referring the case with the right of the court to try the whole claim *de novo*. Pike vigorously opposed this last measure on the ground that a Senate adjudication could not be thus set aside by Congress, but in the end the House bill was adopted March 3, 1881.[51]

The drafting of the briefs for the case brought another violent argument between Pike and the attorneys. Pike would have pleaded that the award of 1859 was final and irrevocable, but the others overruled him and presented the whole claim *de novo*. Meanwhile, Pitchlynn died in 1881 leaving Folsom in charge. Folsom now complained that Pike should not appear prominent in the case because he had been a Confederate and would prejudice the case. Pike "permitted the old fool to have his way," and engaged Gen. James W. Denver of Ohio, a prominent Washington attorney, to appear for him, agreeing to give him half his fee. Through Denver, Pike filed a brief in defense of the award of 1859, but the court of claims decreed January 25, 1886, that the act assigning the case to the court had destroyed "the sanctity of the award of the Senate under the treaty of 1855"; and furthermore that under the treaty of 1830 the Choctaw Nation was not entitled to the net proceeds of its lands ceded to the United States. Pike felt quite justly that the attorneys had thrown way what he had worked over a quarter century to obtain.[52]

Meanwhile Pike's Masonic duties were demanding an increasing amount of his time. By the late seventies he feared that the Northern Supreme Council had intentions of encroaching upon the domain of the Southern Jurisdiction. He needed to travel into the western states and territories to build up the Scottish Rite and to establish control of his Supreme Council over the whole region west of the Mississippi and south of the Ohio,[53] but he was desperately poor and could not do it with his own means. Four times—in 1876, 1878, 1879, and 1880—he went on extensive western and southern visitations into the Southern Jurisdiction at the expense of the Supreme Council, and three times on returning home he found himself without money to buy bread. On these occasions he had borrowed from the funds of the Supreme Council hoping that he would be able to repay it in a short time.

Pride and the illusory hope that Congress might pay the Choctaw claim had prevented him, in 1878, from confessing his poverty to the Supreme Council and asking for a salary. But the hardship of the next two years broke down his resistance. On October 18, 1880, he wrote a confidential letter to the members of the Supreme Council, then in session at Washington. He had, he said, hoped for five years that a payment of the Choctaw claim or other success in his profession

> would enable me to escape from the painful and mortifying necessity of saying to you, that to be enabled to continue the duties of your Grand Commander, no alternative was left me but to consent to receive some pecuniary compensation.

It had always been his pride and desire "to serve the order without fee or reward," and it had been his wish to be able to shortly return all that he had ever received of the Supreme Council for travel and living expenses. However, the war had impoverished him, his business since had not prospered, he had been brought in arrears to the Supreme Council and others, and what he "hoped were certainties" had repeatedly ended in disappointments. He was old and "sick and sore and weary" of the fruitless efforts to obtain justice for the Choctaws; he was also tired of practicing law:

> I wish to devote what remains of my life to the propagation of the Rite, by such personal exertions as I have used since our last session, and to my studies, which have already borne fruit embodied in our Degrees.

Others must speak of the extent and value of his past labor for the order, but he would say that it had been so extended that for the future it would require much of his time. He must "continue to conduct the correspondence, maintain our intercourse with foreign Powers, resist encroachments on our jurisdiction, and travel largely, to incite the Brethren and encourage them, and to gain new members."[54]

The Supreme Council treated Pike charitably, voting him an annuity of $1800 a year from October 1879, for the remainder of his life. They made the salary retroactive for one year to enable him to pay all his indebtedness except that which he owed to the treasury of the Supreme Council. But in spite of the generosity of his brethren Pike could not avoid the feeling that they considered him "a pensioner on the bounty of the Order." Consequently on May 14, 1881, he devised his library, valued by him at $25,000 or more, to the Supreme Council, stipulating that it should be accepted in full repayment of all his indebtedness, of his right to live in the quarters of the Supreme Council, and of the annuity voted him for life the previous fall. This conveyance was ratified at the biennial session of 1882. "I think I need not assure you," he said in presenting it, "that I shall continue to labour diligently and zealously for the Rite, as if I were being paid a salary twice as large as the annuity; while I shall feel that I have a home in which I have bought and paid for the right to live."[55]

Pike lived from 1880 to 1883 in the Supreme Council rooms at 218 Third Street. He traveled much of the time during spring, summer, and fall of these years visiting and organizing bodies of the rite. A seven-thousand-mile itinerary of 1880 took him to Minnesota, Iowa, Kansas, New Mexico, Colorado, Wyoming, and Missouri. The next year he journeyed over twelve thousand miles, going in the spring to the midwestern states and territories of the trans-Mississippi and in the fall into Tennessee, Arkansas, Texas, Louisiana, Mississippi, Alabama, Florida, Georgia, South and North Carolina, and Virginia.[56]

He had looked forward for years to a trip to Arkansas and a fall hunt in the Indian country with former cronies of Van Buren and Fort Smith.[57] His first opportunity came during his visitation of 1881. After having become "perfectly worn out with work, late hours and heat" in Tennessee, Pike arrived at Van Buren on the night of October 15. He had not stopped at Little Rock because "the place and the people are so changed that I do not like to see it"; and all the way across the state he had not seen a single person he knew until he got off the train in Van Buren to find his old friend Dr. Richard Thurston waiting for him. "So it is," he told Vinnie, "that an old man comes to be of another generation."[58]

Though he was unwell, and it was still very hot, Pike left with Dr. Thurston on the morning of the seventeenth for an outing of thirteen days. Four of Pike's friends, whom he had counted on going along, were engaged in court and a fifth was sick. He was disappointed that they could not go, but was "very glad to have got there. It is like being young again; and in the woods I shall be happy. Nature is there, just as she was fifty years ago."[59] Yes, nature had not changed, but Pike had, and the hunt was not pleasant. It rained two days of the thirteen they were out, and the "Lord's mercy did not save me from the gout; for I had a fit of it the very day I returned." It took him nearly a week to recover. He then took up his visitation to Texas and the states of the South.[60]

Pike returned to the South on visitations in the spring of 1882, working at Jacksonville and Pensacola in Florida, at Albany, Macon, Atlanta, and Savannah in Georgia, and at Montgomery in Alabama. The hot season forced him to abandon the South but in the fall he returned to Alabama to complete unfinished work.[61] The spring of 1883 found him on a trip to the Pacific Coast by way of New Orleans, El Paso, New Mexico, and Arizona. At Tucson, where he stopped on April 18 to organize a Lodge of Perfection, he came down with fever and gout. He was disabled for a week, during which a furious sand storm lashed Tucson. "I would not give one month of life in Washington for a year in any of these dry, dusty, sandy, treeless, grassless regions," he confessed to a lady friend. He had not wanted

> to take this journey, but it had to be done, and I take it as a penance for my sins that I have to forego all home comforts, indure fatigue, eat wretched food, lie on hard beds, and having no loving eyes to look into, and hear no kind words from lips that I love, during four long months or more.[62]

By the fourth of May he had recovered and had proceeded by way of Los Angeles to San Francisco.[63] He worked in and near that city until sometime after the middle of June and then sailed to Portland, Oregon, and thence to Seattle, Washington, where he labored until August. From Seattle he went to Helena, Montana, and from there he returned by way of Minnesota and Iowa to Washington, D.C., reaching there late in September.[64] He then moved himself and library into a building that he and William M. Ireland, Grand Secretary, had purchased for the Supreme Council the previous March. The address was 433 Third Street, N.W., and the edifice standing on that site, a commodious, three-story, red-brick residence, was known thereafter as the House of the Temple, and here Pike spent the remainder of his days.[65]

The lengthy and arduous trip of 1883, the backlog of correspondence that awaited him at its end, and the worry and confusion connected with moving to a new place had a telling effect upon Pike. All during late November and December he was beset by nervous indigestion. "I have no appetite," he wrote two days before Christmas; "nothing tastes right or well; smoking hurts me, whiskey scorches, and I steadily lose flesh." He planned, however, to drink punch New Year's Eve with three or four cronies, "though it will not, I know, do *my* stomach any good."[66] In May he was much as he had been "three months ago, dyspeptic, and living on bread and milk." But he had no pain, could work, and had "no right to complain."[67]

By June he had become adjusted to his new surroundings and was quite content among his books and birds—he always had over fifty caged songbirds near him in these last years. He was still on "a bread-and-milk diet," he wrote Vinnie on June 8, but he had no pain and could sit and work well enough. He consoled himself with the thought that he had had his

> share of the comforts and pleasures of life; and if I *am* dyspeptic and likely to be, by and by, light enough to be blown away, there are many worse and more painful maladies that I might have instead; and if I have not many more years to live, I have lived longer than I had a right to expect, have worked to some purpose, [and] have loved and been loved.[68]

In the fall of 1884 he went on a visitation to Arkansas, Texas, Louisiana, Alabama, and North Carolina. "I am entirely rid of dyspepsia," he wrote from Galveston on December 5, "and in better health than I was before I had it, though 75 pounds lighter."[69] Returning to Washington in late December or early January, he had a good winter. But in April he was set back by a three-week siege of gout.[70] He shook it off quickly, however, and in the summer of 1885 went on an extensive trip into Nebraska, Missouri, Wyoming, Utah, Montana, North Dakota, Minnesota, and Iowa. He wrote on June 14, 1885 from Omaha that he had been "*perfectly* well since leaving home"; however, he wrote a few days later from Kansas City that he should be glad to get home. "Traveling does me good; but I am weary of it. I want to be among my books and to see and hear my birds."[71] He was home again by September, worn out and sick.[72]

A month of rest relieved his illness, and he was overjoyed to learn in October that Vinnie would be in Washington shortly for a brief visit. Though she was now married to Capt. Richard Leveridge Hoxie, U.S. Army Engineers, she and Pike had continued to correspond and see each other under the same intimate relationship that they had known from the beginning. Captain Hoxie had no objection apparently; for he and Pike were fast friends by 1885. It had not been so at first, at least on Pike's part, for he had been extremely jealous of Vinnie's affection for the captain. Once he saw, however, that she was seriously in love and intended to marry, he gave the union his blessing, kept Vinnie's affection, and cultivated and won the captain's confidence and friendship. "What a grand thing it is to have a good true loving husband," Pike wrote Vinnie after her and Captain Hoxie's visit in 1885. "I am glad that you were so wise a little woman as to choose out of the many who loved you or thought they did, the best one and truest one of all."[73]

From 1885 to the end, Pike's letters are a melancholy chronicle of the tribulations of infirm old age. His body was continually racked with neuralgia, gout, dyspepsia, and other ailments in these years, and he knew more suffering than he had ever known. Lilian must have seen that he was slipping, for she moved into the House of the Temple in the spring of 1886 to be near him and help look after him. He worked when he was able, but he soon wearied of intense concentration even when well.[74]

He had no serious financial worriers, though he was keenly disappointed in the spring of 1886 when the court of claims set aside the Senate award of 1859. He prepared a brief to file in the appeal to the Supreme Court, but General Denver was absent from the city and did not come back in time to participate in the case. Nevertheless, when the Supreme Court decided, November 15, 1886, that the award was unimpeachable and reversed the decision of the court of claims, Pike assumed that he had won a great moral victory; he had, he boasted, gotten the Senate award of 1859 in the first place. His fee should have been nearly $80,000 but neither McKee, the principal attorney, nor the Choctaws ever paid him a cent. And Pike was too apathetic, if not senile, to care whether he got it or not. "Thank heavens," he told Vinnie in February, 1887, "I never counted upon getting it, and don't count upon getting it now, nor care whether I ever get a cent of it or not."[75]

Virtually a recluse by 1887, he never went into the sunlight, and he rarely went anywhere at night. His wakeful hours he spent in answering letters and in reading. Ever creative, Vinnie began about 1886 to write poetry and send it to him for corrections and criticism. He enjoyed the work but did not value his advice highly, confessing once in 1888 that he could "see what a poem *ought* to be, while unable to make it such. And because I have always known my own inability to produce a poem not full of imperfection, I have refused to *publish* to the world my attempts and failures as a poet, in a book."[76] His birds were very dear to him; it was their dependence on him, "the sense of protecting them, the caring for them, and seeing them grateful for it, that endears them to me."[77] Though many of them had been sent to him from Australia, Africa, and India, at great cost, he was fondest of the southern mockingbird. Vinnie had promised to look for one for him in New York City in 1888, and he wrote her not to buy a northern one; he had once paid twenty-five dollars for one raised in New York and it was "no singer at all." He believed that a mocker, to be a good singer, had to be reared in the South where it could learn to sing from older birds.[78] Next to his birds and books came his pipes, for he confessed to one habit, that many will term a vice,—that of smoking to excess. I have an affection for my pipes. They are indispensable to my well-being. Except when sleeping or eating, or in places where it would be improper, I smoke all the time. I smoke walking, sitting or reclining, while I talk and while I write. And yet one hardly knows in what charm of smoking consists. The act itself is but drawing smoke into the mouth, and permitting it to escape from it; and yet what a pleasure it is idly to lie and watch the blue rings of the smoke revolve, recede and disappear! It soothes and quiets and consoles us, this seemingly useless habit, and none is more general, nor, on the whole, more harmless.[79]

The year of 1889 was the worst one yet. He was harassed by a succession of ailments—gout, fever, boils, dyspepsia, headache, rheumatism, neuralgia, and lumbago—and the intervals between attacks were but a day or two.[80] He had hoped all year to be able to visit Vinnie in New York in the fall, but in August he refused, stating that she would find him "a very unsatisfactory guest, disinclined to locomotion, without appetite and wishing only to sit still and sleep. When one has come to that condition, he is wise if he lets his friends remember him as he was, and does not make them wish that he had stayed at home."[81] By the spring of 1890, after a winter of torment, he was very feeble. "I have not," he wrote Vinnie in early March, "had energy and spirit enough to write letters, or anything to write about, or any thoughts in the semitorpid condition of my intellect, worth putting on paper."[82] Tortured by a vicious attack of rheumatism and neuralgia all that spring and summer, he was unable to write except with excruciating pain, and he failed rapidly.[83] At the biennial session of the Supreme Council in October he "looked worn and haggard, . . . the voice was husky, and it was difficult to readily understand what he said." He presided over its meetings but had to have someone read for him his lengthy allocution.[84]

Exhausted by the exertion of attending the session, he took to his bed as soon as the Supreme Council adjourned. After this he occasionally sat up for an hour or two, but was unable to sit at his desk and write or read. His voice continued to be husky and he had great difficulty swallowing even water. His doctor came to see him five times at the end of October, twenty times in November, and twenty-three times in December, and almost daily, both night and day, thereafter. Two other doctors came for consultation; they both agreed with Pike's physician that there was a stricture of the oesophagus. Pike would not permit them to probe in an attempt to dilate the stricture, though he was able to swallow only liquids. In January and February he suffered several bad attacks of gout, fever, and rheumatism and grew weaker and weaker. March 21 the stricture closed completely, and he consented to five probings that were ineffectual. He was too weak and emaciated to withstand a major operation, and there was no remedy. He must literally starve to death.[85]

He accepted the judgment like a stoic, turning over the commandership of the Supreme Council to Lieutenant Grand Commander James C. Batchelor on March 23: "The good of the Order requires you to come here without delay and take my place," he told his old friend.[86] Starving to death might have taken several days, but on March 31 a new and alarming condition developed. The glands of his throat began to swell and choke him. April 1 the "heavy breathing of the sick man could be heard all over the spacious house." Yet when Pike aroused that night he said he was not in pain. He then dropped off to sleep with the same labored breathing. At three o'clock in the morning of April 2 he awoke, asked the time, and dozed off again. Arousing a few times between three and five, he held water in his mouth to relieve his thirst. He asked, at five o'clock, that the shutters be opened to let in "the light of the returning day." Dozing again, he awoke at six, took from a shelf by his bed a half sheet of note paper and a pencil and wrote a short memorandum relating to the bequest of personalty. This was his last conscious mental act, for he then dropped into a coma. He was still alive at seven that evening, though death was expected momentarily. At eight "the flame began to quiver." Hamilton, Lilian, and Yvon, his faithful black servant, Edward Kenney, and some nine Masonic friends now gathered by his bed, their eyes "riveted on the emaciated body of the great man." The breathing became fainter and fainter, and at last was still. Several of the men took out their watches to note the time. It was exactly eight o'clock.[87]

For five days he lay in state in the House of the Temple, while Masonic dignitaries met with the family to make arrangements for a funeral.[88] On the night of April 7 the Albert Pike Consistory Number 1 of the District of Columbia escorted him to the Scottish Rite Cathedral. There he lay in state two more days. At midnight on April 9 the Consistory escorted him to the Congregational Church, where the Kadosh funeral ceremony was performed. Next day, accompanied by his children, the members of the Supreme Council, and a numerous concourse of Masons and non-Masons, and escorted by the consistory, he was carried to the Church of the Ascension for the burial service of the Episcopal Church. Then the procession moved through the city to Oak Hill Cemetery, where he was temporarily interred in a vault. On April 16 Hamilton and Yvon and Acting Grand Commander Batchelor had him removed from the vault and placed in a grave on a hillside of the cemetery. In 1917 Yvon marked the grave with a modest stone:

ALBERT PIKE
Born: December 29, 1809
Died: April 2, 1891
Vixit.
Laborum Ejus Superstites Sunt Fructus.[89]

Notes

Chapter I

1. *Boston Evening Transcript*, Mar. 15, 1937, May 2, 7, 1938; "Will of John Pike, Sr.," *Essex Antiquarian* 20 (Apr. 1905): 64–65; notes on the ancestry of Albert Pike and on the family of Albert Pike furnished me by the late Mrs. Roscoe M. Packard, West Newton, Mass. (hereafter cited as Packard Notes); Duane Hamilton Hurd, *History of Essex County, Massachusetts, with Biographical Sketches of Many of Its Pioneers and Prominent Men* (2 vols., Philadelphia, 1888), 2: 1150–51; Joshua Coffin, *A Sketch of the History of Newbury, Newburyport, and West Newbury, from 1635 to 1845* (Boston, 1845), 16–17, 25, 26.

2. James Shepherd Pike, *The New Puritan, New England Two Hundred Years Ago* (New York, 1879); Hurd, *Essex County*, 2: 1151; *Dictionary of American Biography*, s.v. "Pike, Robert."

3. Hurd, *Essex County*, 2: 1150–51; *Boston Transcript*, May 2, 1938; Packard Notes; *Dictionary of American Biography*, s.v. "Pike, Zebulon Montgomery."

4. *Dictionary of American Biography*, s.v. "Pike, Nicholas," "Pike, James Shepard"; Packard Notes.

5. *Boston Transcript*, May 2, 7, 9, 13, 14, June 6, 1938; "Will of John Pike, Sr.," *Essex Antiquarian* 20 (Apr. 1905): 64–65; Thomas Hutchinson, *The History of the Colony and Province of Massachusetts-Bay*, ed. Lawrence Shaw Mayo (3 vols., Cambridge, Mass., 1936), II, 62; John Lewis Ewell, *The Story of Byfield, A New England Parish* (Boston, 1904), 125; Coffin, *Newbury, Newburyport, and West Newbury*, 314.

6. Francis B. Heitman, *Historical Register of the Officers of the Continental Army during the Revolution, April, 1775 to December, 1783* (Reprint, Baltimore, 1967), 246, 442; *Massachusetts Soldiers and Sailors of the Revolutionary War* (17 vols., Boston, 1896–1908), XII, 409; Packard Notes; Christopher Ward, *The War of the Revolution* (2 vols., New York, 1952), I, 86, 215, 222; Allen French, *The First Year of the American Revolution* (Boston, 1934), 66, 71, 225, 244, 247, 302, 724. Albert Pike's daughter, Lilian, in 1891 became a charter member of the Daughters of the American Revolution as a result of Thomas Pike's service in the Revolution. Mary S. Lockwood, *Lineage Book of the Charter Members of the Daughters of the American Revolution* (rev. ed., Harrisburg, Pa., 1895), 96.

7. Packard Notes; "Autobiographical Memorandum by Albert Pike," in W. M. Griswold, ed., *Passages from the Correspondence of Rufus W. Griswold* (Cambridge, Mass., 1898), 71–72, is a sketch Pike wrote in 1841 for use with a selection of his poetry in Rufus Wilmot Griswold, *The Poets and Poetry of America* (Philadelphia, 1842), the original manuscript of which Pike sketched is in Rufus Wilmot Griswold Manuscript, Boston Public Library; "Autobiography of General Albert Pike from stenographic notes furnished by himself, April 26, 1886," in Albert Pike Papers, Library of Scottish Rite Supreme Council, House of the Temple, Washington, D.C. (hereafter cited as Autobiography, Pike Papers); *A Volume of Records Relating to the Early History of Boston, Containing Boston Marriages from 1752 to 1809* (Boston, 1903), 499.

8. Lilian Pike Roome, *General Albert Pike's Poems* (Little Rock, 1900), 9–10; "Autobiographical Memorandum," in Griswold, *Griswold Correspondence*, 71–72; Albert Pike, *Essays to Vinnie*, Essay 26, "Of Chance and School-Teaching," Pike Papers (29 essays found in five

manuscript volumes containing in all 2,166 pages autobiographical in form, in Pike's hand, written in Washington, D.C., about 1870–1873, and dedicated to his friend Vinnie Ream the sculptress, who listened to him read most if not all of them during frequent visits with him). (Hereafter cited as *Essays to Vinnie*, with number and title of essay, Pike Papers.)

9. Autobiography, Pike Papers; *Essays to Vinnie*, Essay 1, "Of Content in Old Age," Pike Papers; *Boston Directory* (1810), 156; *Boston Directory* (1813), 204; Samuel Eliot Morison, *The Maritime History of Massachusetts, 1783–1860* (Boston, 1941), 124–28; American Guide Series, *Massachusetts: A Guide to Its Places and People* (Boston, 1937), 152.

10. Packard Notes, for facts on the Benjamin Pike family history.

11. "Autobiographical Memorandum," in Griswold, *Griswold Correspondence*, 71–72; Autobiography, Pike Papers; *Essays to Vinnie*, Essay 26, "Of Chance and School-Teaching," Pike Papers.

12. Alfred W. Pike to the Rev. James Walker, Somerville, Mass., May 26, 1859, and Alfred W. Pike to Mrs. Benjamin Pike, Brunswick, Maine, Oct. 6, 1843, both in papers lent to me by the late Mrs. Roscoe M. Packard, West Newton, Mass. Alfred W. Pike, Albert's cousin, was a pious congregationalist. John James Currier, *History of Newburyport, Mass., 1764–1909* (2 vols., Newburyport, 1906–1909), II, 558.

13. *Essays to Vinnie*, Essay 26, "Of Chance and School-Teaching," Pike Papers, relates something of the character of Benjamin. Also of use is "Autobiographical Memorandum," in Griswold, *Griswold Correspondence*, 71–72.

14. Autobiography, Pike Papers; *Essays to Vinnie*, Essay 1, "Of Content in Old Age," Essay 5, "Of Wrecks and Waifs of Poetry," Essay 26, "Of Chance and School-Teaching," Pike Papers; Morison, *Maritime History of Massachusetts*, 151–52; John L. Thomas, *The Liberator: William Lloyd Garrison, A Biography* (Boston, 1963), 16–53, gives valuable information on Newburyport between 1805 and 1826, the years of Garrison's residence there.

15. Morison, *Maritime History of Massachusetts*, 152–55; Thomas, *Garrison*, 16–53; *Little Rock (Ark.) Advocate*, Sept. 25, 1835 (hereafter cited as *Advocate*).

16. Raymond P. Holden, *The Merrimack* (New York, 1958), 133–46; [Mrs. Euphemia V. Blake], *History of Newburyport; for the Earliest Settlement of the Country to the Present Time, with a Biographical Appendix* (Newburyport, 1854); Caleb Cushing, *The History of the Present State of the Town of Newburyport* (Newburyport, 1826), a political pamphlet with cogent analysis of the town's problems; *And Account of the Great Fire, Which Destroyed about 250 Buildings in Newburyport, on the Night of the 31st of May, 1811* (2d ed., Improved, Newburyport, 1811); "The Restoration of Newburyport," in *Newburyport Herald*, June 10, 1823; Morison, *Maritime History of Massachusetts*, 216.

17. Autobiography, Pike Papers; *Newburyport Herald*, Feb. 14, 1815; Coffin, *Newbury, Newburyport, and West Newbury*, 278–79.

18. Autobiography, Pike Papers; *Newburyport Herald*, July 4, 16, 1817.

19. Autobiography, Pike Papers; *Newburyport Herald*, Sept. 3, 1824.

20. *Essays to Vinnie*, Essay 1, "Of Content in Old Age," Essay 5, "Of Wrecks and Waifs of Poetry," Pike Papers.

21. *Essays to Vinnie*, Essay 1, "Of Content in Old Age," Pike Papers.

22. *Essays to Vinnie*, Essay 1, "Of Content in Old Age," Essay 5, "Of Wrecks and Waifs of Poetry," Pike Papers.

23. Thomas, *Garrison*, 22.

24. *Essays to Vinnie*, Essay 5, "Of Wrecks and Waifs of Poetry," Pike Papers.

25. *Essays to Vinnie*, Essay 26, "Of Chance and School-Teaching," Pike Papers; Walter Herbert Small, *Early New England Schools* (Boston, 1914), 162–86, 290–304; George Emery Littlefield, *Early Schools and School-Books of New England* (Boston, 1904), 129–266.

26. Pike wrote in 1836: "We were taught in our childhood to reverence the Constitution of the United States. Once a month it was read in the school where we received our early education—and we learned to regard it as the noblest monument of human wisdom...." *Advocate*, Jan. 8, 1836. It may well be that Pike was receiving the Federalist interpretation of the Constitution as a protection for minority rights, for that was the spirit in which he wrote in 1836.

27. Currier, *History of Newburyport*, II, 558, says that Alfred (Mar. 21, 1791–Sept. 6, 1860) was the son of Joseph Pike, Benjamin's uncle.

28. Quoted, with a marginal correction by Mrs. Roscoe M. Packard, in Frederick W. Allsopp, *Albert Pike, A Biography* (Little Rock, Ark. 1928), 14, in a copy belonging to Mrs. Packard (hereafter cited as Packard Marginalia in Allsopp, *Pike*), This Packard copy of the Allsopp book is to be deposited in the Library of the Scottish Rite Supreme Council, House of the Temple, Washington, D.C.

29. Alfred Pike to Walker, May 26, 1859, and Benjamin R. Curtis to James Walker, Boston, May 23, 1859, Harvard University Archives; "Autobiographical Memorandum," in Griswold, *Griswold Correspondence*, 71–72; Albert Pike, "Autobiography," in John Hallum, *Biographical and Pictorial History of Arkansas* (1 vol., no more published, Albany, N.Y., 1887), 1: 216 (hereafter cited as "Autobiography," in Hallum, *History of Arkansas*); Autobiography, Pike Papers.

30. Alfred Pike to Walker, May 26, 1859, Harvard University Archives.

31. Ibid.

32. *Essays to Vinnie*, Essay 26, "Of Chance and School-Teaching," Pike Papers.

33. Ibid.; "Silhouette of myself cut about 1825," and signed "Albert Pike," in possession of Library of the Scottish Rite Supreme Council, House of the Temple, Washington, D.C. In his autobiographical long poem, "Fantasma," written in 1833, Pike describes himself. Albert Pike, *Prose Sketches and Poems Written in the Western Country (With Additional Stories)*, ed. David J. Weber (Albuquerque, N.Mex., 1967), 207–13, which reprints the original Pike book with an introduction and notes as well as an appendix containing (1) Pike's "Crayon Sketches and Journeyings," three letters he wrote in late 1834 for Issac Pray's *The Boston Pearl and Literary Gazette* describing his trip from St. Louis to Taos and Santa Fe in ibid., published, Nov. 8, 22, 1834, and Jan. 10, 1836, respectively; (2) Pike's "A Journey to Xemes," published in *The Boston Pearl*, Feb. 20, 1835, an autobiographical account of a trading trip he made in July 1832 from Santa Fe to Jemez Pueblo in the employ of Bent, St. Vrain, and Company; (3) Pike's "Tales of Character and Country, written for the *Advocate*," four stories based on his New Mexico experiences—"San Juan of the Del Norte," *Advocate*, Nov. 27, 1833; "The Gachupin," ibid., Dec. 11, 1834; "Manuel the Wolf Killer," ibid., Feb. 28, 1834; and "Trappers on the Prairie" (title supplied by Weber), ibid., Apr. 11, 1834. (All citations of Pike's book will hereafter be from the Weber edition.)

34. *Essays to Vinnie*, Essay 26, "Of Chance and School-Teaching," Pike Papers.

35. Ibid.

36. Ibid.

37. Ibid.

38. Ibid.

39. *Essays to Vinnie*, Essay 26, "Of Chance and School-Teaching," Pike Papers; "Autobiography," in Hallum, *History of Arkansas*, 1: 216; Harvard University *Statute and Laws*,

1825, p. 4, 1826, p. 4. In August 1859 the faculty of Harvard conferred upon Pike the honorary degree of A.M. in recognition of merit. Alfred W. Pike, Caleb Cushing, and Benjamin R. Curtis recommended him for the degree, which Pike accepted in a letter to Pres. James Walker, Little Rock, Aug. 25, 1859. Copies of these letters were furnished the writer by Clifford H. Shepton, Custodian of Harvard University Archives.

40. *Essays to Vinnie,* Essay 26, "Of Chance and School-Teaching," Pike Papers.

41. Ibid.

42. Ibid.; Thomas Lawson to Pike, n.p., 1885, Pike Papers, gives information on the Social Club and other clubs in Newburyport at this time.

43. *Essays to Vinnie,* Essay 26, "Of Chance and School-Teaching," Pike Papers; Autobiography, Pike Papers.

44. *Essays to Vinnie,* Essay 26, "Of Chance and School-Teaching," Pike Papers; John Tasker Howard, *Our American Music; Three Hundred Years of It* (3d ed. rev. and reset, New York, 1945), 131, 151, 169–70.

45. *Essays to Vinnie,* Essay 26, "Of Chance and School-Teaching," Pike Papers; Autobiography, Pike Papers.

46. *Essays to Vinnie,* Essay 26, "Of Chance and School-Teaching," Pike Papers.

47. Ibid.; *Neburyport Herald,* Aug. 28, Oct. 1, 1829; "Autobiographical Memorandum," in Griswold, *Griswold Correspondence,* 71–72.

48. *Essays to Vinnie,* Essay 26, "Of Chance and School-Teaching," Pike Papers.

49. *Newburyport Herald,* May 21, 1830. Elsewhere Pike indicated that "the common English branches" included writing, arithmetic, algebra, geometry, trigonometry, surveying, and navigation. Ibid., Sept. 24, 1830.

50. Ibid., Aug. 10, Sept. 24, Oct. 5, 12, 1830.

51. Frederick W. Coburn, "Thomas Bayley Lawson, Portrait Painter of Newburyport and Lowell," *Essex Institute Historical Collections* 83 (Oct. 1947): 357.

52. *Essays to Vinnie,* Essay 11, "Of My Books and Studies," Pike Papers; "Autobiography," in Hallum, *History of Arkansas,* 1: 216.

53. Susan B. Riley, "The Life and Works of Albert Pike to 1860" (unpublished Ph.D. dissertation, Peabody College for Teachers, Nashville, Tenn., 1934), 36–98, discusses and analyzes Pike's writing during this period; Jay B. Hubbell, *The South in American Literature, 1607–1900* (Durham, N.C., 1954), 640–50, is a good critical estimate of Pike's life and writings.

54. *Yankee and Boston Literary Gazette* 2 (Feb. 19, 1829): 64.

55. "Fantasma" in Weber, ed., *Albert Pike Prose Sketches,* 209.

56. *Newburyport Herald,* Oct. 29, 1830; *Advocate,* Mar. 27, 1835. No copy of the magazine has been located.

57. "Fantasma" in Weber, *Albert Pike Prose Sketches,* 211.

58. *Essays to Vinnie,* Essay 26, "Of Chance and School-Teaching," Pike Papers; Autobiography, Pike Papers. In "Fantasma" Pike expresses his torn spirit at this time. "Fantasma" in Weber, *Albert Pike Prose Sketches,* 210–13.

59. *Essays to Vinnie,* Essay 26, "Of Chance and School-Teaching," Pike Papers.

Chapter II

1. Autobiography, Pike Papers; Albert Pike, "Western Traveling," *Hartford Pearl and Literary Gazette* 4 (Sept. 1834): 48; Albert Pike, "A Sketch," *Essayist* 2 (July 1831): 69–70, and "Sketches of Tennessee," in ibid., 80.

2. Autobiography, Pike Papers; Harold H. Dunham, "Charles Bent," in Leroy R. Hafen, ed., *The Mountain Men and the Fur Trade of the Far West* (Glendale, Calif., 1965), II, 27–48, and see also ibid., II, 13, for a portrait of Bent, who was the first American governor of New Mexico in 1846.

3. Autobiography, Pike Papers.

4. Pike, "Crayon Sketches and Journeyings," 223–29.

5. Ibid., 224–25.

6. Ibid., 225.

7. Ibid.

8. Ibid., 228; Dunham, "Charles Bent," 38.

9. Pike, "Crayon Sketches and Journeyings," 228.

10. Ibid., 230.

11. Ibid., 230–31.

12. Josiah Gregg, *Commerce of the Prairies*, ed. Max L. Moorhead (Norman, Okla., 1954), who made his first trip to Santa Fe in 1831 also, points out that this dreaded desert was called the "Water-Scrape" and describes the careful preparation that was made for crossing it. Ibid, 49–50.

13. Pike, "Crayon Sketches and Journeyings," 230–32.

14. Ibid., 232–33.

15. Ibid., 233.

16. Ibid., 233–34.

17. Pike, "Narrative of a Journey in the Prairie," in *Prose Sketches and Poems*, 16.

18. Ibid., 16–17.

19. Ibid., 17.

20. Autobiography, Pike Papers.

21. Pike, "Narrative of a Journey in the Prairie," 18–19.

22. Ibid., 19.

23. Ibid.

24. Autobiography, Pike Papers.

25. Ibid.

26. Pike, "Crayon Sketches and Journeyings," 237–38.

27. Ibid., 237–38.

28. Ibid., 238.

29. "Autobiographical Memorandum by Albert Pike," in Griswold, *Griswold Correspondence*, 71–72; William Waldo, "Recollections of a Septuagenarian," *Missouri Historical Society, Glimpses of the Past* 5 (Apr.–June 1938): 91.

30. Pike, "A Journey to Xemes," 242–43.

31. Pike, *Prose Sketches and Poems*, ix–xxv; Harvey L. Carter, "Albert Pike," in Hafen, ed., *Mountain Men and the Fur Trade of the Far West*, II, 265–74; David Lavender, *Bent's Fort* (Garden

City, N.Y., 1954), 129–30; Mabel Major and T. M. Pearce, *Southwest Heritage, A Literary History with Bibliographies* (3d ed., rev. and enl., Albuquerque, N.Mex., 1972), 77.

32. Pike, "The Inroad of the Nabajo," in *Prose Sketches and Poems*, 147–48.

33. Pike, "Refugio," in *Prose Sketches and Poems*, 184; Gregg, *Commerce of the Prairies*, 77, had the same reaction.

34. Pike, "Refugio," 184–85, and "A Journey to Xemes," 241–42; Gregg, *Commerce of the Prairie*, 157, for a description of the siesta.

35. Pike, "Narrative of a Second Journey in the Prairie," in *Prose Sketches and Poems*, 38–39.

36. My sources for this passage are from the prose writings in Pike, *Prose Sketches and Poems*: especially, "A Mexican Tale," 103, 113, 116–17; "Refugio," 185–87; "Crayon Sketches and Journeyings," 237; and "A Journey to Xemes," 241, 242, 247. See also Weber's "Introduction," xv–xvii.

37. My sources for this passage are Weber's "Introduction," xvi–xvii; "A Mexican Tale," 101–2; "The Inroad of the Nabajo," 147–48; "Lines, Written in the Vale of the Picuris, Sept. 3, 1832," pp. 167–71; "Crayon Sketches and Journeyings," 235–36; "A Journey to Xemes," 241–46.

38. Waldo, "Recollections," 90–91.

39. Ibid., 88–91.

40. Ibid., and Pike, "Refugio," 187–91, where Pike describes the life and character of Le Grand; *Handbook of Texas*, s.v. "LeGrand, Alexander."

41. Waldo, "Recollections," 90; Pike, "The Inroad of the Nabajo," 149, and "Refugio," 187–91.

42. Pike, "Refugio," 183–202.

43. Pike, "The Inroad of the Nabajo," 147–49.

44. Waldo, "Recollections," 91.

45. Pike, "Narrative of a Second Journey in the Prairie," 33; *Advocate*, Nov. 7, 1834.

46. Pike, "Narrative of a Second Journey in the Prairie," 35–42; *Advocate*, Nov. 7, 1834; Autobiography, Pike Papers.

47. Pike, "Narrative of a Journey in the Prairie," 4, 28–32; Pike, "Narrative of a Second Journey in the Prairie," 33–79.

48. Pike, "Narrative of a Journey in the Prairie," 29–31; Pike, "Trappers on the Prairie," in *Prose Sketches and Poems*, 281–82.

49. Weber's "Introduction," in Pike, *Prose Sketches and Poems*, xix, 35n.

50. Pike, "Narrative of a Second Journey in the Prairie," 34–35; Pike, "Trappers on the Prairie," 282.

51. Pike, "Narrative of a Second Journey in the Prairie," 42–43; *Handbook of Texas*, s.v. "Comanche Trail," "Comancheros," "Llano Estacado."

52. *Handbook of Texas*, s.v. "Comanche Trail," "Pike, Albert"; David Donaghue, "Explorations of Albert Pike in Texas," *Southwestern Historical Quarterly* 39 (Oct. 1935): 136.

53. Pike, "Narrative of a Second Journey in the Prairie," 42–43, 78.

54. Ibid., 43–45.

55. Ibid., 44–46.

56. Ibid., 46–47.

57. Ibid., 47.

58. Ibid., 47–50.

59. Ibid., 48–50.
60. Ibid., 50–51.
61. Ibid., 51.
62. Ibid., 51–52.
63. *Handbook of Texas*, s.v. "Pike, Albert."
64. Pike, "Narrative of a Second Journey in the Prairie," 52–54.
65. Ibid., 54–57.
66. *Advocate*, Mon. 7, 1834.
67. Pike, "Narrative of a Second Journey in the Prairie," 56–57.
68. Ibid., 57–58, 78–79. In his Autobiography, Pike Papers, Pike says Charles Bent killed "a young man by the name of Titcomb" in New Mexico. It is difficult to believe this was Rufus Titcomb, Pike's friend. On the other hand, Titcomb is not a common name, and it could have been Rufus; that is, if Pike is correct about Bent killing a man there. None of the sources I have read on Bent mention that he killed a Titcomb or any other man.
69. Pike, "Narrative of a Second Journey in the Prairie," 58–59.
70. *Handbook of Texas*, s.v. "Pike, Albert," "Salt Fork of the Brazos."
71. Pike, "Narrative of a Second Journey in the Prairie," 59–62.
72. Ibid., 62–64.
73. Ibid., 63–64.
74. Ibid., 64–73.
75. Ibid., 70–73.
76. Ibid., 73–76; Autobiography, Pike Papers.
77. Autobiography, Pike Papers; Pike, "Narrative of Second Journey in the Prairie," 76–77.
78. Ibid., 77.
79. Ibid.

Chapter III

1. Albert Pike, "Letters from Arkansas, No. I," *New England Magazine* 9 (Oct. 1835): 267.
2. Grant Foreman, *Pioneer Days in the Early Southwest* (Cleveland, Ohio, 1926), 33–34, 63–64; W. David Baird, "Arkansas's Choctaw Boundary: A Study of Justice Delayed," *Arkansas Historical Quarterly* 28: 203–22 and "Fort Smith and the Red Man," ibid., 30 (winter 1971): 337–48.
3. Ed Bearss and Arrell M. Gibson, *Fort Smith: Little Gibraltar on the Arkansas* (Norman, Okla., 1969), 8.
4. *Essays to Vinnie*, Essay 24, "Of Pleasant and Sad Remembrances," Pike Papers.
5. Bearss and Gibson, *Fort Smith*, 113–36.
6. Pike, "Letters from Arkansas," *New England Magazine* 9: 267.
7. Baird, "Fort Smith and the Red Man."
8. Elsa Vaught, "Captain John Rogers: Founder of Fort Smith," *Arkansas Historical Quarterly* 17 (autumn 1958): 239–64; Bearss and Gibson, *Fort Smith*, 31, 101, 104, 124, 130–33, 137–38, 149, 152, 157, 166, 172, 174–77, 200; *Essays to Vinnie*, Essay 24, "Of Pleasant and Sad Remembrances," Pike Papers.

9. *Essays to Vinnie*, Essay 24, "Of Pleasant and Sad Remembrances," Pike Papers.
10. *Essays to Vinnie*, Essay 13, "Of Rowing against the Stream," Pike Papers.
11. Pike, "Letters from Arkansas," *New England Magazine* 9: 265.
12. *Essays to Vinnie*, Essay 13, "Of Rowing against the Stream," Pike Papers.
13. Ibid.
14. Ibid.
15. Ibid., Essay 27, "Of Chance and School-Teaching," Pike Papers.
16. Ibid.
17. Ibid.
18. Albert Pike to John [Lewis] Cass, Secretary of War, Van Buren, Arkansas Territory, Mar. 16, 1833, Indian Office, Western Superintendency, 1833, Retired Classified Files. (Photostatic copy in Archives Collection, University of Texas.)
19. Albert Pike to George W. Light, Van Buren, Arkansas Territory, May 25, 1833, original in Yale University Library, New Haven, Conn.
20. Taken from "Los Tiempos," in *Advocate*, Mar. 13, 1833.
21. Pike to Light, Van Buren, Arkansas Territory, May 25, May 26, 1833.
22. Ibid., May 26, 1833.
23. Ibid.
24. Albert Pike, "To the Public," in *Advocate*, Mar. 7, 1834, gives the account of this affair.
25. Albert Pike, "Letter from Arkansas, No. 11," *American Monthly Magazine* 1 (Jan. 1836): 25.
26. Ibid., 28.
27. *Essays to Vinnie*, Essay 26, "Of Chance and School-Teaching," Pike Papers.
28. Ibid. My account of the history of the Crittenden-Sevier rivalry prior to Pike's arrival in Little Rock is based on an exhaustive reading of the extant files of the *Gazette* and the *Advocate* plus two vital books: Margaret Ross, *Arkansas Gazette, the Early Years 1819–1866: A History* (Little Rock, Ark., 1969) and Lonnie J. White, *Politics on the Southwestern Frontier: Arkansas Territory, 1819–1836* (Memphis, Tenn., 1964), hereafter cited as *Politics in Arkansas Territory*.
29. Orval W. Baylor, *John Pope, Kentuckian, His Life and Times, 1770–1845* (Cynthiana, Ky., 1943) is a good work to consult on Pope's career in *Arkansas Territory*.
30. Pike, "Letters from Arkansas, No. 1," *New England Magazine* 9: 267.
31. Ibid. Sinclair was Robert Sinclair; Bates was James Woodson Bates; Brown was Richard Conway Sevier Brown; and Martin was Bennett H. Martin. All were candidates for the legislature that year.
32. Ibid.
33. Pike, "Letters from Arkansas, No. 11," *American Monthly Magazine* 1: 30. Again, my account of the origin of the rivalry among Arkansas's early newspapers is based on Ross, *Gazette*, and White, *Politics in Arkansas Territory*.
34. John Lewis Ferguson, "William E. Woodruff and the Territory of Arkansas, 1819–1836" (unpublished Ph.D. dissertation, Tulane University, 1960) is a careful study of Woodruff's early career in Arkansas. Again, Ross, *Gazette*, and White, *Politics in Arkansas Territory*, are my principal sources for the *Gazette–Advocate* rivalry.
35. Margaret Smith Ross, "The Cunninghams: Little Rock's First Family," *Pulaski County Historical Review* 2 (June 1953): 11ff.

36. Margaret Smith Ross, "Jesse Brown," *Pulaski County Historical Review* 2 (Dec. 1954): 5ff.

37. Albert Pike, "Robert Crittenden," in Hallum, *History of Arkansas*, 1: 65.

38. Ibid.; Griswold, *Poets and Poetry of American* 392, states that Bertrand was impressed with the poetry that Pike had sent to the *Advocate* during the spring and summer of 1833, and consequently had sent for Pike to come to Little Rock to be his partner. This poetry may have influenced Bertrand in part, for Pike had written several cantos of "Los Tiempos," for the *Advocate* during July and Aug., 1833, are Pike's; "Official Return for Delegate," in *Gazette*, Sept. 18, 1833, gives the election results.

39. Susan B. Riley, "Albert Pike as an American Don Juan," *Arkansas Historical Quarterly* 19 (autumn 1960): 207–24. Susan B. Riley, "The Life and Works of Albert Pike to 1860" (unpublished Ph.D. dissertation, Peabody College for Teachers, Nashville, Tenn., 1934), is a good study of Pike's early literary career and an exhaustive compilation of his fugitive poetry.

40. Riley, "Albert Pike as an American Don Juan," 10: 220–21.

41. Pike, "Robert Crittenden," in Hallum, *History of Arkansas*, 1: 65; Pike, "Letters from Arkansas, no. II," *American Monthly Magazine* 1: 28; *Essays to Vinnie*, Essay 26, "Of Chance and School-Teaching," Pike Papers.

42. Pike, "Letters from Arkansas, No. II," *American Monthly Magazine* 1: 29.

43. "Autobiography," *New Age Magazine* 37: 719.

Chapter IV

1. *Essays to Vinnie*, Essay 13, "Of Rowing against the Stream," Pike Papers.

2. Ibid.

3. *Advocate*, July 25, 1834.

4. Walter Lee Brown, Review of Ira Don Richards, *Little Rock in the Nineteenth Century*, *Arkansas Historical Quarterly* 29 (spring 1970): 85–86.

5. Margaret Smith Ross, "Cadron: An Early Town That Failed," *Arkansas Historical Quarterly* 16 (spring 1957): 3–27; White, *Politics in Arkansas Territory*, 30–32; Ross, *Gazette*, 22, 24, 35–39, 41, 72; Ira Don Richards, *Story of a Rivertown, Little Rock in the Nineteenth Century* (n.p., 1969), 1–11.

6. Pike, "Letters from Arkansas, No. 11," *American Monthly Magazine* 1: 30; "Letters from Arkansas," *American Monthly Magazine*, New Series 1 (Jan. 1836): 29–30.

7. Albert Pike, "Life in Arkansas," *American Monthly Magazine*, New Series 1 (Mar. 1836): 300.

8. *Essays to Vinnie*, Essay 13, "Of Rowing against the Stream," Pike Papers.

9. *Advocate*, Nov. 20, 1833.

10. Ibid., Dec. 1833.

11. Pike, "Life in Arkansas," *American Monthly Magazine* 1: 302.

12. *Advocate*, Oct. 16, 23, 30, 1833; *Gazette*, Oct. 16, 23, 30, Nov. 6, 1833.

13. *Advocate*, Oct. 30, 1833.

14. *Gazette*, Nov. 6, 1833.

15. *Advocate*, Nov. 13, 20, 27, 1833.

16. Ibid., Feb. 28, 1834.

17. In *Advocate*, Mar. 7, 1834.

18. Ibid.

19. See John Harris to Pike, Van Buren, Ark., Mar. 20, 1834; George M. Aldridge to Pike, Van Buren, Mar. 21, 1834; Thomas Phillips to Pike, Van Buren, Mar. 21, 1834, and B.[ennett] H. Martin to Pike, Spadre Bluff, Ark., Mar. 27, 1834, all in the *Advocate*, Apr. 4, 1834.

20. Albert Pike, "To the Public," in ibid., Apr. 11, 1834.

21. *Advocate*, Mar. 21, 1834.

22. Ibid., July 4, 1834.

23. Ibid., June 13, 1834.

24. Ibid., May 2, 9, 1834.

25. Ibid., May 9, 1834.

26. Ibid., Jan. 30, 1835.

27. Ibid., June 27, July 4, 1834.

28. Ibid., July 11, 1834.

29. "Oration Delivered before the Little Rock Debating Society, July 4th, 1834 by Albert Pike," in *Advocate*, July 18, 1834.

30. *Advocate*, May 2, 1833, contains the first number of "The Walking Gentleman."

31. Ibid., Aug. 1, 1834, "The Walking Gentleman, no. X."

32. Ibid.

33. Ibid., Aug. 8, 1834, "The Walking Gentleman, no. XI."

34. *Advocate*, Oct. 3, 1834.

35. Ibid., Sept. 26, 1834.

36. Ibid., Oct. 31, Nov. 7, 28, 1834.

37. "Autobiography," in Hallum, *History of Arkansas*, 1: 216.

38. Ibid., *Essays to Vinnie*, Essay 13, "Of Rowing against the Stream," Pike Papers; "Autobiography," *New Age Magazine* 37: 720; *Advocate*, Aug. 22, 1834, carried Pike's first card as an "attorney at law."

39. *Advocate*, Apr. 18, July 11, Aug. 1, 1834.

40. "Autobiography" in Hallum, *History of Arkansas*, 1: 216; *Essays to Vinnie*, Essay 13, "Of Rowing against the Stream," Pike Papers.

41. "Autobiography," *New Age Magazine* 37: 720; Roome, *General Albert Pike's Poems*, 12.

42. "Autobiography," *New Age Magazine* 37: 720; Probate Record AA, pp. 112, 118, 200, 236–37, Probate Record 1-A, pp. 88–89, 100, 103, 133, 192–94, Arkansas County, in County Clerk's Office, DeWitt, Ark.; and Deed Record E, pp. 308–11, Arkansas County, in Circuit Clerk's Office, Dewitt, Ark., covers Mary Ann Hamilton's Guardianship and her estate.

43. *Gazette*, Sept. 2, 1820, Jan. 20, 27, Feb. 9, Apr. 9, 1822, Dec. 23, 1828; Pike, "Terence Farrelly," in Hallum, *History of Arkansas*, 1: 87; see also the information in the official records in the preceding note.

44. Pike to Light, Little Rock, Aug. 18, 1834, letter pasted in cover of copy of Pike, *Prose Sketches and Poems*, in J. N. Heiskell Collection, Little Rock.

Chapter V

1. Pike to Jesse Turner, Little Rock, Oct. 6, 1834, Jesse Turner Papers, Duke University; *Essays to Vinnie*, Essay 13, "Of Rowing against the Stream," Pike Papers.

2. *Essays to Vinnie*, Essay 13, "Of Rowing against the Stream," Pike Papers; "Autobiography," in Hallum, *History of Arkansas*, 1: 217.

3. Hallum, *History of Arkansas*, 1: 87–88, 101–2.

4. Ibid.

5. Ibid., 87–88.

6. Boyd Johnson, "Frederick Notrebe," *Arkansas Historical Quarterly* 21 (autumn 1962): 269–83; *The Western Journals of Washington Irving*, ed. John Francis McDermott (Norman, Okla., 1944), 168.

7. Hallum, *History of Arkansas*, 1: 82–83, 108.

8. Boyd Johnson, "Benjamin Desha," *Arkansas Historical Quarterly* 19 (winter 1960): 348–60.

9. Ibid., Hallum, *History of Arkansas*, 1: 87–88.

10. The date in "Autobiography," in Hallum, *History of Arkansas*, 1: 217, is Oct. 10, 1834. But in Pike's Bible preserved in the Supreme Council the date is Nov. 18, as it is in *Advocate*, Nov. 28, 1824, and *Gazette*, Dec. 2, 1834.

11. *Advocate*, Nov. 28, 1834.

12. *Essays to Vinnie*, Essay 13, "Of Rowing against the Stream," Pike Papers; "Autobiography," *New Age Magazine* 37: 720; "Autobiography," in Hallum, *History of Arkansas*, 1: 217.

13. *Advocate*, Jan. 2, 1835; *Essays to Vinnie*, Essay 13, "Of Rowing against the Stream," Pike Papers.

14. Deed Record H, 214, 224–26, Pulaski County, Circuit Clerk's Office, Little Rock; Deed Record E, 308–11, Arkansas County, Circuit Clerk's Office, DeWitt, Ark.

15. *Advocate*, Jan. 23, 1835.

16. Ibid.

17. Ibid.

18. Ibid.

19. "Autobiography," in Hallum, *History of Arkansas*, 1: 217.

20. Pike to John Neal, Little Rock, Mar. 8, 1835, Neal Papers, Harvard University Library.

21. *Advocate*, July 24, 1835.

22. Ibid., Sept. 4, 1835.

23. Ibid., Nov. 25, 1836.

24. Ibid., Apr. 10, 1835.

25. Ibid., Sept. 11, 1835.

26. Ibid., Dec. 11, 1835.

27. *Little Rock Times*, Dec. 7, 1835.

28. Ibid.

29. *Advocate*, Dec. 11, 1835.

30. The vital statistics of Ben Desha are in conflict. The Pike Family Bible preserved in the Albert Pike Room, Library of the Supreme Council, gives Ben Desha, born Dec. 2, 1835, died in

Feb., 1838; Albert, born Feb. 23, 1837, died Feb. 25, 1837. But the *Advocate*, Mar. 11, 1836, says Ben Desha died Mar. 3, 1836, and ibid., Feb. 24, 1837, says Albert died on Feb. 19, 1837. The Bible in question was an edition of 1848, wherefore one would presume that Pike entered the dates prior to that from memory. The grave marker for the Albert Pike burial plot in Mount Holly Cemetery, Little Rock, Ark., erected by the Scottish Rite Masons of the Valley of Little Rock early in this century, gives the death dates of Ben Desha as Feb. 17, 1836, aged two months, fifteen days, and of Albert as Feb. 23, 1837. There is no conflict on Hamilton's vital record.

31. Information obtained by a personal tour and interview in June 1953 with Mrs. David O. Terry, who then owned the Pike house and resided there; Pike to William M. Ireland, Tucson, Ariz., Apr. 26, 1883, Pike Papers, SCSR; Deed of Conveyance (Albert Pike to Mary Ann Pike), Oct. 29, 1857, Record Book B, No. 2, pp. 20–27, Circuit Clerk's Office, Pulaski County, Little Rock; Bobbie Sue Hood, "The Albert Pike Home," *Arkansas Historical Quarterly* 13 (spring 1954): 123–26. Dr. Francis J. Scully, Hot Springs, Ark., in a letter to the writer of Apr. 23, 1954, says that Pike acquired Block 61, on which the house is built, from Chester Ashley in 1839, paying $1,500 for it. Dr. Scully also furnished the writer with a typescript copy of the Deed of Conveyance (1957) referred to above in this note. The Pike-Fletcher-Terry mansion is presently the home of the Decorative Arts Museum, a division of the Arkansas Arts Center, Little Rock.

32. Pike, "An Evening Conversation," in *Hymns to the Gods and Other Poems by Gen. Albert Pike*, ed. Mrs. Lilian Pike Roome (Little Rock, Ark., 1916), 131–32.

33. Pike Family Bible, in SCSR; Pike Marker, Mount Holly Cemetery in Little Rock.

34. Pike, "An Invitation," in *Hymns to the Gods and Other Poems*, 233–36.

35. Ibid., 233.

36. Ibid., 235.

37. Ibid., 235–36.

38. Pike, "An Evening Conversation," 120–33.

39. Ibid., 121.

40. Ibid., 130.

41. Ibid., 133.

Chapter VI

1. *Advocate*, July 24, Aug. 28, Sept. 11, Oct. 16, Nov. 20, 1835, July 22, 1836.

2. Ibid., Nov. 13, 1835.

3. Ibid., Jan. 30, 1835.

4. Ibid.

5. Ibid.

6. Ibid.

7. Ibid., Feb. 13, 1835.

8. Ibid., Feb. 6, 1835.

9. Ibid.

10. Ibid.

11. Ibid.

12. Ibid., Jan. 23, 1835.
13. Ibid., June 3, 1836.
14. Ibid.
15. Ibid.
16. Ibid., July 15, Aug. 12, 1836.
17. Ibid., Aug. 21, 1835.
18. Ibid.
19. Ibid., Feb. 6, 1835.
20. Ibid., Feb. 13, 1835.
21. Ibid.
22. Ibid.
23. Ibid., Apr. 10, 17, 1835.
24. Ibid., Apr. 17, 1835.
25. Ibid.
26. Ibid., Feb. 27, 1835.
27. Ibid.
28. Ibid.
29. Ibid., Feb. 20, Mar. 13, 1835; James Kent, *Commentaries on American Law* (2 vols., 2d ed., New York, 1832), 2: 291–92, 240–41.
30. Kent, *Commentaries*, 2: 291–92.
31. Ibid.
32. *Advocate*, Feb. 20, 1835.
33. Ibid.
34. Ibid., Feb. 27, 1835.
35. Ibid., Mar. 6, 1835.
36. Ibid.
37. Ibid.
38. Ibid.
39. Ibid., Mar. 27, 1835.
40. Ibid.
41. Ibid., Mar. 13, 1835.
42. Ibid., Apr. 24, 1835.
43. Ibid., May 6, 1835.
44. Ibid., Aug. 14, 1835.
45. Ibid.
46. Ibid.
47. Ibid., Aug. 21, 1835.
48. Ibid.
49. Ibid., Sept. 25, 1835.
50. Ibid., Nov. 20, 1835.
51. Ibid., Jan. 1, 1836.

52. Ibid., June 5, 1835.

53. Ibid., Sept. 18, 1835.

54. Ibid., Oct. 2, 1835.

55. Ibid., Feb. 26, 1836.

56. Ibid., Nov. 20, 1835.

57. Ibid., Dec. 18, 1835.

58. Ibid., Feb. 19, 1836.

59. Lonnie J. White, "Disturbances on the Arkansas-Texas Border, 1827–1831," *Arkansas Historical Quarterly* 19 (spring 1960): 109–10.

60. *Advocate*, Mar. 17, 1837.

61. Ibid.

62. Ibid., Mar. 20, 1835.

63. Ibid., Aug. 21, 1835.

64. *Little Rock Times and Advocate*, July 24, 1835 (hereafter cited as *Times and Advocate*).

65. Ibid.

66. *Advocate*, July 17, 24, 31, 1835; *Little Rock Times*, July 25, Aug. 1, Sept. 5, 1835; *Gazette*, July 28, 1835.

67. *Advocate*, July 24, 31, 1835.

68. Ibid., July 31, 1835.

69. Ibid.

70. Ibid.

71. Ibid.

72. Ibid.

73. Ibid.

74. Ibid.

75. Ibid.

76. Ibid., Aug. 7, 1835.

77. Ibid., Apr. 10, 1835.

78. Ibid., May 22, 1835.

79. Ibid., July 24, 1835.

Chapter VII

1. White, *Politics in Arkansas Territory*, 164–69, 172–73.

2. *Gazette*, Mar. 31, Apr. 7, 1835; *Advocate*, Jan. 23, May 8, 29, June 12, July 3, 1835; William Savin Fulton to President Jackson, Little Rock, Aug. 22, 1835, in Clarence Edwin Carter, *The Territorial Papers of the United States*, vol. 21, *Arkansas Territory, 1823–1836* (Washington, D.C., 1954), 1074. (Hereinafter cited as *Territorial Papers*, vol. number and page.)

3. *Gazette*, May 26, June 9, 16, 23, 30, July 7, 21, 28, Aug. 25; *Advocate*, May 29, June 19, July 17, 24, Aug. 28, 1835.

4. *Advocate*, June 19, 26, 1835.

5. Ibid., July 17, 24, 1835.

6. Ibid., July 31, 1835.

7. Ibid., Aug. 7, 1835; *Gazette*, Aug. 4, 1835.

8. *Advocate*, Aug. 14, 1835.

9. Ibid., Sept. 4, 11, 1835.

10. Ibid., Sept. 11, 1835.

11. Ibid., Oct. 9, 1835.

12. Ibid.; *Gazette*, Oct. 6, 1835.

13. *Advocate*, Oct. 9, 23, 1835.

14. Since the journals of the council and the house of the territorial general assembly for 1835 were not published, it is necessary to follow the legislative proceedings as published in the *Advocate*, Oct. 9, 16, 23, 30, 1835; *Gazette*, Oct. 6, 13, 20, 27, Nov. 3, 1835; *Little Rock Times*, Oct. 3, 10, 19, 26, Nov. 2, 9, 16, 23, 30, 1835.

15. My view of the sectional division and the political-economic structure of Arkansas in 1835–1836 is based on my own observations and study as well as influences by White, *Politics in Arkansas Territory*, and two articles by Ted R. Worley, "Arkansas and the Money Crisis of 1836–1837," *Journal of Southern History* 15 (May 1949): 178–91, and "The Control of the Real Estate Bank of the State of Arkansas, 1836–1855," *Mississippi Valley Historical Review* 37 (Dec. 1950): 403–26.

16. Absalom Fowler, "To the Freemen of the Counties of White, Saline, & Pulaski," Dec. 3, 1835, in *Advocate*, Dec. 4, 1835; *Advocate*, Oct. 23, 1835.

17. *Advocate*, Oct. 23, 1835.

18. Ibid., Oct. 23, 30, 1835.

19. Ibid., Oct. 30, 1835.

20. *Gazette*, Oct. 27, Nov. 3, 1835; *Advocate*, Nov. 20, Dec. 4, 1835.

21. *Advocate*, Oct. 30, Nov. 6, 1835; *Gazette*, Nov. 3, 1835.

22. *Advocate*, Oct. 30, 1835.

23. Ibid.

24. *Little Rock Times*, Nov. 2, 1835.

25. *Advocate*, Nov. 6, 1835.

26. Ibid., Dec. 11, 1835.

27. *Little Rock Times*, Nov. 2, 23, 30, Dec. 7, 21, 1835.

28. *Advocate*, Dec. 11, 1835.

29. Ibid.

30. Ibid.

31. Ibid., Dec. 11, 18, 1835.

32. Ibid., Dec. 11, 18, 1835.

33. Ibid., Jan. 8, July 29, 1836.

34. Ibid., Jan. 29, July 29, 1836; White, *Politics in Arkansas Territory*, 185–89.

35. *Advocate*, Jan. 15, 1836.

36. Ibid.

37. Ibid., Jan. 15, Feb. 5, 26, 1836.

38. *Advocate*, Jan. 15, 1836.

39. Ibid., Feb. 5, 12, 1836.

40. *Gazette*, Feb. 4, 9, 1836.

41. Ibid.; *Advocate*, Feb. 5, 12, 1836.

42. *Gazette*, Feb. 9, 1836.

43. Ibid.

44. Ibid., Feb. 9, 16, 23, 1836.

45. Ibid.

46. *Advocate*, Feb. 12, 1836.

47. Ibid.,

48. Ibid., Feb. 19, 26, Feb. 11, 18, 25, 1836; *Gazette*, Feb. 16, 23, Mar. 1, 18, 15, 22, 29, 1836; *Little Rock Times*, Feb. 15, 1836.

49. Ross, *Gazette*, 132–34; White, *Politics in Arkansas Territory*, 192.

50. Ross, *Gazette*, 134; White, *Politics in Arkansas Territory*, 192–200.

51. *Advocate*, Mar. 4, 1836.

52. *Territorial Papers*, vol. 21: 1133, 1140, 1180, 1201, 1209, 1210.

53. *Advocate*, Apr. 29, 1836.

54. *Territorial Papers*, 21: 1074, 1169, 1174–76. *Times and Advocate*, June 4, 1838, reveals how Woodruff was replaced by Pew.

55. *Territorial Papers*, 21: 1207–8.

56. Ibid., 1208.

57. *Advocate*, May 13, 1836; *Gazette*, May 10, 17, July 26, 1836. See *Times and Advocate*, June 4, 1838, for an interesting partisan account of Pew's coming to the *Gazette*. Ross, *Gazette*, 134–60, covers the period of Pew's editorship of the *Gazette*.

58. *Advocate*, June 24, July 1, 8, 1836.

59. Ross, *Gazette*, 131.

60. *Gazette*, June 28, July 5, 1836.

61. *Advocate*, July 1, 1836; Hempstead, *Historical Review*, 1: 134–35.

62. *Advocate*, July 15, 1836.

63. Ibid., July 15, 22, 1836.

64. Ibid., July 22, 1836.

65. Ibid., July 22, 29, 1836.

66. Ibid., July 22, 1836.

67. Ibid., Aug. 5, 26, 1836; *Gazette*, Nov. 29, Dec. 6, 1836.

68. *Advocate*, Aug. 5, 12, 1836.

69. Ibid., Aug. 12, 1836.

70. Ibid., Aug. 26, 1836.

71. Ibid.

Chapter VIII

1. *Advocate*, Aug. 5, 12, 19, 1836.
2. Ibid., Aug. 12, 1836.
3. *Gazette*, Aug. 9, Sept. 6, 1836; *Advocate*, Aug. 26, Sept. 16, 23, 1836.
4. *Advocate*, Aug. 26, Sept. 2, 9, 16, 1836.
5. Ibid., Sept. 16, 1836.
6. Pike, "William Cummins," in Hallum, *History of Arkansas*, 1: 82–83.
7. *Advocate*, Nov. 18, 25, 1836; *Gazette*, Aug. 16, 1836.
8. *Advocate*, Sept. 16, 1836; *Gazette*, Sept. 13, 1836.
9. *Advocate*, Sept. 23, Nov. 4, 1836; *Gazette*, Nov. 8, 1836.
10. Ibid., Oct. 30, Nov. 27, 1836.
11. Ibid., Oct. 21, 1836.
12. *Territorial Papers*, 21: 1126–27.
13. *Advocate*, May 23, 30, 1838, Nov. 4, 11, 25, 1836; Worley, "Arkansas and the Money Crisis of 1836–1837," 181.
14. *Advocate*, Oct. 16, 23, 30, 1835; *Gazette*, May 30, June 14, 1836.
15. Worley, "The Control of the Real Estate Bank of the State of Arkansas, 1836–1855," 403–5.
16. Ibid., 404–5.
17. *Arkansas Acts* (1836), pp. 17–24.
18. Ibid., 3–16, contains the terms of the Real Estate Bank charter as discussed in the following paragraphs.
19. Arkansas *Senate Journal* (1836), 138–39; Arkansas *House Journal* (1836), 187–89; *Advocate*, Nov. 4, 1836; *Gazette*, Nov. 8, 1836.
20. *Advocate*, Nov. 4, 1836; *Gazette*, Nov. 8, 1836. Pike later revealed that Brown C. Roberts was one drunk legislator that Ashley rousted out of his room to vote for him. *Advocate*, Jan. 20, 1837.
21. Charles Fenton Mercer Noland, "To the Voters of Independence County," Little Rock, Nov. 10, 1836, in *Advocate*, Nov. 11, 1836.
22. Ibid.
23. Casca to Sam C. Roane, in *Advocate*, Dec. 9, 1836.
24. Ibid.
25. *Advocate*, Sept. 30, Oct. 14, 21, 1836.
26. Ibid., Oct. 21, 1836.
27. Ibid., Oct. 21, 28, 1836.
28. Ibid., Nov. 11, 25, 1836, *Gazette*, Nov. 25, 1836.
29. Brian G. Walton, "The Second Party System in Arkansas, 1836–1848," *Arkansas Historical Quarterly* 28 (summer 1969): 120–55; Brian G. Walton, "Ambrose Hundley Sevier in the United States Senate, 1836–1848," *Arkansas Historical Quarterly* 32 (spring 1973): 25–60.
30. Walton, "Second Party System in Arkansas," 125–27.
31. Hallum, *History of Arkansas*, 1: 105–8, 154–56.
32. *Arkansas Historical Quarterly* 11 (spring 1952): on Keatts, 31–32; 12 (spring 1953), 62;

ibid., 12 (spring 1953): 66; ibid., 20 (spring 1961): on Newton, 36; on Trapnall, in Hallum, *History of Arkansas*, 1: 150, 160, 218, in *Essays to Vinnie*, Essay 12, "Of the Law and Lawyers," Pike Papers; on John W. Cocke, in Hallum, *History of Arkansas*, 1: 218, and *Essays to Vinnie*, Essay 12, "Of the Law and Lawyers," Pike Papers.

33. *History of Benton, Washington, Carroll, Madison, Crawford, Franklin, and Sebastian Counties* (Chicago: Goodspeed Co., 1889), 1205–6; Hallum, *History of Arkansas*, 1: 244–52; *Essays to Vinnie*, Essay 12, "Of the Law and Lawyers," Pike Papers.

34. *Times and Advocate*, Mar. 5, 1838.

35. *Essays to Vinnie*, Essay 24, "Of Pleasant and Sad Remembrances," Pike Papers.

36. Ibid.

37. "The Life and Letters of Judge David Walker of Fayetteville," comp. and ed. W. J. Lemke (Fayetteville, Ark.: Washington County Historical Society, 1957); "The Walker Family Letters," ed. W. J. Lemke (Fayetteville, Ark.: Washington County Historical Society Bulletin No. 21, 1956); Hallum, *History of Arkansas*, 1: 102–5, 119, 245, 250–51.

38. Ted R. Worley, "An Early Arkansas Sportsman: C. F. M. Noland," *Arkansas Historical Quarterly* 11 (spring 1959): 25–39, is the source for the information on Noland.

39. Hallum, *History of Arkansas*, 1: 42; Walton, "Second Party System in Arkansas," 123–27.

40. Hallum, *History of Arkansas*, 1: 42–44, 45–59, 137–44; Josiah M. Shinn, *Pioneers and Makers of Arkansas* (Little Rock, Ark., 1908), 94, 183, 206–16, 239.

41. Hallum, *History of Arkansas*, 1: 158–63; Shinn, *Pioneers and Makers of Arkansas*, 202–5.

42. Hallum, *History of Arkansas*, 1: 242–44, 404–11; Shinn, *Pioneers and Makers of Arkansas*, 370–410.

43. Hallum, *History of Arkansas*, 1: 86–87, 110–19.

44. Ibid., 121–32.

45. Shinn, *Pioneers and Makers of Arkansas*, 9–23.

46. *Gazette*, Aug. 3, 10, 17, 24, 31, Sept. 7, 14, 1836.

47. Walton, "Second Party System in Arkansas," 123–55, especially Table 1, p. 125.

48. "Autobiography," *New Age Magazine* 37: 720–21.

Chapter IX

1. *Advocate*, Apr. 27, 1837.

2. Ibid., Jan. 23, 1835.

3. Ibid., Nov. 20, 1835, Feb. 24, Mar. 10, 1837.

4. Ibid., Mar. 31, Apr. 10, 1837.

5. Ibid., Apr. 27, 1837; *Times and Advocate*, May 1, 1837.

6. *Times and Advocate*, May 1, 8, 1837; *Gazette*, May 2, 9, 1838.

7. *Advocate*, Jan. 13, 1837.

8. Ibid., Mar. 3, 24, 1837; *Times and Advocate*, May 28, 1837.

9. *Advocate*, Feb. 13, 1837.

10. *Advocate*, July 15, 1836.

11. *Gazette*, Aug. 2, 1836.

12. *Advocate*, Aug. 12, 1836.
13. Ibid., Nov. 25, 1836.
14. Ibid., Mar. 3, 1837.
15. Ibid.
16. Ibid., Apr. 10, 1837.
17. Worley, "Arkansas and the Money Crisis of 1836–1837," 183–84.
18. See letter of William D. Ferguson, n.d., quoted in *Gazette*, Jan. 3, 1837, and in *Advocate*, Jan. 6, 1837; *Advocate*, Jan. 13, 20, Feb. 17, Mar. 3, 24, 1837.
19. *Advocate*, Dec. 9, 1836, June 26, July 17, 24, 1837; *Gazette*, Nov. 22, 1836, Oct. 3, 1838.
20. *Advocate*, July 31, 1837; *Gazette*, Feb. 21, Aug. 1, Nov. 14, Dec. 19, 1837.
21. *Gazette*, Jan. 10, 1837.
22. Ibid., Mar. 28, 1837; *Advocate*, Apr. 20, 1837.
23. *Gazette*, Jan. 31, Feb. 17, 1837.
24. Ibid., Oct. 25, 1836.
25. *Report of the Treasurer of the State of Arkansas* (Little Rock, Ark., 1837), 1–8; see also *Times and Advocate*, Dec. 4, 1837; Arkansas *House Journal*, 1837–1838, pp. 196–200, and Abstract C following, unpaged. Woodruff's account of his difficulties in collecting the surplus revenue is based on these reports.
26. See tabular statements accompanying above report for these facts.
27. *Times and Advocate*, May 22, 1837.
28. Ibid.
29. Ibid.
30. Ibid.
31. Ibid., June 19, 1837.
32. Ibid.
33. Ibid., July 10, 1837, quoting *Louisville Journal*, June 28, 1837.
34. Ibid.
35. Ibid.
36. *Times and Advocate*, Jan. 6, 13, 20, 27, May 29, June 12, 1837.
37. Ibid., June 12, 19, 1837.
38. Ibid., Apr. 27, May 1, 8, June 12, 1837; see ibid., July 17, Aug. 21, 1837, for other versions of the McWilliams-Pew encounter.
39. Ibid., June 12, 19, 26, July 3, 1837.
40. Ibid., June 19, 26, July 3, 1837.
41. Ibid., June 26, July 3, 17, 1837.
42. "C." to Col. A. H. Sevier, in *Gazette*, July 25, 1837.
43. Ibid.
44. Ibid.
45. *Times and Advocate*, Aug. 14, 1837.
46. Ibid.
47. Ibid., Aug. 18, 1837.

Chapter X

1. *Gazette*, Aug. 22, 1837.
2. Ibid.
3. Ibid., Aug. 28, 1837.
4. Ibid., Sept. 5, 1837.
5. Ibid.
6. *Times and Advocate*, Sept. 11, 1837.
7. The truth was that northern Whigs objected to the southerner Cummins and wanted a northerner to oppose Yell. Absalom Fowler to Jesse Turner, Little Rock, Aug. 10, 1837, in Allsopp Collection, University of Arkansas at Little Rock (also published in *Pulaski County Historical Review* 7 [June 1958]: 35–36); also letter in Pike's hand on behalf of Whig State Central Committee to James Wooddon Bates, Jesse Turner, et al., Little Rock, Sept. 2, 1837, Turner Papers.
8. *Times and Advocate*, Sept. 25, 1837.
9. Ibid.
10. Ibid.
11. Ibid.; *Gazette*, Aug. 15, 22, Sept. 12, 19, 26, 1837.
12. *Times and Advocate*, Mar. 10, Sept. 25, 1837.
13. Ibid., Sept. 4, 1837.
14. *Gazette*, Mar. 7, Sept. 26, Oct. 3, 1837.
15. *Times and Advocate*, Sept. 25, 1837.
16. Ibid., Oct. 16, 23, Nov. 6, 13, 27, 1837; *Gazette*, Oct. 3, Nov. 7, 21, 1837.
17. *Gazette*, Oct. 17, 1837; *Times and Advocate*, Oct. 23, Nov. 6.
18. The account that follows is based on the copy in *Times and Advocate*, Oct. 16, 1837.
19. These remarks refer to Yell's early residence in Arkansas Territory, where he served in 1831–1833 as a Jacksonian appointee as receiver at the Little Rock Land Office and from Mar. 3, 1833, until Oct. 15, 1836, again as a Jackson appointee on the superior court of the territory. In October 1836 Yell was, of course, elected to represent his newly adopted state in the National House. Yell seemingly liked Pike and sometimes wrote him concerning public affairs in Arkansas. A telling excerpt was Yell's remark in a letter to Pike dated Washington, Dec. 16, 1836: "Since I have got to be a *public man, my private letters seem to be public property*—so I shall write nothing but what may at all times be made public." *Advocate*, Jan. 20, 1837, italics in original.
20. "Autobiography" in Hallum, *History of Arkansas*, 1: 217. In the file of the *Times and Advocate* in the Library of Congress, Pike and Reed last appeared as editors and publishers of the paper on Oct. 3, 1837. The issue of Oct. 9 is missing, but the issue of Oct. 16 lists Reed as sole editor and publisher.

Chapter XI

1. *Advocate*, Jan. 13, 20, Mar. 3, 10, 1837; *Times and Advocate*, June 26, July 17, 24, 31, Aug. 7, 14, 21, Sept. 4, 11, Nov. 13, 29, Dec. 4, 1837.
2. Worley, "The Control of the Real Estate Bank of the State of Arkansas, 1836–1855," 403–26, is the standard history of the Real Estate Bank.

3. *Times and Advocate*, Aug. 7, 21, Sept. 18, 25, Oct. 23, Nov. 13, 1837.

4. The Charter, from which my description of the bank is taken, can be found in *Arkansas Acts* (1836), 3–16.

5. *Report of the Accountants, appointed under the Act of January 15, 1855, to Investigate the Affairs of the Real Estate Bank of Arkansas* (Little Rock, Ark., 1856), 138, 140, 150, 178.

6. Ibid., 116, 122, 124, 140, 141–42.

7. Ibid., 122, 130, 140–42, 170.

8. *Times and Advocate*, Oct. 6, Nov. 13, 27, 1837; *Gazette*, Nov. 7, 14, 21, 1837; Arkansas *House Journal*, 1837, pp. 132–35, 177–86, 197–200, 206, 245.

9. *Times and Advocate*, Dec. 4, 11, 1837.

10. Arkansas *House Journal*, 1837, pp. 247, 311–12, 319, 321, 333, 338, 339, 340, 345, 346–47, 348; W. H. Halli Burton, *A Topographical Description and History of Arkansas County, Arkansas from 1541 to 1875* (DeWitt? 1903), says Eugene Notrebe, the first cashier, resigned Apr. 3, 1838, and Luther Chase was on Apr. 25, 1838, appointed to succeed him.

11. Arkansas *Senate Journal*, 1837, pp. 184, 220, 236–37; *Gazette*, Nov. 21, 1837.

12. Ibid., 26–27, 236–37.

13. Arkansas *House Journal*, 1837, pp. 213, 223, 260; *Gazette*, May 23, 1838, printed in testimony of the Wilson trial; it was reprinted in the *Times and Advocate*, May 28, 1838.

14. Arkansas *House Journal*, 1837, pp. 278–82; *Gazette*, December 12, 1837.

15. Arkansas *House Journal*, 1837, pp. 298–99, 300; Gazette, May 23, 30, June 20, 1838; *Times and Advocate*, May 28,m 1838; Pope, *Early Days in Arkansas*, 22–25; Powell Clayton, *The Aftermath of the Civil War in Arkansas* (New York, 1915), 15–16; Alfred W. Arrington, *The Lives and Adventures of the Desperadoes of the South-West* (New York, 1849), 65–66. The two accounts in the *Gazette* and the reprint of them in the *Times and Advocate* are purported to be based on actual testimony in the trial in Saline County submitted by J. C. Anthony, a relative of the deceased. Worley, "Control of the Real Estate Bank," 408–11, first connected the killing of Anthony by Wilson to their quarrel over the Real Estate Bank.

16. See the sources in footnote 15 above. The quoted material is in *Gazette*, May 23, 1839.

17. Arkansas *House Journal*, 1837, p. 299.

18. Ibid., 299–301; *Gazette*, Dec. 12, 1837, May 23, 30, July 4, 1838; *Times and Advocate*, Dec. 11, 1837, May 28, 1838.

19. Arkansas *House Journal*, 1837, pp. 299–300, 317, 321, 330–31, 340, 355, 361; *Times and Advocate*, Nov. 13, 1837.

20. *Gazette*, Nov. 21, 28, Dec. 5, 12, 1837.

21. *Times and Advocate*, Jan. 8, 15, 22, 1838.

22. Ibid., Jan. 22, 1838; in his later "History of the Real Estate Bank," ch. 3, published in the *Gazette*, Mar. 8, 1843, Pike listed the principal bank directors elected in 1837 as I have given them in the text here. He said John Wilson was elected president on Nov. 11, 1837, after a long contest between Messrs. A. H. Davies and Roswell Beebe for that office. After he killed Anthony and was indicted, Wilson resigned as president and was succeeded by Anthony H. Davies, elected Feb. 5, 1838. Pike wrote his "History of the Real Estate Bank" after he and the Whigs bought the *Gazette* early in 1843, and Pike wanted to inform the public about the true history of the institution.

23. V.V. [Pike] to editor, *Gazette*, Oct. 5, 1842; Chester Ashley to the editor, *Gazette*, May 1, 1839, confesses his early opposition to the "cumbrous machinery provided in the charter" of the Real Estate Bank.

24. *Gazette*, Nov. 28, Dec. 5, 12, 1837, Jan. 2, 1838.

25. *Times and Advocate*, Jan. 8, 15, 22, Feb. 12, 1838; *Gazette*, Feb. 7, 1838.

26. *Arkansas Acts*, 1837, pp. 74–77.

27. *Times and Advocate*, Feb. 5, 12, 1838; *Gazette*, Mar. 7, 1838; Sevier to Robert W. Johnson, Washington, D.C., Jan. 31, 1843, in *Gazette*, Mar. 1, 1843, explains his appointment and conduct as a Real Estate Bank bond commissioner in 1838; Sevier to Anthony H. Davies, Washington, D.C., Mar. 18, 1838, in Arkansas *House Journal*, 1842–1843, appendix, 81–82.

28. *Times and Advocate*, May 21, June 4, 1838.

29. Ibid., June 4, 1838. Pew became assistant agent for distributing Indian rations. Ibid., Aug. 6, 1838.

30. *Advocate*, Sept. 9, Oct. 21, 28, 1836; *Gazette*, Oct. 11, 1836.

31. *Advocate*, Oct. 28, Dec. 2, 9, 16, 1836, Jan. 27, Feb. 17, June 26, 1837; *Gazette*, Dec. 6, 20, 1836, Apr. 11, 25, June 2, 1837.

32. The relevant sources for this account are A. Fowler "To the People of Arkansas," in *Advocate*, Feb. 17, 1837, in which Pike devoted two full pages to his friend's statement; Robert W. Jamison, "To the People of Arkansas," in *Gazette*, Apr. 11, 1837; Samuel M. Hays, "To the Public," in *Gazette*, Apr. 25, 1837; James S. Conway to Messrs. Woodruff & Pew, in *Gazette*, June 20, 1837, including General Arbuckle's response to Conway on the "late Lieutenant Colonel," of Arkansas; and A. Fowler, "To the Editors of the *Times and Advocate*," Little Rock, Ark., June 21, 1837, in *Times and Advocate*, June 26, 1837.

33. *Times and Advocate*, Nov. 6, 27, 1837.

34. Ibid., Dec. 4, 1837.

35. Ross, *Gazette*, 155.

36. Ibid., 152–55; *Times and Advocate*, July 3, 24, 1837, Feb. 26, 1838; C. F. M. Noland and Thomas M. Collins to the editors, Little Rock, Ark., Mar. 1, 1838, in *Times and Advocate*, Mar. 5, 1838; *Gazette*, Feb. 28, 1838, contains an exchange between Woodruff and Speaker of the House Grandison D. Royston over Fowler's criticism of Treasurer Woodruff's action in paying Ball and Roane.

37. *Times and Advocate*, Mar. 12, 1838.

38. Ibid.; *Arkansas Acts*, 1837, pp. 144–46.

39. *Times and Advocate*, Feb. 12, 1838.

Chapter XII

1. *Times and Advocate*, Feb. 19, 1838.

2. Ibid., Feb. 19, 26, 1838.

3. Ibid., Feb. 26, 1838.

4. Ibid.

5. Ibid., Jan. 29, Feb. 26, 1838.

6. Ibid., Feb. 26, 1838.

7. The relevant sources for the Douglass-Howell affair and the Douglass trial are *Gazette*, Mar. 21, 28, May 2, 9, 1838; *Times and Advocate*, Apr. 30, May 7, 1838; Pope, *Early Days in Arkansas*, 234–41.

8. *Gazette*, Apr. 25, 1838.

9. *Ark. Rev. Stat.*, 1838, p. 306.

10. *Gazette*, May 23, 1838.

11. Ibid.

12. Ibid.

13. Ibid.

14. Ibid.

15. Arkansas *House Journal*, 1838, pp. 178–91, containing Pike's report to the legislature on his work on the Revised Code; *Newburyport Daily Herald*, June 6, 29, 1838; *Times and Advocate*, Oct. 1, 1838.

16. *Times and Advocate*, May 28, July 2, 9, 16, 23, 30, Aug. 6, 13, Sept. 3, 10, 24, Oct. 1, 1838; *Gazette*, May 23, June 6, 27, July 11, Aug. 9, 15, 29, Sept. 12, 19, 26, Oct. 3, 1838.

17. *Times and Advocate*, July 2, 9, 1838.

18. Ibid., Sept. 3, 1838; Ross, *Gazette*, 157–58.

19. Cummins, "To the People of Arkansas," in *Times and Advocate*, Sept. 3, 1838; Cross, "To the People of Arkansas," Little Rock, Sept. 12, 1838, in *Gazette*, Sept. 19, 1838. The congressional election results are in *Times and Advocate*, Oct. 8, 15, 1838; *Gazette*, Oct. 3, 31, Nov. 14, 21, 1838.

20. *Times and Advocate*, Oct. 1, 8, 1838; *Gazette*, Oct. 3.

21. "Revised Code," Arkansas *House Journal*, 1838, pp. 178–81, containing Pike's Nov. 10, 1838, report on his work on the code and a copy of his contract with Weeks, Jordan & Co., for printing and binding the Code in 2,500 copies.

22. Ibid.

23. Ibid.

24. "Report of the Joint Committee on the Judiciary" on the Revised Code, in Arkansas *House Journal*, 1838, pp. 248–50; also "Report of the Minority on the New Code," in ibid., pp. 251–55.

25. *Times and Advocate*, Nov. 12, Dec. 10, 17, 1838, Feb. 4, Mar. 25, Aug. 12, 1839.

Chapter XIII

1. *Gazette*, Oct. 3, 24, Nov. 14, 28, Dec. 12, 19, 1838.

2. "A Democratic Stockholder" to editor, *Gazette*, May 10, 1839, explained this action and listed the stockholders affected by it. Dr. William P. Reyburn of Chicot County, a director of the Columbia branch bank, was "Stockholder's" source.

3. Ibid.; Chester Ashley to editor, ibid., May 1, 1839.

4. "V. V. [Pike]," Number 2, in *Gazette*, Oct. 5, 1842; "An Old Observer [Williams Cummins]" to the editors, *Times and Advocate*, May 27, 1839; *Gazette*, Oct. 17, 1837, Nov. 28, Dec. 5, 1838, Jan. 9, June 5, 1839.

5. Ibid.; *Gazette*, Jan. 9, 1839; "An Old Observer [Cummins]" to editor, *Times and Advocate*, May 27, 1839, explained how the Ashleyites carried the election.

6. "An Old Observer" to editors, *Times and Advocate*, May 27, June 10, 1839; "V. V." in *Gazette*, Oct. 5, 1842.

7. "V. V." in *Gazette*, Oct. 5, 1842.

8. Ibid.; *Gazette*, May 22, 1839, carries the opinion in full; see also the editorial in ibid., May 15, 1839.

9. *Gazette*, May 22, 1839; see resolution of the central board in ibid., May 29, 1839.

10. *Gazette*, June 5, 1839.

11. "An Old Observer" in *Times and Advocate*, May 27, June 10, 1839; *Gazette*, May 29, June 5, 12, 1839; Apr. 15, 1840; *Times and Advocate*, June 3, 10, 17, 1839; see "A Card" in *Times and Advocate*, June 17, 1839, and Eli Colby to Jessie Turner, Little Rock, June 19, 1839, Turner Papers, for information on the Cummins-DeBaun quarrel.

12. Ibid., July 10, 17, Nov. 6, 1839; "V. V." in *Gazette*, Oct. 5, 1842.

13. "V. V." in *Gazette*, Oct. 5, 1842.

14. *Gazette*, May 22, 1844. In this issue is a letter from Pike to the editor telling when he became attorney. In ibid., Oct. 5, 1842, Pike over the signature "V. V." relates his resentment over Cummins's handling of the quo warranto case in 1839, and tells how the principal bank directors removed Cummins as attorney.

15. *Times and Advocate*, Dec. 31, 1838.

16. Ibid., Dec. 17, 1838.

17. Ibid., Feb. 4, Apr. 8, June 3, 1839; Albert Pike et al. to Jessie Turner et al., Little Rock, Apr. 29, 1839, in Heiskell Collection; Absalom Fowler to Jessie Turner, Little Rock, June 26, 1839, in Heiskell Collection; "L." to editors, *Times and Advocate*, May 20, 1839; Colby to Turner, Little Rock, June 19, 1839, Turner Papers; Ross, *Gazette*, 168–69.

18. Pike et al. to Turner et al., Little Rock, Apr. 29, 1839, Heiskell Collection; "Prospectus of the Arkansas Star" in Heiskell Collection; "L." to editors, *Times and Advocate*, May 20, 1839; *Times and Advocate*, June 17, 1839; Pike to Turner, Little Rock, June 21, 1839, in Heiskell Collection.

19. Albert Pike to Jesse Turner, Little Rock, June 21, 1839, in J. N. Heiskell Collection, Little Rock; Eli Colby to Jesse Turner, Little Rock, June 19, 1839, Jesse Turner Papers, Duke University Library.

20. Pike to Turner, Little Rock, June 21, 1839, Heiskell Collection, Little Rock.

21. *Times and Advocate*, July 29, Aug. 5, 12, 1839; *Gazette*, July 31, Aug. 7, 14, 21, 1839.

22. *Gazette*, Aug. 21, 1839, Mar. 11, 1840.

23. Ibid., June 10, 1840.

24. Noland to Turner, Batesville, June 11, 1840, Jessie Turner Papers.

25. *Gazette*, June 10, 17, July 1, 1840.

26. Ibid., July 1, 1840.

27. Ibid., July 8, 1840.

28. See Colby's reply to "B." in *Times and Advocate*, July 13, 1840.

29. "Phocion" in *Gazette*, Jan. 29, 1840; also "Harrison meeting" in ibid.

30. "Timon" in *Gazette*, Feb. 26, Mar. 4, 1840.

31. Ibid., Mar. 4, 1840.

32. *Helena Southern Shield*, Mar. 28, 1840; *Gazette*, Nov. 6, 1839, Mar. 18, 25, 1840.

33. "Phocion" in *Gazette*, Apr. 1, 1840.

34. *Gazette*, Mar. 25, 1840.

35. "Phocion" in *Gazette*, Apr. 1, 1840.

36. Ibid., Mar. 11, 1840. William Brown Sr. and Jesse Brown were both prominent Little Rock Whigs about this time. See *Times and Advocate*, Dec. 4, 1843, Jan. 22, 1844.

37. *Gazette*, Apr. 1, 15, June 17, 1840; "Demetrious" in ibid., Apr. 22, 1840; *Times and Advocate*, July 13, 1840, carried the names of Bertrand and Dr. Gibson but not that of his enemy Cummins.

38. *Gazette*, Feb. 26, 1840.

39. "Phocion," in ibid., Mar. 11, 1840.

40. *Gazette*, Apr. 29, May 13, 1840; "Cyrus" in ibid., May 27, 1840.

41. *Little Rock Arkansas Star*, Feb. 13, Mar. 5, May 14, 1840; *Gazette*, July 15, 1840; *Times and Advocate*, July 13, 20, 1840; Pope, *Early Days in Arkansas*, 243–44.

42. *Times and Advocate*, July 13, 20, 1840; *Helena Southern Shield*, July 31, 1840; *Batesville News*, July 23, 1840; *Gazette*, July 15, 1840; Pope, *Early Days in Arkansas*, 244.

43. *Gazette*, Oct. 14, Nov. 11, 25, Dec. 9, 1840.

44. Noland to Turner, Batesville, June 11, 1840, Turner Papers.

45. *Gazette*, Sept. 1, 1841.

46. *Essays to Vinnie*, Essay 24, "Of Pleasant and Sad Remembrances," Pike Papers.

47. Ibid.

Chapter XIV

1. Albert Pike, "Life in Arkansas," *American Monthly Magazine* 1 (Mar. 1836): 299; *Essays to Vinnie*, Essay 12, "Of the Law and Lawyers," Pike Papers.

2. Pike, "Life in Arkansas," 299; *Essays to Vinnie*, Essay 12, "Of the Law and Lawyers," Pike Papers.

3. *Essays to Vinnie*, Essay 12, "Of the Law and Lawyers," Pike Papers.

4. Albert Pike, "The Superior Court," in Hallum, *History of Arkansas*, 1: 76–77.

5. *Essays to Vinnie*, Essay 12, "Of the Law and Lawyers," Pike Papers.

6. Ibid.; "Trapnall Hall, Ante-Bellum Showplace," *Pulaski County Historical Review* 3(4) (Dec. 1955): 59–62; Margaret Ross, "Daniel Ringo, Pulaski County Pioneer," *Pulaski County Historical Review* 2(3) (Sept. 1954): 10–16; *Advocate*, Feb. 17, 1837, carried the announcement of their partnership in the law. John W. Cocke was not related, so far as I know, to Dr. John H. Cocke, who was a People's party representative from Pulaski County in 1836 and who died Oct. 10, 1837, while visiting at Washington, Texas. *Times and Advocate*, Nov. 6, 27, 1837.

7. *Essays to Vinnie*, Essay 12, "Of the Law and Lawyers," Pike Papers.

8. Ibid.

9. Ibid.

10. Ibid.

11. Pike to Hallum, Washington, D.C., Aug. 15, 1886, in Hallum, *History of Arkansas*, 1: 217; *Essays to Vinnie*, Essay 3, "Of Self-Education" and Essay 11, "Of My Books and Studies," Pike Papers; lists of books either purchased or ordered during this period are in Pike to Gould, Banks & Co., Little Rock, Jan. 2, 1841, New York Public Library; Pike to Gould, Banks & Co., Little Rock, Mar. 2, 1843, Huntington Library, San Marino, California; Pike to Gould, Banks & Co., Little

Rock, Dec. 27, 1841, Historical Society of Pennsylvania, Philadelphia; Pike to T. & J. W. Johnson, Little Rock, July 8, 1841, Mar. 2, 1842, Historical Society of Pennsylvania, Philadelphia.

12. *Times and Advocate*, Feb. 4, Aug. 12, 1839; *The Evil and the Remedy*, by Sabinus [Albert Pike] (Little Rock, Ark., 1844), 115.

13. Albert Pike, *The Arkansas Form Book* (Little Rock, Ark., 1842); see issues of *Gazette*, Sept. 21, 28, 1842, for announcements of its publication, and throughout 1843 and 1844 for advertisements of its sale. *Gazette*, Mar. 2, 1855, announced: "The edition of Pike's Form Book is exhausted. There are none of them for sale."

14. *Arkansas Reports*, 1–5 (1840–1845), vol. 1 (Little Rock, Ark.: Budd and Colby, 1840); vol. 2 (Little Rock, Ark.: George H. Burnett, 1841); vol. 3 (Little Rock, Ark.: Wm. E. Woodruff, 1842); vol. 4 (Little Rock, Ark.: 1843); and vol. 5 (Little Rock, Ark.: B. J. Borden, 1845).

15. Having given the printing of the first volume to his former partner in the *Times and Advocate*, John Reed, who was succeeded by Budd and Colby before the book was finished, Pike refused to give Colby a chance at the second and succeeding volumes. He based his action on an alleged long delay in getting the first volume out and on an inferior job of printing, but Colby, who in 1842 attempted unsuccessfully to have the supreme court replace Pike through legislative petition to the judges, claimed Pike's true motive was part and parcel with "his determination to 'break down the *Times and Advocate*.'" *Times and Advocate*, Nov. 21, Dec. 12, 1842, and *Gazette*, Dec. 7, 1842, are the sources for this controversy.

16. Pike to Gould, Banks & Co., Little Rock, Jan. 2, 1841, New York Public Library, and same to same, Little Rock, Dec. 27, 1841, Historical Society of Pennsylvania, shows how Pile exchanged the *Arkansas Reports* for other law books.

17. This is based on an examination of the five volumes of Pike's reports. Of 71 cases argued before the Supreme Court in 1837–1839 Pike took part in 23. For the longer period from 1837 through the January term 1846, he appeared in 194 cases, or 31.3 percent of all cases reported. His banner year was during the three terms of July 1840, Jan. 1841, and July 1841, when he participated in 41.4 percent of the cases that came before the Supreme Court.

18. *Essays to Vinnie*, Essay 11, "Of My Books and Studies," Essay 12, "Of the Law and Lawyers," Pike Papers; Pike, "Autobiography," in Hallum, *History of Arkansas*, 1: 217, 218, 222.

19. *Essays to Vinnie*, Essay 11, "Of My Books and Studies," Pike Papers.

20. *Times and Advocate*, July 5, 1839, July 20, 1840, July 11, 1842; *Gazette*, July 5, 1843, July 3, 10, 1844.

21. *Gazette*, June 14, 1843.

22. Ibid., May 31, 1843, carried a notice signed by Pike as president that the next topic of discussion would be on the true policy of the United States in regard to a tariff. Some of the books in the Library of the Supreme Council, Washington, D.C., are inscribed: "Presented to the Club of Forty by A. Pike."

23. Walter Moffatt, "First Theatrical Activities in Arkansas," *Arkansas Historical Quarterly* 12 (winter 1953): 327–32; D. Allen Stokes, "The First Theatrical Season in Arkansas: Little Rock, 1838–1839," *Arkansas Historical Quarterly* 23 (summer 1964): 166–83.

24. *Gazette*, Jan. 23, 1839, carried the "Address, on the opening of the Little Rock Theatre. By Albert Pike."

25. Ibid., Feb. 26, 1840. Two weeks earlier, Edward Cole had announced: "We are requested by Albert Pike, Esq., to mention that the farce of 'Master and Man,' &c., to be performed on Thursday evening for the Benefit of Mr. Douglas, is not written entirely by him; but that a great part of it is

borrowed and dramatized; and he does not wish to seem to claim to be the *author* of that which he has merely endeavored to adapt to the stage. In part it is his own—in part borrowed." Ibid., Feb. 12, 1840.

26. *Gazette*, Apr. 1, 29, 1840; Ross, *Gazette*, 165; Pope, *Early Days in Arkansas*, 226–27.

27. *Gazette*, Apr. 1, June 10, Aug. 19, Nov. 4, 11, 1840; *Little Rock Star*, July 30, 1840, Jan. 21, 1841.

28. Pike, "Letters from Arkansas," *American Monthly Magazine* 1: 30.

29. *Dictionary of American Biography*, s.v. "Pray, Isaac C."; Isaac C. Pray to S. L. Fairfield, Hartford, Conn., May 14, 1834, Allsopp Collection, Larson Memorial Library, University of Arkansas at Little Rock, in which Pray proposes reviewing Pike's *Prose Sketches and Poems* for Fairfield's *North American Magazine*.

30. Albert Pike, "Hymns to the Gods," *Blackwood's Edinburgh Magazine* 45 (June 1839): 819–30. A copy of Pike's cover letter appears at the conclusion of the poems, together with an editor's note signed "C.N.," that is, Christopher North. Hallum, *History of Arkansas*, 1: 222–23, contains copies of both.

31. *Blackwood's Edinburgh Magazine* 45: 829–30.

32. Albert Pike to Carey and Hart, Little Rock, July 22, 1841, Huntington Library.

33. Albert Pike to John Tomlin (Postmaster, Jackson, Tenn.), Little Rock, June 8, 1843, Heiskell Collection. Tomlin, a poet and writer, had inquired about inditing a series of articles on certain poets and wished to include Pike.

34. Albert Pike, *Nugae*. Printed for private distribution (Philadelphia: C. Sherman, printer, 1854).

35. Griswold, "Albert Pike," in *Poets and Poetry of America*, 392.

36. See "Ode" [written for the Fourth of July], in *Gazette*, July 10, 1839; "To the Mocking Bird," *Blackwood's Edinburgh Magazine* 47 (Mar. 1840): 354–55; "Fancies on Fame," *Ladies Companion* 14 (Nov. 1840): 41–42; "Fanny," *Knickerbocker* 25 (May 1845): 387; "To My Wife," ibid., 26 (Sept. 1845): 202; "Isadore," *New Mirror* 2 (Oct. 1843): 20–21. This last poem has a peculiar history. John H. Ingram, an eminent Poe scholar of England, holds in his biography of Poe (1880) that the latter received inspiration for his best known work, "The Raven," from Pike's "Isadore." Ingram bases his belief on the fact that both Poe and Pike were contributing to the *New Mirror* in 1843, and that Pike's poem is suggestive not only of the same theme—"a lover lamenting his deceased mistress,"—and the same refrain—"forever, Isadore,"—but also of the similar wording and rhythm as that used two years later (1845) by Poe in "The Raven." *Edgar Allen Poe, His Life, Letters, and Opinions* (2 vols., London, 1880), I, 277–81. Curiously, Pike on the eve of a visit "Eastward" and to New York, wrote: "I shall also, I presume, see Mr. Poe—an occurrence that would be most gratifying to me." Pike to Tomlin, Little Rock, June 8, 1843, Heiskell Collection. Since Pike's "Isadore" appeared in *New Mirror* in Oct. 1843, he may well have delivered the poem in person to the magazine, and, if he did not meet Poe that summer, may well have shown him "Isadore."

37. Pike to Tomlin, Little Rock, June 8, 1843, Heiskell Collection.

38. *Little Rock Star*, Mar. 5, May 7, 1840; Hallum, *History of Arkansas*, 1: 106, 108–9.

39. *Gazette*, Jan. 12, 1842, Mar. 23, 1848; Hempstead, *Pictorial History of Arkansas*, 784; "Pulaski County Marriages," *Pulaski County Historical Review* 3(1) (Mar. 1955): 14.

40. Pike to Borden, Little Rock, May 22, 1844, in *Gazette*, May 22, 1844, gives a brief history of his early attorneyship for the Real Estate Bank.

41. Ibid.

42. *Gazette*, Oct. 30, Nov. 6, 13, 1839; *Times and Advocate*, Nov. 18, 1839, contains the Harris report.

43. "Historical Sketch" in *Report of the Accountants Appointed under the Act of January 15, 1855, to Investigate the Affairs of the Real Estate Bank of Arkansas* (Little Rock, Ark., 1856), 11–19; Worley, "Control of the Real Estate Bank of the State of Arkansas," 414.

44. The sources for the account that follows are C. A. Harris and H. L. Briscoe, "Caution to the Public," New York, Sept. 3, 1841, in *Gazette*, Oct. 13, 1841, quoting *New York Herald*, n.d.; Thos. G. Talmage, President, North American Trust and Banking Company, "To the Public—North American Trust Company," ibid.; C. A. Harris to the Editor, Little Rock, Oct. 19, 1841, in *Gazette*, Oct. 20, 1841; C. A. Harris and H. L. Briscoe, "To the Public," Little Rock, Nov. 12, 1841, together with "Resolutions adopted by the Central Board of the Real Estate Bank of the State of Arkansas, on the 8th day of November, 1841," and "Report" of the stockholders, Nov. 8, 1841, and A. Yell to Messrs. Talmage, Holford, & Co., Little Rock, Nov. 10, 1841, all in *Gazette*, Nov. 24, 1841; A. Yell to Jas. Holford, Little Rock, Mar. 20, 1842, in *Times and Advocate*, Apr. 18, 1842. See also *Times and Advocate*, Oct. 18, Nov. 8, 15, 29, 1841.

45. Pike was the original source for the figure of $121,336.50, but in old age he sometimes deviated from it because of faulty memory. Allsopp, *Albert Pike*, 85; W. D. Blocher, *Arkansas Finances* (Little Rock, Ark., 1876), 7; Worley, "Control of the Real Estate Bank of the State of Arkansas," 414–15; *Report of the Accountant of the Real Estate Bank*, 17.

46. C. A. Harris and H. L. Briscoe to Holford & Co., New York, July 12, 1841, pp. 85–86, Arkansas History Commission, Little Rock, in which they offered to pay Holford the amount owed by the Real Estate Bank to North American Trust and Banking Company in return for the 500 bonds.

47. *Gazette*, May 19, July 21, Aug. 27, Sept. 1, 8, 29, Oct. 1, 6, 13, Nov. 10, 17, 1841, June 29, 1842; *Times and Advocate*, Aug. 9, 30, Nov. 8, 15, 1841, May 9, July 4, 1842.

48. *Gazette*, Feb. 3, 10, 17, 24, Mar. 3, 17, May 19, June 30, Oct. 20, 27, Nov. 3, 1841; *Times and Advocate*, Feb. 15, Apr. 19, May 10, Aug. 23, 30, Oct. 25, Nov. 15, 22, 29, Dec. 13, 20, 1841. See especially Archibald Yell to "My Fellow Citizens," Little Rock, July 19, 1841, in *Gazette*, July 21, 1841.

49. Ross, *Gazette*, 178–80.

50. *Gazette*, Jan. 5, Feb. 2, 23, Mar. 2, Apr. 6, 27, 1842. See also *Times and Advocate*, Jan. 17, 1842.

51. *Times and Advocate*, Jan. 17, Feb. 7, 21, 1842.

52. Ibid., Feb. 21, 28, Apr. 11, 18, May 2, 1842.

53. Much of the account that follows is based on a series of articles Pike published in the *Gazette* over the signature V. V. ("Vice Versa") in Aug.–Oct. 1842, in which he set forth much early history of the Real Estate Bank, the reasons for its insolvency, the assignment case, and his side of the controversy with Cummins that followed the court decision. Pike's "History of the Real Estate Bank," in the *Gazette*, Jan. 18, 25, Mar. 8, 1843, narrated the role of the bond commissioners, especially Senator Sevier's role as bond commissioner, for the bank.

54. *Times and Advocate*, Feb. 28, 1842, carried President Carey A. Harris's notice that the central board would meet at the principal bank on the fourth Monday in March—March 28. "Full and punctual attendance is desirable, as business of great importance will be brought before the Board." ibid. "Pulaski" in *Gazette*, Mar. 2, 1842, said that the stockholders and directors were ready to with-

draw the branches and close up and wind up the Real Estate Bank. "This should be done," he wrote, "and without *coercion*."

55. Pike's "V. V." article in *Gazette*, Sept. 26, 1842, describes the financial insolvency and the conditions that caused the bank to go into liquidation.

56. "Deed of Assignment" in *Gazette*, Apr. 20, 1842, and in *Times and Advocate*, Apr. 25, 1842. Pike asserted in 1879 that the bank actually received only about $95,000 for the hypothecated bonds, an amount that Thomas W. Newton arrived at on checking the books of North American Trust and Banking Company in 1843. Albert Pike to Richard H. Johnson, Washington City, Mar. 4, 1879, in *Gazette*, Mar. 8, 1879; also in Allsopp, *Albert Pike*, 85–87. The bonds were placed last in the scheduled order of payments for the simple reason that the central board and Pike did not believe there would be any assets with which to redeem them. Ibid. Judge Lacy found the phrase of "whatever legal amount shall be found due upon the bonds" as freeing the deed of assignment of any intended fraud against Holford's claim. 4 *Arkansas Reports* 363–64.

57. "Pulaski" in the Democratic organ the *Little Rock Banner*, May 29, June 19, 1844.

58. Pike to Borden, Little Rock, May 22, 1844, in *Gazette*, May 24, 1844; "Deed of Assignment" in *Gazette*, Apr. 20, 1842.

59. V. V. in *Gazette*, Oct. 5, 12, 1842.

60. V. V. in *Gazette*, Oct. 12, 1842.

61. Ibid.; *Times and Advocate*, Oct. 31, 1842, which says Washington branch bank stockholders (Thomas T. Williamson, M. Wright, and Judge Lewis B. Fort) were in Little Rock representing southern stockholders of the Real Estate Bank and to confer with the legislature on how to put the entire bank in liquidation. The Washington branch, the article said, had "stopped" the assignment at that bank.

62. V. V. in *Gazette*, Oct. 12, 1842.

63. Ibid.; *Gazette*, June 29, 1842.

64. V. V. in *Gazette*, Oct. 12, 1842.

65. *Times and Advocate*, Apr. 11, May 2, 1842; *Gazette*, May 4, 1842.

66. A copy of the resolves is in *Gazette*, Apr. 27, 1842, and in *Times and Advocate*, May 2, 1842.

67. "Publius" in *Gazette*, Apr. 27, 1842, and in *Times and Advocate*, May 2, 1842.

68. Ibid.

69. Ibid.

70. Ibid.

71. *Gazette*, Apr. 27, 1842.

72. "One of the People" in *Gazette Extra*, Apr. 28, 1842, as quoted in full in *Times and Advocate*, May 2, 1842.

73. *Times and Advocate*, May 2, 1842.

74. Ibid., May 16, 1842, quoting *Van Buren (Ark.) Intelligencer*, n.d.

75. *Gazette*, May 4, 1842; *Times and Advocate*, Aug. 22, 1842; V. V. in *Gazette*, Oct. 12, 1842; *James S. Conway and Others, Ex Parte* (1842), 4 *Arkansas Reports* 305–12.

76. V. V. in *Gazette*, Oct. 12, 1842. Pike had frequently clashed in court with Ringo and was a severe critic of the chief justice, and, quite correctly, did not wish to risk the loss of his case by appealing to him alone. *Essays to Vinnie*, Essay 12, "Of the Law and Lawyers," Pike Papers; Hallum, *History of Arkansas*, 1: 146–52; Ross, "Daniel Ringo," 10–16.

77. V. V. in *Gazette*, Oct. 12, 1842.

78. *Gazette*, May 4, 1842.

79. Hallum, *History of Arkansas*, 1: 82–85, 94, 105–10, 122–32; Hempstead, *Pictorial History of Arkansas*, 763–64, 769–70; V. V. in *Gazette*, Oct. 5, 1842; *Essays to Vinnie*, Essay 12, "Of the Law and Lawyers," Pike Papers.

80. "Abstract of the concluding argument of Albert Pike, Esq. in the case of *James B. Conway and Others Ex Parte*," 4 *Arkansas Reports*, Appendix (p. 12).

81. V. V. in *Gazette*, Aug. 24, Oct. 12, 26, 1842.

82. *Times and Advocate*, May 9, 16, 1842.

83. Ibid., May 23, 1842.

84. Ibid., May–Dec. 1842, Jan.–Mar. 1843. "Anti-Bank Man" said that it was thought that the establishment of the Real Estate Bank would prove a benefit to the state. "I have no doubt that some individuals have been benefited; that Little Rock has been improved by the addition of some fine dwellings [which obviously included Pike's recently completed mansion]; but are the mechanics and farmers of the state *now* benefited by the bank?" His answer was "no," since they were getting thirty cents on a dollar for labor. Ibid., May 16, 1842. For Colby's appeal to class antagonism on the subject of the state banks, see his editorial "A Contrast," in ibid., May 30, 1842, in which he draws a comparison between a poor widowed seamstress with six children to support and her "fat and fair" customer who is a bloated "debtor to the Banks" and a speculator in "Arkansas money."

85. V. V. in *Gazette*, Oct. 12, 1842. Pike did refer, in his concluding argument, to his opponent's remark "that we have read fifty law books." 4 *Arkansas Reports*, Appendix (pp. 6–7).

86. "Quis. Quis." to Editor, New Orleans, Aug. 31, 1842, in *Gazette*, Sept. 21, 1842.

87. Ibid. "Quis. Quis." went on to say: "The assignment was sustained. The author of an 'ode to Bacchus' triumphed, but, I am glad to learn, was not mobbed, according to the wishes of my erratic friend."

88. 4 *Arkansas Reports* 375–76, 376–92.

89. Ibid., 374–75.

Chapter XV

1. *Gazette*, Aug. 17, 24, 31, Sept. 21, 28, 1842; V. V. in ibid., Aug. 24, Sept. 28, Oct. 5, 12, 26, Nov. 16, 1842; X. in ibid., Sept. 7; X. in *Times and Advocate*, Aug. 22, Sept. 12, 19, Oct. 3, 24, 31, 1842.

2. *Gazette*, Sept. 21, 28, 1842; *Times and Advocate*, Oct. 3, 1842; V. V. in *Gazette*, Oct. 26, 1842; X. in *Times and Advocate*, Oct. 24, 31, 1842.

3. X. in *Times and Advocate*, Aug. 22, 1842.

4. V. V. in *Gazette*, Aug. 24, Oct. 26, 1842.

5. Ibid., Aug. 24, 1842.

6. Ibid.

7. *Times and Advocate*, Aug. 29.

8. X. to editor, replying to V. V. in *Gazette*, Aug. 24, 1842.

9. V. V. in *Gazette*, Sept. 28, Oct. 5, 12, 26, Nov. 9, 16, 1842.

10. V. V. in *Gazette*, Nov. 16, 1842.

11. *Times and Advocate*, Sept. 5, 21, 1842.

12. *Gazette*, Mar. 16, 30, Apr. 6, June 8, Aug. 31, 1842; *Times and Advocate*, Nov. 4, 1846.

13. *Times and Advocate*, Sept. 5, 13, Oct. 3, 1842; *Gazette*, Sept. 14, 21, 1842.

14. *Gazette*, Sept. 14, 21, 1842.

15. Ibid., Sept. 12, 1842.

16. Ibid., Sept. 14, 1842.

17. Ibid.

18. *Gazette*, Oct. 5, 12, 26, 1842.

19. *Times and Advocate*, Oct. 31, 1842.

20. Ibid.

21. Ibid., Feb. 20, 1843.

22. Ibid., Mar. 21, Apr. 25, May 2, 9, 16, 1842.

23. Ibid., Mar. 21, Apr. 25, May 2, 9, 16, 1842.

24. Ibid., May 9, 16, 23, June 6, 13, 20, 1842. My abbreviated account is based on Colby's article "The Meeting on Saturday," in ibid., June 20, 1842, in which he says a rain and the influence of some Whig and Democratic bankites reduced attendance at the meeting on June 18. Charles P. Bertrand, a Whig legislative incumbent, spoke to the assembly and asked it not to nominate a ticket. Samuel H. Hempstead, a Little Rock Democratic lawyer, wrote a similar appeal in a speech before the gathering. Jared C. Martin, a Democrat who won a house seat that year in Pulaski County, denounced the Real Estate Bank and opposed straight party tickets, as did a majority of those present, it seems. But Woodruff of the *Gazette* hotly opposed a "Union ticket." See *Gazette*, June 22, 29, July 6, 1842.

25. *Times and Advocate*, June 20, 1842; *Gazette*, June 15, 22, Sept. 28, 1842; Byrd is identified as "a National Bank Man" in *Times and Advocate*, Oct. 17, 1842.

26. *Gazette*, June 22, 29, July 6, Sept. 28, 1842.

27. *Times and Advocate*, Oct. 10, 1842; *Gazette*, Oct. 12, 1842.

28. *Times and Advocate*, July 11, 1842.

29. *Gazette*, July 20, 27, Aug. 3, 1842.

30. Ibid.

31. *Gazette*, July 27, 1842. The writer could have been Pike, but I have no evidence, except conjecture, to prove it.

32. *Times and Advocate*, Aug. 3, 1842.

33. Ibid.

34. Ibid., Sept. 12, 1842, announced such a Whig meeting for Sept. 19. The author has found no record of the proceedings.

35. *Gazette*, Sept. 28, 1842.

36. *Times and Advocate*, Oct. 3, 1842.

37. *Gazette*, Oct. 5, 12, Nov. 2, 1842.

38. *Times and Advocate*, Oct. 10, 31, 1842.

39. Ibid., Oct. 10, 1842.

Chapter XVI

1. Anthony Davies to J. D. Beers, Dec. 6, 1842, quoted in Reginald C. McGrane, *Foreign Bondholders and American State Debts* (New York, 1935), 257–58.

2. *Gazette,* Dec. 21, 1842, contains a table listing members of the house and senate by name, age, place of birth, and occupation. I have furnished party affiliation from data in ibid. and in the *Times and Advocate,* Oct. 17, 24, 1837. One warning, because Eli Colby, the estranged Whig editor of the *Times and Advocate,* was at war with Whigs who had pledged themselves during the legislative canvass to vote for Senator Sevier, the incumbent Democrat, he listed them as Democrats.

3. The editorials and correspondence of the *Gazette* and the *Times and Advocate,* as well as the exchange between Pike and Cummins, are filled with discussion of the two judges and their alleged fate at the hands of the legislature.

4. Townsend Dickinson and Thomas J. Lacy to James Kent, Little Rock, Ark., Aug. 23, 1842, Papers of James Kent, Vol. 10, 1841–1846, Library of Congress; James Kent to Albert Pike, New York, Oct. 17, 1842, in *Gazette,* Nov. 9, 1842; Joseph Story to Townsend Dickinson and Thomas J. Lacy, Cambridge, Mass., Oct. 15, 1842, in ibid.; Pike, *Evil and the Remedy,* 130–31; Pike, "Thomas J. Lacy," in Hallum, *History of Arkansas,* 1: 80. Among the Pike papers in possession of the late Mrs. Roscoe M. Packard, West Newton, Mass., is the original manuscript opinion of Kent, dated New York, Oct. 17, 1842. Pike obviously was responsible for Dickinson's and Lacy's letters to Kent and Story. *Times and Advocate,* Jan. 23, Feb. 20, 1843.

5. Pike, *Evil and the Remedy,* 130–31; Arkansas *House Journal,* 1842–1843, pp. 99–106; Arkansas *Senate Journal,* 1842–1843, pp. 56–61.

6. *Times and Advocate,* Nov. 7, 1842.

7. Ibid., Nov. 7, 14, 1842; *Gazette,* Nov. 9, 16, 1842. These numbers cover the Colby-Weller exchange over the position of the *Gazette* on the trustees and the attack on the independence of the judiciary.

8. *Times and Advocate,* Nov. 28, 1842.

9. *Governor's Message* in Arkansas *House Journal,* 1842–1843, Appendix, 4.

10. Ibid., 6–8.

11. Ibid., 8.

12. Ibid.

13. Ibid.

14. Ibid.

15. Arkansas *House Journal,* 1842–1843, pp. 17–18, 21–22; *Gazette,* Dec. 28, 1842, for identification of legislators.

16. Arkansas *House Journal,* 1842–1843, pp. 17–18, 21.

17. *Times and Advocate,* Nov. 14, 1842.

18. Arkansas *House Journal,* 1842–1843, pp. 21–22, 23, 29–31, 36; Arkansas *Senate Journal,* 1842–1843, pp. 18–21, 23–34.

19. Arkansas *House Journal,* 1842–1843, pp. 65–75.

20. Ibid., 71.

21. Ibid.

22. Ibid.; *Gazette*, Nov. 23, 1842.

23. Arkansas *House Journal*, 1842–1843, pp. 37–38.

24. Ibid., 38–39.

25. Arkansas *Senate Journal*, 1842–1843, p. 11.

26. Arkansas *House Journal*, 1842–1843, pp. 39–40.

27. "Publius" in *Times and Advocate*, Nov. 21, 1842.

28. Ibid.

29. Ibid.

30. Ibid.

31. Arkansas *House Journal*, 1842–1843, p. 100; Hallum, *History of Arkansas*, 1: 45–59; *Times and Advocate*, Nov. 7, 14, 21, 1842; *Batesville News*, Nov. 24, 1842.

32. Arkansas *House Journal*, 1842–1843, pp. 100–106; Arkansas *Senate Journal*, 1842–1843, pp. 56–61.

33. See sources in footnote 32 above.

34. Pike, *Evil and the Remedy*, 131.

35. *Times and Advocate*, Dec. 5, 1842.

36. Ark. Const. (1836), Art. IV, Sec. 27.

37. Arkansas *House Journal*, 1842–1843, pp. 150–53.

38. Ibid.

39. Ibid.

40. Ibid.

41. Ibid.

42. Ibid.

43. Ibid., p. 185.

44. Pike, *Evil and the Remedy*, 133.

45. Arkansas *House Journal*, 1842–1843, pp. 237–38.

46. Ibid., 237–38, 301–2.

47. Pike, *Evil and the Remedy*, 130–31.

48. Ibid., 131–32.

49. Ibid., 132–34.

50. Arkansas *House Journal*, 1842–1843, p. 168.

51. Ibid., 169–73, Appendix, pp. 76–95, containing the Field committee report and supporting documents.

52. Ibid., Appendix, 76–80.

53. Ibid., 80–81.

54. *Gazette*, Jan. 18, 1843, reports the speech of William H. Gaines of Scott County, a Whig, who served on the Field committee and who described the committee's in-fighting.

55. Ibid.

56. Arkansas *House Journal*, 1842–1843, pp. 239–40, 248.

57. Arkansas *Senate Journal*, 1842–1843, pp. 148, 155, 158–65.

58. Arkansas *House Journal*, 1842–1843, pp. 249, 254, 256, 260–69, 288–91; see Appendix, 56–59, for the Arrington (Pike) substitute and Appendix, 128–31 for Field's minority report.

59. Arkansas *Senate Journal*, 1842–1843, pp. 240, 243; *Arkansas Acts*, 1842–1843, pp. 89–104; Jan. 23, 1843, G. to Colby, ibid.

60. Arkansas *Senate Journal*, 1842–1843, pp. 273–74; *Times and Advocate*, Mar. 6, 13, 20, 1843; *Gazette*, Mar. 8, 1843.

61. "To the Public, Protest of the Trustees of the Real Estate Bank," in *Gazette*, Apr. 5, 1843.

62. Ibid.

63. *Arkansas Acts*, 1842–1843, pp. 100–101; Arkansas *Senate Journal*, 1842–1843, pp. 61–66; *Times and Advocate*, Mar. 6, 1843.

64. *The State vs. The Real Estate Bank* (1844), 5 *Arkansas Reports* 595–608; *Gazette*, Aug. 14, 1844.

65. Worley, "Control of the Real Estate Bank of the State of Arkansas, 1836–1855," 420.

66. Arkansas *Senate Journal*, 1842–1843, p. 118.

67. *Times and Advocate*, Jan. 9, Feb. 20 (W. D. to Colby, Pope County, Ark., Feb. 10, 1843, and Colby's answer), 1843.

68. My account is based on Ross, *Gazette*, 190–94, who exhaustively researched the history of the sale.

69. Ibid.; Pike to Borden in *Gazette*, May 22, 1844.

70. *Gazette*, Jan. 4, 11, 1843; Ross, *Gazette*, 193–96.

71. *Gazette*, Jan. 4, 11, 1843.

72. "History of the Real Estate Bank," in *Gazette*, Jan. 18, 25, 1843.

73. Pike, *Evil and the Remedy*, 3–9; *Gazette*, May 22, 1843.

74. *Gazette*, Dec. 21, 28, 1842.

75. Ibid., Jan. 4, 11, Feb. 8, 1843.

76. *Times and Advocate*, Feb. 27, 1843.

77. *Gazette*, Feb. 15, 22, Mar. 1, 8, 15, 22, Apr. 26, 1843.

78. Ibid., Aug. 9, 1843; *Times and Advocate*, July 10, Aug. 7, Sept. 4, 1843.

79. Ross, *Arkansas Gazette*, 195–203.

80. *Gazette*, Jan. 3, 10, 17, 24, 31, Feb. 7, 1844.

81. Ibid., Dec. 13, 1843, Jan. 10, 24, 1844; *Little Rock Banner*, Dec. 9, 1843, Jan. 9, Feb. 6, Apr. 17, 24, May 1, 29, June 5, 12, 1844.

82. *Nashville (Tenn.) Whig Banner*, Aug. 31, 1844.

83. *Gazette*, Sept. 18, 1844; "Autobiography," in Hallum, *History of Arkansas*, 1: 220.

84. My source for Ashley's election to the Senate in 1844 is Ross, *Arkansas Gazette*, 205–6.

85. *Little Rock Banner*, Nov. 6, 20, 1844; *Gazette*, Nov. 6, 13, 27, 1844; Arkansas *Senate Journal*, 1844, pp. 3–4; Arkansas *House Journal*, 1844, pp. 4–5.

86. Worley, "Control of the Real Estate Bank of the State of Arkansas, 1836–1855," 421–23, discusses and casts doubt on these attacks on Pike; Arkansas *House Journal*, 1844, pp. 48–49, 50, 144; Arkansas *Senate Journal*, 1844, pp. 40–41, 139; *Gazette*, Dec. 16, 1844.

87. *Little Rock Banner*, Nov. 20, 1844; *Gazette*, Nov. 27, 1844.

Chapter XVII

1. See files of the *Advocate* and *Gazette* for 1836. To offset Indian depredations on the frontier the president requested the governor of Arkansas to raise a regiment of mounted riflemen, who manned Fort Towson on Red River in the Indian Territory until 1837.

2. *Advocate,* Sept. 2, 1836.

3. Pike commanded the company on July 4, 1837. See "Fourth of July" in *Gazette,* July 11, 1837; Pope, *Early Days in Arkansas,* 222.

4. Pope, *Early Days in Arkansas,* 222–23.

5. *Gazette,* July 11, 1837, Nov. 5, 1840, June 30, 1841; see also other accounts of the Independence Day celebrations from 1837 to 1845 in the *Gazette;* Pope, *Early Days in Arkansas,* 222, 251–52.

6. "The 4th of July, '45" in *Gazette,* July 7, 1845.

7. *Gazette,* May 25, 1846.

8. W. L. Marcy, secretary of war, to Thomas S. Drew, governor of Arkansas, War Department, Washington, D.C., May 15, 1846, in *Gazette,* June 1, 1846.

9. *Gazette,* June 1, 1846.

10. Pike, *The Evil and the Remedy,* 183; Albert Pike to Jessie Turner, Washington [Ark.], July 13, 1846, Turner Papers. Pike requested Turner to assume responsibility for his cases during his absence and informed him that "Circumstances forced me to this expedition. . . ."

11. Albert Pike, "To the Little Rock Guards," May 29, 1846, in *Gazette,* June 1, 1846.

12. *Gazette,* June 8, 1846.

13. *Gazette,* June 15, 22, 1846.

14. Ibid., July 13, 1846.

15. G. B. B., "To the Editor," Washington, Ark., July 7, 1846, in ibid.

16. Josiah Gregg, the famed author of *Commerce of the Prairies,* who accompanied the Arkansas volunteers as a sort of "interpreter-scout," considered Colonel Yell "a very clever, pleasant, sociable fellow, but decidedly out of his element" as a military leader. Gregg thought Pike was the "best disciplinarian and drill officer in the corps . . . and decidedly 'number one' in point of talent and acquirements"; but he considered Pike, in despite of his superior ability, "too stiff and aristocratic in his manner to be popular . . . [and doubted] if he could be elected by a general vote to any office in the regiment." Maurice Garland Fulton, ed., *Diary and Letters of Josiah Gregg* (2 vols., Norman, Okla., 1941), 1: 218–19.

17. *Gazette,* July 13, 1846; see also a copy of the petition of Pike's men in ibid.

18. Ibid., July 20, 27, 1846.

19. Fulton, *Diary and Letters of Gregg,* 1: 208; *Senate Executive Document 32,* 31st Cong., 1st Sess., Serial No. 558, p. 5; George Lockhart Rives, *The United States and Mexico, 1821–1848* (2 vols., New York, 1913), 2: 195–219.

20. Fulton, *Diary and Letters of Gregg,* 1: 201, 206–17.

21. Solon Borland to Maj. William Field, Camp Yell, San Antonio, Tex., Sept. 28, 1846, in *Little Rock Banner,* Nov. 11, 1846; "Autobiography," *New Age Magazine* 37: 142.

22. "Autobiography," *New Age Magazine* 37: 142.

23. Borland to Field, Sept. 28, 1846, in *Little Rock Banner,* Nov. 11, 1846.

24. Augustus Frederick Ehinger, Manuscript Diary of his travels from Illinois to Mexico . . . as a member of Comp. H., Second Regiment Illinois Volunteers, during the Mexican War, [June 15, 1846–June 28, 1847], Dec. 16th, [1846]. Translated from the German script and owned by Col. Charles F. Ward, Roswell, New Mexico. Hereafter cited as Ehinger Diary. Also in Fulton, *Diary and Letters of Gregg*, 1: 261, quoting the unpublished diary of Ehinger.

25. Albert Pike to "L.," Patos, Mexico, Dec. 31, 1846, in *Gazette*, Feb. 6, 1847.

26. An extract from a letter of a member of Pike's company written on Sept. 3, 1846, states that "we have been drilling on the road while other companies have been doing nothing." *Gazette*, Oct. 14, 1846.

27. Borland to Major Fields, Sept. 28, 1846, in *Little Rock Banner*, Nov. 11, 1846.

28. This division of the Arkansas Horse was doubtlessly a result of a quarrel between Major Borland and Colonel Yell. See Fulton, *Diary and Letters of Gregg*, 1: 218–19.

29. *Sen. Ex. Doc. 32*, 31st Cong., 1st Sess., Serial No. 558, p. 18.

30. "Letter from Presidio," Oct. 12, 1846, in *Little Rock Banner*, Nov. 25, 1846.

31. John Preston, "To a Friend," Camp near Presidio, Mexico, Oct. 14, 1846, in *Gazette*, Dec. 5, 1846; *Sen. Ex. Doc. 32*, 31st Cong., 1st Sess., Serial No. 558, pp. 18–21; "Autobiography," *New Age Magazine* 37: 142.

32. *Sen. Ex. Doc. 32*, 31st Cong., 1st Sess., Serial No. 558, p. 22; "Autobiography," *New Age Magazine* 37: 142.

33. Ibid., 26.

34. *H.R. Ex. Doc. 60*, 30th Cong., 1st Sess., Serial No. 520, p. 361.

35. Ibid., 377.

36. *Sen. Ex. Doc. 32*, 31st Cong., 1st Sess., Serial No. 558, p. 28.

37. "Had Santa Anna," says Robert Selph Henry, "left San Luis on the sixth, as was reported, Wool's small force would have been in a perilous position, since they were not only 120 miles from the nearest U.S. force but would also have to march for the last twenty of those miles on the same road which would be used by advancing Mexicans. It would have been entirely possible for Santa Anna to thrust a force between Wool and Worth and destroy them individually and in detail." Robert Selph Henry, *The Story of the Mexican War* (New York, 1950), 196.

38. Pike to "L.," Patos, Mexico, Dec. 31, 1846, in *Gazette*, Feb. 6, 1847. John C. Peay, a member of Pike's company, wrote home to a friend that the origin of this last alarm was "from Dyer, our butcher man. He on the authority of one of his Mexican 'helps,' told General Wool, that on the previous night, one of Santa Anna's sergeants had been in camp, and told the aforesaid Mexican 'help' that he [Santa Anna] would be down on the General the next day." Peay to D. F. Shall, 45 miles from Saltillo, Dec. 25, 1846, in *Little Rock Banner*, Feb. 10, 1847.

39. Peay to Shall, Dec. 26, 1846, in *Little Rock Banner*, Feb. 6, 1847.

40. Pike to "L.," Dec. 31, 1846, in *Gazette*, Feb. 6, 1847.

41. Gen. J. V. Minon, the commander of Santa Anna's cavalry.

42. Albert Pike, "To a Friend in Little Rock," Las Palomas, Mexico, Feb. 14, 1847, in *Little Rock Banner*, Mar. 31, 1847.

43. *H.R. Ex. Doc. 60*, 30th Cong., 1st Sess., Serial No. 520, pp. 1106–9, 1112–3, 1183–4. "It is reported," said General Wool, "they were surprised early in the morning, while asleep, with no pickets or sentinels to guard against surprise." Ibid., 1107.

44. Danley himself had been captured with Borland on Jan. 22.

45. Fulton, *Diary and Letters of Gregg*, 2: 36–37, 39–40.

46. Ibid., 2: 40; Ehinger Diary, Feb. 11, 13, 1847; *H.R. Ex. Doc. 60*, 30th Cong., 1st Sess., Serial No. 520, p. 1138; W. S. Henry, *Campaign Sketches of the War with Mexico* (New York, 1847), 308–9; for a quarrel that developed between Pike and Edward Hunter over this affair, see *Little Rock Banner*, Mar. 31, 1847, and *Gazette*, July 22, 27, 1847.

47. *H.R. Ex. Doc. 60*, 30th Cong., 1st Sess., Serial No. 520, pp. 1106, 1109–11, 1113; Henry, *Campaign Sketches*, 309; John S. Jenkins, *History of the War between the United States and Mexico* (Auburn, N.Y., 1851), 215–16.

48. James Henry Carleton, *The Battle of Buena Vista* (New York, 1848), 1–26, 176–86.

49. Albert Pike, "Buena Vista Letter," Saltillo, Mexico, Mar. 8, 1847, in *Gazette*, Apr. 24, 1847.

50. Henry, *Campaign Sketches*, 309, 311–13; Carleton, *Battle of Buena Vista*, 32, 33–34; Jenkins, *History of the War between the United States and Mexico*, 218–19.

51. Pike, "Buena Vista Letter," Mar. 8, 1847, in *Gazette*, Apr. 24, 1847.

52. Carleton, *Battle of Buena Vista*, 36–37, 43–45; Henry, *Campaign Sketches*, 313; Pike, "Buena Vista Letter," Mar. 8, 1847, in *Gazette*, Apr. 24, 1847.

53. Carleton, *Battle of Buena Vista*, 66–67.

54. Ehinger Diary, Feb. 11, 13, 1847.

55. Ibid., Mar. 7, 1847. Ehinger wrote on Apr. 7, 1847, that "Companies B and G, Arkansas Volunteers who behaved so shamefully at Agua Nueva, and who were so cowardly during the Battle of Buena Vista, were today sent to the mouth of the Rio Grande for punishment." Ibid.

56. Fulton, *Diary and Letters of Gregg*, 2: 48.

57. Pike, "Buena Vista Letter," Mar. 8, 1847, in *Gazette*, Apr. 24, 1847.

58. Henry, *Campaign Sketches*, 393; Fulton, *Diary and Letters of Gregg*, 2: 48–49; Carleton, *Battle of Buena Vista*, 70–72.

59. Henry, *Campaign Sketches*, 316–17; Carleton, *Battle of Buena Vista*, 89–94; Fulton, *Diary and Letters of Gregg*, 2: 49–51.

60. Josiah Gregg, who observed this charge and saw Colonel Yell immediately afterward, said that he was killed by a lance wound in the breast and that his upper lip was cleft by a severe cut. Gregg also took occasion to point out that Yell was "brave even to temerity, but lacked a sufficient degree of prudence." "The truth is," said Gregg, "he mistook his talent, when he entered the army—he was much better suited to politics." Fulton, *Diary and Letters of Gregg*, 2: 49.

61. Pike, "Buena Vista Letter," Mar. 8, 1847, in *Gazette*, Apr. 24, 1846/7. "Some," said Josiah Gregg, "have since endeavored (especially Captain Pike himself) to give much credit to the *charge* of Col. May's command in this case. For my own part, I saw nothing praiseworthy in the affair, and, if justice could be meted out with impartiality, I fear the reverse would be the result." Fulton, *Diary and Letters of Gregg*, 2: 49. For different views, see Henry, *Campaign Sketches*, 316–17; Carleton, *Battle of Buena Vista*, 89–94.

62. Carleton, *Battle of Buena Vista*, 94–126; Henry, *Campaign Sketches*, 315–16, 319–21; *Sen. Ex. Doc. I*, 30th Cong., 1st Sess., Serial No. 503, pp. 97–210, containing General Taylor's report of the battle, with the subreports from his officers. In this last charge of the day, Pike said, that while "the two Illinois, the Mississippi, the Kentucky, and Col. Lane's regiments deserved immortal honor ... the palm belongs to the artillery. They won the battle. Our flank was turned and but for the brilliant operation of the artillery ... in stopping that movement we were lost." Pike, "Buena Vista Letter," Mar. 8, 1847, in *Gazette*, Apr. 24, 1847.

63. Ibid.

64. Ibid.; Carleton, *Battle of Buena Vista*, 126–32.

65. J. T. S. [James T. Stevenson] to his father, Arispi's Mills, Mexico, Apr. 17, 1847, in *Gazette*, May 15, 1847; Stevenson, a member of Pike's squadron, wrote that he had endeavored to keep his two brothers, John and Henry, from going with Pike on this "precarious trip," in which "but little was to be gained and much might be lost." See also *H.R. Ex. Doc. 60*, 30th Cong., 1st Sess., Serial No. 520, pp. 1127–29, 1136; Fulton, *Diary and Letters of Gregg*, 2: 79, 89. An excellent account of Doniphan's march from Missouri and his action in New Mexico will be found in Horatio O. Ladd, *History of the War with Mexico* (New York, 1883).

66. Josiah Gregg, who accompanied the party to Chihuahua, wrote an elaborate account of this affair; a copy of the surrender terms appears in Fulton, *Diary and letters of Gregg*, 2: 95–96. "Only think!" exclaimed Gregg, "a city capitulating to 42 Americans." Ibid., 96.

67. Ibid., 98–100.

68. Henry, *Story of the Mexican War*, 236.

69. Ibid., 237.

70. *H.R. Ex. Doc. 60*, 30th Cong., 1st Sess., Serial No. 520, p. 1175. The Arkansas regiment was discharged at Carmago, Mexico, a few days later. Ibid.

71. Pope, *Early Days in Arkansas*, 276; "Return of the Volunteers," in *Little Rock Banner*, July 12, 1847.

72. Pike, "Buena Vista Letter," Mar. 8, 1847, in *Gazette*, Apr. 24, 1847.

73. Albert Pike to Brigadier General Wool, Camp at Arispi's Mills, May 23, 1847, in *Gazette*, July 22, 1847. Same in General Wool's Orders 297, 301, Adjutant General's Office, R.G. 94, 3 vols., National Archives.

74. See *Gazette*, July 22, 1847, for the record of this court of inquiry.

75. See extracts of a letter from Roane, Camp Taylor, Mexico, Feb. 27, 1847, in *Little Rock Banner*, Apr. 21, 1847; Edward Hunter, "To the People of Arkansas," in *Little Rock Banner*, July 19, 1847. This last letter also in *Clarksville (Tex.) Northern Standard*, July 17, 1847. See also John C. Peay, J. B. Borden, and R. C. Farrelly to Capt. E. Hunter, Little Rock, July 23, 1847, in *Gazette*, July 29, 1847.

76. Fletcher, *Arkansas*, 121–22. Pope, *Early Days in Arkansas*, 281, asserts that Roane challenged Pike after Pike had severely criticized the conduct of the Arkansas regiment in the columns of the *Gazette*. For proof that Pike was the challenger, see "The Recent Duel," in *Little Rock Banner*, Aug. 5, 1847. Allsopp, *Albert Pike*, 131–32, leans toward the Pope version, and is puzzled upon discovering that Dr. James A. Dibrell, Pike's surgeon at the affair, said Pike was the challenger.

77. Quoted in Pope, *Early Days in Arkansas*, 282–83. For additional proof that Burton and Dibrell were responsible for securing a settlement of the affair at this point, see a statement bearing the signatures of the seconds and surgeons in "The Recent Duel," in *Little Rock Banner*, Aug. 9, 1847. J. A. Dibrell Sr. to the editor of the *Gazette*, in *Gazette*, Apr. 2, 1893, adds interesting information to the story.

78. "The Recent Duel," in *Little Rock Banner*, Aug. 9, 1847; "Affair of Honor," in *Gazette*, Aug. 5, 1847, quoting *Van Buren (Ark.) Intelligencer*, n.d.; see also *Clarksville (Tex.) Northern Standard*, Aug. 21, 1847.

79. H. M. Rector to John Hallum, Little Rock, Ark., Apr. 16, 1887, in Hallum, *History of Arkansas*, 1: 230. Something of a tension accompanying the duel may be inferred from the silence

of the newspapers in regard to the affair, aside from a few factual lines. So thankful were the citizens of the state that the fight had not resulted in the death of either combatant that they readily and faithfully cooperated in forever burying the subject of the dispute.

Chapter XVIII

1. Pike, *Evil and the Remedy*, 176–77.

2. This statement is based on an examination of Assessment Books for Pulaski County, 1835–39, 1841, 1843, 1845–49, in Arkansas History Commission Library, Little Rock. Pike's city property in the forties was at times of considerable size and value. In 1841 he had $10,715 worth of taxable property: 30 lots valued at $7,100; 3 slaves at $2,400; 3 horses at $600; household furniture at $600; and milk cow at $15. (Taxable slaves in Arkansas in the forties were over eight and under sixty years of age.) He paid in state and county taxes $16.16 on this property. In 1843 his listings were 30 lots at $2,450; 2 horses at $300; 2 carriages at $400; 1 mule at $70; 1 cow at $10; and 4 slaves at $1,350; in all $6,080, paying $32.80 in taxes. For 1845 his listings showed 18 lots at $2,000; 2 slaves at $800; furniture at $1,500; 2 carriages at $400; 2 horses over three at $250; 1 mule at $50; and 2 head of cattle at $60; a total of $5,060 on which he paid $26.32 in taxes. By 1846 Pike had no real estate except Block 61 (12 lots) on which his house was built, listed at $1,500, but he added an additional slave valued at $400. The remainder of his assessment was the same as 1845. In 1847 Block 61 was evaluated at $15,000, while other property was listed at $3,960, making a total of $18,960, for which he paid $98.80 in taxes. By 1848 he had acquired an additional lot, his listing showing 13 lots at $20,000; 2 slaves at $1,000; household furniture over $200 in value at $1,200; 2 carriages at $400; 2 horses at $200; value of gold watches and jewelry at $300; totalling $23,100, with taxes of $116.50. In 1849 his evaluations and assessments were greatly reduced: 13 lots at $10,300; furniture at $1,000; 1 carriage at $150; 4 horses at $100; 2 horses at $100; 1 cow at $40; 25 cows at $100; 2 slaves at $900; a total of $13,670 and taxes of $70.36.

3. Pike, *Evil and the Remedy*, 178. One might suppose from the phrasing that Pike was suggesting that he did not approve of "slavery in the abstract."

4. Ibid., 178.

5. These themes crop up time and time again in his *Evil and the Remedy*, and in other writings and speeches of the period 1836 to 1860.

6. "As I said, some time ago, there are but two things that keep us out of entire skepticism and anarchy; and these two are, the Constitution of the United States, and the common law. . . .

"I pity the man who sees in our Constitution nothing but a mere formula of words. I look upon it as a political gospel, for the gift of which I cannot be thankful enough; which embodies a wisdom far, far above my erring and clouded intellect, and to which it would be profanation for me to think of adding, or in which altering, a single word." Pike, *Evil and the Remedy*, 71.

7. *Essays to Vinnie*, Essay 11, "Of My Books and Studies," Pike Papers.

8. Lists of certain of the books Pike purchased during this period are in Pike to Messrs. Gould, Banks & Company, Little Rock, Jan. 2, 1841, New York Public Library; Pike to Messrs. Gould, Banks & Co., Little Rock, Mar. 2, 1843, Huntington Library, San Marino, Calif.; Pike to Gould, Banks & Co., Little Rock, Dec. 27, 1841, Historical Society of Pennsylvania, Philadelphia; Pike to Messrs. T & J. W. Johnson, Little Rock, July 8, 1841, Historical Society of Pennsylvania; same to same, Little Rock, Mar. 2, 1843, ibid. For other lists of books and journals which Pike owned but

had "lost or loaned," see *Gazette*, Apr. 26, 1843. In the Library of the Supreme Council at Washington are copies of books that Pike willed to the Supreme Council. Many of these, still in the original expensive leather bindings with Pike's name stamped in gold upon the backs, testify to his taste for finery.

9. *Gazette*, June 14, 1843.

10. Some of these are in the Library of the Supreme Council, Washington, and are inscribed "Presented to the Club of Forty by A. Pike."

11. *Gazette*, May 31, 1843, carried a notice signed by Pike, president, and L. J. Reardon, secretary, that the next discussion would be on the true policy of the United States in regard to a tariff.

12. Albert Pike to Messrs. C. C. Little & Co., Little Rock, June 4, 1840, New York Public Library; Pike to Gould, Banks & Co., Little Rock, Mar. 2, 1843, Huntington Library, San Marino, Calif.; Pike to T. S. & J. W. Johnson, Little Rock, Mar. 2, 1843, Historical Society of Pennsylvania.

13. Pike to Gould, Banks & Co., Little Rock, Dec. 27, 1841, New York Public Library.

14. *Essays to Vinnie*, Essay 12, "Of the Law and Lawyers," Essay 11, "Of My Books and Studies," Pike Papers. The discussion in this paragraph is based also upon a study of *Sixth Census or Enumeration of the Inhabitants of the United States, as Corrected at the Department of State in 1840* (Washington, D.C., 1841), 432–33; *Compendium of the Enumeration of the Inhabitants and Statistics of the United States, as Obtained at the Department of State . . . /1840/* (Washington, D.C., 1841), 2; and J. D. B. Debow, *Statistical View of the United States . . . a Compendium of the Seventh Census* (Washington, D.C., 1854), 194–95, 200–201, 196–97, 202–3, 198–99, 204–5.

15. "Autobiography," *New Age Magazine* 38: 144, 211–12, 345–46.

16. *Little Rock State Gazette*, June 15, 1848.

17. Ibid., *Essays to Vinnie*, Essay 12, "Of the Law and Lawyers," Pike Papers.

18. F. W. Trapnall, Albert Pike, and C. P. Bertrand, to Jesse Turner, Little Rock, June 20, 1848, Turner Papers. This letter is in Pike's hand.

19. *Little Rock State Gazette*, June 22, 1848.

20. Ibid., July 27, 1848.

21. Ibid., Aug. 3, 1848.

22. *Little Rock Banner*, Sept. 19, 1848.

23. *Little Rock State Gazette*, Aug. 10, 1848.

24. *Van Buren (Ark.) Intelligencer*, Aug. 12, 1848.

25. Ibid.

26. *Little Rock State Gazette*, Oct. 12, 1848.

27. *Little Rock Banner*, Nov. 28, 1848.

28. *Little Rock State Gazette*, Nov. 23, 1848, carries his "Taylor Song" and "Song."

29. Pike to Taylor, Washington City, Mar. 6, 1849, Thomas Ewing Papers, Letters Received, Box 6, June 1849–Nov. 1850, p. 125, Library of Congress.

30. Pike to Turner, Little Rock, Apr. 9, 1849, Turner Papers.

31. See undated lists in Pike's hand and signed by him, Ewing Papers, Letters Received, Box 6, pp. 52, 123–24, 152.

32. Pike to Turner, Little Rock, Apr. 9, 1849, Turner Papers.

33. Ibid.; Thomas W. Newton to Ewing, Little Rock, June 5, 1849, Ewing Papers, Letters Received, Box 6, p. 70; Newton to Ewing, Little Rock, July 5, 1849, ibid., 115; C. P. Bertrand to

Ewing, Little Rock, May 2, 1849, ibid., 127; John Preston Jr. to Pike, Helena, Ark., June 19, 1849, ibid., 128; Pike to Ewing, Little Rock, July 2, 1849, ibid., 129.

34. Pike to Turner, Little Rock, Apr. 9, 1849, Turner Papers; *Little Rock State Gazette and Democrat,* May 24, 1849, Oct. 18, 1850.

35. Pike to Turner, June 7, Sept. 17, 1849, Turner Papers.

36. Pike to Turner, Little Rock, Dec. 20, 1849, ibid. Pike surmised incorrectly, for John Bell of Tennessee probably secured the appointment for Ringo. F. W. Trapnall to Hon. John Bell, Little Rock, June 22, 1849, *Ewing Papers,* Book of Letters Received, 1849–1850, [p. 143]; Bell to Ewing, Nashville, Tenn., Nov. 3, 1849, ibid., [p.144]; F. W. Trapnall to Ewing, Little Rock, Oct. 14, 1849, ibid., [p. 191].

37. J. P. Davis, *The Union Pacific Railway* (Chicago, 1894), 13.

38. Ibid., 13–37.

39. Robert R. Russell, *Improvement of Communication with the Pacific Coast as an Issue in American Politics, 1783–1864* (Cedar Rapids, Iowa, 1948), 12–13.

40. Ibid., 13–16.

41. Robert R. Russell, *Economic Aspects of Southern Sectionalism, 1840–1861* (University of Illinois Studies in the Social Sciences, vol. 11, no. 1, Urbana, 1924); Russell, *Improvement of Communication with the Pacific Coast,* 24–25.

42. Thomas, *Arkansas and Its People,* 3: 93.

43. *Little Rock Banner,* Jan. 2, 1849.

44. Proceedings and resolutions of this meeting are in ibid., Jan. 23, 1849.

45. Ibid., Mar. 6, Apr. 17, 24, May 1, 1849; *Little Rock State Gazette,* Mar. 15, 1849.

46. Reprinted in full in *Little Rock Banner,* May 8, 1849.

47. *Little Rock Banner,* Apr. 17, 1849, quoting *Richmond Enquirer,* n.d.

48. Ibid., May 8, 1849, quoting *New Orleans Daily Crescent,* n.d.

49. Ibid., June 12, 1849.

50. Ibid.

51. *Little Rock State Gazette,* June 14, Sept. 13, quoting *Memphis Eagle,* Sept. 6, 1849; *De Bow's Review* 7 (Aug. 1849): 188.

52. *Little Rock State Gazette,* June 14, Oct. 4, 1849.

53. *Little Rock Banner,* Oct. 30, 1849.

54. *New Orleans Daily Delta,* Nov. 6, 1849.

55. The resolutions are in *De Bow's Review* 7 (Dec. 1849): 551–52; resolutions of St. Louis convention in ibid., 7 (Aug. 1849): 188.

56. *Little Rock Banner,* Dec. 18, 1849.

57. Ibid. carried the speech in full.

58. Ibid.

59. Ibid.

60. Ibid.

61. Ibid.

62. Ibid. This address was also printed in full in the *Little Rock State Gazette,* Dec. 13, 1849, and as a pamphlet under title *National Plan of an Atlantic and Pacific Railroad, and Remarks of Albert Pike,*

Made Thereon, at Memphis, November 1849 (Little Rock, 1849). The pamphlet is on microfilm in the University of Texas Library.

63. *Little Rock Banner*, Dec. 4, 18, 1849; *Little Rock State Gazette*, Dec. 20, 1849.

Chapter XIX

1. *Little Rock Banner*, Feb. 12, 1850.
2. Ibid., Mar. 20, 1849.
3. R. W. Johnson to the Citizens of Arkansas, Washington, D.C., Jan. 29, 1850, in *Little Rock Banner*, Feb. 19, 1850.
4. Ibid.
5. Ibid.
6. Ibid.
7. [Pike] to Johnson, Little Rock, Mar. 1850, in *Little Rock State Gazette and Democrat*, Mar. 22, 1850. For proof that Pike was the author of this letter, see *Little Rock Whig*, July 31, 1851.
8. *Little Rock Whig*, July 31, 1851.
9. Ibid.
10. Ibid.
11. Ibid.
12. Ibid.
13. Ibid.
14. Ibid.
15. Ibid.
16. Johnson to the Corps Editorial of the State of Arkansas, House of Representatives, Washington, D.C., Feb. 1, 1850, in *Little Rock Banner*, Feb. 26, 1850.
17. Ibid., Mar. 5, 1850.
18. Johnson to the Editors of the *National Intelligencer*, Washington, D.C., Mar. 24, 1850, in ibid., Apr. 16, 1850; same in *Little Rock State Gazette and Democrat*, Apr. 19, 1850.
19. *National Intelligencer,,* Apr. 16, 1850.
20. Johnson to Reardon and Whiteley, Washington, D.C., Apr. 30, 1850, in ibid., May 14, 1850.
21. *Little Rock State Gazette and Democrat*, Mar. 22, 1850; see Demetrius [Pike] to Editor, in *Little Rock Whig*, July 31, 1851, for evidence of this.
22. See Demetrius [Pike] to Editor, in *Little Rock Whig*, July 31, 1851.
23. *Little Rock Banner*, Apr. 9, 30, 1850.
24. Ibid., Apr. 30, 1850.
25. Johnson to Reardon and Whiteley, Washington, D.C., Apr. 30, 1850, in ibid., May 14, 1850.
26. *Little Rock State Gazette and Democrat*, May 14, 1850.
27. *Little Rock Banner*, Apr. 16, 1850, citing *El Dorado Union*, n.d.
28. *Helena Southern Shield*, May 11, 1850, quoting *Camden Herald*, n.d.

29. *Little Rock Banner*, May 14, 1850.

30. Ibid., May 28, 1850.

31. *Little Rock State Gazette and Democrat*, May 31, 1850.

32. According to the proceedings in the *Little Rock Banner*, June 18, 1850, only J. H. Powell was present from Arkansas on June 4, but apparently either John Selden Roane or Sam C. Roane, or perhaps both, took seats on the following day. *Little Rock State Gazette and Democrat*, June 21, 28, 1850.

33. *Little Rock State Gazette and Democrat*, June 21, 1850.

34. *Little Rock Banner*, June 18, 1850.

35. Ibid., July 2, 1850.

36. *Little Rock State Gazette and Democrat*, June 21, 1850.

37. Ibid., June 28, 1850.

38. Richard Harrison Shryrock, *Georgia and the Union in 1850* (Durham, N.C., 1926), 302–34.

39. Johnson to Reardon and Whiteley, House of Representatives, July 19, 1850, in *Little Rock Banner*, Aug. 13, 1850; "Address from the Hon. R. W. Johnson, Washington, September 6, 1850," in ibid., Oct. 1, 1850; *Dictionary of American Biography*, X, 117.

40. *Little Rock Banner*, Oct. 8, Dec. 31, 1850.

41. Ibid., Apr. 29, 1851; Demetrius [Pike] to Editor, *Little Rock Whig*, July 31, 1851; Johnson to the Editor of the *Little Rock Banner*, Pine Bluff, June 11, 1851, in *Little Rock Banner*, June 17, 1851.

42. Demetrius [Pike] to Editor, *Little Rock Whig*, July 31 and Sept. 20, 1851; and *Little Rock State Gazette and Democrat*, Aug. 31, 1855, for Pike's views on Johnson. Chicot Planter to Editor, in *Little Rock State Gazette and Democrat*, July 25, Aug. 8, 1851, and "Demetrius" in *Little Rock Whig*, Aug. 14, 1851, for the attack on Pike.

43. Pike's ideas concerning the formation of this new party were set forth in a series of articles entitled "Disunion," which he published over the signature of Demetrius in the *Little Rock Whig*, July 3, 10, 24, 31, Aug. 7, 1851. For proof that Pike was the writer, see Demetrius to Editor, ibid., July 31, 1853.

44. Johnson had announced his schedule on May 27, 1851, which included the counties of Perry, Conway, Pope, Yell, Johnson, Franklin, Crawford, Sebastian, Washington, Benton, Madison, Carroll, Newton, Searcy, Van Buren, and Pulaski, in that order. *Little Rock Banner*, May 27, June 17, 1851.

45. John Rust to *Little Rock Banner*, Rockport, Ark., July 11, 1851, in ibid., July 15, 1851.

46. "The Speaking at Rock Port," in ibid., July 29, 1851.

47. The account of the campaign has been based on the *Little Rock Whig*, June 26–Aug. 14, 1851; *Little Rock Banner*, June 17, Aug. 12, 1851; *Little Rock State Gazette and Democrat*, June 13–Aug. 16, 1851.

48. John Rust to the *Little Rock Banner*, Rockport, Ark., July 22, 1851, in *Little Rock Banner*, July 29, 1851.

49. Governor Roane's Proclamation and the Election Returns by Counties is in ibid., Sept. 16, 1851.

50. *Little Rock State Gazette and Democrat*, July 18, 1851.

Chapter XX

1. Pike participated in some forty-nine cases before the Arkansas Supreme Court, July term, 1847, through the July term, 1850. *Arkansas Reports,* VIII, IX.

2. A. W. Bishop, *Loyalty on the Frontier, or Sketches of Union Men of the South-West; with Incidents and Adventures in Rebellion on the Border* (St. Louis, Mo., 1863), 151; Hempstead, *Historical Review of Arkansas,* I, 437–38. See also "A Rebel Opinion of Albert Pike," by Maj. George A. Gallagher, Arkansan, a newspaper clipping in the American Antiquarian Society Library, Worcester, Mass.

3. *Little Rock State Gazette,* Mar. 23, 1848, carried a card announcing the dissolution.

4. A photostat of the original certificate issued to Pike is in Pike Room, Library of the Supreme Council 33°, Washington, D.C. His petition was moved by Attorney General Reverdy Johnson, and he was "duly admitted and qualified as an Attorney and Counsellor of the Supreme Court of the United States, on the 9th day of March . . . [1849]."

5. *Little Rock State Gazette,* July 19, 1849.

6. *Little Rock Banner,* Sept. 25, 1849; *Little Rock State Gazette,* May 24, 1850; Pike to [Gould, Banks & Co. ?], Little Rock, Mar. 6, 1850, in Historical Society of Pennsylvania, Philadelphia.

7. The Pulaski County Assessment Book for 1851, in Arkansas History Commission Library, Little Rock, lists Pike's taxable property as 13 lots valued at $15,500; 9 slaves at $4,850; household furniture over $200 at $2,000; 3 carriages at $500; 5 horses at $350; 1 horse at $30; 4 neat cattle over two years at $55; 14 neat cattle over two years at $102; and gold watches and jewelry at $350. On this total of $23,737 he paid a state tax of $47.81 and a county tax of $61.76.

The manuscript return for Little Rock, Pulaski County, of Schedule 1, Free Inhabitants, Seventh Census of the United States, 1850, lists under Family No. 655 the eight members of the Pike family and William Winter, aged 32, gardener, born in Germany. The enumeration is dated Dec. 1850. Schedule 2, Slave Inhabitants, Pike with six slaves: a mulatto woman, aged 37; a black man and a black boy, aged 25 and 17; a mulatto girl, aged 16; a black girl, aged 11; and a mulatto girl, aged 6. Microfilm copies of these schedules are in the University of Texas Library.

8. *New Orleans Daily Delta,* Jan. 31, 1851; same quoted in *Little Rock State Gazette and Democrat,* Feb. 14, 1851.

9. "Report of the Joint Committee on the Affairs of the Real Estate Bank," in Arkansas *House Journal,* 1856–1857, appendix, 376–77; same in *Little Rock True Democrat,* May 12, 1857.

10. Under the assignment the number of trustees had been reduced on Apr. 2, 1844 from fifteen to five.

11. *Little Rock Banner,* Oct. 1, 1850, quoting *London Times,* July 22, 1850, via *New York Post,* n.d.

12. *Arkansas Acts,* 1853, pp. 195–96, 196–97.

13. *Message of Elias N. Conway, Governor of Arkansas, to Both Houses of the General Assembly; November 7, 1854* (Little Rock, 1854), 12, 30–31, 33–37; *In the Pulaski Circuit Court, in Chancery; The State of Arkansas vs. The Trustees of the Real Estate Bank of the State of Arkansas* [Little Rock, 1854], 3, 19, 28–29, 31–32. Allen, *Arkansas Imprints,* 78–79, dates the pamphlet in 1855; for proof that it was 1854, see *Governor's Message, November 7, 1854,* pp. 12–13.

14. *The State of Arkansas vs. The Trustees of the Real Estate Bank,* 3–37.

15. *Governor's Message, November, 7, 1854,* pp. 12–13; *Little Rock State Gazette and Democrat,* June 9, 1854.

16. *Governor's Message, November 7, 1854*, pp. 13–14.

17. *Arkansas Acts*, 1855, pp. 142–43; *Acts of the General Assembly of the State of Arkansas, Relative to the Real Estate Bank of the State of Arkansas*, 57–58.

18. *Arkansas Acts*, 1855, pp. 137–41; not in *Acts of the General Assembly of the State of Arkansas, Relative to the Real Estate Bank of the State of Arkansas*.

19. *Little Rock State Gazette and Democrat*, May 4, 1855.

20. Ibid., Apr. 20, 1855.

21. Copies of the opinion and decree are printed in ibid., May 4, 1855; see also ibid., Apr. 27, 1855.

22. "Opinion," in *Little Rock State Gazette and Democrat*, May 4, 1855.

23. *Little Rock Chronicle*, Nov. 15, 1855; *Report of the Accountants, Appointed under the Act of January 15, 1855, to Investigate the Affairs of the Real Estate Bank of Arkansas* (Little Rock, 1856), 3, 19. Hereafter cited as *Report of Accountants*.

24. *Little Rock True Democrat*, Nov. 20, 1855.

25. *Little Rock State Gazette and Democrat*, Nov. 30, 1855.

26. Ibid., Aug. 31, 1855.

27. Ibid.

28. Worley, "Control of the Real Estate Bank of the State of Arkansas, 1836–1855," 425n.

29. *Little Rock State Gazette and Democrat*, Aug. 31, 1855. For proof that Conway did have the bill in chancery printed, see *Governor's Message, November 7, 1854*, p. 13.

30. "Historical Sketch," in *Report of Accountants*, 11–19.

31. Ibid., 56.

32. Ibid., 55.

33. Ibid., 30, 37.

34. Ibid., 28, 37.

35. *Report of Gordon N. Peay, as Receiver in Chancery of the Real Estate Bank, 1st October, 1858* (Little Rock, Ark., 1858), 5.

36. *Report of Accountants*, 38–39.

37. Ibid., 39.

38. Ibid., 39–41.

39. Ibid., 41–42, 68–72.

40. Ibid., 44–45.

41. *Little Rock True Democrat*, July 1, 1856.

42. *Little Rock State Gazette and Democrat*, Aug. 31, 1855.

43. Reginald C. McGrane, *Foreign Bondholders and American State Debts* (New York, 1935), 250–51, 254–62.

44. "Report of the Joint Committee on the Affairs of the Real Estate Bank," in Arkansas *House Journal*, 1856–1857, appendix, 381–82.

45. Ibid.

46. *Platenius as Ad. v. The State* (1856), 17 *Arkansas Reports*, 518–23.

47. Report of the Joint Committee on the Affairs of the Real Estate Bank in Arkansas *House Journal*, 1856–1857, appendix, 381–82.

48. *Arkansas Acts*, 1855, p. 17.

49. *Platenius as Ad. v. The State* (1856), 17 *Arkansas Reports*, 520–23.

50. *Little Rock State Gazette and Democrat*, Dec. 14, 1855, carried the announcement of dissolution.

51. *Ark. Rev. Stats.* (1838), 961.

52. Pike and Cummins, In the Supreme Court of Arkansas, July Term A.D. 1855, The President and Directors of the Bank of Washington, and James Holford's Administrators, appellants, vs. Appeal from the Chancery Court of Pulaski Co., The State of Arkansas, and the Trustees of the Real Estate Bank of the State of Arkansas, appellees [Little Rock? 1855?]. The case was not heard until the January term, 1856, by which time Pike and Cummins had dissolved their partnership. Pike therefore deleted Cummins's name from the brief used in the appeal. See the copy in the Library of the Supreme Council. The brief is on microfilm in the University of Texas Library.

53. *Platenius as Ad. v. The State* (1856), 17 *Arkansas Reports*, 523–28.

54. Albert Pike, *Supreme Court of the United States, December Term, 1856, The President and Directors of the Bank of Washington, vs. The State of Arkansas and the Trustees of the Real Estate Bank of the State of Arkansas, Defendants, Error to the Supreme Court of Arkansas Argument for the Plaintiffs in Error* (Washington, D.C., [1856?]). The original brief is in the Library of the Supreme Council; it is on microfilm in the University of Texas Library.

55. *Joseph D. Beers, use of William A. Platenius, as Administrator of James Holford, deceased, Plaintiff in Error v. The State of Arkansas; William A. Platenius, Administrator of James Holford, deceased, Plaintiff in Error v. The State of Arkansas; same v. same* (1858), 15 L. Ed. 991–93; 20 Howard 527. The cases, depending upon the same principles, were grouped together for the convenience of the court.

56. *Little Rock True Democrat*, July 1, 1856.

57. Report of the Joint Committee on the Affairs of the Real Estate Bank, in Arkansas *House Journal*, 1856–1857, appendix, 382; Johnson also printed the report in *Little Rock True Democrat*, May 12, 1857.

58. Arkansas *House Journal*, 1856–1857, appendix, 383.

59. Ibid.

60. Ibid., 383–84.

61. *Report of Accountants*, 41–42.

62. Ibid., 48.

63. Worley, "Control of the Real Estate Bank of the State of Arkansas, 1836–1855," 420, 425–26.

64. See above, 279.

65. Ibid., 421–23, 425n.

66. The extant records of the Real Estate Bank in the Arkansas History Commission Library, Little Rock, are either too incomplete or in many cases too damaged to permit an adequate re-study of the period of the trusteeship. Two surviving letters that show Pike conscientiously protecting the bank are Pike to Trustees of Real Estate Bank, Little Rock, June 24, 1853, Gulley Collection, Arkansas History Commission; and Pike to M.[ichael] Bozeman, Esq., Little Rock, Dec. 23d, 1851, Allsopp Collection, Larson Memorial Library, Little Rock Junior College.

67. *Report of Accountants*, 4–5.

68. Ibid., 9–10, 26.

Chapter XXI

1. *Little Rock Banner*, Apr. 18, 25, 1848, July 16, 1850; *Little Rock State Gazette and Democrat*, Nov. 7, 1854; Albert Pike, *An Address Delivered . . . to the Young Ladies of the Tulip Female Seminary, and Cadets of the Arkansas Military Institute: at Tulip, on June 4, 1852* (Little Rock, 1852).

2. *Little Rock State Gazette and Democrat*, Apr. 23, 1852; R. W. Johnson to Editor of Banner, Washington, Feb. 25, 1852, in *Little Rock Banner*, Mar. 16, 1852. From 1848 to 1850 he was a strong backer and stockholder in the Little Rock Bridge Company, established to bridge the Arkansas at the state capital. *Little Rock State Gazette and Democrat*, July 13, 1845, Feb. 8, Mar. 22, 1850.

3. Demetrius (Pike) to Robert C. Farrelly, New York, Sept. 20, 1851, in *Little Rock Whig*, Oct. 16, 1851; ibid., Nov. 13, Dec. 11, 1851.

4. "Plain Talk, Starvation, Emigration or Railroads, No. I," *Little Rock Whig*, Dec. 25, 1851. The other four numbers appeared in ibid., Jan. 1, 8, 15, 29, 1852.

5. Ibid., Jan. 8, 15, 29, 1852.

6. *De Bow's Review* 12 (Mar. 1852): 315; *Little Rock Whig*, Jan. 22, 29, 1852.

7. Robert R. Russel, *Improvement of Communication with the Pacific Coast, as an Issue in American Politics, 1783–1864* (Cedar Rapids, Iowa, 1948), 110–15.

8. Both the *Little Rock State Gazette and Democrat*, July 30, 1852, and the *Washington (Ark.) Telegraph*, Aug. 18, 1852, carried Pike's speech in full; proceedings of the convention are in *Little Rock Whig*, July 8, 1852.

9. *Little Rock Whig*, July 8, 15, 1852.

10. *Cong. Globe*, 37th Congress, 1st Sess., 54, 782, 1004, 1686, 2387; *Little Rock State Gazette and Democrat*, Feb. 18, 1853. For discussions of why Cairo was designated the terminal of the road, see Frank H. Hodder, "The Pacific Railroad Background of the Kansas-Nebraska Act," *Mississippi Valley Historical Review* 12 (June 1925): 13, and Russel, *Improvement of Communication with the Pacific Coast*, 118–22.

11. *Cong. Globe*, 32d Cong., 1st Sess., 2438, 2463–64. Borland's Senate Bill was never taken up in the House, probably because Johnson knew it would not pass.

12. *Arkansas Acts*, 1853, pp. 108–9, 130–37, 176–80.

13. Russel, *Improvement of Communication with the Pacific Coast*, 119.

14. *Cong. Globe*, 32d Cong., 1st Sess., 514–16, 672–75.

15. Ibid., 672–75; *Little Rock Whig*, Feb. 24, 1853.

16. P.[ike] to Butler, Washington City, Feb. 11, 1853, in *Little Rock Whig*, Mar. 3, 1853.

17. Albert Pike to Col. J. T. Trezevant, Washington City, Feb. 6, 1853, in *Little Rock Whig*, Mar. 3, 1853, quoting *Memphis Appeal*, n.d. To Butler, Pike had said in like vein: "The passage of this bill, (and this is far from being *my* opinion alone,) settles the question as to the Pacific road, and secures a *Southern* route, by Fort Smith or Fulton, and Albequerque [sic] or El Paso. P.[ike] to Butler, Washington City, Feb. 11, 1853, in *Little Rock Whig*, Mar. 3, 1853.

18. *Memphis Tennessean Daily Appeal*, Apr. 20, 1853, quoted in Russel, *Improvement of Communication with the Pacific Coast*, 122; *Little Rock State Gazette and Democrat*, Apr. 8, May 13, 1853.

19. Demetrius (Pike) to Farrelly, New York, Sept. 20, 1851, in *Little Rock Whig*, Oct. 16, 1851; "Starvation, Emigration or Railroads," Nos. IV, V, in *Little Rock Whig*, Jan. 15, 29, 1852.

20. *Little Rock State Gazette and Democrat*, July 30, 1852; *Washington Telegraph*, Aug. 18, 1852.

21. *Little Rock Whig*, July 8, 15, Aug. 19, Sept. 23, 30, Nov. 18, 1852, Feb. 17, 1853; *Little Rock State Gazette and Democrat*, July 30, Aug. 27, Sept. 3, 1852.

22. *Little Rock Banner*, July 13, 1852.

23. Russel, *Improvement of Communication with the Pacific Coast*, 122.

24. *Little Rock State Gazette and Democrat*, June 3, 10, 17, July 12, 22, 29, 1853; *Arkansas Acts*, 1855, pp. 172–75.

25. Russel, *Improvement of Communication with the Pacific Coast*, 165–66, says that Pike was one of the "alert Southerners outside Congress" who recognized what Russel regards as the "immediate purpose and larger implications of the Kansas-Nebraska bill," namely, to secure the organization of territory west of the Mississippi River through which the Pacific railroad could run.

26. Herbert Wender, *Southern Commercial Conventions 1837–1859* (Johns Hopkins University Studies in Historical and Political Science, vol. XLVIII, no. 4, Baltimore, 1930), 87–118; Russel, *Economic Aspects of Southern Sectionalism, 1840–1861*, 123–33; Russel, *Improvement of Communication to the Pacific*, 24–27.

27. *New York Weekly Mirror* 1 (Dec. 21, 1844): 42; *Knickerbocker* 22 (Nov. 1843): 502; 44 (July 1854): 81–84; 53 (Apr. 1859): 429; S. M. Todd as quoted by Charles S. Lobingier, "Albert Pike, the Comparative Lawyer," *American Law Review* 61 (May–June 1927): 394; *New Orleans Daily Delta*, Jan. 31, 1851; *Little Rock Whig*, Feb. 17, 1853, quoting Washington correspondent of the *Van Buren Intelligencer*, n.d.; *Little Rock Whig*, June 29, 1854, quoting *Helena Southern Shield*, n.d.

28. Alfred Bunn, *Old England and New England, in a Series of Views Taken on the Spot* (2 vols., London, 1853), I, 253–60, for a glowing tribute to Pike by an English traveler who met him at a dinner in Washington in the winter of 1852; *Des Arc (Ark.) Citizen*, Dec. 25, 1858; Ben Perley Poore, *Reminiscences of Sixty Years in the National Metropolis* (2 vols., Philadelphia, 1886), I, 542; Todd quoted Lobingier, "Albert Pike, the Comparative Lawyer," *American Law Review* 61: 394.

29. J. H. Easterby, "The Charleston Commercial Convention of 1854," *South Atlantic Quarterly* 25 (Apr. 1926): 183, quoting and citing *Charleston Courier*, "beginning the first week in April," *Journal of Proceedings of the Commercial Convention of the Southern and Western States, Held in the City of Charleston, South-Carolina, during the Week Commencing on Monday, 10th April, 1854* (Charleston, 1854), 3–7.

30. *Journal of Charleston Commercial Convention*, 6, 31–32.

31. Ibid., appendix, xvi–xvii, carries Pike's resolution; same in *De Bow's Review* 16 (June 1854): 636–37.

32. *Journal of Charleston Commercial Convention*, 67; *De Bow's Review* 17 (Aug. 1854): 210.

33. Ibid., 64–70; synopsis of the speech is in *De Bow's Review* 17 (Aug. 1854): 208–12.

34. Andrew F. Muir, *The Thirty-Second Parallel Pacific Railroad in Texas to 1872* (Ph.D. dissertation, University of Texas, 1949), 37–38, is the best authority on this act.

35. *Journal of Charleston Commercial Convention*, 32–33, 60–63; *De Bow's Review* 17: 206–8.

36. *Journal of Charleston Commercial Convention*, 126; *De Bow's Review* 17 (Oct. 1854): 408–9.

37. *Journal of Charleston Commercial Convention*, 132–34; *De Bow's Review* 17 (Nov. 1854): 492–93.

38. *Journal of Charleston Commercial Convention*, 135–36; *De Bow's Review* 17: 494–95.

39. *Journal of Charleston Commercial Convention*, 138–39; *De Bow's Review* 17: 496.

40. *Journal of Charleston Commercial Convention*, 136–38; *De Bow's Review* 17: 495–96.

41. *Journal of Charleston Commercial Convention*, 139–42; *De Bow's Review* 17: 497–99.

42. *Journal of Charleston Commercial Convention*, 142–50; *De Bow's Review* 17: 496–99.

43. *Journal of Charleston Commercial Convention*, 150–51.

44. Ibid.

45. Quoted in *Little Rock True Democrat*, Nov. 2, 1854.

46. Russel, *Economic Aspects of Southern Sectionalism, 1840–1861*, p. 135.

47. Pike presented the proposed charter to the South Carolina legislature because the Virginia legislature did not meet in 1854. *Little Rock State Gazette and Democrat*, July 7, 1854, quoting *New Orleans Picayune*, June 25, 1854. The memorial which accompanied the measure is in *De Bow's Review* 17 (Dec. 1854): 593–99. Allen, *Arkansas Imprints*, 73, lists a printed memoir on behalf of the Southern Commercial Convention, *To the honorable principal chief of the* [blank space] *Nation: Sir . . .* [Little Rock? 1854.], which he says was inscribed in "Pike's hand, September 25, 1854, with the blank space filled in by hand with the word 'Choctaw.'" The present writer has not seen the memoir.

48. South Carolina *House Journal*, 1854, pp. 25, 42.

49. *Little Rock True Democrat*, Nov. 8, 15, 29, 1854. The letter quoted is from the issue of Nov. 29.

50. The proceedings are in *New Orleans Daily Picayune*, Jan. 9–14, 16, 1855; *New Orleans Daily Crescent*, Jan. 9–13, 15–16, 1855.

51. Pike, *Address on the Southern Pacific Railroad: Delivered in the Hall of the House of Representatives of the State of Louisiana* (New Orleans, 1855). Pike took strong sectional grounds as the basis for his argument. "We think that the South can build her own road to the Pacific. . . . We do not propose to wait until the new free States of Nebraska, Kansas, Oregon, and Washington, and the four or five more that the prophetic eye of Mr. [Thomas Hart] Benton already sees carved out of the great Northwestern Territory, with their dozen or more senators, take the moneys from the treasury of the nation, and lay down the rails across the continent far in the frozen north." Ibid., 14.

52. *Louisiana Acts*, 1855, pp. 233–42.

53. For the interest in this new road, see *New Orleans Daily Crescent*, Feb. 27, 1855; *New Orleans Daily Picayune*, Feb. 1, 1855; *De Bow's Review* 20 (May 1857): 509; Muir, *Thirty-Second Parallel Pacific Railroad in Texas to 1872*, pp. 79–86.

54. The proceedings of the Savannah convention are in *De Bow's Review* 22 (Jan.–Mar. 1857): 81–105, 216–24, 307–18; see page 311 for Pike's speech on the Pacific railroad.

55. "M." to *Little Rock Whig*, May 25, 1854.

Chapter XXII

1. *Essays to Vinnie*, Essay 23, "Of the Ability to Say 'No,'" Pike Papers.

2. *Essays to Vinnie*, Essay 12, "Of the Law and Lawyers," Pike Papers; *Sen. Rep. No. 1978*, 29th Cong., 2d Sess., Serial No. 2458, p. 33.

3. *Sen. Rep. No. 1978*, 49th Cong., 2d Sess., Serial No. 2458, p. 33; *Letter of Albert Pike to the Choctaw People* (Washington, D.C., 1872), 3–4. Among the Pike Papers in the Library of the Supreme Council are copies of a bill of complaint filed by John D. MacPherson, executor of the John T. Cochrane estate, in the Supreme Court of the District of Columbia in Aug. 1877, a subpoena, dated Aug. 7, 1877, from the court demanding Pike's answer to the bill, and Pike's reply

thereto, undated. The complainant demanded an accounting by Pike for fees collected in 1861–1862 in the Choctaw case. Pike's answer was an elaborate summary of his connection with the Creek and Choctaw claims and of his relationship with Cochrane and other attorneys and agents in the cases. With the bill of complaint and Pike's reply are copies of accounts, letters, and documents in support of statements made by Pike and MacPherson which throw much light on the Creek case as well as the Choctaw case. These will be cited hereafter by title under MacPherson vs. Pike, Equity Docket No. 5742, Supreme Court District of Columbia, 1877, Pike Papers, SCSR; they are on microfilm in the University of Texas Library.

4. Edward Hanrick Papers, University of Texas Library.

5. This oral agreement as described here is nowhere set down in as complete form as I have made it sound, for I have been forced to piece isolated bits and scraps of information together to reach a conclusion as to Pike's share in the fee. In 1877 Pike states that he and Raiford "were jointly to prosecute the case, he to receive one-third of the fee," from which it is concluded that Pike was to get two-thirds since there is no evidence a third party was concerned in the claim. Pike's answer to Bill of Complaint, MacPherson vs. Pike, Equity Docket No. 5742, Supreme Court District of Columbia, 1877, Pike Papers, SCSR. See also Pike, *Letter to Choctaw People*, 4; Cochrane to Pike, Washington, D.C., May 13, 1859, in Pike, *Letter to Choctaw People*, appendix E, 11–12.

6. *Sen. Rep. No. 1978*, 49th Cong., 2d Sess., Serial No. 2458, p. 33.

7. Albert Pike, *Memorial of the Muscogee or Creek Nation of Indians, to the Congress of the United States*, (Washington, D.C., 1853?), pp. 1–3. Hereafter cited as *Memorial of the Muscogee Nation* (1853). See also *Cong. Globe*, 33d Cong., 1st Sess., 1059–60.

8. Pike, *Memorial of the Muscogee Nation* (1853), 3–6, 8–21; *Cong. Globe*, 33d Cong., 1st Sess., 1089–90, 1135–41, 1261–67, 1282–85; Commissioner of Indian Affairs Luke Lee to R. W. Johnson, Chairman, Committee on Indian Affairs, H.R. Department of the Interior, Office Indian Affairs, Jan. 17, 1853, *H.R. Misc. Doc. No. 10*, 32 Cong., 2d Sess., Serial No. 683, p. 4.

9. Albert Pike, *Memorial of the Muscogee or Creek Nation of Indians to the Honorable the Senate and House of Representatives of the United States of America* (Little Rock, Ark., 1852), p. 58.

10. *House Journal*, 32d Cong., 2d Sess., Serial No. 672, p. 76.

11. Ibid.

12. Luke Lea was later an advocate in the Choctaw case, hired by Cochrane. *Sen. Rep. No. 1978*, 49th Cong., 2d Sess., Serial No. 2458, p. 58.

13. Lea to Johnson, Jan. 17, 1853; *H.R. Misc. Doc. No. 10*, 32d Cong., 2d Sess., Serial No. 685, pp. 2–5.

14. Lea to Secretary of the Interior, A. H. H. Stuart, Office of Indian Affairs, Jan. 21, 1853, in Pike, *Memorial of the Muscogee Nation* (1853), [appendix], pp. 14–15. His estimate was based on prices paid other tribes for lands bought by the United States.

15. Alex. H. H. Stuart to Johnson, Department of Interior, Washington, D.C., Jan. 27, 1853, in ibid., [appendix], p. 15.

16. *Cong. Globe*, 32d Cong., 2d Sess., 758–59, 778–81, 806–7.

17. Ibid., 807–10.

18. Pope, *Early Days in Arkansas*, 79.

19. *Essays to Vinnie*, Essay 24, "Of Pleasant and Sad Remembrances," Pike Papers.

20. Ibid.

21. Bunn, *Old England and New England*, I, 253. In 1895 John F. Coyle, editor of the *Washington National Intelligencer* in the 1850s and close friend of Pike, testified: "In 1852 and 1853 when he [Pike] first came here they had a whole house. General Pike, Senator [William K.] Sebastian, Robert W. Johnson, Mr. [Luther] Chase, Mr. [Ben. T.] Duvall and Mr. Henry Rector and Elias Rector occupied the house on four and a half street, which they had rented from Mrs. Holmead. These people were all connected with Indian affairs and the house was called the wigwam." Testimony of John F. Coyle, in *Yvon Pike et al. vs. The Choctaw Nation*, General Jurisdiction Case No. 19384 (1895), United States Court of Claims Records, National Archives. Cited hereafter as *Yvon Pike et al. vs. The Choctaw Nation*, G. J. C., No. 19384 (1895), CCRNA.

22. "Pike, his X mark, Principal Comanche; [Thompson B.] Flournoy, his x mark, Oussache; [Elias] Rector, his x mark, Apsarookee; [Luther] Chase, his x mark, Piankeshaw; [William M.] Burwell, his x mark, Kickapoo; [William K.] Sebastian, his x mark, Quapaw; [Henry L.] Biscoe, his x mark, Arapaho; [and] [Doctor William P.] Reyburn, Gros Ventre." Bunn, *Old England and New England*, I, 253–54.

23. Ibid., 254–55.

24. In ibid., 256, Bunn had a curious explanatory note attached to Arkansas: "Arkansas as it now is, not as it was, in the days of that highly respectable adage.

    'One year credit, one year law

    The next year off to Arkansas!'"

25. Ibid., 256.

26. Ibid., 256–60; *Essays to Vinnie*, Essay, 24, "Of Pleasant and Sad Remembrances," Pike Papers.

27. *Spirit of the Times*, May 7, 1853, quoting *Missouri Republican*, n.d.; *New Orleans Weekly Delta*, Apr. 17, 1853; *Little Rock Whig*, Apr. 28, 1853; *Waverly Magazine* 6 (June 18, 1853): 395–97; Bunn, *Old England and New England*, I, 257–60; the poem was republished by "request of several old subscribers" in *Spirit of the Times*, Mar. 28, 1857; three verses from it are quoted in Clement Eaton, *A History of the Old South* (New York, 1949), 451.

28. These were four additional "Hymns to the Gods": "To Juno," "To Minerva," "To Flora," and "To Mars," *Knickerbocker* 35 (Apr.–June 1850): 326–27, 443–45, 490–91; 36 (Aug. 1850): 130–31.

29. Pike, *Nugae*, prefatorial statement. Only 150 copies were printed. Most of the 79 poems in the volume had appeared either in *Prose Sketches and Poems Written in the Western Country* or in periodicals. The 12 "Hymns to the Gods" are all in the book, and all the poems in *Nugae* are in Roome, ed., *Hymns to the Gods and Other Poems* and *Lyrics and Love Songs*.

30. Willis Gaylord Clark, an old and dear acquaintance to whom Pike sent a copy, reviewed it at length in the *Knickerbocker* 44 (July 1854): 81–84. "We think Mr. Pike has made a slight mistake in keeping his private 'I' from the *public* eye, in this attractive volume. One who can write as *he* has written, whose verse is a pellucid stream, through which his heart shines like a diamond, need not have permitted his modesty to do the public an injustice. However, his 'private distribution,' if it embraces all his friends, will exhaust a large edition." Ibid., 84. No other review has been found.

31. Pike refused to write the biography but did send Simms a copy of *Nugae*, "'the Multiplied Manuscripts' of my trash." Pike to Simms, Little Rock, Sept. 27, 1854, Ducykinck Collection, New York Public Library; see also Simms to Evert A. Ducykinck, n.p., n.d. [but prior to Sept. 27, 1854], and Simms to Evert A. Ducykinck, "Woodlands," [South Carolina], Nov. 27, 1854, ibid. In Evert A. and George L. Ducykinck, *Cyclopaedia of American Literature* (2 vols., New York, 1856), II,

520–21, the biographical information on Pike was taken from the earlier sketch which Pike wrote for Griswold's *Poets and Poetry of America* in 1841. Two of Pike's poems, "To Ceres," and "Farewell to New England" appear in the *Cyclopaedia*.

32. Pike to John F. Coyle, Little Rock, Apr. 20, 1855, Pike Papers, Duke University.

33. From Pike's "To the Mocking Bird," composed in 1834 when he was twenty-five, which Thompson considered his best poem. Pike "never afterward," he said, "wrote anything half so good." Maurice Thompson, "A Southern Pioneer Poet," *Independent* 50 (Nov. 17, 1898): 1397–98.

34. Pike's prefatory statement in *Prose Sketches and Poems Written in the Western Country* says: "What I have written has been a transcript of my own feelings,—too much so, for the purposes of fame. Writing has always been to me a communion with my own soul."

35. Dr. Gotfried Hult, "'Albert Pike,' Delivered at the Pike Memorial Service in Fargo, North Dakota," *New Age Magazine* 21 (May 1910): 438–46.

36. Edd Winfield Parks, *Southern Poets* (New York, 1936), 389, note 72, says that of "the numerous attempts to write a literary 'Dixie,' the one of Albert Pike is the most successful and best known. It appeared first in the *Natchez Courier*, April 30, 1861." The poem is found at pp. 138–40 of Parks's book. The poem also appeared in *Van Buren (Ark.) Press*, May 29, 1861, introduced with the following: "Through the kindness of a Lady friend, we are favored with a copy of the following lines, from the pen of a gifted son of Arkansas, which we with pleasure give a place in our paper."

37. Roone, *Lyrics and Love Songs*, 229–30; for the other poems mentioned, see ibid., 201–8, 212–21.

38. Pike's answer to Bill of Complaint, McPherson vs. Pike, Equity Docket No. 5742, Supreme Court District of Columbia, 1877, Pike Papers, SCSR; Pike, *Letter to Choctaw People*, 4; *Sen. Rep.* 1978, 49th Cong. 2d Sess., Serial No. 2458, p. 33.

39. He was appointed July 6, 1853, by Governor Conway to succeed Solon Borland, who had resigned on accepting a presidential appointment as "Minister Plenipotentiary of the United States for Central America." *Governor's Message, November 7, 1854*, p. 25.

40. Pike, *Memorial of the Muscogee Nation* (1853).

41. *Senate Journal*, 33d Congress, 1st Sess., Serial No. 689, p. 41.

42. *Sen. Rep. Com. No. 323*, 33d Cong., 1st Sess., Serial No. 707.

43. Ibid.

44. *Cong. Globe*, 33d Cong., 1st Sess., 1089–90.

45. Ibid., 1059; *Senate Journal*, 33d Cong., 1st Sess., Serial No. 689, p. 408.

46. *Cong. Globe*, 33d Cong., 1st Sess., 1059–60, 1089–91, 1135–41, 1145, 1187, 1261–67, 1282–85.

47. Ibid., 1137–39; see also the pages cited above for his other speech against the measure.

48. Ibid., 1285. Only three members of the Indian committee, Sebastian and Walker and Thomas J. Rusk of Texas, voted for the amendment. Stephen Adams of Mississippi and Robert Toombs of Georgia voted against it, and James Cooper of Pennsylvania did not vote. Others who voted for it were George E. Badger of North Carolina, Bell of Tennessee, Brown of Mississippi, Cass of Michigan, John M. Clayton of Delaware, Johnson of Arkansas, Truman Smith of Connecticut, and John B. Thompson of Kentucky.

49. Ibid., 1511; *Senate Journal*, 33d Cong., 1st Sess., Serial No. 689, p. 458; *Sen. Rep. Com. No. 323*, 33d Cong., 1st Sess., Serial No. 707, is the report which accompanied the bill and which was ordered printed.

50. *Sen. Rep. 1978*, 49th Cong., 2d Sess., Serial No. 2458, p. 58. Lea had been replaced by George W. Manypenny under the Pierce administration.

51. *Acts and Resolutions of the General Council of the Choctaw Nation, from 1852 to 1857, both inclusive* (Fort Smith, Ark., 1858), 54–55, the law which created the delegation in 1855. The other members were Israel Folsom, Samuel Garland, and Dixon W. Lewis, all prominent then and later in Choctaw affairs.

52. *Sen. Rep. 1978*, 49th Cong., 2d Sess., Serial No. 2458, pp. 14, 15, 33–34; Pike, *Letter to Choctaw People*, 4; Pike's answer to Bill of Complaint, McPherson vs. Pike, Equity Docket No. 5472, Supreme Court District of Columbia, 1877, Pike Papers, SCSR; see also copy of John T. Cochrane, contract as attorney for Choctaw Nation, Feb. 13, 1855, in folder labeled "Choctaw Case," Pike Papers, SCSR.

53. Pike's answer to Bill of Complaint, McPherson vs. Pike, Equity Docket No. 5742, Supreme Court District of Columbia, 1877, Pike Papers, SCSR.

54. This was probably C. Voorhies, then associate justice on the court.

55. These were the Pandects of Justinian, Byzantine emperor (527–65), under whom Roman law was codified into the Justinian Code or the Pandects of Justinian. The writer has been unable to establish which edition of the Pandects Pike read. It may have been the translation of P. A. Tissat, *Lee douze livres du Code de l'empereur Justinien* (4 vols., Metz, 1807–1810), but was more probably Robert Joseph Pothier's famous *Pandectae Justinianae in novum ordinem* (5 vols., Paris, 1818–1825), a scientific arrangement of Roman law, the first edition (1748–1752), which was the chief source used by the compilers of the Code of Napoleon.

56. "Autobiography," in Hallum, *History of Arkansas*, 1: 219. The works here referred to are undoubtedly A. Duranton's *Cours de droit francois suivant le code civil* (4 ed., 22 vols., Paris, 1844), said to be the first complete treatise on the civil law; M. Dupin's edition of *Oeuvres de Pothier* (11 vols., neuv. ed., Paris, 1835) or M. Bugret's edition of *Oeuvres de Pothier. . .* (11 vols., Paris, 1845–1848); and Victor Marcade's and ―― Pont's *Explication theorique et practique du code civil*, which began to appear "in 1842 and passed through several editions." For these and other citations on the civil law the writer is indebted to George Wilfred Stumberg, *Guide to the Law and Legal Literature of France* (Washington, D.C., 1931), passim.

57. A photostat of the original certificate issued to Pike is in Pike Room, Library of Supreme Council, Washington, D.C.

58. "Autobiography," in Hallum, *History of Arkansas*, 1: 219.

59. The editor of the *Little Rock State Gazette and Democrat*, Mar. 16, 1855, noted that "Capt. Pike has again returned to Little Rock, where he will remain until the April term of the Federal Court; after which he will remove to New Orleans, whither he is going, to locate and practice his profession."

60. Pike to Coyle, Little Rock, Apr. 20, 1855, Pike Papers, Duke University.

61. *New Orleans Daily Picayune*, May 15, 1855, carried the notice and purpose of his arrival. He stopped at the St. Charles Hotel.

62. Pike, *Letter to Choctaw People*, 5, 9; *Cong. Globe*, 33d Cong., 2d Sess., 639.

63. *New Orleans Daily Picayune*, June 28, 1855.

64. *Little Rock State Gazette and Democrat*, Dec. 14, 1855.

65. ―― to Pike, Grand Lake, July 5, 1858, reverse side of p. 1969, *Maxims of Military Science and Art*, Pike Papers, SCSR; *Little Rock True Democrat*, July 14, 1858, noticed his permanent return to Arkansas.

66. *Little Rock True Democrat,* July 14, 1858; "Autobiography," in Hallum, *History of Arkansas,* 1: 219–20.

67. "Autobiography," in Hallum, *History of Arkansas,* 1: 219–20.

68. Lobingier, *Supreme Council, 33°,* 237; see also Lobingier, "Comparative Lawyer of the Nineteenth Century," *American Bar Association Journal* 13: 205–12, on Pike and civil law.

Chapter XXIII

1. Pike, *Letter to Choctaw People,* 4–5.

2. *Sen. Mis. Doc. No. 31,* 34th Cong., 1st Sess., Serial No. 835, pp. 1–5.

3. Pike, *Letter to Choctaw People,* 4–5; Cochrane to Pike, Washington, D.C., Sept. 14, 1854, in ibid., appendix, 1–5.

4. Choctaw Delegates to Manypenny, Washington City, Apr. 5, 1854, Records of the Office of Indian Affairs, Choctaw, 1854, p. 200, National Archives, Washington, D.C. Cited hereafter as O.I.A. The letters cited in this chapter are on microfilm in the University of Texas Library.

5. Manypenny to McClelland, Office Indian Affairs, Apr. 13, 1854, O.I.A., Choctaw, 1854, C826; McClelland to Manypenny, Department of Interior, Apr. 15, 1854, O.I.A., Choctaw, 1854, I532; Manypenny to Cooper, O.I.A., Apr. 20, 1854, O.I.A., Choctaw, 1854, C826.

6. Cochrane to Pike, Washington, D.C., Sept. 14, 1854, in Pike, *Letter to Choctaw People,* appendix, 1–2; Choctaw Delegation to Cooper, Washington City, May 1, 1854, O.I.A., Choctaw, 1854, C826.

7. Cooper to Manypenny, Washington, D.C., May 25, 1854, O.I.A., Choctaw, 1854, C826.

8. McClelland to Charles E. Mix, Acting Commissioner of Indian Affairs, Washington, D.C., June 20, 1854, O.I.A., Choctaw, 1854, I599; Mix to McClelland, Washington, D.C., July 10, 1854, O.I.A., Choctaw, 1854, I704; Choctaw Delegation to Mix, Washington, D.C., July 11, 1854, O.I.A., Choctaw, 1854, P241; McClelland to Mix, Washington, D.C., Sept. 25, 1854, O.I.A., Choctaw, 1854, I704.

9. Cochrane to Pike, Washington, D.C., Sept. 14, 1854, in Pike, *Letter to Choctaw People,* appendix, 4–5.

10. Pike, *Letter to Choctaw People,* 5–6.

11. Copy of John T. Cochrane, contract as attorney for Choctaw Nation, Feb. 13, 1855, in folder labeled "Choctaw Case," Pike Papers, SCSR; see same in *Sen. Rep. No. 1978,* 49th Cong., 2d Sess., Serial No. 2458, pp. 116–18.

12. Pike, *Letter to Choctaw People,* 5–6, 7–9. John B. Luce of Sebastian County, Ark., who came into the case in Dec. 1855, hired by Cochrane, testified in Jan. 1887, before the Senate Committee on Indian Affairs that "When I first came, when Mr. Cochrane first wrote to me to come here to Washington, General Pike was in New Orleans. He had gone there and was absent, and Mr. Cochrane told me that one of the difficulties he had to contend with was that General Pike was the original contractor, and that he found it absolutely necessary to make a new contract in order to bring in other parties, Luke Lea being the principal one." "Testimony of John B. Luce," in *Sen. Rep. No. 1978,* 49th Cong., 2d Sess., Serial No. 2458, p. 58.

13. McClelland to Manypenny, Washington, D.C., Mar. 28, 1855, O.I.A., Choctaw, 1855, 1927.

14. Cooper to Choctaw Delegation, Washington City, Apr. 9, 1855, in *Sen. Mis. Doc. No. 31,* 34th Cong., 1st Sess., Serial No. 835, pp. 49–50.

15. "Testimony of John B. Lice," in *Sen. Rep. No. 1978*, 49th Cong., 2d Sess., Serial No. 2458, p. 58.

16. For the lengthy correspondence connected with the negotiations, see *Sen. Mis. Doc. No. 31*, 34th Cong., 1st Sess., Serial No. 835, pp. 50–88.

17. 11 *U.S. Stat. at L.* (1855), 611–19; Charles J. Kappler, *Indian Affairs, Laws and Treaties* (4 vols., Washington, D.C., 1904–1929), II, 706–14.

18. *Senate Executive Journal, 1855–1858*, p. 33; Pike, *Letter to the Choctaw People*, 9; Pike's Answer to Bill of Complaint, McPherson vs. Pike, Equity Docket No. 5742, Supreme Court District of Columbia, 1877, Pike Papers, SCSR.

19. *Senate Executive Journal, 1855–1858*, pp. 49, 53.

20. Pike's Answer to Bill of Complaint, McPherson vs. Pike, Equity Docket No. 5742, Supreme Court District of Columbia, 1877, Pike Papers, SCSR; Pike, *Letter to the Choctaw People*, 9.

21. 11 *U.S. Stat. at L.* (1856), 699–701; *Senate Executive Journal, 1855–1858*, pp. 140, 142, 150.

22. *Senate Journal*, 34th Cong., 1st Sess., Serial No. 809, p. 633; *House Journal*, 34th Cong., 1st Sess., Serial No. 838, p. 1518.

23. Cochrane to Pike, Washington, D.C., Oct. 2, 1856, in Pike, *Letter to Choctaw People*, 5–8.

24. Pike, *Letter to Choctaw People*, 11.

25. Cochrane to Pike, Fort Towson, Nov. 18, 1856, in ibid., appendix, 8–9.

26. "Notes Upon the Choctaw Question," in [Albert Pike], *The Choctaw Nation vs. The United States* (Washington, D.C., 1872), 27–45. At the top of page 27 is a note, probably written July 27, 1890, in Pike's hand and signed by him: "Wholly prepared by me, in 1856." A copy of this brief was lent the writer by the late Mrs. Roscoe M. Packard, West Newton, Massachusetts. See also, Pike, *Letter to Choctaw People*, 12, in which he says, in part: "I prepared the 'Notes Upon the Choctaw Question,' showing . . . that you were entitled to the net proceeds of your lands. This was placed in the possession of the committee; but we did not succeed in having any action upon it, in consequence of the shortness of the session."

27. 11 *U.S. Stat. at L.* (1857), 169. For a bitter commentary on the governmental policy which made it necessary for the Indians to employ counsel to collect just claims, and which then, once a claim was to be paid, attempted to force the Indians to defraud their counsel of compensation, see *Essays to Vinnie*, Essay 10, "Of Indian Nature and Wrongs," Pike Papers.

28. *Little Rock State Gazette and Democrat*, Apr. 25, May 9, 1857.

29. Ted R. Worley, "An Early Arkansas Sportsman: C. F. M. Noland," *Arkansas Historical Quarterly* 11 (spring 1952): 25–39.

30. *Little Rock State Gazette and Democrat*, May 23, 1857.

31. *Van Buren Intelligencer*, June 5, 1857.

32. Pike to Albert G. Mackey, Creek Agency West of Arkansas, July 8, 1857, in *Official Bulletin of the Supreme Council of the 33rd Degree for the Southern Jurisdiction of the United States* (10 vols., New York, 1870–1892), VII, 358. Hereafter cited as *Official Bulletin*.

33. *Vocabularies of Indian Languages*, Pike Papers, SCSR. The preface to this manuscript, written by Pike perhaps about 1874 or 1875, when it was submitted to the Smithsonian Institution for publication, is the source for the origin of these vocabularies.

34. Ibid.

35. Dr. J. H. McCormick, "General Pike—the Linguist," *New Age Magazine* 12 (Mar. 1910): 260–61.

36. John R. Swanton, *Social Organization and Social Usages of the Indians of the Creek Confederacy* (Forty-Second Annual Report of the Bureau of American Ethnology, 1924–1925; Washington, D.C., 1928), 91, 92; James Constantine Pilling, *Bibliography of the Muskhogean Languages* (American Bureau of Ethnology, *Bulletin* [No. 9]; Washington, D.C., 1889), 63, 69–70.

37. Autograph note, by Albert Pike, Jan. 12, 1887, bound in fly leaf of *Vocabularies of Indian Languages*, Pike Papers, SCSR; Pike to John Hammond Trumbull, Washington, D.C., Mar. 31, 1880, Albert Pike Papers, Duke University Library. Apparently one of the tables prepared by Pike in 1861, a four-page manuscript of Muscogee and other Indian place names, and containing other information, was not returned to Pike, for it was still in the library of the Bureau of Ethnology in 1889. See Pilling, *Bibliography of the Muskhogean Languages*, 63.

38. Pike to Mackey, Creek Agency, 8th July, 1857, *Official Bulletin*, VII, 358.

39. Pike, *Letter to Choctaw People*, 12–13.

40. *Essays to Vinnie*, Essay 10, "Of Indian Nature and Wrongs," Pike Papers.

41. Testimony of Albert Pike, *Sen. Rep. No. 1978*, 49th Cong., 2d Sess., Serial No. 2458, p. 34: "Q. How much did you get in that [Creek] case?—A. I think we got $120,000. I got a million dollars for them. . . . But they came to me after I went out to the Indian country in the summer of 1857 and proposed to me to take less than the amount we were entitled to, on the ground that they had not got as much as they expected, and I voluntarily agreed to take $40,000 less. I took $120,000. . . ." The editors of the *New York City Home Journal*, Nov. 8, 1856, referred to Pike as having "recently gained a suit at law for which he gets the comfortable fee of one hundred and sixty thousand dollars." They may have had reference to the Creek case. In a letter in 1859 Pike said that "after working five years for the Creek Indians, they cheated me out of $20,000," and that at the session of 1857–1858 Congress had failed to appropriate $200,000 due the Creeks under the treaty of 1856 "out of which they owe me a large fee." (Pike to T. V. J. W. Johnson, Washington, D.C., Jan. 28, 1859, Pike Papers, SCSR.) Another inexplicable piece of evidence is the fact that Cochrane wrote Pike on Nov. 18, 1856, that he had "learned from a Choctaw residing near Tuckabatche, where the Creeks hold their council, that they have [sic] voted your fee on $800,000, viz, $200,000." (Cochrane to Pike, Fort Towson, Nov. 18, 1856, in Pike, *Letter to Choctaw People*, appendix, 9.) Unless the letter, the original of which cannot be located, is misdated, and assuming the rumor to be true, the Creeks had approved Pike's fee before Congress appropriated the treaty money. The compromise which Pike described in 1887, when his memory was very bad, may well have been based upon a fee of $200,000, or 25 percent of $800,000, rather than upon $160,000 as Pike implied.

42. *Essays to Vinnie*, Essay 10, "Of Indian Nature and Wrongs," Pike Papers; Pike, *Letter to Choctaw People*, 13, 15–16.

43. Testimony of Albert Pike, *Sen. Rep. No. 1978*, 49th Cong., 2d Sess., Serial No. 2458, p. 34; Cochrane to Pike, Washington, D.C., May 13, 1859, in Pike, *Letter to Choctaw People*, appendix, 8–9, 11–12. Pike's answer to Bill of Complaint, McPherson vs. Pike, Equity Docket No. 5742, Supreme Court District of Columbia, 1877, Pike Papers, SCSR; *Essays to Vinnie*, Essay 10, "Of Indian Nature and Wrongs," Pike Papers; Pike to Edward Hanrick, Little Rock, Apr. 17, 1859, and Cochrane to Hanrick, Washington, D.C., Aug. 25, 1859, Hanrick Papers.

44. *Little Rock State Gazette and Democrat*, Sept. 26, 1857.

45. Pike, *Letter to Choctaw People*, 13; Cochrane to Pike, Washington, D.C., Jan. 18, 1858, in ibid., appendix, 9–11; Cochrane to Hanrick, Washington, D.C., Feb. 3, 1858, Hanrick Papers.

46. Cochrane to Hanrick, Washington, D.C., Feb. 3, 1858, Hanrick Papers.

47. Ibid.

48. Pike, *Letter to Choctaw People*, 13.

49. *Little Rock True Democrat*, July 14, 1858.

50. Ibid.

51. Ibid., May 18, 1858; family notes lent the writer by the late Mrs. Roscoe M. Packard, West Newton, Mass. Among the Pike books in the Library of the Supreme Council is a copy of *Nugae* which Pike had inscribed, Little Rock, Mar. 10, 1855, to Albert Holden, to be given him when he was of age.

52. Pike to Mackey, Little Rock, Sept. 20, 1858, *Official Bulletin*, VII, 362; *Van Buren Intelligencer*, Oct. 1, 1858; Pike, *Letter to Choctaw People*, 13.

53. *Essays to Vinnie*, Essay 10, "Of Indian Nature and Wrongs," Pike Papers.

54. Ibid.

55. "Col. Albert Pike.—This gentleman has been announced dead again by one of the Mobile papers, and the usual honors to the departed duly attended to. This is the third attempt during the year 1858, to 'kill him off.' At last accounts Col. Pike was in the enjoyment of reasonable health, and about to engage in a Buffalo hunt, in the wild region west of Fort Smith. . . ." *Des Arc (Ark.) Citizen*, Dec. 25, 1858. The rank of "colonel" was an editorial gratuity.

56. Ibid., Jan. 9, 1859, stated: "Capt. Pike not dead. He ate a hearty breakfast at Gayoso House, Memphis, on Christmas a.m. and he expects to eat many more Christmas breakfasts." Pike was then on his way to Washington.

57. Ibid.; Pike to Mackey, Washington, D.C., Dec. 31, 1858, *Official Bulletin*, VII, 362.

58. *Essays to Vinnie*, Essay 24, "Of Pleasant and Sad Remembrances," Pike Papers.

59. Ibid.

60. *Dictionary of American Biography*, XII, 96–97.

61. Quoted in *The Life Wake of the Fine Arkansas Gentleman Who Died before His Time* (Washington, D.C., 1859), 39–54.

62. Ibid., 51–53.

63. Testimony of John F. Coyle, in *Yvon Pike et al vs. The Choctaw Nation*, G. J. C. No. 19384 (1895), CCRNA. Coyle said Pike kept this house from 1854–1855 until 1861; no number is given.

64. *Philadelphia Press*, Jan. 22, 1859, quoted in *Life Wake of the Fine Arkansas Gentleman*, 53.

65. *Dictionary of American Biography*, V, 313–14.

66. *Life Wake of the Fine Arkansas Gentleman*, 7–12; *Essays to Vinnie*, Essay 24, "Of Pleasant and Sad Remembrances," Pike Papers.

67. *Life Wake of the Fine Arkansas Gentleman*, 12–16.

68. *Dictionary of American Biography*, XVI, 388–89.

69. Charles W. Boteler, Walter Lenox, Jack Savage, William M. Burwell, A. S. H. White, George S. Gideon, Phillip Barton Key, Jonah D. Hoover, James D. McGuire, R. Shelton MacKenzie, Alexander Dimitry, N. Beverly Tucker, George French, Ben. Perley Poore, Hugh Caperton, Arnold Harris, Robert W. Johnson, "the very bravest of the brave, the truest of the true; impulsive, generous, fearless, frank, the Senate Paladin, Who never did ungenerous act a victory to win," are listed in the poem.

70. *Life Wake of the Fine Arkansas Gentleman*, 16–31.

71. "Editor's Table," *Knickerbocker* 53 (Apr. 1859): 429–31.

72. Ben. Perley Poore, *Reminiscences of Sixty Years in the National Metropolis*, I, 542.

73. Pike, *Letter to Choctaw People*, 13–15.

74. Ibid., 14; in "Testimony of John B. Luce," *Sen. Rep. No. 1978*, 49th Cong., 2d Sess., Serial No. 2458, p. 58, Luce states that he actually "withdrew" from the case in "the summer of 1858" but that "the case as presented to the Senate was substantially prepared by General Pike and myself." In "Pike's Answer to Bill of Complaint," McPherson vs. Pike, Equity Docket No. 5742, Supreme Court District of Columbia, 1877, Pike Papers, SCSR, Pike declared that Luce supplied the facts with which he won the case in the Senate Committee on Indian Affairs.

75. Pike, *Letter to Choctaw People*, 14; "Memorandums of Particulars in which the Choctaw Nation and Individuals are entitled to relief and compensation in case they are not paid the net proceeds of their lands, ceded by the Treaty of September 27, 1830," in [Pike], *The Choctaw Nation vs. The United States* (1872), pp. 46–105. At top of p. 46 of this brief is a note, undated but written probably on July 17, 1890, in Pike's hand and signed by him: "Prepared by me, with the aid of data obtained by John B. Luce from the Indian and General Land Offices."

76. Pike, *Letter to Choctaw People*, 14; *Senate Journal*, 35th Cong., 2d Sess., Serial No. 973, pp. 319, 493; *Sen. Rep. No. 374*, 35th Cong., 2d Sess., Serial No. 994; *Cong. Globe*, 35th Cong., 2d Sess., 1691.

77. Pike to Mackey, Washington, D.C., Feb. 8, 1859, *Official Bulletin*, VII, 366.

78. *Little Rock State Gazette and Democrat*, Apr. 14, 23, 1859; Pike to Hanrick, Little Rock, Apr. 17, 1859, Hanrick Papers, says in part: "I left Rector in Washington. He reached here yesterday, with the Creek money. I will leave here in two weeks from yesterday, for Fort Smith. It will be just about one month from this, when the money is paid; and that is as near as I can guess at it." Rector had recently secured the removal of Billy Bowlegs' band of seminoles from Florida to Indian Territory. Annie Heloise Abel, *The Slaveholding Indians* (3 vols., Cleveland, 1915–1925), I, 20, n.7. The $200,000, reserved until Bowlegs' removal, had been appropriated Mar. 3, 1859, and was now to be paid over by Rector. 11 *U.S. State at L.* (1859), 409.

79. *Little Rock True Democrat*, June 8, 1859, citing *Fort Smith Times*, n.d.; Abel, *Slaveholding Indians*, I, 52–56, and nn.

80. *Little Rock True Democrat*, July 13, 1859, citing *Fort Smith Times*, n.d.

81. *Little Rock True Democrat*, July 27, 1859, citing *Fort Smith Herald*, n.d.; *Van Buren Press*, July 13, 20, Aug. 10, 31, 1859; Cochrane to Hanrick, Washington, D.C., Aug. 25, 1859, Hanrick Papers. At his trial in Dec. 1859, Hurst was sentenced to three years in the penitentiary for manslaughter. *Van Buren Press*, Dec. 2, 9, 1859.

82. *Little Rock State Gazette and Democrat*, Aug. 27, 1859.

83. Pike, *Letter to Choctaw People*, 16.

84. *Senate Journal*, 36th Congress, 1st Sess., Serial No. 1022, p. 437; *House Journal*, 36th Cong., 1st Sess., Serial No. 1042, p. 819.

85. *H.R. Ex. Doc. No. 82*, 36th Cong., 1st Sess., Serial No. 1056.

86. Pike, *Letter to Choctaw People*, 16.

87. *Senate Journal*, 36th Cong., 1st Sess., Serial No. 1022, pp. 652, 697.

88. *Cong. Globe*, 36th Cong., 1st Sess., 2935–36.

89. For an excellent discussion of Toombs's views on and opposition in the fifties to nearly all claims against the United States, see Ulrich Bonnell Phillips, *The Life of Robert Toombs* (New York, 1913), 130–54.

90. In *Letter to Choctaw People*, 14–15, Pike in 1872 remembered himself as having "discussed the case fully ... with Senator Toombs of Georgia, and convinced him of its justice and induced him to support it"—a statement that resulted from faulty memory.

91. *Cong. Globe*, 36th Cong., 1st Sess., 2935–37.

92. Ibid., 2959–63. George E. Pugh of Ohio, Albert G. Brown of Mississippi, and James F. Simmons of Rhode Island spoke in favor of the measure.

93. Ibid., 2963.

94. Ibid. Of the members of the Indian committee only Graham N. Fitch voted against the measure, and he said he had not been present when the matter was heard in committee. Ibid., 2962. A notable vote in favor of the amendment was that of Benjamin Fitzpatrick of Alabama, who in 1854 had strongly opposed the Creek bill. His different attitude toward the Choctaw measure may reflect the work of Hanrick. Cochrane to Hanrick, Washington, D.C., Feb. 3, 1858, and Nov. 18, 1859, Hanrick Papers, offer evidence of Hanrick's influence with the Alabama delegation in Congress.

95. *Senate Journal*, 36th Cong., 1st Sess., Serial No. 1022, p. 697; *Sen. Rep. Com. No. 283*, 36th Cong., 1st Sess., Serial No. 1040.

96. Pike, *Letter to Choctaw People*, 16; see also P. P. Pitchlynn to Hon. C. P. Shanks, Washington, D.C., Feb. 5, 1872, written by Pike for Pitchlynn in opposition to the committee deductions, in [Pike], *The Choctaw Nation vs. The United States* (1872), 203–5.

97. Abel, *Slaveholding Indians*, I, 57–58, and footnote.

98. "Memorandum in regard to the amount found due the Choctaws under the award of the Senate, made Mar. 9, 1859, pursuant to the eleventh article of the treaty of 1855 with the Choctaws and Chickasaws," signed by P. P. Pitchlynn, Choctaw Delegate, Washington City, Dec. 28, 1860, in *Cong. Globe*, 36th Cong., 2d Sess., 1290, and in [Pike], *The Choctaw Nation vs. The United States* (1872), 197–201. Cochrane probably wrote this for Pitchlynn. See also the memorial of Peter Folsom, President of the Choctaw Senate, and William Roebuck, Speaker of the Choctaw House, *Sen. Mis. Doc. No. 9*, 36th Cong., 2d Sess., Serial No. 1098; *Senate Journal*, 36th Cong., 2d Sess., Serial No. 1077, pp. 78, 94; Pitchlynn to Acting Commissioner of Indian Affairs Mix, Washington, D.C., Sept. 12, 1860, in Washington, D.C., *National Intelligencer*, Sept. 21, 1860. For influencing friends in Congress and for printing and writing on behalf of the Choctaw claim, John F. Coyle of the *National Intelligencer*, engaged by Pike for that purpose, was to receive some $2,500. Testimony of John F. Coyle, in *Yvon Pike et al. vs. The Choctaw Nation*, G. J. C. No. 19384 (1895), CCRNA; Pike to Coyle, [Washington], Mar. 20, 1861, Pike Papers, Duke University.

99. *Cong. Globe*, 36th Cong., 2d Sess., 704.

100. Ibid., 704–8.

101. Ibid., 824–830; *Senate Journal*, 36th Cong., 2d Sess., Serial No. 1077, pp. 207–8.

102. *House Journal*, 36th Cong., 2d Sess., Serial No. 1091, p. 314, 352, 369.

103. Ibid., 369, 436, 357, 475, 476, 482; *Senate Journal*, 36th Cong., 2d Sess., Serial No. 1077, pp. 344, 361, 369; *Cong. Globe*, 36th Cong., 2d Sess., 1155–57, 1287–91, 1336, 1340, 1341, 1357, 1414, 1427–29; 12 *U.S. State at L.* (1861), 221–39.

104. In Cochrane to C. B. Johnson, Esq., Washington, D.C., Apr. 19, 1861, Charles B. Johnson Papers, Edward E. Ayer Collection, Newberry Library, Chicago, Illinois (Ramsdell Microfilms, University of Texas, Roll 372B), Cochrane states Pike left Washington, D.C. on Mar. 26. On Apr. 1 Pike was at New Orleans for the opening of the session of the Supreme Council. *Transactions of the Supreme Council of the 33d Degree, Ancient and Accepted Scottish Rite of Free-Masonry, for the*

Southern Jurisdiction of the United States of America (Reprinted, Washington, D.C., 1878), 193, hereafter cited as Supreme Council *Transactions, 1857–1866* (Reprint); *New Orleans Daily Picayune,* Apr. 2, 3, 4, 1861.

105. Breckinridge was a member of the Supreme Council of the Scottish Rite of Freemasonry, Southern Jurisdiction, of which Pike was Grand Commander in 1861. Lobingier, *Supreme Council,* 274–75. Supreme Council *Transactions, 1857–1866* (Reprint), 82–83, 125, 153.

106. Pike, *Letter to Choctaw People,* 16–17. Senate members of the first committee were Daniel Clark, James A. Pearce of Maryland, and Lazarus W. Powell of Kentucky; those of the second were James R. Doolittle of Wisconsin, A. O. P. Nicholson of Tennessee, and George E. Pugh of Ohio. *Senate Journal,* 36th Cong., 2d Sess., Serial No. 1077, pp. 344, 361. For proof that the last named Senators forced the House members to agree to the compromise appropriation, see statement of Howard in *Cong. Globe,* 36th Cong., 2d Sess., 1427–29.

107. Pike, *Letter to Choctaw People,* 17; Pike's Answer to Bill of Complaint, McPherson vs. Pike, Equity Docket No. 5742, Supreme Court District of Columbia, 1877, Pike Papers, SCSR. See also, printed affidavit of P. P. Pitchlynn, Choctaw Delegate, executed in 1872, in which he says in part that "it was wholly owing" to Pike "that the appropriation of $250,000 in money and $250,000 in bonds was obtained in March, 1861." *Sen. Rep. No. 1978,* 49th Cong., 2d Sess., Serial No. 2458, p. 65.

108. Second Auditor of the Treasury, E. B. French to Secretary of the Treasury, Washington, D.C., Jan. 13, 1871, O.I.A., Choctaw, 1871, C1078; Pike to Coyle, [Washington], Mar. 20, 1861, Pike Papers, Duke University; Cochrane to C. B. Johnson, Washington, D.C., Apr. 19, 1861, Johnson Papers; Cochrane to Hanrick, Apr. 8, 27, 1861, Hanrick Papers.

109. Cochrane to Hanrick, Washington, D.C., Apr. 27, 1861, Hanrick Papers; *H.R. Rep. No. 98,* 42nd Cong., 3d Sess., Serial No. 1578, pp. 61–70; *Sen. Rep. No. 1978,* 49th Cong., 2d Sess., Serial No. 2458, p. 35.

Chapter XXIV

1. *Little Rock Whig,* Aug. 14, 1851; *Little Rock State Gazette* and *Democrat,* Aug. 31, 1855. Pike stated in 1855 that the Arkansas Whigs "read me out" of their party "because I did not choose to give my countenance to charges against a political opponent, that I thought unjust." [Albert Pike], *Address by the President of the State Council of Arkansas; Delivered at the First Annual Session, on the 30th April, 1855* (Little Rock, 1855), 7. Allen, *Arkansas Imprints,* 78, attributes this address to Andrew J. Hutt, first president of the State Council, but internal evidence proves that it was by Pike, president of the provisional council. See especially p. 14. Pope, *Early Days in Arkansas,* 303–4, gives additional evidence of Pike's authorship.

2. P.[ike] to Butler, Washington, D.C., Feb. 3, 1853, in *Little Rock Whig,* Feb. 24, 1853.

3. Ibid. Pike agreed with the sentiments expressed by Robert Toombs, Georgia Whig. Cf., Toombs to John J. Crittenden, Roanoke Plantation, Stewart County, Georgia, Dec. 15, 1852, in Ulrich Bonnell Phillips, ed., *The Correspondence of Robert Toombs, Alexander H. Stephens, and Howell Cobb,* American Historical Association *Annual Report,* 1911, II (Washington, D.C., 1913), 322.

4. Dix did not accept a place in the cabinet; Davis became secretary of war.

5. P.[ike] to Butler, Washington, D.C., Feb. 3, 1853, in *Little Rock Whig,* Feb. 24, 1853.

6. A full-scale review of the Kansas-Nebraska matter may be had in Allan Nevins, *Ordeal of the Union* (2 vols., New York, 1948), II, 78–159, 301–46.

7. P.[ike] to Butler, Washington, D.C., Feb. 3, 1853, in *Little Rock Whig*, Feb. 24, 1853; *Little Rock State Gazette and Democrat*, Aug. 31, 1855.

8. *Memphis Daily Appeal*, Feb. 26, 1868.

9. P.[ike] to Butler, New York, Feb. 5, 1852, in *Little Rock Whig*, Feb. 26, 1852; *Little Rock State Gazette and Democrat*, Aug. 24, 1855; [Pike], *Address by the President of the State Council of Arkansas . . . 1855*, 10–11; *Journal of the Charleston Convention*, 66–67.

10. *Little Rock State Gazette and Democrat*, Aug. 24, 1855.

11. James Ford Rhodes, *History of the United States from the Compromise of 1850* (7 vols., New York, 1893–1906), II, 87–88; W. Darrell Overdyke, *The Know-Nothing Party in the South* (Baton Rouge, La., 1950), 36, 56.

12. *New Orleans Daily Delta*, July 12, 1855; *Little Rock True Democrat*, Aug. 14, 1855, quoting *Washington (D.C.) Union*, n.d.; *Memphis Daily Appeal*, Feb. 26, 1868.

13. M. W. Cluskey, *Political Text-Book or Encyclopedia* (Washington, D.C., 1857), 47–58, contains a copy of the ritual and plan of organization of the party.

14. In the course of a speech at New Orleans, July 12, 1855, Pike related how he had organized the order in Arkansas. *New Orleans Daily Delta*, July 12, 1855.

15. *Ark. State Gazette and Democrat*, Aug. 24, 1855; Pope, *Early Days in Arkansas*, 304, remembered incorrectly that "The 'Knownothing' party captured the Legislature in 1854."

16. Overdyke, *Know-Nothing Party in the South*, 72.

17. Richard H. Johnson, editor of the *Little Rock True Democrat*, had bitterly denounced, Mar. 14, 1855, the party both nationally and locally as an abolitionist scheme, and attempted unsuccessfully to draw the editor of the *Little Rock Whig* into a dispute by accusing him of defending the election of Henry Wilson, Massachusetts Abolitionist, to the U.S. Senate by Know Nothings in that state. The editor of the *Whig* refused, however, to be entrapped by such arguments and flatly denied Johnson's accusations, indicating that he was not a member of the order in Arkansas. But neither editor seems to have been aware that the Know Nothings had organized the Arkansas State Council under their very noses. Ibid., Mar. 21, 28, Apr. 17, 24, May 1, 8, 1855.

18. [Pike], *Address by the President of the State Council of Arkansas . . . 1855* (Little Rock, 1855), 3–4.

19. Ibid., 4–12.

20. Ibid., 14.

21. Ibid.

22. *New York Daily Times*, June 8, 1855; *New York Tribune*, June 7, 1855.

23. James K. Greer, *Louisiana Politics, 1845–1861* (Baton Rouge, La., 1930), 126, 129–30.

24. *Little Rock True Democrat*, July 24, 1855, quoting *New Orleans Daily Picayune*, n.d.

25. Greer, *Louisiana Politics*, 129–30; Overdyke, *Know-Nothing Party in the South*, 128, states that the five Protestant members of the delegation took seats on June 10, but fails to cite his authority.

26. *New York Daily Times*, June 9, 1855, reported this speech in full. See also ibid., June 8; *New York Daily Tribune*, June 8, 1855; *New York Weekly Herald*, June 9, 1855.

27. *New York Daily Tribune*, June 9, 1855.

28. Overdyke, *Know-Nothing Party in the South*, 128.

29. *Little Rock State Gazette and Democrat*, Aug. 24, 1855.

30. Ibid.

31. Ibid.

32. Overdyke, *Know-Nothing Party in the South*, 131.

33. *New York Daily Tribune*, June 13, 15, 1855, Feb. 18, 1856.

34. *New York Daily Times*, June 15, 16, 1855; *Little Rock State Gazette and Democrat*, June 24, 1855.

35. *New York Daily Times*, June 15, 1855.

36. *Little Rock State Gazette and Democrat*, Aug. 24, 1855.

37. Ibid.

38. Ibid.

39. Elias Nason and Thomas Russell, *Henry Wilson* (Philadelphia, 1876), 121.

40. *New York Daily Tribune*, June 15, 1855; Overdyke, *Know-Nothing Party in the South*, 132–33.

41. Ibid., June 19, 20, 1855; *New York Weekly Herald*, June 23, 1855; *New Orleans Daily Picayune*, July 12, 1855.

42. *New York Weekly Herald*, June 23, 1855; *Little Rock True Democrat*, July 17, 1855.

43. *New Orleans Daily Picayune*, July 10, 1855.

44. Ibid., June 28, 1855.

45. *New Orleans Daily Delta*, July 10, 1855.

46. Ibid., July 12, 1855. The Louisiana platform accepted the National platform but submitted a reservation in opposition to the "proscription clauses against the professors of the Roman Catholic faith." Greer, *Louisiana Politics*, 130.

47. *Little Rock True Democrat*, Mar. 1, July 24, Aug. 21, 1855.

48. Ibid., Aug. 7, Sept. 4, Oct. 23, 1855.

49. Ibid., Aug. 14, Sept. 4, 11, Oct. 23, 1855; *Little Rock State Gazette and Democrat*, Aug. 31, 1855.

50. *Little Rock State Gazette and Democrat*, June 15, 1855; *Little Rock True Democrat*, Apr. 17, 1855.

51. *Little Rock State Gazette and Democrat*, Aug. 31, 1855.

52. Ibid., Aug. 24, 31, Sept. 7, 14, 21, 1855.

53. Ibid., Nov. 2, 1855; *Little Rock True Democrat*, Nov. 6, 1855.

54. *Little Rock True Democrat*, Oct. 2, 9, 23, Nov. 6, 1855. These letters were reprinted in pamphlet form and circulated as a campaign document under the pseudonym Peter Farrell, *Letters Addressed to the Unprejudiced People of Arkansas, or Captain Pike's Misrepresentations of Catholic Principles, and Apology for the Proscription of Catholics and Foreigners* [Little Rock, 1855]. See *Publications of the Arkansas Historical Association*, II, 439–40, for proof that "Petricula" and "Peter Farrell" were Bishop Byrne.

55. Overdyke, *Know-Nothing Party in the South*, 216–17.

56. *Little Rock True Democrat*, Apr. 1, 1856.

57. *New York Daily Tribune*, Feb. 18, 1856.

58. *Philadelphia North American* and *United States Gazette*, Feb. 18, 1856.

59. *New York Daily Tribune*, Feb. 19–22, 1855.

60. Ibid., Feb. 21, 1855; *Little Rock True Democrat*, Apr. 1, 1856.

61. *New York Daily Tribune*, Feb. 23, 25; *Philadelphia North American* and *United States Gazette*, Feb. 26, 1856.

62. *Little Rock True Democrat*, Apr. 1, 1856; *New York Herald*, Feb. 24, 1856.

63. Ibid., A copy of the pamphlet is in Library of the Supreme Council of the Scottish Rite, Washington, D.C., and it is on microfilm in the University of Texas Library.

64. *Little Rock True Democrat*, Apr. 8, 1856. A copy of the pamphlet is in the Library of the Supreme Council of the Scottish Rite, Washington, D.C., and it is on microfilm in the University of Texas Library.

65. *Little Rock State Gazette and Democrat*, Apr. 12, 19, 1856.

66. Ibid., Apr. 26, May 3, 1856.

67. Pike, *To the American Party South*.

68. Albert Pike to the Editors of the *Memphis Appeal*, Helena, Ark., Oct. 17, 1856, in *Little Rock True Democrat*, Nov. 4, 1856, quoting *Memphis Appeal*, Nov. 3, 1856.

Chapter XXV

1. By A.[lbert] P.[ike], [Washington, D.C., 1856].

2. A.[lbert] P.[ike], *Letters to the People of the Northern States*, 1–16.

3. Ibid., 20.

4. Ibid., 18.

5. Ibid., 28–29.

6. Ibid., 20–23.

7. Ibid., 23.

8. Ibid., 31.

9. Ibid., 31–32.

10. Ibid., 35.

11. *Proceedings of the Convention at Savannah* [Savannah, 1856?], 30–31.

12. Ibid., 31–32.

13. "Autobiography," in Hallum, *History of Arkansas*, 1: 220–21.

14. *Proceedings of the Convention at Savannah*, 39–40.

15. [Albert Pike], *Kansas State Rights, an Appeal to the Democracy of the South, By a Southern State-Rights Democrat* (Washington, D.C., 1857), 21–35.

16. [Albert Pike], *Thoughts on Certain Political Questions, by a Looker-On* (Washington, D.C., 1859), 65–67.

17. Ibid., 67–68.

18. Ibid., 103.

19. Pike to Messrs. Read Fletcher, J. C. Murray, R. W. Millsap, and others [Pine Bluff Committee], Little Rock, July 31, 1860, in *Little Rock True Democrat*, Aug. 18, 1860. Hereafter cited as "Pine Bluff Letter." Same in *Fort Smith (Ark.) Times*, Aug. 30, 1860.

20. *Little Rock True Democrat*, Aug. 18, 1860.

21. *Fort Smith Times*, Aug. 16, 23, 30, 1860.

22. *Washington Telegraph*, Aug. 29, 1860, quoted in *Little Rock True Democrat*, Sept. 8, 1860.

23. *Little Rock True Democrat*, Sept. 8, 1860.

24. Pike, "Pine Bluff Letter," in ibid., Aug. 18, 1860.

25. [Pike], *Thoughts on Certain Political Questions*, 18–19.

26. Pike, "Pine Bluff Letter," in *Little Rock True Democrat*, Aug. 18, 1860.

27. *Inaugural Address of Henry M. Rector, Delivered before the General Assembly of Arkansas, 15th November, 1860* (n.p., n.d.); Arkansas *House Journal*, 1860–1861, pp. 103–5; *Little Rock State Gazette*, Nov. 24, 1860; *Little Rock Old Line Democrat*, Nov. 22, 1860.

28. Arkansas *House Journal*, 1860–1861, pp. 290–96.

29. Ibid., 300–305; *Special Message of the Governor on Federal Relations, 1860* (n.p., n.d.), 7 p.

30. Arkansas *House Journal*, 1860–1861, pp. 407–10.

31. Arkansas *Senate Journal*, 1860–1861, pp. 373, 392–292.

32. Arkansas *House Journal*, 1860–1861, p. 427; *Little Rock State Gazette*, Dec. 29, 1860; *Little Rock True Democrat*, Dec. 29, 1860.

33. *Little Rock State Gazette*, Dec. 29, 1860; *Little Rock True Democrat*, Dec. 29, 1860; *Van Buren Press*, Jan. 4, 1861.

34. *Little Rock State Gazette*, Jan. 5, 12, 19, 1861.

35. Arkansas *Senate Journal*, 1860–1861, pp. 215, 240, 290, 292, 324–25, 328–29, 336–38, 340, 365, 379, 385–86, 392–93, 419–20, 422, 425–26, 431–32, 433–35.

36. Ibid., 469–70, 479–88, 504, 513, 521, 522, 528, 530–31, 540–41, 549.

37. Albert Pike, *State or Province? Bond or Free? Addressed Particularly to the People of Arkansas* (n.p., 1861). Internal evidence shows that Pike wrote sometime between Jan. 26 and Feb. 1, the date of Texas' secession, of which he had not heard. He was in Washington as early as Feb. 7 and probably before that. Ibid., 30; *The War of the Rebellion: A Compilation of the Official Records of the Union and Confederate Armies* (70 vols. in 128, Washington, D.C., 1880–1901), ser. 1, vol. I, 682 (hereafter cited as *Official Records*). The editor of the *Des Arc Constitutional Union*, Mar. 1, 1861, in reviewing the work declared that it had resulted from Pike's "observation at the Federal capital."

38. Pike, *State or Province?*, 28–41.

39. *Official Records*, ser. 1, vol. I, 681–82, vol. LIII, 617; *Little Rock State Gazette*, Feb. 9, 16, 1861.

40. David Hubbard to Andrew B. Moore, governor of Alabama, Kinloch, Alabama, Jan. 3, 1861, William R. Smith, *History and Debates of the Convention of the People of Alabama, January 7, 1861* (Montgomery, 1861), 35; *Little Rock State Gazette*, Mar. 9, 1861.

41. Rector to Ross, Little Rock, Jan. 29, 1861, *Official Records*, ser. 1, vol. I, 683–84, XIII, 490–91; Ross to Rector, Tahlequah, Cherokee Nation, Feb. 22, 1861, ibid., XIII, 491–92.

42. Jack B. Scruggs, "Arkansas in the Secession Crisis," *Arkansas Historical Quarterly* (autumn 1953): 207; *Little Rock State Gazette*, Feb. 2, 16, 1861.

43. *Journal of Both Sessions of the Convention of the State of Arkansas* (Little Rock, 1861), 90–91.

44. Albert Pike, *State or Province? Bond or Free?*, Appendix (n.p., 1861). On his way home from Washington, D.C., Pike stopped for a Masonic meeting in New Orleans and there handed out a few copies of the original forty-page edition of the pamphlet. From this fact it may be inferred that he did not write the appendix until his return to Little Rock. *New Orleans Daily Crescent*, Apr. 8, 1861; *New Orleans Daily Picayune*, Apr. 7, 1861. Allen, *Arkansas Imprints, 1819–1876*, p. 111, gives

Little Rock as the place of imprint. The copy in the Library of the Supreme Council is bound with a copy of the original edition under a single cover.

45. S. R. Cockrell to L. P. Walker, Nashville, Tenn., Apr. 21, 1861, *Official Records*, ser. 1, vol. I, 686.

46. *Journal of the Convention*, 113–14, 121–24.

47. [Albert Pike], *Draught of a Declaration of Independence, Proposed to the Convention of the State of Arkansas, and Withdrawn from Its Consideration* (Little Rock, 1861).

48. *Journal of the Convention*, 184–87.

Chapter XXVI

1. Federal troops evacuated Fort Smith, Apr. 23; Fort Washita, Apr. 17; Fort Arbuckle, May 5; and Fort Cobb, about May 5. *Official Records*, ser. I, vol. I, 648–53.

2. Pike to Johnson, Little Rock, May 11, 1861, *Official Records*, ser. I, vol. III, 572–74; in this letter Pike says he had written Toombs to the same effect, but the Toombs letter has not been found.

3. Ibid.; Pearce to President Davis, Little Rock, May 13, 1861, ibid., 576.

4. James M. Mathews, ed., *The Statutes at Large of the Provisional Government of the Confederate States of America 1861 . . . 1862, Inclusive* (Richmond, Va., 1864), 68; Walker to Davis, Richmond, Apr. 27, 1861, *Official Records*, ser. IV, vol. I, 248; *Journal of the Congress of the Confederate States of America, 1861–1865* (7 vols., Washington, D.C., 1904), I, 211; Pike to Toombs, Little Rock, May 20, 1861, *Official Records*, ser. I, vol. III, 580–81; Pike to D. N. Cooley, Memphis, Tennessee, Feb. 1866, in Abel, *Slaveholding Indians*, I, 135.

5. Pike to Johnson, Little Rock, May 20, 1861, *Official Records*, ser. I, vol. III, 573.

6. Pike to Toombs, Little Rock, May 20, 1861, ibid., 580–81.

7. S. Cooper, Adj. & Insp. Gen., to McCulloch, Montgomery, Ala., May 13, 1861, ibid., 575–76.

8. Abel, *Slaveholding Indians*, I, 128 and footnote.

9. Walker to Hubbard, Montgomery, Ala., May 14, 1861, *Official Records*, ser. I, vol. III, 576–78.

10. Engrossed bill, passed May 17, 1861, in Records of the Confederate Congress, War Department Collection of Confederate Records, National Archives, Washington, D.C. A microfilm copy of this bill is in the University of Texas Library. Only the last three sections of the act have been printed. *Journal of the Confederate Congress*, I, 244, 263. (Unfortunately the original engrossed bill apparently was stolen from the National Archives after 1953 when I copied it.)

11. Pike to Johnson, Little Rock, May 11, 1861, *Official Records*, ser. I, vol. I, 573–74.

12. *Little Rock State Gazette*, May 25, 1861; *Van Buren Press*, June 5, 1861.

13. Pike to Toombs, Little Rock, May 20, 1861, *Official Records*, ser. I, vol. III, 580–81.

14. *Journal of the Convention*, 294; Pike to Toombs, Fort Smith, May 29, 1861, *Official Records*, ser. IV, vol. I, 361; ibid., ser. I, vol. LIII, 688.

15. *Journal of the Convention*, 225, 297, 298, 299; McCulloch to Walker, Little Rock, May 23, 1861, *Official Records*, ser. I, vol. III, 583; *Van Buren Press*, May 29, 1861.

16. *Little Rock State Gazette*, May 25, 1861; McCulloch to Walker, Fort Smith, May 28, 1861, *Official Records*, ser. I, vol. III, 587–88; *Van Buren Press*, May 29, 1861.

17. Pike to Toombs, Fort Smith, May 29, 1861, *Official Records*, ser. IV, vol. I, 360–61.

18. Pike to Leeper, Fort Smith, May 26, 1861, O.I.A. CPWA, 1861.

19. Pike to Toombs, Fort Smith, May 29, 1861, *Official Records*, ser. IV, vol. I, 359–61.

20. Ibid., 360–61.

21. Ibid., 359. Ross had declared to Governor Rector to Col. J. R. Kannady, Confederate commander of Fort Smith, and to a petition from the citizens of Boonsborough, Arkansas, that the Cherokees were firmly determined to remain outside in the struggle between the North and South. Ross to Rector, Tahlequah, Cherokee Nation, Feb. 22, 1861, ibid., ser. I, vol. XIII, 491–92; Mark Bean and others to Ross, Boonsborough, Ark., May 9, 1861, ibid., 493–94; Kannady to Ross, Fort Smith, May 15, 1861, and Ross to Kannady, Park Hill, Cherokee Nation, May 17, 1861, and enclosures, John Ross Papers, Phillips Collection, University of Oklahoma, Norman.

22. Pike to Cooley, Memphis, Feb. 17, 1866, quoted in full in Abel, *Slaveholding Indians*, I, 134–40.

23. *Van Buren Press*, June 12, June 18, 1861.

24. McCulloch to Walker, Fort Smith, May 28, June 12, 1861, *Official Records*, ser. I, vol. III, 587, 590–91.

25. Pike to Cooley, Memphis, Feb. 17, 1866, in Abel, *Slaveholding Indians*, I, 135–36; McCulloch to Walker, Fort Smith, June 12, 1861, *Official Records*, ser. I, vol. III, 590–91; McCulloch to Ross, Fort Smith, June 12, 1861, ibid., 591–92.

26. *Van Buren Press*, June 12, 1861.

27. Ibid., June 12, 19, 1861.

28. Pike to Toombs, Fort Smith, May 29, 1861, *Official Records*, ser. IV, vol. I, 360.

29. *Essays to Vinnie*, Essay 10, "Of Indian Nature and Wrongs," Pike Papers; Abel, *Slaveholding Indians*, I, 193n.

30. Grant Foreman, *A History of Oklahoma* (Norman, Okla., 1942), 103.

31. Pike to Cooley, Memphis, Feb. 17, 1866, in Abel, *Slaveholding Indians*, I, 136.

32. Quesenbury, who was to replace Garrett, had agreed to become Pike's secretary and to allow Garrett to continue as Creek Agent under the Confederacy. Pike to Walker, Seminole Agency, July 31, 1861, *Official Records*, ser. I, vol. III, 623–24; see also Creek Treaty, ibid., ser. IV, vol. I, 439.

33. *Van Buren Press*, June 19, 1861; Gov. Thomas O. Moore of Louisiana to Jefferson Davis, May 31, 1861, *Official Records*, ser. I, vol. XIII, 588. Before the Creek Delegation reached Montgomery the Confederate capital was moved to Richmond, to which place they went to consult Confederate officials.

34. *Van Buren Press*, June 19, 1861.

35. Pike to Cooley, Memphis, Feb. 17, 1866, quoted in Abel, *Slaveholding Indians*, I, 136–37.

36. Lobingier, *Supreme Council*, 216, citing and quoting Pike's official report to President Davis on his negotiations. This report, which was not printed in the *Official Records* but which Lobingier used in the War Department Collection of Confederate Records, National Archives, could not be located in the summer of 1953. In 1968 Pike's rare pamphlet, *Message of the President, and Report of Albert Pike, Commissioner of the Confederate States to the Indian Nations West of Arkansas, of the*

Results of His Mission (Richmond, Va., 1861) was reprinted with the cover title *Report of Albert Pike on Mission to the Indian Nations, Richmond, 1861* (Washington, D.C., 1968).

37. Abel, *Slaveholding Indians*, I, 57–59.

38. Lobingier, *Supreme Council*, 216–17, citing and quoting Pike's official report on negotiations.

Chapter XXVII

1. W. S. Robertson to Secretary of the Interior, Wineconne, Wis., Jan. 7, 1862, O.I.A., *Southern Superintendency*, 1862, R1664.

2. Copies of the Creek Treaty are to be found in *Official Records*, ser. IV, vol. I, 426–43; Matthews, ed., *Statutes at Large of the Provisional Government of the Confederate States*, 289–310.

3. Angie Debow, *The Rise and Fall of the Choctaw Republic* (Norman, Okla., 1934), 80–82.

4. *Official Records*, ser. I, vol. I, 682.

5. Ibid., 648–53. Cooper, a Mississippian, was empowered by the Confederate War Department to raise and command a mounted regiment among the Choctaws and Chickasaws. Walker to Cooper, Montgomery, May 13, 1861, ibid., ser. I, vol. III, 574–75. He accepted the commission and worked actively thereafter for secession. McCulloch to Walker, Fort Smith, May 28, 1861, ibid., 587; Pike to Toombs, Fort Smith, May 29, 1861, ibid., ser. IV, vol. I, 560; and proclamation by Chief Hudson, ibid., ser. I, vol. III, 593–94.

6. Orlando Lee to Commissioner of Indian Affairs Williams P. Dole, Huntington, Long Island, N.Y., Mar. 15, 1862, O.I.A., *Southern Superintendency*, 1862, L632. Lee, a former missionary teacher at Spencer Academy, Choctaw Nation, left the Choctaw Nation on June 24, 1861; he appears in this letter to be writing mostly from hearsay. He said Pitchlynn favored neutrality when he returned from Washington to the Choctaw Nation in May 1861, and induced Principal Chief Hudson to "prepare a message recommending neutrality" to the special session of the National Council, called to meet June 1. But Lee said that by the time the council met a vigilance committee from Texas had quieted Pitchlynn and Hudson was frightened by "a furious speech" of Robert M. Jones, Choctaw slaveholder and ardent secessionist, into presenting a message recommending secession, negotiation with the Confederacy, and immediate organization of Colonel Cooper's Confederate regiment.

7. Pike to the General Council of the Choctaw Nation, [Little Rock? May 1861], O.I.A., *Choctaw*, 1861, C1078. From internal evidence it is apparent that the letter was written between May 11 and May 21, 1861.

8. Proclamation of Chief Hudson, Doaksville, Choctaw Nation, June 14, 1861, *Official Records*, ser. I, vol. III, 593–94.

9. Resolutions of the Chickasaw Legislature, Tishomingo, Chickasaw Nation, May 25, 1861, ibid., 585–87.

10. *Official Records*, ser. 4, vol. I, 445–66; Matthews, *Statutes at Large of the Provisional Government of the Confederate States*, 311–31. In 1887 Pike testified before a Senate committee "that in the treaty which I made in 1861 as commissioner of the Confederate States of America, with the Choctaw Nation, the payment to that nation of the full amount" of the Net Proceeds claim as adjudicated by the U.S. Senate in 1859 "was expressly provided for." He said, also, that he "informed the President and Provisional Congress of those states that I had been counsel and attorney of the

Choctaws in obtaining that adjudication and decision; and with full knowledge of that fact the President recommended the ratification of the treaty, and the Provisional Congress ratified it." *Sen. Rep. No. 1978,* 49th Cong., 2d Sess., Serial No. 2458, p. 56.

   11. Pike to Rector, North Fork of Canadian River, July 5, 1861, O.I.A., CPAS, 1861; same to same, ibid.

   12. Ibid.; Pike to Cooley, Memphis, Feb. 17, 1866, in Abel, *Slaveholding Indians,* I, 136.

   13. Abel, *Slaveholding Indians,* I, 211, cites figures from the U.S. commissioner of Indian affairs giving the Seminole census as 2,267 in 1861.

   14. Rutherford to Rector, Fort Smith, Dec. 7, 1861, O.I.A., CPAS, 1861.

   15. E. H. Carruth to Office of Indian Affairs, n.p., July 11, 1861, O.I.A., *Southern Superintendency,* 1861, C1348; Evan Jones to Commissioner of Indian Affairs W. P. Dole, Lawrence, Kans., Dec. 14, 1861, ibid., J530; Geo. A. Cutler to Dole, Leroy, Kans., Nov. 4, 1861, and enclosures, ibid., C1400; Rutherford to Rector, Fort Smith, Dec. 27, 1861, O.I.A., CPAS, 1861; Pike to Walker, Seminole Agency, July 31, 1861, *Official Records,* ser. I, vol. III, 624.

   16. *Official Records,* ser. IV, vol. I, 513–27; Matthews, *Statutes at Large of the Provisional Government of the Confederate States,* 311–31.

   17. Pike to Hon. Mr. Miles, Chairman Com. on Mil. Affs., Richmond, Dec. 9, 1861, AGPR.

   18. Pike to Walker, Seminole Agency, July 31, 1861, *Official Records,* ser. I, vol. III, 624.

   19. *Essays to Vinnie,* Essay 10, "Of Indian Nature and Wrongs," Pike Papers.

   20. Pike to Cooley, Memphis, Feb. 17, 1866, in Abel, *Slaveholding Indians,* I, 136.

   21. Leeper to Rector, Wichita Agency, L. D., Dec. 12, 1861, O.I.A., CPAS, 1861; *Essays to Vinnie,* Essay 10, "Of Indian Nature and Wrongs," Pike Papers.

   22. *Essays to Vinnie,* Essay 10, "Of Indian Nature and Wrongs," Pike Papers.

   23. Kekarewa, Principal Chief of the Pen-e-tegh-ca Bank of Comanches, had settled his band on the leased districts in 1859.

   24. *Official Records,* ser. IV., vol. I, 542–554; Matthews, *Statutes at Large of the Provisional Government of the Confederate States,* 542–54.

   25. *Essays to Vinnie,* Essay 10, "Of Indian Nature and Wrongs," Pike Papers.

   26. Ibid.

   27. Leeper to Rector, Wichita Agency, Oct. 21, Dec. 12, 1861, O.I.A., CPAS; Pike to Miles, Richmond, Dec. 9, 1861, AGPR; H. P. Jones to Pike, May 8, 1862, O.I.A., CPAS.

   28. Pike to Cooley, Memphis, Feb. 17, 1856, in Abel, *Slaveholding Indians,* I, 136.

   29. Meetings and Proceedings of the Executive Council of the Cherokee Nation, July 2, 1861, O.I.A., *Cherokee,* 1861, C515.

   30. Pike to Ross, Seminole Agency, Aug. 1, 1861, in *Van Buren Press,* Aug. 28, 1861; Ross to Hubbard, Park Hill, June 17, 1861, *Official Records,* ser. I, vol. XIII, 498–99; Ross to McCulloch, Park Hill, June 17, 1861, ibid., III, 596–97.

   31. McCulloch to Walker, Fort Smith, June 22, 29, 1861, *Official Records,* ser. I, vol. III, 595–96, 600.

   32. Meetings and Proceedings of the Cherokee Executive Council, Aug. 1, 1861, O.I.A., *Cherokee,* 1861, C515.

   33. Pike to Ross, Seminole Agency, Aug. 1, 1861, in *Van Buren Press,* Aug. 28, 1861.

34. For the complete address see *Official Records*, ser. I, vol. III, 673–75; same in *Van Buren Press*, Aug. 28, 1861.

35. *Official Records*, ser. I, vol. III, 673, 675–76, 690–91, vol. XIII, 499–502.

36. Pike to Cooley, Memphis, Feb. 17, 1866, in Abel, *Slaveholding Indians*, I, 136–37; *Official Records*, ser. I, vol. VIII, 720; "Address of John Ross . . . 19th December, 1862," in *H.R. Ex. Doc. 1*, 39th Cong., 1st Sess., Serial No. 1248, p. 539.

37. *Essays to Vinnie*, Essay 10, "Of Indian Nature and Wrongs," Pike Papers.

38. Pike apparently sent Andrew J. Dorn, Confederate agent for the Osages, Senecas, Shawnees, and Quapaws, to urge the attendance of his wards' chieftains at the Park Hill council. He may also have sent messengers to the disaffected Creeks under Opoth le Yahola. Ross had communicated with the Osages, Senecas, and disaffected Creeks, and perhaps others. Baptiste Peoris to G. A. Colton, Paola, Kans., May 1, 1862, *H.R. Ex. Doc. 1*, 37th Cong. 3rd Sess., Serial No. 1157, pp. 317–19; statement and testimony of Isaac Warrior, Chief of the Senecas, Sept. 11, 1865, at Fort Smith Council, *H.R. Ex. Doc. 1*, 39th Cong., 1st Sess., Serial No. 1248, p. 505; "Address of John Ross . . . 19th December, 1862," ibid., 540; Ross to Opoth le Yahola and others, Park Hill, Sept. 19, 1861, and same to same, Tahlequah, Oct. 8, 1861, ibid., 337–38.

39. *Essays to Vinnie*, Essay 10, "Of Indian Nature and Wrongs," Pike Papers.

40. *Official Records*, ser. IV, vol. I, 636–46, 647–66; Matthews, *Statutes at Large of the Provisional Government of the Confederate States*, 363–93.

41. "Address of John Ross . . . 19th December, 1862," *H.R. Ex. Doc. 1*, 39th Cong., 1st Sess., Serial No. 1248, p. 539; *Official Records*, ser. IV, vol. I, 669.

42. *Official Records*, ser. IV, vol. I, 669–87; Matthews, *Statutes at Large of the Provisional Government of the Confederate States*, 394–411. All five of the Civilized Tribes could become a part of the proposed Indian State.

43. McCulloch to Ross, Fayetteville, Ark., Sept. 1, 1861, *Official Records*, ser. I, vol. III, 690; McCulloch to Drew, Fayetteville, Sept. 1, 1861, ibid., 69 McCulloch to Walker, Fayetteville, Sept. 1, 1861, ibid., 692, estimated Watie's force at 300 men.

44. W. P. Adair and James M. Bell to Watie, Grand River, Aug. 29, 1861, in Edward Everett Dale and Gaston Litton, eds., *Cherokee Cavaliers, Forty Years of Cherokee History as Told in the Correspondence of the Ridge-Watie-Boudinot Family* (Nov. 1940), 108–10.

45. Eaton, *John Ross and the Cherokee Indians*, 186; Elias Boudinot to Stand Watie, Honey Creek, Oct. 5, 1861, in Dale and Litton, eds., *Cherokee Cavaliers*, 110–11. McCulloch had already recommended to the Confederate War Department that Watie be given "a battalion separate from the Cherokee regiment under Colonel Drew," and that it be attached to his own command. McCulloch to Walker, Fayetteville, Ark., Sept. 2, 1861, *Official Records*, ser. I, vol. III, 692. After the meeting at Park Hill, Watie received the regiment and was placed under McCulloch. McCulloch to Price, Pineville, Mo., Oct. 22, 1861, ibid., 721; Clement Eaton, *A History of the Southern Confederacy* (New York, 1954), 157 and footnote.

46. Pike to Cooley, Memphis, Feb. 17, 1866, in Abel, *Slaveholding Indians*, I, 137.

47. Pike to Benjamin, Fort Smith, Oct. 13, 1861, War Department Register of Letters Received, War Department Collection of Confederate Records, ch. IX, vol. XXI, entry no. 6847, National Archives; Pike to Benjamin, Richmond, Dec. 25, 1861, *Official Records*, ser. I, vol. VIII, 720; *Van Buren Press*, Oct. 31, 1861; Toombs to Walker, Richmond, Aug. 7, 1861, *Official Records of the Union and Confederate Navies in the War of the Rebellion* (30 vols. and index, Washington, D.C., 1894–1927), ser. II, vol. III, 235.

48. He must have heard of his appointment while at Park Hill or before. President Davis recommended him for commission on Aug. 13, and on Aug. 16 the Senate approved. *Journal of the Congress of the Confederate States*, I, 343, 363. *Van Buren Press*, Aug. 28, 1861, noted the senatorial confirmation, and by Sept. 1, McCulloch had learned of it. McCulloch to Ross, Fayetteville, Ark., Sept. 1, 1861, *Official Records*, ser. I, vol. III, 691; Cooper to McCulloch, Richmond, Sept. 5, 1861, ibid., 698.

49. Pike to Benjamin, Fort Smith, Oct. 14, 1861, War Department Register of Letters Received, War Department Collection of Confederate Records, ch. IX, vol. XXI, entries no. 6988, 6989, National Archives; Pike to Cooper, Fort Smith, Oct. 14, 1861, Adjutant and Inspector General's Office Register of Letters Received, War Department Collection of Confederate Records, ch. I, vol. XLVII, entry no. 370, National Archives.

50. Pike to Benjamin, Fort Smith, Oct. 13, 14, War Department Register of Letters Received, War Department Collection of Confederate Records, ch. IX, vol. XXI, entries no. 6982–84, 6986, National Archives; a copy of the ration contract with Johnson is in O.I.A., Confederate Papers, 1861–1862, Drawer 26, folder labeled "Miscellaneous Papers; Licenses to trade, Invoices, Receipts, &c."

51. "Address of John Ross . . . 19th December, 1862," in *H.R. Ex. Doc. 1*, 39th Cong., 1st Sess., Serial No. 1248, p. 540; Ross to Opoth le Yahola, Park Hill, Sept. 19, 1861, ibid., 337–38; *Official Records*, ser. I, vol. VIII, 5; Pike to Cooley, Memphis, Feb. 17, 1866, in Abel, *Slaveholding Indians*, I, 140.

52. *Van Buren Press*, Nov. 7, 1861.

53. Ross to Opoth le Yahola and others, Tahlequah, Oct. 8, 1861, in *H.R. Ex. Doc. 1*, 39th Cong., 1st Sess., Serial No. 1248, p. 338.

54. *Van Buren Press*, Nov. 7, 1861. Carruth to Hopoeithleyohola [sic], Barnsville, Kans., Sept. 10, 1861, *Official Records*, ser. I, vol. VIII, 25; Abel, *Slaveholding Indians*, I, 244–47 and footnotes.

55. "Address of John Ross . . . 19th December, 1862," in *H.R. Ex. Doc.*, 39th Cong., 1st Sess., Serial No. 1248, pp. 540–41.

56. *Official Records*, ser. I, vol. VIII, 5, 719–20. The Indian forces then organized consisted of three regiments and one battalion, all mounted.

Chapter XXVIII

1. The session had opened on Nov. 18, 1861. *Journal of the Congress of the Confederate States*, I, 467.

2. Pike to Benjamin, Richmond, Nov. 25, 1861, CR RLRWD, ch. IX, vol. 21, Entry No. 7827. The report and treaties are presumably in the National Archives, but they could not be located during the summer of 1953.

3. *Official Records*, ser. I, vol. VIII, 690.

4. Pike to Benjamin, Richmond, Nov. 25, 28, 1861, Adjutant and Inspector General's Office Register of Letters Received, War Department Collection of Confederate Records, ch. I, vol. XLVII, entries no. 482, 484, 498–99, 521, National Archives; *Journal of the Congress of the Confederate States*, I, passim.

5. Pike to Cooper, Fort Wachita, Choctaw Nation, Aug. 3, 1862, *Official Records*, ser. I, vol. XIII, 975; Pike to Randolph, Fort McCulloch, June 27, 1862, ibid., 847, 847–48; *Journal of the Congress of the Confederate States*, I, 810, 814.

6. Special Orders, No. 271, Adj. and Insp. General's Office, Richmond, Dec. 20, 1861, *Official Records*, ser. I, vol. LIII, 764, Special Orders, No. 16, Adj. and Insp. General's Office, Richmond, Jan. 20, 1862, ibid., 770.

7. *Official Records*, ser. I, vol. VIII, 690.

8. Pike to Benjamin, Richmond, Nov. 27, 1861, ibid., 697–98.

9. Benjamin to Pike, Richmond, Dec. 2, 1861, ibid., 699–700.

10. Pike to Benjamin, Richmond, Dec. 28, 1861, ibid., vol. LIII, 764; Quesenbury to Leeper, Fort Gibson, Cherokee Nation, Nov. 28, 1861, O.I.A., CPAS.

11. Leeper wrote Rector on Oct. 21 that "the Kiowas and all the Southern bands of the Comanches" were "encamped on the North Canadian within four days ride of this place; they say that their intention is to be here at the falling of the leaves, to conclude a treaty with Capt. Pike. The Kiowas inform us that they received the white beads and tobacco from Capt. Pike and that they desire to be on terms of friendship with us." Leeper to Rector, Wichita Agency, L.D., Oct. 21, 1861, O.I.A., CPAS.

12. Albert Pike, Commissioner of the Confederate States to the Indian Tribes west of Arkansas, to Maj. Elias Rector, Superintendent of Indian Affairs, Richmond, Nov. 21, 1861, O.I.A., CPAS.

13. S. S. Scott, Acting Commissioner of Indian Affairs, to Maj. Elias Rector, Superintendent of Indian Affairs, Richmond, Dec. 2, 1861, O.I.A., CPAS.

14. *Journal of the Congress of the Confederate States*, I, 544.

15. Pike to Miles, Richmond, Dec. 9, 1861, AGPF.

16. Benjamin to Davis, Richmond, Dec. [14?], 1861, *Official Records*, vol. I, 792. Editor's brackets.

17. *Official Records*, ser. IV., vol. I, 785–86.

18. For evidence that they were working together, see Pike to Johnson, Columbia, S.C., Jan. 5, 1862, ibid., ser. I, vol. LIII, 795, 796.

19. *Journal of the Congress of the Confederate States*, I, 564, 565.

20. Ibid., 590–91, 595–96.

21. Ibid., 590–91.

22. Ibid., 595–96.

23. Ibid., 601–2, 610, 611, 632–35.

24. Cooper's official report, *Official Records*, ser. I, vol. VIII, 5–12; Colonel Drew's report, ibid., 16–18; *Little Rock Daily State Journal*, Dec. 28, 1861, quoting *Fort Smith News*, Dec. 24, 1861.

25. Pike to Benjamin, Richmond, Dec. 25, 1861, *Official Records*, ser. I, vol. VIII, 719.

26. *Journal of the Congress of the Confederate States*, I, 607, 620, 621.

27. Pike to Benjamin, Richmond, Dec. 25, 1861, *Official Records*, ser. I, vol. VIII, 719–22.

28. Pike to Hon. R. W. Johnson, Columbia, S.C., Jan. 5, 1862, ibid., ser. I, vol. LIII, 795.

29. Pike to Rector, Richmond, Dec. 29, 1861, O.I.A., CPAS.

30. Scott to Rector, Richmond, Jan. 1, 1862., O.I.A., CPAS.

31. Pike to Johnson, Columbia, S.C., Jan. 5, 1862, *Official Records*, ser. I, vol. LIII, 795.

32. Pike to Adjutant General S. Cooper, Fort Washita, Choctaw Nation, Aug. 3, 1862, ibid., ser. I, vol. XIII, 975; Pike to Randolph, Fort McCulloch, June 27, 1862, ibid., 847.

33. Pike to Randolph, Fort McCulloch, June 26, 1862, ibid., 842–43.

34. Pike to Rector, Richmond, Dec. 29, 1861, O.I.A., CPAS; Scott to Rector, Richmond, Jan. 23, 1862, ibid.; Pike to Rector, Little Rock, Jan. 28, 1862, ibid.

35. Pike had signed a blank account and submitted it in November to the secretary of war, stating that it "was not my intention to accept any remuneration, but the great length of time during which I found it necessary to remain in the Indian Country caused me such losses and so interfered with my business that I am constrained unwillingly to present this account. I leave it to the President or to Congress to fix the sum that shall be paid me." Pike to Benjamin, Richmond, Nov. 25, 1861, Confederate State Department Records, Library of Congress, quoted in Abel, *Slaveholding Indians,* II, 175n.

36. Pike to Rector, Richmond, Dec. 29, 1862, O.I.A., CPAS.

37. *Statutes of the Provisional Congress,* Stat. V, ch. XXVII, 232–37.

38. Scott to Rector, Richmond, Jan. 23, 1862, O.I.A., CPAS; E. C. Elmore, Treasurer C. S., to Rector, Richmond, Jan. 23, 1862, ibid.; Rector to Elmore, Fort Smith, Feb. 28, 1862, ibid.

39. W. H. S. Taylor, Auditor, to General Albert Pike, Agent for the War Department for delivery of . . . funds to Elias Rector, Supt. Ind. Affairs, now in Richmond, Va., Treasury Department, C.S.A., Second Auditor's Office, Richmond, Dec. 31, 1861, O.I.A., CPAS; Scott to Rector, Richmond, Jan. 1, 1862, ibid.

40. Pike to Secretary of War, Fort McCulloch, Apr. 22, 1862, CRLR.

41. Ibid.; Pike to Johnson, Columbia, Jan. 5, 1862, *Official Records,* ser. I, vol. LIII, 796.

42. Pike to Secretary of War, Apr. 22, 1862, CRLR; see also *Account and Vouchers, The Confederate States of America* (Bureau of Indian Affairs) to Albert Pike, Agent of the War Department, dated January 1862 to Feb. 25, 1862, Pike Papers, SCSR, hereafter cited as Account and Vouchers, Agent Pike. A microfilm copy of the Account and Vouchers is in the University of Texas Library.

43. *Little Rock Daily State Journal,* Jan. 28, 1862.

44. *Van Buren Press,* July 3, 1861; McCulloch to Adjutant General S. Cooper, *Official Records,* ser. I, vol. III, 106–7.

Chapter XXIX

1. Pike to Secretary of War, Apr. 22, 1862, CRLR.

2. *Little Rock Daily State Journal,* Dec. 18, 1861.

3. Special Orders No. 8, Adjt. and Insp. Gen.'s Office, Richmond, Jan. 10, 1862, *Official Records,* ser. I, vol. VIII, 734. For the dispute between McCulloch and Price, see ibid., vol. III, passim; vol. VIII, passim; vol. LIII, passim; *Journal of the Congress of the Confederate States,* I, 488, 510, 637.

4. *A Soldier's Honor, with Reminiscences of Major-General Earl Van Dorn. By His Comrades* (New York, 1902), 35–42; *Essays to Vinnie,* Essay 10, "Of Indian Nature and Wrongs," Pike Papers; Abel, *Slaveholding Indians,* I, 55 and footnotes; *Official Records,* ser. I, vol. XIII, 954; Walter P. Webb, *The Texas Rangers* (Boston, 1935), 160.

5. General Orders No. 1, Hdqrs. Trans-Miss. Dist., Dept. No. 2, Little Rock, Ark., Jan. 29, 1862, *Official Records,* ser. I, vol. VIII, 745–46.

6. Pike to Davis, Fort Washita, Ind. T., July 31, 1862, ibid., XIII, 861; Pike to Secretary of War, Fort McCulloch, May 4, 1862, ibid., 819; Van Dorn to Price, Jacksonport, Ark., Feb. 7, 1862, ibid., vol. VIII, 749; Van Dorn to Price, Pocahontas, Ark., Feb. 14, 1862, ibid., VIII, 750–51.

7. Ibid., VIII, 749. Van Dorn most surely was confusing what Pike had with what he expected to have. At the time Van Dorn was in Little Rock, Pike was advertising in the newspapers of the state trying to raise the two regiments of infantry and two companies of artillery authorized by Benjamin in early December. See *Van Buren Press*, Jan. 9, 1862; *Washington Telegraph*, Jan. 15, 1862; *Little Rock Daily State Journal*, Jan. 9, 1862. These advertisements continued until late February, and in early March the troops still had not reached Pike. See proclamation of Governor Rector, Little Rock, Jan. 31, 1862, *Official Records*, ser. I, vol LIII, 776–79, for further proof of this.

8. *Official Records*, ser. I, vol. VIII, 750–51.

9. Ibid., 59, 462, 513–14, 516, 525, 550–51, 553, 756–57.

10. Price estimated his strength at 6,818 on Mar. 4, which was approximately the same as on Feb. 12. Curtis's report of Feb. 12 listed 12,095 as his "effective force," while Hallack estimated Curtis's army at 16,000–17,000 men. Ibid., 305, 554, 555.

11. Ibid., 558, 559, 560, 561–63, 756–57.

12. Ibid., 283 Neither the order to McCulloch nor the one to Pike is in the *Official Records*, nor have they been found in the National Archives. For evidence that such orders were sent, see Van Dorn to Mackall, Jacksonport, February 24, 1862, ibid., McCulloch to Van Dorn, Headquarters McCulloch's Division [Boston Mountains], March 1, 1862, ibid., 763, acknowledging receipt of the order; Pike to Secretary of War, for McCulloch, April 22, 1862, CRLR.

13. *Official Records*, ser. I, vol. VIII, 283, 755, 763–65.

14. Pike to Rector, Little Rock, Jan. 28, 1862, O.I.A., CPAS; Pike to Secretary of War, Fort McCulloch, Apr. 22, 1862, CRLR.

15. *Little Rock Daily State Journal*, Feb. 4, 1862; Account and Vouchers, Agent Pike, Pike Papers, SCSR.

16. Pike to Secretary of War, Fort McCulloch, Apr. 22, 1862, CRLR.

17. *Official Records*, ser. I, vol XIII, 821.

18. Rector to Scott, Fort Smith, Feb. 1862, O.I.A., CPAS; Rector to George Hudson, Chief of Choctaw Nation, Fort Smith, Feb. 1862, ibid.; Rector to Scott, [Fort Smith?], Mar. 4, 1862, ibid. The last letter is unsigned but is in Rector's hand, and is apparently a copy.

19. Pike to Secretary of War, Fort McCulloch, Apr. 22, 1862, CRLR; Pike to Secretary of War, Fort McCulloch, May 4, 1862, *Official Records*, ser. I, vol. XIII, 819; Albert Pike, comp., Maxims of Military Science and Art . . . with Occasional Illustrations and Applications (preface dated Ark.: July 1, 1863), p. 1519, Pike Papers, SCSR.

20. Pike to Secretary of War, Fort McCulloch, Apr. 22, 1862, CRLR; Pike to Secretary of War, Fort McCulloch, May 4, 1862. *Official Records*, ser. I, vol. XIII, 819. Drew's regiment had been refilled after the disaster at Bird Creek, *Little Rock Daily State Journal*, Dec. 28, 1861, quoting *Fort Smith News*, Dec. 24, 1861.

21. Pike to Rector, Mouth of Canadian, Feb. 23, 1862, O.I.A., CPAS; Pike to Secretary of War, Fort McCulloch, Apr. 22, 1862, CRLR.

22. Pike to Rector, Mouth of Canadian, Feb. 23, 1862, O.I.A., CPAS.

23. Pike to Secretary of War, Apr. 22, 1862, CRLR.

24. Ibid.

25. See above, 390, for the origin of this order.

26. Pike to Secretary of War, Apr. 22, 1862, CRLR.

27. *Official Records*, ser. I, vol. VIII, 286–87.

28. Ibid., 283.

29. Ibid., 197.

30. Ibid., 209–10, 283.

31. Ibid., 196.

32. Ibid., 197–99; *New York Times*, Mar. 20, 1862.

33. *Official Records*, ser. I., vol. VIII, 197–99.

34. Ibid., 283.

35. Ibid., 316–17.

36. W. L. Gammage, *The Camp, the Bivouac, and the Battle Field. Being a History of the Fourth Arkansas Regiment* (Selma, Ala., 1864), 25. Gammage was surgeon of the Fourth Arkansas Infantry.

37. Ibid., 25; *Official Records*, ser. I, vol. VIII, 287.

38. *Official Records*, ser. I, vol. VIII, 284, 287; Gammage, *Camp and Bivouac*, 25–26.

39. *Official Records*, ser. I, vol. VIII, 198–99.

40. Ibid., 199.

41. Ibid., 217, 287.

42. Ibid., 217, 233–34, 287–88.

43. Ibid., 288.

44. Ibid., 217–18.

45. Ibid., 288.

46. Ibid., 218–19, 246–47.

47. Ibid., 289–90, 292.

48. Ibid., 290, 293, 301, 318.

49. Ibid., 200–201, 219–20.

50. Ibid., 284, 290, 293–94.

51. Ibid., 290.

52. Ibid., 195, 284.

53. Ibid., 284.

54. Ibid., 290.

55. Pike to Charles B. Johnson, Esq., Fort McCulloch, Choctaw Nation, May 29, 1862, in *Little Rock State Gazette*, June 28, 1862.

56. Ibid.

57. *Official Records*, ser. I, vol. VIII, 290.

58. Ibid., 290–91; Pike to Johnson, Fort McCulloch, May 29, 1862, in *Little Rock State Gazette*, June 28, 1862.

59. Pike to Johnson, Fort McCulloch, May 29, 1862; in *Little Rock State Gazette*, June 28, 1862.

60. *Official Records*, ser. I, vol. VIII, 290, 292.

61. *Washington Telegraph*, Mar. 26, 1862.

62. For Pike's official report, see *Official Records*, ser. I, vol. VIII, 286–92.

Chapter XXX

1. *Memphis Daily Appeal*, Apr. 4, 1867.

2. "Statement of Albert Pike, as to his connection, in the Civil and Military Service of the Confederate States, with the Indian Tribes," sworn and notarized at Ottawa, Canada, Aug. 4, 1865, Pike Amnesty Papers, SCSR. Hereafter cited as Statement of Albert Pike, Ottawa, Canada, Aug. 4, 1865.

3. Ibid.

4. Special Order No. ____. Headquarters Department of Indian Territory, Dwight Mission, Mar. 15, 1862, quoted in *Memphis Daily Appeal*, Apr. 4, 1867.

5. Pike to Curtis, Cantonment Davis, Mar. 23, 1862, in *Memphis Daily Appeal*, Apr. 4, 1867. The accused man was acquitted because of insufficient evidence. Statement of Albert Pike, Ottawa, Canada, Aug. 4, 1865, Pike Amnesty Papers, SCSR.

6. For this exchange, in which Curtis reported that "many of the Federal dead . . . were tomahawked, scalped, and their bodies shamefully mangled," and in which Van Dorn charged that Federal troops, "alleged to be Germans," had shot in cold blood Confederate prisoners taken during the battle, see *Official Records*, ser. I, vol. VIII, 193–95.

7. Curtis to Pike, Cross Timber, Ark., Mar. 29, 1862, ibid., ser. I, vol. III, 410; same in *Memphis Daily Appeal*, Apr. 4, 1867.

8. The correspondence mentioned is in *Official Records*, ser. I, vol. VIII, 25–26. For Indian participation on the Federal side in the Civil War, see Abel, *Slaveholding Indians*, I–III, passim.

9. Pike cited as evidence of this the use by the Kiowas of U.S. rifles of recent makes and of ammunition marked "U.S." Certainly the Kickapoos, Delawares, and Osages, considered wild tribes at the time, were in the Federal Indian Expedition in 1862. Abel, *Slaveholding Indians*, II, 115. The writer has seen no information of the use or non-use of Kiowas, Comanches, and Wichitas by the United States.

10. Reprinted in *Memphis Daily Appeal*, Apr. 4, 1867. The original publication has not been located.

11. *New York Herald*, Mar. 14, 1862; *Boston Evening Transcript*, Mar. 14, 1862.

12. Quoted in Frank Moore, *The Rebellion Record* (11 vols., New York, 1861–1868), IV, 100; Abel, *Slaveholding Indians*, II, 31n. For other accounts and views of Pike, see *New York Herald*, Mar. 14, 17, 19, 23, 1862; *New York Times*, Mar. 20, 1862; *Philadelphia Forney's War Press*, Mar. 29, 1862; *Washington Daily Intelligencer*, Mar. 21, 1862; *Philadelphia Inquirer*, Mar. 20, 24, 1862.

13. *Report of the Joint Committee on the Conduct of the War* (In three parts, Washington, D.C., 1863), pt. III, 449. (*Sen. Rep. Com. No. 108*, 37th Cong., 3d Sess., Serial No. 1151–54.) Hereafter cited as C.C.W.

14. William Whatley Pierson Jr., "The Committee on the Conduct of the Civil War," *American Historical Review* 23 (Apr. 1918): 550–76; T. Harry Williams, "The Committee on the Conduct of the War, An Experiment in Civilian Control," *Journal of the American Military Institute* 3 (fall 1939): 139–56.

15. C.C.W., pt. I, 92.

16. Curtis to Wade, Camp near Batesville, Ark., May 21, 1862, C.C.W., pt. III, 490; same in *Official Records*, ser. I, vol. VIII, 206.

17. C.C.W., pt. I, 98, pt. III, 457, 490–91.

18. It is curious that Bussey reported to Curtis on Mar. 14, nearly two months before when the events were fresh, that he had returned to the field after his men were buried and learned that eight of the men had been scalped. Then, he said, "I had the dead exhumed, and on personal examination I found that it was a fact beyond dispute that 8 of the killed of my command had been scalped. The bodies of many of them showed unmistakable evidence that the men had been murdered after they were wounded. . . ." *Official Records*, ser. I, vol. VIII, 236. For further divergence in Bussey's memory, see his *The Pea Ridge Campaign Considered* (Military Order of the Loyal Legion of the United States, Commandery of the District of Columbia, War Papers, [No.] 60, Washington, D.C., 1905), 23.

19. For Curtis's letter, the statements, and the affidavits, see C.C.W., pt. III, 490–91; *Official Records*, ser. I, vol. VIII, 205–7.

20. Lobingier, *Supreme Council*, 220–21.

21. Abel, *Slaveholding Indians*, II, 30–31, 32.

22. *Official Records*, ser. I, vol. VIII, 195, 289. The only evidence that the present writer has seen that imputes the alleged atrocities to the Cherokees in Colonel Drew's regiment is in a statement by Elias Boudinot, Drew's personal political enemy, before the Fort Smith Peace Convention of 1865. *Little Rock Daily Pantograph*, Oct. 6, 1865; *Memphis Daily Appeal*, Apr. 4, 1867.

23. *Official Records*, ser. I, vol. VIII, p. 662.

Chapter XXXI

1. Pike to Secretary of War, Apr. 20, 1862, CRLR.

2. Pike to Watie, North Fork Village, Apr. 1, 1862, in Dale and Litton, *Cherokee Cavaliers*, 115–17.

3. Special Orders, Headquarters, Dept. of Ind. Ter., Cantonment Davis, Mar. 21, 1862, Orders of Brigadier General Albert Pike, 1862, War Department Collection of Confederate Records, National Archives.

4. Pike to Watie, North Fork Village, Apr. 1, 1862, Dale and Litton, *Cherokee Cavaliers*, 115–17.

5. Foreman, *History of Oklahoma*, 110.

6. *Official Records*, ser. I, vol. VIII, 795–96.

7. Ibid., vol. XIII, 864–65, 868, 870.

8. Pike to Watie, North Fork Village, Apr. 1, 1862, in Dale and Litton, *Cherokee Cavaliers*, 115–17.

9. Ibid., Foreman, *History of Oklahoma*, 110; Ross to Pike, Park Hill, Apr. 10, 1862, in Abel, *Slaveholding Indians*, II, 111 and footnote.

10. William Brown Morrison, *Military Posts and Camps in Oklahoma* (Oklahoma City, 1936), 126–31.

11. William E. Woodruff, *With the Light Guns in '61–'65, Reminiscences of Eleven Arkansas, Missouri and Texas Light Batteries, in the Civil War* (Little Rock, Ark., 1903), 64–67.

12. *Official Records*, ser. I, vol. XIII, 821–22.

13. Ibid., 822–23.

14. Rector to Scott, Fort Smith, Feb. 28, 1862, O.I.A., CPAS, 1862; [Rector to Scott], Office Supt. Ind. Affairs, [Fort Smith], Mar. 4, 1862, ibid.

15. Benjamin to Pike, Mar. 14, 1862, *Official Records*, I, vol. VIII, 780; Pike to Secretary of War, Apr. 22, 1862, CRLR; Abel, *Slaveholding Indians*, II, 181 and footnote; *Official Records*, ser. I, vol. XIII, 964, 976.

16. *Official Records*, ser. I, vol. XIII, 822.

17. Woodruff, *With the Light Guns*, 69–70.

18. Thomas, *Arkansas in War and Reconstruction, 1861–1874* (Little Rock, Ark., 1926), 139–40.

19. *Official Records*, ser. I, vol. X, part 2, p. 547, vol. XIII, 28.

20. Ibid., ser. I, vol. XIII, 830, 934.

21. Ibid., 819–23.

22. Ibid., 827, 828, 935–36.

23. Ibid., 943. Woodruff, *With the Light Guns*, 71–72, stated that Pike was particularly loath to send his artillery, "but finally concluded he would take the sense of the company, and directed the company to take measures accordingly. The company resolved unanimously to return home."

24. *Official Records*, ser. I, vol. XIII, 936–43.

25. Ibid., 947–50.

26. Ibid., 841–44, 846–47, 848–49, 850–51, 852, 946, 967, 968–69.

27. Ibid., 859, 863, 956–57.

28. Frank Lawrence Owsley, *State Rights in the Confederacy* (Chicago, 1925), 150–57, 158–59; *Official Records*, ser. I, vol. XIII, 38–40; Col. John M. Harrell, *Arkansas*, in Clement A. Evans, ed., *Confederate Military History* (12 vols., Atlanta, Ga., 1899), X, 102–3, 115–17, 126.

29. Pike to Davis, Fort McCulloch, Choctaw Nation, July 3, 1862, and Davis to Pike, Richmond, Aug. 9, 1862, in *Essays to Vinnie*, Essay 13, "Of Rowing against the Stream," Pike Papers.

30. Abel, *Slaveholding Indians*, II, 161–63, expresses the view that Hindman may have purposely goaded Pike; the same view is stated in Evans, *Confederate Military History*, X, 125. Hindman never admitted that he wanted Pike to resign, but he did indicate in his official report that he had lost all patience with him by the first week in July. *Official Records*, ser. I, vol. XIII, 40.

31. *Official Records*, ser. I, vol. XIII, 862, 957.

32. Ibid., 854, 856, 860, 867, 973.

33. Ibid., 40–41, 856–57, 859–60, 867, 970, 973.

34. Ibid., 469–71.

35. Abel, *Slaveholding Indians*, II, 167. *Official Records*, ser. I, vol. XIII, passim, contains Confederate and federal reports and correspondence pertaining to the federal expedition into the Cherokee Nation.

36. *Official Records*, ser. I, vol. XIII, 41, 977.

37. *Washington Telegraph*, Aug. 20, 1862; Pike to S. S. Scott, Washington, Ark., Aug. 19, 1862, Pike Papers, SCSR; Pike to Leeper, Washington, Ark., Aug. 19, 1862, O.I.A., CPWA.

38. *Little Rock State Gazette*, Aug. 30, 1862; *Official Records*, ser. I, vol. XIII, 894, 918; Abel, *Slaveholding Indians*, II, 188–90; *Albert Pike's Letter Addressed to Major General Holmes* (Little Rock, Ark., 1862), 1–7.

39. *Charges and Specifications Preferred August 23, 1862, by Brigadier General Albert Pike, Against Major Gen. Thos. C. Hindman* (Richmond, Va., 1863), 13.

40. Pike to Davis, Little Rock, Aug. 25, 1862, AGPF; Pike to Maj. R. C. Newton, Little Rock, Aug. 28, 1862, ibid.

41. Holmes to Davis, Little Rock, Aug. 28, 1862, Private Correspondence of Gen. T. H. Holmes, 1861–64, War Department Collection of Confederate Records, ch. II, vol. CCCLVIII, Military Departments, National Archives.

42. *Official Records*, ser. I, vol. XIII, 903–5.

43. Ibid., 924.

44. Ibid., 44, 905, 924; *Journal of the Congress of the Confederate States*, V, 331, 346; *Little Rock Patriot*, Oct. 5, 1862.

45. *Official Records*, ser. I, vol. XIII, 903–5.

46. Ibid., 42–43, 324–37, 759–61, 892, 907, 908, 910–11, 913, 918, 928.

47. Ibid., 893–94.

48. Ibid., 894.

49. Ibid., 910–11, 913, 919, 923, 927, 980–81. Pike's resignation was accepted on Nov. 11, 1862. Pike to Cooper, Richmond, Apr. 18, 1863, and endorsement, AGPR.

50. *Official Records*, ser. I, vol. XIII, 922, 927.

51. John Gould Fletcher, *Arkansas* (Chapel Hill, N.C., 1947), 166.

52. *Albert Pike's Letter Addressed to Major General Holmes*, 2.

53. Ibid., same printed in *Little Rock Patriot*, Feb. 12, 19, 1863. The pamphlet went through at least three different editions. Allen, *Arkansas Imprints*, 113–14; William L. Boyden, *Bibliography of the Writings of Albert Pike* (Washington, D.C., 1921), 20.

54. Frank A. Rector to Charles B. Johnson, Little Rock, Ark., Jan. 29, 1863; Charles B. Johnson Papers, Edward E. Ayer Collection, Newberry Library, Chicago; microfilm copy in the University of Texas Library.

55. Holmes to Davis, Little Rock, Feb. 12, 1863, *Private Correspondence of Gen. T. H. Holmes, 1861–64*, War Department Collection of Confederate Records, ch. II, vol. 358, Military Departments, National Archives.

56. Thomas, *Arkansas in War and Reconstruction*, 184–85; Joseph Howard Parks, *General Edmund Kirby Smith, C.S.A.* (Baton Rouge, La., 1954), 251–59.

57. *Charges and Specifications Preferred August 23, 1862, by Brigadier General Albert Pike, Against Major General Thomas C. Hindman; Albert Pike, Address to Senators and Representatives of the State of Arkansas in the Congress of the Confederate States*, Richmond, 1863. The last item is signed "Albert Pike, Louisiana, 20th March, 1863," which may indicate a Louisiana imprint. Pike was in Alexandria, Louisiana, during the week of Mar. 20, 1863, probably on the way to Richmond. *Little Rock Patriot*, Apr. 11, 1863.

58. *Richmond Enquirer*, Apr. 17, 21, 1863.

59. *Little Rock Patriot*, July 11, 1863. The letter was printed in a pamphlet entitled *Second Letter to Lieut. General Theophilus H. Holmes* (Richmond, Va., 1863). Boyden, *Writings of Pike*, 20.

60. *Washington Telegraph*, May 27, June 3, 1863.

Chapter XXXII

1. *Washington Telegraph*, May 27, June 3, 1863.

2. Yvon Pike to Fay Hempstead, Washington, D.C., Feb. 28, 1926, in family papers owned by Fred M. Packard, Washington, D.C.

3. *Essays to Vinnie*, Essay 11, "Of My Books and Studies," Pike Papers; "Albert Pike's Second Letter to Lieut. Gen. Theophilus H. Holmes, Richmond, Apr. 20, 1863," in *Little Rock Patriot*, July 11, 1863; Claude Rankin, "The Highland Home of Albert Pike," *Masonic Light* 2 (Jan. 1926): 14; marginal note by Yvon Pike at pp. 226–27 in copy of Allsopp's *Albert Pike* belonging to Fred M. Packard, Washington, D.C.

4. Efforts have been made to prove that Pike wrote *Morals and Dogma of the Ancient and Accepted Scottish Rite of Freemasonry*, his monumental treatise on Scottish Rite philosophy, while residing on the Little Missouri. The present writer has found no evidence to substantiate such a thesis. Allsopp, *Albert Pike*, 226; Charlean Moss Williams, "Where Albert Pike Wrote *Morals and Dogma*," *New Age Magazine* 42 (June 1934): 345–46; Yvon Pike to Hempstead, Washington, D.C., Feb. 28, 1926, in family papers owned by Fred M. Packard.

5. William L. Boyden, "The Masonic Record of Albert Pike," *New Age Magazine* 18 (Jan. 1920): 34–37.

6. Epes W. Sargent, "Some Misconceptions about Masonry," *New Age Magazine* 1 (Aug.–Sept. 1904): 294–96; Albert G. Mackey, *Encyclopedia of Freemasonry and Its Kindred Science* (Philadelphia, 1915), 69, 134, 359, 360, 793–94, 893, 1036.

7. Boyden, "The Masonic Record of Albert Pike," 34–37.

8. Lobingier, *Supreme Council*, 248.

9. Mackey, *Encyclopedia of Freemasonry*, 793–94; Albert Pike, comp., *The Statutes and Regulations, Institutes, Laws and Grand Constitutions of the Ancient and Accepted Scottish Rite* (New York, 1859), 93–137; *Centennial Address by James D. Richardson, 33°, Washington, D.C., October, 1901* (Washington, D.C., 1901), 6–7, 9–13.

10. Lobingier, *Supreme Council*, 6–14, 30–38.

11. Ibid., 60–79.

12. Ibid., 88–182.

13. Ibid., 161, 163.

14. Supreme Council *Transactions, 1857–1866* (reprint), 28–39; *Official Bulletin*, X, 254–58; Lobingier, *Supreme Council*, 187–88, 189.

15. Lobingier, *Supreme Council*, 175–79.

16. Ibid., 248.

17. *Official Bulletin*, VII, 361.

18. Ibid.

19. Ibid.

20. Pike to Mackey, Washington, D.C., Jan. 5, 1859, and Mackey to Pike, Charleston, Feb. 7, 1859, ibid., 363, 365; Lobingier, *Supreme Council*, 249–51.

21. Pike to Mackey, Little Rock, May 23, 1857, Pike Papers, SCSR; Mackey to Pike, Charleston, June 3, 1854, *Official Bulletin*, VII, 353–56; Lobingier, *Supreme Council*, 248, 250.

22. Supreme Council *Transactions, 1857–1866* (Reprint), 46–47; Boyden, "Masonic Record of Albert Pike," 34–37.

23. *Lecture of Bro . . . Albert Pike, Delivered by Special Request before the M. W. Grand Lodge of Louisiana, at Its Forty-Sixth Annual Communication, Held in New Orleans, February, 1858* (New Orleans, La., 1858), 52–68.

24. Ibid., 52–68.

25. Lobingier, *Supreme Council*, 491–519.

26. Ibid., 308.

27. Supreme Council *Transactions, 1870*, pp. 157–59.

28. *Official Bulletin*, VIII, 532; Supreme Council *Transactions, 1857–1866* (reprint), 90.

29. Pike to Mackey, Little Rock, Sept. 13, 1855, *Official Bulletin*, VII, 356.

30. Ibid.; Pike to Mackey, Washington, D.C., Mar. 31, 1857, and New Orleans, Apr. 20, 1857, ibid., 356–58.

31. Pike to Mackey, Washington, D.C., Mar. 31, 1857, *Official Bulletin*, VII, 356–57.

32. Pike to Mackey, New Orleans, Apr. 29, 1857, Creek Agency, July 8, 1857, Washington, D.C., June 3, 1858, Dec. 31, 1858, Feb. 25, 1859, ibid., 357–63, 367.

33. Pike to Mackey, Washington, D.C., Jan. 24, 1859, Pike Papers, SCSR.

34. The proceedings of this session were destroyed during the Civil War.

35. Pike to James C. Batchelor, Washington, D.C., May 29, 1860, Pike Papers, SCSR.

36. Pike to Mackey, New Orleans, Jan. 20, 1858, *Official Bulletin*, VII, 359–360; Supreme Council *Transactions, 1857–1866* (reprint), 86–87.

37. Pike, *Statutes and Regulations, Institutes, Laws and Grand Constitutions of the Scottish Rite*, 157–59.

38. Lobingier, *Supreme Council*, passim.

39. Supreme Council, *Transactions, 1857–1866* (reprint), 90–91.

40. Ibid., 155.

41. Pike to Batchelor, Washington, D.C., June 10, 1860, Pike Papers, SCSR.

42. Pike to Todd, Memphis, Tenn., Mar. 11, 1866, Pike Papers, SCSR.

43. Supreme Council, *Transactions, 1857–1866* (reprint), 203–6.

44. Ibid., 228–29.

Chapter XXXIII

1. Thomas, *Arkansas in War and Reconstruction*, 209–19.

2. Thomas S. Staples, *Reconstruction in Arkansas, 1862–1874* (Columbia University Studies in History, Economics and Public Law, vol. CIX; New York, 1923), 55–56.

3. Ibid., 56–57; Thomas, *Arkansas in War and Reconstruction*, 250–72.

4. Francis J. Scully, "Albert Pike's Home in Montgomery County, Arkansas," *Masonic Review Quarterly* (Mar. 1951): 8–9; Ida Sublette Cobb, "Mountain Legend of Albert Pike's Two Years in the Ouachitas," in *Mena (Ark.) Evening Star*, Apr. 22, 1939.

5. Albert Pike to Mary W. Othick, deed of conveyance, Sevier County, Ark., Mar. 11, 1864; certified and recorded at Washington, Hempstead County, Ark., Apr. 2, 1864, Turner Papers.

6. Adjutant General to Lt. General E. K. Smith, Richmond, Apr. 14, 1864, and endorsement of General Sterling Price, July 5, 1864, Walter L. Pike, AGPR; *Journal of the Congress of the*

Confederate States, June 8, Aug. 9, 1864; Yvon Pike to Hempstead, Washington, D.C., Feb. 28, 1926, Packard Collection; *Memphis Daily Appeal,* Feb. 14, 1867. The Pike gravestone in Mount Holly Cemetery, Little Rock, says Walter Lacy died in April 1863; he probably is buried in the Pike lot in Mount Holly Cemetery. *Memphis Daily Appeal,* Feb. 14, 1867.

7. The original copy of Pike's commission as judge is in Pike Papers, SCSR; it is printed in John H. Caldwell, "Albert Pike, the Lawyer," *Arkansas Research Lodge No. 739 Free & Accepted Masons* 1(3)(1949): 37–38.

8. 24 *Arkansas Reports,* vii; *Trapnall et al v. Burton et al,* (1866), 24 *Arkansas Reports,* 371–402; *Marshall v. Green Exr.* (1866), 24 *Arkansas Reports,* 410–31; *Branch v. Mitchell* (1866), 24 *Arkansas Reports,* 431–56; *Twombly v. Kimbrough* (1866), 24 *Arkansas Reports,* 459–76. The four cases were decided in 1864, but were printed, after review by the loyal court, in the 1866 report; they read "opinion prepared by A. Pike, Esq."

9. Staples, *Reconstruction in Arkansas,* 23–83.

10. *Washington Telegraph,* Aug. 24, 1864.

11. *Memphis Daily Appeal,* Mar. 10, 1867.

12. "Opinion of the Supreme Court of Arkansas Delivered, Aug. 8, 1864. Upon the Nature of the Government, the Rights of the States, and the obligations of Citizens . . . The State of Arkansas vs. Samuel W. Williams. Opinion. By the Court, Mrs. Justice Pike," *Memphis Daily Appeal,* Feb. 26–28, Mar. 1–2, 5–8, 14–16, 19.

13. *Washington Telegraph,* July 27, Aug. 10, 1864.

14. Ibid., July 6, 20, Aug. 10, 1864.

15. Arkansas *Senate Journal* (ms.), 1864, and Arkansas *House Journal* (ms.), 1864, in Library of Congress, Microfilm Collection of Early State Records, Journals, Ark., Senate, Reel 5, and House, Reel 6; microfilm copies in the University of Texas Library.

16. E. A. English and Albert Pike, "Opinion," in *Washington Telegraph,* Sept. 28, 1864. The opinion was also copied into the manuscript journals of the senate and the house.

17. Staples, *Reconstruction in Arkansas,* 57–58; John A. Bering, *History of the Forty-Eighth Ohio Net. Vol. Inf., 1861–1866* (Hillsboro, Ohio, 1880), 237–39, testify to the food shortage at Washington from 1864–1865.

18. Yvon Pike to Hempstead, Washington, D.C., Feb. 28, 1926, Packard Collection.

19. Ibid., "Autobiography," *New Age Magazine* 38 (July 1930): 425.

20. The date of Pike's going to Shreveport is not of record; Herron was there June 6–21, 1865, *Official Records,* ser. I, vol. XLVIII, pt. II, 816–17.

21. *Little Rock Daily Pantograph,* June 27, 1865, reported Pike in New Orleans on June 20.

22. French to the President of the United States, Washington, July 6, 1865, and Worsham and others to the President of the United States, Memphis, Tenn., June 26, 1865, Pike Amnesty Papers, SCSR.

23. The general facts of Pike's trip to Boston, Texas, to Shreveport, New Orleans, and Memphis, are taken from "Autobiography," *New Age Magazine* 38 (July 1930): 425.

24. Pike to the President of the United States, Memphis, Tenn., June 24, 1865, and French to the President of the United States, Washington, July 1, 1865, Pike Amnesty Papers.

25. A copy is in Pike Amnesty Papers, SCSR.

26. Pierson and others to Johnson, New York, July, 1865, Pike Amnesty Papers, SCSR.

27. Albert Pike to the Editors of the *New York Express*, n.p., n.d., in *Washington Telegraph*, Aug. 9, 1865, quoting *New York Express*, n.d.

28. "Autobiography," *New Age Magazine* 38 (July 1930): 425.

29. Pike to Charles C. McClenachan, Ottawa, Canada, July 21, 1865, Carson Collection, Grand Lodge of Massachusetts Library; typescript copy in Library of Supreme Council, Washington, D.C.

30. Pike to McClenachan, Ottawa, Canada, July 29, 1865, Carson Collection.

31. The statement is in Pike Amnesty Papers, SCSR.

32. Pike to Samuel M. Todd, Ottawa, Canada, Aug. 13, 1865, Pike Papers, SCSR.

33. Pike to McClenachan, Ottawa, Canada, July 21, 1865, Carson Collection.

34. Pike to Pierson, Ottawa, Canada, Sept. 11, 1865, Pike Papers, SCSR. A copy of President Johnson's order is printed in [Albert Pike], *Indictment for Treason . . . In the Circuit Court of the United States, for the Eastern District of Arkansas, The United States of America vs. Albert Pike* [n.p., n.d.], 1.

35. Pike to Mackey, New York, July 26, Sept. 22, 1865, Pike to Todd, New York, Oct. 19, 1865, Pike Papers, SCSR; Supreme Council *Transactions, 1857–1866* (reprint), 255; Susan B. RIley, "Albert Pike in Tennessee," *Tennessee Historical Quarterly* 9 (Dec. 1950): 300.

36. John Hallum, *Diary of an Old Lawyer* (Nashville, Tenn., 1895), 277; J. M. Keating, *History of the City of Memphis and Shelby County, Tennessee* (2 vols., Syracuse, N.Y., 1888), II, 83–84; Hallum, *History of Arkansas*, 1: 306–13; Ralph Wooster, "The Arkansas Secession Convention," *Arkansas Historical Quarterly* 13 (summer 1954): 181, 182, Appendix I.

37. Hallum, *Diary of an Old Lawyer*, 277.

38. Yvon Pike to Hempstead, Feb. 28, 1926, Packard Collection; *Little Rock Daily Pantograph*, Nov. 11, 1865.

39. Francis J. Scully, "Interesting Albert Pike Deeds," *Arkansas Research Lodge No. 739 Free & Accepted Masons* 1(5) (1951): 3–14, gives a complete history of this confiscated property.

40. Pike to Todd, New York, Oct. 19, 1865, Pike Papers, SCSR.

41. Pike to French, Little Rock, Dec. 18, 1865, Pike Amnesty Papers, SCSR.

42. Pike to Cooley, Little Rock, Dec. 18, 1865, Heiskell Collection, Little Rock, Ark..

43. Pike to Seward, Little Rock, Dec. 23, 1865, Pike Amnesty Papers, SCSR.

44. [Pike], *Indictment for Treason in the Circuit Court of the United States for the Eastern District of Arkansas, The United States vs. Albert Pike*; Pike, *The Effect of Pardons and Amnesties* [n.p., n.d.], 11p.

45. Scully, "Interesting Albert Pike Deeds," *Arkansas Research Lodge No 739 Free & Accepted Masons* 1(5): 3–4; Assessment Books for Pulaski County, 1862, 1865, 1867, 1878, Arkansas History Commission; *Memphis Daily Appeal*, May 18, 1867.

46. French to Attorney General Speed, Washington, D.C., Jan. 5, 1865 [1866], Taliaferro P. Shaffner to Attorney General Speed, [Washington], Apr. 20, 1866, Andrew King to Attorney General Speed, [Washington], Apr. 22, 1866, and endorsement to Albert Pike File, No. 566, Pike Amnesty Papers, SCSR. See also Lobingier, *Supreme Council*, 226.

47. Pike to Batchelor, Memphis, Tenn., Nov. 1, 1866, Pike Papers, SCSR. A copy of a pardon warrant form identical with the one granted Pike is in Jonathan Truman Dorris, *Pardon and Amnesty under Lincoln and Johnson* (Chapel Hill, N.C., 1953), 143.

Chapter XXXIV

1. *Memphis Daily Appeal*, July 11, 1868.

2. Pike to Mrs. A. P. Foute, Alexandria, Va., Sept. 13, 1875, Pike Papers, SCSR.

3. Albert Pike to Luke E. Barber, deed of conveyance, Little Rock, Oct. 29, 1857, filed and recorded Nov. 3, 1857, Record Book B, No. 2, pp. 20–27, Office of the Clerk of the Pulaski County Circuit Court, Little Rock. The writer is indebted to Dr. Francis J. Scully, Hot Springs, Ark., for a copy of this deed.

4. Yvon Pike to Hempstead, Washington, D.C., Feb. 28, 1926, Packard Papers; marginal notes by Yvon Pike in Allsopp, *Albert Pike*, 216–17, 224–31, in copy belonging to Packard; Pike to Foute, Alexandria, Sept. 13, 1875, Pike Papers, SCSR; Pike to Vinnie Ream Hoxie, Washington, D.C., Aug. 22, 1886, Vinnie Ream Papers, Library of Congress; Albert Pike to Lilian Pike, deed of conveyance, Washington, D.C., D.C., Mar. 27, 1871, Record Book Q2.315, Office of the Clerk of the Pulaski County Circuit Court, Little Rock; Dr. Francis J. Scully to writer, Hot Springs, Apr. 24, 1954. Mrs. Pike died Apr. 14, 1876, and was buried beside her children in Mount Holly Cemetery. Pike did not attend her funeral. The house and grounds in Little Rock then went to Lilian, to whom Pike had deeded his interest in the property in 1871. Lilian sold it in 1886 for $15,000.

5. Gerald M. Capers Jr., *The Biography of a River Town; Memphis: Its Heroic Age* (Chapel Hill, N.C., 1939), 162–63, 183–84.

6. Ibid., 184.

7. E. B. Pickett to Jerry Frazer, Memphis, June 1868, quoted in James Welch Patton, *Unionism and Reconstruction in Tennessee, 1860–1869* (Chapel Hill, N.C., 1934), 239.

8. Patton, *Unionism and Reconstruction in Tennessee*, 104, quoting Brownlow's Proclamation Book, p. 7.

9. E. Merton Coulter, *William G. Brownlow, Fighting Parson of the Southern Highlands* (Chapel Hill, N.C., 1937), 260–400; Patton, *Unionism and Reconstruction in Tennessee*, 226–40; Capers, *Memphis*, 184–85.

10. Pike to Batchelor, Memphis, Aug. 24, Dec. 3, 1866, Jan. 23, 1867, and Pike to Todd, Memphis, Jan. 4, 1867, Pike Papers, SCSR; Pike to T. and J. W. Johnson & Co., Memphis, June 28, 1867, Historical Society of Pennsylvania.

11. Pike to Johnson & Co., Memphis, June 28, 1867, Historical Society of Pennsylvania.

12. *Memphis Daily Appeal*, Feb. 1, 1867, Feb. 26, 1868; Keating, *History of Memphis and Shelby County Tennessee*, 216–17; notes furnished the writer by the late Mrs. Roscoe M. Packard.

13. *Memphis Daily Appeal*, Feb. 5, 1867.

14. Ibid.

15. "Address Read at Centre Hill, Miss. on the 22nd of July 1868, by Albert Pike," in ibid., Aug. 2, 1868; see also file of *Daily Appeal*, Feb. 1, 1867–Aug. 30, 1868.

16. *Memphis Daily Appeal*, May 4, 1867. The unpublished portion of these articles, a mss. of 122 pp., is in the Library of the Supreme Council, Pike Papers.

17. "Address Read at Centre Hill, Miss., July 22, 1868," in ibid., Aug. 2, 1868.

18. *Memphis Daily Appeal*, Feb. 8, 1867.

19. Ibid., Feb. 26, 1867.

20. Ibid., Apr. 16, 18, May 11, July 9, Aug. 3, 1867.

21. Ibid., Aug. 3, 1867.

22. Ibid., Sept. 24, Oct. 9, 12, 1867, Feb. 26, 1868.

23. Ibid., Feb. 26, 1868.

24. Ibid., June 13, 1868.

25. Ibid., July 2, 1868, for proceedings and abstract of a speech by Pike.

26. Ibid., July 11, 1868.

27. Ibid., July 12, 1868, and files of same for July–Nov. 1868.

28. Susan Lawrence Davis, *Authentic History of the Ku Klux Klan, 1865–1877* (New York, 1924), 276; Stanley F. Horn, *Invisible Empire, the Story of the Ku Klux Klan, 1866–1871* (Boston, 1939), 245–62, 335–37; J. C. Lester and D. L. Wilson, *Ku Klux Klan, Its Origins, Growth and Disbandment*, introduction and notes by Walter L. Fleming (New York, 1905), 27.

29. Allen W. Trelease, *White Terror: The Ku Klux Klan Conspiracy and Southern Reconstruction* (Baton Rouge, La., 1971), 20–21.

30. *Memphis Daily Appeal*, Apr. 16, 1868.

31. *Essays to Vinnie*, Essay 24, "Of Pleasant and Sad Remembrances," Pike Papers; *Memphis Daily Appeal*, July 8, 1869; *Edward's Annual Director to the . . . City of Memphis for 1869* (Memphis, Tenn., 1869), 33, 75; *Proceedings of the Grand Lodge of the State of Arkansas . . . 1868* (Little Rock, Ark., 1868), 148.

32. *Essays to Vinnie*, Essay 24, "Of Pleasant and Sad Remembrances," Pike Papers.

33. Ibid.

34. *Memphis Daily Appeal*, Jan. 7, July 21, Aug. 28–31, Sept. 1–2, 1868; Keating, *History of Memphis and Shelby County Tennessee*, 196.

35. Only three weeks before he left Memphis Pike had defended the Scottish Rite and himself from accusations in the *Cincinnati Commercial*, Aug. 10, 1868, that he had used his position in Masonry to advance "his KuKlux notions," and that Scotch Masonry had "too large a proportion of bitter, malignant, unrepentant rebels to be wholesome." *Memphis Daily Appeal*, Aug. 15, 1868.

36. Thomas B. Sultzer, *Pilgrimage of the Sir Knights of Maryland to St. Louis, Missouri, and Interesting Incidents Connected Therewith, During the Second Week of September, 1868* (Baltimore, 1868), 21–24.

37. *Memphis Daily Appeal*, Sept. 25, Oct. 11, 1868; Pike to Ream, Memphis, Oct. 2, 1868, Ream Papers.

38. Horn, *Invisible Empire*, 248–50.

39. Ibid., 250–51.

40. Capers, *Memphis*, 169, 173–74.

41. *Memphis Daily Appeal*, Sept. 2, Nov. 5, 1868.

Chapter XXXV

1. A card announcing this arrangement appeared in *Memphis Daily Appeal*, July 11, 1868.

2. The first notification of the formation of the partnership appeared in ibid., July 11, 1868.

3. Abel, *Slaveholding Indians*, III, 314–15n; *Dictionary of American Biography*, X, 117–18; advertisement of the sale in *Memphis Daily Appeal*, July 1–Aug. 1, 1868.

4. Quoted in *Memphis Daily Appeal*, Sept. 8, 1868.

5. Lobingier, *Supreme Council*, 227.

6. Walter Prescott Webb and H. Bailey Carroll, eds., *The Handbook of Texas* (2 vols., Austin, Tex., 1952), II, 343, 767–68.

7. Albert Pike, Robert W. Johnson, and James Hughes, *In the Supreme Court of the United States, December Term, 1868; The State of Texas, Complainant, vs. George W. White, John Chiles, and Others, Defendants; Original Suit, No. 6, In Equity; Argument for John Chiles, Defendant* [Washington, 1868]. A microfilm copy of this brief is in the University of Texas Library.

8. *Texas v. White* (1869), 19 L. ed. 227; 74 U.S. 700; 7 Wall. 700. The most complete report of the arguments of complainants and defendants is *The State of Texas v. White & Chiles* (1869), 25 Texas Reports (Supplement), 465–621, in which Pike's brief is abstracted at length, pp. 510–54, and Paschal's at pp. 484–510. William Whatley Pierson, *Texas versus White, A Study in Legal History* (Durham, N.C., 1916), is an able and painstaking piece of research.

9. Pierson, *Texas v. White*, 34.

10. *Texas v. White* (1869), 19 L. ed. 227; 74 U.S. 700; 7 Wall. 700; 25 Texas Reports (Supplement), 465.

11. *Essays to Vinnie*, Essay 8, "Of Rowing against the Stream," Pike Papers.

12. *The First National Bank of Louisville v. The Commonwealth of Kentucky* (1870), 19, L. ed. 701, 76 U.S. 353; Albert Pike and Robert W. Johnson, *In the Supreme Court of the United States; First National Bank of Louisville v. The Commonwealth of Kentucky, No. 301, Error to Court of Appeals of Kentucky, Argument for Defendant in Error* [Washington, 1869]. A microfilm copy of this brief is in the University of Texas Library.

13. 19 L. ed. 696; 76 U.S. 339; 9 Wall. 339; James G. Randall, *Constitutional Problems Under Lincoln* (Rev. ed., Urbana, Ill., 1951), 286.

14. 8 D.C. Reports 73.

15. 23 L. ed. 473; 92 U.S. 202; 2 Otto. 202; Albert Pike and Robert W. Johnson, *In the Supreme Court of the United States; Richard L. Wallach and Others, Appellants, vs. John Van Riswick, Appellee, No. 275, Brief for the Appellants* (Washington, D.C., 1874); ibid., *No. 62, Brief for the Appellants in Reply* (Washington, D.C., 1875).

16. Scully, "Interesting Albert Pike Deeds," *Arkansas Research Lodge No. 739, Free and Accepted Masons* 1(5) (1951): 12–14; *Essays to Vinnie*, Essay 12, "Of the Law and Lawyers," Pike Papers.

17. *Hamilton Pike et al. v. Wassell et al.* (1873), 19 Fed. Cas., 689, No. 11, 164 (C.C.E.D. Ark. 1873).

18. *Essays to Vinnie*, Essay 12, "Of the Law and Lawyers," Pike Papers.

19. *Pike et al. v. Wassell et al.* (1877), 24 L. ed. 307; 94 U.S. 711; 4 Otto. 711.

20. Scully, "Interesting Albert Pike Deeds," *Arkansas Research Lodge No. 739, Free and Accepted Masons* 1(5) (1951): 8–9, 13–14.

21. Edward M. Shephard, "The New Madrid Earthquake," *Journal of Geology* 13 (Jan.–Feb. 1905): 45–61; F. A. Sampson, "The New Madrid and Other Earthquakes of Missouri," *Missouri Historical Review* 7 (July 1913): 179–99; 3 *U.S. Stat. at L.* (1815), 211–12; *Hot Springs Cases* (1876), 23 L. ed. 694–95.

22. *Hot Springs Case* (1874), 10 U.S. Ct. Cl. 358.

23. The Arpent de Paris in use in Missouri equaled .84 acres; hence Langlois's 200 arpents equaled about 170 acres.

24. 1 *U.S. Attys. Gen. Opins.* (1820), 361–63, 373–76, 495; *Hot Springs Cases* (1876), 23 L. ed. 695; *The Territorial Papers of the United States*, comp. and ed. Clarence Edwin Carter, vol. XV (Washington, D.C., 1951), 619–24, 702–4.

25. *Territorial Papers of the United States*, vol. XV, 623.

26. 3 *U.S. Stat. at L.* (1822), 668.

27. 4 *U.S. Stat. at L.* (1832), 505.

28. 5 *U.S. Stat. at L.* (1843), 603; *Hot Springs Cases* (1876), 23 L. ed. 695; Thomas H. Blake, Commissioner of the General Land Office, to Secretary of the Treasurer, General Land Office, Feb. 29, 1844, Blake to W. Woodbridge, Chairman of Senate Committee on Public Lands, General Land Office, June 5, 1844, Blake to Henry Rector, General Land Office, Apr. 14, 1845, Henry M. Rector Papers, Ark. History Commission, Little Rock.

29. 5 *U.S. Attys. Gen. Opins.* (1850), 236, 237; 6 ibid. (1854), 697–98; *Little Rock Banner*, Jan. 15, May 7, 1850, Dec. 2, 9, 30, 1851; *Little Rock State Gazette and Democrat*, June 14, 28, 1850.

30. 16 *U.S. Stat. at L.* (1870), 149, *Hot Springs Cases* (1876), 23 L. ed. 691–92.

31. *Hot Springs Cases* (1874), 10 U.S. Ct. Cl. 345–374; Albert Pike and Robert W. Johnson, *In the Court of Claims, No. 6245, Henry M. Rector. vs. The United States; Claim of Title to the Hot Springs of the Ouachita; Argument* (Washington, D.C., 1872), Albert Pike, Robert W. Johnson, and John B. Sanborn, *In the Court of Claims, 6245, Henry M. Rector vs. The United States; Claim of Title to the Hot Springs of the Ouachita: Brief and Argument* (n.p., n.d.), Attorney General of the United States John W. Goforth, *In the Court of Claims of the United States, No. 6245, Henry M. Rector vs. The United States: Brief for Defendants* (n.p., n.d.), and Albert Pike, [Mss.] Petition, dated Aug. 1, 1870, General Jurisdiction Case No. 6245, Records of the United States Court of Claims, National Archives, Washington, D.C. A microfilm copy of the records pertaining to *Henry M. Rector v. The United States*, listed in this note, is in the University of Texas Library.

32. Pike, Johnson, and Sanborn, *Claim of Title to the Hot Springs of the Ouachita: Brief and Argument*, General Jurisdiction Case No. 6245, Records of the Court of Claims, National Archives; *Hot Springs Cases* (1874), 10 U.S. Ct. Cl. 299–314.

33. 10 U.S. Ct. Cl. 371–374. Justice Charles C. Nott delivered the opinion; Justice Edward G. Loring, dissenting, declared that Rector was entitled to the Hot Springs. Ibid., 374–75.

34. Pike to Rector, Alexandria, Va., May 12, 1875, Rector Papers.

35. Pike, Johnson, and Sanborn, *Claim of Title to the Hot Springs of Ouachita: Brief and Argument*, 150–51, General Jurisdiction Case No. 6245, Records of the Court of Claims, National Archives; Albert Pike, Robert W. Johnson, and others, *In the Supreme Court of the United States, No. 646, Henry M. Rector vs. The United States; Argument Upon the Claim Under the New Madrid Location* [n.p., n.d.] same, *In the Supreme Court of the United States, Term of 1875–76, No. 646, Henry M. Rector vs. The United States; Brief for Appellant* [Washington, D.C., 1875].

36. *Hot Springs Cases* (1876), 23 L. ed. 690–97; 92 U.S. 698–716; 2 Otto. 698–716.

37. Pike to Virginia Pike, Alexandria, Va., June 6, 1876, Packard Papers.

38. John H. Caldwell, "Albert Pike, the Lawyer," *Arkansas Research Lodge No. 739, Free and Accepted Masons*, 1(3) (1949): 50.

Chapter XXXVI

1. Pike to Ream, Memphis, Apr. 9, Washington, D.C., June 10, 1869, Ream Papers.
2. Pike to Ream, Washington, D.C., July 8, 1869, ibid.
3. Pike to Ream, Washington, D.C., July 8, 1869, ibid.
4. Ibid.
5. Pike to Batchelor, Washington, D.C., July 12, 1869, Pike Papers, SCSR.
6. Pike to Ream, Washington, D.C., July 14, 1869, Ream Papers. Fletcher, *Arkansas*, 118, states that Isadore "died by her own hand," a phrase that implies suicide. Neither the Pike family correspondence nor the contemporary news reports indicates that her death was anything but accidental. The writer has been informed by two or three physicians that chloroform was commonly used as a household drug in the nineteenth century, and he has seen several accounts of other accidental deaths resulting from imprudent use of the dangerous drug. Pike to Mrs. Foute, Washington, D.C., July 23, 1869, Pike to Batchelor, Washington, D.C., July 12, 1869, Pike Papers, SCSR; *Memphis Daily Appeal*, July 8–9, 1869; *Little Rock Daily Gazette*, July 8, 14, 1869.
7. Pike to Mrs. Foute, Washington, D.C., July 23, 1869, Sept. 18, 1871, Pike Papers, SCSR.
8. Pike to Ream, Washington, D.C., Aug. 15, 1870, Mar. 17, 1871, Ream Papers.
9. Pike to Todd, Washington, D.C., Jan. 8, 1872, Pike Papers, SCSR.
10. Pike to Mrs. Foute, Washington, D.C., Oct. 3, 1877, ibid.
11. Pike to Mrs. Foute, Washington, D.C., Sept. 18, 1871, ibid.
12. *Fort Smith Herald*, Jan. 1, 1867, quoting unidentified Washington, D.C. paper, n.d.; *Dictionary of American Biography*, IX, 317–18; *Who's Who in America, 1914–1915* (Chicago, 1914), 1180; George Brandes, *Recollections of My Childhood and Youth* (London, 1906), 316–24; Lorado Taft, *The History of American Sculpture* (New York, 1903), 212–13; "Obituary," *Washington Post*, Nov. 21, 1914. The bust "minus clothing to the waist" was not of Vinnie but a copy she made of Martial's ancient bust of Sabrina.
13. *Fort Smith Herald*, Jan. 1, 1867.
14. Brandes, *Recollections*, 323.
15. Pike to Ream, Washington, D.C., Mar. 27, 1867, Memphis, Apr. 2, 13, July 6, 29, 1868, Ream Papers.
16. Ibid., Apr. 13, 1868, Ream Papers.
17. Ibid., Oct., 1873, Alexandria, Nov. 6, 1874, Aug. 22, Dec. 16, 1876, Washington, D.C., Aug. 22, 1886, Ream Papers; *Essays to Vinnie*, Introduction, Essay 1, "Of Content in Old Age," Essay 8, "Of the Death of Love," Pike Papers; Roome, *Lyrics and Love Songs*, 7–8, 15–16, 81–82, 87.
18. *Essays to Vinnie*, Essay 25, "Of Sympathy," Pike Papers.
19. *Essays to Vinnie*, Essay 17, "Of Poverty and Its Compensations," Pike Papers.
20. Pike to Ream, Washington, D.C., Feb. 2, 1871, Ream Papers.
21. *New York Daily Tribune*, Feb. 2, 1871.
22. Pike to Ream, Washington, D.C., Feb. 2, 1871, Ream Papers.
23. Pike to Richard Thurston (of Fort Smith, Ark.), Alexandria, Va., Feb. 23, 1874, Turner Papers; Pike to Ream, Alexandria, Nov. 18, 1875, Ream Papers.
24. Ibid.; *Essays to Vinnie*, Essay 11, "Of My Books and Studies," Pike Papers.
25. Letter quoted in Lobingier, *Supreme Council*, 320.

26. Excerpt from Pike's reply in ibid., 320.

27. Lobingier, *Supreme Council*, 321.

28. Ibid., 320–23; *Official Bulletin*, vol. II, pt. II, 17–30.

29. *Official Bulletin*, vol. II, pt. II, 17–20, vol. III, 359–60.

30. Lobingier, *Supreme Council*, 323–24.

31. Ibid., 339–46.

32. *Morals and Dogma of the Ancient and Accepted Scottish Rite of Freemasonry*, Prepared [by Albert Pike] for the Supreme Council of the Thirty-Third Degree, for the Southern Jurisdiction of the United States and published by its authority (Charleston, A . . . M . . . 5641 [1881]), iii–iv, 328.

33. Alfred Moore Waddell, *Some Memories of My Life* (Raleigh, N.C., 1908), 126.

34. Boyden, *Bibliography*, 33–35.

35. *Essays to Vinnie*, Essay 11, "Of My Books and Studies," Pike Papers. Pike's three manuscripts were published by the Supreme Council from 1924–1930: *Irano-Aryan Faith and Doctrine as Contained in the Zend-Avesta*, [By] Albert Pike, 1874 (Louisville, Ky., 1924); *Indo-Aryan Deities and Worship as Contained in the Rig-Veda*, [By] Albert Pike, 1872 (Louisville, Ky., 1930); and *Lectures of the Arya*, [By] Albert Pike, 1873 (Louisville, Ky., 1930).

36. *Essays to Vinnie*, Essay 11, "Of My Books and Studies," Pike Papers.

37. *Essays to Vinnie*, Essay 1, "Of Content in Old Age," Pike Papers.

38. Pike to Todd, [Alexandria], Jan. 22, 1876, Pike Papers, SCSR.

39. Confidential letter of Pike to Supreme Council, Oct. 18, 1880, Pike Papers, SCSR.

40. Pike to Douglas H. Cooper, Washington, D.C., Jan. 19, Oct. 1, 1869, Pike Papers, SCSR; *Sen. Rep. No. 1978*, 49th Cong., 2d Sess., Serial No. 2458, p. 36.

41. Copy of contract printed in *Sen. Rep. No. 1978*, 49th Cong., 2d Sess., Serial No. 2458, pp. 3–4.

42. Pike testified before a Senate committee in 1887 that the Cochrane contract "was rescinded and nullified by the National Council of the Choctaw Nation, at my own special instance . . . because John D. McPherson, executor of Cochrane's will, had transferred it to a third person . . . for the exclusive benefit of the legatees of Cochrane and of Luke Lea." Ibid., p. 55.

43. Debo, *Rise and Fall of the Choctaw Republic*, 206.

44. *Sen. Rep. No. 1248*, 49th Cong., 2nd Sess., Serial No. 2458, pp. 52–54, 64–65.

45. Pike to Coleman, Armstrong Academy, Oct. 6, 1875, Pike Papers, SCSR; Pike to Ream, Midway, Ky., June 8, 1875, Ream Papers, SCSR.

46. Pike to Ream, Midway, Ky., June 8, 1875, Ream Papers.

47. Pike to Cole, Armstrong Academy, Oct. 6, 1875, Pike Papers, SCSR.

48. The affidavits are printed in *Sen. Rep. No. 1978*, 29th Cong., 2nd Sess., Serial No. 2458, pp. 52–54, 64–65.

49. Debo, *Rise and Fall of the Choctaw Republic*, 164–65, 207.

50. *Sen. Misc. Doc. No. 65*, 41st Cong., 3d Sess., Serial No. 1442, *H.R. Doc. No. 164*, 42d Cong., 2d Sess., Serial No. 1526; ibid., *No. 94*, 42d Cong., 3d Sess., Serial No. 1572; ibid., *No. 89*, 43d Cong., 1st Sess., Serial No. 1618; *Sen. Misc. Doc. No. 121*, 43d Cong., 1st Sess., Serial No. 1584.

51. *U.S. Stat. at L.* (1881), 504–505; *Sen. Misc. Doc. No. 34*, 44th Cong., 1st Sess., Serial No. 1665; *H.R. Misc. Doc. No. 40*, 44th Cong., 1st Sess., Serial No. 1698; *Sen. Misc. Doc. No. 34*, 44th Cong., 2d Sess., Serial No. 1722; *H.R. Misc. Doc. No. 14*, 45th Cong., 1st Sess., Serial No. 1774;

Sen. Misc. Doc. No. 59, 45th Cong., 2d Sess., Serial No. 1786; ibid., *No. 32*, 46th Cong., 3d Sess., Serial No. 1943; *Senate Journal*, 46th Cong., 3d Sess., Serial No. 1940, pp. 296, 297, 306, 359, 367–69, 398; *House Journal*, 46th Cong., 3d Sess., Serial No. 1950, pp. 462, 463, 562, 576, 583; *Congressional Record*, 46th Cong., 3d Sess., vol. XI, pts. I–III (Dec. 6, 1880–Mar. 3, 1881), 617, 1402, 1877, 1898–1901, 1965, 2276, 2326, 2364, 2468.

52. *Sen. Rep. No. 1978*, 49th Cong., 2d Sess., Serial No. 2458, p. 38; *The Choctaw Nation v. The United States* (1886), 21 U.S. Ct. Cl. 59–117.

53. Undated confidential report of Pike to Supreme Council at its 1880 session, Pike Papers, SCSR.

54. Confidential letter from Pike to Brethren of the Supreme Council, Washington, D.C., Oct. 18, 1880, Pike Papers, SCSR.

55. Undated confidential letter from Pike to Brethren of Supreme Council presented at the 1882 session, Pike Papers, SCSR; in *Official Bulletin*, vol. VIII, 12, Pike alludes to the motive that led him to devise his library to the Supreme Council.

56. *Official Bulletin*, vol. IV, 418–19; Lobingier, *Supreme Council*, 527; Pike to Ream, Omaha, Nebr., May 29, 1881, Nashville, Tenn., Oct. 5, 1881, Van Buren, Ark., Oct. 16, 1881, Marshall, Tex., Nov. 4, 1881, Ream Papers, SCSR.

57. Pike to Thurston, Alexandria, Feb. 23, 1874, Turner Papers.

58. Pike to Ream, Van Buren, Oct. 16, 1881, Ream Papers.

59. Ibid.

60. Ibid., Marshall, Tex., Nov. 4, 1881, Ream Papers.

61. Ibid., Pensacola, Florida, May 7, 1882, Savannah, June 7, 1882, Ream Papers.

62. Pike to Mrs. Mary Fuller, Tucson, Ariz., Apr. 21, 1883, Pike to William M. Ireland, Tucson, Apr. 20, 1883, Pike Papers, SCSR.

63. Pike to Ireland, San Francisco, May 14, 1820, ibid.

64. Pike to Ream, San Francisco, June 19, 1883, Minneapolis, Sept. 5, 1883, Ream Papers; a memorandum labeled "Visitations to the Pacific Coast, April 1–September 30, 1883," Pike Papers, SCSR.

65. *Official Bulletin*, vol. VII, 9–13; Lobingier, *Supreme Council*, 686–89.

66. Pike to Ream, Washington, D.C., Dec. 23, 1883, Ream Papers.

67. Ibid., May 20, 1884.

68. Ibid., June 8, 1884.

69. Ibid., Dec. 5, 1884.

70. Ibid., Apr. 22, 1885.

71. Ibid., Omaha, Nebr., June 14, 1885, Pike to Mrs. Mary Fuller, Kansas City, [June or July 1885], Ream papers.

72. Pike to Ream, Washington, D.C., Sept. 17, 1885, Ream Papers.

73. Ibid., Alexandria, Dec. 16, 1876; Washington, D.C., Jan., Feb. 7, Mar. 7, 15, 23, Apr. 11, 1877; Denver, Sept. 7; Washington, D.C., Nov. 23, 1878, Dec. 20, 1885, Ream Papers.

74. Ibid., Jan. 5, Feb. 20, Mar. 3, 22, 1886.

75. Ibid., Feb. 5, 1887. Sen. Rep. No. 1978, 49th Cong., 2d Sess., Serial No. 2458, p. 38; *The Choctaw Nation v. The United States*, (1886), 119 U.S. 1–44; 30 L. ed. 306–21. Pike's children forced the Choctaw Nation to pay them $75,000 in an out-of-court settlement in 1896. Debo, *Rise and Fall of the Choctaw Republic*, 209.

76. Pike to Ream, Washington, D.C., Mar. 14, 22, May 3, Aug. 9, Oct. 4, 16, Nov. 16, 1886, Jan. 4, Mar. 7, 15, 1887, Apr. 24, 1888, Ream Papers.

77. Ibid., Oct. 18, 1889.

78. Ibid., Aug. 12, 1888.

79. *Essays to Vinnie,* Essay 7, "Of Habits and Their Slaves," Pike Papers; for a list and description of his pipes, which he gave to the Supreme Council on Feb. 11, 1891, see *Official Bulletin,* vol. X, 424–25. One of these, a finely carved Maltese meerschaum, representing a chamois hunt, took a gold medal at "the Paris Exposition." Ibid., 424.

80. Pike to Ream, Washington, D.C., June 4, Aug. 23, Oct. 1, 16, 18, Dec. 4, Ream Papers.

81. Ibid., Aug. 23, 1889.

82. Ibid., Mar. 6, 1890.

83. Ibid., May 16, June 28, Aug. 19, 1890.

84. Isaac P. Noyes, "The Last Hours of Albert Pike (1809–1891)," *Official Bulletin,* vol. X, 811–12, is an excellent account of Pike's physical decline in these last years by one who knew him personally.

85. Ibid., 812–13; Pike to Ream, Washington, D.C., Nov. 21, 1890, Ream Papers; Pike to Batchelor, Washington, D.C., Nov. 21, 1890, Pike Papers, SCSR; Frederick Webber to the Supreme Council, Washington, D.C., Oct. 1892, encloses a receipt from James Dudley Morgan, M.D., who visited Pike in his last illness; the receipt lists the doctor visits, consultations, and treatments. The letter is in Pike Room, Supreme Council.

86. Pike to Batchelor, Washington, D.C., Mar. 23, 1891, *Official Bulletin,* vol. X, 407–9.

87. Noyes, "Last Hours of Albert Pike," *Official Bulletin,* vol. X, 813–15; ibid., vol. X, 408.

88. Pike had left directions on Feb. 28, 1891, that his body should be cremated and his ashes placed around two acacia trees in front of the House of the Temple; but his children refused to comply with them. *Official Bulletin,* vol. X, 423–24.

89. Lobingier, *Supreme Council,* 566; marginal note by Yvon Pike in Packard's copy of Allsopp, *Albert Pike,* 314–15.

Bibliography

Manuscripts

Records of the Adjutant General's Office, Record Group 94, War Department, National Archives, Washington, D.C. All items described below as having been used in this work are on microfilm in the University of Texas Library.

a) *Letters Received.* This collection contains some material on Pike and officers of the Arkansas troops during the years of the Mexican War, 1846–1848, including two muster rolls of Pike's company, dated Monclova, Mexico, Oct. 31, 1846, and Hacienda de Patos, Mexico, Dec. 31, 1846, respectively.

b) *Letters Sent.* This collection contains three or four important letters from the secretary of war to Gov. Thomas S. Drew of Arkansas during 1846.

c) *Regimental Papers, Mexican War, 1846–1848.* This collection contains one important letter from Pike to Gen. Zachary Taylor, Saltillo, May 23, 1847, and morning and special reports of Colonel Yell and Lt. Col. John S. Roane on the Mounted Regiment of Arkansas.

d) *Mexican War Army of Occupation, Letters Received,* Nov. 1846–May 1847. This collection contains an important letter from Gen. John E. Wool to Maj. W. W. Bliss, Buena Vista, Apr. 8, 1847, relating to sending Pike and twenty-five of his men with a message to Colonel Doniphan at Chihuahua.

e) *General [Zachary] Taylor's Orders and Special Orders, 1847.* These are bound in two volumes; they contain some material on the Arkansas troops in his command.

f) *General [John E.] Wool's Orders, 1846–1848.* These are bound in three volumes, and contain many orders relating to Pike and the officers of the Arkansas Regiment of Wool's command; vol. 2, p. 547, General order No. 297, Buena Vista, May 24, 1847, pertained to a court of inquiry requested by Pike and ordered by Wool.

Fred W. Allsopp Collection, Larson Memorial Library, University of Arkansas at Little Rock, has one letter from Isaac Pray to S. L. Fairfield, Editor of the *North American Magazine,* Hartford, Conn., May 14, 1834, concerning "a full-Essay Review" of Pike's forthcoming *Prose Sketches and Poems Written in the Western Country,* and another concerning Pike's work as attorney for the Real Estate Bank of the State of Arkansas. This collection also has an important letter of Archibald Yell, Feb. 8, 1846, relating to a feud within the Democratic party of Arkansas.

War Department Collection of Confederate Records, Record Group 109, National Archives, Washington, D.C. Copies of all records described below as having been used in this biography are on microfilm in the University of Texas Library.

a) *Letters Received by the Confederate Secretary of War* (1861–1865) [CRLR.] The Pike letters in this collection, except a lengthy report by him of the disposition of Indian moneys, dated Fort McCulloch, Apr. 22, 1862, appear to have been printed in the *Official Records.*

b) *Register of Letters Received by the Confederate Secretary of War* (1861–1865), ch. 9, vols.

21–26 1/2 (1861–1862), contain entries and a brief outline of contents of several important Pike letters that were not printed in the *Official Records* and could not be located in *Letters Received by the Confederate Secretary of War*.

c) *Register of Letters Received by the Confederate Adjutant and Inspector General's Office* (1861–1865), ch. 1, vols. 47–48 (1861–1862), contain important entries for the date and acceptance of Pike's commission in the Provisional Army of the Confederate States, the organization of the Department of Indian Territory, and other matters. Each entry gives a brief summary of contents of each letter, with place and date; many of these letters were printed in *Official Records* but several important ones were not and cannot be located today.

d) *Military Departments* (1861–1865), ch. 2, vol. 358, contains a letter press book labeled "Private Correspondence of Gen. T. H. Holmes" containing copies of a few letters, not published in *Official Records*, of value to this biography. These were written in 1862–1863 while Holmes commanded the Trans-Mississippi Department, headquarters Little Rock and points south. Another collection in this division (ch. 2) is a number of "Orders of Brigadier General Albert Pike, Commanding Department of Indian Territory, Headquarters, Fort McCulloch," printed on Pike's press at that place in 1862. A few of these, not printed in *Official Records*, were of value.

e) *Engrossed Bills of the Confederate Congress* (1861–1865) contains the important bill for "the protection of certain Indian tribes," of May 17, 1861, by which the Confederate States government annexed Indian Territory even though Pike had not yet negotiated treaties. This was a lucky find, since it had never been printed in full. It later was stolen from the National Archives, it is believed; fortunately the original is on microfilm in the University of Texas Library.

Evert A. and George L. Duyckinck Collection, New York Public Library, contains one Pike letter to William Gilmore Simms and two Simms letters to Evert Duyckinck relating to Pike; all in 1854.

Augustus Frederick Ehinger, Diary of His Travels from Illinois to Mexico, and during His Service as a Member of Comp. H., Second Regiment Illinois Volunteers, during the Mexican War. [June 15, 1846–June 28, 1847.] This is a typescript of a translation from the German script. The typescript is owned by Col. Charles F. Ward, Roswell, New Mexico. Ehinger has several important bits of information on the Arkansas volunteers.

Thomas Ewing Papers, Library of Congress, Washington, D.C., six letter-books, 1826–1868, and some 2,000 unbound letters and papers, extending from 1815–1871, contains several important Pike letters and letters from Arkansas Whig leaders relating to federal patronage in the state, 1848–1850. For a complete description, see *Handbook of Manuscripts in the Library of Congress* (Washington, D.C., 1918), 115–17.

Rufus W. Griswold Manuscripts, Boston Public Library, Boston, Mass., contains a two-page MS autobiography of Pike in Pike's hand, written about 1841 for Griswold's use in *Poets and Poetry of America* (Philadelphia, 1842). The MS has been published in full in W. M. Griswold, ed., *Passages from the Correspondence of Rufus W. Griswold* (Cambridge, Mass., 1898).

Edward Hanrick Papers (1831–1865), University of Texas Library, Austin, consist of 252 documents, 610 pages. This collection has one Pike letter and five J. T. Cochrane letters pertaining to the Choctaw Net Proceeds claim in 1858–1861.

Harvard University Archives has one Pike letter to James Walker, president, Aug. 25, 1859, accepting an honorary degree of Master of Arts, and three letters from Alfred W. Pike, Caleb Cushing, and Benjamin R. Curtis to Walker recommending Pike for the degree.

J. N. Heiskell Collection, Little Rock, has four Pike letters, Aug. 18, 1834; June 21, 1839; June 8, 1843; and Feb. 24, 1845. The first letter is pasted on the flyleaf of a choice copy of Pike's *Prose Sketches and Poems Written in the Western Country* (Boston, 1834); the others are filed in the Heiskell Collection under Pike's name. Now owned by the University of Arkansas at Little Rock.

Henry E. Huntington Manuscripts, Huntington Library and Art Gallery, San Marino 15, California, has seven Pike letters (1835–1882), a manuscript poem written and signed by Pike, Mar. 25, 1835, and a letter from John Fox Damon to Pike, Apr. 2, 1877.

Records of the Office of Indian Affairs, Record Group 75, National Archives, Washington, D.C. All material cited below as having been used in this biography are on microfilm in the University of Texas Library.

a) *Cherokee Files* (1861–1862) contain documents and correspondence pertaining to Cherokee neutrality and to the Confederate alliance of 1861.

b) *Choctaw Files* (1853–1895) contain many important letters and documents pertaining to the Net Proceeds claim and to Pike's relations with the Choctaws during the Civil War.

c) *Confederate Papers of the Arkansas Superintendary* (Letters Received and Sent, 1861–1862), in a folder labeled "'Arkansas Suptcy.' (C.S.A.) 1861–1862," in Drawer 26. These were papers found by federal officers in the Confederate Office of the Superintendent Affairs, Fort Smith, during the Civil War. They consist of letters mostly to Elias Rector, Confederate Superintendent, from the Confederate Commissioner of Indian Affairs, S. S. Scott, from Albert Pike, and from various agents and employees in the field. They are extremely valuable for Pike's connection with the Indians from 1861 to 1862. [CPAS]

d) *Confederate Miscellaneous Papers* (1861–1862), in Drawer 26 in a folder labeled "Miscellaneous Papers: Licenses to trade, Invoices, Receipts, etc." These probably came from the Confederate Superintendent of Indian Affairs Office, Fort Smith. Most of the items relate to Indian affairs, and several are signed in Pike's hand.

e) *Confederate Wichita Agency Papers* (Letters Received and Sent, 1861–1862), in Drawer 26, a folder labeled "C.S.A. 'Arkansas Suptcy.,' Wichita Agency." These were papers captured at the Wichita Agency, Leased District during the Civil War. They are mostly letters to Matthew Leeper, Confederate Reserve Indian Agent from 1861–1862, several from Pike to Leeper, one from Pike to Elias Rector. Nearly all relate to Pike's service as Indian Commissioner and Commander. [CPWA]

f) *Miscellaneous Files* (1861–1862) contain a few letters of importance to Pike's relations with the Indians.

g) *Southern Superintendency Files* (1861). These are letters sent by Elias Rector and others from the Southern Superintendency, Fort Smith headquarters, before Arkansas seceded and before Indian Territory was placed under protection of the Confederacy. Elias Rector became Confederate Superintendent in June 1861, and the Southern Superintendency of the United States then became what has been called the "Arkansas Superintendency," or merely the Confederate Superintendency.

h) *Unratified Treaty Files* (1865), containing three folders labeled "Statements, Addresses, and Correspondence." These pertain to the negotiation of Indian Reconstruction treaties with the tribes Pike had as Confederate allies in 1861. Some of the testimony is of value for views of the "Rebel and Union" Indians who attended the Fort Smith Convention in Sept. 1865 when these treaties were negotiated. Only those treaties that were never ratified by the U.S. Senate are in these folders.

Charles B. Johnson Papers (1841–1888), Edward E. Ayer collection of the Newberry Library, Chicago, Ill. These papers (448 documents, 613 pp.) contain a few important letters relating to the Choctaw Net Proceeds Claim, secession in Arkansas, and Indian affairs during the Civil War. A description of the papers is in Ruth Lapham Butler, comp., *A Check List of Manuscripts in the Edward E. Ayer Collection* (Chicago, 1937), 55. All the Johnson Papers are on microfilm in the University of Texas Library.

Charles Colcock Jones Jr. Collection, Duke University Library, contains two unimportant Pike A.L.S., dated Feb. 5, 1887, and June 1890.

James Kent Papers, Library of Congress, Washington, D.C., 1779–1847, bound in eleven volumes, contain one letter (Vol. 10, 1841–1846, August 23, 1842) pertaining to Pike's Deed of Assignment for the Real Estate Bank of the State of Arkansas. For a complete description of the collection, see *Handbook of Manuscripts in the Library of Congress* (1918), 209.

Little Rock City Council Records, 1835–1842, City Clerk's Office, City Hall, Little Rock, contain a motion (p. 172, July 12, 1839) by Alderman Albert Pike concerning fees on bonds of free negroes and mulattoes in Little Rock.

John Neal Papers, Library of Harvard University, The Houghton Library, has three Pike letters to Neal, Feb. 26, 1829; Mar. 8, 1835; and Aug. 24, 1837.

New York Public Library, Manuscript Division, has seven Pike letters (1840–1887), and "Magnolia," a Holograph poem of two pages dated 1862.

Fred M. Packard Collection, Washington, D.C., a descendant of Albert Pike, Packard lent the writer seven family letters, a copy of Allsopp's *Albert Pike*, with marginal notes and corrections by Yvon Pike (Albert's son), and two or three printed items, including a brief *Choctaw Nation v. The United States* (1872) with marginal notes in Albert Pike's hand.

George W. Paschal Papers (1838–1841), Arkansas History Commission Library, Little Rock, consisting of two letter press books (Book 8, Letters of George W. Paschal, 1838–1839; Book 9, Letters of Paschal &. Campbell, 1840–41) has two letters from Paschal to Pike & Cummins, Jan. 1, 1838, and Jan. 4, 1859, and one letter from Paschal to Pike, Mar. 15, 1841, asking legal advice and assistance of Pike & Cummins, and Pike.

Albert Pike Papers (1838–1891), Library of the Supreme Council 33°, Scottish Rite of Freemasonry, Southern Jurisdiction of the United States, House of the Temple, Washington, D.C.

a) [Account as Grand Commander of the Supreme Council, 33°, Southern Jurisdiction, Ancient and Accepted Scottish Rite of Freemasonry, from 1861 to 1878.] This is written in a cashbook of 288 pages with many blank pages and with 44 pages of accounts loosely inserted between the bound pages.

b) [Accounts and Vouchers of Albert Pike, Agent of the Confederate War Department, for expenditures in conveying Indian monies from Columbia, S.C., to Fort Smith, Ark., 1861–1862.] These accounts and vouchers (seventeen pieces) give valuable information on Pike's trip. They are on microfilm in the University of Texas Library.

c) [Ancient Alphabets.] Bound in morocco, each page ruled with border of red ink. Pike cites authorities from which he collected these words and gives information about each word. The words ere probably collected after his removal to Washington in 1869, and used in connection with his work on the Scottish Rite rituals.

d) *Ancient Faith and Worship of the Aryans, as Embodied in the Vedic Hymns*. 2 vols. and supp. vol., Washington, D.C., 1872–1873. Each volume is bound in purple morocco with ornate title pages varying slightly in design and color. There are several illustrations in vols.

1–2 by E. B. MacGrotty, who also ruled the borders of each page in colored inks and underscored many of the words in colored inks. The paper is very heavy with gilt edges.

e) *Autobiography of General Albert Pike from Stenographic Notes Furnished by Himself*, April 26, 1886. These notes were typed up by authority of James D. Richardson, Sovereign Grand Commander, whose signature appears on them. There are eighty-six pages on legal-size paper.

f) *Autograph Letters and Documents of Albert Pike* (1838–1891), collected and arranged by William L. Boyden and others from 1921 to present, consisting of fifteen volumes, over 4,000 pieces. These are in part mounted (by pasting) on folio-size manila sheets bound in buckram, and in part inserted between the sheets. Mr. R. Baker Harris, the librarian, is in the process of removing all these letters from the fifteen Boyden volumes and reorganizing them in new unnumbered volumes. In Boyden's arrangement vols. 1–14 were dated letters and vol. 15 were undated. Though the dated letters extend from 1838 to 1891 the bulk of them fall in the period after 1867, for instance, vol. 1, contained letters from 1838–1867; vol. 2, 1868–1870; vol. 3, 1871–1875; vol. 4, 1874–1878; vol. 5, 1879–1880; vol. 6, 1881–1882; vol. 7, Sept.–Dec., 1882; vol. 8, 1883–Apr., 1884; vol. 9, May, 1884–1885; vol. 10, 1886; vol. 11, 1887; vol. 12, 1888; vol. 13, 1889; vol. 14, 1890–Apr. 2, 1891. The papers before 1867 are not numerous enough to be of much importance, though several in the late fifties throw light on Pike's revision of the Scottish Rite rituals. Most of the letters after 1867 are official correspondence connected with Scottish Rite affairs; some are, however, valuable for the personal side of Pike's life and when supplemented by the *Ream Papers* (Library of Congress) offer a fairly comprehensive calendar of his life in these years. The number of A.L.S. are not so large as one might presume on seeing the total number of items of over 4,000; for a large proportion of the pieces are merely receipts, invoices, etc., signed by Pike. Cited in this work as *Pike Papers*, SCSR.

g) *Commentaries on the Kabbala*. Louisville, Ky., 1878. Not seen by the author; for a description, see Boyden, *Bibliography*, 33.

h) *Essays to Vinnie*. 5 vols., Washington, D.C., 1873–1886. These are written on fine-ruled paper, all pages gilt-edged, bordered in colored inks, and unnumbered. Each volume is bound in blue morocco and lettered on spine "Essays. Pike," with vol. number and number of essays on each; each vol. lettered on front cover, "Vinnie. Pegni d'affetto." These essays are in large degree autobiographical and have been extremely valuable for this biography. They are on microfilm in the University of Texas Library. Extracts from these essays have been printed in *New Age Magazine* 41 (1933): 717–18; 42 (1934): 163–67, 405–10; 43 (1935): 469–74, 529–33, 591–94, 605, 667–71, 733–36; 44 (1936): 35–38.

i) *Excerpts*. N.p., n.d. These are prose and poetry selections from Pike's favorite authors, at home and abroad, ancient and modern. Back side of each page is blank, pages are ruled in colored inks, and many words are underscored in inks. Bound in morocco and lettered on spine "Excerpts." Not paged.

j) *Extracts from and Comments upon the Kabbala*. Translated by Albert Pike, 1860. Not seen by author. This manuscript was probably the basis for Pike's "Gnosticism, the Kabbala and the Mysteries, as Connected with and Illustrating Masonry," *American Quarterly Review of Freemasonry* 1 (1857–1858): 14–38, 160–91, 368–407, 448–60; 2 (1858–1859): 19–33, 162–78, 313–35, 448–67.

k) *Irano-Aryan Theosophy and Doctrine as Contained in the Zend Avesta*. 3 vols., Washington, D.C., 1874. Either all or a large portion of this MS has been published:

Irano-Aryan Faith and Doctrine as Contained in the Zend-Avesta. By Albert Pike, 1874. Louisville, Ky., 1924. For a description of the MS, see Boyden, *Bibliography*, 34.

l) *Lectures of the Arya*. 8 vols., Washington, 1873. Either all or a large part of this MS has been published: *Lectures of the Arya*. By Albert Pike, 1873. Louisville, Ky., 1930. See Boyden, *Bibliography*, 34, for a description of the MS.

m) *Materials for the History of Freemasonry in France and Elsewhere on the Continent of Europe from 1718–1859*. By Albert Pike, 33°. 6 vols., [Washington, D.C.], A∴M∴ 5636 [1876.] For a description, see Boyden, *Bibliography*, 38. Most of vol. 1 of the MS was printed in *New Age Magazine* 1–10 (1904–1909): passim.

n) *Maxims of the Roman Law and Some of the Ancient French Law, as Expounded and Applied in Doctrine and Jurisprudence*. Comp. by Albert Pike. 12 vols. and 1 vol. of appendices, [New Orleans, La., and Washington, D.C., 1855–1876.] The pages are unnumbered, but the maxims are numbered consecutively 1–3,022. There is an index at the end of vol. 12. Each volume is between heavy cardboard covers, tied with string. At front of vol. 1, is a letter of instructions to printer by Pike, dated June 15, 1876.

o) *Maxims of Military Science and Art, from the Writings of Napoleon, Napier, Jomini McDougal, Graham, Mitchell, Suchet, Bisset, Alison and Others*, with *Occasional Illustrations and Applications*. Compiled by Albert Pike. 6 vols., dated Arkansas, July 1, 1863. The pages are placed between heavy cardboards and tied with string into six "volumes." The pages are numbered consecutively. Pike's description of the Pea Ridge campaign was of some value to this biography, and his account of the battles of Prairie Grove and Little Rock are interesting. He intended the work to be used by the officers of the Indian Department, but after his relief from command there he enlarged it, intending to publish it, but apparently found no publisher in the Confederate States.

p) *Notes on the Civil Code of Louisiana Made by Albert Pike in 1855, at New Orleans*. This work, bound in morocco with title page and text pages ruled with a border of red ink, was intended to assist Pike in his New Orleans practice, 1855–1858.

q) *The Past Teaching the Present and Future*. [Memphis, 1867–1868.] These are the unpublished portions of his series of articles under that title for the *Memphis Daily Appeal*, while he was editor of that periodical. Mounted on sheets in the same volume are the clippings of the published portions of the work. These papers are tied in packages between heavy cardboards and have been badly disarranged. The author sued the files of the *Memphis Daily Appeal* on microfilm in the Library of the University of Texas for the published portion of the articles.

r) Albert Pike family Bible, containing information as to births and deaths of the members of his family.

s) *Brig. Gnl. Albert Pike, Provisional Army, C.S.A., in Account with the Confederate States of America*. [1862.] Contains 145 pieces of accounts and receipts pertaining to the payment of treaty monies for the Confederate States in 1862; these are in confused state and part of the receipts have been lost or misplaced. Microfilm copies in the University of Texas Library.

t) *Register of Albert Pike, 33d: Sovereign Grand Inspector General for Arkansas, West Tennessee and the District of Columbia, Commenced the 20th of March, A.D. 1853*. This contains a record of Masonic degrees, offices, and honors conferred on Pike, 1853–1864. The last entry is on page 611, Oct. 1, 1864; balance of pages are blank. Bound in morocco.

u) *Rules and Orders of the Supreme Court of the United States*. [N.p., about 1834.] This is a printed copy of the rules, interleaved with blank pages and with additional blank pages at the back, containing twenty-nine pages of MS notes and amendments by Pike for his private use. It is paged in Pike's hand.

v) "Some Unknown Albert Pike Letters," by Harold V. B. Voorhis, 32°. [C.n.p.] 1932. These are copies of Pike letters written while he was in Canada in the summer of 1864 and after his return to the United States in 1865–1866. They are from the *Carson Masonic Collection*, Grand Lodge of Massachusetts Library.

w) *Subscription List of Official Bulletins [of the Supreme Council], from Vol. 1 to Vol. 7.* [Washington, n.d..] This list was recorded by Pike in a cashbook of 281 pp. The above title was written by Pike on a slip of paper and pasted on the front cover of the cashbook.

x) *Translations from the Rig-Veda, Friends of Indra: Svadha: The Purusha Sukta: Savitri: Names of Rishis*. By Albert Pike. [Washington, D.C., 187–.] For a description, see Boyden, *Bibliography*, 35.

y) *Translations of the Rig-Veda. Consecutive.* [By Albert Pike.] For a description, see Boyden, *Bibliography*, 35.

z) *Translations of the Rig-Veda. Of the Devas Generally and of Passages Which Mention the Arya and Dasyu.* [By Albert Pike, Washington, D.C., 187–.] For a description, see Boyden, *Bibliography*, 36.

aa) *Translation of the Rig-Veda, The Marute.* By Albert Pike. 4 vols. [Washington, D.C., 187–.] For a description, see Boyden, *Bibliography*, 35.

bb) [Vocabularies of Indian Languages. By Albert Pike.] These works were collected and arranged by Pike in 1857 and 1861 in Indian Territory. There are fifty-six pages of Creek Vocabulary, twenty-one pages of tenses and modes of seven verbs in Creek, twenty-seven pages of verb forms of Creek and allied tongues, eleven pages (200 words) of the Osage language, and fourteen pages of words of the Wichita, Caddo, Kichai, Delaware, Comanche, and Tonkawa languages.

cc) [Vocabularies of Sanscrit Words. By Albert Pike.] 7 pts. [Washington, D.C., n.d..] The seven parts are each covered in brown paper and fastened with slips. There are many blank pages interleaved with the seventy-nine pages of written words. The words were probably compiled for use in translating the Rig-Veda and other ancient oriental writings.

Albert Pike Papers (1837–1845), Boston Public Library, Boston, Mass., containing two letters, one to George W. Light dated Little Rock, May 9, 1834, and the other to Ben. Perley Poore, dated Little Rock, June 19, 1845.

Albert Pike Papers (1855–1891), Duke University Library, Durham, N.C., five items.

Albert Pike Papers (1841–1871), Historical Society of Pennsylvania Library, Philadelphia, contain six Pike letters from 1841–1871.

Albert Pike Papers (1860–1884), The New York Historical Society, N.Y., containing three Pike A.L.S., 1860, 1883, 1884.

Albert Pike Papers, Yale University, has five Pike letters (1833–1888) and two manuscript poems by Pike, dated 1846 and 1888.

Pulaski County Assessment Books (1835–1868), Arkansas History Commission Library, Little Rock, containing annual lists of Pike's taxable property and taxes for 1835–1839, 1841, 1843, 1845–1853, 1855–1858, 1861–1863, 1865, 1867–1868.

Records of the Real Estate Bank of the State of Arkansas (1839–1859), Arkansas History Commission Library, Little Rock. Individual Ledger, M to Z, 1843, Central Bank, Little Rock, contains Pike's private account; Cash Book; 1839–1859; Central Bank, Little Rock, carried an account of Pike from 1848–1850; Accounts [Book], 1838–1842, Central Bank, Little Rock, contains an account of Pike from 1839–1840. These records are highly fragmentary; the printed reports of the state legislature are complete. Letters of the Helena Real Estate Bank,

1839–1846, Book 16, contains a few letters of Pike as attorney for the trustees of the Real Estate Bank.

Vinnie Ream Papers (1850–1914), Library of Congress, Washington, D.C., containing some 1,400 letters and documents and two scrapbooks of clippings (1860–1870). This collection contains some 250 Pike letters written to and on behalf of Vinnie Ream from 1867–1890. For a complete description of the Ream Papers, see Solon J. Buck and Dorothy S. Eaton, "Manuscripts," *Library of Congress Quarterly Journal of Current Acquisition* 8(3) (May 1951): 24. The Pike letters of these papers are on microfilm in the University of Texas Library.

Henry M. Rector Papers (1844–1875), Arkansas History Commission Library, Little Rock, contains one Pike letter to Rector, May 12, 1875, relating to Hot Springs Case and three letters of Commissioner of Public Lands Thomas H. Blake (1844–1845) relating to the rejection of Rector's patent to Hot Springs.

John Ross Papers, Phillips Collection, University of Oklahoma Library, Norman, has a few letters concerning Cherokee neutrality in 1861.

Jesse Turner Papers (1827–1910), Duke University Library, Durham, N.C., has 337 items including 33 Pike letters, mostly from Pike to Turner, from 1834–1888, and including a deed, a mortgage, one letter from Pike to James K. Polk, Nov. 30, 1847, and one letter to Dr. Richard Thurston of Fort Smith, Feb. 23, 1874. For a complete description of the Turner collection, see *Guide to the Manuscript Collections in the Duke University Library* (Durham, N.C., 1947), 237.

Records of the United States Court of Claims, Record Group 123, National Archives, Washington, D.C.

a) *General Jurisdiction Case No. 6245. Henry M. Rector v. The United States* (1875), containing a complete record of all beliefs, arguments, testimony, affidavits, and papers filed in the case. There are a total of 584 pp. of printed and MS material in the file. A microfilm copy is in the University of Texas Library.

b) *General Jurisdiction Case No. 12,742. The Choctaw Nation v. The United States* (1883), containing a complete file of all records used in the case, a total of 425 pp. A microfilm copy is in the University of Texas Library.

c) *General Jurisdiction Case No. 19,384. Yvon Pike et al v. The Choctaw Nation* (1895), containing 3,207 pages of printed, written, and typed pages. A microfilm copy is in the University of Texas Library.

Published Writings of Albert Pike

[Pike, Albert.] *Address* [at the celebration of anniversary of St. John the Baptist.] [Little Rock, Ark., 185-.]

An Address Delivered by Albert Pike, Esq., to the Young Ladies of the Tulip Female Seminary and Cadets of the Arkansas Military Institute, at Tulip, on 4th June, 1852. Little Rock, Ark., 1852.

Address, by Albert Pike, Delivered before Western Star Lodge, No. 2, of Ancient, Free and Accepted Masons, June 24, 1851; and at the Laying of the Corner-Stone of the Masons and Odd Fellows' Hall, May 20, 1852, in the City of Little Rock. Little Rock, Ark., 1852.

[Pike, Albert.] *Address by the President of the State Council of Arkansas, Delivered at the First Annual Session on the 30th April, 1855.* Little Rock, Ark., 1855.

[Pike, Albert.] *Address* [on Saint John's College.] [Little Rock, Ark., 1852.]

Address on the Southern Pacific Railroad, Delivered in the Hall of the House of Representatives of the State of Louisiana, by Albert Pike, February 9, 1855. New Orleans, La., 1855.

Pike, Albert. *Address to the Senators and Representatives of the State of Arkansas in the Congress of the Confederate States.* [Richmond, Va., 1863] (Signed: Albert Pike, Louisiana, March 20, 1863.)

P.[ike], A.[lbert.] *To the American Party South.* Washington, D.C., [1856.]

Pike, Albert. *The Arkansas Form Book, Containing a Large Variety of Legal Forms and Instruments, Adapted to Popular Wants and Professional Use, in the State of Arkansas with a Summary of the Principles of Law, of Most Ordinary Application.* Little Rock, Ark., 1842.

Arkansas, Revised Statutes (1838). Preface, notes, and index by Albert Pike.

[Pike, Albert.] "Autobiographical Memorandum (1841)," in W. M. Griswold, ed., *Passages from the Correspondence of Rufus W. Griswold.* Cambridge, Mass., 1898.

Charges and Specifications Preferred August 23, 1862, by Brigadier General Albert Pike, against Major Gen. Thos. C. Hindness. Richmond, Va., 1863.

[Pike, Albert.] *The Choctaw Nation vs. The United States.* Washington, D.C., 1872.

Pike, Albert. "Crayon Sketches and Journeyings, Nos. I–III," *Boston Pearl and Literary Gazette* 4 (Nov. 8, 22, 1834; Jan. 10, 1835): 69–70, 88–89, 143.

[Pike, Albert.] *Draught of a Declaration of Independence, Proposed to the Convention of the State of Arkansas and Withdrawn from Its Consideration.* Little Rock, Ark., 1861.

Pike, Albert. *The Effect of Pardons and Amnesties.* N.p., [1865?.]

[Pike, Albert.] *The Emphatic Remonstrance of the People of the State of Arkansas against Invasion of Their Right of Self-Government; Addressed to the Representatives of the Other United States of America in Congress Assembled.* [Washington, D.C., 1874.]

[Pike, Albert.] *The Evil and the Remedy.* By Sabinus, Little Rock, Ark., 1844. Photostatic copy in the University of Texas Library.

Pike, Albert. *Hymns to the Gods and Other Poems.* Privately printed, pt. 1, [New York], 1873.

Pike, Albert. *Hymns to the Gods and Other Poems.* Privately printed, pt. 2, [New York], 1882.

[Pike, Albert.] *Indictment for Treason . . . In the Circuit Court of the United States, for the Eastern District of Arkansas; The United States of America vs. Albert Pike*, N.p., n.d.

Indo-Aryan Deities and Worship as Contained in the Rig-Veda by Albert Pike, 1872. Louisville, Ky., 1930.

Irano-Aryan Faith and Doctrine as Contained in the Zend-Avesta by Albert Pike, 1874. Louisville, Ky., 1924.

[Pike, Albert.] *Kansas State Rights, An Appeal to the Democracy of the South.* By a Southern State-Rights Democrat. Washington, D.C., 1857.

Lectures of the Arya by Albert Pike, 1873. Louisville, Ky., 1930.

Lecture of Bro. Albert Pike, Delivered by Special Request, before the M. W. Grand Lodge of Louisiana, at Its Forty-Sixth Annual Communication, Held in New Orleans, February, 1858. New Orleans, 1858.

Albert Pike's Letter Addressed to Major General Holmes, Little Rock, December 30, 1862. There are several editions of this pamphlet, varying in number of pages; see Boyden, *Bibliography*, 20.

Letter of Albert Pike to the Choctaw People. Washington, D.C., 1872.

Pike, Albert. "Letters from Arkansas, No. I," *New England Magazine* 9 (Oct. 1835): 263–70.

Pike, Albert. "Letters from Arkansas, No. II," *American Monthly Magazine* 1 (Jan. 1836): 25–32.

Letters to the People of the Northern States. By A.[lbert] P.[ike.] [Washington, D.C., 1856.] (There are two editions of this pamphlet, a thirty-five page one and a forty-eight-page one.)

Pike, Albert. *Letter to the President of the Confederate States*. Fort McCulloch, Indian Territory, July 3, 1862. (Signed: Albert Pike.)

Pike, Albert. *A Letter to the President of the United States*. New York, 1865.

Pike, Albert. "Life in Arkansas," *American Monthly Magazine* 1 (Feb.–Mar. 1836): 154–59, 295–302.

[Pike, Albert.] *Memorial of the Muscogee or Creek Nation of Indians to the Honorable Senate and House of Representatives of the United States of America*. [Little Rock, Ark., 1852.]

Pike, Albert. *Memorial of the Muscogee on Creek Nation of Indians, to the Congress of the United States.* [Washington, D.C.? 1853?]

Mexico, Anniversary of the Capital; The Veteran Celebrate the Event . . . An Oration by General Albert Pike. Reprints from *Washington Chronicle*, Sept. 15, [1875.] [Washington, D.C., 1875.] (Oration by Pike, pp. 2–7.)

[Pike, Albert, comp.] *Morals and Dogma of the Ancient and Accepted Scottish Rite of Freemasonry, Prepared for the Supreme Council of the Thirty-Third Degree, for the Southern Jurisdiction of the United States*. Charleston, A.: M.: 5641 [1881.]

National Plan of an Atlantic and Pacific Railroad, and Remarks of Albert Pike thereon, at Memphis, November, 1849. Little Rock, Ark., 1849.

Pike, Albert. *Nugae*. Printed for private distribution, Philadelphia, 1854.

Pike, Albert. *Oration* [before the Grand Lodge of Odd Fellows, August 8, 1850.] [Little Rock, Ark., 1850.]

[Pike, Albert.] *Overland Route to the Pacific*. By a Citizen of Arkansas. N.p., about 1857.

Pike, Albert. *Prose Sketches and Poems Written in the Western Country*. Boston, 1834.

[Pike, Albert.] *Second Letter Addressed to Lieut. General Theophilus H. Holmes*. [Richmond, Va., 1863.]

Pike, Albert. "A Sketch," *The Essayist* 2 (July 1831): 69–70.

Pike, Albert. "Sketches of Tennessee," *The Essayist* 2 (July 1831): 80.

Southern and Western Commercial Convention. *Resolution of the Charleston Convention upon the Subject of the Southern Pacific Railroad, Adopted April, 1854, [and] Resolutions Adopted by the Southern & Southwestern Commercial Convention, at New Orleans, January, 1855, [together with] A Bill to Create and Incorporate the Southern Pacific Railroad Company. [New Orleans, 1855.]* A committee report presented to the Louisiana Legislature, Feb. 7, 1855, by Albert Pike, chairman.

Pike, Albert. *State or Province? Bond or Free? Addressed Particularly to the People of Arkansas*. N.p., [1861.]

Pike, Albert. *State or Province? Bond or Free? Appendix*. N.p., [1861.]

Pike, Albert, comp. *The Statutes and Regulations, Institutes, Laws and Grand Constitutions of the Ancient and Accepted Scottish Rite*. New York, 1859.

Pike, Albert. *Supreme Court of the United States, December Term, 1856, The President and Directors of the Bank of Washington vs. The State of Arkansas and the Trustees of the Real Estate Bank of the State of Arkansas, Defendants, Error to the Supreme Court of Arkansas: Argument for the Plaintiffs in Error*. Washington, D.C. [1856?]

[Pike, Albert.] *Thoughts on Certain Political Questions*. By a Looker-on. Washington, D.C., 1859.

Pike, Albert. "Western Travelling," *Hartford Pearl and Literary Gazette* 4 (Sept. 1834): 48–49.

Whig Committee Address to the People of Arkansas. Albert Pike, chairman, [Little Rock, Ark., 1838.]

Pike, Albert, and Charles Matthews. *To the People of Arkansas and California*. N.p., [1856.]

Pike, Albert, and Ebenezer Cummins. *In the Supreme Court of Arkansas, July Term, A.D. 1855, The President and Directors of the Bank of Washington, and James Holford's Administrations, Appellants vs. Appeal from the Chancery Court of Pulaski Co., The State of Arkansas, and the Trustees of the Real Estate Bank of the State of Arkansas, Appellees*. [Little Rock, Ark.? 1855?.]

Pike, Albert, Robert W. Johnson, and James Hughes. *In the Supreme Court of the United States, December Term, 1868, The State of Texas, Complainant, vs. George W. White, John Chiles, and Others, Defendant, Original Suit, No. 6, in Equity; Argument for John Chiles, Defendant*. [Washington, D.C., 1868.]

Pike, Albert, and Robert W. Johnson. *In the Supreme Court of the United States, Richard L. Wallach and Others, Appellate, vs. John Van Riswick, Appelle, No. 275; Brief for the Appellate*. Washington, D.C., 1874.

Pike, Albert, and Robert W. Johnson. *In the Supreme Court of the United States, First National Bank of Louisville vs. The Commonwealth of Kentucky, No. 301, Error to Court of Appeals of Kentucky; Argument for Defendant in Error*. [Washington, D.C., 1869.]

Pike, Albert, and Robert Johnson. *In the Supreme Court of the United States, Richard L. Wallach and Others, Appellants, vs. John Van Riswick, Appellee, No. 62, Brief for the Appellate in Reply*. [Washington, D.C., 1875.]

Pike, Albert, Robert W. Johnson, and Others. *In the Supreme Court of the United States, Term of 1875–76, No. 646, Henry M. Rector vs. The United States; Brief for Appellant*. [Washington, D.C., 1875.]

Pike, Albert, and Robert W. Johnson. *The True Merite of the Controversy in Arkansas for the Consideration of Honest Men*. Washington, D.C., 1874–.

Newspapers

Advocate. Little Rock, Ark.

Banner. Little Rock, Ark.

Chronicle. Little Rock, Arkansas.

Daily Appeal. Memphis, Tenn.; five reels of this paper from Jan. 1867–Dec. 31, 1869, are on microfilm in the University of Texas Library.

Daily Crescent. New Orleans, La.

Daily Delta. New Orleans, La.

Daily Enquirer. Richmond, Va.

Daily Examiner. Richmond, Va.

Daily Herald. New York, N.Y.

Daily Intelligencer. Washington, D.C.

Daily Pantograph. Little Rock, Ark.

Daily Picayune. New Orleans, La.

Daily State Journal. Little Rock, Ark.

Daily Times. New York, N.Y.
Daily Tribune. New York, N.Y.
Eagle. Batesville, Ark.
Evening Star. Mena, Ark.
Evening Transcript. Boston, Mass.
Forney's War Press. Philadelphia, Pa.
Gazette. Little Rock, Ark. Title varies: *State Gazette, Arkansas Gazette, State Gazette and Democrat,* and *Daily Arkansas Gazette.*
Herald. Fort Smith, Ark.
Herald. Newburyport, Mass.
Home Journal. New York, N.Y.
Inquirer. Philadelphia, Pa.
Intelligencer. Van Buren, Ark.
National Intelligencer. Washington, D.C.
The New Yorker. New York, N.Y.
News. Batesville, Ark.
North American and United States Gazette. Philadelphia, Pa.
Northern Standard. Clarksville, Tex.
Old Line Democrat. Little Rock, Ark.
Patriot. Little Rock, Ark.
Press. Van Buren, Ark.
Southern Shield. Helena, Ark.
Spirit of the Times. New York, N.Y.
Star. Little Rock, Ark.
State Democrat. Little Rock, Ark.
The Tattler. New York, N.Y.
Telegraph. Washington, Ark.
Times. Fort Smith, Ark.
Times. Little Rock, Ark.
Times and Advocate. Little Rock, Ark.
Tornado. Little Rock, Ark.
Transcript. Boston, Mass.
Tribune. Chicago, Ill.
True Democrat. Little Rock, Ark.
Weekly Delta. New Orleans, La.
Weekly Herald. New York, N.Y.
Whig. Little Rock, Ark.
Whig Banner. Nashville, Tenn.

PERIODICALS

The American Magazine and Repository of Useful Literature Devoted to Science, Literature, and Arts (Albany, N.Y.), 1–2 (1841–1842).

The American Monthly Magazine (Boston), 1–3 (1829–1831).

The American Monthly Magazine (New York), New Series, 1 (1836).

American Quarterly Review of Freemasonry (New York), 1–2 (1857–1859).

Blackwood's Magazine (Edinburgh; London), 45 (1839), 47 (1840).

The Boston Pearl and Literary Gazette, 3–5 (1833–1835).

The Bower of Taste (Boston), 1–3 (1828–1830).

The Essayist (Boston), 1–2 (1829–1831), New Series, 1 (1831–1833).

Graham's Magazine (Philadelphia), 18–21 (1841–1842), 43 (1853).

Hartford Pearl and Library Gazette (Hartford, Conn.), 4 (1834).

Knickerbocker (New York), 22–53 (1844–1859).

Ladies Companion (New York), 12–15 (1839–1841).

Ladies Magazine (Boston), 3 (1830).

The Magnolia (Charleston, N.C.), New Series 1–2 (1842–1843).

National Freemason (Washington, D.C.), 8 (Feb. 2, 1867).

New Age Magazine (Washington, D.C.), 1 (1904).

New England Magazine (Boston), 9 (1835).

The New Mirror (New York), 1–3 (1843–1844).

The New York Mirror 9 (1831).

The New York Weekly Mirror 2 (1845).

The North American Magazine (Philadelphia), 5 (1835).

The Quarterly Journal and Review (Cincinnati, Ohio), 1 (1846).

The Rover, a Weekly Magazine of Tales, Poetry, and Engravings (New York), 2 (1843).

Waverly Magazine (Boston), 6 (June, 1853).

The Western Messenger (Cincinnati, Ohio), 1–8 (1835–1841).

The Yankee and Boston Literary Gazette (Portland, Maine), 2 (1828–1829).

The Young American's Magazine of Self-Improvement (Boston), 1 (1847).

PRINTED SOURCES

Arkansas Bar Association. Constitution of the Bar Association of the State of Arkansas, Adopted at an Aggregate Meeting of the Profession, Held in the City of Little Rock, on the 24th Day of Nov. 1837. Little Rock, 1838.

Arkansas Acts (1843, 1853, 1855).

Arkansas. Acts of the General Assembly of the State of Arkansas, Relative to the Real Estate Bank of Arkansas. Also the Deed of Assignment of Apr. 2d, 1842. Little Rock, Ark., 1855.

Arkansas *House Journal* (1837, 1838, 1842–1843, 1856–1857, 1860–1861).

Arkansas Reports.

Arkansas *Senate Journal* (1860–1861).

[Byrne, Andrew.] *Letters Addressed to the Unprejudiced People of Arkansas, on Captain Pike's Misrepresentations of Catholic Principles, and Apology for the Proscription of Catholics and Foreigners.* By Petricula. Printed at the True Democrat Office for Peter Farrell, [Little Rock, Ark., 1855.]

Choctaw Nation. *Acts and Resolutions of the General Council of the Choctaw Nation, from 1852 to 1857, Both Inclusive.* Fort Smith, Ark., 1858.

Congressional Globe. 32 Cong., 1–2 Sess., Dec. 1, 1851–Aug. 31, 1852, Dec. 6, 1852–Mar. 3, 1853; 33 Cong., 1 Sess., Dec. 5, 1853–Aug. 7, 1854; 34 Cong., 1–2 Sess., Dec. 3, 1855–Aug. 18, 1856, Aug. 21–30, 1856; 35 Cong., 2 Sess., Dec. 6, 1853–Mar. 3, 1859; 36 Cong., 1–2 Sess., Dec. 5, 1859–June 25, 1860, Dec. 3, 1860–Mar. 2, 1861; 37 Cong., Special Sess., Mar. 4–28, 1861.

Congressional Record. 46 Cong., 3 Sess., vol. 11, pts. 1–3 (Dec. 6, 1880–Mar. 3, 1881).

Cooper, Douglas H. *Reply to Charges Made by J. P. C. Shanks . . . in Regard to Matters Connected with Choctaw and Chickasaw Affairs.* Washington, D.C., 1873.

The Cyclopaedia of Wit and Humor. Ed. William E. Burton. 2 vols., New York, 1858.

Dale, Edward Everett, and Gaston Litton, eds. *Cherokee Cavaliers, Forty Years of Cherokee History as Told in the Correspondence of the Ridge-Watie-Boudinat Family.* Norman, Okla., 1940.

De Bow, J. D. B., comp. *Statistical View of the United States . . . a Compendium of the Seventh Census.* Washington, D.C., 1854.

District of Columbia Reports.

"Editor's Table," *Knickerbocker* 52 (Apr. 1859): 429–31.

Edward's Annual Directory to the . . . City of Memphis for 1869. Memphis, Tenn., 1869.

Harvard University. *The Annual Report of the President of Harvard University to the Overseers on the State of the University, for the Academic Year, 1825–6.* Cambridge, Mass., 1827.

Harvard University. *President's Annual Reports, 1825–1831.* N.p., n.d.

Harvard University. *Statutes and Laws of the University in Cambridge, Massachusetts.* Cambridge, Mass., 1825.

Harvard University. *Statutes and Laws of the University in Cambridge, Massachusetts.* Cambridge, Mass., 1826.

Inaugural Address of Henry M. Rector, Delivered before the General Assembly of Arkansas, 15th November, 1860. N.p., n.d.

James, John G. *The Southern Student's Hand-Book of Selections for Reading and Oratory.* New York, 1879.

Journal of Both Sessions of the Convention of the State of Arkansas. Little Rock, Ark., 1861.

Journal of the Congress of the Confederate States of America, 1861–1865. 7 vols., Washington, D.C., 1904–1905.

Kappler, Charles J. *Indian Affairs, Laws and Treaties.* 4 vols., Washington, D.C., 1904–1929.

Life Wake of the Fine Arkansas Gentleman Who Died before His Time. Washington, D.C., 1859.

Louisiana Acts (1855).

Memphis Convention. Minutes and Proceedings of the Memphis [Railroad] Convention, Assembled October 23, 1849. [Memphis, Tenn., 1849.]

Message of Gov. Henry M. Rector to the General Assembly of Arkansas, in extra session, Nov. 6, 1861. Little Rock, Ark., 1861.

Message of Elias N. Conway, Governor of Arkansas, to Both Houses of the General Assembly, November 7, 1854. Little Rock, Ark., 1854.

Moore, Frank, ed. *The Rebellion Record*. 11 vols., New York, 1861–1868.

Official Bulletin of the Supreme Council of the 33rd Degree for the Southern Jurisdiction of the United States. 10 vols., Charleston, S.C., 1870–1892.

Official Records of the Union and Confederate Navies in the War of the Rebellion. 30 vols. and index, Washington, D.C., 1894–1927.

Phillips, Ulrich Bonnell, ed. *The Correspondence of Robert Toombs, Alexander H. Stephens, and Howell Cobb*. American Historical Association Annual Report, 1911, vol. 2. Washington, D.C., 1913.

[Pike, John.] "Will of John Pike, Sr.," *Essex Antiquarian* 9 (Apr. 1904): 64–65.

[Pitchlynn, P. P.] *A Letter from Tushka-Homma to the Choctaw People*. Choctaw Nation, Aug. 1873.

Pitchlynn, P. P. *Reply . . . to a Libellous Pamphlet Published by Douglas H. Cooper*. Washington, D.C., 1873.

Pitchlynn, P. P. *Report . . . to His Excellency the Principal Chief and General Council of the Choctaw Nation*.

Porter, William T., ed. *A Quarter Race in Kentucky and Other Sketches*. Philadelphia, 1847.

Pray, Isaac C., Jr. *Prose and Verse from the Port Folio of an Editor*. Boston, 1836.

Proceedings of the Convention at Savannah. [Savannah, Ga., 1856.]

Proceedings of the Grand Lodge of the State of Arkansas . . . 1868. Little Rock, Ark., 1868.

In the Pulaski Circuit Court, in Chancery. The State of Arkansas vs. The Trustees of the Real Estate Bank of the State of Arkansas. [Little Rock, Ark., 1854.] 37 pp.

[Rector, Henry M.] Special Message of the Governor on Federal Relations, 1860. N.p., n.d.

Report of the Accountants, Appointed under the Act of January 15, 1855, to Investigate the Affairs of the Real Estate Bank of Arkansas. Little Rock, Ark., 1856.

Report of Gordon N. Peay, as Receiver in Chancery of the Real Estate Bank, 1st October, 1858. Little Rock, Ark., 1858.

A Report of the Proceedings of the Occasion of the Reception of the Sons of Newburyport Resident Abroad, July 4th, 1854. Comp. and reported by Joseph H. Brogdon. Newburyport, Mass., 1854.

Report of the Treasurer of the State of Arkansas. Little Rock, 1837.

The Rough and Ready Annual, on Military Souvenir. New York, 1848.

Smith, William R. *History and Debates of the Convention of the People of Alabama, January 7, 1861*. Montgomery, Ala., 1861.

South Carolina House Journal (1854).

Southern Commercial Convention. Proceedings of the Southern Commercial Convention, Held in the City of New Orleans on the 8th, 9th, 10th, 11th, 12th, 13th, and 15th of January, 1855. New Orleans, La., 1855.

Southern Commercial Convention. Proceedings of the Southern Convention at Savannah. [Savannah, Ga., 1856.]

Southern and Western Commercial Convention. *The Journal of Proceedings of the Commercial Convention of the Southern and Western States, Held in the City of Charleston, South Carolina, During the Week Commencing on Monday, 10th April, 1854*. Charleston, S.C., 1854.

The Statutes at Large of the Provisional Government of the Confederate States of America. Ed. by James M. Matthews. Richmond, Va., 1864.

The Territorial Papers of the United States. Comp. and ed. by Clarence Edwin Carter. Vol. 15, Washington, D.C., 1951.

Texas Reports.

Transactions of the Supreme Council of the 33d Degree, Ancient and Accepted Scottish Rite of Free-Masonry, for the Southern Jurisdiction of the United States of America, 1857–1866. Reprint, Washington, D.C., 1878.

U.S. Attorney General Opinions.

U.S. Compendium of the Enumeration of the Inhabitants and Statistics of the United States, as Obtained at the Department of State . . . [1840.] Washington, D.C., 1841.

U.S. Congress. House of Representatives Executive Document 60, 30th Cong., 1st Sess., Serial No. 520. Washington, D.C., 1847–1848.

U.S. Congress. House of Representatives Executive Document No. 82, 36th Cong., 1st Sess., Serial No. 1056. Washington, D.C., 1860.

U.S. Congress. House of Representatives Executive Document 1, 27th Cong., 3d Sess., Serial No. 1157. Washington, D.C., 1863.

U.S. Congress. House of Representatives Executive Document 1, 39th Cong., 1st Sess., Serial No. 12487. Washington, D.C., 1866.

U.S. Congress. House of Representatives Executive Document 10, 42d Cong., 3d Sess., Serial No. 1563. Washington, D.C., 1873.

U.S. Congress. House of Representatives Journal, 19th Cong., 2d Sess., Serial No. 147, Washington, D.C., 1826.

U.S. Congress. House of Representatives Journal, 36th Cong., 1st Sess., Serial No. 1042. Washington, D.C., 1859.

U.S. Congress. House of Representatives Journal, 36th Cong., 2d Sess., Serial No. 1091. Washington, D.C., 1860.

U.S. Congress. House of Representatives Journal, 46th Cong., 3d Sess., Serial No. 1950. Washington, D.C., 1880.

U.S. Congress. House of Representatives Miscellaneous Document No. 10, 32d Cong., 2d Sess., Serial No. 685. Washington, D.C.,1853.

U.S. Congress. House of Representatives Miscellaneous Document No. 89, 43d Cong., 1st Sess., Serial No. 1618. Washington, D.C., 1874.

U.S. Congress. House of Representatives Miscellaneous Document No. 164, 42d Cong., 2d Sess., Serial No. 1526. Washington, D.C., 1872.

U.S. Congress. House of Representatives Miscellaneous Document No. 94, 42d Cong., 3d Sess., Serial No. 1572. Washington, D.C., 1873.

U.S. Congress. House of Representatives Miscellaneous Document No. 89, 43d Cong., 1st Sess., Serial No. 1618. Washington, D.C., 1874.

U.S. Congress. House of Representatives Miscellaneous Document No. 40, 44th Cong., 1st Sess., Serial No. 1698. Washington, D.C., 1876.

U.S. Congress. House of Representatives Miscellaneous Document No. 14, 45th Cong., 1st Sess., Serial No. 1774. Washington, D.C., 1877.

U.S. Congress. House of Representatives Report No. 41, 41st Cong., 3d Sess., Serial No. 1464. Washington, D.C., 1871.

U.S. Congress. House of Representatives Report No. 98, 42d Cong., 3d Sess., Serial No. 1579. Washington, D.C., 1873.

U.S. Congress. Journal of the Executive Proceedings of the Senate. 32 vols., Washington, D.C., 1828–1909.

U.S. Congress. Report of the Joint Committee on the Conduct of the War. In 3 parts, Washington, 1863. (Sen. Ref. Com. No. 108, 37 Cong., 3d Sess., Serial Nos. 1152–1154, Washington, D.C., 1863.)

U.S. Congress. Senate Executive Document No. 1, 30th Cong., 1st Sess., Serial No. 503. Washington, D.C., 1847.

U.S. Congress. Senate Executive Document No. 32, 31st Cong., 1st Sess., Serial No. 558, Washington, D.C., 1850.

U.S. Congress. Senate Journal, 33d Cong., 1st Sess., Serial No. 689. Washington, D.C., 1853.

U.S. Congress. Senate Journal, 35th Cong., 1st Sess., Serial No. 838. Washington, D.C., 1855.

U.S. Congress. Senate Journal, 35th Cong., 2nd Sess., Serial No. 973. Washington, D.C., 1858–1859.

U.S. Congress. Senate Journal, 36th Cong., 1st Sess., Serial No. 1022. Washington, D.C., 1859–1860.

U.S. Congress. Senate Journal, 46th Cong., 3d Sess., Serial No. 1940. Washington, D.C., 1880.

U.S. Congress. Senate Miscellaneous Document No. 31, 34th Cong., 1st Sess., Serial No. 835. Washington, D.C., 1856.

U.S. Congress. Senate Miscellaneous Document No. 9, 36th Cong., 2d Sess., Serial No. 1098. Washington, D.C., 1861.

U.S. Congress. Senate Miscellaneous Document No. 65, 41st Cong., 3d Sess., Serial No. 1442. Washington, D.C., 1871.

U.S. Congress. Senate Miscellaneous Document No. 121, 43d Cong., 1st Sess., Serial No. 1584. Washington, D.C., 1874.

U.S. Congress. Senate Miscellaneous Document No. 34, 44th Cong., 1st Sess., Serial No. 1665. Washington, D.C., 1876.

U.S. Congress. Senate Miscellaneous Document No. 34, 44th Cong., 2d Sess., Serial No. 1786. Washington, D.C., 1877.

U.S. Congress. Senate Miscellaneous Document No. 59, 45th Cong., 2d Sess., Serial No. 1786. Washington, D.C., 1878.

U.S. Congress. Senate Miscellaneous Document No. 32, 46th Cong., 3d Sess., Serial No. 1943. Washington, D.C., 1881.

U.S. Congress. Senate Report Committee No. 323, 33d Cong., 1st Sess., Serial No. 707. Washington, D.C., 1854.

U.S. Senate Report No. 374, 35th Cong., 2d Sess., Serial No. 994. Washington, D.C., 1859.

U.S. Congress. Senate Report Committee No. 283, 36th Cong., 1st Sess., Serial No. 1040. Washington, D.C., 1859–1860.

U.S. Congress. Senate Report Committee No. 108, 37th Cong., 3d Sess., Serial Nos. 1152–1154. Washington, D.C., 1863.

U.S. Congress. Senate Report Committee No. 318, 42d Cong., 3d Sess., Serial No. 1548. Washington, D.C., 1873.

U.S. Congress. Senate Report No. 1978, 49th Cong., 2d Sess., Serial No. 2458. Washington, D.C., 1887.

U.S. Statues at Large.

U.S. Supreme Court Reports.

U.S. Supreme Court Reports, Lawyers Edition.

The War of the Rebellion: A Compilation of the Official Records of the Union and Confederate Armies. 70 vols. in 128, Washington, D.C., 1880–1901.

Abel, Annie Heloise. *The Slaveholding Indians*. 3 vols., Cleveland, Ohio, 1915–1925.

Allen, Albert H. *Arkansas Imprints, 1821–1876*. New York, 1947.

Allibone, S. Austin. *A Critical Dictionary of English Literature and British and American Authors*. Philadelphia, 1870.

Allsopp, Frederick W. *Albert Pike, a Biography*. Little Rock, Ark., 1928.

Allsopp, Frederick W. *The Life Story of Albert Pike*. Little Rock, Ark., 1922.

Allsopp, Frederick W. *The Poets and Poetry of Arkansas*. Little Rock, Ark., 1933.

Baird, W. David. "Arkansas's Choctaw Boundary: A Study of Justice Delayed," *Arkansas Historical Quarterly* 28 (autumn 1969): 203–22.

Baird, W. David. "Fort Smith and the Red Man," *Arkansas Historical Quarterly* 30 (winter 1971): 337–48.

Baird, W. David. *Peter Pitchlynn: Chief of the Choctaws*. Norman, Okla., 1972.

Banks, Charles Edward. *The Planters of the Commonwealth, a Study of the Emigrants and Emigration in Colonial Times*. Boston, 1930.

Barry, William. *A History of Framingham Massachusetts*. Boston, 1847.

Baylor, Orval W. *John Pope, Kentuckian, His Life and Times, 1770–1845*. Cynthiana, Ky., 1943.

Bearss. Ed, and Arvell M. Gibson. *Fort Smith: Little Gibraltar on the Arkansas*. Norman, Okla., 1969.

Benton, Thomas Hart. *Abridgment of the Debater of Congress, 1789–1856*. 16 vols., New York, 1857–1861.

Bering, John A. *History of the Forty-Eighth Ohio Vet. Vol. Inf., 1861–1866*. Hillsboro, Ohio, 1880.

Bishop, A. W. *Loyalty on the Frontier, or Sketches of Union Men of the South-West; with Incidents and Adventures in Rebellion on the Border*. St. Louis, Mo., 1863.

Boyden, William L. *Bibliography of the Writings of Albert Pike*. Washington, D.C., 1921.

Boyden, William L. "The Masonic Record of Albert Pike." *New Age Magazine* 18 (Jan. 1920): 34–37.

Brandes, George. *Recollection of My Childhood and Youth*. London, 1906.

Britton, Wiley. *Civil War on the Border*. New York, 1890.

Bunn, Alfred. *Old England and New England, in a Series of Views Taken on the Spot*. 2 vols., London, 1853.

Bussey, Cyrus. *The Pea Ridge Campaign Considered*. Military Order of the Loyal Legion of the United States, Commandry of the District of Columbia, *War Papers* [No.] 60. Washington, D.C., 1904.

Caldwell, John H. "Albert Pike, Associated Justice Arkansas Supreme Court," *Arkansas Research Lodge No. 739, Free and Accepted Masons*, vol. 1, no. 2 (N.p., 1948), 53–54.

Caldwell, John H. "Albert Pike, the Lawyer," *Arkansas Research Lodge No. 739, Free and Accepted Masons*, vol. 1, no. 3 (N.p., 1949), 28–56.

Capers, Gerald M., Jr. *The Biography of a River Town, Memphis: Its Heroic Age*. Chapel Hill, N.C., 1939.

Carleton, James Henry. *The Battle of Buena Vista, with the Operations of the Army of Occupation for One Month*. New York, 1848.

Carter, Harvey L. "Albert Pike." In Leroy R. Hafen, ed., *The Mountain Men in the Fur Trade of the Far West*. Vol. 2. Glendale, Calif., 1965.

Centennial Address by James D. Richardson, 33° (of Tennessee), Washington, D.C., October, 1901. N.p., 1901.

Cluskey, M. W. *Political Text-book or Encyclopedia*. Washington, D.C., 1857.

Cobb, Ida Sublette. "Mountain Legend of Albert Pike's Two Years in the Ouachitas," in Mena, Ark., *Evening Star*, Apr. 22, 1939.

Coburn, Frederick W. "Thomas Bayley Lawson, Portrait Painter of Newburyport and Lowell," *Essex Institute Historical Collections* 83 (Oct. 1947): 353–76.

Coffin, Joshua. *A Sketch of the History of Newbury, Newburyport, and West Newbury, 1635–1845*. Boston, 1845.

The Confederate Soldier in the Civil War. Ed. Ben La Bree. Louisville, 1897.

Cotterill, R. S. "Memphis Railroad Convention, 1849," *Tennessee Historical Magazine* 4 (June 1918): 83–94.

Coulter, E. Merton. *William G. Brownlow, Fighting Parson of the Southern Highlands*. Chapel Hill, N.C., 1937.

Currier, John James. *History of Newburyport, Mass., 1764–1909*. 2 vols., Newburyport, Mass., 1906–1909.

Daniel, Vivian. *Territorial Development of Arkansas, 1819–1836*. Unpublished M.A. thesis, The University of Texas, Austin, 1929.

Davidson, James Wood. *The Living Writers of the South*. New York, 1869.

Davis, J. P. *The Union Pacific Railway*. Chicago, 1894.

Davis, Sarah Lawrence. *Authentic History of the Ku Klux Klan, 1865–1877*. New York, 1924.

Debo, Angie. *The Rise and Fall of the Choctaw Republic*. Norman, Okla., 1934.

Donoghue, David. "Explorations of Albert Pike in Texas," *Southwestern Historical Quarterly* 39 (Oct. 1935): 135–38.

Donovan, Timothy P., and Willard B. Gatewood Jr., eds. *The Governors of Arkansas, Essays in Political Biography*. Fayetteville, Ark., 1981.

Dorris, Jonathan Truman. *Pardon and Amnesty under Lincoln and Johnson, the Restoration of the Confederates to Their Rights and Privileges, 1861–1898*. Introduction by J. G. Randall. Chapel Hill, N.C., 1953.

Dunham, Harold H. "Charles Bent." In Leroy R. Hafen, ed., *The Mountain Men in the Fur Trade of the Far West*. Vol. 2 (pp. 27–43). Glendale, Calif., 1965.

Duyckinck, Evert A. and George L. *Cyclopaedia of American Literature*. 2 vols., New York, 1856.

Easterly, J. H. "The Charleston Commercial Convention of 1854," *South Atlantic Quarterly* 25 (Apr. 1926): 181–97.

Eaton, Clement. *A History of the Southern Confederacy*. New York, 1954.

Eaton, Rachel Caroline. *John Ross and the Cherokee Indians*. Menasha, Wis., 1914.

Evans, Clement A., ed. *Confederate Military History*. 12 vols., Atlanta, 1899.

Ewell, John Louis. *The Story of Byfield, a New England Parish*. Boston, 1904.

Ferguson, John Lewis. "William E. Woodruff and the Territory of Arkansas, 1819–1836." Unpublished Ph.D. dissertation, Tulane University, 1960.

Fletcher, John Gould. *Arkansas*. Chapel Hill, N.C., 1947.

Ford, Harvey S. "Van Dorn and the Pea Ridge Campaign," *Journal of the American Military Institute* 3 (winter 1939): 222–36.

Foreman, Grant. *A History of Oklahoma*. Norman, Okla., 1942.

Foreman, Grant. *Pioneer Days in the Early Southwest*. Cleveland, Ohio, 1926.

Fulton, Maurice Garland, ed. *Diary and Letters of Josiah Gregg*. 2 vols. Norman, Okla., 1941.

Gammage, W. L. *The Camp, the Bivouac, and the Battle Field, Being a History of the Fourth Arkansas Regiment*. Selma, Ala., 1864.

Grant, Edwin. *History of Education in the United States*. New York, 1916.

Greer, James Kimmins. *Louisiana Politics, 1845–1861*. Baton Rouge, La., 1930.

Gregg, Josiah. *Commerce of the Prairies, of the Journal of a Santa Fe Trader, 1831–1839*. Vols. 19–20 in Reuben Gold Thwaites, ed., *Early Western Travels, 1748–1846*; 32 vols., Cleveland, 1904–1907.

Griswold, Rufus W., ed. *The Poets and Poetry of America*. Philadelphia, 1842.

Hallum, John. *Biographical and Pictorial History of Arkansas*. 1 vol., Albany, N.Y., 1889.

Hallum, John. *The Diary of an Old Lawyer*. Nashville, Tenn., 1895.

Harrell, John M. *The Brooks and Baxter War, a History of the Reconstruction Period in Arkansas*. St. Louis, Mo., 1893.

Hempstead, Fay. *Historical Review of Arkansas*. 3 vols., Chicago, 1911.

Herndon, Dallas T., ed. *Centennial History of Arkansas*. 3 vols., Little Rock, Ark., 1922.

Henry, Robert Selph. *The Story of the Mexican War*. New York, 1950.

Henry, W. S. *Campaign Sketches of the War with Mexico*. New York, 1847.

Hodder, Frank H. "The Pacific Railroad Background of the Kansas-Nebraska Act," *Mississippi Valley Historical Review* 12 (June 1925): 3–22.

Hood, Bobby Sue. "The Albert Pike Home," *Arkansas Historical Quarterly* 13 (spring 1954): 123–26.

Horn, Stanley F. *Invisible Empire, the Story of the Ku Klux Klan, 1866–1871*. Boston, 1939.

Hult, Dr. Gotfried. "'Albert Pike,' Delivered at the Pike Memorial Service in Fargo, North Dakota," *New Age Magazine* 12 (May 1910): 438–46.

Hurd, Duane Hamilton. *History of Essex County, Massachusetts, with Biographical Sketches of Many of Its Pioneers and Prominent Men*. 2 vols., Philadelphia, 1888.

Hutchinson, Thomas. *The History of the Colony and Province of Massachusetts-Bay*. 3 vols., Cambridge, Mass., 1936.

Ingram, John H. *Edgar Allen Poe, His Life, Letters and Opinions*. 2 vols., London, 1880.

Jenkins, John S. *History of the War between the United States and Mexico*. Auburn, N.Y., 1850.

Johnson, Boyd. "Benjamin Desha," *Arkansas Historical Quarterly* 19 (winter 1960): 348–60.

Johnson, Boyd. "Frederick Notrebe," *Arkansas Historical Quarterly* 21 (autumn 1962): 269–83.

Keating, J. M. *History of the City of Memphis and Shelby County Tennessee*. 2 vols., Syracuse, N.Y., 1888.

Kendall, George Wilkins. *Narrative of the Texan Santa Fe Expedition*. 2 vols., New York, 1844.

Kent, James. *Commentaries on American Law*. 2d ed. 2 vols. New York, 1832.

Kvasnicka, Robert M., and Herman J. Viola, eds. *The Commissioners of Indian Affairs, 1824–1977*. Lincoln, Nebr. and London, 1979.

Ladd, Horatio O. *History of the War with Mexico*. New York, 1883.

Lavender, David. *Bent's Fort*. Garden City, N.Y., 1954.

Lemke, W. J., ed. *The Life and Letters of Judge David Walker of Fayetteville*. Fayetteville, Ark: Washington County Historical Society, 1957.

Lemke, W. J., ed. *The Walker Family Letters*. Fayetteville, Ark.: Washington County Historical Society Bulletin No. 21, 1956.

Lester, J. C., and D. L. Wilson. *Ku Klux Klan, Its Origin, Growth and Disbandment*, introduction and notes by Walter L. Fleming. New York, 1905.

Littlefield, George Emery. *Early Schools and School-Books of New England*. Boston, 1904.

Lobingier, Charles Sumner. "Albert Pike, the Comparative Lawyer," *American Law Review* 61 (May–June 1927): 388–409.

Lobingier, Charles Sumner. "A Comparative Lawyer of the Nineteenth Century," *American Bar Association Journal* 13 (Apr. 1927): 205–12.

Lobingier, Charles Sumner. *The Supreme Council, 33°; Mother Council of the World Ancient and Accepted Scottish Rite of Freemasonry, Southern Jurisdiction, U.S.A.* Louisville, Ky., 1931.

Lockwood, Mary S. *Lineage Book of the Charter Members of the Daughters of the American Revolution*. Rev. ed., Harrisburg, Pennsylvania, 1895.

McCormick, J. H. "General Pike—the Linguist," *New Age Magazine* 12 (Mar. 1910): 260–61.

McDermott, John Francis, ed. *The Western Journals of Washington Irving*. Norman, Okla., 1944.

McGrane, Reginald C. *Foreign Bondholders and American State Debts*. New York, 1935.

Major, Mabel, and T. M. Pearce. *Southwest Heritage, A Literary History with Bibliographies*. 3d ed., rev. and enl. Albuquerque, N.Mex., 1972.

McKay, S. S. "Texas and the Southern Pacific Railroad, 1848–1860," *Southwestern Historical Quarterly* 35 (July 1931).

Mackey, Albert G. *Encyclopedia of Freemasonry and Its Kindred Sciences*. Philadelphia, 1915.

Masterson, James Raymond. *Tall Tales of Arkansaw*. Boston, 1943.

Morrison, W. B. "A Journey across Oklahoma Ninety Years Ago," *Chronicles of Oklahoma* 4 (Dec. 1926): 333–37.

Morrison, W. B. *Military Posts and Camps in Oklahoma*. Oklahoma City, 1936.

Muir, Andrew F. *The Thirty-Second Parallel Pacific Railroad in Texas to 1872*. Unpublished Ph.D. dissertation, University of Texas, Austin, 1949.

Nance, Joseph Milton. *The Attitude of New England toward Westward Expansion, 1800–1850*. Unpublished Ph.D. dissertation. University of Texas, Austin, 1941.

Nason, Elias, and Thomas Russell, *Henry Wilson*. Philadelphia, 1876.

Nevins, Allen. *Ordeal of the Union*. 2 vols., 1947.

Nitschke, Mrs. Willard Griffith. *Albert Pike's Service to the Confederacy*. Unpublished M.A. thesis. University of Texas, Austin, 1927.

Overdyke, W. Darrell. *The Know-Nothing Party in the South.* Baton Rouge, La., 1950.

Owsley, Frank Lawrence. *State Rights in the Confederacy.* Chicago, 1925.

Parks, Edd Winfield. *Southern Poets.* New York, 1936.

Parks, Joseph Howard. *General Edmund Kirby Smith, C.S.A.* Baton Rouge, La., 1954.

Patton, James Welch. *Unionism and Reconstruction in Tennessee, 1860–1869.* Chapel Hill, N.C., 1934.

Phillips, Ulrich Bonnell. *The Life of Robert Toombs.* New York, 1913.

Pierson, William Whatley. "The Committee on the Conduct of the Civil War," *American Historical Review* 23 (Apr. 1918): 550–76.

Albert Pike, *Centenary Souvenir of His Birth.* [Washington, D.C., 1909.]

"Robert Pike," *Essex Antiquarian* 4 (Aug. 1900): 113–17.

Pilling, James Constantine. *Bibliography of the Muskhogean Languages.* Bureau of American Ethnology *Bulletin.* [no. 9]; Washington, D.C., 1889.

Poore, Ben. Perley. *Reminiscences of Sixty Years in the National Metropolis.* 2 vols., Philadelphia, 1886.

Porter, William T., ed. *The Big Bear of Arkansas and Other Sketches.* Philadelphia, 1845.

Rankin, Claude. "The Highland Home of Albert Pike," *Masonic Light* 2 (Jan. 1926): 14.

Reynolds, John Hugh. "Papers and Documents of Eminent Arkansans," *Publication of the Arkansas Historical Association* 1: 230–52.

Rhodes, James Ford. *History of the United States from the Compromise of 1850.* 9 vols., New York, 1900–1928.

Richards, Ira Don. *Story of a Rivertown, Little Rock in the Nineteenth Century.* N.p., 1969.

Riley, Susan B. "Albert Pike as an American Don Juan," *Arkansas Historical Quarterly* 19 (autumn 1960): 207–24.

Riley, Susan B. *The Life and Works of Albert Pike to 1860.* Unpublished Ph.D. dissertation. Peabody College for Teachers, Nashville, Tenn., 1934.

Rives, George Lockhart. *The United States and Mexico, 1821–1848.* 2 vols., New York, 1913.

Roome, Lilian Pike, ed. *General Albert Pike's Poems with an Introductory Biographical Sketch.* Little Rock, Ark., 1900.

Roome, Lilian Pike, ed. *Hymns to the Gods and Other Poems by General Albert Pike.* Little Rock, Ark., 1916.

Roome, Lilian Pike, ed. *Lyrics and Love Songs by General Albert Pike.* Little Rock, Ark., 1916.

Ross, Margaret. *Arkansas Gazette, The Early Years 1819–1866: A History.* Little Rock, Ark., 1969.

Ross, Margaret Smith. "Cadron: An Early Town That Failed," *Arkansas Historical Quarterly* 16 (spring 1957): 3–27.

Ross, Margaret Smith. "The Cunninghams: Little Rock's First Family," *Pulaski County Historical Review* 1 (June 1953): 11ff.

Ross, Margaret Smith. "Jesse Brown, Pulaski County Pioneer," *Pulaski County Historical Review* 11 (Dec. 1954): 5–12.

Royce, Charles C. *The Cherokee Nation of Indians: A Narrative of Their Official Relations with the Colonial and Federal Governments.* Bureau of Ethnology *Fifth Annual Report, 1883–1884*, vol. 5, pp. 121–378; Washington, D.C., 1887.

Russel, Robert R. *Economic Aspects of Southern Sectionalism, 1840–1861.* University of Illinois Studies in the Social Sciences, vol. XI; Urbana, Ill., 1923.

Russel, Robert R. *Improvement of Communication with the Pacific Coast as an Issue in American Politics, 1783–1864.* Cedar Rapids, Iowa, 1948.

Sampson, F. A. "The New Madrid and Other Earthquakes of Missouri," *Missouri Historical Review* 7 (July 1913): 179–99. Bibliography, pp. 197–99.

Sargent, Epes W. "Some Misconceptions About Masonry," *New Age Magazine* 1 (Aug.–Sept. 1904): 294–96.

Scroggs, Jack B. "Arkansas in the Secession Crisis," *Arkansas Historical Quarterly* 12 (autumn 1953): 179–224.

Scully, Francis J. "Albert Pike's Home in Montgomery County, Arkansas," *Masonic Review Quarterly* [vol. 1] (Mar. 1951): 8–9.

Scully, Francis J. "Interesting Albert Pike Deeds," *Arkansas Research Lodge No. 739, Free and Accepted Masons.* Vol. 1, no. 5, N.p., 1951.

Shea, William L., and Earl J. Hess. *Pea Ridge, Civil War Campaign in the West.* Chapel Hill, N.C., and London, 1992.

Shepard, Edward M. "The New Madrid Earthquake," *Journal of Geology* 13 (Jan.–Feb. 1905): 45–61.

Shinn, Josiah H. *Pioneers and Makers of Arkansas.* Little Rock, Ark., 1908.

Shinn, Josiah. "Early Arkansas Newspapers," *Publications of the Arkansas Historical Association* 1 (1906): 395–403.

Shryock, Richard Harrison. *Georgia and the Union in 1850.* Durham, 1926.

Small, Walter Herbert. *Early New England Schools.* Boston, 1914.

A Soldier's Honor, with Reminiscences of Major-General Earl Van Dorn. By His Comrades. New York, 1902.

Staples, Thomas S. *Reconstruction in Arkansas, 1862–1874.* Columbia University Studies in History, Economics and Public Law, vol. 109. New York, 1923.

Stedman, Clarence Edmund, and Ellen Mackay Hutchinson, eds. *A Library of American Literature from the Earliest Settlement to the Present Time.* 11 vols. New York, 1891.

Stumberg, George Wilfred. *Guide to the Law and Legal Literature of France.* Washington, 1931.

Sultzer, Thomas D. *Pilgrimage of the Six Knights of Maryland to St. Louis, Missouri, and Interesting Incidents Connected Therewith, During the Second Week of September, 1868.* Baltimore, Md., 1868.

Swanton, John R. *Social Organization and Social Usages of the Indians of the Creek Confederacy.* Bureau of American Ethnology Forty-Second Annual Report, 1924–1925; Washington, D.C., 1928.

Thoburn, Joseph B., ed. "The Cherokee Question," *Chronicles of Oklahoma* 2 (June 1924): 141–242.

Thomas, David Y., ed. *Arkansas and Its People, a History 1561–1930.* 4 vols., New York, 1930.

Thomas, David Y. *Arkansas in War and Reconstruction, 1861–1874.* Little Rock, Ark., 1926.

Thompson, Maurice. "A Southern Pioneer Poet," *Independent* 50 (Nov. 17, 1898): 1396–98.

Trelease, Allen W. *The Ku Klux Klan, Conspiracy and Southern Reconstruction.* Baton Rouge, La., and London, 1971.

Turner, Jesse. "The Constitution of 1836," *Publications of the Arkansas Historical Association* 3 (1911): 74–166.

Vaught, Elsa. "Captain John Rogers: Founder of Fort Smith," *Arkansas Historical Quarterly* 17 (autumn 1958): 239–64.

A Volume of Records Relating to the Early History of Boston, Containing Boston Marriages from 1752 to 1809. Boston, 1903.

Waddell, Alfred Moore. *Some Memories of My Life*. Raleigh, N.C., 1908.

Waldo, William. "Recollections of a Septuagenarian," Missouri Historical Society, *Glimpses of the Past* 5 (St. Louis, Mo., April–June 1988).

Walton, Brian G. "Ambrose Hundley Sevier in the United States Senate, 1836–1848," *Arkansas Historical Quarterly* 32 (spring 1973): 25–60.

Walton, Brian G. "The Second Party System in Arkansas, 1836–1848," *Arkansas Historical Quarterly* 28 (summer 1969): 120–55.

Webb, Walter Prescott. *The Great Plains*. New York, 1931.

Webb, Walter Prescott. *The Texas Rangers*. Boston, 1935.

Webb, Walter Prescott, and H. Bailey Carroll, eds. *The Handbook of Texas*. 2 vols., Austin, Tex., 1952.

Weber, David J., ed. *Albert Pike Prose Sketches and Poems Written in the Western Country (With Additional Stories)*. Albuquerque, N.Mex., 1967.

Wender, Herbert. *Southern Commercial Conventions, 1837–1859*. Johns Hopkins University Studies in Historical and Political Science, vol. 48; Baltimore, Md., 1930.

White, Henry Ford. *The Economic and Social Development of Arkansas Prior to 1836*. Unpublished Ph.D. dissertation. University of Texas, Austin, 1931.

White, Lonnie J. "Disturbances on the Arkansas-Texas Border, 1827–1831," *Arkansas Historical Quarterly* 19 (summer 1960): 95–110.

White, Lonnie J. *Politics on the Southwestern Frontier: Arkansas Territory, 1819–1836*. Memphis, Tenn., 1964.

Wilcox, Cadmus M. *History of the Mexican War*. Washington, D.C., 1892.

Williams, Charlean Moss. "Where Albert Pike Wrote *Morals and Dogma*," *New Age Magazine* 42 (June 1934): 345–46.

Williams, Nathan O. "The Post Office in Early Arkansas," *Publications of the Arkansas Historical Association* 3 (1911): 310–24.

Williams, T. Harry. "The Committee on the Conduct of the War, an Experiment in Civilian Control," *Journal of the American Military Institute* 3 (fall 1939): 139–56.

Woodruff, William E. *With the Light Guns in '61–'65, Reminiscences of Eleven Arkansas, Missouri and Texas Light Batteries, in the Civil War*. Little Rock, Ark., 1903.

Wooster, Ralph. "The Arkansas Secession Convention," *Arkansas Historical Quarterly* 13 (summer 1954): 172–95.

Worley, Ted R. "Arkansas and the Money Crisis of 1836–1837," *Journal of Southern History* 15 (May 1949): 178–91.

Worley, Ted R. "An Early Arkansas Sportsman: C. F. M. Noland," *Arkansas Historical Quarterly* 11 (spring 1952): 25–39.

Worley, Ted R. "The Control of the Real Estate Bank of the State of Arkansas, 1836–1855," *Mississippi Valley Historical Review* 37 (Dec. 1950): 403–26.

Index

Abel, Annie Heloise: unfair use of evidence against Pike at Pea Ridge, 399

Adams, Charles D.: biographical sketch, 431; Pike's law partner at Memphis, 429, 443

Ainslie, John: of *Memphis Daily Appeal*, 435

Aldridge, George M.: Pike works for, 30–31

Alexander, Almarine: commander of Texas Cavalry regiment at Fort McCulloch, 403

American Party: origins, 321; founded by Pike in Arkansas, 273; structure, 321–22

Anderson, Judge, "of Mississippi," 161

Anstell, S. L., 334, 335

Antelope Hills: near Fort Cobb in leased district, 358, 359

Anthony, James C.: director of principal bank of Real Estate Bank, 153

Anthony, Joseph J.: killed by Speaker John Wilson, 150–51; "innocent disciple" of Ashley's war on Real Estate Bank, 154

antigambling affair, 1835, 82–84

Anti-Gaming Association: formed at Little Rock in 1835, 83

Arbuckle, Matthew: commander at Fort Smith, 30; and Fowler affair of 1836–37, 156–58

Arcade Building: used by theater group, 181

Arkansas: endorses a vote on state convention, 349; enters Confederacy, 352; opinion of delegation to Congress in 1850, 255, 263; Texas border trouble, 156; Unionist control of state convention in 1861, 351; violent opposition of to Van Dorn's abandonment in 1862, 405

Arkansas Central Railroad Company: fails to secure land grant for construction in 1855, 285

Arkansas Post: capital of Arkansas, moved to Little Rock, 48; capture in 1863 and clamor against Holmes and Hindman, 415; Pike marries into its close-knit society, 59

Arkansas River: navigation of dangerous, 29

Arkansas Supreme Court: legalizes legitimacy of Confederate state government, 426–28

Arkansas v. Williams (1864): Pike's opinion in, 426–27

Asboth, Alexander: Federal division commander at Pea Ridge, 389

Ashley, Chester, 161, 183; appearance, 192; biographical sketch, 37; called "Talleyrand" by Crittendenites, 43; character in Pike's writing, 133–34; control of Real Estate Bank desired, 148–54; criticized by Pike in 1833, 45; elected to Senate in 1844, 225–26; farcical account by Pike of his election as "head" of Little Rock Regency, 145; identified as "Pulaski" in 1837–38 attack on Real Estate Bank, 154; joins old enemy Cummins in war on Real Estate Bank assignment, 189–97; objects to Real Estate Bank charter provision for electing president of Real Estate Bank, 153–54; Pike sees him as boss of State Bank of Arkansas, 126; Pike sees him as powerful force in Sevier faction, 107–8; Pike's estimate of his ability as a speaker and lawyer, 192; plots to be U.S. senator in place of Fulton, 87; role in Democratic Party of Little Rock, 120–21; role in the rise of Arkansas political factions, 37; secures election of Capt. Jacob Brown as president of State Bank, 114–15; State Bank controlled by, 154; subornation of perjury charge against, 108; suspected of wanting Field elected president of State Bank, 149; war with Cummins over control of principal bank of Real Estate Bank, 155, 167–69; wins election to State Bank directory, 115; wrests control of principal bank of Real Estate Bank from Cummins, 167–68

Astor, John Jacob, 55

Baker, R. B., 342

Baldwin, David J.: Pike's second law partner in 1842, 183, 269

Ball, William McKnight: bank defaulter and embezzler, 185; character in Pike writing, 133–34; codifier of law in 1837–38, 158–59;

Pike alleges Ashley-Woodruff wanted to elbow Yell aside for him, 132; Pike believes Sevier preferred him instead of Fulton as U.S. senator in 1836, 108

Baltimore convention, 346

Bank of the United States (national bank): abolished by Jackson, 73–74; history, 110–11; operated as a central banking institution, 11; Pike blames money crisis of 1836–37 on its destruction, 126; recharter in 1832 vetoed by Jackson, 111–12; removal of federal deposits by Jackson, 112

banks: as Jackson's "deposit banks" of 1837, 126; nature, 110; state chartered and Jackson's deposit plan of 1833–36, 112; suspension of specie payments on federal drafts to Arkansas, 126; bank notes most common money in Arkansas, 111

Banks, Nathaniel P.: leader of Red River Expedition of 1864, 425; defeated, 425

Barber, Luke E.: member of Supreme Council, 422; trustee of Mary Ann Pike, 433

Barrow, Washington, 161

Bartlett, E. B., 333

Batchelor, John R., 422, 423

Bates, James Woodson: breaks with Crittenden, 44; Pike calls him the "Junius of the West," 44

Bean, Mark: with Pike in Cherokee Nation in 1861, 357

Beauregard, Gen. P. G. T.: sends Hindman to Arkansas to replace Van Dorn, 405

Beebe, Roswell: defeated for president of central board of Real Estate Bank and Woodruff attack on Real Estate Bank, 153; director of principal bank of Real Estate Bank and member of central board, 153; resigns from Real Estate Bank central board, 153; satirized by Pike in "Days of the Humbuggers," 145

Bell, John, 300, 346; helps Pike with Arkansas Whig patronage, 246

Belle Point: land feature at Fort Smith, 30

Bent, Charles: Santa Fe trader, 13–17

Bertrand, Arabella June: sister of Charles P. Bertrand, 42

Bertrand, Charles Pierre, 170; biographical sketch, 42–43; editor and founder of *Arkansas Advocate*, 42–43; elected to house in 1840, 173–75; invites Pike to work on *Advocate*, 45; offers to sell *Advocate* to Pike, 61; stepson of Dr. Matthew Cunningham, 42

Bertrand, Eliza (Wilson): mother of Charles P. Bertrand, 42

Bertrand, Pierre: father of Charles P. Bertrand, 42

Biddle, Nicholas: and Bank of the United States, 111, 135

Bigelow v. Forrest (1870): and Confiscation Act of 1862, 447

Big Rock: land feature above Little Rock, Arkansas, 48

Bird Creek: engagement at led to desertion of much of Drew's regiment of Cherokees, 378

Biscoe, Henry L.: trustee of Real Estate Bank in 1850, 270

Blunt, James G.: and net proceeds claim, 460

Borden, Benjamin J.: Whig purchaser of *Gazette* in 1842–43, 221–22

Borland, Solon: imported from Tennessee to edit *Arkansas Banner*, 224; major of Yell's Mexican War regiment captured, 230; in U.S. Senate, 284

Boston, Mass., 2

Boswell, Hartwell: register of public lands at Batesville and brother-in-law of Benjamin Desha, 60

Bowlegs, Billy: Seminole who remained neutral, 364

Bradbury, Daniel: and Indian activities at Pea Ridge, 398

Bradley, Joseph P.: of U.S. Supreme Court and opinion in *Hot Springs Cases*, 452

Bragg, Braxton: captain and artillery commander under Taylor, 234

Brazos River, 1, 23–26

Breckinridge, John C., 346; member of Scottish Rite Supreme Council, 422; vice president and Choctaw "corn money" of 1861, 318

Brown, Albert G., 300

Brown, Capt. Jacob: elected president of State Bank of Arkansas, 114–15; finds market for $300,000 of State Bank bonds with federal government, 127; Pike and Reed attack him for illegally holding a state office while in U.S. Army, 127

Brown, Thomas, 422

Brownlow, "Parson" William G.: radical Republican leader of Tennessee, 434

Bryan, Joseph: and Creek claim, 294, 295

Bryant, William: and net proceeds claim, 461

Buena Vista: battle of, 234–37; behavior of Yell's troops at, 235–36; description of site by Pike, 234

Buffalo Hump, 365

Bunker Hill, battle of, 3

Bunn, Alfred, 296

Burton, Dr. Phillip: at Pike-Roane duel, 240

Burwell, William M., 296; at Pike's "Life Wake," 311

Bussey, Col. Cyrus: and Pea Ridge atrocities, 398

Byfield Church, at Rowley, Massachusetts, 3

Byrd, Richard C.: "Union" candidate for senate in 1838, 166

Byrne, Andrew J.: author of "Petricula" letters on Pike, 332–33

Cadron, Ark.: mentioned by Pike, 45

Caldwell, Charles: and Ashley's Union Bank of Arkansas Territory bill, 110; character in Pike's writing, 133–34; elected to council in 1835, 87, 88; presides as judge over Wilson trial, 161–63

Calhoun, John A., 342

Calhoun, John C., 262

Campbell, Benjamin R., 422

Campbell, Richard: fur trapper and trader joined by Pike, 21–22

Campbell-Harris, expedition of 1832, 30

Camp Stephens: Van Dorn's headquarters northeast of Bentonville, 388

Cantonment Davis: Pike's headquarters in Creek Nation on west bank of Arkansas, 376

Carlisle, J. W.: and *Texas v. White*, 444

Carr, Eugene A.: Federal division commander at Pea Ridge, 388

Cass, Lewis, 300; Pike proposes mission to Comanches to, 33

Cerneau, Joseph: enemy of Southern Supreme Council, 420

Charleston convention, 345

Chase, Luther: boyhood friend of Pike, 9, 10, 11; cashier of Arkansas Post branch of State Bank, 150; and Choctaw net proceeds claim, 300; companion on travel to Santa Fe, 12, 21; joins Pike in Arkansas, 67–68; Pike's "more than friend," 296; second to Pike to duel with Roane, 244

Chase, Salmon P.: chief justice and *Texas v. White*, 446

Cherokee Indians: Chief Ross declares neutrality, 357; division between Ross and Ridge factions, 357, 371; and founding of Fort Smith, 29; Pike treaty with in 1861, 369, 370–71

Chickasaw Indians: legislature declares independence and joins C.S.A., 326

Childress, Robertson C., 161

Chisholm, Jesse: mixed Choctaw-Cherokee trader as Pike's interpreter to Indians in leased district, 365, 367; nurses Pike in illness, 367

Choctaw Indians: and Arkansas border, 29; treaty with Pike, 362

Choctaw Nation v. United States (1886), 557n

Choctaw National Council: declares nation independent of United States and joins C.S.A., 362

Choctaw net proceeds claim: "corn money" relief paid in 1861, 316–18; legal contracts with attorneys for, 300; meaning of "net proceeds," 303; wins new chance when United States negotiates 1855 treaty, 304

Cimarron River: a site on Santa Fe Trail, 15

Clark, Daniel: and Choctaw award of 1859, 316; and Choctaw "corn money" of 1861, 318

Clark, Willis Gaylord: and Pike's "Life Wake," 314

Clarke, Maj. George W., 375

Clendenin, John: censures Cummins and Ashley for "scurrilous cross-bill" in his court, 195; denies Pike injunction in Real Estate Bank assignment case, 191; Pike appeals for writ of mandamus against him, 191; prosecutes Douglass for murder of Dr. Howell, 161; and Wilson trial, 161

Clermont: Osage band chief becomes tribal chief, 370

Cloud, George: town chief of Seminoles, 364

Cochrane, John T., 342; and Choctaw net proceeds claim, 300, 303, 304; and Creek claim, 294; excludes Pike from 1855 Choctaw contract, 304; fails to win Pierce administration's support for net proceeds claim, 304

Cocke, Dr. John H.: death, 155, 157; elected to legislature in 1836, 105

Cocke, John W.: biographical sketch of early life, 178; helps found *Star*, 170; John Field seeks house order to compel him to testify against Lacy, 216–17; only Whig elected from Pulaski County to legislature of 1842, 203; Pike's favorite companion on the law circuits, 118, 177–78; as Whig, pledges to vote for Sevier for Senate, 201–2; Whig elector in 1840, 172

Coinage Act of 1834: terms, 73

Colby, Eli: antibank union party of in 1842, 201–6; editor of *Times and Advocate*, 163–64; estranged Whig editor in 1840, 173–75; gullible in supporting Byrd in 1838, 164; happy over Lambert's departure, 171; identifies Whig Cocke as Democrat for Sevier pledge in 1842, 203; physical clash with Lambert of *Star*, 171; prints "Old Observer" attack on bankites in legislature of 1842–43, 207–8; refuses Whig offer to sell interest in *Times and Advocate*, 170; resents Little Rock Whigs dictating to him, 170; urges run on State and Real Estate Banks, 193; wars on Real Estate Bank trustees, 189–97, 211–12

Cole, Coleman: Choctaw chief and net proceeds claim, 461–62

Cole Edward: new owner-editor of *Gazette* and quarrel with Cummins in 1839, 169

Comanche Indians: Pike treated with, 365–66

Comancheros: New Mexican traders with Comanche Indians, 23

Compromise of 1850: Clay proposes, 259–60

Confederate States of America: Arkansas enters, 352; commissions Pike as "special agent" to Indian tribes west of Arkansas, 353; Congress, 352; Congress passes act for protection of Indian Territory, 354; formation of, 352

Congress, U.S.: "Panic Session" of, 132

Conway, Elias Nelson: of Democratic dynasty, 39; and Real Estate Bank, 271, 273–74

Conway, Henry: death of and Sevier's rise to power, 39; delegate to Congress, 37; resigns as receiver at Batesville, 60

Conway, James Sevier: calls special election for Congress in July 1837, 132; and Democratic dynasty, 39–40; elected governor in 1836, 102, 104–5; and Fowler militia affair, 156–58

Cooley, Dennis N.: Pike asks for his support for a pardon, 432

Cooper, Douglas H.: Choctaw agent defects to C.S.A., 356, 362; and Choctaw net proceeds claim, 300; Indian regiment of at Pea Ridge, 391; Pike puts in command of troops in Indian Territory, 373; raises first regiment of Choctaw and Chickasaw riflemen (C.S.A.), 362; regiment of mustered, 364; reported drunk and unfit for duty at Fort Wayne, 413; succeeds Pike as commander of Indians, 408–9; suppresses Pike's address and orders his arrest, 409; tries to put down Creek rebellion, 378; and trouble with Opoth le Yahola, 373

Cooper, Samuel: adjutant and inspector general of Confederate army, 371

Copp, William: spokesman for Mississippi gamblers in Little Rock, 82–84

Coulter, Archibald: Pike's partner on *Advocate*, 123

Council Grove: on the Neosho River as site on Santa Fe Trail, 15

Cousins, William H.: second lieutenant in Pike's Mexican War company, 229

Coyle, John F.: editor of *National Intelligencer* and Pike's friend, 301; gives Pike a "life wake" for turning up "alive," 310

Crawford, John: asked to continue as agent of Cherokee under C.S.A., 356

Creek Agency: located on west bank of Arkansas west of Fort Gibson, 358

Creek Claim: history, 294

Creek Indians: Confederate troops raised among, 364; history of division among, 358; treaty with Pike, 361

Crittenden, John Jordan: Kentucky brother of Robert Crittenden, 40

Crittenden, Robert: attacked for leaving Arkansas Territory in absence of governor, 38; cabal against, 38–39; called "Cardinal Wolsey" by Ashley, 44; candidate against Sevier, 1833, 40; death as personal loss to Pike, 61; and election of 1833, 36; force behind *Advocate*, 43; plans to sell his house to territory foiled, 40; quarrel with Conway, 39; removed as territorial secretary, 40; rises to political power, 37; rivalry with Governor Pope, 40

Crittenden-Conway duel, 39

Crittenden-Sevier factions: in Arkansas Territory, 37–45
Cross, Edward: defeats Cummins for Congress in 1838, 164; reelected to Congress in 1840, 172–75; Sevier wants him appointed surveyor general of Arkansas, 102–3
Cross Hollows: in White River Mountains, 385
Cross Timbers: Pike's party crosses in 1832, 27
Cummins, Ebenezer, 302; brother and law partner of William, 185; law partner of Pike, 269
Cummins, William: advocates "district representation" in convention of 1836, 92; author of "An Old Observer" account of quo warranto victory, 1839, 169; break with Eli Colby of *Times and Advocate*, 170–71; candidate for Congress in 1836, 104; candidate for Congress in 1838, 159–60, 165–67; candidate for Congress in 1842, 196–200; celebrates bank victory over Ashley in 1839, 169; continues as opponent of Real Estate Bank in 1842–43, 212; declines to make Pike partner, 61; defeated by Ashley for director of State Bank, 115; declines to run for Congress in October 1837, 140; denounces Pike as attorney, 195; director of principal bank of Real Estate Bank, 153; elected to house in 1840, 173–75; estranged from Colby's *Times and Advocate*, 163–64; feud with Colby in 1840, 173–74; and Howell murder case, 161; law partner of Pike, 60; loses to Edward Cross in 1838, 164; opponent of Real Estate Bank assignment, 188–97; and People's Party, 103; Pike's estimate of his ability as a speaker and lawyer, 192; Pike's law partner and house member in territorial legislature of 1835, 87; removal from directory of principal bank of Real Estate Bank in 1839, 167–70; supports slaveholders' interests in 1835–36, 90–94; votes for Fowler's compromise bill of 1835, 93
Cunningham, Chester Ashley: son of Dr. Matthew Cunningham, 43
Cunningham, Dr. Matthew: biographical sketch, 42; "first family" of Little Rock, 43; joins anti-Crittenden cabal, 39
Curran, James M.: files complaint in 1854 to divest Real Estate Bank trustees of assets, 271
Curran, Thomas: partner of Farrelly, 59
Curtis, Samuel Ryan: changes front to meet Van Dorn's attack, 389–90; concentrates army against Van Dorn, 391; defensive position at Little Sugar Creek, 385, 388; exchange with Pike over Indian allies, 395; expects Van Dorn attack on Sugar Creek works, 389; forces Price into Arkansas, 385; orders Dodge to block Bentonville detour, 389; suppresses letters of Van Dorn and Pike in report to Committee on Conduct of the War, 398
Cushing, Caleb, 320; opinion as U.S. attorney general on Hot Springs title, 450

Da Costa, Isaac, 418
Dalcho, Frederick: and Supreme Council, 418
Danley, Christopher C.: a man in his company murdered, 233
Davies, Anthony: chairman of board of managers of Real Estate Bank, 148; explains antibank attitude of legislature of 1842–43, 205; replaced Wilson as president of Real Estate Bank, 155; and state banking in 1836, 110; testimony in Wilson trial, 162–63; writes charter of Real Estate Bank, 153
Davis, Jefferson, 319, 320; approves Pike's financial obligations under Indian treaties, 377; and Buena Vista, 234; and Choctaw award of 1859, 316; disapproves certain features of Pike's Indian treaties, 377; ignores Pike's protest against Hindman's policies, 408; signs Pike's commission as agent to Indians, 353
Davis, Jefferson C.: Federal division commander at Pea Ridge, 388
Dawson, Charles L.: commands Arkansas infantry regiment at Fort McCulloch, 403
Dawson, James, 300
DeBaun, James: duel with Cummins narrowly avoided in 1839, 169
Democratic Party: bossed by Sevier and his relatives, 40
Denver, James W.: and net proceeds claim, 462
Department of Indian Territory: creation with Pike assigned to command, 375
Desha, Capt. Benjamin: becomes receiver of public lands at Batesville, 60; biographical sketch, 59–60; opposes Sevier for delegate to Congress in 1831, 60; Pike on his courage, 60; serves as second to Crittenden in duel with Conway, 60

Dexter, "Lord" Timothy, 4

Dibnell, Dr. James A.: his account of Pike-Roane duel, 240; Pike's surgeon in duel with Roane, 244

Dickinson, Daniel S., 324

Dickinson, Townsend: censures Governor Yell for judicial interference, 195; Pike's injunction in Real Estate Bank assignment case approved, 191, 194; purged by legislature for Real Estate Bank assignment decision, 205, 213–14

Dillard, John: stockholder in Real Estate Bank, 148

Dillon, John Forrest: federal judge, rules in *Pike v. Wassell,* 448

Dimitry, Prof. Alexander: and Pike's "Life Wake," 311

Distribution, or Deposit, Act of 1836: Treasury to deposit surplus with states, 124

Dix, John A., 319; and warning to Pike to leave New York City in 1865, 430

Dodge, Augustus C., 320

Donelson, Andrew Jackson, 334

Doniphan, Col. Alexander W.: Pike sent to guide him, 237–38

Doolittle, James R.: and Choctaw award of 1859, 316; and Choctaw "corn money" of 1861, 318

Dorn, Andrew J.: Indian agent, 387

Douglas, Stephen A., 346; break with Buchanan, 344–45; and Compromise of 1850, 264; and Kansas-Nebraska Act, 319–20; and Lecompton constitution, 344; and Pacific railroad, 247; and popular sovereignty, 344

Douglass, David S.: trial for murder of Howell, 161

Drennen, John: Pike secures Whig office for, 246; owns stock in Real Estate Bank, 148; second to Pike in Roane duel, 244; trustee of Real Estate Bank in 1850, 270; and Van Buren branch of Real Estate Bank, 154–55; Whig leader at Van Buren, 118–19

Drew, John: Cherokee regiment of, 366, 369; escorts Pike to Park Hill, 369; and Pea Ridge, 390; Pike overtakes his regiment at Osage Springs, 388; troops dissent and go over to Union, 409

"Editor's Table, The": Pike's continuing column in the *Advocate,* 69–85

education, in Arkansas: Pike stresses need of tax-supported public schools in, 281

election of 1833, 36, 41–43

election of 1835: Pike backs winning slate in Pulaski County, 87

election of 1836, 103–6, 116–17

election of 1837: for Congress, 139–43

election of 1838, 163

election of 1840, 172–75; Whig division in campaign, 173–75

election of 1842, 197–203

election of 1844, 224–26, 228–30

election of 1848, 244–46

election of 1856, 336

election of 1860, 345–46, 348

election of 1868, 442

election of delegates to constitutional convention, 1835, 94, 96

English, Elbert H.: chief justice of state supreme court in 1864, 426–28

Erwin, James: director of principal bank of Real Estate Bank, 153

Ewing, Thomas: secretary of interior under Taylor helps Pike, 246

Fairchild, Hulbert F.: chancellor of special court of chancery at Little Rock and Real Estate Bank, 272

Farrelly, Pat: at Pike-Roane duel, 240

Farrelly, Terence: Ashley engineers his defeat for State Bank presidency, 114; biographical sketch, 59–60; council member in 1833, 57; Crittendenite, 62; and election of 1838, 159; guardian of Mary Ann Hamilton, 57–58; secures State Bank branch at Arkansas Post, 149–50, 153, 154–55

Faulkner, Sanford C.: member of Pike's treaty party, 355; trustee of Real Estate Bank in 1850, 270

Ferguson, William D.: becomes Whig in 1836–37, 148; defeats McCamy resolution on Real Estate Bank, 150; testimony in Wilson trial, 163

Field, John: Whig partisan in persecuting Judge Lacy, 217–18

Field, William: Byrd supporter in 1838, 164–65; chair of Sevier censure committee, 218–19; Democratic stockholder in Real Estate Bank, 148; nephew of Governor Pope and rise as Democrat, 148; principal bank director and Real Estate Bank trustee, 188

Fillmore, Millard, 334

"Fine Arkansas Gentleman, The," by Pike, 297

First National Bank of Louisville v. Kentucky (1870): Pike's and Johnson's part in, 446–47

Fitzhugh, R. H., 375

Fitzpatrick, Benjamin, 293, 300

Flanagin, Harris: appoints Pike to state supreme court, 426

Flatrock Creek: tributary of Arkansas River east of Van Buren, 32

Flint, Timothy: Pike corrects his description of Santa Fe, 18–19

Folsom, Peter: and net proceeds claim, 462

Folsom, Sampson H.: and his Choctaw battalion, 386

Forrest, Nathan Bedford: alleged head of KKK and leader of raid on *Hesper*, 442

Fort Arbuckle, 363, 368

Fort Gibson: in Cherokee Nation, 29; Pike visits, 32

Fort McCulloch: location and construction, 403

Fort Smith, Ark.: Territory, described by Pike, 29

Fort Smith, post of: and whiskey smuggling, 29

Fort Smith, town of, 29

Fort Smith Times: endorses Pike's "Pine Bluff Letter" of 1860, 347

Fort Sumter: capture leads to secession of Arkansas, 351–52

Fort Washita, 363

Foulhouze, James: adherent of Cerneauism, 420

Fowler, Absalom, 161, 334, 335; attacks Ball and Roane for bad work on law code, 158–59; biographical sketch, 87–88; breaks with Cummins over "district representation," 92; candidate for Congress in 1840, 172–75; candidate for governor in 1836, 104–5; chairs joint committee drafting bill, 1835, 90; coauthor of compromise convention bill, 1835, 93; default charges against Woodruff in 1837–38, 158; defeat of his first convention bill, 91; helps found *Star* at Little Rock, 170; and Howell trial, 163; "Knight of the Wooden Horse, The," 157; and People's Party, 103; quarrel with Governor Conway in 1836–37, 156–57; reelected to house in 1838, 164; success of convention compromise on basis of representation, 90–94, 97; wins election of territorial legislature in 1835, 87

Framingham Academy, 7

Frederick II: and Scottish Rite, 418

Freemasonry: three basic degrees, 417

Free Soilers in 1852, 319

French, Benjamin B., 422; federal commissioner of public buildings and Supreme Council member, 429; Pike requests help in getting pardon, 432

frontier: Pike as a farm worker on, 31

Fulton, Dr. John: and Howell murder case, 160

Fulton, William Savin: death in 1844, 225; election to U.S. Senate in 1836, 109; refuses to call special session for statehood, 88; replaces Crittenden as territorial secretary, 40; secures replacement of Woodruff by Pew, 103; will not hinder statehood, 89

Gaines, Edmund Pendleton: commander of military department in 1836–37, 157

Garland, Augustus Hill: elected to Provisional Congress of the Confederacy, 352

Garrison, William Lloyd: Pike's view of, 79

Garrison Creek: tributary of Arkansas River west of Van Buren, Arkansas, 31

Georgia Platform, 264, 267

Gibson, Dr. Lorenzo: drafts report censuring Sevier and Williamson in 1842, 218–19; elected to house in 1838, 164; elected to house in 1840, 173–75; as Whig leader, 118

Gideon, George S.: and Pike's "Life Wake," 311

Gill, E. H., 422

Glorieta Pass: in Sangre de Cristo mountains of New Mexico, 17

Gorgas, Josiah: chief of ordnance of C.S.A. promises Pike rifles, 380

Gouge, William M., 273

Gouldin, William B., 342

Gouley, George Frank: of Missouri and quarrel with Pike over York and Scottish rituals, 457–58

Grand Prairie of Arkansas: Pike's prediction it will one day be settled, 72
Gray, Alexander T.: writes opinion of United States in U.S. Court of Claims on Hot Springs, 451
Great Bend: on Arkansas River as a site on the Santa Fe Trail, 15
Green, Martin E.: his Missouri militia guarded Van Dorn's train, 389
Greenwood, Alfred Burton: and Choctaw net proceeds claim, 315
Gregg, Josiah: with Pike in Mexico, 238
Grier, Robert C.: dissent in *Texas v. White*, 446
Griswold, Rufus Wilmot: publishes Pike's poems in his *Poets and Poetry of America* (1842), 183

Halleck, Henry W.: and Department of Missouri, 385
Hamilton, Druscilla: mother of Mrs. Albert Pike, 58
Hamilton, James: father of Mrs. Albert Pike, 58
Hamilton, Margaret: sister of Mrs. Albert Pike, 58
Hamilton, Mary Ann: biographical sketch, 58; courted by Pike, 1833–34, 57
Hanly, Thomas B.: Democratic partisan's role in Lacy investigation of 1842–43, 216
Hanrick, Edward: and the Creek claim, 294
Harris, Carly A.: cashier and secretary of Real Estate Bank central board, 184
Harris, John: trapper and fur trader of Missouri at Taos, 21
Harrison, William Henry: had following in Arkansas, 117; Whig candidate for president in 1836, 102
Hempstead, Samuel Hutchinson: Democratic stockholder in Real Estate Bank, 148; testimony in Wilson trial, 162
Herron, Francis J.: Federal general allows Pike to go north without a pass, 429
Hesper, steamboat: and Clayton's militia arms at Memphis, 442
Hewson, M. Butt, 290
Hill, George: trustee of Real Estate Bank in 1850, 270

Hillyer, Giles M.: member of Supreme Council, 422, 423
Hindman, Thomas Carmichael, 405–16; ignores Pike's plea to be left alone in Indian country, 406; placed in command of Trans-Mississippi District, 405; relieves Pike of command and to report to Little Rock, 408; sends Dodge to take Pike's Parrott guns, 408; wants to withdraw Pike's resignation and court-martial him, 409
Hogan, J. S. C.: and *Memphis Daily Appeal*, 435
Holbrook, Moses, 419
Holford, James: London banker and Real Estate Bank, 184
Holmes, Robert D.: Masonic Grand Master of New York signs petition for Pike's pardon, 430
Holmes, Theophilus Hunter: backs Hindman against Pike, 410; commander of Trans-Mississippi Department but keeps Hindman in Arkansas, 409; endorses Pike's resignation, 411; retained by Kirby Smith in District of Arkansas, 415
Hornebrook, James H., and Miles Q. Townsend: and Pike's property, 448
Hot Springs, Ark.: reserved from public sale, 63
Hot Springs Cases (1876): Pike's part in, 448–52
House of the Temple, on Third Street N.W., Washington, D.C., 465
Houston, Sam, 33
Howard, Volney E., 295
Howell, Dr. Thomas: and his brother's murder, 160
Howell, Dr. William C.: murdered by Douglass, 160–61
Howell, Laban C.: elected colonel of militia, 156
Hubbard, David: Confederate Commissioner of Indian Affairs, 354
Hudson, George: principal chief of Choctaws and Confederate treaty, 362
Hughes, John T.: historian of Doniphan expedition, 238
Hunt, Andrew Jackson: and antigambling movement, 1835, 82–84; editor of the *Times*, Little Rock, 82
Hunter, Edward: commander of company in Arkansas regiment, 233; falsehood about Pike, 239

Hunter, Logan: Pike's New Orleans law partner, 301
Hurst, Asa P.: kills Wharton Rector at Wichita Agency in 1859, 315
"Hymns to the Gods": Pike poems published in *Blackwood's Magazine*, 181–82

Independent Treasury: origin of plan, 137
Indian Service: at Fort Smith, 30
Indian Territory: its defense, 353
Indian vocabularies: Pike's collection in 1857, 307–8
industrialism in Arkansas: Pike urges it, 281–82
Irwin: Pike's companion on the Campbell-Harris expedition and trouble, 35
Ives, Edward, 422
Izard, Gov. George: and the birth of the Crittenden-Sevier factions, 37
Izard, Mark: attacks Real Estate Bank and demands full report from President Wilson, 150

Jackson, Andrew, 30; removal of deposits from Bank of the United States., 73–74; vetoes repeal of Specie Circular, 127; war on the Bank of the United States, 110–12
Jemez, Pueblo: visited by Pike, 18
Jesup, Gen. Thomas S.: inspects Pike's Little Rock Guards in 1845, 228
Johnson, Andrew: Pike writes him petitioning for a pardon, 429; signs presidential order assuring Pike of his personal liberty, 431
Johnson, Benjamin, 39; endorses legality of Real Estate Bank assignment, 206; impeachment charges against foiled by Sevier, son-in-law, 40; Sevier wants him appointed federal judge at Little Rock, 102; state director of Real Estate Bank principal bank, 153; territorial superior court judge, 39
Johnson, Charles B., 356, 365, 372; Fort Smith Indian trader, 364
Johnson, Reverdy: estimate of Pike's ability as a lawyer, 444; opinion as U.S. attorney general on Hot Springs title, 450
Johnson, Richard Henry: editor of *True Democrat* attacks Pike for hostility to his paper, 330
Johnson, Richard Menton: Kentuckian with family connections in Arkansas, 39
Johnson, Robert Ward: attacked as Pike's "sub-attorney" in Creek claim, 335; and Choctaw award payment in 1861, 317; and Clay's proposed compromise, 260–61; and Creek claim of 1852, 295–96; and Creek claim, 300; and crisis of 1850, 255–56, 261; death, 452; defeated in 1878 for Senate, 452; delegate to Provisional Congress and chairman of the Committee on Indian Affairs, 377; dispels disunionist charges in 1857, 266–67; elected to Provisional Congress of C.S.A., 352; expedites ratification of Pike's Indian treaties, 377–78; invites Pike to attend Nashville convention, 256; and law partnership with Pike, 443–44; member of "Wigwam Club," 296; not a candidate for Senate in 1860, 348; and Pike-Roane duel, 240; Pike writes him about Indian Territory defense, 353; post–Civil War life, 443–44; reelected to Congress in 1851, 264–67; role in "family dynasty," 120; skill as stump speaker, 266
Johnson, William Warren, 375; and Pike treaty party, 355
Joint Committee on the Conduct of the War: investigates whether "Indian savages" were used by rebels, 397–98
Jumper, John: principal chief of Seminoles and Confederate treaty, 364, 365

Kansas, 319–20, Lecompton constitution, 343–44; rivalry for political control, 337; southern reaction concerning, 344; Walker as governor, 343
Kavanaugh, John: elected major of militia, 156
Keating, John M.: buys Pike's share of *Daily Appeal*, 441
Keatts, James B.: Whig leader at Little Rock, 117
Kendall, Amos: Pike attacks him for interfering with mail, 80
Kent, James: Pike's admiration for his conservative views, 74–75; supports legality of bank assignment, 206
Kinnaird, Moty, 364, 367
Kiowa Indians: Pike never treated with, 368
Kirby Smith, Edmund: forces Steele back into Little Rock lines in 1864, 425; replaces Holmes, 415

Kirkland, John T.: Harvard president, 7
Knight, John Elliott: editor of *Gazette* and 1850 crisis, 261
Know Nothing Party. *See* American Party
Ku Klux Klan: in Tennessee, 439–40
Kuykendall, Amos: councilman from Conway County, 1833, and "wolf bill," 49

Lacy, Judge Thomas J.: attempt to "address" him from state supreme court, 194; Governor Pope secures his appointment to superior court, 57; opinion on mandamus case in 1842, 194; purge attempt by legislature, 205
Lafayette, Marquis de: meets Pike, 5
Laffon de Ladebat, Charles: disputes Pike's Scottish rituals, 421–22
Lambert, David: cowhided by Cole of *Gazette*, 171; flees to Kentucky with Whig money, 171; founds *Star*, 170
Lane, Joseph, 346; rumored to be planning Kansas expedition to Indian Territory, 363–64
Lanegan, Francis, 375
Langlois, Francis: New Madrid land warrant and *Hot Springs Cases*, 448–49
Latrobe, John H. B.: hired by Choctaws to handle claim, 460
Lawson, John H.: and Indian atrocities at Pea Ridge, 398
Lawson, Thomas Bayley: Pike's boyhood friend, 9
Lea, Luke, 299; and Creek claim of 1852, 295; and Choctaw claim, 305; share of fee in Choctaw claim, 305
Leeper, Matthew: continues as agent of Wichitas and others in leased district, 355–56, 365
legislature, session of 1837, 147
legislature of 1835: fight over basis of representation in constitutional convention, 90–94
legislature of 1842–43: antibank session, 205; determined to purge Judges Dickinson and Lacy, 205; party makeup, 205
LeGrand, Alexander: Santa Fe resident and Pike, 19–21
Lenox, William H.: stepfather of Mrs. Albert Pike, 58
Lewis, Aaron B., 28; fur trapper and Pike, 22, 33
Lewisburg, Ark.: mentioned by Pike, 45

Light, George W.: Pike writes him of his coming marriage, 58; publisher of Pike's book, 11, 35
Lincoln, Abraham, 346
Little Piney Creek: tributary of Arkansas River in Johnson County, 36
Little Rock, Ark.: arsenal seized, 351; capital of Arkansas Territory described by Pike, 48; captured in 1863, 425; how named, 48; key site on Arkansas River, 48; meeting of territorial legislature, 48–49
Little Rock and Fort Smith Road, 48; Pike travels on to Little Rock in 1833, 45
Little Rock Arkansas Advocate: anti-Sevier and anti-Jackson paper, 43; moved by Pike to Markham Street, 81
Little Rock Arkansas Banner: formed by dynasty Democrats in 1843 as its organ, 224–25
Little Rock Arkansas Gazette: assaults charter of Real Estate Bank in 1837–38, 153–55; first newspaper in Arkansas, 30; removal of Woodruff as editor, 103; rivalry with *Arkansas Advocate*, 41; sold by Woodruff to Whigs in 1842–43, 225–28
Little Rock Arkansas Star: office destroyed by tornado, 171; Whig paper, 170–71
Little Rock Arkansas Times and Advocate: formed by merger, 123; Reed sells his interest in to Colby and Steck, 163
Little Rock Debating Society: Pike supports, 54
Little Rock Regency: the Democratic machine of Ashley, 131–32; heals 1838 Democratic breach, 164; Pike says it wants to replace Yell with Ball, 132; Yell as tool of, 140
Little Rock Theater: wrecked by storm while under construction, 181
Little Rock True Democrat: editor welcomes Pike as Democrat in 1860, 347
Little Rock Whig: established in 1851, 265
Llano Estacado: described by Albert Pike, 23
Lobingier, Charles S.: his estimate of Pike's ability as a lawyer and writer, 302
Logan, James, 334, 335
"Los Tiempos," by Albert Pike, 33
Lucas, James H.: performs Pike-Hamilton wedding, 60–61
Luce, John B.: and Choctaw net proceeds claim, 308
Lunt, George: Pike's boyhood friend, 9

McCamy, Robert: 150, 163
McClellan, Capt. David: Choctaw sub-agent in 1832, 28
McClelland, Robert: secretary of interior and Choctaw net proceeds claim, 303–4
McCulloch, Benjamin: C.S.A. brigadier general to command troops in Indian Territory, 354; death at Pea Ridge, 391; joins Pike in visit to Ross in 1861, 357; joins Price in 1862 in Boston Mountains below Fayetteville, 385; and Pea Ridge, 389, 390–91; quarrel with Price over military policy, 383; scout for Taylor in 1847, 234
McCurdy, Samuel: works on *Star*, 171
McDaniel, John Robin, 419
McIntosh, Chilly: of Creeks, 364, 365
McIntosh, David N.: Creek regiment of, 386, 391
McIntosh, James McQueen: brigadier general under McCulloch, killed, 39
McKee, Henry E.: and net proceeds claim, 460
McKee, William F.: hanged for murder of Beaufort P. Scott, 132
MacKenzie, Robert Shelton: British writer's account of banquet given Pike at Roast Oyster Club, 310–11
Mackey, Albert Gallatin: and place in Scottish Rite history, 419; work for Supreme Council, 421–22
Mackey, Thomas J., 375
McLain, John: defeated by Colby treachery in 1838, 164–65, elected as Whig to state senate in 1836, 105
McSweany, George W.: apprentice to Pike on *Advocate*, 61
McWilliams, Dr. F. A., Pulaski County sheriff and Pew affair, 132–33
Magnet Cove, Ark.: site of magnetized lodestone, 63
Mansen, Andy: Pike boards with on Flat Rock Creek, 32
Manypenny, George W.: and Choctaw net proceeds claim, 303
Martin, Bennett H., 161
Massie, Dr. Edward L.: Pike's surgeon at Pea Ridge and Indian scalpings, 395
Mathews, Charles, 334

May, Charles: lieutenant colonel of squadron of dragoons under Taylor, 234
Mayers, Abram G.: Democrat refuses to sustain vote censuring Sevier in 1842, 219
Maynard, Horace: and Choctaw award of 1859, 317
Mellen, William P., 422
Memphis, Tenn.: conditions in 1865, 433–34; Southwestern Convention and Pacific railroad, 247
Memphis and Little Rock Road: at Little Rock, 48
Memphis and Little Rock Railroad: completed on January 26, 1862, 381
Memphis Pacific Railroad Convention: Pike and, 248–51
Memphis Avalanche: opposes Pike's *Daily Appeal*, 441
Middle Spring of the Cimarron: a site on the Santa Fe Trail, 16
Mighill, Thomas, 2
Miller, Samuel F.: of U.S. Supreme Court and *Hot Springs Cases*, 447, 451; and *Texas v. White*, 446
Miller, William Read, 273
Missouri Compromise: line of and 1850 crisis, 263; repeal of slavery restriction, 320
Missouri-Texas Road: crossed Arkansas at Cantonment Davis, 376
Mitchell, John: and Supreme Council, 418
Monroe, James: Pike remembers seeing him at Newburyport, 5
Moore, James W.: and *Texas v. White*, 444
Mosely, Mary: widow who married Terence Farrelly, 59
Murrell, John: black accomplices hanged, 79

Nashville, Tenn.: convention at, 255, 259, 263
Neal, John, 11, 85
Nebraska, 319–20
net proceeds claim: Pike and after Civil War, 460–62, 466
Nettie Jones: tugboat in *Hesper* incident of Clayton's militia arms, 442
Newbury, Mass., 2

Newburyport, Mass.: history, 4–5

New Orleans Daily Delta: attack on Pike and exchange, 328–29

Newton, Thomas Willoughby: called "the Knight of the Hornslow Heath" by Bates, 44; candidate for Congress in 1848, 245–46; cashier and secretary of trustees of Real Estate Bank, 187; duel with Sevier, 39; Whig leader, 117, 120

Noah, Mordecai: Pike's "beau ideal" of a Whig editor, 69

Noble, John W.: and Pea Ridge atrocities, 398

Noland, Charles Fenton Mercer ("Fent"), 290; appointed receiver of Real Estate Bank assets in 1855, 272; attacks Governor Conway for politicizing bank war, 274; and Ashley's intrigue to control State Bank, 115; dismissed as Real Estate Bank receiver, 273; and Fowler attack on Ball-Roane code, 158, 165–66; messenger to convey Arkansas constitution to Washington, 101; recounts how Lambert fled with Whig money, 171; Whig friend of Pike, 119–20

Norris, J. C., 419

North Fork Village: location, 358, 359

Northern Supreme Council of Scottish Rite, 418–19

Northrop, Lucius B.: run in with Pike over commissary supplies, 380

Notrebe, Col. Frederick: biographical sketch, 59–60

Notrebe, Francine: wife of William Cummins, 60

Oden, Robert H.: defeated in 1827 by Henry Conway, 39

Opoth le Yahola: leader of Upper Creeks and Pike, 358, 363–64, 372, 378–79

Osage Indians: and Fort Smith, 29; treaty with Pike, 369–70

Osage Springs: site southeast of Bentonville, 385

Osterhaus, Peter J.: Federal commander at Pea Ridge, 389, 390

Ostinelli, Eliza: daughter of Louis, European opera singer, 10

Ostinelli, Louis: Italian violinist, 10

O'Sullivan, Anthony, 422

Otis, Harrison Gray, 3

Ouachita Mountains: at Little Rock, 48

Ozark, Ark.: town founded by Yell, 143, 145

Panic of 1837: onset, 124; followed by economic depression, 183–84

Parvin, Theodore S., 422

Paschal, George Washington: elected supreme court judge in 1842, 213–14; Pike's opponent in *Texas v. White,* 444

Pas-co-fa: town chief of Seminoles, 364

Pearce, Nicholas Bartlett: brigadier general of Arkansas militia in western divisions, 353, 355, 375

Peay, Gordan N.: leads Capital Guards as Pike's escort, 355

Penn, James, 422

People's Party: Pike's name for the Crittenden faction in 1836, election, 103

Perkins, Elizabeth: Pike's first love, 12, 35

Pettigrew, Charles: elected lieutenant colonel of militia in place of Fowler, 156

Pew, Thomas Jefferson: controversy with Sheriff McWilliams, 132; declares "basic question" of 1835–36 and "exploded local question in Arkansas," 142; defends Jackson's hard money policies in 1837, 124–25; and election of 1836, 103–5; offended by Pike's having *Revised Statutes* printed in Boston, 158; replaces Woodruff as editor of *Gazette,* 103, 107–8; reshipped to Washington in 1838, 156

Phelps, John S.: opposes Choctaw payment of 1861, 317

Phillips, Philip: and *Texas v. White,* 444

Pierce, Franklin, 319

Pike, Albert:
    abandons Cantonment Davis as untenable, 401;
    abolition as a state question to be decided by the people of a state, 78–79;
    abolition in North denounced, 78;
    accepts company flag from ladies of his soldiers in Little Rock, 228;
    acclimatizes himself to Little Rock's weather, 47;
    accused of seeking personal fame on Pacific railroad question, 284;

Albert Pike: (cont.)
- address of the chief of Five Civilized Tribes, purpose of, 408–9;
- addresses Arkansas state council of American Party, 323–24;
- addresses letter through Rector to Indian tribes on treaty ratification, 380;
- administers oath of office to Governor Conway in 1836, 109;
- admitted to Arkansas bar, 57;
- admitted to bar of U.S. Supreme Court, 246;
- admitted to Louisiana bar, 269, 301;
- advertises for lost books, 81–82;
- *Advocate* duties, 47;
- *Advocate* given a literary character, 55;
- *Advocate*, history of his purchase, 61;
- *Advocate* home moved, 81;
- *Advocate* merged with Reed's *Times*, 123;
- *Advocate* office becomes a public library, 81;
- *Advocate* ownership brings him in touch with Crittendenites, 62;
- *Advocate* under his ownership, 61;
- and affection of women, 454–55;
- at Agua Nueva near Saltillo with Yell's regiment, 232–33;
- alarmed by split in Democratic Party, 344–45;
- alarmed over growth of sectional Republican Party, 342–43;
- and American Party in Arkansas, 273, 322–24;
- American Party member in 1954, 321;
- *Ancient Faith and Worship of the Aryans as Embodied in the Vedic Hymns*, 459–60;
- anecdote about pay for hired horses, 367;
- anecdote of collecting Creek fee from Opoth le Yahola, 309–10;
- announces law partnership with Adams, 431;
- and antigambling affair in Little Rock, 82;
- apologizes for criticism of Postmaster General Amos Kendall, 80;
- appeals to Davis for free hand in managing Indian country, 404;
- appearance, 17, 19–20, 28, 61;
- applauds bill of rights in Arkansas Constitution of 1836, 98;
- applauds destruction of abolitionist tracts received in mail at Little Rock, 80;
- applauds Jackson's payment of national debt, 71;
- appointed associate justice of Arkansas Supreme Court in 1864, 426;
- appointed "superintendant" of printing Ball-Roane code, 158;
- *Form Book, The*, 179;
- Arkansas visit of 1881, 464;
- Arkansas's mild winters enjoyed, 70;
- arranges for defense of Indian Territory by Indian troops, 364;
- arrest avoided in Indian Territory, 409;
- arrested at Fayetteville and returned to Van Buren for trial, 35;
- arrested in Indian Territory and released at Washington, Arkansas, in 1862, 414;
- arrested near Tishomingo by force sent by Hindman, 414;
- arrival in Richmond, 375;
- arrives at Little Rock for first time, 45;
- artillery company of volunteers as mounted company for Mexican War, 228–29, 233;
- and Ashley as evil force in Democratic Party, 107–8;
- Ashley covets Senate seat in 1836, 108;
- Ashley's role in controlling election of State Bank director, 115–16;
- asks Indian leaders with powers to ratify amendments to meet him at Cantonment Davis, 380;
- asks Supreme Council to pay him an annuity to live on, 463–64;
- asserts neutrality in 1856 election, 335–36;
- assistant secretary of legislative council, 1833, 49;
- assumes command of Fort Washita, 411–14;
- attacked by *Gazette* for break with American Party, 335;
- attends American Party National Council, 1855, 324–28;
- author of "The Review, or The Days of the Humbuggers," 143;
- authorized to raise as many companies or regiments of Indians as he could arm, 375;
- backs long terms for judges of courts, 97;

Albert Pike: (cont.)
 becomes accustomed to language in West, 50;
 becoming a southerner, 241–43;
 belief in limited powers for the governor, 76–77;
 Bent, Saint Vrain and Company employee, 18;
 "the biggest pig owner in Johnson County," 45;
 birth, 3;
 birth of children, 64;
 boyhood in Newburyport, 4–7;
 breaks with Southern Convention over slavery fervor, 342;
 Buena Vista, battle of and, 235–37;
 builder of Scottish Rite in Louisiana, 420;
 Bulwer's *England and the English* a favorite work, 56;
 burlesque of Sevier and others, 143–46;
 called "Capting Bostin," 172;
 calls for revision of criminal code in Arkansas, 77;
 camp chest, described by Noland, 307;
 capture of Federal battery at Pea Ridge, 390;
 "Casca" letters expose Servier's support for Ashley, 108;
 ceases to be Whig after 1852, 319;
 Cerneausim in Louisiana defeated, 420;
 challenges Roane to duel for falsehoods about his service at Buena Vista, 239;
 champions southeast slaveholders' interest in convention bill of 1835, 91;
 charges Hindman with usurpation in Arkansas, 410–11;
 charges against Hindman and Holmes not sustained in Congress, 416;
 charter member of new Blue Lodge, Magnolia Lodge Number 60, in 1852, 417;
 children of Albert Pike, 269;
 children with him in Memphis after 1868, 433;
 Christmas 1861 report to Benjamin on needs in Indian Department, 379;
 Choctaw contract of revoked in 1855, 304;
 Choctaw fee for Treaty of 1855, 306;
 Choctaw net proceeds claim and, 300;
 Choctaw net proceeds claim and settlement with Pike's heirs, 557n;
 cites Opoth le Yahola as evidence of Federal use of Indian allies, 396;
 Clay's distribution of public land's proceeds at first opposed, 71;
 close observer of convention work in 1836, 97;
 close observer of legislature of 1835 on statehood, 89;
 close reader of *Federalist Papers*, 94;
 Cochrane and Treaty of 1855, 303;
 Colby publishes "Old Snooks's" letter, 204–7;
 collector of Indian vocabularies, 307–8;
 commissioned brigadier general in provisional army of the Confederacy, 372;
 confiscation of his Little Rock property, 432;
 Congress and the establishment of public schools in a state, 71;
 Coinage Act of 1834 opposed, 73;
 commander Arkansas Whig squadron at Presidio, 232;
 commands Captain Pike's Artillery, 180, 227–28;
 complains about high cost of vegetables and produce at Little Rock, 63;
 condemns scalping and shooting wounded soldiers, 395;
 consciousness of being charged with approving Indian atrocities and his pardon, 430–31;
 conveys treaty money to Rector at Fort Smith, 379;
 cooperates with McCulloch in Indian country, 355;
 "corn money" won for Choctaws by Johnson, he says, cotton crops concerned, 64;
 counsels against immediate secession in 1860, 349;
 court of inquiry for at Buena Vista, 239;
 "corn money" won for Choctaws by Johnson, 318;
 and Creek claim, 305–6;
 Creek claim fees, 1857, 306;
 Creek claim in 1859, 314;
 Creek claim legal contracts, 294;

Albert Pike: (cont.)
    Creek claim low fees, distribution, 308;
    Creek claim, origin of his connection with, 293;
    Creek treaty of 1856, his crucial work for, 305–6;
    Creek treaty, 361;
    Crittenden impressed by, 44;
    Crockett dinner at Little Rock attended, 80;
    Cummins and Real Estate Bank case of 1839, 167;
    Cummins partnership dissolved, 302;
    Cummins's political break with, 199–203;
    date of arrival in Arkansas territory, 1;
    daughters residence in Lafayette County during Civil War, 433;
    death, 467–68;
    debates Thomas Pew of *Gazette* on causes of Panic of 1837, 124;
    decides to go to the West, 12;
    defends Arkansas to his northern readers, 85;
    defends independent federal judiciary, 75;
    defends location of Fort McCulloch, 401–3;
    defends minority rights of southeast against Reed, 94–96;
    defends states' rights theory, 346;
    defends Walker's work in Kansas, 344;
    defies Van Dorn's orders for Indian defense, 402;
    delivers agency funds in Rector's name, 401;
    Democratic National Convention condemned, 71;
    denies Democratic charges of misuse of Real Estate Bank funds, 274;
    denies in sworn statement all charges of approving Indian atrocities, 430;
    denounces popular sovereignty, 346–47;
    describes electioneering in 1833, 41–42;
    describes Little Rock in 1833, 47–48;
    devises his library to Supreme Council, 463–64;
    discouraged over Van Dorn's withdrawal from line of Boston Mountains in Arkansas, 401;
    dismissed as headmaster of Newburyport, 10;
    dispute with Charles Laffon de Ladebat of Louisiana over rituals, 421–22;
    disunion spirit feared, 54;
    Doniphan guided from Chihuahua to Saltillo, 237–38;
    Douglass trial and, 161;
    "Down East" accent ridiculed, 172;
    defends Dred Scott decision, 346;
    duel with Roane, 239–40;
    ease of treaty negotiations with Choctaw and Chickasaw Indians, 362–63;
    editorial and publishing problems, 69;
    education, 6–7;
    education at Framingham Academy, 7;
    education by county governments, 53;
    education by property tax defended, 53, 281;
    education in Arkansas needed, 70;
    elected by American Party state council as delegate to National Council, 324;
    elected captain of mounted company in Yell's cavalry regiment, 228–29;
    and election of 1835, 88–89;
    and election of 1868, 441;
    endorses a city code to control free persons of color, 79;
    endorses Cummins's "district representation," 93;
    Episcopalian, 4;
    "Epitaphs Conned in a Church-Yard," 45;
    "Essays to Vinnie," 456;
    estimates little opposition to a constitutional convention in 1835, 90;
    Evil and the Remedy, The, by Sobinus, 222–23;
    experiences on the Great Plains of Texas, 23–26;
    fails to be elected to Confederate Congress, 352;
    fails to convince Ross to make treaty, 357;
    father of the Scottish Rite in Arkansas, 419–20;
    fears sectionalism will defeat statehood movement, 91;
    federal system of public schools, endorsed, 71;
    federal system of schools in Mexico praised, 71;

Albert Pike: (cont.)
"Fine Arkansas Gentleman, The," introduced, 297;
first formal speech, in Little Rock, 54;
first lieutenant of artillery battery in 1836, 109;
first letter of resignation captured en route to Richmond, 411;
first letter of resignation endorsed by Hindman and sent to Davis, 408;
flew unique Confederate States of America flag at Park Hill, 369;
forced to flee Montgomery County in early 1864, 425–26;
free public schools proposed, 107;
"frolic" at the surveyor general's office and, 64;
funeral, 468;
Gazette purchased by Whigs and Pike's role, 221–22;
goes to leased district to treat with Reserve Indians, 364;
goes with Comanche chiefs to select their reservation, 367;
Gouley's objection to Scottish rituals, 457–58;
governor's limited veto power approved, 98;
governor's veto opposed, 76–77;
Greasy Cove farm on Little Missouri River purchased, 417;
Halford Bond case against state, 276–78;
Hamilton Pike becomes partner, 443;
Harvard fees too high for him, 7, 8;
Harvard studies for junior-senior years completed on his own, 11;
Hamilton and the national debt, 71;
health, 47, 454, 464, 465, 466–68;
heirs win $75,000 in out-of-court settlement with Choctaws, 557n;
helps found Saint John's Masonic College, 417;
"History of the Real Estate Bank," 222;
holds powwow at Fort McCulloch with Comanche chiefs, 404–5;
"Hymns to the Gods" published, 172;
Hot Springs Cases, argument in, 451–52;
Hot Springs Cases, his bitterness over losing, 452;
Hot Springs described, 63;
"Hotch Pot" party denounced, 223;
historian of Harris expedition of 1832, 23;
home life in Little Rock, 62, 66–68;
home described, 65–66;
homesteads for actual settlers endorsed, 71;
his travels among Indians, 22–28;
hotly denies he is a "federalist," 77;
"Hymns to the Gods" originated, 11;
ignores instructions from Confederate States of America War Department on treaties, 359;
incensed by Van Dorn's ingratitude over Indians at Pea Ridge, 405;
and Independence Day, 227–28;
industrial development supporter, 281;
"Intercepted Letters," 51;
inveterate smoker of cigars and pipes, 70;
invited to Little Rock to work on *Advocate*, 45;
Irano-Aryan Theosophy and Doctrine as Contained in the Zend-Avesta, 459–60;
issued special order against scalping, 395;
opposes Jackson, 70;
attacks Jackson's gold policies in Arkansas, 73;
Jackson's "hard money" commented on, 53;
Jackson's monetary policies ridiculed, 125–26;
Jackson's veto of Specie Circular repeal attacked, 127;
Jacksonians' hard money ideas opposed, 72;
Jeffersonian Republican-Democrat in youth, 70;
joins Charles Bent's Santa Fe expedition, 13;
joins friend George Lunt in *Scrap Book*, 12;
joins fur trapping expedition to Great Plains, 21–22;
judges elected on nonpartisan basis, 109;
and Ku Klux Klan, 439–40;
labor for Scottish Rite in 1868–70, 457;
Lacy investigation denounced, 217–18;
"Las Tiempos" poem excerpted, 34;
"Las Tiempos" poem evaluated, 45;

Albert Pike: (cont.)
>law practice, 57, 58, 62, 63, 161, 177, 183, 246, 269, 301–2, 431;
>learning in judges, how secured, 75–76;
>learns that Holmes has replaced Hindman and visits him, 409;
>leaves Harris expedition for Fort Towson, 26;
>leaves Tahlequah for Fort Gibson, 358;
>*Lecturer of the Arya*, 459–60;
>legend as "rebel renegade," 398;
>*Letter Addressed to Major General Holmes*, 414;
>*Letter to the Choctaw People*, 461;
>*Letters to the People of the Northern States*, 337–41;
>library moved to Pike County in 1862, 417, 433;
>"Life Wake" by Coyle, 310–14;
>loss of German and Italian readers for Know Nothingism, 441;
>love of his smoking pipes, 466–67;
>makes Luke E. Barber trustee of property ceded to Mary Ann, 433;
>malaria attributed to "miasma" from plowed fields, 64;
>marriage ceremony, 60–61;
>marriage, 57–58;
>"masterly inactivity" recommended to southern people in regard to reconstruction, 435;
>*Maxims of the Roman Law and Some of the Ancient French Law, as Expounded and Applied in Doctrine and Jurisprudence*, among his unpublished mss., 302;
>meets Crittenden in 1833, 44;
>*Memphis Daily Appeal*, editor-in-chief, 435;
>*Memphis Daily Appeal*, share sold, 441;
>*Memphis Daily Appeal*, writings for, 436–39;
>money and banking ideas, 72–74;
>*Morals and Dogma of the Ancient and Accepted Scottish Right of Freemasonry*, 458–59;
>mounted company mustered at Washington, Arkansas, 229;
>mourns death of daughter Isadore, 453–54;
>moves from Webster's to Calhoun's theory of Union, 241, 243;
>national bank supported, 62;
>national bank with proper restrictions needed, 70;
>"National Plan of an Atlantic and Pacific Railroad," presented at Memphis, 251–52;
>national system of internal improvement supported, 70, 251, 281–82;
>nationalist in spirit, 56;
>needs power to negotiate treaties, 356;
>net proceeds claim, 460–62, 466;
>net proceeds claim of Choctaws and victory of March 9, 1859, 314;
>neutrality on national frontier, 320–21;
>new national theory of Union expounded to President Johnson, 429;
>no party label in 1835, 70;
>northern accounts of Pike's approving Indian atrocities at Pea Ridge, 396–97;
>northern experience and nationalism, 241–43;
>"Notes on the Choctaw Question" filed with Sebastian, 306;
>*Notes on the Civil Code of Louisiana*, among his unpublished mss., 302;
>*Nugae* published 183;
>nullification opposed, 241;
>oath of allegiance taken in New York and forwarded to Washington, 430;
>opposes Mexican War, 229;
>opposes popular election of judges in state, 75;
>opposes reopening slave trade in 1856, 341;
>opposes special session of American National Council in 1856, 333;
>opposes tying Indian Territory to Western Arkansas, 402;
>organizes a Creek-Seminole company as escort to leased district, 365;
>organizer of American Party in Arkansas, 322;
>Pacific railroad convention of 1849 proposed, 247–50;
>Pacific railroad plan, compromise nature, 253;
>Pacific railroad plan approved at Charleston, 285–89, 290;

Albert Pike: (cont.)
"Pacific Railroad" through Arkansas proposed, 248;
past differences with Van Dorn, 383–84;
"Past Teaching the Present and the Future, The," discussed, 436;
patriotism as a theme in speeches, 54;
partnership with Johnson dissolved, 452;
and Pea Ridge, 388, 389, 390–91; 392–94;
penitentiary system for Arkansas endorsed, 78;
permanent residence in Washington, 454;
Pierson supports a pardon for Pike, 430;
Pine Bluff letter and Democracy, 346;
plans move to New Orleans, 300–301;
plans trip to Richmond, 372;
poetry, 11, 182–83; 297–99;
political base of Whigs and of *Gazette* alleged, 226;
political leadership and need for Whig paper, 203;
political leadership and Tippecanoe Club, 171;
political leadership, 159–60;
political leadership in rallying Crittendenites, 62;
political strife eschewed, 67;
political trip to Tennessee and Kentucky in 1844, 224–25;
praised by Secretary of War Benjamin for Indian mission, 377;
praised for leadership qualities as a military officer, 229–30;
praises a two-house Congress, 75;
predicts defeat of Democratic Party in 1860, 345;
predicts Grand Prairie of Arkansas will one day be settled as rich agricultural area, 72;
prefers charges against General Holmes, 414;
and Prentice dispute of 1854, 290;
president should serve only one term, 70;
printer to convention of 1836, 96–97;
property at Little Rock in 1840s, 242;
Prose Sketches and Poems Written in the Western Country completed and mailed, 35;
protective tariff opposed, 62;
protective tariff would hurt the South, 70;
protests Hindman's subordinating him to junior officers, 407;
protests to Davis Hindman's illegalities in Arkansas, 407–8;
protests to Hindman the withdrawal of white troops from Indian territory, 405–6;
publishes James W. Robinson as liar and slanderer, 53;
publishes order and correspondence with Curtis over alleged Indian atrocities, 396;
publishes protest of American Party platform of 1856, 334;
quarrel with Woodruff over printing costs, 98–100;
railroad project proposed, 1836, 72;
railroad urged by Pike in 1836 out of surplus revenue, 71–72;
railroads for state proposed, 107;
rains contempt on Van Buren administration for sticking by Specie Circular, 126;
reader of Arkansas newspapers, 41–42;
Real Estate Bank and denial of political use, 273–74;
Real Estate Bank and history of attorneyship, 270–71, 273–74;
Real Estate Bank attorney, 183–84, 187–94;
Real Estate Bank attorney and legislature of 1842–43, 205–6;
Real Estate Bank case of 1839, 167–69;
Real Estate Bank deed of assignment case and, 187–94;
Real Estate Bank deed of assignment case and Cummins, 195–97;
Real Estate Bank lobbying, 206–8;
Real Estate Bank memorial to legislature written, 211–12;
Real Estate Bank political use of by Governor Conway, 274;
Real Estate Bank principal bank and Cummins-Ashley war over, 167–69;
Real Estate Bank principal bank wrested from director, 195;
Real Estate Bank principal bank's attorney, 169;

Albert Pike: (cont.)
>Real Estate Bank used for alleged evil ends, 226;
>Real Estate Bank war and, 155–56;
>receives Van Dorn's order at Cantonment Davis to join him at Bentonville, 387;
>recommends abolishing public hangings in Arkansas, 77;
>recommends abolishing public whippings in Arkansas, 77;
>recommends legislative program for state, 107;
>reelected to American National Council and National Convention, 332;
>refuses Hindman's order to report to Little Rock, 408;
>refuses pardon from President Johnson, 432;
>refuses to attend American National Convention in 1856, 334;
>refuses Van Dorn–Roane order, 405;
>rejoins Yell's regiment at Parras, 232;
>reply to *True Democrat* attack, 331;
>report on Indian mission to Confederate War Department, 375;
>reply to Representative Johnson on Nashville convention, 256–59, 261;
>reported that after Pea Ridge Van Dorn seized money and supplies of Indians, 404;
>reporter of state supreme court, 158, 179–80;
>reports speech of Amos Kuykendall on wolf bill, 49;
>reports to Richmond on his planned defense of Indian Territory, 403–4;
>reports to Van Dorn in Little Rock, 384;
>reprints subornation of perjury charge against Ashley, 108;
>requests Davis to restore Department of Indian Territory, 404;
>resents Hindman's order to send all his white troops to Arkansas, 405;
>residence in *Advocate* office, 47;
>residence in Alexandria, Virginia, 457;
>residence in Memphis in 1868, 433, 440–41;
>residence in New Orleans, 269, 302;
>residence in quarters of Supreme Council after 1876, 460;
>residence in Washington, Arkansas, 1864, 426;
>residence near Rondo, then in Lafayette County, 428;
>residence of 1880–83, 464;
>return to Cantonment Davis, paying treaty money in Rector's name, 401;
>return to Memphis in spring of 1869, 453;
>revised law code needed, 70;
>revised law code urged, 107;
>*Revised Statutes*, his labor on, 165;
>*Revised Statutes* delayed by Boston printer, 165–66;
>Rice lost as *Advocate* printer, 123;
>and Robert Johnson's election of 1851, 265;
>rumored killed in Indian country in 1858, 310;
>Santa Fe described, 18–19;
>Santa Rosa surrendered to Pike's squadron, 232;
>school teaching at Flat Rock Creek near Van Buren, 32;
>school teaching on Little Piney Creek, 36;
>Scottish Rite degrees conferred on, March 20, 1853, 418;
>Scottish Rite expansion under 462–64;
>Scottish Rite expansion main motive in seeking pardon, 431;
>Scottish Rite printing done in New York in 1865, 431;
>Scottish Rite rituals revised, 421, 423–24;
>Scottish Rite rituals revised in Greasy Cove home in 1863–64, 417;
>Scottish Rite Sovereign Grand Commander, 419;
>Scottish Rite Supreme Council members in 1860, 422;
>Scottish Rite Supreme Council membership expanded under, 422–23;
>Scottish Rite to be exclusive in nature, 423;
>secessionism and, 350;
>second letter of resignation endorsed by Holmes and forwarded to Davis, 411;
>*Second Letter to Lieutenant General Theophilus H. Holmes* (1863), 416;

Albert Pike: (cont.)
- seeks Taylor's help with Arkansas Whig patronage, 246;
- sells his share of *Times and Advocate* to John Reed, 146;
- separation from Mary Ann in 1857, 433;
- Sevier and "C" letter, 135–36;
- Sevier opposed, 50–52;
- Sevierites charged with political trickery, 106;
- view of Sevier's party, 107;
- Shakespeare and Byron compared, 56;
- speaks at New Orleans in 1855, 330;
- Specie Circular criticized, 125–26;
- speech at El Dorado on southern question, 262–63;
- sportsman in Arkansas, 180;
- "Spree at Johnny Coyle's," 313–14;
- squadron escorts topographical engineers of Wool from Presidio to Santa Rosa, 232;
- "Starvation, Emigration, or Railroads," 281–82;
- *State or Province? Bond or Free?*, 350–51;
- and statehood movement in 1835, 87–88;
- State University urged, 107;
- states' rights doctrine, 77;
- street improvement needed in Little Rock, 53;
- stubborn adherence to proslavery plank of American platform, 333–34;
- student of English poets, 11;
- studies for admission to Louisiana bar, 300–302;
- suggests "conservative" constitutional union party in South in 1851, 265–66;
- superstitions among western people, 53;
- and Supreme Council meeting at Charleston in 1865, 431;
- supports a national bank, 74;
- supports Lambert in starting *Arkansas Star*, 170–71;
- supports legislative election of judges in state, 76;
- supports statehood by early 1835, 74;
- supports two state banks in 1836, 107;
- Surplus Revenue Act endorsed, 71;
- surplus revenue share for Arkansas should go to schools, 71;
- surprised at proslavery fervor, 342;
- surrounds himself with caged birds, 465, 466;
- takes three basic Masonic degrees in 1850 at Western Star Lodge Number 2, Little Rock, 417;
- teacher assistant at Newburyport grammar school, 9;
- teacher at Fairhaven, Massachusetts, 10;
- teacher at Gloucester, Massachusetts, 7–8;
- teacher at Knowlton's Cove, Massachusetts, 8;
- teacher at Newburyport, 9–10;
- Texans on Arkansas border viewed negatively, 80;
- Texas annexation divides Whig Party, 81;
- Texas Cavalry under Welch and Quayle with him at Pea Ridge, 387, 391;
- Texas independence and statehood at first endorsed, 80;
- theater in Little Rock supported, 56;
- threatens to shoot neighbors' hogs, 62–63;
- *Times and Advocate* "senior editor," 123;
- tomato extolled, 63;
- *To the American Party South*, 334–35;
- travels from Arkansas to Boston, Texas, in 1865, 429;
- travels from Arkansas to Richmond in 1863, 416;
- travels from Boston to Saint Louis, 13;
- travels from Independence to Santa Fe, 13–18;
- travels from Little Rock to Cantonment Davis, 386–87;
- travels from New York to Ottawa to avoid arrest in 1865, 430;
- travels from Richmond to Arkansas in 1863, 416;
- travels from Richmond to Little Rock in 1862, 381;
- travels from Saltillo to Las Palomas for sentry duty, 233;
- travels in the West, 13;
- travels to join Van Dorn at Pea Ridge, 387–88;

Albert Pike: (cont.)
- travels to Memphis in 1865 to seek help in getting a pardon, 429;
- travels to New Orleans in 1835, 64;
- travels to Shreveport and New Orleans in 1865, 429;
- travels with company from Arkansas to San Antonio, 230;
- travels with squadron from Santa Rosa to Monclova and Parras, 232;
- treated as an apprentice by Bertrand, 47;
- treaties submitted for ratification, 375;
- treaty party of 1861, 355;
- trees on lawn named for his children, 66–67;
- Trousdale dismissed from *Daily Appeal*, 441;
- unionist views in 1850, 259;
- U.S. Senate as bastion of southern rights, 95;
- U.S. Senate nominee in 1842, 211;
- uplands along Arkansas Valley described, 64;
- Van Buren attacked as anti-western, 69;
- Van Dorn knew Indians could not be removed from their country without tribal consent, 385;
- Van Dorn's misunderstanding of Pike's forces, 384–85;
- view on Fitz-Greene Halleck, 55–56;
- view on James Gates Percival, 55–56;
- view on Mrs. Lydia Sigourney as poet, 55–56;
- view on Nathaniel Parker Willis, 55–56;
- view on William Cullen Bryant, 55–56;
- views on American poets and poetry, 55–56;
- views on limiting power of people under state government. 74;
- violin player with Louis Ostinelli, 10;
- visits family in Little Rock late in 1865, 432;
- visits mother in Newburyport, 163;
- visits Nashville, Tennessee, in 1831, 13;
- "Walking Gentleman, The" is used for literary criticism, 55;
- wants to occupy Federal posts in Indian Territory, 353;
- wants to save his books from confiscation, he tells President Johnson, 429;
- "Whig Address of 1838," 159–60;
- and Whig campaign of 1848, 245–46;
- and Whig patronage in 1848–49, 246–47;
- white troops authorized at Richmond, 375;
- Wilson trial for killing Anthony, 161;
- withdraws from American National Council over repeal of proslavery section, 334;
- women appealed to in speeches, 54;
- Woodruff as subject of editorial, 50–51;
- Woodruff attacked in poetry, 51;
- Woodruff Junior's service under, 402;
- Woodruff opens *Gazette* to attack on Pike by Robinson, 52–53;
- Woodruff's collecting of Arkansas's share of surplus revenue attacked, 127–31;
- Woodruff's referendum on statehood plan endorsed, 87;
- work for American Party in 1855, 328–30;
- work for Grand Lodge of Arkansas, 417;
- works to organize his military department, 375;
- works to secure funds under Indian treaties, 376;
- writes critical estimate of Yell's and Roane's poor leadership at Buena Vista, 238–39;
- writes French for help in securing pardon in 1865, 429;
- writes Hindman of Van Dorn's contemptuous indignity to Pike, 406;
- writes of New Mexico, 20–21;
- writes opinion in *Arkansas v. Williams* in 1864;
- writes political farce about Little Rock Regency of 1837, 132–35;
- writes to Rector to arrange gifts to Indians, 380;
- writing at Van Buren, 33–35;
- writings in *Advocate* that won him attention of Crittendenites, 45;
- writings on liberty and freedom in state government, 74;
- writings on Louisiana and French law, 302;
- Yell criticized as military leader, 230–31;
- York Right degree conferred on, 418;
- York Rite meeting at Saint Louis attended in 1868, 441

Pike, Albert: Albert Pike's grandfather, 2, 5–6
Pike, Albert: Albert Pike's son, 65
Pike, Albert Holden: Albert Pike's son, 66, 269
Pike, Alfred W.: Albert Pike's cousin and teacher, 7
Pike, Ann: Albert Pike's sister, 3
Pike, Benjamin: Albert Pike's father, 3, 6
Pike, Benjamin Desha: Albert Pike's son, 64
Pike, Benjamin Jr.: Albert Pike's brother, 3
Pike, Capt. John, 2
Pike, Clarence: Albert Pike's son, 66
Pike, Dorothy Day, 1
Pike, Eustace: Albert Pike's son, 66
Pike, Frances Haskell: Albert Pike's sister, 3
Pike, Hamilton: Albert Pike's son, 381, 426
Pike, Isadore: Albert Pike's daughter, birth, 66, 269, 381, 426; death, 453–54
Pike, John, 1, 2
Pike, Joseph, 2
Pike, Lilian: Albert Pike's daughter, 66, 269, 381, 426, 447–48
Pike, Luther Hamilton: Albert Pike's son, 65, 269, 314
Pike, Nicholas, 2, 6
Pike, Mary Ann Hamilton: Albert Pike's wife, 61, 79, 243, 351, 426, 433
Pike, Richard: Albert Pike's uncle, 3
Pike, Robert, 1
Pike, Sarah: Albert Pike's sister, 3
Pike, Sarah Andrews: Albert Pike's mother, 3
Pike, Sarah Little, 2
Pike, Sarah Moody, 2
Pike, Walter Lacy: Albert Pike's son, 65, 66, 269, 314, 355, 381, 426
Pike, Yvon: Albert Pike's son, 66, 269, 381, 426, 428, 433
Pike, Zebulon, 2
Pike, Zebulon Montgomery, 2
Pike v. Wassell (1877): Pike's part in, 447–48
Pierson, Azariah T. C., 422
Pioneering: on the Arkansas frontier, 31
Pitchlynn, Peter Perkins: and Choctaw net proceeds claim, 300, 460–62; defects to Confederacy and supports Pike treaty, 362
Platenius, William A.: administrator in the United States of estate of James Holford, 277

Plumb Island: at Newburyport, Mass., 6
Point of Rocks: a site on Santa Fe Trail, 16
Polk, James Knox: friend of Yell of Arkansas, 108
Pope, John: Kentuckian as governor of Arkansas Territory, 40, 45, 133; and "Pope's Folly" on Arkansas State House, 109
Pope, William C., 160–61
"Pope's Folly": reference to governor Pope's construction of capitol, 48
Porter, David D.: admiral leads fleet on Red River in 1864, 425
Porter, William T.: editor of *Spirit of the Times* and Pike's friend, 297
Powell, Maj. John Wesley: offends Pike over use of Indian vocabularies, 308
Prairie Grove: battle of helps destroy Hindman and Holmes in Arkansas, 415
Pray, Isaac C.: Pike's New York literary friend, 182
Prentice, George D.: attacks Treasurer Woodruff for trying to collect specie in Kentucky in 1837, 131; Pike's admiration for as Whig editor, 69; Pike as settler of dispute, 290
Prentiss, Sargent S., 174
Presidio, Mexico: site of Wool's crossing of Rio Grande, 232
Preston, John Jr.: commander of Helena Whig company in Pike's squadron in Mexico, 231, 233, 235–37; candidate for Congress in 1851, 265–67;
Price, Sterling, 385, 425

Quayle, William: lieutenant colonel of Ninth Texas Cavalry under Pike at Pea Ridge, 373, 390
Quesenbury, William: accepts Creek Agency under C.S.A., 355; Pike's brigade quartermaster, 375
Quitman, John Anthony, 419

Raiford, Philip H.: Creek agent and Pike, 290, 293
railroads to Pacific: Mexican War lands enhance southern route, 247; Pike's interest in, 247–54; Pike's plan for South to build its own, 283; sectionalism and, 247–54

railroads in Arkansas: extolled in 1852 by Pike, 281; intrastate rivalry over, 283–85
Rapley, Charles, 153
Raynes, Kenneth: and American Party, 322
Real Estate Bank of the State of Arkansas: act creating in 1836, 112; act to liquidate protested by trustees, 219–20, 225–26; attacked by Ashley-Woodruff junto, 152, 154; bill to liquidate discussed, 219–20; board of managers award stock in, 147–49; charges brought against trustees in 1854–55, 271–72; charter provisions, 113–14; comes under attack in 1841–42, 185–94; control of principal bank by large Whig stockholders in 1838, 167; deed of assignment to trustees, 186–87; first directory of Real Estate Bank principal bank of 1837–38, 167; history of the quo warranto case of 1839, 167–69; hypothecation of 500 state bonds by the North American Trust and repudiation of, 184–85; interest rate on state banks of increases to 6 percent, 152; involved in Wilson trial of 1838, 162; John Reed defends it in 1837–38 against Ashley-Woodruff assault, 152–54; large Democratic stockholder of, 149; members of first central board, 153; members of Real Estate Bank principal bank directory, 153; move to stack stockholder voting in 1839, 167; new elections ordered by supreme court in 1839, 169; principal bank at Little Rock put into operation in 1838, 167; provisions of deed of assignment by central board, 187–88; purging of Ashley and Cummins from Real Estate Bank principal bank directory, 272–73; put in state receivership, 272–73; putting Real Estate Bank into operation, 147–49; residuary trustees of in 1850, 270; retains Pike as Real Estate Bank attorney after 1841, 183–84; subject of legislative controversy in 1837, 149; supreme court upholder of Real Estate Bank charter and power of central board in 1839 care, 168–69; suspends specie payments in 1839, 184; trustees divested of assets in 1853, 271; trustees protest liquidation of 1843, 220–21; Van Buren branch of approved in 1838, 152, 154–55
Ream, Vinnie: biographical sketch of early life, 455–56; commissioned to sculpt Lincoln statue, 455–56; married to Captain Hoxie but still loyal Pike friend, 465–66; Pike's friendship with, 455–56

reconstruction: in Tennessee, 434
Rector, Ann: wife of Thomas Conway who fathered the Conway brothers of Arkansas, 120
Rector, Elias: father of Henry Massey Rector, 449
Rector, Elias: member of family dynasty, 120
Rector, Elias: of Fort Smith (called "Major"): head of Southern Superintendency of Indians, 306, 355; member of Pike treaty party, 364, 365, 367; personal description, 296; quarrel with Pike over treaty payments, 379, 386–87, 404; subject of Pike's song "The Fine Arkansas Gentleman," 297
Rector, Frank A.: nephew of Maj. Elias Rector and stabbed at Wichita Agency, 315; Pike wants his infantry regiment in Indian Territory, 379
Rector, Henry Massie: Civil War governor, 40, 348; claim to Hot Springs, 63; and election of state convention of 1861, 351; goes over to secession, 348; and *Hot Springs Cases*, 448–52; and Pike-Roane duel, 240
Rector, Wharton: brother of Ann (Rector) Conway, 39–40
Rector, Wharton: brother of Maj. Elias Rector and cousin of Sevier and Conway brothers, 102, 120
Rector, Wharton Jr.: nephew of Maj. Elias Rector, killed at Wichita Agency, 315
Rector, William, surveyor general of Missouri, Illinois, and Arkansas (called "General"): and birth of "dynasty," 40, 120
Red River: navigation on, 29
Reed, John: attacks Pike for having Ball-Roane code printed in Boston, 158; buys control of *Times*, 103; comments on Pike-Woodruff conflict over convention printing charges, 100; editorial attacker on Pike's view of "basic question" in 1835, 153–55; endorses White in 1836, 103; informs Woodruff that he, not Pike, is editor and publisher of *Times and Advocate*, 123
Report of the Accountants, Appointed under the Act of January 15, 1855, to Investigate the Affairs of the Real Estate Bank of Arkansas (Little Rock, 1856): biased nature, 274–80
Revised Statutes of the State of Arkansas (1838): declared in effect "as printed and reported" by Pike, 166; Pike's work on, 165–66

Reynolds, Hamilton: first lieutenant in Pike's Mexican War Company, 229

Rhett, Robert B., 345

Rice, Charles E.: leaves *Advocate* to join Houston's army in Texas, 123; printer on *Advocate* staff, 61

Richmond convention, 346

Riley, Susan B.: on Pike's poetry, 45

Ringgold, John: biographical sketch, 110; runs for congress in October 1837, 140; runs on People's ticket but his measures are Whig, 141; supporter of state banking in 1836, 110; Whig election in 1840, 172

Ringo, Chief Justice Daniel: his capricious views on common law and equity pleadings, 191

Rio de Santa Fe: described by Albert Pike, 18

Rio Fernando de Taos: at Taos, New Mexico, 17

Roane, John Selden: attacks Real Estate Bank trustees, 270; duel with Pike, 239–40; orders Pike to send white troops to Arkansas on Van Dorn's authority, 405

Roane, Samuel Calhoun: and law code of 1838, 158–59; Pike berates him for voting for Ashley, 115–16

"Roast Oyster Club": successor to "Wigwam Club," 310

Rockwell, William Spencer, 419

Rogers, John: Fort Smith founder, 30; biographical sketch, 30

Rogers, Mary: wife of John Rogers, 30

Ross, John: defects to Confederacy in 1861, 369; offers to treat with Pike, 368; Pike's first visit to in 1861, 356–57; rejects Governor Rector's approach on secession, 351; suspected of anti-C.S.A. feelings, 359; Wilson's Creek and, 368–69

Rowley, Mass., 2

Royston, Grandison D.: replaces Wilson as speaker of house, 152

Rust, Albert, 352; Democrat refuses to sustain vote to censure Sevier in 1842, 219

Rutherford, Samuel N., 355, 364, 387

Salt Fork of the Brazos: named by Pike, 26

Sangre de Cristo Mountains of New Mexico, 19

Schwarzmann, G. A., 375

Scott, Beaufort P.: murdered in Little Rock, 132

Scott, Charles, 422

Scott, Judge Andrew: Pike's neighbor in Pope County, 36, 37

Scott, William C.: lawyer, 161

Scott, Winfield, 319; suppresses Pike's censure of Van Dorn for attack on Comanches in 1858, 384

Scottish Rite of Freemasonry, 417–18; history in United States, 418–19; Pike after Civil War seeks pardon so that he might extend the Rite, 431

scrip: a common form of paper money in Arkansas, 111

Sebastian, William King: Arkansas senator and Creek claim, 299–300; attacked as Pike's "sub-attorney" on Creek claim, 355; and net proceeds claim of Choctaws, 315–16

secession: feeling in Arkansas, 348, 351–52

sectionalism in Arkansas: based on slaveholders versus nonslaveholders, 90–97

Seminole Indians: closely tied to Creeks, 363; treaty with Pike, 364

Seneca Indians: treaty with Pike, 369–70

Sevier, Ambrose Hundley: and anti-Crittenden faction, 40; appointed bond commissioner of Real Estate Bank by Davies, 155; blamed for Governor Pope's state house "folley," 133; called "Don Ambrosia" by enemies, 44; "C" letter to in 1837, 135–36; duel with Thomas Newton, 1827, 39; elected delegate to Congress, 1827, 39; and election of 1833, 36; and election to U.S. Senate, 1836, 109; forces legislative repeal in 1844 of house censure, 226; legislative investigation of his role as board broker for state banks, 209–11; letter to Jackson on appointments in Arkansas, 102–3; Pike criticizes his view on northern fanticism, 79; Pike satirizes, 51–52; reaction to house censure in 1842–43, 223–26; reelection in 1842 and state banks, 205, 209–11; reverses stand against statehood, 1833, 51; role in "family dynasty," 120; saves Judge Johnson from impeachment, 40; secures replacement of Woodruff by Pew, 103; and statehood movement, 87–88; threatens to ask Pike for "Casca's" name, 108–9

Shawnee Indians: treaty with Pike, 369–70

Sherman, John: helps secure defeat of Choctaw award of 1861, 317
Sherman, Thomas W.: captain and artillery commander under Taylor, 234
Sigel, Franz: almost trapped at Bentonville by Van Dorn, 388; led Osterhaus's division at Leetown, 389–90
Simms, William Gilmore: and Pike, 297
slavery: issue in 1849–50, 255; and sectionalism, 241–44, 252–54
Smith, Abram T.: Pike's landlord at Little Piney, 36, 41, 44
Smith, James M. C.: raises security force for Missouri-Texas Road, 364
Smith, James M. G., 364
Smith, Jefferson: co-owner of the *Times*, 89
Smith, Thomas L. "Peg-leg": Pike describes him at Taos in 1832, 22
Smithson, Bryan H.: independent Democrat for Congress in 1840, 175
Southern Commercial Convention: holds annual sessions in 1852–59, 285, 286; Pike at 1854 Charleston session, 285–89
southern sectionalism: economic decline of South and, 247–48; enhanced by Mexican War, 243–44; origin and growth, 241–54
Southern Supreme Council of Scottish Rite, 418–19
Southwest Military Road: crosses Arkansas at Little Rock, 48
Spadre, Ark.: a settlement in Johnson County, 44
Specie Circular, or Treasury Order of 1836, 112, 124
State Bank of Arkansas: Brown markets $300,000 of state bonds, 127; charter, 113; contest in legislature for political control, 114–16; created in 1836, 112; intrastate rivalry over principal bank, 142; Pike criticizes Democratic control, 126; rate of interest on bonds too low, 127; and special session of legislature, 1837, 147
state deposit banks: Pike opposes, 73, 112–13; Van Buren abandons in 1837, 137
statehood: delegate Sevier fails to get enabling act in 1833–34, 87; Pike endorses, 1835, 74
State House: capitol building described by Pike, 48; readying for new state government, 109

Steele, Frederick: Federal general occupies Little Rock, 1863–65, 425; occupies Camden, 425; uses Pike home as headquarters, 425
Steuart, John M., 161
Stevenson, William W.: director of principal bank of Real Estate Bank, 153
Stidham, George W., 310, 375; educated Creek who aided Pike in collecting vocabulary, 307
Stone, B. Warren: colonel of Sixth Texas Cavalry at Pea Ridge, 391
Stone, Cornelius: works on *Star*, 171
Story, Joseph: U.S. Supreme Court justice supports equality of assignment, 206
Strong, William: opinion in *Wallach v. Van Riswick*, 447
Stuart, Alexander H. H., 295, 299
Suggett, Baptiste: apprentice to Pike on *Advocate*, 61
superstitions: Pike writes on those in the west, 53
Surplus Revenue Act: established deposit distribution of U.S. Treasury surplus among states, 71, 124, 126, 127
Swayne, Noah H.: and *Texas v. White*, 446

Taney, Roger B.: opinion in Pike's Holford bond case, 177–78
Taos, New Mexico: visited by Pike, 17
Taylor, John M., 161
Taylor, Robert H.: commands Texas cavalry regiment at Fort McCulloch, 403
Taylor, Zachary: and crisis of 1850, 255–60; death, 264; had following in Arkansas, 117, 245; marches to Saltillo, 234; opposes Clay compromise plan, 264; Pike applies to for Arkansas federal patronage, 246; prepares to meet Santa Anna at Buena Vista, 234–35; stationed at Fort Gibson, 227–28
Tennessee: reconstruction, 434
Texas: annexation and Mexican War, 226; and crisis of 1850, 264; Pike opposes annexation, 81; under Mexican-Texan rule, 80–81
Texas Road. *See* Missouri-Texas Road
Texas v. White (1869): Pike's part in, 444–46
Thespian Society of Little Rock: Pike helps found, 56

Thommason, Hugh F., 352

Thompson, Maurice: critic of Pike's poetic ability, 297–98

Thurston, Dr. Richard, 464; at Pike-Roane duel, 240

Titcomb, Henry: friend of Albert Pike, 11

Titcomb, Joseph: Pike's boyhood friend, 9, 10

Titcomb, Rufus: Pike's boyhood friend, 9; Pike's companion to the west, 12

Toombs, Robert, 264, 293; and defense of Indian Territory, 353; and Senate attack on net proceeds award of 1859, 316

Tosawi: Comanche chief, 367

Totten, Capt. James: withdraws from arsenal at Little Rock, 351

Trans-Mississippi Department: surrendered by Kirby-Smith on May 26, 1865, 428

Trans-Mississippi District of Department No. 2: supposedly made Department of Indian Territory subordinate to Van Dorn, 393

transportation in Arkansas: criticized by Pike, 281–82

Trapnall, Frederick W.: biographical sketch, 178; helps found *Star*, 170; Whig leader at Little Rock, 117

Treaty of 1855: Choctaw net proceeds claim referred by the Senate, 305

Treaty of Dancing Rabbit Creek: and Choctaw net proceeds claim, 300

Triplett, Hedgeman C.: Pike anecdote, 179

Triplett, William: town loafer at Little Rock, 178–79

Trumbull, John Hammond: and Pike's Indian vocabularies, 308

Tucker, Sterling H., 173

Tully, Lewis B.: rebel Democrat in race for Congress in 1838, 163–64

Turner, Jesse: of Van Buren, 62; Pike fails to make him federal judge, 247; solicited by Pike in behalf of *Star*, 170–71; Whig leader, 118, 174–75

Union Bank of Arkansas Territory: defeated, 110

Upper Spring of the Cimarron: a site on the Santa Fe Trail, 16

U.S. Court of Claims: rules against Rector in 1874, 450–51

Van Buren, Martin: national Whig strategy against in 1836, 102; succession to Jackson assured, 69

Van Buren, Ark.: Pike at, 31, 32; Pike describes road to, 1835, 64

Van Dorn, Earl: advances on Curtis, 385, 388; authorizes white troops for Pike, 384; commander of Trans-Mississippi District of Department No. 2, 383; elaborates plan for taking St. Louis, 385; leaves Arkansas weakened by move to Mississippi, 403; march from Boston Mountains to Bentonville, 388; orders Pike to Arkansas, 385; and Pea Ridge, 389; plans turning movement of Curtis's position, 389; retreats from Pea Ridge, 392; rides from Jacksonport to Boston Mountains and takes command of Price and McCulloch, 385

Van Horne, Francis M.: jocular comment on Pike's suit in chancery court, 191

Vann, Joseph: Cherokee chief, 372–73

Waite, Morrison R.: chief justice and *Pike v. Wassell*, 448

Walker, David, 62; breaks with Cummins over "district representation," 92; leader of northwestern faction in legislature of 1835, 90–94; president of 1861 state convention, 351–52; revised harsh language of Gibson report on censure of Sevier and Williamson, 219; Whig leader at Fayetteville, 118, 119

Walker, Isaac P.: 299, 300

Walker, James H.: of Hempstead County: council member, 1835, opposes statehood, 90; Pike opposes his obstruction of statehood, 91

Walker, Leroy P.: Confederate secretary of war and Indian Affairs, 354

Wallach v. Van Riswick (1876): Pike's part in, 447

Walters, Ebenezer: trustee of Real Estate Bank in 1850, 270

Ware, Katherine A.: publisher of Pike's early poems, 11

Washington Telegraph: regrets Pike conversion to Democratic Party in 1860, 347

Wassell, John: and Pike's confiscated land, 447–48

Waters, Sam: and Little Rock Theater, 180–81

Watie, Stand: Cherokee regiment, 386; Cherokee regiment at Pea Ridge, 390; fears being put under Drew's command, 371; leads anti-Ross Cherokee faction, 368, 369; Pike meets regiment at Cincinnati, Ark., 387

Watkins, W. W., 352

Watkins, George C.: law partner of Ashley, 183

Watson, Hugh Parks, 422

Webster, Daniel: admired by Pike, 241; Whig presidential candidate in 1836, 102

Welch, Capt. O. L.: commands 200 Texas cavalrymen under Pike at Pea Ridge, 387, 390

Weller, Cyrus W.: editor of *Gazette* in 1842 and Democrats, 197–203; shocked over Woodruff's sale of *Gazette* to Whigs, 22; supports Pike against Cummins and Colby in 1842, 198–203

Whig Party in Arkansas: breach in Little Rock leadership in 1838–39, 170–71; and crisis of 1850, 262, 265; and election of 1842, 197–99; and election of 1844, 225–26; minority party in Arkansas, 120; origins in Arkansas, 116–17; presidential election in 1848, 246; source of its popularity in Arkansas, 117; Young Men's Convention in 1840, 174–75

Whig Party in south: weakened by crisis of 1850, 265–66

White, Edward L.: Pike's boyhood friend, 9, 10

White, Emeline: wife of Phineas White at Van Buren, 175

White, Hugh Lawson: endorsed by Pike, 69, 70, 102

White, Phineas H.: Pike's friend at Van Buren, 175

White Hair: Osage chief yields to Clermont, 370

Whitfield, John W.: McCulloch's cavalry leader informs Pike of deaths of McCulloch and McIntosh, 391

Whitney, Asa: and Pacific railroad, 247

Whittington, Hiram, 62

Wichita Agency: Pike's destination in leased district, 365

"Wigwam Club": Pike association with, 296

Wiley, J. McCaleb, 422

Williams, Bill: Pike relates his ability as a hunter, 22–23

Williamson, Thomas T.: appointed bond commissioner of Real Estate Bank, 155; stockholder in Real Estate Bank, 148

Willis, Nathaniel Parker: publisher of Pike's poetry, 11

Wilmot Proviso: Pike attacks, 252; Arkansas delegation to Congress and, 255–56

Wilson, Henry, 328

Wilson, John: carries pistol to seek satisfaction against Sen. Robert McCamy, 162; expelled from house, 152; murder trial of 1838 moved to Benton, 161; speaker of house, kills Anthony, 150–52; trial, 161–63

Wilson, John ("Christopher North"): editor of *Blackwood's Magazine*, 182

Wilson's Creek: battle affects Ross, 369

Woodbridge, N. J., 2

Woodruff, William Edward, 160, 161; alleged motive for selling *Gazette* to Whigs in 1842–43, 221; attacked by Pike, 45, 51; attacks Pike for printing charges in 1836, 98–100; biographical sketch, 38, 42; botched collection of surplus revenue, 133; and crisis of 1850, 261; default as state treasurer, 157–58; director of principal bank and member of central board of Real Estate Bank, 153; drives last spike completing Memphis and Little Rock Railroad, 381; and election of 1835, 88; endorses city code for free blacks, 79; expresses surprise at Clendenin's refusing injunction to Pike, 192; *Gazette* founder, 38; leans toward Pike's defense of Real Estate Bank assignment, 189–94; and legislature of 1835, 89; *Gazette* copy of constitution reaches Sevier before Noland arrives, 102; mistakenly calls Pike "senior editor" of *Times and Advocate*, 123; Pike sees Chester Ashley as controlling him, 107–8; Pike's conflict with over antigambling movement, 82–84; proposes Pacific railroad through Arkansas, 248; resigns from Real Estate Bank central board to attack Real Estate Bank, 153; role in Democratic Party, 121; state treasurer's role in collecting surplus revenue, 126, 127–31; strong supporter of statehood, 90; suspected of being anti-Jackson, 42

Woodruff, William Edward Jr.: captain commanding two artillery companies at Fort McCulloch, 403; describes Pike's powwow with Comanche chiefs, 404–5

Worsham, John Jennings: Scottish Rite Mason secures petition for Pike's pardon at Memphis, 429

Yancey, William L., 345

Yell, Archibald: attacked by Pike and Reed for supporting Jackson–Van Buren money policies, 134; and battle of Buena Vista, 235–36; blames Panic of 1837 on banks and extravagances of people, 139; character in Pike's writing, 133–34; candidate for Congress in 1837, 139; candidate for Congress in 1844, 225–26; death, 238; defeats Ringgold in 1837, 142–43; elected to Congress in 1836, 104–5; elected to Congress in 1844, 119; foils plot of Ashley-Woodruff to put Ball in his place in Congress, 132–34; independent force in Arkansas politics, 120; interferes in assignment case, 195; message in 1842 on Real Estate Bank, 206, 208–9, 212–13; his "mounted devils" and General Wool, 231; notorious for poor spelling, 144; resigns congressional seat to command Arkansas cavalry regiment in Mexican War, 230; runs afoul of General Wool, 230–31; says Congress should coerce deposit banks to pay specie, 140; special election in 1837, 132

Yell, James: a member of American Party, 274

York Rite of Freemasonry, 417–18